BENSON and HEDGES
CRICKET YEAR

EIGHTH EDITION

SEPTEMBER 1988 to SEPTEMBER 1989

EDITOR – DAVID LEMMON

PELHAM BOOKS/STEPHEN GREENE PRESS

Editor's note

The aim of *Benson and Hedges Cricket Year* is that the cricket enthusiast shall be able to read through the happenings in world cricket, from each October until the following September (the end of the English season). Form charts are printed and a player's every appearance will be given on these charts, and date and place allow these appearances to be readily found in the text.

The symbol * indicates 'not out' or 'wicket keeper' according to the context and the symbol † indicates captain.

The editor wishes to express his deepest thanks to Brian Coudy, Les Hatton, Victor Isaacs, Anthony Lalley, Qamar Ahmed, Graeme Wright and the late Peter Sichel, to whose memory this volume is dedicated.

PELHAM BOOKS/STEPHEN GREENE PRESS

Published by the Penguin Group
27 Wrights Lane, London W8 5TZ, England
Viking Penguin Inc., 40 West 23rd Street, New York, New York 10010, USA
The Stephen Greene Press Inc., 15 Muzzey Street, Lexington, Massachusetts 02173, USA
Penguin Books Australia Ltd, Ringwood, Victoria, Australia
Penguin Books Canada Ltd, 2801 John Street, Markham, Ontario, Canada L3R 1B4
Penguin Books (NZ) Ltd, 182–190 Wairau Road, Auckland 10, New Zealand

Penguin Books Ltd, Registered Offices: Harmondsworth, Middlesex, England

First published 1989

Typeset by Goodfellow and Egan, Cambridge
Printed and bound in Great Britain by
Richard Clay Ltd, Bungay, Suffolk

A CIP catalogue record for this book is available from the British Library
ISBN 0 7207 1900 3

PREVIOUS PAGES: *Worcestershire* v. *Australia at Worcester in May. (Adrian Murrell/Allsport)*

Sponsor's message

As the final ball of the 1989 Benson and Hedges Cup Final raced to the boundary and Eddie Hemmings celebrated Nottinghamshire's victory in flamboyant style it was possible for the briefest of moments to forget the frailties inherent within the English game.

Unfortunately, over the past summer, such pleasant occasions were in short supply. The announcement of the South African Tour Party, a one-day loss by an English team at the hands of the Netherlands, and of course the miserable 4–0 Test series defeat against the Australians, have brought us all back to earth with a jolt. However, new teams and new series bring fresh optimism and we all wish Graham Gooch, Mark Nicholas and their respective tour parties the best of fortune over the coming months.

Whilst our cricketers battle it out in India, the West Indies and Zimbabwe, the Eighth Edition of the *Benson and Hedges Cricket Year* will provide a comprehensive review of all first-class cricket played around the world over the past 12 months.

Supplying clear statistical analysis, supported by superb photography and informed comment, I am sure the Year Book will prove both a vital source of reference and a most enjoyable read.

BARRY JENNER
Marketing Manager
Benson and Hedges

Contents

Comment

At the end of 1987, Raman Subba Row had to fly to Pakistan in an attempt to restore some harmony to a tour which was threatened by player rebellion and disintegration. There had been arguments with umpires and dissension at decisions. The players could bear only part of the blame, for they had been subjected to provocation, but that they violated certain basic principles of the game, such as staying at the wicket after being given out, was undeniable. To placate them, one has to choose a word carefully, Subba Row awarded the players on that tour their full bonus for satisfactory behaviour. He might now care to ponder the fact that eight of those players who received the bonus have now decided to turn their backs on the England Test team and go to South Africa. Those who put money into the game, either by sponsorship or payment at the turnstiles, may well ask now what they got for their money.

One reflects on these incidents only because they emphasize the need for strength, courage and objectivity in management. Short-term unpopularity is often necessary if one is to achieve a more lasting good. In 1989, English cricket paid the full price for the lack of firm government in the previous two or three years.

The season began with a fanfare which promised a new era. Ted Dexter was made cricket supremo in what amounted to a palace coup, and then the same faces appeared, and within weeks we realized that the TCCB, and many of us with them, had become victims of their own publicity. It is too early to judge Dexter, but one despairs that none of the lessons that should have been learned from defeats at the hands of India, New Zealand, Pakistan and West Indies had been learned. There still seemed to be a caucus in the England side which remained immune to any loss of form, while others, eager and enthusiastic, beat on the walls in vain and, if they were allowed in, were put out of doors again if they did not achieve instant success. Stability in a Test side is desirable, but Test selection is an honour that has to be earned and should never be seen as an inalienable right. Perhaps it was ever thus. C.B. Fry was told nearly a century ago that 'It takes a long time to become recognized in big cricket and just as long to be dropped from it.'

The greater concern, however, is the continuing lack of self-assessment in attitudes and technique that is prevalent. Failure at Test level brings the constant demand for scapegoats. The selectors are, of course, the first targets, but that is incumbent with their job, and, unlike the press, they cannot conveniently forget that they advocated the choice of a man who has been proved palpably out of his depth. What is more disturbing is the tendency to blame one-day cricket, too much cricket, the lack of four-day cricket or anything else that springs conveniently to mind. These are windmills. None of them should be tilted at, for that would dissipate the energy that should be spent on self-questioning by those who run and play the game.

The confusion among the administrators is alarming. In 1989, we had a county deprived of the championship because they were subtracted 25 points for a sub-standard pitch. There is no complaint here if that rule had been applied consistently, but it was not. The county who gained from this penalty had produced one of the worst pitches of the season for the opening match against the Australians, after which they had stated that they had inherent problems, called in the TCCB's pitch adviser and thereby made themselves immune from prosecution. When one county captain drew an umpire's attention to a sub-standard pitch and asked why he was not going to report it, the umpire replied that it had not been done on purpose by the county concerned so he would not report it – a clear misinterpretation of the law.

At the end of the season, when it was decided to dispense with David Gower as England captain and to choose someone else to lead the side to West Indies, the man who was, one believes, the first choice and who was contacted, was then deemed to be ineligible even though he has played for England, attended a British university and holds a British passport.

Earlier, hours had been spent persuading Ian Botham to change his mind and agree to tour West Indies. Botham had shown no form to suggest that he should be selected for England but, having been persuaded, he had every right to believe he would be selected automatically. He was not.

While these confusions, and others, remain at the highest level of administration, how can we hope to succeed on the field? And how long will the paying-customer put up with these vagaries? We ignore him at our peril.

Last year, in these pages, I cried for the smack of firm government. Now, together with intelligence and sensitivity, it is needed more than ever.

DAVID LEMMON

Foreword by Mark Nicholas

'There must be a deep down love for the game. The batsman must want to bat and score many runs, the bowlers want to bowl whether or not they are getting the correct results. A deep down love for the game is a must. Without this, no amount of coaching will achieve the correct results.'

WILF SLACK, COACHING NOTES 1983

Wilf Slack died suddenly last winter. He is missed more than has been documented; he, more than most, would have been hurt by the events of the last few months. Wilf's successful career was based on a deep affection for the game of cricket and his simple words mean more than the thousands of others written in judgement of this summer past.

Media attention has focused on our national game as never before. Solutions to the problems in English cricket have bounced like a pinball from column to column. Cries for heads have been as plentiful in France's bicentenary year as they may have been at the time of the revolution itself.

Accusations of poor technique and a lack of dedication have rankled with players, wet the lips of officials and misled laymen. In truth much has been glossed over. We have an indiscriminate domestic game designed to wear the enthusiasm of the most eager protagonist and to test the patience of the keenest follower.

In addition, South Africa, the predator whose keen eye picks out vulnerable targets, attacked when our national spirit could least cope. Their prize was announced the day the Ashes were relinquished. By mid-August English cricket was on the canvas.

Realistically much of the plight of the national team is due to a shift in the balance of power of world cricket. The West Indies, with their uncompromising approach, have turned the torture screw on almost everyone. Pakistan have built authority around the pillars of Imran Khan, Abdul Qadir and Javed Miandad. India have discovered solidarity and a seam bowler or two. New Zealand have Hadlee and Crowe to provide the creativity in a team of defenders and hard-running midfield players who are hungry for the world stage. Australia have re-emerged as a real force with baggy caps and gum chewers and a steel in the eye missing since first Packer, then South Africa tugged at the guts of their foundations and found them as shaky and uncertain as England's appear now.

All these countries won their last Test series in England and are increasingly difficult to beat. In our own backyard we are humiliated by fresh, motivated tourists who still see England's scalp as the one most fit to set before their own gloating supporters.

So what to do? The South Africans pose a threat, and who can blame them? Their cricket is run by a few shrewd, innovative administrators. They cannot be blamed for

Mark Nicholas holding the 1988 Benson and Hedges Cup trophy. On his left Stephen Jefferi.

considering their own interests. The danger is that they may choose to recruit further, thus diminishing the number of worthy cricketers in the county game available to play for England. Legislation (not retrospective) may be necessary. Imagine a Middlesex team with Gatting and Emburey (already signed up), Fraser, Downton and Ramprakesh (hypothetical possibilities) and Haynes all ineligible. No fault of Middlesex nor of the players, but a headache for national selectors. The most valued cricketers will have to be on long contracts otherwise the law courts may again be called to judge upon issues of restraint of trade as the TCCB seeks to control the exodus. There can be no apathy to South Africa's whip-hand.

In our domestic structure the main problem is the poor quality of pitches. Just as Ivan Lendl may find it hard to make a spectacle of a match against Boris Becker on a court of bad bounce and inconsistent pace, so cricketers suffer on surfaces which are under-prepared, or worse still, doctored. To deduct 25 points from the team at the head of the championship may appear unjust but a kick on the backside is needed and we are, for the moment, bereft of another cure.

The 1989 Australians played on good pitches virtually wherever they went. As a consequence, their confidence and form was excellent before each Test match. Only twice did they encounter rogue pitches and on these they played poorly, losing once and winning by five runs on the other occasion. Their buoyant confidence was momentarily shaken, their jauntiness deflated. County players confront these rogue pitches each week. It is on these that current and future international players prepare. It will not do. Groundsmen can prepare good surfaces – they do so for touring teams – it must become an obligation to do the same for all other first-class cricket.

We must search for a system in which players want for victory, triumph and recognition more than they want for anything. Flair must be chivvied, charisma respected. Cart-horses must come second to stallions. Rewards should be high for achievers and minimal for under-achievers. The game must be played with passion and ambition not mediocrity and indifference.

English cricket needs leadership and imagination. The raw materials remain, as they have always done, but they urgently need direction. We must rebuild thoughtfully and quickly so as not to spend too long in our own epitaph.

MARK NICHOLAS

World XI

For the second year in succession we offer the *Benson and Hedges Cricket Year* World XI. Once again it is likely to produce debate and disappointment and even, on the evidence of reactions to last year's side, anger. For this we apologize in advance, but then cricket is a game which thrives on armchair debate and which rouses deep passions among its followers.

One of the criticisms levelled at last year's side was that it lacked balance and was short of a bowler, but this, one must emphasize, is to miss the point. Eleven players have been chosen this year on the strength of their performances throughout the cricket year from September 1988, to September 1989, and to leave one out to make room for a lesser player who would give this selection more balance or supply a missing ingredient would defeat the purpose of the exercise.

On the strength of his batting against England many

ABOVE: *Desmond Haynes. (Adrian Murrell/Allsport)*

LEFT: *Mark Taylor. (Adrian Murrell/Allsport)*

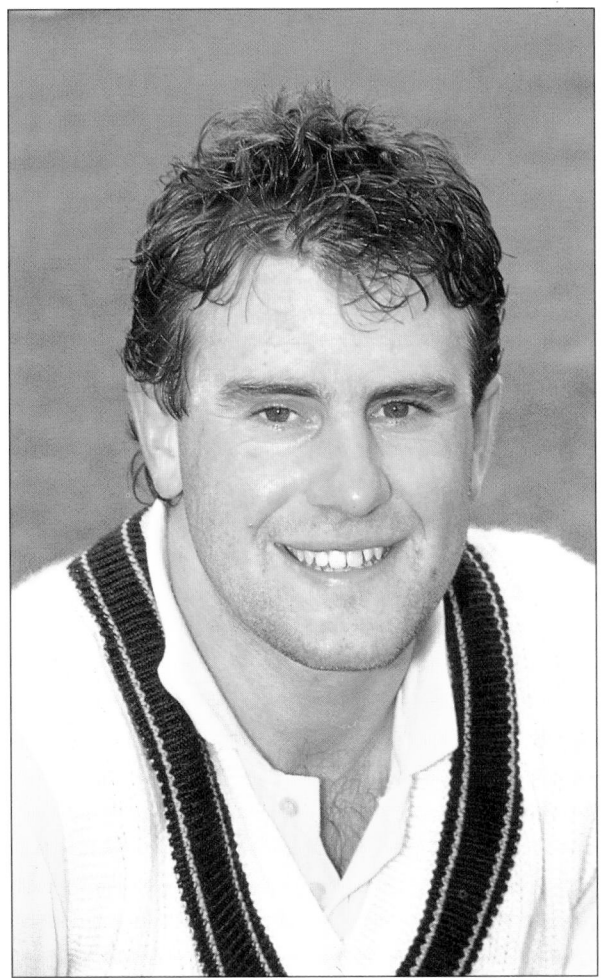

would advocate that Dean Jones should be in the eleven, but he had a pretty miserable season in Australia and won his place in the side to tour England only on the strength of his double century in the final Test against West Indies. Before that he had done little, and it would be unfair to omit a player who shone throughout the year in order to accommodate him.

Jim Cook is another who may be considered very unlucky, for he was the most consistent batsman in county cricket in 1989, but his record in the South African season, 1988–9, while good, was not outstanding enough to demand his inclusion.

There will, no doubt, be raised eyebrows at the exclusion of the great Viv Richards, but, when on form, which of the batsmen could be left out to make room for him?

ABOVE: *Richie Richardson. (Alan Cozzi)*

ABOVE RIGHT: *Graeme Hick. (Adrian Murrell/Allsport)*

The same comment must apply to Allan Border. He performed splendidly in England and bravely against West Indies, but he is not the power he once was, and he cannot be placed ahead of any of the six front-line batsmen chosen. I would like to make him non-playing captain with Bobby Simpson as manager.

The final position rested between two bowlers, Abdul Qadir and Curtly Ambrose. Qadir was not the force that he had been in recent years, and so the place went to Ambrose, who was devastating in Australia if he did show a little weariness by the time he arrived in Northampton.

This means that there is no first-rank spinner in the eleven, but is there a front-rank spinner in the world, save Qadir, and are we likely to see one emerge with Test cricket played as it is at present? India offers the hope with Arshad Ayub, who has had a fine year, and Hirwani, who tasted failure for the first time in West Indies and who has proved totally ineffective in domestic cricket in India. He is very young, however, and with sympathetic captaincy and careful handling he could thrive.

Desmond Haynes (West Indies)

Desmond Haynes maintained his consistently high standard as an opening batsman throughout Australia, West Indies and even the ravages of an English domestic season. His certainty of technique and admirable temperament allow him to conquer in all forms of cricket.

Mark Taylor (Australia)

Mark Taylor's splendid season for New South Wales was rewarded with a place in the Australian side for the last two Tests against West Indies and in the party to tour England. He revealed himself as a most accomplished and sound opening batsman, with an eye ever open for runs. Only Bradman has scored more in a Test series against England. He has now played eight Test matches against West Indies and England and has yet to finish on a losing side.

Richie Richardson (West Indies)

Against Australia and India Richardson scored prolifi-

LEFT: *Javed Miandad. (Chris Cole/Allsport)*

BELOW LEFT: *Steve Waugh. (Ben Radford/Allsport)*

cally, and he is now close to assuming the mantle that has belonged for many years to Viv Richards.

Graeme Hick (Northern Districts and Worcestershire)

The brilliance of Hick's batting has yet to be tested at international level, but he has continued to dominate in New Zealand and England. There were those in England who thought that he did not show the form of the previous season, but, although hampered by the doubtful wickets at New Road for the first half of the season, he still scored more than 1,800 runs and finished high in the averages. Hick's off-break bowling also became increasingly effective.

Javed Miandad (Pakistan)

Probably the finest batsman in world cricket at the present time, Javed continued to amass runs against all opposition in Pakistan and in New Zealand. Not since Bradman has a batsman looked so determined to complete a second hundred once he has reached the first.

Ian Smith. (David Munden)

Steve Waugh (Australia)

Steve Waugh batted with great courage and determination against West Indies and he graced the English summer in a manner never to be forgotten. His medium-pace bowling troubled the West Indians although he was less successful in England. His New South Wales colleague Greg Matthews prophesied that Steve Waugh would score more than 5,000 runs for Australia in Test cricket, and there is no reason now to question that assessment, which was made before Waugh had played Test cricket.

Ian Smith (New Zealand)

The consistency and durability of Ian Smith earn him the wicket-keeping position. He is adept at keeping to all kinds of bowling, and he is a powerful batsman who is capable of bringing out his best when it is most needed. Russell, after one series, is a strong challenger for the position as is, inevitably, Dujon, who was not, however, at his most consistent in 1988–9.

Kapil Dev (India)

Kapil Dev shouldered the Indian attack in 1988–9 and bowled magnificently in the West Indies. He remains a most powerful hitter, who is capable of changing the course of a game with his batting. His achievements as a bowler are remarkable when one considers how little support he has had over the past decade.

Malcolm Marshall (West Indies)

If there were times when Marshall appeared weary of county cricket, he remains the most potent fast bowler in world cricket. He claimed his 300th Test wicket against Australia and led the rout of India.

Curtly Ambrose (West Indies)

The most controversial choice for the eleven is Ambrose, as after an outstanding tour of Australia he tended to fall away a little. One feels, however, that he poses one of the greatest threats to batsmen at the highest level, with his height and pace.

Terry Alderman (Australia)

Alderman's return to Test cricket was marked with success against West Indies. He bowled with consistent hostility in the Sheffield Shield, and against England he swept all before him.

It is interesting to compare the *Benson and Hedges Cricket Year* World XI with the Deloitte Ratings. The top six batsmen in the Deloitte Ratings at the end of the English season were:

1 Javed Miandad
2 Richie Richardson
3 Dilip Vengsarkar

BELOW: *Kapil Dev. (David Munden)*

RIGHT: *Malcolm Marshall. (David Munden)*

Curtly Ambrose. (Adrian Murrell/Allsport)

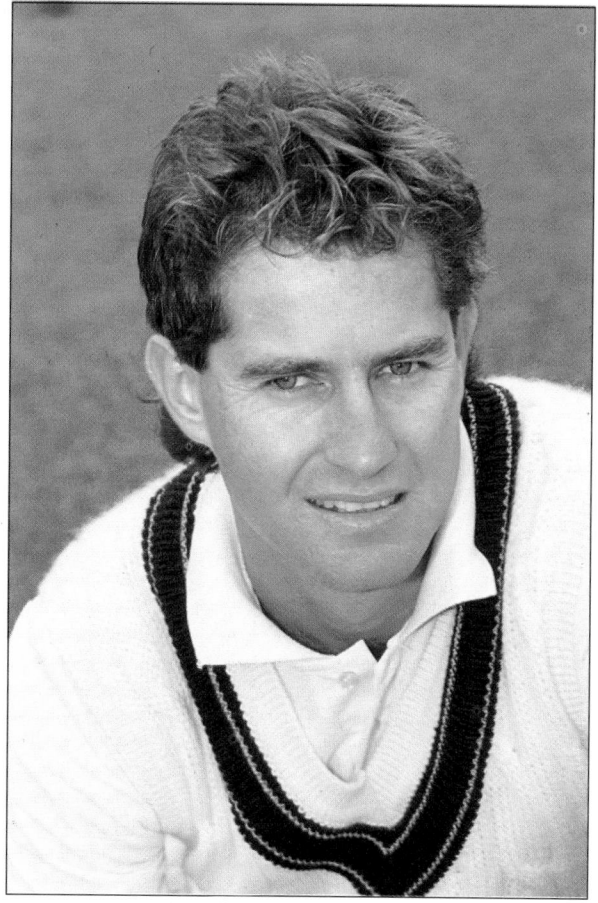

Terry Alderman. (Adrian Murrell/Allsport)

    4 Viv Richards
    5 Martin Crowe
    6 Allan Border

The ratings of those in the *Benson and Hedges Cricket Year* World XI not in the top six were:

Mark Taylor	7
Desmond Haynes	9
Steve Waugh	10

Graeme Hick has not played Test cricket so has no rating.

One feels that there is insufficient evidence on which to return Martin Crowe to the top bracket as yet while Vengsarkar, on recent form, is in a false position.

Wicket-keepers are not ranked by Deloitte, but the places in the batting ratings of the three contenders for the post were:

    22 Russell
    29 Dujon
    30 Smith

The top four bowlers in the Deloitte Ratings were:

    1 Richard Hadlee
    2 Malcolm Marshall
    3 Imran Khan
    4 Terry Alderman

Kapil Dev was rated at number 5 and Curtly Ambrose at number 9.

Surfeiting the Appetite

The season in Australia.
Sheffield Shield. FAI Insurance Cup.
West Indian tour and Tests.
Benson and Hedges World Series,
Australia, West Indies and Pakistan.
Form charts.
First-class averages.
Review of the season by
Chris Harte.

Melbourne Cricket Ground. The attraction of the one-day game. (Allsport)

Australian cricket had seemed to revive in 1987–8 with the triumph in the World Cup followed by success against New Zealand, but the experiences in Pakistan and the arrival of the West Indians tended to lessen the euphoria. Nevertheless, the Australians faced the West Indian challenge not without hope. It would appear that the great problem confronting the Australian Board is to excite as great an interest in the Sheffield Shield and in Test cricket as there is in the one-day international matches which continue to dominate the fixture list.

The advent to the season had seen casualties in the struggle to control the game in Australia. Fred Bennett and Dick Guy lost their positions in the New South Wales administration, and Norman McMahon, for 21 years chairman of the Queensland association, failed to gain re-election. In Western Australia, Bert Rigg, long-serving vice-president, lost his seat after an acrimonious struggle.

On the happier side, Simon O'Donnell, after exhaustive cancer therapy treatment, returned to first-class cricket as captain of Victoria. New South Wales appointed Greg Dyer as captain while their former leader, Dirk Wellham, renounced his retirement to take up the challenging post of trying to turn Tasmania into a winning combination. Wellham was to have the help of David Gilbert who joined Tasmania from New South Wales, but Lillee, Woolley and Davison had all retired. Greg Shipperd of Western Australia also moved to Tasmania, but Western Australia, so rich in talent, were still fancied to take the Sheffield Shield. Queensland, their nearest challengers for the past two seasons, lost Ian Botham and wicket-keeper Peter Anderson. Anderson had moved to South Australia, whose one loss was Michael Haysman, who had returned to South Africa.

26 October 1988

at Perth

West Indians 143 for 6
Western Australia 144 for 6

Western Australia won by 4 wickets

A boundary by Brayshaw off the last ball of the 30 overs gave Western Australia victory over the tourists. A power strike reduced what was originally a 50-over day/night match to 30 overs. Western Australia needed 20 from the last two overs and 12 from the last, but the West Indian bowling was wayward throughout.

28, 29, 30 and 31 October 1988

at Woolloongabba, Brisbane

New South Wales 291 (S.R. Waugh 118, G.R.J. Matthews 108, C.J. McDermott 5 for 85) and 249 (M.A. Taylor 85)
Queensland 212 (P.E. Cantrell 52) and 329 for 8 (G.M. Ritchie 92, G.S. Trimble 62)

Queensland won by 2 wickets
Queensland 6 pts, New South Wales 0 pts

at Adelaide

Victoria 231 (G.M. Watts 80, P.W. Gladigau 4 for 53, T.B.A. May 4 for 56) and 177
South Australia 287 (A.M.J. Hilditch 65, D.W. Hookes 58, P.C. Nobes 56, P.W. Jackson 6 for 55) and 122 for 2

South Australia won by 8 wickets
South Australia 6 pts, Victoria 0 pts

at Perth

West Indians 213 (C.L. Hooper 83, C.D. Matthews 5 for 84) and 236 (R.A. Harper 67 not out, C.D. Matthews 4 for 75)
Western Australia 247 (T.M. Moody 59, I.R. Bishop 5 for 27, C.E.L. Ambrose 4 for 64) and 206 for 3 (M.R.J. Veletta 81 not out, T.M. Moody 78)

Western Australia won by 7 wickets

Queensland made an emphatic start to their bid for the Sheffield Shield when they gained a thrilling victory over New South Wales after trailing by 79 on the first innings. New South Wales were 29 for 4, but were rallied by Steve Waugh and Greg Matthews who added 195. Peter Taylor with 34 was the only other visiting batsman to reach double figures. The Queensland innings, too, was uneven, with Barsby and debutant Peter Cantrell giving the side a sound start before three wickets fell for 12 runs. Healy's 44 not out boosted the lower order. Left-handed opener Mark Taylor seemed to have put New South Wales in an impregnable position as Queensland were left to make 329 to win. At 117 for 4, they looked beaten, but Ritchie and Trimble added 134 in 115 minutes. From the last 20 overs, 100 were needed, and the winning hit came when Tazelaar hit Lawson over point with two balls of the match remaining.

Victoria were 100 for 0 at lunch on the opening day at Adelaide, but Gladigau and May brought about a collapse. In spite of a career-best bowling performance by left-arm spinner Paul Jackson, South Australia took a first-innings lead of 46. Hookes hit Jackson for 14 in one over, but Jackson had his revenge when he caught and bowled Hookes and finished with a remarkable 6 for 55. Victoria contributed to their own downfall with three run outs in their second innings, and the home state moved to a comfortable victory.

Western Australia gave Australian cricket another boost when they beat the West Indian tourists for the second time in five days. Put in to bat, the West Indians struggled against Chris Matthews on a doubtful wicket. They were 72 for 6, and were saved from total embarrassment only by Carl Hooper's fluent innings. In contrast, the state side gave a gritty batting display after being 44 for 3. Ambrose and Bishop were most impressive, but Western Australia took a lead of 34. Matthews sent back Haynes without a run scored at the end of the second day, and he quickly claimed Richardson and Arthurton on the third morning. Harper revived West Indies with some powerful hitting, but Western Australia were left to make 203 in 65 overs. Veletta and Moody put on 132 for the second wicket and victory came with 4.2 overs to spare.

4, 5, 6 and 7 November 1988

at Woolloongabba, Brisbane

Tasmania 405 (D.M. Wellham 92, R.E. Soule 80 not out, G. Shipperd 53, D. Tazelaar 4 for 117)
Queensland 406 for 7 (S.G. Law 179, A.R. Border 52)

Match drawn
Queensland 2 pts, Tasmania 0 pts

at Sydney

Victoria 175 and 331 for 7 dec (G.M. Watts 135, J.D. Siddons 63, A.I.C. Dodemaide 54 not out)
New South Wales 173 (G.C. Dyer 69, S.P. O'Donnell 6 for 54, A.I.C. Dodemaide 4 for 48) and 312 for 7 (M.A. Taylor 73, T.H. Bayliss 70 not out)

Match drawn
Victoria 2 pts, New South Wales 0 pts

at Adelaide

West Indians 593 for 8 dec (C.G. Greenidge 213, I.V.A. Richards 136, D.L. Haynes 79, P.R. Sleep 4 for 207)
South Australia 163 and 410 (P.C. Nobes 95, A.M.J. Hilditch 64, C.L. Hooper 4 for 163)

West Indians won by an innings and 20 runs

No play on the third day in Brisbane meant that Queensland and Tasmania could contest only first-innings points. Three Tasmanian debutants, Wellham, Shipperd and Gilbert, 3 for 146, all performed well, and Soule hit a career best in an even batting display which was boosted by Soule's last-wicket stand of 116 with Greg Campbell, who hit a career-best 41. Stuart Law, in his second first-class match, dominated the Queensland innings. He and Border added 143 for the fourth wicket, and Law, a 20-year-old right-handed batsman, batted 417 minutes and hit a six and 17 fours in his 179.

Having chosen to bat first, Victoria gave a poor display in Sydney, but Simon O'Donnell produced the best bowling performance of his career to bring them back into the game. Four wickets fell with the score at 37, three of them, the Waugh twins and Smith, in one over to O'Donnell. At 71 for 8, New South Wales faced humiliation, but Greg Dyer and Geoff Lawson added 87. Victoria still claimed first-innings points and built on their position when Watts and Whatmore began their second innings with a stand of 117. Gary Watts went on to hit the fourth hundred of his career, and O'Donnell declared early on the last day. After Dyson had been forced to retire hurt at two, Taylor and Mark Waugh gave New South Wales a spirited chance of victory with another 106 runs before they were separated, but a mid-innings collapse against debutant off-spinner Mark Osborne halted their advance, and a fine game ended in a draw.

ABOVE: *Geoff Marsh (George Herringshaw)*

RIGHT: *. . . and Mike Veletta shared two opening stands of more than 300 for Western Australia within five days at the beginning of November 1988. (Allsport)*

West Indians came back to form with the second highest score a West Indian side has ever made in Australia. Gordon Greenidge reached his first century in Australia and went on to make 213. Viv Richards hit his 99th first-class hundred. Greenidge and Haynes put on 169 for the first wicket, and Greenidge and Richards 169 for the fourth. South Australia were forced to follow-on, but they gave a brave showing in their second innings, with Paul Nobes hitting 95 in 188 minutes in what was his fourth first-class innings.

Kemplast-Kallis Cup
WESTERN AUSTRALIA v. TAMIL NADU

An interesting challenge match between the Sheffield Shield and Ranji Trophy holders resulted in an over-whelming victory for the Australian champions. Vasude-van asked Western Australia to bat when he won the toss and must have regretted his decision when the home side ended the first day on 400 for 1. Geoff Marsh and Mike Veletta put on 374 for the first wicket, which was a Western Australia record for any wicket. Marsh reached the first double century of his career.

Wood declared early on the second morning, and Tamil Nadu were 25 for 1 in their second innings by the end of

the day. Matthews again showed fine form and was well supported by left-arm pace bowler Alan Mullally who, in the second innings, returned the best figures of his brief career. Only Venkataraman Sivaramakrishnan batted with any authority in what was a most disappointing display by the Indians.

As the match ended a day early, a one-day limited-over game was played on the scheduled fourth day, and this was again won by Western Australia.

11, 12, 13 and 14 November 1988

at St Kilda, Melbourne

Victoria 103 (D. Tazelaar 5 for 25, J.N. Maguire 4 for 21) and 281 (D.F. Whatmore 90, D. Tazelaar 5 for 55)
Queensland 260 (T.J. Barsby 92, A.R. Border 57, M.G. Hughes 7 for 81) and 125 for 6 (T.J. Barsby 55)

Queensland won by 4 wickets
Queensland 6 pts, Victoria 0 pts

at Bellerive Oval, Hobart

Tasmania 213 and 108 for 1 (D.C. Boon 61 not out)
Western Australia 502 for 2 dec (G.R. Marsh 223, M.R.J. Veletta 157, T.M. Moody 112 not out)

Match drawn
Western Australia 2 pts, Tasmania 0 pts

KEMPLAST-KALLIS CUP – WESTERN AUSTRALIA v. TAMIL NADU
4, 5 and 7 November 1988 at WACA Ground, Perth

WESTERN AUSTRALIA

	FIRST INNINGS	
G.R. Marsh	c L. Sivaramakrishnan, b Arun	209
M.R.J. Veletta	not out	166
C.D. Matthews	c Raman, b Venkatarama	50
K.H. MacLeay	not out	0
G.M. Wood†		
T.M. Moody		
W.S. Andrews		
T.J. Zoehrer*		
T.G. Hogan		
A.D. Mullally		
T.M. Alderman		
Extras	b 1, lb 10, nb 2	13
	(for 2 wkts, dec)	438

TAMIL NADU

	FIRST INNINGS		SECOND INNINGS	
V. Chandrasekhar	c Matthews, b Mullally	6	c Wood, b MacLeay	9
B. Arun	b Matthews	24	c Moody, b Matthews	21
W.V. Raman	c Zoehrer, b Alderman	0	(4) lbw, b Mullally	21
P.C. Prakash	c Alderman, b Mullally	37	(5) lbw, b Mullally	7
V. Sivaramakrishnan	c Veletta, b Matthews	19	(6) c Alderman, b MacLeay	75
Robin Singh	b Mullally	30	(7) c Mullally, b Alderman	26
L. Sivaramakrishnan	c Zoehrer, b Hogan	9	(8) run out	7
D. Girish*	c Hogan, b Matthews	14	(9) not out	14
M. Venkatarama	c Marsh, b Matthews	2	(10) c Hogan, b Mullally	2
D. Vasu	not out	5	(3) b Moody	34
S. Vasudevan†	st Zoehrer, b Hogan	1	c Zoehrer, b Mullally	0
Extras	lb 8, nb 4	12	b 4, lb 2, nb 6	12
		159		228

	O	M	R	W
Arun	18	2	75	1
Vasu	15	2	58	–
Vasudevan	23	4	80	–
Robin Singh	4	1	19	–
L. Sivaramakrishnan	3	–	13	–
Venkatarama	26	3	116	1
Raman	12	–	66	–

	O	M	R	W	O	M	R	W
Mullally	18	7	44	3	22	6	71	4
Alderman	11	3	28	1	17	11	25	1
Matthews	18	4	55	4	11	–	40	1
MacLeay	11	6	12	–	14	7	19	2
Hogan	13.1	9	12	2	18	5	56	–
Moody					5	2	11	1

FALL OF WICKETS
1–374, 2–437

FALL OF WICKETS
1–6, 2–6, 3–44, 4–70, 5–99, 6–112, 7–133, 8–135, 9–158
1–10, 2–34, 3–63, 4–72, 5–147, 6–189, 7–204, 8–220, 9–228

Umpires: G.J. Bibby & R.J. Evans

Western Australia won by an innings and 51 runs

Dirk Wellham led Tasmania in a most inspirational manner. (Allsport)

at Sydney

New South Wales 401 for 8 dec (M.A. Taylor 82, J. Dyson 79, S.B. Smith 63, P.L. Taylor 50 not out) and 261 for 1 dec (M.E. Waugh 103 not out, J. Dyson 100 not out)
West Indians 329 (I.V.A. Richards 101, G.F. Lawson 5 for 69) and 156 for 4 (K.L.T. Arthurton 57 not out, D.L. Haynes 52)

Match drawn

In miserable conditions at St Kilda, Queensland swept to their second Shield victory of the season and moved to the top of the embryo table. Left-arm pace bowler Dirk Tazelaar gave further indication that he was ready for Test selection by routing Victoria on the opening day when he was ably supported by Maguire. Trevor 'Tank' Barsby, holding the opening spot because of Kerr's injury, played two excellent innings in the game, and his 92 on the first and second day took Queensland to a strong position which Tazelaar saw that they did not relinquish. What-more played a brave innings for Victoria, but Queensland moved to a comfortable win after a slight scare when they slipped from 73 for 1 to 106 for 6. This fright was brought about by Mervyn Hughes who returned a career best in the first innings, 7 for 81, and turned it into a best match analysis with 3 for 40 in the second innings.

Geoff Marsh and Mike Veletta followed their opening stand of 374 against Tamil Nadu with a stand of 310 against Tasmania. Marsh reached the highest score of his career in just over eight hours with a six and 22 fours. It was his second double century in successive innings. Veletta's 157 came off 343 balls, and Tom Moody hit 5 sixes and 8 fours in his 112 not out. Heavy rain ruled out play on the last day and frustrated Western Australia's bid for victory.

New South Wales ran to a good score against the West

BELOW: *New South Wales' skipper Greg Dyer congratulates Viv Richards on reaching his 100th hundred. Dyer was later to lose the captaincy of the state side to Geoff Lawson. (Allsport)*

BELOW RIGHT: *Boon leg before wicket to Marshall for 10, and West Indies take a quick grip on the match. (David Cannon/Allsport)*

Indian tourists, and there were exciting centuries from Mark Waugh and Dyson on the last day, but the highlight of the match at Sydney was Viv Richards' 100th hundred. He hit a six and 15 fours and faced 175 deliveries to become the 22nd batsman to reach 100 hundreds. Only Bradman, Hutton, Compton and Boycott reached the mark in fewer innings than Richards' 658.

18, 19, 20 and 21 November 1988

at Bellerive Oval, Hobart

South Australia 382 (P.R. Sleep 100, A.K. Zesers 80) and 19 for 1
Tasmania 312 (G.A. Hughes 126, D.M. Wellham 67, P.R. Sleep 4 for 109)

Match drawn
South Australia 2 pts, Tasmania 0 pts

The tedium of the batting condemned this match to a draw. Sleep and Zesers put on 171 for South Australia's eighth wicket, but the first day brought only 200 runs and the second only 194. Hughes hit his second Shield century, but Zesers was injured and unable to bowl. All-rounder Joe Scuderi from the Australian Cricket Academy made his first-class debut for South Australia and took 3 for 60 in 43 overs.

First Test Match
AUSTRALIA v. WEST INDIES

Australia remained faithful to the players who had toured Pakistan. Chris Matthews, who replaced the injured Bruce Reid, was the only member of the side who had not been in the party for Pakistan. Mike Veletta was preferred to Dean Jones who was badly out of form.

Choosing to bat first on a greenish wicket, Australia were soon struggling against the West Indian pacemen. Patterson retired from the attack with a knee injury, but Marshall, Ambrose and Walsh posed sufficient problems to have Australia in total disarray, and it was only some spirited batting by Healy and Dodemaide at the close of

Ambrose, the scourge of Australia all season, has Wood caught by Greenidge. (David Cannon/Allsport)

FIRST TEST MATCH – AUSTRALIA *v.* WEST INDIES
18, 19, 20 and 21 November 1988 at Woolloongabba, Brisbane

AUSTRALIA

	FIRST INNINGS		SECOND INNINGS	
G.R. Marsh	c Logie, b Ambrose	27	(2) lbw, b Ambrose	2
D.C. Boon	lbw, b Marshall	10	(1) c Dujon, b Marshall	12
M.R.J. Veletta	b Hooper	37	c Hooper, b Walsh	10
G.M. Wood	c Greenidge, b Ambrose	6	(5) lbw, b Walsh	0
A.R. Border†	c Dujon, b Ambrose	4	(6) c Haynes, b Ambrose	41
S.R. Waugh	lbw, b Marshall	4	(4) c Haynes, b Marshall	90
I.A. Healy*	c Logie, b Walsh	27	c Ambrose, b Marshall	28
A.I.C. Dodemaide	c Richards, b Walsh	22	c Richards, b Marshall	7
C.J. McDermott	c Logie, b Walsh	2	not out	32
C.D. Matthews	c Dujon, b Walsh	1	c sub (Arthurton), b Walsh	32
T.B.A. May	not out	4	c Hooper, b Ambrose	5
Extras	b 1, lb 5, w 1, nb 16	23	b 4, lb 5, nb 21	30
		167		289

	O	M	R	W	O	M	R	W
Marshall	18	3	39	2	26	2	92	4
Patterson	3.1	1	5	–				
Ambrose	16.5	5	30	3	26.1	5	78	3
Walsh	18.3	3	62	4	19	3	61	3
Hooper	12	2	24	1	4	–	23	–
Richards	1	–	1	–	11	4	26	–

FALL OF WICKETS
1–19, 2–52, 3–64, 4–76, 5–86, 6–126, 7–138, 8–140, 9–150
1–14, 2–16, 3–65, 4–65, 5–157, 6–199, 7–212, 8–212, 9–270

WEST INDIES

	FIRST INNINGS		SECOND INNINGS	
C.G. Greenidge	b May	80	c Healy, b Dodemaide	16
D.L. Haynes	c Healy, b Waugh	40	not out	30
R.B. Richardson	lbw, b Dodemaide	81	not out	7
C.L. Hooper	c Border, b Waugh	1		
I.V.A. Richards†	c McDermott, b May	68		
A.L. Logie	c Border, b May	19		
P.J.L. Dujon*	c May, b McDermott	27		
M.D. Marshall	c Border, b McDermott	11		
C.E.L. Ambrose	not out	19		
C.A. Walsh	lbw, b McDermott	0		
B.P. Patterson	lbw, b Dodemaide	0		
Extras	b 5, lb 9, w 6, nb 28	48	lb 4, w 3, nb 3	10
		394	(for 1 wkt)	63

	O	M	R	W	O	M	R	W
McDermott	28	3	99	3	4	–	12	–
Matthews	21	3	62	–	3.5	1	18	–
Dodemaide	16.4	2	60	2	5.2	1	15	1
May	29	6	90	3				
Waugh	18	2	61	2	6	–	14	–
Border	1	–	8	–				

FALL OF WICKETS
1–135, 2–156, 3–162, 4–270, 5–307, 6–359, 7–361, 8–389, 9–393
1–43

Umpires: A.R. Crafter & P.J. McConnell

West Indies won by 9 wickets

the innings which lifted Australia as high as 167. The innings ended when Dodemaide attempted to hook Walsh and gave Richards a simple running catch. It was his 100th catch in Test cricket in his 100th Test match.

In 13 overs before the end of the first day, Greenidge and Haynes put on 39. They extended their stand to 135 on the second day, by the end of which West Indies were 366 for 7 and in total command. They had been well served, not only by the openers but by Richardson, who played a studious innings, and Richards, who hit 68 in 78 minutes. The pair added 108 in 25 overs.

The Australian cause was not advanced by some poor catching and some wretchedly wayward bowling. Matthews had a nightmare match. He was the leading bowler in Australia in 1987–8 and had started the current campaign in top form, but his Test match bowling was without control, wides, no-balls and deliveries of assorted length being splayed in all directions. He limped out of the match with an injured side in the second innings after three more wides and another no-ball, and there were many who doubted that he would be seen again in Test cricket.

The West Indian innings was over within an hour on the third morning, but Border added to his woes by breaking the forefinger of his right hand in catching Marshall. He had entered the match with a chipped right thumb.

LEFT: *Hat-trick hero Courtney Walsh. (Dan Smith/Allsport)*

BELOW: *Steve Waugh in his brave but vain attempt to save Australia. (Allsport)*

Off-spinner May could draw some comfort from his performance, and Craig McDermott, like May, took three wickets, but none of the Australian pace bowlers could make the ball rear in the way that Ambrose had done to the discomfort of the Australian batsmen.

Marsh and Boon had proved a dependable opening pair for 18 months, and hopes were rested on them, but with only 16 scored, both were out, and Australia faced defeat in three days. Veletta and Steve Waugh, who had come in above the injured Border, took the score to 65 at which point Walsh was brought into the attack. Veletta pulled his first delivery into the hands of mid-on, and the next had Graeme Wood leg-before, so giving the Jamaican fast bowler a hat-trick, for he had dismissed Dodemaide with the last ball of the first innings.

Border showed great pluck and resilience and helped Waugh to add 92. Ambrose returned and again showed the ability to make the ball rear uncomfortably to have Border taken at backward short-leg, and Waugh, in sight of his first Test century, hit Marshall straight to cover. The day ended with Australia 200 for 6, and Marshall quickly made this 212 for 8 on the fourth morning. McDermott and Matthews offered some rustic aggression, which ensured that West Indies would have to bat again.

There was more nightmare for Matthews, followed by injury, a wicket for Dodemaide, and West Indies swept to victory in 81 minutes with a day and a half to spare. Like England a few months earlier, Australia had suffered a chastening experience.

Greg Campbell, 5 for 44 for Tasmania against New South Wales, 25 November. He finished his first full season with 36 wickets and won a place on the trip to England. (David Munden)

25, 26, 27 and 28 November 1988

at Adelaide

Western Australia 268 (M.R.J. Veletta 69, T.B.A. May 5 for 92) and 131 (J.C. Scuderi 5 for 51, T.B.A. May 4 for 49)
South Australia 325 (P.C. Nobes 79, P.W. Anderson 52 not out) and 75 for 7 (T.M. Alderman 5 for 29)

South Australia won by 3 wickets
South Australia 6 pts, Western Australia 0 pts

at Devonport

New South Wales 228 (S.B. Smith 77, G.D. Campbell 5 for 44) and 157 for 1 (M.E. Waugh 100 not out, J. Dyson 53 not out)
Tasmania 360 (R.E. Soule 99, D.C. Boon 98, B.A. Cruse 64, G.A. Hughes 50)

Match drawn
Tasmania 2 pts, New South Wales 0 pts

at MCG, Melbourne

Victoria 385 (W.N. Phillips 111, M. Osborne 58 not out, R.A. Harper 5 for 78)
West Indians 328 (A.L. Logie 134, C.L. Hooper 64)

Match drawn

South Australia beat Western Australia for the first time since January 1985, in an enthralling match at Adelaide. Put in to bat, Western Australia were held together by the stolid Veletta, but May's off-spin troubled all batsmen, and the visitors were all out early on the second morning. The home state batted consistently to take a first-innings lead of 57. Nobes again impressed, and Anderson, who kept wicket splendidly, batted with great resource, cajoling 102 runs from the last four wickets. Scuderi, in his second match, had also batted well, and he now joined with May on the third day to rout the visitors. Carew, like Scuderi a Queenslander with the Cricket Academy, made his first appearance for South Australia, who tried to force victory on the third day, but needed 13 minutes, 2.5 overs, of the fourth.

Tasmania took their first points of the season when, having put New South Wales in to bat, they took first-innings lead in a high scoring match at Devonport. Greg Campbell produced the best bowling performance of his career and joined with Faulkner and Gilbert to dismiss New South Wales after much of the first day had been lost. Boon and Hughes began Tasmania's reply with a stand of 79, but the highlight of the innings was a seventh-wicket stand of 110 between Cruse and Soule, both of whom hit their highest scores. Soule was run out by Dyson in going for the run that would have brought him his maiden century. Mark Waugh and Dyson shared an unbroken second-wicket stand of 154 when New South Wales batted again, Waugh hitting the sixth century of his career.

Wayne Phillips, a young, fair-haired, right-handed batsman, hit 111 against the West Indians on the occasion of his first-class debut. Another young player, Osborne, made the highest score of his brief career, and Hooper and Logie added 169 after the tourists had been 4 for 3, but the match was ruined by rain.

2, 3, 4 and 5 December 1988

at Newcastle Sports Ground

New South Wales 269 (M.E. Waugh 69, T.M. Alderman 4 for 42) and 279 for 7 dec (M.A. Taylor 83, J. Dyson 78)
Western Australia 164 and 250 (W.S. Andrews 69)

New South Wales won by 134 runs
New South Wales 6 pts, Western Australia 0 pts

A second defeat for Western Australia left them surprisingly adrift at the bottom of the Sheffield Shield table. Put in to bat, New South Wales were again well served by Mark Waugh, and there were useful contributions from Bayliss and Greg Matthews. Western Australia collapsed before a varied attack, left-arm paceman Whitney, medium-pacer Jones, 3 for 18, the best figures of his career, and off-spinner Taylor each took three wickets, and New South Wales led by 105 runs. Dyson and Mark Taylor consolidated the advantage with an opening stand of 130. Alderman again bowled well, and Zoehrer took four catches, but Dyer was able to declare with more than an hour of the third day left, and debutant medium-pace bowler Stobo captured the wicket of Gonnella before the close. Reid and Mullally hit the highest scores of their careers and added 46 for the last wicket, but New South Wales won with an hour to spare.

Second Test Match
AUSTRALIA v. WEST INDIES

West Indies were unchanged from the side that won the first Test while Australia recalled Geoff Lawson for the injured Matthews and preferred Mervyn Hughes to Craig McDermott. Bruce Reid was not considered to be fit enough for a five-day Test.

Border won the toss and asked West Indies to bat, but his efforts to claim quick wickets were nullified by missed

Desmond Haynes. The delight of a man who scored runs against Australia consistently in all forms of cricket.

chances. Lawson had three catches put down off his bowling, and each of the first five West Indian batsmen benefited from being dropped. Hughes did trap Haynes leg-before with the score on 16, but the missed chances allowed West Indies to finish the first day on 280 for 4.

Richards duly completed his 23rd Test century off the third ball of the second day and then launched a violent attack on the bowling. He and Logie, who again just missed his century, took their stand to 163, and Richards' 146 came off 150 balls and included 3 sixes and 21 fours. The last five wickets went down for 28 runs, and Hughes, who had bowled with tireless aggression, ended the innings when he had Ambrose caught with the last ball of his 36th over and Patterson caught off the first ball of his 37th.

Boon and Marsh gave Australia a solid start, and although Marsh fell to Walsh, they ended the day happily on 119 for 1. They slumped to 167 for 4 next morning before Wood, who had entered the game under enormous pressure, his place in jeopardy, played a positive innings and, in conjunction with Waugh, added 200 to raise Australian hopes.

Wood batted for four hours for his ninth Test hundred

Australian folk hero Mervyn Hughes, 13 wickets in the second Test, including the hat trick, but he still finished on the losing side. (David Cannon/Allsport)

before falling to Ambrose, and, disappointingly, Waugh soon followed. It was Ambrose who moved the game back in West Indies' favour. He produced a spell of 3 for 10 which gave him his first five-wicket haul in a Test innings and reduced Australia to 395 for 8. Lawson lost sight of the second ball he received from Ambrose, which rose sharply and broke his jaw. He also fell on his wicket, but he was ruled 'retired hurt' and carried from the field on a stretcher.

Border declared, leaving West Indies four overs to negotiate. In the absence of Lawson, Hughes took first over and had Greenidge leg-before with his first ball, so emulating Walsh's performance in the first Test by completing the hat trick. Hughes was to continue to bowl manfully, but with little support of quality. Haynes reached his tenth Test hundred. Hooper, batting with a runner, hit 2 sixes and 6 fours, and West Indies forged further ahead.

They closed the fourth day on 331 for 8 and rather surprisingly batted on for 20 minutes on the last morning, during which time Hughes took his eighth wicket, his 13th in the match, both being the best performances of his career.

Australia were set the impossible task of scoring 404 to win. Boon, Marsh and Veletta were out before lunch so that Australia's chances of survival lessened. Waugh started with three boundaries, but was caught at slip. Wood

also started aggressively, but he was taken at square-leg. Border had gone at 93, and at 140 for 6, Lawson injured, Australia still had nearly 50 overs to bat in order to save the game. Healy, with his first Test fifty, and Dodemaide showed spirit, but there were still 25 overs remaining when Ambrose had Hughes taken at short-leg and ended the match.

1 December 1988

at Cairns

Pakistanis 300 for 7 (Saleem Malik 126, Saeed Anwar 59)
North Queensland 204 for 7 (W. London 52)

Pakistanis won by 96 runs

3 December 1988

at Mackay

Queensland 196 for 9 (T.J. Barsby 81)
Pakistanis 192 (Rameez Raja 75)

Queensland won by 4 runs

4 December 1988

at Mackay

Pakistanis 229 for 8 (Moin-ul-Atiq 57)
Queensland 192 for 9 (G.M. Ritchie 66)

SECOND TEST MATCH – AUSTRALIA v. WEST INDIES
2, 3, 4, 5 and 6 December 1988 at WACA Ground, Perth

WEST INDIES

	FIRST INNINGS		SECOND INNINGS	
C.G. Greenidge	b Lawson	40	lbw, b Hughes	0
D.L. Haynes	lbw, b Hughes	11	c Healy, b Hughes	100
R.B. Richardson	c Boon, b Hughes	66	c Healy, b Hughes	48
C.L. Hooper	c Boon, b Lawson	26	c Dodemaide, b Hughes	64
I.V.A. Richards†	c Dodemaide, b Lawson	146	lbw, b Hughes	5
A.L. Logie	c Waugh, b May	93	b Hughes	30
P.J.L. Dujon*	c Veletta, b May	32	c Dodemaide, b Hughes	9
M.D. Marshall	c Veletta, b Hughes	4	c Healy, b Dodemaide	23
C.E.L. Ambrose	c Healy, b Hughes	8	c Wood, b Hughes	15
C.A. Walsh	not out	0	not out	17
B.P. Patterson	c Dodemaide, b Hughes	1	not out	6
Extras	b 1, lb 12, nb 9	22	b 14, lb 9, nb 9	32
		449	(for 9 wkts, dec)	349

	O	M	R	W	O	M	R	W
Lawson	32	7	97	3				
Hughes	36.1	7	130	5	37	9	87	8
Dodemaide	17	1	79	–	24	2	101	1
Waugh	28	3	90	–	23	1	70	–
May	10	3	40	2	14	1	68	–

FALL OF WICKETS
1–16, 2–82, 3–126, 4–180, 5–343, 6–421, 7–426, 8–440, 9–448
1–0, 2–103, 3–216, 4–236, 5–246, 6–259, 7–300, 8–310, 9–341

AUSTRALIA

	FIRST INNINGS		SECOND INNINGS	
G.R. Marsh	c Richardson, b Walsh	30	(2) c Logie, b Marshall	6
D.C. Boon	c Logie, b Ambrose	80	(1) b Patterson	4
M.R.J. Veletta	run out	11	c Dujon, b Marshall	13
G.M. Wood	c Richardson, b Ambrose	111	c Greenidge, b Walsh	42
A.R. Border†	c Dujon, b Ambrose	6	b Hooper	26
S.R. Waugh	c Dujon, b Ambrose	91	c Hooper, b Patterson	26
I.A. Healy*	lbw, b Marshall	8	c Logie, b Ambrose	52
A.I.C. Dodemaide	not out	7	lbw, b Ambrose	11
T.B.A. May	c Richards, b Ambrose	2	not out	8
G.F. Lawson	retired hurt	0	absent injured	–
M.G. Hughes			(10) c Logie, b Ambrose	0
Extras	b 6, lb 8, nb 35	49	b 5, lb 4, nb 37	46
	(for 8 wkts, dec)	395		234

	O	M	R	W	O	M	R	W
Marshall	23	3	84	1	12	–	50	2
Patterson	16	1	95	–	14	2	58	2
Walsh	19	3	58	1	15	1	46	1
Ambrose	23.3	3	72	5	17	1	66	3
Richards	14	–	43	–				
Hooper	5	–	29	–	5	2	5	1

FALL OF WICKETS
1–83, 2–139, 3–152, 4–167, 5–367, 6–374, 7–388, 8–395
1–14, 2–14, 3–46, 4–93, 5–138, 6–140, 7–190, 8–232, 9–234

Umpires: R.C. Bailhache & T.A. Prue

West Indies won by 169 runs

Pakistanis won by 37 runs

The Pakistanis played three country games in Queensland as part of their preparation for the Benson & Hedges World Series Cup.

8 December 1988

at Canberra

Prime Minister's XI v. West Indians
Match abandoned

10, 11, 12 and 13 December 1988

at Woolloongabba, Brisbane

Queensland 351 (G.M. Ritchie 101, P.J. Drinnen 74, T.J. Barsby 53, J.C. Scuderi 5 for 66)
South Australia 201 and 141 for 2 (P.C. Nobes 81 not out)

Match drawn
Queensland 2 pts, South Australia 0 pts

at MCG, Melbourne

Tasmania 428 for 9 dec (G. Shipperd 155 not out, R.E. Soule 57, R.C.A.M. McCarthy 4 for 84) and 94 for 0
Victoria 397 (D.F. Whatmore 69, R.C.A.M. McCarthy 61, S.P. O'Donnell 60)

Match drawn
Tasmania 2 pts, Victoria 0 pts

On the eve of being swamped by the one-day international carnival, the Sheffield Shield produced two matches of great tedium. At Brisbane, Greg Ritchie, leading Queens-

Steve Waugh in action in the day/night match, Australia v. West Indies at Melbourne, 13 December 1988. His 40 brought his side close to victory, but West Indies won by one run. (David Cannon/Allsport)

land, hit his first century of the season, but it was debutant wicket-keeper Peter Drinnen who captured the attention. Drinnen, from the Cricket Academy, faced 371 balls and batted for 421 minutes for his 74. It is believed to be the slowest fifty in the history of the Sheffield Shield. The Queensland innings lasted for 686 minutes, runs coming at less than two an over, and although South Australia failed by one run to avoid the follow-on, a draw always seemed inevitable.

The match at Melbourne was almost as slow. Tasmania took 663 minutes, 170 overs, to make 428. Shipperd, formerly of Western Australia, batted with a runner for the last 130 runs of his innings, having injured a calf muscle. Tucker, formerly of New South Wales, made his debut for Tasmania and hit a career-best 39. Darren Walker made his debut for Victoria.

Benson and Hedges World Series

First One-Day International
WEST INDIES v. PAKISTAN

The Benson and Hedges World Series opened with an embarrassingly easy win for West Indies over Pakistan. Imran won the toss and asked West Indies to bat first,

BENSON AND HEDGES WORLD SERIES   FIRST ONE-DAY INTERNATIONAL – WEST INDIES v. PAKISTAN
10 December 1988 at Adelaide Oval

WEST INDIES			
C.G. Greenidge	b Abdul Qadir		70
D.L. Haynes	c Aaqib Javed, b Imran Khan		111
R.B. Richardson	c Saleem Yousuf, b Aaqib Javed		1
I.V.A. Richards†	lbw, b Abdul Qadir		1
C.L. Hooper	c Wasim Akram, b Tauseef		15
A.L. Logie	c Saleem Yousuf, b Tauseef		14
M.D. Marshall	b Imran Khan		20
W.K.M. Benjamin	lbw, b Wasim Akram		0
D. Williams*	c Saleem Yousuf, b Abdul Qadir		5
C.E.L. Ambrose	not out		0
C.A. Walsh	not out		1
Extras	b 7, lb 15, w 2, nb 7		31
(47 overs)	(for 9 wkts)		269

	O	M	R	W
Imran Khan	10	–	47	2
Wasim Akram	10	–	45	1
Aaqib Javed	9	–	49	1
Tauseef Ahmed	9	–	72	2
Abdul Qadir	9	–	34	3

FALL OF WICKETS
1–169, 2–174, 3–181, 4–217, 5–218, 6–240, 7–241, 8–262, 9–263

PAKISTAN			
Rameez Raja	not out		69
Sajid Ali	c Greenidge, b Marshall		2
Saleem Malik	b Marshall		7
Javed Miandad	c Williams, b Walsh		38
Ijaz Ahmed	c Williams, b Marshall		26
Wasim Akram	b Marshall		9
Imran Khan†	c Richards, b Benjamin		8
Saleem Yousuf*	c Richards, b Ambrose		6
Abdul Qadir	not out		4
Tauseef Ahmed			
Aaqib Javed			
Extras	lb 5, w 2, nb 4		11
(47 overs)	(for 7 wkts)		180

	O	M	R	W
Marshall	10	1	34	4
Ambrose	8	2	22	1
Benjamin	9	–	30	1
Walsh	10	–	41	1
Richards	9	–	43	–
Hooper	1	–	5	–

FALL OF WICKETS
1–3, 2–17, 3–81, 4–129, 5–141, 6–152, 7–166

Umpires: A.R. Crafter & R.J. Evans

Man of the Match: D.L. Haynes

West Indies won by 89 runs

presumably hoping that he and his pace bowlers would be able to exploit the cloudy conditions. Imran's optimism proved to be unfounded as Haynes and Greenidge began the West Indian innings with a stand of 169 off 158 balls.

Abdul Qadir, the tidiest of the Pakistan bowlers, broke the stand when he bowled Greenidge in his third over, and a minor collapse followed. Richardson was caught behind off the 16-year-old pace bowler Aaqib Javed, who was making his international debut and who performed creditably, but Haynes went on to reach his 11th hundred in limited-over internationals. He hit 11 fours and 2 sixes. In contrast, Rameez Raja, who batted throughout Pakistan's 47 overs, hit only one boundary, and it proved to be the only boundary of a miserable Pakistan innings which was a mixture of unprofitable defence and wild slogs.

Javed and Saleem Malik were going sweetly did they look like an international side. Javed was hit on the foot and then bowled by McDermott, and there was some flourish from Ijaz and Imran after Saleem Malik had been run out by Marsh, but the score of 177 never seemed likely to give Australia problems. So it proved.

Marsh and Boon began with a competent stand, and Dean Jones, recalled to the side after his loss of form had cost him his place, batted well after an uncertain start. He and Marsh shared an unbeaten second wicket stand of 126, which took their side to victory.

Australia gave one-day international debuts to Merv Hughes and Mark Waugh, who joined his twin brother Steve in the side. Hughes took the individual award in his first match.

Benson and Hedges World Series

Second One-Day International
AUSTRALIA v. PAKISTAN

No doubt relieved to be free from the batterings of the West Indian pace bowlers, Australia added to Pakistan's unhappy weekend with a substantial victory which came with 5.2 overs and nine wickets to spare. Imran again won the toss and chose to bat on this occasion, but his batsmen looked ill-prepared for the encounter, and only when

Benson and Hedges World Series

Third One-Day International
AUSTRALIA v. WEST INDIES

The first day/night match in the series was a most thrilling affair. The game began in a familiar pattern as Haynes and Greenidge put on 90 in 19 overs after Richards had won the toss, but some excellent slow bowling by Peter Taylor on a slow pitch brought Australia back into the match. Taylor's off-spin accounted for Greenidge, caught on the

BENSON AND HEDGES WORLD SERIES SECOND ONE-DAY INTERNATIONAL – AUSTRALIA v. PAKISTAN
11 December 1988 at Adelaide Oval

PAKISTAN			
Rameez Raja	b Hughes	3
Sajid Ali	b McDermott	15
Saleem Yousuf*	run out	12
Javed Miandad	b McDermott	18
Saleem Malik	run out	44
Ijaz Ahmed	b Hughes	37
Imran Khan†	not out	23
Wasim Akram	b Taylor	7
Abdul Qadir	lbw, b Hughes	10
Tauseef Ahmed	b Alderman	1
Aaqib Javed	lbw, b S.R. Waugh	0
Extras	lb 2, w 2, nb 3	7
(45.4 overs)		177

	O	M	R	W
Alderman	9	3	15	1
Hughes	10	1	30	3
McDermott	10	–	51	2
S.R. Waugh	7.4	–	27	1
Taylor	9	–	52	1

FALL OF WICKETS
1–5, 2–30, 3–42, 4–71, 5–114, 6–146, 7–155, 8–174, 9–175

AUSTRALIA		
G.R. Marsh	not out	86
D.C. Boon	run out	27
D.M. Jones	not out	55
M.E. Waugh		
A.R. Border†		
S.R. Waugh		
I.A. Healy*		
C.J. McDermott		
P.L. Taylor		
M.G. Hughes		
T.M. Alderman		
Extras	b 4, lb 3, w 1, nb 2	10
(42.4 overs)	(for 1 wkt)	178

	O	M	R	W
Imran Khan	10	3	33	–
Aaqib Javed	9	–	45	–
Wasim Akram	7	–	22	–
Abdul Qadir	7	–	36	–
Tauseef Ahmed	9	–	31	–
Saleem Malik	0.4	–	4	–

FALL OF WICKET
1–52

Umpires: L.J. King & T.A. Prue

Man of the Match: M.G. Hughes

Australia won by 9 wickets

BENSON AND HEDGES WORLD SERIES THIRD ONE-DAY INTERNATIONAL – AUSTRALIA v. WEST INDIES
13 December 1988 at SCG, Sydney

WEST INDIES		
C.G. Greenidge	c M.E. Waugh, b Taylor	52
D.L. Haynes	c and b Hughes	78
R.B. Richardson	b Taylor	12
I.V.A. Richards†	st Healy, b Taylor	12
C.L. Hooper	c Healy, b Hughes	20
A.L. Logie	c and b Border	8
P.J.L. Dujon*	c Boon, b Border	0
M.D. Marshall	c sub (Wood), b McDermott	17
W.K.M. Benjamin	b Hughes	6
C.E.L. Ambrose	not out	1
C.A. Walsh	b McDermott	2
Extras	lb 8, nb 4	12
(48 overs)		220

	O	M	R	W
Alderman	7	–	30	–
Hughes	10	–	48	3
S.R. Waugh	4	–	15	–
McDermott	7	–	37	2
Taylor	10	–	50	3
Border	10	–	32	2

FALL OF WICKETS
1–90, 2–114, 3–144, 4–182, 5–189, 6–190, 7–199, 8–127, 9–217

AUSTRALIA		
D.C. Boon	b Marshall	71
G.R. Marsh	c Ambrose, b Walsh	19
D.M. Jones	lbw, b Walsh	1
S.R. Waugh	run out	40
M.E. Waugh	b Benjamin	18
A.R. Border†	run out	8
I.A. Healy*	not out	23
P.L. Taylor	c Hooper, b Benjamin	16
C.J. McDermott	c Richards, b Ambrose	6
M.G. Hughes		
T.M. Alderman		
Extras	b 6, lb 6, w 4, nb 1	17
(50 overs)	(for 8 wkts)	219

	O	M	R	W
Walsh	10	–	36	2
Marshall	10	–	40	1
Richards	10	–	46	–
Benjamin	10	1	44	2
Ambrose	10	1	41	1

FALL OF WICKETS
1–50, 2–54, 3–141, 4–144, 5–158, 6–177, 7–207, 8–219

Umpires: P.J. McConnell & R.J. Evans

Man of the Match: D.L. Haynes

West Indies won by 1 run

long-on boundary, Richardson, bowled behind his legs, and Richards, stumped having a wild fling. Border, too, produced a testing spell, relying on slow accuracy rather than on spin, and West Indies were blunted in mid-innings. The Australian cause was helped by some excellent ground fielding and good catching.

Needing 221 to win, Australia were given a good start by Boon and Marsh, but Jones went quickly, and it was left to Steve Waugh to partner the solid Boon and give Australia a glimpse of victory. At 102 for 2 in 30 overs, the game was nicely balanced, and Steve Waugh was beginning to show great authority. Marshall bowled Boon at 141, and Mark Waugh, batting for Australia for the first time, immediately ran out his twin brother. At 158, he accounted for Border in the same way, the Australian captain just failing to beat Logie's throw, but Mark Waugh, in spite of these lapses, still looked a useful player.

Australia needed to score 71 from the last 10 overs, and 41 from the last five. Healy, with his highest score in his brief one-day international career, and Taylor kept Australia's hopes alive, and Ambrose began the last over with the home side needing six to win with three wickets in hand. The first five balls produced only four runs, so accurately and sensibly did Ambrose bowl, so that McDermott had to hit two off the last ball to win the match. Unaccountably, Ambrose produced his first bad ball, a full toss. A mixture of glee and surprise saw McDermott clout the ball hard over the bowler's head, but Richards, who

had positioned himself on the edge of the circle in a spot closer to mid-on than mid-wicket, took the catch, and West Indies were victors by one run.

13 and 14 December 1988

at Adelaide

Pakistanis 336 for 9 (Saleem Yousuf 102, Javed Miandad 57)
Australian Cricket Academy 299 (B. Williams 96, J. Cox 74)

Pakistanis won by 67 runs

Williams and Cox, both of whom were to play Sheffield Shield cricket later in the season, put on 174 for the Academy's first wicket. Saleem Yousuf batted for three hours and hit 13 fours.

Benson and Hedges World Series

Fourth One-Day International
AUSTRALIA v. WEST INDIES

The second day/night match, this time in Melbourne, again ended in favour of West Indies, although this time the issue was not in doubt until the last ball, as it had been at Sydney. Australia began well, the prolific Haynes being dismissed in the 10th over and Richardson in the 12th. Both men fell to Craig McDermott, who cut down his speed to concentrate on accuracy, with good effect. Greenidge was caught off Taylor at 89, but Logie and

---

BENSON AND HEDGES WORLD SERIES   FOURTH ONE-DAY INTERNATIONAL – AUSTRALIA v. WEST INDIES
15 December 1988 at MCG, Melbourne

WEST INDIES				AUSTRALIA			
C.G. Greenidge	c Boon, b Taylor	57		G.R. Marsh	c Hooper, b Ambrose	6
D.L. Haynes	c Alderman, b McDermott	8		D.C. Boon	c Dujon, b Benjamin	20
R.B. Richardson	b McDermott	5		D.M. Jones	lbw, b Richards	43
A.L. Logie	c and b Border	44		S.R. Waugh	run out	54
I.V.A. Richards†	c Healy, b S.R. Waugh	58		M.E. Waugh	b Ambrose	32
C.L. Hooper	c Boon, b S.R. Waugh	17		A.R. Border†	run out	12
P.J.L. Dujon*	c Healy, b S.R. Waugh	3		I.A. Healy*	c Ambrose, b Benjamin	3
M.D. Marshall	b McDermott	19		P.L. Taylor	b Ambrose	4
W.K.M. Benjamin	lbw, b McDermott	0		C.J. McDermott	c Dujon, b Ambrose	2
C.E.L. Ambrose	not out	12		M.G. Hughes	not out	4
C.A. Walsh	run out	1		T.M. Alderman	b Ambrose	0
Extras	lb 5, w 5, nb 2	12		Extras	b 4, lb 7, w 10, nb 1	22
(49.2 overs)		236		(47.2 overs)		202

	O	M	R	W		O	M	R	W
Alderman	7	1	22	–	Marshall	10	–	39	–
Hughes	8	–	39	–	Ambrose	8.2	1	17	5
McDermott	9.2	2	38	4	Walsh	10	–	45	–
S.R. Waugh	10	–	57	3	Benjamin	9	–	35	2
Taylor	10	–	52	1	Richards	10	–	55	1
Border	5	–	23	1					

FALL OF WICKETS
1–33, 2–45, 3–89, 4–162, 5–194, 6–202, 7–203, 8–203, 9–235

FALL OF WICKETS
1–25, 2–53, 3–110, 4–168, 5–184, 6–190, 7–192, 8–197, 9–202

Umpires: R.C. Bailhache & C.D. Timmins

Man of the Match: C.E.L. Ambrose

West Indies won by 34 runs

Richards, more circumspect than usual, began a stand which contained many strokes of delight. They were not parted until the 36th over, by which time they had added 73. Ten overs later, West Indies, thanks to some accurate medium-pace bowling by Steve Waugh, had been reduced to 203 for 8, and the game had swung very much in favour of Australia. The 32 runs which Ambrose and Marshall plundered for the ninth wicket were to prove to be decisive.

Australia began slowly, Boon took 17 overs to score 20, but Jones scampered well, and the Waugh twins showed class and authority. At 168 for 3 in the 40th over, Australia seemed to have the ideal platform for victory. Then Steve Waugh pulled at Richards, survived the appeal for lbw and moved up the wicket. His brother sent him back, but substitute Harper's throw to Dujon was too quick for him. Worse was to follow as Mark Waugh encouraged Border to take a second run to Walsh at deep mid-on, and once again the Australian captain was run out. Mark Waugh was leg before to Ambrose, who now took four wickets for five runs in the space of 10 balls to end the match with indecent haste.

Benson and Hedges World Series

Fifth One-Day International
WEST INDIES v. PAKISTAN

For the third time in a week, Desmond Haynes took the individual award as he notched a record 12th century in limited-over internationals. West Indies owed much to Haynes and Dujon, promoted to number three, who added 145 in 22 overs.

Pakistan suffered early set-backs as Mudassar, Rameez and Saleem Yousuf were dismissed with only 25 scored, but a partnership of 122 in 23 overs between Javed Miandad and Saleem Malik restored Pakistan's pride, even if it could not give them any real hope of victory. Imran hit 37 off 19 balls, taking 15 off Ambrose's last over, but it was merely a gallant dying gesture.

With the first round of matches completed, West Indies already seemed certain of a place in the final, having won all four of their matches. Pakistan, on the other hand, suffered their third defeat in as many matches and looked to have a difficult task if they were to revive their chances of making a serious challenge in the competition.

17, 18, 19 and 20 December 1988

at WACA Ground, Perth

South Australia 128 (K.H. MacLeay 4 for 24) and 104 (T.M. Alderman 5 for 26)
Western Australia 335 for 8 dec (J.A. Brayshaw 81, T.J. Zoehrer 63, T.M. Moody 64, P.W. Gladigau 4 for 78)

Western Australia won by an innings and 103 runs
Western Australia 6 pts, South Australia 0 pts

at Woolloongabba, Brisbane

Queensland 157 for 7 dec (G.M. Ritchie 58 not out)
Victoria 122 (P.E. Cantrell 4 for 52)

BENSON AND HEDGES WORLD SERIES   FIFTH ONE-DAY INTERNATIONAL – PAKISTAN v. WEST INDIES
17 December 1988 at Bellerive Oval, Hobart

WEST INDIES				PAKISTAN			
D.L. Haynes	lbw, b Imran Khan	101		Mudassar Nazar	lbw, b Walsh		12
R.B. Richardson	c Wasim Akram, b Mudassar	8		Rameez Raja	c Logie, b Marshall		3
P.J.L. Dujon*	c and b Wasim Akram	63		Saleem Yousuf*	c sub (Arthurton), b Walsh		9
A.L. Logie	not out	40		Javed Miandad	c Hooper, b Ambrose		62
I.V.A. Richards†	c Tauseef Ahmed, b Imran Khan	10		Saleem Malik	c Logie, b Richards		68
R.A. Harper	not out	0		Ijaz Ahmed	c Harper, b Richards		12
C.L. Hooper				Imran Khan†	c Walsh, b Benjamin		37
M.D. Marshall				Wasim Akram	c Hooper, b Benjamin		17
C.E.L. Ambrose				Abdul Qadir	not out		2
W.K.M. Benjamin				Tauseef Ahmed	not out		0
C.A. Walsh				Aaqib Javed			
Extras	lb 12, w 8, nb 2	22		Extras	lb 4, w 1		5
(43 overs)	(for 4 wkts)	244		(43 overs)	(for 8 wkts)		227

	O	M	R	W		O	M	R	W
Imran Khan	9	1	49	2	Marshall	9	1	31	1
Wasim Akram	9	–	35	1	Ambrose	9	3	46	1
Mudassar Nazar	7	–	36	1	Walsh	8	1	23	2
Aaqib Javed	8	–	48	–	Benjamin	9	1	52	2
Abdul Qadir	6	–	36	–	Richards	6	–	48	2
Tauseef Ahmed	4	–	28	–	Harper	2	–	23	–

FALL OF WICKETS
1–28, 2–173, 3–219, 4–238

FALL OF WICKETS
1–9, 2–23, 3–25, 4–147, 5–170, 6–170, 7–225, 8–226

Umpires: S.G. Randell & C.D. Timmins

Man of the Match: D.L. Haynes

West Indies won by 17 runs

Match drawn
Queensland 2 pts, Victoria 0 pts

19, 20 and 21 December 1988

at Bellerive Oval, Hobart

West Indians 409 (R.B. Richardson 121, C.G. Greenidge 84, K.L.T. Arthurton 72, A.J. de Winter 5 for 88) and 112 for 0 (C.G. Greenidge 58 not out, P.J.L. Dujon 53 not out)
Tasmania 320 (B.A. Cruse 98, D.J. Buckingham 69)

Match drawn

at Sydney

Pakistanis 191 (M.R. Whitney 4 for 34) and 198 for 8 dec (Mudassar Nazar 66, M.R. Whitney 5 for 66)
New South Wales 175 (T.H. Bayliss 52, Wasim Akram 4 for 40) and 150 for 2 (M.E. Waugh 63 not out, M.A. Taylor 62)

Match drawn

Western Australia clambered back into a challenging position in the Sheffield Shield when they trounced early season leaders South Australia in Perth inside three days. Western Australia welcomed back Capes and Reid after injury, but it was Alderman and MacLeay who did the damage in the first innings. Geoff Marsh was out for 0, but Veletta and Moody added 109. Three wickets went down for nine runs, but Brayshaw and Zoehrer played sensible cricket to take the home side to a commanding lead. South Australia fared even worse in their second innings than they had done in their first, and there was encouragement

for the Australian selectors as Bruce Reid marked his return with figures of 3 for 28.

There was no play possible on the first three days in Brisbane because of rain, and the match became a struggle for first-innings points on a treacherous wicket on the last day. Ritchie's determined innings, and some good off-break bowling from Cantrell, brought the points to Queensland.

Greenidge and Richardson began the match at Hobart with a stand of 165. For Tasmania, Cruse hit his highest score and de Winter took five wickets in an innings for the first time.

In their only first-class match of their tour, the Pakistanis came close to defeat as Mark Waugh and Mark Taylor added 104 for the second wicket when New South Wales were chasing 215 for victory.

Third Test Match
AUSTRALIA v. WEST INDIES

Allan Border's decision to ask West Indies to bat first when he won the toss seemed to have been the correct one when his medium-pace trio, Alderman, McDermott and Steve Waugh, took advantage of a well-grassed pitch of

Steve Waugh receives the congratulations of Healy, Hughes and Jones. Twice in the match he dismissed Viv Richards, who walks away disconsolately. (David Cannon/Allsport)

ABOVE: *Australian batsmen were subjected to a torrid time as they attempted to fend off a series of short-pitched deliveries. Graeme Wood is the sufferer. (David Cannon/ Allsport)*

RIGHT: *Malcolm Marshall – 300 Test wickets (David Cannon/Allsport)*

uneven bounce to reduce West Indies to 199 for 8. At this point, Walsh and Ambrose hit their highest scores in Test cricket as they added 60 invaluable runs and took the West Indian innings into the second day.

Australia began well enough, with Boon and Marsh putting on 40 for the first wicket and Marsh and Jones taking the score past 100, before the second wicket fell. At the end of the second day, having withstood a barrage of short-pitched and often unpleasant bowling, Australia were 121 for 4 with Wood and Waugh undefeated.

It was on the third day that the game began to tilt positively in favour of West Indies. Wood hung on doggedly until falling to the hostile Patterson, but Ambrose bowled Border for 0, and Ian Healy quickly followed. Some lusty blows from Hughes and McDermott kept alive Australia's hopes and took them to within 38 runs of West Indies. One pull from Hughes hit Gus Logie, who was fielding at short leg, and Logie was led from the field.

Haynes and Greenidge began to build on West Indies' lead, but Haynes was bowled at 38, and Greenidge was forced to retire hurt when the score was 69. Hooper did not last long, but, on a wicket which was never easy for the batsmen, Richie Richardson played with masterly assurance and Viv Richards delighted a holiday crowd by hitting 63 off 70 deliveries. Richardson's seventh Test hundred took West Indies to an impregnable position, and, in all, he faced 288 balls, batted for 391 minutes and hit 14 fours.

Border is bowled by Ambrose for 0. It was the first time that the Australian captain had failed to score in 89 consecutive Test innings. (David Cannon/Allsport)

Richards declared at the end of the fourth day and left Australia the last day in which to score 400 to win. Their only realistic hope was survival, but that hope was soon in tatters as Patterson bowled Marsh and Marshall had Boon leg before to claim his 300th Test wicket. Jones fell to a magnificent catch at slip by substitute Harper, who also accounted for Waugh, but not before Waugh had suffered nasty knocks on his chest. Border, playing his 100th Test match, also received some unpleasant blows in making the innings equal top score, 20. Border's first innings 0 had been the first time he had failed to score after 89 consecutive Test innings.

Shocked and shattered, Australia were bowled out for their lowest score in a Test against West Indies at Melbourne, and West Indies took a winning 3 – 0 lead in the series which now took a rest to allow for the completion of the one-day tournament.

27 December 1988

at Newcastle

Pakistanis 290 for 4 (Rameez Raja 74, Ijaz Ahmed 69, Saeed Anwar 65, Javed Miandad 54 not out)
New South Wales Invitation XI 286 (M.A. Taylor 99, M.W. Waugh 58, Abdul Qadir 4 for 66)

Pakistanis won by 4 runs

Taylor and Mark Waugh added 123 for the second wicket in this 50-over match.

31 December 1988, 1, 2 and 3 January 1989

at Woolloongabba, Brisbane

Queensland 184 (P.A. Capes 4 for 36, K.H. MacLeay 4 for 48) and 254 (P.S. Clifford 61, K.H. MacLeay 4 for 48)
Western Australia 293 (W.S. Andrews 82, T.M. Moody 69, M.R.J. Veletta 59, C.G. Rackemann 6 for 65) and 146 for 4

Western Australia won by 4 wickets
Western Australia 6 pts, Queensland 0 pts

Western Australia entered 1989 with a convincing win, which placed them in a good position to defend the Sheffield Shield of which they were the holders. Unfortunately, during the course of the match, Reid and Chris Matthews, the Western Australian pacemen, both broke down with recurrence of injuries. It was Capes and MacLeay who skittled out Queensland on the opening day, and Moody and Andrews who took Western Australia to a commanding lead on the second. The encouragement for Queensland was the bowling of Carl Rackemann, who took 6 for 65 and showed that he was fully recovered from injury. Queensland batted dourly in their second innings, taking 137 overs to score 254 runs. The rearguard action had the effect of making Western Australia's task

---

THIRD TEST MATCH – AUSTRALIA v. WEST INDIES
24, 26, 27, 28 and 29 December 1988 at MCG, Melbourne

WEST INDIES

	FIRST INNINGS		SECOND INNINGS	
C.G. Greenidge	c Healy, b Alderman	49	not out	36
D.L. Haynes	c Boon, b McDermott	17	lbw, b Alderman	23
R.B. Richardson	c Taylor, b Alderman	26	c and b Waugh	122
C.L. Hooper	c Border, b McDermott	38	lbw, b Alderman	4
I.V.A. Richards†	c Border, b Waugh	12	(6) lbw, b Waugh	63
A.L. Logie	lbw, b Alderman	10	(10) c Border, b Waugh	17
P.J.L. Dujon*	c Healy, b Waugh	26	(5) c Wood, b Alderman	46
M.D. Marshall	c Jones, b Waugh	7	(7) c Alderman, b Waugh	19
C.E.L. Ambrose	lbw, b McDermott	44	(8) c Marsh, b McDermott	5
C.A. Walsh	not out	30	(9) c Marsh, b Waugh	6
B.P. Patterson	lbw, b Alderman	13	not out	3
Extras	b 1, lb 4, nb 3	8	lb 1, nb 16	17
		280	(for 9 wkts, dec)	361

	O	M	R	W	O	M	R	W
Hughes	14	3	52	–	24	8	71	–
Alderman	32.1	9	68	4	36	12	78	3
McDermott	19	3	62	3	26	3	78	1
Waugh	21	3	77	3	24	5	92	5
Taylor	7	3	16	–	9	1	41	–
Border					1	1	0	–

AUSTRALIA

	FIRST INNINGS		SECOND INNINGS	
D.C. Boon	run out	23	(2) lbw, b Marshall	20
G.R. Marsh	b Patterson	36	(1) b Patterson	1
D.M. Jones	b Ambrose	28	c sub (Harper), b Ambrose	18
G.M. Wood	c Haynes, b Patterson	12	c Ambrose, b Walsh	7
A.R. Border†	b Ambrose	0	c Haynes, b Patterson	20
S.R. Waugh	c Greenidge, b Ambrose	42	c sub (Harper), b Ambrose	3
I.A. Healy*	lbw, b Patterson	4	c Hooper, b Walsh	8
P.L. Taylor	c Greenidge, b Ambrose	14	not out	18
C.J. McDermott	c Marshall, b Patterson	28	c sub (Arthurton), b Patterson	0
M.G. Hughes	not out	21	c Dujon, b Patterson	4
T.M. Alderman	b Walsh	3	c Dujon, b Patterson	0
Extras	b 2, lb 14, nb 15	31	b 4, lb 5, nb 6	15
		242		114

	O	M	R	W	O	M	R	W
Marshall	30	8	68	–	9	3	12	1
Ambrose	27	7	60	4	13	5	21	2
Walsh	17.3	3	49	1	16	7	21	2
Patterson	20	2	49	4	15.1	3	39	5
Richards					4	1	12	–

FALL OF WICKETS
1–68, 2–68, 3–114, 4–137, 5–147, 6–166, 7–185, 8–199, 9–256
1–38, 2–92, 3–191, 4–284, 5–317, 6–324, 7–324, 8–335, 9–356

FALL OF WICKETS
1–40, 2–103, 3–117, 4–117, 5–155, 6–161, 7–186, 8–190, 9–234
1–7, 2–30, 3–56, 4–58, 5–64, 6–75, 7–104, 8–104, 9–114

Umpires: A.R. Crafter & P.J. McConnell

West Indies won by 285 runs

more difficult, for they were left 41 overs in which to score 146 to win. They had little trouble, and the match was won with 8.3 overs to spare. It was Western Australia's first win in Brisbane for 17 years, and Queensland's first defeat in a Sheffield Shield game at Brisbane for five years.

Benson and Hedges World Series

Sixth One-Day International
WEST INDIES v. PAKISTAN

The wicket at Perth, like that at Melbourne, came in for some harsh words from both captains as West Indies recorded their fifth win in as many matches in the competition, and claimed a place in the final. The West Indies decision to include young pace bowler Ian Bishop proved to be a stroke of genius. He took three wickets as Pakistan collapsed to 32 for 5 in the first 12 overs, and his 5 for 27, among the best performances in the history of the competition, contained only 17 runs from the bat. Javed had little option but to bat out the 50 overs and take his side to some respectability. Their total was never going to be enough to trouble West Indies, however.

Benson and Hedges World Series

Seventh One-Day International
AUSTRALIA v. PAKISTAN

For the first time in the tournament, Pakistan built an innings of some substance. They owed much to Aamer Malik who, in his first match in the World Series, hit 90 between the 10th and 48th overs. It was a tenacious innings on a wicket which did not encourage free scoring and against fielding which was always keen. The usually fluent Javed showed the difficulties involved by taking 23 overs to make 31.

Needing 217 to win, Australia were given a sound start by Boon and Marsh, who put on 46. They then lost six wickets while 56 runs were scored. Three of the wickets went to the young and very promising Aaqib, and two to Aamer, very much Man of the Match. Australian hopes were revived by Simon O'Donnell, who was returning to international cricket for the first time since his successful fight against cancer. He was given a wonderful reception by the record crowd of 27,385 and was missed twice at the start of his innings. He played some skimming drives, and Healy added 50, before Wasim Akram returned to take 4 for 12 in 18 balls and give Pakistan their first win in the competition.

Benson and Hedges World Series

Eighth One-Day International
AUSTRALIA v. WEST INDIES

A crowd of more than 66,000 gave a thankful welcome to an Australian victory, a victory which increased their chances of qualifying to meet West Indies in the final. Richards won the toss and asked Australia to bat first. They began enterprisingly, with Marsh and Jones bustling well between the wickets. Steve Waugh and Graeme Wood put on 58 in seven overs, and Australia passed 200

BENSON AND HEDGES WORLD SERIES   SIXTH ONE-DAY INTERNATIONAL – PAKISTAN v. WEST INDIES
1 January 1989 at WACA Ground, Perth

PAKISTAN				WEST INDIES			
Rameez Raja	lbw, b Bishop	6		C.G. Greenidge	c Tauseef, b Aaqib Javed	13
Saleem Yousuf*	b Bishop	2		D.L. Haynes	c Saleem Yousuf, b Wasim Akram	23
Saeed Anwar	c Hooper, b Marshall	3		R.B. Richardson	not out	50
Javed Miandad	not out	63		P.J.L. Dujon*	c Wasim Akram, b Aaqib Javed	10
Saleem Malik	c Richards, b Bishop	1		C.L. Hooper	not out	33
Ijaz Ahmed	c Greenidge, b Bishop	1		I.V.A. Richards†		
Imran Khan†	c Dujon, b Walsh	7		R.A. Harper		
Wasim Akram	c Dujon, b Hooper	13		M.D. Marshall		
Tauseef Ahmed	run out	12		W.K.M. Benjamin		
Mohsin Kamal	b Bishop	1		I.R. Bishop		
Aaqib Javed	not out	0		C.A. Walsh		
Extras	b 1, lb 8, w 13, nb 9	31		Extras	lb 3, w 3, nb 7	13
(50 overs)	(for 9 wkts)	140		(38.2 overs)	(for 3 wkts)	142

	O	M	R	W		O	M	R	W
Marshall	7	–	17	1	Imran Khan	9	2	23	–
Bishop	10	1	27	5	Mohsin Kamal	9.2	–	56	–
Walsh	10	2	21	1	Wasim Akram	10	–	27	1
Benjamin	10	3	17	–	Aaqib Javed	10	–	33	2
Hooper	8	–	28	1					
Richards	5	–	21	–					

FALL OF WICKETS
1–12, 2–20, 3–21, 4–22, 5–32, 6–59, 7–94, 8–135, 9–139

FALL OF WICKETS
1–30, 2–44, 3–61

Umpires: R.C. Bailhache & T.A. Prue

Man of the Match: I.R. Bishop

West Indies won by 7 wickets

Terry Alderman. A most impressive return to international cricket. (Allsport)

with six overs still remaining. They should have plundered more than 26 in those last six overs, but they tended to panic, and the final score fell short of what had been hoped.

There was tremendous encouragement for Australia when Greenidge and Haynes were dismissed cheaply, but Richardson batted delightfully, and Dujon, too, was in his best form. In the 28th over, at 113, Dujon gave Border a simple return catch. Richardson, too, fell to a caught and bowled, a difficult chance to Peter Taylor, who had been brought into the side in place of Hughes and well justified his selection with an admirable spell of bowling.

Richards was perhaps guilty in part of Richardson's dismissal, for he denied Richardson the strike when he was in his very best form and eager for runs. Richards was to have a charmed life, being dropped four times in his 72-minute innings, but it was an outstanding catch by Steve Waugh, running back and taking the ball over his shoulder at long-off to dismiss Harper, which finally turned the game in Australia's favour. West Indies needed 14 off the last over, but Terry Alderman showed a calm temperament and immaculate control to steer Australia to victory.

BENSON AND HEDGES WORLD SERIES   SEVENTH ONE-DAY INTERNATIONAL – AUSTRALIA v. PAKISTAN
2 January 1989 at WACA Ground, Perth

PAKISTAN				AUSTRALIA			
Moin-ul-Atiq	c Healy, b McDermott		8	D.C. Boon	c Ijaz Ahmed,		
Saeed Anwar	c Border,				b Aaqib Javed		24
	b Alderman		15	G.R. Marsh	c Saleem Yousuf,		
Aamer Malik	c O'Donnell,				b Aaqib Javed		24
	b McDermott		90	D.M. Jones	run out		13
Javed Miandad	c Alderman,			G.M. Wood	c and b Aamer Malik		2
	b O'Donnell		31	A.R. Border†	c Javed Miandad,		
Saleem Malik	c Healy, b Waugh		0		b Aamer Malik		11
Ijaz Ahmed	c Border, b Hughes		17	S.R. Waugh	b Aqib Javed		12
Imran Khan†	c Healy, b Waugh		23	S.P. O'Donnell	b Wasim Akram		46
Wasim Akram	not out		5	I.A. Healy*	c Saleem Yousuf,		
Saleem Yousuf*	not out		1		b Wasim Akram		16
Tauseef Ahmed				C.J. McDermott	c Ijaz Ahmed,		
Aaqib Javed					b Wasim Akram		0
Extras	b 1, lb 3, w 16, nb 6		26	M.G. Hughes	c Ijaz Ahmed,		
					b Wasim Akram		8
(49 overs)	(for 7 wkts)		216	T.M. Alderman	not out		0
				Extras	lb 10, w 4, nb 8		22
				(46.1 overs)			178

	O	M	R	W
Alderman	10	1	32	1
Hughes	10	1	49	1
McDermott	10	2	38	2
O'Donnell	10	–	45	1
S.R. Waugh	9	–	48	2

	O	M	R	W
Imran Khan	8	–	30	–
Wasim Akram	8.1	–	25	4
Aaqib Javed	10	1	28	3
Aamer Malik	10	1	35	2
Tauseef Ahmed	6	–	29	–
Saleem Malik	4	–	21	–

FALL OF WICKETS
1–30, 2–30, 3–113, 4–118, 5–154, 6–200, 7–209

FALL OF WICKETS
1–46, 2–67, 3–73, 4–79, 5–98, 6–102, 7–152, 8–152, 9–174

Umpires: R.J. Evans & P.J. McConnell

Man of the Match: Aamer Malik

Pakistan won by 38 runs

BENSON AND HEDGES WORLD SERIES   EIGHTH ONE-DAY INTERNATIONAL – AUSTRALIA v. WEST INDIES
5 January 1989 at MCG, Melbourne

AUSTRALIA				WEST INDIES			
G.R. Marsh	run out		52	C.G. Greenidge	b McDermott		11
D.C. Boon	b Ambrose		8	D.L. Haynes	c Border, b Alderman		0
D.M. Jones	lbw, b Richards		43	R.B. Richardson	c and b Taylor		63
G.M. Wood	c Hooper, b Bishop		39	P.J.L. Dujon*	c and b Border		39
S.R. Waugh	b Ambrose		34	I.V.A. Richards†	c Marsh, b Alderman		48
A.R. Border†	run out		13	C.L. Hooper	c McDermott, b Taylor		14
S.P. O'Donnell	run out		1	R.A. Harper	c Waugh, b McDermott		15
I.A. Healy*	b Ambrose		1	C.E.L. Ambrose	not out		7
P.L. Taylor	c Dujon, b Bishop		7	W.K.M. Benjamin	b Alderman		7
C.J. McDermott	not out		2	I.R. Bishop	not out		4
T.M. Alderman	b Bishop		0	C.A. Walsh			
Extras	b 3, lb 11, w 6, nb 6		26	Extras	lb 9, w 1		10
	(47.4 overs)		226		(48 overs)	(for 8 wkts)	218

	O	M	R	W		O	M	R	W
Ambrose	9	2	26	3	Alderman	9	1	30	3
Bishop	9.4	–	50	3	McDermott	8	–	54	2
Walsh	10	–	30	–	O'Donnell	8	–	35	–
Benjamin	6	–	35	–	S.R. Waugh	10	–	36	–
Harper	8	–	42	–	Taylor	10	–	36	2
Richards	5	–	29	1	Border	3	–	18	1

FALL OF WICKETS
1–26, 2–106, 3–144, 4–202, 5–202, 6–207, 7–217, 8–220, 9–226

FALL OF WICKETS
1–9, 2–21, 3–113, 4–127, 5–160, 6–189, 7–202, 8–213

Umpires: A.R. Crafter & L.J. King

Man of the Match: S.R. Waugh

Australia won by 8 runs

BENSON AND HEDGES WORLD SERIES   NINTH ONE-DAY INTERNATIONAL – PAKISTAN v. WEST INDIES
7 January 1989 at Woolloongabba, Brisbane

PAKISTAN				WEST INDIES			
Rameez Raja	c Dujon, b Ambrose		5	C.G. Greenidge	b Aaqib Javed		46
Moin-ul-Atiq	c Richards, b Marshall		2	D.L. Haynes	b Aaqib Javed		26
Aamer Malik	c Richards, b Ambrose		75	R.B. Richardson	c Aaqib Javed, b Wasim Akram		17
Javed Miandad	c Benjamin, b Bishop		38	P.J.L. Dujon*	c and b Aamer Malik		0
Saleem Malik	c Hooper, b Bishop		3	I.V.A. Richards†	run out		18
Imran Khan†	not out		67	C.L. Hooper	b Wasim Akram		18
Ijaz Ahmed	c Bishop, b Ambrose		3	R.A. Harper	b Saleem Malik		6
Wasim Akram	run out		2	M.D. Marshall	b Wasim Akram		39
Saleem Yousuf*	not out		4	W.K.M. Benjamin	c Javed Miandad, b Imran Khan		0
Abdul Qadir				C.E.L. Ambrose	b Imran Khan		2
Aaqib Javed				I.R. Bishop	not out		0
Extras	b 8, lb 10, w 37, nb 4		59	Extras	lb 15, w 13, nb 3		31
	(50 overs)	(for 7 wkts)	258		(40.4 overs)		203

	O	M	R	W		O	M	R	W
Marshall	10	–	34	1	Imran Khan	9.4	–	42	2
Ambrose	10	–	39	3	Aaqib Javed	10	1	49	2
Benjamin	9	1	64	–	Wasim Akram	7	–	27	3
Bishop	10	–	51	2	Aamer Malik	4	–	20	1
Harper	6	1	31	–	Abdul Qadir	7	–	28	–
Richards	5	–	21	–	Saleem Malik	3	–	22	1

FALL OF WICKETS
1–9, 2–20, 3–127, 4–137, 5–197, 6–220, 7–240

FALL OF WICKETS
1–34, 2–63, 3–64, 4–131, 5–131, 6–150, 7–196, 8–199, 9–202

Umpires: R.C. Bailhache & C.D. Timmins

Man of the Match: Imran Khan

Pakistan won by 35 runs

Benson and Hedges World Series

Ninth One-Day International
WEST INDIES v. PAKISTAN

Pakistan kept alive their hopes of ousting Australia for a place in the final by beating West Indies in a match which was marred by complaints at the umpires' over zealous desires to signal wides. Aamer Malik played another excellent innings, but it was Imran's fierce hitting – he hit 50 off 33 balls and helped add 106 in 10 overs – that gave Pakistan the edge. West Indies never seemed to have a heart for the contest, and after Richards was run out by substitute Shoaib, it was only the hitting of Marshall that kept their hopes alive before Wasim returned to end resistance.

Benson and Hedges World Series

Tenth One-Day International
AUSTRALIA v. PAKISTAN

Some splendidly controlled bowling by Terry Alderman, who bowled Rameez Raja and Aamer Malik with the first two balls of the match, set up Australia's crucial victory over Pakistan. The visitors recovered well enough through Javed and Ijaz, to reach 124 for 3 in the 24th over, but Javed was run out, and O'Donnell held a good return catch to account for the dangerous Saleem Malik, and the innings began to stutter. Imran again showed bright form, but Australia were faced with a meagre target.

An opening partnership of 100 in 24 overs between

Boon and Marsh put the game firmly under Australia's control, and McDermott was promoted to number three to hit quick runs in case run rate should become an issue in qualifying for the final. He responded well to his task, hitting 32 off 36 balls, but Pakistan looked a team of crocks. Australia moved to victory with 5.1 overs to spare and seemed certain to meet West Indies in the final.

6, 7, 8 and 9 January 1989

at Adelaide

South Australia 506 (A.M.J. Hilditch 168, P.R. Sleep 90, J.C. Scuderi 67, D.S. Lehmann 51, M.R. Whitney 4 for 104) and 90 for 2 (G.A. Bishop 54)
New South Wales 423 (G.R.J. Matthews 104, M.A. Taylor 86, J. Dyson 55, G.F. Lawson 71, T.B.A. May 7 for 146)

Match drawn
South Australia 2 pts, New South Wales 0 pts

at Devonport

Queensland 305 (S.G. Law 73, T.J. Barsby 66, A.B. Henschell 61) and 153 for 3 dec (P.S. Clifford 71 not out)
Tasmania 263 (T.V. Hohns 5 for 50) and 107 for 1

Match drawn
Queensland 2 pts, Tasmania 0 pts

Two Sheffield Shield matches wedged into the glut of one-day internationals did little to alter the balance of power as Queensland, South Australia and Western Australia remained the three sides for whom a place in the final offered a realistic prospect. On a perfect batting

---

BENSON AND HEDGES WORLD SERIES   TENTH ONE-DAY INTERNATIONAL – AUSTRALIA v. PAKISTAN
8 January 1989 at Woolloongabba, Brisbane

PAKISTAN					AUSTRALIA			
Rameez Raja	b Alderman	0			D.C. Boon	c Ijaz Ahmed,		
Shoaib Mohammad	c Marsh,					b Aaqib Javed	45	
	b O'Donnell	29			G.R. Marsh	b Aaqib Javed	41	
Aamer Malik	b Alderman	0			C.J. McDermott	b Abdul Qadir	32	
Javed Miandad	run out	54			D.M. Jones	b Wasim Akram	16	
Ijaz Ahmed	c Boon, b Taylor	41			G.M. Wood	run out	8	
Saleem Malik	c and b O'Donnell	22			A.R. Border†	not out	18	
Imran Khan†	c Border,				S.R. Waugh	not out	22	
	b Alderman	28			S.P. O'Donnell			
Saleem Yousuf*	c McDermott,				I.A. Healy*			
	b O'Donnell	2			P.L. Taylor			
Wasim Akram	c and b Taylor	4			T.M. Alderman			
Abdul Qadir	not out	9			Extras	b 4, lb 6, w 12	22	
Aqib Javed								
Extras	b 1, lb 4, w 7, nb 2	14			(44.5 overs)	(for 5 wkts)	204	
(50 overs)	(for 9 wkts)	203						

	O	M	R	W		O	M	R	W
Alderman	9	2	27	3	Imran Khan	10	–	33	–
McDermott	10	–	45	–	Aaqib Javed	10	1	38	2
O'Donnell	10	1	31	3	Aamer Malik	1	–	9	–
S.R. Waugh	9	–	35	–	Wasim Akram	8.5	–	70	1
Taylor	10	–	48	2	Abdul Qadir	10	1	26	1
Border	2	–	12	–	Shoaib Mohammad	5	–	18	–

FALL OF WICKETS
1–0, 2–0, 3–64, 4–124, 5–152, 6–158, 7–167, 8–173, 9–203

FALL OF WICKETS
1–100, 2–100, 3–128, 4–164, 5–168

Umpires: L.J. King & S.G. Randell

Man of the Match: T.M. Alderman

Australia won by 5 wickets

Tim May, 7 for 146 in 67.4 overs for South Australia against New South Wales at Adelaide, January 1989. It was a career-best bowling performance by the off-spinner, who finished the season with 50 wickets and was named as Sheffield Shield Player of the Year. (Adrian Murrell/ Allsport)

wicket in Adelaide, Andrew Hilditch batted well into the second day to record his 12th first-class hundred. Peter Sleep continued to show that he was now a batsman rather than an all-rounder, and Darren Lehmann was run out in unfortunate circumstances after colliding with Geoff Lawson. Lawson himself was one of the New South Wales batting successes, hitting the highest score of his career. Mark Taylor and Jeff Dyson put on 124 for New South Wales' first wicket, and Greg Matthews hit his second century of the season. Tim May bowled a marathon spell of 67.4 overs to return the best figures of his career, 7 for 146.

Poor weather on the last day at Devonport frustrated both sides. At 256 for 5, Tasmania looked certain to take first-innings points, but leg-spinner Trevor Hohns took 4 for 7 in 25 balls, to bring the points to Queensland.

Benson and Hedges World Series

Eleventh One-Day International
AUSTRALIA v. PAKISTAN

Australia duly qualified to meet West Indies in the final of the Benson and Hedges World Series when they beat Pakistan under the floodlights at the MCG. Geoff Marsh underlined his position as Australia's leading batsman in limited-over cricket with his sixth international century. He and Border added 114 for the second wicket, and Australia moved to an impressive 258 for 4 in a mere 43 overs.

On current form this looked to be a target well beyond the capabilities of Pakistan, but the weather intervened. Pakistan had performed miserably in the field, not for the first time in the series, and had lost Saeed Anwar to the second ball of their innings, when rain arrived to halt play. When it was decided to resume, at 9.00 p.m., conditions looked totally unsatisfactory for the fielding side and Pakistan received the bonus of having their target reduced to 115 in 19 overs. When Imran and Wasim Akram were together adding 38 in four overs it looked as if Pakistan might snatch victory. The last over began with Pakistan on 104 for 5, but Terry Alderman again produced an over which left the batsmen searching vainly for runs, and justice was done as Australia claimed victory. The last over began with Pakistan on 104 for 5, but Terry Alderman again produced an over which left the batsmen searching vainly for runs, and justice was done as Australia claimed victory.

Benson and Hedges World Series

Twelfth One-Day International
AUSTRALIA v. WEST INDIES

With both sides having qualified for the final, the last of the preliminary matches had little meaning, but a crowd of more than 45,000 was still happy to see Australia claim a comfortable win over West Indies.

Dean Jones, somewhat hesitantly, and the Waugh twins took Australia to a good score as West Indies failed to exploit a pitch that was helpful to spinners. The one spinner in their side, Harper, bowled far too short and suffered in consequence. Australia, on the other hand, had two spinners, Taylor and Border, who used the conditions admirably and pointed to a way in which Australia could possibly have the better of West Indies when the two sides met on the same ground in the fourth Test match later in the month.

Benson and Hedges World Series

Final Table

	P	W	L	Pts	R/R
West Indies	8	5	3	10	4.50
Australia	8	5	3	10	4.48
Pakistan	8	2	6	4	4.24

Benson and Hedges World Series

First Final
AUSTRALIA v. WEST INDIES

A crowd of 73,760 saw Australia begin badly in the first final. After 12 overs they were 34 for 3, but Border, whose best form had been seeping back to him, played the pace bowlers with calm authority, and he and Jones, another to be refinding form, added 99. Steve Waugh and Simon O'Donnell also made useful contributions, but Australia's 204 hardly looked to be a winning score.

The West Indies had done themselves few favours by their behaviour in the field, where they seemed incensed

BENSON AND HEDGES WORLD SERIES ELEVENTH ONE-DAY INTERNATIONAL – AUSTRALIA v. PAKISTAN
10 January 1989 at MCG, Melbourne

AUSTRALIA				PAKISTAN		
G.R. Marsh	not out		125	Javed Miandad	c Taylor, b Hughes	16
D.C. Boon	c Wasim Akram,			Saeed Anwar	run out	0
	b Imran Khan		11	Ijaz Ahmed	c S.R. Waugh,	
A.R. Border†	c Aamer Malik,				b O'Donnell	7
	b Javed		60	Imran Khan†	run out	42
M.E. Waugh	b Tauseef Ahmed		12	Saleem Malik	c and b Taylor	11
S.R. Waugh	lbw, b Tauseef Ahmed		0	Aamer Malik*	c and b Border	5
G.M. Wood	not out		24	Wasim Akram	b Alderman	17
S.P. O'Donnell				Shoaib Mohammad	not out	2
I.A. Healy*				Abdul Qadir	not out	1
P.L. Taylor				Tauseef Ahmed		
M.G. Hughes				Aaqib Javed		
T.M. Alderman				Extras	b 2, lb 4, w 1	7
Extras	b 5, lb 12, w 5, nb 4		26			
				(19 overs)	(for 7 wkts)	108
(43 overs)	(for 4 wkts)		258			

	O	M	R	W
Imran Khan	7	–	36	1
Aaqib Javed	10	3	40	–
Wasim Akram	9	–	59	–
Tauseef Ahmed	7	–	43	2
Abdul Qadir	7	–	35	–
Javed Miandad	3	–	28	1

	O	M	R	W
Alderman	4	–	22	1
O'Donnell	4	–	15	1
S.R. Waugh	4	–	27	–
Hughes	4	–	18	1
Taylor	2	–	16	1
Border	1	–	4	1

FALL OF WICKETS
1–22, 2–136, 3–178, 4–178

FALL OF WICKETS
1–0, 2–13, 3–37, 4–59, 5–68, 6–105, 7–106

Umpires: A.R. Crafter & S.G. Randell

Man of the Match: G.R. Marsh

Australia won on faster scoring rate

BENSON AND HEDGES WORLD SERIES TWELFTH ONE-DAY INTERNATIONAL – AUSTRALIA v. WEST INDIES
12 January 1989 at SCG, Sydney

AUSTRALIA			WEST INDIES		
D.C. Boon	c Arthurton,		D.L. Haynes	st Healy, b Border	58
	b Marshall	6	P.J.L. Dujon*	c Taylor,	
G.R. Marsh	c Arthurton,			b S.R. Waugh	17
	b Bishop	24	R.B. Richardson	c Border,	
D.M. Jones	b Ambrose	77		b McDermott	8
M.E. Waugh	c Haynes, b Marshall	42	K.L.T. Arthurton	b Border	22
S.R. Waugh	not out	40	I.V.A. Richards†	c Marsh, b Taylor	3
A.R. Border†	b Marshall	3	A.L. Logie	not out	29
S.P. O'Donnell	not out	3	R.A. Harper	lbw, b Border	1
I.A. Healy*			M.D. Marshall	lbw, b Taylor	1
P.L. Taylor			C.E.L. Ambrose	c Border, b Taylor	6
C.J. McDermott			I.R. Bishop	not out	4
M.G. Hughes			B.P. Patterson		
Extras	lb 7, w 4, nb 9	20	Extras	lb 4, nb 1	5
(48 overs)	(for 5 wkts)	215	(48 overs)	(for 8 wkts)	154

	O	M	R	W
Marshall	10	3	25	2
Patterson	9	–	50	–
Bishop	10	1	34	1
Ambrose	9	–	42	2
Harper	9	–	51	–
Richards	1	–	6	–

	O	M	R	W
O'Donnell	7	–	22	–
Hughes	7	1	26	–
McDermott	7	–	26	1
S.R. Waugh	3	–	13	1
Taylor	10	2	22	3
Border	10	1	33	3
Jones	4	–	8	–

FALL OF WICKETS
1–9, 2–59, 3–137, 4–191, 5–211

FALL OF WICKETS
1–49, 2–63, 3–107, 4–110, 5–124, 6–125, 7–126, 8–134

Umpires: P.J. McConnell & T.A. Prue

Man of the Match: P.L. Taylor

Australia won by 61 runs

every time a wide was called, and some of this lack of discipline may have found its way into their batting. West Indies floundered against the opening bowlers, Hughes and Alderman, and when these two were rested after 16 overs, Greenidge, Haynes, Logie and Richards were back in the pavilion and only 41 runs on the board.

Merv Hughes, the local hero, was in fiery form, and his performance raised the crowd to a state of feverish excitement. O'Donnell and Taylor kept up the pressure, and at 129 for 7, West Indies looked well beaten. The seventh wicket to fall was that of Marshall, adjudged run out although he claimed that Healy had broken the wicket after he had dropped the ball. This was another umpiring decision that upset the tourists, and Marshall later apologized for showing dissent, but one felt that Healy should perhaps have offered an apology for his appeal.

Ambrose and Bishop came together at 148 for 8 and, with some fierce hitting, took the score to 196 before O'Donnell bowled Ambrose in the penultimate over. Hughes bowled the last over, and Walsh needed to hit him for four off the final ball to win the match. He hit a good cover drive, but the ball went straight to Border, and West Indies had suffered their fifth defeat in a row. Australia, on the other hand, were playing their best cricket of the season.

Simon O'Donnell is bowled by Malcolm Marshall for 10 in the first Benson and Hedges World Series Final at Melbourne. O'Donnell's return to the Australian one-day side after his fight against cancer was one of the happiest events of the Australian season. (David Cannon/Allsport)

BENSON AND HEDGES WORLD SERIES   FIRST FINAL – AUSTRALIA v. WEST INDIES
14 January 1989 at MCG, Melbourne

AUSTRALIA				WEST INDIES			
G.R. Marsh	lbw, b Ambrose	18			C.G. Greenidge	c Healy, b Hughes	5
D.C. Boon	c Dujon, b Ambrose	0			D.L. Haynes	lbw, b Hughes	6
G.M. Wood	c Logie, b Marshall	6			R.B. Richardson	c Healy, b O'Donnell	24
A.R. Border†	c Greenidge, b Ambrose	78			A.L. Logie	lbw, b Alderman	4
D.M. Jones	c Logie, b Walsh	36			I.V.A. Richards†	c Border, b Alderman	14
S.R. Waugh	c and b Ambrose	33			C.L. Hooper	c Jones, b Taylor	33
S.P. O'Donnell	b Marshall	10			P.J.L. Dujon*	c Jones, b Taylor	27
I.A. Healy*	not out	3			M.D. Marshall	run out	18
P.L. Taylor	run out	0			C.E.L. Ambrose	b O'Donnell	23
M.G. Hughes	lbw, b Ambrose	0			I.R. Bishop	not out	33
T.M. Alderman					C.A. Walsh	not out	3
Extras	lb 9, w 6, nb 5	20			Extras	b 3, lb 6, w 3	12
(50 overs)	(for 9 wkts)	204			(50 overs)	(for 9 wkts)	202

	O	M	R	W		O	M	R	W
Marshall	9	1	31	2	Alderman	10	2	29	2
Ambrose	10	2	26	5	Hughes	10	1	34	2
Bishop	10	–	37	–	O'Donnell	7	–	36	2
Walsh	10	–	45	1	S.R. Waugh	10	–	43	–
Richards	10	–	48	–	Taylor	10	2	35	2
Hooper	1	–	8	–	Border	3	–	16	–

FALL OF WICKETS
1–15, 2–26, 3–34, 4–133, 5–176, 6–200, 7–202, 8–202, 9–204

FALL OF WICKETS
1–14, 2–16, 3–23, 4–41, 5–76, 6–108, 7–129, 8–148, 9–196

Umpires: L.J. King & S.G. Randell

Australia won by 2 runs

Healy and Marsh are jubilant as Marshall is given run out in the first Benson and Hedges World Series Final. Marshall turns to debate the point with umpire Randell, insisting that Healy did not have the ball in his gloves when he broke the wicket. (David Cannon/Allsport)

Benson and Hedges World Series

Second Final
AUSTRALIA v. WEST INDIES

West Indies roused themselves from their slumbers to gain a convincing win over Australia and force a deciding third final. Australia brought in Greg Matthews to bolster their spin attack on a wicket which was believed to assist the slow bowlers, but, by the time he came on to bowl, West Indies were well in charge, and Matthews did not have a happy match.

Richards won the toss, and West Indies batted. Greenidge and Haynes had 50 on the board from only 51 balls. Hughes, the hero of Melbourne, was hit for 4 fours in an over by Haynes, who also pulled Alderman over square-leg for six. The rate of scoring dropped when Haynes began to feel ill, but Viv Richards, appearing in the 35th over, hit 53 off 40 deliveries. Three times he hit Matthews for six. Richards was finally bowled slogging at Hughes, who benefited from bowling at the close of the innings, by which time West Indies had thrown off any hint of caution.

There seemed little realistic chance of Australia matching West Indies' huge score, but, after a solid start, Boon, Marsh and Jones hit 84 in one period of nine overs, and West Indies threatened to disintegrate. They did not, thanks to old heads and wise counselling, Bishop sent back both Boon and Jones, and Australia succumbed much as had been expected.

BENSON AND HEDGES WORLD SERIES SECOND FINAL – AUSTRALIA v. WEST INDIES
16 January 1989 at SCG, Sydney

WEST INDIES				AUSTRALIA			
C.G. Greenidge	c Jones, b Taylor	46		D.C. Boon	c Richardson,		
D.L. Haynes	c S.R. Waugh,				b Bishop	36	
	b Border	62		G.R. Marsh	run out	22	
R.B. Richardson	c M.E. Waugh,			D.M. Jones	c sub (Harper),		
	b S.R. Waugh	55			b Bishop	27	
A.L. Logie	c and b Border	18		A.R. Border†	c Richardson,		
I.V.A. Richards†	b Hughes	53			b Bishop	10	
C.L. Hooper	c M.E. Waugh,			M.E. Waugh	c and b Bishop	22	
	b Hughes	12		S.R. Waugh	st Dujon, b Hooper	8	
M.D. Marshall	b Hughes	4		G.R.J. Matthews	run out	4	
P.J.L. Dujon*	b Hughes	5		I.A. Healy*	run out	7	
C.E.L. Ambrose	not out	7		P.L. Taylor	not out	13	
I.R. Bishop	run out	0		M.G. Hughes	b Hooper	13	
C.A. Walsh				T.M. Alderman	b Hooper	0	
Extras	b 5, lb 9, w 1	15		Extras	b 1, lb 10, w 9, nb 3	23	
(50 overs)	(for 9 wkts)	277		(40 overs)		185	

	O	M	R	W		O	M	R	W
Alderman	8	–	42	–	Marshall	5	1	30	–
Hughes	7	–	44	4	Ambrose	6	1	30	–
Matthews	7	–	62	–	Bishop	10	–	52	4
S.R. Waugh	8	–	45	1	Walsh	9	1	40	–
Taylor	10	–	31	1	Hooper	10	2	22	3
Border	10	–	39	2					

FALL OF WICKETS
1–99, 2–120, 3–166, 4–246, 5–258, 6–263, 7–270, 8–277, 9–277

FALL OF WICKETS
1–57, 2–94, 3–100, 4–133, 5–137, 6–149, 7–149, 8–162, 9–185

Umpires: P.J. McConnell & T.A. Prue

West Indies won by 92 runs

Third Final
AUSTRALIA v. WEST INDIES

The deciding match in the Benson and Hedges World Series was sadly disrupted by rain. There were two stoppages which cost three hours 35 minutes of playing time, and the second stoppage undoubtedly cost Australia the match.

Batting first, Australia reached 83 for 2 off 23.1 overs before the first stoppage. When they resumed their number of overs had been reduced from 50 to 38, and, from the 14.5 of their quota that remained to them, they plundered 143 runs at an astounding rate of 9.64 runs an over. Dean Jones confirmed his rehabilitation with a brilliantly aggressive innings. At 15 not out at the break, he advanced to 93 off another 54 balls, batting with aggression but never resorting to wild slogging.

West Indies needed to score at 5.97 runs an over to win, and after five balls from Alderman they were 4 for 2. Viv Richards countered this crisis with immediate attack, once

Curtly Ambrose, the destroyer of Australia, 21 wickets in the Benson and Hedges World Series and 26 in the Tests. (Allsport)

BENSON AND HEDGES WORLD SERIES – AVERAGES

AUSTRALIA BATTING

	M	Inns	NOs	Runs	HS	Av	100s	50s
D.M. Jones	10	10	2	404	93*	50.50		3
G.R. Marsh	11	11	2	448	125*	49.77	1	2
S.R. Waugh	11	10	3	270	54	38.57		1
A.R. Border	11	10	1	245	78	27.22		2
D.C. Boon	11	11		264	71	24.00		1
M.E. Waugh	7	6		131	42	21.83		
S.P. O'Donnell	7	4	1	60	46	20.00		
G.M. Wood	5	5	1	79	39	19.75		
I.A. Healy	11	6	2	53	23*	13.25		
C.J. McDermott	7	5	1	42	32	10.50		
P.L. Taylor	10	5	1	40	16	10.00		
M.G. Hughes	9	4	1	25	13	8.33		
T.M. Alderman	10	4	1	0	0*	0.00		

Played in one match: G.R.J. Matthews 4

WEST INDIES BATTING

	M	Inns	NOs	Runs	HS	Av	100s	50s
D.L. Haynes	11	11	1	513	111	51.30	2	3
I.R. Bishop	7	5	4	41	33*	41.00		
C.G. Greenidge	9	9		304	70	33.77		3
A.L. Logie	8	7	2	157	44	31.40		
I.V.A. Richards	11	10	1	277	60*	30.77		3
R.B. Richardson	11	11	1	243	63	24.30		3
C.L. Hooper	10	8	1	162	33*	23.14		
C.E.L. Ambrose	10	8	5	58	23	19.33		
P.J.L. Dujon	9	9		164	63	18.22		1
M.D. Marshall	10	7		118	39	16.85		
R.A. Harper	5	4	1	22	15	7.33		
C.A. Walsh	9	4	2	7	3*	3.50		
W.K.M. Benjamin	7	5		13	7	2.60		

Played in two matches: D. Williams 5
Played in one match: K.L.T. Arthurton 22; B.P. Patterson did not bat

AUSTRALIA BOWLING

	Overs	Mds	Runs	Wkts	Av	Best	4/inns
A.R. Border	44	1	177	10	17.70	3/33	
T.M. Alderman	77	10	271	13	20.84	3/27	
M.G. Hughes	69	4	309	14	22.07	4/44	1
C.J. McDermott	61.2	4	289	13	22.23	4/38	1
P.L. Taylor	83	4	365	16	22.81	3/22	
S.P. O'Donnell	47	1	196	7	28.00	3/31	
S.R. Waugh	78		373	8	46.62	3/57	

Bowled in one innings: G.R.J. Matthews 7–0–62–0; D.M. Jones 4–0–8–0

WEST INDIES BOWLING

	Overs	Mds	Runs	Wkts	Av	Best	4/inns
C.E.L. Ambrose	87.2	13	334	21	15.90	5/17	2
I.R. Bishop	66.4	2	283	15	18.86	5/27	2
C.L. Hooper	25	2	101	5	20.20	3/22	
M.D. Marshall	88	8	326	12	27.16	4/34	1
W.K.M. Benjamin	62	6	277	7	39.57	2/35	
C.A. Walsh	84	4	320	8	40.00	2/36	
I.V.A. Richards	64		329	5	65.80	2/48	
R.A. Harper	25	1	147	0	–	0/23	

Bowled in one innings: B.P. Patterson

AUSTRALIA FIELDING FIGURES

12 - A.R. Border; 12 - I.A. Healy (ct 10/st 2); 5 - P.L. Taylor; 4 - D.C. Boon and S.R. Waugh; 3 - G.R. Marsh, D.M. Jones and M.E. Waugh; 2 - S.P. O'Donnell, T.M. Alderman and C.J. McDermott; 1 - M.G. Hughes and sub (G.M. Wood)

WEST INDIES FIELDING FIGURES

8 - P.J.L. Dujon (ct 7/st 1); 7 - C.L. Hooper; 6 - I.V.A. Richards; 4 - A.L. Logie; 3 - C.G. Greenidge, R.B. Richardson, C.E.L. Ambrose and K.L.T. Arthurton (one as sub); 2 - I.R. Bishop, D. Williams and R.A. Harper (one as sub); 1 - D.L. Haynes, C.A. Walsh and W.K.M. Benjamin

BENSON AND HEDGES WORLD SERIES THIRD FINAL – AUSTRALIA v. WEST INDIES
18 January 1989 at SCG, Sydney

AUSTRALIA			
G.R. Marsh	run out		31
D.C. Boon	b Walsh		16
D.M. Jones	not out		93
A.R. Border†	c Richardson, b Richards		32
M.E. Waugh	b Hooper		5
S.R. Waugh	not out		27
S.P. O'Donnell			
I.A. Healy*			
P.L. Taylor			
M.G. Hughes			
T.M. Alderman			
Extras	b 6, lb 9, w 4, nb 3		22
(38 overs)	(for 4 wkts)		226

	O	M	R	W
Marshall	8	–	45	–
Ambrose	8	1	45	–
Bishop	7	–	32	–
Walsh	7	–	39	1
Hooper	5	–	38	1
Richards	3	–	12	1

FALL OF WICKETS
1–40, 2–70, 3–137, 4–152

WEST INDIES			
C.G. Greenidge	c S.R. Waugh, b Alderman		4
D.L. Haynes	not out		40
R.B. Richardson	c Healy, b Alderman		0
I.V.A. Richards†	not out		60
A.L. Logie			
C.L. Hooper			
M.D. Marshall			
D. Williams*			
C.E.L. Ambrose			
I.R. Bishop			
C.A. Walsh			
Extras	lb 6, w 1		7
(13.2 overs)	(for 2 wkts)		111

	O	M	R	W
Alderman	4	–	22	2
Hughes	3	–	21	–
S.R. Waugh	3.2	–	27	–
Taylor	2	–	23	–
O'Donnell	1	–	12	–

FALL OF WICKETS
1–4, 2–4

Umpires: P.J. McConnell & T.A. Prue

Men of the Finals: A.R. Border & D.L. Haynes

West Indies won on faster scoring rate

BENSON AND HEDGES WORLD SERIES – AVERAGES

PAKISTAN BATTING

	M	Inns	NOs	Runs	HS	Av	100s	50s
Javed Miandad	8	8	1	320	63*	45.71		3
Aamer Malik	4	4		170	90	42.50		2
Imran Khan	8	8	2	235	67*	39.16		1
Shoaib Mohammad	2	2	1	31	29	31.00		
Abdul Qadir	6	5	4	26	10	26.00		
Saleem Malik	8	8		156	68	19.50		1
Ijaz Ahmed	8	8		144	41	18.00		
Rameez Raja	6	6	1	86	69*	17.20		1
Wasim Akram	8	8	1	74	17	10.57		
Sajid Ali	2	2		17	15	8.50		
Saleem Yousuf	7	7	2	36	12	7.20		
Tauseef Ahmed	6	3	1	13	12	6.50		
Saeed Anwar	3	3		18	15	6.00		
Moin-ul-Atiq	2	2		10	8	5.00		
Aaqib Javed	8	2	1	0	0*	0.00		

Played in one match: Mohsin Kamal 1; Mudassar Nazar 12

PAKISTAN BOWLING

	Overs	Mds	Runs	Wkts	Av	Best	4/inns
Aamer Malik	15	1	64	3	21.33	2/35	
Wasim Akram	69		310	11	28.18	4/25	1
Aaqib Javed	76	6	330	10	33.00	3/28	
Imran Khan	72.4	6	293	7	41.85	2/42	
Saleem Malik	7.4		47	1	47.00	1/22	
Abdul Qadir	46	1	195	4	48.75	3/34	
Tauseef Ahmed	35		203	4	50.75	2/43	

Bowled in one innings: Javed Miandad 3–0–28–1; Shoaib Mohammad 5–0–18–0; Mohsin Kamal 9.2–0–56–0; Mudassar Nazar 7–0–36–1

PAKISTAN FIELDING FIGURES
6 - Saleem Yousuf; 5 - Wasim Akram; 4 - Ijaz Ahmed; 3 - Aamer Malik;
2 - Javed Miandad, Tauseef Ahmed and Aqib Javed

---

lifting Alderman into the pavilion, but at 47 for 2 off 6.4 overs, the rain returned. When play resumed West Indies' target was reduced, so that they were asked to make another 61 in 11.4 overs, a task that was considerably easier than the 179 from 31.2 overs that they had needed before the interruption. Richards continued in dominant form, and West Indies won with ease, although Australia could feel themselves a little hard done by. Haynes ended the match when he hit a six over square-leg off Steve Waugh.

20, 21, 22 and 23 January 1989

at WACA Ground, Perth

Western Australia 273 (T.J. Zoehrer 71, P. Gonnella 65 not out, D.R. Gilbert 5 for 88) and 312 for 8 dec (W.S. Andrews 121, T.J. Zoehrer 67, G.R. Marsh 51, G.D. Campbell 5 for 69)
Tasmania 237 (D.M. Wellham 90 not out, P.A. Capes 5 for 95, T.M. Alderman 4 for 49) and 200 for 7 (G.A. Hughes 65, P.A. Capes 5 for 69)

Match drawn
Western Australia 2 pts, Tasmania 0 pts

at MCG, Melbourne

Victoria 238 (G.R. Parker 56, W.J. Holdsworth 6 for 55) and 304 for 9 dec (J.D. Siddons 81, W.N. Phillips 72, M.G. Dimattina 66 not out, M.R. Whitney 4 for 49)
New South Wales 151 (M. Osborne 4 for 17) and 191 (P.A. Emery 83, M.G. Hughes 6 for 36)

Victoria won by 200 runs
Victoria 6 pts, New South Wales 0 pts

at Woolloongabba, Brisbane

West Indians 316 (R.A. Harper 82, A.L. Logie 67, W.K.M. Benjamin 50) and 332 (A.L. Logie 110 not out, D.L. Haynes 102, T.V. Hohns 5 for 71)
Queensland 240 (T.J. Barsby 67, C.L. Hooper 5 for 33) and 124 for 3

Match drawn

Set to make 349 in 77 overs, Tasmania were content to battle for a draw after left-arm pace bowler Peter Capes had caused them early discomfort. Capes took 10 wickets in a match for the first time in his career and returned his best figures in the second innings. Alderman had helped him to bowl Western Australia to first-innings points in spite of a courageous knock from Tasmanian skipper Dirk Wellham. The highlight of Western Australia's second innings was a century in under three hours by left-hander Wayne Andrews. He shared a sixth-wicket stand of 130 with Tim Zoehrer, who batted with great panache in both innings. David Gilbert and Greg Campbell bowled impressively for Tasmania.

On the eve of the game at Melbourne, New South Wales decided to drop skipper Greg Dyer. Philip Emery, who was to hit a career-best 83, was brought in as wicket-keeper, and Geoff Lawson was appointed captain. It was a bitter experience for Dyer, who only 12 months earlier had been Australia's first choice keeper. The changes brought

David Boon putting Australia emphatically in command. (Dan Smith/Allsport)

little joy to New South Wales, who were well beaten and so provided Victoria with their first win of the season. There was some comfort for New South Wales in the performance of debutant quick bowler Wayne Holdsworth, who bowled Dav Whatmore with his first ball in first-class cricket and had Jamie Siddons caught in the same over. He finished with 6 for 55, but New South Wales batted poorly, and the home side were quick to build upon their substantial first-innings lead and put the game out of New South Wales' reach. Merv Hughes then tore the heart out of the visitors' batting.

In their last first-class game outside the Test matches, West Indies enjoyed some healthy batting practice and Carl Hooper returned his best bowling figures.

27, 28, 29 and 30 January 1989

at WACA Ground, Perth

Victoria 395 for 9 dec (J.D. Siddons 156, G.M. Watts 70) and 275 for 6 dec (W.N. Phillips 76, S.P. O'Donnell 52, J.D. Siddons 51)
Western Australia 436 for 3 dec (T.M. Moody 202, G.M. Wood 138 not out) and 235 for 4 (M.R.J. Veletta 100, P. Gonnella 56)

Western Australia won by 6 wickets
Western Australia 6 pts, Victoria 0 pts

Although weakened by Test calls, Western Australia recorded a good win over Victoria and moved ominously to the top of the Sheffield Shield table. Put in to bat, Victoria fared well with Siddons, who had not enjoyed a happy season after being with the Australian side in Pakistan, hitting the eighth century of his career, his first of the summer. Western Australia gave a first-class debut to 29-year-old pace bowler Ken Lilly, and he took three wickets on the second morning, including that of Siddons, to halt Victoria's advance. Western Australia's reply revolved around a massive third-wicket stand of 264 between Tom Moody and Graeme Wood. Wood, whose form in Shield matches places him without a superior in Australia, reached the 30th century of his career while Moody, pressing for a place in the Test side, hit the highest score of his career. The surprise arrived when O'Donnell declared Victoria's second innings closed and left Western Australia 40 overs in which to score 235. The home side accepted the challenge gleefully. Gonnella and Veletta, one of Australia's forgotten men, put on 137 for the first wicket at a brisk rate to set up a victory for their side with 2.2 overs to spare. Queensland were said to be not amused with O'Donnell's declaration.

Fourth Test Match
AUSTRALIA v. WEST INDIES

Australia gave first Test caps to Queensland leg-spinner Trevor Hohns and to New South Wales left-handed opening batsman Mark Taylor who had enjoyed such a successful season. The inclusion of the veteran Hohns was an indication that Australia expected the wicket to assist the spinners. Peter Taylor gained the off-spinner place ahead of Tim May, who was handicapped by a damaged finger.

Richards won the toss, and Greenidge and Haynes

began in their usual confident fashion. Even the introduction of Peter Taylor into the attack in the seventh over did not disturb them, and they lunched at 67 for 0. It was Peter Taylor who broke the opening stand, but a partnership of 54 between Richardson and Haynes gave no indication of the collapse that was to follow. It was the unlikely slow left-arm bowling of Allan Border which brought about the decline as he induced mishits and indecision with almost every ball he bowled. As the wickets tumbled, so his confidence grew. He realized that his bowling had been blessed with a golden day and that for the West Indians all 'bushes' had now become 'bears'. Full tosses and long-hops brought wickets as well as balls which were generously flighted and appreciably turned. By 5.53 p.m. in the 100th over, West Indies were out for 224, and Allan Border had taken a career-best 7 for 46, as much to his own astonishment as anyone else's.

Australia began to grind out a determined reply. By lunch on the second day, they had scored just 39 for the loss of Marsh. Mark Taylor's gritty debut innings lasted for more than two hours, but his departure saw an acceleration in the scoring as Jones lofted Hooper into the outfield and David Boon began to play some belligerent strokes. Jones was bowled by Richards who, confronted by a situation which demanded more than four pace

Desmond Haynes' magnificent innings is brought to an end when he is caught Mark Taylor, bowled Allan Border for 143. (Dan Smith/Allsport)

bowlers and bat-pad catchers, displayed tactical limitations as a captain. At tea, Australia had advanced to 131 for 3, and by the close they were a commendable 200 for 3 with David Boon 110 not out, an innings of great character.

Boon's 499-minute innings ended on the third day. He hit 11 fours before being caught behind to become Walsh's 100th Test victim. Border continued to grind his way to the

FOURTH TEST MATCH – AUSTRALIA v. WEST INDIES
26, 27, 28, 29 and 30 January 1989 at SCG, Sydney

WEST INDIES

	FIRST INNINGS			SECOND INNINGS	
C.G. Greenidge	c Waugh, b P. Taylor	56		c and b Hughes	4
D.L. Haynes	c Boon, b Hohns	75		c M. Taylor, b Border	143
R.B. Richardson	c P. Taylor, b Border	28		c Hughes, b P. Taylor	22
C.L. Hooper	c Marsh, b Border	0		c Jones, b Hohns	35
I.V.A. Richards†	c Boon, b Border	11		c Jones, b Hohns	4
A.L. Logie	b Border	0		c P. Taylor, b Hohns	6
P.J.L. Dujon*	c Hughes, b Border	18		run out	9
R.A. Harper	c P. Taylor, b Border	17		lbw, b Border	12
M.D. Marshall	c Marsh, b Border	9		c P. Taylor, b Border	3
C.E.L. Ambrose	c Jones, b P. Taylor	1		c Boon, b Border	5
C.A. Walsh	not out	4		not out	7
Extras	b 1, w 1, nb 3	5		b 1, w 1, nb 4	6
		224			**256**

	O	M	R	W	O	M	R	W
Alderman	10	2	17	–	2	–	6	–
Hughes	10	3	28	–	18	6	29	1
P.L. Taylor	25.2	8	65	2	29	4	91	1
Hohns	24	8	49	1	34	11	69	3
Border	26	10	46	7	18.4	3	50	4
Waugh	4	–	18	–	3	–	10	–

FALL OF WICKETS
1–90, 2–144, 3–156, 4–174, 5–174, 6–174, 7–199, 8–213, 9–220
1–17, 2–56, 3–167, 4–188, 5–198, 6–225, 7–232, 8–244, 9–247

AUSTRALIA

	FIRST INNINGS			SECOND INNINGS	
G.R. Marsh	c Dujon, b Marshall	2	(2) b Richards	23
M.A. Taylor	b Ambrose	25	(1) c Haynes, b Ambrose	3
D.C. Boon	c Dujon, b Walsh	149	c Harper, b Marshall	10
D.M. Jones	b Richards	29	not out	24
A.R. Border†	b Marshall	75	not out	16
S.R. Waugh	not out	55		
I.A. Healy*	c Logie, b Marshall	11		
P.L. Taylor	lbw, b Marshall	0		
T.V. Hohns	b Marshall	0		
M.G. Hughes	c Dujon, b Walsh	12		
T.M. Alderman	run out	9		
	b 6, lb 14, nb 14	34	b 3, lb 1, nb 2	6
		401	(for 3 wkts)	**82**

	O	M	R	W	O	M	R	W
Marshall	31	16	29	5	8	2	17	1
Ambrose	33	5	78	1	7	1	16	1
Harper	37	9	86	–				
Walsh	22.5	5	48	2	3	–	9	–
Hooper	37	10	72	–	10.3	2	24	–
Richards	31	1	68	1	7	2	12	1

FALL OF WICKETS
1–14, 2–43, 3–114, 4–284, 5–335, 6–355, 7–357, 8–357, 9–388
1–3, 2–16, 3–55

Umpires: L.J. King & T.A. Prue

Australia won by 7 wickets

TEST SERIES
The BENSON and HEDGES Company

HEDGES TEST SERIES
The BENSON and HEDGES Company

ABOVE LEFT: *Allan Border spinning Australia to victory with the best bowling performance of his career. (Allsport)*

BELOW LEFT: *Trevor Hohns appeals enthusiastically in his first Test match, but this time without success. (Dan Smith/Allsport)*

RIGHT: *Allan Border raises his bat in triumph as Australia beat West Indies by seven wickets. (Dan Smith/Allsport)*

slowest half-century by an Australian in Test cricket, 310 minutes, 262 balls, and, in all, he batted for 386 minutes, hitting 5 fours. Marshall returned, most belatedly, to sweep away the tail, but the West Indian Achilles' heel had long been disclosed, the spinners, Harper, Hooper and Richards taking 1 for 226 in 105 overs on a wicket on which the Australian spinners had claimed 10 for 160 in 75.2 overs.

The Australian innings ended when Alderman injured himself as he unsuccessfully tried to avoid being run out. Alderman was later able to bowl only two overs and was forced to withdraw from the final Test. Greenidge was quickly dismissed, but Haynes was at his most authoritative, displaying a technique and temperament which places him high among world cricketers. He and Hooper, who had had a poor tour, added 111 in 138 minutes, but Trevor Hohns regained the initiative for Australia when he dismissed Hooper, Richards and Logie in quick succession. Border then came into the action again. By the end of the day, West Indies were 254 for 9. Border had taken 3 for 6 in 29 balls as seven wickets fell for 80 runs. Haynes was one of Border's victims after an innings which had lasted 268 balls and contained 16 fours.

Border ended the West Indian innings with the 16th ball of the final day. It gave him match figures of 11 for 96, figures bettered by only three other Test captains, Fazal Mahmood, Imran Khan and Arthur Gilligan.

It was appropriate that it should be Border who made the winning hit some quarter of an hour after lunch on the final day, as Australia moved to victory without too many alarms.

Fifth Test Match
AUSTRALIA v. WEST INDIES

West Indies reverted to the side which had won the first three Tests, Patterson returning in place of Harper, who seemed to have lost form completely, while Australia brought back Tim May in place of Peter Taylor and called up Mike Whitney as an emergency replacement for Terry Alderman. It was the fourth time that Whitney had been drafted into the Australian side, and all his appearances had been as a late replacement.

Border was delighted to win the toss and for Australia to bat first on a placid pitch. Two wickets for Ambrose, Man of the Series, and a run out caused Australia early discomfort, but by the end of the day, Dean Jones had

reached his fourth Test hundred and Australia were 283 for 3. Border added only three to his overnight score before being bowled by Marshall, and Walsh tilted the match in favour of West Indies with three wickets in 17 balls, but May helped Jones to add 50 in under an hour.

At 383 for 8, Australia were well placed, but they now took total command of the match as the swashbuckling Merv Hughes joined Jones in a riotous ninth-wicket record stand of 114. Hughes reached his highest score in first-class cricket and hit 6 fours and a six off 118 balls. Jones' second double hundred in Test cricket was ended when he was run out by Haynes. He batted for 538 minutes, faced 346 balls and hit 16 fours.

RIGHT: *Dean Jones during his innings of 216, which put Australia in an impregnable position and marked his return to his very best form. (David Cannon/Allsport)*

FIFTH TEST MATCH – AUSTRALIA v. WEST INDIES
3, 4, 5, 6 and 7 February 1989 at Adelaide Oval

AUSTRALIA

	FIRST INNINGS		SECOND INNINGS	
G.R. Marsh	c Dujon, b Ambrose	21	c Dujon, b Ambrose	79
M.A. Taylor	run out	3	run out	36
D.C. Boon	c Richardson, b Ambrose	34	not out	55
D.M. Jones	run out	216	lbw, b Richards	6
A.R. Border†	b Marshall	64	(6) not out	6
S.R. Waugh	c Dujon, b Walsh	12	(5) run out	8
I.A. Healy*	lbw, b Walsh	0		
T.V. Hohns	c Hooper, b Walsh	9		
T.B.A. May	c Richardson, b Ambrose	24		
M.G. Hughes	not out	72		
M.R. Whitney	c Dujon, b Patterson	2		
Extras	lb 18, nb 40	58	b 11, lb 13, nb 10	34
		515	(for 4 wkts, dec)	224

WEST INDIES

	FIRST INNINGS		SECOND INNINGS	
C.G. Greenidge	b Whitney	12	c Boon, b May	104
D.L. Haynes	run out	83	c Healy, b Whitney	15
R.B. Richardson	c Jones, b Whitney	106	c Border, b Whitney	22
C.L. Hooper	c Healy, b Whitney	2	b May	0
I.V.A. Richards†	c Boon, b Whitney	69	not out	68
A.L. Logie	c Healy, b Hohns	21	not out	2
P.J.L. Dujon*	b Hohns	28		
M.D. Marshall	c Marsh, b Whitney	0		
C.E.L. Ambrose	c Boon, b Whitney	9		
C.A. Walsh	c Healy, b Whitney	4		
B.P. Patterson	not out	9		
Extras	b 6, lb 10, nb 10	26	b 3, lb 7, w 1, nb 11	22
		369	(for 4 wkts)	233

	O	M	R	W	O	M	R	W
Marshall	23	3	67	1	12	2	30	–
Patterson	30.5	1	130	1	8	1	29	–
Ambrose	26	4	93	3	15	2	44	1
Walsh	33	5	120	3	13	2	26	–
Hooper	3	–	14	–	3	1	7	–
Richards	25	1	73	–	24	3	64	1

	O	M	R	W	O	M	R	W
Hughes	15	–	86	–	9	5	20	–
Whitney	30	6	89	7	20	4	60	2
May	16	6	42	–	23	2	60	2
Waugh	3	–	17	–	9	3	23	–
Hohns	47.4	9	106	2	15	3	56	–
Border	10	2	13	–	5	3	4	–

FALL OF WICKETS
1–7, 2–64, 3–75, 4–289, 5–311, 6–311, 7–333, 8–383, 9–497
1–98, 2–176, 3–187, 4–213

FALL OF WICKETS
1–19, 2–186, 3–190, 4–231, 5–293, 6–315, 7–315, 8–331, 9–346
1–21, 2–87, 3–89, 4–212

Umpires: R.J. Evans & P.J. McConnell

Match drawn

LEFT: *Gus Logie survives an attempted run out by Ian Healy. (David Cannon/Allsport)*

RIGHT: *Viv Richards saves the game for West Indies. David Boon is at short-leg. (David Cannon/Allsport)*

West Indies' reply was founded on a second-wicket partnership of 167, a record for West Indies against Australia. Richardson, looking a far better player than he had done in England, reached his eighth Test hundred off 137 balls. Australia, too, had their hero in Mike Whitney, the left-arm pace bowler, who bowled with great heart and fire on an unresponsive wicket to capture seven wickets for 89, an outstanding performance which, unaccountably, did not earn him a place on the tour to England.

West Indies avoided the follow-on, and Border left them the last day in which to score 371 to win. Mark Taylor achieved the rare feat of being run out in both innings of a Test match, and Whitney claimed two more wickets. Greenidge hit his first Test century in Australia, but West Indies never mounted a serious challenge, and the often bad tempered series, marked by constant criticism of the umpires and unrelenting short-pitched bowling by the West Indian pace bowlers whom, seemingly, no one

AUSTRALIA v. WEST INDIES – TEST MATCH AVERAGES

AUSTRALIA BATTING

	M	Inns	NOs	Runs	HS	Av	100s	50s
D.M. Jones	3	6	1	321	216	64.20	1	
D.C. Boon	5	10	1	397	149	44.11	1	2
S.R. Waugh	5	9	1	331	91	41.37		3
M.G. Hughes	4	5	2	109	72*	36.33		1
A.R. Border	5	10	2	258	75	32.25		2
G.M. Wood	3	6		178	111	29.66	1	
G.R. Marsh	5	10		227	79	22.70		1
C.J. McDermott	2	4	1	62	32*	20.66		
M.R.J. Veletta	2	4		71	37	17.75		
I.A. Healy	5	8		138	52	17.25		1
P.L. Taylor	2	3	1	32	18*	16.00		
A.I.C. Dodemaide	2	4	1	47	22	15.66		
T.B.A. May	3	5	2	43	24	14.33		
T.V. Hohns	2	2		9	9	4.50		
T.M. Alderman	2	3		12	9	4.00		

Played in one Test: M.R. Whitney 2; G.F. Lawson 0*; C.D. Matthews 1 & 32

WEST INDIES BATTING

	M	Inns	NOs	Runs	HS	Av	100s	50s
D.L. Haynes	5	10	1	537	143	59.66	2	2
R.B. Richardson	5	10	1	528	122	58.66	2	2
I.V.A. Richards	5	9	1	446	146	55.75	1	4
C.G. Greenidge	5	10	1	397	104	44.11	1	2
A.L. Logie	5	9	1	198	93	24.75		1
P.J.L. Dujon	5	8		195	46	24.37		
C.A. Walsh	5	8	5	68	30*	22.66		
C.L. Hooper	5	9		170	64	18.88		1
C.E.L. Ambrose	5	8	1	106	44	15.14		
B.P. Patterson	4	6	3	32	13	10.66		
M.D. Marshall	5	8		76	23	9.50		

Played in one Test: R.A. Harper 17 & 12

AUSTRALIA BOWLING

	Overs	Mds	Runs	Wkts	Av	Best	10/m	5/inns
A.R. Border	61.4	19	121	11	11.00	7/46	1	1
M.R. Whitney	50	10	149	9	16.55	7/89		1
T.M. Alderman	80.1	23	169	7	24.14	4/68		
G.F. Lawson	32	7	97	3	32.33	3/97		
C.J. McDermott	77	9	251	7	35.85	3/62		
M.G. Hughes	163.1	41	503	14	35.92	8/87	1	2
T.B.A. May	92	18	300	7	42.85	3/90		
T.V. Hohns	120.4	31	280	6	46.66	3/69		
S.R. Waugh	139	17	472	10	47.20	5/92		1
A.I.C. Dodemaide	63	6	255	4	63.75	2/60		
P.L. Taylor	70.2	16	213	3	71.00	2/65		
C.D. Matthews	24.5	4	80	0	–			

WEST INDIES BOWLING

	Overs	Mds	Runs	Wkts	Av	Best	10/m	5/inns
C.E.L. Ambrose	204.3	38	558	26	21.46	5/72		1
M.D. Marshall	192	42	488	17	28.70	5/29		1
C.A. Walsh	176.5	32	500	17	29.41	4/62		
B.P. Patterson	107.1	11	405	12	33.75	5/39		1
C.L. Hooper	79.3	17	198	2	99.00	1/5		
I.V.A. Richards	117	12	299	3	99.66	1/12		
R.A. Harper	37	9	86	0	–			

AUSTRALIA FIELDING FIGURES
12 - I.A. Healy; 9 - D.C. Boon; 7 - A.R. Border; 5 - D.M. Jones, G.R. Marsh and P.L. Taylor; 4 - A.I.C. Dodemaide; 3 - M.G. Hughes and S.R. Waugh; 2 - G.M. Wood and M.R.J. Veletta; 1 - M.A. Taylor, C.J. McDermott, T.B.A. May and T.M. Alderman

WEST INDIES FIELDING FIGURES
15 - P.J.L. Dujon; 8 - A.L. Logie; 5 - D.L. Haynes and C.L. Hooper; 4 - C.G. Greenidge and R.B. Richardson; 3 - I.V.A. Richards and R.A. Harper (two as sub); 2 - C.E.L. Ambrose and sub (K.L.T. Arthurton); 1 - M.D. Marshall

Mike Whitney, called up as a late replacement, took nine wickets in the fifth Test. The left-arm fast medium bowler performed outstandingly for New South Wales throughout the season and his 58 wickets placed him far ahead of other bowlers, but he was a surprise omission from the Australian party to tour England. (David Cannon/Allsport)

is able or even wants to control or discipline, drifted to a close.

Desmond Haynes was named international cricketer of the year, an honour well deserved, not only because of his outstanding achievements with the bat, but because he always carries himself with dignity, good humour and no hint of rancour.

9, 10, 11 and 12 February 1989

at Sydney

South Australia 356 (D.W. Hookes 83, D.S. Lehmann 79, P.C. Nobes 58, G.A. Bishop 57, G.F. Lawson 5 for 72) and 245 for 9 (A.M.J. Hilditch 101, D.S. Lehmann 60)
New South Wales 357 for 6 dec (P.L. Taylor 84, G.R.J. Matthews 76 not out, M.A. Taylor 69)

Match drawn
New South Wales 2 pts, South Australia 0 pts

New South Wales introduced 38-year-old spinner Steve Whitfield to first-class cricket, but the match in which Geoff Lawson surpassed Richie Benaud's record of 266 Sheffield Shield wickets for New South Wales had little to commend it. Hookes was angered by Lawson's failure to declare on the third morning, and negative bowling and slow scoring brought the game to a tedious end.

FAI Insurance Group Cup

11 February 1989

at Bellerive Oval, Hobart

Tasmania 121
Western Australia 125 for 2 (G.R. Marsh 66 not out)

Western Australia (2 pts) won by 8 wickets

12 February 1989

at Woolloongabba, Brisbane

Victoria 216 for 7
Queensland 114

Victoria (2 pts) won by 102 runs

With the international season at an end, Australia was able to concentrate on the domestic competitions. The 50-over tournament, under new sponsors, began with comfortable wins for Western Australia and Victoria. Victoria gave a fine all-round team performance in Brisbane with Siddons winning the individual award for his innings of 45.

15, 16, 17 and 18 February 1989

at Adelaide

South Australia 292 (D.W. Hookes 71, J.C. Scuderi 59) and 308 for 6 dec (D.W. Hookes 73, G.A. Bishop 57)
Queensland 164 (J.C. Scuderi 6 for 53) and 330 for 8 (I.A. Healy 90, T.J. Barsby 85)

Match drawn
South Australia 2 pts, Queensland 0 pts

at Perth

New South Wales 326 (M.A. Taylor 107, K.H. MacLeay 4 for 65) and 303 for 4 dec (M.A. Taylor 152 not out)
Western Australia 235 and 327 (T.J. Zoehrer 163, W.S. Andrews 78, G.F. Lawson 5 for 51)

New South Wales won by 67 runs
New South Wales 6 pts, Western Australia 0 pts

at Launceston

Victoria 224 for 4 dec (G.M. Watts 79, J.D. Siddons 59, G.R. Parker 52 not out) and 263 (W.N. Phillips 73)
Tasmania 226 for 5 dec (D.M. Wellham 68 not out, R.J. Tucker 63, G.A. Hughes 58) and 265 for 4 (D.C. Boon 90, R.J. Tucker 64, G.A. Hughes 57)

Tasmania won by 6 wickets
Tasmania 6 pts, Victoria 0 pts

South Australia edged closer to a place in the Sheffield Shield final by taking first-innings points in the match

Mark Taylor – a century in each innings for New South Wales against Western Australia at Perth gave his side a surprise victory, 15–18 February 1989. (USPA)

Tim Zoehrer hit two mighty centuries for Western Australia in the closing weeks of the season, finished fourth in the first-class batting averages and was the leading wicket-keeper in Australia. (Adrian Murrell/Allsport)

against Queensland, but with each side still having two matches to play, there were still three teams competing for the two places in the final. Splendid all-round cricket by Joe Scuderi, who had match figures of 9 for 115 and a career-best 6 for 53 in the first innings, put South Australia very much on top, and Queensland were left to make 437 to win. In spite of a fine career-best 90 off 122 balls by Ian Healy, Queensland seemed to be facing defeat when their eighth wicket fell at 308, but Hohns and Maguire survived for nearly 19 overs to save the game.

A century in each innings by Mark Taylor and eight wickets from Geoff Lawson helped New South Wales inflict upon Western Australia their first home defeat for six years. Western Australia were left more than a day in which to score 395, but they slumped to 64 for 5. A sixth-wicket stand of 152 between Wayne Andrews and Tim Zoehrer gave the innings respectability, and Zoehrer went on to reach the highest score of his career.

There was no play on the first day at Launceston because of rain, and the game was kept alive by declarations. An opening stand of 121 and a fine 90 from David Boon took Tasmania to their first victory of the season with 17 balls to spare.

FAI Insurance Group Cup
19 February 1989

---

at Adelaide

Queensland 258 for 3 (G.M. Ritchie 114, P.E. Cantrell 100)
South Australia 212 (A.M.J. Hilditch 106, D.S. Lehmann 55, C.G. Rackemann 7 for 34)

Queensland (2 pts) won by 46 runs

at Perth

New South Wales 170 (M.E. Waugh 51)
Western Australia 173 for 7

Western Australia (2 pts) won by 3 wickets

There was a remarkable contest in the second round of matches when Queensland won at Adelaide. Ritchie and Cantrell put on 233 for Queensland's second wicket, Hilditch became the third centurion of the match, and Carl Rackemann established a record for limited-over cricket in Australia with 7 for 34 in 9.2 overs.

22, 23, 24 and 25 February 1989

at Sydney

New South Wales 278 (S.B. Smith 61, P.L. Taylor 57, G.R.J. Matthews 55, G.D. Campbell 4 for 58) and 253 for 4 dec (J. Dyson 112 not out, M.E. Waugh 85)
Tasmania 153 (R.J. Tucker 82 not out, G.F. Lawson 6 for 36) and 309 for 9 (D.C. Boon 132)

Match drawn
New South Wales 2 pts, Tasmania 0 pts

at MCG, Melbourne

Victoria 284 (M.G. Dimattina 113, S.P. O'Donnell 55, J.C. Scuderi 4 for 64) and 3T2 (W.N. Phillips 62, T.B.A. May 7 for 93)
South Australia 510 (D.W. Hookes 133, D.S. Lehmann 87, P.C. Nobes 67, C.R. Miller 59, A.M.J. Hilditch 60, A.I.C. Dodemaide 5 for 94) and 40 for 2

Match drawn
South Australia 2 pts, Victoria 0 pts

24, 25, 26 and 27 February 1989

at Perth

Queensland 291 (G.M. Ritchie 140, P.A. Capes 5 for 74) and 17 for 2
Western Australia 294 for 7 dec (G.M. Wood 119 not out, K.H. MacLeay 70)

Match drawn
Western Australia 2 pts, Queensland 0 pts

Rain interrupted play on the second and third days at Perth and reduced the game to a battle for first-innings points. Greg Ritchie carried the Queensland innings on his shoulders, receiving help only from the tail-enders while, inevitably, Graeme Wood led his side to success and shared a vital seventh-wicket stand of 131 with MacLeay.

The two points that Western Australia gained gave them an almost certain place in the final, while South Australia drew level on points with Queensland by taking a first-innings lead over Victoria. Mike Dimattina, the Victorian wicket-keeper, hit a maiden century on the first day to effect a recovery for his side, but brilliant batting by David Hookes, who hit a hundred before lunch on the third day, and consistently aggressive batting, took South Australia to a commanding lead. Colin Miller, formerly of Victoria, marked his début for South Australia with 59 off 38 balls as he and Gladigau added 76 for the last wicket. Tim May produced the best bowling performance of his career when Victoria batted again, but South Australia found the task of scoring 87 in seven overs to win beyond them.

Fine bowling by Lawson and an excellent century by John Dyson gave New South Wales the edge over Tasmania, who were set to make 379 in just under four sessions. David Boon scored a masterful 132, and at 209 for 2, Tasmania looked likely to pull off a remarkable victory, but they collapsed before Mike Whitney and Steve Waugh, and it was left to Gilbert and Soule to bat out the last five overs to save the game.

FAI Insurance Group Cup

26 February 1989

at Sydney

Tasmania 188 for 6 (G.A. Hughes 50)
New South Wales 189 for 1 (S.R. Waugh 81 not out, S.B. Smith 60 not out)

New South Wales (2 pts) won by 9 wickets

at MCG, Melbourne

South Australia 185
Victoria 186 for 3 (G.M. Watts 71, D.M. Jones 56 not out)

Victoria (2 pts) won by 7 wickets

Emphatic victories for New South Wales and Victoria confirmed their places in the semi-final. South Australia struggled woefully in Melbourne and had four men run out.

FAI Insurance Group Cup – Qualifying Tables

Group A

	P	W	L	Pts
Victoria	2	2	–	4
Queensland	2	1	1	2
South Australia	2	–	2	0

Group B

	P	W	L	Pts
Western Australia	2	2	–	4
New South Wales	2	1	1	2
Tasmania	2	–	2	0

FAI Insurance Group Cup Semi-Finals

4 March 1989

at MCG, Melbourne

Victoria 228 for 9 (G.R. Parker 83, W.N. Phillips 50, G.F. Lawson 4 for 31)
New South Wales 179 (M.A. Taylor 61)

Victoria won by 49 runs

5 March 1989

at WACA Ground, Perth

Queensland 238 for 8 (T.J. Barsby 58)
Western Australia 222 for 6 (G.R. Marsh 64, T.M. Moody 53)

Queensland won by 16 runs

Another emphatic team performance took Victoria into the one-day final. Phillips and Parker put on 97 for the second wicket, and Dean Jones scored at a brisk pace, but it was pace bowler Fleming who took the individual award after sending back Steve Smith and Steve Waugh with only one run scored.

Queensland scored consistently in Perth, but the later Western Australian batsmen failed to capitalize on a second-wicket stand of 105 between Marsh and Moody.

10, 11,12 and 13 March 1989

at Sydney

New South Wales 301 for 6 dec (M.A. Taylor 132, S.B. Smith 54) and 198 for 5 dec (M.E. Waugh 58)
Queensland 230 for 6 dec (P.E. Cantrell 105, R.B. Kerr 69) and 266 for 8 (P.E. Cantrell 71, R.B. Kerr 57, S.R. Waugh 6 for 51)

Match drawn
New South Wales 2 pts, Queensland 0 pts

at MCG, Melbourne

Western Australia 533 for 6 dec (T.J. Zoehrer 168, T.G. Hogan 115 not out, M.R.J. Veletta 64, T.M. Moody 59, G.R. Marsh 55)
Victoria 343 for 3 (G.M. Watts 121, D.M. Jones 102 not out)

Match drawn
No points

at Adelaide

South Australia 455 (D.S. Lehmann 89, B. Williams 77, P.C. Nobes 71, D.W. Hookes 66, G.D. Campbell 5 for 138) and 172 for 4 dec (P.C. Nobes 52)
Tasmania 356 (R.J. Tucker 98, D.M. Wellham 94, D.C. Boon 56) and 272 for 4 (J. Cox 82 not out, G.A. Hughes 62, R.J. Tucker 55 not out)

Tasmania won by 6 wickets
Tasmania 6 pts, South Australia 0 pts

Western Australia and South Australia reached the Sheffield Shield final almost by default. At Melbourne, on a perfect wicket and with most of the third day lost to rain, Western Australia and Victoria could not even resolve first-innings points. Zoehrer and Hogan added 231 for Western Australia's sixth wicket. Zoehrer reached his highest score in first-class cricket, bettering by five runs his score of a month earlier, and almost certainly forced himself into the party to tour England. Hogan reached a maiden century. For Victoria, Watts hit his fifth first-class hundred, and Jones followed his double century in the Adelaide Test with his best Shield score of the season.

Only an outright victory would have given New South Wales a place in the final, and a win for Queensland would have confirmed their place in the final, but a tense game at Sydney ended in a draw. The prolific Mark Taylor took New South Wales to 301 with his third century in five innings. In reply, Robbie Kerr showed a welcome return to form for Queensland, for whom Peter Cantrell hit a maiden century. The problem was that Cantrell's hundred took 392 minutes, and he was passive on 96 for almost an hour. Eventually, Lawson asked Queensland to make 270 off 73 overs. With Cantrell batting with more dash, Queensland looked set for victory, but a collapse followed and, with three overs remaining, 18 were needed with four wickets in hand. Two more wickets fell as Steve Waugh returned career-best bowling figures, and the last ball arrived with Ian Healy needing to hit it for four to win. He missed, and the game was drawn.

South Australia believed that they needed to beat Tasmania to reach the final. They batted with great conviction and led by 99 on the first innings in spite of Rod Tucker's career best and another stirling knock from Dirk Wellham. Hookes set Tasmania the task of scoring 272 in 74 overs, and they responded in fine fashion, with Cox

hitting a career best and Tucker again batting well, so that victory was achieved with 19 balls to spare.

It transpired that this defeat did not prevent South Australia from competing in the final, for they had edged out Queensland, who had the same number of points, with their faster run rate.

Sheffield Shield – Final Table					
	P	W	L	D	Pts
Western Australia	10	3	3	4	24
South Australia	10	2	2	6	20
Queensland	10	2	1	7	20
New South Wales	10	2	2	6	18
Tasmania	10	2	–	8	15.5
Victoria	10	1	4	5	7.9
(Tasmania had 0.5 points and Victoria 0.1 points deducted for slow over rates)					

FAI Insurance Cup Final
VICTORIA v. QUEENSLAND

Having performed so well in the qualifying rounds, with teenage pace bowler Damien Fleming showing outstanding form, Victoria gave a bitterly disappointing display in the final, which turned out to be a most one-sided affair.

Border won the toss and chose to bat first. Again Queensland showed consistency, and with Border and Ritchie adding 97, they reached a formidable 253. With his best bowling performance in one-day cricket, Dirk Tazelaar wrecked the Victorian innings, and the Queensland pace quartet proved far too strong for the home side. Only a highest score from Damien Fleming helped Victoria from complete despair.

Rackemann's three wickets brought his total for the season's competition to a record 14.

Sheffield Shield Final
WESTERN AUSTRALIA v. SOUTH AUSTRALIA

The South Australian team flew back to Perth on 23 March knowing that they had to defeat Western Australia outright to win the Shield for the first time since 1981–2. A draw would be of no use to them.

On the morning of the match, David Hookes won the toss and decided to field. It was his only real option, even though the pitch was dry and lacked bounce. Western Australia replied with 287 for 2, which included a splendid unbeaten 123 from Tom Moody, ironically born in Adelaide 23 years earlier.

Next day, Western Australia went on to record their highest total against South Australia, reaching 535 with Moody, 162, and Wood, 68, breaking the third-wicket record partnership in games between the two teams. Their 230 in 280 minutes was broken by medium-pace Colin Miller, who eventually finished with 7 for 112. The visitors had time to score 30 from six overs before stumps.

The holiday Monday crowd of 9251 saw a day of

FAI INSURANCE CUP FINAL – VICTORIA v. QUEENSLAND
19 March 1989 at MCG, Melbourne

QUEENSLAND			
T.J. Barsby	run out		35
P.E. Cantrell	b O'Donnell		25
R.B. Kerr	run out		30
G.M. Ritchie	b Hughes		60
A.R. Border†	not out		77
S.G. Law	not out		17
I.A. Healy*			
C.J. McDermott			
D. Tazelaar			
J.N. Maguire			
C.G. Rackemann			
Extras	lb 7, w 2		9
(50 overs)	(for 4 wkts)		253

	O	M	R	W
Hughes	10	1	49	1
Fleming	10	–	44	–
Dodemaide	10	1	43	–
O'Donnell	10	–	58	1
Jackson	10	–	52	–

FALL OF WICKETS
1–51, 2–75, 3–108, 4–205

VICTORIA			
W.N. Phillips	b Tazelaar		3
G.M. Watts	c Cantrell, b Tazelaar		7
G.R. Parker	c Healy, b Tazelaar		2
D.M. Jones	c Kerr, b Rackemann		18
J.D. Siddons	c Healy, b Maguire		5
S.P. O'Donnell†	b Rackemann		3
A.I.C. Dodemaide	b Rackemann		1
M.G. Dimattina*	lbw, b Maguire		17
M.G. Hughes	c Tazelaar, b Maguire		4
D.W. Fleming	not out		18
P.W. Jackson	run out		1
Extras	lb 3, w 4, nb 4		11
(32.4 overs)			90

	O	M	R	W
McDermott	6	–	19	–
Tazelaar	7	1	18	3
Rackemann	8	3	9	3
Maguire	9	1	30	3
Ritchie	2.4	–	11	–

FALL OF WICKETS
1–3, 2–7, 3–22, 4–37, 5–42, 6–45, 7–46, 8–53, 9–71

Umpires: R.C. Bailhache & L.J. King

Man of the Match: A.R. Border

Queensland won by 163 runs

SHEFFIELD SHIELD FINAL – WESTERN AUSTRALIA v. SOUTH AUSTRALIA
25, 26, 27, 28 and 29 March 1989 at WACA Ground, Perth

WESTERN AUSTRALIA

	FIRST INNINGS		SECOND INNINGS	
G.R. Marsh	c Hilditch, b Scuderi	55	not out	105
M.R.J. Veletta	c Hookes, b Scuderi	26	lbw, b Scuderi	5
T.M. Moody	lbw, b May	162	lbw, b Williams	155
G.M. Wood†	b Miller	68		
W.S. Andrews	b Miller	75		
T.J. Zoehrer*	lbw, b Miller	81		
P. Gonnella	c Scuderi, b Miller	10	(4) not out	11
K.H. MacLeay	c Sleep, b Miller	10		
P.A. Capes	c May, b Miller	4		
A. Mullally	c Williams, b Miller	0		
T.M. Alderman	not out	1		
Extras	b 6, lb 29, w 4, nb 4	43	b 5, lb 4, nb 4	13
		535	(for 2 wkts)	289

	O	M	R	W	O	M	R	W
Gladigau	38	8	92	–	16	3	47	–
Miller	35.3	7	112	7	14	1	63	–
Scuderi	41	8	159	2	23	5	68	1
May	43	15	94	1	9	2	32	–
Sleep	9	–	43	–	3	–	23	–
Williams					7	2	21	1
Hilditch					4	–	8	–
Anderson					4	–	7	–
Lehmann					1	–	5	–

FALL OF WICKETS
1–65, 2–116, 3–346, 4–503, 5–510, 6–526, 7–532, 8–535, 9–535
1–10, 2–236

SOUTH AUSTRALIA

	FIRST INNINGS	
B.D. Williams	lbw, b MacLeay	69
A.M.J. Hilditch	c Marsh, b Alderman	41
P.C. Nobes	c Marsh, b MacLeay	18
D.W. Hookes†	c Alderman, b Capes	24
D.S. Lehmann	c Veletta, b Alderman	17
P.R. Sleep	not out	146
J.C. Scuderi	lbw, b Moody	11
P.W. Anderson*	c Wood, b Alderman	38
T.B.A. May	c and b Alderman	34
P.W. Gladigau	st Zoehrer, b Andrews	45
C.R. Miller	c Marsh, b Andrews	0
Extras	b 5, lb 13, nb 33	51
		494

	O	M	R	W
Capes	38	10	115	1
Alderman	43	7	117	4
Mullally	34	4	106	–
MacLeay	34	9	96	2
Moody	9	3	23	1
Andrews	2.3	–	19	2

FALL OF WICKETS
1–118, 2–147, 3–156, 4–189, 5–202, 6–231, 7–341, 8–409, 9–494

Umpires: P.J. McConnell & A.R. Crafter

Match drawn – Western Australia win Shield by virtue of heading league

Tom Moody – a century in each innings of the Sheffield Shield Final. (George Herringshaw)

frenzied inactivity as 245 runs came from 87 overs with six wickets falling. Western Australia really won the Shield in the middle session of play, when they bowled 27 overs and conceded only 62 runs: Capes, Alderman, Mullally and MacLeay were on top form – and the South Australian batsmen became increasingly frustrated as they let the game slip.

Peter Sleep, with a career-best unbeaten 146, saw his side to 494 on the fourth day – just 41 runs behind the home team. But now it was just a matter of playing out time as Marsh and Moody ambled to 26 for 1 at the close. Tom Moody dominated the final day, scoring 155 – including 98 before lunch – to become only the third Western Australian to score a century in each innings of a first-class match, following Alan Edwards and Peter Kelly. Geoff Marsh stayed through the day unbeaten on 105 as the total ended on 289 for 2 to make three titles in a row for Graeme Wood and his team.

Chris Harte

First-Class Averages

BATTING

	M	Inns	NOs	Runs	HS	Av	100s	50s
B.D. Williams	2	3		186	77	62.00		2
T.M. Moody	13	20	1	1175	202	61.84	4	5
R.J. Tucker	7	12	3	548	98	60.88		5
T.J. Zoehrer	13	16	3	779	168	59.92	2	4
R.E. Soule	11	12	5	408	99	58.28		3
D.M. Wellham	11	13	4	555	94	55.50		5
P.J. Drinnen	3	4	1	150	74	50.00		1
M.A. Taylor	14	26	1	1241	152*	49.64	3	7
J. Cox	3	6	2	194	82*	48.50		1
W.N. Phillips	8	12		580	111	48.33	1	4
M.R.J. Veletta	14	23	2	1004	166*	47.80	3	4
A.B. Henschell	2	4	1	140	61	46.66		1
G.R. Marsh	15	25	1	1092	223	45.50	3	4
D.C. Boon	13	23	2	939	149	44.71	2	6
G.M. Wood	14	21	6	670	138*	44.66	3	1
D.W. Hookes	12	21	3	762	133	42.33	1	5
G.R.J. Matthews	12	17	3	588	108	42.00	2	2
P.R. Sleep	12	17	3	587	146*	41.92	2	1
G.A. Hughes	11	18	1	711	126	41.82	1	5
W.S. Andrews	13	18	2	668	121	41.75	1	4
P.C. Nobes	12	21	1	811	95	40.55		9
M.E. Waugh	11	21	3	727	103*	40.38	2	4
D.M. Jones	11	19	2	679	216	39.94	2	
D.S. Lehmann	7	13	1	478	89	39.83		5
A.M.J. Hilditch	12	21	1	796	168	39.80	2	3
J. Dyson	12	22	3	742	112*	39.05	2	4
G.M. Ritchie	11	17	1	624	140	39.00	2	2
G.M. Watts	11	18		694	135	38.55	2	3
G. Shipperd	9	12	2	382	155*	38.20	1	1
P.L. Taylor	12	18	6	429	84	35.75		1
S.G. Law	10	16	3	452	179	34.76	1	1
B.A. Cruse	5	6		205	98	34.16		2
J.D. Siddons	11	18	1	564	156	33.17	1	4
G.R. Parker	5	9	1	256	56	32.00		2
T.G. Hogan	7	8	2	192	115*	32.00	1	
T.J. Barsby	11	19		588	92	30.94		6
S.B. Smith	11	19	1	557	77	30.94		4
S.R. Waugh	14	24	1	711	118	30.91	1	3
P.S. Clifford	6	11	2	271	71*	30.11		2
M.G. Dimattina	11	16	2	416	113	29.71	1	1
T.H. Bayliss	6	10	2	237	70*	29.62		2
D.J. Buckingham	8	11	2	266	69	29.55		1
I.A. Healy	13	19	5	407	90	29.07		2
P.A. Emery	5	6	2	116	83	29.00		1
D.F. Whatmore	8	13		376	90	28.92		2
G.A. Bishop	10	20	2	504	57	28.00		3
P.E. Cantrell	10	17	1	436	105	27.25	1	2
S.P. O'Donnell	11	17	1	428	60	26.75		3
A.K. Zesers	6	8	1	187	80	26.71		1
A.R. Border	12	21	2	506	75	26.63		4
J.C. Scuderi	9	13	1	309	67	25.75		2
R.B. Kerr	4	6		153	69	25.50		2
G.C. Dyer	7	10	2	204	69	25.50		1
P. Gonnella	8	14	2	303	65*	25.25		2
J.A. Brayshaw	5	5		125	81	25.00		1
M.G. Hughes	13	17	5	272	72*	22.66		1
G.S. Trimble	4	7		157	62	22.42		1
G.F. Lawson	11	11	3	169	71	21.12		1
M. Osborne	7	10	5	101	58*	20.20		1
P.W. Gladigau	12	15	4	210	47*	19.09		
P.W. Anderson	12	16	3	240	52*	18.46		1
W.B. Phillips	5	8	1	129	36	18.42		
K.H. MacLeay	13	15	3	219	70	18.25		1
A.I.C. Dodemaide	12	19	3	290	54*	18.12		1
M.D. Taylor	7	7		122	32	17.42		
T.B.A. May	14	19	7	206	37	17.16		
W.G. Ayres	3	6		101	41	16.83		
C.D. Matthews	6	7		112	50	16.00		1
C.J. McDermott	9	14	2	188	35	15.66		5
J.N. Maguire	9	10	3	107	32	15.28		
T.V. Hohns	10	13	2	161	35	14.63		
G.D. Campbell	11	11	3	112	41	14.00		
P.I. Faulkner	8	9		119	43	13.22		

(Qualification – 100 runs, average 10.00)

BOWLING

	Overs	Mds	Runs	Wkts	Av	Best	10/m	5/inns
A.R. Border	78.4	22	182	12	15.16	7/46	1	1

	Overs	Mds	Runs	Wkts	Av	Best	10/m	5/inns
T.M. Alderman	442.1	122	1005	48	20.93	5/26		2
T.M. Moody	97	25	231	11	21.00	3/24		
G.F. Lawson	405.1	112	1005	45	22.33	6/36		4
M.R. Whitney	460.3	110	1370	58	23.62	7/89		2
D. Tazelaar	335.4	71	889	36	24.69	5/25	1	2
M. Osborne	122.3	26	433	16	27.06	4/17		
K.H. MacLeay	410.4	133	897	33	27.18	4/24		
J.C. Scuderi	367.3	105	910	33	27.57	6/53		3
J.N. Maguire	251.2	49	647	21	30.80	4/21		
S.R. Waugh	365	68	1114	36	30.94	6/51		2
C.G. Rackemann	269	61	748	24	31.16	6/65		1
B.A. Reid	134.4	25	348	11	31.63	3/28		
P.A. Capes	286.5	61	894	28	31.92	5/69	1	3
T.B.A. May	634.3	160	1601	50	32.02	7/93		3
M.G. Hughes	442.3	97	1330	41	32.43	8/87	2	4
A.D. Mullally	241.5	51	755	23	32.82	4/71		
G.D. Campbell	426	91	1209	36	33.58	5/44		3
C.J. McDermott	259.4	38	885	26	34.03	5/85		1
T.V. Hohns	391.5	102	942	27	34.88	5/50		2
A.K. Zesers	185	63	435	12	36.25	3/41		
T.G. Hogan	198.1	51	511	14	36.50	3/78		
R.J. Tucker	184.3	34	518	14	37.00	3/38		
P.W. Gladigau	417	103	1099	29	37.89	4/53		

	Overs	Mds	Runs	Wkts	Av	Best	10/m	5/inns
A.I.C. Dodemaide	388	81	1147	30	38.23	5/94		1
C.D. Matthews	182	30	613	16	38.31	5/84		1
A.J. de Winter	257.3	48	728	19	38.31	5/88		1
D.R. Gilbert	325.1	49	1019	26	39.19	5/88		1
G.R.J. Matthews	447.3	128	1111	28	39.67	3/43		
P.L. Taylor	378.1	101	1029	24	42.87	3/35		
P.E. Cantrell	224	39	658	15	43.86	4/52		
P.W. Jackson	300	99	764	17	44.94	6/55		1
S.P. O'Donnell	286.2	55	836	16	52.25	6/54		1
P.R. Sleep	296	77	895	14	63.92	4/109		
P.I. Faulkner	319	91	720	11	65.45	3/60		

(Qualification – 10 wickets)

LEADING FIELDERS

45 – T.J. Zoehrer (ct 41/st 4); 38 - I.A. Healy (ct 36/st 2); 32 - P.W. Anderson (ct 30/st 2); 29 - M.G. Dimattina (ct 24/st 5); 22 - M.A. Taylor; 21 - R.E. Soule and G.C. Dyer (ct 20/st 1); 20 - G.R. Marsh; 18 - D.W. Hookes; 17 - M.R.J. Veletta; 16 - P.A. Emery (ct 15/st 1); 14 - P.L. Taylor; 13 - D.C. Boon, D.M. Jones, P.E. Cantrell and A.R. Border; 12 - S.R. Waugh and P.S. Clifford; 11 - P.R. Sleep, W.S. Andrews, J. Dyson, A.I.C. Dodemaide and K.H. MacLeay; 10 - G.R.J. Matthews, M.E. Waugh, T.H. Bayliss and P.J. Drinnen.

AUSTRALIAN SHEFFIELD SHIELD SEASON 1988–9
by Chris Harte

Late in the afternoon of Wednesday 29th March 1989, Western Australian captain Graeme Wood proudly raised the Sheffield Shield to indicate to Australian cricket, yet again, his State's superiority in the competition.

For five months the title had been in doubt as fortunes ebbed and flowed. Had Queensland batsman Ian Healy been able to hit a boundary from New South Wales bowler Peter Taylor's final delivery of their match in Sydney, then Queensland would have hosted the final against Western Australia in Brisbane. As it was, Healy failed in his attempt and so South Australia went to Perth to face Graeme Wood and his men.

So much of Australian cricket's main decisions seemed to be made off the field before and during the 1988–9 season. On 16 June 1988 at a Melbourne hotel, Greg Chappell, looked upon by many as the potential saviour of the domestic game, tipped a monumental bucket on cricket administration at the State level.

Chappell, in announcing his resignation from all cricket administration, stated that he was 'beating his head against a brick wall'. He added: 'The system of administration of Australian cricket is archaic. The wrong people are getting involved in the game, and it is very difficult for the right people to get in.' Turning to the State Associations, Chappell said they were 'generally poorly administered', with Queensland being the least enlightened of the lot'.

He concluded: 'Queensland has never won a Sheffield Shield, but even in my time there, since moving from South Australia in 1973, if the place was properly run we probably could have won six.'

In many ways Chappell was reiterating the forthright views of another Australian captain, Richie Benaud, who had been saying similar things for nearly three decades. In spite of those views, any reaction to Greg Chappell's comments appeared lost on most States, the majority of whom blundered their way through the season. The glowing exception, Western Australia, showed on the field how a good administration can breed a confidence and pride throughout a State squad.

Maybe, someday, the rest will follow.

The 1988–9 Sheffield Shield season started on 28 October in Adelaide when South Australia, guided by new coach Barry Richards, took on Victoria under recently appointed captain Simon O'Donnell. The Victorian selectors had dumped last season's skipper, Dean Jones, and gambled on O'Donnell, recently recovered from cancer, a natural team leader and now an inspiration to thousands of fellow sufferers. Having ballooned to 17 stone and suffered the loss of his hair through chemotherapy treatment, O'Donnell was now fit and raring to go.

He won the toss, elected to bat on a typically perfect pitch and watched as openers Davenell Whatmore and Gary Watts put on a century partnership in the first session. Richards read the riot act to his charges during the interval, which had the desired effect as Victoria lost their next eight wickets for 88 runs, being dismissed early on the second morning for 231. When O'Donnell walked to the crease in mid-afternoon he was given a rousing standing ovation by the large Friday crowd. It was an emotional reception which O'Donnell acknowledged with good grace. From the centre he could see the SACA committee room, and his heart no doubt missed a beat when he saw the greatest of all cricketers standing, amongst others, applauding him.

South Australia gained a first-innings lead of 56 as a result of half centuries from Andrew Hilditch (65), David Hookes (58) and Paul Nobes (56), who was making his début. Three run outs broke the back of the Victorian second innings, with Dean Jones' dismissal being highly unusual. Noticing that Jones was batting out of his crease, South Australian captain, Hookes, told his medium-fast bowler Andrew Zesers to bowl a delivery wide of the off stump – which he duly did. Hookes gathered the ball and threw down the stumps with a direct hit, an action which saw the out-of-form Jones trudge dejectedly from the field.

Only a big hitting last-wicket partnership, mainly due to Australia's new cult hero Merv Hughes, who remained unbeaten on 32, saw Victoria reach 177. South Australia struggled early on in chasing 122 for victory, but when Hookes came to the crease the final 51 runs came in 23 minutes, as the home team won by eight wickets.

In Brisbane, Greg Dyer won the toss and batted in 30° C heat, and must have rued his decision when New South Wales were 24 for four. Then a flu-stricken Steve Waugh and Greg Matthews (108) hammered centuries and shared a five-hour partnership of 195. Waugh scored his 118 in 272 minutes from 187 balls with 14 fours. Paceman Craig McDermott (5 for 85) mopped up the tail as the Queensland batsmen prepared to chase 291. A top-order collapse saw them at 133 for 6 until new Australian wicket-keeper Ian Healy saved the day with a fighting knock.

Having gained a first-innings lead of 79, New South Wales went for the runs, aided by some sloppy homeground fielding. Five catches went down and, had it not been for three spells of tight accurate bowling by Craig McDermott, New South Wales would have added considerably to their 249. Needing 329 to win in 91 overs on the final day, Queensland claimed full points with two balls to go and with only two wickets remaining.

Captain Allan Border described the victory as 'a nail-biting thriller', and 'one of the best wins I have had in six years at the helm'. Greg Ritchie (92) and Glenn Trimble (62) blazed a 134-run fifth-wicket partnership in 115 minutes to set up a challenge for the lower order batsmen. On their departure 100 were needed in the final 20 overs. Trevor Hohns and Ian Healy then put on 53 in eight overs and, on Hohn's departure, McDermott joined Healy for a 29-run effort in seven overs. Umpires Col Timmins and Peter Parker then offered the batsmen the opportunity to leave the field because of deteriorating light, a move which was promptly rejected. With three runs needed from the final over, paceman Geoff Lawson watched agonizingly as his first three deliveries went past Dirk Tazelaar's off stump, with his fourth slashed through mid-off to bring a home success.

New South Wales travelled home for their match against Victoria four days later, to be played on a pitch about which the politest comment was from Simon O'Donnell, who described it as 'a minefield'. The visitors batted first, taking six hours to reach 174 for 8. Dav Whatmore, usually a dashing opening batsman, took 3½ hours to score 38 runs, including 39 stagnant minutes when it seemed he would never progress beyond seven. Tony Dodemaide took half a day to also make 38, while the New South Wales bowlers sent down 96 overs, of which Michael Whitney bowled 21 to take 3 for 24.

Victoria added only a single before their innings folded on the second morning; then the New South Wales batsmen hit a horror patch. From 35 without loss, they had five wickets go down for the addition of only two runs, and lost eight for 36 before Greg Dyer (69) and Geoff Lawson (32) added 87 for the ninth wicket in even time. Dyer's innings took exactly two hours with seven boundaries. For Victoria, O'Donnell claimed career-best figures of 6 for 54

and must have been relieved as his team gained a two-run first-innings lead.

Watts and Whatmore saw the score to 42 at stumps, continuing on in front of a good Sunday crowd as the pitch became easier. Whatmore (42) went at 117, but Gary Watts carried on to post his third Shield century, finishing with 135 made in 343 minutes with 14 boundaries from 276 balls. His third-wicket partnership of 119 with Jamie Siddons (63) was the highlight of the day's play. O'Donnell declared at 331 for seven, which left New South Wales needing 334 for victory.

Try as hard as they could, New South Wales just could not force the pace on the final day. The spin pair of Paul Jackson and Mark Osborne stifled any hope Greg Dyer's team had of victory and the match finished in a draw with New South Wales still 22 runs short.

The benefit of the new National Cricket Academy bore fruit for Queensland in their match against Tasmania in Brisbane. The visitors were sent in to bat, and took a day and a half to score 405. New captain Dirk Wellham made 92, and Richard Soule an unbeaten 80. At 289 for 9, Tasmania could have hoped for 300. As it was, Soule, along with Greg Campbell, added 116 for the last wicket in 158 minutes.

Queensland plodded to 125 for 3 at the end of Saturday's play, and with Sunday washed out by a typical Brisbane November rainstorm, it was up to overnight-batsmen Stuart Law (21 not out) and Allan Border (12 not out) to take the fight to the Tasmanian bowlers. Law, playing in only his second first-class match, had spent the past six months in Adelaide being specially coached at the Academy by Jack Potter and his assistant, Peter Spence. Resuming with Border, the pair added a record 143 for the fourth wicket, with Law at one stage telling his captain, 'not to worry, I'll take on (Dave) Gilbert'. The maturity of Law impressed Border – who did as he was told. Law then added 78 with Glenn Trimble, and 62 with Ian Healy, before falling at 400, still six runs in arrears. Law scored 179, described by Border as 'a fantastic performance'. He took just under seven hours, and hit 17 fours (10 of which were driven through the covers) and 1 six off Peter Faulkner, which landed in a rubbish bin.

While all this was going on, a first-class match was taking place in Perth between Western Australia, as Sheffield Shield champions, and Indian Ranji Trophy holders Tamil Nadu. Geoff Marsh and Mike Veletta opened with a partnership of 374 with Marsh scoring a career-best 209.

Six days later at Bellerive Oval, Hobart, the pair put on 310 for the first wicket against Tasmania, with Marsh exceeding his best with 223 made in a fraction over nine hours, with 22 fours and a six. Mike Veletta added to his unbeaten 166 in Perth by scoring 157, added to which big-hitting Tom Moody savaged the Tasmanian bowling with 112 containing 8 fours and 5 sixes in even time as Western Australia made 502 for 2 declared.

Tasmania had already batted, scoring 213, and in reply were 108 for 1, when overnight rain caused the game to be abandoned early on the final day.

Queensland scored a fine four-wicket victory over Victoria at St Kilda's Junction Oval in their match which started on 11 November. Put in to bat, the Victorians had no answer to the pace attack of Dirk Tazelaar (5 for 25) and John Maguire (4 for 21), and were dismissed before tea for 103. Queensland overtook this score with only two wickets down, Trevor Barsby making 92, Border 57, and Greg Ritchie 46. Great credit went to paceman Merv Hughes, who, on a docile pitch, bowled with guile and fire to take 7 for 81. Victorian coach Ian Redpath was pleased with his charges and said of Hughes: 'He put some welcome steel back into the side, and did well to keep bowling at off stump and not drift to leg as he had done before.'

As Queensland's last wicket fell at 260, so the ground announcer read the Australian team for the first Test against the West Indies in Brisbane. Merv was in the squad along with fellow Victorian Tony Dodemaide, who had claimed the other three Queensland wickets. For the rest of Saturday, and all day on Sunday, Victoria laboured in their second innings, Davenell Whatmore's 90 took 400 minutes; Simon O'Donnell took 133 minutes for his 44, and the third day ended at 270 for seven.

Monday dawned wet and miserable, but play started on time. Dirk Tazelaar took the remaining three wickets to finish with 5 for 55, leaving Queensland to score 125 for victory. Hughes was not going to allow the visiting batsmen any room for manoeuvre as he thumped the ball in with accuracy. From 73 for 1, five wickets fell for 33 and the game was evenly poised. However, Stuart Law came to the rescue and Queensland gained full points in the gloom and persistent rain.

The following weekend saw only one Shield match scheduled. Originally South Australia were to play Tasmania in Launceston, but the poor quality of the centre square saw the match transferred to Hobart. Dirk Wellham won the toss and asked the visitors to bat on a greenish pitch. In the opinion of South Australian coach Barry Richards, 'The Tasmanians bowled very well and Wellham is to be praised for a good tactical display.' This was after the visitors had struggled to 200 for 6 from the first day's 95 overs.

The second day was a very different ball game. After losing a wicket early, Peter Sleep (100) and Andrew Zesers (80) proceeded to add a record breaking 171 for the eighth wicket to frustrate the Tasmanian attack, with the innings finally ending at 382.

Wellham knew the match would be only a first-innings affair and gave his batsmen instructions to play cautiously. They did, to such an extent that the score mounted by only two runs an over. Glenn Hughes (126) and Richard Bennett (34) broke the first-wicket record partnership for matches against South Australia as Tasmania plodded to 244 for 4 at stumps on day three. The collapse came next morning as the final six wickets fell in the space of 42 runs and the game then petered out to its predictable conclusion.

The Tasmanians then went north to Devonport to face New South Wales the following weekend. Once again Wellham won the toss and decided to field. Only an hour's play was possible because of rain, by which time New South Wales were 50 for 2. Rain still persisted on the Saturday but most of the day saw the game continue. It was left to the dashing Steve Smith to bolster New South Wales with a sparkling 77, which contained 5 fours and 2 sixes, Greg Campbell took 5 for 44 with his medium pace as New South Wales reached 228.

Tasmania, 54 without loss overnight, fairly rattled along. David Boon scored 98; Glenn Hughes and Bruce Cruse made half-centuries and, tragedy of tragedies, portly wicket-keeper Richard Soule was run out by John Dyson, when on 99 and going for his maiden first-class century. But Tasmania had the points, and, as so often happened during the season, this was sufficient for them to then play for a draw. Not, however, before New South Wales opener Mark Waugh had cracked an unbeaten century.

With the inter-island jealousy that is a regular part of Tasmanian life, cricket suffers as much as any other sport. In Hobart the Shield crowds were good considering the population. To programme matches in Devonport, just to stop the natives becoming restless, is downright stupid. On the final day the biggest crowd was in the press-box with less than two dozen spectators paying at the gate.

Adelaide's second Shield match saw Western Australia bat for all the first day to be 258 for 7, with Mike Veletta top scoring with 69 made in 249 minutes of slow grind. Off-spinner Tim May wrapped up the innings for 268 next day, finishing with 5 for 92. The home reply was a mixed bag: Paul Nobes taking 230 minutes for his 79, and Peter Anderson 141 minutes for his unbeaten 52. The Western Australians had gambled by bringing in injured Test fast bowler Bruce Reid, but to no avail, as it was obvious he was far from effective.

Gaining a 57-run lead, South Australia would have expected a hard fight to prise out the visitors a second time. But, in an unusual move, off-spinner Tim May was brought on for the fifth over and bowled unchanged, initially with Peter Gladigau, the promising local paceman, and then with Joe Scuderi, one of the leading players from the National Cricket Academy.

Suddenly from 50 without loss, Western Australia crumbled. May took 4 for 49 and Scuderi, with a top-class display of controlled medium-paced deliveries, 5 for 51, and South Australia needed only 75 to win with three and a half sessions in which to get them.

Then came the shock. On an unresponsive pitch Western Australian seamer Terry Alderman took 5 for 29 in nine overs and South Australia were reeling. At stumps they were 68 for 6, still needing seven runs to win. Next morning in front of 122 spectators, who saw 13 minutes of play, the home side gained the points and a three-wicket victory.

Western Australia then made their way to Newcastle to play New South Wales. Marsh, Veletta and Wood went home to Perth for the second Test, with Wood's replacement being Kim Hughes, a shadow of his former self and now barely a fringe Shield player. Hughes, who had lost everything in the stock market crash, was working as a builder's labourer for his brother-in-law: a far cry from the national hero-worshipping of a few seasons earlier.

Acting-captain Terry Alderman gambled by sending New South Wales in to bat on a flat pitch which was evenly paced. After John Dyson fell early, it was the exciting

Mark Waugh, with 10 boundaries, who took control for New South Wales. His 69 was elegantly made and should have been many more had he not miscued a hook from Bruce Reid. Alderman again did well with 4 for 42 from 21 controlled overs and on stumps New South Wales were dismissed for 269.

Most of the local players then spent the evening at one of Newcastle's best sea-food restaurants, which seems to have been a team get-together to repair harmony which had been lacking behind the scenes. Maybe it worked, temporarily, as the following day the bowling and fielding were of the highest order. Western Australia had only Peter Gonnella (45) getting past the twenties as Mike Whitney, Peter Taylor and Andrew Jones each took three wickets as the visitors fell for 164.

John Dyson and Mark Taylor opened, and continued their stand to 130 before Dyson played back to Alderman and was bowled for 78. Taylor went from 55 to 83 in 38 minutes after lunch before he edged Bruce Reid to wicket-keeper Tim Zoehrer, to give the Western Australian the first of his four catches for the innings. The New South Wales batsmen then hit out, and an hour before the close Dyer declared at 279 for 7, leaving the visitors to score 385 for victory.

Gonnella went in Richard Stobo's first over to give the New South Wales paceman his initial wicket in his début match, and at stumps Western Australia had moved to 41 for 1.

The final day saw some unwanted histrionics from New South Wales off-spinner Greg Matthews as Western Australia slowly but surely fell to defeat. Ken MacLeay and Tom Moody fell in the first hour, both to Mike Whitney, and only determined batting from vice-captain Wayne Andrews (69 in 169 minutes) made any impression. When the final wicket fell 15 minutes into the last hour, New South Wales had won by 134 runs, with Western Australia suffering the rare occurrence of two outright defeats in 11 days.

Two matches were played from 10 to 13 December, both ending in tame draws. At the Melbourne Cricket Ground, Tasmania took first use of the pitch against Victoria. The previous day had seen flash flooding in parts of the city, with grade cricket matches already abandoned, yet the match started on time and in hot sunshine: bearing out the adage that Melbourne's weather can produce all four seasons in one day!

Victoria had a good morning, having the Tasmanians at 71 for 4 at lunch. But then Greg Shipperd came to the crease and consolidation began. Dirk Wellham (38), Rod Tucker (39), Richard Soule (57) and Greg Campbell (37) all stayed with the diminutive batsman – who is also the Tasmanian assistant coach – with the last three wickets adding 290 runs on the second day.

Shipperd's unbeaten 155 took an amazing 546 minutes, with poor Mick Taylor acting as his runner for seven hours after Shipperd damaged a hamstring. Wellham declared at 428 for 9 towards the end of the sixth session to give himself just over two days to dismiss the Victorians.

The reply was bitty. Dav Whatmore top-scored with 69, two players made sixties, and there were three run outs as Victoria reached 397 from 151 overs. Tasmania batted out

time facing part-time bowling and that was that.

Prior to the game in Brisbane between Queensland and South Australia, a most unusual fight had been going on between the States over who had the right to select the talented Joe Scuderi. Born in North Queensland, Scuderi had come up through the ranks of Queensland Country cricket and in junior representative matches. When the Cricket Academy, based in Adelaide, looked for its first intake of students, Joe Scuderi was one of the Queenslanders selected.

Having settled in Adelaide, Scuderi (and a number of other students) found the life-style very acceptable and let it be known, privately, that he was seriously considering staying in South Australia. Then the South Australia selectors chose him for the away match against Tasmania, and subsequently the home fixture with Western Australia. In Tasmania he had made 17 (before being given out caught off his pad) and had bowled 43 overs, taking 3 for 60. Against Western Australia it was 39 and 1, with bowling 1 for 61 from 22 overs followed by 5 for 51.

The Queensland selectors took note, for under the rules of the Academy a player's home State had first call on him unless he had played three times for South Australia. Scuderi had played twice.

Scuderi met the cricketing media late on the third day of the Western Australia match. 'I haven't heard anything from Queensland', he said. 'But I enjoy playing for South Australia and I'd be very disappointed if I wasn't with them in Brisbane in a couple of weeks' time. In so far as I have any say in the matter I want to play for South Australia. They have given me the chance; if I was in Queensland now I don't even think I would be a net bowler. I know the South Australian players and I don't know the Queensland guys. They don't really mean anything to me whereas the South Australian players have been really good to me, full of advice and encouragement since I came here. I feel at home, so why should I want to play for Queensland?' Scuderi concluded: 'South Australia picked me and gave me a chance. I think they should get the benefit of that.'

The following day Scuderi was chosen by the Queensland selectors to play in two one-day matches against Pakistan in Mackay. He said on hearing of his selection: 'Obviously I can't do a lot about it. If I have to play for Queensland then that's all there is to it.'

In the first match on 3 December, Scuderi was run out without scoring and bowled five overs for 27 runs. Overnight he was taken ill and missed the second game. Queensland Cricket Association chairman Alan Pettigrew flew north from Brisbane to Mackay to see Scuderi to discuss his future. A lot of hot air was spoken to the media about 'securing Scuderi's future in Queensland', but as is so often the case nothing came of it.

Next day moves were made behind the scenes. Australian Cricket Board delegate Colin Egar from South Australia spoke to Pettigrew and others, pointing out that Scuderi was an Australian and had suffered enough through inter-state parochialism. In a press release issued later that night, the Queensland selection panel said it felt that 'it was in Scuderi's best interests he not be picked for the State against South Australia'.

New South Wales 1988–9

First-Class Matches

BATTING

Matches (two innings each — 1st / 2nd):
1. v. Queensland (Brisbane) 28–31 October 1988
2. v. Victoria (Sydney) 4–7 November 1988
3. v. West Indians (Sydney) 11–14 November 1988
4. v. Tasmania (Devonport) 25–8 November 1988
5. v. Western Australia (Newcastle) 2–5 December 1988
6. v. Pakistanis (Sydney) 19–21 December 1988
7. v. South Australia (Adelaide) 6–9 January 1989
8. v. Victoria (Melbourne) 20–3 January 1989
9. v. South Australia (Sydney) 9–12 February 1989
10. v. Western Australia (Perth) 15–18 February 1989

BATTING	1a	1b	2a	2b	3a	3b	4a	4b	5a	5b	6a	6b	7a	7b	8a	8b	9a	9b	10a	10b
M.A. Taylor	2	85	28	73	82	49	10	0	28	83	0	62	86	—	40	4	69	—	107	152*
J. Dyson	5	14	8	16	79	100*	40	53*	8	78	34	8	55	—	4	0	25	—	26	15
S.B. Smith	0	29	0	17	63	—	77	—	12	4	26	3*			45	32	38	—	35	41
S.R. Waugh	118	5	0	24	21	—	39	—	69	39	0	63*			7	5	29	—	38	37
M.E. Waugh	0	18	0	46	9	103*	0	100*	69	39	0	63*			7	5	29	—	38	37
G.R.J. Matthews	108	32	12	11	26*	—	6	—	40	5	0	—	104	—	34	36	76*	—	5	—
T.H. Bayliss	0	3	14	70*	9	—			39	26	52	5*	19	—						
P.L. Taylor	34	12	1	44	50*	—	0	—	21	19*	6*	—	22	—	0	10*	84	—	9	—
G.C. Dyer	0	19	69	3*	33	—	22	—	14	16	6*	—	71	—	0	5			38	—
G.F. Lawson	0*	10	32	—	9	—	4*	—					0*	—	0*	0			22*	—
M.R. Whitney	1	6*	2*	—	0*	—	6	—			0	—			0*	0				
R.A. Jones								14	21*	—	0	—	3							
R.J. Stobo											0	—	42	3						
M.D. O'Neill													5	27						
G.J. Robertson													11	—						
J.D. Kenny															0	83	4*	—	10	—
P.A. Emery															0	0			0	—
W.J. Holdsworth																			—	—
S.B.J. Whitfield																			—	—

	1a	1b	2a	2b	3a	3b	4a	4b	5a	5b	6a	6b	7a	7b	8a	8b	9a	9b	10a	10b
Byes			4	1	8	1	3		1		4		4	4	2	2	5		4	
Leg-byes	6	6	3	7	6	6	2		4		4		5	5	7	1	4	3	9	15
Wides																1			1	2
No-balls	17	10			6	2	5	4	8	5	1		10		1	1			11	9
Total	291	249	173	312	401	261	228	157	269	279	175	150	423	—	151	191	357	—	326	303
Wickets	10	10	10	7	8	1	10	1	10	7	10	2	10	—	10	10	6	—	10	
Result	L		D		D		D		W		D		D		L		D		W	
Points	0		0		—		0		6		—		0		0		2		6	

Fielding Figures

21 – M.A. Taylor and G.C. Dyer (ct 20/st 1)
16 – P.A. Emery (ct 15/st 1)
12 – S.B. Smith
11 – J. Dyson

10 – G.R.J. Matthews, M.E. Waugh and T.H. Bayliss
9 – P.L. Taylor and S.R. Waugh
3 – G.F. Lawson

2 – M.D. O'Neill, M.R. Whitney, R.J. Stobo and W.J. Holdsworth
1 – J.D. Kenny, G.J. Robertson and S.B.J. Whitfield

BOWLING

	G.F. Lawson	M.R. Whitney	S.R. Waugh	G.R.J. Matthews	M.E. Waugh	P.L. Taylor	S.B. Smith	R.A. Jones
v. Queensland (Brisbane) 28–31 October 1988	18–5–39–3	15–1–53–0	22–7–48–3	14–5–22–2	3–0–21–0	11.3–3–20–2		
	21.4–5–77–3	15–2–52–2	22–2–79–2	18–3–55–0	3–0–15–0	11–1–41–0		
v. Victoria (Sydney) 4–7 November 1988	23.2–9–31–2	21–11–24–3	17–9–21–2	19–8–38–2		19–7–45–1		
	28–11–32–3	31–7–91–3	17–1–81–0	18–6–61–1	7–2–23–0	18–7–38–0		
v. West Indians (Sydney) 11–14 November 1988	24.2–10–69–5	21–3–82–2	10–2–22–0	23–4–77–2		21–4–72–1		
	4–0–24–0	5–1–19–1		15–4–41–1		17–5–65–2	~ 1–0–4–0	
v. Tasmania (Devonport) 25–8 November 1988	26.4–8–63–3	36–7–90–2	29–7–68–2	16–4–34–0	7–0–21–0	20–6–39–0		16–3–38–1
v. Western Australia (Newcastle) 2–5 December 1988		13–4–44–3		7–2–15–1		16–5–35–3		10–3–18–3
		26–7–80–3		27–8–53–2		24.2–5–49–2		14–1–45–1
v. Pakistanis (Sydney) 19–21 December 1988		15.5–5–34–4		18–6–47–1	13–4–46–1			6–0–24–0
		21.1–3–66–5		13–1–32–2	8–1–24–0			
v. South Australia (Adelaide) 6–9 January 1989	30–5–95–1	39.1–14–104–4		32–8–118–2				
	4–0–14–0	6–0–20–0						
v. Victoria (Melbourne) 20–3 January 1989	12.1–0–42–1	12–4–26–0	6–1–21–0	20–6–52–1		21–9–41–2		
	21–3–52–0	14–4–49–4	11–4–17–1	21–3–64–1		15–3–48–1		
v. South Australia (Sydney) 9–12 February 1989	27–7–72–5	21.4–6–71–2	21–5–54–1	22–8–57–0		1–0–9–0		
	17–9–30–1	14–3–42–1		39–15–77–3		18–6–52–2		
						19–8–38–1		
v. Western Australia (Perth) 15–18 February 1989	21–6–49–3	15–1–59–1	13–0–49–3	21.3–8–43–3				
	24.5–10–51–5	9–0–53–1	16–1–68–3	17–2–49–0	1–0–4–0	17–2–55–1		
v. Tasmania (Sydney) 22–5 February 1989	19.1–6–36–6	13–5–32–2	6–1–21–0	14–5–31–1		11–5–25–1		
	22–4–64–0	19–5–51–3	14–7–21–3	35–11–63–2		7–2–27–0		
v. Queensland (Sydney) 10–13 March 1989	18–4–29–1	13.4–2–52–3	12–4–21–0	24–8–43–1		21–5–42–1		
	11–3–39–0	9–3–27–0	10–0–51–6	14–3–39–0		21–2–84–1		
	373.1–105–908–42	406.3–98–1221–49	226–51–642–26	447.3–128–1111–28	43–7–163–1	307.5–85–816–21	1–0–4–0	46–7–125–5
	av. 21.61	av. 24.91	av. 24.69	av. 39.67	av. 163.00	av. 38.85	—	av. 25.00

Four days later Scuderi tore the heart out of Queensland's middle order batsmen, taking 3 for 40 off 17 overs as the home side scored 170 for 6 in a full day's play. The struggle went on next day with Queensland making just two runs an over and finishing at 351, Scuderi 5 for 66.

A strange record was broken during the innings. Back in 1965–6 the then New South Wales wicket-keeper Brian Taber did not concede a bye while his bowlers went for 1,580 runs. Now, South Australian keeper Peter Anderson had pushed the Australian record to 1,635 before Dirk Tazelaar confused him into letting through four byes from off-spinner Tim May.

South Australia faltered in their reply, reaching 201 and being asked to follow-on. They made 141 for 2 mid-way through the final day, before bad light brought an obvious draw to an early end.

The South Australian team flew home for a day before going on to Perth to play Western Australia, but not before the selectors did the seemingly impossible: they dropped former Test batsman/wicket-keeper Wayne Phillips for the first time since 1980, replacing him with the hugely talented Darren Lehmann.

Put in to bat by Western Australia's captain Graeme Wood, South Australia scrambled to 37 for 4 in the first hour before rain and bad light put an end to the day's proceedings. The humid, overcast conditions carried over to the second morning, when South Australia fell for 128 from 56 overs. Western Australia lost Marsh in the first over but then had Mike Veletta and Tom Moody add 109 in 117 minutes before three quick wickets fell and Western Australia were 156 for 4 at the close.

South Australia capitulated late the next day after Western Australia had declared at 335 for 8. Terry

Batting

		v.Tasmania (Sydney) 22–5 February 1989	v.Queensland (Sydney) 10–13 March 1989	M	Inns	NOs	Runs	HS	Av
44	11	132	27	12	22	1	1174	152*	55.90
4	112*	21	37	12	22	3	742	112*	39.05
61	20	54	0	11	19	1	557	77	30.94
14	21	4	44	9	15	—	380	118	25.33
19	85	2	58	11	21	3	727	103*	40.38
55	—	23	15*	12	17	3	588	108	42.00
				6	10	2	237	70*	29.62
57	—	43*	13*	10	15	5	397	84	39.70
				7	10	2	204	69	25.50
0	—	—	—	10	10	2	169	71	21.12
7	—	—	—	12	12	6	48	22*	8.00
				3	3	1	35	21*	17.50
				2	2	—	3	3	1.50
				2	2	—	45	42	22.50
				2	2	—	32	27	16.00
				1	1	—	11	11	11.00
6	—	13*	—	5	6	2	116	83	29.00
				2	3	—	0	0	0.00
1*	—	—	—	3	1	1	1	1*	
2									
5	4	5	2						
3									
		4	2						
278	253	301	198						
10	4	6	5						
D		D							
2		2							

Bowling

R.J. Stobo	G.J. Robertson	M.D. O'Neill	T.H. Bayliss	J. Dyson	W.J. Holdsworth	S.B.J. Whitfield	Byes	Leg-byes	Wides	No-balls	Total	Wkts
							1	8	4	10	212	10
							1	9		5	329	8
							6	10			175	10
								5		2	331	7
								7		1	329	10
							2	1			156	4
								7		4	360	10
13–2–48–0							2	2		3	164	10
10–6–16–1								7		4	250	10
		14–5–17–2	6–1–19–1				1	3		2	191	10
		16–2–53–1	2–0–17–0				1	5		2	198	8
30–9–84–0	31–5–100–1							5	1	1	506	10
12–3–27–1	10–3–29–0		1–1–0–0	0.1–0–0–1						1	90	2
					14–1–55–6			1		9	238	10
					19–2–65–1			9		4	304	9
						5–0–32–0	8	1		5	356	10
						34–17–54–2		4	1	1	245	9
				5–1–30–0			4	1	6	11	235	10
				9–3–38–0				9	1	3	327	10
						2–1–8–0				1	153	10
						25–7–72–1	7	4		6	309	9
				3–1–8–0	23–11–28–0		1	6		4	230	6
						8–1–18–0	3	5		2	266	8
65–20–175–2	71–15–199–4	8–1–36–1	1–1–0–0	3.1–1–8–1	47–7–188–7	97–37–212–3						
av. 87.50	av. 49.75	av. 36.00	—	av. 8.00	av. 26.85	av. 70.66						

Queensland 1988–9

First-Class Matches

BATTING	v. New South Wales (Brisbane) 28–31 October 1988		v. Tasmania (Brisbane) 4–7 November 1988		v. Victoria (St Kilda) 11–14 November 1988		v. South Australia (Brisbane) 10–13 December 1988		v. Victoria (Brisbane) 17–20 December 1988		v. Western Australia (Brisbane) 31 December 1988 – 3 January 1989		v. Tasmania (Devonport) 6–9 January 1989		v. West Indians (Brisbane) 20–3 January 1989		v. South Australia (Adelaide) 15–18 February 1989		v. Western Australia (Perth) 24–8 February 1989	
T.J. Barsby	22	41	26	—	92	55	53	—	7	—	4	10	66	0	67	18	11	85	13	0
P.E. Cantrell	52	8	41	—	0	6	5	—	26	—	1	0			1	31*	47	19	14	9
S.G. Law	4	24	179	—	0	14*	3	—	8	—			73	—	0	36*	24	35	0	8*
G.M. Ritchie	0	92	8	—	46	3	101	—	58*	—	31	17	3	38	18	—	8	12	140	—
A.R. Border	38	14	52	—	57	9			2	—							0	21	12	—
G.S. Trimble	1	62	43	—	11	22					7	11								
T.V. Hohns	24	11	6	—	22	5*	2	—					35	—	10	—	11	23*		
I.A. Healy	44*	26*	14*	—	0	—			11	—					15	—	33	90	24	—
C.J. McDermott	3	21	6*	—	12	1			35	—					26	—	20	0	2	—
D. Tazelaar	0	15*	—	—	2*	—	12	—	0*	—	13	15	3	—	1	—			16*	—
J.N. Maguire	1	—			4	—	18	—	—	—	23	22*	0*	—			0	7*	32	—
M.A. Polzin			—	—																
R.B. Kerr							10	—	2	—	12	3								
P.S. Clifford							19	—			24	61	22	71*	35	8	0	25	6	0*
P.J. Drinnen							74	—			26*	45	5	—						
C.G. Rackemann							31*	—	—	—	8	0	0	—	4*	—	0*	—	0	—
A.B. Henschell											7	41	61	31*						
J.W. Walker													23	1	41	22				
Byes	1	1	3			1	4						1	7	4		1	1		
Leg-byes	8	9	9		9	7	6		3		10	9	5	3	8	7	3	6	7	
Wides	4		1			2	3		1		3	3						1	1	
No-balls	10	5	18		5		10		4		15	17	8	2	10	2	6	5	24	
Total	212	329	406		260	125	351		157		184	254	305	153	240	124	164	330	291	17
Wickets	10	8	7		10	6	10		7		10	10	10	3	10	3	10	8	10	2
Result	W		D		W		D		D		L		D		D		D		D	
Points	6		2		6		2		2		0		2		—		0		0	

Fielding Figures

26 – I.A. Healy (ct 24/st 2)
13 – P.E. Cantrell
10 – P.J. Drinnen
8 – G.M. Ritchie
7 – G.S. Trimble
6 – A.R. Border
5 – S.G. Law and T.J. Barsby
4 – P.S. Clifford, R.B. Kerr, J.N. Maguire and C.J. McDermott
3 – D. Tazelaar
2 – T.V. Hohns
1 – A.B. Henschell and C.G. Rackemann

BOWLING	C.J. McDermott	D. Tazelaar	J.N. Maguire	T.V. Hohns	P.E. Cantrell	G.S. Trimble	M.A. Polzin
v. New South Wales (Brisbane)	31.4–6–85–5	24–7–56–2	17–4–51–2	12–0–43–0	16–3–50–1		
28–31 October 1988	20–6–35–3	11–2–59–1	12.2–0–26–1	18–6–45–1	23–2–62–2	7–3–16–1	
v. Tasmania (Brisbane)	7–0–29–1	43.4–8–117–4		20–5–41–0	34–6–75–3	16.4–5–42–0	33–6–95–2
4–7 November 1988							
v. Victoria (St Kilda)	13–3–49–1	13–3–25–5	16.2–7–21–4		4–1–8–0		
11–14 November 1988	30–9–74–0	39.3–15–55–5	37–12–60–1	34–13–67–3	7–5–9–1		
v. South Australia (Brisbane)		20–2–37–3	23–8–45–1	19–5–41–2	12–2–30–2		
10–13 December 1988		9–4–15–0	15.2–4–34–0	12–4–27–0	12–4–41–0		
v. Victoria (Brisbane)	5–1–15–1	10–2–31–2	2.5–0–5–2		16–2–52–4		
17–20 December 1988							
v. Western Australia (Brisbane)		23–5–57–3	13–0–54–0		32–7–72–0		
31 December 1988–3 January 1989		7–1–27–0	8–0–37–4		4–0–21–0		
v. Tasmania (Devonport)		25–3–64–2	27–4–60–0	26.1–5–50–5			
6–9 January 1989		6–1–21–0	9–2–21–1	13–1–33–0			
v. West Indians (Brisbane)	14–0–91–2	19–4–53–1		14–3–59–2	10–2–36–2		
20–3 January 1989	15–0–65–1	17.3–3–59–1		35–10–71–5	15–1–71–0		
v. South Australia (Adelaide)	18–3–77–3		16–1–68–2	21–10–28–2	6–0–33–0		
15–18 February 1989	15–1–54–0		14.3–2–35–2	22–4–80–1	5–0–25–0		
v. Western Australia (Perth)	14–0–60–2	19–3–75–2	16–4–54–0		12–2–21–0		
24–9 February 1989							
v. New South Wales (Sydney)		30–7–86–2	18–1–49–0	14–3–36–0	16–2–52–0		
10–13 March 1989		19–1–52–3	6–0–27–1	11–2–41–0			
	182.4–29–634–19 *av.* 33.36	335.4–71–889–36 *av.* 24.69	251.2–49–647–21 *av.* 30.80	271.1–71–662–21 *av.* 31.52	224–39–658–15 *av.* 43.86	23.4–8–58–1 *av.* 58.00	33–6–95–2 *av.* 47.50

Alderman, bowling his perfect seamers, took 5 for 26 to add to his first innings 3 for 16 as the visitors crumbled for 104 in a pathetic display. Coach Barry Richards would crack the whip before the next match three weeks later.

Victoria, meanwhile, had gone to Brisbane only to spend the first three days of their match against Queensland watching the rain pour down. Play was possible on the last scheduled day, with both captains willing to gamble for first-innings points.

Queensland, sent in to bat on a seaming wicket, declared at 157 for 7 after 48 overs had been bowled, Craig McDermott hitting 35 off 33 deliveries in 32 minutes immediately prior to the declaration. Victoria went for the runs and all seemed well at 58 for 2. Then came the slump, starting with the needless run out of Siddons, and finishing on 122 to give Queensland the points.

New Year's Eve saw the start of Brisbane's last Shield match of the minor round. This time Western Australia were the visitors under the captaincy of Mike Veletta, who sent Queensland in to bat. On a green-tinged pitch which provided ample movement off the seam, visiting fastmen Peter Capes and Ken MacLeay picked up four wickets each as Queensland reached 184. A second-wicket stand of 134 between Veletta (59) and Tom Moody (69) saw Western Australia off to an ideal start, after which Wayne Andrews (82) consolidated the innings on a still awkward pitch to gain a 109-run first-innings lead. Queensland then inexplicably started to lose wickets, with Greg Ritchie's controversial run out adding to their woes. Ritchie, in the second over after lunch, turned Capes behind square-leg and ran hard for two runs. Bruce Reid fielded the ball and threw it on the bounce to wicket-keeper Tim Zoehrer, who removed the bails. The contentious issue was whether Zoehrer had the ball in his gloves when shattering the

Batting

v. New South Wales (Sydney) 10–13 March 1989		M	Inns	NOs	Runs	HS	Av
1	17	11	19	—	588	92	30.94
105	71	10	17	1	436	105	27.25
14	30	10	16	3	452	179	34.76
23	26	11	17	1	624	140	39.00
7	36	7	11	—	248	57	22.54
		4	7	—	157	62	22.42
—	3	8	11	2	152	35	16.88
0*	12*	8	11	5	269	90	44.83
		7	10	1	126	35	14.00
—	4*	10	11	5	81	16*	13.50
—	0	9	10	3	107	32	15.28
		1					
69	57	4	6	—	153	69	25.50
		6	11	2	271	71*	30.11
		3	4	1	150	74	50.00
—	—	8	7	3	43	31*	10.75
		2	4	1	140	61	46.66
		2	4	—	87	41	21.75
1	3						
6	5						
4	2						
230	266						
6	8						
D							
0							

Bowling

A.R. Border	C.G. Rackemann	A.B. Henschell	G.M. Ritchie	Byes	Leg-byes	Wides	No-balls	Total	Wkts
				6			17	291	10
				6			10	249	10
				6			14	405	10
							9	103	10
3–1–7–0				5	4	2	28	281	10
	29.4–14–44–1			1	3		8	201	10
	12–2–21–1				3			141	2
	7–3–18–0				1		2	122	10
	29.1–9–65–6	11–2–37–0		6	2		18	293	10
	13.3–1–58–0			2	1		5	146	4
	24–5–55–3	10–3–23–0		3	8		12	263	10
	6–1–14–0	3–0–9–0		3	6		2	107	1
	19.1–2–72–2				5		17	316	10
	16–4–57–2			4	5		19	332	10
	25–5–79–3				7		3	292	10
8–1–37–1	23–1–69–1			4	4		3	308	6
2–0–9–0	21.3–6–66–2			4	5		19	294	7
1–0–4–0	28–8–69–3			5			4	301	6
31–1–4–0	15–0–61–0		2–0–11–0	2			2	198	5
17–3–	269–61–	24–5–	2–0–						
61–1	748–24	69–0	11–0						
av. 61.00	av. 31.16	—	—						

South Australia 1988–9
First-Class Matches

BATTING	v. Victoria (Adelaide) 28–31 October 1988		v. West Indians (Adelaide) 4–7 November 1988		v. Tasmania (Hobart) 18–21 November 1988		v. Western Australia (Adelaide) 25–8 November 1988		v. Queensland (Brisbane) 10–13 December 1988		v. Western Australia (Perth) 17–19 December 1988		v. New South Wales (Adelaide) 6–9 January 1989		v. New South Wales (Sydney) 9–12 February 1989		v. Queensland (Adelaide) 15–18 February 1989		v. Victoria (Melbourne) 22–5 February 1989	
A.M.J. Hilditch	65	36*	8	64	37	0	22	4	47	12	2	1	168	—	13	101	21	48	60	—
G.A. Bishop	7	43	12	45	34	10*	22	10	2	38	27	32	9	54	57	0	24	57	0	21*
P.C. Nobes	56	1	34	95	57	—	79	7	27	81*	1	0	8	29	58	20	6	44	67	—
D.W. Hookes	58	39*	8	47	15	—	28	18	16	7*	6	15	21	—	83	1	71	73	133	0
W.B. Phillips	0	—	18	36	18	8*	14	23	12	—										
P.R. Sleep	48*	—	28	19	100	—	23	3	25	—	31	0	90	—	4	6	5	32*	22	—
P.W. Anderson	12	—	21	6	7	—	52*	4*	15	—	7	12*	17	—	13	0	7	—	24	—
C.M. Killen	1	—	6	32	5*	—			9*	—										
P.W. Gladigau	4	—	6	16			16		8		0*	0	47*	—	0	5*	6	—	26*	—
A.K. Zesers	12	—	4*	25	80	—							1	—	15	38	12	—		
T.B.A. May	5	—	—	7*			7	3*	4	—	4	3	20	—	1*	8*	26*	—	4	—
J.C. Scuderi			17	—			39	1	24	—			67	—	19	0	59	42	6	—
P.J. Carew							2	—												
D.S. Lehmann											0	24	51	6*	79	60	45	1	87	16
D.B. Scott											35	1								
D. Clarke											2	10								
C.R. Miller																			59	—
B.D. Williams																				
D.S. Chyer																				
Byes	8		5			1	1		1						8			4	3	
Leg-byes	7	3	5	9	6		1	2	3	3	8	2	5		1		4	7	4	14
Wides					4										1		1			
No-balls	4		8	9		2	19		8		5	4	1	1	5	1	3	3	5	2
Total	287	122	163	410	382	19	325	75	201	141	128	104	506	90	356	245	292	308	510	40
Wickets	10	2	9†	10	10	1	10	7	10	2	10	10	10	2	10	9	10	6	10	2
Result	W		L		D		W		D		L		D		D		D		D	
Points	6		—		2		6		0		0		2		0		2		2	

Fielding Figures

32 – P.W. Anderson (ct 30/st 2)
18 – D.W. Hookes
11 – P.R. Sleep
7 – G.A. Bishop
6 – P.C. Nobes
5 – J.C. Scuderi
4 – D.S. Lehmann, P.W. Gladigau and W.B. Phillips
3 – A.M.J. Hilditch, B.D. Williams and T.B.A. May
2 – C.M. Killen
1 – A.K. Zesers and D. Clarke

†T.B.A. May absent injured

BOWLING	P.W. Gladigau	C.M. Killen	A.K. Zesers	T.B.A. May	P.R. Sleep	D.W. Hookes	J.C. Scuderi
v. Victoria (Adelaide) 28–31 October 1988	18–5–53–4	18–5–49–0	24–9–45–2	33–9–66–4	2–1–7–0		
	12–2–38–1	8.2–4–15–2	10–4–17–0	30–9–61–3	25–16–31–1	2–0–5–0	
v. West Indians (Adelaide) 4–7 November 1988	33–6–99–1	24–2–112–0	43–12–139–3		52–8–207–4	4–0–28–0	
v. Tasmania (Hobart) 18–21 November 1988	31–10–72–1	22.2–5–58–2			59–20–109–4	1–0–7–0	43–15–60–3
v. Western Australia (Adelaide) 25–8 November 1988	18–5–34–2			33.3–4–92–5	10–4–34–1		22–5–61–1
	12–4–28–0			26–10–49–4			16.3–5–51–5
v. Queensland (Brisbane) 10–13 December 1988	37–14–48–3		27–11–45–1	49–13–101–1	34–10–81–0		31.1–7–66–5
v. Western Australia (Perth) 17–19 December 1988	25–4–78–4			33–6–102–2	11–1–45–0	4–0–10–0	
v. New South Wales (Adelaide) 6–9 January 1989	28–7–71–0		35–12–54–1	67.4–18–146–7	21–3–82–1	4–1–15–0	19–6–44–1
v. New South Wales (Sydney) 9–12 February 1989	30–12–74–3		34–13–78–3	23–6–54–0	12–1–67–0	3–1–5–0	25–8–65–0
v. Queensland (Adelaide) 15–18 February 1989	13–4–27–1		17–5–41–3	19–6–39–0			23.3–10–53–6
	21–2–71–1		22–8–61–0	49–12–125–3	7–6–4–1		30–12–62–3
v. Victoria (Melbourne) 22–5 February 1989	25–6–68–2			22–4–51–1	14–5–20–1	4–0–14–0	27.3–4–64–4
	24–5–88–3			40.4–14–93–7	17–2–50–0		21–6–55–0
v. Tasmania (Adelaide) 10–12 March 1989	26–6–67–3			39.4–11–93–3	10–0–48–0	1–0–9–0	27–11–57–2
	10–0–44–0			25–2–103–2	10–0–44–1		17.5–3–45–0
v. Western Australia (Perth) 25–9 March 1989	38–8–92–0			43–15–94–1	9–0–43–0		41–8–159–2
	16–3–47–0			9–2–32–0	3–0–23–0		23–5–68–1
	417–103–	99.4–27–	185–63–	542.3–141–	296–77–	23–2–	367.3–105–
	1099–29	279–5	435–12	1301–43	895–14	93–0	910–33
	av. 37.89	av. 55.80	av. 36.25	av. 30.25	av. 63.92	—	av. 27.57

stumps. Umpire Peter Parker, after a long consultation, finally raised his finger in a situation of very grave doubt. Within a week, a worse wicket-keeping furore would arise.

Queensland made 254, which left Western Australia plenty of time to get 146 for 4 and record its first outright win in Brisbane since 1971. The beaten side then moved south, across Bass Strait to Devonport to take on Dirk Wellham's Tasmanians. Sent in on a slow track of uneven bounce, the visitors scored 248 for 5 at the close with Trevor Barsby (66) and Brett Henschell (61) taking the batting honours, which was extended to 305 at lunch on the second day.

The pitch was starting to favour the bowlers, and curator Peter Apps predicted it would crack up further over the final two days and be of far more assistance to the spinners. Not heeding the warning, Tasmania ambled along to 183 for 3 by the end of the first hour of the third day. Then leg-spinner Trevor Hohns came on to bowl and the batsmen started to falter. The scoring became progressively slower until, at 263 for 5, Hohns did his job, taking 4 for 7 off 25 balls to send Tasmania tumbling to 263.

Acting Queensland captain Greg Ritchie let his batsmen amble in their second innings with the delayed declaration coming at 153 for 3. Needing 196 from 41 overs was always going to be beyond the Tasmanians, with rain and bad light bringing the game to a merciful end.

Drama and gamesmanship soiled the first day of New South Wales' match in Adelaide. Batting first on a good track and in front of an unusually large Friday crowd, South Australia stuttered early, losing three wickets for 92 before veteran opener Andrew Hilditch was joined by batting prodigy Darren Lehmann. The fourth-wicket

Batting

v. Tasmania (Adelaide) 10-13 March 1989	v. Western Australia (Perth) 25-9 March 1989		M	Inns	NOs	Runs	HS	Av
9	37	41	—	12	21	1	796	168	39.80
				10	20	2	504	57	28.00
71	52	18	—	12	21	1	811	95	40.55
66	33*	24	—	12	21	3	762	133	42.33
				5	8	1	129	36	18.42
5	—	146*	—	12	17	3	587	146*	41.92
5	—	38	—	12	16	3	240	52*	18.46
				4	5	2	53	32	17.66
31	—	45	—	12	15	4	210	47*	19.09
				6	8	1	187	80	26.71
37	—	34	—	11	14	5	163	37	18.11
23	1*	11	—	9	13	1	309	67	25.75
				1	1		2	2	2.00
89	3	17	—	7	13	1	478	89	39.83
				1	2	—	36	35	18.00
				1	2	—	12	10	6.00
		0	—	2	2	—	59	59	29.50
77	40	69	—	2	3	—	186	77	62.00
13*	—			1	1	1	13	13*	—
3		5							
16	4	13							
1									
9	2	33							
455	172	494							
10	4	10							
L		L							
0		—							

Bowling

P.J. Carew	D. Clarke	D.B. Scott	C.R. Miller	D.S. Chyer	B.D. Williams	A.M.J. Hilditch	P.W. Anderson	D.S. Lehmann	Byes	Leg-byes	Wides	No-balls	Total	Wkts
										11	1	3	231	10
									3	7			177	10
										8	1	2	593	8
										6		2	312	10
-1-43-1										4		8	268	10
										3		2	131	10
									4	6	3	10	351	10
	14-5-48-0	8-1-40-1							2	10		11	335	8
									4	7	1	10	423	10
									5	9	1	1	357	6
									1	3		6	164	10
			24-7-59-2						1	6	1	5	330	8
			11-4-21-0							8		7	284	10
				20-4-65-1	4-2-6-0				4	1		7	312	10
				8-1-31-1					2	9	1	1	356	10
			35.3-7-112-7						1	4		3	272	4
			14-1-69-0						6	29	4	4	535	10
					7-2-21-1	4-0-8-0	4-0-7-0	1-0-5-0	5	4		4	289	2
-1-	14-5-	8-1-	84.3-19-	28-5-	11-4-	4-0-	4-0-	1-0-						
-1	48-0	40-1	261-9	96-2	27-1	8-0	7-0	5-0						
43.00	—	av. 40.00	av. 29.00	av. 48.00	av. 27.00	—	—	—						

Tasmania 1988–9
First-Class Matches

BATTING	v. Queensland (Brisbane) 4–7 November 1988		v. Western Australia (Hobart) 11–14 November 1988		v. South Australia (Hobart) 18–21 November 1988		v. New South Wales (Devonport) 25–8 November 1988		v. Victoria (Melbourne) 10–13 December 1988		v. West Indians (Hobart) 19–21 December 1988		v. Queensland (Devonport) 6–9 January 1989		v. Western Australia (Perth) 20–3 January 1989		v. Victoria (Launceston) 16–18 February 1989		v. New South Wales (Sydney) 22–5 February 1989	
D.C. Boon	8	—	21	61*			98	—			1	—			26	4	10	90	11	132
G.A. Hughes	36	—	18	45	126	—	50	—	27	8*	20	—	37	39	8	65	58	57	2	43
G. Shipperd	53	—	10	—	39	—			155*	—			23	—	17	4	1*	—	5	27
M.D. Taylor	32	—	15	—	3	—	17	—	8	—	32	—	15	—						
D.M. Wellham	92	—	27	—	67	—	0	—	38	—	2	—	46	—	90*	23*	68*	—	2	6
D.J. Buckingham	16	—	36	—	2	—	0	—	19	43*	69	—	48	10*	2	21				
P.I. Faulkner	15	—	43	—	9	—	1	—	0	—	6	—	0	—	3	42				
R.E. Soule	80*	—	12*	—	7	—	99	—	57	—	26*	—	0	—	39	19*	—	—	22	20*
A.J. de Winter	5	—			14	—	14	—			14	—	0	—			0	4*	8	4
D.R. Gilbert	7	—	5	—	2	—	5	—	20*	—					2	—	—	—	0	0*
G.D. Campbell	41	—	7	—	1*	—	1*	—	37	—	3	—	2*	—	0	—	—	—	6	1
S.L. Saunders			9	—													—	1	9	12
R.J. Bennett					34	—			11	39*										
B.A. Cruse							64	—			98	—	22	—	13	1				
R.J. Tucker									39	—	24	—	47	47*	22	3	63	64	82*	4
J. Cox																	19	29*	5	43
Byes									4		2		3	3		8	2	6		7
Leg-byes	6		9	1	6		7		7		10		8	6	2	1	2	12		4
Wides																		1		
No-balls	14		1	1	2		4		6	4	13		12	2	13	9	3	1	1	6
Total	405		213	108	312		360		428	94	320		263	107	237	200	226	265	153	309
Wickets	10		10	1	10		10		9	0	10		10	1	10	7	5	4	10	9
Result	D		D		D		D		D		D		D		D		W		D	
Points	0		0		0		2		2		—		0		0		6		0	

Fielding Figures 21 – R.E. Soule
7 – G. Shipperd
6 – G.A. Hughes and M.D. Taylor
5 – R.J. Tucker, D.J. Buckingham and S.L. Saunders
4 – D.C. Boon and D.M. Wellham
3 – A.J. de Winter
2 – P.I. Faulkner, R.J. Bennett and subs
1 – J. Cox and D.R. Gilbert

BOWLING	D.R. Gilbert	A.J. de Winter	P.I. Faulkner	G.D. Campbell	G.A. Hughes	S.L. Saunders	D.C. Boon
v. Queensland (Brisbane) 4–7 November 1988	39.5–4–146–3	16–2–44–0	43–14–86–2	20–2–81–2	19–6–37–0		
v. Western Australia (Hobart) 11–14 November 1988	38–10–104–1		31–9–93–0	36–9–79–0	26–3–116–1	19–0–93–0	3–0–13–0
v. South Australia (Hobart) 18–21 November 1988	44–4–115–3 4–0–8–1	40.5–8–103–3 0.1–0–0–0	46–14–72–2	44–11–80–2 3.5–1–10–0	2–0–6–0 1–1–0–0		
v. New South Wales (Devonport) 25–8 November 1988	25–5–73–2 10–0–30–1	16–2–46–0 6–0–11–0	22–7–60–3 10–3–16–0	17.3–5–44–5 14–5–46–0	8–2–21–0		
v. Victoria (Melbourne) 10–13 December 1988	25.1–1–100–1		40–12–69–1	42.3–9–112–2	24–10–57–2		
v. West Indians (Hobart) 19–21 December 1988		25–4–88–5 4–1–8–0	18–5–74–0 11–2–35–0	24–4–69–2 5–1–13–0	21–2–74–0		4–1–13–0
v. Queensland (Devonport) 6–9 January 1989		27.3–5–76–3 8–1–16–0	27–5–69–2 34–12–56–1	29–9–72–3 11–1–42–1	3–2–2–0 2–1–1–0		
v. Western Australia (Perth) 20–3 January 1989	27.4–6–88–5 24–4–85–3		25–6–48–0 12–2–42–0	26–9–64–1 23–6–69–5	4–2–3–0 8–0–43–0		
v. Victoria (Launceston) 16–18 February 1989	12–1–40–1 23–6–68–1	6–1–18–0 17–4–41–2		17–2–61–1 24–1–79–1	6–1–15–0 6–1–14–0	10–0–54–1 1–0–16–0	
v. New South Wales (Sydney) 22–5 February 1989	25–4–71–3 17.3–3–57–1	22–6–60–1 21–5–53–0		23.1–6–58–4 19–3–61–1	7–2–18–0 9–3–20–0	9–1–36–0	
v. South Australia (Adelaide) 10–13 March 1989	10–1–34–0	30–7–96–3 18–2–68–2		39.2–5–138–5 7.4–2–31–1	30–7–71–0 1–0–4–0		
	325.1–49–1019–26 *av.* 39.19	257.3–48–728–19 *av.* 38.31	319–91–720–11 *av.* 65.45	426–91–1209–36 *av.* 33.58	177–43–502–3 *av.* 167.33	39–1–199–1 *av.* 199.00	7–1–26–0 —

v. South Australia (Adelaide) 10–13 March 1989		M	Inns	NOs	Runs	HS	Av
56	24	8	13	1	542	132	45.16
10	62	11	18	1	711	126	41.82
20	28	9	12	2	382	155*	38.20
		7	7	—	122	32	17.42
94	—	11	13	3	555	94	55.50
		8	11	2	266	69	29.55
		8	9		119	43	13.22
27	—	11	12	5	408	99	58.28
2	13	8	11	1	78	14	7.80
0*	—	9	9	3	41	20*	6.83
13	—	11	11	3	112	41	14.00
		3	4	—	31	12	7.75
		2	3	1	84	39*	42.00
7	—	5	6	—	205	98	34.16
98	55*	7	12	3	548	98	60.88
16	82*	3	6	2	194	82*	48.50
2	1						
9	4						
1							
1	3						
356	272						
10	4						
	W						
	6						

partnership of 74 had Hilditch scoring 18, plus five leg-byes: Lehmann got the rest.

Starting slowly, Lehmann scored a single from his first 24 deliveries, then 50 from the remaining 29. His seven boundaries and general stroke-play caused South Australia coach Barry Richards to say: 'His batting is sensational. He is the most exciting young batsman I have seen in years.'

Lehmann was tearing the Test attack of Lawson, Whitney and Matthews to shreds. Then Geoff Lawson decided to bowl around the wicket from the southern end of Adelaide Oval. The second ball of his 15th over was pushed into the covers by Hilditch. Lawson ran to collect and in doing so slowed up when he ran in front of Lehmann, who was backing up. The youngster was tripped up and sent sprawling as the ball was returned to wicket-keeper/captain Greg Dyer, who immediately whipped off the bails.

Dyer appealed; the crowd were stunned, and even Greg Matthews put his hands over his face. Lawson started to gesticulate to Hilditch, as umpires Daryl Harper and Max O'Connell conferred. Harper, who was at square-leg, walked over to Dyer and gave him the opportunity to withdraw his appeal. Reaching the height of unsportsmanlike conduct, Dyer refused, and the bemused Lehmann walked back to the pavilion to a standing ovation.

The reaction of the crowd was stunning. Even the mildest mannered of octogenarians, who said later he had last raised his voice 'at Mr Jardine', vented his spleen at Dyer. Coming off the ground at the tea interval, the New South Wales captain had a number of things explained to him. The upshot of the incident was a report made to the New South Wales Cricket Association, who nine days later

B.A. Cruse	R.J. Tucker	D.J. Buckingham	M.D. Taylor	Byes	Leg-byes	Wides	No-balls	Total	Wkts
				3	9	1	18	406	7
					4		3	502	2
					6	4	2	382	10
				1				19	1
5–0–33–0				3	2		5	228	10
	19–2–49–1						4	157	1
					10	3	25	397	10
6–1–12–1	24.5–6–66–2				13		3	409	10
12–3–51–0		1–0–2–0	1–0–2–0		1			112	0
13–1–43–0	21–5–37–1			1	5		8	305	10
12–2–23–0	5–2–5–0			7	3		2	153	3
6–0–16–1	19–4–47–3				7		3	273	10
9–1–32–0	6–1–27–0			3	11		7	312	8
	11–2–32–1				4		5	224	4
	20.2–6–38–3			3	4	1	10	263	10
	20–3–64–1			2	5	3		278	10
	8–0–22–0				4			253	4
7–0–31–0	19–3–66–1			3	16	1	9	455	10
	11.2–0–65–1				4		2	172	4
70–8–	184.3–34–	1–0–	1–0						
241–2	518–14	2–0	2–0						
av. 120.50	av. 37.00	—	—						

Victoria 1988–9
First-Class Matches

BATTING

Each match column shows the two Victoria innings (1st and 2nd). "—" = did not bat; blank = did not play.

BATTING	v. South Australia (Adelaide) 28–31 Oct 1988	v. New South Wales (Sydney) 4–7 Nov 1988	v. Queensland (St Kilda) 11–14 Nov 1988	v. West Indians (Melbourne) 25–8 Nov 1988	v. Tasmania (Melbourne) 10–13 Dec 1988	v. Queensland (Brisbane) 17–20 Dec 1988	v. New South Wales (Melbourne) 20–3 Jan 1989	v. Western Australia (Perth) 27–30 Jan 1989	v. Tasmania (Launceston) 16–18 Feb 1989	v. South Australia (Melbourne) 22–5 Feb 1989
D.F. Whatmore	41 10	38 43	3 90	31 —	69 —	5 —	14 0	22 10		
G.M. Watts	80 13	3 135	2 29	15 —	35 —	9 —	35 28	70 7	79 10	0 23
D.M. Jones	0 43	13 2	33 12	42 —		37 —			2 42	3 27
J.D. Siddons	21 10	13 63	2 5	9 —	8 —	18 —	0 81	156 51	59 15	0 40
W.G. Ayres	8 16	41 4	13 19							
S.P. O'Donnell	11 5	0 0	27 44	33 —	60 —	1 —	20 4	3 52	23* 41	55 49
A.I.C. Dodemaide	7 0	38 54*	9 15	2 —		4 —	9 11	36 37*	— 4	6 11
M.G.D. Dimattina	9 24	11 19	0 22	14 —	45 —	9 —	38 66*	17 10*	— 17	2* 9
P.W. Jackson	11* 4	0* —	3* 3	2 —	2 —	15* —	4* 4*	0* —		
P.R. Reiffel	12 10		0 2		15* —			0* —		
M.G. Hughes	16 32*	1 —	2 1*	24 —		10* —	6 9	0 9*	— 24	2 36
M. Osborne		1 4*		58* —						29 0*
W.N. Phillips				111 —	45 —	6 —	46 72	21 76	0 73	20 62
M.B. Quinn					19 —					
D.K. Walker					0 —					
R.C.A. McCarthy					61 —	20 —		12 —		
G.R. Parker							56 16	18 0	52* 13	39 30
P.E. McIntyre										
Byes		3 6	— 5	6					1 3	— 4
Leg-byes	11 7	10 5	4 7	10	1	1	1 9	10 7	4 4	8 1
Wides	1		— 2	2	3			— 1	— 1	
No-balls	3	— 2	9 28	29	25	2	9 4	20 24	5 10	7 7
Total	231 177	175 331	103 281	385	397	122	238 304	395 275	224 263	284 312
Wickets	10 10	10 7	10 10	10	10	10	10 9	9 6	4 10	10 10
Result	L	D	L	D	D	D	W	L	L	D
Points	0	2	0	—	0	0	6	0	0	0

Fielding Figures

29 – M.G. Dimattina (ct 24/st 5)
9 – J.D. Siddons
8 – D.M. Jones
7 – G.M. Watts, D.F. Whatmore, S.P. O'Donnell and A.I.C. Dodemaide
4 – G.R. Parker, M.G. Hughes and P.W. Jackson
3 – W.N. Phillips
1 – R.C.A. McCarthy, M. Osborne, M.B. Quinn, W.G. Ayres and P.R. Reiffel

BOWLING

Match	M.G. Hughes	A.I.C. Dodemaide	P.R. Reiffel	P.W. Jackson	S.P. O'Donnell	D.M. Jones	W.G. Ayres
v. South Australia (Adelaide) 28–31 October 1988	24-6-66-1 / 5-0-17-0	29-8-61-2 / 4-1-11-0	16-1-59-0 / 9-2-35-1	36-17-55-6 / 14-5-37-1	12-4-24-0 / 5-0-17-0	1-0-7-0	0.2-0-2-0
v. New South Wales (Sydney) 4–7 November 1988	14-3-40-0 / 16-2-59-0	24-7-48-4 / 12-2-48-0		7-0-24-0	16-2-54-6 / 11-3-39-0		
v. Queensland (St Kilda) 11–14 November 1988	26.3-0-81-7 / 18-3-40-3	20-4-37-3 / 15-8-29-1	20-6-62-0 / 8-1-23-1		15-3-31-0 / 14-3-40-0	0.1-0-0-0	
v. West Indians (Melbourne) 25–8 November 1988	27-6-82-2	28-9-55-3			24-7-68-0 / 21.2-2-52-2		
v. Tasmania (Melbourne) 10–13 December 1988			31-3-79-1 / 7-0-22-0	36-14-67-1 / 13-4-30-0	30-9-53-1 / 14-7-25-0		
v. Queensland (Brisbane) 17–20 December 1988	12-2-41-2	14-3-44-3			12-3-28-1		
v. New South Wales (Melbourne) 20–3 January 1989	19-7-46-1 / 23.2-10-36-6	16-4-42-1 / 15-5-28-0		9.4-6-14-2 / 24.2-11-46-0	12-3-26-1 / 16-4-31-2		
v. Western Australia (Perth) 27–30 January 1989		28-2-114-0 / 8-0-44-0	20-4-70-1 / 11.4-0-48-0		27-4-83-1 / 7-0-39-0		
v. Tasmania (Launceston) 16–18 February 1989	11-3-47-1 / 9.1-0-48-1	20-5-58-1 / 22-5-59-1		15-1-53-2 / 8-1-55-1	9-0-34-1 / 16-3-66-0		
v. South Australia (Melbourne) 22–5 February 1989	36-6-114-1 / 3.2-0-17-1	33-5-94-5 / 3-0-22-0		29-9-104-2	26-3-106-1		
v. Western Australia (Melbourne) 10–13 March 1989	35-8-93-1	34-7-98-2		35-10-87-1	30-1-96-0		
Totals	279.2-56- / 827-27 / av.30.62	325-75- / 892-26 / av.34.30	122.4-17- / 398-4 / av.99.50	300-99- / 764-17 / av.44.94	286.2-55- / 836-16 / av.52.25	1.1-0- / 7-0 / av.—	0.2-0- / 2-0 / av.—

v. Western Australia (Melbourne) 10–13 March 1989	M	Inns	NOs	Runs	HS	Av
	8	13	—	376	90	28.92
21 —	11	18	—	694	135	38.55
02* —	8	13	1	358	102*	29.83
13* —	11	18	1	564	156	33.17
	3	6	—	101	41	16.83
— —	11	17	1	428	60	26.75
— —	10	15	2	243	54*	18.69
— —	11	16	2	416	113	29.71
— —	9	12	6	61	17	10.16
	4	6	2	39	15*	9.75
— —	9	12	3	163	36	18.11
	7	10	5	101	58*	20.20
48 —	8	12	—	580	111	48.33
	1	1	—	19	19	19.00
	1	1	—	0	0	0.00
	3	3	—	93	61	31.00
32 —	5	9	1	256	56	32.00
— —	1					
8						
8						
11						
343						
3						
D						
0						

requested Greg Dyer to attend their central Sydney offices. He was then informed that he was not only being relieved of the New South Wales captaincy after one and a half seasons, but he was also dropped from the team. Geoff Lawson was appointed in his stead.

Suddenly, all life had gone out of the contest. Andrew Hilditch batted on into the second afternoon to record his eighth century for South Australia. His 168 took 531 minutes, came from 411 deliveries with 10 fours and a six. Peter Sleep added 90, while Joe Scuderi had the Saturday crowd purring with pleasure at his 67. The last-wicket pair of Peter Gladigau and Tim May then hit out, only to fall two runs short of Clarrie Grimmett and Tim Wall's 1930 record. Chasing 506, New South Wales made a valiant effort to reach 423 aided by Matthews 104, Mark Taylor 86 and a career-best 71 from Lawson. Tim May bowled himself back into Test contention with his best effort of 7 for 146 from 68 overs. The match then petered out into a draw best forgotten.

Two matches started on 20 January. The first, at the Melbourne Cricket Ground, saw Victoria fall to the pace of débutant bowler Wayne Holdsworth. The young New South Welshman became the 11th Australian in first-class cricket to take a wicket with his first ball (Whatmore) and then dismissed Siddons with his fifth. At lunch Victoria were 78 for 4 and only a stand between Wayne Phillips (a first-season player from South Melbourne) and Geoff Parker of 77 gave the final total of 238 some respectability. Holdsworth went on to claim 6 for 55 in a most impressive display.

New South Wales looked set for first-innings points at 147 for 5, but then came an amazing collapse as the final five wickets fell for just four runs to the spin pair of Paul Jackson and Mark Osborne. Victoria then had to build up

M. Osborne	R.C.A. McCarthy	D.K. Walker	W.N. Phillips	D.F. Whatmore	J.D. Siddons	G.R. Parker	P.E. McIntyre	Byes	Leg-byes	Wides	No-balls	Total	Wkts
								8	7		4	287	10
									3			122	2
1–1–0–0								4	3			173	10
24–4–67–3								1	7			312	7
									9		5	260	10
								1	7	2		125	6
16–1–56–2								6	9		2	328	10
	31–5–84–4	38–9–117–2	4–0–17–0					4	7		6	428	9
	3–0–7–0	3–0–8–0	2–2–0–0	1–0–2–0							4	94	0
	10–0–41–1								3	1	4	157	7
11–7–17–4								2	4			151	10
13.4–3–34–1			2–0–2–0		1–0–9–0	1–1–0–0		2	3		1	191	10
26–6–74–1	20–1–67–0		6–2–15–0			2–0–5–0		3	5		17	436	3
8–0–61–4	3–0–27–0							4	12	1	1	235	4
7.1–2–30–0								2	2		3	226	5
3–0–19–0								6	12	1	1	265	4
12.4–2–75–1								3	14		5	510	10
									1		2	40	1
			3–0–7–0		3–0–22–0		40–11–109–2	5	16	2	12	533	6
122.3–26–433–16 av.27.06	67–6–226–5 av.45.20	41–9–125–2 av.62.50	17–4–41–0 –	1–0–2–0 –	4–0–31–0 –	3–1–5–0 –	40–11–109–2 av.54.50						

Western Australia 1988–9
First-Class Matches

BATTING

BATTING	v. West Indians (Perth) 28–31 October 1988		v. Tamil Nadu (Perth) 4–8 November 1988		v. Tasmania (Hobart) 11–14 November 1988		v. South Australia (Adelaide) 25–8 November 1988		v. New South Wales (Newcastle) 2–5 December 1988		v. South Australia (Perth) 17–19 December 1988		v. Queensland (Brisbane) 31 December 1988 – 3 January 1989		v. Tasmania (Perth) 20–3 January 1989		v. Victoria (Perth) 27–30 January 1989		v. New South Wales (Perth) 15–18 February 1989	
G.R. Marsh	27	21	209	—	223	—	6	35			0	—			11	51			30	16
M.R.J. Veletta	11	81*	166*	—	157	—	69	18			43	—	59	44	12	8	44	100	22	0
T.G. Hogan	0	—	—	—	—	—	1	8	24	24					8	12*				
T.M. Moody	59	78	—	—	112*	—	46	10	22	23	64	—	69	20	8	0	202	19	49	5
G.M. Wood	39	11*	—	—	3*	—	39	3			0	—			39	0	138*	16*	2	5
W.S. Andrews	15	3	—	—	—	—	45	32	0	69	24	—	82	24*	20	121	17*	22	20	78
J.A. Brayshaw	2	—							19	17	81	—	6	—						
T.J. Zoehrer	49*	—	—	—	—	—	29	1	29	1	63	—	23	9*	71	67		4*	5	163
K.H. MacLeay	3	—	0*	—	—	—	9	0	10	24	27*	—	5	—	9	7			13	24
C.D. Matthews	0	—	50	—	—	—							2	—					13	14
T.M. Alderman	12	—	—	—	—	—	8	0	3	3	9*	—			10	—				
A.D. Mullally			—	—	—	—	2*	1	0	21*										
B.A. Reid							2	18*	0*	30	—		0*	—						
P. Gonnella									45	1			2	31	65*	14	10	56	45	7
K.J. Hughes									5	26			14	10						
P.A. Capes											1	—	5	—	10	11*			10	2*
K.E. Lilly																	—	—	4*	0
Byes	10	4	1				2				2		6	2	3	3	4		4	
Leg-byes	5		10		4		4	3	2	7	10		2	1	7	11	5	12	1	9
Wides																		1	6	1
No-balls	15	8	2		3		8	2	3	4	11		18	5	3	7	17	1	11	3
Total	247	206	438		502		268	131	164	250	335		293	146	273	312	436	235	235	327
Wickets	10	3	2		2		10	10	10	10	8		10	4	10	8	3	4	10	10
Result	W		W		D		L		L		W		W		D		W		L	
Points	—		—		2		0		0		6		6		2		6		0	

Fielding Figures

45 – J.T. Zoehrer (ct 41/st 4)	5 – G.M. Wood
15 – G.R. Marsh and M.R.J. Veletta	4 – P. Gonnella
13 – T.M. Alderman	2 – T.M. Moody
11 – W.S. Andrews and K.H. MacLeay	1 – C.D. Matthews and A.D. Mullally
6 – T.G. Hogan and J.A. Brayshaw	

BOWLING

BOWLING	C.D. Matthews	T.M. Alderman	K.H. MacLeay	T.G. Hogan	J.A. Brayshaw	A.D. Mullally	T.M. Moody
v. West Indians (Perth) 28–31 October 1988	25.4–5–84–5 / 21–7–75–4	17–6–50–1 / 26.4–5–61–3	10–3–34–2 / 21–8–31–1	12–2–40–2 / 16–4–24–1	9–0–34–1		
v. Tamil Nadu (Perth) 4–8 November 1988	18–4–55–4 / 11–0–40–1	11–3–28–1 / 17–11–25–1	11–6–12–0 / 14–7–19–2	13.1–9–12–2 / 18–5–56–0		18–7–44–3 / 22–6–71–4	5–2–11–1
v. Tasmania (Hobart) 11–14 November 1988	21.3–2–66–1 / 7–1–30–0	17–5–35–3 / 11–2–36–0	13–5–16–1	16–4–37–1 / 11.3–4–16–1		24–6–50–1 / 10–2–24–0	2–2–0–1 / 1–0–1–0
v. South Australia (Adelaide) 25–8 November 1988		18–2–65–1 / 9–0–29–5	17–5–35–1	27.3–4–78–3		24–7–82–3 / 4.5–0–18–2	3–1–2–1
v. New South Wales (Newcastle) 2–5 December 1988		21–10–42–4 / 32–7–80–3	18–6–30–1 / 15–4–34–0	14–2–61–2 / 8–2–36–0		18–3–69–2 / 18–2–55–2	3–0–11–0
v. South Australia (Perth) 17–19 December 1988		17–7–16–3 / 11.2–1–26–5	10.3–3–24–4 / 8–3–21–1				
v. Queensland (Brisbane) 31 December 1988 – 3 January 1989	12–0–45–0 / 4–0–10–0		30–12–48–4 / 43–23–48–4			3–0–16–0	4.2–2–11–1 / 8–3–12–0
v. Tasmania (Perth) 20–3 January 1989		27–9–49–4 / 20–5–43–1	24–3–54–0 / 12–3–27–1	14–4–26–0 / 14–4–31–0			2–0–11–0 / 5.4–2–13–0
v. Victoria (Perth) 27–30 January 1989			39–7–114–2 / 19–4–68–3		2–0–11–0	31–9–97–2 / 14–3–49–1	6–1–19–0
v. New South Wales (Perth) 15–18 February 1989	23–5–75–1 / 14–2–53–0		25.1–8–65–4 / 14–2–63–0				17–6–24–3 / 9–1–37–1
v. Queensland (Perth) 26–9 February 1989		34–8–73–1	18–6–32–0			24–2–90–3	7–0–15–1 / 5–1–14–1
v. Victoria (Melbourne) 10–13 March 1989		30–11–61–1	15–6–26–0	34–7–94–2			10–1–27–0
v. South Australia (Perth) 25–9 March 1989		43–7–117–4	34–9–96–2			34–4–106–0	9–3–23–1
	157.1–26–533–16 av.33.31	362–99–836–41 av.20.39	410.4–133–897–33 av.27.18	198.1–51–511–14 av.36.50	14–0–61–1 av.61.00	241.5–51–755–23 av.32.82	97–25–231–11 av.21.00

v. Queensland (Perth) 24–8 February 1989		v. Victoria (Melbourne) 10–13 March 1989		v. South Australia (Perth) 25–9 March 1989		M	Inns	NOs	Runs	HS	Av
21	—	55	—	55	105*	10	15	1	865	223	61.78
4	—	64	—	26	5	12	19	2	933	166*	54.88
		115*	—			7	8	2	192	115*	32.00
13	—	59	—	162	155	13	20	1	1175	202	61.84
119*	—	10*	—	68	—	11	15	6	492	138*	54.66
2	—	19	—	75		13	18	2	668	121	41.75
						5	5	—	125	81	25.00
16	—	168	—	81		13	16	3	779	168	59.92
70	—	8*	—	10	—	13	15	3	219	70	18.25
						5	5	—	79	50	15.80
—	—			1*	—	10	8	2	46	12	7.66
—	—			0	—	7	5	2	24	21*	8.00
						4	5	3	50	30	25.00
6	—	0	—	10	11*	8	14	2	303	65*	25.25
						2	4	—	55	26	13.75
15*	—	—	—	4	—	8	8	3	58	15*	11.60
						2	2	1	4	4*	4.00
4		5		6	5						
5		16		29	4						
		2		4							
19		12		4	4						
294		533		535	289						
7		6		10	2						
	D		D		D						
2		0		—							

a substantial first-innings lead in order for O'Donnell to declare and try for the outright win. All went well until the final session, with Siddons pounding 81 and Phillips 72. Then something seemed to go amiss, with only 46 runs added in an hour and a half until the declaration. But the Victorians need not have worried. Only new New South Wales wicket-keeper Phil Emery, with a patient 331-minute occupation of the crease for 83, stood in the way of a home victory. Merv Hughes claimed 6 for 36 with two devastating spells of bowling to prove, yet again, his authority as one of Australia's top pacemen.

Tasmania flew to Perth without star player Mick Taylor, who was having a bad run. His replacement, medium-pace bowler Rod Tucker, immediately showed his worth by claiming three of the first four Western Australian wickets to fall. However, Tasmania's luck changed for the bad at 133 for 5 when Western Australia's wicket-keeper Tim Zoehrer was adjudged not to have edged a Dave Gilbert delivery to Richard Soule. As the slips cordon shouted loudly on two occasions umpire Graham Bibby remained unmoved. Zoehrer (36) went on to make 71, and Gilbert to take 5 for 88 as Western Australia reached 273.

Without Taylor, the Tasmanian middle-order looked brittle, and only an undefeated 90 from Dirk Wellham saw them to 237. Yet again it was the home pace attack which did the damage: Alderman 4 for 49 and Capes 5 for 95 from 27 overs each.

From 22 for 3 in their second innings, Western Australia went on a scoring spree. Graham Marsh hit a quickfire 51, Wayne Andrews 121 and Zoehrer 67, but yet again a declaration was delayed, this time by Graeme Wood, for

B.A. Reid	W.S. Andrews	P.A. Capes	K.E. Lilly	G.M. Wood	G.R. Marsh	T.J. Zoehrer	Byes	Leg-byes	Wides	No-balls	Total	Wkts
								5	1	5	213	10
							4	7		2	236	10
								8		4	159	10
							4	2		6	228	10
								9		1	213	10
								1		1	108	1
18–1–61–1							1	1		19	325	10
5–0–26–0								2			75	7
20–3–62–1							1	4		8	269	10
21–3–57–2	1–0–2–0							4		5	279	7
15–3–35–1		13–3–45–2						8		5	128	10
13–4–28–3		6–1–27–1						2		4	104	10
9.4–3–26–1	6–1–8–0	22.3–9–36–4						10	3	15	184	10
33–8–53–2	16–8–19–1	30–6–87–1						9	3	17	254	10
		27.4–4–95–5						2		13	237	10
	2–1–8–0	24–5–69–5					8	1		9	200	7
	1–1–0–0	26–7–83–1	24–5–72–3					10	1	20	395	9
	16–8–29–1	13–2–42–0	15–3–68–1				1	7		24	275	6
		21–5–83–1	12–0–60–1				4	15	2	11	326	10
	5–0–20–0	19.4–2–71–2	9–0–55–1					4		9	303	4
	1–1–0–0	21–1–74–5						7	1	24	291	10
	5–4–3–1										17	2
	10–3–25–0	25–6–67–0		3–0–23–0	1–0–3–0	1–0–1–0	8	8		11	343	3
	2.3–0–19–2	38–10–115–1					5	13		33	494	10
134.4–25–	65.3–27–	286.5–61–	60–8–	3–0–	1–0–	1–0–						
348–11	133–5	894–28	255–6	23–0	3–0	1–1						
av.31.63	av.26.60	av.31.92	av.42.50	–	–	–						

West Indians in Australia 1988-9
First-Class Matches

BATTING

BATTING	v. Western Australia (Perth) 28–31 Oct 1988		v. South Australia (Adelaide) 4–7 Nov 1988		v. New South Wales (Sydney) 11–14 Nov 1988		FIRST TEST MATCH (Brisbane) 18–21 Nov 1988		v. Victoria (Melbourne) 25–8 Nov 1988		SECOND TEST MATCH (Perth) 2–6 Dec 1988		v. Tasmania (Hobart) 19–21 Dec 1988		THIRD TEST MATCH (Melbourne) 26–9 Dec 1988		v. Queensland (Brisbane) 20–3 Jan 1989		FOURTH TEST MATCH (Sydney) 26–30 Jan 1989	
C. G. Greenidge	24	23	213	—			80	16	1	—	40	0	84	58*	49	36*			56	4
D. L. Haynes	4	0	79	—	13	52	40	30*			11	100			17	23	0	102	75	143
R. B. Richardson	9	15	35	—	41	15	81	7*	2		66	48	121	—	26	122			28	22
C. L. Hooper	83	35	14	—	22	27	1	—	64	—	26	64	25	—	38	4	46	21	0	35
K. L. T. Arthurton	5	18			7	57*			0	—			72	—			20	3		
P. J. L. Dujon	5	24	39	—			27	—	10		32	9	19	53*	26	46	23	22	17	12
R. A. Harper	0	67*	21*	—	46	0*			9				25*	—			82	9		
M. D. Marshall	31	1	21*	—			11	—			4	23			7	19			9	3
C. E. L. Ambrose	30	28	4				19*				8	15			44	5			1	5
I. R. Bishop	5*	12			20				20				0		5*	2				
B. P. Patterson	6	0			11	—	0	—	18*		1	6*	5	—	13	3*	1	0		
I. V. A. Richards			136	—	101	—	68	—			146	5			12	63			11	4
A. L. Logie			32		28	2	19	—	134		93	30	30	—	10	17	50	12	0	6
W. K. M. Benjamin			9*		28*	—			39				3							
C. A. Walsh			—		—	0	0	—			0*	17*		9	30*	6	0	12	4*	7*
D. Williams					4	—			14				9				0	11		
Byes	5	4				2	5	6			1	14		1			4		1	1
Leg-byes		7	8		7	1	9	4	9		12	9	13	1	4	1	5	5		
Wides	1		1				6	3											1	1
No-balls	5	2	2		1		28	3	2		9	9	3		3	16	17	19	3	4
Total	213	236	593		329	156	394	63	328		449	349	409	112	280	361	316	332	224	256
Wickets	10	10	8		10	4	10	1	10		10	9	10	1	10	9	10	10	10	10
Result	L		W		D		W		D		W		D		W		D		L	

Fielding Figures
- 20 – P. J. L. Dujon (ct 19/st 1)
- 12 – R. B. Richardson
- 10 – A. L. Logie
- 9 – C. L. Hooper
- 8 – R. A. Harper (and 2 as sub)
- 7 – D. L. Haynes
- 6 – D. Williams (ct 5/st 1)
- 5 – C. G. Greenidge, W. K. M. Benjamin and I. V. A. Richards
- 3 – C. E. L. Ambrose and K. L. T. Arthurton (and 2 as sub)
- 2 – C. A. Walsh
- 1 – B. P. Patterson, I. R. Bishop and M. D. Marshall

BOWLING

	B. P. Patterson	C. E. L. Ambrose	M. D. Marshall	I. R. Bishop	C. L. Hooper	R. A. Harper	C. A. Walsh
v. Western Australia (Perth) 28–31 October 1988	19–3–58–1 / 9–1–28–1	24.2–4–64–4 / 14–6–33–0	19–5–54–0 / 10–1–36–0	16–5–27–5 / 10–1–37–0	2–0–7–0 / 4–0–15–0	6–2–22–0 / 13.4–0–53–2	
v. South Australia (Adelaide) 4–7 November 1988			12–2–32–1 / 12–4–42–1	13–2–31–1 / 9–2–42–0	10.2–3–27–2 / 51–8–163–4		11–3–26–3 / 18–4–51–1
v. New South Wales (Sydney) 11–14 November 1988	19–5–52–1 / 17–3–36–0			21–4–53–2 / 12–0–51–0	9–0–23–0 / 5–0–10–0	42–6–118–1 / 20–0–86–0	
FIRST TEST MATCH (Brisbane) 18–21 November 1988	3.1–1–5–0	16.5–5–30–3 / 26.1–5–78–3	18–3–39–2 / 26–2–92–4		12–2–24–1 / 4–0–23–0		18.3–3–62–4 / 19–3–61–3
v. Victoria (Melbourne) 25–8 November 1988	22–2–78–1			25–2–88–1	12.5–3–25–1	31–9–78–5	
SECOND TEST MATCH (Perth) 2–6 December 1988	16–1–95–0 / 14–2–58–2	23.3–3–72–5 / 17–1–66–3	23–3–84–1 / 12–0–50–2		5–0–29–0 / 5–2–5–1		19–3–58–1 / 15–1–46–1
v. Tasmania (Hobart) 19–21 December 1988	16–2–65–3			13–1–69–2	16.3–3–30–2	32–5–91–3	
THIRD TEST MATCH (Melbourne) 24–9 December 1988	20–2–49–4 / 15.1–3–39–5	27–7–60–4 / 13–5–21–2	30–8–68–0 / 9–3–12–1				17.3–3–49–1 / 16–7–21–2
v. Queensland (Brisbane) 20–3 January 1989	9–2–35–1 / 11–4–29–2			9–1–43–0 / 14–3–40–0	14.3–4–33–5 / 6–3–6–0	11–1–31–0 / 9–2–15–0	13–0–44–2
FOURTH TEST MATCH (Sydney) 26–30 January 1989		33–5–78–1 / 7–1–16–1	31–16–29–5 / 8–2–17–1		37–10–72–0 / 10.3–2–24–0	37–9–86–0	22.5–5–48–2 / 3–0–9–0
FIFTH TEST MATCH (Adelaide) 3–7 February 1989	30.5–1–130–1 / 8–1–29–0	26–4–93–3 / 15–2–44–1	23–3–67–1 / 12–2–30–0		3–0–14–0 / 3–1–7–0		33–5–120–3 / 13–2–26–0
	229.1–33– / 786–22 / av. 35.72	266.5–54– / 729–32 / av. 22.78	243–52– / 651–18 / av. 36.16	120–17– / 408–10 / av. 40.80	210.4–40– / 537–16 / av. 33.56	201.4–34– / 580–11 / av. 52.72	218.5–39– / 621–23 / av. 27.00

a T.B.A. May absent injured
b G.F. Lawson absent injured

Fifth Test Match (Adelaide) 3–7 February 1989		M	Inns	NOs	Runs	HS	Av
12	104	9	16	2	800	213	57.14
83	15	9	17	1	787	143	49.18
106	22	10	17	1	766	122	47.87
2	0	11	18	—	507	83	28.16
		5	8	1	182	72	26.00
28	—	10	16	1	390	53*	26.00
		6	10	3	267	82	38.14
0	—	7	11	1	129	31	12.90
9	—	7	11	1	168	44	16.80
		5	7	2	64	20	12.80
9*	—	9	13	4	73	18*	8.11
69	68*	7	11	1	683	146	68.30
21	2*	10	16	2	601	134	42.92
		5	6	2	141	50	35.25
4	—	7	10	5	80	30*	16.00
		4	5	—	38	14	7.60
6	3						
10	7						
	1						
10	11						
369	233						
10	4						
D							

fear of losing those two valuable points gained for a first-innings lead.

Tasmania had five hours in which to save the match, and with Glenn Hughes (65) and Peter Faulkner (42) stone-walling, the visitors were 200 for 7 at the close. Capes, with 5 for 69, recorded match figures of 10 for 164, which brought his three-match haul to 18 wickets at an average of 19.94.

There were two more matches to be played to level up the sides at seven games each before the final set of matches in the run home to the final.

In Perth, Victoria were the visitors in late January and took first use of the pitch on being sent in to bat. Whatmore and Phillips went cheaply, but then Gary Watts (70) and the stylish Jamie Siddons started to pile up the runs. At the end of the first day Victoria were 292 for 5, which they extended to 395 for 9 before Simon O'Donnell declared at lunch on day two. Siddons went on to make 156 in 311 minutes with 23 boundaries and some sensational straight driving. He fell, going for one drive too many, and snicked a Ken Lilly leg-cutter to Ken MacLeay at gully.

Then it was Western Australia's turn. Gonnella (10) fell at 22; Veletta (44) at 133, and on came the Tom Moody show. The six-feet-eight-inch giant opened up his great shoulders and hit the Victorian attack to shreds. His quite outstanding 202 came in 6½ hours, with 24 fours, and became Western Australia's 13th individual double century made in first-class cricket.

Moody and his State captain Graeme Wood shared a

W.K.M. Benjamin	I.V.A. Richards	K.L.T. Arthurton	P.J.L. Dujon	D.L. Haynes		Byes	Leg-byes	Wides	No-balls	Total	Wkts
						10	5		15	247	10
15–3–33–2	3–1–4–0					4			8	206	3
7–3–25–1	25–2–78–3					5	5		8	163	9a
26–7–73–1	19–5–46–2	7–0–22–0					9		9	410	10
11–2–26–0	4.1–0–13–0	9–0–32–0				8	6		6	401	8
						1	6		2	261	1
	1–0–1–0					1	5	1	16	167	10
	11–4–26–0					4	5		21	289	10
26–1–101–1		2–1–2–0				6	7	2	29	385	10
	14–0–43–0					6	8		35	395	8
13–2–53–0						5	4		37	234	9b
						2	10		13	320	10
						2	14		15	242	10
15–2–42–2	4–1–12–0					4	5		6	114	10
8–4–8–1		8–1–15–0	1–0–1–0	1–0–3–0		4	8		10	240	10
							7		2	124	3
	31–1–68–1					6	14		14	401	10
	7–2–12–1					3	1		2	82	3
	25–1–73–0							18	40	515	10
	24–3–64–1					11	13		10	224	4
121–24–	168.1–20–	26–2–	1–0–	1–0–							
361–8	440–8	71–0	1–0	3–0							
av. 45.12	av. 55.00	—	—	—							

third-wicket partnership of 264 in 272 minutes which saw the bat completely dominate the ball. Wood went on to an unbeaten 138 with 15 boundaries made in 316 minutes before declaring at 436 for 3. No wonder the crowd of 9,885 enjoyed it!

Ken MacLeay captured two Victorian wickets before the close at 61 for 2 on the third day. Victoria, with half-centuries from Phillips, Siddons and O'Donnell, then declared at tea at 275 for 6, which left Western Australia a target of 235 in the final session at a rate in excess of six runs an over.

Gonnella (56) and Veletta ripped into Victoria before the first wicket fell at 137. Veletta went with the score 219 but only after he had made exactly 100 from 110 balls with 8 fours and a six. Western Australia won by six wickets, with 2.2 overs to spare, having scored at a pace reminiscent of a limited-overs fixture.

Whenever New South Wales and South Australia meet there appears to be controversy, and the early February clash in Sydney was no exception. David Hookes won the toss and batted on an unusually even SCG track. Glenn Bishop (57) and Paul Nobes (58) set the scene for Hookes and teenage prodigy Darren Lehmann to add 137 for the fourth wicket in 79 minutes before Hookes (83) was caught behind off opposing captain Geoff Lawson. Next morning, after Lehmann (79) departed, the tail collapsed as South Australia reached 356.

New South Wales plodded to 170 for 4 at stumps with only Mark Taylor (69) making any impression. Then at lunch on the third day, another slow session had seen the score to 234 for 5. During the interval Lawson, using the internal telephone system, contacted the South Australian dressing room and let it be known: 'We will have a slap about a bit, and take a look at things after 20 minutes.' So Hookes gave away some easy runs, with batsmen Greg Matthews and Peter Taylor scoring freely as well as expecting the imminent declaration. After an hour, as Hookes said: 'A word of trust has been broken', or as Stephen Waugh later put it: 'It was the greatest set-up since The Sting.'

Feelings then started to run high: Hookes instructed his pace attack of Scuderi and Gladigau to bowl wide of the leg-stump and the 'promised' declaration came 90 minutes later than agreed, and only when New South Wales had gained a first-innings lead.

Hookes then made it known he was going to kill the game – and he did. For the next four sessions of play, South Australia plodded along to score 245 for 9 (Hilditch 101, Lehmann 60) and see the match to a draw.

Three days later in Adelaide, Hookes won the toss and batted against the strong Queensland line-up. It was even play, with South Australia 56 for 3, until Lehmann joined Hookes. The master had to bow to his apprentice in the 104-run fourth-wicket partnership, which took just over an hour. In that time, the batsmen had between them scored 19 fours and a six: 82 in boundaries. It was sensational cricket and more in the mode of the one-day run rates. Hookes (71), Lehmann (45) and latterly Joe Scuderi (59) saw South Australia to 292. In reply Queensland had only Cantrell (47) and Healy (33) to thank for their score looking respectable at 164. Scuderi took career-best

figures of 6 for 53 for South Australia to gain a most welcome 128-run first-innings lead.

Then South Australia turned on an awesome display of batting. Hilditch (48) and Bishop (57) put on an opening stand of 99, following which Hookes (73) and Nobes (44) added 96 for the third wicket in just under the hour. The Friday crowd were once again treated to some short but effective Joe Scuderi stroke-play before the teenager was bowled by Maguire for 42 as Hookes declared.

Needing 437 for victory from 129 overs was always going to be beyond the visitors. At 172 for 5 matters looked decidedly poor, but Ian Healy came to the rescue with a career-best 90 and Queensland hung on to draw the game.

In Perth, Graeme Wood did his usual unconventional trick: win the toss, put the opposition in – and try to snatch an outright victory. It had worked nine times in the previous 15 matches but not this time against Geoff Lawson's New South Wales team. A first-day score of 304 for 8 – including 107 from Mark Taylor with 14 fours – which then became 326, gave New South Wales a strong base from which to attack Western Australia.

Lawson and Steve Waugh took three wickets each as the home team stumbled to 235. Lawson gave a splendid display of controlled seam bowling and could so well have doubled his tally of wickets. New South Wales then went for the runs, with Mark Taylor completing his second century of the match to become the 25th batsman in the 97-year history of the Sheffield Shield to achieve such a feat. Taylor's unbeaten 152 was scored in 282 minutes with 22 boundaries and concluded when Lawson declared at 303 for 4 – a lead of 394.

The 1,605 crowd were then stunned into silence as Western Australia crashed to the visitors' pace attack. At 27 for 4 the match looked effectively over, which was reflected by attendance on the last day.

If ever there was a case for showing how unpredictable the game of cricket could be – and how predictable the paying public were – then the weekend of 18 and 19 February was a prime example. On Saturday, the final day of the match, a crowd of exactly 617 souls turned up to watch Western Australia bat nearly six hours, only to fail at the very last to win an absorbing contest. The next day the two teams met again in a one-day match with 12,103 present to watch a predictable limited-overs fixture go through its dull schedule.

For Western Australia, Wayne Andrews (78) and Tim Zoehrer added 152 for the sixth wicket, after which the 27-year-old Zoehrer went on to score a career-best 163 in 250 minutes with 22 fours. He fell to the penultimate ball of the innings as New South Wales went on to victory by 67 runs. It was Western Australia's first defeat in Perth for six years and 51 Shield matches.

The other Shield fixture of the weekend was in Launceston, where Tasmania and Victoria sat out a frustrating first day as the rain poured down. Had the parochial in-fighting which has always dogged Tasmanian cricket been able to apply itself to sanity, the match should have been played in Hobart on a perfect cricket pitch. Now the two teams had to play a contrived version of the game before a dozen men and a dog in three days of some farce.

Simon O'Donnell won the toss, decided to bat and closed at tea with Victoria 224 for 4 from 62 overs. Next day, by sheer coincidence, Tasmania were on exactly the same score from the same number of overs. However, Dirk Wellham did not enter into the spirit of things: he declared one ball and two runs later, much to the open disgust of the Victorian fieldsmen.

Victoria's second innings became bogged down after little Wayne Phillips, the South Melbourne rookie, had knocked up a classy 73. From 144 for 4 overnight, it took Tasmania until after lunch on the final day to dismiss the visitors for 263.

David Boon and Glenn Hughes took the score to 71 by tea, with Hughes, when 21, notching up his 2,000 first-class runs for Tasmania. After the break, and with the benefit of certain dubious umpiring decisions, the home team began the run chase. Boon (90) led the way as 194 runs came in 147 minutes from 35 overs for Tasmania to record their first victory of the season by six wickets.

By now each team had played eight matches with all, theoretically, in with a chance to contest the Shield final. The following weekend's round of fixtures, therefore, took on an air of extra enthusiasm.

The pitch at the Sydney Cricket Ground for the visit of Tasmania was green and under-prepared, with the mown outfield looking like a harshly sacrificed wheat paddock, but there were few dangers for the batsmen. New South Wales batted first, losing John Dyson early, which brought Steve Smith to the crease. For just over two hours he played one of the most delightful innings seen on the ground during the season, only to end prematurely his knock of 61 with a hasty cover drive to a rising half-volley off Dave Gilbert which went straight to cover point.

As New South Wales poked around, their former captain, now leading Tasmania, showed a superb tactical hand. Wellham knew his former team well and set his fields accordingly. At the end of the first day New South Wales were 268 for 8, adding only 10 further runs the following morning. All Wellham's effort came to nought as opposing captain Lawson took 6 for 36 later in the day and Tasmania fell for 153, of which former New South Wales batsman Rod Tucker contributed an unbeaten 82. Lawson's haul saw him pass 300 wickets for New South Wales and 500 wickets in all first-class cricket.

New South Wales then scored slowly with opener Dyson making an unbeaten 112 in 323 minutes with 11 fours before Lawson declared just after tea on the third day at 253 for 4. Set 379 to win, Tasmania clawed their way to 46 without loss at stumps. The final day's crowd of 1,155 saw 100 overs bowled in just six hours as Tasmania fought valiantly for a draw. David Boon took all but half an hour of the day to score 132, with the burly Richard Soule holding up an end for an unbeaten 20 as New South Wales tried unsuccessfully for 33 minutes to claim the last wicket and a near certain place in the Shield final.

In Melbourne, South Australia's David Hookes put Victoria in to bat on a slow, moist pitch, a move which paid off with three wickets within the first 22 minutes. From 101 for 6, Victoria escaped from the quagmire as O'Donnell (55) and Osborne (29) helped Michael Dimattina (113) to his maiden first-class century.

Victoria's 284 had taken exactly a day and a half with Joe Scuderi's 4 for 64 causing most damage. After Hilditch (60) and Nobes (67) had seen South Australia to 144 for 3, it was time to sit back and watch the brilliance of Darren Lehmann.

His partner David Hookes – no slouch with the bat himself – had a 51-minute start in their partnership. Just 56 minutes later, at stumps on the second day, Hookes had gone from 17 to 24 while Lehmann had reached his 50 from 46 balls with 7 fours. 'He's just brilliant', said Hookes later in the evening.

Next day the pair took their fourth-wicket stand to 178 from just 194 balls in 128 minutes before Lehmann fell for 87. Hookes, however, was in one of his scoring moods, going from 24 to 133, as South Australia scored 170 runs for the loss of one wicket off 28 overs in the pre-lunch session. To rub salt into the wound, last batsman Colin Miller, on his debut, scored 59 in a 10th-wicket partnership of 76 with Peter Gladigau as the score mounted to 510.

The innings had been marred by Victorian paceman Merv Hughes' on-field antics, which at one time included nine successive short-pitched deliveries to Hookes. Umpires Robin Bailhache and David Holden laid two misconduct charges against Hughes, who after the match was fined heavily by Code of Behaviour Commissioner Gordon Lewis.

In search of survival Victoria lost Gary Watts before the close, and took nearly all of the final day to reach 312, with off-spinner Tim May claiming new career-best figures of 7 for 93. Needing 87 to win in just 28 minutes, South Australia gave up the chase at 40 for 2.

Two days after everybody else had started, Queensland captain Allan Border decided on first use of the Perth pitch when he won the toss against Graeme Wood – who would have fielded in any case. A superb spell of seam bowling by Terry Alderman saw the visitors struggle all day, just getting to 200 for 8 at the close. With disharmony in the Queensland camp, resulting from typical administration blunders and nepotism back in Brisbane, Border spent most of the day fighting off media questions rather than concentrating on the match at hand.

Then came a quite unexpected happening for Perth in February – freakish, unseasonable rain. Play was washed out for all of the second day and most of the third. However, on the third morning Queensland had managed to reach 291, mainly thanks to a fine 140 from Test-discard Greg Ritchie.

The last day saw the chase for first-innings points, Western Australia slumped to 75 for 5, then 118 for 6, until Wood and Ken MacLeay took charge. Their 131-run seventh-wicket stand in even time saw them only 43 runs short when MacLeay (70) sent a return catch to Craig McDermott. In gathering gloom, Peter Capes helped his captain knock off the runs to claim those two precious points. Graeme Wood remained unbeaten on 119 scored in 321 minutes with 14 fours and a six.

With a single round of matches to go, one thing was sure: neither Victoria nor Tasmania would be in the final. As for the remaining teams – it was anyone's guess. And as for the venue: it was favoured to be Adelaide, Perth or Sydney – in that order.

Carl Rackemann returned from injury to bowl well enough for Queensland to win a place in the side to tour England. (Adrian Murrell/Allsport)

Friday 10 March saw fixtures start in Melbourne, Adelaide and Sydney. Each day was tension-filled with fortunes swaying. Simon O'Donnell, after having had a row with his selectors over the composition of his Victorian team, sent Western Australia in to bat, on a green Melbourne pitch. O'Donnell's point was made as the two spinners forced onto him proved totally useless in the conditions.

The visiting batsmen opened cautiously, adding 133 for the first wicket. March (55), Veletta (64) and Moody (59)

took things easily with the stumps score being 257 for 5. Then the following day produced a quite remarkable display as night-watchman Tom Hogan scored an unbeaten career-best 115 whilst Tim Zoehrer broke his personal best with 168. The sixth-wicket record partnership of 231 helped Wood declare at 533 for 6. If nothing else, O'Donnell had won the battle, if not the war, with his selectors.

Victoria, with aid from rain delays, then took the rest of the match to score 343 for 3 with centuries from Gary Watts (121) and Dean Jones (102 not out). With neither side gaining any points, the spotlight fell on Adelaide.

There the first day of the match against Tasmania had seen South Australia score at a cracking pace. On his debut 21-year-old Brett Williams scored 77, Paul Nobes 71 and David Hookes 66. But yet again, the privileged few were able to watch Darren Lehmann in action. His unbeaten 71 was sheer brilliance, with boundaries all around the ground, which caused visiting captain Dirk Wellham to employ six fielders on the ropes for most of Lehmann's innings.

On the second day Lehmann fell for 89 as South Australia reached 455. Then came the Tasmanian fightback as Tucker (98) and Wellham (94) strived for first-innings points. As it was, Tasmania fell well short at 356. Hookes then took his gamble: quick runs and a tantalizing declaration.

Starting their second innings on the third afternoon, South Australia were 61 for 1 overnight before Hookes declared half an hour before lunch on the final day at 172 for 4. This left Tasmania a target of 272 from 73 overs to claim their first ever victory over South Australia in the 112 years of matches between the two sides. The home attack lacked penetration as the visitors' score mounted. Glenn Hughes made 62, but it was left to Jamie Cox (82) and Rod Tucker (55) to see Tasmania home by six wickets. South Australia then faced an agonizing wait to hear the result from Sydney where New South Wales were playing Queensland.

In that match, Allan Border had won the toss and put New South Wales in to bat. Mark Taylor had thanked his Australian skipper by scoring 132 as New South Wales moved to 254 for 6 at the end of the first day. The score moved to 301 without further loss before Geoff Lawson declared at tea on a day interrupted by rain.

Queensland, desperate for points, were then bogged down by the spin of Matthews and Whitfield struggling to 83 for 1 at the close. Throughout the Sunday morning session Border was content to allow his batsmen to proceed with caution towards a first-innings lead, gambling that Tasmania would achieve the same in Adelaide.

At one stage, the Queenslanders asked for the Tasmanian score to be flashed up on the Sydney Cricket Ground scoreboard every 10 minutes while their coach, John Bell, checked with the Bureau of Meteorology for the weather forecasts around the country. But Border was forced to reassess his position after Tasmania's challenge began to falter during the second session. Opener Peter Cantrell – who had been stuck on 92 for 51 minutes – mercifully completed one of the dreariest first-class centuries on record. He faced 316 deliveries in 392 minutes at the crease – second only to the slowest century recorded at the SCG by England's Derek Randall, who took 406 minutes in the 1978–9 Test against Australia.

Border then gambled by declaring 71 runs behind New South Wales. The gauntlet had been thrown down, and New South Wales to their credit took up the challenge. From 111 for 3 overnight, they went to 198 for 5 before Lawson declared exactly half an hour before lunch on the final day. Queensland needed 270 runs from 73 overs to win. If they succeeded, the final would be in Brisbane; if they failed, they would not play in the final at all.

The question in hindsight is: Did Allan Border err in not changing his batting order? Cantrell's first-innings 105 in 413 minutes was followed by 71 in 214 minutes, which was exactly the opposite of what was required. In the end it came down to 113 runs from the final 20 overs.

The slog was now on. Steve Waugh picked up 6 for 51 as wickets fell. The final over saw nine runs still required with two wickets standing, but Ian Healy and Dirk Tazelaar could only manage five. Queensland were out.

In Melbourne, Graeme Wood was pacing around like a caged lion for 68 minutes, having left the ground at 5.30 p.m., and enduring the Sydney match on the dressing-room television monitor. When Healy failed to score that final boundary, the Western Australian team erupted. They had their home match.

With the half-an-hour time-zone difference in Adelaide, the wait for South Australia was only nine minutes. Hundreds of spectators huddled in groups to listen to the final tense moments on radio. It was agony for coach Barry Richards and his team. Then it was all over, South Australia would play Western Australia in the Sheffield Shield final in Perth from 25 to 29 March 1989.

The Australian season had lacked flair during the International matches, with the West Indies becoming increasingly unpopular as their tour progressed. Only on their departure did the Shield regain the media attention it deserved and only then because the jaded senior cricket scribes were away from domestic reporting. The build-up matches to the final could not have been scripted in a better fashion, and once again in Australia it was very noticeable that attendance figures were high for Shield encounters. South Australian captain David Hookes remarked: 'I wonder if Australian cricket would benefit from having a season of purely domestic cricket.' His thoughts were echoed around the country, as it was becoming quite obvious that international visiting teams were losing their glamour and appeal.

Overall, the 1988–9 season was good for Australian cricket. Western Australia emerged from the pack at the end to confirm their superiority and depth, especially when Test duties saw them having to call up good quality reserves.

Barry Richards pulled South Australia into line fairly quickly, and early in the season was virtually in a position of non-playing captain. Gradually David Hookes understood what was required and their team-work saw the side rise from fifth to second in a good effort.

Queensland were wracked by off-field problems all year, with Allan Border's end-of-season Australian Cricket Board contract of $300,000 being his only ray of sunshine.

New South Wales also had their share of dark days, especially the mid-season change of captaincy and the reasons for it. Tasmania were more than pleased with their initial season of Dirk Wellham at the helm. Unbeaten for the first time, the bubbling enthusiasm in Hobart will be rewarded by their first Test match in early 1990.

What can one say about Victoria? Bottom of the Shield table – very undeservedly – but with the potential of an exciting captain in Simon O'Donnell. Do not write off Victoria, for as these notes are being read they could be astride the Shield table once more.

As a postscript last year the names of six young cricketers were mentioned as being worthy of noting. Two were short-listed, subsequently, for the England tour; five played first-class cricket, with the sixth (Berry) expected to do so very soon. There are more on the horizon: the future of the game in Australia looks to be in good shape. If only the administration could follow suit.

Too Many Disappointments for Comfort

The season in New Zealand.
Shell Cup. Shell Trophy.
Test and One-Day series, New Zealand *v.* Pakistan.
First-class averages. Form charts.
Review of the season by Don Cameron.

Batsman of the Year – Andrew Jones. (Simon Bruty/Allsport)

After 35 years as a top cricket administrator, Bob Vance retired as Chairman of the New Zealand Cricket Council. He was succeeded by Barry Paterson, a capable man, but none would deny the fact that Vance's retirement brought to an end a highly successful period in New Zealand cricket history. The tour to India had been generally satisfactory, and Richard Hadlee had returned as the most successful bowler in the history of Test cricket, but there was a certain unease that no one had yet established a positive claim to be recognised as his successor. New Zealand cannot hope to have Hadlee in their side for very many years to come, and Chatfield and Wright are other leading players whose careers must be nearing an end. On top of these concerns was the continuing worry over the health of Martin Crowe, who was unable to make the trip to India and who had slipped from the world cricket scene at a time when he seemed about to become the most dominant of batsmen.

For New Zealand cricket the time had arrived for young players like Greatbatch, Blain, Thomson and Watson to assert themselves and assure the followers of the game that standards and traditions would be maintained.

Northern Districts welcomed back Graeme Hick and looked to Chris Cairns for an advance after his season in Nottingham. Central Districts had changes in administration, but the team remained much as it had done the previous season except that Derek Stirling had moved to Wellington.

With the arrival of Stirling, the recovery from injury of Beyeler and the development of Millmow as a genuine pace bowler, Wellington looked strong in bowling. Stephen Hotter, a young left-arm bowler of promise, was likely to challenge Evan Gray, and there was much competition for batting places. Robert Vance stood down as captain, and McSweeney was appointed in his place.

Otago were able to call upon two players registered with English counties, Neil Mallender of Somerset and Kassem Ibadulla of Gloucestershire, but they would miss Warren Lees, who had retired. Canterbury also had an English county player in Northamptonshire's Mark Robinson, and much was hoped for Stu Roberts.

Auckland looked towards a season of more stability when, hopefully, they would not have to call upon as many as the 27 players that they had used in 1987–8 in an effort to find, without success, a winning team. Jeff Crowe remained optimistic, and there was general optimism that he would refind form and favour with the selectors.

Shell Cup

27 December 1988

at Levin

Central Districts 213 (P.S. Briasco 57 not out)
Northern Districts 147

Central Districts (2 pts) won by 66 runs

at Auckland

Otago 122 for 9
Auckland 123 for 4 (R.B. Reid 59)

Auckland (2 pts) won by 6 wickets

at Christchurch

Wellington 157
Canterbury 145 (E.J. Gray 4 for 27)

Wellington (2 pts) won by 12 runs

The neatly organized New Zealand season began with the one-day competition, the Shell Cup. A powerful all-round performance by Gary Robertson, who hit 40 and took 3 for 16 in eight overs, earned him the individual award and Central Districts victory at Levin. Scott Briasco, too, had a fine match, hitting a brisk 57 not out and capturing the vital wicket of Graeme Hick.

On a difficult pitch, Otago could manage only 16 runs from their first 10 overs and eventually laboured to 122 for 9 in 50 overs. Auckland bowled and fielded well, and Man of the Match Richard Reid hit 59 in under 25 overs to take them to victory with ease.

Evan Gray bowled Wellington to victory after Canterbury had looked to be in a strong position.

29 December 1988

at Basin Reserve, Wellington

Wellington 196 for 5 (R.H. Vance 99 not out, B.A. Edgar 60)
Auckland 176 (D.G. Scott 55)

Wellington (2 pts) won by 20 runs

at Tauranga

Otago 148
Northern Districts 149 for 4

Northern Districts (2 pts) won by 6 wickets

at Ashburton

Canterbury 184 for 8 (P.E. McEwan 71)
Central Districts 157 for 8

Canterbury (2 pts) won by 27 runs

After two rounds of matches Wellington were the only unbeaten side. Robert Vance played a sparkling innings to take them to a commanding score against Auckland. He and Bruce Edgar put on 170 for the second wicket, and Auckland rarely looked like matching their score. Vance was denied his century when Grant Cederwall ran one short.

Otago were again caught on a difficult pitch, and rain added to their woes. Northern mastered the conditions much better and won with 10 overs to spare. Derek Beard, 3 for 21, took the individual award.

Paul McEwan led Canterbury to a formidable score, and, when Martin Crowe was stumped for 49, Central's challenge faded.

31 January 1988

at Alexandra

Central Districts 280 for 6 (M.D. Crowe 125, C.J. Smith 84)
Otago 162 (K.J. Burns 52)

Central Districts (2 pts) won by 118 runs

at Auckland

Auckland 163 (R.B. Reid 54, M.W. Priest 5 for 26)
Canterbury 164 for 4 (D.J. Boyle 52)

Canterbury (2 pts) won by 6 wickets

at Basin Reserve, Wellington

Northern Districts 198 (S.A. Thomson 52, E.J. Chatfield 4 for 43)
Wellington 200 for 7

Wellington (2 pts) won by 3 wickets

The year 1988 was not a good one for Martin Crowe, but he said farewell to it in regal manner. He hit 125 off 118 balls in 147 minutes and hit 3 sixes and 7 fours. He and John Smith put on 154 for the second wicket, and Central Districts moved to a crushing win over Otago.

Slow left-arm bowler Mark Priest spun Canterbury to victory at Eden Park. Remarkable bowling, which brought him 5 for 26 in 10 overs, reduced Auckland to 163 all out after they had been 95 for 2, and Canterbury sailed to victory with 4.5 overs to spare after Boyle and Wright had put on 71 for the first wicket.

Wellington took a strong hold on the cup with a thrilling victory over Northern Districts. Wicket-keeper-captain Ervin McSweeney was Man of the Match with six catches and an innings of 36 not out, which saw his side home with five balls to spare. Earlier, Northern had been saved from rout by Shane Thomson and Grant Bradburn, who came together at 97 for 6 and added 81. McSweeney and Beyeler had to score 19 from the last 18 deliveries, but some blistering shots from McSweeney eased the pressure.

2 January 1989

at Alexandra

Otago 113 (K.J. Burns 52)
Wellington 117 for 4 (B.A. Edgar 68 not out)

Wellington (2 pts) won by 6 wickets

at New Plymouth

Central Districts 78 (D.K. Morrison 4 for 21)
Auckland 81 for 0

Auckland (2 pts) won by 10 wickets

at Mount Maunganui

Northern Districts 90 for 5
v. Canterbury

Match abandoned
Canterbury 1 pt, Northern Districts 1 pt

Another dismal collapse by Otago gave Wellington a simple task at Alexandra, and Bruce Edgar took them to victory with 7.4 overs to spare. This win gave Wellington the cup, for rain caused the abandonment of Canterbury's game at Mount Maunganui.

Martin Crowe and Gary Robertson were the only batsmen to reach double figures as Central Districts wilted before Danny Morrison. Richard Reid and Phil Horne took Auckland to victory in 18 overs.

3 January 1989

at Christchurch

Otago 238 for 7 (B.R. Blair 91)
Canterbury 180

Martin Crowe – a hundred for Central Districts in the Shell Cup match at Alexandra on the last day of 1988 indicated the return to fitness and form that all New Zealand looked for. (David Munden)

Otago (2 pts) won by 58 runs

at Hamilton 263 for 4

Auckland 263 for 4 (D.N. Patel 94)
Northern Districts 149

Auckland (2 pts) won by 114 runs

4 January 1989

at Palmerston North

Wellington 150 (E.J. Gray 51, G.R. Logan 4 for 12)
Central Districts 132

Wellington (2 pts) won by 18 runs

The Otago batsmen at last found their form and took their side to their first win in the competition. Bruce Blair was in devastating form and moved from 57 to 91 in 13 deliveries. Boyle and McEwan gave Canterbury hope in a second-wicket stand of 58, but Blair bowled Boyle and McEwan fell to Lindsay. McEwan became the first Otago batsman to reach 1,000 runs in Shell Cup cricket.

With Dipak Patel scoring an elegant 94 and sharing a fourth-wicket stand of 112 with Pringle, Auckland overwhelmed Northern Districts.

On a difficult pitch, Evan Gray gave a fine all-round

Shell Cup – Final Table					
	P	*W*	*L*	*Ab*	*Pts*
Wellington	5	5	–	–	10
Auckland	5	3	2	–	6
Canterbury	5	2	2	1	5
Central Districts	5	2	3	–	4
Northern Districts	5	1	3	1	3
Otago	5	1	4	–	2

performance. His 51 held Wellington together as Greg Logan took 4 for 12 in 10 overs of left-arm medium pace. Gray then took 3 for 16 in his 10 overs and, with Grant Cederwall, took Wellington to victory and a hundred per cent record for the competition.

Shell Trophy

6, 7 and 8 January 1989

at Lancaster Park, Christchurch

Wellington 330 for 5 dec (B.A. Edgar 150, R.H. Vance 51, A.H. Jones 50) and 204 for 9 dec (E.B. McSweeney 67 not out)
Canterbury 257 (P.E. McEwan 99, M.W. Priest 79, E.J. Gray 4 for 42) and 55 for 0

Match drawn
Wellington 4 pts, Canterbury 0 pts

at Eden Park, Auckland

Otago 174 (R.N. Hoskin 71, W. Watson 5 for 36)
v. Auckland

Match drawn
Auckland 2 pts, Otago 2 pts

at McLean Park, Napier

Central Districts 252 (C.J. Smith 65, B.P. Bracewell 5 for 45) and 329 for 5 dec (P.S. Briasco 154 not out, T.E. Blain 69, M.R. McKinnon 4 for 131)
Northern Districts 316 for 8 dec (D.J. White 77, G.A. Hick 57, G.E. Bradburn 54 not out) and 259 (G.A. Hick 105, D.J. White 73)

Central Districts won by 6 runs
Central Districts 12 pts, Northern Districts 4 pts

The New Zealand first-class season began with rain. Play was possible only on the last day at Auckland, when Willie Watson did enough to show that he would be challenging for a Test place.

Bruce Edgar again made the New Zealand selectors rue the fact that he had turned his back on Test cricket with an innings of 150 in 316 minutes that dominated the Wellington innings at Christchurch. He and Vance put on 141 for the first wicket, and Jones joined him in a second-wicket stand of 127. Gray and Stirling bowled Wellington to first-innings points, but the visitors slumped to 93 for 7 in their second innings before McSweeney and Stirling hit them out of trouble. McSweeney made a challenging declaration, but rain intervened.

Central Districts trailed by 64 on the first innings at Napier after Brendon Bracewell, still short of his 30th birthday and still a likely candidate for a recall to the national side, had bowled well on the opening day. Central's second innings was dominated by Scott Briasco, who had missed the previous season and who marked his return with the fourth century of his career. Tony Blain also batted well, hitting 69 in 103 minutes with a six and 6 fours. Martin Crowe declared, setting Northern Districts to score 266 at 4½ an over. Hick and White seemed to have made victory inevitable with a second-wicket stand of 182 in 150 minutes. Hick's 105 came off 131 balls and included 13 fours, but thereafter Northern lost their way, Briasco following his fine innings with three wickets. In a mad dash at the end, Brendon Bracewell hit Unwin for six

Bruce Edgar – three centuries for Wellington in the opening Shell Trophy matches of the season. (Alan Cozzi)

and then was bowled, while Spragg was run out first ball to give Central an exciting victory with only two balls to spare.

10, 11 and 12 January 1989

at Lancaster Park, Christchurch

Canterbury 362 for 6 dec (L.K. Germon 106 not out, M.W. Priest 85, B.R. Hartland 73) and 214 for 5 dec (P.E. McEwan 116, R.T. Latham 51 not out)
Central Districts 216 for 5 dec (M.J. Greatbatch 78, M.W. Douglas 71) and 191 for 3 (P.S. Briasco 100 not out)

Match drawn
Canterbury 4 pts, Central Districts 0 pts

at Basin Reserve, Wellington

Auckland 333 (P.A. Horne 86, D.N. Patel 77, M.C. Snedden 58) and 312 for 2 dec (J.J. Crowe 156, T.J. Franklin 133 not out)
Wellington 334 for 1 dec (A.H. Jones 177, B.A. Edgar 147 not out) and 217 for 8 (A.H. Jones 66, D.N. Patel 4 for 16)

Match drawn
Wellington 4 pts, Auckland 0 pts

at Harry Barker Reserve, Gisborne

Otago 129 (B.P. Bracewell 4 for 49) and 208 (G.E. Bradburn 4 for 62)
Northern Districts 240 (B.A. Young 68, S.L. Boock 4 for 63) and 98 for 2

Northern Districts won by 8 wickets
Northern Districts 16 pts, Otago 0 pts

A maiden first-class century by wicket-keeper Lee Germon and a career-best 85 from Mark Priest set Canterbury on the way to a big score. Martin Crowe kept the game alive by declaring as soon as the follow-on had been avoided. Paul McEwan hit 116 off 153 balls with 3 sixes and 12 fours when Canterbury batted again, and Latham declared, setting Central to make 361 in 94 overs. Briasco hit his second century in successive matches, but the run rate lapsed after the loss of early wickets, and the last 20 overs went unused.

Auckland batted consistently to reach 333 by the end of the first day at Wellington. Edgar and Jones responded with an opening stand of 333, which beat by 95 runs the previous best opening stand for Wellington by Dempster and Dustin 57 years ago. Auckland, not to be outdone, produced a record second-wicket partnership of 241 between Jeff Crowe and Trevor Franklin when they batted again. Set to make 312 in 62 overs, Wellington lost their way against the spin of Dipak Patel, 4 for 16 in 14 overs, and the match was drawn.

Otago's limp batting surrendered to the pace trio of Brendon Bracewell, Thomson and Chris Cairns, and the batting of Young and Bradburn took Northern Districts to a first-innings lead of 111 at Gisborne. Otago fared only marginally better when they batted again, and Northern moved to a comfortable win.

14, 15 and 16 January 1989

at Basin Reserve, Wellington

Wellington 198 (R.H. Vance 69, A.H. Jones 62, B.P. Bracewell 6 for 49) and 448 for 1 (R.H. Vance 254 not out, B.A. Edgar 140)
Northern Districts 370 (G.A. Hick 121 not out, S.A. Thomson 65, D.J. White 64, G.N. Cederwall 7 for 97) and 231 for 7 (G.W. McKenzie 71, D.J. White 50, E.J. Gray 4 for 71)

Match drawn
Northern Districts 4 pts, Wellington 0 pts

at Eden Park, Auckland

Auckland 304 (J.J. Crowe 115, I.D.S. Smith 50, A.J. Nuttall 4 for 80) and 125 for 7
Canterbury 120 (D.N. Patel 4 for 27) and 307 (J.G. Wright 149 not out, R.T. Latham 64, J.G. Bracewell 5 for 90, D.N. Patel 4 for 93)

Auckland won by 3 wickets
Auckland 16 pts, Canterbury 0 pts

at Molyneux Park, Alexandra

Otago 404 for 6 dec (K.R. Rutherford 179, B.R. Blair 118, S.W. Duff 4 for 87)
Central Districts 156 (M.J. Greatbatch 67, N.A. Mallender 5 for 38, S.L. Boock 5 for 51) and 245 (T.E. Blain 80, G.K. Robertson 52, N.A. Mallender 5 for 69, T.J. Wilson 4 for 75)

Otago won by an innings and 3 runs
Otago 16 pts, Central Districts 0 pts

With no side being able to establish a commanding lead in the early stages of the Shell Trophy, Northern Districts edged just four points clear by virtue of their first-innings lead over Wellington. Another stirring performance by

Brendon Bracewell brought about a Wellington collapse, the last nine wickets going down for 71 runs. Graeme Hick's second century of the season and some hard hitting from Shane Thomson, a six and 13 fours in his 65, took Northern to a big lead. Vance and Edgar countered with an opening stand of 310, the second triple century opening stand by Wellington openers in a week. Bob Vance reached the first double century of his career. His 254 came off 348 balls and included 6 sixes and 31 fours. Edgar hit his third century of the season, the 22nd of his career, and the partnership of 310 took only 289 minutes. Set to make 277 at nearly five an over, Northern floundered against Gray although Grant Cederwall, who had returned career-best figures in the first innings, went wicketless. Bradburn and Chris Cairns batted out time after seven wickets had fallen for 204.

Jeff Crowe signalled a complete return to form with his second century in successive innings, and the spin duet of John Bracewell and Dipak Patel forced Canterbury to follow-on. The spinners bowled effectively in the second innings, too, but John Wright carried his bat, facing 384 balls and staying for 369 minutes to force Auckland to bat

Robert Vance threw off the caution of previous seasons to become a batsman of great attacking flair. He hit 254 not out for Wellington against Northern Districts, 15 January, and was to complete 1,000 runs in the season. (Simon Bruty/Allsport)

Auckland 1989
First-Class Matches

BATTING

	Otago (A) 6–8 Jan		Wellington 10–12 Jan		Canterbury (A) 14–16 Jan		Central Districts (Nelson) 18–20 Jan		Northern Districts (A) 29–31 Jan		Central Districts (A) 2–4 Feb		Northern Districts (Ham.) 6–8 Feb		Otago (Dun.) 16–18 Feb		M	Inns	NOs	Runs	HS	Av
P.A. Horne	—	—	86	10	15	0	82	21	209	—	54	—	23	2	11	22*	8	12	1	535	209	48.63
R.B. Reid	—	—	20	8*	20	1	36	34	6	90	37	—	7	54			7	11	1	313	90	31.30
J.J. Crowe	—	—	33	156	115	35	66	4	54	86					95	—	6	9	—	644	156	71.55
D.N. Patel	—	—	77	—	21	3	0	31	20	41*					30	—	6	8	1	223	77	31.85
M.R. Pringle	—	—	5	—	29	22	3	2	11	—	89*	—	0	60	8	—	8	10	1	229	89*	25.44
I.D.S. Smith	—	—	0	—	50	6	64	—	21*	—							5	5	1	141	64	35.25
J.G. Bracewell	—	—			5	4*	26	22*	0						35*	—	5	6	3	92	35*	30.66
M.C. Snedden	—	—	58	—	21	—	8*	—	—	—							6	3	1	87	58	43.50
S.R. Gillespie	—	—															1					—
D.K. Morrison	—	—	16	—							0	—	6*	0	—	—	7	4	1	22	16	7.33
W. Watson	—	—	2	—	0*	—											6	2	1	2	2	2.00
T.J. Franklin			16	133*	13	36	—	15*	2	30	67	—	7	23	58	25*	7	12	3	425	133*	47.22
R.P. de Groen	0*	—									0	—	1	0*			3	4	2	1	1	0.50
W.P. Fowler					0	4*					14	—	10	3			3	5	1	31	14	7.75
S.W. Brown											12	—	1	50	7*	—	3	4	1	70	50	23.33
P.J. Hounsell											5	—	22	1			2	3	—	28	22	9.33
P.J. Kelly											0	—	7	21			2	3	—	28	21	9.33
P.S. Neutze											3	—	0	0			2	3	—	3	3	1.00
A. Parore															—	—	1					—
Byes	3			2	4	3					4		3	1	2							
Leg-byes	9			4	8	1	4	4	10	11	5		7	12								
Wides	2			1					1		6		1									
No-balls	6		4	9	2	6	3	13	8		9		6	3								
Total	333		312	304	125	296	136	340	265	296	107		229	261	47							
Wickets	10		2	10	7	7	5	7	3	10	10		10	5	0							
Result	Ab.		D		W		W		L		D		L		W							
Points	2		0		16		16		4		4		0		16							

Fielding Figures

19 – I.D.S. Smith (ct 18/st 1)
10 – P.A. Horne
9 – P.J. Kelly (ct 8/st 1)
8 – J.J. Crowe
7 – M.R. Pringle
6 – A. Parore
5 – D.N. Patel
4 – T.J. Franklin, D.K. Morrison, R.B. Reid and J.G. Bracewell
3 – P.J. Hounsell
2 – W.P. Fowler and W. Watson
1 – S.W. Brown, M.C. Snedden, P.S. Neutze and sub.

BOWLING

	D.K. Morrison	S.R. Gillespie	M.C. Snedden	W. Watson	J.G. Bracewell	R.P. de Groen	D.N. Patel	P.A. Horne
v. Otago (Auckland) 6–8 January	14–3–29–0	11.1–4–17–2	20–8–30–2	25–10–36–5	14–2–60–1			
v. Wellington (Wellington) 10–12 January	17.2–1–68–0 / 14–2–53–0		23–7–57–0 / 7–1–35–1	18–0–87–1 / 15–3–57–1		15–1–50–0 / 11–1–39–1	19–3–66–0 / 14–8–16–4	1–0–5–1
v. Canterbury (Auckland) 14–16 January			2–0–7–0 / 8–3–22–0	12–6–18–1 / 14–2–47–0	26–11–42–3 / 50.3–18–90–5		11.4–5–27–4 / 39–12–93–4	
v. Central Districts (Nelson) 18–20 January	13–2–42–0 / 14–3–46–1		22.2–6–54–4 / 28–6–71–3	25–6–51–6 / 26–3–97–3	2–0–3–0 / 20.4–5–48–3		7–3–5–0	
v. Northern Districts (Auckland) 29–31 January	24.4–4–85–5 / 13.5–0–89–1		27–8–58–3 / 24–8–71–2	14–4–40–1 / 25–3–93–1	26–6–71–1 / 12–0–55–1		5–0–21–0	
v. Central Districts (Auckland) 2–4 February	21–5–39–3 / 11–1–30–0					16–1–54–1 / 8–1–17–0		
v. Northern Districts (Hamilton) 6–8 February	22–5–94–3 / 5–0–33–2					26–11–41–1 / 2–0–14–0		
v. Otago (Dunedin) 16–18 February	12–1–34–0 / 11.3–6–16–5		17–5–47–0 / 13–5–14–4	18–3–40–1 / 7–2–18–0	31–11–47–4		16–3–37–2	
	193.2–33–658–20 av. 32.90	11.1–4–17–2 av. 8.50	191.2–57–466–19 av. 24.52	199–42–584–20 av. 29.20	182.1–53–416–18 av. 23.11	78–15–215–3 av. 71.66	111.4–34–265–14 av. 18.92	1–0–5–1 av. —

again. Wright hit a six and 22 fours. Under no undue pressure, Auckland made hard work of reaching the target of 328.

Otago's batsmen arrived and helped their side to an innings victory at Alexandra. Ken Rutherford and Bruce Blair put on 227 for the third wicket, so beating the record of Blunt and McMullan, which had stood for 60 years. The pace of Mallender and the spin of Boock twice accounted for Central Districts.

18, 19 and 20 January 1989

at Trafalgar Park, Nelson

Central Districts 153 (W. Watson 6 for 51, M.C. Snedden 4 for 54) and 278 (M.W. Douglas 67, T.E. Blain 59)
Auckland 296 for 7 dec (P.A. Horne 82, J.J. Crowe 66, I.D.S. Smith 64, G.R. Logan 5 for 60) and 136 for 5

Auckland won by 5 wickets
Auckland 16 pts, Central Districts 0 pts

at Carisbrook, Dunedin

Wellington 220 (V.F. Johnson 4 for 44) and 173 (B.A. Edgar 78, S.L. Boock 4 for 46)
Otago 111 (E.J. Chatfield 4 for 29) and 225 (B.R. Blair 70, E.J. Chatfield 5 for 36, D.A. Stirling 4 for 66)

Wellington won by 57 runs
Wellington 16 pts, Otago 0 pts

at Seddon Park, Hamilton

Northern Districts 342 for 4 dec (G.A. Hick 145, C.M. Kuggeleijn 101 not out) and 313 for 5 dec (D.J. White 110, G.A. Hick 71)
Canterbury 343 for 4 dec (R.T. Latham 121 not out, P.E. McEwan 66) and 181 for 8 (J.G. Wright 53)

Match drawn
Canterbury 4 pts, Northern Districts 0 pts

Auckland moved 10 points clear at the top of the table with a convincing win over Central Districts. The pace bowling of Snedden and Watson bundled out Central for 153 in 263 minutes, and Auckland were 124 for 1 by the end of the first day. Jeff Crowe, again in good batting form, declared with a comfortable lead, but by the end of the second day, Central were 39 runs ahead with 6 second-innings wickets standing and Douglas and Blain in full flow. Blain went without addition on the last morning, and Auckland moved to a comfortable win.

Wellington maintained their challenge by beating Otago at Carisbrook in a match in which bowlers were always on top. Chatfield had match figures of 9 for 65 and Stirling 6 for 98.

Centuries by Hick and Kuggeleijn could not bring Northern Districts first-innings points on a batsman's paradise at Seddon Park. Skipper Rod Latham took his side into the lead, but Northern hit fiercely in their second innings in an attempt to force victory. Set to make 319 in 58 overs, Canterbury collapsed, but Nuttall batted an hour for 5 not out to stave off defeat.

18, 19 and 20 January 1989

at Pukekura Park, New Plymouth

Pakistanis 329 for 9 dec (Mudassar Nazar 82, Saleem Malik 69, Shoaib Mohammad 62, R.P. de Groen 4 for 50) and 124 for 1 (Shoaib Mohammad 55 not out, Saleem Malik 50 not out)
New Zealand Second XI 126 (S.W. Brown 64)

Match drawn

This match was added to the Pakistanis' tour programme as they had finished their tour of Australia earlier than anticipated. There was no play on the second day because of rain. The tourists opted for batting practice in a match which was not granted first-class status.

W.P. Fowler	S.W. Brown	P.S. Neutze	T.J. Franklin		Byes	Leg-byes	Wides	No-balls	Total	Wkts
						2		5	174	10
					2	4		4	334	1
					8	4		3	217	8
11–4–24–2						2			120	10
15–3–47–1					4	4		2	307	10
						3	1	5	153	10
					3	8	1	9	278	10
					4	6			285	10
					3	13			324	5
15–8–15–2	13–4–23–0	26.2–11–41–4				2		1	174	10
28–13–38–3		34–13–71–3				1		2	157	6
6–2–7–0	35–9–102–4	11–3–16–2				.14		6	274	10
	2–0–14–0		0.1–0–4–0					5	65	2
	15–2–39–2				11	2		6	257	9
						2		6	50	10
75–30–	65–15–	71.2–27–	0.1–0–							
131–8	178–6	128–9	4–0							
av. 16.37	av. 29.66	av. 14.22	—							

Canterbury 1989
First-Class Matches

BATTING

Match key (each match shown as two innings columns):
1. v. Wellington (Christchurch) 6–8 January
2. v. Central Districts (Christchurch) 10–12 January
3. v. Auckland (Auckland) 14–16 January
4. v. Northern Districts (Hamilton) 18–20 January
5. v. Wellington (Wellington) 22–4 January
6. v. Pakistanis (Christchurch) 29–31 January
7. v. Otago (Christchurch) 4–6 February
8. v. Otago (Oamaru) 11–13 February
9. v. Northern Districts (Christchurch) 16–18 February

BATTING	Well(Ch)	Well(Ch)	CD(Ch)	CD(Ch)	Auck	Auck	ND(H)	ND(H)	Well(W)	Well(W)	Pak	Pak	Otago(Ch)	Otago(Ch)	Otago(Oam)	Otago(Oam)	ND(Ch)	ND(Ch)
B.R. Hartland	21	22*	73	26	5	22	32	10	9	20			3	39	7	9	42	3
P.G. Kennedy	19	—	10	2					5	18	68	24	29*	27	0	37	28	2
P.E. McEwan	99	—	27	116	32	8	66	27	55	65	13	16	22	1	137	6	68	0
R.T. Latham	0	—	26	51*	10	64	121*	8	0	0	24	4	24*	50	45	90	98	142*
M.W. Priest	79	—	85	6	0	17	44*	47	66	33	5*	24	11*	37	31	24	1	92*
L.K. Germon	0	—	106*	2*	27	0	—	4	16	22	5*	20	—	11	9	20	13	—
C.W. Flanagan	17	—	6*		13	25	—	6			—	0	—	4				
A.J. Nuttall	2	—	—	—	0*	0	—	5*	33	9	—	9*	9	3	31	0	7	—
S.J. Roberts	0	—	—	—	0	8	—	0*	29	5	—	6*	—	0	11	6	—	—
M.A. Robinson	0*	—	—	—	0	0	—	—	9*	0*	—	—	—	—	—	2	—	—
J.G. Wright					12	149*	23	53	13	81								
D.J. Boyle	2	31*	21	0	19	4	40	17	108	6	46	54	48*	0*				
R.G. Petrie													—	8				
B.Z. Harris											45	6			20	10	9	0
R.M. Ford															10*	8*	21*	—
M.C. Chamberlain																	20*	—
R.J. Hadlee													—	37				
Byes	2					4	4		3	1	4	7	4				10	7
Leg-byes	10	1	8	7	2	4	6		16	2	2	9	5	10	12	3	7	7
Wides				1			1		3				1					
No-balls	6			4		2	6	4	16	5	7	3	5	5	2	3	19	4
Total	257	55	362	214	120	307	343	181	381	267	219	219	161	195	315	218	343	257
Wickets	10	0	6	5	10	10	4	8	10	10	5	9	3	10	9	10	8	4
Result	D		D		L		D		Tie		D		L		L		W	
Points	0		4		0		4		8		—		0		4		16	

Fielding Figures

28 – L.K. Germon (ct 25/st 3)
9 – P.E. McEwan
7 – R.T. Latham
6 – B.R. Hartland
4 – C.W. Flanagan
3 – B.Z. Harris, S.J. Roberts and A.J. Nuttall
2 – M.W. Priest, P.G. Kennedy and M.A. Robinson
1 – J.G. Wright, D.J. Boyle and sub

BOWLING

BOWLING	S.J. Roberts	M.A. Robinson	C.W. Flanagan	A.J. Nuttall	M.W. Priest	R.T. Latham	D.J. Boyle	J.G. Wright
v. Wellington (Christchurch) 6–8 January	15-2-55-0	17.3-2-62-3	16-3-55-0	27-5-76-1	9-2-46-0	10-2-24-1		
	17-4-46-3	18.2-2-52-3	3-0-6-0	10-2-26-0	24-5-71-3			
v. Central Districts (Christchurch) 10–12 January	14-3-35-2	16-4-49-0	6-3-9-0	18-5-47-2	18-3-53-1	10-4-17-0		
	12-3-48-1	20-6-42-1	7-3-21-0	16-9-33-1	18-8-38-0	1-0-5-0		
v. Auckland (Auckland) 14–16 January	13-1-59-2	18-3-56-1		35-9-80-4	24-1-103-3			
	6-1-14-1			29-14-40-2	23-7-52-3	1-0-7-0		
v. Northern Districts (Hamilton) 18–20 January	15-1-61-2	29-3-114-1	6-1-32-0	28.4-7-86-1	7-1-39-0			
	5-4-6-0	8-1-28-1	19-2-72-1	12-1-49-0	25-5-84-2		8-1-68-0	
v. Wellington (Wellington) 22–4 January	20-1-115-5	21.2-2-71-2		44-10-123-1	19-4-44-0	10-3-33-0		
	6-1-41-1	12-2-40-2		8-4-32-0	19-4-48-1	13-2-41-0		5-0-44-0
v. Pakistanis (Christchurch) 29–31 January	14-0-74-2		16-2-53-2	12-2-48-1	17-5-39-0			
	9-0-82-1		20-9-37-1	6-1-27-0	12-1-57-0			
v. Otago (Christchurch) 4–6 February	15-3-54-2		19-5-50-2	11-3-32-0	27-7-70-1	9-1-19-0		
	11-2-43-1		14-2-39-2			4-0-9-0		
v. Otago (Oamaru) 11–13 February	14-1-68-2	23.2-10-47-1		15-2-49-1	16-5-51-3	6-0-34-1		
	2-0-16-0	14-5-48-0		7-1-33-0	16-2-77-1			
v. Northern Districts (Christchurch) 16–18 February	21-4-51-2			4-1-16-1	18-5-35-0	10-7-15-1		
	5-1-38-0			18-1-74-4		5-1-31-0		
	214-32–	197.3-40–	126-30–	300.4-71–	316.1-69–	79-20–	8-1–	5-0–
	906-27	609-15	374-8	871-19	999-24	235-3	68-0	44-0
	av. 33.55	*av. 40.60*	*av. 46.75*	*av. 45.84*	*av. 41.62*	*av. 78.33*	–	–

M	Inns	NOs	Runs	HS	Av
8	16	1	343	73	22.86
7	13	1	269	68	22.41
9	17	—	758	137	44.58
9	17	4	757	142*	58.23
9	17	4	602	92*	46.30
9	14	3	255	106*	23.18
6	7	1	71	25	11.83
9	12	3	108	33	12.00
9	10	2	65	29	8.12
6	6	3	11	9*	3.66
3	6	1	331	149*	66.20
7	14	3	396	108	36.00
1	1	—	8	8	8.00
3	6	—	90	45	15.00
2	3	3	39	21*	—
1	1	1	20	20*	—
1	1	—	37	37	37.00

22 January 1989

at Eden Park, Auckland

Pakistanis 48 (M.C. Snedden 4 for 7, D.K. Morrison 4 for 18)
Auckland Invitation XI 49 for 3

Auckland Invitation XI won by 7 wickets

The match was reduced to 45 overs because of rain, but the Pakistanis were bowled out in 26.1 overs, and the home side reached their target in 17 overs.

22, 23 and 24 January 1989

at Basin Reserve, Wellington

Wellington 398 (T.D. Ritchie 106, A.H. Jones 97, G.R. Larsen 82, R.H. Vance 51, S.J. Roberts 5 for 115) and 250 for 4 dec (A.H. Jones 181 not out)
Canterbury 381 (D.J. Boyle 108, M.W. Priest 66, P.E. McEwan 55) and 267 (J.G. Wright 81, P.E. McEwan 65, E.J. Gray 4 for 77)

Match tied
Wellington 8 pts, Canterbury 8 pts

at Fitzherbert Park, Palmerston North

Central Districts 424 for 3 dec (M.J. Greatbatch 202 not out, P.S. Briasco 89, M.D. Crowe 74)
Otago 193 (K.J. Burns 56, P.D. Unwin 6 for 42) and 332 for 8 (K.B.K. Ibadulla 69, K.J. Burns 66, K.J. McKnight 56 not out, P.D. Unwin 4 for 110)

Match drawn
Central Districts 4 pts, Otago 0 pts

The strong Wellington batting line-up seemed to have taken them to a good position against Canterbury. With Tim Ritchie hitting the third century of his career, they moved to 336 for 3, but collapsed to 398 all out. Canterbury's reply was inconsistent and was boosted by a fifth-wicket stand of 117 between Mark Priest and David Boyle,

R.G. Petrie	P.E. McEwan	R.M. Ford	M.C. Chamberlain	R.J. Hadlee	Byes	Leg-byes	Wides	No-balls	Total	Wkts
					4	8		12	330	5
						3		6	204	9
						6		2	216	5
					2	2	4	4	191	3
					2	4		9	304	10
					4	8		2	125	7
					4	6	1	13	342	4
					3	3		5	313	5
					2	10		15	398	10
				17–6–40–1		4		2	250	4
				14–5–25–1		7		5	235	3
20–10–44–0	5–2–17–0				3	10	1	8	299	6
8–0–45–2						6		1	142	5
		19–6–39–2			5	7	1	8	300	10
		15.1–2–48–0			8	4		3	234	1
		17–4–37–3	17.2–2–65–3		1	5		3	225	3
		7–0–50–0	4–1–24–0		1	3		3	313	10
28–10–89–2	5–2–17–0	58.1–12–174–5	21.2–3–89–3	31.11–65–2						
av. 44.50	av. —	av. 34.80	av. 29.66	av. 32.50						

Central Districts 1989
First-Class Matches

BATTING	v. Northern Districts (Napier) 6–8 January		v. Canterbury (Christchurch) 10–12 January		v. Otago (Alexandra) 14–16 January		v. Auckland (Nelson) 18–20 January		v. Otago (Palmerston North) 22–4 January		v. Wellington (New Plymouth) 29–31 January		v. Auckland (Auckland) 2–4 February		v. Wellington (Wellington) 16–18 February		M	Inns	NOs	Runs	HS	Av
P.S. Briasco	2	154*	3	100*	1	16	39	13	89	—	22	42	3	22	97	2	8	15	2	605	154*	46.53
C.J. Smith	65	8	14	3	8	29	5	32	18	—	20	30	30	28	70	62	8	15	—	422	70	28.13
M.J. Greatbatch	2	39	78	1	67	2	2	4	202*	—	17	59					6	11	1	473	202*	47.30
M.D. Crowe	16	3	—	44	5	3	29	5	74	—	141*	—			51	2	7	11	1	373	141*	37.30
M.W. Douglas	37	34	71	31*	4	5	24	67	17*	—	0	73*	0	0	39	0	8	15	3	402	73*	33.50
T.E. Blain	28	69	29*	—	1	80	12	59	—	—	19	108	5	51*	36*	43	8	13	3	540	108	54.00
S.W. Duff	5	6*	6	—	40*	21	11	8	—	—	23	—	52*	32	—	64	8	11	3	268	64	33.50
G.K. Robertson	48*	—	7*	—	12	52	11	29			28	—	50	1*	—	10	7	10	3	248	52	35.42
P.D. Unwin	1	—	—	—	—	0	26*	—	—	0	—	9	—				6	5	1	36	26*	9.00
G.R. Logan	9	—	—	—	7	19*	9*	8	—	—	3	—	0	—			7	7	2	55	19*	11.00
T.M. McKenna	3	—	—	—	0	2	2	6	—	—	8	—	2	—	—	8*	8	8	1	31	8*	4.42
K.A. O'Dowda					0	0			—	—							2	2	—	0	0	0.00
R.K. Brown											1	18			—	12	2	3	—	31	18	10.33
D.J. Finlay															—	39	1	1	—	39	39	39.00
P.J. Baker															—	6	1	1	—	6	6	6.00
D.J. Guthardt													19	2			1	2	—	21	19	10.50
Byes	1	3		2		5		3	2		3											
Leg-byes	10	5	6	2	4	7	3	8	13		7	3	2	1	1	8						
Wides	4	5		4			1	1	1		1											
No-balls	21	3	2	4	7	4	5	9	8		1	4	1	2	11	1						
Total	252	329	216	191	156	245	153	278	424		290	322	174	157	305	257						
Wickets	10	5	5	3	10	10	10	10	3		10	4	10	6	4	10						
Result	W		D		L		L		D		W		D		L							
Points	12		0		0		0		4		12		0		0							

Fielding Figures

- 13 – T.E. Blain
- 11 – M.W. Douglas
- 9 – M.J. Greatbatch
- 8 – P.D. Unwin
- 7 – S.W. Duff
- 5 – T.M. McKenna
- 4 – P.S. Briasco
- 3 – subs
- 2 – G.K. Robertson, C.J. Smith, G.R. Logan, D.J. Guthardt and R.K. Brown
- 1 – P.J. Baker and K.A. O'Dowda

BOWLING	G.K. Robertson	G.R. Logan	S.W. Duff	T.M. McKenna	P.D. Unwin	P.S. Briasco	K.A. O'Dowda	M.W. Douglas
v. Northern Districts (Napier) 6–8 January	20–3–44–0	16–8–26–0	40–18–81–3	15–6–33–3	30–6–103–1	7–1–20–1		
	8–0–30–1	8–2–22–0	12–2–63–1	6–0–38–1	10.4–1–54–2	14–0–47–3		
v. Canterbury (Christchurch) 10–12 January	19–5–57–0	27–9–79–3	19–6–46–2	14–4–54–0	20–2–93–1	11–4–25–0		
	15–2–49–3	17–6–60–0	10–2–29–1	5–0–15–0	12–0–47–1	1–0–7–0		
v. Otago (Alexandra) 14–16 January	21–3–61–0	26–9–52–0	26–4–87–4	21–5–69–0		10–4–14–0	22–4–75–2	1–0–7–0
v. Auckland (Nelson) 18–20 January	21–2–86–0	23–7–60–5	16–6–30–1	15–1–47–0	14.2–0–55–1	3–0–14–0		
	4.5–1–15–1	20.2–3–65–3		15.1–2–52–1				
v. Otago (Palmerston North) 22–4 January		13–5–25–0	35–8–89–2	8–2–23–1	21.4–6–42–6		5–1–10–0	
		14–2–44–0	60–17–114–2	15–7–20–2	45–15–110–4	2–0–2–0	8–1–23–0	
v. Wellington (New Plymouth) 29–31 January	15–3–41–1	20–6–50–0	20.5–6–59–0	15–3–45–1	13.3–1–69–1	7–0–22–0		
	9–2–32–1	10–0–43–0	23–3–90–4	7.5–1–26–1	23–5–91–4			
v. Auckland (Auckland) 2–4 February	14–2–58–3	19–8–23–1	37–13–68–3	13.5–4–40–2	23–2–92–1			
v. Wellington (Wellington) 16–18 February	16–4–49–1		17–6–49–1	16–1–55–1				
	11–0–47–0		18.5–2–106–3			3–0–13–0		
	173.5–27–569–11 av. 51.72	213.2–65–549–12 av. 45.75	334.4–93–911–27 av. 33.74	166.5–36–517–13 av. 39.76	213.1–38–756–22 av. 34.36	58–9–164–4 av. 41.00	35–6–108–2 av. 54.00	1–0–7–0 av. —

who hit the second century of his career. A stunning innings of 181 off 183 balls in just over three hours by Andrew Jones, who hit 4 sixes and 25 fours, enabled McSweeney to declare, and set Canterbury to make 268 off 68 overs. Wright and Hartland began the chase with a stand of 75 in 71 minutes. McSweeney kept the carrot dangling as he relied almost entirely on the left-arm spin of Evan Gray and the very occasional spin of Andrew Jones. Jones dismissed both openers and took 3 for 104 in 19 overs, but Canterbury lost their way and in the dash for runs McEwan was run out after hitting 65 off 58 balls, and Roberts was run out as he went for what would have been the winning run, so that the match was tied.

Mark Greatbatch hit the first double century of his career and took Central Districts to a massive score against Otago, who were forced to follow-on. Consistent batting in the second innings enabled Otago to force a draw. Paul Unwin returned the best figures of his career for innings and match.

25, 26 and 27 January 1989

at Seddon Park, Hamilton

Pakistanis 302 for 6 dec (Aamer Malik 88, Moin-ul-Atiq 66, Javed Miandad 63) and 108 for 3
President's XI 261 for 5 dec (J.G. Wright 73, J.J. Crowe 58)

Match drawn

Rain curtailed play in the Pakistanis' first first-class match of the tour. Brendon Bracewell, Nuttall, Chris Cairns and Johnson were an interesting selection as the President's XI main attack.

29, 30 and 31 January 1989

at Pukekura Park, New Plymouth

Central Districts 290 (M.D. Crowe 141 not out, E.J. Chatfield 4 for 72) and 322 for 4 dec (T.E. Blain 108, M.W. Douglas 73 not out, M.J. Greatbatch 59)

Mark Greatbatch hit the first double century of his career, Central Districts v. Otago, 22 January 1989. (David Munden)

M.D. Crowe	M.J. Greatbatch	D.J. Finlay	P.J. Baker		Byes	Leg-byes	Wides	No-balls	Total	Wkts
					5	4		7	316	8
						5		1	259	10
						8			362	6
						7		4	214	5
7–0–34–0					3	2		5	404	6
					3	1	1	6	296	7
						4		3	136	5
						4	1	3	193	10
	2–1–6–0				5	8		1	332	8
					3	3		3	292	3
						6		2	288	10
					4	11			296	10
		20.3–5–76–1	23–5–73–1			7		1	309	5
		5–0–25–0	10–0–61–0			2		1	254	3
7–0–34–0 —	2–1–6–0 —	25.3–5–101–1 av. 101.00	33–5–134–1 av. 134.00							

Northern Districts 1989
First-Class Matches

BATTING

	v. Central Districts (Napier) 6–8 January	v. Otago (Gisborne) 10–12 January	v. Wellington (Wellington) 14–16 January	v. Northern Districts (Hamilton) 18–20 January	v. Auckland (Auckland) 29–31 January	v. Wellington (Morrinsville) 2–4 February	v. Auckland (Hamilton) 6–8 February	v. Canterbury (Christchurch) 16–18 February	M	Inns	NOs	Runs	HS	Av
L.M. Crocker	11 0	12 32*	8 13	2 24	28 6	0 0			6	12	1	136	32*	12.36
B.T. Spragg	10 0	27 0							2	4	—	37	27	9.25
D.J. White	77 73	3 4*	64 50	37 110	16 18	27 1	0 17*	1 62	8	16	2	560	110	40.00
G.A. Hick	57 105	12 44*	121* 1	145 71	27 211*	144 132	49 33	41 35	8	16	3	1228	211*	94.46
C.M. Kuggeleijn	49 17	38 —	0 21	101* —	76 33	13 18*	22 —	49 43	8	13	2	480	101*	43.63
B.A. Young	0 7	68 —	11 23	30* 39	26 0	5 23*	4 5	43 97	8	15	2	381	97	29.30
G.E. Bradburn	54* 15	44 —	6 20*	— 44*			5	30	5	8	3	218	54*	43.60
S.A. Thomson	15 23	1 —	65 18	— 7*	68* 31*	19 1	2 5*	21 2	8	14	4	278	68*	27.80
C.L. Cairns	21 4	6* —	32 5*	— 8	— 7	— 110	— 10	3	8	10	2	206	110	25.75
B.P. Bracewell	6* 9	11 8	0 —	— —	4 —	22 —	4 8		7	9	1	72	22	9.00
M.R. McKinnon	— 0*	0 —	0 —		0	1* —			5	5	2	1	1*	0.33
G.W. McKenzie			31 71	3 7	9 9	2 4	2 —		5	9	—	138	71	15.33
A. Somani			—	—		15	11	7	3	3	—	33	15	11.00
M.L. Sua					13 —	19* 30			2	3	1	62	30	31.00
B.J. Barrett						3 —	5* 0*	2	3	4	2	10	5*	5.00
K.A. Weallans							23 —	31 17*	2	3	1	71	31	35.50
Byes	5	6	2 1	4	3 4	3	1	1 1						
Leg-byes	4 5	10 1	3 3	6 3	6 13	3 1	14	5 3						
Wides		1	1	1		1								
No-balls	7	1 1	7 27	6 13	5	8 2	6 5	3 3						
Total	316 259	240 98	370 231	342 313	285 324	252 213	274 65	225 313						
Wickets	8 10	10 2	10 7	4 5	10 5	9 6	10 2	10 10						
Results	L	W	D	D	W	D	W	L						
Points	4	16	4	0	12	0	16	0						

Fielding Figures
18 – B.A. Young
8 – G.A. Hick
6 – D.J. White and C.L. Cairns
5 – G.E. Bradburn and G.W. McKenzie
4 – B.P. Bracewell and S.A. Thompson
2 – C.M. Kuggeleijn and B.T. Spragg
1 – K.A. Weallans, M.R. McKinnon, M.L. Sua and L.M. Crocker

BOWLING

	C.L. Cairns	S.A. Thomson	B.P. Bracewell	M.R. McKinnon	G.E. Bradburn	C.M. Kuggeleijn	G.W. McKenzie	G.A. Hick
v. Central Districts (Napier)	20.5–1–87–3	16–2–64–1	18–3–45–5	16–4–42–1	2–1–3–0			
6–8 January	3–0–16–0	4–0–18–0	14–2–42–1	51–10–131–4	38–9–112–0	3–2–2–0		
v. Otago (Gisborne)	10.1–3–20–3	17–4–47–3	18–6–49–4	18–1–64–2		1–0–6–0		
10–12 January	14–4–40–3	10–1–31–0	6–4–6–0		15.4–2–62–4			
v. Wellington (Wellington)	18–4–56–3	11–3–45–1	19.3–5–49–6	4–1–9–0	7–1–16–0	6–0–17–0		
14–16 January	18–2–69–0	4–0–24–0	22–4–76–0	20–1–84–0	17.4–2–93–0		16–3–70–0	12–7–15–1
v. Canterbury (Hamilton)	14–1–48–0		22–3–74–1		32–5–119–1	4–0–11–0	3–0–24–0	
18–20 January	10–2–38–0	4–2–4–1	17–2–60–3		4–0–12–1	11–2–32–2		3–2–7–0
v. Auckland (Auckland)	15–1–53–1		22.1–5–63–2	23–1–112–3		10–0–31–0	3–0–23–0	
29–31 January	12.1–0–41–1		16–5–36–0	21–3–98–2			7–1–21–0	
v. Wellington (Morrinsville)	23–2–70–2	6–0–18–0		14–2–36–2		17–6–31–1		
2–4 February	3–1–7–1					1–0–8–0		
v. Auckland (Hamilton)	8–0–17–0		18–8–33–2			11–5–17–3		
6–8 February	16–3–47–0	5–1–16–0	21.3–2–55–4			19–12–16–2	5–2–12–1	2–0–6–0
v. Canterbury (Christchurch)	23–4–76–1		16–5–52–2		24–7–67–1		3–1–18–0	
16–18 February	12–4–45–2	2–1–2–0	19.4–5–48–2		4–0–25–0			
	220.1–32–730–20	79–14–269–6	249.5–58–688–32	171–25–579–14	116.2–20–417–6	111–34–263–9	34–6–150–1	20–10–46–1
	av. 36.50	*av.* 44.83	*av.* 21.50	*av.* 41.35	*av.* 69.50	*av.* 29.22	*av.* 150.00	*av.* 46.00

Wellington 292 for 3 dec (R.H. Vance 116 not out, G.R. Larsen 72 not out, B.A. Edgar 57) and 288 (R.H. Vance 123, B.A. Edgar 87, S.W. Duff 4 for 90, P.D. Unwin 4 for 91)

Central Districts won by 32 runs
Central Districts 12 pts, Wellington 4 pts

at Eden Park, Auckland

Auckland 340 for 7 dec (P.A. Horne 209, J.J. Crowe 54) and 265 for 3 dec (R.B. Reid 90, J.J. Crowe 86)
Northern Districts 285 (C.M. Kuggeleijn 76, S.A. Thomson 68 not out, D.K. Morrison 5 for 85) and 324 for 5 (G.A. Hick 211 not out)

Northern Districts won by 5 wickets
Northern Districts 12 pts, Auckland 4 pts

at Lancaster Park, Christchurch

Pakistanis 258 for 7 dec (Saleem Malik 69) and 235 for 3 dec (Javed Miandad 101 not out, Aamer Malik 80)
Canterbury 219 for 5 dec (P.G. Kennedy 68) and 219 for 9 (D.J. Boyle 54, Abdul Qadir 4 for 55)

Match drawn

On the eve of the first Test, there was much to encourage New Zealand. Martin Crowe and Tony Blain hit fine centuries for Central Districts, who gained an unexpected win over Wellington. Blain's 108 was made off 105 balls and contained 5 sixes and 13 fours. There is no more attractive batsman in New Zealand than Tony Blain when he is in form. Robert Vance continued his outstanding season with a century in each innings. When, set a target of 321, Wellington were 202 for 1, Vance and Edgar having added 190 for the second wicket, the visitors looked sure of victory, but Unwin and Duff brought about a collapse and the last six wickets fell for 30 runs.

Phil Horne hit a career-best 209 in 346 minutes to put Auckland in a strong position against Northern Districts, who fell to the ever improving Danny Morrison. Jeff Crowe and Reid scored briskly so that Auckland were able to declare and leave Northern Districts the daunting task

of scoring 321 to win. At 69 for 3, their challenge looked forlorn, but Graeme Hick ravished the bowling. He hit 173 runs in the last session, and his 211 came off 241 balls with 2 sixes and 27 fours. The next highest scorer in the Northern innings was Kuggeleijn with 33.

In the tourists' match, Javed Miandad and Abdul Qadir showed their worth, and the Pakistanis came close to snatching victory in an entertaining game.

Ewen Chatfield's four wickets at New Plymouth brought his total to 396 wickets for Wellington, a New Zealand provincial record.

2, 3 and 4 February 1989

at Eden Park, Auckland

Central Districts 174 (S.W. Duff 52 not out, G.K. Robertson 50, P.S. Neutze 4 for 41) and 157 for 6 (T.E. Blain 51 not out)
Auckland 296 (M.R. Pringle 89 not out, T.J. Franklin 67, P.A. Horne 54)

Match drawn
Auckland 4 pts, Central Districts 0 pts

at Morrinsville Recreation Ground, Morrinsville

Northern Districts 252 for 9 dec (G.A. Hick 144, E.J. Gray 4 for 68) and 213 for 6 dec (G.A. Hick 132)
Wellington 257 for 9 dec (E.J. Gray 59) and 38 for 1

Match drawn
Wellington 4 pts, Northern Districts 0 pts

Auckland maintained a two-point lead over Wellington by claiming a first-innings lead over Central Districts in a game which was ruined by rain on the last day. Martin Pringle hit a career best for Auckland.

Graeme Hick hit his sixth and seventh centuries of the season and reached 1,000 runs, but Wellington took the first-innings points at Morrinsville. Hick's second-innings 132 was made off 153 balls in 154 minutes and included 3 sixes and 12 fours.

D.J. White	A. Somani	M.L. Sua	B.J. Barrett	Byes	Leg-byes	Wides	No-balls	Total	Wkts
				1	10	4	21	252	10
				3	5	5	3	329	5
					4		7	129	10
				3	2	2		208	10
				4	2	2	11	198	10
2-0-12-0					5		4	448	1
1-1-0-0	12-2-57-1			4	6	1	6	343	4
	10-5-28-1						4	181	8
		12-0-54-1					13	340	7
		14-1-59-0			10		8	265	3
		16-2-46-2	16.5-3-45-2	11		1	14	257	9
		2-0-20-0		3				38	1
			14.5-5-32-4	3	5	6	9	107	10
	9-0-36-1		21-9-33-1	1	7	1	6	229	10
	6-1-26-1		26-2-87-3	10	7		19	343	8
1-0-17-0	11-0-56-0		14-1-50-0	7	7			257	4
4-1-	48-8-	44-3-	92.4-20-						
29-0	203-4	179-3	247-10						
—	av. 50.75	av. 59.66	av. 24.70						

Otago 1989
First-Class Matches

BATTING	v. Auckland (Napier) 6–8 January		v. Northern Districts (Gisborne) 10–12 January		v. Central Districts (Alexandra) 14–16 January		v. Wellington (Dunedin) 18–20 January		v. Central Districts (Palmerston North) 22–4 January		v. Canterbury (Christchurch) 4–6 February		v. Canterbury (Oamaru) 11–13 February		v. Auckland (Dunedin) 16–18 February		M	Inns	NOs	Runs	HS	Av
K.J. Burns	11	—	5	9	25	—	9	4	56	66	15	3	73	—	89	6	8	13	—	371	89	28.53
P.W. Dobbs	2	—	7	40	35	—	0	5	20	37	69	15	38	86*	1	0	8	14	1	355	86*	27.30
S.J. McCullum	5	—					5	49	14	30	43	23	38	75	69	14	6	11	—	365	75	33.18
K.R. Rutherford	17	—	18	25	179	—	20	4	20	16	125	47	21	58*	1	0	8	14	1	551	179	42.38
B.R. Blair	34	—	8	2	118	—	0	70	6	0	3	30	61	—	52	2	8	13	—	386	118	29.69
R.N. Hoskin	71	—	1	0	1	—	27	11									4	6	—	111	71	18.50
J.K. Lindsay	13	—	2	21	7	—			23	3							4	6	—	69	23	11.50
N.A. Mallender	4	—	20	38	25*	—	14	43	2	23	13*	—			9*	0	7	11	3	191	43	23.87
P.W. Hills	8	—	29	32									14	—	0	0	4	6	—	83	32	13.83
S.L. Boock	0	—	13	0	—	—	21	15			—	—	27	—	0	5	7	8	—	81	27	10.12
V.F. Johnson	2*	—	0*	25*	—	—	7*	3*	0	18*	—	—	5*	—	0	0	8	10	7	60	25*	20.00
K.J. McKnight			15	9	—	—	6	2	3	56*	5*	—					5	7	2	96	56*	19.20
T.J. Wilson					4*	—	0	4	10	—	—	7*	0	—	1*	8*	6	8	4	34	10	8.50
K.B.K. Ibadulla									31*	69	4	10*	2	—	16	7	4	7	2	139	69	27.80
J.R. Murtagh													0	—			1	1	—	0	0	0.00
Byes				3	3					5	3		5	8	11							
Leg-byes	2		4	2	2			5	4	8	10	6	7	4	2	2						
Wides				2			2	1	1		1		1									
No-balls	5		7		5			9	3	1	8	1	8	3	6	6						
Total	174		129	208	404		111	225	193	332	299	142	300	234	257	50						
Wickets	10		10	10	6		10	10	10	8	6	5	10	1	9	10						
Result	Ab.		L		W		L		D		W		W		L							
Points	2		0		16		0		0		16		12		0							

Fielding Figures

12 – K.J. McKnight (ct 10/st 2)
8 – K.R. Rutherford
7 – S.J. McCullum (ct 6/st 1)
5 – S.L. Boock
4 – P.W. Dobbs
3 – K.J. Burns
2 – K.B.K. Ibadulla, V.F. Johnson, P.W. Hills, T.J. Wilson, J.R. Murtagh and subs
1 – N.A. Mallender and J.K. Lindsay

BOWLING	N.A. Mallender	P.W. Hills	V.F. Johnson	S.L. Boock	J.K. Lindsay	T.J. Wilson	B.R. Blair	K.B.K. Ibadulla
v. Auckland (Auckland) 6–8 January								
v. Northern Districts (Gisborne) 10–12 January	20–6–44–1	8–0–39–1	24–11–40–3	27.5–10–63–4	15–5–38–1			
	10–6–18–0		5–0–30–0	18.1–7–39–2	4–1–8–0			
v. Central Districts (Alexandra) 14–16 January	17–4–38–5		5–0–19–0	31–12–51–5	15–4–33–0	4–1–11–0		
	29–5–69–5		3–0–4–0	67.5–31–75–4	34–8–74–1	3–1–6–0	1–0–5–0	
v. Wellington (Dunedin) 18–20 January	27–1–55–2		24–7–44–4	23–11–37–1		29.1–8–72–3	1–0–2–0	
	14–4–41–3		11–3–29–0	26–8–46–4		20–2–49–3		
v. Central Districts (Palmerston North) 22–4 January	17–4–33–0		30–1–101–0		6–0–27–0	28–5–110–2		15–1–77–0
v. Canterbury (Christchurch) 4–6 February	17–2–62–0		13–4–29–0			22–6–61–3		
	15.1–5–34–3		9–1–26–2	26–8–67–4		12–0–58–1		
v. Canterbury (Oamaru) 11–13 February		27.3–4–91–4	15–2–61–0	35–16–80–1		14–4–46–0		8–4–13–2
		15–3–50–2	10–0–38–1	30–13–43–5		20–7–55–2		7–3–29–0
v. Auckland (Dunedin) 16–18 February	11–1–26–1	8–2–29–0	14–4–39–0	30–8–70–2		13–2–40–1		14–5–43–1
	6–1–17–0	2–0–13–0	1–0–6–0	4–1–10–0			0.2–0–1–0	
	183.1–39–427–20 av. 21.35	60.3–9–222–7 av. 31.71	164–33–466–10 av. 46.60	318–125–581–32 av. 18.15	74–18–180–2 av. 90.00	165.1–36–508–15 av. 33.86	2.2–0–8–0 —	44–13–162–3 av. 54.00

A maiden century for Chris Cairns, Northern Districts v. Auckland, 4 February. He showed encouraging form as an all-rounder throughout the season. (Tom Morris)

First Test Match
NEW ZEALAND v. PAKISTAN

The match at Carisbrook was abandoned without a ball being bowled. This was the fourth time in the history of Test cricket that weather has caused such an abandonment.

It was decided to play a one-day international on what would have been the fourth day of the Test match. J.G. Bracewell, who had been in New Zealand's twelve for the Test, was twelfth man for the one-day game. In the Pakistan side, Rameez Raja, Rizwan-uz-Zaman and Saleem Jaffer, who were in the twelve for the Test, did not play in the one-day international, while Ijaz Ahmed and Sikhander Bakht, who were not in the Test twelve, were in the side for the one-day game.

Wright won the toss and asked Pakistan to bat first. They were soon in trouble, and only a brisk 83 from Saleem Malik saved them from complete humiliation.

Wright and Vance gave New Zealand a fine start, and Jones took them to victory with nine balls to spare.

4, 5 and 6 February 1989

at Lancaster Park, Christchurch

Otago 299 for 6 dec (K.R. Rutherford 125, P.W. Dobbs 69) and 142 for 5 dec
Canterbury 161 for 3 dec and 195 (R.T. Latham 50, S.L. Boock 4 for 67)

Otago won by 85 runs
Otago 16 pts, Canterbury 0 pts

6, 7 and 8 February 1989

at Seddon Park, Hamilton

Northern Districts 274 (C.L.Cairns 110, S.W. Brown 4 for 102) and 65 for 2
Auckland 107 (B.J. Barrett 4 for 32) and 229 (M.R. Pringle 60, R.B. Reid 54, S.W. Brown 50, B.P. Bracewell 4 for 55)

Northern Districts won by 8 wickets
Northern Districts 16 pts, Auckland 0 pts

Otago kept alive their faint hopes of winning the Shell Trophy with a convincing win at Christchurch. Ken Rutherford reminded the Test selectors of his qualities with an innings of 125 off 129 balls in 2¼ hours. He hit 20 fours. Rain claimed much of the second day, but Latham and Burns kept the game alive with declarations that left Canterbury to score 281 to win. A combination of Mallender's pace and Boock's spin proved too much for them, and they never looked like reaching their target.

Northern Districts moved to the top of the Shell Trophy table with an important win over Auckland. Put in to bat, Northern were struggling at 93 for 6 when Chris Cairns came to the wicket. In a style reminiscent of his father, he hit 110 off 149 balls, with 2 sixes and 9 fours. It was his maiden first-class hundred. Auckland collapsed before Chris Kuggeleijn and Brian Barrett, whose 4 for 32 was a career best. At 22, Barrett is a pace bowler who could serve New Zealand well in the near future. Northern Districts had moved to a strong position even though much of the first day had been lost to rain, but they still faced a race against time. Eventually, they had to make 63 in 10

K.R. Rutherford	Byes	Leg-byes	Wides	No-balls	Total	Wkts
						Ab.
	6	10	1	1	240	10
	2	1		7	98	2
			4	7	156	10
	5	7		4	245	10
			10	11	220	10
	4	4		8	173	10
14–0–61–1	2	13	1	8	424	3
	4	5	1	5	161	3
			10		5	195	10
1–0–12–1			12		2	315	9
			3		3	218	10
	2	12		3	261	5
					47	0
15–0– 73–2 av. 36.50						

Wellington 1989
First-Class Matches

BATTING

BATTING	v. Canterbury (Christchurch) 6–8 January	v. Auckland (Wellington) 10–12 January	v. Northern Districts (Wellington) 14–16 January	v. Otago (Dunedin) 18–20 January	v. Canterbury (Wellington) 22–4 January	v. Central Districts (New Plymouth) 29–31 January	v. Northern Districts (Morrinsville) 2–4 February	v. Central Districts (Wellington) 16–18 February	M	Inns	NOs	Runs	HS	Av
B.A. Edgar	150	29 147*	23 0	140 15	78 8	4 57	87 24	—	7	13	1	762	150	63.50
R.H. Vance	51	7 —	19 69	254* 7	0 51	9 116*	123	38 144	7	13	2	888	254*	80.72
A.H. Jones	50	1 177	66 62	45* 22	0 97	181*			5	10	2	701	181*	87.62
T.D. Ritchie	14 16	—	40 9	— 0	0 106	15 15	5 44	6 84 37*	8	14	1	391	106	30.07
E.J. Gray	17* 17	—	14* 2	— 30	0 12*	—	3 59	— 40 27	8	11	4	194	59	27.71
G.R. Larsen	6 3	0* 11 0	— 29	47 82	23 72*	17 12	— 40	27	8	14	2	369	82	30.75
E.B. McSweeney	18* 67*	—	2 13	— 35	1 13	— —	14 20	19* 1 27*	8	12	4	230	67*	28.75
F. Beyeler	— 11	—	1 4	— 34	12 4	10* —	— 7	2* — —	8	8	—	109	34	13.62
D.A. Stirling	— 38	—	26 3	— 9	9 10*	— —	1	— —	7	8	2	104	38	17.33
J.P. Millmow	— 6	—	0*	—	0	—	2*	— —	5	4	1	7	6	2.33
E.J. Chatfield	— —	— 0*	— 0* 2*	—	2*	— —			6	4	4	4	2*	—
G.N. Cederwall		17	—	0* 14*		38	10* 14*	—	4	5	2	79	38	26.33
S.J. Hotter				18 8					1	2	—	26	18	13.00
G.P. Burnett						23	4 0	— 84 16	3	5	—	127	84	25.40
B.R. Williams									2	—	—	—	—	—
S.C.W. Hainsworth							6		1	1	—	6	6	6.00
Byes	4	2	8 4		4 2	3	2							
Leg-byes	8	3 4	4 2	5 10	4 10	4 3	6 11	1 7 2						
Wides			2				1	1						
No-balls	12	6 4	3 11	4 11	8 15	2 3	2 14	1 1						
Total	330	204 334	217 198	448 220	173 398	250 292	288 257	38 309 254						
Wickets	5	9 1	8 10	1 10	10 10	4 3	10 9	1 5 3						
Result	D	D	D	W	Tie	L	D	W						
Points	4	4	0	16	8	4	4	16						

Fielding Figures
25 – E.B. McSweeney (ct 21/st 4)
10 – E.J. Gray
9 – T.D. Ritchie
7 – G.R. Larsen and R.H. Vance
4 – D.A. Stirling, F. Beyeler, A.H. Jones and B.A. Edgar
3 – E.J. Chatfield and J.P. Millmow
2 – B.R. Williams and G.P. Burnett
1 – S.J. Hotter

BOWLING

BOWLING	J.P. Millmow	E.J. Chatfield	F. Beyeler	D.A. Stirling	E.J. Gray	A.H. Jones	G.R. Larsen	B.A. Edgar
v. Canterbury (Christchurch) 6–8 January	13–2–53–1 5–1–10–0	22–4–65–0 4–0–13–0	12–1–32–0 3–0–14–0	13–1–42–3 7–1–17–0	18.5–8–42–4	4–1–11–2		
v. Auckland (Wellington) 10–12 January	11–2–35–0	27–5–69–1 17–2–71–0	14–3–35–1 9–2–30–0	18–2–62–1 10–2–67–1	28–8–84–2 15–4–49–0	3.5–0–12–2 9–0–34–1	13–4–24–1 3–0–8–0	3–1–12–0
v. Northern Districts (Wellington) 14–16 January		27–8–61–0 7–0–19–0	17–3–66–1 9–1–43–2	11.4–2–48–2 4–0–17–0	23–11–70–0 24–6–71–4	2–0–16–0	3–0–8–0	
v. Otago (Dunedin) 18–20 January		14–6–29–4 21.4–8–36–5	16–4–45–3 9–0–30–0	13.2–4–32–2 23–5–66–4	16–4–49–1	5–0–19–0		
v. Canterbury (Wellington) 22–4 January	17–6–42–1 5–0–25–0		17–2–71–3 5–0–21–0	8–0–51–0	36.5–15–69–3 23–1–77–4	16–4–32–0 19–0–104–3	3–0–15–0 5–1–19–0	
v. Central Districts (New Plymouth) 29–31 January	15–2–47–0 5–1–14–0	31–10–72–4 14–4–34–0	15–7–35–3 9–4–25–0	16–1–78–3 11–0–72–1	29–9–51–0 9–2–81–0		14–2–69–1 1–0–9–0	1–0–6–0
v. Northern Districts (Morrinsville) 2–4 February			11–3–36–1 9–5–14–3	4–1–11–0 4–0–12–0	44–19–68–4 16–3–54–1	9–1–37–1	6–2–9–0	
v. Central Districts (Wellington) 16–18 February	10.5–1–40–1 16–5–33–2	21–2–59–2 23–3–57–3	9–0–30–0 21.4–5–64–4	21.4–5–64–4	9–1–37–1 20–5–50–0			
	97.5–20– 299–5 av. 59.80	228.4–52– 585–19 av. 30.78	185.4–40– 591–21 av. 28.14	143–19– 575–17 av. 33.82	311.4–96– 852–24 av. 35.50	58.5–5– 228–8 av. 28.50	45–9– 153–2 av. 76.50	4–1– 18–0 av. —

overs. With Hick hitting 33 off 23 balls, they won with five balls to spare.

Shoaib Mohammad – a record partnership and a tedious 163 in the second Test match. (Adrian Murrell/Allsport)

Second Test Match
NEW ZEALAND v. PAKISTAN

Pakistan gave a Test debut to Aaqib Javed who at 16 years and 189 days, was the second youngest player in Test history to appear in Test cricket. On a wicket that was to play slowly but safely, Imran elected to field first. He had immediate success when first change Mudassar had both openers caught behind.

Andrew Jones, however, had enjoyed a magnificent season at the Basin Reserve, and it was to continue. He and Martin Crowe, who was playing his first Test for a year, added 149 in 201 minutes. Jones was to prove to be the only batsman in the match with a willingness to play his shots. He hit with power and grandeur through the off side, and it came as a surprise when he hit a short ball into the hands of point after batting for 213 minutes and hitting 8 fours. Crowe, seeking rehabilitation, moved remorselessly to his century. He batted for nearly 10 hours in all, reaching his 10th Test hundred. It was his first against Pakistan and the highest score by a New Zealander against that country. He was given good support by brother Jeff in a stand of 114. New Zealand were all out by the end of the second day, by which time Smith and Chatfield had offered some welcome late-order fireworks.

Pakistan were to bat for 2¼ days. Hadlee and Morrison made early inroads for New Zealand, but Shoaib Mohammad and Javed Miandad then settled to a stand of 220 in 360 minutes. The stand was a record for either side in the series, and Javed reached his 20th Test hundred. Shoaib went on to play the longest innings in the history of first-class cricket in New Zealand. He reached his highest score in Test cricket with what was his second century and was at the crease for 720 minutes. He hit a six and 17 fours

R.H. Vance	G.N. Cederwall	T.D. Ritchie	S.J. Hotter	B.R. Williams	S.C.W. Hainsworth	Byes	Leg-byes	Wides	No-balls	Total	Wkts
						2	10			257	10
							1	1		55	0
8–0–49–0						3	9	2	6	333	10
	22–2–97–7							1	4	312	2
	9–0–66–0	3–1–12–1				1	3	1	27	370	10
							3		6	231	7
			3–1–5–1					2		111	10
			4–0–20–0				5	1	9	225	10
	14–0–82–2					3	16	3	16	381	10
	3–0–18–0					1	2		5	267	10
							7	1		290	10
		2–0–21–1				3	3		4	322	4
	17–1–75–2			20–8–44–2			3	1	8	252	9
	9–5–14–0	5–0–31–1		12–3–30–0	5–0–56–0				2	213	6
	16–0–74–0			19–3–55–0		1			11	305	4
2–1–7–0	12–4–27–1			4–1–11–0			8		1	257	10
10–1–	102–12–	10–1–	7–1–	55–15–	5–0–						
56–0	453–12	64–3	25–1	140–2	56–0						
—	av. 37.75	av. 21.33	av. 25.00	av. 70.00	—						

ONE-DAY INTERNATIONAL – NEW ZEALAND v. PAKISTAN
6 February 1989 at Carisbrook, Dunedin

PAKISTAN			
Mudassar Nazar	c J.J. Crowe, b Snedden		14
Shoaib Mohammad	c Smith, b Hadlee		0
Aamer Malik	run out		2
Javed Miandad	c Smith, b Watson		16
Saleem Malik	c sub (J.G. Bracewell), b Hadlee		83
Imran Khan†	c J.J. Crowe, b Hadlee		22
Ijaz Ahmed	b Hadlee		9
Saleem Yousuf*	c Smith, b Hadlee		2
Abdul Qadir	run out		9
Sikhander Bakht	not out		6
Aaqib Javed	not out		1
Extras	lb 4, w 1, nb 1		6
(48 overs)	(for 9 wkts)		170

	O	M	R	W
Hadlee	10	–	38	5
Watson	10	1	32	1
Snedden	9	2	18	1
Chatfield	10	2	36	–
Patel	9	1	42	–

FALL OF WICKETS
1–2, 2–14, 3–21, 4–75, 5–119, 6–129, 7–139, 8–160, 9–165

NEW ZEALAND			
J.G. Wright†	c Ijaz Ahmed, b Sikhander		35
R.H. Vance	b Imran Khan		46
A.H. Jones	not out		55
M.D. Crowe	not out		17
J.J. Crowe			
D.N. Patel			
R.J. Hadlee			
I.D.S. Smith*			
M.C. Snedden			
E.J. Chatfield			
W. Watson			
Extras	lb 11, w 9, nb 1		21
(46.3 overs)	(for 2 wkts)		174

	O	M	R	W
Imran Khan	10	–	42	1
Sikhander Bakht	8.3	–	43	1
Aaqib Javed	8	1	26	–
Mudassar Nazar	10	1	23	–
Abdul Qadir	10	–	29	–

FALL OF WICKETS
1–73, 2–113

Umpires: R.S. Dunne & S.J. Woodward

Man of the Match: R.J. Hadlee

New Zealand won by 8 wickets

SECOND TEST MATCH – NEW ZEALAND v. PAKISTAN
10, 11, 12, 13 and 14 February 1989 at Basin Reserve, Wellington

NEW ZEALAND

	FIRST INNINGS		SECOND INNINGS	
R.H. Vance	c Yousuf, b Mudassar	5	(2) lbw, b Imran	44
J.G. Wright†	c Yousuf, b Mudassar	7	(1) c Javed, b Imran	19
A.H. Jones	c Shoaib, b Jaffer	86	c sub (Rameez Raja), b Saleem Jaffer	39
M.D. Crowe	c Javed, b Jaffer	174	lbw, b Saleem Jaffer	0
D.N. Patel	lbw, b Imran Khan	0	c Yousuf, b Jaffer	2
J.J. Crowe	b Abdul Qadir	39	b Saleem Jaffer	23
J.G. Bracewell	b Imran Khan	15	lbw, b Saleem Jaffer	0
R.J. Hadlee	c Rizwan, b Jaffer	32	c sub (Ijaz Ahmed), b Imran Khan	7
I.D.S. Smith*	not out	40	not out	29
D.K. Morrison	lbw, b Imran Khan	0	not out	1
E.J. Chatfield	run out	14		
Extras	b 10, lb 14, nb 11	35	b 10, lb 6, nb 6	22
		447	(for 8 wkts)	186

	O	M	R	W	O	M	R	W
Imran Khan	46.4	18	75	3	17	7	34	3
Saleem Jaffer	34	5	94	3	17	4	40	5
Mudassar Nazar	22	5	59	2				
Aaqib Javed	34	5	103	–	13	1	57	–
Abdul Qadir	29	4	83	1	14	3	39	–
Aamer Malik	4	1	9					

FALL OF WICKETS
1–13, 2–18, 3–167, 4–168, 5–282, 6–321, 7–389, 8–398, 9–399
1–36, 2–107, 3–108, 4–117, 5–128, 6–132, 7–140, 8–180

PAKISTAN

	FIRST INNINGS	
Mudassar Nazar	c and b Morrison	6
Rizwan-uz-Zaman	lbw, b Hadlee	18
Shoaib Mohammad	b Hadlee	163
Javed Miandad	lbw, b Hadlee	118
Saleem Malik	c Smith, b Bracewell	38
Imran Khan†	b Chatfield	71
Aamer Malik	not out	8
Saleem Yousuf*	c Jones, b Hadlee	4
Abdul Qadir	not out	0
Saleem Jaffer		
Aaqib Javed		
Extras	b 1, lb 8, nb 3	12
	(for 7 wkts, dec)	438

	O	M	R	W
Hadlee	54	14	101	4
Morrison	36	10	96	1
Chatfield	53	21	82	1
Bracewell	40	8	123	1
Patel	12	3	27	–

FALL OF WICKETS
1–14, 2–54, 3–274, 4–325, 5–422, 6–430, 7–437

Umpires: R.S. Dunne & S.J. Woodward

Match drawn

and faced 516 balls. Between lunch and tea on the third day he scored 10 runs.

Shoaib was eventually bowled by Hadlee on the last morning, and six minutes later, Imran declared. The game had looked destined for a draw for the best part of four days, but New Zealand contrived to lose wickets to Saleem Jaffer, who returned his best figures in Test cricket at a time when most had lost interest. Only two wickets had fallen on the third and fourth days, but 11 went down on the last day. There were a few seconds of anxiety for New Zealand, but Ian Smith was again in fierce form and broke the mood of the match by hitting 29 off 28 balls before time was called.

11, 12 and 13 February 1989

at Centennial Park, Oamaru

Canterbury 315 for 9 dec (P.E. McEwan 137, P.W. Hills 4 for 91) and 218 (R.T. Latham 90, S.L. Boock 5 for 43)
Otago 300 (K.J. Burns 73, B.R. Blair 61) and 234 for 1 (P.W. Dobbs 86 not out, S.J. McCullum 75, K.R. Rutherford 58 not out)

Otago won by 9 wickets
Otago 12 pts, Canterbury 4 pts

Another fine innings by Paul McEwan enabled Canterbury to reach a good score, but a fourth-wicket stand of 123 between Blair and Burns kept Otago in touch. Canterbury threatened to crumble in their second innings, and only Rod Latham's forceful knock helped them to survive against the wiles of Stephen Boock, who took 5 for 43 in 30 overs, 13 of which were maidens. Otago were left to make 234 in 57 overs, and they were given a resounding start by Dobbs and McCullum, who hit 145 in as many minutes. Rutherford kept the momentum going with a six and 6 fours, and Otago won with 17 balls to spare.

Otago's win meant that, with one round of matches to go, only Canterbury and Central Districts could not win the Trophy.

16, 17 and 18 February 1989

at Lancaster Park, Christchurch

Canterbury 343 for 8 dec (R.T. Latham 98, P.E. McEwan 68) and 257 for 4 dec (R.T. Latham 142 not out, M.W. Priest 92 not out)
Northern Districts 225 and 313 (B.A. Young 97, D.J. White 62, M.W. Priest 6 for 92, A.J. Nuttall 4 for 74)

Canterbury won by 62 runs
Canterbury 16 pts, Northern Districts 0 pts

at Basin Reserve, Wellington

Central Districts 305 for 4 dec (P.S. Briasco 97, C.J. Smith 70, M.D. Crowe 51) and 257 (S.W. Duff 64, C.J. Smith 62, F. Beyeler 4 for 64)
Wellington 309 for 5 dec (G.P. Burnett 84, T.D. Ritchie 84) and 254 for 3 (R.H. Vance 144)

Wellington won by 7 wickets
Wellington 16 pts, Central Districts 0 pts

at Carisbrook, Dunedin

Otago 257 for 9 dec (K.J. Burns 89, S.J. McCullum 69, B.R. Blair 52, J.G. Bracewell 4 for 47) and 50 (D.K. Morrison 5 for 16, M.C. Snedden 4 for 14)

Ian Smith, a consistently efficient wicket-keeper and an aggressive batsman. (George Herringshaw)

Auckland 262 for 5 dec (J.J. Crowe 95, T.J. Franklin 58) and 47 for 0

Auckland won by 10 wickets
Auckland 16 pts, Otago 0 pts

Northern Districts' hopes of taking the Shell Trophy disappeared at Lancaster Park, where Mark Priest produced career-best performances with bat and ball to wreck them. McEwan and Latham gave the Canterbury first innings solidity with a fourth-wicket partnership of 118, and Chamberlain, Ford and Roberts kept Northern in check, both Hick and Kuggeleijn being cut short when they looked likely to play long innings. Northern seemed well on top, however, when Chris Cairns and Brendon Bracewell reduced Canterbury to 5 for 4 in their second innings, but Latham and Priest added 252 in 219 minutes. Both batsmen hit the highest scores of their careers. Latham's declaration left Northern to make 376 in 148 minutes plus 20 overs. It was a mighty task, but they died bravely. Bryan Young and David White gave them a fine start with 118 in 85 minutes, but Priest's slow left-arm bowling tamed them and gave his side victory.

Wellington played splendid cricket to beat Central Districts, who raced to 305 on the opening day thanks to a first-wicket partnership of 173 between Scott Briasco and John Smith. The home side's powerful batting, even without Jones, took them into a first-innings lead, and

ABOVE: *The season was a triumph for Jeff Crowe. He led Auckland to the Shell Trophy and won back his place in the Test side. (Alan Cozzi)*

RIGHT: *Ewen Chatfield set up a record for Wellington, but it appeared that his international career was drawing to a close. (Simon Bruty/Allsport)*

Beyeler and Chatfield finally bowled out Central after some durable batting. Needing to score 254 at nearly five runs an over, Wellington were given a marvellous start by Rob Vance. He capped a memorable season in which he had become the first Wellington player to score a century in each innings, and in which he had reached his highest score by hitting a century off 81 balls in 82 minutes. The stodgy batsman of past years had become a faded memory as Vance hit a spectacular 144 off 130 balls with 2 sixes and 21 fours. When he was third out only 48 were needed, and

Ritchie and McSweeney saw Wellington to victory with ease.

Their win had come in vain, for Auckland took the Shell Trophy with a resounding win at Carisbrook. McCullum and Burns added 147 for Otago's second wicket, but Jeff Crowe guided his side to first-innings points. Morrison and Snedden then destroyed Otago, and Franklin and Horne hit off the required runs in 13.2 overs to win the Shell Trophy for Auckland.

19, 20 and 21 February 1989

at McLean Park, Napier

Pakistanis 282 for 9 dec (Imran Khan 104, Aamer Malik 81,

Shell Trophy – Final Table (1988 positions in brackets)							
					1st inns		
	P	W	L	D	lead	Ab	Pts
Auckland (2)	8	3	2	1	5	1	58
Wellington (4)	8	2	1	5*	6	–	56
Northern Districts (3)	8	3	2	3	4	–	52
Otago (1)	8	3	3	1	2	1	46
Canterbury (6)	8	1	3	4*	4	–	36
Central Districts (5)	8	2	3	3	1	–	28
*includes a match tied – 8 points							

Shoaib Mohammad 56, G.K. Robertson 5 for 44) and 198 for 4 dec (Mudassar Nazar 97)
Shell XI 196 for 5 dec (T.E. Blain 79 not out) and 152 (Abdul Qadir 7 for 31)

Pakistanis won by 130 runs

After a bright century by Imran Khan on the opening day, the last match before the final Test threatened to die of boredom on the second day when the Shell XI batted in turgid fashion. The innings was enlivened at last by a sixth-wicket stand between Blain and Kuggeleijn, who declared with his side still 86 runs behind. Mudassar scored briskly, and on the last afternoon Abdul Qadir produced an outstanding performance to take 7 for 31 in 18 overs and bowl his side to victory. The Shell XI went from 79 for 2 to 152 all out, and Pakistan gained much encouragement on the eve of the third Test match.

Third Test Match
NEW ZEALAND v. PAKISTAN

Believing that the Eden Park wicket would encourage spin bowling, the New Zealand selectors persuaded Stephen Boock to recant his decision that he had retired from Test cricket and to return to the New Zealand side. Boock must later have regretted being persuaded to change his mind.

Hadlee began the Test needing five wickets to become the first bowler in history to capture 400 Test wickets, but, like Boock, he was to end the game a rather disappointed man. He did have the encouragement of an early wicket, as did Boock, and Pakistan, having elected to bat when they won the toss, were 44 for 2. At this point, Javed joined Shoaib, and the pair proceeded to beat the third-wicket record that they had established at Wellington. They moved at a much brisker rate. Shoaib's 112 came off 254 balls, contained 17 fours and was made in 350 minutes. Javed's sixth Test double century was the highest score ever made in a Pakistan–New Zealand Test and took him 558 minutes. He faced 465 balls and hit 5 sixes and 28 fours. He shared a stand of 147 for the fourth wicket with Aamer Malik, and Saleem Malik and Imran Khan added an unbeaten 136 as Pakistan batted into the third afternoon, reached the highest total ever made in Tests between the two countries, and put the game right out of New Zealand's reach.

Finishing on 69 not out, Imran became only the third player in Test history to complete 3,000 runs and 300 wickets, the first two being Ian Botham and Kapil Dev.

Imran quickly brought his spinners into the attack, and Tauseef soon accounted for Wright. Vance and Jones added 109 in positive style. Vance completed his 1,000 runs for the season, but he was out when he rashly attempted to hit Abdul Qadir over cover. In Qadir's next over, Martin Crowe set off on a sharp single, changed his mind and sent Jones back, but Jaffer's throw from mid-off hit the wicket and Jones was run out. This was a dreadful waste of New Zealand's most dangerous batsman. Nightwatchman Boock was adjudged caught bat and pad before the close, which came with New Zealand on 133 for 4.

Only three wickets fell on the fourth day, so that New Zealand seemed safe from defeat, mainly as a result of a fifth-wicket stand of 154 between Martin Crowe and Mark

Javed Miandad – 271 in the third Test match. It was the sixth time that this supreme batsman had scored a double century in a Test match. (Adrian Murrell/Allsport)

Greatbatch. By now, however, the game had degenerated, with Pakistan making constant vociferous appeals and the umpires being put under much pressure. Intikhab complained about the standard of umpiring; and the New Zealand Cricket Council expressed dismay at the behaviour of the Pakistan players. A sadly familiar pattern was unfolding.

New Zealand were dismissed just before lunch on the last morning, and for the 15th time in a Test innings, Abdul Qadir took five or more wickets. New Zealand followed-on, but they never looked to be in danger of defeat, and another very drab series came to an end.

First One-Day International
NEW ZEALAND v. PAKISTAN

Pakistan were without Javed Miandad, who had a recurrence of his back injury, while the ankle injury which Richard Hadlee had suffered in the third Test had ended his cricket for the season. New Zealand also left out Ewen Chatfield, preferring to trust to their younger bowlers, and

THIRD TEST MATCH – NEW ZEALAND v. PAKISTAN
24, 25, 26, 27 and 28 February 1989 at Eden Park, Auckland

PAKISTAN

	FIRST INNINGS	
Mudassar Nazar	lbw, b Hadlee	5
Rizwan-uz-Zaman	c J.J. Crowe, b Boock	15
Shoaib Mohammad	run out	112
Javed Miandad	c Smith, b Chatfield	271
Aamer Malik	c J.J. Crowe, b Bracewell	56
Saleem Malik	not out	80
Imran Khan†	not out	69
Saleem Yousuf*		
Abdul Qadir		
Tauseef Ahmed		
Saleem Jaffer		
Extras	lb 7, nb 1	8
	(for 5 wkts, dec)	616

	O	M	R	W
Hadlee	28	7	68	1
Chatfield	65	14	158	1
Boock	70	10	229	1
Bracewell	37	4	138	1
Jones	3	–	16	–

FALL OF WICKETS
1–10, 2–44, 3–292, 4–439, 5–480

NEW ZEALAND

	FIRST INNINGS		SECOND INNINGS	
R.H. Vance	c Shoaib, b Qadir	68	(2) c Yousuf, b Mudassar	31
J.G. Wright†	c Rizwan, b Tauseef	2	(1) c Yousuf, b Qadir	36
A.H. Jones	run out	47	c Yousuf, b Mudassar	0
M.D. Crowe	c Yousuf, b Jaffer	78	not out	9
S.L. Boock	c Mudassar, b Qadir	8		
M.J. Greatbatch	b Abdul Qadir	76	(5) not out	13
J.J. Crowe	c Javed, b Qadir	33		
J.G. Bracewell	b Abdul Qadir	0		
I.D.S. Smith*	c Mudassar, b Imran	58		
R.J. Hadlee	not out	14		
E.J. Chatfield	c Aamer, b Qadir	0		
Extras	b 7, lb 2, nb 10	19	nb 10	10
		403	(for 3 wkts)	99

	O	M	R	W	O	M	R	W
Saleem Jaffer	18	6	44	1	8	4	18	–
Imran Khan	34	9	76	1	5.4	1	13	–
Tauseef Ahmed	69	28	106	1	12	4	23	–
Abdul Qadir	58.1	17	160	6	16	7	27	1
Shoaib Mohammad	2	1	1	–	1	–	5	–
Mudassar Nazar	3	1	7	–	8	2	13	2

FALL OF WICKETS
1–13, 2–122, 3–123, 4–132, 5–286, 6–294, 7–294, 8–388, 9–388
1–68, 2–71, 3–76

Umpires: B.L. Aldridge & S.J. Woodward

Match drawn

NEW ZEALAND v. PAKISTAN – TEST MATCH AVERAGES

NEW ZEALAND BATTING

	M	Inns	NOs	Runs	HS	Av	100s	50s
I.D.S. Smith	2	3	1	127	58	127.00		1
M.D. Crowe	2	4	1	261	174	87.00	1	1
A.H. Jones	2	4		172	86	43.00		1
R.H. Vance	2	4		148	68	37.00		1
J.J. Crowe	2	3		95	39	31.66		
R.J. Hadlee	2	3	1	53	32	26.50		
J.G. Wright	2	4		64	36	16.00		
E.J. Chatfield	2	2		14	14	7.00		
J.G. Bracewell	2	3		15	15	5.00		

Played in one Test: M.J. Greatbatch 76 & 13*; S.L. Boock 8; D.N. Patel 0 & 2; D.K. Morrison 0 & 1*

PAKISTAN BATTING

	M	Inns	NOs	Runs	HS	Av	100s	50s
Javed Miandad	2	2		389	271	194.50	2	
Imran Khan	2	1	1	140	71	140.00		2
Shoaib Mohammad	2	2		275	163	137.50	2	
Saleem Malik	2	2	1	118	80*	118.00		1
Aamer Malik	2	2	1	64	56	64.00		1
Rizwan-uz-Zaman	2	2		33	18	16.50		
Mudassar Nazar	2	2		11	6	5.50		

Played in two Tests: Saleem Yousuf 4; Abdul Qadir 0*; Saleem Jaffer did not bat
Played in one Test: Aaqib Javed and Tauseef Ahmed did not bat

NEW ZEALAND BOWLING

	Overs	Mds	Runs	Wkts	Av	Best	10/m	5/inns
R.J. Hadlee	82	21	169	5	33.80	4/101		
E.J. Chatfield	118	35	240	2	120.00	1/82		
J.G. Bracewell	77	12	261	2	130.50	1/123		

Bowled in one innings: D.K. Morrison 36–10–96–1; S.L. Boock 70–10–229–1; D.N. Patel 12–3–27–0; A.H. Jones 3–0–16–0

PAKISTAN BOWLING

	Overs	Mds	Runs	Wkts	Av	Best	10/m	5/inns
Mudassar Nazar	33	8	79	4	19.75	2/13		
Saleem Jaffer	77	19	196	9	21.77	5/40		1
Imran Khan	103.2	35	198	7	28.28	3/34		
Abdul Qadir	117.1	31	309	8	38.62	6/160		1
Tauseef Ahmed	81	32	129	1	129.00	1/106		
Aaqib Javed	47	6	160	0	–			
Shoaib Mohammad	3	1	6	0	–			

Bowled in one innings: Aamer Malik 4–1–9–0

NEW ZEALAND FIELDING FIGURES
2 - I.D.S. Smith and J.J. Crowe; 1 - D.K. Morrison and A.H. Jones

PAKISTAN FIELDING FIGURES
7 - Saleem Yousuf; 3 - Javed Miandad; 2 - Shoaib Mohammad, Rizwan-uz-Zaman and Mudassar Nazar; 1 - Aamer Malik, sub (Rameez Raja) and sub (Ijaz Ahmed)

Neil Mallender, the Somerset pace bowler, who enjoyed a highly successful season for Otago. (Neal Simpson/ASP)

they were well served. Danny Morrison produced his best figures in a one-day international, and Pakistan did well to recover from the early blows that he dealt them. His figures would have been better but for Ijaz Ahmed taking 20, including 2 sixes off his last over. Unfortunately this led to a confrontation between the two players.

New Zealand began as badly as Pakistan had done, but Jones, who reached a thousand runs in his 25th one-day international, and Martin Crowe put on 103, and Greatbatch then joined Jones in seeing that New Zealand romped to victory with 6.1 overs to spare.

Second One-Day International
NEW ZEALAND v. PAKISTAN

Shoaib Mohammad hit his first century in a one-day international match, and his 126 not out was the highest score made for Pakistan in one of these matches. It was a fine effort and was made off 158 balls as he carried his bat throughout the 50 overs. He and Rameez Raja put on 152 in 114 minutes for the third wicket and seemingly took Pakistan to a very strong position.

Once again, however, Jones launched a blistering attack on the bowling, and his savagery was maintained by Martin Crowe and Ian Smith, who took New Zealand to victory with an unbroken fifth-wicket stand of 108. Martin

FIRST ONE-DAY INTERNATIONAL – NEW ZEALAND v. PAKISTAN
4 March 1989 at Lancaster Park, Christchurch

PAKISTAN				NEW ZEALAND			
Mudassar Nazar	b Morrison	8		J.G. Wright†	c Tauseef Ahmed, b Imran Khan	7
Shoaib Mohammad	c Greatbatch, b Morrison	2		R.H. Vance	c Aamer Malik, b Saleem Jaffer	3
Aamer Malik*	b Morrison	7		A.H. Jones	not out	62
Saleem Malik	lbw, b Robertson	6		M.D. Crowe	c Saleem Malik, b Jaffer	45
Imran Khan†	c M.D. Crowe, b Snedden	38		M.J. Greatbatch	not out	35
Rameez Raja	run out	51		C.M. Kuggeleijn		
Ijaz Ahmed	not out	42		I.D.S. Smith*		
Abdul Qadir	run out	0		G.K. Robertson		
Tauseef Ahmed	not out	8		M.C. Snedden		
Saleem Jaffer				D.K. Morrison		
Aaqib Javed				W. Watson		
Extras	lb 2, w 2, nb 4	8		Extras	b 5, lb 4, w 1, nb 9	19
(47 overs)	(for 7 wkts)	170		(40.5 overs)	(for 3 wkts)	171

	O	M	R	W		O	M	R	W
Morrison	10	2	44	3	Imran Khan	5	–	17	1
Watson	10	1	47	–	Saleem Jaffer	10	–	35	2
Robertson	9	2	21	1	Aaqib Javed	9.5	1	33	–
Snedden	9	1	17	1	Mudassar Nazar	8	–	35	–
Kuggeleijn	9	–	39	–	Tauseef Ahmed	6	–	32	–
					Abdul Qadir	2	–	10	–

FALL OF WICKETS
1–7, 2–14, 3–23, 4–23, 5–101, 6–148, 7–151

FALL OF WICKETS
1–10, 2–12, 3–115

Umpires: B.L. Aldridge & R.L. McHarg

Man of the Match: A.H. Jones

New Zealand won by 7 wickets

SECOND ONE-DAY INTERNATIONAL – NEW ZEALAND v. PAKISTAN
8 March 1989 at Basin Reserve, Wellington

PAKISTAN				NEW ZEALAND			
Mudassar Nazar	c Smith, b Watson		3	R.H. Vance	b Mudassar Nazar		8
Shoaib Mohammad	not out		126	J.G. Wright†	c Aamer Malik,		
Aamer Malik*	run out		3		b Saleem Jaffer		0
Rameez Raja	c Vance,			A.H. Jones	run out		67
	b Robertson		72	M.D. Crowe	not out		87
Saleem Malik	c Vance, b Robertson		9	M.J. Greatbatch	c Saleem Malik,		
Imran Khan†	b Morrison		17		b Tauseef		9
Ijaz Ahmed	c Robertson,			I.D.S. Smith*	not out		62
	b Morrison		2	C.M. Kuggeleijn			
Abdul Qadir	not out		8	G.K. Robertson			
Saleem Jaffer				M.C. Snedden			
Tauseef Ahmed				D.K. Morrison			
Aaqib Javed				W. Watson			
Extras	lb 4, w 7, nb 2		13	Extras	b 9, lb 10, w 2		21
(50 overs)	(for 6 wkts)		253	(46.5 overs)	(for 4 wkts)		254

	O	M	R	W		O	M	R	W
Morrison	10	–	62	2	Imran Khan	9	1	33	–
Watson	10	–	48	1	Saleem Jaffer	9	1	48	1
Snedden	10	–	31	–	Aaqib Javed	8	–	44	–
Robertson	10	–	56	2	Mudassar Nazar	9	1	45	1
Kuggeleijn	10	–	52	–	Abdul Qadir	3.5	–	30	–
					Tauseef Ahmed	8	–	35	1

FALL OF WICKETS
1–15, 2–24, 3–176, 4–192, 5–225, 6–242

FALL OF WICKETS
1–3, 2–56, 3–133, 4–146

Umpires: B.L. Aldridge & S.J. Woodward

Man of the Match: Shoaib Mohammad

New Zealand won by 6 wickets

THIRD ONE-DAY INTERNATIONAL – NEW ZEALAND v. PAKISTAN
11 March 1989 at Eden Park, Auckland

NEW ZEALAND				PAKISTAN			
J.G. Wright†	c Aamer Malik,			Rameez Raja	c J.J. Crowe,		
	b Aaqib Javed		59		b Morrison		101
A.H. Jones	c Aamer Malik,			Shoaib Mohammad	c Kuggeleijn,		
	b Qadir		82		b Snedden		15
M.D. Crowe	b Abdul Qadir		32	Aamer Malik*	run out		23
M.J. Greatbatch	c Ijaz Ahmed,			Imran Khan†	not out		51
	b Tauseef		1	Saleem Malik	not out		56
J.J. Crowe	b Aaqib Javed		27	Ijaz Ahmed			
I.D.S. Smith*	lbw, b Aaqib Javed		8	Mudassar Nazar			
C.M. Kuggeleijn	c Saleem Malik,			Abdul Qadir			
	b Imran Khan		12	Tauseef Ahmed			
G.K. Robertson	b Saleem Jaffer		4	Saleem Jaffer			
M.C. Snedden	b Saleem Jaffer		7	Aaqib Javed			
D.K. Morrison	run out		2	Extras	lb 4, nb 1		5
W. Watson	not out		4	(48.3 overs)	(for 3 wkts)		251
Extras	b 2, lb 4, w 5		11				
(49.5 overs)			249				

	O	M	R	W		O	M	R	W
Imran Khan	10	1	41	1	Morrison	10	1	63	1
Saleem Jaffer	6.5	1	38	2	Watson	9	1	37	–
Aaqib Javed	10	–	48	3	Snedden	9.3	1	57	1
Tauseef Ahmed	10	–	49	1	Robertson	10	1	42	–
Abdul Qadir	10	–	49	2	Kuggeleijn	10	–	48	–
Mudassar Nazar	3	–	18	–					

FALL OF WICKETS
1–94, 2–178, 3–181, 4–182, 5–194, 6–224, 7–236,
8–238, 9–245

FALL OF WICKETS
1–45, 2–106, 3–168

Umpires: R.S. Dunne & R.L. McHarg

Man of the Match: Rameez Raja

Pakistan won by 7 wickets

FOURTH ONE-DAY INTERNATIONAL – NEW ZEALAND v. PAKISTAN
14 March 1989 at Seddon Park, Hamilton

PAKISTAN		
Rameez Raja	c Watson, b Morrison	0
Shoaib Mohammad	c and b Morrison	3
Aamer Malik*	lbw, b Snedden	11
Imran Khan†	c Smith, b Morrison	2
Mudassar Nazar	b Morrison	48
Saleem Malik	lbw, b Snedden	1
Ijaz Ahmed	c Smith, b Robertson	5
Abdul Qadir	c Morrison, b Kuggeleijn	41
Tauseef Ahmed	c Smith, b Watson	13
Saleem Jaffer	not out	3
Aaqib Javed	not out	1
Extras	b 4, lb 1, w 3, nb 2	10
(50 overs)	(for 9 wkts)	138

	O	M	R	W
Morrison	10	1	33	4
Watson	10	3	20	1
Snedden	10	3	14	2
Robertson	10	2	21	1
Kuggeleijn	10	–	45	1

FALL OF WICKETS
1–0, 2–3, 3–17, 4–19, 5–25, 6–40, 7–103, 8–133, 9–137

NEW ZEALAND		
J.G. Wright†	c Saleem Malik, b Imran Khan	1
A.H. Jones	not out	63
M.D. Crowe	c Ijaz Ahmed, b Imran Khan	15
M.J. Greatbatch	b Tauseef Ahmed	6
J.J. Crowe	not out	39
C.M. Kuggeleijn		
I.D.S. Smith*		
M.C. Snedden		
G.K. Robertson		
D.K. Morrison		
W. Watson		
Extras	b 4, lb 7, w 4	15
(39.4 overs)	(for 3 wkts)	139

	O	M	R	W
Imran Khan	10	1	24	2
Saleem Jaffer	8	1	26	–
Aaqib Javed	6.4	1	23	–
Tauseef Ahmed	9	1	29	1
Abdul Qadir	6	–	26	–

FALL OF WICKETS
1–6, 2–28, 3–43

Umpires: G.I.J. Cowan & R.S. Dunne

Man of the Match: D.K. Morrison

New Zealand won by 7 wickets

Crowe's 87 came off 95 balls, while Ian Smith hit 62 off 51 balls.

Third One-Day International
NEW ZEALAND v. PAKISTAN

In spite of Wright and Jones putting on 94 for the first wicket, and Martin Crowe and the irrepressible Andrew Jones adding an exhilarating 84 in 48 minutes, Pakistan won the third one-day international and so kept the series alive. Rameez Raja gave them just the start that they needed, hitting a six and 9 fours in his 101 which came off 114 balls. With such a foundation, Pakistan were able to prosper through Imran and Saleem Malik, who came together with under 11 overs remaining and 82 needed. Saleem hit 56 off 34 balls with 9 fours, and Imran faced 62 balls for his 51. With nine balls left, Imran hit Martin Snedden into the crowd at long-leg to complete his fifty and win the match.

Fourth One-Day International
NEW ZEALAND v. PAKISTAN

Put in to bat on a wicket which gave the seam bowlers encouragement, Pakistan failed miserably. Danny Morrison improved on his best performance of the opening match of the series and set New Zealand on the path to victory by sending back both openers cheaply. Pakistan's only stand of substance was for the seventh wicket, when Mudassar and Abdul Qadir added 63 in 58 minutes, Qadir equalling his highest score in a one-day international.

Wright went early, but Andrew Jones ended the season in the dominant form that he had shown from the start. He hit his sixth fifty in successive matches, and New Zealand romped to victory with 10.2 overs to spare.

The Pakistanis left few friends. The New Zealand Cricket Council issued a statement complaining about their language, behaviour and attitude to umpires. A year ago, one had believed them to be the best side in the world, but their lack of discipline and their perpetual feeling of persecution leaves them now as a team very much in need of self-questioning and a complete change of attitudes. A great corporate talent is being dissipated.

First-Class Averages

BATTING

	M	Inns	NOs	Runs	HS	Av	100s	50s
G.A. Hick	8	16	3	1228	211*	94.46	6	2
A.H. Jones	8	15	2	884	181*	68.00	2	5
R.H. Vance	10	18	2	1037	254*	64.81	4	4
B.A. Edgar	7	13	1	762	150	63.50	3	3
J.J. Crowe	9	13		797	156	61.30	2	5
T.E. Blain	9	15	4	622	108	56.54	1	5
I.D.S. Smith	7	8	3	268	64	53.60		3
R.T. Latham	10	19	4	781	142*	52.06	2	5
M.J. Greatbatch	7	13	2	562	202*	51.09	1	4
M.D. Crowe	9	15	2	634	174	48.76	2	3
P.A. Horne	8	12	1	535	209	48.63	1	3
J.G. Wright	6	11	1	468	149*	46.80	1	3
P.S. Briasco	8	15	2	605	154*	46.53	2	2
T.J. Franklin	8	13	3	448	133*	44.80	1	2
C.M. Kuggeleijn	9	15	3	536	101*	44.66	1	1
P.E. McEwan	9	17		758	137	44.58	2	5

First-Class Averages continued

	M	Inns	NOs	Runs	HS	Av	100s	50s
G.E. Bradburn	5	8	3	218	54*	43.60		1
M.W. Priest	10	18	4	603	92*	43.07		4
K.R. Rutherford	8	14	1	551	179	42.38	2	1
D.J. White	9	18	2	631	110	39.43	1	5
D.J. Boyle	7	14	3	396	108	36.00	1	1
E.B. McSweeney	9	13	5	274	67*	34.25		1
S.W. Duff	8	11	3	268	64	33.50		2
M.W. Douglas	8	15	3	402	73*	33.50		3
S.J. McCullum	6	11		365	75	33.18		2
G.K. Robertson	8	11	3	262	52	32.75		2
R.B. Reid	7	11	1	313	90	31.30		2
T.D. Ritchie	8	14	1	391	106	30.07	1	1
B.R. Blair	8	13		386	118	29.69	1	3
C.L. Cairns	9	11	3	231	110	28.87	1	
K.J. Burns	8	13		371	89	28.53		4
C.J. Smith	8	15		422	70	28.43		3
G.R. Larsen	9	16	2	395	82	28.21		2
S.A. Thomson	8	14	4	278	68*	27.80		2
K.B.K. Ibadulla	4	7	2	139	69	27.80		1
E.J. Gray	8	11	4	194	59	27.71		1
P.W. Dobbs	9	16	1	390	86*	26.00		2
B.A. Young	9	17	2	382	97	25.46		2
M.R. Pringle	8	10	1	229	89*	25.44		2
G.P. Burnett	3	5		127	84	25.40		1
D.N. Patel	8	10	1	225	77	25.00		1
N.A. Mallender	7	11	3	191	43	23.87		
L.K. Germon	9	14	3	255	106*	23.18	1	
B.R. Hartland	8	16	1	343	73	22.86		1
P.G. Kennedy	7	13	1	269	68	22.41		1
R.N. Hoskin	4	6		111	71	18.50		1
J.G. Bracewell	7	9	3	107	35*	17.83		
D.A. Stirling	7	8	2	104	38	17.33		
G.W. McKenzie	5	9		138	71	15.33		1
F. Beyeler	9	9	1	109	34	13.62		
L.M. Crocker	6	12	1	136	32*	12.36		
A.J. Nuttall	10	12	3	108	33	12.00		

(Qualification – 100 runs, average 10.00)

BOWLING

	Overs	Mds	Runs	Wkts	Av	Best	10/m	5/inns
D.N. Patel	123.4	37	292	14	20.85	4/16		
N.A. Mallender	183.1	39	437	20	21.35	5/38	1	2
B.P. Bracewell	286.5	64	799	34	23.50	6/49		2
M.C. Snedden	191.2	57	466	19	24.52	4/14		
S.L. Boock	388.5	135	810	33	24.54	5/43		2
B.J. Barrett	92.4	20	247	10	24.70	4/32		
W. Watson	199	42	584	20	29.20	6/51		2
F. Beyeler	211.4	45	676	21	32.19	4/64		
S.J. Roberts	214	32	906	27	33.55	5/115		1
S.W. Duff	334.4	92	911	27	33.74	4/87		
D.A. Stirling	143	19	575	17	33.82	4/66		
J.G. Bracewell	259.1	65	677	20	33.85	5/90		1
T.J. Wilson	165.1	36	508	15	33.86	3/49		
P.D. Unwin	212.1	38	756	22	34.36	6/42	1	1
E.J. Gray	311.4	96	852	24	35.50	4/42		
D.K. Morrison	229.2	43	754	21	35.90	5/16		2
G.N. Cederwall	102	12	453	12	37.75	7/97		1
G.K. Robertson	202.3	34	654	17	38.47	5/44		1
C.L. Cairns	238.1	33	814	21	38.76	3/20		
E.J. Chatfield	346.4	87	825	21	39.28	5/36		1
T.M. McKenna	166.5	36	517	13	39.76	3/33		
M.W. Priest	360.1	84	1124	28	40.14	6/92		1
M.A. Robinson	197.3	40	609	15	40.60	3/52		
M.R. McKinnon	171	25	579	14	41.35	4/131		
A.J. Nuttall	333	83	991	23	43.08	4/74		
G.R. Logan	213.2	65	549	12	45.75	5/60		1
V.F. Johnson	200	45	550	12	45.83	4/44		

(Qualification – 10 wickets)

LEADING FIELDERS

28 - L.K. Germon (ct 25/st 3) and E.B. McSweeney (ct 24/st 4); 21 - I.D.S. Smith (ct 20/st 1); 18 - B.A. Young; 16 - T.E. Blain; 12 - K.J. McKnight (ct 10/st 2); 11 - J.J. Crowe, G.R. Larsen and M.W. Douglas; 10 - E.J. Gray and P.A. Horne

Paul Unwin – a young spinner of immense promise. (Adrian Murrell/Allsport)

NEW ZEALAND 1988–9
by
DON CAMERON

Even the elevation of Richard Hadlee to become perhaps New Zealand's first genuine Test world recordholder – the collective disaster of 26 in an innings of 1955 must be rather a non-record – could not put a cheerful gloss on what became a rather sad and depressing New Zealand season.

One of the first acts of the season was Hadlee taking nine wickets in an innings against West Zone at Rajkot, with John Bracewell denying Hadlee his first all-ten. The second major achievement came in the first hour of the first Test at Bangalore, when Arun Lal obliged quite quickly with the Test wicket which at last took Hadlee one ahead of Ian Botham.

That Test was eventually lost, mainly because of such a spectacular attack of illness that Jeremy Coney was plucked down from the radio box to be one emergency fielder, and then Ken Nicholson added one indelible mark to his otherwise modest first-class career by abandoning his post as a television producer-director and went out to give Coney and the remaining upright New Zealanders a hand.

This Test was lost. Surprisingly, however, the next was won quite brilliantly at Bombay when the hot and bothered New Zealanders managed at least one heroic recovery operation each day, and had the Test won early on the fifth day.

And that, really, was that for the New Zealand cricket 1988–9 season – there was nothing very remarkable or successful or interesting from about mid-December onward to the end of a wet and dismal summer.

In fact, the New Zealand Cricket Council even managed the impossible: through a combination of wet weather and limp cricket on ordinary pitches the crowds were very small and the NZCC lost money on the home tour by Pakistan. The deficit has not yet been released, but it represents a very sobering passage in New Zealand cricket history. Going back over the last 30 years or so, no other major tour has cost the NZCC money.

But first the good news, which largely centred on Hadlee in India, and on that quite astonishing batsman Andrew Jones whenever he took up his bat, in Shell series, Tests or one-dayers.

The fact that Hadlee was in India was largely an accident. Twelve months before, as Hadlee contemplated breaking the world Test bowling record in the home series against England, he blithely announced that he would not be available for the tour of India. He had once before withdrawn from a Test tour of Pakistan. Hadlee made it quite plain that the rigours of life in Pakistan or India would not be permitted to make any inroads into the Hadlee constitution.

But then Hadlee crocked a knee against England and did not get the Test wicket he needed to pull clear of Botham. Then there came the news that Botham might well recover from his back injury sufficiently to resume Test cricket, and increase his pile of victims.

Never one to miss a chance, Hadlee changed tack quickly, and announced himself available for India. Like his team mates, Hadlee was stocked with umpteen pills, jabbed with about as many needles, and on the rest day of the first Test – the record already in his grasp – he was just as dramatically ill as most of his team mates.

But once past that problem, Hadlee drew deep on his twin wells of skill and spirit, and found to his surprise that India could be quite enjoyable. In other words, Hadlee could get wickets, when he had feared there would be nothing for him in the bare and bony pitches which the Indians tend to produce for their spinners.

The challenge drew a remarkable response from Hadlee. He was soon as gaunt and grey about the gills as his team mates. His slim frame looked thin. But the skill was still there, perhaps in greater quantity.

Chris Kuggeleijn. A most effective all-rounder in the one-day game. (Simon Bruty/Allsport)

Hadlee first of all found that he could get some bounce and pace from the pitch, and that the top of the Indian batting could be vulnerable to the occasional flier, and the even more frequent movement in the air or from the seam.

Then Hadlee found that Indians love sports heroes, and positively adore world cricket recordholders. Immediately, Hadlee was the centre of all attention; people rushed to give him compliments and gifts. A local sponsor weighed in with a considerable amount of money, provided Hadlee added the sponsor's logo to his bat, wristbands and eyebrow sweat-bands. Hadlee, and his captain John Wright, got into the newspaper columnist business, which annoyed both the Indian board and the Indian players, for not long beforehand Dilip Vengsarkar, to become the Indian captain, was sacked for writing for the newspapers.

But Hadlee tends to make his own rules in such matters, and he lapped up the hero-worship and attention he received from the home spectators. And how brilliantly he bowled! Hadlee had 10 wickets in the second Test, and Bracewell eight, as the New Zealanders managed to pull off an heroic and brilliant win.

In the three-Test series Hadlee had 18 wickets at 14. The rest of the New Zealanders obtained 22 among them. On pitches designed for them Arshad Ayub had 21 wickets, Narendra Hirwani 20, but they bowled in six full innings, whereas Hadlee bowled in only four. It might also be pointed out that Hadlee had rather more difficulty extracting lbw decisions from the umpires than some of the home players.

So Hadlee had 391 Test wickets and again had the spur that he might well be the first man to 400 on his home soil, perhaps on his favourite Lancaster Park pitch.

Pakistan were scheduled to play three Tests, but at Dunedin, Wellington and Auckland. Suddenly England, with their Test squad idle but still being paid, opened up negotiations to play in New Zealand. Eventually the Pakistan and England tours were arranged, three Tests with Pakistan, two with England, and a three-way one-day series in between.

It was the kind of itinerary to make someone like Hadlee sit up and take notice, given the fact that he would not mind missing the one-day internationals.

Then things began to go irreversibly wrong, for virtually the last three months of the summer season.

The NZCC, under the new chairmanship of Barry Paterson, a Hamilton lawyer without the years of craggy experience gained by Bob Vance, his predecessor, rather let the planning for the England tour come under the influence of the Labour government's Minister of External Affairs, Russell Marshall.

Rather than make the arrangements quietly and then slip them into public view – and England had toured New Zealand the previous summer without any guilt-by-association on the South African question – Paterson and the NZCC guaranteed the planning would have a high profile by including government ministers in the preliminary work.

This alerted the protest movement in New Zealand. Suddenly the Pakistan board, who had approved the idea of the three-way one-day series with New Zealand and England, changed direction and said it could not agree to compete against England in the one-day series.

This series was central, and essential, to the considered success of the twin tours. England might lose money playing late-season Tests after a one-day series, but the one-dayers would have offered the novelty of a three-way competition and would have drawn heavy television fees, sponsorship and gate-takings.

When Pakistan backed off New Zealand had no alternative but to cancel the England tour. The reason, said Paterson, was purely economic. Not too many people accepted that at face value. By including Marshall in the

planning, Paterson and the NZCC had put the England team up as the no. 1 target for protesters and malcontents, for whom there had been precious little to march and wave their banners about in recent times. The England team, and its venues, would have been the focus for all manner of protest, making the whole tour a physical risk.

So what was seen as a bold and interesting enterprise was lost on the altar of compromise, which did not mark a very strong start to Paterson's chairmanship of the NZCC.

However, Hadlee could still eye those 400 wickets, for there were three home Tests against Pakistan.

But then there were two. The first Test was scheduled for Dunedin, where it rained and rained and rained. Eventually the Test was abandoned, a one-day international was played on the fifth day, and, while Hadlee dominated that with three quick wickets, he had lost some of his good humour. All of a sudden five Tests had become two, with nine wickets needed for the 400.

By now Hadlee must have wondered whether the whole home season was something sent to torment him. The second Test was played on the Basin Reserve pitch in Wellington, a place where over the years the batsmen had begun to flourish, but there was usually a stiff tail-wind and some bounce and pace to encourage the quicker bowlers.

But again fate played Hadlee false. In normal times the visiting captain, after winning the toss, would bat first, and take the risk that the pitch might have some life before lunch on the first day. Should Wright win the toss he might very well bowl first and hope for some quick success by Hadlee. Either way the great man seemed sure of the new ball when it would do him and his team the most good.

Imran Khan, the Pakistan captain, had other ideas. On winning the toss Imran made New Zealand bat first. By the time New Zealand had batted the first two days for 447 there was little life left in the pitch, and little prospect that Hadlee might bowl at two Pakistan innings.

And so it proved, with Shoaib Mohammad batting 720 minutes for 163, Javed Miandad 360 minutes for 118, and Pakistan taking 787 minutes over their 437 for seven wickets declared. New Zealand filled in the remaining 270 minutes with 186 for eight wickets.

While the first Test was being washed out, and the second consigned to the dullest of draws, the words coming from Eden Park in Auckland would not have been as soothing music to the Hadlee ears.

Over recent years the Eden Park staff have tried hard to produce pitches with some grass and a reasonable speed and bounce. Sometimes, on a first and steamy morning, the new ball can zip about. Hadlee had taken only four wickets at Wellington, but there might have been the prospect of the remaining five he needed from Eden Park.

Again, alas and alack. Auckland was in the middle of a sad and soggy summer. The pitch block had had to be covered frequently against rain. While covered, some foreign beasty had got to work and killed all the grass.

There was, not surprisingly, a fine old panic about this, and the prospect that the Test be moved from Eden Park to McLean Park in Napier – which is not a fast bowler's home away from home, either!

However, the NZCC stuck with Eden Park, the

Danny Morrison, New Zealand's most successful bowler in the one-day series. (Simon Bruty/Allsport)

went quietly to 99 for three wickets, and what had seemed the longest, slowest, most pointless Test series in New Zealand history was laid to rest – with no mourners.

New Zealand did regain some prestige by dominating the one-day series 3 to 1, and counting the one played instead of the first Test, 4 to 1. But the crowds were not great, and the administrators had to sit down and wonder what had gone wrong, and why one side of the ledger had ended so much out of kilter with the other.

The miscalculation with the England tour was one reason. The wet weather was another. Then there were two or three other factors which rather insisted, from lunch-time on the first day of the second Test at Wellington, that no one was going to win this series.

The pitches used for the Tests in Wellington and Auckland decreed that one side or the other would have to play very, very badly to be beaten by the other.

That was the supreme irony of the rain in Dunedin. In the two recent Tests there New Zealand had scratched home for narrow wins against West Indies and Pakistan. The seamers had dominated those games. A quick look at the Carisbrook pitch before the rain poured down suggested a pitch very much under-prepared. The team making the right decision with the toss and bowling well might well dominate what looked like a three-day Test. No one could exploit such a pitch like Hadlee or his lieutenant, Ewen Chatfield. They had to wait in the rain, and then in the one-day match both were quite often unplayable – Hadlee taking three wickets, Chatfield making the ball perform all manner of tricks.

But the Basin Reserve and Eden Park offered the bowlers no help at all, and, while there were some monumental efforts of concentration, such as Shoaib in Wellington and Miandad in Auckland, the paying spectators in New Zealand are not interested in monuments which move very slowly.

By the end the public and the players, and probably the administrators too, were insisting that by next summer the pitches should promote more action, so that the struggle between batsman and bowler would be rather more even.

Then there will come another problem. During, and not after, the second Test at the Basin Reserve, Intikhab Alam, the Pakistan manager, elected to give me first the information that the Pakistanis were not the slightest bit impressed by the umpires in the second Test, Steve Woodward, the more experienced of the two, and Steve Dunne.

They had, said Intikhab, made several mistakes, and perhaps had tried to compensate by making further bad rulings. His players had quickly lost confidence in the umpires. It was all, said Intikhab, further proof that some form of international panel of the best umpires in the world should be gathered together, and that Test series such as Pakistan v. New Zealand should be umpired by men from other countries.

Considering that his own country had been the focus of two major umpiring rows involving England and then Australia, Intikhab may have appeared to be moving on thin ice. But he was manifestly sincere in his claim for neutral or independent umpires. He may even have been on the side of the truth when he said that Woodward and

groundstaff toiled manfully and they produced what looked like the most un-New Zealand cricket pitch imaginable. It had grass clippings rolled in, which gave the top a greenish tinge and were supposed to bind the surface. Underneath was bare, flat and very hard mud. It looked, to the Pakistani eyes, like something they would recognise at Karachi or Bombay.

It looked even better for Imran when he won the toss and this time batted first. Hadlee raised a glimmer of hope with Mudassar Nazar's wicket when he was five and the total 10. Rizwan went, to Stephen Boock, at 44.

But then nobody went anywhere for a long, long time as Shoaib, this time with 112 in 350 minutes, and Miandad, 271 in 558 minutes, sent the Pakistan total soaring up to 616 for five wickets, and Hadlee's blood pressure must have soared a little too, as he had only one wicket.

As the final indignity to Hadlee, who had probably despaired of getting close to 400 in any case, Imran imposed the follow-on when New Zealand were out for 403; so Hadlee did not have another bowl as New Zealand

Tony Blain finished high in the batting averages, held 16 catches and remains an exciting prospect for the future. (Adrian Murrell/Allsport)

Dunne had not umpired well. They have undoubtedly umpired better.

Naturally, the NZCC was not amused that there should be criticism of the New Zealand umpires, especially when it was laid during the progress of one Test. However, the NZCC and its chairman, Paterson, chose to remain silent, and to try and isolate Intikhab and Imran as critics of the umpires.

This probably suited Intikhab and Imran, for they maintained regular comments about the quality, or lack of it, of the umpiring during and after the third Test, while the NZCC disclaimer that it had complete faith in its umpires was not issued by Paterson until after the one-dayers.

By then the damage had really been done, and the Intikhab–Imran attack had dominated the latter half of the Test series almost to the point of boredom. The NZCC, so the early comment went, was not very eager to have an international panel of independent Test umpires. However, Paterson is a member of an ICC committee looking at that question, and by the end of the summer the NZCC

was beginning to view the idea with some favour – which probably caused a wry smile or two from Imran and Intikhab.

So, at the end of his season, and six months after it had started with nine wickets at Rajkot, Hadlee was left with 396 Test wickets and the concern that Botham, through some medical miracle, might get to 400 first against the Australians.

Graham Dowling, the NZCC executive officer, probably had similarly sad thoughts, for what could have been a very distinctive season turned into a most disappointing one. As the final twist of the knife, what appeared to be a very strong New Zealand Youth team was sent to Australia, and beaten pointless.

The pity of it all was that the one person who was entitled to regard the 1988–9 summer as a totally marvellous experience is a man not given to wide or frequent smiles.

Hadlee got close to 400 wickets and held the world record. Martin Crowe chipped in with another Test century, but without ever looking to be near his peak of classical form.

Andrew Howard Jones, 29 years of curious class, simply went on scoring runs virtually every time he took centre. His Test scores in India were not exactly shattering – 45, 17, 3, 78, 8 and 5 – but this was his first real experience of top-class spin bowling on helpful pitches. Jones moved into better gear with two fifties in the four one-day internationals.

He then came home to thunderous success, turning the Wellington side into his own personal kingdom, with scores of 50, 1, 177, 66, 62, 45, 22, 0, 97 and 181. What is more, Jones scored those runs with the confidence and arrogance of the lord of the manor extracting tribute from the serfs and villeins of the area. Especially on his favourite Basin Reserve, which gave him some pace and a true bounce, Jones simply smashed the bowlers to pieces. He scored the 177 and 66 against Auckland, and the 66 was probably the more pyrotechnical of the two.

Afterwards I compared notes with some rather senior Wellington people. We all agreed. Even the formidable John Reid, the New Zealand captain in the 1950s and 60s, did not hit the ball off the back foot quite so powerfully as did Jones. There could not be higher tribute.

Jones started off with 86 in the second Test against Pakistan and was very annoyed with himself that yet another Basin Reserve century had eluded him. He ended with 86, 39, 47 and 0 in the Tests. The one-dayers were a complete triumph for Jones, with scores of 55 not out, 62 not out, 67, 82 and 63 not out. The beauty of his one-day batting is that while Jones is not a bucolic slogger of the ball, he is seldom at a loss for a scoring stroke.

Compared with the classical elegance of Martin Crowe, or the street-urchin charm of Miandad, Jones looks a cricketer of pawky method, of unglamorous intent. It does not worry him in the slightest. For Jones grew up into

Richard Hadlee, a national hero in sight of becoming the first bowler to capture 400 Test wickets. (Alan Cozzi)

first-class cricket with Central Districts until they spurned him, and then Otago when they eventually wanted him, and then Wellington when he could not be disregarded, and then New Zealand when he could not be left out, dominated by one thought. He did not come from one of the glamorous cricket areas of New Zealand such as Auckland or Christchurch or Wellington.

But, with hard work and a tough competitive mind, Jones would simply score more runs than those from the fancy cities who had scoffed at him. This is the batsman that the Australians mocked the first time they saw him at the Gabba, so he extracted 150 runs of sweet revenge in the next Test at Adelaide.

In 28 one-dayers Jones has had 20 completed innings, 1,225 runs, 15 times past 50, average 61.1. In 10 Tests he has 751 runs.

No one mocks Jones any more. He will never be fashionable but he is fired along by this fierce determination to succeed, to prove he is better than his team mates and the opposing bowler. Who knows, within a year or so Jones may be regarded as the best no. 3 in the world – and then he might have a quiet smile to himself.

On the home front Auckland, who messed up their winning chance by relying on the calculator in their last match in 1987–8, repaired that error by winning the Shell Trophy narrowly in the three-day series, while Wellington won the one-day Shell Cup competition.

The Shell series over the years have been interesting, but have always lacked the real sense of home and away competition. Next summer the six competing associations, at huge risk to their bank accounts, will play a complete home and away series of three-day games, starting in early December. The Shell Cup will have a round-robin series as usual just after Christmas, but will have semifinals and a final in March.

Whether or not the Shell Trophy produces a worthier competition remains to be seen, for there will be considerable interruption from touring international sides.

But the longer series hopefully will produce umpires of longer experience and thus more expertise and poise. Also the need for more first-class pitches might produce at the international grounds Test or one-day pitches of appropriate quality. The summer of 1988–9 had rather too many disappointments for comfort. If 1989–90 produces better umpires and pitches, that will represent a start back to cricket respectability in New Zealand.

Domestic Celebration

The season in South Africa.
Castle Currie Cup. Castle Bowl.
Nissan Shield. Benson and Hedges Trophy.
First-class averages.

*Ken McEwan enjoyed his best ever season in South Africa and
contributed much to Eastern Province winning the
Currie Cup for the first time.*

In 1988–9, South Africa celebrated a centenary of Test cricket. Ironically, the celebration came at a time when the country was excluded from official Test matches and when the ICC took a stronger and more positive line against cricketers who opted to play or coach in the Republic. Yet, in this climate, Joe Pamensky, President of the South African Cricket Union, asserted:

It is generally accepted that very few cricketing countries would have been able to withstand 18 years of international isolation and yet retain as strong a cricketing system as we have in South Africa, which many agree is stronger and more soundly based now than when we were competing officially against our traditional international opponents.

In his speech at the annual *Wisden* dinner in London in April 1989, Ali Bacher re-enforced this point when he claimed that in the past three years a development programme 'has taken the game to more than 60,000 children in the black townships of my country and from this has emerged a burgeoning talent among players, coaches and administrators that is revolutionizing our cricket'.

Whatever the decision of the ICC, the debate will continue. There are some brave men in South Africa who have done much to see that cricket becomes multi-racial and thrives. They achieve much in circumstances which, to say the least, are difficult, and, in the end, their success will depend not upon their own efforts, nor even upon those of administrators in other countries, but upon the attitudes and actions of politicians.

For the first time, the South African Cricket Union instigated an end-of-the-season match to decide promotion and relegation between the Currie Cup and the Bowl.

8, 9 and 10 October 1988

at Buffalo Park, East London

Eastern Province 330 (D.J. Richardson 75, I.L. Howell 4 for 47) and 295 for 3 (K.C. Wessels 146, P.G. Amm 116)
Border 426 (B.M. Osborne 145, E.N. Trotman 97, B.W. Lones 87, D.J. Callaghan 4 for 50, T.G. Shaw 4 for 90)

Match drawn

The season began with a first-class friendly match in which Border, the Castle Bowl side, acquitted themselves with great credit. Bradley Osborne hit the highest score of his career and shared in century stands with Lones and skipper Trotman.

Protea Shield

10 October 1988

at Newlands, Cape Town

Transvaal 174 for 8 (S.J. Cook 72)
Western Province 137 (R.O. Estwick 4 for 8)

Transvaal won by 37 runs

Transvaal comfortably retained the Protea Assurance Challenge Shield in the 55-over match, and suggested that their might was undiminished.

Nissan Shield

15 October 1988

at Newlands, Cape Town

Western Province 276 for 4 (L. Seeff 88, A.P. Kuiper 62, P.N. Kirsten 58)
Northern Transvaal 216 (M. Yachad 93, A.P. Kuiper 4 for 44)

Western Province won by 60 runs

at De Beers Country Club, Kimberley

Border 178 (C.W. Symcox 4 for 35)
Griqualand West 120

Border won by 58 runs

22 October 1988

at Centurion Park, Verwoerdburg

Western Province 242 for 7 (P.N. Kirsten 94, D.J. Cullinan 83)
Northern Transvaal 224 (M.J.R. Rindel 75)

Western Province won by 18 runs

at Buffalo Park, East London

Border 329 for 4 (L.M. Phillips 153 not out, B.M. Osborne 73)
Griqualand West 127

Border won by 202 runs

South Africa's premier one-day competition, the Nissan Shield, began with Western Province winning both games against Northern Transvaal to enter the semi-finals, Kirsten batting well in both matches.

Border maintained the good form that they had shown in the first-class friendly match earlier in the month by twice overwhelming Griqualand West. In the second match, in East London, Leroy Phillips carried his bat and hit 20 fours in an innings lasting 218 minutes. Border's victories earned them a place in the quarter-finals against Eastern Province.

Benson and Hedges Trophy

26 October 1988

at St George's Park, Port Elizabeth

Orange Free State 179 for 8 (P.J.R. Steyn 61, L.J. Wilkinson 50)
Eastern Province 166 (K.C. Wessels 69)

Orange Free State (2 pts) won by 13 runs

28 October 1988

at Centurion Park, Verwoerdburg

Natal 167 for 9 (N.P. Daniels 76, P.S. de Villiers 4 for 32)
Northern Transvaal 152

Natal (2 pts) won by 15 runs

2 November 1988

at Wanderers, Johannesburg

Orange Free State 206 for 9 (W.J. Cronje 63)
Transvaal 212 for 1 (H.R. Fotheringham 129 not out, R.F. Pienaar 66 not out)

Transvaal (2 pts) won by 9 wickets

4 November 1988

at Centurion Park, Verwoerdburg

Eastern Province 201 for 5 (M.W. Rushmere 76)
Northern Transvaal 179 (W.F. Morris 63, M.D. Haysman 59, R.J. McCurdy 5 for 23)

Eastern Province (2 pts) won by 22 runs

The first round of matches in the day and night competition saw Transvaal again assert their strength with a crushing win over Orange Free State, who had earlier beaten Eastern Province. Henry Fotheringham and Roy Pienaar established a Benson and Hedges Trophy record with a second-wicket stand of 211, which took Transvaal to victory by nine wickets. Earlier, Clive Rice had bowled well to restrict the Free State on a good wicket.

Nissan Shield

29 October 1988

at Wanderers, Johannesburg

Transvaal 239 for 9 (S.J. Cook 84, S.J. Base 4 for 36)
Boland 187 (J.P. Stephenson 80)

Transvaal won by 52 runs

5 November 1988

at Oude Libertas, Stellenbosch

Transvaal 193 (C.E.B. Rice 62, S. Botha 4 for 31)
Boland 183 for 9 (O. Henry 59 not out)

Transvaal won by 10 runs

As expected, Transvaal claimed a place in the semi-finals of the Nissan Shield with two wins over Boland. The Bowl side gave a good account of themselves, however, with Essex's John Stephenson batting well in the first match.

Benson and Hedges Trophy

10 November 1988

at Kingsmead, Durban

Impalas 205 for 7 (B.M. Osborne 83)
Natal 192 (P.H. Rayner 64, T.R. Madsen 61, S.J. Base 4 for 20, B.C. Fourie 4 for 24)

Impalas (2 pts) won by 13 runs

11 November 1988

at Harmony Ground, Virginia

Western Province 190 for 8 (A.P. Kuiper 64)
Orange Free State 191 for 5

Orange Free State (2 pts) won by 5 wickets

16 November 1988

at Kingsmead, Durban

Natal 171 for 7 (K.M. Curran 57, R.M. Bentley 51, R.J. McCurdy 4 for 39)
Eastern Province 155

Natal (2 pts) won by 16 runs

18 November 1988

at Centurion Park, Verwoerdburg

Transvaal 178 for 5 (H.R. Fotheringham 81 not out)
Northern Transvaal 180 for 1 (K.D. Verdoorn 78 not out, M. Yachad 50)

Northern Transvaal (2 pts) won by 9 wickets

Another round of matches in the day/night competition left Impalas as the only unbeaten side, and they had played only one match. Natal crushed Transvaal in sensational fashion, having earlier accounted for Eastern Province. Curran produced some fine all-round cricket. Impalas' win was founded on some excellent bowling by Simon Base and Branden Fourie, who performed the hat trick.

Nissan Shield

12 November 1988

at St George's Park, Port Elizabeth

Eastern Province 285 for 2 (M.W. Rushmere 137 not out, K.S. McEwan 109 not out)
Border 191 for 6 (E.N. Trotman 66)

Eastern Province won by 94 runs

19 November 1988

at Buffalo Park, East London

Border 181 for 9
Eastern Province 185 for 2 (M.W. Rushmere 77 not out)

Eastern Province won by 8 wickets

Eastern Province joined Transvaal in the semi-final of the Nissan Shield with two emphatic victories over Border. At Port Elizabeth, Mark Rushmere and Ken McEwan added 204 in 95 minutes for the third wicket. Rushmere's 135 came off 192 balls, and McEwan hit a ferocious 109 off 95 deliveries.

Castle Bowl

18, 19 and 20 November 1988

at Wanderers, Johannesburg

Transvaal 'B' 236 (D.H. Howell 54, R.E. Bryson 5 for 62) and 273 for 8 dec (P.J. Botha 103 not out)
Northern Transvaal 'B' 203 (J. Groenewald 60 not out, A.M. Ferreira 58) and 103 (K.J. Kerr 4 for 24)

Transvaal 'B' won by 203 runs
Transvaal 'B' 23 pts, Northern Transvaal 'B' 8 pts

The first-class competitive season opened with Transvaal 'B' displaying the association's usual strength in depth with what was eventually an easy win. Only Groenewald kept the visitors in touch in the first innings, with a hard-hit 60 which raised his side from 129 for 8 to 202. Botha's century put Transvaal 'B' in a strong position, and he and Kerr bowled them to victory.

Transvaal off-spinner Kevin Kerr, who bowled well throughout the season and helped the 'B' side to the Castle Bowl final. Many felt that he should have had a regular place in the Currie Cup side. (David Munden)

Benson and Hedges Trophy

23 November 1988

at Harmony Ground, Virginia

Orange Free State 205 for 7 (P.J.R. Steyn 55)
Northern Transvaal 198 for 6 (N.T. Day 67)

Orange Free State (2 pts) won by 7 runs

25 November 1988

at St George's Park, Port Elizabeth

Eastern Province 162 for 9 (M.W. Rushmere 58, A.P. Kuiper 4 for 33)
Western Province 163 for 6 (P.N. Kirsten 61)

Western Province (2 pts) won by 4 wickets

Orange Free State took a clear lead in the Benson and Hedges Trophy with a narrow victory over Northern Transvaal. Eastern Province's poor form continued when they lost to Western Province with 7.5 overs to spare.

Castle Bowl

25, 26 and 27 November 1988

at SFW Ground, Stellenbosch

Western Province 'B' 305 for 6 dec (J.B. Commins 78, G. Kirsten 73, L.F. Bleekers 71 not out) and 178 for 6 dec (J.B. Commins 50)
Boland 177 (J.P. Stephenson 63 not out) and 186 (I. Barnes 4 for 71)

Western Province 'B' won by 120 runs
Western Province 'B' 23 pts, Boland 5 pts

26, 27 and 28 November 1988

at Kingsmead, Durban

Border 190 (C.S. Stirk 6 for 58) and 314 for 9 dec (E.N. Trotman 91, B.W. Lones 79, N.R. Boonzaaier 54, M.R. Hobson 4 for 77)
Natal 'B' 207 (M.A. Bowman 59, I.L. Howell 4 for 36) and 185 for 5 (C.S. Stirk 95 not out)

Match drawn
Natal 'B' 8 pts, Border 7 pts

at Wanderers, Johannesburg

Transvaal 'B' 310 (K.J. Rule 75, D.H. Howell 61) and 186 for 7 (N.E. Wright 70, M.W. Pringle 4 for 64)
Eastern Province 'B' 287 (A. van N. Snyman 63, M.B. Billson 52 not out, A.V. Birrell 51, P.J. Botha 5 for 54)

Match drawn
Transvaal 'B' 9 pts, Eastern Province 'B' 8 pts

Boland's batting let them down badly in the match at Stellenbosch, and consistent bowling and batting took Western Province 'B' to victory in their opening match. Wicket-keeper Kevin Bridgens, formerly of Western Province, claimed six victims in the match, five of them in the second innings.

Border's recovery came too late to force victory at Durban. For Natal 'B', Craig Stirk returned the best bowling figures of his career and followed with an innings of 95 not out when his side looked in danger of defeat.

Although Botha's excellent all-round cricket continued for Transvaal 'B', they were thwarted by Eastern Province 'B', for whom Meyrick Pringle took seven wickets.

Nissan Shield

26 November 1988

at UOFS Ground, Bloemfontein

Natal 235 for 7 (A.C. Hudson 70, P.H. Rayner 59)
Orange Free State 236 for 8 (A.A. Metcalfe 59, H.L. Alleyne 4 for 35)

Orange Free State won by 2 wickets

3 December 1988

at Kingsmead, Durban

Natal 199 for 7 (N.P. Daniels 80 not out, T.R. Madsen 72)
Orange Free State 201 for 5 (W.J. Cronje 91 not out)

Orange Free State won by 5 wickets

Orange Free State won the last semi-final place with two comfortable victories over Natal.

Benson and Hedges Trophy

30 November 1988

at Newlands, Cape Town

Western Province 186 for 8
Northern Transvaal 125

Western Province (2 pts) won by 61 runs

2 December 1988

at Wanderers, Johannesburg

Western Province 173 for 8
Transvaal 177 for 3 (R.F. Pienaar 53 not out)

Transvaal (2 pts) won by 7 wickets

A win and a loss kept Western Province's hopes alive in the competition, but a fourth defeat for Northern Transvaal virtually ended their chances of qualifying for the semi-final stage.

Castle Bowl

30 November, 1 and 2 December 1988

at Centurion Park, Verwoerdburg

Northern Transvaal 'B' 282 (M. Ferreira 55, V.F. du Preez 52) and 178
Eastern Province 'B' 300 for 9 dec (P.G. Amm 81) and 161 for 5 (M.W. Pringle 58, M. Michau 50)

Eastern Province 'B' won by 5 wickets
Eastern Province 'B' 25 pts, Northern Transvaal 'B' 8 pts

2, 3 and 4 December 1988

at De Beers Country Club, Kimberley

Transvaal 'B' 274 (K.J. Rule 59) and 114 for 4
Griqualand West 180 (A.J. Moles 83, G.E. McMillan 5 for 28)

Match drawn
Transvaal 'B' 9 pts, Griqualand West 7 pts

Northern Transvaal 'B' suffered their second defeat as Eastern Province 'B' took maximum points at Centurion Park as the result of good all-round team-work.

Griqualand West lost their last six wickets for 40 runs at Kimberley, but rain thwarted Transvaal 'B'.

First-Class Friendly Matches

8, 9 and 10 December 1988

at De Beers Country Club, Kimberley

Eastern Province 289 for 4 dec (P.I. Barclay 76, D.J. Callaghan 64) and 223 for 5 dec (K.C. Wessels 74, I.M. Kidson 4 for 86)
Griqualand West 219 (J.E. Morris 73, J.M. Arthur 69, M.W. Pringle 4 for 37) and 149 (J.E. Morris 52)

Eastern Province won by 144 runs

at Union Ground, Windhoek

Meyrick Pringle. Consistently good medium-pace bowling for Eastern Province 'B' brought him 43 wickets in the season. Only Lindenberg took more. (Steve Lindsell)

Boland 272 (J.D. du Toit 148) and 337 (K.J. Bridgens 71, J.P. Stephenson 68, R. Marais 53, G.J. Turner 4 for 94)
South African Defence Force 306 (H. Donachie 126) and 182 for 6 (J.J. Strydom 61 not out, G.J. Turner 59)

Match drawn

Benson and Hedges Trophy

9 December 1988

at Kingsmead, Durban

Natal 155
Transvaal 157 for 2 (S.J. Cook 87 not out)

Transvaal (2 pts) won by 8 wickets

13 December 1988

at St George's Park, Port Elizabeth

Eastern Province 231 for 6 (M.W. Rushmere 52)
Transvaal 211 for 7 (B. Roberts 66 not out, R.F. Pienaar 51)

Eastern Province (2 pts) won by 20 runs

15 December 1988

at Newlands, Cape Town

Western Province 168 for 8 (R.J. Varner 4 for 34)
Natal 110 (E.O. Simons 4 for 31)

Western Province (2 pts) won by 58 runs

at Victoria Ground, Kingwilliamstown

Orange Free State 88 for 1
v. Impalas

Match abandoned
Impalas 1 pt, Orange Free State 1 pt

The end of the first half of the Benson and Hedges series saw Orange Free State one point ahead of Transvaal and Western Province, all sides having played five matches bar Impalas, who had taken three points from their two matches played.

Friendly

10 December 1988

at Newlands, Cape Town

South African Universities 153 for 9 (P.J.R. Steyn 59)

More success with the bat than with the ball for Anton 'Yogi' Ferreira of Northern Transvaal. (George Herringshaw)

Western Province 156 for 3 (D.J. Cullinan 70 not out, P.N. Kirsten 60)

Western Province won by 7 wickets

Castle Currie Cup

17, 18 and 19 December 1988

at Wanderers, Johannesburg

Northern Transvaal 236 (A.M. Ferreira 71 not out, L.J. Barnard 51, R.O. Estwick 5 for 68, N.V. Radford 4 for 44) and 164 (V.F. du Preez 61, C.E.B. Rice 5 for 22)
Transvaal 230 (R.F. Pienaar 88, B.M. McMillan 58, P.S. de Villiers 4 for 80) and 96 for 4 (P.S. de Villiers 4 for 29)

Match drawn
Transvaal 8 pts, Northern Transvaal 8 pts

at University Ground, Bloemfontein

Orange Free State 178 and 174 (C.J. van Heerden 68 not out, R.J. McCurdy 4 for 39)
Eastern Province 334 (M.W. Rushmere 117, K.S. McEwan 65, C.J.P.G. van Zyl 5 for 95, A.A. Donald 4 for 85) and 19 for 0

Eastern Province won by 10 wickets
Eastern Province 24 pts, Orange Free State 6 pts

at Kingsmead, Durban

Natal 239 (J.N. Rhodes 108, G.S. le Roux 4 for 26) and 212 (D.B. Rundle 4 for 77)
Western Province 255 for 4 dec (T.N. Lazard 85, A.P. Kuiper 80 not out, P.N. Kirsten 53) and 199 for 3 (D.J. Cullinan 55 not out)

Western Province won by 7 wickets
Western Province 24 pts, Natal 5 pts

The first round of matches in the Currie Cup, which celebrates its centenary in 1989–90, brought convincing wins for Western and Eastern Provinces, but holders Transvaal, asked to make 171 at eight runs an over, drew with Northern Transvaal. The visitors did well to recover from the shock of 11 for 3 and even claimed a slender first-innings lead. The magnificent bowling of Clive Rice put Transvaal on top, but time was not on their side.

Orange Free State were lifted from the depths of 92 for 7 by some late-order vigour, but, in spite of some fiery bowling by Donald and van Zyl, Mark Rushmere put Eastern Province well in control of the match with his innings of 117, which included a six and 11 fours. He and McEwan added 126 for the fourth wicket. Orange Free State fared worse in their second innings than they had done in their first, and were 48 for 6 before van Heerden led a spirited revival which was insufficient to prevent Eastern Province from claiming an easy victory.

At Durban, Natal were 39 for 4 when Jonty Rhodes, making his debut, came to the wicket. He hit 108 in 235 minutes and helped his side to recover to 239, but Western Province, having lost Seeff at two, took a first-innings lead with ease, and went on to win with little fuss or doubt.

Castle Bowl

17, 18 and 19 December 1988

at SFW Ground, Stellenbosch

Natal 'B' 185 (A.R. Wormington 53) and 288
Boland 215 (J. de Swardt 60, J.D. du Toit 52, R.K. Illingworth 5 for 69) and 121 for 9 (R.K. Illingworth 6 for 39)

Match drawn
Boland 8 pts, Natal 'B' 7 pts

at Centurion Park, Verwoerdburg

Transvaal 'B' 402 for 3 dec (K.J. Rule 112 not out, M.S. Venter 108, P.J. Botha 106, N.E. Wright 53) and 9 for 0
Northern Transvaal 'B' 177 (M. Ferreira 51, K.J. Kerr 4 for 44) and 233 (A. Geringer 62)

Transvaal 'B' won by 10 wickets
Transvaal 'B' 24 pts, Northern Transvaal 'B' 3 pts

at St George's Park, Port Elizabeth

Griqualand West 155 (R.E.W. Mawhinney 61, M.W. Pringle 6

Cornelius van Zyl bowled wholeheartedly in an Orange Free State side which struggled in the early part of the season, but which recovered to win the Benson and Hedges Trophy. (Sporting Pictures UK Ltd)

for 41) and 323 (B.I. Stott 75, M.A. Fletcher 55, P. McLaren 51)
Eastern Province 'B' 305 (M.B. Billson 106, P. McLaren 4 for 85, C.W. Symcox 4 for 99) and 54 for 0

Match drawn
Eastern Province 'B' 9 pts, Griqualand West 7 pts

With their second victory in four matches, Transvaal 'B' moved well clear of all opposition in the Castle Bowl. They crushed Northern Transvaal 'B', who suffered their third defeat in three matches in the match at Verwoerdburg. Wright and Venter began with a stand of 97, and Venter and Botha then added 118. The third-wicket stand between Botha and Rule realized 149, and three of the first four Transvaal 'B' batsmen hit centuries. For Rule, it was a maiden first-class hundred. The home side battled bravely in their second innings, and just avoided an innings defeat.

Reigning champions Boland, bereft of players like Barnett, Newport and Jones, took a first-innings lead against Natal 'B', but were eventually thankful to escape defeat as Worcestershire's Richard Illingworth returned match figures of 11 for 108 with his left-arm spin.

There was some more good bowling by Meyrick Pringle for Eastern Province 'B' against Griqualand West, but the visitors recovered well in their second innings and saved the match after trailing by 150 runs on the first innings.

21, 22 and 23 December 1988

at RJE Burt Oval, Constantia

Natal 'B' 303 (E.L.R. Stewart 78, I.S. Barnes, 4 for 105) and 256 for 5 (I.B. Hobson 105 not out)
Western Province 'B' 305 (J.H. du Plessis 96 not out, L.F. Bleekers 67, J.B. Commins 58, R.K. Illingworth 5 for 87)

Match drawn
Natal 'B' 6 pts, Western Province 'B' 5 pts

The batsmen dominated at Constantia, in spite of another fine spell of bowling by Richard Illingworth.

Castle Currie Cup

26, 27 and 28 December 1988

at St George's Park, Port Elizabeth

Eastern Province 251 (K.S. McEwan 107, C.J.P.G. van Zyl 4 for 47) and 171 for 7 dec (D.J. Callaghan 66)
Orange Free State 135 (A.L. Hobson 5 for 24) and 98 (P.R. Steyn 57 not out)

Eastern Province won by 198 runs
Eastern Province 22 pts, Orange Free State 4 pts

at Newlands, Cape Town

Western Province 235 (P.N. Kirsten 66, P.S. de Villiers 6 for 47) and 276 for 4 dec (T.N. Lazard 99 not out, L. Seeff 82, A.P. Kuiper 65)
Northern Transvaal 250 (L.J. Barnard 79, M. Yachad 56, M.J.R. Rindel 55, E.O. Simons 4 for 34) and 259 for 9 (M.J.R. Rindel 109)

Match drawn
Western Province 8 pts, Northern Transvaal 8 pts

at Wanderers, Johannesburg

Transvaal 232 (C.E.B. Rice 68, K.M. Curran 7 for 47) and 164 for 6 dec (K.M. Curran 4 for 52)
Natal 94 (B.M. McMillan 4 for 27) and 168

Transvaal won by 134 runs
Transvaal 23 pts, Natal 5 pts

Transvaal and Eastern Province emerged as clear favourites to contest the Currie Cup final after only two rounds of matches. Having lost both openers for six, Eastern Province were revived by Ken McEwan, who hit 14 fours in his 256-minute stay. On a wicket that was always giving some aid to the bowlers, Orange Free State floundered. Needing 288 to win, they were bowled out for 98 in 52.4 overs, with Rudi Steyn carrying his bat through the innings.

Natal also struggled for runs on a green wicket at Wanderers. Natal skipper Kevin Curran returned the best bowling figures of his career, and only Clive Rice batted against him with any confidence, but Natal's batting fared worse than Transvaal's. Against the pace trio of Estwick, Page and Brian McMillan, they performed miserably, and only the last pair, Varner and Packer, saw the follow-on avoided. In spite of some more good bowling from Curran, Transvaal took a firm grip on the match, which they did not relinquish.

There was an exciting finish at Newlands, where

Northern Transvaal finished three runs short of their target, with the last pair together. 'Fanie' de Villiers produced the best bowling performance of his career, as Western Province were dismissed for 235, and the first innings ended on near parity. Western began their second innings in violent mood, with Seeff and Lazard putting on 150, and Kuiper hitting 65 off 45 balls with 5 sixes. Needing 262 to win, Northern Transvaal were in trouble at 82 for 5, but Mike Rindel hit 109 in 208 minutes to produce an exciting finish.

31 December 1988, 1 and 2 January 1989

at Kingsmead, Durban

Natal 259 (M.B. Logan 59, B.J. Whitfield 58, G.J. Parsons 5 for 33) and 243 for 3 dec (B.J. Whitfield 102 not out, K.D. Robinson 65)
Orange Free State 167 (T.J. Packer 5 for 42) and 330 for 9 (C.J. van Heerden 104, R.J. East 68, J.J. Strydom 67, R.K. Illingworth 4 for 87)

Match drawn
Natal 8 pts, Orange Free State 6 pts

at Newlands, Cape Town

Western Province 144 (C.E.B. Rice 4 for 21) and 358 for 3 (D.J. Cullinan 140, T.N. Lazard 122 not out)
Transvaal 389 (R.F. Pienaar 112, S.J. Cook 76)

Match drawn
Transvaal 8 pts, Western Province 3 pts

at St George's Park, Port Elizabeth

Northern Transvaal 290 for 5 dec (M.D. Haysman 78 not out, M.J.R. Rindel 77, M. Yachad 53) and 269 for 6 dec (M. Yachad 121 not out, M.J.R. Rindel 58)
Eastern Province 300 for 4 dec (M.W. Rushmere 92, K.S. McEwan 64, K.C. Wessels 62) and 233 (K.S. McEwan 88, D.J. Callaghan 78, W.F. Morris 6 for 63)

Northern Transvaal won by 26 runs
Northern Transvaal 19 pts, Eastern Province 7 pts

Northern Transvaal's surprising victory over the strong Eastern Province side was the highlight of the traditional New Year matches. A stand of 161 for the fifth wicket between Haysman and Rindel had made possible a Northern Transvaal declaration, but the powerful Eastern batting trio of Rushmere, Wessels and McEwan gained their side a first-innings lead. Yachad's century allowed another declaration, but, with Callaghan and McEwan adding 168 and Eastern Province at 215 for 3 in search of 260, the home side looked certain winners. Then, as Willie Morris dismissed Callaghan, Richardson and Shaw with successive deliveries to perform the hat trick, four wickets fell with the score on 215. Two more went down at 225, and when Morris had Pringle stumped Northern Transvaal had completed an amazing victory.

Orange Free State came close to recording another sensational victory in Durban. In spite of Gordon Parsons' 5 for 33 in 22 overs, Natal always seemed on top, and, thanks to Brian Whitfield's 10th first-class hundred, Curran was able to declare and ask Orange Free State to make 336 in 281 minutes plus 20 overs. At 60 for 4, the Free State looked beaten, but Strydom, East and van Heerden, who hit a maiden first-class hundred, all batted well and, in an exciting finish, the visitors needed 13 to win with four wickets standing. Some desperate running and a loss of nerve denied them victory, and Natal came close to snatching the 15 points.

The retirement of Garth le Roux had not only taken Western Province by surprise, but it had seriously weakened their attack which, with Jefferies unable to recapture his best form, looked rather toothless. An inept first-innings batting display further added to their woes against Transvaal, but a third-wicket stand of 242 in the second innings between Lazard and Cullinan, who hit a career best, saved them from defeat.

Castle Bowl

31 December 1988, 1 and 2 January 1989

at Buffalo Park, East London

Boland 238 (W.K. Watson 5 for 47) and 162 (K.J. Bridgens 99)
Border 197 (E.N. Trotman 77) and 209 for 7 (I.L. Howell 71 not out)

Border won by 3 wickets
Border 22 pts, Boland 8 pts

That Boland were a shadow of the team that had done so well the previous season, was confirmed when Border won a low-scoring contest in East London. Needing 204 to win, Border were struggling at 102 for 6, but skipper Ian Howell hit a lusty 71 and finished the match by hitting Omar Henry for six.

4, 5 and 6 January 1989

at Jan Smuts Stadium, Pietermaritzburg

Natal 'B' 256 (C.S. Stirk 87, O. Henry 4 for 57) and 281 for 9 dec (I.B. Hobson 131, R. Marais 6 for 75)
Boland 265 (J.P. Stephenson 57) and 45 for 1

Match drawn
Natal 'B' 9 pts, Boland 9 pts

A rather unimaginative draw was salvaged by the bowling of Marais and the batting of Hobson, both of whom produced career-best performances.

Roy Pienaar. A stalwart of the Transvaal batting, a century in the New Year game with Western Province. (Tom Morris)

Castle Currie Cup

6, 7 and 8 January 1989

at Centurion Park, Verwoerdburg

Western Province 258 (G. Kirsten 81 not out, L. Seeff 74, A.M. Ferreira 4 for 46) and 211 (E.O. Simons 57, G. Grobler 5 for 56)
Northern Transvaal 295 for 6 dec (M.J.R. Rindel 110 not out, G. Grobler 80) and 177 for 9 (E.O. Simons 4 for 42)

Northern Transvaal won by 1 wicket
Northern Transvaal 24 pts, Western Province 7 pts

at Wanderers, Johannesburg

Transvaal 232 (B.M. McMillan 77, J.G. Thomas 5 for 77) and 231 for 6 (H.R. Fotheringham 64, R.F. Pienaar 52)

Neal Radford, 9 for 102 for Transvaal against Eastern Province in early January, but far too much work fell on his shoulders in a Transvaal side that seemed past its best. (David Munden)

Eastern Province 280 (J.G. Thomas 91, K.C. Wessels 60, N.V. Radford 9 for 102)

Match drawn
Transvaal 8 pts, Eastern Province 7 pts

6, 7 and 9 January 1989

at University Oval, Bloemfontein

Natal 290 for 3 dec (R.M. Bentley 124 not out, K.M. Curran 101 not out)
Orange Free State 80 for 0 (W.J. Cronje 53 not out)

Match drawn
No points

Play was possible only on the last day at Bloemfontein. Bentley and Curran added 222 for the fourth wicket, but no result could be fashioned.

Northern Transvaal moved ahead of Transvaal in the northern section of the Currie Cup with a thrilling win over Western Province. Gary Kirsten, younger brother of Peter, hit a career-best 81, but Anton Ferreira restricted Western Province to 295. Sent in as night-watchman, Gerbrand Grobler played the best innings of his career and shared a fifth-wicket stand of 137 with Mike Rindel, which gave Northern Transvaal a first-innings advantage. Grobler's left-arm fast medium pace then played a prominent part in Western Province's dismissal for 211, so that Northern Transvaal were left 38 overs in which to score 175 to win. They were given a good start by Vernon du Preez, but wickets tumbled in the dash for runs, and it was not until the fourth ball of the last over that de Villiers hit Matthews for four to win the match.

Transvaal looked to be on top in the meeting of the giants at Wanderers. With Neal Radford in devastating form after Estwick had claimed Amm, Eastern Province were tottering at 130 for 7. At this point, Greg Thomas hit a furious 91, and took his side to a first-innings lead. Cook was out for 0 when Transvaal batted again, after which Fotheringham and Pienaar added 103 and the game ambled to a draw.

13, 14 and 15 January 1989

at Newlands, Cape Town

Eastern Province 440 for 8 dec (M.W. Rushmere 140, K.C. Wessels 108, A.V. Birrell 105, E.O. Simons 4 for 99)
Western Province 175 (J.G. Thomas 5 for 45) and 213 for 9 (P.N. Kirsten 55)

Match drawn
Eastern Province 9 pts, Western Province 3 pts

13, 14 and 16 January 1989

at University Oval, Bloemfontein

Transvaal 301 for 5 dec (S.J. Cook 133) and 350 for 2 dec (S.J. Cook 180 not out, H.R. Fotheringham 127)
Orange Free State 303 for 9 dec (G.C. Victor 133) and 242 (D.J. Ferrant 64 not out)

Transvaal won by 106 runs
Transvaal 25 pts, Orange Free State 7 pts

14, 15 and 16 January 1989

at Kingsmead, Durban

Natal 242 (J.N. Rhodes 78, P.S. de Villiers 4 for 52) and 255 for 8 dec (B.J. Whitfield 51, P.H. Rayner 50, K.M. Curran 50 not out)
Northern Transvaal 237 (V.F. du Preez 57) and 158 (M.J.R. Rindel 52, R.M. Bentley 4 for 33)

Natal won by 102 runs
Natal 23 pts, Northern Transvaal 8 pts

Adrian Birrell hit a career-best 105 and shared a second-wicket partnership of 218 with Mark Rushmere, who also hit the highest score of his career. Skipper Kepler Wessels followed with a punishing century, and Eastern Province reached a massive 440. The bowling of Greg Thomas, Rod McCurdy and Tim Shaw proved too much for the fragile Western Province batting, and they followed-on 265 in arrears. The home side batted grimly in their second innings, scoring at under two runs an over, but the ninth wicket fell at 197. Rundle and Barnes hung on through the closing overs to save the game for Western Province.

In spite of failing to beat Western Province, Eastern Province looked certain to head the southern section. Natal, with a surprising win in Durban over Northern Transvaal, remained 28 points adrift in second place, and had little hope of catching Eastern Province. A solid team performance took them to victory over Northern Transvaal, and one of the highlights of the match was the medium-pace bowling of Rob Bentley, who took a career-best 4 for 33, which included one spell of 3 for 3.

Northern Transvaal's defeat allowed Transvaal to climb back to the top of the northern section. Jim Cook hit a century in each innings, and, in the second innings, he and Henry Fotheringham put on 290 for the first wicket. Orange Free State had fought well until this point, with Gavin Victor hitting 133 off 151 balls on his debut. He hit 4 sixes and 17 fours. The attack of Estwick, Radford and James proved too much for the Free State at the second attempt, however, and Transvaal ran out easy winners and looked likely to be Eastern Province's opponents in the final.

Castle Bowl

13, 14 and 15 January 1989

at SFW Ground, Stellenbosch

Boland 318 (W.S. Truter 80, H.C. Lindenberg 5 for 95) and 205 (O. Henry 64, J. de Swardt 55)
Border 207 (E.N. Trotman 73, M. Erasmus 5 for 76) and 281 (B.W. Lones 82, O. Henry 4 for 69, W. Radford 4 for 119)

Boland won by 35 runs
Boland 22 pts, Border 7 pts

14, 15 and 16 January 1989

at Centurion Park, Verwoerdburg

Northern Transvaal 'B' 294 (M. Ferreira 100, A. Geringer 57, I.M. Kidson 6 for 53) and 290 (J. Groenewald 64, R.A. Cobb 55, A. Geringer 55, P.L. Symcox 4 for 82)
Griqualand West 387 for 6 dec (A.J. Moles 230 not out) and 170 for 7 (B.M. Arthur 80)

Match drawn
Griqualand West 9 pts, Northern Transvaal 'B' 7 pts

Eastern Province captain Kepler Wessels. A year of triumph. (Adrian Murrell/Allsport)

In the Castle Bowl, in which teams played only those within their own section, Boland gained revenge on Border and registered their first win of the season. It was essentially the result of fine team work, with the bowling of Henry and Erasmus proving decisive.

Andy Moles bettered his career-best score of the previous season when he hit 230 not out as Griqualand West dominated the early stages of the match against Northern Transvaal 'B'. Ferreira hit a maiden first-class hundred on the opening day of the match, but Moles' innings put Griqualand West in total control. Northern Transvaal 'B' fought back doggedly, and Griqualand West were left to make 198 in 21 overs to win the match, a task which was just beyond them.

17, 18 and 19 January 1989

at RJE Burt Oval, Constantia

Border 154 (B.W. Lones 61 not out, J.E. Nolte 6 for 57) and 333 for 9 dec (E.N. Trotman 111, B.M. Osborne 76)
Western Province 'B' 223 and 107 (H.C. Lindenberg 7 for 31)

Border won by 157 runs
Border 22 pts, Western Province 'B' 8 pts

18, 19 and 20 January 1989

at Wanderers, Johannesburg

Transvaal 'B' 193 (H.A. Page 55, P. McLaren 4 for 53) and 158 (P. McLaren 4 for 50)

Griqualand West 271 (A.J. Moles 97, J.E. Morris 57, B.I. Stott 50, H.A. Page 4 for 64) and 85 for 2

Griqualand West won by 8 wickets
Griqualand West 24 pts, Transvaal 'B' 7 pts

Border moved to the top of the southern section table with a splendid win over Western Province 'B' after trailing by 69 runs on the first innings. Their major heroes were Osborne and West Indian Trotman, who shared a third-wicket stand of 184 in the second innings, and Hugo Lindenberg, who took a career-best 7 for 31 with his slow left-arm bowling to win the match.

Those who query the validity of granting first-class status to Bowl matches were given extra ammunition by events at Wanderers. Having taken four wickets in Griqualand West's first innings, Hugh Page was withdrawn from the match so that he could play in Transvaal's Currie Cup side. He was 21 not out at the time, and his place was taken by Kourie, who not only bowled in the second innings, but was allowed to bat in continuation of Page's innings, which tends to make nonsense of the laws of the game. Nothing, however, should detract from Griqualand West's excellent cricket, which deservedly brought them a surprise first victory of the season.

Castle Currie Cup

20, 21 and 22 January 1989

at Centurion Park, Verwoerdburg

Transvaal 269 (R.F. Pienaar 118, S.J. Cook 53, P.S. de Villiers 5 for 81) and 237 for 5 (H.R. Fotheringham 104)
Northern Transvaal 439 (M.J.R. Rindel 97, N.T. Day 92, A.M. Ferreira 71, M. James 4 for 124)

Match drawn
Northern Transvaal 10 pts, Transvaal 7 pts

at Newlands, Cape Town

Western Province 301 for 7 dec (D.J. Cullinan 100 not out, A.P. Kuiper 67) and 196 for 6 (T.N. Lazard 51)
Orange Free State 449 (P.J.R. Steyn 178, A.A. Metcalfe 64, L.J. Wilkinson 53)

Match drawn
Orange Free State 7 pts, Western Province 5 pts

at St George's Park, Port Elizabeth

Natal 391 for 7 dec (B.J. Whitfield 161, K.M. Curran 115, R.M. Bentley 54) and 10 for 0
Eastern Province 382 for 5 dec (M.W. Rushmere 88, K.C. Wessels 85, K.S. McEwan 85)

Match drawn
Natal 4 pts, Eastern Province 3 pts

The penultimate round of matches in the Currie Cup could not produce a winner, but Northern Transvaal had the better of the drawn match with northern section leaders Transvaal and so kept alive their hopes of winning a place in the final. They savaged the Transvaal attack after dismissing the visitors for 269, of which Cook and Pienaar, in consistently good form, had made 105 for the second wicket. Northern's strength came from their late-order batting, with Day and Anton Ferreira adding 133 for the seventh wicket after Rindel had hit 97 at number six.

Batting again, Transvaal took no risks, and, inspired by Fotheringham, they easily saved the day.

There was a run feast at Port Elizabeth, where Whitfield and Curran added 215 in 204 minutes for Natal's fourth wicket. The daunting trio of Rushmere, Wessels and McEwan was able to counter for Eastern Province, and honours were shared, although each side gained only one bowling point.

Cullinan's fine batting form continued for Western Province, but Orange Free State had by far the better of the match at Newlands, thanks mainly to Rudi Steyn's career-best 178. He and Ashley Metcalfe added 131 for the third wicket, Metcalfe batting at number four.

27, 28 and 29 January 1989

at Wanderers, Johannesburg

Western Province 103 (N.V. Radford 5 for 22) and 130 (P.N. Kirsten 61)
Transvaal 224 (S.J. Cook 110, D.B. Rundle 4 for 29, E.O. Simons 4 for 66) and 12 for 1

Transvaal won by 9 wickets
Transvaal 23 pts, Western Province 6 pts

at Kingsmead, Durban

Eastern Province 412 for 5 dec (K.S. McEwan 180 not out, P.G. Amm 158, H.L. Alleyne 4 for 74) and 180 for 7 dec (K.C. Wessels 69)
Natal 278 for 9 dec (B.J. Whitfield 91, A.L. Hobson 4 for 75) and 284 for 9 (B.J. Whitfield 92, K.D. Robinson 61)

Match drawn
Eastern Province 11 pts, Natal 5 pts

at Centurion Park, Verwoerdburg

Orange Free State 160 (P.S. de Villiers 5 for 44) and 169 (T. Bosch 4 for 49)
Northern Transvaal 250 and 82 for 3

Northern Transvaal won by 7 wickets
Northern Transvaal 24 pts, Orange Free State 7 pts

A gem of an innings by Ken McEwan who, in under 3¼ hours, hit 180 off 147 balls with 8 sixes and 23 fours, and a welcome first century of the season from Phillip Amm, took Eastern Province to six batting points and a place in the Currie Cup final. Their opponents, inevitably, but rather fortunately, were to be Transvaal.

On a green-top wicket in Johannesburg, the Transvaal pace attack, spearheaded by Neal Radford, bundled out Western Province for 103. There followed a masterly display of batting by Jim Cook, whose patience and technical strength enabled him to combat the vagaries of the pitch while others faltered. The quality of his innings can be seen from the fact that as soon as he was dismissed Transvaal lost their last seven wickets for 30 runs. Nevertheless, their first-innings lead of 121 was to prove decisive, and they ran out easy winners, claiming 23 points.

Meanwhile, Northern Transvaal were beating Orange Free State. 'Fanie' de Villiers and Tertius Bosch, the medium-pace attack, proved to be too much for the Free State at Centurion Park, but Northern Transvaal struggled in their turn. With Donald, van Zyl and Parsons in menacing form, the home side lost eight wickets before taking a first-innings lead, and it was only a ninth-wicket stand of 89 between de Villiers and Anton Ferreira that gave the innings any substance. Bosch helped de Villiers to see them to a fourth batting point before falling to van Heerden. This brave effort was insufficient, for, although Northern Transvaal eventually won with ease, they finished one point adrift of Transvaal in the northern section.

Castle Currie Cup – Final Tables

Northern Section

	P	W	L	D	Btg Pts	Blg Pts	Pts
Transvaal	7	3	–	4	26	31	92
Northern Transvaal	7	3	1	3	24	32	91
Western Province	7	1	2	4	18	23	56

Southern Section

	P	W	L	D	Btg Pts	Blg Pts	Pts
Eastern Province	7	2	1	4	25	28	83
Natal	7	1	2	4	15	20	50
Orange Free State	7	–	4	3	16	21	37

Castle Bowl

27, 28 and 29 January 1989

at Newlands, Cape Town

Boland 300 (J.P. Stephenson 118, C.C. Lillie 4 for 59) and 140 (I.S. Barnes 5 for 39, L.J. Ryan 4 for 64)
Western Province 'B' 212 (L.J. Koen 55) and 279 for 5 (L.J. Koen 54 not out, O. Henry 4 for 100)

Western Province won by 5 wickets
Western Province 23 pts, Boland 9 pts

at St George's Park, Port Elizabeth

Northern Transvaal 'B' 214 (S. Elworthy 56, C. Roelofse 4 for 46) and 91 (P.A. Rayment 6 for 30)
Eastern Province 'B' 105 (D.W. McCosh 8 for 39) and 193 (P.A. Amm 76, D.W. McCosh 6 for 40)

Northern Transvaal 'B' won by 7 runs
Northern Transvaal 'B' 23 pts, Eastern Province 'B' 6 pts

Boland's last game of the season ended in defeat, and so they lost their chance of again competing in the Bowl Final. They batted well in their first innings, with Essex's John Stephenson hitting a maiden first-class century. They seemed secure with a first-innings lead of 88, but a second-innings collapse against Barnes and Ryan, and a sensible approach to a target of 229 by Western Province 'B', gave success to the home side. The win meant that the southern section had become a straight fight between Western Province 'B' and Border.

A remarkable bowling performance by the newcomer, medium-pace bowler McCosh, took Northern Transvaal 'B' to victory at Port Elizabeth. His eight-wicket haul in the first innings gave his side a 109-run lead, but a best bowling performance by Paul Rayment helped to shoot out Northern Transvaal 'B' for 90 when they batted for a second time. Needing 201 to win, Eastern Province 'B' looked beaten at 161 for 9, but Bryson and Roelofse put

Hugh Page returned to Transvaal after a season of injury. He bowled splendidly for the 'B' side, but he could find no regular place in the Currie Cup side. (Adrian Murrell/ Allsport)

up spirited resistance, to add 32, before Bryson became McCosh's 14th victim of the match.

3, 4 and 5 February 1989

at Buffalo Park, East London

Border 403 for 6 dec (E.N. Trotman 131, B.W. Lones 102, I.L. Howell 53 not out) and 222 (D. Norman 5 for 77, R.K. McGlashan 5 for 89)
Natal 'B' 205 (P.P.H. Trimborn 80 not out) and 456 for 8 dec (A.J. Forde 120, G.M. Walsh 100, I.B. Hobson 99, M.A.W. Bowman 63 not out)

Natal 'B' won by 36 runs
Natal 'B' 21 pts, Border 10 pts

at De Beers Country Club, Kimberley

Griqualand West 217 (J.M. Arthur 51, A.J. Moles 50, R.E. Bryson 7 for 68) and 194 (R.E. Bryson 5 for 65, M.W. Pringle 4 for 62)

Eastern Province 'B' 139 (G.P. van Rensburg 5 for 41) and 159 (C.W. Symcox 6 for 36)

Griqualand West won by 113 runs
Griqualand West 22 pts, Eastern Province 'B' 6 pts

Natal 'B' won a remarkable match at East London to dent Border's chances of reaching the Bowl Final. A third-wicket stand of 217 between Bryan Lones and Emmerson Trotman, enjoying a splendid season, took Border to a massive 403 and five batting points. Natal 'B' were 88 for 6, but recovered to score 205, thanks to a sprightly innings of 80 not out from wicket-keeper Trimborn. They did not, however, save the follow-on, but a second-wicket stand of 151 between Walsh and Hobson in their second innings helped wipe out the arrears. Then Forde and Bowman added 143 for the fifth wicket, and Bowman was able to declare and set Border to make 259 at five runs an over. With Lones and Osborne adding a brisk 96 for the second wicket, they looked capable of reaching their target, but collapse followed, and Natal 'B' became only the seventh side in South African cricket history to win after following-on. By coincidence, the last time this happened in South Africa was when Natal 'B' beat Orange Free State at Bloemfontein 13 years ago.

Griqualand West were given a fine start at Kimberley, with Moles and Arthur putting on 105. They kept their hold on the match in spite of outstanding bowling by Rudi Bryson, whose 7 for 68 in the first innings and 12 for 133 in

Jon Hardy, 80 for Western Province as they won the Nissan Shield. (George Herringshaw)

the match were both career-best performances. Griqualand West's victory was their second in succession and kept them in contention with Transvaal 'B' in the northern section.

Benson and Hedges Trophy

8 February 1989

at Victoria Ground, Kingwilliamstown

Northern Transvaal 181 (M.J.R. Rindel 59)
Impalas 181 for 7 (K.J. Bridgens 55 not out, P.S. de Villiers 4 for 16)

Impalas (2 pts) won by virtue of having lost fewer wickets with scores level

The Benson and Hedges Trophy reawoke with an exciting win for Impalas off the last ball of the match. This win placed Impalas in a good position to qualify for the semi-finals.

Nissan Shield

Semi-Finals – First Leg

11 February 1989

at Newlands, Cape Town

Western Province 221 for 5 (P.N. Kirsten 108)
Eastern Province 131 for 7

Western Province won by 90 runs

at UOFS Ground, Bloemfontein

Orange Free State 162 for 3 (A.A. Metcalfe 75 not out)
v. Transvaal

Match abandoned

After a lean season in which he had appeared to lose confidence, Peter Kirsten played a splendid innings to take Western Province to victory in the first leg of their semi-final with Eastern Province, whose batsmen failed to live up to their reputation on this occasion. The game at Bloemfontein was abandoned, so that the second leg at Johannesburg became a straightforward cup tie.

Benson and Hedges Trophy

16 February 1989

at Wanderers, Johannesburg

Transvaal 174 for 9 (K.J. Rule 67)
Impalas 160

Transvaal (2 pts) won by 14 runs

A good all-round performance by Clive Rice, who hit 49 and took three wickets, helped to inflict a first defeat on Impalas. Transvaal's win assured them of a place in the semi-finals.

Nissan Shield

Semi-Finals – Second Leg

18 February 1989

at St George's Park, Port Elizabeth

Western Province 248 for 6 (L. Seeff 88, D.J. Cullinan 79)
Eastern Province 170 (M.W. Rushmere 73)

Western Province won by 78 runs

at Wanderers, Johannesburg

Transvaal 247 for 4 (H.R. Fotheringham 88)
Orange Free State 175

Transvaal won by 72 runs

Finding their form late in the season, Western Province gave another exhilarating batting display, in which they crushed Eastern Province and entered the Nissan Shield final. As expected, their opponents were to be Transvaal, who had been in the final six times in the previous seven years and had won the Shield four times in succession between 1983 and 1986.

Castle Bowl

17, 18 and 19 February 1989

at De Beers Country Club, Kimberley

Northern Transvaal 'B' 114 (P.J. Grobler 52, P.McLaren 5 for 28) and 213 (M. Ferreira 61, B.I. Stott 4 for 44)
Griqualand West 114 (K.T. Medlycott 4 for 25) and 214 for 9 (K.T. Medlycott 6 for 83)

Griqualand West won by 1 wicket
Griqualand West 21 pts, Northern Transvaal 'B' 6 pts

at Uitenhage

Transvaal 'B' 181 (B. McBride 53, B.E. van der Vyver 5 for 33) and 188 for 7
Eastern Province 'B' 113 (K.J. Kerr 4 for 35) and 157 (K.J. Kerr 4 for 60)

Transvaal 'B' won by 99 runs
Transvaal 'B' 22 pts, Eastern Province 'B' 6 pts

at Buffalo Park, East London

Western Province 'B' 312 (P.W. Martin 119, J.B. Commins 78) and 111 (H.C. Lindenberg 6 for 34)
Border 254 for 5 dec (E.N. Trotman 106 not out, I.L. Howell 101 not out) and 170 for 3 (E.N. Trotman 91)

Border won by 7 wickets
Border 22 pts, Western Province 'B' 5 pts

Griqualand West gained a fine win over Northern Transvaal 'B' in an exciting game at Kimberley, but it was not enough to give them a place in the Bowl Final. In a match in which bowlers were always on top, and in which Keith Medlycott in only his second game of the season excelled, Griqualand West, needing 214 to win, had scored 204 when their ninth wicket fell. Gert van Rensburg was their hero. He had come in at 151 for 8, added 53 with Symcox, and then, with Kidson, scored the last 13 needed for victory.

Griqualand West had taken maximum bowling points

from all their matches, but only 15 batting points left them four adrift of Transvaal 'B', who beat Eastern Province 'B' with ease.

In the southern section, Border won a splendid victory over Western Province 'B' to guarantee themselves a place in the final as the opponents of Transvaal 'B'. Martin and Commins had taken the visitors to a commendable score, and Border were 68 for 5 when skipper Howell joined Emmerson Trotman. The West Indian's run of mighty form continued as he hit his third century of the season. He and Ian Howell put on 186 before Howell declared. Western Province 'B' were then bowled out cheaply, with Hugo Lindenberg producing another excellent bowling performance. Needing to score at nearly six an over to win, Border were led to victory by another astonishing innings from Trotman, who scored 91 out of a third-wicket partnership of 126 with Lones.

21, 22 and 23 February 1989

at Kingsmead, Durban

Western Province 'B' 427 for 6 dec (G. Kirsten 159, J.B. Commins 138)
Natal 'B' 179 (A.C. Hudson 61, M.B. Minnaar 5 for 57) and 94 for 5

Match drawn
Western Province 'B' 10 pts, Natal 'B' 4 pts

Needing seven batting points, that is 400 runs in 85 overs, maximum bowling points and a victory to overtake Border, Western Province 'B' made a brave but unsuccessful effort in the final Bowl match. Gary Kirsten and John Commins shared a fourth-wicket stand of 223, and both men hit the highest scores of their careers.

Castle Bowl – Final Tables

Northern Section

	P	W	L	D	Btg Pts	Blg Pts	Pts
Transvaal 'B'	6	3	1	2	19	30	94
Griqualand West	6	3	–	3	15	30	90
Eastern Province 'B'	6	1	3	2	15	30	60
Northern Transvaal 'B'	6	1	4	1	16	23	54

Southern Section

	P	W	L	D	Btg Pts	Blg Pts	Pts
Border	6	3	2	1	18	27	90
Western Province 'B'	6	2	2	2	19	25	74
Boland	6	1	3	2	18	28	61
Natal 'B'	6	1	–	5	17	23	55

Benson and Hedges Trophy

22 February 1989

at Victoria Ground, Kingwilliamstown

Impalas 219 for 8 (B.W. Lones 97)
Eastern Province 197 (K.S. McEwan 82)

Impalas (2 pts) won by 22 runs

23 February 1989

at Harmony Ground, Virginia

Natal 136
Orange Free State 141 for 6

Orange Free State (2 pts) won by 4 wickets

1 March 1989

at Newlands, Cape Town

Western Province 178 (A.P. Kuiper 59, P.N. Kirsten 58, P. McLaren 4 for 21)
Impalas 81

Western Province (2 pts) won by 97 runs

When Impalas beat Eastern Province at the Victoria Ground the four semi-finalists for the Benson and Hedges Trophy were decided, for the last two matches had the effect only of determining venues.

Benson and Hedges Trophy – Final Table					
	P	*W*	*L*	*Ab*	*Pts*
Orange Free State	6	4	1	1	9
Transvaal	6	4	2	–	8
Western Province	6	4	2	–	8
Impalas	6	3	2	1	7
Natal	6	2	4	–	4
Eastern Province	6	2	4	–	4
Northern Transvaal	6	1	5	–	2

Nissan Shield Final
WESTERN PROVINCE v. TRANSVAAL

The Nissan Shield Final was played over two legs in 1988–9, and Western Province, having struggled for most of the season and having been much weakened by the retirement of Garth le Roux, saved their best until the last.

Transvaal got off to a good start in the first match at Newlands, with Cook and Fotheringham putting on 71 for the first wicket in a match which was reduced to 51 overs. Off-break bowler Rundle dismissed them both and bowled with great economy, and, although several batsmen promised a substantial innings, all were cut down just as they looked set. Western Province, too, started well, but were in some trouble when Hardy and Seeff were run out in quick succession. Daryll Cullinan came in to play just the innings that was needed. He and Kirsten added 37, but three wickets fell for 27 runs, and the game was very much in the balance. Cullinan then found a good partner in Simons, and they took Western Province to victory with two balls to spare.

In the second leg at Wanderers, Hardy and Kirsten put on 135 for the second wicket to lay the basis of a commanding score. Kuiper hit well towards the end of the 55 overs, and Western Province reached an impressive 241. Despite Cook's fine effort, Transvaal never quite seemed in touch until Clive Rice began to bat with authority. Unfortunately for Transvaal, he could find no adequate support, and Simons returned to bowl a restricting spell

alongside the admirable Kuiper, whose bowling and leadership did much to clinch the trophy for Western Province.

Castle Bowl Final
BORDER v. TRANSVAAL 'B'

Throughout the season Border had shown great spirit and tenacity in their cricket, and never were these qualities shown to better advantage than in the Bowl Final. Transvaal 'B' fielded a strong side with Vorster, Roberts, Page and Kerr all players of Currie Cup experience, and all, in the opinion of many, wrongly omitted from the 'A' side. Vorster and Roberts in particular had suffered the humiliation of being left out of the Currie Cup side after a lean patch, to be replaced by older men.

It was Hugh Page who upset Border on the opening day. He quickly accounted for Lones, and seemed to capture a wicket every time Transvaal 'B' needed it most. Wilmot promised a durable innings, but he was left without partners as the last seven Border wickets fell for 69.

Transvaal 'B' started badly, losing Whyte, Botha and Cresswell with only 42 scored. When Jacobs was seventh out they still held only a slender lead, but McBride found an admirable partner in Kerr, and they added 77. Hooper went quickly, but James helped McBride to put on 35 for the last wicket, and enabled the wicket-keeper to reach a maiden first-class century. The 30-year-old Bruce McBride had made his first-class debut nine years earlier and had assisted Glamorgan Second Eleven in 1980.

With a first-innings lead of 171, Transvaal 'B' seemed in an impregnable position, and Border lost five wickets in clearing off the arrears. For skipper Ian Howell the cause was not lost, however, and the left-hander had ample support from Boonzaaier and the later order so that Transvaal 'B' were left with the task of scoring 146 to win.

With Cresswell in top form, they seemed to be strolling to victory at 96 for 1. The Border attack had variety, however, and was intelligently used by Howell. Slow left-arm spinner Hugo Lindenberg, who had enjoyed an excellent season, bowled with relentless accuracy, and medium pacers Watson and Fourie bowled with great energy. Transvaal 'B' could find no one after Cresswell who could keep his head and bat with the necessary good sense. Eight wickets fell for 28 runs, and Border claimed an historic victory and the Castle Bowl.

Promotion/Relegation Play-Off
ORANGE FREE STATE v. BORDER

Having finished with the smallest number of points in the Currie Cup, Orange Free State had to play off with Border for the right to remain in the premier competition. They entered the match with confidence, for they had found their form late in the season, while Border had only just emerged from their great struggle in the Bowl Final.

Border had a quick success, but Steyn and Strydom added 134 for the second wicket, and the Free State's innings was further boosted by a fourth-wicket stand of 104 between English county players, Metcalfe and

NISSAN SHIELD FINAL – FIRST LEG – WESTERN PROVINCE v. TRANSVAAL
25 February 1989 at Newlands, Cape Town

TRANSVAAL

S.J. Cook	c Jefferies, b Rundle	28
H.R. Fotheringham	c Simons, b Rundle	58
R.F. Pienaar	b Jefferies	23
K.J. Rule	c Simons, b Kuiper	28
C.E.B. Rice†	c and b Simons	23
M.S. Venter	c Seeff, b Simons	31
G.E. McMillan	not out	0
R.V. Jennings*	not out	8
N.V. Radford		
R.O. Estwick		
R.P. Snell		
Extras		17
(51 overs)	(for 6 wkts)	216

WESTERN PROVINCE

J.J.E. Hardy	run out	19
L. Seeff	run out	49
P.N. Kirsten	c Jennings, b Estwick	19
D.J. Cullinan	not out	75
A.P. Kuiper†	c Jennings, b McMillan	0
L.F. Bleekers*	b Rice	14
J.H. du Plessis	b McMillan	3
E.O. Simons	not out	24
D.B. Rundle		
S.T. Jefferies		
J.E. Nolte		
Extras		14
(50.4 overs)	(for 6 wkts)	217

	O	M	R	W
Simons	11	1	40	2
Nolte	10	1	45	–
Jefferies	10	–	38	1
Kuiper	8	1	38	1
Rundle	10	2	31	2
Kirsten	2	–	16	–

	O	M	R	W
Radford	9.4	2	25	–
Estwick	10	1	44	1
Rice	10	2	43	1
Snell	7	–	31	–
McMillan	11	1	31	2
Pienaar	3	–	24	–

FALL OF WICKETS
1–71, 2–98, 3–140, 4–155, 5–208

FALL OF WICKETS
1–67, 2–79, 3–116, 4–121, 5–143

Western Province won by 4 wickets

NISSAN SHIELD FINAL – SECOND LEG – TRANSVAAL v. WESTERN PROVINCE
4 March 1989 at Wanderers, Johannesburg

WESTERN PROVINCE

J.J.E. Hardy	b Estwick	80
L. Seeff	c Fotheringham, b B.M. McMillan	10
P.N. Kirsten	c Venter, b Estwick	73
D.J. Cullinan	c Venter, b Estwick	3
A.P. Kuiper†	not out	42
J.B. Commins	c Jennings, b Rice	2
E.O. Simons	not out	6
L.F. Bleekers*		
S.T. Jefferies		
D.B. Rundle		
J.E. Nolte		
Extras		25
(55 overs)	(for 5 wkts)	241

TRANSVAAL

S.J. Cook	c Bleekers, b Kuiper	79
H.R. Fotheringham	lbw, b Kuiper	21
R.F. Pienaar	run out	16
K.J. Rule	c Bleekers, b Simons	9
C.E.B. Rice†	b Simons	53
B.M. McMillan	b Kuiper	18
M.S. Venter	b Simons	14
G.E. McMillan	b Kuiper	1
R.V. Jennings*	c Jefferies, b Kuiper	1
R.O. Estwick	not out	1
N.V. Radford	c Kuiper, b Simons	0
Extras		22
(55 overs)		235

	O	M	R	W
Radford	11	5	14	–
Estwick	11	–	49	3
B.M. McMillan	11	2	47	1
G.E. McMillan	7	–	30	–
Rice	11	–	71	1
Pienaar	4	–	16	–

	O	M	R	W
Simons	11	–	44	4
Nolte	11	–	50	–
Jefferies	11	1	44	–
Kuiper	11	2	47	5
Rundle	11	1	35	–

FALL OF WICKETS
1–31, 2–166, 3–177, 4–210, 5–213

FALL OF WICKETS
1–62, 2–103, 3–128, 4–138, 5–185, 6–218, 7–219, 8–221, 9–235

Western Province won by 6 runs

Western Province won the Shield by 2 – 0

CASTLE BOWL FINAL – BORDER v. TRANSVAAL 'B'
3, 4, 5 and 6 March 1989 at Buffalo Park, East London

BORDER

	FIRST INNINGS		SECOND INNINGS	
B.W. Lones	c Vorster, b Page	8	c Whyte, b Hooper	10
R. Moult	c McBride, b Jacobs	34	c Roberts, b Hooper	60
B.M. Osborne	b Page	33	b Jacobs	26
E.N. Trotman*	c Cresswell, b Jacobs	15	c Whyte, b Hooper	8
A.L. Wilmot	not out	36	c Jacobs, b James	11
N.R. Boonzaaier	b Page	0	c and b James	50
I.L. Howell†	c Roberts, b Hooper	2	c McBride, b Page	65
F.D. Toppin	c McBride, b Jacobs	15	b Page	34
W.K. Watson	lbw, b Page	1	not out	32
B.C. Fourie	run out	0	c Cresswell, b Jacobs	2
H.C. Lindenberg	c McBride, b Hooper	9	b Jacobs	0
Extras	b 1, lb 7, w 2	10	b 3, lb 12, nb 3	18
		163		316

TRANSVAAL 'B'

	FIRST INNINGS		SECOND INNINGS	
V.G. Cresswell	lbw, b Watson	10	b Fourie	70
B. Whyte	c Wilmot, b Lindenberg	7	c Boonzaaier, b Lindenberg	13
P.J. Botha	c Trotman, b Toppin	18	run out	13
L.P. Vorster†	c Trotman, b Toppin	48	b Boonzaaier	5
B. Roberts	c Moult, b Fourie	37	(11) c Trotman, b Lindenberg	0
B. McBride*	c Boonzaaier, b Fourie	101	(5) c Osborne, b Lindenberg	17
H.A. Page	c Trotman, b Fourie	26	(6) c Trotman, b Fourie	0
S. Jacobs	c Lones, b Howell	7	(7) run out	5
K.J. Kerr	c Trotman, b Watson	45	(8) lbw, b Watson	0
J.J. Hooper	c Lindenberg, b Watson	4	(10) not out	0
M. James	not out	17	(9) c Trotman, b Watson	4
Extras	b 2, lb 10, nb 2	14	lb 2	2
		334		129

	O	M	R	W	O	M	R	W
Page	19	6	41	4	27	9	67	2
Hooper	13.1	–	49	2	37	6	106	3
Jacobs	15	3	63	3	13.3	4	29	3
James	1	–	2	–	29	14	56	2
Kerr					14	4	34	–
Botha					3	–	9	–

	O	M	R	W	O	M	R	W
Watson	34	7	68	3	10	2	20	2
Fourie	19.3	3	51	3	7	1	11	2
Lindenberg	26	9	84	1	24.1	11	44	3
Toppin	29	4	86	2	5	1	15	–
Howell	21	10	22	1	5	–	21	–
Osborne	6	2	11	–				
Boonzaaier					8	2	16	1

FALL OF WICKETS
1–23, 2–80, 3–80, 4–94, 5–97, 6–117, 7–118, 8–119, 9–121
1–37, 2–79, 3–95, 4–118, 5–124, 6–225, 7–251, 8–296, 9–316

FALL OF WICKETS
1–16, 2–26, 3–42, 4–110, 5–132, 6–181, 7–204, 8–281, 9–299
1–62, 2–96, 3–101, 4–107, 5–107, 6–118, 7–125, 8–129, 9–129

Umpires: S.F. Marais & R. Brooks

Border won by 16 runs

Moores, the Sussex wicket-keeper, who was making his one appearance of the season.

Border struck back and captured five wickets while only 30 runs were scored, but van Zyl and Gordon Parsons dealt them a crushing blow with a violent stand of 78 for the ninth wicket, to take Orange Free State to a daunting 386.

This time there was to be no recovery by Border, who struggled against the pace of van Zyl and Donald and only narrowly avoided an innings defeat; so Orange Free State preserved their place in the Currie Cup.

Castle Currie Cup Final
EASTERN PROVINCE v. TRANSVAAL

The stranglehold that Transvaal, winners of the Currie Cup five times in the previous six years, had held on South African cricket was finally broken by Eastern Province.

For much of the season it had seemed that Clive Rice no longer had at his disposal the ammunition that he had had in the past. For various reasons, Clarke, Kallicharran,

M.D. Haysman, the Australian batsman who made a few appearances for Leicestershire, left his own country and played for Northern Transvaal. (George Herringshaw)

PROMOTION/RELEGATION PLAY-OFF – ORANGE FREE STATE v. BORDER

10, 11, 12 and 14 March 1989 at UOFS Ground, Bloemfontein

ORANGE FREE STATE

	FIRST INNINGS		SECOND INNINGS	
P.J.R. Steyn	c Osborne, b Lindenberg	70		
W.J. Cronje	c Boonzaaier, b Watson	6	(1) not out	1
J.J. Strydom†	c Watson, b Lindenberg	61		
A.A. Metcalfe	c Boonzaaier, b Watson	66		
P. Moores*	c and b Toppin	50		
L.J. Wilkinson	b Watson	1		
C.J. van Heerden	c Trotman, b Toppin	8		
D.J. Ferrant	c Trotman, b Toppin	4		
C.J.P.G. van Zyl	not out	54		
G.J. Parsons	c Osborne, b Howell	27	(2) not out	4
A.A. Donald	run out	4		
Extras	b 17, lb 7, w 4, nb 7	35	b 1	1
		386	(for no wkt)	6

BORDER

	FIRST INNINGS		SECOND INNINGS	
B.W. Lones	c Wilkinson, b van Zyl	7	c Moores, b van Zyl	47
R. Moult	c Moores, b Donald	4	c Moores, b Donald	0
B.M. Osborne	lbw, b Parsons	13	b Donald	0
E.N. Trotman*	b van Heerden	16	c van Heerden, b Donald	15
A.L. Wilmot	c Metcalfe, b van Zyl	20	b Ferrant	20
N.R. Boonzaaier	c Moores, b van Heerden	20	b Ferrant	49
I.L. Howell†	not out	22	c Strydom, b van Zyl	22
F.D. Toppin	c sub, b Donald	9	b van Heerden	4
W.K. Watson	lbw, b van Zyl	26	c Moores, b Donald	35
A.W. Schoeman	b van Zyl	0	b Donald	17
H.C. Lindenberg	lbw, b van Zyl	4	not out	1
Extras	b 4, lb 2, nb 11	17	b 4, lb 2, w 4, nb 9	19
		158		229

	O	M	R	W	O	M	R	W
Watson	26	5	63	2				
Toppin	30	3	80	4				
Lindenberg	51	14	121	2				
Schoeman	12	1	40	–				
Howell	16	7	34	1				
Boonzaaier	4	–	24	–				
Wilmot					0.3	–	5	–

	O	M	R	W	O	M	R	W
Donald	15	3	49	2	13	1	46	5
van Zyl	16.3	3	51	5	14	1	44	2
Parsons	5	2	22	1	8	2	29	–
van Heerden	8	2	16	2	11	1	46	1
Ferrant	5	2	14	–	12	1	54	2
Wilkinson					5	2	4	–

FALL OF WICKETS
1–9, 2–143, 3–158, 4–262, 5–272, 6–273, 7–289, 8–292, 9–370

FALL OF WICKETS
1–5, 2–29, 3–29, 4–60, 5–72, 6–101, 7–118, 8–151, 9–151
1–2, 2–2, 3–24, 4–86, 5–99, 6–135, 7–141, 8–210, 9–219

Umpires: C.J. Mitchley & S.B. Lambson

Orange Free State won by 10 wickets

Pollock, McKenzie and Kourie had moved on or retired. Page, following injury, had lost some of his fire and had spent most of the season in the 'B' side, as had Kerr. Both Vorster and Roberts, so promising a year earlier, had been dropped to the 'B' side after a loss of form, and had been replaced by players who were, in the opinion of many, not of the same quality. There was an ageing look about the Transvaal side, and the attack relied heavily on Neal Radford, who had benefited from the green-top wickets at Wanderers.

Eastern Province, on the other hand, had shown a tremendous resurgence in 1987–8 under the leadership of Kepler Wessels, and the return home of Ken McEwan after his years in the west had been a great boost. The enthusiasm for cricket in the province reached a climax in March 1989, when the Currie Cup was won for the first time.

Things had not gone well for Eastern Province at the start of the Currie Cup final, as Rushmere and Wessels, both prolific scorers in the earlier part of the season, were dismissed with only 42 scored. There then followed one of the most glorious displays of batting seen in South Africa for many years as Phil Amm and Ken McEwan added 337 in 437 minutes. This constituted a record for the third wicket in the Currie Cup.

McEwan's innings, his highest in South Africa, contained a six and 25 fours, while Amm went on to reach the first double century of his career. He batted for 687 minutes and hit 2 sixes and 18 fours. Michau plundered runs later, and Eastern Province placed themselves in an impregnable position by reaching 561.

Fotheringham, Venter and Cook all went quickly, and Transvaal never effectively recovered. There was resistance from Rice and Pienaar, and, when forced to follow-on, inevitably it was Rice who raised hopes that Transvaal might save the game. The lively and eager Eastern Province pace attack was not to be denied, however, and the home side swept to their first Currie Cup triumph in style as the slow left-arm bowling of Tim Shaw reduced Transvaal to impotence.

Benson and Hedges Trophy

Semi-Finals – First Leg

7 March 1989

at Wanderers, Johannesburg

Transvaal 134 (E.O. Simons 4 for 21)
Western Province 137 for 7 (L. Seeff 71)

Western Province won by 3 wickets

CASTLE CURRIE CUP FINAL – EASTERN PROVINCE v. TRANSVAAL
10, 11, 12, 13 and 14 March 1989 at St George's Park, Port Elizabeth

EASTERN PROVINCE

	FIRST INNINGS	
M.W. Rushmere	lbw, b Radford	3
P.G. Amm	st Jennings,	
	b Eksteen	214
K.C. Wessels†	c Jennings, b James	11
K.S. McEwan	c Venter,	
	b McMillan	191
D.J. Callaghan	b Eksteen	10
M. Michau	c Eksteen,	
	b McMillan	79
D.J. Richardson*	lbw, b Radford	12
T.G. Shaw	c Jennings,	
	b McMillan	10
J.G. Thomas	c Jennings, b Radford	0
A.L. Hobson	not out	7
R.J. McCurdy	c Venter, b Radford	10
Extras	b 5, lb 9	14
		——
		561

TRANSVAAL

	FIRST INNINGS		SECOND INNINGS	
S.J. Cook	lbw, b Hobson	29	b Shaw	28
H.R. Fotheringham	c Richardson,		c and b McCurdy	33
	b Thomas	15		
M.S. Venter	lbw, b Thomas	0	lbw, b Thomas	8
R.F. Pienaar	b Shaw	50	c Michau,	
			b McCurdy	30
C.E.B. Rice†	c Michau, b Shaw	33	c Michau, b Hobson	75
K.J. Rule	lbw, b McCurdy	1	c Richardson,	
			b McCurdy	0
B.M. McMillan	b Shaw	16	c Shaw, b Thomas	32
R.V. Jennings*	not out	33	c Richardson, b Shaw	27
C.E. Eksteen	c Richardson,		lbw, b Shaw	0
	b McCurdy	12		
N.V. Radford	c Thomas, b Hobson	2	b Thomas	6
M. James	c Callaghan, b Hobson	2	not out	0
Extras	lb 5, w 3, nb 2	10	b 4, lb 4, w 4, nb 4	16
		——		——
		203		255

	O	M	R	W
Radford	35.2	12	77	4
Rice	25	7	50	–
McMillan	31	4	95	3
James	48	12	135	1
Eksteen	42	7	155	2
Fotheringham	1	–	3	–
Pienaar	9	1	32	–

	O	M	R	W	O	M	R	W
Thomas	22	6	49	2	26	6	68	3
McCurdy	22	6	30	2	28	9	55	3
Shaw	46	28	38	3	46	31	32	2
Hobson	33.3	9	65	3	35	10	81	1
Callaghan	7	2	16	–	5	1	7	–
Michau					4	2	4	–

FALL OF WICKETS
1–12, 2–42, 3–379, 4–397, 5–490, 6–525, 7–542, 8–542, 9–546

FALL OF WICKETS
1–27, 2–31, 3–52, 4–120, 5–123, 6–135, 7–158, 8–185, 9–201
1–35, 2–58, 3–85, 4–113, 5–113, 6–174, 7–249, 8–249, 9–249

Umpires: K.E. Liebenberg & J.W. Peacock

Eastern Province won by 103 runs

---

at Kingwilliamstown

Orange Free State 174 for 9
Impalas 163

Orange Free State won by 11 runs

Semi-Finals – Second Leg

16 March 1989

at Newlands, Cape Town

Western Province 195 for 5 (P.N. Kirsten 86)
Transvaal 163 (S.J. Cook 75)

Western Province won by 32 runs

17 March 1989

at Harmony Ground, Virginia

Impalas 210 for 9 (E.N. Trotman 72)
Orange Free State 211 for 7 (W.J. Cronje 105 not out)

Orange Free State won by 3 wickets

Western Province's two wins over Transvaal not only put them in the final of the Benson and Hedges Trophy, but meant that Transvaal would finish the season without a trophy of any kind, the first time that this had happened since 1977–8.

Orange Free State qualified to meet Western Province in the final, and in the second match owed much to Wessel Cronje, who hit 105 off 141 balls with 2 sixes and 6 fours.

Benson and Hedges Trophy

Final

22 March 1989

at Newlands, Cape Town

Orange Free State 213 for 8 (W.J. Cronje 73, A.A. Metcalfe 71)
Western Province 152 (P.N. Kirsten 72, A.A. Donald 4 for 18)

Orange Free State won by 61 runs

Cronje and Metcalfe put on 115 for the Free State's second wicket, and the Yorkshireman hit 71 off 85 balls to put his

Allan Donald – devastating bowling against Border in the promotion/relegation battle helped to keep Orange Free State in the Currie Cup. (Ken Kelly)

side in a strong position. Allan Donald proved too much for the Western Province, and so Orange Free State, after a disappointing season in which they had had to fight for their Currie Cup status, took the last of South Africa's four trophies. As each trophy had been won by a different side, it suggested a healthy competitive state in the Republic's cricket.

First-Class Averages

BATTING

	M	Inns	NOs	Runs	HS	Av	100s	50s
K.S. McEwan	9	13	2	885	191	80.45	3	4
J.H. du Plessis	5	8	5	214	96*	71.33		1
B.J. Whitfield	6	10	1	609	161	67.66	2	4
M.J.R. Rindel	7	13	2	711	110*	64.33	2	5
A.J. Moles	6	11	1	627	230*	62.70	1	3
C.S. Stirk	2	4	1	187	95*	62.33		2
K.C. Wessels	10	15	1	806	146	57.57	2	5
S.J. Cook	8	14	1	721	180*	55.46	3	2
E.N. Trotman	9	17	1	871	131	54.43	3	5
J.B. Commins	5	8		428	138	53.50	1	4
P.G. Amm	10	16	1	755	214	50.33	3	
I.B. Hobson	6	12	1	537	131	48.81	2	1
P.S. de Villiers	7	9	6	143	46*	47.66		
B.W. Lones	9	17	2	685	102	45.66	1	4
A.J. Forde	2	4		179	120	44.75		1
I.L. Howell	9	16	5	481	101*	43.72	1	3
R.F. Pienaar	8	15	1	610	118	43.57	2	3
B.M. McMillan	8	12	4	337	77	42.12		2
K.M. Curran	7	12	2	421	115	42.10	2	1
T.N. Lazard	7	14	2	499	122*	41.58	1	3
P.J.R. Steyn	8	13	2	453	178	41.18	1	2
M.W. Rushmere	10	16	1	609	140	40.60	2	2
M.B. Billson	6	10	2	323	106	40.37	1	1
R.M. Bentley	4	6	1	201	124*	40.20	1	1
A.M. Ferreira	9	16	4	475	71*	39.58		3
H.R. Fotheringham	8	14		547	127	39.07	2	1
C.E.B. Rice	8	13	3	376	75	37.00		2
H.A. Page	9	12	5	263	55	37.57		1
J.P. Stephenson	7	13	1	442	118	36.83	1	3
M. Ferreira	6	12		442	100	36.83	1	3
G.C. Victor	3	5		184	133	36.80	1	
D.J. Cullinan	7	14	2	437	140	36.41	2	1
M. Yachad	7	13	1	435	121*	36.25	1	2
L.F. Bleekers	4	7	1	217	71*	36.16		2
K.J. Rule	7	12	1	378	112*	34.36	1	2
A.P. Kuiper	7	13	2	377	80*	34.27		3
G. Kirsten	11	17	2	512	159	34.13	1	2
P.W. Martin	5	8		271	119	33.87	1	
P.J. Botha	6	11	2	300	106	33.33	2	
A.R. Wormington	7	10	3	232	53	33.14		1
K.D. Robinson	8	14		464	65	33.14		2
D.J. Richardson	10	13	4	298	75	33.11		1
K.J. Bridgens	7	14	1	428	99	32.92		2
E.L.R. Stewart	3	6	1	164	78	32.80		1
V.G. Cresswell	3	6	1	163	70	32.60		1
B.M. Osborne	9	17		550	145	32.35	1	2
J.N. Rhodes	7	11	1	321	108	32.10	1	1
P.N. Kirsten	7	14		442	66	31.57		4
J.E. Morris	7	13	1	336	73	30.50		3
V.F. du Preez	9	17	1	487	61	30.43		3
L. Seeff	7	14		425	82	30.35		3
G.M. Walsh	2	4		121	100	30.25	1	
B. McBride	6	9		270	101	30.00	1	1
A. Geringer	5	10		295	62	29.50		3
P.P.H. Trimborn	3	5	1	116	80*	29.00		1
L.J. Koen	6	10	1	261	55	29.00		2
D.J. Callaghan	10	14	1	372	78	28.61		3
S. Elworthy	3	6		169	56	28.16		1
O. Henry	7	13	2	309	64	28.09		1
J.J. Strydom	9	14	2	334	67	27.83		3
J.D. du Toit	6	11		304	148	27.63	1	1

	M	Inns	NOs	Runs	HS	Av	100s	50s
N.E. Wright	5	10	1	244	70	27.11		2
D.J. Ferrant	7	10	3	188	64*	26.85		1
R. Marais	6	11	1	267	53	26.70		1
M. Michau	7	11		290	79	26.36		2
J.M. Arthur	7	13	1	311	80	25.91		3
P.J. Grobler	2	4		102	52	25.50		1
W.K. Watson	8	13	5	204	35	25.50		
A. van N. Snyman	5	8	1	175	63	25.00		1
C.J. van Heerden	5	9		224	104	24.88	1	1
G.E. McMillan	6	9	2	171	41	24.42		
C.J.P.G. van Zyl	8	12	3	216	54*	24.00		1
M.S. Venter	7	14	1	312	108	24.00	1	
R.J. Varner	5	7	1	144	36	24.00		
A.A. Metcalfe	8	12		282	66	23.50		2
A.C. Hudson	5	10		235	61	23.50		1
J.G. Thomas	8	8	1	163	91	23.28		1
P.I. Barclay	4	6	1	116	76	23.20		1
B.E. van der Vyver	4	7	1	139	58	23.16		1
D.H. Howell	6	11	1	225	61	22.50		2
P.A. Amm	6	10		224	81	22.40		2
T.G. Shaw	10	10	4	131	35*	21.83		
E.O. Simons	7	10	1	196	57	21.77		1
P.H. Rayner	7	12		259	50	21.58		1
B.I. Stott	5	10		210	75	21.00		2
L.J. Wilkinson	8	12		252	53	21.00		1
A.L. Hobson	8	9	4	105	24	21.00		
M.A. Fletcher	5	8	1	146	55	20.85		1
B. Roberts	8	14	1	269	37	20.69		
R.K. Illingworth	9	11	2	186	42	20.66		
C.M. Lister-James	5	9	1	165	33	20.62		
W.S. Truter	6	11	1	205	80	20.50		1
A.L. Wilmot	9	17	1	321	39	20.06		
R.A. Cobb	4	8		159	55	19.87		1
C.L. Inglis	4	6		117	40	19.50		
P. McLaren	6	10	2	156	51	19.50		1
M.D. Haysman	7	13	1	233	78*	19.41		1
N.R. Boonzaaier	9	17	1	302	54	18.87		2
A.V. Birrell	10	14		262	105	18.71	1	1
R.J. East	7	11	1	180	68	18.00		1
R.E.W. Mawhinney	6	10	1	161	61	17.88		1
M.A.W. Bowman	6	12	2	178	63*	17.80		2
L.J. Barnard	7	13		230	79	17.69		2
F.D. Toppin	8	14	1	226	49	17.38		
D.B. Rundle	7	10	3	121	39	17.28		
A.L. de Swardt	7	14		240	60	17.14		2
L.M. Fuhri	4	8		136	45	17.00		
J. Groenewald	6	12	1	186	64	16.90		2
K.J. Kerr	7	10	2	121	45	15.12		
N.T. Day	7	12		179	92	14.91		1
W.J. Cronje	8	14	2	177	53*	14.75		1
R.V. Jennings	8	10	3	103	33*	14.71		
M.W. Pringle	10	13	2	155	45	14.09		
L.P. Vorster	8	15	1	193	48	13.78		
I. Human	7	11	2	120	28	13.33		
A. da Costa	5	10		133	29	13.30		
M.P. Stonier	5	8		104	34	13.00		
G.J. Parsons	8	13	1	150	44	12.50		
G. Grobler	9	14		167	80	11.92		1
W.F. Morris	7	10	1	105	27	11.66		

(Qualification – 100 runs, average 10.00)
(Played in one match – H. Donachie 126 and 1)

Omar Henry – another fine all-round season. (Ken Kelly)

Andy Moles hit the highest score of his career during the South African season, but he could not find consistent form on his return to Warwickshire. (Ken Kelly)

First-Class Averages continued

BOWLING

	Overs	Mds	Runs	Wkts	Av	Best	10/m	5/inns
G.P. van Rensburg	62.2	18	131	12	10.91	6/36	1	2
S. Jacobs	72.3	22	186	13	14.30	3/21		
K.J. Kerr	157.2	54	388	27	14.37	4/24		
R.E. Bryson	147.4	22	401	27	14.85	7/68	1	3
K.T. Medlycott	50	11	150	10	15.00	6/83	1	1
D.W. McCosh	107.2	17	383	25	15.32	8/39	1	1
N.V. Radford	200	52	511	33	15.48	9/102		2
P. McLaren	162	37	467	29	16.10	5/28		1
G.E. McMillan	112.3	41	206	12	17.16	5/28		1
P.J. Botha	98	16	314	18	17.44	5/54		1
B.I. Stott	94.1	33	192	10	19.20	4/44		
W.K. Watson	230.2	52	582	30	19.40	5/47		1
B.E. van der Vyver	80	11	237	12	19.75	5/33		1
P.S. de Villiers	284	45	873	43	20.30	6/47		3
E.O. Simons	209	43	613	30	20.43	4/34		
K.M. Curran	138.2	36	394	19	20.73	7/47	1	1
O. Henry	315.3	97	855	41	20.85	5/59		1
J.G. Thomas	306.5	72	817	39	20.94	5/45		2
H.C. Lindenberg	366.5	110	986	47	20.97	7/31		3
R.O. Estwick	216.2	54	554	26	21.30	5/68		1
M.W. Pringle	323	52	923	43	21.46	6/41		1
R. Marais	107.5	19	368	17	21.64	6/75		1
C. Roelofse	233.5	84	451	19	23.73	4/46		
M.R. Hobson	110.2	23	357	15	23.80	4/77		
C.E.B. Rice	118	34	239	10	23.90	5/22		1
T.G. Shaw	467	197	829	34	24.38	4/90		
I.M. Kidson	143.1	29	418	17	24.58	6/53		1
T. Bosch	66.4	8	250	10	25.00	4/49		
C.J.P.G. van Zyl	260.3	60	705	28	25.17	5/51		2
J.D. du Toit	117	29	303	12	25.25	3/24		
B.M. McMillan	200.2	38	537	21	25.57	4/27		
R.M. Bentley	94.2	15	257	10	25.70	4/33		
H.A. Page	218.5	50	681	26	26.19	4/41		
P.A. Rayment	158.1	37	448	17	26.35	6/30		1
R.J. McCurdy	217.5	57	533	20	26.65	4/39		
I.S. Barnes	203.5	39	673	25	26.92	5/39		1
L.J. Ryan	165	32	472	17	27.76	4/64		
R.K. Illingworth	373.3	123	851	30	28.36	6/39	1	3
D.B. Rundle	256.4	59	683	24	28.45	4/29		
J.E. Nolte	224.1	46	604	21	28.76	6/57		1
B.A. Matthews	208.4	54	461	16	28.81	3/28		
W.F. Morris	195	47	577	20	28.85	6/63		1
A.A. Donald	260	55	815	28	29.10	5/46		1
F.D. Toppin	245.4	51	682	23	29.65	4/80		
C.W. Symcox	180.5	29	653	22	29.68	4/99		
I.L. Howell	305	108	669	22	30.40	4/36		
P.L. Symcox	119.4	35	304	10	30.40	4/82		
G. Grobler	279.2	56	893	29	30.79	5/56		1
S.J. Base	148.1	38	403	13	31.00	3/34		
D.J. Callaghan	130	27	350	11	31.81	4/50		
A.L. Hobson	303.2	75	777	24	32.37	5/24		1
B.C. Fourie	119.3	14	406	12	33.83	3/51		
C.C. Lillie	106.1	21	342	10	34.20	4/59		
A.M. Ferreira	124	26	393	11	35.72	4/46		
S.T. Jefferies	144.5	29	427	11	38.61	3/55		
C.R. Matthews	128	18	397	10	39.70	2/39		
G.J. Parsons	196	41	556	14	39.71	5/33		1
R.K. McGlashan	96	9	442	10	44.20	5/89		1
D.J. Ferrant	191.1	51	613	13	47.15	3/57		
M. James	230.3	55	682	14	48.71	4/124		

(Qualification – 10 wickets)

LEADING FIELDERS

42 - E.N. Trotman (ct 33/st 9); 35 - D.J. Richardson (ct 34/st 1); 34 - R.V. Jennings (ct 32/st 2); 27 - I. Human (ct 26/st 1); 26 - N.T. Day (ct 24/st 2) and B. McBride (ct 20/st 6); 25 - K.J. Bridgens (ct 22/st 3); 17 - R.J. Ryall (ct 16/st 1), L.F. Bleekers, M. Michau and N.R. Boonzaaier; 16 - R.J. East (ct 15/st 1), J.E. Morris and P.A. Tullis; 15 - A. da Costa and A.R. Wormington; 12 - O. Henry and K.C. Wessels; 11 - D.J. Callaghan and M.D. Haysman; 10 - M.B. Billson and H.R. Fotheringham

Unaffected by Time

The season in India.
Duleep Trophy. Irani Cup.
India *v.* New Zealand Test
series and one-day international series.
Richard Hadlee's world record.
Deodhar Trophy.
Ranji Trophy.
First-class averages.

Men at work. Ground preparations for the first Test match between India and New Zealand at Bangalore. (Simon Bruty/Allsport)

In spite of the cancellation of the England tour, the Indian season was still a very full one, with the New Zealanders as visitors and Richard Hadlee in search of a record number of Test wickets. The national side was to be engaged not only against New Zealand, but was to participate in one-day international tournaments in Sharjah and Bangladesh, and was to fly to the Caribbean in March before the completion of the Ranji Trophy. The season began with the Duleep Trophy.

Duleep Trophy

Quarter-Final

10, 11, 12 and 13 September 1988

at Sher-i-Kashmir Stadium, Srinagar

East Zone 369 for 5 dec (J. Arun Lal 103, I.B. Roy 81, S.S. Karim 63 not out)
Central Zone 322 (Padam Shastri 64, N.K. Churi 63, P.K. Amre 57, N. Venkatram 5 for 93)

Match drawn
East Zone entered semi-final by virtue of first-innings lead

There was no play on the first day because of rain, but on the second day, East Zone skipper Arun Lal hit his fourth successive century in the Duleep Trophy, so that his side finished the day on a commanding 208 for 3. Arun Lal, who was dropped three times, was ably assisted by Duleep Trophy debutant, I.B. Roy of Bengal. The pair added 186 for the second wicket. Arun Lal declared East Zone's innings closed 15 minutes after tea on the third day, and Randhir Singh captured Hignekar at 10. Chasing a target of 370, Central reached 74 for the loss of one wicket, and at 268 for 4, they looked comfortable first-innings winners, but the later batsmen wilted under pressure after Amre had been run out.

Semi-Finals

16, 17, 18 and 19 September 1988

at Patiala C.A. Stadium, Patiala

North Zone 400 for 5 dec (M.B. Amarnath 149 not out, Ajay Sharma 100 not out, N.S. Sidhu 52) and 64 for 1
East Zone 253 (J. Arun Lal 58, Maninder Singh 4 for 37)

Match drawn
North Zone entered final by virtue of first-innings lead

at Mayur Stadium, Faridabad

West Zone 395 (R.J. Shastri 87 not out, S.J. Kalyani 69, L.S. Rajput 68, C.S. Pandit 57, M. Venkataramana 4 for 97) and 192 for 7 (D.B. Vengsarkar 128 not out)
South Zone 335 (W.V. Raman 94, V.B. Chandrasekhar 80)

Match drawn
West Zone entered final by virtue of first-innings lead

With no play possible on the first day at Patiala, North Zone were in total command at the end of the third, with Mohinder Amarnath and Ajay Sharma sharing an unbeaten sixth-wicket partnership of 224, and Amarnath able to declare on 400 just after Ajay Sharma had completed his first Duleep Trophy century. East Zone lost

Mohinder Amarnath. A brilliant start to the season and then controversy with the Indian Board of Control, which could mean that a distinguished Test career is at an end. (Adrian Murrell/Allsport)

Dubey before the close and never looked likely to match the North's score on the final day as Maninder Singh and Kirti Azad bowled with great skill and economy.

The West Zone had a greater struggle at Faridabad after starting well and being 253 for 4 at stumps on the first day. Shastri dominated the later stages of the innings, and West reached a formidable 395, but South were undaunted. Srikkanth and Chandrasekhar began with a stand of 78, and Chandrasekhar gained in confidence to share a second-wicket stand of 83 with Raman, which threatened to put South Zone in command. Although he lost Chandrasekhar early on the third morning, Raman continued to flourish and to give his side every hope of a first-innings lead. The 22-year-old left-hander faced 228 balls in his 328 minutes at the wicket, but when he was caught off Ranjane, South's hopes vanished. Vengsarkar showed a welcome return to form with an elegant century on the last day.

Duleep Trophy Final
NORTH ZONE v. WEST ZONE

The cancellation of the England tour had left the Indian selectors and administrators the opportunity to concentrate their attentions more fully on the domestic competitions, something which had been needed for some time, and the selectors stated that they were using the Duleep Trophy as a means of determining the form of those under consideration for the series against New Zealand. Unfortunately, the Duleep Trophy Final was totally ruined by rain. Only 10 minutes' play was possible on the first day and 25 minutes on the second. There was two hours' cricket on the third day, and 50 minutes was lost after lunch on the fourth day. No play was possible on the scheduled fifth day. There were, however, some commendable performances, although the abandonment of the match meant that West and North Zone shared the trophy.

Kapil Dev bowled quite splendidly to reduce West Zone to 88 for 4 at the end of the third day. Kiran More, coming to the wicket at 117 for 5, quickly saw Shastri leave, but Radia helped him in a stand of 55. Rashid Patel batted with dogged defence while More played some exciting shots, and the pair added 87 for the eighth wicket. More was last out, caught bat-pad, having faced 134 balls and batted for 214 minutes. His 113 included 4 sixes and 12 fours and his innings breathed life into West Zone, but the rain returned.

Irani Cup
TAMIL NADU v. REST OF INDIA

Having suffered both criticism and embarrassment in the early stages of the match, Tamil Nadu pulled off a quite remarkable victory over the Rest of India to take the Irani Cup in dramatic fashion.

With players anxious to impress selectors, the select side crawled to 243 for 4 off 101 overs on the opening day. Sidhu and Roy began with a record opening stand of 158, surpassing the previous best in the Irani Cup set up 15 years earlier by seven runs. Three wickets fell quickly, but Kalyani showed great patience, and on the second day the Rest moved to a strong position.

Faced by a score of 433, Tamil Nadu began sketchily. Srikkanth showed a blend of defence and aggression, but Ghopal Sharma, bowling a tight line on or outside the off stump, troubled all batsmen, and it was only the enterprise of Venkataraman Sivaramakrishnan and Girish that saved Tamil Nadu from complete humiliation. The left-handed Sivaramakrishnan was particularly effective against Hirwani, and it was interesting to read that one Indian commentator felt that Hirwani's 'worth in domestic cricket is a doubtful quantity'.

Surprisingly, and wrongly, for Ghopal Sharma was relishing bowling, Arun Lal did not enforce the follow-on. As it transpired, his batsmen collapsed against a varied attack, which Srikkanth handled in his customary fidgety manner, ringing frequent changes.

In spite of the success of their bowlers, Tamil Nadu were still faced with the daunting task of scoring 340 to win on a

---

DULEEP TROPHY FINAL – NORTH ZONE v. WEST ZONE
22, 23, 25, 26 and 27 September 1988 at Ferozshah Kotla, Delhi

WEST ZONE					NORTH ZONE			
L.S. Rajput	st Vinayak, b Maninder	53			M. Prabhakar	not out	8
C.S. Pandit	b Kapil Dev	0			R. Lamba	not out	5
S.J. Kalyani	c Vinayak, b Kapil Dev	13			Gursharan Singh		
D.B. Vengsarkar†	b Kapil Dev	4			K.P. Bhaskar		
S.V. Manjrekar	c Gursharan, b Maninder	5			M.B. Amarnath		
R.J. Shastri	lbw, b C.J. Sharma	28			R.N. Kapil Dev†		
K.S. More*	c Kapil Dev, b Maninder	113			Kirti Azad		
B. Radia	c A.K. Sharma, b Prabhakar	21			Maninder Singh		
R.G. Patel	b Kirti Azad	13			C.J. Sharma		
S.V. Ranjane	lbw, b Kirti Azad	4			A.K. Sharma		
A. Kher	not out	0			R. Vinayak*		
Extras	b 1, lb 3, w 2, nb 17	23			Extras	nb 5	5
	penalty runs	8					
		285				(for no wkt)	18

	O	M	R	W		O	M	R	W
Kapil Dev	24	8	43	3	Patel	2	–	12	–
Prabhakar	16	4	45	1	Ranjane	2	–	6	–
C.J. Sharma	19	3	84	1					
Maninder Singh	30.2	10	67	3					
Amarnath	3	1	6	–					
Kirti Azad	9	4	26	2					
Ajay Sharma	4	2	2	–					

FALL OF WICKETS
1–5, 2–35, 3–41, 4–63, 5–117, 6–123, 7–178, 8–265, 9–269

Umpires: S.K. Ghosh & R.S. Rathore

Match abandoned

Dilip Vengsarkar hit a century for West in the Duleep Trophy semi-final and led India to victory in the Test series, but he did not reach his best form. (Simon Bruty/Allsport)

pitch which offered the spinners assistance. The Ranji Trophy holders got off to a magnificent start. For once, Srikkanth was put in the shade. He hit 52 off 77 balls but, by the time he was out, Chandrasekhar had hit 101 off 59 balls, the fastest century, in terms of balls received, ever made in a first-class match in India. In all, he batted for 123 minutes, hit 8 sixes and 11 fours and faced 78 balls for his 119. Essentially a front foot player, he dictated length to the spinners and, although he fell to Hirwani, caught in the deep, he gave the young leg-spinner and Jeshwant, the other spinner, a most depressing time.

There was much to do after Chandrasekhar's dismissal, but Venkataraman Sivaramakrishnan again played with great good sense. Arun, too, played resourcefully, and Tamil Nadu gained an historic victory by three wickets. Unfortunately, the selectors named the national side before the completion of the match, and only Srikkanth of the Tamil Nadu side was chosen. Ghopal Sharma set up an Irani Cup record with 12 wickets in the match.

New Zealand Tour

1, 2 and 3 November 1988

at Municipal Ground, Rajkot

West Zone 253 (S.J. Kalyani 82, T. Arothe 56, R.J. Hadlee 9 for 55)
New Zealanders 338 for 7 (J.G. Wright 104, T.J. Franklin 72)

Match drawn

The failure of the New Zealand kit to arrive at the ground on time caused the start of the opening match of the tour to be delayed, but Richard Hadlee was soon in top form, claiming all four wickets on the first day as West Zone slumped to 23 for 4. Kalyani and Arothe added 129, and Radia and Sulakshan Kulkarni put on 69 for the seventh

wicket. The honours went to Richard Hadlee, however, who gave an outstanding display of fast bowling on a placid pitch. Trevor Franklin dominated an opening stand of 118 with John Wright, the New Zealand captain, who went on to make an accomplished century with a six and 13 fours as the match was drawn, New Zealand drawing much comfort from their performance.

6, 7 and 8 November 1988

at Nahar Singh Stadium, Faridabad

New Zealanders 389 for 7 dec (J.G. Wright 123, K.R. Rutherford 59, C.M. Kuggeleijn 54 not out, J.G. Bracewell 50 not out, C.J. Sharma 4 for 87)
North Zone 362 (K.P. Bhaskar 111, Kirti Azad 79, D.K. Morrison 4 for 87)

Match drawn

John Wright hit his second century in succession, but batting was rather laboured as North Zone matched the tourists. Bhaskar Pillai played a fine innings for the North Zone, but once again he failed to force his way into the Test side. Mohinder Amarnath was also omitted from the chosen fourteen, and another Test discard, Kirti Azad, hit 5 sixes and 5 fours in his 79 made off 128 deliveries.

First Test Match
INDIA v. NEW ZEALAND

The main interest at the beginning of the first Test centred on Richard Hadlee and whether or not the great fast bowler would become the leading wicket-taker in Test history. He had drawn level with Ian Botham's 373 wickets at Melbourne in December 1987, but injury had kept him out of the series against England which followed, and he had to wait more than 10 months to beat Botham's record. The record was not long delayed in what was Hadlee's 75th Test. Vengsarkar won the toss and elected to bat. With his 13th ball of the match, Hadlee found the edge of Arun Lal's bat, and Chris Kuggeleijn, making his Test debut, held the catch at slip. In his next over, he bowled Srikkanth with a ball at which the batsman offered no stroke, but this was almost the last joy that the New Zealanders would find in the match.

Sidhu and Vengsarkar added 174 before the Indian captain had to retire with cramp when he had scored 73. Sidhu played with great confidence and virtuosity to reach a maiden Test hundred. He hit 4 sixes, off Evan Gray, and 12 fours, thereby blunting any threat that the New Zealand spinners might have posed. Sidhu's previous Test experience had been against West Indies in 1983.

Shastri, who was under much pressure to produce the form of which people knew he was capable, but of which so little had been seen in recent matches, batted with great caution, but More, relishing in a freedom of stroke-play, hit 46 off 97 balls.

RIGHT: *Richard Hadlee leaps in joy as Chris Kuggeleijn catches Arun Lal at slip. This wicket was Hadlee's 374th in Test cricket and constituted a new world record. (Simon Bruty/Allsport)*

IRANI CUP – TAMIL NADU v. REST OF INDIA
1, 2, 4, 5 and 6 October 1988 at M.A. Chidambaram Stadium, Madras

REST OF INDIA

	FIRST INNINGS		SECOND INNINGS	
I.B. Roy	c Girish, b Venkataramana	60	c L. Sivaramakrishnan, b Vasudevan	1
N.S. Sidhu	c Chandrasekhar, b Vasudevan	86	absent hurt	0
J. Arun Lal†	c Girish, b Vasudevan	5	c V. Sivaramakrishnan, b Raman	16
S.J. Kalyani	c and b Robin Singh	93	c Robin Singh, b Raman	17
N.K. Churi	c V. Sivaramakrishnan, b Raman	30	c Girish, b Vasudevan	23
S. Viswanath*	lbw, b Venkataramana	22	b Vasudevan	32
K. Jeshwant	c Venkataramana, b Vasudevan	62	c V. Sivaramakrishan, b Srikkanth	6
S.K. Sharma	st Girish, b Vasudevan	34	b Srikkanth	22
G. Sharma	not out	12	lbw, b Srikkanth	7
R.G. Patel	c Venkataramana, b Vasudevan	1	c Venkataramana, b Vasudevan	1
N.D. Hirwani	lbw, b Venkataramana	0	not out	2
Extras	b 14, lb 7, nb 7	28	b 1, lb 1, nb 3	5
		433		**132**

	O	M	R	W	O	M	R	W
Arun	15	3	36	–	5	1	4	–
Robin Singh	14	2	35	1	2	–	6	–
Vasudevan	47	13	116	5	17	5	42	4
Venkataramana	43.2	7	118	3	13	2	40	–
L. Sivaramakrishnan	11	–	54	–				
Raman	19	7	43	1	8	2	24	2
Srikkanth	7	2	10	–	4.2	–	14	3

FALL OF WICKETS
1–158, 2–160, 3–169, 4–226, 5–266, 6–367, 7–419, 8–420, 9–433
1–10, 2–36, 3–41, 4–93, 5–94, 6–109, 7–125, 8–126, 9–132

TAMIL NADU

	FIRST INNINGS		SECOND INNINGS	
K. Srikkanth†	lbw, b G. Sharma	57	c S.K. Sharma, b G. Sharma	52
V.B. Chandrasekhar	lbw, b Patel	0	c Patel, b Hirwani	119
W.V. Raman	c Churi, b G. Sharma	19	b G. Sharma	25
M. Senthilnathan	c Viswanath, b G. Sharma	6	b G. Sharma	2
Robin Singh	run out	6	c Arun Lal, b G. Sharma	21
V. Sivaramakrishnan	c Patel, b G. Sharma	37	not out	49
L. Sivaramakrishnan	c G. Sharma, b Jeshwant	29	b G. Sharma	18
B. Arun	lbw, b G. Sharma	7	not out	37
D. Girish*	not out	39	c Kalyani, b G. Sharma	15
M. Venkataramana	c Arun Lal, b G. Sharma	13		
S. Vasudevan	run out	3		
Extras	b 5, lb 1, nb 4	10	b 3, lb 2	5
		226	(for 7 wkts)	**343**

	O	M	R	W	O	M	R	W
Patel	11	1	43	1	3	1	10	–
S.K. Sharma	5	1	15	–	4	–	32	–
G. Sharma	32	7	69	6	33.3	4	133	6
Hirwani	24.3	6	70	–	17	1	82	1
Jeshwant	15	4	23	1	13	1	59	–
Arun Lal					9	–	22	–

FALL OF WICKETS
1–1, 2–40, 3–50, 4–88, 5–130, 6–137, 7–155, 8–186, 9–214
1–154, 2–178, 3–184, 4–217, 5–222, 6–252, 7–291

Umpires: R.B. Gupta & P.D. Reporter

Tamil Nadu won by 3 wickets

John Wright, a most durable and valiant skipper throughout the series. Kapil Dev is the fielder. (Simon Bruty/Allsport)

New Zealand were hampered by a mystery illness which seeped through the side, and were clearly not at their best, although Hadlee managed to claim five wickets in a Test innings for the 33rd time.

Wright and Franklin gave their side a dour start, but, once Arshad Ayub and Hirwani found their rhythm, New Zealand looked a harassed side. On the third day, during which New Zealand scored 136 runs as six wickets fell, 50 maiden overs were bowled. The illness gripped the side on the rest day; Hadlee collapsed, being unable to continue his innings on the fourth morning, and Kuggeleijn was too ill to bat. Ian Smith and Bracewell resumed, and Smith hit lustily, but he was leg before to Kapil Dev, who dismissed the stricken Kuggeleijn first ball with a dipping full toss. Hadlee hobbled to the wicket, saved the hat trick and edged a four, which avoided the follow-on, but New Zealand surrendered a first-innings lead of 195 to the Indians.

As India began their second innings New Zealand fielded five substitutes, and the batsmen made merry at five runs an over. Vengsarkar declared early on the fourth afternoon, and New Zealand were left with the daunting task of scoring 337 to win or simply surviving for a day and a half.

Wright and Franklin batted stoically, and at the end of the day they had 73 on the board and had made an Indian victory appear less likely. Hirwani and Arshad Ayub bowled unchanged on the last day, and they soon confirmed that New Zealand were doomed. Hirwani's flipper accounted for Franklin, and Wright added only a boundary to his overnight score before falling leg before to the leg-spinner whose second Test success was almost as amazing as his first against West Indies the previous season. Four wickets fell with the score at 113, Kuggeleijn bagged a 'pair' on his Test debut and 10 wickets fell for 87 runs. The combination of Arshad's off-breaks and Hirwani's leg-breaks on a wicket which gave them assistance was altogether too much for the New Zealanders.

Arshad bowled most impressively to return match figures of 8 for 104, while Hirwani's eight wickets gave him 24 wickets in his first two Tests and five wickets in an innings three times in those two Tests.

Hirwani bowls Franklin in New Zealand's second innings, and India are on their way to victory. (Simon Bruty/ Allsport)

FIRST TEST MATCH – INDIA v. NEW ZEALAND
12, 13, 14, 16 and 17 November 1988 at Chinnaswamy Stadium, Bangalore

INDIA

	FIRST INNINGS		SECOND INNINGS	
K. Srikkanth	b Hadlee	1	not out	58
J. Arun Lal	c Kuggeleijn, b Hadlee	6	c and b Gray	33
N.S. Sidhu	c Jones, b Gray	116	not out	43
D.B. Vengsarkar†	b Hadlee	75		
M. Azharuddin	c Smith, b Hadlee	42		
W.V. Raman	b Hadlee	3		
R.J. Shastri	c Rutherford, b Gray	54		
R.N. Kapil Dev	c Jones, b Chatfield	24		
K.S. More*	lbw, b Kuggeleijn	46		
Arshad Ayub	not out	2		
N.D. Hirwani	not out	0		
Extras	b 4, lb 4, nb 7	15	b 5, lb 2	7
	(for 9 wkts, dec)	384	(for 1 wkt, dec)	141

NEW ZEALAND

	FIRST INNINGS		SECOND INNINGS	
J.G. Wright†	c Arun Lal, b Ayub	22	(2) lbw, b Hirwani	58
T.J. Franklin	c Azharuddin, b Ayub	28	(1) b Hirwani	16
A.H. Jones	c Srikkanth, b Ayub	45	lbw, b Hirwani	17
M.J. Greatbatch	c Srikkanth, b Raman	14	c Kapil Dev, b Ayub	10
K.R. Rutherford	c Arun Lal, b Hirwani	14	(6) lbw, b Hirwani	0
E.J. Gray	lbw, b Hirwani	1	(5) c Srikkanth, b Hirwani	2
R.J. Hadlee	b Kapil Dev	5	(8) not out	13
J.G. Bracewell	c More, b Ayub	3	(10) c Arun Lal, b Ayub	11
I.D.S. Smith*	lbw, b Kapil Dev	30	lbw, b Hirwani	25
E.J. Chatfield	not out	4	(11) c Vengsarkar, b Ayub	0
C.M. Kuggeleijn	lbw, b Kapil Dev	0	(7) c More, b Ayub	0
Extras	b 6, lb 8, nb 9	23	b 10, nb 2	12
		189		164

	O	M	R	W	O	M	R	W
Hadlee	30	10	65	5				
Chatfield	30	12	53	1	14	–	61	–
Kuggeleijn	13	2	50	1				
Gray	45	8	128	2	6	–	39	1
Bracewell	24	1	80	–	8	–	34	–

	O	M	R	W	O	M	R	W
Kapil Dev	9.3	4	24	3	4	–	16	–
Arshad Ayub	48	21	51	4	35.4	12	53	4
Hirwani	31	12	62	2	30	10	59	6
Shastri	14	8	11	–	7	1	21	–
Srikkanth	3	2	1	–				
Raman	17	8	26	1	2	–	5	–

FALL OF WICKETS
1–9, 2–10, 3–236, 4–244, 5–254, 6–258, 7–294, 8–378, 9–384
1–64

FALL OF WICKETS
1–58, 2–62, 3–119, 4–128, 5–135, 6–140, 7–149, 8–183, 9–183
1–77, 2–92, 3–107, 4–113, 5–113, 6–113, 7–113, 8–143, 9–164

Umpires: S.K. Ghosh & P.D. Reporter

India won by 172 runs

19, 20 and 21 November 1988

at Bandodkar Ground, Panaji

New Zealanders 288 for 5 dec (T.E. Blain 108, C.M. Kuggeleijn 101 not out) and 231 for 9 (I.D.S. Smith 69, M.J. Greatbatch 53, Arun Kumar 4 for 49)
Tamil Nadu 289 for 7 dec (P.C. Prakash 71, Arjan Kripal Singh 52)

Match drawn

Tony Blain and Chris Kuggeleijn, returned to fitness, shared a fifth-wicket partnership of 166, which dominated the match. It was the second century of Kuggeleijn's career.

Second Test Match
INDIA *v.* NEW ZEALAND

New Zealand made two changes for the second Test: Blain replaced the injured Gray, and Morrison came in for Kuggeleijn. India gave a first Test cap to left-arm medium-pace bowler Rashid Patel, who came in for Raman.

Wright won the toss, but New Zealand struggled painfully against the spinners on the opening day, and at tea they were 161 for 8, with India very much in control. The last session of the day proved to be decisive for New Zealand. They did not lose another wicket as Bracewell and Morrison batted with dash to take their side to 231 at the close. They added only three more runs on the second

morning, but their ninth-wicket stand of 76 was a New Zealand record against India, and the New Zealand total of 236 was far beyond what had been expected earlier.

Hadlee and Chatfield made quick breakthroughs to keep New Zealand on top, but Srikkanth played with uncharacteristic restraint to keep out Hadlee, while hitting savagely at Bracewell and the other bowlers. He and Vengsarkar appeared to be taking India to a strong position until the Indian captain threw away his wicket with a rash stroke. Hadlee returned to destroy the middle order in spite of some resolute defence from Shastri, who bowled and batted well, but remained the butt of the crowd. Hadlee's magnificent bowling gave his side a first-innings lead of two runs and a great psychological boost.

The quick dismissal of Franklin pushed the advantage back again in favour of India, but Wright was as steadfast as ever, and Jones showed enterprising footwork in stands with both his captain and Greatbatch. Then Hirwani and Arshad Ayub began to torment the New Zealand batsmen as they had done in the first Test, and the visitors ended the third day on 182 for 8, another Indian victory looming.

Once again India's failure to finish off the innings proved costly, and Ian Smith and John Bracewell batted

John Wright is caught behind off Hirwani. Kapil Dev joins in the appeal. (Simon Bruty/Allsport)

ABOVE: *Franklin is stumped by More off the bowling of Arshad Ayub. (Simon Bruty/Allsport)*

BELOW: *New Zealand hero John Bracewell. The off-spinner claimed 6 for 51 in India's second innings. (Simon Bruty/Allsport)*

Indian debutant Rashid Patel, one of three medium-pace bowlers to share the new ball with Kapil Dev during the three-Test series. (Simon Bruty/Allsport)

bravely to take their stand to 69. Bracewell, who was twice missed by More, and Chatfield added an invaluable 29 runs for the last wicket, before Bracewell became Arshad Ayub's fifth victim. It was the first time that the off-spinner had taken five wickets in a Test innings.

Needing 282 to win, India had the worst possible start as Srikkanth padded up to Hadlee's first delivery, an in-swinger. Sidhu was bowled by Bracewell, whose aggressive off-spin now became the dominant factor in a match in which he had already played such an important part. He bowled Vengsarkar for nought, and the Indian batting fell

ABOVE: *Shastri is caught behind by a jubilant Ian Smith off the bowling of Richard Hadlee, and New Zealand are in sight of victory. (Simon Bruty/Allsport)*

BELOW: *Arshad Ayub, India's hero. Seven wickets in the third Test and 21 in the series. (Simon Bruty/Allsport)*

TOP: *Another wicket for Hirwani as Rutherford falls to a catch at short-leg by Srikkanth. (Simon Bruty/Allsport)*

ABOVE: *Hadlee traps Srikkanth lbw with the first ball of the second innings. (Simon Bruty/Allsport)*

apart. There were some lusty blows from Kapil Dev, but Hadlee and Bracewell shared the wickets, the last seven falling as only 56 runs were added.

For the ninth time, Hadlee took 10 wickets in a Test match, but John Bracewell had an outstanding all-round match and was the key to New Zealand's victory. It was the first time they had drawn level in a three-Test series in India after losing the first Test.

Third Test Match
INDIA v. NEW ZEALAND

India introduced another medium-pace bowler to Test cricket as Kapil Dev's partner by bringing in Sanjeev Sharma in place of Patel. New Zealand brought back Kuggeleijn for Rutherford and brought in Snedden for Morrison.

SECOND TEST MATCH – INDIA v. NEW ZEALAND
24, 25, 26, 27 and 29 November 1988 at Wankhede Stadium, Bombay

NEW ZEALAND

	FIRST INNINGS		SECOND INNINGS	
T.J. Franklin	st More, b Ayub	18	c More, b Kapil Dev	2
J.G. Wright†	c More, b Hirwani	33	lbw, b Hirwani	36
A.H. Jones	lbw, b Kapil Dev	3	lbw, b Ayub	78
M.J. Greatbatch	lbw, b Shastri	46	b Hirwani	31
K.R. Rutherford	c Srikkanth, b Hirwani	6	c Arun Lal, b Ayub	17
T.E. Blain	c Kapil Dev, b Shastri	16	lbw, b Ayub	5
R.J. Hadlee	c Patel, b Hirwani	10	c Vengsarkar, b Hirwani	1
I.D.S. Smith*	b Shastri	13	c Vengsarkar, b Ayub	54
J.G. Bracewell	c More, b Shastri	52	(10) c and b Ayub	32
D.K. Morrison	not out	27	(9) c More, b Hirwani	0
E.J. Chatfield	b Kapil Dev	0	not out	2
Extras	lb 5, nb 7	12	b 4, lb 8, w 1, nb 8	21
		236		279

INDIA

	FIRST INNINGS		SECOND INNINGS	
K. Srikkanth	c Franklin, b Hadlee	94	lbw, b Hadlee	0
J. Arun Lal	lbw, b Hadlee	9	c Greatbatch, b Hadlee	47
N.S. Sidhu	lbw, b Chatfield	6	b Bracewell	14
D.B. Vengsarkar†	c Blain, b Bracewell	25	b Bracewell	0
M. Azharuddin	c Greatbatch, b Bracewell	9	c Rutherford, b Bracewell	21
R.J. Shastri	b Chatfield	32	c Smith, b Hadlee	6
R.N. Kapil Dev	b Hadlee	7	c Wright, b Bracewell	36
K.S. More*	b Hadlee	28	b Bracewell	2
Arshad Ayub	c Bracewell, b Hadlee	10	not out	4
R.G. Patel	c Rutherford, b Hadlee	0	c Smith, b Hadlee	0
N.D. Hirwani	not out	2	c Chatfield, b Bracewell	3
Extras	lb 5, nb 7	12	b 5, lb 4, nb 3	12
		234		145

	O	M	R	W	O	M	R	W
Kapil Dev	15.3	4	48	2	24	5	52	1
R.G. Patel	4	–	14	–	10	–	37	–
Arshad Ayub	25	10	42	1	33	11	50	5
Hirwani	31	6	82	3	38	7	93	4
Shastri	18	1	45	4	10	1	35	–

	O	M	R	W	O	M	R	W
Hadlee	20.5	5	49	6	16	3	39	4
Morrison	16	1	58	–	6	1	27	–
Chatfield	18	6	41	2	10	1	19	–
Bracewell	21	6	81	2	17.4	3	51	6

FALL OF WICKETS
1–36, 2–43, 3–67, 4–83, 5–110, 6–121, 7–141, 8–158, 9–234
1–2, 2–73, 3–149, 4–163, 6–169, 6–176, 7–176, 8–181, 9–250

FALL OF WICKETS
1–26, 2–34, 3–134, 4–150, 5–150, 6–172, 7–209, 8–224, 9–229
1–0, 2–48, 3–54, 4–89, 5–89, 6–134, 7–134, 8–141, 9–142

Umpires: R.B. Gupta & V.K. Ramaswamy

New Zealand won by 136 runs

Wright won the toss, but New Zealand were in trouble as soon as Arshad Ayub and Hirwani came into the attack. Ayub sent back the first three batsmen in quick succession. Hirwani accounted for Blain and the luckless Kuggeleijn, and Ayub had Hadlee taken at slip to reduce New Zealand to 91 for 6. Greatbatch had been dropped by Azharuddin before he had scored, and Smith was missed at slip by Kapil Dev. Benefiting from these lapses, the two batsmen played with some panache, and they remained undefeated at the close, Greatbatch 76, Smith 78, and the score 228.

Hopes of them continuing in the same vein on the second morning were dashed when Smith reported sick. He decided to continue his innings, but he lasted only a few minutes before falling to Kapil Dev. Smith and Greatbatch had added 139, the first century stand of the series by the New Zealanders, but Sanjeev Sharma soon ended the innings with three quick wickets, Greatbatch being left undefeated for a most valiant 90.

Arun Lal and Sidhu went cheaply, but Srikkanth hit Bracewell for 3 sixes and bristled with aggression. By the end of the day, India were only 43 runs behind, with six wickets standing, and, although Shastri left after only six runs had been added on the third morning, Azharuddin continued in flowing style and was ably supported by Kapil Dev. There were valuable contributions from the tail, and India moved to a commanding lead of 104.

Franklin, Jones and Snedden were out before the close of the third day, and New Zealand still trailed by 39 runs.

Wright alone seemed to offer the necessary determination and technique to cope with the varied Indian attack in which the spinners again dominated. He hit 10 fours and batted for 230 minutes, but the last seven wickets fell for the addition of only 53 runs, and India needed a meagre 21 to win. Srikkanth, as ever, was in a hurry to finish the match.

New Zealand had given a creditable account of themselves in a good series. Hadlee bowled magnificently and made history, but the honours went to Arshad Ayub and Hirwani who, having played in four Test matches, had 36 Test wickets to his credit by the end of the series. In tandem with Arshad Ayub, he provided one of the most lethal spinning combinations in the world, certainly on wickets in the Indian subcontinent.

First One-Day International
INDIA v. NEW ZEALAND

Sent in to bat, New Zealand soon lost Wright, but Jones and Rutherford added 113 for the second wicket. They launched a fierce attack on the spinners and hit 94 runs off 20 overs. It was Maninder, however, who broke the stand as Jones lifted him to long-off. Greatbatch was run out first ball by Srikkanth, who was then immediately introduced into the attack with devastating effect.

He bowled Rutherford, and then had Franklin caught. In his next over, he bowled Smith, took a return catch to

THIRD TEST MATCH – INDIA v. NEW ZEALAND
2, 3, 4 and 6 December 1988 at Lal Bahadur Shastri Stadium, Hyderabad

NEW ZEALAND

	FIRST INNINGS		SECOND INNINGS	
T.J. Franklin	c Arun Lal, b Ayub	7	c Kapil Dev, b Hirwani	15
J.G. Wright†	c and b Ayub	17	c and b Shastri	62
A.H. Jones	c Kapil Dev, b Ayub	8	c Vengsarkar, b Ayub	5
M.J. Greatbatch	not out	90	(5) lbw, b Hirwani	5
T.E. Blain	b Hirwani	15	(6) c Arun Lal, b Hirwani	0
C.M. Kuggeleijn	c Vengsarkar, b Hirwani	7	(7) c Sharma, b Ayub	0
R.J. Hadlee	c Azharuddin, b Ayub	1	(8) c More, b Kapil Dev	31
I.D.S. Smith*	c Srikkanth, b Kapil Dev	79	(9) b Kapil Dev	0
J.G. Bracewell	c Vengsarkar, b Sharma	3	(10) lbw, b Kapil Dev	0
M.C. Snedden	lbw, b Sharma	0	(4) lbw, b Ayub	0
E.J. Chatfield	c Srikkanth, b Sharma	0	not out	0
Extras	b 8, lb 11, w 1, nb 7	27	lb 1, w 5	6
		254		124

	O	M	R	W	O	M	R	W
Kapil Dev	26	6	71	1	10	3	21	3
S.K. Sharma	17	4	37	3	4	–	13	–
Arshad Ayub	30	9	55	4	25	12	36	3
Shastri	6	2	15	–	3.3	1	10	1
Hirwani	15	2	51	2	23	10	43	3
Srikkanth	1	–	6	–				

FALL OF WICKETS
1–25, 2–33, 3–38, 4–82, 5–90, 6–91, 7–230, 8–246, 9–248
1–49, 2–58, 3–60, 4–71, 5–75, 6–80, 7–118, 8–118, 9–124

INDIA

	FIRST INNINGS		SECOND INNINGS	
K. Srikkanth	c Bracewell, b Snedden	69	not out	18
J. Arun Lal	c Greatbatch, b Hadlee	8	not out	0
N.S. Sidhu	c Franklin, b Snedden	19		
D.B. Vengsarkar†	c Hadlee, b Chatfield	32		
R.J. Shastri	c Franklin, b Chatfield	42		
M. Azharuddin	c Smith, b Chatfield	81		
R.N. Kapil Dev	c Wright, b Hadlee	40		
K.S. More*	c Bracewell, b Snedden	0		
Arshad Ayub	c Smith, b Hadlee	19		
S.K. Sharma	not out	18		
N.D. Hirwani	c and b Snedden	17		
Extras	lb 9, nb 4	13	nb 4	4
		358	(for no wkt)	22

	O	M	R	W	O	M	R	W
Hadlee	34	7	99	3				
Chatfield	33	6	82	3	1	–	5	–
Snedden	18.3	3	69	4	1	–	13	–
Bracewell	18	1	86	–				
Kuggeleijn	3	–	13	–	0.1	–	4	–

FALL OF WICKETS
1–17, 2–48, 3–116, 4–150, 5–217, 6–279, 7–281, 8–310, 9–322

Umpires: S.K. Ghosh & R.B. Gupta

India won by 10 wickets

INDIA v. NEW ZEALAND – TEST MATCH AVERAGES

INDIA BATTING

	M	Inns	NOs	Runs	HS	Av	100s	50s
K. Srikkanth	3	6	2	240	94	60.00		3
N.S. Sidhu	3	5	1	198	116	49.50	1	
M. Azharuddin	3	4		153	81	38.25		1
R.J. Shastri	3	4		134	54	33.50		1
D.B. Vengsarkar	3	4		132	75	33.00		1
R.N. Kapil Dev	3	4		107	40	26.75		
J.Arun Lal	3	6	1	103	47	20.60		
K.S. More	3	4		76	46	19.00		
Arshad Ayub	3	4	2	35	19	17.50		
N.D. Hirwani	3	4	2	22	17	11.00		

Played in one Test: W.V. Raman 3; R.G. Patel 0 & 0; S.K. Sharma 18*

NEW ZEALAND BATTING

	M	Inns	NOs	Runs	HS	Av	100s	50s
M.J. Greatbatch	3	6	1	196	90*	39.20		1
J.G. Wright	3	6		228	62	38.00		2
I.D.S. Smith	3	6		201	79	33.50		2
A.H. Jones	3	6		156	78	26.00		1
J.G. Bracewell	3	6		101	52	16.83		1
T.J. Franklin	3	6		86	28	14.33		
R.J. Hadlee	3	6	1	61	31	12.20		
K.R. Rutherford	2	4		37	17	9.25		
T.E. Blain	2	4		36	16	9.00		
E.J. Chatfield	3	6	3	6	4*	2.00		
C.M. Kuggeleijn	2	4		7	7	1.75		

Played in one Test: E.J. Gray 1 & 2; D.K. Morrison 27* & 0; M.C. Snedden 0 & 0

INDIA BOWLING

	Overs	Mds	Runs	Wkts	Av	Best	10/m	5/inns
Arshad Ayub	196.4	75	287	21	13.66	5/50		1
S.K. Sharma	21	4	50	3	16.66	3/37		
N.D. Hirwani	168	47	390	20	19.50	6/59		1
R.N. Kapil Dev	89	22	232	10	23.20	3/21		
R.J. Shastri	58.3	14	137	5	27.40	4/45		
W.V. Raman	19	8	31	1	31.00	1/26		
K. Srikkanth	4	2	7	0	–	0/2		
R.G. Patel	14		51	0	–	0/14		

NEW ZEALAND BOWLING

	Overs	Mds	Runs	Wkts	Av	Best	10/m	5/inns
R.J. Hadlee	100.5	25	252	18	14.00	6/49	1	2
M.C. Snedden	19.3	3	82	4	20.50	4/69		
J.G. Bracewell	88.4	11	332	8	41.50	6/51		1
E.J. Chatfield	106	25	261	6	43.50	3/82		
E.J. Gray	51	8	167	3	55.66	2/128		
C.M. Kuggeleijn	16.1	2	67	1	67.00	1/50		
D.K. Morrison	22	2	85	0	–	0/27		

INDIA FIELDING FIGURES
8 - K.S. More (ct 7/st 1); 6 - K. Srikkanth, D.B. Vengsarkar and J. Arun Lal; 4 - R.N. Kapil Dev; 2 - M. Azharuddin and Arshad Ayub; 1 - R.J. Shastri, S.K. Sharma and R.G. Patel

NEW ZEALAND FIELDING FIGURES
5 - I.D.S. Smith; 3 - K.R. Rutherford, J.G. Bracewell, T.J. Franklin and M.J. Greatbatch; 2 - J.G. Wright and A.H. Jones; 1 - T.E. Blain, E.J. Gray, M.C. Snedden and C.M. Kuggeleijn

dismiss Kuggeleijn and had Bracewell caught behind. This unexpected success by an occasional bowler sent New Zealand floundering, and they made only 196 off their 50 overs, which was very disappointing after their good form earlier.

Srikkanth, partnered by Chandrasekhar, who was included after his wonderful innings in the Irani Cup, immediately attacked the bowling, and, with Azharuddin also in fine form, India raced to victory with 22 balls to spare.

Second One-Day International
INDIA *v.* NEW ZEALAND

In a match reduced to 45 overs in anticipation of poor light, India were always on top once Maninder Singh had broken the promising opening partnership between Wright and Jones. From 52 for 0, New Zealand collapsed to 67 for 4, and only some dogged batting by Gray, and some more adventurous batting by Bracewell, took the visitors past 150.

In spite of the early loss of Srikkanth and Chandrasekhar, India always had the game in control, with Sidhu in particularly impressive form.

Srikkanth – as belligerent as ever. In the one-day series, his medium-pace bowling had a devastating effect upon the New Zealanders, as well as his batting. (Simon Bruty/ Allsport)

CHARMINAR CHALLENGE CUP – FIRST ONE-DAY INTERNATIONAL – INDIA *v.* NEW ZEALAND
10 December 1988 at Indira Priyadarshinee Stadium, Viskhapatnam

NEW ZEALAND				INDIA			
J.G. Wright†	c Vengsarkar, b Kapil Dev	2		K. Srikkanth	c Chatfield, b Bracewell	70	
A.H. Jones	c S.K. Sharma, b Maninder Singh	63		V.B. Chandrasekhar	lbw, b Watson	10	
K.R. Rutherford	b Srikkanth	70		N.S. Sidhu	run out	25	
M.J. Greatbatch	run out	0		D.B. Vengsarkar†	run out	0	
T.J. Franklin	c S.K. Sharma, b Srikkanth	21		M. Azharuddin	not out	48	
I.D.S. Smith*	b Srikkanth	5		R.N. Kapil Dev	c Greatbatch, b Watson	22	
J.G. Bracewell	c Pandit, b Srikkanth	13		C.S. Pandit*	c Rutherford, b Snedden	2	
C.M. Kuggeleijn	c and b Srikkanth	4		A.K. Sharma	not out	3	
M.C. Snedden	not out	6		Arshad Ayub			
W. Watson	b Kapil Dev	1		S.K. Sharma			
E.J. Chatfield	not out	0		Maninder Singh			
Extras	lb 4, w 5, nb 2	11		Extras	lb 14, w 1, nb 2	17	
(50 overs)	(for 9 wkts)	196		(46.2 overs)	(for 6 wkts)	197	

	O	M	R	W		O	M	R	W
Kapil Dev	7	–	16	2	Chatfield	8	–	38	–
S.K. Sharma	6	–	13	–	Watson	10	–	36	2
Azharuddin	2	–	11	–	Snedden	4.2	–	20	1
Maninder Singh	10	–	49	1	Rutherford	4	–	25	–
Arshad Ayub	10	–	45	–	Bracewell	10	1	36	1
A.K. Sharma	8	–	31	–	Kuggeleijn	10	1	28	–
Srikkanth	7	–	27	5					

FALL OF WICKETS
1–2, 2–115, 3–115, 4–163, 5–168, 6–176, 7–182, 8–191, 9–194

FALL OF WICKETS
1–16, 2–79, 3–79, 4–129, 5–180, 6–188

Umpires: S. Banerjee & R.V. Ramani

Man of the Match: K. Srikkanth

India won by 4 wickets

CHARMINAR CHALLENGE CUP – SECOND ONE-DAY INTERNATIONAL – INDIA v. NEW ZEALAND
12 December 1988 at Barabati Stadium, Cuttack

NEW ZEALAND				INDIA			
J.G. Wright†	b Maninder Singh		39	K. Srikkanth	lbw, b Watson		5
A.H. Jones	c Srikkanth,			V.B.Chandrasekhar	b Kuggeleijn		9
	b Maninder Singh		16	N.S. Sidhu	c Smith, b Watson		67
K.R. Rutherford	lbw, b Arshad Ayub		4	D.B. Vengsarkar†	c Smith, b Bracewell		15
M.J. Greatbatch	run out		1	M. Azharuddin	c Bracewell, b Gray		32
E.J. Gray	b Kapil Dev		38	R.N. Kapil Dev	not out		27
I.D.S. Smith*	lbw, b A.K. Sharma		9	A.K. Sharma	not out		2
C.M. Kuggeleijn	c S.K. Sharma,			C.S. Pandit*			
	b Srikkanth		9	S.K. Sharma			
J.G. Bracewell	not out		24	Arshad Ayub			
M.C. Snedden	not out		2	Maninder Singh			
W. Watson				Extras	lb 4		4
E.J. Chatfield							
Extras	b 4, lb 9, w 4, nb 1		18	(41.3 overs)	(for 5 wkts)		161
(45 overs)	(for 7 wkts)		160				

	O	M	R	W		O	M	R	W
Kapil Dev	7	–	29	1	Chatfield	9	2	23	–
S.K. Sharma	5	–	19	–	Watson	7.3	–	33	2
Maninder Singh	9	2	23	2	Kuggeleijn	9	–	29	1
Arshad Ayub	9	–	23	1	Snedden	5	–	11	–
A.K. Sharma	7	–	25	1	Bracewell	5	–	37	1
Srikkanth	8	–	28	1	Gray	6	–	24	1

FALL OF WICKETS
1–52, 2–64, 3–65, 4–67, 5–90, 6–109, 7–156

FALL OF WICKETS
1–5, 2–30, 3–69, 4–117, 5–159

Umpires: D.N. Dotiwala & S.B. Kulkarni

Man of the Match: N.S. Sidhu

India won by 5 wickets

CHARMINAR CHALLENGE CUP – THIRD ONE-DAY INTERNATIONAL – INDIA v. NEW ZEALAND
15 December 1988 at Nehru Stadium, Indore

INDIA				NEW ZEALAND			
K. Srikkanth	b Snedden		23	J.G. Wright†	c Arshad Ayub,		
V.B. Chandrasekhar	b Kuggeleijn		53		b Maninder		43
N.S. Sidhu	c Rutherford,			A.H. Jones	c Pandit,		
	b Kuggeleijn		14		b S.K. Sharma		6
D.B. Vengsarkar†	c Jones, b Gray		14	K.R. Rutherford	c Kapil Dev,		
M. Azharuddin	c Bracewell, b Gray		17		b S.K. Sharma		6
R.N. Kapil Dev	c Blain, b Snedden		11	M.J. Greatbatch	c Kapil Dev,		
A.K. Sharma	not out		52		b Srikkanth		64
C.S. Pandit*	not out		19	T.E. Blain*	c Maninder,		
S.K. Sharma					b Srikkanth		17
Arshad Ayub				C.M. Kuggeleijn	run out		0
Maninder Singh				J.G. Bracewell	b Srikkanth		7
Extras	b 1, lb 12, w 6		19	E.J. Gray	st Pandit, b Srikkanth		3
				M.C. Snedden	c Pandit, b Srikkanth		6
(45 overs)	(for 6 wkts)		222	W. Watson	not out		3
				E.J. Chatfield	not out		0
				Extras	lb 10, w 2, nb 2		14
				(45 overs)	(for 9 wkts)		169

	O	M	R	W		O	M	R	W
Chatfield	7	2	23	–	Kapil Dev	9	2	18	–
Watson	5	1	30	–	S.K. Sharma	7	–	22	2
Snedden	8	–	43	2	Maninder Singh	9	1	28	1
Kuggeleijn	9	2	31	2	Arshad Ayub	9	–	27	–
Rutherford	3	–	16	–	A.K. Sharma	5	–	32	–
Bracewell	8	–	40	–	Srikkanth	6	–	32	5
Gray	5	–	26	2					

FALL OF WICKETS
1–59, 2–91, 3–105, 4–125, 5–141, 5–168

FALL OF WICKETS
1–12, 2–24, 3–75, 4–125, 5–129, 6–144, 7–154,
8–161, 9–168

Umpires: R.B. Gupta & R.S. Rathore

Man of the Match: A.K. Sharma

India won by 53 runs

Third One-Day International
INDIA v. NEW ZEALAND

A damp outfield delayed the start and reduced the game to 45 overs, but some consistent batting took India to a good total. Chandrasekhar hit his first fifty in international cricket. His innings contained 7 fours and lasted for 75 balls, but it was Ajay Sharma who stole the limelight with 50 off 31 balls, including 3 fours and 3 sixes, one of them off the last ball of the innings.

Wright reached 3,000 runs in his 113th one-day international, but it was Greatbatch who offered New Zealand hope with his highest score in limited-over international matches. He fell to the off-spin of Srikkanth, however, and the Tamil Nadu captain went on to have another amazing success with the ball, finishing with 5 for 32, his second five-wicket haul in three matches.

Fourth One-Day International
INDIA v. NEW ZEALAND

Having given their best batting performance of the series, New Zealand were beaten by an innings of genius from Azharuddin. Wright chose to bat first on a fine wicket, and he and Jones gave New Zealand an excellent start with a partnership of 140. This was followed by a blistering innings by Mark Greatbatch. He hit his highest score in one-day internationals, his 84 not out coming off 65 balls and including 2 sixes and 8 fours.

New Zealand looked totally secure with their total of 278, particularly when Chandrasekhar and Raman were out cheaply and Pandit soon followed. Manjrekar and Vengsarkar helped repair the damage with a stand of 68, but it was Mohammed Azharuddin and Ajay Sharma who made victory possible. Sharma's fifty came off 35 balls and included 5 fours, and he and Azharuddin added 127. Sharma was out in the 45th over, but Azharuddin romped to the fastest hundred in limited-over international cricket, 62 balls, and his 108 came off 65 balls to take India to a dramatic victory with 17 balls to spare.

The fifth one-day international at Jammu was scheduled for 19 December 1988, but it was abandoned without a ball being bowled, so leaving India 4 to 0 winners of the series.

Deodhar Trophy

Quarter-Final

22 January 1989

at Indore

East Zone 204 for 8 (J. Arun Lal 52)
Central Zone 208 for 2 (J. Mathur 66 not out, S.S. Khandkar 64)

Central Zone won by 8 wickets

In the first match of India's first limited-over competition of the season, Central Zone won with ease, reaching their target with 29 balls of their 50 overs remaining.

CHARMINAR CHALLENGE CUP – FOURTH ONE-DAY INTERNATIONAL – INDIA v. NEW ZEALAND
17 December 1988 at Moti Bagh Palace Stadium, Baroda

NEW ZEALAND						INDIA					
J.G. Wright†	st Pandit, b Venkataramana			68		V.B. Chandrasekhar	c Bracewell, b Morrison			1
A.H. Jones	c Pandit, b Venkataramana			57		C.S. Pandit*	b Snedden			30
K.R. Rutherford	c Manjrekar, b C.J. Sharma			32		W.V. Raman	run out			5
M.J. Greatbatch	not out			84		S.V. Manjrekar	c Chatfield, b Morrison			52
T.E. Blain	not out			11		D.B. Vengsarkar†	b Kuggeleijn			28
I.D.S. Smith*						M. Azharuddin	not out			108
C.M. Kuggeleijn						A.K. Sharma	c Jones, b Morrison			50
J.G. Bracewell						S.K. Sharma	run out			0
M.C. Snedden						C.J. Sharma	c Smith, b Snedden			0
D.K. Morrison						M. Venkataramana	not out			0
E.J. Chatfield						R.G. Patel				
Extras	b 1, lb 13, w 7, nb 5			26		Extras	b 2, lb 5, w 1			6
(50 overs)	(for 3 wkts)			278		(47.1 overs)	(for 8 wkts)			282

	O	M	R	W			O	M	R	W
C.J. Sharma	10	–	54	1		Morrison	10	–	50	3
Patel	10	1	58	–		Chatfield	10	–	61	–
S.K. Sharma	10	–	74	–		Snedden	9	–	51	2
Venkataramana	10	–	36	2		Bracewell	10	–	49	–
A.K. Sharma	9	1	31	–		Kuggeleijn	8.1	–	64	1
Raman	1	–	11	–						

FALL OF WICKETS
1–140, 2–155, 3–211

FALL OF WICKETS
1–3, 2–12, 3–50, 4–118, 5–133, 6–260, 7–263, 8–278

Umpires: P.G. Pandit & V.K. Ramaswamy

Man of the Match: M. Azharuddin

India won by 2 wickets

Mohammed Azharuddin followed his fine innings in the third Test with the fastest hundred in limited-over international cricket in the one-day game at Baroda. (Adrian Murrell/Allsport)

Semi-Finals

24 January 1989

at Kanpur

West Zone 224 for 4 (S.V. Manjrekar 66 not out)
South Zone 228 for 4 (R.M.H. Binny 62 not out, M. Azharuddin 58)

South Zone won by 6 wickets

at Vidarbha CA Ground, Nagpur

North Zone 301 for 7 (R.N. Kapil Dev 111, K.P. Bhaskar 77, S. Srinavasan 4 for 48)
Central Zone 118

North Zone won by 183 runs

A disappointing batting display by West Zone gave the South a comparatively easy task at Kanpur, and with Azharuddin and Binny adding 94 for the fourth wicket, South Zone won a lacklustre match with 7.2 overs to spare.

North Zone's victory was even more decisive as Kapil Dev hit a century off 43 balls, and his side overwhelmed Central Zone.

Final

28 January 1989

at Kanpur

South Zone 239 for 8 (Abdul Azeem 63, M. Azharuddin 50 not out)
North Zone 243 for 6 (Ashwini Kapoor 62)

North Zone won by 4 wickets

North Zone won the Deodhar Trophy for the third year in succession, so confirming their supremacy in limited-over cricket. Their victory came with five overs to spare. Prabhakar had a fine all-round match, and there was another punishing innings from Kapil Dev. Bhaskar Pillai was outstanding in the field.

Wills Trophy

Quarter-Finals

12 March 1989

at Visakhapatnam

Baroda 138 for 9
Wills XI 139 for 2

Wills XI won by 8 wickets

at Chinnaswamy Stadium, Bangalore

Tamil Nadu 109
Delhi 111 for 2

Delhi won by 8 wickets

A damp pitch after heavy rain caused the match at Visakhapatnam to be reduced to 30 overs, and Baroda failed to come to terms with the situation. They lost three batsmen, run out in a mad dash for runs, and Pandit's aggression took the Wills XI to an easy victory.

Tamil Nadu surrendered meekly to Delhi, giving a most inept display.

Semi-Finals

15 March 1989

at Hyderabad

Railways 261 (Durga Prasad 77, Raju Kulkarni 4 for 51)
BCCI President's XI 211 (Ashwini Kapoor 80)

Railways won by 50 runs

at Visakhapatnam

Delhi 277 for 7 (K.P. Bhaskar 56, M. Nayyar 54)
Wills XI 226 (L.S. Rajput 81)

Delhi won by 51 runs

Railways entered the Wills final for the first time when, having been put in, they reached a commendable score thanks mainly to an intelligent innings from Durga Prasad after a good opening stand of 56 by Yusuf Ali Khan and Radhakrishnan. Prasad followed his fine knock with 3 for 22 in 7.1 overs.

Delhi were equally emphatic winners, although Rajput and Gursharan Singh added 100 for Wills XI's third wicket. The dismissal of Rajput, 81 off 87 balls, Gursharan Singh and Gunjal within the space of 37 deliveries turned the match in favour of Delhi.

Final

19 March 1989

at Madras

Railways 200 (Yusuf Ali Khan 71, P. Jain 4 for 51)
Delhi 205 for 2 (R. Lamba 116 not out, M. Prabhakar 71)

Delhi won by 8 wickets

Put in to bat, Railways began well enough. Stands of 54 between Yusuf Ali Khan and Radhakrishnan, and 70 between Yusuf Ali Khan and Durga Prasad, took them to 143 for 2, but collapse followed, and, in the post-lunch period, Delhi dominated the game. Lamba and Prabhakar added 174 in 35.5 overs for the second wicket, and Delhi raced to victory with 5.5 overs to spare.

Ranji Trophy

North Zone

13, 14 and 15 October 1988

at Sher-I-Kashmir Stadium, Srinagar

Services 230 (Chinmoy Sharma 84, Abdul Qayyum 4 for 63) and 240 for 5 dec (Bhaskar Ghosh 100 not out, A.S. Bajwa 64)
Jammu and Kashmir 201 (Shahid Pervez 75, Ashwini Gupta 51, Vilas Kadam 6 for 61) and 183 for 5 (Ashwini Gupta 55 not out)

Match drawn
Services 13 pts, Jammu and Kashmir 10 pts

India's premier domestic competition began with the North Zone match at Srinagar. Put in to bat, Services struggled against debutant medium-pace bowler Abdul Qayyum, but Chinmoy Sharma held the middle order together only to see the last five wickets go down for 28 runs. Vilas Kadam's medium pace troubled Jammu, and only a fourth-wicket stand of 116 between Gupta and Pervez saved them from complete annihilation. After skipper Bhaskar Ghosh had hit a century for Services, Jammu were set to make 270 at more than five an over, a task that was beyond them.

18, 19 and 20 October 1988

at Bikram Park, Udhampur

Jammu and Kashmir 123 (M. Prabhakar 4 for 40) and 135
Delhi 320 for 8 dec (K.P. Bhaskar 93, M. Nayyar 61, Kirti Azad retired hurt 58, Ajay Sharma 57, Sanjay Sharma 4 for 62)

Delhi won by an innings and 62 runs
Delhi 23 pts, Jammu and Kashmir 3 pts

Delhi gained their expected resounding victory over Jammu and Kashmir after Madan Lal had won the toss and, in combination with Prabhakar, had bowled Jammu out on the opening day. In spite of losing Lamba and Prabhakar for 44, Delhi never looked like relinquishing their hold on the match, with Bhaskar Pillai again in fine form and pressing for a Test place.

Manoj Prabhakar – an outstanding all-round season for Delhi, but no place in the national side. (Sporting Pictures UK Ltd)

23, 24 and 25 October 1988

at Sher-I-Kashmir Stadium, Srinagar

Jammu and Kashmir 154 (C.J. Sharma 5 for 55) and 291 (Shahid Pervez 63)
Haryana 348 (Yashpal Sharma 78 not out, Deepak Sharma 76, Ajay Jadeja 69, Amarjeet Kaypee 57, Asif Peerjada 6 for 144) and 98 for 0

Haryana won by 10 wickets
Haryana 18 pts, Jammu and Kashmir 5 pts

Fine bowling by Chetan Sharma and Deepak Sharma bundled out Jammu on the opening day, by the close of which Haryana had taken a nine-run lead for the loss of only one wicket. Haryana consolidated their position on the second day with some sound batting after losing two wickets early on, and, by the end of the day, Jammu were fighting for survival, having conceded a first-innings lead of 194 and being 150 for 4 in their second. Jammu fought back bravely on the last day, but Haryana duly accomplished victory. One consolation for Jammu was that Asif Peerjada returned the best bowling figures of his career.

28, 29 and 30 October 1988

at Sher-I-Kashmir Stadium, Srinagar

Punjab 480 for 7 dec (Gursharan Singh 152, D. Pandove 137, Ashwini Kapoor 60, Arun Sharma 52 not out, Abdul Qayyum 4 for 160)
Jammu and Kashmir 316 (Sudarshan Mehta 86, Ashwini 72, Bhupinder Singh 6 for 40) and 156 (Krishna Mohan 6 for 43)

Punjab won by an innings and 8 runs
Punjab 22 pts, Jammu and Kashmir 6 pts

Punjab gained a dramatic victory over Jammu and Kashmir at Srinagar, the home side suffering their third substantial defeat in succession. Partnerships of 145 for the second wicket between Dhruv Pandove and Ashwini Kapoor, and 137 for the third wicket between Pandove and Gursharan Singh, took Punjab to 372 for 5 on the opening day after they had been put in to bat. Ghai declared at lunch on the second day and Bhupinder made the early breakthrough for Punjab when he bowled Rahil Habib, the debutant wicket-keeper opening batsman. Ashwini Gupta and Sudarshan Mehta shared a fourth-wicket partnership of 106, however, and Jammu closed the day on 229 for 4, looking sure to save the follow-on and the match. It was right-arm medium-pace bowler Bhupinder Singh who gave the advantage to Punjab when he claimed four of the last five wickets while only 47 were added. Bhupinder returned the best bowling figures of his career, 6 for 40. Jammu, forced to follow-on, batted doggedly for survival, but spinner Krishna Mohan bowled better than at any time in his brief career, to reduce them to 122 for 9. Sanjay Sharma and Asif Peerjada joined in a courageous last-wicket stand, which threatened to deny Punjab, but, with the fourth ball of the last over of the match, Bhupinder had Sharma lbw to give Punjab victory.

5, 6 and 7 November 1988

at Indira Stadium, Una

Punjab 393 for 8 dec (Sapan Chopra 88, Ashwini Kapoor 71, Jaspal Singh 50 not out, Jaswant Rai 4 for 91)
Himachal Pradesh 144 (M.I. Singh 6 for 63) and 203 (Rajkumar 57, Jaspal Singh 5 for 43)

Punjab won by an innings and 16 runs
Punjab 20 pts, Himachal Pradesh 3 pts

Punjab moved to the top of the North Zone table with their second-innings victory in two matches. Consistent batting took Punjab to a commanding 393 for 8, and Mahesh Inder Singh's off-breaks and Jaspal Singh's career-best second-innings bowling proved too much for Himachal Pradesh.

11, 12 and 13 November 1988

at Indira Stadium, Una

Haryana 351 (Yashpal Sharma 153, Anil Sen 4 for 93) and 99 for 2 dec
Himachal Pradesh 262 (R. Nayyar 110) and 72 for 6

Match drawn
Haryana 13 pts, Himachal Pradesh 9 pts

at Army Headquarters, Delhi

Punjab 316 for 7 dec (Vikram Rathore 128, Ashwini Kapoor 109) and 295 for 2 (Ashwini Kapoor 135 not out)
Services 321 (Chinmoy Sharma 78 not out, Bhaskar Ghosh 74, Arjit Ghosh 53, M.I. Singh 4 for 47)

Match drawn
Punjab 13 pts, Services 11 pts

Both Haryana and Punjab were held in matches which they would have expected to win. The bigger upset was at Una, where Yashpal Sharma hit a fine 153 to help his side to a score which looked sufficient to win the match, but Haryana dropped vital catches at the start of the Himachal Pradesh innings and the home side finished the second day on 176 for 5. The last day was historic for Himachal Pradesh, for, batting with great restraint and good sense, Rajiv Nayyar became the first of their batsmen to hit a century in the Ranji Trophy. The follow-on was saved, and Haryana were thwarted again when they set Himachal 50 minutes and 20 overs in which to score 189. Rajiv Nayyar is the son of Major S.C. Nayyar, who captained Himachal Pradesh in the first Ranji Trophy match in 1985.

In the match at Delhi, Punjab were in a strong position at the end of the first day. Ashwini Kapoor and Vikram Rathore had both hit centuries and shared a fifth-wicket partnership of 208, 122 of which had come between lunch and tea, and the score was 292 for 6 at the close. Gursharan Singh declared early next morning, but, in spite of the early loss of Bajwa, Services moved doggedly to a first-innings lead. The Ghosh brothers, Arjit and Bhaskar, proved particularly defiant, and Punjab coach and manager Bishen Bedi circled the field in frustration as his pupils failed to gain the necessary breakthrough. He gained some consolation on the last day when Ashwini Kapoor became the only batsman during the season to hit a century in each innings.

14, 15 and 16 November 1988

at Ferozeshah Kotla Ground, Delhi

Punjab 221 (Arun Sharma 54) and 219 for 8 dec (Gursharan Singh 60, Shankar Saini 5 for 52)
Delhi 337 (Bantoo Singh 83, Ajay Sharma 70, R. Lamba 60) and 26 for 0

Match drawn
Delhi 13 pts, Punjab 7 pts

At 104 for 7, Punjab looked in deep despair on the opening day against Delhi, but a stand of 83 between Arun Sharma and Bhupinder Singh gave them some encouragement and helped them to 221, a more respectable score than had been anticipated. Nevertheless, Delhi's consistent batting strength took them to a first-innings lead for the loss of only two wickets. Batting for a second time, 116 runs in arrears, Punjab could try only to avoid defeat and this they did through a resolute sixth-wicket partnership between Gursharan Singh and Arun Sharma.

16, 17 and 18 November 1988

at Race Course Ground, Delhi

Services 211 (Chetan Sharma 4 for 112) and 115 (Chetan Sharma 5 for 49)
Haryana 446 for 8 dec (D. Sharma 143, A. Jadeja 58, Amarjeet Kaypee 58)

Haryana won by an innings and 120 runs
Haryana 24 pts, Services 5 pts

at Indira Stadium, Una

Jammu and Kashmir 327 (Ashwini Gupta 60, S. Mehta 58, Z. Bhatt 56) and 34 for 0.
Himachal Pradesh 146 (B. Dhar 4 for 28) and 280 for 8 dec (V. Sen 90, R. Nayyar 78)

Match drawn
Jammu and Kashmir 12 pts, Himachal Pradesh 5 pts

Fine medium-pace bowling by Chetan Sharma and an excellent century by opening batsman Deepak Sharma took Haryana to a resounding victory over Services and mounted their challenge for a place in the later stages of the competition.

Meanwhile, in the wooden spoon match at Una, Himachal Pradesh were forced to follow-on, but recovered sufficiently through a 145-run fourth-wicket partnership between Nayyar and Sen to save the game.

20, 21 and 22 November 1988

at Air Force Station, Palam, Delhi

Himachal Pradesh 271 (Jaswant Rai 53, Ramesh Dutta 51, G. Radkar 4 for 64) and 242 for 9 (R. Nayyar 77, V. Sen 53, M.V. Rao 4 for 69)
Services 449 for 9 dec (A. Ghosh 109, B. Ghosh 102, R. Nayyar 7 for 93)

Match drawn
Services 13 pts, Himachal Pradesh 7 pts

at Nahar Singh Stadium, Faridabad

Haryana 303 (Yashpal Sharma 111, Amarjeet Kaypee 75, C.J. Sharma 60, P. Jain 5 for 42) and 206 for 7 (D. Sharma 58, A. Jadeja 52)
Delhi 399 for 7 dec (R. Lamba 138, M. Prabhakar 106, K.P. Bhaskar 69 not out)

Match drawn
Delhi 14 pts, Haryana 9 pts

Rajiv Nayyar followed his performance in becoming the first Himachal Pradesh player to score a century with a match-saving innings against Services and figures of 7 for 93, the best ever recorded for Himachal. His first wicket came when he bowled Arjit Ghosh who, with his brother Bhaskar, had added 179 for the second wicket. Both brothers completed centuries, a remarkable achievement.

Haryana moved to the top of the table after drawing with Delhi. Another splendid innings from Yashpal Sharma, who shared a fourth-wicket stand of 134 with skipper Amarjeet Kaypee, put Haryana in a good position, although batting was slow. Lamba reached a hundred in under three hours in contrast, moving to his century by hitting off-spinner Deepak Sharma for four, six and one off successive deliveries. He and Prabhakar

batted into the last day to add 220 for the second wicket, by which time the match was destined to be drawn.

24, 25 and 26 November 1988

at Ferozeshah Kotla Ground, Delhi

Delhi 448 for 3 dec (M. Prabhakar 229 not out, R. Lamba 118, K.P. Bhaskar 64)
Himachal Pradesh 102 (S. Saini 6 for 21) and 78 (M. Prabhakar 6 for 36)

Delhi won by an innings and 268 runs
Delhi 24 pts, Himachal Pradesh 1 pt

In gaining the biggest victory of the season inside two days, Delhi recorded a number of notable performances. Lamba and Prabhakar hit centuries for the second match in succession and shared a second-wicket stand of 280. Prabhakar hit the highest score of his career and completed an outstanding all-round performance with seven wickets in the match, six of them for 36, a career-best, in the second innings. Another career-best bowling performance came from Shankar Saini. The medium pacer took 6 for 21 in the first innings and ended the innings when he dismissed Dutt and Anil Sen with successive balls. Brought into the attack for the 19th over of the second innings, with the score at 71 for 6, he had Shakti Singh caught with his first delivery and bowled Satish Mehra with his next to give him four wickets in four balls. Delhi's win placed them top of the table, with qualification for the knock-out stage a certainty, while Himachal Pradesh were condemned to the wooden spoon.

25, 26 and 27 November 1988

at Punjab Agricultural University, Ludhiana

Punjab 183 (D. Sharma 6 for 48, V. Dutt 4 for 63) and 273 for 9 dec (R.S. Ghai 64, V. Rathore 57, A. Singla 4 for 35)
Haryana 111 (K. Mohan 4 for 29, M.I. Singh 4 for 40) and 180 (Yashpal Sharma 65 not out, B. Vij 5 for 32, M.I. Singh 4 for 90)

Punjab won by 165 runs
Punjab 15 pts, Haryana 7 pts

In an exciting match at Ludhiana, Punjab finally claimed victory and so qualified for the knock-out stage of the Ranji Trophy. Batting first on a wicket which encouraged the spinners, Punjab were bowled out for 183, off-spinners Deepak Sharma and Vinay Dutt sharing the 10 wickets. Haryana closed the day on 60 for 3, but collapsed next morning against spinners Mohan and M.I. Singh. Left-arm spinner Arun Singla bowled well for Haryana, but Punjab batted with great consistency and determination to build upon their first-innings lead of 72. Krishna Mohan and Ghai, whose batting has advanced as his bowling has diminished in effectiveness, were particularly resourceful in the late middle order, and Ghai was able to declare and set Haryana a daunting target of 346. They ended the second day on 30 for 1, but they were all out within 200 minutes on the last day, only Yashpal Sharma showing any spirit. Mahesh Singh claimed four wickets, the last of which, Vinay Dutt, gave him 100 wickets in Ranji Trophy cricket. There was also some excellent bowling from slow left-armer Bharati Vij, who claimed a career-best 5 for 32.

28, 29 and 30 November 1988

at Ferozeshah Kotla Ground, Delhi

Services 227 (B. Ghosh 70, M. Prabhakar 5 for 17) and 275 (B.R. Singh 81)
Delhi 287 (R. Lamba 56, M.V. Rao 4 for 105) and 232 for 2 (R. Lamba 70, M. Nayyar 67, M. Prabhakar 61 not out)

Delhi won by 8 wickets
Delhi 20 pts, Services 7 pts

Delhi gained their expected win over Services to claim the North Zone title, but only after a few alarms. Manoj Prabhakar gave another fine all-round display, taking 8 for 79 in the match. Delhi owed much to determined late-order batting; their last four wickets added nearly a hundred valuable runs. Chinmoy Sharma and B.R. Singh held up Delhi with a sixth-wicket stand of 120, but Nayyar, Lamba and Prabhakar made up the time lost by racing to victory at nearly eight runs an over.

North Zone Final Table					
	P	*W*	*L*	*D*	*Pts*
Delhi	5	3	–	2	94
Punjab	5	3	–	2	77
Haryana	5	2	1	2	71
Services	5	–	2	3	49
Jammu and Kashmir	5	–	3	2	36
Himachal Pradesh	5	–	2	3	25

Central Zone

13, 14 and 15 November 1988

at Digvijay Stadium, Rajnandagon

Madhya Pradesh 165 and 150 (S. Vyas 5 for 48, Y. Mathur 4 for 39)
Rajasthan 122 (R. Chauhan 7 for 39) and 63 (S.M. Patil 5 for 9, R. Chauhan 4 for 30)

Madhya Pradesh won by 130 runs
Madhya Pradesh 17 pts, Rajasthan 5 pts

at Vidarbha CA, Nagpur

Vidarbha 499 (S. Phadkar 203, S. Hujar 115, G. Pandey 4 for 82) and 49 for 1 dec
Uttar Pradesh 355 (R. Sapru 87, Indrapal Singh 73, S.S. Khandkar 62, H.R. Wasu 5 for 78) and 82 for 4

Match drawn
Vidarbha 13 pts, Uttar Pradesh 8 pts

In a match in which Suhail Ansari's 47 was the highest score and 165 the highest team score, Madhya Pradesh still managed to win by 130 runs. There were two outstanding performances. On the occasion of his debut, Chauhan returned match figures of 11 for 69, the best of the season, and skipper Sandeep Patil, once of India and Bombay, had second-innings figures of 5.2–3–9–5 as Rajasthan were bowled out for the lowest score of the season.

In contrast, at Nagpur, Gujar and Phadkar put on 315 for Vidarbha's fifth wicket, the fourth highest partnership for this wicket in the history of the competition and a Vidarbha record for any wicket. Phadkar went on to reach the first double century hit for the association, but Uttar Pradesh replied with some solid batting and the match was drawn.

19, 20 and 21 November 1988

at Karnail Singh Stadium, Delhi

Madhya Pradesh 241 (K.K. Sharma 4 for 78, S. Srinivasan 4 for 87) and 215 (A. Varia 93, Rattan Singh 7 for 48)
Railways 315 (P.K. Amre 110, N.K. Churi 57, T.A. Sekhar 6 for 109) and 64 for 2

Match drawn
Railways 14 pts, Madhya Pradesh 10 pts

at Vidarbha CA, Nagpur

Vidarbha 336 (H.R. Wasu 69, U. Phate 54, P. Vaidya 53 not out) and 174 for 7 dec (R. Pankule 71, Yogesh Mathur 5 for 55)
Rajasthan 402 for 9 dec (S. Vyas 128, S. Mudkavi 84, Amar Singh Negi 79, H.R. Wasu 4 for 120) and 84 for 3 (Jaideep Mathur 56 not out)

Match drawn
Rajasthan 12 pts, Vidarbha 9 pts

Slow left-arm bowler Rattan Singh produced a career-best bowling performance for Railways, for whom Churi and Amre shared a century stand, but his side had insufficient time in which to force a win.

Vidarbha's chances of reaching the knock-out stage of the competition suffered a severe set-back when they failed to beat Rajasthan. Vidarbha slumped to 195 for 7, and they were saved only by some late-order hitting, Wasu and Vaidya putting on 100 for the ninth wicket. Vyas, Negi and Mudkavi took Rajasthan to a first-innings lead, however, and they even attempted to score the 109 runs in the last 10 overs that they needed to win the match.

Sandeep Patil changed his allegiance to Madhya Pradesh and, with some fine all-round cricket, played an important part in their qualifying from the Central Zone for the knock-out stage of the Ranji Trophy. (Adrian Murrell/ Allsport)

25, 26 and 27 November 1988

at Kanla Club, Kanpur

Uttar Pradesh 361 (S.S. Khandkar 82, Ghopal Sharma 82, R. Venkatesh 5 for 101) and 178 for 8 dec (R. Venkatesh 5 for 58)
Railways 237 (Yusuf Ali Khan 114, G. Sharma 6 for 73) and 115 for 1

Match drawn
Uttar Pradesh 12 pts, Railways 10 pts

at Grasim Industries Ground, Nagda

Madhya Pradesh 423 (S.M. Patil 100, P. Divedi 90, A. Vijayavargiya 63, P. Laghate retired hurt 53, H.R. Wasu 4 for 72)
Vidarbha 149 (U. Phate 55, T.A. Sekhar 7 for 54) and 214 (P. Hingnikar 98, S. Lahore 4 for 68)

Madhya Pradesh won by an innings and 60 runs
Madhya Pradesh 21 pts, Vidarbha 2 pts

A second win in three matches made Madhya Pradesh favourites to reach the later stages of the Ranji Trophy. Sandeep Patil played a fine captain's innings and was ably supported by Divedi, Vijayavargiya and Laghate. Vidarbha were routed by former Tamil Nadu and Indian Test player Tirumalai Sekhar, who returned match figures of 10 for 98.

Uttar Pradesh batted consistently against Railways, but a dour second innings left them insufficient time in which to press for victory.

2, 3 and 4 December 1988

at Roop Singh Stadium, Gwalior

Railways 499 for 7 dec (P.K. Amre 214 not out, S.M.H. Kirmani 103)
Vidarbha 330 (S. Gujar 64, U. Ghani 61, S. Takle 55, Rattan Singh 4 for 56) and 138 for 3 (P. Hingnikar 52)

Match drawn
Railways 12 pts, Vidarbha 9 pts

at Mansingh Stadium, Jaipur

Rajasthan 246 (S. Mudkavi 78, Mazhar Ali 5 for 68) and 206 (R. Sapru 5 for 30)
Uttar Pradesh 430 (S. Chaturvedi 118, S.S. Khandkar 88, V. Vats 77) and 23 for 3

Uttar Pradesh won by 7 wickets
Uttar Pradesh 17 pts, Rajasthan 5 pts

Syed Kirmani hit his first century for Railways. It was the ninth century of the 37-year-old former Test wicket-keeper's career, and he shared a fourth-wicket partnership of 201 with Amre, who hit the highest score of his career. Rattan Singh again bowled effectively, and Vidarbha were forced to follow-on, but they had no difficulty in saving the game.

In contrast, Rajasthan were well beaten by Uttar Pradesh, who thereby moved into a strong position to qualify for the quarter-finals. Khandkar and Chaturvedi put on 156 for the third wicket, and Uttar Pradesh's only moment of concern was, when chasing a meagre 23 to win, they lost three wickets to Vyas.

9, 10 and 11 December 1988

at Mansingh Stadium, Jaipur

Railways 206 (S. Vyas 4 for 62) and 255 for 7 dec (K. Bharathan 98, Yusuf Ali Khan 60)
Rajasthan 99 (Rattan Singh 5 for 18) and 260 (Rattan Singh 5 for 89)

Railways won by 102 runs
Railways 16 pts, Rajasthan 6 pts

at Kamla Club, Kanpur

Uttar Pradesh 266 (R. Sapru 90, S.M. Patil 5 for 54, R. Chauhan 5 for 92) and 141 for 8 dec
Madhya Pradesh 147 (G. Sharma 6 for 43) and 111 (G. Sharma 5 for 26, M.A. Ansari 4 for 27)

Uttar Pradesh won by 149 runs
Uttar Pradesh 17 pts, Madhya Pradesh 6 pts

A fine victory over Rajasthan proved to be insufficient to earn Railways a place in the knock-out stage of the competition. Uttar Pradesh beat Madhya Pradesh to clinch the second qualifying place by the narrowest of margins, with Madhya earning themselves just enough points in defeat. Rattan Singh again bowled splendidly for Railways, but their failure to score runs quickly enough, or take wickets soon enough in the second innings, cost them dearly.

Uttar Pradesh's 266 in 85.4 overs gave them a vital extra point, and Madhya Pradesh gained all their points with their bowling, the young discovery, Chauhan, having another fine match with 8 for 144.

Central Zone Final Table

	P	W	L	D	Pts
Madhya Pradesh	4	2	1	1	54
Uttar Pradesh	4	2	–	2	54
Railways	4	1	–	3	52
Vidarbha	4	–	1	3	33
Rajasthan	4	–	3	1	28

South Zone

22, 23 and 24 November 1988

at Gymkhana Ground, Secunderabad

Hyderabad 425 for 9 dec (K.A. Qayyum 106, V. Jaisimha 90, Arun Paul 73, Ehtesham Ali Khan 64)
Kerala 248 (S. Ramesh 84) and 123 (M.V. Narasimha Rao 4 for 42)

Hyderabad won by an innings and 42 runs
Hyderabad 24 pts, Kerala 5 pts

Big stands for the second and fourth wickets and a thoroughly good team performance gave Hyderabad a comfortable win in the opening South Zone match. Only Ramesh and debutant Padmanabhan, with a ninth-wicket stand of 84, threatened Hyderabad's supremacy.

26, 27 and 28 November 1988

at Panjim Gymkhana, Panaji

Goa 371 (S. Dhuri 141, S. Shinde 101, A.R. Bhat 4 for 111) and 87 for 1 dec

Karnataka 373 for 6 dec (Madhu Vijay 110, Ramesh Rao 80, R.M.H. Binny 66, S. Viswanath 53 not out) and 20 for 2

Match drawn
Karnataka 10 pts, Goa 7 pts

With G.R. Viswanath and Brijesgh Patel having retired and Kirmani having opted to play for Railways, Karnataka began the season with problems, but they could hardly have expected the stiff opposition that they received from Goa, whom they had beaten by an innings the previous season. A century by Shinde on the opening day was followed by a maiden century from Sandeep Dhuri, and Goa moved to an impressive total. Karnataka's first-innings lead was due to some excellent batting after the loss of Saldanha and Arjun Raja for 97. The dominant force was debutant Madhu Vijay, who hit a very fine hundred, the fourth Karnataka batsman to achieve this feat on his debut. Vijay and Ramesh Rao added 126 for the third wicket, and Binny and Viswanath batted in lively fashion, but Goa continued to frustrate their illustrious opponents who had to settle for 10 points.

29, 30 and 31 November 1988

at Police Parade Ground, Guntur

Kerala 243 (Ranganathan 73, Chakradhar Rao 4 for 81) and 174 (P.T. Subramaniam 85)
Andhra 341 (V. Chamundeswaranath 125, P.T. Subramaniam 5 for 86) and 78 for 2

Andhra won by 8 wickets
Andhra 19 pts, Kerala 6 pts

In spite of a brave display of all-round cricket from Subramaniam, Kerala were well beaten by Andhra. A maiden century from skipper Vankenna Chamundeswara-nath, who made his first-class debut in 1978, was the highlight of the Andhra innings. He added 131 for the sixth wicket with wicket-keeper Krishna Mohan.

3, 4 and 5 December 1988

at Chamundi Vihar Stadium, Mysore

Hyderabad 208 (Abdul Azeem 76, R. Ananth 5 for 60) and 113 (A.R. Bhat 6 for 29)
Karnataka 138 (N.S. Yadav 4 for 30) and 187 for 5 (S. Viswanath 59 not out)

Karnataka won by 5 wickets
Karnataka 15 pts, Hyderabad 8 pts

Debutant off-spinner Ananth gave an impressive perform-ance on the opening day and was mainly responsible for Hyderabad being bowled out for 208. In reply, Karnataka were 50 for 3, and they slumped to 138 all out on the second day, with veteran off-spinner Shivlal Yadav doing most of the damage. Trailing by 70 runs, Karnataka clawed their way back into the game by capturing seven Hyderabad wickets for 91 runs before the end of the second day. Left-arm spinner Raghuram Bhat brought about the rout, and he was ably assisted by another left-arm spinner, Jeshwant, who took the last three wickets for nine runs. Needing to score 184 to win, Karnataka were given a good start by Saldanha and Vijay, but four men were out for 91. It was Sadanand Viswanath

who brought victory, with a confident 2¼-hour innings. The win was a great encouragement to a Karnataka side which, under Binny's leadership, is in the process of rebuilding.

10, 11 and 12 December 1988

at Gymkhana Ground, Secunderabad

Hyderabad 268 (R.A. Swarup 82, K.A. Qayyum 62, S. Subramaniam 4 for 67) and 128 (Arun Kumar 4 for 29, M. Venkataramana 4 for 33)
Tamil Nadu 168 (N.S. Yadav 6 for 44) and 53 for 3

Match drawn
Hyderabad 13 pts, Tamil Nadu 12 pts

at Bahadur Shastri Stadium, Quilon

Goa 216 (S. Shinde 72, V. Hariharan 4 for 48) and 339 for 5 dec (S. Kangralkar 138 not out, D. Bangera 121)
Kerala 427 for 7 dec (Ranganathan 92, P.T. Subramaniam 72 not out, Thomas Mathew 66, P.G. Sunder 55) and 6 for 0

Match drawn
Kerala 15 pts, Goa 7 pts

Tamil Nadu, the reigning champions, made a distinctly unspectacular entry into the Ranji Trophy as they strug-gled for most of the match against Hyderabad. Hyderabad won the toss and began with a flourish, but the later batsmen failed to exploit the advantage that they had been given. Sunil Subramaniam made an excellent debut for Tamil Nadu with his left-arm spin, and it was he who dismissed Rajesh Yadav just in time to give his side the fourth bowling point. The wicket offered the spinners assistance from the start, and Hyderabad owed much to the experienced pair of Khalid Abdul Qayyum and Nara-simha Rao, who added 71 for the fifth wicket. Just how valuable their stand had been could be seen on the second day, when the bowlers dominated, 18 wickets fell, and Shivlal Yadav returned his best figures in the Ranji Trophy. At the end of the day, Hyderabad were 113 for 8, a commanding lead of 213, but rain on the last day denied them victory.

Goa showed their vast improvement with a fighting performance on the matting at Quilon. With Thomas Mathew and P. Ranganathan putting on 162 for the first wicket, Kerala took a first-innings lead of 211. When Goa slipped to 59 for 4 in their second innings, defeat looked imminent, but Kangralkar and Bangera added 236 for the fifth wicket, a record for Goa for any wicket, and the match was saved.

17, 18 and 19 December 1988

at Kakinda

Hyderabad 344 (M.V. Sridhar 74, Ehtesham Ali Khan 75 not out, R.A. Swarup 69, B.S. Mangesh 5 for 108) and 262 for 3 dec (M.V. Sridhar 129 not out, R.A. Swarup 66)
Andhra 273 (K.V.S.D. Kamaraju 138, R. Yadav 6 for 87, V. Raju 4 fo 63) and 130 for 4

Match drawn
Hyderabad 19 pts, Andhra 10 pts

at Lal Bahadur Shastri Stadium, Quilon

Karnataka 184 (V. Hariharan 7 for 60) and 330 for 7 dec (R.M.H. Binny 140)
Kerala 301 (P.G. Sunder 71, P.T. Subramaniam 62) and 171 for 5 (P. Ranganathan 101 not out)

Match drawn
Karnataka 13 pts, Kerala 13 pts

An impressive debut by Sridhar, 203 runs for once out in the match, could not bring Hyderabad victory at Kakinda, but they enjoyed a profitable draw. Rajesh Yadav showed a return to his best form with his medium pace, and only Kamaraju coped with him adequately.

It was the medium pace of Hariharan, who had a career-best performance on the matting at Quilon, which shattered Karnataka, but Roger Binny played a captain's innings to bring his side back into the game. Nevertheless, Kerala were only 44 runs short of victory, with five wickets standing when time ran out. They owed much to a maiden century by Ranganathan.

24, 25 and 26 December 1988

at Maharaja College Ground, Ernakulam

Tamil Nadu 419 for 7 dec (Robin Singh 123 not out, W.V. Raman 90, K. Arun Kumar 51 not out)
Kerala 197 (B. Arun 5 for 72, Robin Singh 4 for 50) and 205 (P.G. Sunder 69 not out, B. Arun 6 for 79)

Tamil Nadu won by an innings and 17 runs
Tamil Nadu 24 pts, Kerala 7 pts

at Nehru Stadium, Bidar

Karnataka 419 (R.M.H. Binny 138, Ramesh Rao 79)
Andhra 239 (K.V.S.D. Kamaraju 78, K. Jeshwant 4 for 45, A.R. Bhat 4 for 95) and 347 for 5 (V. Chamundeswaranath 108, M.F. Rehman 81, S. Reddy 54)

Match drawn
Karnataka 13 pts, Andhra 9 pts

25, 26 and 27 December 1988

at Gymkhana Ground, Secunderabad

Hyderabad 394 (M. Azharuddin 105, Abdul Azeem 89, R.A. Swarup 53, U. Naik 6 for 103) and 213 for 3 (Abdul Azeem 64, R.A. Swarup 54)
Goa 255 (J. Fernandez 70, Arshad Ayub 5 for 69)

Match abandoned
Hyderabad 14 pts, Goa 10 pts

Splendid all-round cricket by left-handed batsman and right-arm medium-pace bowler, Rabindra (Robin) Singh, who was actually born in Trinidad, helped Tamil Nadu to maximum points against Kerala. Raman was also in fine form with the bat, and Bharathi Arun produced the best bowling spell of his career, taking 6 for 79 in the second innings and claiming 11 wickets with his medium pace.

Like Tamil Nadu, Hyderabad welcomed back their Test players, and Mohammed Azharuddin, leading the side, celebrated his return with a century. Arshad Ayub claimed five wickets and bowled Hyderabad to a first-innings lead, but play was abandoned after lunch on the third day because of political disturbances. The 14 points that Hyderabad earned, however, were enough to give them a place in the final stages of the competition, as Karnataka

failed to beat Andhra.

Binny hit his second century in succession and shared a fourth-wicket stand of 176 with Ramesh Rao to take Karnataka to a commanding score. The combined left-arm spin of Bhat and Jeshwant forced Andhra to follow-on, but Chamundeswaranath hit his second hundred of the season and saved the match.

31 December 1988, 1 and 2 January 1989

at Chidambaram Stadium, Madras

Tamil Nadu 447 (Robin Singh 131 not out, P.C. Prakash 58, M. Sharath 51) and 4 for 0
Andhra 173 (S. Subramaniam 7 for 44) and 276 (M.F. Rehman 83, M. Venkataramana 5 for 83, S. Subramaniam 4 for 109)

Tamil Nadu won by 10 wickets
Tamil Nadu 16 pts, Andhra 3 pts

Some more fine batting by Robin Singh, and some wonderfully impressive bowling by Sunil Subramaniam, took Tamil Nadu to a comfortable victory over Andhra and to the verge of the quarter-finals. The young left-arm spinner took 11 for 153 in what was only his third first-class match.

8, 9 and 10 January 1989

at Bandodkar Stadium, Panaji

Andhra 354 (V. Chamundeswaranath 144, K.V.S.D. Kamaraju 65, K.B.R. Murthy 55, V. Korgaonkar 5 for 60) and 239 (K.V.S.D. Kamaraju 115, V. Korgaonkar 4 for 40)
Goa 451 for 9 dec (S. Dhuri 108, V. Pednekar 99, S. Kangralkar 61, G.V. Gopal Raju 4 for 102) and 39 for 1

Match drawn
Goa 14 pts, Andhra 10 pts

The improvement of Goa was confirmed when they enjoyed the better of a draw with Andhra on an excellent batting wicket at Panaji. The third, and highest, century of the season for Chamundeswaranath took Andhra to a good score, but Pednekar and Dhuri ensured a commanding lead for Goa. Trailing by 97 runs, Andhra lost two cheap wickets and looked likely to lose, but Kamaraju and some forceful batting by the tail took them to safety.

15, 16 and 17 January 1989

at Chidambaram Stadium, Madras

Karnataka 98 (M. Venkataramana 4 for 13, Robin Singh 4 for 39) and 220 (C. Saldanha 83, S. Subramaniam 5 for 67)
Tamil Nadu 441 (Robin Singh 101, B. Arun 59, V. Sivaramakrishnan 77, V.B. Chandrasekhar 58, R. Anant 4 for 123)

Tamil Nadu won by an innings and 123 runs
Tamil Nadu 21 pts, Karnataka 1 pt

With Subramaniam looking like a Test-class bowler in his first season, and Robin Singh hitting his third hundred in succession, Tamil Nadu overwhelmed Karnataka. There was some encouraging bowling by the young spinner Anant and a good knock from Saldanha, whom many had believed would be on the verge of the Indian side in 1989, but Tamil Nadu were superior in all departments.

20, 21 and 22 January 1989

at Bandodkar Stadium, Panaji

Tamil Nadu 912 for 6 dec (W.V. Raman 313, Arjan Kripal Singh 302 not out, L. Sivaramakrishnan 100 not out, Robin Singh 69)
Goa 230 for 6 (Prasad Amonkar 74)

Match drawn
Tamil Nadu 8 pts, Goa 6 pts

The last match in the South Zone provided the sensation of the season. Tamil Nadu were 1 for 1, 12 for 2, 35 for 3 and 95 for 4 before Raman and Robin Singh added 165. Robin Singh was run out, and Raman and Kripal Singh then added 356, the second highest partnership for the fifth wicket in the history of the competition. When Raman was bowled by Angle for 313, the highest score ever made for Tamil Nadu, and the seventh highest in the tournament's history, Kripal Singh joined in an unbroken stand of 244 with Laxman Sivaramakrishnan. Tamil Nadu's 912 for 6 equalled Holkar's 912 for 8 made in 1945, which was the highest score made in the Ranji Trophy. It is the fifth highest score in the history of cricket, and is the first occasion that two batsmen have scored a triple century in the same innings. All 11 of the Goa side bowled, and they were penalized 52 runs for bowling 13 overs fewer than they should have done in the time. Tamil Nadu faced 191.2 overs, and Laxman Sivaramakrishnan, who was leading the side, declared when he reached his century off the bowling of Pednekar, the 11th man used. Goa had the consolation of going through the season unbeaten.

South Zone Final Table					
	P	*W*	*L*	*D*	*Pts*
Tamil Nadu	5	3	–	2	81
Hyderabad	5	1	1	3	78
Karnataka	5	1	1	3	52
Andhra	5	1	1	3	51
Kerala	5	–	3	2	46
Goa	5	–	–	5	44

West Zone

10, 11 and 12 December 1988

at GSFC Ground, Fertilizer Nagar, Baroda

Baroda 488 (T. Arothe 100, R. Parikh 86, A.D. Gaekwad 82, R. Jadeja 5 for 121)
Saurashtra 440 for 9 (B. Jadeja 190, K. Chauhan 101, A. Pandya 87 not out)

Match drawn
Baroda 6 pts, Saurashtra 6 pts

at Wankhede Stadium, Bombay

Gujarat 140 (A. Sabnis 5 for 41, P.N. Kasliwal 4 for 28) and 306 (B. Mistry 120, P.N. Kasliwal 4 for 84)
Bombay 394 for 6 dec (A. Sippy 127, S.R. Tendulkar 100 not out, L.S. Rajput 99) and 43 for 2

Match drawn
Bombay 13 pts, Gujarat 4 pts

A century by left-hander Tushar Arothe and solid batting from Gaekwad and Parikh put Baroda in an unassailable position in spite of some good bowling by paceman Rajendra Jadeja. Saurashtra countered well, with Kirit Chauhan and Bimal Jadeja adding 240 for the second wicket. Left-handed Bimal Jadeja hit the highest score of his career, but a draw had long been the obvious outcome of the match.

Bombay quickly disposed of Gujarat on the opening day at Wankhede Stadium and took the lead for the loss of only one wicket. Rajput and Sippy added 159 for the second wicket, and Sippy and Tendulkar 155 for the third. Rajput delayed his declaration until debutant Tendulkar had reached his century, and the understandable delay may have cost Bombay a chance of victory. Led by left-hander Bharat Mistry, who hit a maiden first-class hundred, Gujarat fought back well, and Bombay were left with seven overs in which to score 53 to win, a task they failed to accomplish.

17, 18 and 19 December 1988

at Nehru Stadium, Pune

Gujarat 341 (B. Mistry 90, M. Parmar 85, B. Patel 58, J. Zinto 52, S. Ankola 6 for 108) and 194 for 6 (N. Laliwala 52)
Maharashtra 516 for 7 dec (S.J. Kalyani 115, M.D. Gunjal 109, S. Sugwekar 85, J. Saigal 4 for 145)

Match drawn
Maharashtra 13 pts, Gujarat 8pts

at Municipal Ground, Rajkot

Bombay 252 (S.S. Hattangadi 103, S.R. Tendulkar 58, Ashok Patel 4 for 73, B. Radia 4 for 74) and 250 for 5 dec (S.R. Tendulkar 89, S.S. Hattangadi 76, V. Gohil 4 for 72)
Saurashtra 297 (B. Radiyani 77, B. Jadeja 61, S.V. Nayak 4 for 85, K.D. Mokashi 4 for 95) and 76 for 4

Match drawn
Saurashtra 12 pts, Bombay 11 pts

In a good season for newcomers, Ankola took six wickets on his debut for Maharashtra. He added further glory by dismissing Zinto, Saigal and D. Patel with the second, third and fourth balls of his 24th over to complete a hat trick, a most memorable achievement in his first match. Kalyani and Gunjal hit centuries to take Maharashtra to an impressive score, but Gujarat had no difficulty in drawing the match.

Bombay had a surprisingly hard struggle against Saurashtra, in spite of the continued good form of Tendulkar. He and Hattangadi held Bombay together when Rajput and Sippy were out to Rajendra Jadeja without a run scored, but Saurashtra still took a first-innings lead, and Bombay had to be content with what extra bowling points they could manage in the second innings.

31 December 1988, 1 and 2 January 1989

at Municipal Ground, Rajkot

Maharashtra 500 for 5 dec (S. Sugwekar 155 not out, S. Bhave 116, M.D. Gunjal 93, N. Phadnis 62) and 37 for 1 dec
Saurashtra 351 (R. Badiyani 119, B. Pujara 68, A. Pandya 58, S.J. Jadhav 5 for 115) and 81 for 3

Match drawn
Maharashtra 13 pts, Saurashtra 7 pts

at Dadoji Konddeo Stadium, Thane

Baroda 313 (K.S. More 77, K. Chavan 67, R.R. Kulkarni 4 for 99) and 114 for 6 dec
Bombay 332 (Iqbal Khan 76, D.B. Vengsarkar 54) and 5 for 1

Match drawn
Bombay 14 pts, Baroda 10 pts

The third round of matches still failed to produce a result. Maharashtra again scored heavily, but Radiyani and Radia added 121 for Saurashtra's ninth wicket, and Mehta helped Radia, 43 not out, to add the 10 runs that were needed to save the follow-on.

Bombay recovered after an uncertain start, to take four first-innings batting points against Baroda.

7, 8 and 9 January 1989

at Moti Baug, Baroda

Baroda 182 (R. Parikh 52, S. Ankola 6 for 51) and 195 for 3 dec (R. Parikh 99, B. Adiacha 81)
Maharashtra 323 (S. Bhave 110, S.J. Jadhav 56, S.J. Kalyani 54, T. Arothe 5 for 100) and 55 for 1

Maharashtra won by 9 wickets
Maharashtra 16 pts, Baroda 5 pts

at GNFC Ground, Bharuch

Gujarat 394 (M. Parmar 83, B. Patel 121, C. Mankad 5 for 82)
Saurashtra 136 (B. Pujara 58, D. Patel 5 for 57) and 231 for 1 (B. Pujara 112 not out, B. Jadeja 72 not out)

Match drawn
Gujarat 12 pts, Saurashtra 6 pts

By beating Baroda and claiming the first win in the West Zone, Maharashtra assured themselves of a quarter-final place. They won in most extraordinary circumstances. Ankola's fine bowling and an excellent century by Bhave gave them a commanding first-innings lead of 141, but Parikh and Adiacha put on 170 for Baroda's second wicket in the second innings, and the game seemed destined to be drawn. No doubt in hope of gaining some extra bowling points, Gaekwad declared and left Maharashtra six overs in which to score 55 to win. It proved to be a generous declaration, and Bhave hit 43 not out as Maharashtra reached their target with three balls to spare.

Gujarat did make Saurashtra follow-on, but Pujara and Bimal Jadeja thwarted them with a second-wicket stand which was worth 175 when the game ended.

21, 22 and 23 January 1989

at Pithawala Stadium, Bhimpore

Baroda 346 (R. Parikh 128, K.S. More 61, J. Zinto 5 for 88) and 197 for 2 (K. Chavan 85, R. Parikh 68)
Gujarat 316 (M. Parmar 78, S. Talati 57, T. Arothe 4 for 59)

Match drawn
Baroda 12 pts, Gujarat 8 pts

at Marathwada University Ground, Aurangabad

Maharashtra 575 (S. Bhave 274, N. Phadnis 65, R.J. Shastri 4 for 120) and 22 for 0 dec

Bombay 435 (C.S. Pandit 103, S.R. Tendulkar 81, R.R. Kulkarni 61, S.V. Manjrekar 60, L.S. Rajput 51, S.J. Jadhav 5 for 97) and 49 for 2

Match drawn
Maharashtra 13 pts, Bombay 8 pts

A lucklustre West Zone competition came to an end with two more drawn matches. Gujarat and Baroda proved to be evenly matched, and Maharashtra once again reached a massive score. Surendra Bhave hit the highest score of his career and shared an opening partnership of 171 with Phadnis, while Pandit shared in two century partnerships for Bombay, who looked nothing like the strong team of former years.

West Zone Final Table					
	P	*W*	*L*	*D*	*Pts*
Maharashtra	4	1	–	3	55
Bombay	4	–	–	4	46
Baroda	4	–	1	3	33
Gujarat	4	–	–	4	32
Saurashtra	4	–	–	4	31

East Zone

25, 26 and 27 November 1988

at Railway Stadium, Guwahati

Bengal 413 for 4 dec (S. Ganguly 127, Raja Venkat 117, A.O. Malhotra 61 not out)
Assam 182 (A. Bhattacharjee 4 for 33, S.M. Sensharma 4 for 67) and 265 for 7 (Rajinder Singh 68, Rajesh Bora 55)

Match drawn
Bengal 14 pts, Assam 5 pts

With Venkat and Ganguly sharing a third-wicket stand of 182, Bengal had much the better of the opening game in the East Zone, but they were unable to force victory.

2, 3 and 4 December 1988

at NF Railway Stadium, Maligaon

Bihar 325 (B.S. Gossain 176 not out)
Assam 95 (N. Venkatram 5 for 39) and 175 for 5 (Rajesh Bora 81)

Match drawn
Bihar 13 pts, Assam 6 pts

at Eden Gardens, Calcutta

Bengal 348 for 3 dec (I.B. Roy 152, Raja Venkatram 147 not out)
Tripura 80 (Satyendra Singh 5 for 31) and 145 (Satyendra Singh 4 for 42)

Bengal won by an innings and 123 runs
Bengal 22 pts, Tripura 1 pt

Assam again produced a great escape. Skipper Baldev Singh Gossain played a remarkable innings for Bihar, hitting 176 out of 289, with Karim, 28, the next highest scorer. Assam were shot out by Venkatram, but loss of play through rain and a 103 second-wicket partnership between Bora and Das thwarted Bihar after they had enforced the follow-on.

A second-wicket stand of 290 between Raja Venkatram and the left-handed Indu Bhushan Roy put Bengal on the path to victory over lowly Tripura, who succumbed twice to the medium pace of Satyendra Singh.

9, 10 and 11 December 1988

at Hazaribagh Stadium, Hazaribagh

Bihar 99 (Sushil Kumar 8 for 22) and 222 (P. Khanna 56)
Orissa 155 (N. Venkatram 4 for 33) and 85 for 3

Match drawn
Orissa 10 pts, Bihar 6 pts

Sushil Kumar produced the best bowling performance of the season to bundle out Bihar on the first day, but he was badly let down by his batsmen. In 115.2 overs, Orissa scored just 155 runs. Off-spinner Venkatram had figures of 32.2–17–33–4 while slow left-arm bowler Abinash Kumar took 3 for 33 in 45 overs, of which 29 were maidens. It was grim stuff and condemned the game to a draw. It took Bihar 102 overs to score 222 in their second innings, and when Orissa were left 40 overs in which to score 167, they managed 85 for 3.

27, 28 and 29 December 1988

at Ispat Stadium, Rourkela

Tripura 153 (S. Chowdhary 52) and 109 (Amiya Roy 5 for 27)
Orissa 430 (Amiya Roy 100, Ranjit Biswal 70, Debashish Mohanty 69, A. Das 4 for 119)

Orissa won by an innings and 168 runs
Orissa 24 pts, Tripura 3 pts

Scoring at four runs an over in contrast to their efforts in the previous match, and with Amiya Roy in fine all-round form, Orissa took maximum points against Tripura.

6, 7 and 8 January 1989

at Eden Gardens, Calcutta

Orissa 264 (Amiya Roy 86, S. Chowdhary 60, S. Sen Sharma 5 for 64) and 201 (S. Das 63, Satyendra Singh 4 for 41)
Bengal 304 for 7 dec (A.O. Malhotra 117, S. Ganguly 86, J. Mukherjee 54, Rajesh Singh 4 for 40) and 162 for 7 (I.B. Roy 72, S. Mohapatra 4 for 65)

Bengal won by 3 wickets
Bengal 18 pts, Orissa 9 pts

at Giridih

Tripura 101 (Abinash Kumar 5 for 32) and 77 (N. Venkatram 4 for 30)
Bihar 274 (Abinash Kumar 71, Rajiv Arora 57, S. Chowdhary 4 for 84)

Bihar won by an innings and 78 runs
Bihar 22 pts, Tripura 4 pts

Bengal's victory over Orissa assured them of a place in the final stages of the competition. A fifth-wicket stand of 159 between Malhotra and Ganguly took Bengal into a first-innings lead and helped them to four batting points, and, led by Indu Roy, they scored at nearly five an over to win the match.

Having produced another weak batting performance, Tripura fought back strongly after Bihar had been 101 for 2, taking seven wickets for 49 runs, but Sanjay Ranjan and Abinash Kumar put on 120 for the last wicket with some bold hitting, and a dispirited Tripura collapsed in their second innings.

12, 13 and 14 January 1989

at Railway Stadium, Maligaon

Assam 306 (Rajinder Singh 80, S. Mahapatra 5 for 68) and 91 (S. Kumar 5 for 28)
Orissa 159 (I.M. Kakoti 4 for 23, H. Barua 4 for 48) and 251 for 5 (Amiya Roy 76 not out)

Orissa won by 5 wickets
Orissa 17 pts, Assam 10 pts

at Eden Gardens, Calcutta

Bengal 468 for 6 dec (J. Arun Lal 91, I.B. Roy 88, C.J. Venkatraman 75, A.O. Malhotra 78) and 183 for 4 (J. Arun Lal 66, I.B. Roy 62)
Bihar 410 (H. Gidwad 152, B.S. Gossain 60, S.S. Karim 59, D.J. Mukherjee 5 for 83, Arup Bhattacharjee 5 for 101)

Match drawn
Bengal 11 pts, Bihar 10 pts

While Bihar could take only 10 points from the run-saturated match at Eden Gardens, Orissa pulled off a dramatic victory over Assam to qualify for the quarter-final stage of the Ranji Trophy. Batting first, Assam reached a commendable 306 after losing seven wickets for 191. Orissa never recovered from a bad start and only 40 penalty runs awarded for Assam bowling 10 overs below the required rate took them past the point of having to follow-on. Spinners Mahapatra and Kumar routed Assam when they batted again, but Orissa still had to score 239 at four an over to win. At 157 for 5, the game was in the balance, but Amiya Roy and Randhir Singh took Orissa to victory. Assam conceded another 12 runs by bowling three overs short, although this had no influence on the outcome of the match.

17, 18 and 19 January 1989

at Nehru Stadium, Guwahati

Tripura 134 (A. Das 54) and 195 (S. Chowdhary 73, A. Das 50, N. Konwar 5 for 47)
Assam 275 for 7 dec (Rajkumar Das 87) and 59 for 1

Assam won by 9 wickets
Assam 16 pts, Tripura 3 pts

Assam's comfortable win over the luckless Tripura could do nothing to lift them in the East Zone table.

East Zone Final Table

	P	W	L	D	Pts
Bengal	4	2	–	2	65
Orissa	4	2	1	1	60
Bihar	4	1	–	3	51
Assam	4	1	1	2	37
Tripura	4	–	4	–	11

Pre-Quarter-Finals

3, 4, 5 and 6 February 1989

at Gymkhana Ground, Secunderabad

Hyderabad 270 (M.V. Narasimha Rao 66 not out, M. Azharuddin 52, K.D. Mokashi 4 for 65, R.J. Shastri 4 for 91) and 268 (Arshad Ayub 69, M. Azharuddin 65, K.D. Mokashi 5 for 109)

Bombay 283 (D.B. Vengsarkar 64, S.R. Tendulkar 59, R.S.L. Venkatapathy 4 for 98, Arshad Ayub 6 for 129) and 256 for 4 (S.V. Manjrekar 80 not out, R.J. Shastri 50 not out, L.S. Rajput 50)

Bombay won by 6 wickets

at Nehru Stadium, Pune

Madhya Pradesh 261 (S.M. Patil 68, S. Ansari 53, S. Ankola 5 for 93, G. D'Monte 4 for 74) and 177 (P. Divedi 50, G. D'Monte 5 for 60)

Maharashtra 700 (S. Sugwekar 299 not out, M.D. Gunjal 159, B. Joglekar 52)

Maharashtra won by an innings and 262 runs

Hyderabad and Bombay met for the seventh time in the history of the Ranji Trophy, and the seventh meeting ended as the previous six had done in victory for Bombay. Hyderabad were handicapped by the absence of regular skipper Shivlal Yadav, and Mohammed Azharuddin led the side. He won the toss and decided to bat first, but no one batsman was able to establish himself against the Bombay spinners, and it was left to Narasimha Rao to play some attractive shots towards the end of the innings and boost the score. Bombay themselves started circumspectly, with Arshad Ayub and Venkatapathy Raju troubling all batsmen, and they closed at 90 for 4. Not-out batsmen Vengsarkar and Tendulkar took their partnership to 118 the next morning, but Ayub and the slow left-arm bowler Venkatapathy kept Hyderabad in touch and restricted Bombay's lead to 13. It seemed immense when four Hyderabad second-innings wickets fell for 50, but Azharuddin and Vivek Jaisimha took them to the close at 121 for 4. Both batsmen were out on the Sunday morning with the score on 144, but Narasimha Rao, Arshad Ayub and Ehtesham Ali Khan all batted with resolution to take Hyderabad to 268 and leave Bombay with the task of scoring 256 to win and the game still in the balance. Attacking bowling and fielding reduced Bombay to 115 for 3 at the end of the third day, and Tendulkar went early on the last morning, but Manjrekar imposed an authority on the match which no other batsman had done, and Shastri, too, was in fine form. They shared an unbeaten stand of 128 to win the match.

The contest at Pune was more one-sided. Patil waged almost a lone battle against the opening Maharashtra bowlers, Gregory D'Monte and Salil Ankola, on the first day, and, boosted by 16 penalty runs, Madhya Pradesh reached 261. Bhave, Phadnis and Kalyani were all back in the pavilion with only 16 scored, but Sugwekar and Gunjal moved to the end of an absorbing first day without further trouble, and Maharashtra ended with 95 for 3. Thirteen wickets fell on the first day, but only two fell on the second as Maharashtra plundered 388 runs. Gunjal and Sugwekar

added 321 for the fourth wicket, before Milind Gunjal was bowled by Nilosey. The youthful Shantanu Sugwekar batted into the third day and took out his bat for 299, the third highest score ever hit for Maharashtra, beaten only by Nimbalkar and V.S. Hazare. By the time he left the field, the game had long been out of Madhya Pradesh's reach.

Quarter-Finals

17, 18, 19 and 20 February 1989

at Chidambaram Stadium, Madras

Tamil Nadu 507 (W.V. Raman 200 not out, V.B. Chandrasekhar 65, Robin Singh 63, K. Srikkanth 57, S.C. Gudge 5 for 122) and 247 (Arjan Kripal Singh 89, R. Hazare 7 for 68)

Maharashtra 382 (S. Bhave 128, S.J. Kalyani 106, S. Subramaniam 7 for 107) and 333 (S.J. Jadhav 86, R. Hazare 54, B. Arun 4 for 75)

Tamil Nadu won by 39 runs

at Eden Gardens, Calcutta

Bengal 594 for 8 dec (A.O. Malhotra 200, I.B. Roy 126, C. Raja Venkatram 90, J. Mukherjee 58) and 66 for 2

Punjab 551 (Gursharan Singh 298 not out, Krishna Mohan 112, Satyendra Singh 4 for 94)

Match drawn
Bengal qualified for semi-final on first-innings lead

at Wankhede Stadium, Bombay

Bombay 234 (S.S. Hattangadi 140, L.S. Rajput 59, G. Sharma 4 for 81) and 422 (S.V. Manjrekar 131, L.S. Rajput 98, S.R. Tendulkar 75, G. Sharma 7 for 113)

Uttar Pradesh 137 and 295 (R. Sapru 92 not out, Inderpal Singh 57, K.D. Mokashi 4 for 104)

Bombay won by 224 runs

at Ferozeshah Kotla, Delhi

Orissa 161 (M. Prabhakar 6 for 65) and 262 (S. Chowdhary 79, A. Jayaprakasham 70, M. Prabhakar 4 for 42)

Delhi 638 for 6 (R. Lamba 180, M. Nayyar 146, Ajay Sharma 130, Kirti Azad 112 not out)

Delhi won by an innings and 215 runs

A splendid game of cricket in Madras saw Tamil Nadu, the defending champions, enter the semi-finals after a great struggle. Batting first, Tamil Nadu were indebted to Woorkeri Raman, who became the first Tamil Nadu player to hit a double century in the knock-out stage of the Ranji Trophy. He also became the leading run-getter in a season for the association, passing Rajagopal's 729 runs made in 1967–8. He batted for 443 minutes, faced 341 deliveries and hit 20 fours. Tamil Nadu seemed in an impregnable position, but Maharashtra fought back bravely. On the Saturday afternoon, Surendra Bhave and Srikant Kalyani put on 222 for the second wicket to keep their side's hopes alive. The 23-year-old Bhave hit his fourth century of the season and, like Kalyani, reached three figures in under three hours. The brilliance of their batting was not sustained on the Sunday, which belonged to left-arm spinner Sunil Subramaniam, who not only bowled his side to a first-innings lead of 125, but also held two catches, one to dismiss the dangerous Sugwekar. Maharashtra were all out half an hour after lunch on the third day, by the end of which Tamil Nadu were 164 for 4, a lead of 289. On the last day, they lost their last six wickets for 83 runs, with Ramesh Hazare returning his best figures in three years in first-class cricket. His performance left Maharashtra to score 373 to win in a little over four hours, a daunting task which seemed near to impossible when four men were out in the first 11 overs as 64 were scored. At 182 for 7, Maharashtra looked well beaten, but Srikant Jadhav and Ramesh Hazare launched a violent attack which brought 124 runs in 86 minutes, at a rate of more than five runs an over. This violent stand threatened to bring Maharashtra a sensational victory, but it was ended when Arun, who earlier had taken 1 for 61 in eight overs, was brought back and bowled both batsmen.

Bengal ran to 342 for 4 on the opening day in Calcutta, with Roy and Raja Venkatram adding 162 for the second wicket. On the second day, Ashok Malhotra reached an attractive double century, and it was apparent that the game would be decided on the first innings. Punjab reached 285 for 5 on the third day, after losing four wickets before lunch. They had been revived by a splendid innings from Gursharan Singh, who batted with immense resource and courage into the last day. He and Krishna Mohan put on 320 for the sixth wicket, a record for Punjab and the fourth highest sixth-wicket stand in the history of the competition. Gursharan Singh reached the highest score ever made for Punjab, but his courageous effort was to no avail as he ran out of partners when Punjab were still 43 runs short of the Bengal total.

Rajput and Hattangadi began the match at Bombay with a stand of 145, but no one else reached double figures, and the last six wickets fell for 50 runs. Uttar Pradesh fared even worse and, by the end of the second day, Bombay were in total control, having 213 for 2 in their second innings, an overall lead of 310. Manjrekar, a most impressive batsman, and Rajput took their stand to 180 the next day, and Bombay ended as comfortable winners.

Delhi crushed Orissa. Prabhakar, the most successful pace bowler of the season, took 10 for 107 in the match, and Lamba and Nayyar began Delhi's innings with a stand of 339. There were four centuries in Delhi's innings. Ajay Sharma's 130 came off 150 balls and contained 19 fours. Included in the Delhi side was Mohinder Amarnath, who had not appeared in the zonal matches after his argument with the Indian Board. Surinder Khanna, who had transferred to Bengal, decided to return to Delhi for the knock-out stage of the competition, but the Bengal Cricket Association refused to agree to his return to his old state.

Semi-Finals

3, 4 and 5 March 1989

at Wankhede Stadium, Bombay

Delhi 409 (M. Prabhakar 123, M. Nayyar 105, R.R. Kulkarni 5 for 90) and 176 for 5

Bombay 321 (S.R. Tendulkar 78, S.S. Hattangadi 68, Maninder Singh 7 for 105)

Match drawn
Delhi qualified for final on first-innings lead

at Eden Gardens, Calcutta

Bengal 596 for 8 dec (Rajinder Singh 148, S. Banerjee 140, S. Ganguly 81, G. Shome jnr 54, Arup Bhattacharjee 52 not out) and 76 for 1
Tamil Nadu 535 (W.V. Raman 238, K. Arun Kumar 95 not out, P.C. Prakash 75, G. Shome 4 for 135)

Match drawn
Bengal qualified for final on first-innings lead

In a year when so many matches in the knock-out stage had produced results, Delhi and Bengal both qualified for the final by virtue of their first-innings lead. A stomach upset meant that Lamba could not open for Bombay in the clash of the titans at the Wankhede Stadium, so Manoj Prabhakar moved up to partner Manu Nayyar. At the end of a rather dour first day, they had scored 225 against a listless attack which desperately needed another seam bowler to partner Raju Kulkarni, well as Nayak bowled in the circumstances. Having failed to take a wicket on the

Ashok Malhotra. His consistently brilliant batting helped Bengal to the Ranji Trophy final. (Adrian Murrell/Allsport)

first day, Bombay bowled out Delhi on the second. Kulkarni bowled Nayyar at 232, and he continued to disturb all batsmen, giving his best bowling display of the season. His efforts were nullified on the third day, when Maninder Singh bowled Delhi to a position of strength. Saini made the initial breakthrough when he bowled Rajput, who lost concentration and lifted his head as he attempted to drive. Maninder then had Sanghani stumped and worked his way through a batting order that was minus Vengsarkar, Shastri and Manjrekar, all on their way to the Caribbean. Bombay, 258 for 7 at the end of the third day, added only 39 the next morning, and even the award of 24 penalty runs could not help them to save the match.

Playing his 50th Ranji Trophy match, Bengal skipper S. Banerjee hit his first century in the competition in the game in Calcutta. He put his side in a strong position at the end of the first day against the reigning champions. He batted throughout the day to score 101 out of Bengal's 252 for 4. Left-hander Snehashish Ganguly helped him in a third-wicket stand of 169, and his 155-run partnership with Rajinder Singh, formerly of Delhi, lasted until after lunch on the second day, which ended with Bengal on 574 for 8. Tamil Nadu's one consolation was that V. Sivaramakrishnan, playing his 80th Ranji Trophy match, took his 100th catch when he caught Gautan Shome junior at gully.

Unfortunately, V. Sivaramakrishnan failed with the bat, but, inspired by Raman, Tamil Nadu relinquished their hold on the trophy only after a very brave struggle. Batsman of the season, Raman, who, inexplicably, had been omitted from the Indian side which was chosen to tour West Indies, reached his third double century of the season and became the only batsman to score a thousand runs. He shared century partnerships with Vasu and Prakash, but seven wickets fell for 72 runs to blunt his efforts before Arun Kumar arrived to give renewed hope. He hit 95 off 89 balls, with 3 sixes and 11 fours, but, when Sanjay was dismissed 85 minutes after lunch on the last day, Kumar had run out of partners, and Bengal were in their first final for 17 years.

Ranji Trophy Final
DELHI v. BENGAL

The Ranji Trophy was decided on the first day, when Bengal, deciding to bat first when they won the toss, were bowled out for 167, the last eight wickets adding only 95 runs. Delhi suffered a shock when Sen Sharma, bowling a lively medium pace, sent back both Nayyar and Prabhakar with only two scored, and Lamba fell to Das. The day ended with the favourites on 91 for 3. This was the end of

---

RANJI TROPHY FINAL – DELHI v. BENGAL
22, 23, 25, 26 and 27 March 1989 at Ferozeshah Kotla Ground, Delhi

BENGAL

	FIRST INNINGS		SECOND INNINGS	
S. Banerjee†*	lbw, b Prabhakar	55	(7) c Bhaskar, b Maninder	38
I.B. Roy	lbw, b Madan Lal	18	b Madan Lal	23
C.R. Raja Venkat	c Lamba, b Madan Lal	1	(1) lbw, b Prabhakar	1
S. Ganguly	lbw, b Saini	7	(4) c Vinayak, b Madan Lal	36
A.O. Malhotra	run out	13	(5) b Maninder	69
Rajinder Singh	b Prabhakar	18	(6) c Bantoo, b Maninder	79
G. Shome jnr	b Maninder	25	(3) b Prabhakar	19
A. Bhattacharjee	b Prabhakar	5	lbw, b Kirti Azad	13
S. Sen Sharma	c Rajkumar, b Prabhakar	6	c Madan Lal, b Kirti Azad	16
Satyendra Singh	run out	0	c sub, b Kirti Azad	5
Anup Das	not out	0	not out	0
Extras	lb 4, nb 11	15	b 2, lb 5, w 1, nb 9	17
	penalty runs	4	penalty runs	28
		—		—
		167		344

DELHI

	FIRST INNINGS	
M. Nayyar	lbw, b Sen Sharma	0
R. Lamba	b Das	35
M. Prabhakar	lbw, b Sen Sharma	0
Bantoo Singh	c Banerjee, b Sen Sharma	179
K.P. Bhaskar	c Bhattacharjee, b Das	199
Kirti Azad	c Shome, b Das	158
U.S. Madan Lal†	c Shome, b Satyendra Singh	13
R. Vinayak*	not out	103
Maninder Singh	c Venkat, b Bhattacharjee	1
S. Saini	c Ganguly, b Bhattacharjee	0
Rajkumar Sharma	c Banerjee, b Bhattacharjee	7
Extras	b 11, lb 8, w 1, nb 6	26
		—
		721

	O	M	R	W	O	M	R	W
Madan Lal	16	4	33	2	17	3	72	2
Prabhakar	20.2	5	40	4	18	4	67	2
Saini	8	1	41	1	8	–	36	–
Maninder Singh	18	7	45	1	20	4	81	3
Rajkumar Sharma					6	1	25	–
Kirti Azad					5.4	–	28	3

	O	M	R	W
Sen Sharma	31	6	94	3
Shome	30	4	94	–
Satyendra Singh	22	3	92	1
Anup Das	36	4	148	3
Rajinder Singh	17	3	57	–
Bhattacharjee	42.1	5	149	3
Ganguly	13	–	68	–

FALL OF WICKETS
1–50, 2–59, 3–68, 4–94, 5–118, 6–143, 7–151, 8–163, 9–163
1–5, 2–29, 3–56, 4–159, 5–163, 6–256, 7–294, 8–296, 9–316

FALL OF WICKETS
1–1, 2–2, 3–78, 4–406, 5–445, 6–487, 7–687, 8–695, 9–695

Umpires: D.N. Dotiwala & R.S. Rathore

Delhi won by an innings and 210 runs

Bengal's joy. They went through two sessions on the second day without taking a wicket as, in blustery conditions, Bhaskar Pillai and Bantoo ground the attack into the dust while sharing a fourth-wicket record stand for Delhi of 318. Bhaskar was the more adventurous and looked certain to reach a double century, but failed to do so when he mis-hit an attempted fifth six. As well as his 4 sixes, he hit 20 fours. He faced 278 balls. Bantoo Singh, who had a torrid time against Shome early in his innings, was more circumspect, and his 179 occupied 456 minutes, 362 balls. He hit 24 fours and a straight six.

Delhi had both hands on the trophy by the end of the

second day, when they were 445 for 5, and they moved relentlessly to 721 on the third day, with Kirti Azad hitting his second century of the season and Rajiv Vinayak reaching a maiden first-class hundred. Delhi's 721 was the highest score that they had made in the Ranji Trophy, but Bengal gave a spirited display when they batted again, although they had no chance of avoiding defeat. So Delhi won the Ranji Trophy for the fifth time, their first victory having come as late as 1978–9, and it was fitting that Madan Lal, who celebrated his 38th birthday on the second day of the match, should be the one to receive the trophy.

First-Class Averages

BATTING

	M	Inns	NOs	Runs	HS	Av	100s	50s		M	Inns	NOs	Runs	HS	Av	100s	50s
M.B. Amarnath (Delhi)	3	2	1	164	149*	164.00	1		S.J. Kalyani (Maharashtra)	10	14	1	627	115	48.23	2	4
S. Sugwekar (Maharashtra)	6	8	3	669	229*	133.80	2	1	S.V. Manjrekar (Bombay)	7	12	3	433	131	48.11	1	3
K. Arun Kumar (Tamil Nadu)	6	5	3	212	95*	106.00		2	K. Srikkanth (Tamil Nadu)	8	13	2	518	94	47.09		6
W.V. Raman (Tamil Nadu)	10	13	2	1159	313	105.36	3	2	Amiya Roy (Orissa)	5	8	1	325	100	46.42	1	2
Gursharan Singh (Punjab)	7	9	2	660	298*	94.28	2	1	R. Sapru (Uttar P.)	5	10	3	324	92*	46.28		3
S. Banerjee (Bengal)	7	7	4	280	140	93.33	1	1	A. Sippy (Bombay)	2	3		138	127	46.00	1	
Ajay Sharma (Delhi)	6	5	1	366	130	91.50	2	2	M. Nayyar (Delhi)	8	11	1	460	146	46.00	2	2
S. Bhave (Maharashtra)	6	10	2	730	274	91.25	4		S.G. Gujar (Vidarbha)	4	7	1	276	115	46.00	1	1
Yashpal Sharma (Haryana)	5	7	2	452	153	90.40	2	2	U.S. Phate (Vidarbha)	4	8	2	274	55	45.66		2
A. Kripal Singh (Tamil Nadu)	5	7	1	538	302*	89.66	1	2	K.A. Qayyum (Hyderabad)	6	11	3	363	106	45.37	1	1
P.K. Amre (Railways)	5	7	2	425	214*	85.00	2	1	R. Swarup (Hyderabad)	4	8		357	82	44.62		5
B.S. Gossain (Bihar)	3	4	1	251	176*	83.66	1	1	S.S. Hattangadi (Bombay)	6	10		430	140	43.00	2	2
Rajinder Singh (Bengal)	2	3		245	148	81.66	1	1	P. Subramaniam (Kerala)	5	9	1	340	85	42.50		3
Kirti Azad (Delhi)	11	10	3	517	158	73.85	2	2	Amarjeet Kaypee (Haryana)	6	9	2	295	75	42.14		3
A.O. Malhotra (Bengal)	7	9	1	577	200	72.12	2	3	S.J. Jadhav (Maharashtra)	6	7	1	251	86	41.83		2
K. Bhaskar Pillai (Delhi)	11	12	2	718	199	71.80	2	3	Ashwini Gupta (Jammu & K.)	5	9	1	328	72	41.00		4
B.K. Patel (Gujarat)	4	6	2	287	121	71.75	1	1	A. Pandya (Saurashtra)	5	7	2	202	87*	40.40		1
R.B. Parikh (Baroda)	4	7		478	128	68.28	1	4	L.S. Rajput (Bombay)	10	17	2	602	99	40.13		7
K.V.S.D. Kamaraju (Andhra)	5	10	1	596	138	66.22	2	2	M.F. Rehman (Andhra)	5	10	1	355	83	39.44		2
Bantoo Singh (Delhi)	6	7	2	329	179	65.80	1	1	D.B. Vengsarkar (Bombay)	8	11	1	394	128*	39.40	1	3
M.D. Gunjal (Maharashtra)	6	8	1	458	159	65.42	2	1	D. Bangera (Goa)	5	7	2	197	121	39.40	1	
S.R. Tendulkar (Bombay)	7	11	2	583	100*	64.77	1	6	V.B. Chandrasekhar								
M.V. Sridhar (Hyderabad)	3	6	1	323	129*	64.60	1	1	(Tamil Nadu)	9	12	1	433	119	39.36	1	3
M. Prabhakar (Delhi)	10	13	4	581	229*	64.55	3	1	S.S. Khandkar (Uttar P.)	5	10		392	88	39.20		3
R. Lamba (Delhi)	11	14	2	771	180	64.25	3	1	Bhupinder Singh (Punjab)	6	7	4	116	42*	38.66		
A. Kapoor (Punjab)	6	9	1	511	135*	63.87	2	2	P.C. Prakash (Tamil Nadu)	7	8		308	75	38.50		3
Robin Singh (Tamil Nadu)	9	12	3	569	131*	63.22	3	2	V. Rathore (Punjab)	4	7		269	128	38.42	1	1
Yusuf Ali Khan (Railways)	4	7	2	315	114	63.00	1	1	K. Chauhan (Saurashtra)	4	7	1	230	101	38.33	1	
S.Y. Dhuri (Goa)	5	5		311	141	62.20	2		K. Bharatan (Railways)	3	4		153	98	38.25		1
M. Parmar (Gujarat)	3	4		246	85	61.50		3	S. Viswanath (Karnataka)	6	9	2	262	59*	37.42		1
Bhaskar Ghosh (Services)	5	8	1	430	102	61.42	2	2	S. Chopra (Punjab)	3	3		112	88	37.33		1
P.G. Sunder (Kerala)	3	5	1	237	71	59.25		3	R. Nayyar (Himachal P.)	5	10		372	110	37.20	1	2
V. Chamundeswaranath									H. Gidwani (Bihar)	5	6		223	152	37.16	1	
(Andhra)	5	9	1	472	144	59.00	3		Rajesh Bora (Assam)	4	7		259	81	37.00		2
I.B. Roy (Bengal)	10	16	1	843	152	56.20	2	6	S. Mehta (Jammu & K.)	3	5		182	86	36.40		2
B.M. Jadeja (Saurashtra)	4	7	1	337	190	56.16	1	2	B. Joglekar (Maharashtra)	4	5		182	52	36.40		1
N.S. Sidhu (Punjab)	5	7	1	336	116	56.00	1	2	B. Adiacha (Baroda)	3	5		181	81	36.20		1
P.V. Ranganathan (Kerala)	4	8	2	333	101*	55.50	1	2	D. Pandove (Punjab)	6	8		288	137	36.00	1	
R. Badiyani (Saurashtra)	4	5	1	221	119	55.25	1	1	J. Mukherjee (Bengal)	7	8	2	216	58	36.00		2
Deepak Sharma (Haryana)	5	9	2	378	143	54.00	1	2	S. Chaturvedi (Uttar P.)	5	10	1	322	118	35.77	1	
C. Raja Venkat (Bengal)	7	12	2	529	147*	52.90	2	2	D. Mohanty (Orissa)	5	9	1	283	69	35.37		1
S.K. Ganguly (Bengal)	7	9	1	420	127	52.50	1	2	B.R. Singh (Services)	5	8		282	81	35.25		1
S. Shinde (Goa)	4	7	2	262	101	52.40	1		Sanjeev K. Sharma (Delhi)	4	4	1	105	34	35.00		
S.J. Phadkar (Vidarbha)	4	6	1	262	203	52.40	1		N.K. Churi (Railways)	6	10	1	314	63	34.88		2
S.S. Karim (Bihar)	5	6	2	209	63*	52.25		2	J.K. Mathur (Rajasthan)	4	8	1	243	56*	34.71		1
B. Mistry (Gujarat)	4	6		311	120	51.83	1	1	Shahid Pervez (Jammu & K.)	5	10	1	312	75	34.66		1
M. Azharuddin (Hyderabad)	6	9		413	105	51.62	1	3	J. Fernandez (Goa)	4	3		104	70	34.66		1
S. Kangralkar (Goa)	5	6	1	256	138*	51.20	1	1	M.V. Narasimha Rao								
Zahir Alam (Assam)	2	4	1	153	47	51.00			(Hyderabad)	5	8	3	173	66*	34.60		1
T. Arothe (Baroda)	5	8	2	305	100	50.83	1		Chinmoy Sharma (Services)	5	8	1	240	84	34.28		2
R.M.H. Binny (Karnataka)	6	9		457	140	50.77	2	1	V. Sivaramakrishnan								
B. Pujara (Saurashtra)	4	7	1	295	112*	49.16	1	2	(Tamil Nadu)	7	10	1	308	77	34.22		1
Arjit Ghosh (Services)	4	5		245	109	49.00	1	1	R. Vinayak (Delhi)	9	7	3	136	103*	34.00	1	

First-Class Averages continued

	M	Inns	NOs	Runs	HS	Av	100s	50s
R. Venkatesh (Railways)	3	4	1	101	42	33.66		
U.I. Ghani (Vidarbha)	2	3		101	61	33.66		1
K.S. More (Baroda)	9	12		402	113	33.50	1	2
G. Shome jnr (Bengal)	2	4	1	100	54	33.33		1
J. Arun Lal (Bengal)	9	15	1	466	103	33.50	1	2
P. Rao Ramesh (Karnataka)	5	8		266	80	33.25		2
P. Divedi (Madhya P.)	3	5		165	90	33.00		2
A.R. Bhattacharjee (Bengal)	9	11	4	231	52*	33.00		1
A.D. Gaekwad (Baroda)	4	5	1	130	82	32.50		1
R.J. Shastri (Bombay)	8	12	2	324	87*	32.40		3
Abdul Azeem (Hyderabad)	6	11		356	89	32.36		3
S. Chowdhary (Orissa)	5	9	1	258	79	32.25		2
S.V. Mudkavi (Rajasthan)	4	8	1	222	84	31.71		2
Iqbal Khan (Bombay)	4	6	2	125	76	31.25		1
S.M.H. Kirmani (Railways)	4	5		156	103	31.20	1	
S.M. Patil (Madhya P.)	5	9		278	100	30.88	1	1
R.N. Kapil Dev (Haryana)	5	5		154	47	30.80		
D. Raj Kumar (Assam)	2	4		121	87	30.25		1
S.M. Vyas (Rajasthan)	4	7	1	181	128	30.16	1	
V. Pednekar (Goa)	5	7		210	99	30.00		1
C.S. Pandit (Bombay)	7	11		328	103	29.81	1	1
P. Khanna (Bihar)	4	5		149	56	29.80		1
H. Wasu (Vidarbha)	4	5	1	119	69	29.75		1
V. Madhu (Karnataka)	5	8		237	110	29.62	1	
K. Chavan (Baroda)	4	7		206	85	29.42		2
Sudhakar Reddy (Andhra)	4	7	1	176	54	29.33		1
V. Vats (Uttar P.)	3	5		146	77	29.20		1
Krishna Mohan (Punjab)	5	6		174	112	29.00	1	
Amar Singh Negri (Rajasthan)	3	6		174	79	29.00		1
Jaswant Rai (Himachal P.)	5	10		289	53	28.90		1
N. Laliwala (Gujarat)	4	6		173	52	28.83		1
A. Vijayavargiya (Madhya P.)	5	9		259	93	28.77		2
C. Saldanha (Karnataka)	5	9	1	226	83	28.25		1
A. Jayaprakasham (Orissa)	5	8		226	70	28.25		1
P.B. Hingnikar (Vidarbha)	5	8		223	98	27.87		2
Arun Sharma (Punjab)	5	7	1	166	54	27.66		2
A. Jadeja (Haryana)	5	8		221	69	27.62		3
Rajinder Singh (Assam)	4	8	1	193	80	27.57		2
S.S. Talati (Gujarat)	3	4		110	57	27.50		1
V. Jaisimha (Hyderabad)	6	10		275	90	27.50		1
Ehtesham A. Khan (Hyderabad)	6	9	1	217	75*	27.12		2
S. Krishna Mohan (Andhra)	4	6	1	135	48*	27.00		
P.S. Vaidya (Vidarbha)	4	6	1	134	53*	26.80		1
L. Sivaramakrishnan (Tamil Nadu)	8	10	1	239	100*	26.55	1	
N. Phadnis (Maharashtra)	6	7		185	65	26.42		2
A.S. Bajwa (Services)	5	8		211	71	26.37		2
S. Dutta (Assam)	3	6	1	131	40	26.20		
K.S.B. Ramamurthy (Andhra)	5	9	2	178	55	25.42		1
S. Paul (Tripura)	4	8		201	44	25.12		
Ramesh Dutta (Himachal P.)	4	8		198	51	24.75		1
Akhtar Aijaz (Jammu & K.)	5	9		218	48	24.22		
B. Arun (Tamil Nadu)	9	11	2	216	59	24.00		1
S. Ansari (Madhya P.)	5	9		213	53	23.66		1
Indrapal Singh (Uttar P.)	5	10		236	73	23.60		2
V. Sen (Himachal P.)	4	8		187	90	23.37		2
S. Ramesh (Kerala)	4	6		140	84	23.33		1
K. Jeshwant (Karnataka)	7	11	1	225	62	22.50		1
C.J. Sharma (Haryana)	8	8	1	157	60	22.42		1
Abhijit Das (Tripura)	4	8	1	157	54	22.42		2
A. Laghate (Madhya P.)	4	7	1	132	53*	22.00		1
S.P. Takle (Vidarbha)	4	6		131	55	21.83		1
Arshad Ayub (Hyderabad)	6	8	2	131	69	21.83		1
V. Yadav (Haryana)	5	7		152	50	21.71		1
J.J. Zinto (Gujarat)	4	6	1	107	52	21.40		1
V.S. Yadav (Uttar P.)	6	11	1	211	45	21.10		
S. Mahadevan (Goa)	5	5		105	45	21.00		
P.M. Pankule (Vidarbha)	4	8		167	71	20.87		1
S. Chowdhary (Tripura)	4	8		166	73	20.75		2
B. Radia (Saurashtra)	7	8	2	124	43*	20.66		
S. Das (Orissa)	3	6		122	63	20.33		1
Ghopal Sharma (Uttar P.)	7	11	2	179	82	19.88		1
R. Pratap Singh (Uttar P.)	6	9	1	156	48	19.50		
R.S. Ghai (Punjab)	4	6		114	64	19.00		1
Sanjay Sharma (Jammu & K.)	5	8	1	132	29*	18.85		
U.S. Madan Lal (Delhi)	9	8	1	132	40	18.85		
A. Asawa (Rajasthan)	4	7		132	41	18.85		
C.P. Singh (Madhya P.)	4	7		129	46	18.42		
Vidya Bhaskar (Jammu & K.)	4	8		147	51	18.37		1
K.N.A. Padmanabhan (Kerala)	3	6		109	27	18.16		
Rajesh Singh (Orissa)	5	9	2	124	46	17.71		
Padam Shastri (Rajasthan)	5	9		158	64	17.55		1
P.S. Karkera (Railways)	4	7		116	36	16.57		
Sushil Kumar (Orissa)	5	9		149	33	16.55		
R. Kalsi (Punjab)	6	9		143	36	15.88		
M. Venkataramana (Tamil Nadu)	9	7		111	37	15.85		
N. Kutty (Kerala)	4	8		126	39	15.75		
Raj Kumar (Himachal P.)	5	10		157	57	15.70		
S. Lahore (Madhya P.)	5	8		121	32	15.12		
N. Goel (Haryana)	4	8	1	103	44*	14.71		
L.K. Adisheshu (Andhra)	5	10		146	40	14.60		
R.R. Kulkarni (Bombay)	8	9		129	61	14.33		1
Brijender Sharma (Himachal P.)	5	10	2	108	27	13.50		

(Qualification – 100 runs, average 10.00)

BOWLING

	Overs	Mds	Runs	Wkts	Av	Best	10/m	5/inns
N. Konwar (Assam)	82	24	181	13	13.92	5/47		1
N.S. Yadav (Hyderabad)	81	20	181	12	15.08	6/44		1
M. Prabhakar (Delhi)	236.3	53	630	41	15.36	6/36	1	3
Rattan Singh (Railways)	179	49	396	24	16.50	7/48	1	3
R. Nayyar (Himachal P.)	43.2	1	169	10	16.90	7/93		1
Y. Mathur (Rajasthan)	75.3	12	188	11	17.09	5/55		1
R. Yadav (Hyderabad)	119.4	21	350	20	17.50	6/87		1
R. Venkatesh (Railways)	136	28	333	18	18.50	5/58	1	3
V. Venkatram (Bihar)	181.4	41	468	25	18.72	5/39		2
M.I. Singh (Punjab)	200	61	434	23	18.86	6/63		1
Maninder Singh (Delhi)	176.1	54	418	22	19.00	7/105		1
Ghopal Sharma (Uttar P.)	366	80	939	49	19.16	7/113	3	6
Arun Singla (Haryana)	98.2	26	254	13	19.53	4/35		
S. Subramaniam (Tamil Nadu)	261.4	59	793	40	19.82	7/44	1	3
Arshad Ayub (Hyderabad)	358.3	116	698	35	19.94	6/129		1
S. Ankola (Maharashtra)	139.5	14	545	27	20.18	6/51		3
T.A. Sekhar (Madhya P.)	126.2	14	452	22	20.54	7/54	1	2
P. Jain (Delhi)	129.4	37	298	14	21.28	5/42		1
S.M. Patil (Madhya P.)	107	26	263	12	21.91	5/9		2
S. Vyas (Rajasthan)	165	30	424	19	22.31	5/48		1
R. Chauhan (Madhya P.)	165	37	471	21	22.42	7/39	1	2
K.D. Mokashi (Bombay)	252	59	707	31	22.80	5/109		1
Bhupinder Singh (Punjab)	172	55	389	17	22.88	6/40		1
R.N. Kapil Dev (Haryana)	121	32	298	13	22.92	3/21		
V. Korgaonkar (Goa)	57.4	2	253	11	23.00	5/60		1
Satyendra Singh (Bengal)	156.1	33	461	20	23.05	5/31		1

First-Class Averages continued

	Overs	Mds	Runs	Wkts	Av	Best	10/m	5/inns
R. Venkatapathy (Hyderabad)	230.5	65	555	24	23.12	4/63		
S. Saini (Delhi)	144	25	465	20	23.25	6/21		2
T.B. Arothe (Baroda)	89	18	280	12	23.33	5/100		1
Krishna Mohan (Punjab)	131.1	35	332	14	23.71	6/43		1
A.R. Bhat (Karnataka)	224.3	41	605	25	24.20	6/29		1
C.J. Sharma (Haryana)	192	28	682	28	24.35	5/49		2
U.S. Madan Lal (Delhi)	224.1	44	672	27	24.88	3/29		
H. Wasu (Vidarbha)	132	20	376	15	25.06	5/78		1
Sushil Kumar (Orissa)	197.3	45	530	21	25.23	8/22	1	2
Deepak Sharma (Hyderabad)	207.2	57	483	19	25.42	6/48		1
V. Kadam (Services)	77.3	11	282	11	25.63	6/61		1
K. Jeshwant (Karnataka)	193.5	47	462	18	25.66	4/45		
Abinash Kumar (Bihar)	188	69	339	13	26.07	5/32		1
V. Hariharan (Kerala)	147.4	26	523	20	26.15	7/60	1	1
G. D'Monte (Maharashtra)	69	10	315	12	26.25	5/60		1
B. Arun (Tamil Nadu)	169.1	26	609	23	26.47	6/79	1	2
S. Lahore (Madhya P.)	148.2	40	347	13	26.69	4/68		
Kirti Azad (Delhi)	199.2	42	529	19	27.84	3/28		
M. Ansari (Uttar P.)	164.5	36	390	14	27.85	5/68		1
D. Mukherjee (Bengal)	155	28	531	19	27.94	5/83		1
R.J. Shastri (Bombay)	225.1	39	597	21	28.42	4/45		
V. Dutt (Haryana)	123	27	346	12	28.83	4/63		
Robin Singh (Tamil Nadu)	123.1	17	437	15	29.13	4/39		
S.J. Jadhav (Maharashtra)	187.5	35	499	17	29.35	5/97		2
R. Ananth (Karnataka)	143.4	23	442	15	29.46	5/60		1
N.D. Hirwani (Madhya P.)	266.3	69	680	23	29.56	6/59		1
S. Sen Sharma (Bengal)	178	31	652	22	29.63	5/64		1
A. Sabnis (Bombay)	100.3	9	393	13	30.23	5/41	1	2
M. Venkataramana (Tamil Nadu)	313.4	75	916	30	30.53	5/83		1
S. Mohapatra (Orissa)	186.3	28	679	22	30.86	5/68		1
W.V. Raman (Tamil Nadu)	131	44	342	11	31.09	2/10		
A. Bhattacharjee (Bengal)	315.3	76	765	24	31.87	5/101		1
K. Arun Kumar (Tamil Nadu)	131	25	388	12	32.33	4/29		
P. Subramaniam (Kerala)	88.3	14	356	11	32.36	5/86		1
R.R. Kulkarni (Bombay)	136.1	29	488	15	32.53	5/90		1
B.S. Mangesh (Andhra)	166.1	24	522	16	32.62	5/37		2
Ajay Verma (Kerala)	86.1	7	368	11	33.45	3/71		
R.S. Hazare (Maharashtra)	131	22	403	12	33.58	7/68		1
S. Srinivasan (Railways)	87.4	11	374	11	34.00	4/87		
J. Zinto (Gujarat)	134.3	37	375	11	34.09	5/88		1
S.V. Nayak (Bombay)	244	68	590	17	34.70	4/85		
Y. Chakradhar Rao (Andhra)	77.1	10	353	10	35.30	4/81		
Abdul Qayyum (Jammu & K.)	154.3	21	569	16	35.56	4/63		
D. Patel (Gujarat)	108	15	392	11	35.63	5/57		1
Asif Peerzada (Jammu & K.)	115.1	10	518	14	37.00	6/144		1
B. Radia (Saurashtra)	208.5	39	572	15	38.13	4/74		
M.V. Rao (Services)	132.5	13	531	13	40.84	4/69		
Rashid Patel (Baroda)	129.4	17	500	12	41.66	3/77		
Pratap Singh (Uttar P.)	133	24	480	10	48.00	3/67		
U. Naik (Goa)	150	13	590	11	53.63	6/103		1

LEADING FIELDERS

22 - S. Banerjee (Bengal) (ct 21/st 1); 21 - K.S. More (Baroda) (ct 19/st 2); 19 - A. Panicker (Kerala) (ct 18/st 1) and R. Vinayak (Delhi) (ct 17/st 2); 18 - P.L. Bose (Orissa) (ct 11/st 7) and C.S. Pandit (Bombay); 16 - N. Phadnis (Maharashtra) (ct 12/st 4); 15 - Ehtesham A. Khan (Hyderabad) (ct 14/st 1); 13 - S. Chowdhary (Jammu & Kashmir) (ct 11/st 2), M. Sanjay (Tamil Nadu) (ct 11/st 2), V. Sivaramakrishnan (Tamil Nadu) and K. Arun Sharma (Punjab) (ct 11/st 2); 12 - M.F. Rehman (Andhra), M. Venkataramana (Tamil Nadu), Robin Singh (Tamil Nadu) and C.R. Venkatraman (Bengal); 11 - D.S. Bangera (Goa) (ct 10/st 1), V. Yadav (Haryana), D. Jain (Rajasthan) (ct 8/st 3) and A. Bhattacharjee (Bengal); 10 - S. Viswanath (Karnataka) (ct 6/st 4), J. Arun Lal (Bengal), K. Bhaskar Pillai (Delhi), M.D. Gunjal (Maharashtra) and P.B. Hinganikar (Vidarbha) (ct 8/st 2)

The Asia Cup in Bangladesh

Ravi Ratnayeke (Sri Lanka). (Adrian Murrell/Allsport)

In spite of the country experiencing the worst floods in years only a few weeks earlier, the Bangladesh Cricket Board bravely went ahead with the organization of the Asia Cup, which was held by Sri Lanka. One-day international cricket was staged for the first time in Bangladesh, in the capital city of Dhaka and the port of Chittagong. Unfortunately, there were disturbances and unrest resulting from the sale of tickets shortly before the tournament began, for it had aroused tremendous interest.

The tournament followed close upon the Champions' Trophy in Sharjah, and for the Pakistan side it meant a third international competition in a third country within the space of three weeks, which sounds like indigestion.

Match One
PAKISTAN v. SRI LANKA

The first international match to be staged on Bangladesh soil produced a surprise as a travel weary Pakistan side were convincingly beaten by Sri Lanka. Put in to bat, Pakistan struggled on a pitch on which the moisture gave Sri Lanka some encouragement. Labrooy and newcomer Wijegunawardene sent back Rameez Raja, Aamer Malik and Shoaib Mohammad for 35. Saleem Malik fell at 98, by which time Javed Miandad had been forced to retire with a back injury which was to keep him out of the rest of the tournament.

Pakistan were revived by Ijaz Ahmed, who hit 54 off 58 balls, and by Saleem Yousuf, 31 off 24 balls, after the first 22 overs had yielded just 52 runs. It was the fifth-wicket

stand of 57, followed by some late blows, which gave the Pakistan score its only semblance of respectability.

It proved totally insufficient, however, as Mahanama and Kuruppu gave their side a flying start with a 72-run partnership. Mendis and Aravinda de Silva maintained the brisk rate of scoring, and Sri Lanka romped to victory with 5.3 overs to spare.

Match Two
BANGLADESH v. INDIA

The host country, an associate member of the ICC, proved to be no match for India, as had been expected. Invariably, when club or minor county cricketers are up against first-class opposition they reveal the capacity to survive, but not to score runs quickly. So it was with Bangladesh. Following two early disasters, they batted dourly and lost only six more wickets in their 45 overs, but they managed only 99 runs. India raced home at four an over.

Match Three
SRI LANKA v. INDIA

Sri Lanka took full advantage of winning the toss and batting first on a perfect wicket. With Samarasekera hitting his highest score in a one-day international and sharing a stand of 126 for the third wicket with Aravinda de Silva, Sri Lanka reached a formidable 271 in their 45 overs, even though they were without injured skipper Madugalle.

ASIA CUP – MATCH ONE – PAKISTAN v. SRI LANKA
27 October 1988 at National Stadium, Dhaka, Bangladesh

PAKISTAN				SRI LANKA			
Rameez Raja	b Labrooy		3	R.S. Mahanama	c Saleem Malik, b Wasim Akram		55
Aamer Malik	c Mahanama, b Wijegunawardene		11	D.S.B.P. Kuruppu*	c and b Abdul Qadir		35
Shoaib Mohammad	b Wijegunawardene		10	M.A.R. Samarasekera	c Saleem Yousuf, b Manzoor		10
Javed Miandad†	retired hurt		25	P.A. de Silva	c Tauseef, b Wasim Akram		48
Saleem Malik	c Mahanama, b Labrooy		30	A. Ranatunga	run out		7
Ijaz Ahmed	c Kuruppu, b Labrooy		54	L.R.D. Mendis	not out		21
Saleem Yousuf*	c sub, b J.R. Ratnayeke		31	J.R. Ratnayeke	not out		2
Manzoor Elahi	c Mahanama, b J.R. Ratnayeke		12	R.S. Madugalle†			
Wasim Akram	not out		9	G.F. Labrooy			
Abdul Qadir	not out		3	S.D. Anurasiri			
Tauseef Ahmed				K.I.W. Wijegunawardene			
Extras	w 1, nb 5		6	Extras	b 1, lb 9, w 3, nb 4		17
(44 overs)	(for 7 wkts)		194	(38.3 overs)	(for 5 wkts)		195

	O	M	R	W
J.R. Ratnayeke	9	1	27	2
Labrooy	8	1	36	3
Wijegunawardene	8	1	35	2
Samarasekera	9	1	34	–
Anurasiri	4	–	22	–
Ranatunga	3	–	27	–
de Silva	3	–	13	–

	O	M	R	W
Wasim Akram	7.3	–	31	2
Manzoor Elahi	8	–	43	1
Aamer Malik	2	–	12	–
Abdul Qadir	8	–	48	1
Tauseef Ahmed	9	–	27	–
Shoaib Mohammad	4	–	24	–

FALL OF WICKETS
1–3, 2–24, 3–35, 4–98, 5–155, 6–180, 7–187

FALL OF WICKETS
1–72, 2–100, 3–116, 4–138, 5–192

Umpires: R.B. Gupta & V.K. Ramaswamy

Man of the Match: R.S. Mahanama

Sri Lanka won by 5 wickets

ASIA CUP – MATCH TWO – BANGLADESH v. INDIA
27 October 1988 at Chittagong Stadium, Chittagong, Bangladesh

BANGLADESH			
Azhar Hussain Shantu	lbw, b Sharma		1
Harunur Rashid Liton	b Kapil Dev		0
Gazi Ashraf Lipu†	b Maninder Singh		11
Athar Ali Khan	c Kapil Dev, b Amarnath		16
Minhazul Abedin Nannu	b Arshad Ayub		22
Aminul Islam Bulbul	lbw, b Arshad Ayub		10
Zahid Razzak	b Arshad Ayub		6
Ghulam Faruq Suru	c Sidhu, b Hirwani		4
J.S. Badsha	not out		7
Nasir Nasu*	not out		9
G.M. Nausher Prince			
Extras	b 1, lb 6, w 5, nb 1		13
(45 overs)	(for 8 wkts)		99

	O	M	R	W
Kapil Dev	6	2	14	1
S.K. Sharma	9	2	22	1
Amarnath	6	1	8	1
Maninder Singh	9	6	9	1
Arshad Ayub	9	2	20	3
Hirwani	6	–	19	1

FALL OF WICKETS

1–1, 2–2, 3–33, 4–40, 5–64, 6–72, 7–79, 8–79

INDIA			
K. Srikkanth	c Athar Ali Khan, b Shantu		24
N.S. Sidhu	not out		50
M.B. Amarnath	not out		19
D.B. Vengsarkar†			
R.N. Kapil Dev			
M. Azharuddin			
K.S. More*			
Arshad Ayub			
S.K. Sharma			
Maninder Singh			
N.D. Hirwani			
Extras	lb 4, w 3		7
(26 overs)	(for 1 wkt)		100

	O	M	R	W
Prince	6	2	15	–
Suru	4	–	19	–
Badsha	6	1	16	–
Shantu	7	–	30	1
Athar Ali Kahn	2	–	12	–
Nannu	1	–	4	–

FALL OF WICKET

1–47

Umpires: K.T. Francis & Tariq Ata

Man of the Match: N.S. Sidhu

India won by 9 wickets

ASIA CUP – MATCH THREE – INDIA v. SRI LANKA
29 October 1988 at National Stadium, Dhaka, Bangladesh

SRI LANKA			
R.S. Mahanama	lbw, b Amarnath		21
D.S.B.P. Kuruppu*	b Sharma		16
M.A.R. Samarasekera	b Srikkanth		66
P.A. de Silva	lbw, b Arshad Ayub		69
A. Ranatunga†	not out		49
L.R.D. Mendis	c Amarnath, b Kapil Dev		19
J.R. Ratnayeke	b Kapil Dev		16
H.P. Tillekeratne	not out		2
H.C.P. Ramanayake			
W.R. Madurasinghe			
K.I.W. Wijegunawardene			
Extras	lb 9, w 1, nb 3		13
(45 overs)	(for 6 wkts)		271

	O	M	R	W
Kapil Dev	9	–	39	2
S.K. Sharma	8	1	44	1
Amarnath	4	–	27	1
Maninder Singh	5	–	26	–
Hirwani	4	–	38	–
Arshad Ayub	9	–	58	1
Srikkanth	6	–	30	1

FALL OF WICKETS

1–35, 2–52, 3–178, 4–184, 5–216, 6–269

INDIA			
K. Srikkanth	c Mahanama, b Ranatunga		42
N.S. Sidhu	c Kuruppu, b Ranatunga		50
M.B. Amarnath	run out		31
D.B. Vengsarkar†	c Wijegunawardene, b de Silva		34
R.N. Kapil Dev	lbw, b Wijegunawardene		7
M. Azharuddin	c Madurasinghe, b Ratnayeke		34
K.S. More*	c Ratnayeke, b Wijegunawardene		6
Arshad Ayub	run out		9
S.K. Sharma	c Madurasinghe, b Wijegunawardene		28
Maninder Singh	c de Silva, b Wijegunawardene		7
N.D. Hirwani	not out		1
Extras	lb 1, w 3, nb 1		5
(44 overs)			254

	O	M	R	W
J.R. Ratnayeke	8	–	47	1
Ramanayake	8	–	36	–
Wijegunawardene	9	–	49	4
Samarasekera	2	–	17	–
Ranatunga	5	–	27	2
de Silva	6	–	36	1
Madurasinghe	6	–	41	–

FALL OF WICKETS

1–89, 2–96, 3–146, 4–166, 5–167, 6–182, 7–195, 8–224, 9–252

Umpires: Salim Badar & Tariq Ata

Man of the Match: P.A. de Silva

Sri Lanka won by 17 runs

Maninder Singh (India). (David Munden)

India, too, prospered and were given an exciting start by Srikkanth and Sidhu. At 146 for 2, they were well placed, but Wijegunawardene, in only his second international, produced a fine spell of bowling which gnawed into the middle order and tilted the game in favour of Sri Lanka.

This victory assured Sri Lanka of a place in the Asia Cup Final.

Match Four
BANGLADESH v. PAKISTAN

A massive stand of 205 for the third wicket between centurions Moin-ul-Atiq and Ijaz Ahmed effectively put the game well beyond the reach of Bangladesh. Once more the host nation elected for survival rather than attempting a run rate which was way beyond their capabilities.

Match Five
INDIA v. PAKISTAN

The decisive match of the tournament was the meeting of the Asian giants, India and Pakistan, in the last round of the group matches. It seemed that the game was heading

for an anti-climax when Pakistan, having been put in to bat, were bundled out for a miserable 142, but Abdul Qadir and Tauseef Ahmed, the Pakistan spinners, bowled their side back into contention, only to find that the total that they were defending was too small even for their wiles.

Pakistan had begun well enough, but as Maninder Singh and Arshad Ayub came into the attack, they faltered. Arshad's off-spinners proved devastating, and the last seven Pakistan wickets went down for 35 runs.

Sidhu went quickly, and the dismissal of Vengsarkar for nought caused a tremor in the Indian ranks as they set out in search of their moderate target. The loss of three wickets for six runs brought them to a point of crisis, but Mohinder Amarnath played a fine innings, keeping his head when those about him were losing theirs. He hit 6 fours in his 74, which came off 122 balls and occupied 166 minutes. He was given resolute support by Pandit, who offered sensible defence at a time when it was most needed and allowed Amarnath as much of the strike as possible.

India won with 5.2 overs to spare and qualified for the final.

Match Six
BANGLADESH v. SRI LANKA

With Sri Lanka already assured of a place in the final, the last group match had no importance save for prestige. To their credit, Bangladesh recovered from the despair of 8

ASIA CUP – MATCH FOUR – BANGLADESH v. PAKISTAN
29 October 1988 at Chittagong Stadium, Chittagong, Bangladesh

PAKISTAN				BANGLADESH			
Rameez Raja	c Nasu, b Prince		10	Azhar Hussain Shantu	c Saleem Yousuf, b Iqbal Qasim		10
Moin-ul-Atiq	lbw, b Athar Ali Khan		105	Faruque Ahmed	lbw, b Iqbal Qasim		14
Saleem Malik	c and b Shantu		15	Gazi Ashraf Lipu†	b Iqbal Qasim		10
Ijaz Ahmed	not out		124	Athar Ali Khan	c Rameez Raja, b Abdul Qadir		22
Shoaib Mohammad	not out		7	Minhazul Abedin Nannu	lbw, b Shoaib Mohammad		11
Manzoor Elahi				Aminul Islam Bulbul	b Abdul Qadir		0
Saleem Yousuf*				J.S. Badsha	not out		8
Wasim Akram				Akram Hussain Khan	not out		21
Abdul Qadir†				Nasir Nasu*			
Iqbal Qasim				G.M. Nausher Prince			
Tauseef Ahmed				Wahidul Ghani			
Extras	b 3, lb 6, w 14		23	Extras	b 4, lb 6, w 4, nb 1		15
(45 overs)	(for 3 wkts)		284	(45 overs)	(for 6 wkts)		111

	O	M	R	W		O	M	R	W
Prince	6	–	55	1	Wasim Akram	6	2	11	–
Badsha	9	1	53	–	Manzoor Elahi	4	1	7	–
Athar Ali Khan	9	–	54	1	Tauseef Ahmed	8	2	12	–
Shantu	6	–	24	1	Iqbal Qasim	9	3	13	3
Wahidul Ghani	6	–	32	–	Shoaib Mohammad	8	–	21	1
Akram Hussain Khan	5	–	28	–	Abdul Qadir	9	–	27	2
Nannu	2	–	17	–	Rameez Raja	1	–	10	–
Bulbul	2	–	12	–					

FALL OF WICKETS
1–43, 2–72, 3–277

FALL OF WICKETS
1–30, 2–39, 3–54, 4–82, 5–82, 6–82

Umpires: R.B. Gupta & S. Poonadurai

Man of the Match: Moin-ul-Atiq

Pakistan won by 173 runs

ASIA CUP – MATCH FIVE – PAKISTAN v. INDIA
31 October 1988 at National Stadium, Dhaka, Bangladesh

PAKISTAN				
Rameez Raja	lbw, b Arshad Ayub			33
Moin-ul-Atiq	b Maninder Singh			38
Saleem Malik	lbw,			
	b Maninder Singh			19
Ijaz Ahmed	b Kapil Dev			14
Aamer Malik*	lbw, b Arshad Ayub			2
Shoaib Mohammad	b Arshad Ayub			2
Naved Anjum	lbw, b Arshad Ayub			1
Wasim Akram	b Arshad Ayub			4
Abdul Qadir†	run out			3
Haafiz Shahid	b Kapil Dev			2
Tauseef Ahmed	not out			7
Extras	b 1, lb 7, w 8, nb 1			17
(42.2 overs)				142

	O	M	R	W
Kapil Dev	6.2	1	16	2
S.K. Sharma	7	–	26	–
Amarnath	5	–	29	–
Maninder Singh	9	1	25	2
Arshad Ayub	9	–	21	5
A.K. Sharma	5	–	15	–
Srikkanth	1	–	2	–

FALL OF WICKETS
1–62, 2–91, 3–97, 4–107, 5–112, 6–116, 7–124,
8–128, 9–133

INDIA				
K. Srikkanth	b Abdul Qadir			23
N.S. Sidhu	b Naved Anjum			3
M.B. Amarnath	not out			74
D.B. Vengsarkar†	lbw, b Abdul Qadir			0
M. Azharuddin	lbw, b Wasim Akram			15
R.N. Kapil Dev	st Aamer Malik,			
	b Abdul Qadir			2
A.K. Sharma	b Wasim Akram			2
C.S. Pandit*	not out			5
S.K. Sharma				
Arshad Ayub				
Maninder Singh				
Extras	b 2, lb 5, w 5, nb 7			19
(39.4 overs)	(for 6 wkts)			143

	O	M	R	W
Wasim Akram	9	–	29	2
Naved Anjum	7.4	–	30	1
Abdul Qadir	9	3	27	3
Haafiz Shahid	3	–	17	–
Tauseef Ahmed	9	–	22	–
Shoaib Mohammad	1	–	6	–
Saleem Malik	1	–	5	–

FALL OF WICKETS
1–13, 2–76, 3–76, 4–110, 5–113, 6–116

Umpires: K.T. Francis & S. Poonadurai

Man of the Match: Arshad Ayub

India won by 4 wickets

ASIA CUP – MATCH SIX – BANGLADESH v. SRI LANKA
2 November 1988 at National Stadium, Dhaka, Bangladesh

BANGLADESH				
Faruque Ahmed	c de Silva,			
	b Ratnayeke			0
Harunur Rashid Liton	c Kuruppu,			
	b Ratnayeke			0
Azhar Hussain Shantu	lbw, b Ratnayeke			3
Gazi Ashraf Lipu†	b Ramanayake			2
Athar Ali Khan	st Kuruppu,			
	b de Silva			30
Minhazul Abedin Nannu	c Anurasiri,			
	b Madurasinghe			10
Akram Hussain Khan	c Kuruppu,			
	b Anurasiri			9
Aminul Islam Bulbul	c Anurasiri,			
	b Ratnayeke			27
Ghulam Faruq Suru	not out			23
Nasir Nasu*	not out			2
G.M. Nausher Prince				
Extras	b 1, lb 2, w 5, nb 4			12
(45 overs)	(for 8 wkts)			118

	O	M	R	W
J.R. Ratnayeke	8	1	23	4
Ramanayake	6	2	6	1
Wijegunawardene	6	1	21	–
Samarasekera	2	–	11	–
Anurasiri	9	2	18	1
Madurasinghe	9	–	11	1
de Silva	5	1	25	1

FALL OF WICKETS
1–1, 2–2, 3–8, 4–8, 5–42, 6–62, 7–68, 8–114

SRI LANKA				
D.S.B.P. Kuruppu	not out			58
J.R. Ratnayeke†	lbw, b Shantu			17
M.A.R. Samarasekera	not out			38
P.A. de Silva				
L.R.D. Mendis				
H.P. Tillekeratne				
S.H.U. Karnain				
H.C.P. Ramanayake				
W.R. Madurasinghe				
S.D. Anurasiri				
K.I.W Wijegunawardene				
Extras	b 1, lb 4, w 1, nb 1			7
(30.4 overs)	(for 1 wkt)			120

	O	M	R	W
Prince	4	1	15	–
Suru	8	1	34	–
Athar Ali Khan	4	–	17	–
Shantu	6.4	–	20	1
Bulbul	6	–	23	–
Akram Hussain Khan	2	–	6	–

FALL OF WICKETS
1–57

Umpires: V.K. Ramaswamy & Salim Bardar

Man of the Match: J.R. Ratnayeke

Sri Lanka won by 9 wickets

Graeme Labrooy (Sri Lanka). (David Munden)

for 4, brought about mainly by Ravi Ratnayeke, to reach their highest score of the tournament. It mattered little as Sri Lanka rushed to victory with more than 14 overs to spare.

Asia Cup Final
INDIA v. SRI LANKA

Having played so well in the earlier stages of the competition, Sri Lanka disappointed in the final and came

Final League Table

	P	W	L	Pts	R/R
Sri Lanka	3	3	–	6	5.13
India	3	2	1	4	4.53
Pakistan	3	1	2	2	4.72
Bangladesh	3	–	3	0	2.42

nowhere near to showing the form that they had shown in beating India and Pakistan in the qualifying round. Put in to bat, they began briskly, and the running between the wickets by Mahanama and Kuruppu was a joy. Kuruppu did not hit the first boundary of the day until the tenth over, by which time the score was already 42, so fleet had been the running. The fifty came up in 12.3 overs without any hint of the disasters that lay ahead. Even when Kuruppu and Mahanama were out in quick succession, the run rate did not slacken as de Silva and Samarasekera unleashed a barrage of strokes. Then both batsmen were run out in wasteful fashion, and the next six overs produced only 12 runs and saw another silly run out, the

ASIA CUP FINAL – INDIA v. SRI LANKA
4 November 1988 at National Stadium, Dhaka, Bangladesh

SRI LANKA			
R.S. Mahanama	lbw, b Amarnath		23
D.S.B.P. Kuruppu*	st Pandit,		
	b Maninder Singh		21
M.A.R. Samarasekera	run out		26
P.A. de Silva	run out		18
A. Ranatunga†	run out		5
L.R.D. Mendis	c Amarnath,		
	b Srikkanth		36
J.R. Ratnayeke	run out		7
S.H.U. Karnain	c Pandit, b Srikkanth		11
G.F. Labrooy	b Kapil Dev		1
K.I.W. Wijegunawardene	not out		8
W.R. Madurasinghe	b Srikkanth		2
Extras	lb 5, w 7, nb 6		18
(43.2 overs)			176

INDIA			
K. Srikkanth	run out		23
N.S. Sidhu	b Wijegunawardene		76
M.B. Amarnath	st Kuruppu,		
	b Madurasinghe		7
D.B. Vengsarkar†	not out		50
M. Azharuddin	c Kuruppu,		
	b Wijegunawardene		0
R.N. Kapil Dev	not out		12
A.K. Sharma			
C.S. Pandit*			
S.K. Sharma			
Arshad Ayub			
Maninder Singh			
Extras	b 1, lb 6, w 2, nb 3		12
(37.1 overs)	(for 4 wkts)		180

	O	M	R	W
Kapil Dev	7	–	30	1
S.K. Sharma	5	–	20	–
Amarnath	6	–	21	1
Maninder Singh	9	–	35	1
Arshad Ayub	9	–	24	–
A.K. Sharma	4	–	29	–
Srikkanth	3.2	–	12	3

	O	M	R	W
J.R. Ratnayeke	9	1	35	–
Labrooy	5	–	30	–
Ranatunga	1	–	12	–
Madurasinghe	9	–	33	1
de Silva	4	–	28	–
Wijegunawardene	9	1	31	2
Mahanama	0.1	–	4	–

FALL OF WICKETS
1–53, 2–57, 3–97, 4–105, 5–113, 6–130, 7–164,
8–165, 9–166

FALL OF WICKETS
1–45, 2–69, 3–155, 4–155

Umpires: Tariq Ata & Saleem Badar (Pakistan)

Man of the Match: N.S. Sidhu

India won by 6 wickets

valuable wicket of Ranatunga. The insanity continued as Ravi Ratnayeke was also run out, and at 130 for 6 from 34 overs, Sri Lanka had virtually given the game to India.

Duleep Mendis raised spirits when he hit left-arm spinner Ajay Sharma for a six and 2 fours in the same over. Four overs yielded 30 runs, but the recovery was to be a brief one as three wickets went down for two runs. Srikkanth ended the innings with his occasional off-breaks, taking 3 for 12 in 20 balls. One of his victims was Mendis, whose 36 off as many deliveries gave some light in the Sri Lankan gloom.

The asking rate of 3.93 was never likely to trouble India, and Sidhu and Srikkanth gave them an explosive start. Srikkanth hit 2 successive fours off Ravi Ratnayeke, and

Sidhu greeted Ranatunga with a four and a massive six over long-on. Having made 23 off 28 balls, Srikkanth was brilliantly run out by Karnain's direct throw, and the Sri Lankan fielding was of exceptional quality. Amarnath was very well stumped by the agile Kuruppu, but Sidhu was in irresistible form and claimed the individual awards for both the match and the series. When he departed, Vengsarkar finished the job.

If the Sri Lankans had failed to do themselves justice with the bat, they had done enough in the competition to show the immense talent that they possess, and one can only hope that the rest of the cricketing world will treat them with more sympathy and understanding and grant them the tours that they need to develop that talent.

SECTION F

Balance of Power

The season in Pakistan.
Test series and One-Day
International *v.* Australia.
The Wills Cup. Patron's Trophy,
Quaid-e-Azam Trophy and
Sri Lanka 'B' tour.
First-class averages.

*Leading wicket-taker Iqbal Qasim – 75 wickets in the
Pakistan season. (Adrian Murrell/Allsport)*

A new cricket administration in Pakistan decided on yet another change of structure in the first-class game in the country in order to give the first-class competitions more credibility, but, as the leading players were again to be absent abroad for much of the season, it was still hard to give the domestic tournaments the substance that they urgently need. The season in Pakistan began earlier than usual with the tour by the Australians. Imran Khan, who declined to play against the Australians, voiced the opinion that the tour was a mistake, for the weather was inappropriate and the series clashed with the Olympic Games. The lack of interest in the tour and the seemingly inevitable complaints from the visitors about umpiring and state of pitches were to give support to Imran's opinion.

5, 6 and 7 September 1988

at Qaddafi Stadium, Lahore

Australians 317 for 3 dec (G.R. Marsh 136, D.C. Boon 76, G.M. Wood 66 not out) and 194 for 6 dec (P.L. Taylor 50 not out, Nadeem Ghauri 4 for 72)
BCCP Patron's XI 246 (Ijaz Ahmed 97, P.R. Sleep 4 for 65) and 85 for 5

Match drawn

Under the management of C.J. Egar, and with Bobby Simpson as cricket manager, the Australians began their tour in promising fashion. Marsh, Boon and Wood, whose form in the Sheffield Shield had earned him a recall to the national squad, all batted well, and there was some very good bowling from Reid, hopefully restored to full fitness, Sleep and Taylor. Ijaz Ahmed hit 97 off 98 balls for the Patron's XI, and Nadeem Ghauri, the left-arm spinner from Habib Bank, gave further evidence that he was worthy of Test recognition.

9, 10 and 12 September 1988

at Ayub Stadium, Quetta

Australians 288 for 8 dec (G.M. Wood 91, J.D. Siddons 60, P.R. Sleep 52) and 156 for 2 dec (M.R.J. Veletta 72 not out)
Baluchistan Governor's XI 260 for 9 dec (Raees Ahmed 77, A.I.C. Dodemaide 4 for 46) and 78 for 4

Match drawn

In their only other match before the first Test, the Australians gave another satisfactory display with Siddons hitting a six and 5 fours in his 60 which was made in 144 minutes, and Graeme Wood scoring 91 in 226 minutes. Veletta also batted well, but, like Siddons and Sleep, who had another good match, he was unable to find a place in the side for the first Test. McDermott, too, was omitted.

First Test Match
PAKISTAN v. AUSTRALIA

Australia brought back Graeme Wood to Test cricket after a three-year absence and gave a first Test cap to Ian Healy, who had been selected as the only wicket-keeper for the tour although he had come late into the Queensland side as a replacement for the injured Anderson. Pakistan were weakened by the absence of their first choice opening attack, Imran Khan and Wasim Akram, who was convalescing.

Javed won the toss and Pakistan batted first on a wicket that was expected to take spin. Australia had a most encouraging start when Bruce Reid bowled Mudassar behind his legs with the second ball of the day. There was further success for Reid when Rameez edged a ball to Healy, who took the catch diving in front of first slip. That was to be Australia's last success for nearly five hours. Shoaib Mohammad, who has at last blossomed into a batsman of Test quality, played splendidly, and Javed was soon into his stride. The pair added 196 in 279 minutes, blending caution with strokes of great authority. Both batsmen were aided by some poor catching, and Javed survived several confident appeals for lbw. The refusal of these appeals was to bring bitter protest from the Australian management, who cited figures that Javed had been given out leg before many more times overseas than he had been in Tests in Pakistan. Such figures, however, can be interpreted in two ways, and the umpires for the first Test were Khizar Hayat and Mahboob Shah, who were highly praised for their work in the World Cup a year earlier.

Shoaib played a masterly innings, batting for 64 overs and hitting 15 fours before playing back to Waugh and being deceived by a slower delivery. The close came with Pakistan on 227 for 3, with Javed Miandad 95 not out.

Australia had erred in the field on the first day; on the second they became wretched as four straightforward catches were put down. Javed reached the highest score made by a Pakistani against Australia and, in doing so, scored the fifth Test double century of his career. He hit a six and 29 fours and batted for 590 minutes, facing 439 deliveries. He was given splendid support by Tauseef Ahmed, who made his highest Test score. Saleem Malik, who was dropped twice in quick succession, joined Javed in a fifth-wicket stand of 114 in three hours. Both batsmen were finally caught by Boon, but Pakistan closed the day on 438 for 6.

Javed declared after his side had batted for 37 minutes on the third morning. Tim May finished with his best figures in Test cricket, but the Australian spinners had failed badly to exploit a pitch which offered them assistance. The Pakistani spinners were to give them a lesson as to how to bowl on such a wicket. They demoralized and destroyed the Australian upper order. The veteran left-arm spinner Iqbal Qasim, in particular, bowled in masterly fashion and enjoyed one spell of 4 for 14. The day ended with Australia on 116 for 7, still 154 runs short of avoiding the follow-on. The Australian problems did not end there, for their management chose to criticize umpire Mahboob Shah and the Karachi wicket. There were even threats of calling off the tour and returning home. The West Indies were to issue similar complaints about Australian umpires and pitches when they were beaten at Sydney a few months later.

Mr Egar's outbursts were unwise and unfortunate. Javed Miandad responded by saying that Pakistan would play the remaining Tests with the Australians providing whomever they liked as umpires, and that Pakistan would offer no complaint of any kind. The Australian raging could not conceal the technical deficiencies of their batting. In spite of Peter Taylor's maiden Test fifty and some

Bruce Reid; prominent for Australia in the Test series, but he broke down with a recurrence of his back injury when he returned home. (Adrian Murrell/Allsport)

more resolute batting by the late order, they were forced to follow-on and were soon in trouble again. At the end of the fourth day, they were 66 for 5.

The game lasted only 90 minutes more on the last morning. The Australians were still in an angry mood at the end of the match, believing that they were beaten by a conspiracy, and suggesting that neutral umpires were the only cure for the dissension. It should be remembered that it was Pakistan who first suggested the use of neutral umpires in Test matches some years ago, and their idea was rejected by England and Australia, in particular. Peter Taylor had batted nearly five hours for his first innings fifty. Had some of the other Australian batsmen shown some of his backbone and had the Australians held their catches, there might have been less cause for complaint by the visitors, who were subject to the largest defeat ever inflicted on Australia by a Pakistan side.

Second Test Match
PAKISTAN v. AUSTRALIA

Both sides made one change from their elevens for the first Test. Pakistan brought in pace bowler Saleem Jaffer for Aamer Malik while Australia brought in leg-spinner Peter

---

FIRST TEST MATCH – PAKISTAN v. AUSTRALIA
15, 16, 17, 19 and 20 September 1988 at National Stadium, Karachi

PAKISTAN

	FIRST INNINGS	
Mudassar Nazar	b Reid	0
Rameez Raja	c Healy, b Reid	9
Shoaib Mohammad	b Waugh	94
Javed Miandad†	c Boon, b Reid	211
Tauseef Ahmed	c Boon, b May	35
Saleem Malik	c Boon, b May	45
Ijaz Ahmed	c Boon, b Reid	12
Aamer Malik	not out	17
Saleem Yousuf*	c Wood, b May	5
Abdul Qadir	c Marsh, b May	8
Iqbal Qasim		
Extras	b 16, lb 12, nb 5	33
	(for 9 wkts, dec)	469

AUSTRALIA

	FIRST INNINGS		SECOND INNINGS	
G.R. Marsh	b Iqbal Qasim	8	lbw, b Tauseef	17
D.C. Boon	b Abdul Qadir	14	(3) b Iqbal Qasim	4
D.M. Jones	lbw, b Iqbal Qasim	3	(4) c Ijaz, b Qadir	4
G.M. Wood	c Qasim, b Tauseef	23	(5) lbw, b Qasim	15
A.R. Border†	c Aamer, b Qasim	4	(6) b Qasim	18
S.R. Waugh	lbw, b Iqbal Qasim	0	(7) st Yousuf,	
			b Qasim	13
P.L. Taylor	not out	54	(2) c Ijaz, b Aamer	2
I.A. Healy*	c Ijaz, b Mudassar	26	c Shoaib, b Qadir	21
A.I.C. Dodemaide	c Ijaz, b Saleem Malik	8	st Yousuf, b Tauseef	2
T.B.A. May	c Yousuf, b Qadir	6	lbw, b Qadir	0
B.A. Reid	lbw, b Iqbal Qasim	0	not out	8
Extras	b 12, lb 7	19	b 6, lb 6	12
		165		116

	O	M	R	W
Reid	41	10	109	4
Dodemaide	29	13	35	–
Waugh	26	3	94	1
May	40.5	10	97	4
Taylor	16	2	73	–
Border	17	7	33	–

	O	M	R	W	O	M	R	W
Mudassar Nazar	10	3	15	1	3	–	5	–
Aamer Malik	2	–	6	–	2	2	0	1
Iqbal Qasim	39	24	35	5	25	14	49	4
Abdul Qadir	37	16	54	2	13	4	34	3
Tauseef Ahmed	26	15	28	1	21.4	13	16	2
Shoaib Mohammad	2	1	1	–				
Saleem Malik	6	4	7	1				

FALL OF WICKETS
1–0, 2–21, 3–217, 4–284, 5–398, 6–428, 7–444, 8–457, 9–469

FALL OF WICKETS
1–19, 2–23, 3–40, 4–48, 5–54, 6–64, 7–106, 8–139, 9–162
1–4, 2–10, 3–15, 4–46, 5–50, 6–80, 7–93, 8–104, 9–104

Umpires: Khizar Hayat & Mahboob Shah

Pakistan won by an innings and 188 runs

SECOND TEST MATCH – PAKISTAN v. AUSTRALIA
23, 24, 25, 27 and 28 September 1988 at Iqbal Stadium, Faisalabad

PAKISTAN

	FIRST INNINGS		SECOND INNINGS	
Mudassar Nazar	c Marsh, b Reid	9	c Border, b May	27
Rameez Raja	lbw, b Dodemaide	0	c Boon, b Waugh	32
Shoaib Mohammad	b Dodemaide	11	st Healy, b May	74
Javed Miandad†	c Boon, b May	43	lbw, b Reid	107
Saleem Malik	b Dodemaide	0	c Border, b Reid	10
Ijaz Ahmed	b Reid	122	c Healy, b Reid	0
Saleem Yousuf*	c Boon, b Dodemaide	62	not out	66
Abdul Qadir	b Reid	6	(10) c Reid, b May	13
Tauseef Ahmed	not out	35	(8) c Waugh, b Dodemaide	2
Iqbal Qasim	c and b Sleep	16	(9) lbw, b Reid	28
Saleem Jaffer	lbw, b Sleep	0		
Extras	b 2, lb 6, nb 4	12	lb 6, nb 13	19
		316	(for 9 wkts, dec)	378

	O	M	R	W	O	M	R	W
Reid	31	8	92	3	30	6	100	4
Dodemaide	34	6	87	4	20	4	48	1
Waugh	11	3	36	–	18	6	44	1
Sleep	5.5	1	24	2	13	4	51	–
May	19	3	58	1	34.4	7	126	3
Border	6	1	11	–	1	–	3	–

FALL OF WICKETS
1–4, 2–20, 3–24, 4–25, 5–144, 6–255, 7–255, 8–267, 9–316
1–64, 2–64, 3–236, 4–264, 5–265, 6–269, 7–274, 8–344, 9–378

AUSTRALIA

	FIRST INNINGS		SECOND INNINGS	
D.C. Boon	b Mudassar Nazar	13	(2) c Mudassar, b Tauseef	15
G.R. Marsh	b Tauseef Ahmed	51	(1) b Abdul Qadir	9
D.M. Jones	lbw, b Abdul Qadir	16	not out	21
G.M. Wood	lbw, b Saleem Jaffer	32	(5) not out	2
A.I.C. Dodemaide	c Ijaz, b Mudassar	19		
A.R. Border†	not out	113	(4) c and b Shoaib	19
S.R. Waugh	st Yousuf, b Tauseef	1		
P.R. Sleep	b Tauseef	12		
I.A. Healy*	c Iqbal, b Jaffer	27		
T.B.A. May	c sub (Moin-ul-Atiq), b Abdul Qadir	14		
B.A. Reid	c Yousuf, b Qasim	1		
Extras	b 4, lb 15, w 1, nb 2	22	b 1	1
		321	(for 3 wkts)	67

	O	M	R	W	O	M	R	W
Saleem Jaffer	29	7	69	2	2	–	8	–
Mudassar Nazar	17	4	39	2	2	–	5	–
Abdul Qadir	34	5	84	2	10	1	34	1
Tauseef Ahmed	35	10	73	3	11	4	17	1
Iqbal Qasim	14.5	4	37	1				
Shoaib Mohammad					1	–	2	1

FALL OF WICKETS
1–24, 2–65, 3–122, 4–122, 5–167, 6–170, 7–204, 8–256, 9–318
1–18, 2–30, 3–65

Umpires: Mahboob Shah & Tariq Ata

Match drawn

THIRD TEST MATCH – PAKISTAN v. AUSTRALIA
7, 8, 9, 10 and 11 October 1988 at Qaddafi Stadium, Lahore

AUSTRALIA

	FIRST INNINGS		SECOND INNINGS	
D.C. Boon	c Shoaib, b Jaffer	43	(2) c Javed, b Jaffer	28
G.R. Marsh	st Yousuf, b Qasim	64	(1) not out	84
D.M. Jones	lbw, b Tauseef	0	lbw, b Saleem Jaffer	0
A.R. Border†	c Yousuf, b Tauseef	75	c Yousuf, b Tauseef	20
G.M. Wood	lbw, b Mudassar	15		
P.L. Taylor	st Yousuf, b Qadir	29	(5) not out	25
S.R. Waugh	c Ijaz, b Qasim	59		
I.A. Healy*	lbw, b Abdul Qadir	0		
A.I.C. Dodemaide	c Qasim, b Qadir	14		
T.B.A. May	not out	13		
B.A. Reid	c Mudassar, b Tauseef	8		
Extras	b 4, lb 12, nb 4	20	lb 4	4
		340	(for 3 wkts, dec)	161

	O	M	R	W	O	M	R	W
Saleem Jaffer	33	9	82	1	14	2	60	2
Mudassar Nazar	15	6	23	1	3	–	8	–
Abdul Qadir	37	10	88	3	4	1	26	–
Tauseef Ahmed	50	20	85	3	17	2	48	1
Iqbal Qasim	22	6	42	2	3	–	15	–
Shoaib Mohammad	1	–	4	–				

FALL OF WICKETS
1–87, 2–88, 3–155, 4–200, 5–231, 6–241, 7–241, 8–294, 9–331
1–71, 2–71, 3–108

PAKISTAN

	FIRST INNINGS		SECOND INNINGS	
Mudassar Nazar	c Boon, b May	27	c Border, b Taylor	49
Rameez Raja	c Healy, b Reid	64	c Boon, b May	21
Shoaib Mohammad	run out	13	lbw, b May	3
Javed Miandad†	c Healy, b Reid	27	c Border, b May	24
Saleem Malik	c and b Dodemaide	26	c Healy, b Taylor	13
Ijaz Ahmed	lbw, b Dodemaide	23	c Taylor, b Dodemaide	15
Saleem Yousuf*	c Healy, b Reid	1	c Waugh, b Taylor	2
Abdul Qadir	lbw, b Dodemaide	18	st Healy, b Taylor	6
Iqbal Qasim	lbw, b May	14	not out	10
Tauseef Ahmed	c Boon, b May	3	not out	1
Saleem Jaffer	not out	0		
Extras	lb 6, nb 11	17	b 6, lb 1, nb 2	9
		233	(for 8 wkts)	153

	O	M	R	W	O	M	R	W
Reid	23	3	53	3				
Waugh	18	4	34	–	5	1	8	–
Dodemaide	26	6	56	3	12	5	20	1
May	27.2	6	73	3	35	20	39	3
Taylor	4	2	11	–	28	9	78	4
Border					4	3	1	–

FALL OF WICKETS
1–80, 2–104, 3–118, 4–172, 5–172, 6–173, 7–206, 8–228, 9–232
1–36, 2–48, 3–86, 4–107, 5–123, 6–125, 7–131, 8–147

Umpires: Khizar Hayat & Saleem Badar

Match drawn

Sleep for off-spinner Peter Taylor. Javed again won the toss, but Pakistan began disastrously.

In the first 50 minutes of the match, Australia captured four wickets. The main honours went to Tony Dodemaide, who took 3 for 23 in 11 overs of accurate and hostile bowling. Reid, too, bowled well, but after the early moisture had gone from the pitch the Australian attack struggled.

Javed was subdued early on, but Ijaz Ahmed took the attack to the Australians from the start, driving in an upright and regal manner and displaying remarkable authority in one so young. Ijaz and Javed added 119 before Javed hit May low to short-leg. Ijaz had reached 51 out of 64 in 21 overs, and he continued to play an array of exciting shots. He hit Sleep out of the attack with two vast sixes in the leg-spinner's first two overs, and his innings also included 17 fours.

Saleem Yousuf gave Ijaz excellent support after an uncertain start. He was ever eager to hit the ball, and Pakistan ended the first day on a relieved 244 for 5.

Ijaz was out without addition to his overnight score, but, when Australia again threatened to take control of the game, Tauseef batted with great resolution, and he and Iqbal added valuable runs. The wicket held none of the devils that the Karachi pitch had held, but Australia ended the second day on a rather uncertain 128 for 4.

The fifth-wicket stand had realized 45 when Dodemaide was splendidly caught at short-leg by Ijaz off Mudassar, and, with Waugh well stumped off Tauseef, Australia had lost two wickets in 12 balls and slumped to 170 for 6. That they regained the initiative was thanks entirely to Allan Border, who batted for six hours, hit 12 fours and reached his 23rd Test century. He was given good support by Healy and the tail, and Australia closed the third day and their first innings just five runs ahead.

What hopes Australia had of winning the match and levelling the series were dashed on the fourth day, when a good holiday crowd of 12,000 revelled in a third-wicket stand of 172 between Javed and the ever-improving Shoaib. Javed moved to his 19th Test hundred with a blistering cover drive for four off May, and he ended the day with 107 and Pakistan on 264 for 3. The grandeur of Javed and Shoaib's batting could not be denied, but the paucity of the Australian spin attack, and the plethora of dropped catches, with wicket-keeper Healy a prime offender, did not help the visitors' cause.

Javed was not to add to his score on the last morning, but Saleem Yousuf again batted with panache, and Javed did not declare until after lunch, so that a draw was inevitable.

2, 3 and 4 October 1988

at Arab Niaz (Shahi Bagh) Stadium, Peshawar

Australians 472 for 8 dec (G.R. Marsh 106, P.L. Taylor 83, G.M. Wood 70, D.C. Boon 65, D.M. Jones 60)
NW Frontier Governor's XI 343 for 7 (Saeed Anwar 127, Anil Dalpat 51)

Match drawn

The first one-day international scheduled for Gujranwala on 30 September was cancelled because of extensive flooding in the Punjab province, so that the Australians were left with only the game in Peshawar between the second and third Tests. Geoff Marsh led the tourists and celebrated with his second century of the tour. He hit a six and 15 fours. Boon, Jones, Wood and later Taylor, who hit 13 boundaries in his 80, all enjoyed the batting practice. The Governor's XI was well served by Saeed Anwar, the slim left-hander, who played a glorious innings, hitting 23 fours and reaching his hundred off 112 deliveries. His 127 came in 272 minutes.

Third Test Match
PAKISTAN v. AUSTRALIA

Australia reverted to the side which had lost the first Test; Pakistan remained unchanged. Winning the toss for the first time, Border saw his openers give Australia their best start of the series, but they laboured to establish themselves against some naggingly accurate bowling. At lunch, after 2½ hours' play, the score was only 69, and when Boon was caught at point 45 minutes after lunch the partnership had realized 87. Jones padded up to a straight ball from Tauseef one run later, but Border showed majestic form from the start of his innings to end Pakistan's hopes of bringing about a collapse. Marsh was stumped in the last session, but Border was dominant until the close at 175 for 3.

Australia's chances of building a huge score were thwarted by the Pakistan spinners on the second day. They exerted a frustrating stranglehold on the batting, conceding less than two runs an over, and the visitors could add only 165 runs in the day before being all out just before the close. Pakistan scored six in the one over available to them.

Mudassar and Rameez took their opening stand to 80 on the third morning, but three quick wickets gave Australia hope of bringing about a collapse. Again they were badly let down by their catching, and Pakistan ended the day on 165 for 3 with Javed, 24 not out, having passed 7,000 runs in Test cricket, the first Pakistani to achieve this feat. The Australian cause was not helped when 22 overs were lost to a thunderstorm.

Early on the fourth morning three wickets in successive overs heralded Australia's best day of the tour. Reid had Javed caught behind in his second over, and Saleem Malik was brilliantly caught and bowled one-handed by Dodemaide, the bowler clinging on to a fierce drive as he followed through. Reid also dismissed Saleem Yousuf, but then he left the field with a recurrence of the back injury which had kept him out of most of the 1987–8 season. Dodemaide filled the breach manfully, and May took two late wickets, so that Australia claimed a first-innings lead of 107. The lead was increased to 239 by the close with Marsh and Taylor at the crease, and the problem confronting Border was how to force a victory.

In three overs on the last morning, Marsh and Taylor added 29, and Border declared, setting Pakistan to make 269 in a minimum of 75 overs. They began confidently enough, but Border soon introduced May into the attack, and he had Rameez Raja taken at forward short-leg. The quick dismissal of Shoaib gave the Australians encourage-

Ijaz Ahmed – a brilliant and exciting century for Pakistan in the Second Test. (David Munden)

ment. Javed was caught at slip, and Saleem Malik was spectacularly caught on the leg side by Healy. In 14 deliveries after tea, Taylor took three wickets for eight runs. He ended Mudassar's four-hour innings, had Saleem Yousuf taken at long-off and had Qadir stumped. Once more, Ijaz showed great maturity, however, and when he was caught Iqbal and Tauseef survived the last five overs. Australia had lost the series, but they had regained some pride and honour, and their spinners had at last shown something close to the form expected of international bowlers.

One-Day International
PAKISTAN v. AUSTRALIA

With the first one-day international cancelled because of floods and the second and third at Karachi and Hyderabad cancelled because of riots and the resultant curfew, only one limited-over match could be scheduled, and that was played at Lahore as the last match of the Australian tour.

Australia, put in to bat, gave games to all those who had not played in the Test series. Healy and Siddons made their debuts in one-day international cricket. Wasim Akram returned to the Pakistan side and maintained a good line, which made him the most successful of the home bowlers. Boon and Marsh gave the visitors a fine start, and Marsh's innings lasted until the 42nd over. Veletta and Siddons also batted well.

Mudassar proved to be the backbone of the Pakistan innings, and he and Saleem Malik added 88 in 15 overs for the second wicket to put Pakistan well on the road to victory. Mudassar hit 9 fours in a sparkling display, and he was out when McDermott blocked a hard drive and threw down the wicket before Mudassar could regain his ground. Javed and Manzoor Elahi followed in quick succession, but Ijaz Ahmed stroked Pakistan close to victory before playing on in the penultimate over, with four runs needed for victory.

The last over began with only two needed, and Saleem Yousuf took a single off the first ball to level the scores. Wasim blocked and swung alternately before being caught off a skimming drive, with one ball of the match remaining. Qadir padded away the last ball of Dodemaide's over, and Pakistan won by virtue of having lost seven wickets to Australia's eight.

So Australia returned home from a tour which, in spite of the crowd of 20,000 at the one-day international, had been a financial disaster, without a win in seven matches. Pakistan's national side flew off to Sharjah for the Champions' Trophy and the next round of the international circus. The Sharjah tournament was to begin only two days after the game in Lahore.

ONE-DAY INTERNATIONAL – PAKISTAN v. AUSTRALIA
14 October 1988 at Qaddafi Stadium, Lahore

AUSTRALIA			
D.C. Boon	lbw, b Mudassar Nazar		38
G.R. Marsh	b Wasim Akram		89
A.R. Border†	b Mudassar Nazar		11
M.R.J. Veletta	c Javed Miandad, b Abdul Qadir		18
J.D. Siddons	c Shoaib Mohammad, b Wasim Akram		32
S.R. Waugh	run out		7
P.L. Taylor	not out		12
C.J. McDermott	lbw, b Wasim Akram		6
I.A. Healy*	run out		1
A.I.C. Dodemaide	not out		5
T.B.A. May			
Extras	lb 3, w 6, nb 1		10
(45 overs)	(for 8 wkts)		229

PAKISTAN			
Mudassar Nazar	run out		76
Rameez Raja	c Dodemaide, b May		24
Saleem Malik	c Border, b McDermott		44
Javed Miandad†	lbw, b Taylor		10
Ijaz Ahmed	b Waugh		39
Manzoor Elahi	run out		13
Saleem Yousuf*	not out		4
Wasim Akram	c Border b Dodemaide		1
Abdul Qadir	not out		0
Shoaib Mohammad			
Mohsin Kamal			
Extras	b 4, lb 9, nb 5		18
(45 overs)	(for 7 wkts)		229

	O	M	R	W
Wasim Akram	9	–	38	3
Mohsin Kamal	5	–	39	–
Manzoor Elahi	7	–	23	–
Mudassar Nazar	9	–	40	2
Abdul Qadir	7	–	36	1
Shoaib Mohammad	1	–	6	–
Javed Miandad	7	–	44	–

	O	M	R	W
McDermott	9	–	43	1
Dodemaide	8	–	36	1
May	9	1	31	1
Waugh	8	–	42	1
Taylor	9	–	48	1
Border	2	–	16	–

FALL OF WICKETS
1–71, 2–94, 3–146, 4–196, 5–199, 6–208, 7–216, 8–217

FALL OF WICKETS
1–53, 2–141, 3–168, 4–170, 5–204, 6–226, 7–229

Umpires: Mian Mohammad Aslam & Ikram Rabbani

Man of the Match: Mudassar Nazar

Pakistan won by losing fewer wickets with scores level

PAKISTAN v. AUSTRALIA – TEST MATCH AVERAGES

PAKISTAN BATTING

	M	Inns	NOs	Runs	HS	Av	100s	50s
Javed Miandad	3	5		412	211	82.40	2	
Shoaib Mohammad	3	5		195	94	39.00		2
Ijaz Ahmed	3	5		172	122	34.40	1	
Saleem Yousuf	3	5	1	136	66*	34.00		2
Tauseef Ahmed	3	5	2	76	35*	25.33		
Rameez Raja	3	5		126	64	25.20		1
Iqbal Qasim	3	4	1	68	28	22.66		
Mudassar Nazar	3	5		112	49	22.40		
Saleem Malik	3	5		94	45	18.80		
Abdul Qadir	3	5		51	18	10.20		
Saleem Jaffer	2	2	1	0	0*	0.00		

Played in one Test: Aamer Malik 17*

AUSTRALIA BATTING

	M	Inns	NOs	Runs	HS	Av	100s	50s
A.R. Border	3	5	1	230	113*	57.50	1	1
P.L. Taylor	2	4	2	110	54*	55.00		1
G.R. Marsh	3	6	1	233	84*	46.60		3
G.M. Wood	3	5	1	87	32	21.75		
D.C. Boon	3	6		117	43	19.50		
I.A. Healy	3	4		74	27	18.50		
S.R. Waugh	3	5		92	59	18.40		1
T.B.A. May	3	4	1	33	14	11.00		
A.I.C. Dodemaide	3	4		43	19	10.75		
D.M. Jones	3	6	1	44	21*	8.80		
B.A. Reid	3	4	1	17	8*	5.66		

Played in one Test: P.R. Sleep 12

PAKISTAN BOWLING

	Overs	Mds	Runs	Wkts	Av	Best	10/m	5/inns
Aamer Malik	4	2	6	1	6.00	1/0		
Shoaib Mohammad	4	1	7	1	7.00	1/2		
Iqbal Qasim	103.5	48	178	12	14.83	5/35		1
Mudassar Nazar	50	13	95	4	23.75	2/39		
Tauseef Ahmed	160.4	64	267	11	24.27	3/73		
Abdul Qadir	135	37	320	11	29.09	3/34		
Saleem Jaffer	78	18	219	5	43.80	2/60		

Bowled in one innings: Saleem Malik 6–4–7–1

AUSTRALIA BOWLING

	Overs	Mds	Runs	Wkts	Av	Best	10/m	5/inns
B.A. Reid	125	27	354	14	25.28	4/100		
A.I.C. Dodemaide	121	34	246	9	27.33	4/87		
T.B.A. May	156.5	46	393	14	28.07	4/97		
P.R. Sleep	18	5	75	2	37.50	2/24		
P.L. Taylor	48	13	162	4	40.50	4/78		
S.R. Waugh	78	17	216	2	108.00	1/44		
A.R. Border	28	11	48	0	–	0/1		

PAKISTAN FIELDING FIGURES

9 – Saleem Yousuf (ct 4/st 5); 6 – Ijaz Ahmed; 3 – Shoaib Mohammad and Iqbal Qasim; 2 – Mudassar Nazar; 1 – Javed Miandad, Aamer Malik and sub (Moin-ul-Atiq)

AUSTRALIA FIELDING FIGURES

10 – D.C. Boon; 8 – I.A. Healy (ct 6/st 2); 4 – A.R. Border; 2 – G.R. Marsh and S.R. Waugh; 1 – G.N. Wood, P.L. Taylor, P.R. Sleep, A.I.C. Dodemaide and B.A. Reid

Wills Cup One-Day Tournament

The competition began in a sensational manner. On the opening day, 8 November, at Peshawar, Habib Bank's left-arm spinner Anwar Miandad established a tournament record when he took seven Lahore wickets for 20 runs in 6.3 overs to give his side victory by 16 runs.

The bowling award for the competition, however, went to Rizwan Qazi of Lahore. Shoaib Mohammad was named as the best batsman. Didar Malik of Multan took the wicket-keeping award, and Tahir Shah of National Bank won the fielding prize.

In the first semi-final, in Karachi, PIA bowled out National Bank for 171 in 41.1 overs and won by five wickets. Shoaib Mohammad hit 69. In the other semi-final, at Peshawar, Tauseef Ahmed bowled his side to an exciting 14-run win over ADBP by completing the hat trick with the last three deliveries of the 45-over quota.

Wills Cup – Final Tables

Group A			
	P	W	L	Pts
PIA	5	4	1	8
United Bank	5	4	1	8
PNSC	5	3	2	6
Karachi	5	2	3	4
Multan	5	2	3	4
Muslim Commercial Bank	5	–	5	0
Group B			
ADBP	5	4	1	8
National Bank	5	4	1	8
Habib Bank	5	4	1	8
Lahore	5	1	4	2
Rawalpindi	5	1	4	2
HBFC	5	1	4	2

Wills Cup Final
PAKISTAN INTERNATIONAL AIRLINES v. UNITED BANK

The final had to be delayed for a day as rain prevented play on 25 November.

Sikhander Bakht won the toss and asked PIA to bat first, but United Bank had no immediate success. Rizwan and Shoaib began steadily, and they reached 50 in the 14th over. At this point, Ali Zia, bowling medium-pace, had both Shoaib and Aamer Malik caught behind to tilt the game in United Bank's favour.

Asif Mujtaba helped Rizwan to rebuild the innings and never lost a chance to punish the loose ball. His 42 came off 50 deliveries. He was out with the score on 143, and, 49 runs later, Rizwan's fine innings came to an end when he was run out. His century included six boundaries, and he faced 140 balls.

Quick runs were supplied by Wasim Akram, who hit 2 sixes and 2 fours, but two unnecessary run outs at the end of the innings were to prove costly to PIA.

WILLS CUP FINAL – PAKISTAN INTERNATIONAL AIRLINES v. UNITED BANK
26 November 1988 at Qaddafi Stadium, Lahore

PIA				UNITED BANK			
Rizwan-uz-Zaman	run out		100	Moin-ul-Atiq	c Zulfiqar Ali,		
Shoaib Mohammad†	c Ashraf Ali,				b Rashid Khan		31
	b Ali Zia		13	Raees Ahmed	b Wasim Akram		94
Aamer Malik	c Ashraf Ali, b Ali Zia		0	Mansoor Akhtar	c and		
Asif Mujtaba	c Ashraf Ali,				b Zahid Ahmed		26
	b Masood Anwar		42	Inzamam-ul-Haq	run out		5
Wasim Haider	b Masood Anwar		10	Saeed Anwar	c Rizwan,		
Wasim Akram	c Saeed Anwar,				b Zahid Ahmed		36
	b Kamal Merchant		33	Ali Zia	c and b Wasim Akram		6
Zahid Ahmed	c Moin-ul-Atiq,			Ashraf Ali*	not out		7
	b Kamal		1	Masood Anwar	not out		0
Anil Dalpat*	c Ashraf Ali,			Kamal Merchant			
	b Sikhander		8	Sikhander Bakht†			
Rashid Khan	not out		1	Sajid Bashir			
Asif Mohammad	run out		1	Extras	b 5, lb 4, w 11, nb 3		23
Zulfiqar Ali	run out		0				
Extras	lb 6, w 12, nb 1		19	(45 overs)	(for 6 wkts)		228
(45 overs)			228				

	O	M	R	W		O	M	R	W
Sikhander Bakht	7	1	37	1	Wasim Akram	9	–	51	2
Sajid Bashir	5	–	22	–	Zulfiqar Ali	6	–	29	–
Ali Zia	9	–	38	2	Wasim Haider	8	–	39	–
Kamal Merchant	8	–	38	2	Rashid Khan	9	–	39	1
Masood Anwar	9	–	48	2	Zahid Ahmed	9	–	42	2
Raees Ahmed	7	–	39	–	Asif Mujtaba	4	1	19	–

FALL OF WICKETS
1–50, 2–53, 3–143, 4–165, 5–192, 6–216, 7–225, 8–227, 9–228

FALL OF WICKETS
1–74, 2–132, 3–138, 4–192, 5–212, 6–227

Umpires: Khizar Hayat & Mahboob Shah

Man of the Match: Raees Ahmed

United Bank won by virtue of having lost fewer wickets with the scores tied

United Bank required 229 at 5.08 runs an over, and were given a splendid start by Moin-ul-Atiq and Raees Ahmed, who put on 74 in 14.1 overs. Mansoor Akhtar helped Raees to maintain the right tempo, and the pair added 58. Saeed Anwar hit 36 off 34 balls with a massive six and 3 fours.

It was Raees Ahmed who held the innings together. His 94 came off 128 balls, and he was bowled in the last over as he attempted a big hit. Ashraf and Masood kept cool, however, and brought the Cup to United Bank by virtue of losing fewer wickets, the scores being level.

Patron's Trophy

The first of the two first-class competitions in Pakistan began shortly after the final of the Wills Cup. The Patron's Trophy, now sponsored by the Pakistan Tobacco Company, was divided into two grades, but only the first grade was granted first-class status. Grade One was restricted to the major city, zonal or divisional teams of the country, namely, Karachi, Sargodha, Faisalabad, Bahawalpur, Rawalpindi, Peshawar, Multan and Lahore. The Quaid-e-Azam Trophy was to be competed for later by the top commercial organizations. Once again there was to be a second grade which would not be of first-class status.

28, 29, 30 November and 1 December 1988

at Sargodha Stadium

Sargodha 123 (Mohsin Mirza 4 for 49) and 173
Karachi 347 for 8 (Basit Ali 65, Asif Mujtaba 74, Aziz-ur-Rhaman 4 for 125)

Karachi won by an innings and 51 runs
Karachi 14 pts, Sargodha 4 pts

at Rawalpindi Club Ground

Peshawar 240 (Waseem Yousuf 50, Raja Afaq 5 for 93) and 85 (M. Riaz 7 for 27)
Rawalpindi 345 for 5 (Naseer Ahmed 122, Mujahid Hameed 119 not out)

Rawalpindi won by an innings and 20 runs
Rawalpindi 14 pts, Peshawar 5 pts

at Montgomery Biscuit Factory Ground, Sahiwal

Multan 336 (Rizwan Sattar 133, Bilal Rana 74) and 132 for 4 (Rizwan Qazi 4 for 47)
Lahore 181 (Mushtaq Ahmed 4 for 55) and 286 (Rizwan Qazi 88, Hyder Jahangir 68, Bilal Rana 5 for 131)

Multan won by 6 wickets
Multan 14 pts, Lahore 5 pts

28, 29 and 30 November 1988

at Bahawalpur Stadium

Faisalabad 115 (Mohammad Altaf 4 for 34) and 161 (Mohammad Ashraf 65 not out, Mohammad Zahid 5 for 20, Mohammad Altaf 4 for 52)
Bahawalpur 127 (Naved Nazir 5 for 34) and 121 (Naved Nazir 7 for 49)

Faisalabad won by 28 runs
Faisalabad 10 pts, Bahawalpur 4 pts

With the fixtures a mixture of three- and four-day contests, the first innings in three-day matches was restricted to 65 overs and the first innings in four-day matches to 85 overs.

Karachi took maximum points with a fine team effort against Sargodha. Consistent batting and the strength of their spin attack were decisive.

Rawalpindi and Multan also began with maximum point victories. Peshawar batted confidently enough on the first

Forgotten by the Pakistan selectors, Asif Mujtaba showed fine form·for both Karachi and PIA. (Adrian Murrell/ Allsport)

day against Rawalpindi, but a fifth-wicket stand of 222 between Naseer Ahmed and Mujahid Hameed demoralized the visitors who closed the second day at 55 for 6. The game was over early on the third morning, Rawalpindi winning with more than five sessions to spare.

Multan took a commanding grip on the game in Sahiwal on the first day. Rizwan Sattar and Bilal Rana added 157 after four wickets had fallen for 38. Forced to follow-on, Lahore batted with more spirit in their second innings, but Multan were easy victors early on the last day.

A wonderful bowling performance by Naved Nazir gave Faisalabad a thrilling win over Bahawalpur in a low-scoring match.

4, 5, 6 and 7 December 1988

at Iqbal Stadium, Faisalabad

Faisalabad 172 (Iqbal Qasim 4 for 9) and 151 (Iqbal Sikander 4 for 36)
Karachi 121 (Sajid Khan 50 not out, Tanvir Afzal 4 for 31, Wasim Haider 4 for 32) and 179 (Naved Nazir 6 for 56)

Faisalabad won by 23 runs
Faisalabad 11 pts, Karachi 4 pts

at Sargodha Stadium

Bahawalpur 204 (Naeem Taj 64) and 171 (Akram Raza 5 for 50)
Sargodha 269 for 9 (Arshad Pervez 73, Maqsood Ahmed 54) and 108 for 2

Sargodha won by 8 wickets
Sargodha 14 pts, Bahawalpur 6 pts

at Rawalpindi Club Ground

Lahore 296 for 9 (G.A. Pasha 84, Wasim Ali 62, Raja Afaq 5 for 89) and 246 (Babar Zaman 79, Raja Sarfraz 5 for 37)
Rawalpindi 274 (Shahid Ali Khan 6 for 96) and 272 for 6 (Masood Anwar 98, Sabih Azhar 51)

Rawalpindi won by 4 wickets
Rawalpindi 14 pts, Lahore 8 pts

at Arbab Niaz Stadium, Shah Bagh, Peshawar

Peshawar 186 (Rehmat Gul Tajik 77, Mushtaq Ahmed 6 for 42, Bilal Rana 4 for 53) and 141 (Mushtaq Ahmed 8 for 40)
Multan 141 (Zakir Khan 5 for 57, Wahid Khan 5 for 62) and 190 for 2 (Zahoor Elahi 62, Masroor Hussain 50)

Multan won by 8 wickets
Multan 10 pts, Peshawar 5 pts

Faisalabad gained a surprising win over Karachi on a pitch on which bowlers always dominated. Set to make 203 to win, Karachi slumped to 123 for 9 and came close to victory only through a spirited last-wicket stand between Iqbal Qasim and Barkatullah.

Sargodha beat Bahawalpur with considerable ease, but Rawalpindi had a great struggle against Lahore. Trailing by 22 runs on the first innings, they eventually reached a formidable target of 269 with four wickets to spare. They owed much to Masood Anwar, who played the anchor role, and to Sabih Azhar, who hit a brisk 51. They were also much indebted to the bowling of the Raja brothers, Sarfraz and Afaq.

The leg-spin bowling of Mushtaq Ahmed, who had match figures of 14 for 82, was the main reason for Multan's triumph over Peshawar. Left to score 187 to win, they were given a splendid start by Zahoor and Masroor, who put on 111 for the first wicket.

10, 11, 12 and 13 December 1988

at Bahawalpur Stadium

Karachi 180 (Iqbal Sikander 70, Naeem Taj 5 for 51) and 138 (Mansoor Akhtar 51, Mohammad Altaf 4 for 30)
Bahawalpur 130 (Iqbal Qasim 4 for 25, Iqbal Sikander 4 for 32) and 135 (Iqbal Qasim 5 for 40)

Karachi won by 53 runs
Karachi 11 pts, Bahawalpur 4 pts

at Sargodha Stadium

Sargodha 103 (Naved Nazir 5 for 40, Tanvir Afzal 4 for 16) and 164 (Tanvir Afzal 5 for 44)
Faisalabad 177 (Nadeem Arshad 51, Aziz-ur-Rehman 4 for 57, Akram Raza 4 for 63) and 92 for 2 (Wasim Haider 52 not out)

Faisalabad won by 8 wickets
Faisalabad 11 pts, Sargodha 4 pts

at Rawalpindi Club Ground

Rawalpindi 302 for 8 (Shahid Javed 102 not out, Masood

Anwar 76, Bilal Rana 4 for 73) and 376 for 5 dec (Shahid Javed 138, Raja Afaq 92, Bilal Rana 4 for 116)
Multan 229 (Raja Sarfraz 6 for 85) and 120 (Raja Sarfraz 6 for 35, Raja Afaq 4 for 37)

Rawalpindi won by 329 runs
Rawalpindi 14 pts, Multan 7 pts

at Arbab Niaz Stadium, Shah Bagh, Peshawar

Peshawar 163 (Wahid Khan 58, Babar Zaman 5 for 73) and 163 (Shahid Ali Khan 5 for 45)
Lahore 180 (Wasim Ali 53, Farrukh Zaman 5 for 55) and 147 for 5 (Wasim Ali 70 not out)

Lahore won by 5 wickets
Lahore 11 pts, Peshawar 5 pts

The spin combination of skipper Iqbal Qasim and Iqbal Sikander proved too much for Bahawalpur on a doubtful wicket. The two left-arm spinners, Naved Nazir and Tanvir Afzal, were instrumental in bringing about the downfall of Sargodha, but this was to prove Faisalabad's third and last victory of the season.

A century in each innings by Shahid Javed, and 12 wickets from left-arm spin bowler Raja Aarfraz, took Rawalpindi to a massive victory over Multan, while Lahore gained a welcome win over lowly Peshawar.

16, 17, 18 and 19 December 1988

at Qaddafi Stadium, Lahore

Lahore 214 (Wasim Ali 72, Shahid Mahboob 4 for 97) and 111 (Shahid Mahboob 4 for 32)
Karachi 276 (Asif Mujtaba 101, Umar Rasheed 55, Zain-ul-Abedin 4 for 76, Babar Zaman 4 for 83) and 50 for 1

Karachi won by 9 wickets
Karachi 14 pts, Lahore 6 pts

at Montgomery Biscuit Factory Ground, Sahiwal

Multan v. Bahawalpur

Multan awarded a walk-over
Multan 3 pts, Bahawalpur 0 pts

at Sargodha Stadium

Rawalpindi 128 (Akram Raza 5 for 39, Aziz-ur-Rehman 4 for 30) and 244 (Shahid Javed 78, Aziz-ur-Rehman 5 for 76)
Sargodha 182 (Mohammad Anis 73, Mohammad Riaz 7 for 65)

Match drawn
Sargodha 6 pts, Rawalpindi 4 pts

at Arbab Niaz Stadium, Shah Bagh, Peshawar

Faisalabad 206 (Arshad Khan 7 for 59) and 208 for 5 (Aamer Nazir 66, Wasim Haider 57 not out)
Peshawar 128 (Naved Nazir 4 for 38)

Match drawn
Faisalabad 7 pts, Peshawar 4 pts

Rain washed out the last two days' play at Peshawar and the last day at Sargodha. With Bahawalpur defaulting at Sahiwal, the only game in the fourth round of matches to produce a result was that at Lahore, where Karachi took maximum points. Asif Mujtaba hit his first century of the season before being run out, and pace bowler Shahid Mahboob took eight wickets in the match. Lahore were in

Saleem Jaffer, a career-best bowling performance for Karachi against Peshawar, 22 December. His feat earned him a recall to the Pakistan side. (Chris Cole/Allsport)

contention until the third afternoon, when their batting in their second innings collapsed.

22, 23, 24 and 25 December 1988

at National Stadium, Karachi

Peshawar 62 (Saleem Jaffer 7 for 29) and 137 (Zaffar Sarfraz 57, Haaris Khan 6 for 45)
Karachi 315 for 5 dec (Mohammad Aslam 77, Sajjad Abbas 52 not out, Ishtiaq Ahmed 52)

Karachi won by an innings and 116 runs
Karachi 14 pts, Peshawar 2 pts

at Rawalpindi Club Ground

Bahawalpur 255 (Naeem Taj 84 not out) and 132 (Raja Sarfraz 7 for 49)
Rawalpindi 321 (Sabih Azhar 60, Shahid Javed 56) and 69 for 2

Rawalpindi won by 8 wickets
Rawalpindi 14 pts, Bahawalpur 8 pts

at Montgomery Biscuit Factory Ground, Sahiwal

Multan v. Sargodha

Match abandoned
Multan 5 pts, Sargodha 5 pts

at Iqbal Stadium, Faisalabad

Lahore 230 (Rizwan Qazi 64, Naved Nazir 9 for 109) and 78 for 4
Faisalabad 189 (Aamer Nazir 96, Maqsood Rana 7 for 56)

Match drawn
Lahore 8 pts, Faisalabad 5 pts

Rain prevented any play on the first two days at Faisalabad, but the match still produced some performances of individual brilliance. The 18-year-old Naved Nazir, who made a brief first-class appearance in 1986–7, but who was playing his first full season, took a career-best 9 for 109 for Faisalabad. His controlled left-arm spin proved to be the most lethal in the competition. When Faisalabad batted they lost eight wickets for 74 runs before Aamer Nazir hit a marvellous 96. His runs came out of the 131 added for the last four wickets.

Karachi devastated Peshawar, who were put in to bat and bowled out in 25 overs. Their main destroyer was Saleem Jaffer, the left-arm pace bowler, who, returning after injury, bowled unchanged to record the best figures of his career. He was immediately called to reinforce the Pakistan side in Australia. An opening stand of 126 between Mohammad Aslam and Ishtiaq Ahmed took Karachi to an impregnable position, and Iqbal Qasim declared with 12.3 of his side's 85 overs unused. Peshawar were again quickly bowled out, and Karachi claimed maximum points with victory inside two days.

Rawalpindi, with the bowling of Raja Sarfraz again prominent, also claimed maximum points and led the table at the end of the fifth round. Karachi were three points behind in second place.

28, 29, 30 and 31 December 1988

at National Stadium, Karachi

Rawalpindi 273 for 7 (Masood Anwar 59, Naseer Ahmed 54, Sabih Azhar 54 not out, Barkatullah 4 for 97) and 62 (Shakeel Sajjad 6 for 28)
Karachi 172 (Ijaz Faqih 77 not out, Sabih Azhar 6 for 81) and 164 for 3 (Mohammad Aslam 78 not out, Ishtiaq Ahmed 67)

Karachi won by 7 wickets
Karachi 10 pts, Rawalpindi 8 pts

at Bahawalpur Stadium

Peshawar 263 for 9 dec (Haroon Jan 69, Wahid Ali Khan 55 not out, Imran Adil 4 for 68) and 249 (Mohammad Sajid 65, Mohammad Zahid 4 for 69)
Bahawalpur 325 for 8 (Mujahid Usmani 65, Naeem Taj 50, Mohammad Faridoon 4 for 97) and 187

Match tied
Bahawalpur 11 pts, Peshawar 11 pts

at Qaddafi Stadium, Lahore

Sargodha 144 (Rizwan Qazi 4 for 55) and 216 (Maqsood Ahmed 84 not out, Rizwan Qazi 7 for 93)
Lahore 301 for 6 (Rizwan Qazi 89, Haider Jahangir 71) and 63 for 2

Lahore won by 8 wickets
Lahore 14 pts, Sargodha 3 pts

at Montgomery Biscuit Factory, Sahiwal

Faisalabad 230 (Anwar Awais 62) and 334 for 8 dec (Nadeem

Arshad 109, Anwar Awais 76)
Multan 156 (Naved Nazir 5 for 56) and 411 for 2 (Manzoor Elahi 163 not out, Masoor Ahmed 126, Bilal Rana 55 not out)

Multan won by 8 wickets
Multan 11 pts, Faisalabad 7 pts

The top of the table struggle ended in favour of Karachi, who had trailed by 101 runs on the first innings. The game turned on the third morning, when Shakeel Sajjad and Barkatullah bowled unchanged and dismissed Rawalpindi in 25.3 overs. Karachi were victorious by the afternoon.

Peshawar and Bahawalpur, both without a win, engaged in a thrilling tie. Bahawalpur held the edge for most of the game, but, needing 188 to win and with the whole of the last day in which to score the runs, they reached 174 for 6. Three wickets then fell before last man Imran Adil joined wicket-keeper Rana Javed. They added 13 before Imran was bowled by Wahid to tie the match.

Lahore were always too strong for Sargodha, but Multan brought off an amazing win in Sahiwal. Faisalabad, thanks to a century by Nadeem Arshad, were well on top, and Shakir Javed's declaration left his bowlers more than a day to bowl out Multan, who faced the seemingly impossible task of scoring 409 to win. Zahoor Elahi and Masroor Ahmed had 76 on the board in 11 overs before the close. Zahoor went early on the last morning, but skipper Manzoor Elahi joined Masroor in a stand of 178. Naved Nazir dismissed Masroor, but Manzoor and Bilal Rana took Multan to a memorable victory. Dildar Malik, Multan's exciting young wicket-keeper, caught six and stumped one in Faisalabad's first innings, and caught one and stumped one in the second.

3, 4, 5 and 6 January 1989

at National Stadium, Karachi

Multan 139 (Tariq Mahboob 51, Haaris Khan 4 for 44) and 210
Karachi 300 for 4 (Basit Ali 112 not out, Ata-ur-Rehman 71, Shujaat Ali 69) and 50 for 3

Karachi won by 7 wickets
Karachi 14 pts, Multan 2 pts

at Qaddafi Stadium, Lahore

Lahore v. Bahawalpur

Match abandoned
Lahore 5 pts, Bahawalpur 5 pts

at Sargodha Stadium

Peshawar 98 (Aziz-ur-Rehman 6 for 30)
Sargodha 115 for 1

Match drawn
Sargodha 5 pts, Peshawar 0 pts

at Rawalpindi Club Ground

Rawalpindi 262 (Naved Nazir 5 for 95, Fazal Hussain 4 for 60)
Faisalabad 121 for 5 (Aamer Nazir 57)

Match drawn
Rawalpindi 7 pts, Faisalabad 4 pts

With rain badly affecting three of the final round of matches, Karachi clinched first place in the Patron's Trophy Grade One league table with an emphatic win over Multan. Hero of the victory was Basit Ali, who hit an unbeaten century and shared a third-wicket stand of 142 with Shujaat Ali. Basit Ali was later named as captain of Pakistan's Under-19 side for the series against India.

Patron's Trophy Grade One – Final Table						
	P	W	L	D	Tie	Pts
Karachi	7	6	1	–	–	81
Rawalpindi	7	4	1	2	–	75
Lahore	7	2	3	3	–	57
Faisalabad	7	3	1	3	–	53
Multan	7	4	1	2	–	52
Sargodha	7	1	3	3	–	41
Bahawalpur	7	–	5	1	1	38
Peshawar	7	–	4	2	1	32

Karachi 'B' and Gujranwala topped the two groups in Grade Two of the Patron's Trophy, not first-class.

Patron's Trophy Final
KARACHI v. RAWALPINDI

Well as Rawalpindi had played in the league competition, they proved to be no match for the strong Karachi side in the Patron's Final. The weather and the pitch seemed to be in favour of seam bowling, and Raja Sarfraz had little hesitation in asking Karachi to bat first when he won the toss. Appearances were deceptive, for by the end of the first day, Karachi had taken a firm grip on the game, having hit 313 for 3 from 91 overs.

Mohammad Aslam and Basit Ali gave their side a sound start with a partnership of 140, and it was the young Basit Ali who was the dominant partner. He had recently hit a monumental 189 for Pakistan Under-19s against India at Gujranwala, and he continued in the form that he had shown in that match. He batted for 250 minutes, faced 208 balls and hit 17 fours in what was the highest score of his youthful first-class career.

In nine overs on the second morning, Karachi added 57 to their overnight score before Shahid Mahboob declared. The Karachi skipper was to be the main sufferer as his side dropped half a dozen catches when Rawalpindi batted, but, nevertheless, the visitors were soon reduced to 109 for 6. There was a recovery, but they were all out early on the third morning and trailed by 128 on the first innings.

Now came a revival for Rawalpindi as Aftab Abbasi produced the best bowling performance of his career with his medium pace. Only Basit Ali, an exciting young talent, played him with any confidence, but, 207 for 9 at the close of the third day, Karachi had a lead of 335, and the match looked to be theirs.

So it proved to be, but in an unexpected manner. The medium-pace in-swingers of Umar Rasheed caused havoc with the Rawalpindi batting, and the game was all over 50 minutes before the scheduled close of play on the fourth day. Umar, a younger brother of Haroon Rasheed, the former Test cricketer, had improved his bowling in league cricket in England, but never before had he taken five wickets in an innings in his first-class career, let alone 10 in a match.

PATRON'S TROPHY FINAL – KARACHI v. RAWALPINDI
6, 7, 8 and 9 February 1989 at National Stadium, Karachi

KARACHI

	FIRST INNINGS		SECOND INNINGS	
Mohammad Aslam	c Ghyasuddin, b Raja	59	run out	15
Basit Ali	b Jamal	135	c Nadeem, b Aftab	84
Ata-ur-Rehman	c Mujahid, b Shiraz	2	(6) lbw, b Jamal	1
Ishtiaq Ahmed	b Raja Sarfraz	89	c sub (Tariq Javed), b Aftab Abbasi	29
Zafar Ali	c and b Shiraz	52	c and b M. Riaz	17
Shahid Mahboob†	not out	23	(7) b Jamal	0
Shakeel Sajjad	not out	5	(8) b Aftab Abbasi	17
Umar Rasheed			(3) c sub (Shakeel Ahmed), b Aftab	26
Haaris A. Khan			c Nadeem, b Aftab	6
Jalal-ud-Din			c M. Riaz, b Aftab	11
Iftikhar Ahmed*			not out	2
Extras	b 1, lb 1, nb 3	5	b 4, lb 8	12
	(for 5 wkts dec)	370		220

RAWALPINDI

	FIRST INNINGS		SECOND INNINGS	
Jamal Siddiqi	c Iftikhar, b Jalal	36	lbw, b Umar	25
Ghyasuddin Balban	run out	17	b Shahid	7
Naseer Ahmed	c Ishtiaq, b Shahid	12	run out	5
Shahid Javed	c Iftikhar, b Umar	12	b Umar	21
Mujahid Hameed	c Iftikhar, b Umar	8	c Ishtiaq, b Umar	24
Nadeem Abbasi*	c Basit, b Umar	5	b Haaris	53
Shiraz Khan	c Zafar, b Haaris	33	b Umar	4
Mohammad Arif snr	c Iftikhar, b Shahid	28	lbw, b Umar	0
Mohammad Riaz	b Jalal	44	c Shakeel, b Umar	1
Raja Sarfraz†	run out	28	not out	1
Aftab Abbasi	not out	4	lbw, b Umar	0
Extras	b 4, lb 10, nb 1	15	b 8, lb 8	16
		242		157

	O	M	R	W	O	M	R	W
Jamal Siddiqi	14	1	81	1	20	6	66	2
Aftab Abbasi	8	1	42	–	22.3	5	60	6
Shiraz Khan	34	6	83	2	3	3	0	–
Raja Sarfraz	32	4	114	2	9	1	16	–
Mohammad Riaz	12	1	48	–	12	1	39	1
Mohammad Arif snr					12	3	27	–

	O	M	R	W	O	M	R	W
Shahid Mahboob	30	5	92	2	12	3	22	1
Jalal-ud-Din	24	3	55	2	11	–	36	–
Umar Rasheed	13	3	39	3	19.4	6	48	7
Shakeel Sajjad	4	1	6	–	5	1	24	–
Haaris A. Khan	12	3	36	1	13	7	11	–

FALL OF WICKETS
1–140, 2–149, 3–214, 4–331, 5–359
1–59, 2–120, 3–131, 4–168, 5–169, 6–169, 7–196, 8–206, 9–207

FALL OF WICKETS
1–47, 2–71, 3–75, 4–88, 5–94, 6–109, 7–165, 8–165, 9–226
1–13, 2–28, 3–51, 4–68, 5–142, 6–154, 7–154, 8–154, 9–157

Umpires: Mahboob Shah & Feroze Butt

Karachi won by 191 runs

Basit Ali was named Man of the Match for his two fine innings.

Quaid-e-Azam Trophy

Pakistan's senior first-class competition followed a pattern similar to that used in the Patron's Trophy. The eight competing teams were from the main business institutions, although such sides as PACO, Allied Bank and Railways had found themselves relegated to Grade Two, the non first-class competition.

7, 8, 9 and 10 January 1989

at National Stadium, Karachi

Habib Bank 283 for 8 (Shaukat Mirza 61, Tahir Rasheed 58 not out) and 197 for 6 dec (Anwar Miandad 74 not out)
PNSC 169 (Farrukh Bari 52, Nadeem Ghauri 4 for 26, Akram Raza 4 for 41) and 173 (Akram Raza 6 for 41)

Habib Bank won by 138 runs
Habib Bank 14 pts, PNSC 5 pts

at Niaz Stadium, Hyderabad

Muslim Commercial Bank 254 (Ijaz Faqih 85) and 198 (Pervez Shah 63, Babar Basharat 60, Mushtaq Ahmed 5 for 66, Masood Anwar 4 for 54)
United Bank 180 and 183 (Mansoor Akhtar 53, Ijaz Faqih 5 for 61)

Muslim Commercial Bank won by 89 runs
Muslim Commercial Bank 14 pts, United Bank 5 pts

at Qaddafi Stadium, Lahore

HBFC v. PIA

Match abandoned
HBFC 5 pts, PIA 5 pts

at Rawalpindi Club Ground

National Bank 231 for 7 (Ameer Akbar 89)
ADBP 212 (Manzoor Elahi 68, Shahid Tanvir 5 for 71)

Match drawn
National Bank 8 pts, ADBP 5 pts

The Quaid-e-Azam Trophy began in damp weather. There was no play possible in Lahore and a limited amount scattered over the last three days in Rawalpindi. Habib Bank and Muslim Commercial Bank, for whom Ijaz Faqih had a fine all-round match, managed maximum point victories. Akram Raza's off-breaks played a major part in Habib Bank's win over PNSC. He had match figures of 10 for 82.

13, 14, 15 and 16 January 1989

at Qaddafi Stadium, Lahore

PIA 330 for 7 (Asif Mujtaba 141 not out, Hammad Butt 54) and 309 for 8 dec (Zahid Ahmed 113 not out)

National Bank 275 (Muhammad Jamil 82, Tanvir Ali 6 for 68) and 246 for 9 (Saleem Pervez 118, Iqbal Sikander 5 for 57)

Match drawn
PIA 9 pts, National Bank 7 pts

at National Stadium, Karachi

PNSC 126 (Waqar Yunus 6 for 33) and 307 (Mahmood Hamid 116)
United Bank 394 for 2 (Inzamam-ul-Haq 201 not out, Mansoor Akhtar 113) and 40 for 4

United Bank won by 6 wickets
United Bank 14 pts, PNSC 1 pt

at Niaz Stadium, Hyderabad

Habib Bank 270 (Aamer Sohail 79, Farrukh Zaman 5 for 82) and 147 (Ijaz Faqih 7 for 54)
Muslim Commercial Bank 141 (Akram Raza 5 for 51, Nadeem Ghauri 4 for 40) and 178 (Babar Basharat 76, Nadeem Ghauri 5 for 64, Waheed Niazi 4 for 60)

Habib Bank won by 98 runs
Habib Bank 14 pts, Muslim Commercial Bank 4 pts

at Bagh-e-Jinnah Ground, Lahore

HBFC 188 (Saghir Abbas 55, Raja Afaq 6 for 64) and 276 for 9 dec (Munir-ul-Haq 167 not out, Mohammad Riaz 52, Manzoor Elahi 4 for 38)
ADBP 162 and 204 for 6 (Manzoor Elahi 85, Atif Rauf 67 not out, Kazim Mehdi 4 for 62)

Match drawn
HBFC 6 pts, ADBP 5 pts

Habib Bank won their second match in succession when the bowling of Nadeem Ghauri took them to victory over

Ijaz Faqih – fighting cricket for Karachi and for the disappointing Muslim Commercial Bank side. (Patrick Eagar)

Outstanding all-round cricket for Multan and ADBP by Manzoor Elahi, but no recall to the Pakistan side. (Chris Cole/Allsport)

Another splendid knock by Asif Mujtaba, who deserves better treatment by the Pakistan selectors, put Pakistan International Airlines on top against National Bank. Zahid Ahmed's second-innings century confirmed their superiority, and National Bank were left most of the last day in which to score 365 to win. They never approached the target as Iqbal Sikander and Rashid Khan wrought havoc among their batting, and it was only the tenacity of the last pair, Iqbal Qasim and Afzal Butt, that saved them from defeat.

19, 20, 21 and 22 January 1989

at Bagh-e-Jinnah Ground, Lahore

HBFC 257 (Sagheer Abbas 60, Saadat Ali 57, Iqbal Qasim 5 for 112. Hafeez-ur-Rehman 4 for 90) and 192 (Saleem Taj 53, Iqbal Qasim 5 for 15, Tahir Shah 4 for 98)
National Bank 263 for 9 (Ameer Akbar 82) and 187 for 4 (Ameer Akbar 72 not out)

National Bank won by 6 wickets
National Bank 14 pts, HBFC 8 pts

at Model Town, Lahore

ADBP 256 for 7 (Mansoor Rana 113 not out) and 410 (Sabih Azhar 78 not out, Manzoor Elahi 77, Raja Afaq 77, Bilal Ahmed 75, Rashid Khan 4 for 98)
PIA 260 for 8 (Asif Mohammad 77 not out, Zahid Ahmed 52, Khatib Rizwan 5 for 120) and 116 for 2 (Hammad Butt 51 not out)

Match drawn
ADBP 8 pts, PIA 8 pts

at Qaddafi Stadium, Lahore

United Bank 199 (Ashraf Ali 70, Saadat Gul 58 not out) and 169 (Naved Anjum 4 for 60)
Habib Bank 259 for 8 (Arshad Pervez 65, Akram Raza 56 not out, Kamal Merchant 4 for 44) and 112 for 1 (Arshad Pervez 56 not out)

Habib Bank won by 9 wickets
Habib Bank 14 pts, United Bank 5 pts

at Bakhtiari Youth Centre Ground, Karachi

PNSC 266 for 8 (Qaiser Rasheed 74, Abdullah Khan 71, Farrukh Bari 62, Salahuddin 5 for 69) and 278 for 7 (Farrukh Bari 63, Ijaz Faqih 4 for 71)
Muslim Commercial Bank 127 (Sajjad Akbar 4 for 34) and 157 (Rifaqat Ali 55, Amin Lakhani 6 for 34)

PNSC won by 260 runs
PNSC 14 pts, Muslim Commercial Bank 4 pts

Muslim Commercial Bank. Ijaz Faqih strove manfully to bowl his side back into the match, but Muslim Commercial Bank's batting failed twice, and Habib ran out comfortable winners.

United Bank crushed PNSC. Inzamam-ul-Haq and the ever-reliable Mansoor Akhtar put on 187 for United's second wicket, and Inzamam dominated an unfinished third-wicket partnership of 179 with Shafiq Ahmed. Inzamam reached the first double century of the season in the Quaid-e-Azam Trophy.

The two matches in Lahore were drawn. In spite of a fine innings from Manzoor Elahi, ADBP could not reach their target of 303 at more than 3½ runs an over. HBFC had been taken to a position of dominance by Munir-ul-Haq's magnificent innings of 167 not out. He had come to the wicket after two men had been dismissed with only one run on the board, so that he scored his 167 out of 275.

Habib Bank confirmed their position as the strongest side in the competition with a decisive win over United Bank. Once again it was essentially a team performance rather than any individual brilliance which gave them victory. Their attack was varied, and their batting solid.

An opening stand of 136 between Qaiser Rasheed and Abdullah Khan gave PNSC the foundation for a crushing victory over Muslim Commercial Bank, who again showed alarming weaknesses in batting. Farrukh Bari played two innings of substance at number three for PNSC, and the slow left-arm bowling of Amin Lakhani, once on the threshold of the Pakistan Test side, hastened the victory on the third day.

HBFC collapsed against Iqbal Qasim and Tahir Shah on the third afternoon to allow National Bank to sweep to victory early on the last day.

Mansoor Rana seemed to have put ADBP in a strong position with an excellent century, but the consistency of PIA's batting took them to a narrow first-innings lead. Scoring at less than three runs an over, ADBP batted remorselessly into the last day and condemned the match to a draw.

25, 26, 27 and 28 January 1989

at Bagh-e-Jinnah Ground, Lahore

National Bank 179 (Ameer Akbar 77, Nadeem Ghauri 4 for 52, Akram Raza 4 for 57) and 164 (Nadeem Ghauri 8 for 67)
Habib Bank 219 (Agha Zahid 61, Aamer Sohail 53, Iqbal Qasim 4 for 71) and 126 for 1 (Arshad Pervez 57 not out)

Habib Bank won by 9 wickets
Habib Bank 12 pts, National Bank 5 pts

at Qaddafi Stadium, Lahore

PNSC 247 (Abdullah Khan 57, Wasim Haider 5 for 71) and 314 (Abdullah Khan 106)
PIA 281 (Feroze Mehdi 51, Amin Lakhani 4 for 45) and 245 (Feroze Mehdi 65, Asif Mohammad 59, Amin Lakhani 5 for 111, Sajjad Akbar 4 for 78)

PNSC won by 35 runs
PNSC 14 pts, PIA 7 pts

at Iqbal Stadium, Faisalabad

ADBP 320 for 5 (Atif Rauf 50 not out, Manzoor Elahi 50, Mansoor Rana 50) and 335 for 7 dec (Ghaffar Kazmi 76, Mansoor Rana 66, Atif Rauf 50 not out)
Muslim Commercial Bank 248 for 9 (Babar Basharat 90) and 284 for 5 (Babar Basharat 101 not out, Ijaz Faqih 101 not out)

Match drawn
ADBP 9 pts, Muslim Commercial Bank 5 pts

at Jinnah Stadium, Sialkot

United Bank 249 (Shafiq Ahmed 62, Ashraf Ali 54 not out) and 276 for 8 dec (Shafiq Ahmed 71, Mansoor Akhtar 55)
HBFC 147 (Saadat Ali 89, Masood Anwar 4 for 59) and 251 for 4 (Sagheer Abbas 100 not out, Shahid Saeed 94)

Match drawn
United Bank 8 pts, HBFC 4 pts

The continued dominance of Habib Bank received a slight dent when they failed for the first time to reach 250 runs and claim four batting points. Having bowled out National Bank for 179, they were moving serenely towards a big score at 216 for 5, only to lose their last five wickets for the addition of three runs and to be bowled out in 74.5 overs. The off-breaks of Akram Raza and the left-arm spin of Nadeem Ghauri had accounted for National Bank in the first innings, and it was these two who now bowled 88.4 overs between them to exert a stranglehold on National when they batted again. Nadeem returned the remarkable figures of 8 for 67, and Habib Bank completed victory on the third day.

PNSC maintained their place among the challengers with a close victory over PIA, who led by 34 runs on the first innings. A splendid century by Abdullah Khan in the second innings tilted the advantage in favour of PNSC, and PIA were left most of the last day in which to score

281 to win. At 157 for 4, PIA seemed to be well positioned to win, but the persevering left-arm spin of Amin Lakhani allied to the off-breaks of Sajjad Akbar brought victory to PNSC.

Rain curtailed play in Sialkot and thwarted HBFC in their bid for victory. Needing 379 to win, they lost Saleem Taj at 24 and Munir-ul-Haq at 55, but Shahid Saeed and Saghir Abbas added a valiant 164 for the third wicket.

ADBP drew their fourth game in succession, and once again Raja Afaq showed great caution in the timing of his declaration. ADBP batted into the last day, and Muslim Commercial Bank were set the impossible task of scoring 408 at four an over to win. ADBP captured five wickets for 84 runs, but Babar Basharat and Ijaz Faqih shared an unbroken stand of 200 to save the game for Muslim Commercial Bank. Both batsmen reached centuries, but they were aided by some occasional bowling when all hope of a result had vanished.

31 January, 1, 2 and 3 February 1989

at Qaddafi Stadium, Lahore

National Bank 213 (Sajid Bashir 4 for 78) and 287 (Sajid Ali 97, Saleem Pervez 56, Raees Ahmed 5 for 84)
United Bank 288 for 7 (Mansoor Akhtar 117, Saifullah 72, Iqbal Qasim 5 for 77) and 214 for 1 (Mansoor Akhtar 118 not out, Raees Ahmed 57)

United Bank won by 9 wickets
United Bank 14 pts, National Bank 5 pts

at Iqbal Stadium, Faisalabad

Muslim Commercial Bank 174 (Tariq Khan 51) and 230 (Salahuddin 54)
PIA 286 (Zahid Ahmed 108, Feroze Mehdi 59, Farrukh Zaman 4 for 90) and 119 for 3 (Zahid Ahmed 53 not out)

PIA won by 7 wickets
PIA 14 pts, Muslim Commercial Bank 5 pts

at KRL Ground, Rawalpindi

ADBP 211 for 9 (Atif Rauf 76 not out, Nadeem Ghauri 4 for 68) and 192 (Shakeel Khan 4 for 67)
Habib Bank 78 (Zakir Khan 5 for 36, Manzoor Elahi 5 for 37) and 148 (Mohammad Asif 5 for 18)

ADBP won by 177 runs
ADBP 12 pts, Habib Bank 4 pts

at Bagh-e-Jinnah Ground, Lahore

PNSC 188 (Mahmood Hamid 50, Kazim Mehdi 4 for 36) and 210 (Kazim Mehdi 4 for 62)
HBFC 163 (Amin Lakhani 5 for 66, Sajjad Akbar 4 for 54) and 198 (Sagheer Abbas 57, Sajjad Akbar 5 for 75, Amin Lakhani 5 for 95)

PNSC won by 37 runs
PNSC 11 pts, HBFC 5 pts

Habib Bank's run of success came to an end when they were beaten by ADBP in Rawalpindi. Atif Rauf held together the ADBP innings when it was in danger of crumbling, and medium-pace bowlers Zakir Khan and Manzoor Elahi then shot out the league leaders for 78 in 20.2 overs. Showing great determination on a wicket that was never easy, ADBP reached 192 all out in their second innings early on the third day. By the end of the same day they had won the match, Habib Bank falling apart against the occasional spin of Mohammad Asif.

United Bank and PNSC moved to the fore as the main challengers to Habib Bank, with good victories. In a low-scoring match, PNSC had to thank the continued success of their spin pair, Amin Lakhani and Sajjad Akbar. Victory came on the third afternoon. United Bank won in more splendid fashion on the last day in the Qaddafi Stadium.

They owed their victory to the brilliant batting of Mansoor Akhtar. Probably the most technically accomplished of Pakistani batsmen, Mansoor, wrongly rejected by the Test selectors, hit a century in each innings. His second hundred of the match, 118 not out, was made in 49 overs and took United Bank to an emphatic victory.

Zahib Ahmed was another heavy scorer as PIA trounced Muslim Commercial Bank.

6, 7, 8 and 9 February 1989

at Municipal Stadium, Gujranwala

PNSC 183 (Sohail Miandad 59, Barkatullah 4 for 79) and 168 for 1 (Abdullah Khan 101 not out, Farrukh Bari 51 not out)
National Bank 278 for 5 (Sajid Ali 81, Taslim Arif 75)

Match drawn
National Bank 9 pts, PNSC 3 pts

at Pindi Club Ground, Rawalpindi

PIA 197 and 96 (Naved Anjum 5 for 50, Shakeel Khan 4 for 42)
Habib Bank 197 (Akram Raza 57 not out, Rashid Khan 4 for 55) and 97 for 5

Habib Bank won by 5 wickets
Habib Bank 11 pts, PIA 5 pts

at Qaddafi Stadium, Lahore

Muslim Commercial Bank 189 (Ali Ahmed 4 for 90) and 136 (Ali Ahmed 6 for 30)
HBFC 323 (Rafat Alam 110, Munir-ul-Haq 77, Zain-ul-Abedin 6 for 127) and 6 for 0

HBFC won by 10 wickets
HBFC 14 pts, Muslim Commercial Bank 5 pts

at Bagh-e-Jinnah Ground, Lahore

ADBP 317 for 6 (Masood Anwar 146, Mansoor Rana 84) and 278 for 9 dec (Ghaffar Kazmi 67, Mansoor Rana 51, Manzoor Elahi 50)
United Bank 256 (Shahid Butt 71, Ashraf Ali 52 not out, Raja Afaq 4 for 72) and 219 (Mansoor Akhtar 113 not out)

Match drawn
ADBP 9 pts, United Bank 7 pts

Rain in Gujranwala prevented any play on the first day and restricted it on the second, so National Bank were happy to claim first-innings advantage.

Habib Bank's bowlers brought them victory over PIA and virtually assured them of finishing top of the league. At the other end of the table, Muslim Commercial Bank looked certain to end with the wooden spoon after being trounced by HBFC, who recovered from 99 for 5 to reach 323 in 83 overs thanks to a violent century by Rafat Alam.

The strength of ADBP's batting again assured them of the better of a draw. Masood Anwar hit 19 fours in his 146, and, in the second innings, Manzoor Elahi hit a whirlwind

fifty with a six and 7 fours. Eventually, it was another exquisite century from Mansoor Akhtar, who batted through 88 overs, that saved the game for United Bank.

12, 13, 14 and 15 February 1989

at Municipal Stadium, Gujranwala

Muslim Commercial Bank 253 for 9 (Asif Mahmood 58, Anwar-ul-Haq 54 not out, Barkatullah 4 for 38) and 410 for 6 dec (Najeeb Baig 108, Ijaz Faqih 100 not out, Babar Basharat 94, Rifaqat Ali 54 not out)
National Bank 313 for 9 (Saeed Azad 134, Farrukh Zaman 4 for 52, Pervez Shah 4 for 92) and 351 for 4 (Sajad Ali 125, Tahir Shah 88, Saeed Azad 51 not out)

National Bank won by 6 wickets
National Bank 14 pts, Muslim Commercial Bank 8 pts

at National Stadium, Karachi

PIA 292 for 9 (Wasim Haider 105 not out, Hammad Butt 67, Waqar Younus 5 for 99) and 141 for 2 (Nasir Khan 50 not out)
United Bank 260 (Masood Anwar 76 not out, Zulfiqar Ali 7 for 76)

Match drawn
PIA 9 pts, United Bank 8 pts

at Pindi Club, Rawalpindi

HBFC 237 (Tariq Alam 64, Rifat Alam 59, Akram 5 for 57) and 148 (Nadeem Ghauri 7 for 61)
Habib Bank 183 (Kazim Mehdi 5 for 80, Zulfiqar Butt 4 for 73) and 203 for 3 (Arshad Bata 67)

Habib Bank won by 7 wickets
Habib Bank 11 pts, HBFC 7 pts

at Bagh-e-Jinnah Ground, Lahore

PNSC 266 for 9 (Farrukh Bari 82, Mahmood Hamid 58, Mohammad Asif 4 for 107) and 228 (Abdullah Khan 63, Mohammad Asif 6 for 70)
ADBP 259 for 8 (Mansoor Rana 85, Atif Rauf 52) and 236 for 5 (Mansoor Rana 84)

ADBP won by 5 wickets
ADBP 14 pts, PNSC 8 pts

By beating PNSC and preserving their unbeaten record ADBP clinched second place in the league table and qualified to meet Habib Bank in the final. Mohammad Asif's off-spin bowling and the consistently fine batting of Mansoor Rana were major factors in ADBP's victory.

Inevitably it was the spin bowling of Nadeem Ghauri and Akram Raza that brought Habib Bank victory after they had trailed by 54 runs on the first innings. Bad weather affected the match in Karachi, where Wasim Haider hit a remarkable century at number eight after his side had been 48 for 5. Similarly, Masood Anwar, at number nine, helped lift United Bank from the depths of 127 for 7.

Muslim Commercial Bank died bravely in their attempt to avoid bottom place and possible relegation to non-first-

Mansoor Akhtar – still among the most accomplished and technically correct batsmen in Pakistan. (Adrian Murrell/ Allsport)

class cricket. Najeeb Baig and skipper Ijaz Faqih hit second-innings centuries, but Sajad Ali still took National Bank to a resounding win.

Quaid-e-Azam Grade One Championship

	P	W	L	D	Pts
Habib Bank	7	6	1	–	80
ADBP	7	2	–	5	62
National Bank	7	2	2	3	62
United Bank	7	2	2	3	61
PIA	7	1	2	4	57
PNSC	7	3	3	1	56
HBFC	7	1	3	3	49
Muslim Commercial Bank	7	1	5	1	45

PACO won the Grade Two Trophy to earn the right to compete at first-class level in 1989–90.

Quaid-e-Azam Trophy Final
HABIB BANK v. ADBP

Agha Zahid won the toss and asked ADBP to bat first when play eventually began 10 minutes after the tea interval. There had been heavy overnight rain, and the Habib Bank captain considered the batsmen would be at a disadvantage early on, and, in the limited time on the first day, the ball did seem dominant as ADBP closed at 71 for 2.

Consistent batting with the necessary hint of aggression took ADBP to 398 in their allotted 100 overs before the end of the second day. The outstanding performance came from Mansoor Rana, son of umpire Shakoor, who hit 16 fours in a most polished innings. Mansoor had batted splendidly throughout the competition so that his innings came as no surprise, nor did the fact that he was later to win the individual award.

Habib Bank began their first innings shortly before the end of the second day and were 15 for 0 at the close. On the third day, they appeared to take total command of the game. Skipper Agha Zahid led the way with a fine century, and with Naved Anjum and Akram Raza at the crease, they ended the day on 349 for 5 off 88 overs. They were only 50 runs short of the vital first-innings lead and had 12 overs remaining in which to get the runs.

The game took a dramatic turn on the fourth morning when, in 27 balls, Zakir Khan took 4 wickets for 15 runs and bowled one of the finest spells of his first-class career. The last five Habib wickets added a mere 33 runs, and ADBP had snatched the first-innings lead.

Fiery and whole-hearted bowling by the Habib pacemen Naved Anjum and Shakeel Khan brought the Bank side back into contention, but more rain and slippery conditions left them with the task of scoring the 181 runs that they needed to win at a rate of 9.52 an over. They found this beyond them, and they called off the chase after just 12 overs.

ADBP therefore took the trophy by virtue of their

QUAID-E-AZAM TROPHY FINAL – ADBP v. HABIB BANK
14, 15, 16, 17 and 18 March 1989 at Qaddafi Stadium, Lahore

ADBP

	FIRST INNINGS		SECOND INNINGS	
Masood Anwar	c Aamer, b Akram	39	c Tahir, b Waheed	15
Tanvir Ahmed	b Naved	13	c Agha, b Naved	23
Bilal Ahmed*	b Shakeel	24	c Akram, b Naved	0
Qasim Shera	c Tahir, b Naved	49	(9) b Shakeel	10
Mansoor Rana	c Azhar, b Nadeem	90	c and b Naved	48
Manzoor Elahi	c Tahir, b Akram	42	lbw, b Naved	1
Atif Rauf	not out	51	c Naved, b Akram	24
Sabih Azhar	b Waheed	44	(4) c Tahir, b Shakeel	10
Raja Afaq†	b Shakeel	4	(8) c Agha, b Nadeem	11
Khatib Rizwan	c Tahir, b Waheed	17	(11) b Shakeel	2
Zakir Khan			(10) not out	3
Extras	b 8, lb 5, nb 12	25	b 9, lb 2, nb 6	17
	(for 9 wkts)	398		164

HABIB BANK

	FIRST INNINGS		SECOND INNINGS	
Agha Zahid†	lbw, b Zakir	134	(7) not out	1
Arshad Pervez	c Raja, b Sabih	44	c Manzoor, b Zakir	12
Aamer Sohail	run out	43	(1) b Zakir	36
Shaukat Mirza	st Bilal, b Raja	23	(5) not out	22
Azhar Khan	b Qasim	47		
Naved Anjum	c sub (Mohammad Asif), b Zakir	56	(4) run out	0
Akram Raza	b Zakir	0	(6) b Manzoor	2
Tahir Rasheed*	c Zakir, b Manzoor	6	(3) c Atif, b Zakir	3
Shakeel Khan	c Manzoor, b Zakir	6		
Nadeem Ghauri	b Zakir	0		
Waheed Niazi	not out	0		
Extras	b 6, lb 16, w 1	23	lb 4, w 1	5
		382	(for 5 wkts)	81

ADBP bowling

	O	M	R	W	O	M	R	W
Waheed Niazi	17	4	59	2	12	1	35	1
Naved Anjum	23	2	89	2	22	8	52	4
Shakeel Khan	28	6	109	2	23	5	23	3
Nadeem Ghauri	14	1	53	1	21	9	27	1
Akram Raza	13	3	48	2	14	8	16	1
Agha Zahid	5	–	27	–				

HABIB BANK bowling

	O	M	R	W	O	M	R	W
Zakir Khan	25.3	3	90	5	6	–	33	3
Manzoor Elahi	19	2	46	1	6	–	44	1
Qasim Shera	11	2	40	1				
Raja Afaq	22	–	84	1				
Sabih Azhar	11	–	62	1				
Khatib Rizwan	8	–	38	–				

FALL OF WICKETS
1–28, 2–66, 3–120, 4–163, 5–246, 6–292, 7–366, 8–371, 9–398
1–20, 2–21, 3–50, 4–51, 5–51, 6–106, 7–119, 8–155, 9–162

FALL OF WICKETS
1–116, 2–195, 3–259, 4–273, 5–349, 6–350, 7–375, 8–382, 9–382
1–26, 2–39, 3–41, 4–74, 5–79

Umpires: Khizar Hayat & Mian Aslam

Match drawn. ADBP won trophy by virtue of first-innings lead.

Zakir Khan – devastating bowling in the Quaid-e-Azam Trophy Final. (Adrian Murrell/Allsport)

first-innings lead. It was their first Quaid-e-Azam title. Indeed, they have had first-class status only since 1985–6. The consolation for Habib Bank was that four of their premier members, Javed Miandad, Abdul Qadir, Ijaz Ahmed and Saleem Malik were unable to assist them in the tournament as they were on duty with the Pakistan national side.

The final round of first-class matches in the Pakistan season were those which involved the Sri Lanka 'B' team. The tourists played nine matches, of which four were international matches.

17, 18 and 19 February 1989

at National Stadium, Karachi

Karachi 333 for 9 dec (Nadeem-ud-Din 55, Shakeel Sajjad 105 not out, Asif Mujtaba 61) and 131 for 4 dec (Asif Mujtaba 52 not out, Nadeem-ud-Din 51 retired hurt)
Sri Lanka 'B' 247 (A.M. de Silva 53, Shahid Mahboob 6 for 52) and 145 for 3 (S.T. Jayasuriya 102 not out)

Match drawn

The first match of the tour was marked by a brilliant

century by teenager Sanath Teran Jayasuriya from Matara. He had played no first-class cricket before coming to Pakistan.

21, 22 and 23 February 1989

at Pindi Club Ground, Rawalpindi

Rawalpindi 368 for 8 dec (Masood Anwar 201 not out, W.R. Madurasinghe 4 for 111) and 53 for 2
Sri Lanka 'B' 330 (A.C. Alirajah 62, S. Ranatunga 58)

Match drawn

Masood Anwar hit the third and last double century of the season.

26, 27, 28 February and 1 March 1989

at Jinnah Stadium, Sialkot

Sri Lanka 'B' 204 and 156 (Iqbal Qasim 4 for 40, Akram Raza 4 for 52)
Pakistan 'B' 345 for 8 dec (Mansoor Rana 126, Saeed Anwar 82, H.C.P. Ramanayake 4 for 96) and 16 for 0

Pakistan 'B' won by 10 wickets

Iqbal Qasim and Akram Raza, neither of whom was to appear again in the series, spun Pakistan 'B' to victory in the first 'Test'. Iqbal Qasim led a strong side, and Mansoor Rana, the outstanding batsman in the Quaid-e-Azam Trophy, demonstrated the qualities that were to earn him a call to the national side.

4, 5 and 6 March 1989

at Sargodha Stadium

Sri Lanka 'B' 224 for 8 dec (Naved Anjum 4 for 27) and 239 for 7 dec (R.S. Kalpage 66)
Sargodha Commissioner's XI 234 for 7 dec (Arshad Pervez 82, Mohammad Nawaz 70, P.M.V. Deshapriya 5 for 100) and 167 for 4 (Talat Imtiaz 65 not out)

Match drawn

8, 9, 10 and 11 March 1989

at Qaddafi Stadium, Lahore

Sri Lanka 'B' 434 for 7 dec (S.T. Jayasuriya 203 not out, D. Ranatunga 66) and 128 for 1 (D. Ranatunga 62 not out, U.C. Hathurusinghe 58 not out)
Pakistan 'B' 433 (Mansoor Rana 142, Nadeem Abbasi 114, Shaukat Mirza 68, H.C.P. Ramanayake 4 for 85)

Match drawn

Mansoor Rana became the only batsman to reach a thousand runs during the season, and he completed his third century of the summer. His performance was overshadowed, however, by another thrilling innings by Jayasuriya, who reached an unbeaten double century.

14, 15 and 16 March 1989

at National Stadium, Karachi

Pakistan Universities 252 (U.C. Hathurusinghe 4 for 59) and 237 for 5 dec (Sajid Riaz 103 not out, Shakeel Sajjad 77)
Sri Lanka 'B' 181 and 105 for 5 (Nadeem Khan 4 for 30)

Match drawn

Consistent batting for Sri Lanka 'B' by D. Ranatunga. (Michael King/Allsport)

19, 20, 21 and 22 March 1989

at National Stadium, Karachi

Sri Lanka 'B' 390 (S.T. Jayasuriya 207 not out, Iqbal Sikander 4 for 89) and 54 for 2
Pakistan 'B' 193 (M.B. Halangoda 4 for 75) and 248 (Babar Basharat 68, Saeed Anwar 56, H.C.P. Ramanayake 6 for 85)

Sri Lanka 'B' won by 8 wickets

Sanath Jayasuriya's second not out double century put Sri Lanka 'B' in a strong position, and his side never lost a grip on the game. The home side were forced to follow-on, and the bowling of Champaka Ramanayake assured them of victory. Ramanayake, the 24-year-old pace bowler who toured England in 1988, finished with match figures of 9 for 155. He was the outstanding bowler of the tour. Sri Lanka 'B''s victory levelled the series with one match to play.

24, 25 and 26 March 1989

at Quetta

Baluchistan Chief Minister's XI 25 for 1
v. Sri Lanka 'B'

Match abandoned

Only 40 minutes' play on the first day was possible.

29, 30, 31 March and 1 April 1989

at National Stadium, Karachi

Sri Lanka 'B' 266 (D. Ranatunga 70, A.M. de Silva 51, Zakir Khan 5 for 73) and 122 (Naved Anjum 5 for 61, Mushtaq Ahmed 4 for 34)
Pakistan 'B' 427 for 6 dec (Munir-ul-Haq 202 not out)

Pakistan 'B' won by an innings and 39 runs

Pakistan's season ended with the national second eleven beating Sri Lanka 'B' in a decisive manner and so taking the four-match series 2–1. The outstanding performance came from HBFC's Munir-ul-Haq. Pakistan used 31 players in the four matches, and only Saeed Anwar appeared in all four.

For Sri Lanka, Ramanayake confirmed his potential as a pace bowler, but the precocious talent of the young batsman Sanath Jayasuriya was the most heartening aspect of the tour. He hit 643 runs, average 80.37 in all matches, and in the four 'Tests', he scored 486 runs, average 121.50.

First-Class Averages

BATTING

	M	Inns	NOs	Runs	HS	Av	100s	50s
Javed Miandad (Pak)	3	5	0	412	211	82.40	2	
Mansoor Rana (ADBP)	10	17	1	1077	142	67.31	3	7
Atif Rauf (ADBP)	8	15	6	587	76*	65.22		6
Munir-ul-Haq (HBFC)	7	12	2	612	202*	61.20	2	1
Zahid Ahmed (PIA)	6	11	2	530	113*	58.88	2	3
Rizwan Sattar (M)	3	6	2	220	133	55.00	1	
Ashraf Ali (UB)	8	11	4	350	70	50.00		3
Shakeel Sajjad (K)	7	10	4	295	105*	49.16	1	1
Mansoor Akhtar (K/UB)	10	18	2	766	118*	47.87	4	3
Saeed Anwar (UB)	7	8	0	367	127	45.87	1	2
Basit Ali (K)	7	12	1	502	135	45.63	2	2
Sajid Ali (NB)	7	12	0	539	125	44.91	1	2
Abdullah Khan (PNSC)	9	17	3	617	106	44.07	2	3
Asif Mujtaba (K/PIA)	11	19	4	657	141*	43.80	2	3
Saifullah (UB)	5	9	2	302	72	43.14		1
Ijaz Ahmed (Pak)	4	7	0	301	122	43.00	1	1
Sagheer Abbas (HBFC)	6	11	1	428	100*	42.80	1	3
Babar Basharat (MCB)	8	16	1	630	101*	42.00	1	5
Mujahid Hameed (R)	7	11	2	371	119*	41.22	1	1
Manzoor Elahi (M/ADBP)	13	23	1	901	163*	40.95	1	5
Talat Imtiaz (S)	7	12	3	353	65*	39.22		2
Rizwan Qazi (L)	6	11	1	390	89	39.00		3
Inzamam-ul-Haq (M/UB)	7	12	2	387	201*	38.70	1	
Shahid Javed (R)	9	15	2	494	138	38.00	2	2
Ishtiaq Ahmed (K)	5	9	1	304	89	38.00		3
Masood Anwar (R/ADBP)	16	27	1	981	201*	37.73	2	3
Nadeem Abbasi (R)	10	16	1	557	113	37.13	1	1
Ijaz Faqih (K/MCB)	10	17	3	507	101*	36.21	2	2
Aamer Sohail (HB)	7	14	2	431	79	35.91		2
Ameer Akbar (NB)	9	15	1	501	89	35.78		4
Farrukh Bari (PNSC)	7	14	1	458	82	35.23		5
Maqsood Ahmed (S)	6	9	2	246	84*	35.14		2
Wasim Ali (L)	6	12	2	348	72	34.80		4

First-Class Averages continued

	M	Inns	NOs	Runs	HS	Av	100s	50s
Sabih Azhar (R/ADBP)	15	25	7	619	78*	34.38		5
Mohammad Aslam (K)	5	9	1	273	78*	34.12		3
Saleem Pervez (NB)	7	12	1	375	118	34.09	1	1
Azhar Khan (HB)	5	8	1	238	48*	34.00		
Arshad Pervez (S/HB)	13	24	3	709	83	33.76		6
Naeem Taj (B)	6	12	2	337	84*	33.70		3
Bilal Rana (M)	5	10	2	267	74	33.37		2
Wasim Haider (F/PIA)	9	14	4	329	105*	32.90	1	1
Saeed Azad (K/NB)	9	15	2	427	134	32.84	1	1
Aamer Nazir (F)	6	10	0	328	96	32.80		3
Mahmood Hamid (PNSC)	7	13	0	424	116	32.61	1	3
Shaukat Mirza (K/HB)	14	21	4	553	68	32.52		2
Asif Mohammad (PIA)	6	9	1	255	77*	31.87		2
Zahoor Elahi (M/HBFC)	8	13	1	380	62	31.66		1
Hammad Butt (PIA)	6	11	1	316	67	31.60		3
Rafat Alam (HBFC)	5	9	0	282	110	31.33	1	1
Anwar Awais (F)	5	8	0	250	76	31.25		2
Naseer Ahmed (R)	7	11	0	341	122	31.00	1	2
Akram Raza (S/HB)	13	19	7	358	57*	29.83		3
Shafiq Ahmed (UB)	7	11	1	297	71	29.70		3
Agha Zahid (HB)	8	16	1	432	134	28.80	1	1
G.A. Pasha (L)	6	12	2	288	84	28.80		1
Nasir Khan (PIA)	4	8	1	200	50*	28.57		1
Haider Jahangir (L)	6	10	1	257	71	28.55		2
Masroor Hussain (M)	5	10	0	285	126	28.50	1	1
Raja Afaq (R/ADBP)	16	25	5	536	92	26.80		2
Mohammad Nawaz (S/UB)	7	13	0	344	70	26.46		2
Nadeem Arshad (F)	5	8	0	209	109	26.12	1	1
Ghaffar Kazmi (ADBP)	7	13	0	327	76	25.15		3
Feroze Mehdi (PIA)	6	11	0	274	65	24.90		3
Tahir Shah (NB)	7	12	0	279	88	23.25		1
Saleem Taj (B/HBFC)	8	16	0	361	53	22.56		1
Shahid Saeed (HBFC)	6	11	0	237	94	21.54		1
Sajjad Akbar (PNSC)	9	16	4	252	40	21.00		
Tariq Javed (R)	6	11	0	230	48	20.90		
Tahir Rasheed (HB)	9	13	3	205	58*	20.50		1
Anwar-ul-Haq (MCB)	6	12	1	219	54*	19.90		1
Shujaat Ali (K/MCB)	6	12	1	218	69	19.81		1
Babar Zaman (L)	9	16	0	309	79	19.31		1
Wahid Khan (P)	7	12	1	212	58	19.27		2
Pervez Shah (MCB)	7	14	1	241	63	18.53		1
Rifaqat Ali (MCB)	7	13	1	221	55	18.41		2
Anil Dalpat (K/PIA)	11	17	1	287	51	17.93		1
Raees Ahmed (UB)	9	16	0	273	77	17.06		2
Bilal Ahmed (F/ADBP)	14	25	0	424	47	16.96		
Nasir Wasti (PNSC)	7	13	0	213	44	16.38		

(Qualification – 200 runs, average 10.00)

BOWLING

	Overs	Mds	Runs	Wkts	Av	Best	10/m	5/inns
Naved Nazir (F)	265.1	40	711	51	13.94	9/109	2	7
Iqbal Qasim (K/NB/Pak)	653.2	232	1213	75	16.17	5/15	1	5
Mohammad Zahid (B)	132.5	38	314	19	16.52	5/20		1
Akram Raza (S/HB)	572.5	201	1070	64	16.71	6/41	1	5
Raja Sarfraz (R)	254.4	55	640	37	17.29	7/49	1	4
Nadeem Ghauri (HB)	456.4	161	940	54	17.40	8/67	2	3
Mohammad Altaf (B)	195.1	43	447	24	18.62	4/30		
Umar Rasheed (K)	107.4	28	284	15	18.93	7/48	1	1
Shakeel Sajjad (K)	83.3	20	247	13	19.00	6/28		1
Tanvir Afzal (F)	255.5	48	573	29	19.75	5/44		1
Shahid Mahboob (K)	218.4	39	655	33	19.84	6/52		1
Haaris Khan (K)	120.4	26	319	16	19.93	6/45		1
Mohammad Asif (ADBP)	183.2	35	442	22	20.09	6/70	1	2
Kazim Mehdi (HBFC)	242.5	73	586	29	20.20	5/88		1
Aziz-ur-Rehman (S)	254.5	45	666	32	20.81	6/30		2
Naved Anjum (HB)	258.4	35	848	40	21.20	5/50		2
Wasim Haider (F/PIA)	165.1	27	469	22	21.31	5/71		1

	Overs	Mds	Runs	Wkts	Av	Best	10/m	5/inns
Imran Adil (B)	83	20	256	12	21.33	4/68		
Shakeel Khan (HB)	150	21	472	22	21.45	4/42		
Ali Ahmed (HBFC)	187.5	41	500	23	21.73	6/30	1	1
Saleem Jaffer (K/Pak)	102	23	287	13	22.07	7/29		1
Mohammad Riaz (R)	198.3	37	576	26	22.15	7/27	1	2
Waqar Younus (M/UB)	162.5	31	546	24	22.75	6/33		2
Mushtaq Ahmed (M/UB)	381.1	65	1188	52	22.84	8/40	1	3
Asif Mujtaba (K/PIA)	194.1	49	514	22	23.36	3/20		
Shahid A. Khan (L)	250	66	561	24	23.37	6/96		2
Amin Lakhani (PNSC)	300.1	61	831	35	23.74	6/34	1	4
Zulfiqar Ali (PIA)	61.1	8	238	10	23.80	7/76		1
Tauseef Ahmed (Pak)	161.3	64	268	11	24.36	3/73		
Iqbal Sikander (K/PIA)	342.1	93	911	37	24.62	5/57		1
Bilal Rana (M)	254.1	53	672	26	25.84	5/131		1
Raja Afaq (R/ADBP)	524.2	89	1448	56	25.85	6/64		3
Rizwan Qazi (L)	221.4	42	626	24	26.08	7/93	1	1
Manzoor Elahi (M/ADBP)	195.4	25	629	24	26.20	5/37		1
Babar Zaman (L)	152	22	472	18	26.22	5/73		1
Naeem Taj (B)	170.2	36	477	18	26.50	5/51		1
Zakir Khan (P/ADBP)	290.5	50	984	37	26.59	5/36		4
Barkatullah (K/NB)	313.1	46	1151	43	26.76	4/38		
Waheed Niazi (HB)	110	16	376	14	26.85	4/60		
Arshad Khan (P)	149.3	23	465	17	27.35	7/59		1
Pervez Shah (MCB)	142	31	443	16	27.68	4/92		
Azeem Hafeez (PNSC)	132	18	514	18	28.55	3/16		
Zulfiqar Butt (HBFC)	201	48	550	19	28.94	4/73		
Farrukh Zaman (P/MCB)	298.2	34	1073	37	29.00	5/55		2
Wahid Khan (P)	120.3	13	464	16	29.00	5/62		1
Rashid Khan (PIA)	156.3	15	634	21	30.19	4/55		
Jamal Siddiqi (R)	76	12	306	10	30.60	3/40		
Abdul Qadir (Pak)	141	37	348	11	31.63	3/33		
Sajjad Akbar (PNSC)	424.1	108	1111	35	31.74	5/75		1
Masood Anwar (UB)	287	79	774	24	32.25	4/54		
Zain-ul-Abedin (L/MCB)	137.5	15	489	15	32.60	6/127		1
Naseer Shaukat (F)	83	10	329	10	32.92	3/32		
Tanvir Ali (PIA)	167.5	45	428	13	32.92	6/68		1
Sabih Azhar (R/ADBP)	140.2	19	495	15	33.00	6/81		1
Ijaz Faqih (K/MCB)	332.5	62	932	28	33.28	7/54		2
Shahid Tanvir (NB)	138	15	406	11	36.90	5/71		1
Khatib Rizwan (ADBP)	265	64	630	16	39.37	5/110		1
Tahir Shah (NB)	121	18	465	11	42.27	4/98		
Ilyas Khan (MCB)	152.1	15	512	12	42.66	3/18		
Raees Ahmed (UB)	151.2	26	473	10	47.30	5/84		1

(Qualification – 10 wickets)

LEADING FIELDERS

35 – Tahir Rasheed (HB) (ct 32/st 3); 32 – Anil Dalpat (K/PIA) (ct 24/st 8); 23 – Dildar Malik (M) (ct 15/st 8); 22 – Mutahir Shah (PNSC) (ct 17/st 5) and Bilal Ahmed (F/ADBP) (ct 16/st 6); 21 – Nadeem Abbasi (R) (ct 17/st 4); 20 – Haider Jahangir (L) (ct 17/st 3); 19 – Ashraf Ali (UB); 17 – Masood Anwar (R/ADBP); 16 – Imran Zia (B) (ct 11/st 5), Rifaqat Ali (MCB) (ct12/st 4); 15 – Mansoor Akhtar (K/UB) and Asif Mujtaba (K/PIA); 12 – Shujaat Ali (K/MCB), Arshad Pervez (S/HB) and Raja Afaq (R/ADBP); 11 – Iftikhar Shmed (K), Zahoor Elahi (M/HBFC) and Akram Raza (S/HB); 10 – Wasim Yousuf (P) (ct 9/st 1), Anwar Miandad (HB), Munir-ul-Haq (HBFC) and Saeed Azad (K/NB)

Abbreviations of team names: ADBP – Agricultural Development Bank of Pakistan; B – Bahawalpur; F – Faisalabad; HB – Habib Bank; HBFC – House Building Finance Corporation; K – Karachi; L – Lahore; M – Multan; MCB – Muslim Commercial Bank; NB – National Bank; Pak – Test matches for Pakistan; PIA – Pakistan International Airlines; PNSC – Pakistan National Shipping Corporation; P – Peshawar; R – Rawalpindi; S – Sargodha; UB – United Bank.

Firmly Forward

The season in Zimbabwe.
The tour of the Young New Zealand Internationals.
Lancashire in Zimbabwe.
First-class averages.

Barry Dudleston, the former Leicestershire player, who exerted a tremendous influence on cricket in Zimbabwe as the coach to the national side.

Significant changes heralded the arrival of the cricket season in Zimbabwe. Andy Pycroft, the country's most consistent and outstanding batsman since Independence, excepting Hick, who has decided to follow his career elsewhere, announced that he was retiring from first-class cricket. The reason for Pycroft's decision was that he felt a growing sense of disillusionment at Zimbabwe's failure to be accorded full Test status. Although Pycroft's relationships with other players and with officials have not always been harmonious, it was apparent that his presence in the national side would be sorely missed.

Following upon the news of Pycroft's retirement came the request from veteran John Traicos that he be relieved of the captaincy. Traicos, still a fine off-spinner and the only South African Test player remaining in the first-class game, stated that he would continue to be available for selection for the national side.

Peter Rawson, the talented all-rounder, was named as successor to Traicos as Zimbabwe's captain, while Barry Dudleston was appointed coach to the national side. Rawson and Dudleston were to have a dynamic effect on Zimbabwe's showing against the touring New Zealand side, which was led by Robert Vance and included eight players with Test experience, including vice-captain Mark Greatbatch, who had batted so impressively against England earlier in the year.

25 September 1988

at Harare South Country Club

New Zealand Young Internationals 294 for 3 (T.J. Franklin 84, P.A. Horne 76, R.H. Vance 64 not out)
Country Districts 193 (A. Elliott 80, K.R. Rutherford 4 for 44)

New Zealand Young Internationals won by 101 runs

With each of the first four batsmen showing good form, the tourists quickly established themselves and scored at nearly six an over. Alan Elliott's aggressive innings was a consolation for the home side.

27, 28 and 29 September 1988

at Harare South Country Club

Zimbabwe 'B' 347 for 5 dec (C.M. Robertson 95, C.D. James 69, G.A. Briant 58) and 101 for 3
New Zealand Young Internationals 357 for 4 dec (M.R. Pringle 120 not out, P.A. Horne 71)

Match drawn

Although this match was allotted three days, it was not granted first-class status. Glenn Bruk-Jackson, fresh from a season with Leicestershire Second XI, and Gavin Briant gave the home side a fine start with a stand of 107, but it was Colin Robertson who took the eye with 95 off 156 balls, an innings which earned him a recall to the national side. Murray Pringle batted splendidly for the visitors, and he and Tony Blain shared an unbroken stand of 104.

1 October 1988

at Harare Sports Club
Zimbabwe 'B' 197

John Traicos relinquished the captaincy but continued to bowl his off-breaks economically. (Adrian Murrell/ Allsport)

New Zealand Young Internationals 199 for 2 (P.A. Horne 101 not out)

New Zealand Young Internationals won by 8 wickets

Phil Horne dominated the match with a fine century which took his side to victory with 6.3 overs to spare. Horne and Greatbatch added 125 for the second wicket.

First One-Day International
ZIMBABWE v. NEW ZEALAND YOUNG INTERNATIONALS

After a poor start Zimbabwe had to concentrate on rebuilding the innings and Arnott and Houghton erred somewhat on the side of caution. Houghton's 50 took 96 deliveries, but the next 18 runs came off eight balls. It was Robertson who put zest into the Zimbabwe innings with 74 off 79 balls, but even this proved ineffective in the face of the onslaught that was to come. Phil Horne, in magnificent form, again dominated, and he reached 50 off 62 balls. He maintained his aggression, and his 120 came off 154 deliveries and included 9 fours, so that the tourists won with 15 balls to spare.

First International Match
ZIMBABWE *v.* NEW ZEALAND YOUNG INTERNATIONALS

The Zimbabwe Cricket Union's decision to play two of the first-class international matches over four days proved to be a popular one, although the early stages of the first match suggested that four days would not be needed. As David Houghton had expressed an unwillingness to keep wicket in the longer fixtures, Robin Brown, 37 years old, was recalled to act as keeper and sheet anchor to the batting. Competently as Brown performed, his selection emphasized that Zimbabwe are in need of a young wicket-keeper of top quality.

Rawson won the toss and Zimbabwe batted first on a good wicket, but they were dismissed in 43 overs for 139, the pace bowling of Shane Thomson and Willie Watson, ably assisted by wicket-keeper Tony Blain, proving too much for them. Having reached 40 for 1, they lost their next seven wickets for 44 runs and were revived only by some late determination from Rawson and Jarvis. To the delight of Zimbabwe, Horne, who had been scoring so prolifically, was dismissed cheaply, but the New Zealanders finished the first day well placed on 101 for 3.

Duers, Rawson and Jarvis bowled Zimbabwe back into the game on the second morning, and some keen cricket restricted the tourists' lead to 61 runs. This lead had been reduced to six by the close, and Zimbabwe had not lost a

Robin Brown, recalled to keep wicket for Zimbabwe in the first-class matches. (Adrian Murrell/Allsport)

FIRST ONE-DAY INTERNATIONAL – ZIMBABWE *v.* NEW ZEALAND YOUNG INTERNATIONALS
2 October 1988 at Harare Sports Club

ZIMBABWE

K.J. Arnott	c Morrison, b Duff	41
D.G. Goodwin	c Greatbatch, b Watson	2
A.C. Waller	c Franklin, b Watson	3
D.L. Houghton*	b Watson	68
C.M. Robertson	not out	74
G.A. Paterson	not out	22
I.P. Butchart		
P.W.E. Rawson†		
L.L. de Grandhomme		
A.J. Traicos		
K.G. Duers		
Extras	lb 4, w 5	9
(50 overs)	(for 4 wkts)	219

	O	M	R	W
Morrison	8	–	53	–
Watson	10	–	46	3
Thomson	10	3	32	–
Larsen	10	–	35	–
Duff	10	1	36	1
Rutherford	2	–	13	–

FALL OF WICKETS
1–14, 2–29, 3–66, 4–177

NEW ZEALAND YOUNG INTERNATIONALS

P.A. Horne	not out	120
T.J. Franklin	c Rawson, b Traicos	48
K.R. Rutherford	not out	47
R.H. Vance†		
M.J. Greatbatch		
T.E. Blain*		
G.R. Larsen		
S.W. Duff		
S.A. Thomson		
D.K. Morrison		
W. Watson		
Extras	lb 1, w 3, nb 1	5
(47.3 overs)	(for one wkt)	220

	O	M	R	W
Rawson	10	1	40	–
Duers	9.3	–	41	–
Traicos	10	–	43	1
Butchart	8	–	47	–
de Grandhomme	10	–	48	–

FALL OF WICKET
1–129

Umpires: R. Jackson & D.C. Moore-Gordon

New Zealand Young Internationals won by 9 wickets

wicket, but Arnott had been forced to retire hurt with a damaged finger. He resumed at the fall of the seventh wicket, but the injury was to keep him out of the rest of the series.

Robertson was dismissed without addition on the third morning, but Goodwin and Houghton batted with great resolution. Unfortunately, they were poorly supported by the late middle order, and, in spite of the New Zealanders being handicapped by an injury to Thomson, Zimbabwe were bowled out for 214, and the visitors needed only 154 to win. Thomson's injury was to rule him out of the rest of the tour, and Chris Cairns was brought in as a replacement.

The New Zealanders closed the third day on 81 for 3, and the match was seemingly within their grasp, but a middle order collapse brought the game to a dramatic climax. The eighth wicket fell at 129, but Watson batted sensibly for a couple of overs before falling to Traicos, which left the last pair, Duff and Millmow, the task of scoring 14 to win the match.

Millmow played straight and intelligently, while Duff, an accredited batsman, took runs where he could. As the target neared, Duff seemed to lose his nerve and began to sweep at Traicos with an air of desperation. Traicos maintained a relentless length and direction on middle and

off stump, and when Duff swept and missed he was palpably lbw to give Zimbabwe a sensational and totally surprising victory by four runs. It was their first win in a first-class match for 21 games.

Second One-Day International
ZIMBABWE v. NEW ZEALAND YOUNG INTERNATIONALS

Heartened by their success in the first-class match, Zimbabwe gave a spirited display in the second one-day international and levelled the series. They began shakily, but a violent innings from Brandes, who hit 50 off 40 balls, and an equally exhilarating knock by Butchart, 31 off 14 balls, pushed Zimbabwe to a commendable score.

The tourists, too, began badly, and although Vance and Rutherford promised a recovery, both fell to Brandes before they could take a firm grip on the game, and the returning Duers proved too much for the rest of the New Zealand batting.

Second International Match
ZIMBABWE v. NEW ZEALAND YOUNG INTERNATIONALS

Only three days were allocated to the second first-class international match of the tour, and when the whole of the

---

FIRST INTERNATIONAL MATCH – ZIMBABWE v. NEW ZEALAND YOUNG INTERNATIONALS
4, 5, 7 and 8 October 1988 at Harare Sports Club

ZIMBABWE

	FIRST INNINGS		SECOND INNINGS	
K.J. Arnott	c Blain, b Thomson	12	c Pringle, b Watson	24
D.G. Goodwin	c Blain, b Watson	22	b Duff	52
R.D. Brown*	c Blain, b Watson	11	c Rutherford, b Duff	6
C.M. Robertson	c Blain, b Watson	12	c Franklin, b Duff	18
D.L. Houghton	c Pringle, b Thomson	0	c Pringle, b Rutherford	68
G.K. Bruk-Jackson	c Rutherford, b Thomson	2	st Blain, b Duff	7
P.W.E. Rawson†	c Rutherford, b Thomson	31	c sub (Larsen), b Duff	0
I.P. Butchart	c Blain, b Millmow	10	c Vance, b Rutherford	2
A.J. Traicos	c Greatbatch, b Millmow	2	lbw, b Rutherford	0
M.P. Jarvis	b Thomson	28	b Watson	12
K.G. Duers	not out	2	not out	6
Extras	lb 1, nb 6	7	b 3, lb 6, w 1, nb 9	19
		139		214

NEW ZEALAND YOUNG INTERNATIONALS

	FIRST INNINGS		SECOND INNINGS	
P.A. Horne	b Jarvis	12	b Traicos	17
T.J. Franklin	lbw, b Duers	37	b Rawson	27
R.H. Vance†	c Goodwin, b Rawson	40	c Traicos, b Rawson	14
M.J. Greatbatch	c Rawson, b Duers	7	c Brown, b Rawson	22
S.W. Duff	lbw, b Jarvis	46	(9) lbw, b Traicos	23
K.R. Rutherford	c Traicos, b Duers	4	(5) c Goodwin, b Rawson	17
M.R. Pringle	c Goodwin, b Rawson	2	(6) c Brown, b Rawson	4
T.E. Blain*	c Traicos, b Rawson	14	(7) c Rawson, b Duers	6
S.A. Thomson	b Duers	4	(8) c Rawson, b Duers	9
W. Watson	not out	23	c Brown, b Traicos	5
J.P. Millmow	c Arnott, b Traicos	0	not out	1
Extras	lb 5, nb 6	11	b 3, lb 1	4
		200		149

	O	M	R	W	O	M	R	W
Millmow	10	2	32	2	17	3	41	–
Watson	18	5	49	3	29.4	10	60	2
Thomson	12	1	49	5	7	4	10	–
Duff	3	–	8	–	38	10	77	5
Vance					1	–	1	–
Rutherford					8	1	16	3

	O	M	R	W	O	M	R	W
Rawson	24	10	32	3	24	8	44	5
Jarvis	20	4	54	2	2	–	11	–
Duers	23	11	50	4	8	2	22	2
Butchart	8	3	17	–	2	–	5	–
Traicos	29.2	11	42	1	31.3	10	63	3

FALL OF WICKETS
1–35, 2–40, 3–54, 4–55, 5–57, 6–68, 7–82, 8–84, 9–126
1–55, 2–80, 3–81, 4–133, 5–133, 6–151, 7–158, 8–168, 9–199

FALL OF WICKETS
1–20, 2–86, 3–97, 4–110, 5–118, 6–128, 7–161, 8–173, 9–185
1–39, 2–55, 3–60, 4–86, 5–104, 6–105, 7–116, 8–129, 9–140

Umpires: R. Jackson & K. Kanjee

Zimbabwe won by 4 runs

SECOND ONE-DAY INTERNATIONAL – ZIMBABWE v. NEW ZEALAND YOUNG INTERNATIONALS
9 October 1988 at Harare Sports Club

ZIMBABWE

D.L. Houghton*	c Blain, b Morrison	10
D.G. Goodwin	lbw, b Watson	4
C.M. Robertson	b Duff	21
A.C. Waller	c Rutherford, b Larsen	41
G.A. Paterson	c Franklin, b Rutherford	3
G.K. Bruk-Jackson	c Rutherford, b Millmow	21
E.A. Brandes	c Rutherford, b Watson	50
P.W.E. Rawson†	c and b Morrison	22
I.P. Butchart	not out	31
A.J. Traicos	c Greatbatch, b Millmow	11
K.G. Duers	not out	2
Extras	lb 7, w 4, nb 3	14
(50 overs)	(for 9 wkts)	230

	O	M	R	W
Millmow	7	1	45	2
Watson	10	–	45	2
Morrison	8	–	33	2
Larsen	10	–	34	1
Duff	10	2	28	1
Rutherford	5	–	38	1

FALL OF WICKETS
1–9, 2–29, 3–67, 4–79, 5–103, 6–119, 7–180, 8–184, 9–200

NEW ZEALAND YOUNG INTERNATIONALS

P.A. Horne	lbw, b Brandes	15
T.J. Franklin	lbw, b Duers	2
R.H. Vance†	c sub (G.A. Briant), b Brandes	27
K.R. Rutherford	c Traicos, b Brandes	34
M.J. Greatbatch	c Robertson, b Duers	28
T.E. Blain*	c sub (G.A. Briant), b Duers	24
G.R. Larsen	not out	20
S.W. Duff	c Rawson, b Duers	2
D.K. Morrison	c Rawson, b Duers	4
W. Watson	c Brandes, b Butchart	8
J.P. Millmow	not out	4
Extras	lb 3, w 3	6
(50 overs)	(for 9 wkts)	174

	O	M	R	W
Rawson	8	3	24	–
Duers	10	2	24	5
Brandes	10	1	34	3
Traicos	10	–	32	–
Butchart	10	–	51	1
Waller	2	–	6	–

FALL OF WICKETS
1–8, 2–22, 3–77, 4–84, 5–132, 6–138, 7–140, 8–144, 9–160

Umpires: I.D. Robinson & D.C. Moore-Gordon

Zimbabwe won by 56 runs

SECOND INTERNATIONAL MATCH – ZIMBABWE v. NEW ZEALAND YOUNG INTERNATIONALS
11, 12 and 13 October 1988 at Harare Sports Club

NEW ZEALAND YOUNG INTERNATIONALS

T.J. Franklin	c Goodwin, b Traicos	16
R.H. Vance†	lbw, b Rawson	31
M.J. Greatbatch	c Brown, b Rawson	81
K.R. Rutherford	run out	33
M.R. Pringle	c Brandes, b Rawson	52
T.E. Blain*	c Brown, b Duers	13
G.R. Larsen	not out	34
M.W. Priest	st Brown, b Traicos	11
S.W. Duff	c Brown, b Duers	1
W. Watson	c Rawson, b Waller	7
D.K. Morrison		
Extras	lb 4, w 3	7
	(for 9 wkts, dec)	286

	O	M	R	W
Rawson	30.3	13	39	3
Brandes	14.3	1	65	–
Duers	28	7	84	2
Traicos	36	14	74	2
Houghton	7	2	19	–
Waller	0.3	–	1	1

FALL OF WICKETS
1–49, 2–49, 3–90, 4–211, 5–222, 6–238, 7–255, 8–264, 9–286

ZIMBABWE

R.D. Brown*	retired hurt	5
D.G. Goodwin	run out	27
G.K. Bruk-Jackson	c Blain, b Morrison	4
C.M. Robertson	c Larsen, b Morrison	2
A.C. Waller	lbw, b Rutherford	52
D.L. Houghton	c and b Priest	43
G.A. Paterson	not out	2
E.A. Brandes	not out	9
P.W.E. Rawson†		
A.J. Traicos		
K.G. Duers		
Extras	lb 4, w 4, nb 13	21
	(for 5 wkts)	165

	O	M	R	W
Morrison	11	–	45	2
Watson	10	4	22	–
Rutherford	16	2	32	1
Larsen	4	2	3	–
Priest	16	3	54	1
Duff	1	–	5	–

FALL OF WICKETS
1–34, 2–42, 3–66, 4–144, 5–154

Umpires: R. Jackson & I.D. Robinson

Match drawn

THIRD ONE-DAY INTERNATIONAL – ZIMBABWE v. NEW ZEALAND YOUNG INTERNATIONALS
15 October 1988 at Bulawayo Athletic Club

NEW ZEALAND YOUNG INTERNATIONALS

P.A. Horne	c Houghton, b Duers	0
T.J. Franklin	c and b Rawson	10
R.H. Vance†	c Brandes, b Rawson	0
K.R. Rutherford	b Traicos	18
M.J. Greatbatch	c Houghton, b Brandes	20
T.E. Blain*	b Duers	3
G.R. Larsen	c Waller, b Butchart	65
S.W. Duff	lbw, b Brandes	28
C.L. Cairns	c Bruk-Jackson, b Rawson	38
W. Watson	not out	2
D.K. Morrison	not out	0
Extras	lb 5, w 5, nb 3	13
(50 overs)	(for 9 wkts)	197

	O	M	R	W
Rawson	10	3	29	3
Duers	10	2	37	2
Traicos	10	2	19	1
Butchart	9	1	44	1
Brandes	10	–	55	2
Waller	1	–	8	–

FALL OF WICKETS
1–1, 2–5, 3–19, 4–35, 5–52, 6–62, 7–113, 8–185, 9–196

ZIMBABWE

D.G. Goodwin	c Blain, b Watson	16
G.A. Paterson	lbw, b Larsen	20
C.M. Robertson	not out	70
D.L. Houghton*	b Larsen	18
A.C. Waller	c Blain, b Watson	9
G.K. Bruk-Jackson	lbw, b Morrison	2
E.A. Brandes	not out	37
P.W.E. Rawson†		
I.P. Butchart		
A.J. Traicos		
K.G. Duers		
Extras	lb 9, w 8, nb 9	26
(44.5 overs)	(for 5 wkts)	198

	O	M	R	W
Morrison	6.5	–	36	1
Watson	10	1	33	2
Cairns	5	–	28	–
Larsen	10	–	27	2
Duff	10	1	40	–
Rutherford	3	–	25	–

FALL OF WICKETS
1–25, 2–71, 3–103, 4–128, 5–133

Umpires: R. Jackson & E. Gilmour

Zimbabwe won by 5 wickets

FOURTH ONE-DAY INTERNATIONAL – ZIMBABWE v. NEW ZEALAND YOUNG INTERNATIONALS
16 October 1988 at Bulawayo Athletic Club

NEW ZEALAND YOUNG INTERNATIONALS

R.H. Vance†	c Houghton, b Rawson	11
T.J. Franklin	c Brandes, b Duers	15
M.J. Greatbatch	run out	23
K.R. Rutherford	b Duers	3
M.R. Pringle	c sub (Bruk-Jackson), b Brandes	26
G.R. Larsen	run out	49
T.E. Blain*	c Waller, b Rawson	19
C.L. Cairns	c Robertson, b Rawson	19
S.W. Duff	not out	15
W. Watson	not out	1
D.K. Morrison		
Extras	lb 9, w 2	11
(50 overs)	(for 8 wkts)	192

	O	M	R	W
Rawson	10	1	40	3
Jarvis	10	1	36	–
Duers	10	2	26	2
Traicos	10	2	27	–
Brandes	9	–	41	1
Butchart	1	–	13	–

FALL OF WICKETS
1–20, 2–35, 3–47, 4–60, 5–119, 6–146, 7–173, 8–182

ZIMBABWE

D.G. Goodwin	lbw, b Duff	14
G.A. Paterson	c Watson, b Duff	20
C.M. Robertson	run out	20
A.C. Waller	c Larsen, b Duff	13
D.L. Houghton*	c Blain, b Watson	17
E.A. Brandes	c Greatbatch, b Larsen	7
P.W.E. Rawson†	c Blain, b Morrison	24
I.P. Butchart	b Larsen	34
A.J. Traicos	run out	7
M.P. Jarvis	c Blain, b Cairns	10
K.G. Duers	not out	4
Extras	b 1, lb 5, w 6, nb 4	16
(49.3 overs)		186

	O	M	R	W
Watson	10	–	36	1
Cairns	9.3	1	37	1
Duff	10	2	27	3
Morrison	10	1	49	1
Larsen	10	–	31	2

FALL OF WICKETS
1–31, 2–43, 3–68, 4–87, 5–99, 6–112, 7–143, 8–168, 9–175

Umpires: R. Jackson & E. Gilmour

New Zealand Young Internationals won by 6 runs

second day was lost to rain it became obvious that no result could be obtained.

Vance won the toss, and the highlight of the New Zealand innings was some sound batting by Greatbatch and Pringle. The visitors ended the first day on 238 for 5 and continued their innings on the last morning. Houghton and Waller shared a partnership of 78 for Zimbabwe, and Waller hit his first first-class fifty for more than three years.

Third One-Day International
ZIMBABWE *v.* NEW ZEALAND YOUNG INTERNATIONALS

The New Zealanders were soon in grave trouble as Horne and Vance were sent back without scoring and Franklin followed with the score on 19. At 62 for 6, the main batting gone, they looked a well-beaten side, but Larsen played an innings of great enterprise and courage, hitting 65 off 87 balls. Duff and Cairns, in his first match, also batted well, and the final score of 197 was well beyond what the tourists might have expected earlier.

Zimbabwe were never really in danger of not reaching the target, however, once Paterson and Robertson had settled into a solid second-wicket stand. Two quick wickets brought encouragement to the New Zealanders, but Eddo Brandes again showed his ability to hit lustily, and Zimbabwe cruised to victory.

Fourth One-Day International
ZIMBABWE *v.* NEW ZEALAND YOUNG INTERNATIONALS

In the most exciting match of the series, the tourists drew level at two games each when they won by six runs with three balls to spare. It was a brave and determined victory, for once again they had started badly, and once again it was the resolution of Larsen that gave them renewed hope.

It seemed that Zimbabwe would have little trouble in scoring the 193 needed for victory, but the spin of Duff unsettled the early batsmen, and no one was able to establish himself. Rawson and Butchart showed the necessary attacking flair, but once they were dismissed and Traicos was run out, Zimbabwe's chances of clinching the series vanished.

Third International Match
ZIMBABWE *v.* NEW ZEALAND YOUNG INTERNATIONALS

The revitalized and more professional approach to the game that Zimbabwe had shown throughout the New Zealanders' visit was never more in evidence than in the final first-class match, which saw the home side at their best. Winning the toss, the New Zealanders would have been in total disarray but for an outstanding innings by

---

THIRD INTERNATIONAL MATCH – ZIMBABWE *v.* NEW ZEALAND YOUNG INTERNATIONALS
18, 19, 21 and 22 October 1988 at Harare Sports Club

NEW ZEALAND YOUNG INTERNATIONALS

	FIRST INNINGS			SECOND INNINGS	
T.J. Franklin	c Butchart, b Duers	9	(2) b Rawson		39
R.H. Vance†	c Traicos, b Duers	10	(1) lbw, b Rawson		0
M.J. Greatbatch	c Paterson, b Traicos	18	c Waller, b Rawson		28
K.R. Rutherford	not out	144	lbw, b Rawson		9
M.R. Pringle	c Butchart, b Traicos	16	c Goodwin, b Rawson		0
G.R. Larsen	hit wkt, b Brandes	51	c Brown, b Butchart		26
T.E. Blain*	c Waller, b Brandes	0	c Brown, b Butchart		20
M.W. Priest	lbw, b Brandes	0	(9) c Goodwin, b Brandes		1
S.W. Duff	c Brown, b Rawson	9	(8) lbw, b Rawson		9
W. Watson	b Duers	0	not out		13
D.K. Morrison	lbw, b Rawson	0	lbw, b Rawson		8
Extras	b 4, lb 1, w 1, nb 1	7	b 1, lb 7, nb 1		9
		264			162

ZIMBABWE

	FIRST INNINGS		SECOND INNINGS	
D.G. Goodwin	b Morrison	17	lbw, b Watson	42
G.A. Paterson	c Blain, b Morrison	34	c Blain, b Duff	6
R.D. Brown*	c Greatbatch, b Larsen	74		
C.M. Robertson	c Blain, b Larsen	5	(3) c Morrison, b Watson	15
D.L. Houghton	run out	90	(4) not out	21
A.C. Waller	c Blain, b Watson	20	(5) not out	12
P.W.E. Rawson†	lbw, b Watson	28		
E.A. Brandes	c Priest, b Duff	14		
I.P. Butchart	c Greatbatch, b Duff	4		
A.J. Traicos	not out	17		
K.G. Duers	c Greatbatch, b Duff	8		
Extras	b 7, lb 4, w 1, nb 7	19	lb 1, w 1, nb 2	4
		330	(for 3 wkts)	100

	O	M	R	W	O	M	R	W
Rawson	22.2	6	40	2	24.5	7	41	7
Duers	29	8	58	3	12	3	21	–
Brandes	13	2	50	3	11	3	28	1
Traicos	33	8	73	2	24	6	49	–
Butchart	6	1	26	–	6	2	15	2
Houghton	3	–	12	–				

	O	M	R	W	O	M	R	W
Morrison	21	3	56	2	2	–	14	–
Watson	34	9	76	2	10	1	36	2
Duff	25.2	8	56	3	10	–	49	1
Larsen	31	10	54	2				
Rutherford	11	4	20	–				
Priest	21	6	57	–				

FALL OF WICKETS
1–10, 2–27, 3–63, 4–112, 5–229, 6–229, 7–229, 8–252, 9–264
1–0, 2–71, 3–71, 4–75, 5–80, 6–127, 7–130, 8–133, 9–150

FALL OF WICKETS
1–26, 2–66, 3–79, 4–181, 5–215, 6–273, 7–294, 8–299, 9–302
1–30, 2–65, 3–70

Umpires: R. Jackson & I.D. Robinson

Zimbabwe won by 7 wickets

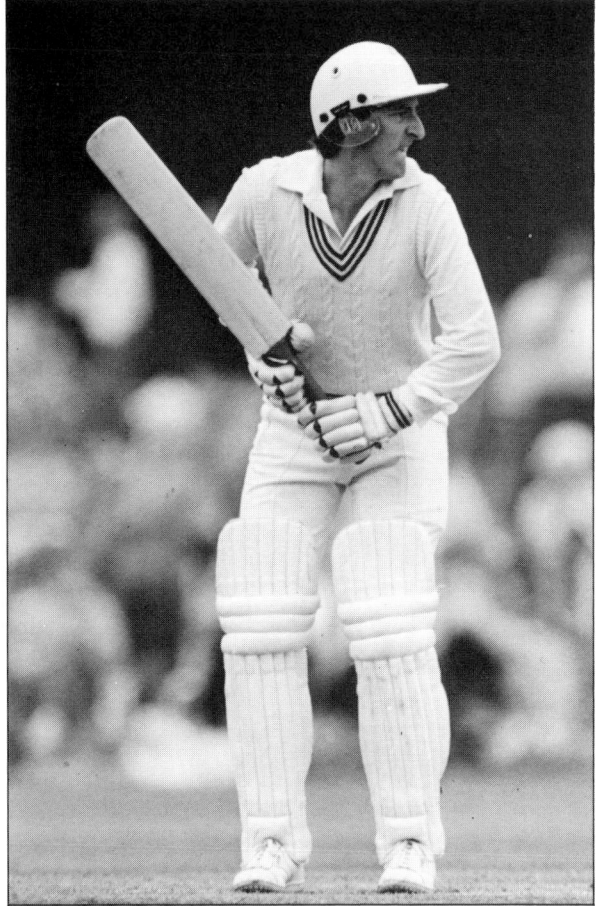

New Zealander Ken Rutherford played an outstanding innings of 144 not out in the final international of the tour. (Adrian Murrell/Allsport)

Rutherford. He batted into the second day, and his 144 was made off 266 balls. The only adequate support he received came from Gavin Larsen, who, like Duff, was one of the all-round successes of the tour. Larsen helped Rutherford to add 117 for the fifth wicket, but his dismissal brought about a collapse. Larsen hit his wicket and Blain was taken at short-leg first ball. With his next delivery Eddo Brandes had Priest leg before, so completing the first hat trick ever taken for Zimbabwe in a first-class match. Brandes was, in fact, bowling his first over with the second new ball, and his tenth of the match.

Zimbabwe quickly lost Goodwin, but by the end of the second day they were 155 for 3 with Brown and Houghton showing fine form. Brown reached his first fifty in first-class cricket for five years and provided the innings with a solid base, his 74 coming off 230 balls. Houghton batted in an equally uncompromising manner and looked set for a century before running himself out after he had faced 264 deliveries. Houghton was seventh out, by which time Zimbabwe had already taken a 30-run lead. The tail did

not succumb meekly, and Zimbabwe eventually claimed a valuable 66-run advantage on the first innings.

Vance was out before the close, but Franklin and Greatbatch wiped out the arrears without further problems. Then Rawson returned for a second spell and bowled with great passion and aggression with the old ball. He dismissed Greatbatch and Franklin at the same score, and four wickets fell for nine runs. Larsen and Blain suggested resistance with a stand of 47, but Butchart, who had not had a good series with the ball, accounted for both of them, and three wickets fell for six runs. Rawson's relentlessly hostile and inspiring bowling continued, and he finished with 7 for 41, the best figures of his career.

Zimbabwe were left to make 97 in even time to win the match. Darrell Goodwin gave them a fine start, and there was never any doubt that they would clinch the series with a memorable victory and time to spare.

Fifth One-Day International
ZIMBABWE v. NEW ZEALAND YOUNG INTERNATIONALS

Wet conditions delayed the start of the deciding one-day international, and the match was reduced to 47 overs. The tourists began confidently, and, after a hesitant period in which three wickets fell quickly, the confidence was reasserted. As the later batsmen attempted to increase the scoring rate, Brandes claimed five wickets, but the New Zealanders' total of 222 at 4.72 an over was still a formidable one.

Zimbabwe started briskly enough, but Goodwin and Paterson were out in quick succession, and it was Robertson and Houghton who revived the home side with a stand of 71. At 190 for 3, Zimbabwe were well set for victory, but the dismissal of Waller brought about a minor collapse, and it was left to Butchart, missed early in his innings in the gathering gloom, and the cool Traicos to take Zimbabwe to victory with 10 balls to spare.

It was only the second time since Independence that Zimbabwe had beaten a touring side in both the one-day and first-class series; the other occasion being when the Young West Indians were overcome in 1983–4. Great credit is due to Rawson, who bowled better than at any time in his career and who was an inspiring captain. His bowling was sharp, accurate and aggressive, and he was very well supported by Brandes and the economic Traicos.

In batting, Dave Houghton confirmed his authority and status, and Colin Robertson finally proved his worth after some seasons of uncertainty, but generally success was founded on a team effort.

25 October 1988

at Mutare Sports Club

New Zealand Young Internationals 216 for 6 (M.J. Greatbatch 74 not out)
Young Zimbabwe 217 for 8 (G.A. Briant 72, C.L. Cairns 4 for 44)

Young Zimbabwe won by 2 wickets

A surprise victory by the Young Zimbabwe team ended the New Zealand tour. The visitors were well served by

Greatbatch and Blain, but a fifth-wicket stand of 87 between Briant and James set up the home side's win with one of their 50 overs unused.

The Zimbabwe selectors had been criticized for their conservative policy in relying on the same players for the national side who had given service for some seasons, and the success of Young Zimbabwe proved that there is a nucleus of young talent in the country.

The problem that constantly confronts cricket in Zimbabwe is that of finding first-class opposition. Invitations to the Indian Test side and to the Indian 'B' side to tour in 1989 were turned down, and attention was then switched to encouraging an English county, Middlesex or Lancashire, to make a pre-season tour of Zimbabwe, but, as the New Zealanders departed, the Zimbabwe cricketers remained uncertain as to who their opponents would be in the second half of the season.

It transpired that Lancashire were the visitors to Zimbabwe in the second half of the season. With respect to Lancashire, this was something of a disappointment for the cricket enthusiasts of Zimbabwe who, following the success against the New Zealand side, had looked forward to a visit from a powerful Indian side, perhaps even the full Indian Test side on their way to the West Indies. Communication with the Indian cricket authorities, however, remains only marginally easier than communication with Mars, and it proved impossible to arrange anything definite with them. Fortunately for Zimbabwe, Lancashire were looking for a brief tour as a prelude to the English season.

Anticlimax was inevitable, and there was worry that Zimbabwe might perform indifferently, but Rawson's energetic leadership kept Zimbabwe on top. They won the first-class game and both one-day matches against the county side. Rawson himself bowled magnificently and was ably assisted by Duers and Traicos. The fielding was of the very highest quality, and the batting, if inconsistent, was adequate.

Lancashire, looking for nothing more than a stimulating warm-up, did not enter the series with the same fierce competitiveness shown by Zimbabwe. They were without Patterson and Wasim Akram and never fielded their strongest side from the players available, but they were likeable and courteous opponents.

FIFTH ONE-DAY INTERNATIONAL – ZIMBABWE v. NEW ZEALAND YOUNG INTERNATIONALS
23 October 1988 at Harare Sports Club

NEW ZEALAND YOUNG INTERNATIONALS

Batsman	Dismissal	Runs
P.A. Horne	c Waller, b Rawson	26
T.J. Franklin	st Houghton, b Traicos	29
K.R. Rutherford	c Houghton, b Brandes	23
M.J. Greatbatch	c Duers, b Jarvis	47
R.H. Vance†	c Houghton, b Brandes	0
G.R. Larsen	c sub (Bruk-Jackson), b Butchart	34
T.E. Blain*	c Houghton, b Brandes	24
C.L. Cairns	c sub (Bruk-Jackson), b Brandes	12
S.W. Duff	c Houghton, b Brandes	7
W. Watson	not out	2
D.K. Morrison	not out	1
Extras	lb 11, w 6	17
(47 overs)	(for 9 wkts)	222

ZIMBABWE

Batsman	Dismissal	Runs
D.G. Goodwin	b Larsen	25
G.A. Paterson	c Horne, b Watson	8
C.M. Robertson	c Blain, b Morrison	38
D.L. Houghton*	run out	61
A.C. Waller	c Cairns, b Morrison	38
P.W.E. Rawson†	c Vance, b Watson	0
E.A. Brandes	run out	5
I.P. Butchart	not out	12
A.J. Traicos	not out	6
M.P. Jarvis		
K.G. Duers		
Extras	lb 7, w 14, nb 9	30
(45.2 overs)	(for 7 wkts)	223

Bowler	O	M	R	W
Rawson	10	3	25	1
Jarvis	8	–	47	1
Duers	8	–	59	–
Traicos	10	1	23	1
Brandes	9	–	47	5
Butchart	2	–	10	1

Bowler	O	M	R	W
Cairns	8	–	47	–
Watson	10	2	35	2
Morrison	9	–	37	2
Larsen	10	–	40	1
Duff	6	2	38	–
Rutherford	2.2	–	19	–

FALL OF WICKETS
1–50, 2–76, 3–89, 4–100, 5–147, 6–195, 7–201, 8–218, 9–219

FALL OF WICKETS
1–40, 2–43, 3–114, 4–190, 5–190, 6–202, 7–202

Umpires: R. Jackson & K. Kanjee

Zimbabwe won by 3 wickets

1 April 1989

at Harare South Country Club

Lancashire 188 for 8 (N.J. Speak 62)
Mashonaland Country Districts 159 for 6 (G.K. Bruk-Jackson 97 not out)

Mashonaland Country Districts won on faster scoring rate

Rain interrupted play in mid-afternoon and reduced the home side's overs from 50 to 36. Glen Bruk-Jackson dominated the game with an innings of 97 off 117 balls. Only Speak and Hughes mastered the Country Districts' bowling.

2 April 1989

at Harare Sports Club

Zimbabwe 198 (A.C. Waller 56, P.J.W. Allott 4 for 35)
Lancashire 131 (K.G. Duers 4 for 38)

Zimbabwe won by 67 runs

Put in to bat, Zimbabwe batted inconsistently, but their 198, although looking insufficient, proved too much for Lancashire, for whom only Jack Simmons, 26 not out off 18 balls, and David Hughes offered much resistance.

4, 5 and 6 April 1989

at Harare Sports Club

Lancashire 325 (N.H. Fairbrother 54, J.D. Fitton 52, W.K. Hegg 50, I. Folley 50, D.B. Lake 4 for 50) and 144 for 6 dec
Zimbabwe 'B' 198 (M. Watkinson 5 for 34) and 124 for 5 (I.D. Austin 4 for 19)

Match drawn

Lancashire struggled to 230 for 8, but fine innings by Hegg, Fitton and Folley rallied them. Only a determined sixth-wicket stand between Brent and James saved the follow-on for Zimbabwe, and, with Lancashire seemingly intent on batting practice, the match was drawn.

8, 10 and 11 April 1989

at Harare Sports Club

Lancashire 86 (P.W.E. Rawson 7 for 30) and 206 (G. Fowler 76)
Zimbabwe 275 (A.C. Waller 99, D.G. Goodwin 85, P.A.J. DeFreitas 4 for 73) and 19 for 0

Zimbabwe won by 10 wickets

The only first-class match of the tour was a complete triumph for Zimbabwe. With Butchart injured, Jon Brent was brought into the side to make his first-class debut after his fine performances for Zimbabwe 'B'.

Hughes won the toss, but he must have regretted his decision to bat first when Rawson, extracting a great deal of life and movement from the pitch, had Mendis caught in the slips off his first ball in the match. Fowler and Hayhurst struggled for survival, and once Fowler was taken at short-leg off Rawson with the score on 21, a collapse followed. By the end of his 13th over, Rawson had the remarkable figures of 4 for 8. Tiring, he conceded 13 runs in two overs, mainly to Warren Hegg, who added 42 for the sixth wicket with Hayhurst.

ABOVE: *A career-best 99 for Andy Waller against Lanca-shire. (David Munden)*
RIGHT: *An inspiring captain, Peter Rawson enjoyed a magnificent season as a bowler, capturing 30 first-class wickets at under 10 runs each. (Ken Kelly)*

Rawson returned for a second spell before lunch and dismissed Allott and Simmons. Traicos had already sent back Hegg and DeFreitas so that Lancashire were 78 for 9. Seven minutes after lunch, Rawson caught and bowled Folley and so improved on his career-best figures in first-class cricket achieved against the New Zealanders earlier in the season.

Zimbabwe struggled at the beginning of their innings with only a leg-bye and the wicket of Arnott on the score-board after eight overs. Goodwin found his touch and, aided by debutant left-hander Flower, added 86. Robertson and Houghton fell to successive balls and in identical fashion, padding up to DeFreitas, but Waller, first with Goodwin and then with Rawson, moved to his highest first-class score and was last man out when he hit high to cover in a desperate attempt to reach his century.

Lancashire, with the exception of Fowler, who batted for 326 minutes and was ninth out, offered little resistance as Zimbabwe moved inexorably to victory. Goodwin hit 4 fours as he scored all 19 that Zimbabwe needed to win off just 11 balls.

9 April 1989

at Harare Sports Club

Zimbabwe 236 for 7
Lancashire 228 for 8 (N.H. Fairbrother 85, T.E. Jesty 56)

Zimbabwe won by 8 runs

A consistently sound batting display took Zimbabwe to a good score. As long as Fairbrother was at the wicket, Lancashire had a chance of victory for he was in regal form. He was eventually caught on the long-on boundary, and although Simmons made an heroic effort to score 37 runs off the last 23 balls, Zimbabwe were not to be denied.

So ended an encouraging season, and Zimbabwe looked to the ICC to see how seriously their claim for Test status would be treated when they renewed their application.

The fear is that a further delay could prove counterproductive.

First-Class Averages

BATTING

	M	Inns	NOs	Runs	HS	Av	100s	50s
A.C. Waller	3	4	1	183	99	61.00		2
D.G. Goodwin	4	7	1	274	85	45.66		2
D.L. Houghton	4	6	1	222	90	44.40		2
R.D. Brown	3	4	1	96	74	32.00		1
P.W.E. Rawson	4	4		104	45	26.00		

(Qualification – 50 runs, average 10.00)

BOWLING

	Overs	Mds	Runs	Wkts	Av	Best	10/m	5/inns
P.W.E. Rawson	165.5	55	297	30	9.90	7/31	1	3
K.G. Duers	125	39	289	13	22.23	4/50		
A.J. Traicos	191.5	74	332	11	30.18	3/63		
E.A. Brandes	64.2	13	218	6	36.33	3/50		

(Qualification – 4 wickets)

LEADING FIELDERS

10 - R.D. Brown (ct 9/st 1); 8 - A.J. Traicos and D.G. Goodwin; 5 - P.W.E. Rawson; 4 - A.C. Waller

Golden Handshakes

The Champions' Trophy and the Sharjah Cup.
Cricket in the United Arab Emirates.

Double prize winner Saleem Malik of Pakistan.
(Adrian Murrell/Allsport)

Sharjah once again offered lucrative prizes and generous donations to beneficiaries, Mohsin Khan, Ravi Shastri, Munir Malik and Bhagwat Chandrasekhar as the United Arab Emirates staged the Champions' Trophy with Pakistan, India and West Indies as the participating teams. Each side was to play the others with the top team qualifying for the final and the other two sides competing in the semi-final for the right to meet them.

Champions' Trophy – Match One
INDIA v. WEST INDIES

Although without Richards and Marshall, the West Indies were otherwise at full strength, while Vengsarkar returned to lead India who had a side full of exciting young talent.

Put in to bat, India began sedately against Patterson and Ambrose and only 14 runs came from the first 10 overs. By the 19th over, both Sidhu and Amarnath were out with 42 scored, but Srikkanth was moving into top gear. He hit Harper for 3 sixes over long-on in one over, and his fourth century in one-day internationals came off 113 balls with 5 sixes and 10 fours. He had an attack of cramp and batted with a runner for the latter part of his innings. He shared a stand of 120 with Vengsarkar who hit a six and 6 fours in what was his 100th one-day international.

The leg-spin bowling of Hirwani proved as effective for India in one-day cricket as it had done in Test cricket. (Simon Bruty/Allsport)

CHAMPIONS' TROPHY – MATCH ONE – INDIA v. WEST INDIES
16 October 1988 at Sharjah Cricket Association Stadium

INDIA				WEST INDIES			
	K. Srikkanth	b Hooper	112		C.G. Greenidge†	c Kapil Dev, b Sharma	27
	N.S. Sidhu	c Dujon, b Patterson	3		D.L. Haynes	b Kapil Dev	87
	M.B. Amarnath	run out	7		R.B. Richardson	c Vengsarkar, b Hirwani	38
	D.B. Vengsarkar†	not out	76		C.L. Hooper	c More, b Hirwani	25
	R.N. Kapil Dev	c Logie, b Hooper	3		A.L. Logie	c Kapil Dev, b Hirwani	3
	R.J. Shastri	c Greenidge, b Hooper	17		P.J.L. Dujon*	b Hirwani	10
	M. Azharuddin	not out	5		R.A. Harper	b Sharma	4
	K.S. More*				C.E.L. Ambrose	not out	2
	S.K. Sharma				W.K.M. Benjamin	lbw, b Sharma	0
	Maninder Singh				C.A. Walsh	c Sidhu, b Sharma	2
	N.D. Hirwani				B.P. Patterson	b Sharma	2
	Extras	b 4, lb 5, w 5, nb 1	15		Extras	b 1, lb 12, w 2	15
	(50 overs)	(for 5 wkts)	238		(48.3 overs)		215

	O	M	R	W		O	M	R	W
Patterson	9	2	37	1	Kapil Dev	9	2	24	1
Ambrose	9	1	38	–	S.K. Sharma	7.3	–	26	5
Walsh	10	1	35	–	Shastri	10	–	41	–
Benjamin	10	–	49	–	Maninder Singh	10	–	50	–
Harper	5	–	38	–	Hirwani	10	1	50	4
Hooper	7	–	32	3	Srikkanth	2	–	11	–

FALL OF WICKETS
1–12, 2–42, 3–162, 4–170, 5–218

FALL OF WICKETS
1–42, 2–134, 3–142, 4–178, 5–192, 6–208, 7–210, 8–210, 9–212

Umpires: H.D. Bird & D.R. Shepherd

Man of the Match: K. Srikkanth

India won by 23 runs

Greenidge and Haynes gave West Indies a good start before Greenidge lofted Sharma to mid-off. This was the first of five wickets taken by Sanjeeva Sharma, but it was a splendid spell of leg-spin bowling by Hirwani which put India on top. Logie and Dujon slogged against the spin, and Hooper charged down the wicket and touched the ball to the keeper. Richardson, too, fell victim to the leg-spinner who thus became the first bowler to take four wickets in three successive one-day internationals.

Maninder and Shastri were less effective, but Kapil Dev bowled a fine, controlled spell, and in his seventh over Sanjeeva Sharma took three wickets. He bowled Patterson in his next over to give India victory, and he had taken the last four wickets in nine balls for two runs.

Champions' Trophy – Match Two
PAKISTAN v. WEST INDIES

Fresh from their victory over Australia in Lahore and showing no signs of jet lag, Pakistan, having been put in to bat, made the highest score recorded in the Sharjah Stadium with some consistently aggressive batting. Mudassar was in particularly fine form and hit 6 fours in his 64, which came off 100 balls. Rameez Raja's 64 came off 84 balls, and the pair gave Pakistan a scintillating start with a stand of 113. Javed and Saleem Malik maintained the momentum, Javed hitting 3 sixes and 3 fours in his 68-ball innings, and Saleem clouting a six and 4 fours in his 42 off 37 deliveries.

Pakistan set a pace which West Indies could never match, especially after Wasim Akram had reduced them to 24 for 3 with a fine opening spell. In his 100th one-day international, Greenidge opted for batting practice and laboured to his 10th hundred in this form of international cricket.

Champions' Trophy – Match Three
PAKISTAN v. INDIA

Put in to bat, Pakistan began uncertainly when Rameez Raja fell to Sharma in the second over of the match. Mudassar Nazar was the next to go, the first of four Pakistani batsmen to be run out, but Saleem Malik was in his very best form, and he and Javed added 126 for the third wicket. Javed, in particular, swept the Indian spinners much as Gooch had done in the World Cup semi-final 12 months earlier, but it was Saleem Malik who took the batting honours with his highest score in limited-over internationals.

Well as Pakistan had scored, the target that faced India

Champions' Trophys Final League Table

	P	W	L	Pts	R/R
Pakistan	2	2	–	4	5.4
India	2	1	1	2	4.5
West Indies	2	–	2	0	4.3

CHAMPIONS' TROPHY – MATCH TWO – PAKISTAN v. WEST INDIES
18 October 1988 at Sharjah Cricket Association Stadium

PAKISTAN				WEST INDIES			
Mudassar Nazar	st Dujon, b Hooper	64		C.G. Greenidge†	not out		102
Rameez Raja	st Dujon, b Harper	64		D.L. Haynes	c and b Wasim Akram		1
Javed Miandad†	c Hooper, b Walsh	79		R.B. Richardson	c Javed Miandad, b Wasim		6
Saleem Malik	c Dujon, b Patterson	42		C.L. Hooper	c Saleem Yousuf, b Wasim		0
Ijaz Ahmed	c Patterson, b Ambrose	16		A.L. Logie	run out		12
Manzoor Elahi	c Bishop, b Ambrose	12		P.J.L. Dujon*	c Wasim Akram, b Mudassar		37
Wasim Akram	not out	2		R.A. Harper	not out		22
Saleem Yousuf*	not out	0		C.E.L. Ambrose			
Shoaib Mohammad				C.A. Walsh			
Abdul Qadir				B.P. Patterson			
Tauseef Ahmed				I.R. Bishop			
Extras	b 2, lb 8, w 3, nb 2	15		Extras	b 1, lb 17, w 2, nb 10		30
(50 overs)	(for 6 wkts)	294		(50 overs)	(for 5 wkts)		210

	O	M	R	W
Patterson	8	–	72	1
Ambrose	9	3	41	2
Walsh	7	–	36	1
Bishop	6	–	47	–
Harper	10	–	40	1
Hooper	10	–	48	1

	O	M	R	W
Wasim Akram	9	–	37	3
Manzoor Elahi	10	–	40	–
Tauseef Ahmed	10	–	21	–
Mudassar Nazar	10	–	48	1
Abdul Qadir	10	–	35	–
Javed Miandad	1	–	11	–

FALL OF WICKETS
1–113, 2–153, 3–252, 4–278, 5–281, 6–294

FALL OF WICKETS
1–12, 2–24, 3–24, 4–74, 5–146

Umpires: H.D. Bird & D.R. Shepherd

Man of the Match: Wasim Akram

Pakistan won by 84 runs

was by no means an impossible one. Their failure was due in part to the fact that Dilip Vengsarkar took 71 balls to make 51 and could never find his touch, while Azharuddin, Sidhu and Shastri played some exotic and attractive shots, but failed to work the singles that would have kept the score moving at the necessary rate.

Champions' Trophy – Semi-Final
INDIA v. WEST INDIES

Electing to bat first on a perfect wicket, India gave a poor display, and their 169 for 7 never looked likely to offer West Indies any problems. Ambrose and Patterson gained considerable lift, which negated quick scoring early on, and Walsh produced a fine spell of bowling in which he moved the ball appreciably and took the wickets of Amarnath and Vengsarkar. Shastri looked the soundest of the Indian batsmen until he swung Harper into the hands of Logie, and it was left to Pandit and More to bat in a way which put the earlier batsmen to shame.

An opening partnership of 165 between Greenidge and

Mudassar Nazar shared a century opening partnership for Pakistan against West Indies with Rameez Raja, 18 October. The veteran is still a most accomplished all-rounder. (George Herringshaw)

CHAMPIONS' TROPHY – MATCH THREE – INDIA v. PAKISTAN
19 October 1988 at Sharjah Cricket Association Stadium

PAKISTAN				INDIA			
Mudassar Nazar	run out		11		K. Srikkanth	lbw, b Wasim Akram	19
Rameez Raja	c Maninder Singh, b Sharma		2		N.S. Sidhu	run out	38
Saleem Malik	c More, b Maninder Singh		101		M.B. Amarnath	run out	15
Javed Miandad†	run out		52		D.B. Vengsarkar†	c Javed Miandad, b Wasim Akram	51
Abdul Qadir	c Kapil Dev, b Maninder Singh		1		M. Azharuddin	c Saleem Malik, b Abdul Qadir	26
Wasim Akram	b Maninder Singh		2		R.J. Shastri	c sub (Shoaib), b Saleem Jaffer	33
Ijaz Ahmed	c Azharuddin, b Kapil Dev		26		R.N. Kapil Dev	c Manzoor Elahi, b Saleem Jaffer	3
Manzoor Elahi	run out		9		S.K. Sharma	not out	8
Saleem Yousuf*	c Hirwani, b Kapil Dev		25		K.S. More*	c sub (Shoaib), b Saleem Jaffer	2
Tauseef Ahmed	run out		2		Maninder Singh	not out	6
Saleem Jaffer	not out		0		N.D. Hirwani		
Extras	lb 11, w 1, nb 3		15		Extras	lb 5, w 4, nb 2	11
(49.1 overs)			246		(50 overs)	(for 8 wkts)	212

	O	M	R	W		O	M	R	W
Kapil Dev	9.1	2	31	2	Wasim Akram	10	1	39	2
S.K. Sharma	8	–	51	1	Saleem Jaffer	9	–	37	3
Amarnath	5	–	20	–	Manzoor Elahi	3	–	22	–
Maninder Singh	10	–	47	3	Mudassar Nazar	10	–	38	–
Shastri	10	–	45	–	Tauseef Ahmed	10	–	37	–
Hirwani	7	–	41	–	Abdul Qadir	8	–	34	1

FALL OF WICKETS
1–3, 2–41, 3–167, 4–171, 5–179, 6–180, 7–200, 8–229, 9–239

FALL OF WICKETS
1–40, 2–70, 3–75, 4–132, 5–183, 6–196, 7–196, 8–201

Umpires: H.D. Bird & D.R. Shepherd

Man of the Match: Saleem Malik

Pakistan won by 34 runs

Haynes, aided by a couple of missed chances, put the issue beyond doubt, and West Indies won with 10 overs to spare. So they entered the final even though they had lost their first two matches.

Champions' Trophy – Final
PAKISTAN v. WEST INDIES

Sent in to bat, West Indies made the quickest start of the tournament as Greenidge and Haynes put up the fifty in 60 balls. The fall of three wickets slowed the run rate, but Keith Arthurton, making his one-day international début at the expense of Gus Logie, and Carl Hooper added a valuable 67 for the fourth wicket. The elegant Hooper reached 62 off 71 deliveries, and with Dujon and Harper plundering well, West Indies reached a commendable, but not unbeatable, 235.

Curtley Ambrose began at a fiery pace and bowled both Pakistan openers with only 20 scored. When Shoaib fell to Walsh at 49, Pakistan looked well beaten, but, inevitably, it was Javed who rallied them. Batting with a great sense of responsibility, and curbing his naturally aggressive tendencies, he hit only one four in his fifty which he reached off 74 balls as he and Saleem Malik added 79 in 17 overs. Saleem Malik fell to Hooper, and Ijaz Ahmed, after a brief flurry, became Bishop's first victim. With 10 overs remaining and five wickets in hand, Pakistan needed 64 to

Man of the Series in the Champions' Trophy – Gordon Greenidge, West Indies. (Gray Mortimore/Allsport)

CHAMPIONS' TROPHY – SEMI-FINAL – INDIA v. WEST INDIES
21 October 1988 at Sharjah Cricket Association Stadium

INDIA

K. Srikkanth	c Dujon, b Ambrose	6
R.J. Shastri	c Logie, b Harper	35
M.B. Amarnath	c Dujon, b Walsh	20
D.B. Vengsarkar†	b Walsh	3
M. Azharuddin	c Harper, b Hooper	25
R.N. Kapil Dev	c Greenidge, b Hooper	0
C.S. Pandit	not out	31
K.S. More*	c Logie, b Ambrose	30
S.K. Sharma	not out	13
Maninder Singh		
N.D. Hirwani		
Extras	b 2, lb 4	6
(50 overs)	(for 7 wkts)	169

WEST INDIES

C.G. Greenidge†	not out	77
D.L. Haynes	b Sharma	85
R.B. Richardson	c More, b Sharma	0
C.L. Hooper	not out	2
A.L. Logie		
P.J.L. Dujon*		
R.A. Harper		
C.E.L. Ambrose		
C.A. Walsh		
I.R. Bishop		
B.P. Patterson		
Extras	lb 6, w 1, nb 4	11
(40 overs)	(for 2 wkts)	175

	O	M	R	W
Patterson	9	–	39	–
Ambrose	9	2	31	2
Walsh	6	–	19	2
Bishop	6	–	13	–
Harper	10	–	28	1
Hooper	10	1	33	2

	O	M	R	W
Kapil Dev	4	–	14	–
S.K. Sharma	6	–	25	2
Maninder Singh	10	–	32	–
Shastri	6	–	31	–
Hirwani	10	–	49	–
Srikkanth	4	–	18	–

FALL OF WICKETS
1–16, 2–41, 3–45, 4–85, 5–86, 6–93, 7–144

FALL OF WICKETS
1–165, 2–165

Umpires: H.D. Bird & D.R. Shepherd

Man of the Match: D.L. Haynes

West Indies won by 8 wickets

CHAMPIONS' TROPHY – FINAL – PAKISTAN v. WEST INDIES
22 October 1988 at Sharjah Cricket Association Stadium

WEST INDIES			
C.G. Greenidge†	c Manzoor Elahi, b Mudassar		37
D.L. Haynes	c Saleem Malik, b Shoaib		45
R.B. Richardson	b Abdul Qadir		2
C.L. Hooper	c Ijaz Ahmed, b Abdul Qadir		62
K.L.T. Arthurton	c Saleem Yousuf, b Wasim Akram		27
P.J.L. Dujon*	not out		21
R.A. Harper	c Abdul Qadir, b Tauseef Ahmed		16
C.E.L. Ambrose	not out		3
C.A. Walsh			
B.P. Patterson			
I.R. Bishop			
Extras	b 3, lb 10, w 3, nb 6		22
(50 overs)	(for 6 wkts)		235

PAKISTAN			
Mudassar Nazar	b Ambrose		9
Rameez Raja	b Ambrose		4
Shoaib Mohammad	c Bishop, b Walsh		15
Javed Miandad†	b Ambrose		76
Saleem Malik	c Harper, b Hooper		38
Ijaz Ahmed	lbw, b Bishop		17
Manzoor Elahi	b Patterson		33
Saleem Yousuf*	run out		0
Wasim Akram	b Ambrose		1
Abdul Qadir	b Bishop		10
Tauseef Ahmed	not out		0
Extras	b 1, lb 13, w 5, nb 2		21
(49.4 overs)			224

	O	M	R	W
Wasim Akram	10	–	45	1
Manzoor Elahi	3	–	20	–
Mudassar Nazar	10	–	41	1
Abdul Qadir	10	–	41	2
Tauseef Ahmed	10	–	49	1
Shoaib Mohammad	7	–	26	1

	O	M	R	W
Patterson	8	–	40	1
Ambrose	10	–	29	4
Walsh	10	–	42	1
Bishop	8.4	–	38	2
Harper	6	–	26	–
Hooper	7	–	35	1

FALL OF WICKETS
1–74, 2–79, 3–118, 4–185, 5–190, 6–228

FALL OF WICKETS
1–8, 2–20, 3–49, 4–128, 5–159, 6–192, 7–192, 8–202, 9–218

Umpires: H.D. Bird (Fareed Malik) & D.R. Shepherd

Man of the Match: C.E.L. Ambrose

West Indies won by 11 runs

win, and at 189 for 5 in the 43rd over, Pakistan were as West Indies had been at the same stage. In the next over, Javed, having played impeccably for 116 balls, was bowled by the towering Ambrose. Later the same over, Saleem Yousuf was run out, and the Pakistan slide had begun.

Umpire Bird had retired with heat exhaustion, and local umpire Fareed Malik deputized as David Shepherd took the major role at each end. When Wasim Akram was bowled by Ambrose three wickets had fallen for 10 runs, but still Pakistan had a chance of victory. It vanished when Patterson bowled Manzoor Elahi, and 18 from the last over with the last pair at the wicket was beyond even Abdul Qadir's bravery.

The West Indians took home 30,000 US dollars as first prize, Pakistan 20,000 and India 15,000. Each Man of the Match won 500 dollars and Gordon Greenidge, who scored 243 runs, average 121.50 in the competition, claimed the Man-of-the-Series prize and 2,500 dollars. The beneficiaries were awarded 50,000 and 15,000 dollars. Cricket in Sharjah is a lucrative business.

Sharjah Cup – Match One
PAKISTAN v. SRI LANKA

With India and West Indies engaged in a Test series in the Caribbean, Australia declining an invitation because of the coming tour of England, and England withdrawing when they believed they would be playing in New Zealand, the Sharjah Cricket Association was left with two nations, Pakistan and Sri Lanka, to compete for the Sharjah Cup. Two matches were arranged on successive days and, as ever, capacity crowds flocked to see them. Sri Lanka recalled Roy Dias to their party, but he did not appear in either match.

Ranatunga won the toss and asked Pakistan to bat first. A second-wicket stand of 127 between Shoaib Mohammad and Saleem Malik gave substance to the Pakistan innings, although the later batsmen failed to capitalize on a strong position as well as might have been expected, and the score of 237 for 8 was something of a disappointment after such a strong start.

Sri Lanka, however, could find no one to play the innings of length and power that was necessary if they were to win the match in spite of the fact that Abdul Qadir, who, as the main beneficiary, received 50,000 United States dollars from the tournament, had to retire hurt after bowling 4.3 overs. He damaged his hand in attempting to take a return catch.

Most impressive were debutant pace bowler Mushtaq Ahmed and young Aaqib Javed. Mushtaq's two wickets tilted the game in favour of Pakistan, and Aaqib bowled with great economy.

Brave batting for Sri Lanka by Brendon Kuruppu in the Sharjah Cup. (Patrick Eagar)

Sharjah Cup – Match Two
PAKISTAN v. SRI LANKA

Sri Lanka gave an international début to Nilantha Ratnayake, and the new pace bowler was to give his side hope of victory when he bowled Rameez Raja with Pakistan's score on 18. Aamer Malik also went quickly, so that Pakistan faced a stiff task in overhauling Sri Lanka's 244, a score built on consistently enterprising and aggressive batting.

It was Shoaib Mohammad and Saleem Malik who once again proved to be the scourge of Sri Lanka. They added 102 to put Pakistan back on course, and Imran then joined Saleem. On the third ball of the 45th over, Saleem flicked Ravi Ratnayeke to leg to take the score to 215 and so ensure the Cup for Pakistan, and, by the beginning of the 48th over, Pakistan had reached 235 with Saleem on 99. After a few anxious moments he took the single off Nilantha Ratnayake to reach his hundred, and Imran then

---

SHARJAH CUP – MATCH ONE – PAKISTAN v. SRI LANKA
23 March 1989 at Sharjah Cricket Association Stadium

PAKISTAN				SRI LANKA			
Rameez Raja	b J.R. Ratnayeke	13		R.S. Mahanama	c Mushtaq Ahmed, b Aaqib Javed	14
Shoaib Mohammad	st Kuruppu, b Ranatunga	76		D.S.B.P. Kuruppu*	b Mushtaq Ahmed	22
Saleem Malik	st Kuruppu, b E.A.R. de Silva	71		M.A.R. Samarasekera	lbw, b Imran Khan	7
Imran Khan†	b E.A.R. de Silva	16		P.A. de Silva	c and b Mushtaq Ahmed	48
Ijaz Ahmed	b Ranatunga	18		A. Ranatunga†	c Saleem Malik, b Jaffer	23
Aamer Malik*	run out	14		L.R.D. Mendis	c sub (Mansoor Rana), b Jaffer	17
Abdul Qadir	b Labrooy	7		H.P. Tillekeratne	b Imran Khan	26
Mushtaq Ahmed	c Kuruppu, b J.R. Ratnayeke	0		J.R. Ratnayeke	run out	8
Tauseef Ahmed	not out	6		G.F. Labrooy	b Tauseef Ahmed	7
Saleem Jaffer	not out	10		E.A.R. de Silva	not out	19
Aaqib Javed				K.I.W. Wijegunawardene	b Aaqib Javed	0
Extras	lb 3, w 2, nb 1	6		Extras	b 4, lb 8, w 3, nb 1	16
(50 overs)	(for 8 wkts)	237		(48.4 overs)		207

	O	M	R	W		O	M	R	W
J.R. Ratnayeke	10	–	31	2	Imran Khan	8	–	31	2
Labrooy	8	–	41	1	Aaqib Javed	6.4	–	15	2
E.A.R. de Silva	10	–	47	2	Abdul Qadir	4.3	–	15	–
Wijegunawardene	4	–	21	–	Saleem Jaffer	10	–	50	2
P.A. de Silva	3	–	19	–	Tauseef Ahmed	10	–	51	1
Samarasekera	5	–	28	–	Mushtaq Ahmed	9.3	1	33	2
Ranatunga	10	–	47	2					

FALL OF WICKETS
1–31, 2–158, 3–174, 4–183, 5–201, 6–221, 7–221, 8–221

FALL OF WICKETS
1–18, 2–29, 3–82, 4–109, 5–141, 6–148, 7–162, 8–175, 9–206

Umpires: V.K. Ramaswamy & R.B. Gupta

Man of the Match: Shoaib Mohammad

Pakistan won by 30 runs

cracked successive boundaries to bring himself a deserved fifty and Pakistan the match.

Saleem Malik took the generous monetary awards as Man of the Match and Man of the Series.

Abdulrehman Bukhatir announced that Pakistan, India, England and West Indies had been invited to compete for the Champions' Trophy in October 1989. Iqbal Qasim, Fazal Mahmood, Srikkanth and M.J. Gopalan are to be the beneficiaries.

SHARJAH CUP – MATCH TWO – PAKISTAN v. SRI LANKA
24 March 1989 at Sharjah Cricket Association Stadium

SRI LANKA			
R.S. Mahanama	b Shoaib Mohammad		35
D.S.B.P. Kuruppu*	st Saleem Yousuf, b Shoaib Mohammad		63
P.A. de Silva	run out		60
M.A.R. Samara-sekera	c Aamer Malik, b Saleem Jaffer		15
A. Ranatunga†	c Aaqib Javed, b Imran Khan		20
L.R.D. Mendis	run out		10
G.F. Labrooy	b Imran Khan		0
H.P. Tillekeratne	not out		10
J.R. Ratnayeke	c Mushtaq Ahmed, b Imran Khan		18
E.A.R. de Silva			
N.L.K. Ratnayake			
Extras	lb 11, w 2		13
(50 overs)	(for 8 wkts)		244

	O	M	R	W
Imran Khan	10	–	49	3
Aaqib Javed	9	–	32	–
Saleem Jaffer	7	–	36	1
Tauseef Ahmed	8	–	39	–
Shoaib Mohammad	10	–	42	2
Mushtaq Ahmed	6	–	35	–

FALL OF WICKETS
1–74, 2–127, 3–157, 4–197, 5–211, 6–211, 7–219, 8–244

PAKISTAN			
Rameez Raja	b N.L.K. Ratnayake		5
Shoaib Mohammad	c Tillekeratne, b J.R. Ratnayeke		65
Aamer Malik	b E.A.R. de Silva		20
Saleem Malik	not out		100
Imran Khan†	not out		50
Ijaz Ahmed			
Saleem Yousuf*			
Mushtaq Ahmed			
Tauseef Ahmed			
Saleem Jaffer			
Aaqib Javed			
Extras	b 1, lb 5, w 1, nb 1		8
(47.5 overs)	(for 3 wkts)		248

	O	M	R	W
J.R. Ratnayeke	9	–	35	1
N.L.K. Ratnayake	9.5	–	59	1
E.A.R. de Silva	10	–	38	1
Labrooy	6	–	42	–
Samarasekera	2	–	15	–
Ranatunga	9	–	42	–
P.A. de Silva	2	–	11	–

FALL OF WICKETS
1–18, 2–46, 3–148

Umpires: V.K. Ramaswamy & R.B. Gupta

Man of the Match: Saleem Malik

Pakistan won by 7 wickets

Victory Parade

The season in the West Indies.
Red Stripe Cup.
India *v.* West Indies,
One-Day series and Test series.
First-class averages.
Form charts.

Richie Richardson. Man of the Series against India, he is slowly donning the mantle of Viv Richards. (Adrian Murrell/Allsport)

Once again the domestic season in West Indies began with the leading players in action overseas. Nevertheless, the Red Stripe Cup again excited great interest and gave the opportunity to several players to re-establish their claims for Test recognition.

Guystac Trophy

19, 20, 21 and 22 October 1988

at Bourda, Georgetown, Guyana

Demerara 163 for 1 (S.N. Mohammed 79, N. McKenzie 53 not out)
v. Berbice

Match abandoned

Only 58.1 overs on the first day were possible in the Guystac Trophy match.

Red Stripe Cup

20, 21, 22 and 23 January 1989

at Guaracara Park, Pointe-à-Pierre, Trinidad

Trinidad and Tobago 310 (B.C. Lara 127, M.P. Carew 56, K.A. Williams 51) and 86 (C.G. Butts 4 for 18, L.A. Joseph 4 for 43)
Guyana 185 (S. Dhaniram 54, R. Dhanraj 5 for 69) and 213 for 5 (A.F.D. Jackman 106 not out)

Guyana won by 5 wickets
Guyana 16 pts, Trinidad and Tobago 5 pts

The opening match of the Red Stripe tournament saw Guyana effect a remarkable recovery to win comfortably after trailing by 125 runs on the first innings. Brian Lara and Kelvin Williams put on 120 for the home side's third wicket to put them well in control, and Lara's hundred included 15 fours and was made off 277 balls. Guyana succumbed to the leg-break bowling of Rajindra Dhanraj, who returned the best figures of his brief career. Pace bowler Linden Joseph also returned a career-best performance as he and Clyde Butts shot out Trinidad in 32.1 overs in their second innings. Andrew Jackman, who added 130 for the fifth wicket with Sheikh Mohammed, guided Guyana to a fine win.

26, 27, 28 and 29 January 1989

at Mindoo Phillip Park, Castries, St Lucia

Leeward Islands 239 for 9
v. Windward Islands

Match abandoned
Windward Islands 4 pts, Leeward Islands 4 pts

27, 28, 29 and 30 January 1989

at Kensington Oval, Bridgetown, Barbados

Barbados 289 (A.L. Grant 88, L.K. Puckerin 79, R. Dhanraj 6 for 75, R. Nanan 4 for 65) and 287 for 5 dec (C.A. Best 157 not out, M.H.W. Inniss 64)
Trinidad and Tobago 272 (B.C. Lara 77, E. Jordan 4 for 53) and 203 (D.I. Mohammed 87 not out, M.A. Small 6 for 55)

Barbados won by 101 runs
Barbados 16 pts, Trinidad and Tobago 0 pts

28, 29, 30 and 31 January 1989

at Sabina Park, Kingston, Jamaica

Jamaica 338 (D.S. Morgan 122, C.A. Davidson 57 not out, B. St A. Browne 4 for 75)
Guyana 144 (N.O. Perry 4 for 35) and 145 (N.O. Perry 8 for 45)

Jamaica won by an innings and 49 runs
Jamaica 16 pts, Guyana 0 pts

There was limited play on the first and last days in Castries and no play at all on the second and third days.

In Bridgetown, in spite of Dhanraj bettering his career-best performance of the opening match, Trinidad suffered their second defeat. Carlisle Best and Michael Inniss began Barbados' second innings with a stand of 148, which put the home side in control of the match. This was followed by some excellent pace bowling from Milton Small, who had virtually disappeared from first-class cricket after being a member of the West Indian side in England in 1984. Having recovered from injury, he showed that he had lost none of his fire and bowled Barbados to an emphatic victory.

Delroy Morgan hit the second century of his career to help Jamaica to a substantial first-innings score at Sabina Park, but the honours of the game went to Nehemiah Perry, who took 12 for 80 in the match with his off-breaks. His second-innings figures of 28.4–11–45–8 represented the best bowling of his career.

3, 4, 5 and 6 February 1989

at Kensington Oval, Bridgetown, Barbados

Windward Islands 231 (D.A. Joseph 128) and 284 (L.D. John 67, D.A. Joseph 52, G.L. Linton 5 for 78)
Barbados 366 (C.A. Best 136, T.R.O. Payne 70, T.Z. Kentish 5 for 110) and 151 for 2 (M.H.W. Inniss 68 not out)

Barbados won by 8 wickets
Barbados 16 pts, Windward Islands 0 pts

at Sabina Park, Kingston, Jamaica

Jamaica 523 for 9 dec (C.A. Davidson 200 not out, D.S. Morgan 111, M.A. Tucker 61)
Leeward Islands 243 (R.M. Otto 67, N.O. Perry 5 for 74) and 250 (A.L. Kelly 77, R.M. Otto 74, N.O. Perry 4 for 66)

Jamaica won by an innings and 30 runs
Jamaica 16 pts, Leeward Islands 0 pts

Second wins for both Barbados and Jamaica placed them well ahead in the race for the Red Stripe Cup. Dawnley Joseph hit the highest score of his career, but Carlisle Best scored his second century in as many matches and added 108 for the third wicket with Thelston Payne, who had relinquished wicket-keeping duties to concentrate on his batting. Barbados took a first-innings lead of 105, and George Linton's leg-break and googly bowling kept them on top.

Like Carlisle Best, Delroy Morgan hit his second century in successive matches, but the Man of the Match in Kingston was Cleveland Davidson, who reached the first double century of his career in 421 minutes. He hit 20

Carlisle Best flexes his muscles. He hit centuries in success-ive Red Stripe Cup matches for Barbados. (Adrian Murrell/Allsport)

fours. Perry was again in splendid form with his off-breaks as Jamaica swept to victory.

10, 11, 12 and 13 February 1989

at Grove Park, Nevis

Leeward Islands 219 (L.L. Harris 68 not out) and 148 (R. Dhanraj 5 for 58)
Trinidad and Tobago 67 (E.A.E. Baptiste 6 for 26) and 114 (E.A.E. Baptiste 5 for 42)

Leeward Islands won by 186 runs
Leeward Islands 16 pts, Trinidad and Tobago 0 pts

at Bourda, Georgetown, Guyana

Guyana 238 for 1 dec (C.B. Lambert 105 not out, S. Dhaniram 93)
Barbados 65 for 1

Match abandoned
Guyana 4 pts, Barbados 4 pts

11, 12, 13, and 14 February 1989

at Sabina Park, Kingston, Jamaica

Jamaica 384 (A.G. Daley 79, D.S. Morgan 70, M.C. Neita 55, I.A. Allen 5 for 102) and 223 for 5 dec (W.W. Lewis 103, W.W. Thomas 4 for 73)
Windward Islands 334 (L.C. Sebastien 91, N.O. Perry 4 for 91) and 104 for 2 (L.D. John 63 not out)

Match drawn
Jamaica 8 pts, Windward Islands 4 pts

While rain restricted play in Guyana to two days, and no result could be obtained, Jamaica had the better of a draw with Windward Islands and moved ahead of Barbados in the Red Stripe Cup. Morgan and Perry again performed well for Jamaica, and Wayne Lewis hit the third century of his career, but runs never came quickly and a draw always looked probable.

Dhanraj once more spun his leg-breaks to great effect, but he could not save Trinidad and Tobago from crashing to another big defeat. They were twice routed by Eldine Baptiste, who had match figures of 11 for 68, and Leeward Islands won in three days.

17, 18, 19 and 20 February 1989

at Recreation Ground, St John's, Antigua

Leeward Islands 207 (K.L.T. Arthurton 85, M.A. Small 4 for 32) and 155 for 9
Barbados 205 (C.A. Best 53, E.A.E. Baptiste 5 for 46)

Match drawn
Leeward Islands 8 pts, Barbados 4 pts

at Bourda, Georgetown, Guyana

Windward Islands 133 (C.G. Butts 4 for 36) and 237 (J.J. Pierre 54)
Guyana 252 for 8 dec (A.F.D. Jackman 71, C.B. Lambert 57, S. Dhaniram 52) and 121 for 4

Guyana won by 6 wickets
Guyana 16 pts, Windward Islands 0 pts

18, 19, 20 and 21 February 1989

at Guaracara Park, Pointe-à-Pierre, Trinidad

Jamaica 261 (J.C. Adams 63, C.A. Davidson 63, M.A. Tucker 52) and 71 (I.R. Bishop 6 for 41, A.H. Gray 4 for 29)
Trinidad and Tobago 256 (R. Nanan 56, R.C. Haynes 4 for 76) and 77 for 0

Trinidad and Tobago won by 10 wickets
Trinidad and Tobago 16 pts, Jamaica 5 pts

Barbados were once again unlucky as the first day's play in Antigua was lost. Arthurton, one of several Test players to be available for this penultimate round of matches, rallied Leeward Islands after four men had gone for 69. Eldine Baptiste was once more in devastating form, and nine Barbados wickets fell for 178. Milton Small, who had bowled splendidly, and Jordan added 27 and looked likely to take their side to first-innings points, but Small was leg before to Ferris when Barbados were still two short of the Leeward total. After that, time was against Barbados, and they could earn only the four points from the drawn match.

Barbados 1989
First-Class Matches

BATTING

BATTING	v. Trinidad & Tobago (Bridgetown) 27–30 January	v. Windward Islands (Bridgetown) 3–6 February	v. Guyana (Bourda) 10–13 February	v. Leeward Islands (St John's) 17–20 February	v. Jamaica (Bridgetown) 24–7 February	M	Inns	NOs	Runs	HS	Av
C.A. Best	42 157*	136 22	5 —	53 —	7 —	5	7	1	422	157*	70.33
M.H.W. Inniss	31 64	27 68*	27* —			3	5	2	217	68*	72.33
R.I.C. Holder	11 0	19 36	26* —	15 —		4	6	1	107	36	21.40
T.R.O. Payne	14 32	70 17*	— —	0 —	53 —	5	6	1	186	70	37.20
A.L. Grant	88 6*	32 —	— —	25 —	0 —	5	5	1	151	88	37.75
L.K. Puckerin	79 —	25 —	— —	9 —		4	3	—	113	79	37.66
A.C. Cummins	5 20	4 —				2	3	—	29	20	9.66
H.W. daC. Springer	2 —	19 —				2	2	—	21	19	10.50
A.L. Johnson	1 1	9 —	— —			3	3	—	11	9	3.66
M.A. Small	8 —	1 —	— —	15 —	7 —	5	4	—	31	15	7.75
E. Jordan	1* —			24* —	1 —	4	3	2	26	24*	26.00
G.L. Linton		7* —	— —	30 —	24 —	4	3	1	61	30	30.50
J.V. Harris			— —	4 —		2	1	—	4	4	4.00
M.L. Sealy				5 —	6 —	2	2	—	11	6	5.50
V. deC. Walcott				6 —	5* —	2	2	1	11	6	11.00
C.G. Greenidge					0 —	1	1	—	0	0	0.00
D.L. Haynes					82 —	1	1	—	82	82	82.00
M.D. Marshall					89 —	1	1	—	89	89	89.00
Byes		1 1		9	9						
Leg-byes	1 4	6 2	1	6	6						
Wides					2						
No-balls	6 3	10 5	6	4	23						
Total	289 287	366 151	65	205	314						
Wickets	10 5	10 2	1	10	10						
Result	W	W	Ab.	D	D						
Points	16	16	4	4	8						

Fielding Figures
13– L.K. Puckerin (ct 12/st 1)
9– C.A. Best
7– T.R.O. Payne (ct 6/st 1)
5– A.L. Grant
3– M.H.W. Inniss, G.L. Linton and M.A. Small
1– H.W. daC. Springer, A.C. Cummins,
A.L. Johnson, E. Jordan, J.V. Harris,
V. deC. Walcott, R.I.C. Holder, C.G.
Greenidge and sub (Harrison)

BOWLING

BOWLING	M.A. Small	E. Jordan	A.C. Cummins	A.L. Johnson	H.W. daC. Springer	C.A. Best	G.L. Linton	J.V. Harris
v. Trinidad & Tobago (Bridgetown) 27–30 January	23–4–53–1 / 20–3–55–6	22–7–53–4 / 11.2–3–34–1	18–1–64–1 / 15–4–41–2	17.5–4–32–1 / 6–3–7–0	19–2–65–3 / 12–1–44–1	10–3–18–0		
v. Windward Islands (Bridgetown) 3–6 February	17–0–68–2 / 23–7–51–2		9–0–33–1 / 10–2–26–0	10–2–42–3 / 29–5–76–1	10.3–1–32–3	16–4–43–2	13–2–51–1 / 32.2–4–78–5	
v. Guyana (Bourda) 10–14 February	9–0–18–0	9–0–53–0		10–1–33–1		6–2–22–0	11–0–35–0	26–2–65–0
v. Leeward Islands (St John's) 17–20 February	15.4–4–32–4 / 11–1–45–2	13–1–39–0 / 3–2–2–0				2–0–6–1	19–1–71–3 / 14–1–42–3	4–0–9–0 / 3–2–2–0
v. Jamaica (Bridgetown) 24–7 February	16–2–51–0 / 26–4–68–3	12.5–3–31–2 / 23–3–52–1				2–0–13–0 / 19.4–2–41–1	27–6–80–5 / 44–16–92–1	
	160.4–25– 441–20 av. 22.05	94.1–19– 264–8 av. 33.00	52–7– 164–4 av. 41.00	72.5–15– 190–6 av. 31.66	41.3–4– 141–7 av. 20.14	55.4–11– 143–4 av. 35.75	160.2–30– 449–18 av. 24.94	33–4– 76–0 —

A return to form and to international cricket for Eldine Baptiste of Leeward Islands. (Tony Edenden)

Meanwhile, Jamaica were taking five points for their narrow first-innings lead over Trinidad, who brought about a remarkable reversal to win the match in three days. Jamaica were routed in their second innings by Ian Bishop and Tony Gray. The visitors were all out in 17.2 overs, and Trinidad reached their meagre target in exactly the same number of overs. Bishop finished with match figures of 9 for 90 and Gray, named Man of the Match, had 7 for 93.

Guyana kept alive their faint hopes of winning the title by beating Windward Islands. They owed much to Lambert and Dhaniram, who gave their innings a sound foundation with an opening stand of 103.

24, 25, 26 and 27 February 1989

at Kensington Oval, Bridgetown, Barbados

Jamaica 287 (D.S. Morgan 99, G.L. Linton 5 for 80) and 331 for 8 (P.J.L. Dujon 64, J.C. Adams 55, M.A. Tucker 52 not out)
Barbados 314 (M.D. Marshall 89, D.L. Haynes 82, T.R.O. Payne 53)

Match drawn
Barbados 8 pts, Jamaica 4 pts

25, 26, 27 and 28 February 1989

at Bourda, Georgetown, Guyana

Leeward Islands 419 (K.L.T. Arthurton 154, R.M. Otto 116, L.A. Joseph 4 for 91) and 415 (E.A.E. Baptiste 95, W.K.M. Benjamin 85, K.L.T. Arthurton 62)
Guyana 415 (R. Seeram 96, S. Dhaniram 71, R.A. Harper 51, E.A.E. Baptiste 4 for 75)

Match drawn
Leeward Islands 8 pts, Guyana 4 pts

at Queen's Park, St George's, Grenada

Windward Islands 318 (D.A. Joseph 87, J.J. Pierre 73, W.W. Thomas 69, I.R. Bishop 4 for 61) and 234 (L.D. John 63, R. Nanan 5 for 41)
Trinidad and Tobago 415 (K.A. Williams 167, R. Nanan 59, A.L. Logie 50) and 55 for 3

Match drawn
Trinidad and Tobago 8 pts, Windward Islands 4 pts

The final round of matches in the Red Stripe Cup saw Barbados needing to beat Jamaica to take the trophy. Best won the toss and asked Jamaica to bat first, but there was no immediate reward, and the Jamaican innings was held together by Delroy Morgan, who was run out one short of his third century of the season. Morgan was fifth out at 221, after which Jamaica collapsed before the leg-breaks of George Linton. Barbados quickly lost Greenidge and Best, but Haynes and Payne, who had reassumed the

V. deC. Walcott	M.D. Marshall	A.L. Grant	D.L. Haynes	Byes	Leg-byes	Wides	No-balls	Total	Wkts
				3	2	4	3	272	10
				1	3	2	3	203	10
				1	4		8	231	10
					10	1	9	284	10
				2	10	1	4	238	1
15–2–55–2					1	2	2	207	10
13–0–55–3				2	1		5	155	9
13–1–46–0	18–3–59–1			5	2	1	12	287	10
23–3–62–1	1–0–1–0	2–0–2–0	6–4–2–1	3	8	1	15	331	8
64–6–	19–3–	2–0–	6–4–						
218–6	60–1	2–0	2–1						
av. 36.33	av. 60.00	—	av. 2.00						

wicket-keeping duties, put on 124. Then a whirlwind 89 from Malcolm Marshall brought them a first-innings lead. Jamaica needed only to avoid defeat to win the Red Stripe Cup, and when Dujon and Adams added 107 for the third wicket they moved into an impregnable position.

In a high scoring game at Bourda, Guyana were thwarted by a fourth-wicket stand of 242 between Keith Arthurton and Ralston Otto. Arthurton hit a six and 20 fours in the highest score of his career, and his stand with Otto was the only double-century partnership of the season in the Red Stripe Cup. Guyana batted consistently in reply, but Baptiste again bowled finely and completed an excellent all-round match in the second innings with a hard-hit 95.

Dawnley Joseph and James Pierre put on 152 for Windwards' second wicket at St George's, but the highlight of the match was Kenneth Williams' career-best 167, an innings which included 4 sixes and 15 fours.

Guyana 1989
First-Class Matches

BATTING	v. Trinidad & Tobago (Pointe-à-Pierre) 20–3 January		v. Jamaica (Kingston) 28–31 January		v. Barbados (Bourda) 10–13 February		v. Windward Islands (Bourda) 17–20 February		v. Leeward Islands (Bourda) 25–8 February		M	Inns	NOs	Runs	HS	Av
C.B. Lambert	49	21	40	33	105*	—	57	2	40	—	5	8	1	347	105*	49.57
S. Dhaniram	54	16	6	15	93	—	52	3	71	—	5	8	—	310	93	38.75
A.F.D. Jackman	1	106*	21	19*	23*	—	71	46*	11	—	5	8	4	298	106*	74.50
R. Seeram	18	4	9	40	—	—	10	25	96	—	5	7	—	202	96	28.85
J.A. Angus	2	—	3	1	—	—	—	—	33	—	5	4	—	39	33	9.75
C.B. Burnett	13	3	2	13	—	—	—	—	—	—	2	4	—	31	13	7.75
S.N. Mohammed	9	43	1	0	—	—	1*	—	2	—	5	6	1	56	43	11.20
C.G. Butts	3	—	33	1	—	—	—	—	1	—	5	4	—	38	33	9.50
G.E. Charles	16*	8*	—	—	—	—	4	—	28	—	4	4	2	56	28	28.00
L.A. Joseph	8	—	4	1	—	—	—	—	11*	—	5	4	1	24	11*	8.00
B. St A. Browne	0	—	0*	0	—	—					3	3	1	0	0*	0.00
D.I. Harper			14	16							1	2	—	30	16	15.00
N.A. Hafiz					—	—	—	5*	30	—	3	2	1	35	30	35.00
R.A. Harper							43	32	51	—	2	3	—	126	51	42.00
Byes	6	2			2		1	5	14							
Leg-byes	1	6	5	4	10		9	1	12							
Wides					1				1							
No-balls	5	4	6	2	4		4	2	14							
Total	185	213	144	145	238		252	121	415							
Wickets	10	5	10	10	1		6	4	10							
Result	W		L		Ab.		W		D							
Points	16		0		4		16		4							

Fielding Figures
8 – S.N. Mohammed (ct 6/st 2)
6 – R. Seeram
5 – C.B. Lambert
3 – R.A. Harper, L.A. Joseph and N.A. Hafiz
2 – C.G. Butts, A.F.D. Jackman and S. Dhaniram
1 – J.A. Angus, C.B. Burnet, and D.I. Harper (plus one as sub)

BOWLING	L.A. Joseph	G.E. Charles	B.St A. Browne	C.G. Butts	J.A. Angus	C.B. Burnett	S. Dhaniram	D.I. Harper
v. Trinidad & Tobago (Pointe-à-Pierre) 20–3 January	15–6–33–3	8–3–19–0	18–4–61–0	48–13–96–2	28.5–6–78–3	3–1–10–0	1–0–6–0	
	16.1–5–43–4		7–1–17–2	9–3–18–4				
v. Jamaica (Kingston) 28–31 January	24–5–66–2		25.5–4–75–4	41–13–67–2	11–2–35–0	4–1–7–0		29–6–57–2
v. Barbados (Bourda) 10–13 February	5–0–28–0	3–0–11–0	4–0–19–1	1–0–2–0	3–2–1–0			
v. Windward Islands (Bourda) 17–20 February	11–3–39–1	5–0–21–0		21.4–10–36–4				
	14–2–36–3			33–10–79–3	15–2–60–3		1–0–2–0	
v. Leeward Islands (Bourda) 25–8 February	22–2–91–4	18–0–75–2		41–6–105–0	19.1–3–65–2			
	3–0–31–1	14–0–63–0		31–6–61–2	25–6–67–2		10.4–0–55–2	
	110.1–23–367–18	48–3–189–2	54.5–9–172–7	225.4–61–464–17	102–21–306–10	7–2–17–0	12.4–0–63–2	29–6–57–2
	av. 20.38	av. 94.50	av. 24.57	av. 27.29	av. 30.60	av. —	av. 31.50	av. 28.50

LEFT: *Milton Small reasserted a claim for international recognition with fine bowling for Barbados. (Adrian Murrell/Allsport)*

BELOW: *George Ferris. His opportunities were limited, but he bowled well for Leeward Islands. (David Munden)*

Red Stripe Cup – Final Table

	P	W	L	D	Nr	Pts
Jamaica (1)	5	2	1	2		49
Barbados (4)	5	2	–	2	1	48
Guyana (5)	5	2	1	1	1	40
Leeward Islands (2)	5	1	1	2	1	36
Trinidad and Tobago (3)	5	1	3	1		29
Windward Islands (6)	5	–	2	2	1	12

(1988 positions in brackets)

A.F.D. Jackman	R.A. Harper	R. Seeram	C.B. Lambert	N.A. Hafiz		Byes	Leg-byes	Wides	No-balls	Total	Wkts
						2	5		3	310	10
						1	7		9	86	10
						19	12	5		338	10
1–0–3–0							1		6	65	1
	14–3–26–3					7	4	1	1	133	10
	25–7–38–1					18	4		7	237	10
	31–6–70–1					2	11		5	419	10
	17–3–41–2	9–0–59–0	4–0–21–1	3–0–6–0		6	5		6	415	10
1–0–	87–19–	9–0–	4–0–	3–0–							
3–0	175–7	59–0	21–1	6–0							
—	av. 25.00	—	av. 21.00	—							

Jamaica 1989
First-Class Matches

BATTING

	v. Guyana (Kingston) 28–31 January		v. Leeward Islands (Kingston) 3–6 February		v. Windward Islands (Kingston) 11–14 February		v. Trinidad & Tobago (Pointe-à-Pierre) 18–21 February		v. Barbados (Bridgetown) 24–7 February		v. Indians (Kingston) 22–5 April		M	Inns	NOs	Runs	HS	Av
W.W. Lewis	21	—	7	—	32	103	0	11	27	32	0	—	6	9	—	233	103	25.88
D.S. Morgan	122	—	111	—	70	8	0	0	99	25	19	—	6	9	—	454	122	50.44
R.C. Haynes	1	—	36	—	21	9	1	0	24	36		—	5	8	—	128	36	16.00
J.C. Adams	27	—	6	—	25	34	63	10	48	55	38	—	6	9	—	306	63	34.00
M.C. Neita	49	—	3	—	55	24	36	4			36	—	5	7	—	207	55	29.57
C.A. Davidson	57*	—	200*	—	8	29*	63	2	43	13	74	—	6	9	3	489	200*	81.12
M.A. Tucker	0	—	61	—	31	5*	52	0	0	52*	18	—	6	9	2	219	61	31.28
A.G. Daley	9	—	0	—	79	—							3	3	—	88	79	29.33
M.A. Holding	7	—	15	—	14*	—	12	12	0	11			5	7	1	71	15	11.83
N.O. Perry	9	—	47	—	16	—	0	4	0	—	24		6	7	—	100	47	14.28
P.A. Gayle	0	—	1*	—	12	—							3	3	1	13	12	6.50
C.A. Walsh							8*	12*	21*	16			2	4	3	57	21*	57.00
B.P. Patterson							5	7	0	—			2	3	—	12	7	4.00
P.J.L. Dujon									5	64			1	2	—	69	64	34.50
R. Samuels											46	—	1	1	—	46	46	46.00
C. Carter											35*	—	1	1	1	35	35*	—
S. Gordon											12	—	1	1	—	12	12	12.00
C. Banton											0	—	1	1	—	0	0	0.00
Byes	19		10		4	2	3		5	3	6							
Leg-byes	12		15		4	7	9	1	2	8	8							
Wides	5		2						1	1	7							
No-balls			9		13	2	9	8	12	15	7							
Total	338		523		384	223	261	71	287	331	330							
Wickets	10		9		10	5	10	10	10	8	10							
Result	W		W		D		L		D		D							
Points	16		16		8		5		4		—							

Fielding Figures
11 – M.A. Holding
7 – D.S. Morgan
6 – J.C. Adams
5 – P.A. Gayle (ct 4/st 1)
4 – C.A. Davidson and W.W. Lewis
3 – M.C. Neita and N.O. Perry
2 – R.C. Haynes and P.J.L. Dujon
1 – S. Gordon and C. Banton

BOWLING

	M.A. Holding	A.G. Daley	M.A. Tucker	R.C. Haynes	N.O. Perry	C.A. Davidson	B.P. Patterson	C.A. Walsh
v. Guyana (Kingston) 28–31 January	12–1–36–2	14–1–31–1	4–3–5–0	22–6–32–3	17–5–35–4			
	10–5–16–0	10–1–25–1	4–0–14–0	25–8–41–1	28.4–11–45–8			
v. Leeward Islands (Kingston) 3–6 February	13–3–35–1	13–2–51–1	6–3–7–1	13–2–59–2	26.1–6–74–5			
	11–2–45–2	12–4–39–1		32–12–85–3	26–4–66–4			
v. Windward Islands (Kingston) 11–14 February	18–3–52–1	12–0–48–1	23–6–49–1	28.5–7–81–3	42–7–91–4	7–0–31–1		
		3–0–17–0		6–3–29–0	10–2–26–1			
v. Trinidad & Tobago (Point-à-Pierre) 18–21 February	10–0–40–2		7–3–13–0	29–4–76–4	16–2–47–2		13–2–50–1	12–4–20–1
				5–1–24–0	5.2–0–13–0		4–0–17–0	3–0–20–0
v. Barbados (Bridgetown) 24–7 February	18–1–44–2		21–5–37–1	16–4–42–1	10–2–23–0		17–0–64–3	28–5–89–3
v. Indians (Kingston) 22–5 April			34–2–115–2		37.3–6–110–2	7–0–27–0		
					4–0–7–0	1–1–0–0		
	92–15–	64–8–	99–22–	176.5–47–	222.4–45–	15–1–	34–2–	43–9–
	268–10	211–5	240–5	469–17	537–30	58–1	131–4	129–4
	av. 26.80	av. 42.20	av. 48.00	av. 27.58	av. 17.90	av. 58.00	av. 32.75	av. 32.25

2, 3, 4 and 5 March 1989

at Kensington Oval, Bridgetown, Barbados

Indians 365 (R.J. Shastri 57, M. Azharuddin 52) and 307 (R.N. Kapil Dev 97, R.J. Shastri 65, D.B. Vengsarkar 60)
President's XI 246 (C.A. Best 104 not out, R.N. Kapil Dev 6 for 27) and 183 for 3 (P.V. Simmons 116 not out)

Match drawn

The opening match of the Indian tour saw them perform commendably against a strong President's XI. On the opening day they batted solidly although they failed to build on a substantial opening. Kapil Dev then produced one of his finest spells of bowling to rout the President's XI, for whom skipper Carlisle Best alone stood firm, carrying his bat for 104. Kapil Dev emphasized his all-round qualities with 97 off 102 balls when the tourists batted again. Set to make 418, the President's XI clearly had no hope of victory, but Phil Simmons made a most welcome and aggressive century to confirm that he was once again contending for a Test place after his fearful injury on the tour of England in 1988.

First One-Day International
WEST INDIES v. INDIA

Baptiste returned to international cricket after his fine season in the Red Stripe Cup. He replaced the injured Benjamin. Hooper and Marshall were also missing from the West Indian side, and Arthurton and Bishop took their places.

Vengsarkar won the toss and asked West Indies to bat first, but Haynes pulled Sanjeeva Sharma to the boundary three times in his first over, so that although Kapil Dev bowled Greenidge for four, knocking out his middle stump, West Indies were quickly into their stride. Richardson was taken at deep gully off a hard slash, and Arthurton was aided by being missed behind the wicket and dropped off a simple caught and bowled chance.

Viv Richards, on his 37th birthday, was far from fit, but he helped Haynes to add 79. It was Haynes who totally dominated the innings, hitting 5 sixes and 8 fours in his 13th century in one-day internationals.

One of the happiest stories of the West Indian season – Phil Simmons, captain of Trinidad, celebrated his return to full fitness with a century for the President's XI in the opening match of the Indian tour. Simmons received a serious head injury against Gloucestershire in 1988. (Adrian Murrell/ Allsport)

C. Banton	S. Gordon	S. Carter	M.C. Neita	Byes	Leg-byes	Wides	No-balls	Total	Wkts
					5		6	144	10
					4		2	145	10
				13	4		16	243	10
				2	13		9	250	10
				9	4		14	334	10
					1		8	104	2
				8	2		17	256	10
					3		3	77	0
				9	6	2	23	314	10
19–2–81–1	22–2–103–2	35–3–129–2	4–1–16–0	2	3		19	586	10
11–2–39–1	8–0–26–2	10–3–20–0	3–2–4–0	4	4		5	104	3
30–4–	30–2–	45–6–	7–3–						
120–2	129–4	149–2	20–0						
av. 60.00	av. 32.25	av. 74.50	—						

Leeward Islands 1989
First-Class Matches

BATTING	v. Windward Islands (Castries) 26–9 January		v. Jamaica (Kingston) 3–6 February		v. Trinidad & Tobago (Nevis) 10–12 February		v. Barbados (St John's) 17–20 February		v. Guyana (Bourda) 25–8 February		M	Inns	NOs	Runs	HS	Av
A.L. Kelly	14	—	21	77	12	3			6	0	4	7	—	133	77	19.00
L.L. Lawrence	36	—	18	14	7	21	4	0			4	7	—	100	36	14.28
A.C.H. Walsh	34	—	3	6	27	0			1	27	4	7	—	98	34	14.00
S.C. Williams	5	—	3	13	11	22	0	10			4	7	—	64	22	9.14
R.M. Otto	40	—	67	74	14	2	9	28	116	13	5	9	—	363	116	40.33
E.A.E.Baptiste	25	—	10	15	18	4	26	7	31	95	5	9	—	231	95	25.66
L.L. Harris	6	—	42*	5	68*	31	43	33			4	7	2	228	68*	45.60
N.C. Guishard	32	—	11	10	15	13			32	29	4	7	—	142	32	20.28
T.A. Merrick	17*	—	29	0							2	3	1	46	29	23.00
K.C.G. Benjamin	4	—	6	11	12	3			12	26*	4	7	1	74	26*	12.33
G.J.F. Ferris	11*	—	0	1*	1	20*	6*	11*			4	7	5	50	20*	25.00
E.T. Willett					5	17					1	2	—	22	17	11.00
L.A. Harrigan							5	9			1	2	—	14	9	7.00
K.L.T. Arthurton							85	10	154	62	2	4	—	311	154	77.75
C.E.L. Ambrose							17	34			1	2	—	51	34	25.50
W.K.M. Benjamin							3	5	36	85	2	4	—	129	85	32.25
J.D. Thompson							4	0*	2*	26	2	4	2	32	26	16.00
R.B. Richardson									0	14	1	2	—	14	14	7.00
F.A. Buffonge									11	21	1	2	—	32	21	16.00
Byes	1		13	2	11	6		2	2	6						
Leg-byes	2		4	13	9	2	1	1	11	5						
Wides						1	2									
No-balls	12		16	9	8	4	2	5	5	6						
Total	239		243	250	219	148	207	155	419	415						
Wickets	9		10	10	10	10	10	9	10	10						
Result	Ab.		L		W		D		D							
Points	4		0		16		8		8							

Fielding Figures
7 – L.L. Harris
5 – A.L. Kelly and R.M. Otto
4 – E.A.E. Baptiste
2 – N.C. Guishard and J.D. Thompson
1 – R.B. Richardson, L.L. Lawrence and sub
 (L.A. Harrigan)

BOWLING	T.A. Merrick	G.J.F. Ferris	K.C.G. Benjamin	E.A.E. Baptiste	N.C. Guishard	R.M. Otto	E.T. Willett	C.E.L. Ambrose
v. Windward Islands (Castries) 26–9 January								
v. Jamaica (Kingston) 3–6 February	26–2–90–1	25–3–117–3	30–4–92–1	23–3–83–1	33–3–109–3	3–1–7–0		
v. Trinidad & Tobago (Nevis) 10–12 February		8–3–16–3	9–1–24–1	10.1–3–26–6				
v. Barbados (St John's) 17–20 February		6–1–14–2	8–0–18–2	16.1–5–42–5			13–1–28–1	
		15.1–3–49–2		20–6–46–5				20–3–44–2
v. Guyana (Bourda) 25–8 February			23–0–76–1	30.2–5–75–4	33–6–87–3			
	26–2–90–1 av. 90.00	54.1–10–196–10 av. 19.60	70–5–210–5 av. 42.00	99.4–22–272–21 av. 12.95	66–9–196–6 av. 32.66	3–1–7–0 —	13–1–28–1 av. 28.00	20–3–44–2 av. 22.00

FIRST ONE-DAY INTERNATIONAL – WEST INDIES v. INDIA
7 March 1989 at Kensington Oval, Bridgetown, Barbados

WEST INDIES			
C.G. Greenidge	b Kapil Dev		4
D.L. Haynes	not out		117
R.B. Richardson	c Sidhu, b Kapil Dev		18
K.L.T. Arthurton	c Srikkanth, b Shastri		25
I.V.A. Richards†	b A.K. Sharma		40
A.L. Logie	not out		19
P.J.L. Dujon*			
E.A.E. Baptiste			
C.E.L. Ambrose			
I.R. Bishop			
C.A. Walsh			
Extras	b 5, lb 13, w 3, nb 4		25
(48 overs)	(for 4 wkts)		248

INDIA			
R.J. Shastri	b Walsh		23
K. Srikkanth	c Richardson, b Bishop		18
N.S. Sidhu	c Baptiste, b Richards		22
D.B. Vengsarkar†	b Richards		23
M. Azharuddin	c and b Baptiste		10
R.N. Kapil Dev	c and b Richards		0
A.K. Sharma	not out		43
K.S. More*	c Richards, b Baptiste		31
S.K. Sharma	b Bishop		6
Arshad Ayub	not out		4
C.J. Sharma			
Extras	lb 7, w 3, nb 8		18
(48 overs)	(for 8 wkts)		198

	O	M	R	W
Kapil Dev	9	–	28	2
S.K. Sharma	8	–	55	–
C.J. Sharma	6	–	32	–
Shastri	10	–	43	1
Arshad Ayub	10	2	46	–
A.K. Sharma	5	–	26	1

	O	M	R	W
Ambrose	10	–	42	–
Bishop	9	–	30	2
Walsh	10	1	30	1
Baptiste	9	–	42	2
Richards	10	–	47	3

FALL OF WICKETS
1–26, 2–51, 3–116, 4–195

FALL OF WICKETS
1–40, 2–60, 3–91, 4–100, 5–103, 6–107, 7–179, 8–186

Umpires: D.A. Archer & L.H. Barker

Man of the Match: D.L. Haynes

West Indies won by 50 runs

India never looked likely to reach the target of 249 in a contest which had been reduced to 48 overs. They scored soundly enough, but there was never a hint of acceleration. Richards added three wickets and a brilliant diving catch in the gully to his 40 off 38 balls, and West Indies ran out easy winners.

The seventh-wicket stand of 72 between More and Ajay Sharma was a record for the series.

Second One-Day International
WEST INDIES v. INDIA

India brought in leg-spinner Hirwani, but they fared even more miserably than they had done in the first match of the series. Put in to bat, India could muster only 42 runs for the loss of three wickets in the first 20 overs of their innings, and, in spite of a late flurry by Kapil Dev, they could never break the restrictions that the West Indian bowling and fielding placed upon them.

Greenidge hit a six and 2 fours in Chetan Sharma's opening over, and he continued to dominate until he became one of Srikkanth's three victims in mid-innings. Richards came in to dispel any doubts as to the outcome of the match that may have arisen because of Srikkanth's three wickets. He hit a six and a four, and West Indies won with 9.2 overs to spare.

W.K.M. Benjamin	J.D. Thompson	K.L.T. Arthurton		Byes	Leg-byes	Wides	No-balls	Total	Wkts
									Ab.
				10	15	2	9	523	9
					1		4	67	10
				4	8		3	114	10
20–3–34–1	9–2–17–0			9	6		4	205	10
23–2–83–1	16–3–51–1	4–0–17–0		14	12	1	14	415	10
43–5–	25–5–	4–0–							
117–2	68–1	17–0							
av. 58.50	*av.* 68.00	—							

Trinidad and Tobago
First-Class Matches

BATTING

BATTING	v. Guyana (Pointe-à-Pierre) 20–3 January		v. Barbados (Bridgetown) 27–30 January		v. Leeward Islands (Nevis) 10–12 February		v. Jamaica (Pointe-à-Pierre) 18–21 February		v. Windward Islands (St George's) 25–8 February		M	Inns	NOs	Runs	HS	Av
P.V. Simmons	16	30	44	12	0	6	14	46*	0	21	5	10	1	189	46*	21.00
H. Gangapersad	21	1	11	6	0	7					3	6	—	46	21	7.66
K.A. Williams	51	4	0	1	11	4	11	—	167	9	5	9	—	258	167	28.66
B.C. Lara	127	4	77	48	11	9	36	—	24	—	5	8	—	336	127	42.00
D.I. Mohammed	1	12	20	87*	15	17	26	—	38	10*	5	9	2	226	87*	32.28
M.P. Carew	56	4	10	21	0	11					3	6	—	102	56	17.00
K.C. Williams	8	6	0	4	11	27					3	6	—	56	27	9.33
R. Nanan	6	0	36*	13	1	16	56	—	59	—	5	8	1	187	59	26.71
A.H. Gray	6	1			1	1*	47	—	14	—	4	6	1	70	47	14.00
R. Dhanraj	4	6	47	1	7*	1	5*	—	30*	—	5	8	3	101	47	20.20
A. Dwarika	4*	1*	0	1							2	4	2	6	4*	3.00
D.V. St Hilaire			15	0							1	2	—	15	15	7.50
S. Ragoonath					5	0	17	25*	5	7	3	6	1	59	25*	11.80
R. Mahabir							0	—			1	1	—	0	0	0.00
D. Williams							9	—	10	—	2	2	—	19	10	9.50
I.R. Bishop							8	—	2	—	2	2	—	10	8	5.00
A.L. Logie									50	6*	1	2	1	56	50	56.00
Byes	2	1	3	1		4	8		1							
Leg-byes	5	7	2	3	1	8	2	3	10	1						
Wides			4	2												
No-balls	3	9	3	3	4	3	17	3	5	1						
Total	310	86	272	203	67	114	256	77	415	55						
Wickets	10	10	10	10	10	10	10	0	10	3						
Result	L		L		L		W		D							
Points	5		0		0		16		8							

Fielding Figures
9 – P.V. Simmons
6 – B.C. Lara and H. Gangapersad (ct 1/st 5)
5 – D.I. Mohammed and R. Nanan
4 – D. Williams
3 – M.P. Carew, S. Ragoonath, A.H. Gray and
  R. Dhanraj
2 – K.C. Williams
1 – A. Dwarika, K.A. Williams, R. Mahabir and
  I.R. Bishop

BOWLING

BOWLING	A.H. Gray	K.C. Williams	R. Nanan	R. Dhanraj	A. Dwarika	P.V. Simmons	D.V. St Hilaire	I.R. Bishop
v. Guyana (Pointe-à-Pierre) 20–3 January	6–0–45–0	3–0–22–0	29–12–42–3	27–8–69–5	1.1–1–0–2			
	8–1–22–0	15–2–35–3	25–4–56–1	15–1–45–0	11–1–44–0	1–0–3–0		
v. Barbados (Bridgetown) 27–30 January		21–1–65–0	26.5–8–65–4	29–7–75–6	14–2–35–0		11–2–48–0	
		12–0–63–0	37–6–97–1	25–1–81–3	6–0–28–0		4–0–14–0	
v. Leeward Islands (Nevis) 10–12 February	14–2–38–2	11.1–2–29–3	28–11–58–3	24–5–58–2		6–2–16–0		
	10–1–22–1	12–2–27–2	18–6–33–2	23.4–4–58–5				
v. Jamaica (Pointe-à-Pierre) 18–21 February	14–4–64–3		19–4–42–1	24–3–76–2				18.4–2–49–3
	8.2–1–29–4							9–1–41–6
v. Windward Islands (St George's) 25–8 February	18.1–3–75–1		30–7–78–3	27–2–97–2				27–4–61–4
	15–4–48–0		31.2–11–41–5	15–4–43–1		8–4–19–1		26–5–62–3
	93.3–16– 343–11 av. 31.18	74.1–7– 241–8 av. 30.12	244.1–69– 512–23 av. 22.26	209.4–35– 602–26 av. 23.15	32.1–4– 107–2 av. 53.50	15–6– 38–1 av. 38.00	15–2– 62–0 av. —	80.4–12– 213–16 av. 13.31

SECOND ONE-DAY INTERNATIONAL – WEST INDIES v. INDIA
9 March 1989 at Queen's Park Oval, Port of Spain, Trinidad

INDIA			
R.J. Shastri	c Richardson,		
	b Baptiste		10
K. Srikkanth	c Dujon, b Ambrose		5
N.S. Sidhu	run out		12
D.B. Vengsarkar†	c and b Richards		7
M. Azharuddin	c Richardson,		
	b Baptiste		19
R.N. Kapil Dev	c Logie, b Richards		44
A.K. Sharma	b Richards		5
K.S. More*	c and b Richards		7
S.K. Sharma	c Dujon, b Bishop		14
C.J. Sharma	run out		15
N.D. Hirwani	not out		0
Extras	b 1, lb 7, w 1, nb 1		10
(48 overs)			148

	O	M	R	W
Ambrose	9	2	22	1
Bishop	9	1	22	1
Walsh	10	1	31	–
Baptiste	10	1	21	2
Richards	10	–	44	4

FALL OF WICKETS
1–13, 2–22, 3–32, 4–43, 5–69, 6–81, 7–107, 8–118, 9–144

WEST INDIES		
C.G. Greenidge	lbw, b Srikkanth	69
D.L. Haynes	c More, b Shastri	8
R.B. Richardson	not out	36
A.L. Logie	c and b Srikkanth	0
K.L.T. Arthurton	c S.K. Sharma,	
	b Srikkanth	15
I.V.A. Richards†	not out	11
P.J.L. Dujon*		
E.A.E. Baptiste		
C.E.L. Ambrose		
I.R. Bishop		
C.A. Walsh		
Extras	lb 8, w 1, nb 3	12
(38.4 overs)	(for 4 wkts)	151

	O	M	R	W
Kapil Dev	7	4	4	–
C.J. Sharma	7	–	27	–
A.K. Sharma	2	–	5	–
Shastri	8	–	36	1
Hirwani	10	–	45	–
Srikkanth	4.4	1	26	3

FALL OF WICKETS
1–38, 2–110, 3–110, 4–139

Umpires: Muhammed Hossein & C.E. Cumberbatch

Man of the Match: C.G. Greenidge

West Indies won by 6 wickets

Richards' bowling performance of 4 for 44 took him past 100 wickets in one-day internationals.

Third One-Day International
WEST INDIES v. INDIA

India chose to bat first when they won the toss, a decision which surprised many as there was early life in the pitch, but they began well enough. Against fine bowling and tenacious fielding India could not hope to score quickly, and wickets tumbled towards the close of the innings as they pressed for runs.

Kapil Dev and Chetan Sharma, not as quick as the West Indian pace bowlers, performed gallantly for India and sent back both openers. Richardson and Arthurton set West Indies on course for victory before Richardson was run out by Azharuddin. With 92 runs needed for victory and 12 overs remaining, Hirwani caught and bowled Richards to send a shiver of apprehension through the West Indian ranks. Had Arthurton been stumped in the same over as he should have been, India might well have snatched victory, but the chance was missed and Arthurton and Logie took their side to victory.

Robin Singh made his international debut, but he was

R. Mahabir		Byes	Leg-byes	Wides	No-balls	Total	Wkts
		6	1		5	185	10
		2	6		4	213	5
			1		6	289	10
			4		3	287	5
		11	9	1	8	219	10
		6	2		4	148	10
6–1–18–0		3	9		9	261	10
			1		8	71	10
		3	4	2	9	318	10
		12	9	1	6	234	10
6–1– 18–0 —							

given little opportunity to show his worth.

14, 15 and 16 March 1989

at Basseterre, St Kitts

Indians 411 for 6 dec (N.S. Sidhu 114, S.V. Manjrekar 109) and 39 for 0
West Indies Under-23 XI 405 (B.C. Lara 182, S. Dhaniram 61, N.D. Hirwani 5 for 150)

Match drawn

The tourists gave outings to all those who had not played in the one-day internationals, so that Manjrekar, wicket-keeper Saba Karim and spinner Venkataramana all took the field. Manjrekar hit a polished century and added 17 for the third wicket with Sidhu who, benefiting from being missed early on, hit 7 sixes and 8 fours and reached the first hundred of the tour. The West Indian youngsters gave an emphatic reply, particularly the left-handed captain Lara, who hit a dazzling 182 with 21 fours and a six. He was severe on Hirwani, but the leg-spinner came through well to capture five wickets.

Windward Islands
First-Class Matches

BATTING	v. Leeward Islands (Castries) 26–9 January	v. Barbados (Bridgetown) 3–6 February		v. Jamaica (Kingston) 11–14 February		v. Guyana (Bourda) 17–20 February		v. Trinidad & Tobago (St George's) 25–8 February		M	Inns	NOs	Runs	HS	Av
J.D. Charles	—	—	13	48*	47	—	6	41	7	11	5	7	1	173	48*	28.83
L.D. John	—	—	24	67	26	63*	3	6	0	63	5	8	1	252	67	36.00
D.T. Telemaque	—	—	0	44	13	20	24	1			4	6	—	102	44	17.00
D.A. Joseph	—	—	128	52	28	3	43	24	87	23	5	8	—	388	128	48.50
L.C. Sebastien	—	—	5	7	91	—	11	31	2	4	5	7	—	151	91	21.57
J.R. Murray	—	—	8	2	21	—	0	28	31	4	5	7	—	94	31	13.42
D.J. Collymore	—	—	4	25					5	14	3	4	—	48	25	12.00
W.W. Thomas	—	—	4	11	28	—	9	9	69	30	5	7	—	160	69	22.85
T.Z. Kentish	—	—	19	7	2	—	0	7	17	24*	5	7	1	76	24*	12.66
J.T. Etienne	—	—	12	0	6*	—	6	5			4	5	1	29	12	7.25
I.A. Allen	—	—	1*	1	0	—	7*	2*	7	4	5	7	3	22	7*	5.50
J.J. Pierre					45	9*	11	54	73	27	3	6	1	219	73	43.80
D. Lewis									2*	2	1	2	1	4	2*	4.00
Byes		1		9		7	18	3	12							
Leg-byes		4	10	4	1	4	4	4	9							
Wides			1			1		2	1							
No-balls		8	9	14	8	1	7	9	6							
Total		231	284	334	104	133	237	318	234							
Wickets		10	10	10	2	10	10	10	10							
Result	Ab.	L		D		L		D								
Points	4	0		4		0		4								

Fielding Figures 9 – J.R. Murray (ct 8/st 1)
5 – L.D. John
4 – W.W. Thomas and D.A. Joseph
1 – J.T. Etienne, J.J. Pierre, T.Z. Kentish, I.A. Allen,, J.D. Charles and sub (D. Lewis)

BOWLING	I.A. Allen	D.J. Collymore	W.W. Thomas	J.T. Etienne	T.Z. Kentish	J.D. Charles	L.D. John	D. Lewis
v. Leeward Islands (Castries) 26–9 January	14–4–47–0	14–0–35–2	16.2–2–50–1	32–11–63–3	16–1–41–1			
v. Barbados (Bridgetown) 3–6 February	17–2–56–1 14–0–50–1	12–0–40–0	13–0–56–1 2–0–18–0	35–7–76–1 10–0–34–0	43.5–7–110–5 12–1–32–1	4–0–21–1 4–0–10–0	0.2–0–4–0	
v. Jamaica (Kingston) 11–14 February	37–5–102–5 23–2–54–0		22.1–3–78–2 23–0–73–4	37–6–113–3 19–3–55–1	45–11–83–0 19–7–32–0			
v. Guyana (Bourda) 17–20 February	10.3–0–52–3 4–0–23–1		10–0–55–0 4–1–23–1	23–4–53–1 8–0–52–1	21–2–74–2 9–0–17–1	2–1–8–0		
v. Trinidad & Tobago (St George's) 25–8 February	26–5–95–2 10–1–28–1	19–2–49–2	19–2–73–2		33.2–6–94–2	8–0–25–0		14–0–68–1 10–1–26–2
	155.3–19– 507–14 *av.* 36.21	45–2– 124–4 *av.* 31.00	109.3–10– 426–11 *av.* 38.72	164–31– 446–10 *av.* 44.60	209.1–35– 483–12 *av.* 40.25	18–1– 64–1 *av.* 64.00	0.2–0– 4–0 —	24–1– 94–3 *av.* 31.33

THIRD ONE-DAY INTERNATIONAL – WEST INDIES *v.* INDIA
11 March 1989 at Queen's Park Oval, Port of Spain, Trinidad

INDIA			
K. Srikkanth	c Ambrose, b Walsh		17
N.S. Sidhu	c Ambrose, b Richards		50
M.Azharuddin	run out		36
D.B. Vengsarkar†	c Richards, b Ambrose		38
R.N. Kapil Dev	c Arthurton, b Ambrose		12
Robin Singh	b Richards		3
R.J. Shastri	c Richardson, b Bishop		3
A.K. Sharma	c Richards, b Bishop		9
K.S. More*	c and b Bishop		4
C.J. Sharma	not out		2
N.D. Hirwani	b Bishop		0
Extras	b 2, lb 10, w 1, nb 5		18
(49.5 overs)			192

	O	M	R	W
Ambrose	10	1	29	2
Bishop	9.5	1	33	4
Walsh	10	–	22	1
Baptiste	10	–	49	–
Richards	10	1	47	2

FALL OF WICKETS
1–47, 2–113, 3–115, 4–147, 5–156, 6–175, 7–177, 8–186, 9–190

WEST INDIES			
C.G. Greenidge	lbw, b Kapil Dev		3
D.L. Haynes	c Srikkanth, b C.J. Sharma		18
R.B. Richardson	run out		30
K.L.T. Arthurton	not out		76
I.V.A. Richards†	c and b Hirwani		3
A.L. Logie	not out		45
P.J.L. Dujon†			
E.A.E. Baptiste			
I.R. Bishop			
C.E.L. Ambrose			
C.A. Walsh			
Extras	b 2, lb 7, w 2, nb 7		18
(47.2 overs)	(for 4 wkts)		193

	O	M	R	W
Kapil Dev	9	–	35	1
C.J. Sharma	8	–	23	1
A.K. Sharma	5	–	24	–
Shastri	10	1	32	–
Hirwani	10	–	44	1
Srikkanth	4	–	19	–
Robin Singh	1.2	–	7	–

FALL OF WICKETS
1–11, 2–34, 3–83, 4–101

Umpires: C.E. Cumberbatch & G. Johnson

Man of the Match: K.L.T. Arthurton

West Indies won by 6 wickets

Fourth One-Day International
WEST INDIES *v.* INDIA

After their brief excursion into first-class cricket, India returned to the serious grind of the one-day international series, sponsored by Cable and Wireless. Winning the toss, they batted first but quickly lost Srikkanth and Arun Lal. Vengsarkar at last gave something of a glimpse of his best, however, and shared with Shastri a stand of 107 for the fourth wicket, a record for India against West Indies in one-day internationals. India eventually reached their highest score of the series on a wicket which, after a lively first hour, settled down to become a paradise for batsmen.

Gordon Greenidge confirmed the serenity of the wicket with a ferocious display of strokes. His 117 occupied only 37 overs, and he hit 8 sixes and 6 fours. His 8 sixes constituted a new record for a one-day international. India were blasted to defeat with 40 balls to spare.

Fifth One-Day International
WEST INDIES *v.* INDIA

Even though their innings was cut short by rain, West Indies raced to a massive 289 at more than 6½ runs an over. Greenidge, who hit a six and 9 fours, and Haynes put on a record 185 for the first West Indian wicket. Haynes went on to reach the highest of his 14 centuries in one-day internationals, and his 152 came from 126 balls and contained 6 sixes and 12 fours.

India never looked likely to approach the West Indian score, but far more serious than their humiliating 5–0 defeat in the series was the loss of Srikkanth, who suffered a broken left forearm when hit by a ball from Bishop. Srikkanth was flown back to India, and Raman, desperately unlucky not to be in the original party, came to the Caribbean as replacement.

The loss of Srikkanth was a dreadful blow to India's

	Byes	Leg-byes	Wides	No-balls	Total	Wkts
	1	2		12	239	9
	1	6		10	366	10
	1	2		5	151	2
	4	4		13	384	10
	2	7		2	223	5
	1	9		4	252	6
	5	1		2	121	4
	1	10		5	415	10
		1		1	55	3

FOURTH ONE-DAY INTERNATIONAL – WEST INDIES v. INDIA
18 March 1989 at Recreation Ground, St John's, Antigua

INDIA			
K. Srikkanth	c Dujon, b Bishop		7
J. Arun Lal	c Arthurton, b Bishop		1
M. Azharuddin	run out		27
D.B. Vengsarkar†	c Arthurton, b Bishop		88
R.J. Shastri	c and b Richards		44
R.N. Kapil Dev	c Greenidge, b Ambrose		12
A.K. Sharma	c Richards, b Ambrose		29
Robin Singh	not out		10
K.S. More*	c sub (W.K.M. Benjamin), b Bishop		0
Arshad Ayub	not out		1
C.J. Sharma			
Extras	lb 12, w 2, nb 4		18
(50 overs)	(for 8 wkts)		237

	O	M	R	W
Ambrose	10	1	42	2
Bishop	10	1	46	4
Walsh	10	–	53	–
Baptiste	10	–	35	–
Richards	10	–	49	1

FALL OF WICKETS
1–9, 2–11, 3–62, 4–169, 5–185, 6–201, 7–229, 8–231

WEST INDIES			
C.G. Greenidge	c Kapil Dev, b A.K. Sharma		117
D.L. Haynes	run out		42
R.B. Richardson	not out		58
P.J.L. Dujon*	not out		11
I.V.A. Richards†			
K.L.T. Arthurton			
A.L. Logie			
E.A.E. Baptiste			
C.E.L. Ambrose			
I.R. Bishop			
C.A. Walsh			
Extras	lb 6, w 1, nb 5		12
(43.2 overs)	(for 2 wkts)		240

	O	M	R	W
Kapil Dev	6	–	26	–
C.J. Sharma	7.2	–	52	–
Azharuddin	2	–	10	–
A.K. Sharma	10	–	47	1
Shastri	5	–	36	–
Arshad Ayub	10	–	36	–
Srikkanth	3	–	27	–

FALL OF WICKETS
1–86, 2–216

Umpires: A.E. Weekes & S. Bucknor

Man of the Match: C.G. Greenidge

West Indies won by 8 wickets

FIFTH ONE-DAY INTERNATIONAL – WEST INDIES v. INDIA
21 March 1989 at Bourda, Georgetown, Guyana

WEST INDIES			
C.G. Greenidge	c C.J. Sharma, b A.K. Sharma		80
D.L. Haynes	not out		152
R.B. Richardson	c Sidhu, b C.J. Sharma		42
K.L.T. Arthurton	not out		0
I.V.A. Richards†			
A.L. Logie			
P.J.L. Dujon*			
E.A.E. Baptiste			
C.E.L. Ambrose			
C.A. Walsh			
I.R. Bishop			
Extras	lb 7, w 2, nb 6		15
(43.5 overs)	(for 2 wkts)		289

	O	M	R	W
Kapil Dev	8	2	39	–
C.J. Sharma	7.5	1	38	1
A.K. Sharma	7	–	42	1
Azharuddin	2	–	23	–
Shastri	7	–	52	–
Arshad Ayub	8	–	55	–
Srikkanth	4	–	33	–

FALL OF WICKETS
1–185, 2–280

INDIA			
K. Srikkanth	retired hurt		17
J. Arun Lal	c Logie, b Bishop		6
N.S. Sidhu	c Dujon, b Ambrose		4
D.B. Vengsarkar†	c Baptiste, b Walsh		22
M. Azharuddin	b Walsh		19
R.N. Kapil Dev	b Richards		38
R.J. Shastri	run out		3
A.K. Sharma	c Walsh, b Richards		30
K.S. More*	not out		20
Arshad Ayub	lbw, b Richards		2
C.J. Sharma	not out		6
Extras	b 2, lb 16, w 1, nb 2		21
(44 overs)	(for 8 wkts)		188

	O	M	R	W
Ambrose	5	–	18	1
Bishop	5	1	15	1
Richards	10	1	43	3
Walsh	9	–	26	2
Arthurton	3	–	10	–
Baptiste	10	–	47	–
Richardson	2	–	11	–

FALL OF WICKETS
1–10, 2–33, 3–61, 4–84, 5–96, 6–141, 7–162, 8–166

Umpires: L.H. Barker (sub – R. Haynes) & C. Duncan

Man of the Match: D.L. Haynes

West Indies won by 101 runs

Ian Bishop had an outstanding debut Test series for West Indies. (Adrian Murrell/Allsport)

Richardson was finally broken when Greenidge dragged a ball from Chetan Sharma into his stumps. Twelve runs later, Keith Arthurton, playing his first Test in the Caribbean, was brilliantly run out by substitute Robin Singh fielding at cover. The run rate now dropped considerably, and Richards batted for over an hour for five before being bowled by a ball which cut back sharply and hit his leg stump. Bishop was lbw first ball, and the day ended with Richardson 143, Logie 2, and West Indies 273 for 5. India had clawed their way back into the game.

That they had done so was due mainly to Kapil Dev, who had a confident appeal for leg before against Richardson rejected shortly before the close, a rejection which caused angry reaction from the Indian pace bowler.

Richardson reasserted the West Indian dominance on the second day when he took his score to 194, the highest of his nine Test centuries. He hit 20 fours and shared stands of 87 with Logie and 55 with Dujon. The last four wickets fell cheaply, and Arshad Ayub ended with the commendable figures of 5 for 104.

India lost Arun Lal at 14, but Sidhu and Shastri played confidently until the close. Then it rained, and for most of the remaining scheduled time for the match, much of the playing area was under water.

Kapil Dev retained all his old fire as India's new-ball bowler, but he carried the attack alone at times. (Adrian Murrell/Allsport)

hopes for the Test series, for he is not only a very fine player of fast bowling, but also one of the most experienced of the Indian batsmen.

First Test Match
WEST INDIES v. INDIA

With Malcolm Marshall still suffering from a wrist injury, West Indies brought in Ian Bishop for his first Test cap. Vengsarkar won the toss and asked West Indies to bat first although it was difficult to follow the reasoning behind his decision. There was an early success when Haynes saw a ball from Arshad Ayub spin back onto his stumps after a defensive prod, but at lunch, 91 for 1, Greenidge and Richardson were in total command.

That situation had been confirmed by tea, at which time West Indies were 207 for 1. India would have been in a far happier position had Vengsarkar not dropped Richie Richardson at slip off Kapil Dev when the batsman had scored six. The partnership between Greenidge and

FIRST TEST MATCH – WEST INDIES v. INDIA
25, 26, 27, 28, 29 and 30 March 1989 at Bourda, Georgetown, Guyana

WEST INDIES FIRST INNINGS

C.G. Greenidge	b C.J. Sharma	82
D.L. Haynes	b Arshad Ayub	20
R.B. Richardson	c Shastri, Arshad Ayub	194
K.L.T. Arthurton	run out	9
I.V.A. Richards†	b Kapil Dev	5
I.R. Bishop	lbw, b Kapil Dev	0
A.L. Logie	c and b Hirwani	46
P.J.L. Dujon*	lbw, b Arshad Ayub	31
C.E.L. Ambrose	not out	13
W.K.M. Benjamin	c C.J. Sharma, b Arshad Ayub	7
C.A. Walsh	b Arshad Ayub	6
Extras	lb 5, w 4, nb 15	24
		437

	O	M	R	W
Kapil Dev	28	8	67	2
C.J. Sharma	20	2	68	1
Shastri	33	6	87	–
Arshad Ayub	30.5	4	104	5
Hirwani	29	2	106	1

FALL OF WICKETS
1–41, 2–219, 3–231, 4–270, 5–270, 6–357, 7–412, 8–413, 9–423

INDIA FIRST INNINGS

J. Arun Lal	c Richards, b Walsh	9
N.S. Sidhu	not out	42
R.J. Shastri	not out	29
D.B. Vengsarkar†		
M. Azharuddin		
S.V. Manjrekar		
R.N. Kapil Dev		
K.S. More*		
Arshad Ayub		
C.J. Sharma		
N.D. Hirwani		
Extras	lb 1, nb 5	6
	(for 1 wkt)	86

	O	M	R	W
Ambrose	3	2	6	–
Bishop	9	3	16	–
Benjamin	11	2	27	–
Walsh	6	–	12	1
Richards	7	1	17	–
Arthurton	3	–	7	–

FALL OF WICKETS
1–14

Umpires: D.M. Archer & L.H. Barker

Match abandoned as a draw

Ravi Shastri – a brave all-round series for India. (Alan Cozzi)

1, 2, 3 and 4 April 1989

at Kingstown, St Vincent

Indians 103 for 9 dec (B.P. Patterson 5 for 47)
West Indies Board XI 185 for 3 (C.A. Best 58, C.L. Hooper 54 not out)

Match drawn

India's preparations for the second and third Test matches suffered a serious blow when rain prevented play on the first day of their match against the strong Board XI led by Roger Harper. Only 90 minutes play before lunch was possible on the second day, and there was no play on the third day. Patrick Patterson advanced his claim for a place in the West Indian Test side with a fierce bowling display, while Carl Hooper indicated his return to fitness with an unbeaten fifty on a last afternoon in which there was little else of consequence.

Second Test Match
WEST INDIES v. INDIA

Malcolm Marshall returned to the West Indian side and played a major part in his side's victory. It was not Marshall, however, who made the initial breakthrough after Richards had won the toss and asked India to bat first. Coming on as first change, Ian Bishop captured his first Test wicket with his first delivery, a ball which moved late and lifted sharply to find the edge of Arun Lal's bat. Shastri and Sidhu followed quickly as the result of poor shots and, at 27 for 3, India were in deep trouble.

Vengsarkar and Azharuddin added 41 in 70 minutes, but, since his elevation to the captaincy, Vengsarkar has inspired confidence neither as a leader nor as a batsman, and he was frequently beaten by Bishop before running himself out while attempting a second run to Curtly Ambrose at long-leg.

Sanjay Manjrekar immediately showed a quality of batsmanship that mocked the situation. Staunch in defence and positive in attack, with some flowing shots through the off-side field, he shared partnerships of 71 in 18 overs with Azharuddin and 79 in 12 overs with Kapil Dev. Kapil Dev's 34 off 26 balls brought him on a par with Ian Botham as the second of only two men to have taken 300 wickets and scored 4000 runs in Test cricket.

Bishop accounted for both Azharuddin and Kapil Dev. Azharuddin nudged at a short-pitched delivery, and Kapil Dev cut lazily and disappointingly into the hands of gully. More was soon out, and it was left to Arshad Ayub to help Manjrekar to the close, which came at 281 for 7, with Manjrekar seven short of his century.

In reaching three figures on the second morning, Sanjay Manjrekar earned just reward for an innings of calm

delight and authority which recalled memories of his father, the great Vijay Manjrekar. Arshad Ayub batted with much sense, and helped Manjrekar to add 84 for the eighth wicket, so that India reached 321 before being bowled out shortly before lunch.

Manjrekar, who batted for 5¾ hours and hit 15 fours, was one of Ian Bishop's six victims. He fended off a bouncer and was taken at third slip. Bishop bowled splendidly. He was quick, and his late outswinger brought five of his wickets as catches in the area between gully and the wicket-keeper.

Greenidge and Haynes began the West Indian innings in ideal circumstances, but India missed a glorious opportunity when Greenidge, on eight, mishooked Chetan Sharma to Arshad Ayub on the fine-leg boundary, but the fielder missed a simple chance. Greenidge went on to reach his 17th Test century, and he and Richardson put on 117 for the second wicket. Greenidge was caught at mid-wicket when he mis-hit another hook against Chetan Sharma. Hirwani bowled Arthurton first ball, and the leg-break bowler had Richards taken at short-leg off the last ball of the same over. Gus Logie swept at the final ball of the day's play and was caught at backward square-leg, so that West Indies were 246 for 5, and India were back in contention.

It was Richie Richardson who rebuilt the West Indian innings on the third morning, adding 79 with the fluent

SECOND TEST MATCH – WEST INDIES v. INDIA
7, 8, 9, 11 and 12 April 1989 at Kensington Oval, Bridgetown, Barbados

INDIA

	FIRST INNINGS			SECOND INNINGS	
J. Arun Lal	c Dujon, b Bishop	8	c Haynes, b Walsh	15
N.S. Sidhu	c Richards, b Walsh	9	c Logie, b Marshall	0
R.J. Shastri	c Richardson, b Bishop	6	c sub (Herbert), b Ambrose	107
D.B. Vengsarkar†	run out	20	c Dujon, b Bishop	6
M. Azharuddin	c Ambrose, b Bishop	61	c Dujon, b Marshall	14
S.V. Manjrekar	c Greenidge, b Bishop	108	c Logie, b Ambrose	3
R.N. Kapil Dev	c Richardson, b Bishop	34	c Dujon, b Marshall	1
K.S. More*	c Dujon, b Marshall	1	b Marshall	50
Arshad Ayub	c Richards, b Bishop	32	b Marshall	0
C.J. Sharma	not out	12	c Dujon, b Ambrose	21
N.D. Hirwani	c Haynes, b Walsh	1	not out	1
Extras	b 2, lb 5, nb 22	29	b 16, lb 4, nb 13	33
		321		251

WEST INDIES

	FIRST INNINGS			SECOND INNINGS	
C.G. Greenidge	c Hirwani, b Sharma	117	lbw, b Sharma	6
D.L. Haynes	c Manjrekar, b Shastri	27	not out	112
R.B. Richardson	c Sidhu, b Ayub	93	b Ayub	59
K.L.T. Arthurton	b Hirwani	0	not out	11
I.V.A. Richards†	c sub (Robin Singh), b Hirwani	1		
A.L. Logie	c Manjrekar, b Shastri	26		
P.J.L. Dujon*	c Manjrekar, b Shastri	33		
M.D. Marshall	not out	40		
C.E.L. Ambrose	c Kapil Dev, b Shastri	3		
I.R. Bishop	lbw, b Kapil Dev	8		
C.A. Walsh	b Kapil Dev	0		
Extras	lb 7, nb 22	29	lb 5, nb 3	8
		377	(for 2 wkts)	196

	O	M	R	W	O	M	R	W
Marshall	22	–	56	1	26	5	60	5
Ambrose	26	5	84	–	21.4	3	66	3
Bishop	25	5	87	6	24	7	55	1
Walsh	23.2	5	69	2	20	6	34	1
Richards	9	3	18	–	6	–	16	–
Arthurton					1	1	0	–

	O	M	R	W	O	M	R	W
Kapil Dev	24.5	3	68	2	8	–	42	–
C.J. Sharma	18	1	86	1	4	–	19	1
Arshad Ayub	17	1	55	1	14	4	26	1
Hirwani	24	1	83	2	11	–	56	–
Shastri	28	7	78	4	11	2	41	–
Manjrekar					1	–	7	–

FALL OF WICKETS
1–14, 2–22, 3–27, 4–68, 5–139, 6–218, 7–219, 8–303, 9–320
1–0, 2–23, 3–32, 4–53, 5–62, 6–63, 7–195, 8–195, 9–245

FALL OF WICKETS
1–84, 2–201, 3–201, 4–203, 5–246, 6–325, 7–325, 8–354, 9–377
1–14, 2–142

Umpires: D.M. Archer & L.H. Barker

West Indies won by 8 wickets

Jeff Dujon – more dismissals than any other West Indian wicket-keeper in Test history. (Adrian Murrell/Allsport)

More. Shastri had come to the wicket without a run on the board, but he battled away for seven hours and 20 minutes to reach his eighth Test century before being last out. He batted in his usual calm and cultured manner and added 132 with More for the seventh wicket. Shastri was later to be named Man of the Match for his resolute efforts with both bat and ball.

India were all out five minutes after tea on the fourth day. Greenidge was leg before to Sharma in the third over of the West Indian second innings when a delivery kept low, but Haynes and Richardson scored at a furious pace. They added 126 in 106 minutes, before Richardson had his off bail clipped by a ball from Arshad Ayub. Haynes, 80 at the close of the fourth day, reached his 12th Test century on the last morning with a four and a six off Hirwani, and West Indies needed only 12 overs to score the last 42 runs that they needed to complete an emphatic victory.

Third Test Match
WEST INDIES v. INDIA

India's miserable tour continued with the loss of Azharuddin from their side with a groin strain shortly before the third Test match. His place was taken by Raman, who had been flown out as a replacement for the injured Srikkanth.

Vengsarkar won the toss and asked West Indies to bat first. The home side had to struggle hard against the Indian spinners on the opening day, but although Ayub, Hirwani and Shastri turned the ball sharply, they bowled far too many loose deliveries, of which the West Indian batsmen took full advantage. It was Kapil Dev who made the early breakthrough with a fine away swinger, but Arshad Ayub immediately turned the ball a considerable amount, and it was he who bore the burden of the attack. He had Richardson caught off an attempted sweep, and the same shot was the undoing of Haynes, who had played well until that point. He swept at Shastri and was well caught by Raman running in from the boundary and diving forward. The fielder injured himself in the process. Richards, too, was out before tea when he tried to cut at Ayub's off-spin, and was bowled. The off-break bowler also captured the wicket of Arthurton before the close, which came with West Indies on 237 for 5.

Arthurton played with great care for 3½ hours to give the West Indian innings some stability, but it was Gus Logie who breathed life into it. He hit 7 fours and was quick to attack when given the opportunity. He was out shortly before lunch on the second morning, caught behind off a widish leg-break, but he had taken West Indies to a position of some strength on a wicket which always encouraged the bowlers.

Sidhu and Arun Lal negotiated 13 overs without too much trouble, but Marshall cut down his pace and began to move the ball back off the pitch or swing it away in the air. Sidhu's middle and off stumps were knocked back, and Shastri was taken at bat and pad. Vengsarkar dragged a ball from Richards onto his stumps, and Marshall struck again when he had Arun Lal taken at slip. The carnage continued, and Walsh supported Marshall with late wickets, so that India closed at 122 for 8, their plight desperate.

Dujon. Both batsmen were dismissed at the same total, 325, but Marshall struck some lusty blows to give West Indies a 56-run advantage on the first innings. Shastri, with 4 for 78, bowled better than he had done in a Test match for some considerable time.

India had seemingly recovered from their desperate plight in the early stages of the match, but they were soon plunged back into despair as Marshall had Sidhu taken at short-leg before a run was scored. Arun Lal batted with great resolution for 74 minutes before lashing out at a ball from Walsh and being taken in the gully. Vengsarkar's stay was brief. He fell to an enormous outswinger from Bishop.

Azharuddin and Shastri added 21 in half an hour, before Malcolm Marshall returned for his second spell. With his fifth ball he persuaded Azharuddin to nibble at an outswinger, and Dujon took a tumbling catch. It was Marshall's 310th wicket in Test cricket and took him ahead of Lance Gibbs' record number of wickets by a West Indian in Test cricket.

Kapil Dev was out in the same way as Azharuddin, and Manjrekar was taken at short-leg off Ambrose. India ended the third day at 81 for 6, defeat and despair imminent.

That India died bravely was entirely due to Shastri and

Marshall was not needed on the third morning, as Walsh ended Indian resistance after Arshad Ayub and Chetan Sharma had batted with spirit. Under heavy cloud, Sharma and Kapil Dev then gave the West Indian batsmen a torrid time to give hope of an Indian revival. Sharma took three wickets in his first 10 overs, and West Indies were reduced to 26 for 4. They were rescued by Richardson and Logie, and by the end of the day West Indies were 199 for 7, and the match was almost out of reach of India.

The day was not without controversy. Kapil Dev and the Indians did not disguise their disgust when Richardson was given not out to leg before appeals, and Vengsarkar later complained that his side had been robbed by bad umpiring.

It was Kapil Dev who ended the West Indian innings on the fourth day, giving himself five or more wickets in a Test innings for the 20th time. His victims included Richie Richardson, bowled round his legs by the second new ball, but Richardson's innings and his ninth-wicket stand of 46 with the impressive Bishop had taken the game way out of India's reach.

Needing 431 to win, India temporarily lost Arun Lal with a blow on the ear off one of the rare short deliveries. Sidhu was out when he drove at Ambrose and sliced the ball to Dujon, but there were no further mishaps until after tea when, in four consecutive overs, India lost four wickets and collapsed to 75 for 5. Raman was leg before to

a ball of very full length, and Shastri and Kapil Dev edged outswingers to the wicket-keeper. Only Manjrekar, who was leg before to a ball that shot along the ground, could blame the pitch for his dismissal.

Arun Lal became the fifth victim in an hour, caught behind off a splendid ball from the irrepressible Marshall. Vengsarkar, not without some luck, and More stayed together until the close, 161 for 6. More spent two brave hours over his 42 before offering no stroke to a Marshall in-swinger, and Vengsarkar was last out, caught at short-leg. Marshall, 11 for 89, was the undisputed Man of the Match.

22, 23, 24 and 25 April 1989

at Sabina Park, Kingston, Jamaica

Indians 586 (N.S. Sidhu 286, D.B. Vengsarkar 111, S.V. Manjrekar 57, A.K. Sharma 57) and 104 for 3
Jamaica 330 (C.A. Davidson 74, S.K. Sharma 4 for 61)

Match drawn

With the Test series already lost, the Indian tourists played the penultimate match of the trip against the Red Stripe Cup winners, who did not field their front line attack. Navjot Singh Sidhu hit 286, the highest score by an Indian on tour. He opened the innings and was ninth out at 568. His innings included 2 sixes and 27 fours. The tourists took

---

THIRD TEST MATCH – WEST INDIES v. INDIA
15, 16, 17, 19 and 20 April 1989 at Queen's Park Oval, Port of Spain, Trinidad

WEST INDIES

	FIRST INNINGS			SECOND INNINGS	
C.G. Greenidge	c More, b Kapil Dev	21	c More, b Sharma		5
D.L. Haynes	c Raman, b Shastri	65	c Shastri, b Sharma		6
R.B. Richardson	c Hirwani, b Ayub	15	b Kapil Dev		99
K.L.T. Arthurton	c sub (Robin Singh), b Ayub	37	lbw, b Kapil Dev		1
I.V.A. Richards†	b Ayub	19	c Manjrekar, b Sharma		0
A.L. Logie	c More, b Hirwani	87	c and b Hirwani		38
P.J.L. Dujon*	c Raman, b Ayub	5	b Shastri		3
M.D. Marshall	st More, b Ayub	18	lbw, b Kapil Dev		26
C.E.L. Ambrose	c More, b Kapil Dev	12	c More, b Kapil Dev		16
I.R. Bishop	not out	11	not out		30
C.A. Walsh	c Arun Lal, b Hirwani	6	b Kapil Dev		4
Extras	b 7, lb 5, nb 6	18	b 3, lb 24, w 1, nb 10		38
		314			**266**

INDIA

	FIRST INNINGS			SECOND INNINGS	
J. Arun Lal	c Richards, b Marshall	30	(2) c Dujon, b Marshall		18
N.S. Sidhu	b Marshall	11	(1) c Dujon, b Ambrose		1
R.J. Shastri	c Logie, b Marshall	8	c Dujon, b Bishop		15
D.B. Vengsarkar†	b Richards	2	(5) c Logie, b Marshall		62
W.V. Raman	c Dujon, b Walsh	17	(4) lbw, b Marshall		15
S.V. Manjrekar	lbw, b Marshall	0	lbw, b Marshall		1
R.N. Kapil Dev	c Dujon, b Marshall	16	c Dujon, b Bishop		4
K.S. More*	b Walsh	2	lbw, b Marshall		42
Arshad Ayub	b Walsh	29	c Richards, b Bishop		1
C.J. Sharma	not out	19	b Marshall		7
N.D. Hirwani	lbw, b Walsh	0	not out		1
Extras	b 2, lb 5, w 1, nb 8	16	b 7, lb 15, nb 24		46
		150			**213**

	O	M	R	W	O	M	R	W
Kapil Dev	19	6	45	2	25	5	58	5
C.J. Sharma	6	1	23	–	13	–	54	3
Arshad Ayub	52	11	117	5	18	1	50	–
Shastri	27	8	58	1	18	3	32	1
Hirwani	19.3	1	59	2	19	4	40	1
Raman					3	1	5	–

	O	M	R	W	O	M	R	W
Ambrose	9	1	28	–	15	8	23	1
Bishop	11	4	16	–	25	8	81	3
Walsh	18	5	37	4	10	4	15	–
Marshall	17	7	34	5	19.5	2	55	6
Richards	12	3	28	1	8	–	13	–
Arthurton					4	2	4	–

FALL OF WICKETS
1–33, 2–80, 3–118, 4–146, 5–216, 6–238, 7–269, 8–294, 9–302
1–17, 2–18, 3–23, 4–26, 5–100, 6–119, 7–180, 8–204, 9–250

1–32, 2–47, 3–50, 4–61, 5–68, 6–89, 7–93, 8–99, 9–148
1–20, 2–60, 3–64, 4–66, 5–75, 6–92, 7–190, 8–194, 9–212

Umpires: C.E. Cumberbatch & A. Weekes

West Indies won by 217 runs

Navjot Singh Sidhu, 286 v. Jamaica, the highest score by an Indian on tour, was followed by a brave century in the final Test. (Adrian Murrell/Allsport)

a first-innings lead of 256, but they did not enforce the follow-on, and the match ended in a tame draw.

<hr>

Fourth Test Match
WEST INDIES v. INDIA

West Indies were unchanged for the third Test match in succession. India had Azharuddin fit again in place of Raman, and brought in Venkataramana for his first Test match in place of Hirwani, who was not fully fit and had been poorly handled by Vengsarkar throughout the series.

Richards asked India to bat first when he won the toss, but the tourists batted courageously in a hostile pre-lunch spell and lost only the wicket of Arun Lal, who had defended stubbornly for 72 minutes. Shastri was out immediately after lunch when he drove at Bishop and was caught at slip at the second attempt by Richards. Vengsarkar and Azharuddin were also out in the afternoon session, but Sidhu battled on bravely in spite of receiving some painful blows, and reached his second Test hundred. Another blow on the hand forced him to retire hurt shortly before the close with his score on 116, and Manjrekar and More continued to the end of the day and took the score to 226.

Walsh brought the Indian innings to a close on the second day to finish with 6 for 62, his best performance in Test cricket. One of his victims was Sidhu, who failed to add to his score when he returned to the crease after his retirement through injury.

CABLE AND WIRELESS TEST SERIES AVERAGES – WEST INDIES v. INDIA

WEST INDIES BATTING

	M	Inns	NOs	Runs	HS	Av	100s	50s
R.B. Richardson	4	7		619	194	88.42	2	3
D.L. Haynes	4	7	1	280	112*	46.66	1	1
A.L. Logie	4	6	1	214	87	42.80		1
C.G. Greenidge	4	7		243	117	34.71	1	1
M.D. Marshall	3	4	1	84	40*	28.00		
I.R. Bishop	4	5	3	55	30*	27.50		
I.V.A. Richards	4	5		135	110	27.00	1	
P.J.L. Dujon	4	5		83	33	16.60		
K.L.T. Arthurton	4	7	2	78	37	15.60		
C.E.L. Ambrose	4	5	1	54	16	13.50		
C.A. Walsh	4	5		20	6	4.00		

Played in one Test: W.K.M. Benjamin 7

INDIA BATTING

	M	Inns	NOs	Runs	HS	Av	100s	50s
S.V. Manjrekar	4	6		200	108	33.33	1	
N.S. Sidhu	4	7	1	179	116	29.83	1	
R.J. Shastri	4	7	1	170	107	28.33	1	
M. Azharuddin	3	4		113	61	28.25		1
C.J. Sharma	4	6	2	86	21	21.50		
D.B. Vengsarkar	4	6		110	62	18.33		1
K.S. More	4	6		103	50	17.16		1
J. Arun Lal	4	7		113	30	16.14		
R.N. Kapil Dev	4	6		91	34	15.16		
Arshad Ayub	4	6		78	32	13.00		
N.D. Hirwani	3	4	2	3	1*	1.50		

Played in one Test: W.V. Raman 17 & 15; M. Venkataramana 0* & 0*

WEST INDIES BOWLING

	Overs	Mds	Runs	Wkts	Av	Best	10/m	5/inns
C.A. Walsh	123.2	33	268	18	14.88	6/62	1	1
M.D. Marshall	111.2	18	290	19	15.26	6/55	1	3
I.R. Bishop	137	38	371	16	23.18	6/87		1
C.E.L. Ambrose	95	20	273	5	54.60	3/66		
I.V.A. Richards	51	8	128	1	128.00	1/28		
K.L.T. Arthurton	14	3	37	0	–	–		

Bowled in one innings: W.K.M. Benjamin 11-2-27-0

INDIA BOWLING

	Overs	Mds	Runs	Wkts	Av	Best	10/m	5/inns
R.N. Kapil Dev	151.5	31	386	18	21.44	6/84		2
Arshad Ayub	171.4	33	451	14	32.21	5/104		2
C.J. Sharma	90	6	366	8	45.75	3/54		
R.J. Shastri	137	29	339	7	48.42	4/78		
N.D. Hirwani	102.3	8	344	6	57.33	2/59		
M. Venkataramana	11.4	1	58	1	58.00	1/10		

Bowled in one innings: W.V. Raman 3-1-5-0; S.V. Manjrekar 1-0-7-0

WEST INDIES FIELDING FIGURES

14 – P.J.L. Dujon; 10 - I.V.A. Richards; 5 - A.L. Logie; 3 - D.L. Haynes and C.G. Greenidge; 2 - R.B. Richardson, K.L.T. Arthurton and C.E.L. Ambrose; 1 - sub (Herbert)

INDIA FIELDING FIGURES

11 - K.S. More (ct 8/st 3); 4 - S.V. Manjrekar and N.D. Hirwani; 3 - R.J. Shastri; 2 - J. Arun Lal, W.V. Raman and sub (Robin Singh); 1 - N.S. Sidhu, M. Azharuddin, C.J. Sharma, R.N. Kapil Dev and M. Venkataramana

FOURTH TEST MATCH – WEST INDIES v. INDIA
28, 29 and 30 April, 2 and 3 May 1989 at Sabina Park, Kingston, Jamaica

INDIA

	FIRST INNINGS		SECOND INNINGS	
N.S. Sidhu	c Richards, b Walsh	116	(2) c Greenidge, b Walsh	0
J. Arun Lal	c Richards, b Marshall	7	(1) c Greenidge, b Bishop	26
R.J. Shastri	c Richards, b Bishop	5	lbw, b Bishop	0
D.B. Vengsarkar†	c Dujon, b Bishop	12	(5) b Bishop	8
M. Azharuddin	c Richards, b Walsh	25	(6) b Walsh	13
S.V. Manjrekar	c Logie, b Walsh	47	(4) c Haynes, b Walsh	41
K.S. More*	hit wkt, b Walsh	6	(8) c Dujon, b Walsh	2
R.N. Kapil Dev	c Ambrose, b Walsh	23	(7) c Richards, b Bishop	13
Arshad Ayub	c Arthurton, b Walsh	2	run out	14
C.J. Sharma	c Arthurton, b Ambrose	6	b Marshall	21
M. Venkataramana	not out	0	not out	0
Extras	b 1, lb 7, w 1, nb 31	40	b 1, lb 2, nb 11	14
		289		152

	O	M	R	W	O	M	R	W
Ambrose	13.2	1	46	1	7	–	20	–
Bishop	26	8	55	2	17	3	61	4
Walsh	29	6	62	6	17	7	39	4
Marshall	19	4	56	1	7.3	–	29	1
Richards	9	1	36	–				
Arthurton	6	–	26	–				

FALL OF WICKETS
1–35, 2–64, 3–97, 4–142, 5–252, 6–252, 7–256, 8–279, 9–285
1–0, 2–1, 3–75, 4–75, 5–88, 6–100, 7–107, 8–113, 9–150

WEST INDIES

	FIRST INNINGS		SECOND INNINGS	
C.G. Greenidge	c Arun Lal, b Kapil Dev	0	c More, b Kapil Dev	12
D.L. Haynes	c Shastri, b Kapil Dev	15	st More, b Venkataramana	35
R.B. Richardson	b Kapil Dev	156	st More, b Shastri	3
K.L.T. Arthurton	c Azharuddin, b Sharma	20	not out	0
I.V.A. Richards†	c More, b Kapil Dev	110		
A.L. Logie	lbw, b Kapil Dev	11	(5) not out	6
P.J.L. Dujon*	b Ayub	11		
M.D. Marshall	b Kapil Dev	0		
C.E.L. Ambrose	c More, b Sharma	10		
I.R. Bishop	not out	6		
C.A. Walsh	c Venkataramana, b Ayub	4		
Extras	b 10, lb 9, w 3, nb 19	41	lb 3, nb 1	4
		384	(for 3 wkts)	60

	O	M	R	W	O	M	R	W
Kapil Dev	38	7	84	6	9	2	22	1
C.J. Sharma	27	2	100	2	2	–	16	–
Arshad Ayub	39.5	12	99	2				
Venkataramana	11	1	48	–	0.4	–	10	1
Shastri	13	1	34	–	7	2	9	1

FALL OF WICKETS
1–1, 2–32, 3–86, 4–321, 5–343, 6–344, 7–344, 8–364, 9–378
1–31, 2–50, 3–54

Umpires: D.M. Archer & S. Bucknor

West Indies won by 8 wickets

Kapil Dev, who bowled manfully throughout the series, made an immediate breakthrough for India when he had Greenidge caught at slip off the last ball of his opening over. Kapil added Haynes' wicket in his fifth over. Arthurton spent 90 minutes in scoring 20, and when he was out at 86 India seemed to have the advantage. Richards began uncertainly – he had scored only 25 runs in four innings in the series – but he stayed with Richie Richardson until the close, when the score was 170 for 3.

Richards refound his authority on the third day, moving from 50 to 110 off only 68 balls. He and Richardson, the outstanding batsman of the series, added 235 and took West Indies into the lead, before Richards was adjudged caught behind off Kapil Dev, although there was debate between the two umpires, and it seemed that the ball had brushed the West Indian captain's pad. He reacted angrily to the decision and was later fined for his show of dissent. The crowd reacted with some bottle-throwing, which Richards himself had to quell.

The dismissal of Richards brought about a collapse, but it was apparent that the West Indian lead of 95 would prove a major obstacle to India's hopes of saving the game. The home side owed a vast amount to Richardson, who batted for nearly eight hours and hit 20 fours in what was his 10th Test century, his fourth in his last seven Test matches. The size of the West Indian lead became magnified when India lost Sidhu and Shastri in the first two overs of their second innings. They should have lost Arun Lal, too, but he was dropped in the slips off Bishop and stayed until the close with Manjrekar.

The pair batted for an hour on the fourth morning and took their partnership to 74 before Walsh and Bishop scythed through the spineless Indian batting. Six wickets fell for 38 runs, and only Arshad Ayub and Chetan Sharma offered further resistance. Walsh captured 10 wickets in a Test match for the first time, and bad weather brought play to an end, with West Indies 31 for 1, still 27 short of victory.

Their third win in four matches in the series came after 40 minutes on the last day, when Logie hit Venkataramana for six in the same over in which he had just captured his first Test wicket.

West Indies had reasserted their claim to be the world's leading Test side in a series from which India could draw little comfort, and which left one with the feeling that the tourists were desperately in need of positive and responsible leadership.

First-Class Averages

BATTING

	M	Inns	NOs	Runs	HS	Av	100s	50s
C.A. Davidson	7	9	3	490	200*	81.66	1	3
C.A. Best	7	10	2	600	157*	75.00	3	2
M.H.W. Inniss	3	5	2	217	68*	72.33		2
R.B. Richardson	5	9		633	194	70.33	2	3
A.F.D. Jackman	7	10	5	333	106*	66.60	1	1
D.L. Haynes	5	8	1	362	112*	51.71	1	2
B.C. Lara	8	11		567	182	51.54	2	1
D.S. Morgan	7	10		493	122	49.30	2	2
C.B. Lambert	7	9	1	374	105*	46.75	1	1
D.A. Joseph	6	9		419	128	46.55	1	2
L.L. Harris	4	7	2	228	68*	45.60		1
A.L. Logie	5	8	2	270	87	45.00		2
J.J. Pierre	3	6	1	219	73	43.80		2
M.D. Marshall	4	5	1	173	89	43.25		1
R.A. Harper	3	3		126	51	42.00		1
S. Dhaniram	7	9		371	93	41.22		5
R.M. Otto	5	9		363	116	40.33	1	2
K.L.T. Arthurton	7	13	2	441	154	40.09	1	2
A.L. Grant	5	5	1	151	88	37.75		1
L.K. Puckerin	4	3		113	79	37.66		1
T.R.O. Payne	5	6	1	186	70	37.20		2
L.D. John	5	8	1	252	67	36.00		3
D.I. Mohammed	5	9	2	226	87*	32.28		1
P.V. Simmons	7	13	2	346	116*	31.45	1	
M.A. Tucker	6	9	2	219	61	31.28		3
J.C. Adams	7	10		307	63	30.70		2
C.G. Greenidge	5	8		243	117	30.37	1	1
M.C. Neita	5	7		207	55	29.57		1
R. Seeram	6	7		202	96	28.85		1
J.D. Charles	5	7	1	173	48*	28.83		
K.A. Williams	5	9		258	167	28.66	1	1
W.K.M. Benjamin	5	5		136	85	27.20		1
I.V.A. Richards	4	5		135	110	27.00	1	
R. Nanan	5	8	1	187	59	26.71		2
W.W. Lewis	6	9		233	103	25.88	1	
E.A.E. Baptiste	5	9		231	95	25.66		1
W.W. Thomas	5	7		160	69	22.85		1
S.N. Mohammed	6	7	1	135	79	22.50		1
P.J.L. Dujon	5	7		152	64	21.71		1
L.C. Sebastien	5	7		151	91	21.57		1
R.I.C. Holder	4	6	1	107	36	21.40		
N.C. Guishard	4	7		142	32	20.28		
R.C. Haynes	6	10	1	176	46	19.55		
A.L. Kelly	4	7		133	77	19.00		1
C.E.L. Ambrose	5	7	1	105	34	17.50		
D.T. Telemaque	4	6		102	44	17.00		
M.P. Carew	3	6		102	56	17.00		1
R. Dhanraj	6	9	3	102	47	17.00		
L.L. Lawrence	4	7		100	36	14.28		
N.O. Perry	8	9		128	47	14.22		
J.R. Murray	6	8		108	31	13.50		

(Qualification: 100 runs, average 10.00)

BOWLING

	Overs	Mds	Runs	Wkts	Av	Best	10/m	5/inn
E.A.E. Baptiste	99.4	22	272	21	12.95	6/26	1	3
M.D. Marshall	130.2	21	350	20	17.50	6/55	1	3
C.A. Walsh	166.2	42	397	22	18.04	6/62	1	1
I.R. Bishop	212.4	50	584	32	18.25	6/41		2
N.O. Perry	297.4	62	763	35	21.80	8/45	1	2
M.A. Small	160.4	25	441	20	22.05	6/55		1
L.A. Joseph	135.1	25	443	20	22.15	4/43		
R. Nanan	244.1	69	512	23	22.26	5/41		2
G.L. Linton	160.2	30	449	18	24.94	5/78		2
G.J.F. Ferris	92.1	17	347	13	26.69	3/16		
M.A. Holding	92	15	268	10	26.80	2/36		
R. Dhanraj	240.4	39	730	27	27.03	6/75		3
C.G. Butts	225.4	61	464	17	27.29	4/18		
R.C. Haynes	232.4	56	601	22	27.31	4/76		
A.H. Gray	157.4	27	548	20	27.40	4/29		
J.A. Angus	120	25	350	11	31.81	3/60		
I.A. Allen	174.3	21	564	15	37.60	5/102		1
W.W. Thomas	109.3	10	426	11	38.72	4/73		
T.Z. Kentish	209.1	35	483	12	40.25	5/110		1
J.T. Etienne	164	31	446	10	44.60	3/63		

(Qualification – 10 wickets)

LEADING FIELDERS

17 - P.J.L. Dujon; 13 - L.K. Puckerin (ct 12/st 1); 11 - M.A. Holding; 10 I.V.A. Richards, C.A. Best and P.V. Simmons; 9 - D. Williams and J.R. Murray (ct 8/st 1); 8 - J.C. Adams, B.C. Lara and S.N. Mohammed (ct 6/2)

New Era Postponed

The season in England. Benson and Hedges Cup.
Britannic Assurance County Championship.
Refuge Assurance League and Cup.
NatWest Bank Trophy. Tilcon Trophy.
Seeboard Trophy.
Four Counties Tournament.
Cornhill Test Matches, England *v.* Australia.
Texaco Trophy. Form charts. First-class averages.
Review of the season.

Cricket at Cheltenham. (Adrian Murrell/Allsport)

The death of Wilf Slack while playing cricket in Gambia added to the gloom of an English close season which was already cast in shadow. The cancellation of the tour to India was not unexpected, nor was the ICC's decision to ban from international cricket for a period of four years all those who had cricketing links with South Africa after March 1989, but both events continued to cloud the cricket world with a sense of uncertainty and unease.

Peter May retired as chairman of selectors, and in what amounted to a palace coup, Ted Dexter became supremo of English cricket. Many counties were less than happy that his appointment was presented to them as something of a *fait accompli* and that they were asked merely to rubber stamp their approval. David Gower was reinstated as England's captain for the summer, and he, Dexter and Stewart would select the England side. We were told that a new era had begun.

There was the usual crop of 'transfers'. Greg Thomas, having fretted for two or three seasons, decided that he would become a better bowler away from his native county and moved to Northamptonshire. Chris Tavare, still, it seemed, wounded by the loss of the captaincy, chose to go west to Somerset, and DeFreitas went north from Leicestershire to Lancashire, in search of self-discipline, one hopes. Simon Dennis trod the road from Yorkshire to Glamorgan as others had done before him, and Glamorgan also threatened to include Viv Richards in their side later in the summer. Essex, surprisingly, brought Mike Garnham back to first-class cricket, and Sussex signed the much travelled and often troubled David Smith from Surrey, who had also dispensed with the services of another England player, Jack Richards, who did not find another county.

The sun began to shine. There was the round of pre-season lunches, dinners and gatherings, and, on 15 April, the Champion County took the field against MCC, and the cricket season began.

15, 16, 17 and 18 April

at Lord's

Worcestershire 474 for 3 dec (G.A. Hick 173 not out, T.S. Curtis 92, G.J. Lord 80, P.A. Neale 50 not out)
MCC 281 for 4 (A.J. Lamb 67 not out, J.D. Carr 64, R.A. Smith 56)

Match drawn

15, 16 and 17 April

at Cambridge

Glamorgan 307 (H. Morris 102, M.J. Cann 58, M.F. Mullins 5 for 77)
Cambridge University 135 for 6

Match drawn

15, 16 and 18 April

at Oxford

Northamptonshire 356 for 6 dec (W. Larkins 126, E.D. Hester 4 for 91) and 39 for 0
Oxford University 177 (M.J. Kilborn 52, D.J. Capel 4 for 33)

Match drawn

LEFT: *The season begins. MCC v. Worcestershire at Lord's. Gordon Lord and Tim Curtis occupied most of the first day with a stand of 177. Lord turns a ball to leg watched by Lamb, Russell and Carr. (Adrian Murrell/Allsport)*

BELOW LEFT: *Three county captains in action for MCC – Lamb (Northamptonshire), Parker (Sussex) and Chris Cowdrey (Kent). (Adrian Murrell/Allsport)*

BELOW: *Graeme Hick acknowledges the applause as he reaches his century for the Champion County against MCC, 16 April. (Patrick Eagar)*

BELOW RIGHT: *. . . but the season's first centurion was Wayne Larkins, 126 for Northamptonshire against Oxford University in The Parks. (David Munden)*

The doubts that had existed as to whether or not the season at Lord's would begin on time because of the difficulties that the ground staff had had in preparing the wicket disappeared when the sun shone and Curtis and Lord came out to open the Worcestershire innings. They were cast in the role of supporting players as a good sized crowd awaited the arrival of the leading performers, Hick and fit-again Ian Botham. Curtis and Lord, however, were unwilling to accept their subservient roles and occupied much of the Saturday with an opening stand of 177. The second day belonged to Graeme Hick, who indicated that he would continue in the form that he had exhibited in 1988 and in New Zealand, by hitting 173 not out. One hundred and two of his runs came off 92 balls in the second session on Sunday. Monday was lost to rain, and the MCC hopefuls, led, diplomatically, by Paul Parker, batted brightly on the last day.

Rain ruined the matches at Oxford and Cambridge after entertaining play on the Saturday. Wayne Larkins was the season's first centurion, beating Hugh Morris, the Glamorgan captain, by a matter of minutes.

19, 20 and 21 April

at Cambridge

Gloucestershire 345 for 7 dec (P. Bainbridge 97, P.W. Romaines 64, R.C. Russell 59 not out, A.J. Wright 55)
Cambridge University 187 for 6 (J.C.M. Atkinson 51)

Match drawn

at Oxford

Surrey 447 for 6 dec (D.M. Ward 145, I.A. Greig 107 not out, D.J. Bicknell 82) and 119 for 1 dec (K.T. Medlycott 56 not out)

Oxford University 201 (P.D. Lunn 61) and 120 for 4

Match drawn

There was no play on the second day at Oxford, and rain also curtailed play at Fenner's, but there was time enough for David Ward to hit a career-best 145 and for skipper Ian Greig to begin the season with a blistering century. Phil Bainbridge started his benefit year with a flourish.

20, 21, 22 and 24 April

at Derby

Derbyshire 183 (W.W. Davis 4 for 43) and 216 (K.J. Barnett 74, D.J. Capel 5 for 53)
Northamptonshire 161 (G. Cook 53, P.G. Newman 5 for 45, S.J. Base 4 for 61) and 177 for 9

Match drawn
Derbyshire 5 pts, Northamptonshire 5 pts

at Southampton

Somerset 413 (P.M. Roebuck 149, S.J. Cook 85, N.D. Burns 62, M.C.J. Nicholas 6 for 37) and 71 for 1
Hampshire 318 (R.A. Smith 127, R.J. Parks 76 not out, N.A. Mallender 4 for 58)

Match drawn
Somerset 6 pts, Hampshire 4 pts

at Leicester

Leicestershire 190 (S.L. Watkin 6 for 53) and 415 for 9 dec

New Era? David Gower, Ted Dexter and Micky Stewart at the press conference to announce Gower's appointment as England captain. (David Leah/Allsport)

RIGHT: *David Ward began the season with a career-best 145 for Surrey against Oxford University, 19 April. (Adrian Murrell/Allsport)*

(D.I. Gower 228, S.L. Watkin 4 for 130)
Glamorgan 167 (J. Derrick 67, G.J.F. Ferris 4 for 44) and 166 for 4 (A.R. Butcher 84 not out)

Match drawn
Leicestershire 5 pts, Glamorgan 5 pts

at Canterbury

Essex 203 (A.W. Lilley 65, C. Penn 4 for 57) and 224 for 3 dec (J.P. Stephenson 109 not out, G.A. Gooch 55)
Kent 119 (N.A. Foster 4 for 38, T.D. Topley 4 for 39) and 133 for 8 (N.R. Taylor 63, D.R. Pringle 4 for 36)

Match drawn
Essex 6 pts, Kent 4 pts

at Lord's

Middlesex 260 (M.W. Gatting 72, P.W. Jarvis 5 for 77) and 119 for 4
Yorkshire 130 (A.R.C. Fraser 4 for 28)

Match drawn
Middlesex 7 pts, Yorkshire 3 pts

at Trent Bridge

Nottinghamshire 218 (D.W. Randall 73 not out, G.R. Dilley 5 for 42) and 198 (B.C. Broad 61, N.V. Radford 4 for 56)
Worcestershire 291 (T.S. Curtis 68, G.A. Hick 56) and 129 for 3 (G.A. Hick 55 not out)

Worcestershire won by 7 wickets
Worcestershire 22 pts, Nottinghamshire 5 pts

at Edgbaston

Lancashire 259 (G. Fowler 56) and 171 (G.C. Small 5 for 55)
Warwickshire 210 (T.A. Lloyd 65, P.J.W. Allott 4 for 44) and 81 for 4

Match drawn
Lancashire 7 pts, Warwickshire 6 pts

The first round of four-day matches in the Britannic Assurance County Championship produced only one result. Weather deemed that there should be no play on the last day at Lord's or Southampton, and made life rather uncomfortable elsewhere.

Derbyshire were quickly bowled out by Winston Davis and newcomer to the Northamptonshire side Greg Thomas, but the visitors, 45 for 2 at the end of the first day, collapsed on the second and trailed on the first innings. Eventually, Northamptonshire needed 239 to win and began the last day at 47 for 2, but snow and rain delayed the start until 4.00 p.m. and the match died bravely with neither side quite managing victory.

South African Jim Cook made a most impressive debut for Somerset, hitting 129 runs for once out. He and Peter Roebuck began the match at Southampton with a stand of 143. This was followed by a mid-order collapse, but Neil Burns helped Roebuck to add 151 for the sixth wicket, and Somerset reached a commanding 413. The Hampshire attack, without Marshall, Ayling and Tremlett, looked threadbare, and it was left to skipper Mark Nicholas to end the innings with his medium pace. His 6 for 37 was a career-best performance. Robin Smith played a gem of an innings for Hampshire, hitting 18 fours and looking in his very best form, and later Bobby Parks allayed any fears of the follow-on before the rains came and claimed the final day.

The pace bowling of Steve Watkin was a feature at Grace Road, but his bowling was overshadowed by David Gower's second-innings display for the home side. The England captain hit the highest score of his career, with 2 sixes and 24 fours, and when he square cut Steve Barwick for 4 he reached 20,000 runs in first-class cricket. It was an innings of graceful belligerence, and his 228 came off 317 balls in 352 minutes. Rain ended any hope of a result on the Monday.

Rain can be said to have denied Essex victory at Canterbury. Their first innings was held together by a restrained knock from Alan Lilley, and Foster and Topley bowled them to a first-innings lead of 84. Gooch and Stephenson built on this with a powerful opening stand of 114 on the Saturday, and Stephenson went on to reach his first first-class century in England. He moved to three figures with 2 fours and a six off Kelleher, and, in all, he hit 4 sixes and 8 fours. Gooch declared at the Saturday night score. Pringle and Topley had Kent in trouble from the start of the innings, but, with Kent on 133 for 8 and 39 overs still remaining, rain came to the rescue of the home side.

Yorkshire, sadly weakened by injury, had the worst of a rain-reduced struggle against Middlesex, while hail and sleet ended the contest between Lancashire and Warwickshire with honours just about even.

Appropriately, the only winners were the reigning champions, Worcestershire. Neale chose to field first when he won the toss at Trent Bridge but, although Robinson was an early victim of Dilley's, Nottinghamshire passed 100 with only two wickets down. The last seven wickets fell for 88 runs, however, and only a responsible innings by Randall saved the home side from complete disaster. Curtis and Hick gave substance to the Worcestershire innings with a stand of 88 after two wickets had fallen for 47, but then wickets tumbled and eight men were out for 199. At this point Rhodes was joined by the aggressive Radford, and, in a stand which continued into the third morning, they added 86. Radford hit 47, and Rhodes finished with 40 not out. Nottinghamshire again began disastrously, but Broad and Johnson added 78 and wiped out the first-innings arrears. The Worcestershire seam attack was relentless, and the home side were bowled out for 198, leaving the visitors the last day in which to score 126 to win. In fact, with Hick and Curtis batting most sensibly on a wicket which encouraged the bowlers, they reached their target inside two hours.

Refuge Assurance League

23 April

at Derby

Derbyshire v. Northamptonshire

Match abandoned
Derbyshire 2 pts, Northamptonshire 2 pts

at Southampton

Somerset 220 for 8 (C.J. Tavare 120 not out)
Hampshire 221 for 5 (M.C.J. Nicholas 57)

Hampshire (2 pts) won by 5 wickets

at Canterbury

Kent 135
Essex 136 for 4

Essex (2 pts) won by 6 wickets

at Leicester

Leicestershire v. Glamorgan

Match abandoned
Leicestershire 2 pts, Glamorgan 2 pts

at Lord's

Yorkshire 170 for 9 (A.A. Metcalfe 76, P.E. Robinson 55)
Middlesex 162 for 2 (M.W. Gatting 81 not out)

Middlesex (2 pts) won on faster scoring rate

at Trent Bridge

Nottinghamshire v. Worcestershire

Match abandoned
Nottinghamshire 2 pts, Worcestershire 2 pts

at The Oval

Surrey 164 for 5 (D.M. Ward 57)
Gloucestershire 81 (A.J. Murphy 4 for 22)

Surrey (4 pts) won on faster scoring rate

Snow at Derby and rain elsewhere ate into the first round of matches in the Sunday league. Playing his first match for Somerset, Chris Tavare hit 2 sixes and 15 fours and reached his century off 100 balls, but Nicholas and Terry put on 100 for Hampshire's first wicket and the home side won with four balls to spare.

Rain curtailed play at Lord's and The Oval, where Gloucestershire's target was reduced to 87 off 20 overs. Tony Murphy, playing his first game for Surrey since joining them from Lancashire, took four of the first five Gloucestershire wickets and helped his side to win by five runs. Surrey were without Monte Lynch, who had broken a leg in a football match just before the start of the season. The injury was a serious one and threatened to deprive Surrey of his services for at least three months, a grave blow to a young and eager side.

Benson and Hedges Cup

25 April

at Old Trafford

Leicestershire 186 for 6
Lancashire 187 for 3 (G.D. Mendis 82 not out, G. Fowler 78)

Lancashire (2 pts) won by 7 wickets
(Gold Award – G.D. Mendis)

at Cardiff

Glamorgan 82
Kent 83 for 4

Kent (2 pts) won by 6 wickets
(Gold Award – H.L. Alleyne)

25 and 26 April

at Edgbaston

Warwickshire 221 for 7 (P.A. Smith 74, A.I. Kallicharran 50)
Northamptonshire 225 for 6 (A.J. Lamb 84 not out, G. Cook 57)

Northamptonshire (2 pts) won by 4 wickets
(Gold Award – A.J. Lamb)

at Hove

Essex 232 for 7 (P.J. Prichard 73)
Sussex 169

Essex (2 pts) won by 63 runs
(Gold Award – P.J. Prichard)

at Derby

Derbyshire 141
Somerset 142 for 3 (P.M. Roebuck 65)

Somerset (2 pts) won by 7 wickets
(Gold Award – P.M. Roebuck)

at Jesmond

Minor Counties 179 for 6 (N.A. Folland 61)
Yorkshire 181 for 5

Yorkshire (2 pts) won by 5 wickets
(Gold Award – D.L. Bairstow)

26 April

at Fenner's, Cambridge

Combined Universities 116 (M.A. Feltham 5 for 28)
Surrey 107 for 9

Combined Universities (2 pts) won by 9 runs
(Gold Award – J. Boiling)

at Lord's

Worcestershire 115 for 6
Middlesex 114 for 7

Worcestershire (2 pts) won by 1 run
(Gold Award – I.T. Botham)

Uncertain weather greeted the first round of matches in the Benson and Hedges Cup, but the rain failed to stop the competition from getting off to a sparkling start full of exciting cricket. Only two matches could be completed on the scheduled day, and both produced comfortable winners. Hartley Alleyne took 3 for 23 as Glamorgan were bowled out for 82, the fourth time in the history of the Cup that they have failed to reach a hundred, and Kent strolled to victory. Leicestershire batted meekly against Lancashire, who were set on the path to an easy win by Fowler and Mendis, who put on 156 in 44 overs for the first wicket.

A fifth-wicket partnership of 102 in 22 overs by Paul Smith and Alvin Kallicharran lifted Warwickshire from the depths of 66 for 4, but Lamb, relishing his new role as captain, took Northamptonshire to victory with seven balls to spare. Lamb was dropped by Munton off his own bowling early in his innings, and the visitors were allowed to recover from the precarious position of 49 for 3.

Prichard, Pringle and Stephenson took Essex to a winning score after they had been struggling at 54 for 4. The game was virtually decided on the first day, which Sussex ended on 72 for 7 from 31 overs.

A hard-hit 48 not out by David Bairstow took Yorkshire to victory with eight balls to spare over Minor Counties who, put in to bat, were well served by left-hander Nick Folland. He hit 61 off 88 balls. Derbyshire never really recovered from the shock of losing Kim Barnett, caught at deep point, to the first ball of the match, although Somerset laboured somewhat to reach the meagre target of 142.

The match at Lord's was so hit by the weather that it had to be reduced to 31 overs. Tight bowling, by Emburey in particular, restricted Worcestershire to 115 and, when Middlesex reached 66 for 3 in the 21st over, victory seemed to be theirs. Botham produced a spell of gentle medium pace which changed the course of the match. He dismissed Ramprakash with the fifth ball of his first over, and he had Butcher caught at backward point at the beginning of his next over. He caught and bowled Emburey off a skier, and Middlesex reached the last over, the only one to be bowled by Martin Weston, needing 13 runs to win. Botham caught Brown on the boundary, and Sykes was left to hit the last ball for six to win the match. He could manage only a four, and Worcestershire won by one run. Botham, having won six Gold Awards with Somerset, took his first award as a Worcestershire player.

The dramatic events at Lord's were overshadowed by what happened at Fenner's, however. There seemed little chance of any sensation when, in spite of a sound innings of 30 from Speight, Combined Universities were bowled out for 116 in 36.3 overs. There was a quick retort by the Universities when they took the field, Robinson falling to Tolley without scoring. Tolley bowled an admirably accurate spell, and his partner, Hansford, was equally impress-

ive. He bowled a spell of eight overs, four of them maidens, and captured the wickets of Stewart and Ward for 11 runs. When he was taken off, Surrey were 25 for 3 in 15 overs. With Clinton still at the wicket Surrey had little cause for alarm, but James Boiling, a Surrey player, turned his off-breaks on the damp pitch and bowled with intelligence and confidence. He bowled Sadiq and had Greig caught off a quicker ball. In the 27th over he bowled Clinton, and Surrey were 62 for 6. In a match that had been reduced to 37 overs, their position was serious, and they were allowed no recovery. Dale, after an uncertain start, removed Medlycott, Feltham and Martin Bicknell and, in spite of some fierce hitting from Bullen, Combined Universities snatched an historic victory by nine runs. It was their first victory in the competition since they beat Gloucestershire at Bristol in 1984, and it underlined the strength of the side since it had become truly representative of British Universities.

27, 28 and 29 April

at Cambridge

Leicestershire 344 for 8 dec (J.J. Whitaker 89, N.E. Briers 54, C.C. Lewis 54)
Cambridge University 159 for 8

Match drawn

at Oxford

Derbyshire 320 for 5 dec (P.D. Bowler 157) and 143 for 5 dec (B.J.M. Maher 53 not out)
Oxford University 181 for 9 dec (M.A. Crawley 60, S.J. Base 4 for 21)

Match drawn

27, 28, 29 and 30 April

at Edgbaston

Worcestershire 143 (T.A. Munton 4 for 39) and 160 for 5 dec (T.S. Curtis 55 not out)
Warwickshire 99 (G.R. Dilley 5 for 28, N.V. Radford 4 for 43) and 204 for 6 (A.J. Moles 85 not out)

Match drawn
Warwickshire 12 pts, Worcestershire 4 pts

at Bristol

Gloucestershire 265 (K.M. Curran 65, A.J. Wright 61, P. Bainbridge 59, J.G. Thomas 5 for 87, M.A. Robinson 4 for 60) and 291 (A.J. Wright 130, C.W.J. Athey 63, D.J. Capel 4 for 67)
Northamptonshire 505 (R.J. Bailey 100, D.J. Capel 81, G. Cook 76, R.G. Williams 71) and 53 for 0

Northamptonshire won by 10 wickets
Northamptonshire 23 pts, Gloucestershire 4 pts

27, 28, 29 April and 1 May

at Chelmsford

Middlesex 129 (D.R. Pringle 5 for 42) and 85 (D.R. Pringle 5 for 38, N.A. Foster 4 for 42)
Essex 149 (G.A. Gooch 65, N.G. Cowans 5 for 34) and 69 for 1

Essex won by 9 wickets
Essex 20 pts, Middlesex 4 pts

Chris Tavare hit a century in his first match for Somerset, 23 April. (ASP)

at Old Trafford

Lancashire 300 for 6 dec (G.D. Mendis 118, M. Watkinson 61 not out) and 250 for 7 dec (G.D. Mendis 81 not out, W.K. Hegg 50)
Nottinghamshire 283 for 9 dec (M. Newell 99, R.T. Robinson 66, K.P. Evans 55, Wasim Akram 6 for 70) and 147 for 0 (R.T. Robinson 77 not out, B.C. Broad 56 not out)

Match drawn
Lancashire 7 pts, Nottinghamshire 5 pts

at The Oval

Hampshire 198 (V.P. Terry 63) and 215 for 1 dec (C.L. Smith 94 not out, V.P. Terry 88)
Surrey 219 (I.A. Greig 69 not out, M.A. Feltham 64, P.J. Bakker 6 for 81) and 115 for 6

Match drawn
Surrey 6 pts, Hampshire 4 pts

at Hove

Kent 234 (T.R. Ward 64, C.M. Wells 7 for 65) and 252 for 2 dec (T.R. Ward 87 not out, M.R. Benson 74 not out, S.G. Hinks 56)

Sussex 361 (D.M. Smith 68, A.C.S. Pigott 64)

Match drawn
Sussex 7 pts, Kent 5 pts

28, 29, 30 April and 1 May

at Taunton

Glamorgan 118 (V.J. Marks 5 for 38, G.D. Rose 4 for 12) and 260 for 9 dec (H. Morris 96, M.J. Cann 65, G.D. Rose 4 for 46)
Somerset 186 (J.J.E. Hardy 51, S.R. Barwick 7 for 47) and 152 for 6 (S.J. Cook 79)

Match drawn
Somerset 5 pts, Glamorgan 4 pts

Rain curtailed play on the first day of all matches, and there was no play at all at Chelmsford, The Oval, Edgbaston or Fenner's. Essex remained calm at this loss of play and took less than two days to beat Middlesex. Middlesex won the toss and batted, but they collapsed before the Essex seamers, and by the close of play on the Friday Gooch had steered his side into the lead. The match was all over on the Saturday, when 16 wickets fell for 97 runs in 37 overs at one period. Derek Pringle exploited the low cloud and the moisture in the pitch to claim 10 for 80 in the match, and Essex survived the early loss of Gooch to win by nine wickets. Sensing rain, Stephenson hit 49 off 40 balls to take his side to an early victory.

Northamptonshire bowled out Gloucestershire on the opening day at Bristol, with Greg Thomas bowling with great hostility for his new county and impressing Ted Dexter, who was a spectator at the match. Geoff Cook and Robert Bailey added 167 for Northamptonshire's second wicket on the Saturday, and Wild, Capel and Williams all boosted the score with positive innings. Faced with only faint prospects of being able to save the game, Gloucestershire were aided in their cause by the loss of 22 overs on the Monday and by Wright's 5½-hour century. It was David Capel who made the vital, last breakthrough, taking four wickets for one run in 20 balls after tea. Northamptonshire were left needing to make 52 in 13 overs to win, but they needed only 6.5 overs in which to reach their target.

A fine innings by Andy Moles enabled Warwickshire to climb back from a first-innings deficit of 44 and to come close to snatching victory on a fiery wicket. The pace bowlers dominated the early stages of the match and, in a low-scoring game disrupted by the weather, Botham, leading Worcestershire in the absence of Neale, asked Warwickshire to make 205 in 52 overs. With 20 overs remaining, they were 92 for 2 and looked set to win. Thorne gave Moles admirable support, but he was caught off Newport; Kallicharran and Smith were run out, and Moles himself fell to Illingworth. It was Illingworth who bowled the last over, and Small needed to hit two runs off the final ball to win the match, but he could manage only one and Warwickshire had to be content with the extra eight points that they gained for being the side batting second in a drawn match in which the scores finished level.

There was no such excitement at Old Trafford, where Mendis played two fine innings for Lancashire, and Nottinghamshire were set a target of 268 in 55 overs, a target

ABOVE: *Tony Wright hit 130 for Gloucestershire against Northamptonshire at Bristol, 29 April, but his side was well beaten. (ASP)*

RIGHT: *Gehan Mendis – exciting early season form for Lancashire. (Adrian Murrell/Allsport)*

which, to the anger of the crowd, they declined to attempt.

Surrey seemed to have made up for a lost day by bowling out Hampshire for 198, but they struggled in turn and were saved only by Stewart, Feltham and the hard-hitting Greig. Terry and Chris Smith began Hampshire's second innings with a stand of 168, and, set to make 195, Surrey were bewildered by Maru's left-arm spin and were happy to draw. Maru took 3 for 18 in 11 overs.

Colin Wells took a career-best 7 for 65 with his medium pace, but Kent thwarted Sussex through a second-innings opening partnership of 99 between Hinks and Benson, and an unbroken partnership of 117 for the third wicket between Ward and Benson which was highlighted by some long hitting from Ward.

Rose had an excellent game for Somerset against Glamorgan, but the Welsh county recovered sufficiently to earn an honourable draw.

Refuge Assurance League

30 April

at Chelmsford

Middlesex 130
Essex 134 for 2 (G.A. Gooch 76 not out)

Essex (4 pts) won by 8 wickets

at Old Trafford

Nottinghamshire 184 for 5 (B.C. Broad 54)

Lancashire 186 for 3 (N.H. Fairbrother 53)

Lancashire (4 pts) won by 7 wickets

at Leicester

Derbyshire 187 for 6 (K.J. Barnett 77)
Leicestershire 105

Derbyshire (4 pts) won by 82 runs

at The Oval

Hampshire 114 for 9
Surrey 116 for 5

Surrey (4 pts) won by 5 wickets

at Hove

Sussex 110 (A.P. Igglesden 5 for 13)
Kent 114 for 3

Kent (4 pts) won by 7 wickets

Essex continued their persecution of Middlesex. Topley and Stephenson were the main wicket-takers, and Gooch hit a six and 10 fours in his unbeaten 76 which took Essex to victory with 20 balls to spare.

The only other side to come through their second match with a second victory was Surrey. Greig won the toss and asked Hampshire to bat first. Against a varied attack they slumped to 81 for 8 and were lifted to three figures only by late hitting from Jefferies. Surrey did not find runs easy to get and won with five balls to spare, thanks mainly to the careful Clinton, who hit 45.

Benson and Hedges Cup

2 May

at Leicester

Leicestershire 236 for 5 (N.E. Briers 71)
Warwickshire 205 (A.I. Kallicharran 62)

Leicestershire (2 pts) won by 31 runs
(Gold Award – N.E. Briers)

at Perth

Scotland 111 for 9 (O. Henry 58 not out, Wasim Akram 5 for 27, P.A.J. DeFreitas 4 for 13)
Lancashire 114 for 3

Lancashire (2 pts) won by 7 wickets
(Gold Award – P.A.J. DeFreitas)

at Chelmsford

Hampshire 173 for 6 (V.P. Terry 73)
Essex 175 for 3 (G.A. Gooch 100 not out)

Essex (2 pts) won by 7 wickets
(Gold Award – G.A. Gooch)

at Canterbury

Kent 173 for 9
Sussex 176 for 5 (P.W.G. Parker 85 not out)

Sussex (2 pts) won by 5 wickets
(Gold Award – P.W.G. Parker)

at Bristol

Middlesex 149
Gloucestershire 150 for 4

Gloucestershire (2 pts) won by 6 wickets
(Gold Award – P. Bainbridge)

at The Oval

Worcestershire 190 for 7
Surrey 191 for 9 (G.S. Clinton 74, I.T. Botham 4 for 44)

Surrey (2 pts) won by 1 wicket
(Gold Award – G.S. Clinton)

at Taunton

Somerset 205 for 7 (C.J. Tavare 78, S.J. Cook 55)
Minor Counties 170 for 6

Somerset (2 pts) won by 35 runs
(Gold Award – C.J. Tavare)

at Trent Bridge

Derbyshire 178 for 9 (K.J. Barnett 50, F.D. Stephenson 4 for 34)
Nottinghamshire 179 for 5 (D.W. Randall 57 not out, F.D. Stephenson 54)

Nottinghamshire (2 pts) won by 5 wickets
(Gold Award – F.D. Stephenson)

The weather was kind for the second round of matches in the Benson and Hedges Cup. Hampshire, the holders, were brushed aside by Essex, who won with 8.4 overs to spare. Terry faced 155 balls for his 73, and only James gave the Hampshire innings any impetus. In contrast, Gooch, who had bowled economically and taken two wickets, hit his eighth century in the competition. His innings included 2 fours, and he shared brisk half-century partnerships with Hardie and Waugh. Gooch's Gold Award was his 15th in the competition. Barry Wood and Chris Balderstone each won nine awards, but both have now retired from first-class cricket.

Gloucestershire gained a surprisingly easy win over Middlesex. Put in to bat, Middlesex reached 59 for the loss of Downton, but then lost six wickets for 56 runs. They were very much frustrated by Phil Bainbridge, who took one for 12 in 11 overs. Bainbridge followed his economic bowling with a forceful innings of 47. He and Wright added 106 for the second wicket and made Gloucestershire's victory a formality.

Nottinghamshire had to struggle a little harder to beat Derbyshire and were much indebted to all-rounder Franklyn Stephenson, who won his first Gold Award. Facing a total of 178, Nottinghamshire lost Broad, Robinson, Johnson and Newell for 36 before Randall and Stephenson

LEFT: *Kevan James is bowled by Neil Foster as Hampshire crash to Essex in the Benson and Hedges Cup match at Chelmsford, 2 May. (Steve Lindsell)*

RIGHT: *Cricket at The Oval in early May. (Adrian Murrell/ Allsport)*

added 90 in 22 overs. The home side eventually won with 23 balls to spare.

DeFreitas destroyed the early Scottish batting at Perth, so that Lancashire were able to move to the most comfortable of victories, while Somerset had little trouble against Minor Counties and, like Essex and Lancashire, claimed their second win in as many matches.

Sussex and Kent played each other for the sixth day in succession, and on this occasion Sussex won with 8.2 overs to spare. Kent rather lost their way after reaching a hundred with only three wickets down. Nevertheless, their score of 173 began to look immense when Igglesden and Kelleher sent back Smith, Green and Alan Wells with only 10 scored. A superb faultless innings from skipper Paul Parker turned the game in favour of Sussex. He added 90 with Colin Wells, and although Gould was out for nought, Parker steered his side to victory with characteristic charm.

Leicestershire scored soundly at Grace Road, and Ferris made early breakthroughs which ensured that Warwickshire were never really in reach of their target.

The main excitement was at The Oval, where Surrey recovered from the shock of having lost to Combined Universities to snatch a thrilling last-ball victory. Surrey included Sylvester Clarke in their side for the first, and as it transpired last, time in the season. He bowled at a brisk pace, although obviously still troubled by his recent knee operation, and helped to restrict Worcestershire to 190.

Surrey began uncertainly in reply, but Clinton and Stewart added 83 to take the score to 120 before Stewart fell to Dilley. With seven overs remaining and six wickets standing, Surrey needed 29 to win. In the 50th over, Botham had Ward leg before, and the same bowler accounted for the durable Clinton, caught at long-on. Botham also made a spectacular slip catch to dismiss Feltham, and Greig sliced to third man. Botham took another magnificent catch to get rid of Martin Bicknell off the penultimate ball of the match when Surrey were still two short of victory. This brought in the hobbling Clarke, who drove Dilley through the covers. He turned for the second run, but seemed unlikely to make his ground until a final thrust and dive gave Surrey victory.

4, 5, 6 and 8 May

at Chelmsford

Derbyshire 113 (T.D. Topley 5 for 30, N.A. Foster 4 for 39) and 197 (B. Roberts 63, P.G. Newman 57, D.R. Pringle 4 for 63)
Essex 522 for 3 dec (G.A. Gooch 148, A.W. Lilley 113 not out, J.P. Stephenson 94, M.E. Waugh 77, P.J. Prichard 54 not out)

Essex won by an innings and 212 runs
Essex 24 pts, Derbyshire 0 pts

at Cardiff

Gloucestershire 282 (K.M. Curran 93, P. Bainbridge 56, S.J. Dennis 4 for 56) and 381 for 5 dec (A.J. Wright 100, C.W.J. Athey 93 not out, P.W. Romaines 77)

The Australians arrive and meet the press. Allan Border and Bobby Simpson, the men who planned and plotted the rout of England, smile at a question. (Adrian Murrell/ Allsport)

Glamorgan 435 (M.P. Maynard 191 not out, H. Morris 90, A.R. Butcher 69, D.A. Graveney 6 for 128)

Match drawn
Glamorgan 4 pts, Gloucestershire 4 pts

at Southampton

Hampshire 358 (R.A. Smith 182, R.M. Ellison 5 for 98) and 280 for 5 dec (V.P. Terry 96, D.R. Turner 65 not out)
Kent 369 (T.R. Ward 91, N.R. Taylor 78, R.P. Davis 67, R.J. Maru 4 for 64) and 136 (R.J. Maru 8 for 41)

Hampshire won by 133 runs
Hampshire 22 pts, Kent 5 pts

at Lord's

Middlesex 247 (M.R. Ramprakash 69, M.W. Gatting 54) and 348 for 9 dec (R.O. Butcher 126, M.W. Gatting 83, M.P. Bicknell 5 for 99)
Surrey 190 and 280 (D.J. Bicknell 93, K.T. Medlycott 77)

Middlesex won by 125 runs
Middlesex 22 pts, Surrey 5 pts

at Northampton

Leicestershire 208 (J.J. Whitaker 92 not out, J.G. Thomas 6 for 53) and 250 (P. Whitticase 56 not out)
Northamptonshire 185 (W. Larkins 50, C.C. Lewis 4 for 47) and 276 for 9 (A.J. Lamb 148, J.P. Agnew 4 for 80)

Northamptonshire won by 1 wicket
Northamptonshire 21 pts, Leicestershire 6 pts

at Taunton

Sussex 234 (I.J. Gould 84, N.A. Mallender 5 for 30) and 232 (A.P. Wells 58, C.M. Wells 50, N.A. Mallender 7 for 62)
Somerset 229 (S.J. Cook 91, V.J. Marks 59 not out) and 238 for 5 (C.J. Tavare 90 not out)

Somerset won by 5 wickets
Somerset 22 pts, Sussex 6 pts

at Worcester

Lancashire 171 (G. Fowler 60, I.T. Botham 4 for 53) and 231 (G.D. Mendis 69, I.T. Botham 4 for 61, G.R. Dilley 4 for 62)
Worcestershire 166 (Wasim Akram 5 for 52, P.A.J. DeFreitas 4 for 61) and 170 (D.B. D'Oliveira 58, M. Watkinson 5 for 44)

Lancashire won by 66 runs
Lancashire 21 pts, Worcestershire 5 pts

at Leeds

Yorkshire 92 (F.D. Stephenson 7 for 38) and 109 (F.D. Stephenson 6 for 37)
Nottinghamshire 86 (I.M. Priestley 4 for 27) and 119 for 0 (R.T. Robinson 55 not out, B.C. Broad 54 not out)

Nottinghamshire won by 10 wickets
Nottinghamshire 20 pts, Yorkshire 4 pts

4, 5 and 6 May

at Cambridge

Warwickshire 284 for 6 dec (A.J. Moles 66, P.A. Smith 61, D.A. Banks 60 not out) and 263 for 2 dec (J.D. Ratcliffe 127 not out, G.W. Humpage 97)
Cambridge University 276 for 5 dec (S.J. James 151 not out) and 144 for 5

Match drawn

Strong and justified opponents of the four-day game, Essex showed their contempt for the formula by beating Derbyshire in just over two days. The margin of victory and the speed of its attainment emphasized the gap between a county who were certain to be contending strongly for the Britannic Assurance County Championship and one who looked destined to be jostling for the wooden spoon from the start of the season. Electing to bat when they won the toss, Derbyshire were bowled out for 113 in 45.5 overs by the high-class Essex seam attack of Topley, Foster and Pringle. Derbyshire were lifted past three figures only by a last-wicket stand of 28 between Newman and Mortensen. That the pitch was entirely blameless for Derbyshire's lightning dismissal was proved by Gooch and Stephenson, who finished the day with 204 on the board in the 61 overs available to them. Gooch reached the 67th first-class century of his career, but Stephenson was out on the second morning for 94, by which time he and Gooch had put on 254, just 11 short of a new county record. Lilley and Waugh gave an exhilarating display after lunch, with savage treatment of the slow bowling, one cannot use the word spin, of Bowler and Sharma. Lilley made the highest of his three first-class hundreds, and Prichard had a brief flurry before Gooch called a halt. Maher and Morris were bowled by Pringle before the close, and he and Foster finished the job on the Saturday, but not before Childs, 2 for 27 in 24 overs, gave some demonstration of what true spin bowling can be. Essex took maximum points, moved to the top of the embryo championship, and Derbyshire became the first

ABOVE: *A career-best batting performance of 191 not out by Matthew Maynard for Glamorgan against Gloucestershire at Cardiff, 4–8 May, could not bring his side victory. Maynard's later decision to tour South Africa was a surprise and a disappointment. (Sporting Pictures UK Ltd)*

LEFT: *Alan Lilley, a thrilling century as Essex demolished Derbyshire at Chelmsford, 4–8 May. (USPA)*

side to fail to take a point from an uninterrupted four-day match, albeit that it did not last three days.

The match at Headingley did not last two. Choosing to bat first, Yorkshire were bowled out for 92 in hot, sticky weather and low cloud. Franklyn Stephenson, aided by the technical inadequacies of the Yorkshire batsmen, returned the best bowling figures of his career, but he failed to give his side a first-innings lead. Paul Jarvis and Ian Priestley, who was making his debut for the white rose county, bowled out Nottinghamshire in 34.4 overs. Three more Yorkshire wickets fell before the close so that the first day had seen 23 wickets fall for 239 runs. At 61 for 3 overnight, Yorkshire added only another 48 runs on the second morning as Stephenson brought his match figures to 13 for 75, the best figures by a Nottinghamshire bowler since Bruce Dooland's 15 for 193 against Kent at Gravesend in 1956. Broad and Robinson, their confidence boosted by a generous sprinkling of half-volleys, took Nottinghamshire to victory just after lunch on the second day.

The matches at Northampton and Worcester did last into the third day. Botham won the toss at New Road and asked Lancashire to bat first. His decision proved to be correct, for the visitors were bowled out for 171, and their innings was boosted only by a ninth-wicket stand of 45 between Hegg and DeFreitas. Earlier, only Fowler had withstood the ravages of the Worcestershire seam attack. The home side did not find batting easy and finished the first day on 123 for 5, and, with Wasim Akram and DeFreitas again proving to be a formidable combination, they added only another 43 runs on the second morning. Lancashire were then bowled out quickly as Radford and Botham moved the ball appreciably. A target of 237 was never likely to prove easy, but Worcestershire ended the second day with all their wickets intact and 20 runs on the board. On the Saturday, they collapsed to 54 for 5, were revived by a stand of 85 between D'Oliveira and Rhodes, only to lose their last five wickets for 31 runs.

A career-best bowling performance by Greg Thomas seemed to have put Northamptonshire in a good position against Leicestershire, for whom Whitaker, once an England batsman, played the lone innings of defiance. He came in with his side on 32 for 3 – they were soon 34 for 4 – and battled through to the end. Northamptonshire fared no better than the visitors had done and trailed on the first innings. Eventually, Northamptonshire needed 274 to win, and that they reached this target, the highest score of the match, was entirely thanks to Allan Lamb, who reached his century off 81 balls and shared a fifth-wicket stand of 115 in 21 overs with David Capel. After Lamb's dismissal, the home side stuttered to victory. They were 256 for 6, but lost three wickets for 16 runs before Winston Davis clouted the winning four off Lewis.

There was limited excitement at Cardiff. Gloucestershire batted dourly on the opening day, runs coming at barely two an over. Glamorgan showed a little more enterprise. Butcher and Morris put on 168 for the first wicket, and on the Saturday, Matthew Maynard reached the highest score of his career. He dominated a fifth-wicket stand of 159 with Michael Cann. David Graveney bowled 50 overs to take 6 for 126, after which Gloucestershire chose to bat out the game.

Having done well to bowl out Middlesex on the opening day at Lord's, Surrey gave a very limp batting display and surrendered the initiative. Gatting and Butcher put on 155 for Middlesex's fifth wicket when they batted for a second time, and Roland Butcher went on to hit 126 with a six and 18 fours. Surrey had lost the services of Tazelaar in the first innings when he was censured after running on the pitch, but the Australian took three wickets in the second innings and, with Martin Bicknell, helped to keep Surrey in touch. They soon lost touch again when Cowans and Hughes reduced them to 64 for 5 by the end of play on Saturday. A defiant innings by Darren Bicknell, who shared a sixth-wicket stand of 147 with Keith Medlycott, gave Surrey respectability on the Monday, but it could not save them from defeat.

A bubbling innings by Robin Smith took Hampshire to an impressive score against Kent, but the visitors, with Ward and Davis hitting career bests, took a first-innings lead. Nicholas' declaration left Kent a minimum of 55 overs in which to score 270, but they never looked like approaching the target. Slow left-arm spin bowler Rajesh Maru produced the best bowling performance of the

A century for Roland Butcher as Middlesex beat Surrey at Lord's, 4–8 May. Butcher's bright start to his benefit season was not sustained. (David Munden)

season. In 23.4 overs, he took 8 for 41 (12 for 108 in the match) and bowled with intelligence and variety to take his side to victory.

At Taunton, it was the pace bowling of Neil Mallender which took Somerset to victory, and at Cambridge, it was the batting of Jason Ratcliffe and Stephen James which took the eye. Both players made the highest scores of their careers.

5 May

at West Bromwich Dartmouth

Australians 326 for 3 (D.M. Jones 170, G.R. Marsh 101)
League Cricket Conference 161 for 5 (M. Ingham 56 not out, S.P. O'Donnell 52 not out)

Australians won by 165 runs

The Australians could not have hoped for a better start to their tour. They hit 326 in 55 overs against a league eleven which included bowlers of the calibre of Maninder Singh, Ezra Moseley, Brian McMillan and Simon O'Donnell. The league side lost three wickets for nine runs and had no hope of recovery.

7 May

at Arundel

Australians 314 for 6 (D.C. Boon retired hurt 114, T.M. Moody 72, A.R. Border 66)
Lavinia, Duchess of Norfolk's XI 194 for 5 (M.P. Speight 55)

Australians won by 120 runs

The batting power of the Australian tourists was confirmed in their second match at the beautiful ground in the shadow of Arundel Castle. Their 314 was made in 50 overs. Boon retired at lunch-time, and the slaughter was continued by Border and Moody, who hit 72 off 66 balls.

Refuge Assurance League

7 May

at Chelmsford

Essex 154 for 8
Derbyshire 153 for 8 (P.D. Bowler 58)

Essex (4 pts) won by 1 run

at Newport

Glamorgan 171 for 6 (A.R. Butcher 52)
Gloucestershire 173 for 7

Gloucestershire (4 pts) won by 3 wickets

at Southampton

Kent 156
Hampshire 158 for 1 (V.P. Terry 79 not out, M.C.J. Nicholas 52)

Hampshire (4 pts) won by 9 wickets

at Lord's

Middlesex 221 for 5 (J.D. Carr 86, M.W. Gatting 80)
Surrey 161 (J.D. Carr 4 for 21)

Middlesex (4 pts) won by 60 runs

at Northampton

Warwickshire 171 for 9
Northamptonshire 172 for 3 (A.J. Lamb 80 not out)

Northamptonshire (4 pts) won by 7 wickets

at Taunton

Somerset 182 for 9 (R.J. Harden 61, P.M. Roebuck 52)
Sussex 182 for 7

Match tied
Somerset 2 pts, Sussex 2 pts

at Worcester

Lancashire 202 for 8 (N.H. Fairbrother 64)
Worcestershire 188 for 9 (S.J. O'Shaughnessy 69)

Lancashire (4 pts) won by 14 runs

at Leeds

Yorkshire 201 for 4 (D.L. Bairstow 65 not out, R.J. Blakey 61)
Nottinghamshire 141 (D.W. Randall 55)

Yorkshire (4 pts) won by 60 runs

Reigning champions Worcestershire, handicapped by the continued absence of Phil Neale with glandular fever, lost to Lancashire, their arch rivals, in a gripping contest. Allott took 2 for 9 in his eight overs, and DeFreitas bowled Hick and Botham in his first 13 deliveries, but O'Shaughnessy and Radford put on 72 in 10 overs for the eighth wicket and came close to pulling off a spectacular victory.

Essex did pull off a spectacular victory when, defending a very modest 154, they ran out Newman off the last ball of the match as he was going for the run which would have made the scores level. There was a similar finish at Taunton, where Sussex reached the last over needing 10 to win. The over was bowled by Roebuck, and five runs came from the first four balls. Dodemaide drove the fifth ball of the over powerfully through the covers, but Rose stopped the drive on the boundary and the batsmen ran three. Gould drove hard at the last ball, but Dodemaide was run out as he went for the second run that would have won the match. Rose was again the fielder. Marks had restricted Sussex in the earlier part of their innings as he bowled his eight overs for 12 runs and took two wickets.

There were less hectic finishes elsewhere. Terry and Nicholas put on 133 for Hampshire's first wicket, and Carr produced Sunday-best performances with bat and ball as Middlesex trounced Surrey.

9 May

at Hove

Australians 154 (S.R. Waugh 86)
Sussex 158 for 6

Sussex won by 4 wickets

The Australians lost the third of their one-day warm-up matches in an uncomfortable manner. Dean Jones was hit in the face by a ball from Pigott and suffered an injury which was to keep him out of action until the end of the month.

Benson and Hedges Cup

9 May

at Southampton

Hampshire 286 for 3 (R.A. Smith 155 not out, V.P. Terry 76)
Glamorgan 290 for 2 (H. Morris 143 not out, P.A. Cottey 68)

Glamorgan (2 pts) won by 8 wickets
(Gold Award – H. Morris)

at Canterbury

Kent 192 for 7
Essex 196 for 6 (J.P. Stephenson 63 not out)

Essex (2 pts) won by 4 wickets
(Gold Award – J.P. Stephenson)

at Leeds

Somerset 243 for 5 (C.J. Tavare 65, S.J. Cook 62)

A large crowd gathered to see the Australians at Arundel. (Adrian Murrell/Allsport)

LEFT: *Paul Parker hits Tim May for six, Sussex v. Australians, Hove, 9 May. (Patrick Eagar)*

Yorkshire 181 (D.L. Bairstow 51 not out, A.N. Jones 4 for 47)

Somerset (2 pts) won by 62 runs
(Gold Award – C.J. Tavare)

at Oxford

Combined Universities 190 for 9 (M.A. Atherton 66)
Middlesex 194 for 2 (M.W. Gatting 123 not out)

Middlesex (2 pts) won by 8 wickets
(Gold Award – M.W. Gatting)

at Worcester

Gloucestershire 200 for 7 (P. Bainbridge 53)
Worcestershire 152

Gloucestershire (2 pts) won by 48 runs
(Gold Award – K.M. Curran)

at Leicester

Leicestershire 239 for 6 (G.J. Parsons 63 not out)
Scotland 128 (I.L. Phillip 62, G.J. Parsons 4 for 12)

Leicestershire (2 pts) won by 111 runs
(Gold Award – G.J. Parsons)

at Northampton

Northamptonshire 235 for 5 (G. Cook 66)
Lancashire 197 (Wasim Akram 52)

Northamptonshire (2 pts) won by 38 runs
(Gold Award – J.G. Thomas)

at Oxton

Minor Counties 172
Nottinghamshire 175 for 5 (D.W. Randall 52)

Nottinghamshire (2 pts) won by 5 wickets

Robin Smith hit his first century in the Benson and Hedges Cup. Coming in to bat at 6 for 2, Smith shared a stand of 185 in 34 overs with Paul Terry, and then an unbroken stand of 95 with David Turner. Hampshire's 286 for 3 looked likely to be a winning score, except that they had chosen, most unwisely, to omit the successful Maru. Butcher and Morris began Glamorgan's challenge with 79 in 24 overs. Cottey hurried and scurried with Morris to add 125 in the next 23 overs, so that when Maynard joined his captain 63 were needed from eight overs. The accomplished young pair achieved the target with ease, having 11 balls to spare at the end. Morris rightly took the Gold Award for his captain's innings, but one could not help but commiserate with Robin Smith.

John Stephenson, such an improved cricketer, bowled tidily and took Essex to victory over Kent after four wickets had fallen for 65 runs. This win meant that Essex had qualified for the quarter-finals. In Group C, Somerset

ABOVE: *Ian Botham and Steve Rhodes join in vociferous appeal, Worcestershire v. Gloucestershire, Benson and Hedges Cup, 9 May, but Worcestershire were beaten and failed to qualify for the quarter-finals. (Simon Bruty/Allsport)*

RIGHT: *Gordon Parsons produced a spectacular solo performance for Leicestershire against Scotland, 9 May, and won the Benson and Hedges Gold Award. (David Munden)*

qualified with a comfortable win at Headingley, and Nottinghamshire looked most likely to join them after disposing of Minor Counties.

Gatting completed 2,000 runs in the Benson and Hedges Cup as his 123 not out took Middlesex to victory over Combined Universities with eight balls to spare. There was another excellent spell of economic bowling from Tolley.

Gordon Parsons gave a virtuoso performance for Leicestershire against Scotland. He was promoted to number five to boost a sagging scoring rate and hit 63 off 56 balls. He followed this with four wickets, including that of Clive Rice, for 12 runs in eight overs.

Another all-rounder, Kevin Curran, added to Worcestershire's woes. He and Bainbridge put on 63 for the fifth wicket, and he then took 3 for 15 in his 11 overs. Greene also took 3 for 15, and Worcestershire's interest in the competition was virtually at an end.

In Group D, Northamptonshire had a surprisingly easy win over Lancashire, so that both counties and Leicestershire became locked on four points each.

11 May

at Lord's

Australians 309 for 4 (D.C. Boon 166, G.R. Marsh 102, C.S. Cowdrey 4 for 60)
MCC 208 (M.W. Gatting 86, G.D. Mendis 52)

Australians won by 101 runs

What was an eagerly awaited traditional fixture, the first big test of the strength of the touring party, has been relegated to a 55-over thrash, but once again it provided evidence of the power of the Australian batting. Boon's 166 came off as many balls and won him the individual award. He and Marsh put on 277 for the first wicket and virtually assured their side of the inaugural Bass Cup. The MCC side was selected only from those counties who were not engaged in the Benson and Hedges Cup.

Benson and Hedges Cup

11 May

at The Oval

Gloucestershire 286 for 7 (A.W. Stovold 90, P.W. Romaines 76)
Surrey 142

Gloucestershire (2 pts) won by 144 runs (Gold Award – A.W. Stovold)

at Chelmsford

Glamorgan 98
Essex 99 for 0 (G.A. Gooch 69 not out)

Essex (2 pts) won by 10 wickets
Gold Award – G.A. Gooch)

at Edgbaston

Scotland 158 for 6
Warwickshire 159 for 4 (D.A. Thorne 57 not out)

Warwickshire (2 pts) won by 6 wickets
Gold Award – P.A. Smith)

at Hove

Hampshire 242 for 5 (R.A. Smith 96 not out, R.J. Scott 69)
Sussex 177 (P.W.G. Parker 57, C.A. Connor 4 for 19)

Hampshire (2 pts) won by 65 runs
Gold Award – R.A. Smith)

at Worcester

Worcestershire 216 for 8 (G.A. Hick 109)
Combined Universities 217 for 5 (N. Hussain 67, S.P. James 65, N.V. Radford 4 for 38)

Combined Universities (2 pts) won by 5 wickets
Gold Award – G.A. Hick)

at Derby

Minor Counties 149
Derbyshire 150 for 3 (K.J. Barnett 75)

Derbyshire (2 pts) won by 7 wickets
Gold Award – K.J. Barnett)

at Northampton

Northamptonshire 204 for 6 (A.J. Lamb 87 not out)
Leicestershire 11 for 1

Match abandoned
Northamptonshire 1 pt, Leicestershire 1 pt

11 and 12 May

at Trent Bridge

Nottinghamshire 144 (B.C. Broad 53, S. Oldham 4 for 13)
Yorkshire 111 (K.E. Cooper 4 for 9)

Nottinghamshire (2 pts) won by 33 runs
Gold Award – K.E. Cooper)

Bad weather caused the game at Northampton to be abandoned. It proved to be the only abandonment of the 1989 competition. The match at Trent Bridge went into a second day and ended quite sensationally. Steve Oldham, Yorkshire's 40-year-old assistant coach, was recalled to the side after an absence of four years because Yorkshire were so plagued with injuries to their seam bowlers. His four wickets for 13 runs in 11 overs were the main reason that Nottinghamshire were bowled out for a meagre 144. When bad light ended play on the Thursday Yorkshire were 73 for 4 from 38.5 overs, with Love and Bairstow the not-out batsmen. They added 15 careful runs on the Friday morning before Bairstow scooped Pick to mid-wicket. Nine runs later, Love, who batted 26 overs for 30, was well caught behind low down by French off Cooper, who thereby began a remarkable spell which brought victory to his side. He had Jarvis leg before and dismissed Pickles

and Oldham with successive balls. Carrick was caught at short extra cover off Evans, and Yorkshire lost their last six wickets for 23 runs. The win took Nottinghamshire into the quarter-finals along with Somerset from Group C.

There was another Gold Award for Gooch as Essex completed their programme with a fourth win. Glamorgan were dreadful. Foster and Pringle took three wickets each, but they were aided by some wretched batting. Essex romped to victory in 23.2 overs against unsubtle permutations of seam bowling. It was still unclear who would join Essex as qualifiers from Group A as Hampshire beat Sussex with ease to bring the other four sides in the section level on two points each. Robin Smith, thwarted by Glamorgan in the previous round, hit 96 not out off 99 balls, an exciting and entertaining innings.

Gloucestershire qualified from Group B when they overwhelmed Surrey at The Oval. Clarke reported unfit for Surrey, and Gloucestershire celebrated by reaching 195 for 1 off 38 overs at lunch. Wright and Stovold gave them a fine start with an opening stand of 113, and Romaines later plundered runs. Surrey lost Atkins when he was hit in the face, and were reduced to 27 for 3, a depth from which they could not hope to rise.

Steve Oldham, Yorkshire's assistant coach, was forced out of retirement because of his county's long list of injuries. He took 4 for 13 in 11 overs in the Benson and Hedges Cup game at Trent Bridge, 11 May. (Sporting Pictures UK Ltd)

Combined Universities moved into second place in Group B and made history when they became the first universities side to win two matches in the competition in the same season. Worcestershire were eliminated from the tournament and were almost totally humiliated as Dale, Crawley and Hansford captured wickets regularly and sent them tumbling to 137 for 7. Hick had stood firm throughout this slaughter, and he at last found an able partner in Radford, who attacked the bowling from the start. In seven overs, the pair added 74 runs, and Worcestershire reached a commendable 216. Hick's first fifty runs came from 79 balls; his second fifty came from only 39. The Universities were undeterred by the immediate loss of O'Gorman, and even the more serious loss of Atherton at 46 failed to upset their rhythm. James and Hussain seized the advantage and added 106 in 26 overs, and when they were dismissed Speight and Longley were equal to the demands of the occasion, and the Combined Universities swept to an emphatic victory with 11 balls to spare. With a lack of vision characteristic of England captains of the sixties, M.J.K. Smith ignored the claims of James, Hussain and Dale when it came to naming the Gold Award winner.

Benson and Hedges Cup

13 May

at Southampton

Hampshire 235 for 8 (R.J. Scott 54)
Kent 237 for 6 (N.R. Taylor 64)

Kent (2 pts) won by 4 wickets
(Gold Award – N.R. Taylor)

at Leeds

Yorkshire 208 for 5 (A.A. Metcalfe 77)
Derbyshire 201 for 6 (K.J. Barnett 101, S.N. Hartley 4 for 32)

Yorkshire (2 pts) won by 7 runs
(Gold Award – K.J. Barnett)

at Old Trafford

Warwickshire 199 for 8 (A.J. Moles 65)
Lancashire 203 for 5 (N.H. Fairbrother 69 not out)

Lancashire (2 pts) won by 5 wickets
(Gold Award – N.H. Fairbrother)

at Lord's

Middlesex 232 for 9 (D.L. Haynes 59)
Surrey 156

Middlesex (2 pts) won by 76 runs
(Gold Award – D.L. Haynes)

at Glasgow

Scotland 207 for 7
Northamptonshire 210 for 1 (G. Cook 72 not out, R.J. Bailey 69 not out)

Northamptonshire (2 pts) won by 9 wickets
(Gold Award – R.J. Bailey)

at Taunton

Nottinghamshire 202 for 9 (B.C. Broad 78, A.N. Jones 5 for 53)
Somerset 203 for 3 (S.J. Cook 79, C.J. Tavare 59 not out)

Somerset (2 pts) won by 7 wickets
(Gold Award – A.N. Jones)

at Bristol

Combined Universities 223 for 7 (M.A. Crawley 54)
Gloucestershire 227 for 7

Gloucestershire (2 pts) won by 3 wickets
(Gold Award – M.A. Crawley)

13 and 14 May

at Swansea

Sussex 207 for 7 (C.M. Wells 117)
Glamorgan 160

Sussex (2 pts) won by 47 runs
(Gold Award – C.M. Wells)

To the surprise of many people, Kent edged out Sussex for the second place in Group A and so qualified for the quarter-finals. Facing a target of 236, Kent beat Hampshire with three balls to spare, and their scoring rate put them ahead of Sussex who, in spite of Colin Wells' 117, his highest score in the competition, failed to reach four runs an over.

In Group B, Combined Universities continued with most impressive cricket, for, although they were beaten by

Tony Murphy leaps into action for Surrey against Middlesex at Lord's, Benson and Hedges Cup, 13 May. (Tom Morris)

Gloucestershire off the penultimate ball of the match, they qualified for the last eight with a scoring rate far superior to that of Middlesex.

Lancashire beat Warwickshire with considerable ease to claim the second spot in Group D.

Benson and Hedges Cup – Zonal Tables
Final Positions

Group A	P	W	L	N/R	Pts	R/R
Essex	4	4	–	–	8	65.73
Kent	4	2	2	–	4	57.95
Sussex	4	2	2	–	4	57.40
Hampshire	4	1	3	–	2	70.91
Glamorgan	4	1	3	–	2	48.13
Group B						
Gloucestershire	4	4	–	–	8	67.79
Combined Universities	4	2	2	–	4	62.11
Middlesex	4	2	2	–	4	58.99
Worcestershire	4	1	3	–	2	57.22
Surrey	4	1	3	–	2	49.17
Group C						
Somerset	4	4	–	–	8	61.86
Nottinghamshire	4	3	1	–	6	55.96
Yorkshire	4	2	2	–	4	51.91
Derbyshire	4	1	3	–	2	56.11
Minor Counties	4	–	4	–	0	50.75
Group D						
Northamptonshire	4	3	–	1	7	69.86
Lancashire	4	3	1	–	6	61.33
Leicestershire	4	2	1	1	5	65.75
Warwickshire	4	1	3	–	2	64.79
Scotland	4	–	4	–	0	45.00

13, 14 and 15 May

at Worcester

Australians 103 (P.J. Newport 6 for 43) and 205 (S.R. Waugh 63, P.J. Newport 5 for 84, N.V. Radford 4 for 58)
Worcestershire 146 (T.M. Alderman 4 for 33) and 163 for 7 (T.M. Alderman 4 for 61)

Worcestershire won by 3 wickets

The Australians' opening first-class match of the tour was all over in two days. On a pitch of uneven bounce which encouraged the seam bowlers from the start and left the batsmen perplexed and groping, 24 wickets fell on the

ABOVE RIGHT: *Adrian Jones, an aggressive and whole-hearted pace bowler who did much to help Somerset into the final stages of the Benson and Hedges Cup. (David Munden)*

RIGHT: *A shock for the Australians at Worcester – all-out for 103 before lunch on the first day. The scoreboard tells a sorry tale, 1.10 p.m., Saturday, 13 May. (Ken Kelly)*

Saturday while 300 runs were scored. Ten of the wickets went to Phil Newport, who revelled in the conditions, and he was well supported by some fine catching. Alderman, too, bowled splendidly for the Australians, and Taylor looked a slip fielder of high quality. Waugh played the innings of the match, and it was his batting which nearly made Worcestershire's target just a little too great. It took patient innings from Hick and Botham to bring the county within sight of victory, and it was sensible batting by Illingworth, Newport and Rhodes which finally made that victory possible. It was the first time that the county had ever beaten an Australian touring side, but the tourists themselves were not pleased about the standard of the wicket on which the match was played.

Refuge Assurance League

14 May

at Leek

Lancashire 176 for 8
Derbyshire 153 for 9 (I.D. Austin 4 for 28)

Lancashire (4 pts) won by 23 runs

Minor Counties 1989
Benson and Hedges Cup

BATTING	v. Yorkshire (Jesmond) 25 & 26 April	v. Somerset (Taunton) 2 May	v. Nottinghamshire (Oxton) 9 May	v. Derbyshire (Derby) 11 May	Runs
S.R. Atkinson	25			5	30
G.K. Brown	26	34	29	4	93
N.A. Folland	61	25	19	29	134
P.R. Oliver	13	24	9	0	46
S.G. Plumb	1	15	43	3	62
S. Greensword	29*	13*		39	81
N. Priestley	0	32			32
R.A. Evans	2*	13*	2	28*	45
I.E. Conn	—	—	0	0	0
R.C. Green	—				—
N.R. Taylor	—	—	1*	14	15
C.J. Stockdale		1	5		6
A. Wingfield-Digby		—			—
N. O'Brien			17		17
D.A. Hale			11	6	17
A.R. Fothergill			13	4	17
Byes	2			1	
Leg-byes	10	5	15	3	
Wides	10	5	7	9	
No-balls		3	1	4	
Total	179	170	172	149	
Wickets	6	6	10	10	
Result	L	L	L	L	
Points	0	0	0	0	

Fielding Figures 4 – N. Priestley (ct 3/st 1)
2 – N.A. Folland and A.R. Fothergill
1 – S.G. Plumb and R.A.Evans

BOWLING	R.C. Green	N.R. Taylor	I.E. Conn	R.A. Evans	S. Greensword	S.G. Plumb	A. Wingfield-Digby	D.A. Hale
v. Yorkshire (Jesmond) 25 & 26 April	5–0–17–0	10.4–1–33–1	11–2–27–3	11–2–26–0	9–0–35–1	7–2–29–0		
v. Somerset (Taunton) 2 May		11–2–38–3	8–1–32–0	11–2–26–1	6–1–24–0	8–0–48–2	11–3–22–1	
v. Nottinghamshire (Oxton) 9 May		11–1–35–2	7–0–23–0	11–3–21–0		2–0–5–0		7.2–1–37–1
v. Derbyshire (Derby) 11 May		11–2–24–1	11–2–44–0	6–0–39–0		1–0–2–0		5–0–36–2
Wickets	0	7	3	1	1	2	1	3

ABOVE: *Worcestershire* v. *the Australians, May, 1989.*
(Patrick Eagar)

RIGHT: *Worcestershire hero Phil Newport receives the con-*
gratulations of his colleagues as he captures one of his
11 victims in the match against the Australians. Newport's
season was brought to an abrupt halt by injury in June.
(Adrian Murrell/Allsport)

N. O'Brien	G.K. Brown		Byes	Leg-byes	Wides	No-balls	Total	Wkts
			4	10	8		181	5
			9	6			205	7
8–1–32–2	1–0–8–0		3	11	2	3	175	5
				5	2	2	150	3
2	0							

at Chelmsford

Hampshire 156 for 9 (D.R. Turner 66)
Essex 157 for 7 (G.A. Gooch 63, S.T. Jefferies 4 for 39)

Essex (4 pts) won by 3 wickets

at Bristol

Middlesex 202 for 6
Gloucestershire 188 for 7 (A.J. Wright 66, M.W. Gatting 4 for 30)

Middlesex (4 pts) won by 14 runs

at Canterbury

Surrey 195 for 7 (D.M. Ward 62 not out)
Kent 197 for 6

Kent (4 pts) won by 4 wickets

at Leicester

Yorkshire 89 for 9
Leicestershire 92 for 3

Leicestershire (4 pts) won by 7 wickets

Essex, Lancashire and Middlesex moved clear of the pack in the Sunday League. Lancashire owed much to the hitting of Mike Watkinson. He scored 44 off 33 balls on a wicket which did not make stroke play easy. Mike Gatting produced his best bowling performance in the league, and Kent and Leicestershire won with ease. Essex seemed to be cruising to an early and easy victory at Chelmsford, but four wickets in 12 balls by Jefferies changed the outlook of the game. Essex finally won when Lilley drove the last ball of the match into the covers for a single.

16, 17, 18 and 19 May

at Northampton

Yorkshire 191 (W.W. Davis 4 for 48) and 251 (D. Byas 50)
Northamptonshire 418 (D. Ripley 123, D.J. Wild 121, G. Cook 83, C.S. Pickles 4 for 92) and 26 for 4

Northamptonshire won by 6 wickets
Northamptonshire 22 pts, Yorkshire 3 pts

17, 18 and 19 May

at Chesterfield

Leicestershire 274 (N.E. Briers 73) and 12 for 1
Derbyshire 57 (W.K.M. Benjamin 6 for 26, J.P. Agnew 4 for 31) and 228 (J.E. Morris 77, C.C. Lewis 5 for 69)

Leicestershire won by 9 wickets
Leicestershire 23 pts, Derbyshire 4 pts

at Lord's

Hampshire 217 (A.R.C. Fraser 4 for 49) and 176 (D.R. Turner 53)
Middlesex 290 (N.F. Williams 69 not out, D.L. Haynes 67, P.J. Bakker 5 for 52) and 106 for 6

Middlesex won by 4 wickets
Middlesex 23 pts, Hampshire 5 pts

at Hove

Sussex 300 for 7 dec (N.J. Lenham 116, A.P. Wells 103) and 233 for 6 dec (A.P. Wells 54 not out)
Surrey 259 (I.A. Greig 87 not out, A.C.S. Pigott 4 for 91) and

235 for 5 (D.J. Bicknell 101, G.S. Clinton 90 not out)

Match drawn
Sussex 7 pts, Surrey 5 pts

at Old Trafford

Lancashire 261 (P.A.J. DeFreitas 78) and 133 (N.H. Fairbrother 62, A.A. Donald 4 for 23)
Warwickshire 158 (M. Asif Din 67, M. Watkinson 5 for 45, P.A.J. DeFreitas 4 for 65) and 174 (P.A.J. DeFreitas 4 for 47)

Lancashire won by 62 runs
Lancashire 23 pts, Warwickshire 5 pts

at Taunton

Australians 339 for 8 dec (M.A. Taylor 97, D.C. Boon 61) and 144 for 3 dec (M.A. Taylor 58, G.R. Marsh 57)
Somerset 140 and 235 for 3 (P.M. Roebuck 100 not out, S.J. Cook 57)

Match drawn

at Cambridge

Cambridge University 259 (R.J. Turner 58, J.C.M. Atkinson 57, M.D. Harman 4 for 56) and 220 (M.A. Atherton 79, M.D. Harman 5 for 80, R.P. Davis 4 for 68)
Kent 304 (S.G. Hinks 76, G.R. Cowdrey 78, C.S. Cowdrey 59, A.J. Buzza 6 for 102) and 176 for 3 (R.F. Pienaar 75, T.R. Ward 54)

Kent won by 7 wickets

at Oxford

Nottinghamshire 320 for 6 dec (D.W. Randall 100, P. Pollard 72, E.D. Hester 4 for 100) and 194 for 3 dec (P. Johnson 109 not out)
Oxford University 191 (R.E. Morris 55, A.N.S. Hampton 53, R.A. Pick 6 for 52) and 83

Nottinghamshire won by 240 runs

Northamptonshire and Lancashire continued to set the pace in the Britannic Assurance County Championship although both counties had moments of misgiving before they clinched victories. The first day of the four-day game at Northampton belonged entirely to the home side, who won the toss, asked Yorkshire to bat first and dismissed them for 191 in 52.1 overs. By the end of the day, Northamptonshire were 113 for 2 and, seemingly, in complete control of the match. The next morning, however, Yorkshire removed Cook, Capel and Williams within the space of four overs, Northamptonshire were 145 for 5 and the game was in the balance. Ripley now joined the eager Wild in a stand which spread into the third day and which realized 243 runs. Both batsmen were aided by dropped catches, but both played with great zest and no little skill. When they were dismissed the Northamptonshire innings collapsed. For the second time in the match the Yorkshire batting crumbled, and they ended the third day needing five runs to make the home side bat again and with only one wicket standing. The last pair, Pickles and Priestley, restored some pride with a stand of 48, but Northamptonshire were still left with a meagre 25 needed to win. Jarvis and Pickles captured four wickets for 16 runs before Capel and Williams brought back sanity to the batting.

Lancashire were indebted to DeFreitas' all-round ability for their victory over Warwickshire. He and Allott added

Duncan Wild hit 121 and shared a sixth-wicket stand of 243 for Northamptonshire against Yorkshire at Northampton, 16–19 May. (David Munden)

126 in 19 overs after Lancashire had been 125 for 7. DeFreitas then returned match figures of 8 for 112 and with Watkinson and acting skipper Allott took Lancashire to a comfortable win on a pitch on which batting was never easy.

The loss of 45 overs on the second day because of rain, and a more determined second-innings batting performance, saved Derbyshire from the humiliation of a two-day defeat at Chesterfield. Benjamin and Parsons put on 74 for Leicestershire's ninth wicket to lift them from 198 for 8, four wickets having fallen for 22 runs, and then Benjamin combined with Agnew to reduce the home side to 31 for 6 by the close of the first day. There was no effective recovery. Benjamin returned the best bowling figures of his career, and Leicestershire won by nine wickets.

Cowans and Fraser quickly disposed of Hampshire on the first day at Lord's, but Middlesex lost seven middle-order wickets for 41 runs on the second day and regained the initiative only through a ninth-wicket stand of 85 between Fraser and Williams. The pitch was never as difficult as the batsmen would suggest, but Middlesex lost six wickets for 79 runs when they were seeking 104 to win the match, and it needed the application of Emburey and Williams to see them home.

Ian Greig asked Sussex to bat first when he won the toss at Hove, but he must have had regrets as the home side were rescued from 23 for 2 by a third-wicket partnership of 191 between Neil Lenham and Alan Wells. Both batsmen reached excellent hundreds, and for Lenham it was a first in the Championship. Surrey seemed in danger of being overwhelmed until Ian Greig hit a powerful 87 not out at number eight. Colin Wells, leading Sussex in the absence of the injured Parker, ultimately set Surrey the daunting task of scoring 275 in 50 overs. The visitors were given a splendid start by Darren Bicknell and Clinton, who put on 178 for the first wicket, but the target proved too great, and the match was drawn.

The Australians again demonstrated the strength and depth of their batting, but, in spite of some good work by Rackemann and May on the second day, their bowlers failed to exploit conditions on the last day when the wicket was offering help to the spinners. Roebuck played a patient and resolute innings, but May, in particular, proved a disappointment to the Australians and the match was drawn.

Kent were thankful for a last-ball win at Fenner's, and Andy Pick returned career-best bowling figures for Nottinghamshire in The Parks, where the visitors had an easy win in spite of maiden first-class fifties from Hampton and Morris.

20, 21 and 22 May

at Dartford

Derbyshire 416 (B. Roberts 102, S.C. Goldsmith 88, J.E. Morris 55, A.P. Igglesden 4 for 90) and 87 for 2
Kent 210 (N.R. Taylor 74, S.A. Marsh 52, D.E. Malcolm 4 for 69, M.A. Holding 4 for 71) and 292 (C. Penn 60, T.R. Ward 57, D.J.M. Kelleher 53 not out)

Derbyshire won by 8 wickets
Derbyshire 24 pts, Kent 5 pts

at Trent Bridge

Nottinghamshire 331 for 6 dec (B.C. Broad 64) and 214 for 4 dec (R.T. Robinson 73 not out, P. Johnson 64)
Hampshire 300 for 6 dec (R.A. Smith 148, M.C.J. Nicholas 71, F.D. Stephenson 4 for 84) and 172 for 6 (V.P. Terry 82 not out)

Match drawn
Hampshire 6 pts, Nottinghamshire 5 pts

at Lord's

Middlesex 245 (M.W. Gatting 65, C.G. Rackemann 4 for 85)

and 227 (M.W. Gatting 79, G.F. Lawson 5 for 48)
Australians 233 for 2 dec (G.R. Marsh 100 not out, T.M. Moody 60 not out) and 243 for 7 (D.C. Boon 86, A.R. Border 77, A.R.C. Fraser 4 for 89)

Australians won by 3 wickets

20, 22 and 23 May

at Swansea

Glamorgan 290 (M.J. Cann 75 not out, R.J. Shastri 50, N.G.B. Cook 4 for 62) and 214 for 4 dec
Northamptonshire 200 (S.R. Barwick 4 for 34) and 60 (S.L. Watkin 6 for 42)

Glamorgan won by 244 runs
Glamorgan 23 pts, Northamptonshire 6 pts

at Bristol

Essex 178 (G.A. Gooch 63, D.V. Lawrence 4 for 61) and 108
Gloucestershire 80 (N.A. Foster 4 for 14, T.D. Topley 4 for 39) and 90 (N.A. Foster 4 for 35)

Essex won by 116 runs
Essex 21 pts, Gloucestershire 4 pts

at Taunton

Somerset 399 for 4 dec (S.J. Cook 156, C.J. Tavare 153) and 203 for 4 dec (P.M. Roebuck 66)
Lancashire 303 for 8 dec (G. Fowler 96, W.K. Hegg 58) and 302 for 4 (T.E. Jesty 93 not out, M. Watkinson 59 not out, G.D. Mendis 59)

Lancashire won by 6 wickets
Lancashire 21 pts, Somerset 7 pts

at Edgbaston

Surrey 293 (A.J. Stewart 60, P.A. Smith 5 for 82) and 108 (A.A. Donald 5 for 18)
Warwickshire 190 (M.P. Bicknell 6 for 64) and 207 (A.J. Moles 100, M.A. Feltham 4 for 68)

Surrey won by 4 runs
Surrey 23 pts, Warwickshire 5 pts

Northamptonshire's short reign as Championship leaders came to a sensational end. A generally pedestrian first day at Swansea saw Glamorgan bowled out for 290 and Northamptonshire reach 33 without loss. Both openers were soon out on the Monday, Cook being caught behind off Watkin, and Larkins being out when his helmet fell on his wicket. Barwick bowled his off-cutters to good effect and numbered Lamb and Bailey among his four wickets as Glamorgan claimed a first-innings lead of 90. In 82 minutes on the last morning, Glamorgan added 126 runs to their overnight 88 for 2, and Morris declared. Geoff Cook was absent because of an illness in his family, and Lamb opened with Larkins. The Northamptonshire captain was soon out when he prodded Dennis to short leg, but by then his side had already lost Larkins, caught behind on the leg side. Soon, the visitors were 6 for 5, and in an astonishing pre-lunch spell, Steve Watkin took 4 for 9 in 21 deliveries. He eventually took 6 for 42, and his figures would have been even better had it not been for some late-order hitting into the untenanted outfield by Greg Thomas, who did not enjoy a happy time against his old county. So Glamorgan enjoyed their first Championship win of the

Somerset v. the Australians at Taunton. Tim Zoehrer hits out. Neil Burns is the wicket-keeper. (Adrian Murrell/Allsport)

RIGHT: *Derbyshire beat Kent at Dartford, 20–2 May, by eight wickets. They owed their win to some solid batting, tight bowling and good catching. Chris Cowdrey is well caught by former Kent player Steve Goldsmith. (Tom Morris)*

season, and Northamptonshire suffered their first defeat in any competition.

Lancashire took over as leaders when, set to make 300 in 58 overs at Taunton, they won with 19 balls to spare. Somerset were weakened by the absence of Marks, who was attending his father's funeral, and it was difficult for Tavare to judge his declaration on a pitch which offered hope to all batsmen. South African Jim Cook had hit a fine century on the opening day, but it was Jesty and Watkinson who took the final honours with the unbroken stand of 142 in 21 overs which won the match.

Essex were close on the heels of the leaders and beat

Steve Watkin enjoyed an outstanding season for Glamorgan. He took 4 for 9 in 21 balls to bring about the collapse of Northamptonshire at Swansea, 23 May. (Gray Mortimore/Allsport)

Gloucestershire by 116 runs in two days at Bristol in a match in which 178 was the best score. This was the total Essex reached when they were put in to bat on the Saturday, the day on which 24 wickets fell for 276 runs and which Essex ended tottering at 18 for 4. Prichard and Hardie effected a minor recovery on the Monday morning, and the game was over shortly after 5.00 p.m. when Gloucestershire, without the injured Athey, were again bowled out by the Essex seamers for under a hundred. All agreed that the wicket was blameless.

Bruce Roberts, who had had a poor season in South Africa, returned to his best form with an aggressive century against Kent at Dartford. Steve Goldsmith enjoyed batting against his old county and helped Roberts

to add 153 for the fifth wicket. Derbyshire made 416 in 108 overs, and with Malcolm and Holding in good form, they forced Kent to follow-on. The fierce hitting of Penn and Kelleher saved the home county from the indignity of an innings defeat, but there was never any doubt that Derbyshire would claim their first Championship win of the season.

There was another sparkling century from Robin Smith of Hampshire in the game at Trent Bridge, but a draw always seemed probable in a match in which the bat dominated. The one fright that Hampshire had was when they lost four wickets in 11 balls on the last afternoon, but Terry and Tremlett stood firm for the last 14 overs.

Cool captaincy by Ian Greig produced a tense finish at Edgbaston. Perhaps Andy Lloyd misread the wicket when he asked Surrey to bat when he won the toss, for they reached 293 in a rather uneven display. Martin Bicknell put Surrey on top when he captured three Warwickshire wickets before the close on Saturday, and he claimed three more on the Monday as Surrey took a first-innings lead of 103. Donald bowled Warwickshire back into the game with a fiery spell, and the home county were left with just over a day in which to score 212 to win. Moles and Lloyd opened with a stand of 60 and, on a dour last day, runs came at less than two an over. Bicknell bowled manfully and took three more wickets, and Murphy worked very hard on an impressive Championship debut for Surrey to claim three wickets at a crucial time. Feltham, the third seamer, also bowled with great heart, but Moles, who batted for six hours, nearly brought Warwickshire victory with his monumental patience. Thirteen runs were needed from the last five overs with two wickets in hand when Greig was able to take the new ball. Pierson was caught at slip off Feltham with six still needed for victory, and the last over began with Warwickshire still five short of their target. Moles swung at Feltham's second ball and was bowled, and Surrey claimed their first Championship win of the season.

The Australians had their first first-class win, and they owed much to Border's captaincy and enterprise. He declared when his side was still in arrears and concentrated on bowling out Middlesex a second time. This was brought about by Lawson and Alderman, and the tourists were left to make 240 at approximately three runs an over. At tea, they were 103 for 1, and Border and Boon took them to 163 before another wicket fell. Border then decided to juggle his batting order; Angus Fraser bowled splendidly to trouble all batsmen, taking four wickets in five overs, and the Australians had to fight all the way, achieving victory with only three balls to spare when Lawson edged Fraser over the heads of slips for four.

Refuge Assurance League

21 May

at Cardiff

Glamorgan 162 for 7
Northamptonshire 163 for 4 (G. Cook 53, D.J. Wild 52 not out)

Northamptonshire (4 pts) won by 6 wickets

at Bristol

Gloucestershire 167 for 7
Essex 168 for 1 (G.A. Gooch 76, B.R. Hardie 73 not out)

Essex (4 pts) won by 9 wickets

at Taunton

Somerset 244 for 7 (S.J. Cook 123)
Lancashire 245 for 6 (G. Fowler 74, M. Watkinson 57)

Lancashire (4 pts) won by 4 wickets

at Hove

Sussex 208 for 4 (A.P. Wells 69)
Leicestershire 131

Sussex (4 pts) won by 77 runs

at Worcester

Surrey 221 (G.S. Clinton 78, A.J. Stewart 55)
Worcestershire 216 for 8 (D.B. D'Oliveira 91 not out)

Surrey (4 pts) won by 5 runs

at Leeds

Warwickshire 191 for 7 (A.I. Kallicharran 104)
Yorkshire 192 for 5 (R.J. Blakey 94 not out)

Yorkshire (4 pts) won by 5 wickets

Jim Cook hit his second century on successive days for Somerset against Lancashire, but the visitors romped to victory with 10 balls to spare, Watkinson providing some flourishing hitting at the right time. The win kept Lancashire close on the heels of Essex, for whom Gooch and Hardie shared an opening stand of 146 in the triumph over Gloucestershire. The most exciting game of the day was at Worcester, where Surrey, thanks to the stability of Clinton and the later exuberance of Stewart and Ward, made 221 in their 40 overs. Curtis and Botham began the Worcestershire innings with a partnership of 68, but as they pressed for runs Botham was run out and Curtis was caught off Greig. Hick was out for one, but D'Oliveira, who played a marvellous innings, hitting 91 off 80 balls including 2 sixes in the last over off Bicknell, nearly brought Worcestershire a dramatic victory. However, Surrey were not to be denied.

23 May

at Leeds

Australians 297 for 3 (D.C. Boon 172, D.M. Jones 89 not out)
Yorkshire 188 (M.D. Moxon 55)

Australians won by 109 runs

Dean Jones returned after injury to share a second-wicket stand of 184 with Boon. Boon's 172 included 3 sixes and 21 fours and came off only 157 balls. Martyn Moxon played his first game since breaking an arm in the winter and scored an encouraging 55, but Yorkshire were well beaten, and Australia gained much confidence in their last game before the Texaco Trophy.

24, 25 and 26 May

at Leicester

Kent 307 (G.R. Cowdrey 105 not out, M.R. Benson 75) and

133 for 1 dec (T.R. Ward 69)
Leicestershire 201 for 7 dec (L. Potter 56) and 184 for 7

Match drawn
Kent 5 pts, Leicestershire 4 pts

at The Oval

Lancashire 257 (W.K. Hegg 59, D.P. Hughes 50 not out, K.T. Medlycott 4 for 42) and 232 for 4 dec (N.H. Fairbrother 62 not out, G. Fowler 52)
Surrey 200 for 3 dec (D.J. Bicknell 100 not out) and 119 for 3

Match drawn
Surrey 6 pts, Lancashire 4 pts

at Worcester

Worcestershire 209 (T.S. Curtis 50, E.E. Hemmings 4 for 60) and 180 for 3 dec (G.A. Hick 90 not out, P.A. Neale 51 not out)
Nottinghamshire 150 for 3 dec (R.T. Robinson 54 not out) and 238 for 9 (M. Newell 62, P.J. Newport 4 for 64)

Match drawn
Nottinghamshire 5 pts, Worcestershire 3 pts

at Leeds

Derbyshire 178 (A. Sidebottom 5 for 40, P. Carrick 4 for 60) and 189 for 7 (J.E. Morris 70, R. Sharma 53 not out)
Yorkshire 313 (I.G. Swallow 64, A.A. Metcalfe 60, K. Sharp 51, M.D. Moxon 50)

Match drawn
Yorkshire 8 pts, Derbyshire 4 pts

at Cambridge

Cambridge University 133 (M.C. Ilott 4 for 26) and 184 (S.P. James 60, J.H. Childs 7 for 35)
Essex 347 for 6 dec (M.E. Waugh 92, P.J. Prichard 88, J.P. Stephenson 63, M.A. Garnham 55 not out)

Essex won by an innings and 30 runs

at Oxford

Middlesex 358 for 1 dec (I.J.F. Hutchinson 201 not out, M.A. Roseberry 101 not out, J.D. Carr 50) and 173 for 3 dec (K.R. Brown 91)
Oxford University 92 (D. Boden 4 for 11) and 174 for 5 (S.A. Almaer 62)

Match drawn

Rain ate into the Championship matches and not one produced a result in spite of some challenging declarations. At New Road, the last morning saw Johnson and Robinson offer bowling which produced 10 runs an over in order to precipitate a declaration. Nottinghamshire, asked to make 240 in 61 overs, were given a good start by Newell and Broad, who was out to the last ball before tea with the score on 74. When the last 20 overs arrived the visitors were still 111 short of victory, but 17 off the first of these overs gave Nottinghamshire encouragement. Randall was then bowled by Newport, and Newell mis-hit Illingworth to mid-wicket. The climax came with 10 runs or two wickets needed off the last over. Evans lost the strike after seven had been scored, and Radford bowled Scott with the penultimate ball. Pick could manage only a single from the last delivery.

Morris and Sharma rescued Derbyshire from the danger of an innings defeat at Headingley, and Kent's bowlers

could not force victory at Leicester, where Graham Cowdrey hit a fine century.

The other centurion was Darren Bicknell, but, in spite of Ian Greig's efforts to keep the game alive, Lancashire asked Surrey to make 290 in 59 overs, a less than generous declaration, and the match was drawn.

The events on the field at The Oval were overshadowed by the announcement that Sylvester Clarke's contract had been cancelled. He had failed to attend team meetings, had arrived late for a Sunday League game and had generally shown a lack of appetite for the game and for club discipline. The decision that the Surrey Club took was inevitable, and one regrets that Clarke had let down a club and a captain who had treated him generously and with understanding.

As one player left the game, another announced an emphatic arrival. Ian Hutchinson shared a first-wicket stand of 112 with John Carr for Middlesex in The Parks on a fractured first day. On the second day, Mike Roseberry reached a maiden first-class century and Ian Hutchinson extended his maiden century to a double century. He is only the second batsman to have scored a double hundred as a first three-figured first-class innings in England. Roseberry and Hutchinson added 256 without being parted, but, in spite of some lively seam bowling by debutant David Boden, the match was drawn.

Essex claimed the only victory in the six matches, thanks mainly to the bowling of Mark Ilott, who had career-best figures in the first Cambridge innings, and of John Childs whose left-arm spin destroyed the university on the last day.

Texaco Trophy
First Texaco One-Day International
ENGLAND v. AUSTRALIA

The first contest of the summer between England and Australia went most decidedly in favour of England. The match marked the return to international cricket after injury of Ian Botham and the debut of wicket-keeper Steven Rhodes.

Gower won the toss and it was he who opened the innings with Gooch. The England captain batted with a pleasing fluency. He off-drove Alderman for the first boundary of the match and pulled Lawson for six. He had hit 36 off 33 balls when he failed to remove his bat in time from a Rackemann outswinger and was caught behind. This was in Rackemann's first over, and Waugh also took a wicket in his first over when Gatting lofted to cover. Border became the third bowler to claim a wicket in his first over, Gooch top edging the ball to fine-leg.

The wicket had become progressively slower, but Smith

ABOVE LEFT: *Ian Hutchinson, 201 not out for Middlesex against Oxford University at Oxford, 24–6 May. It was Hutchinson's first century in first-class cricket and he and Mike Roseberry put on 256 for the second wicket. (USPA)*

LEFT: *Mike Roseberry – a maiden first-class hundred. (David Munden)*

ABOVE: *David Gower opens the England innings with a flourish. (Ben Radford/Allsport)*

RIGHT: *An early set-back for Australia – Man-of-the-Match DeFreitas knocks David Boon's off stump out of the ground. (Patrick Eagar)*

and Lamb, the former in particular, kept the score moving. There were no boundaries in the last seven overs, but the final over provided something of a pantomime with 10 runs and two dropped catches.

Boon had scored centuries in each of the one-day matches he had played on the tour, and when he was soon bowled by DeFreitas it was a great set-back to Australia. Foster accounted for Jones and Border, and the visitors were in despair. Waugh played some merry shots while Marsh dropped anchor. The Australian vice-captain's innings of 17 spanned 29 overs, and he faced 78 balls.

When Waugh hit DeFreitas high to mid-wicket, where Smith took the catch running in from the boundary, Australia were 85 for 5, and their hopes of scoring six runs an over to win the match were at an end.

Second Texaco One-Day International
ENGLAND *v.* AUSTRALIA

England fielded the side that had won at Old Trafford,

TOP: *A catch for Rhodes on his international debut. Marsh is the victim. (Ben Radford/Allsport)*

ABOVE: *A decisive blow. Border is bowled by Foster. (Adrian Murrell/Allsport)*

RIGHT: *Gatting is bowled by May. (USPA)*

FIRST TEXACO ONE-DAY INTERNATIONAL – ENGLAND v. AUSTRALIA
25 May 1989 at Old Trafford, Manchester

ENGLAND			
G.A. Gooch	c Jones, b Border		52
D.I. Gower†	c Healy, b Rackemann		36
M.W. Gatting	c Boon, b Waugh		3
A.J. Lamb	b Lawson		35
R.A. Smith	c and b Alderman		35
I.T. Botham	c Boon, b Lawson		4
D.R. Pringle	lbw, b Waugh		9
S.J. Rhodes*	b Lawson		8
P.A.J. DeFreitas	not out		17
J.E. Emburey	b Rackemann		10
N.A. Foster	not out		5
Extras	lb 12, w 3, nb 2		17
(55 overs)	(for 9 wkts)		231

AUSTRALIA			
G.R. Marsh	c Rhodes, b Emburey		17
D.C. Boon	b DeFreitas		5
D.M. Jones	c Rhodes, b Foster		4
A.R. Border†	b Foster		4
S.R. Waugh	c Smith, b DeFreitas		35
T.M. Moody	b Emburey		24
M.R.J. Veletta	lbw, b Pringle		17
I.A. Healy*	c Emburey, b Foster		10
G.F. Lawson	c DeFreitas, b Emburey		0
C.G. Rackemann	b Botham		6
T.M. Alderman	not out		0
Extras	b 1, lb 9, w 4		14
(47.1 overs)			136

	O	M	R	W
Alderman	11	2	38	1
Lawson	11	1	48	3
Rackemann	10	1	33	2
Waugh	11	1	45	2
Moody	8	–	37	–
Border	4	–	18	1

	O	M	R	W
Foster	10	3	29	3
DeFreitas	8	1	19	2
Pringle	8	2	19	1
Botham	10.1	1	28	1
Emburey	11	–	31	3

FALL OF WICKETS
1–55, 2–70, 3–125, 4–161, 5–167, 6–179, 7–190,
8–203, 9–220

FALL OF WICKETS
1–8, 2–13, 3–17, 4–64, 5–85, 6–115, 7–119, 8–120,
9–136

Umpires: J.W. Holder & N.T. Plews

Man of the Match: P.A.J. DeFreitas

England won by 95 runs

SECOND TEXACO ONE-DAY INTERNATIONAL – ENGLAND v. AUSTRALIA
27 May 1989 at Trent Bridge, Nottingham

ENGLAND			
G.A. Gooch	c Jones, b Alderman		10
D.I. Gower†	b Waugh		28
M.W. Gatting	b May		37
A.J. Lamb	not out		100
R.A. Smith	st Healy, b May		3
I.T. Botham	run out		8
D.R. Pringle	not out		25
S.J. Rhodes*			
P.A.J. DeFreitas			
J.E. Emburey			
N.A. Foster			
Extras	lb 14, w 1		15
(55 overs)	(for 5 wkts)		226

AUSTRALIA			
D.C. Boon	b Botham		28
G.R. Marsh	lbw, b Emburey		34
D.M. Jones	b Emburey		29
A.R. Border†	c Rhodes, b Pringle		39
S.R. Waugh	run out		43
T.M. Moody	run out		10
I.A. Healy*	not out		26
G.F. Lawson	c Gooch, b Foster		1
T.B.A. May	b DeFreitas		2
C.G. Rackemann	not out		0
T.M. Alderman			
Extras	b 1, lb 6, w 7		14
(55 overs)	(for 8 wkts)		226

	O	M	R	W
Alderman	9	2	38	1
Lawson	11	–	47	–
Rackemann	11	1	37	–
Waugh	11	1	47	1
May	11	1	35	2
Moody	2	–	8	–

	O	M	R	W
Foster	11	2	44	1
DeFreitas	11	–	48	1
Pringle	11	1	38	1
Botham	11	–	42	1
Emburey	11	–	47	2

FALL OF WICKETS
1–30, 2–57, 3–119, 4–123, 5–138

FALL OF WICKETS
1–59, 2–81, 3–116, 4–153, 5–174, 6–205, 7–218,
8–225

Umpires: H.D. Bird & J.H. Hampshire

Man of the Match: A.J. Lamb

Match tied

ABOVE: *England* v. *Australia, Texaco Trophy, at Trent Bridge. (Patrick Eagar)*

LEFT: *Botham is run out for 8. (Adrian Murrell/Allsport)*

while Australia brought in off-spinner May for batsman Veletta. Once again Gower won the toss, but this time the start was less impressive than at Old Trafford. The first 10 overs produced only 27 runs, and Gooch was soon out when he hit the accurate Alderman to mid-wicket. Gower looked as if he might play an innings of substance when he dragged a ball from Waugh onto his off-stump, and Gatting, having completed 2,000 runs in one-day internationals, swung across the line at May and was bowled. The off-spinner bowled an impressive spell and beat Smith through the air when the batsman advanced down the wicket to him. Botham was run out when Lamb left him stranded and Border threw down the wicket at the bowler's end. After 45 overs, England were 147 for 5 and were not finding runs easy to score.

With Pringle giving sensible and meaningful support, Allan Lamb, who had reached 50 off 71 balls, moved to 100 in another 34 balls. He had needed nine runs off the last over to reach his century, and, in spite of losing the strike for one ball, he hit those nine runs, reaching three-figures off the last ball of the innings. It was a well-merited hundred, full of scintillating shots.

Boon and Marsh began Australia's innings in excellent fashion. Boon was going well until he hit rashly across the line. Marsh was out to the first ball after tea. Border and Jones were scoring at a brisk rate and moving their side to a comfortable win when Jones was bowled by Emburey, but Waugh and Border still looked as if they would take Australia to victory. Then Border was caught behind, and Moody, having hit the day's only six, was tardy when Waugh called for a legitimate single and was run out.

Waugh continued to smite all around him, but he was run out when Healy, handicapped by a twisted knee, was slow to respond to a call for a second run. Jones came on as runner for Healy, but he was ordered back to the pavilion when Healy ran as quickly as his runner. Lawson was caught on the boundary, and May was bowled having a slog before Healy and Rackemann ran a bye to the wicket-keeper off the last ball to tie the match.

Third Texaco One-Day International
ENGLAND v. AUSTRALIA

A splendid Texaco series reached a glorious climax on a sun-drenched Bank Holiday Monday at Lord's. Gower's luck with the toss remained. England fielded the same side, and Gower and Gooch put on 123 for the first wicket. Gooch was fortunate to survive an appeal for run out, and Gower surrendered his innings when he flashed at the medium pace of Moody and was excitingly caught by Veletta, who had come into the side as wicket-keeper because both Healy and Zoehrer were unfit. Gooch went on to reach 50 off 76 balls and his hundred off 135. In all,

he faced 162 balls and hit 11 fours before he was yorked when playing an understandably tired shot.

There were gems of innings from Smith and Botham. Smith helped Gooch to add 57 in nine overs and hit one breath-taking cover-drive, while Botham hit a six and 3 fours as he made a highly popular 25 off 11 deliveries. He looked to have helped England to a winning score.

The early part of the Australian innings did nothing to contradict this opinion. Boon began in emphatic style, hitting 3 fours, but he was cut short by an lbw decision. At tea, after 25 overs, Australia were 80 for 1, and Jones, frustrated by Emburey's leg-stump attack, was caught at mid-wicket shortly after the resumption.

It was Border who changed the course of the match. He hit 5 fours and made 53 off 46 balls as he and Marsh added 113 in 17 overs. Marsh had played just the innings that was needed, first standing firm and then gradually accelerating.

From the last 10 overs, 76 were needed. Pringle bowled Border, and had both Marsh and Waugh missed on the mid-wicket boundary in front of the Tavern in successive overs. The dropped catch off Waugh was dramatic and decisive, for the all-rounder celebrated by hitting 2 sixes

England players Gatting, Rhodes and Jarvis watch happily from the balcony. Stewart and Emburey look more serious. Footballer Gary Lineker is enjoying the match and the company. (Adrian Murrell/Allsport)

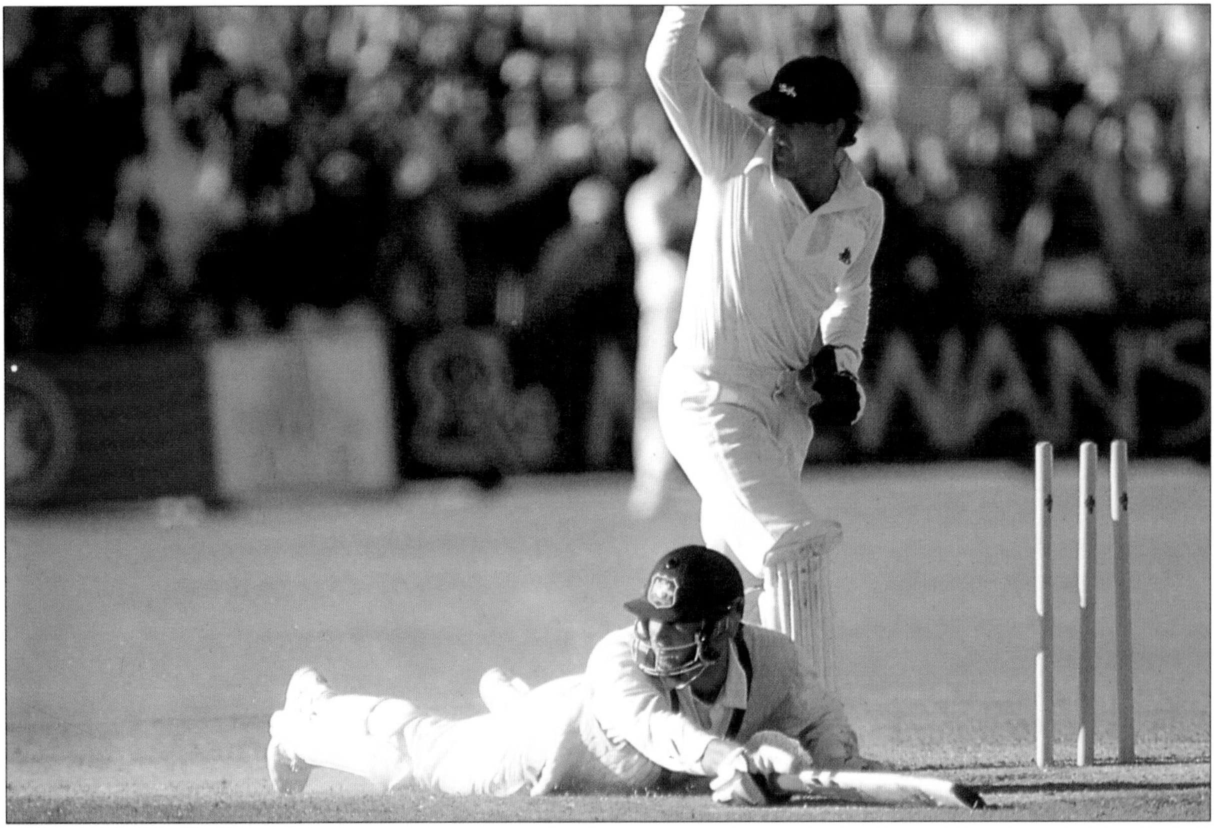

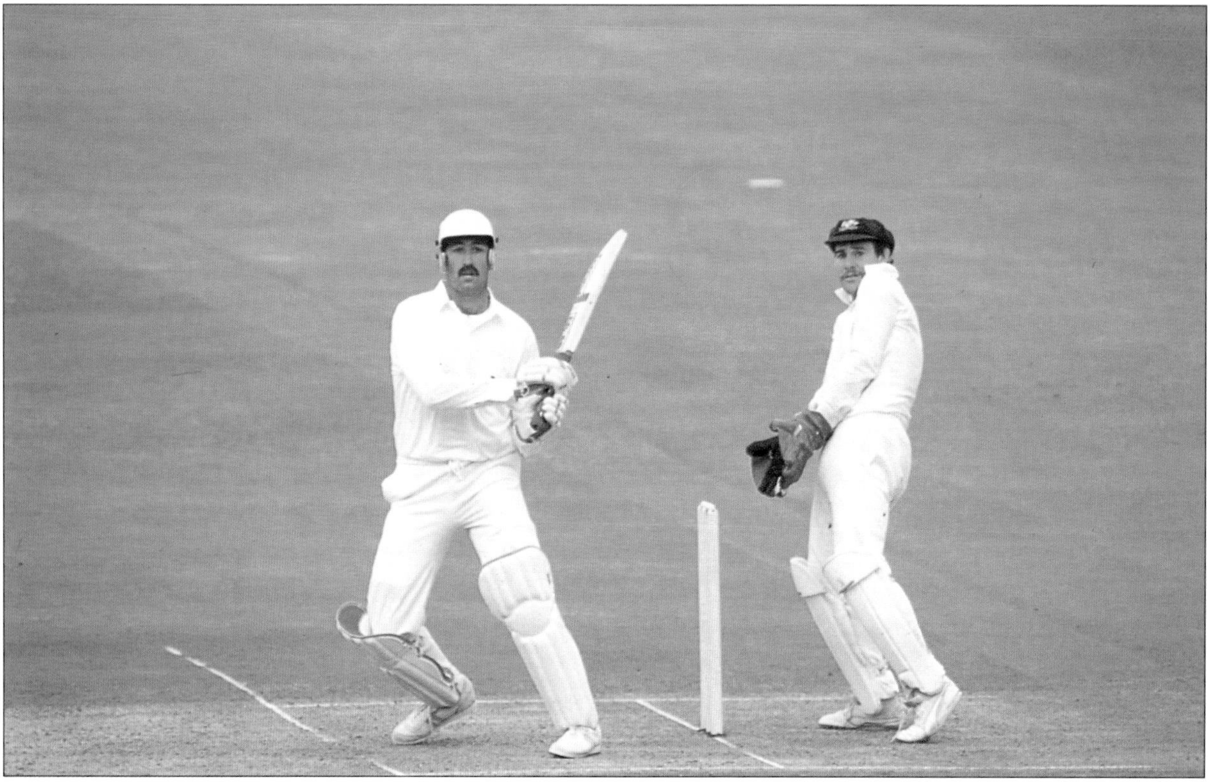

THIRD TEXACO ONE-DAY INTERNATIONAL – ENGLAND *v.* AUSTRALIA
29 May 1989 at Lord's

ENGLAND				AUSTRALIA			
G.A. Gooch	b Alderman		136	G.R. Marsh	not out		111
D.I. Gower†	c Veletta, b Moody		61	D.C. Boon	lbw, b Foster		19
M.W. Gatting	run out		18	D.M. Jones	c Gower, b Emburey		27
A.J. Lamb	lbw, b Alderman		0	A.R. Border†	b Pringle		53
R.A. Smith	b Rackemann		21	S.R. Waugh	c Gooch, b Foster		35
I.T. Botham	not out		25	T.M. Moody	not out		6
P.A.J. DeFreitas	c Rackemann, b Alderman		0	M.R.J. Veletta*			
D.R. Pringle	run out		0	G.F. Lawson			
S.J. Rhodes*	not out		1	T.B.A. May			
J.E. Emburey				C.G. Rackemann			
N.A. Foster				T.M. Alderman			
Extras	lb 14, w 2		16	Extras	lb 18, w 9, nb 1		28
	(55 overs)	(for 7 wkts)	278		(54.3 overs)	(for 4 wkts)	279

	O	M	R	W		O	M	R	W
Alderman	11	2	36	3	DeFreitas	11	1	50	–
Rackemann	11	–	56	1	Foster	11	–	57	2
Lawson	11	–	48	–	Botham	11	–	43	–
Waugh	11	–	70	–	Pringle	10.3	–	50	1
May	6	–	33	–	Emburey	11	–	61	1
Moody	5	–	21	1					

FALL OF WICKETS
1–123, 2–180, 3–182, 4–239, 5–266, 6–266, 7–268

FALL OF WICKETS
1–24, 2–84, 3–197, 4–268

Umpires: B.J. Meyer & D.R. Shepherd

Man of the Match: G.R. Marsh

England won by 6 wickets

LEFT: *Tom Moody – down and out. (Adrian Murrell/ Allsport)*

BELOW LEFT: *Graham Gooch in dominant mood; 136 in the Texaco Trophy match at Lord's. (Adrian Murrell/Allsport)*

and Emburey had seemed to have taken the ball cleanly before it fell to the ground.

Waugh's sixes came in the 52nd over, which Australia began still 36 short of victory. They were struck high and cleanly over Emburey. Eleven runs were needed from 10 deliveries when Waugh again tried to hit Foster for six, but this time to the longest boundary on the ground, and this time he was safely held by Gooch. Marsh hit his 7th four to reduce the target to five from the last over and, although Moody was crowded by fielders, he was equal to the occasion, and Australia won a fine match with three balls to spare.

Marsh was rightly named Man of the Match for his 111 off 162 balls, and Gooch and Waugh were Men of the Series. England took the Texaco Trophy by virtue of having lost fewer wickets at Trent Bridge. A good time was had by all.

An Australian colleague said, 'No matter. Whoever loses the Texaco Trophy always wins the Test series.' We all laughed!

27, 29 and 30 May

at Chelmsford

Essex 327 for 8 dec (J.P. Stephenson 102) and 217 for 3 dec (B.R. Hardie 80, M.E. Waugh 79)
Somerset 280 for 3 dec (S.J. Cook 147 not out, R.J. Harden 101 not out) and 116 for 4 (P.M. Roebuck 65 not out)

Match drawn
Somerset 5 pts, Essex 4 pts

at Cardiff

Nottinghamshire 300 for 6 dec (B.C. Broad 132, P. Johnson 52) and 302 for 3 dec (B.C. Broad 113, P. Johnson 87, R.T. Robinson 63 not out)
Glamorgan 250 for 2 dec (A.R. Butcher 107, R.J. Shastri 54 not out) and 286 for 6 (R.J. Shastri 80, M.P. Maynard 65)

Match drawn
Glamorgan 5 pts, Nottinghamshire 4 pts

at Bristol

Worcestershire 201 (P.A. Neale 70, K.M. Curran 6 for 53, D.V. Lawrence 4 for 62) and 283 for 6 dec (T.S. Curtis 102, G.A. Hick 53)
Gloucestershire 148 (N.V. Radford 5 for 57) and 257 (K.M. Curran 116 not out, P.J. Newport 5 for 73)

Worcestershire won by 79 runs
Worcestershire 22 pts, Gloucestershire 4 pts

at Bournemouth

Hampshire 288 (R.J. Scott 77, K.D. James 68) and 239 for 4 dec (V.P. Terry 68)
Leicestershire 293 (P. Willey 52, T.M. Tremlett 4 for 67) and 115 (K.D. James 4 for 24, M.D. Marshall 4 for 33)

Hampshire won by 119 runs
Hampshire 23 pts, Leicestershire 6 pts

at Liverpool

Sussex 334 for 7 dec (D.M. Smith 101, C.M. Wells 66, A.P. Wells 52) and 185 for 4 dec (A.P. Wells 63 not out)
Lancashire 204 (A.M. Babington 5 for 37) and 266 for 8 (G.D. Mendis 84, T.E. Jesty 50, A.M. Babington 4 for 23)

Match drawn
Sussex 7 pts, Lancashire 4 pts

at The Oval

Surrey 400 for 6 dec (D.J. Bicknell 119, K.T. Medlycott 71, G.P. Thorpe 64 not out, R.I. Alikhan 51) and 177 for 7 dec
Yorkshire 303 for 8 dec (M.D. Moxon 162 not out, P. Carrick 51) and 217 for 6 (D.L. Bairstow 101 not out)

Match drawn
Surrey 6 pts, Yorkshire 6 pts

at Edgbaston

Warwickshire 194 and 112 (A.R.C. Fraser 5 for 20, S.P. Hughes 4 for 23)
Middlesex 199 (R.O. Butcher 58, A.A. Donald 7 for 66) and 108 for 2

Middlesex won by 8 wickets
Middlesex 21 pts, Warwickshire 5 pts

Lancashire maintained their place at the top of the table, but they came close to defeat at the hands of Sussex. On a rather dour first day at Liverpool, David Smith hit a century and there were fifties from the Wells brothers, but Sussex continued their innings on the Monday morning in order to reach a reasonable score. Lancashire fell to Babington, and Parker was able to set the home side a target of 316 in 68 overs after his batsmen had plundered quick runs in their second innings. Mendis and Fowler gave Lancashire a sparkling start with 132 in 38 overs. Jesty hit 50 in 37 minutes, and a Lancashire victory looked

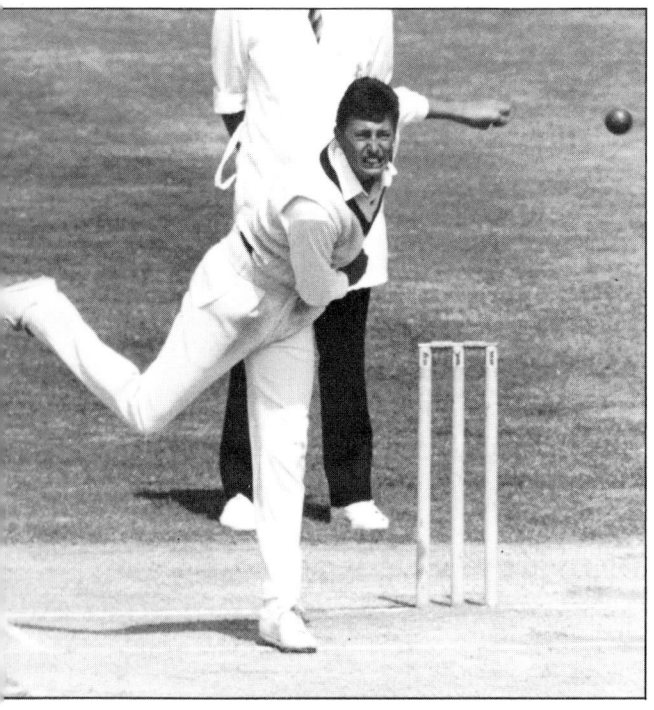

possible when 97 were needed from the last 12 overs with Jesty and Fairbrother together. Babington once again proved to be Lancashire's undoing, for in the space of 15 balls he dismissed Jesty, Hughes, Fairbrother and Watkinson. In the end, Lancashire were indebted to Allott and Fitton for saving the game.

Middlesex climbed level with Northamptonshire in second place by beating Warwickshire at Edgbaston on an erratic pitch which was, at times, dangerous. Two aggressive innings from Roland Butcher tilted the game in Middlesex's favour.

Darren Bicknell hit his third century of the season for Surrey, but on a wicket in which there was little encouragement for bowlers, neither side was bowled out. Surrey came close to winning as they captured six Yorkshire second-innings wickets and Sharp had been forced to retire hurt after being struck in the face, but Bairstow thwarted them. Surrey's bowling resources were greatly depleted since the sacking of Clarke because Dirk Tazelaar was forced to return to Australia with a back injury and Ian Greig's knee prevented him from bowling for long spells.

An heroic performance by Kevin Curran failed to save Gloucestershire from defeat against Worcestershire. He and Lawrence bundled out the reigning champions on the opening day, but Gloucestershire trailed by 53 on the first innings and were ultimately set to make 337 to win in 87 overs. At 116 for 7, they were without hope of victory, but Curran batted for 3½ hours and, first with Graveney and then with Walsh and Lawrence, he threatened to deny Worcestershire. For 19 overs Curran and Lawrence, the last wicket pair, defied the Worcestershire bowlers before Lawrence was caught at silly point off Illingworth. Curran's 116 included 2 sixes and 17 fours.

After first innings at Bournemouth which ended in near parity, Hampshire took command of the game against Leicestershire. The home county batted briskly and boldly in their second innings, and Nicholas set Leicestershire the fair target of 235 in 57 overs. Bakker quickly dismissed Briers and Willey. Kevan James' left-arm seam accounted for the middle order and Malcolm Marshall completed Hampshire's impressive victory with three wickets in 19 balls.

A century in each innings by Chris Broad was the main feature of the game at Cardiff, but Alan Butcher's century and a positive declaration kept Glamorgan in touch with Nottinghamshire. Robinson, who shared a second-wicket partnership of 179 in the second innings with Broad, set Glamorgan the rather daunting target of 353 in 77 overs. To their credit, Glamorgan went after the runs eagerly in spite of the early loss of Butcher and Morris. Maynard, Ontong and Shastri batted with a flourish against a consistently defensive field. From 15 overs, 112 were needed, but when Ontong was caught on the boundary and Shastri was bowled the match was ended as a draw.

There was little hint of excitement at Chelmsford. Essex were well served by Hardie and Stephenson in an opening stand of 101. Stephenson batted with great panache until

Ian Swallow bowling for Yorkshire against Surrey at The Oval, 27–30 May. (Tom Morris)

Chris Broad, a century in each innings for Nottinghamshire against Glamorgan, followed by the Gold Award for his century in the Benson and Hedges quarter-final at Bristol. (Stuart Franklin/ASP)

he became becalmed in the nineties before heaving Roebuck for six to reach an excellent hundred. Hardie, leading Essex in the absence of both Pringle and Gooch, declared at the Saturday evening score and, with Childs at his best, the home side quickly captured three wickets for 51 runs. Richard Harden joined Jim Cook in an unbeaten stand of 229. Cook presented a straight bat to everything in contrast to the wilder Harden, but he failed to increase his scoring rate as the overs ticked away and as Harden became more hesitant when approaching his century. Hardie and Waugh hit fiercely when Essex batted again, and Hardie's generous declaration left Somerset to make 265 at just under five an over. Sadly, having lost Cook and Bartlett for 27, Somerset gave up the chase and condemned the game and the paying-customers to purgatory.

Refuge Assurance League

28 May

at Chelmsford

Essex 218 for 5 (M.E. Waugh 81 not out)
Somerset 171 for 7 (P.M. Roebuck 58)

Essex (4 pts) won by 47 runs

at Llanelli

Glamorgan 172 for 5 (G.C. Holmes 63 not out)
Nottinghamshire 174 for 4 (R.T. Robinson 76 not out)

Nottinghamshire (4 pts) won by 6 wickets

at Bristol

Gloucestershire 221 for 5
Worcestershire 222 for 4 (G.A. Hick 84, T.S. Curtis 50)

Worcestershire (4 pts) won by 6 wickets

at Bournemouth

Leicestershire 107
Hampshire 110 for 3

Hampshire (4 pts) won by 7 wickets

at Canterbury

Kent 201 for 8 (W.W. Davis 4 for 38)
Northamptonshire 205 for 2 (R.J. Bailey 96, G. Cook 66 not out)

Northamptonshire (4 pts) won by 8 wickets

at Old Trafford

Sussex 145 for 9
Lancashire 146 for 7

Lancashire (4 pts) won by 3 wickets

at The Oval

Surrey 238 for 5 (G.S. Clinton 76, I.A. Greig 61 not out)
Yorkshire 206 (R.J. Blakey 50, C.K. Bullen 5 for 31)

Surrey (4 pts) won by 32 runs

at Edgbaston

Warwickshire 196 for 4 (P.A. Smith 93 not out)
Middlesex 167 for 8 (A.A. Donald 4 for 32)

Warwickshire (4 pts) won by 29 runs

A full programme of Sunday league matches saw Essex, with Mark Waugh hitting 81 off 55 balls, and Lancashire maintain their ferocious pace at the top. Sussex fielded two leg-spinners, Clarke and Salisbury, against Lancashire and came close to defending their meagre 145. It was only a violent 44 not out from Wasim Akram that saw Lancashire home. Wasim was awarded his county cap. Northamptonshire also maintained their unbeaten record with a surprisingly easy win over Kent, while Surrey continued to challenge strongly. They owed much to skipper Ian Greig, who hit hard and cleanly at the end of their innings and to Chris Bullen, whose accuracy denied Yorkshire any hope of achieving the required run rate.

31 May, 1 and 2 June

at Edgbaston

Australians 444 for 3 dec (D.M. Jones 248, T.M. Moody 144 not out) and 195 for 4 dec (A.R. Border 69, M.A. Taylor 67)
Warwickshire 235 (G.W. Humpage 58, M. Asif Din 50, T.V. Hohns 4 for 87) and 105 for 3

Match drawn

On the opening day, Dean Jones and Tom Moody put on

349 in 63 overs for the tourists' third wicket. Jones, in what was his first first-class match of the tour, hit 12 sixes and faced 284 balls. It was a mighty performance, but the match was drawn when the Australians opted for batting practice.

Benson and Hedges Cup

Quarter-Finals

31 May

at Chelmsford

Lancashire 246 for 9
Essex 250 for 7 (M.E. Waugh 93, B.R. Hardie 65, Wasim Akram 4 for 54)

Essex won by 3 wickets
(*Gold Award* – M.E. Waugh)

at Bristol

Nottinghamshire 222 for 6 (B.C. Broad 106, K.M. Curran 4 for 41)
Gloucestershire 217 (C.W.J. Athey 54, E.E. Hemmings 4 for 47)

Nottinghamshire won by 5 runs
(*Gold Award* – B.C. Broad)

at Northampton

Kent 208 for 8 (M.R. Benson 55)
Northamptonshire 187 for 8

Kent won by 21 runs
(*Gold Award* – R.M. Ellison)

at Taunton

Somerset 252 for 6 (P.M. Roebuck 102, S.J. Cook 61, M.A. Atherton 4 for 42)
Combined Universities 249 for 9 (N. Hussain 118)

Somerset won by 3 runs
(*Gold Award* – N. Hussain)

The quarter-finals of the Benson and Hedges Cup brought together the two sides who, currently, had the best one-day records in the country, Essex and Lancashire. In the end, Essex were to gain a surprisingly easy victory. Gooch asked Lancashire to bat first when he won the toss, but Essex gained no immediate reward. The beginning was slow, and the first run from the bat did not come until the fourth over. The first boundary, to Mendis, did not come until the 10th over, at the end of which Lancashire were 28 without loss. Nine overs later, the fifty came up. The over was bowled by Stephenson, whose medium pace was to prove a vital part of the Essex success. Fowler was his first victim, lifting the ball into the hands of Gooch at mid-on

and, three overs later, Stephenson bowled Mendis. Hegg was caught behind off Gooch in the 30th over with the score on 87, and Essex had captured the initiative. At lunch, Lancashire were 125 for 3 from 36 overs.

In the afternoon session, Jesty and Fairbrother began briskly, but Pringle bowled Jesty as he was looking particularly menacing. Watkinson became Stephenson's third victim when he was bowled by the first ball of the 43rd over, Stephenson's last, with the score on 150. The next 50 runs came in eight overs, and Fairbrother and Wasim Akram batted with great zest. Both were dismissed, but Hughes, Allott and DeFreitas plundered 39 runs from the last four overs of the innings to take them to 246, a total which, with their strong attack, they looked highly capable of defending.

Essex began disastrously when Gooch hit the first ball of the third over to Mendis at square-leg, who held it at the second attempt. DeFreitas captured his second wicket when he had Lilley caught behind off a ferocious lifter, but there the Lancashire joy ended. In spite of a short stoppage for bad light, Hardie and Waugh batted with total confidence and never allowed the scoring rate to flag. The usually economic Simmons was savagely dealt with, as was Wasim Akram and, when Hardie was caught behind off Watkinson, he and Waugh had added 158 in 31 overs. Mark Waugh, who hit nine fours, and faced 101 balls and batted splendidly, was unlucky to play on to Wasim 20 runs later when seven short of his century.

Any hopes Lancashire may have nursed of recovering their grip on the game were dashed by Stephenson and Prichard, who were particularly severe on Watkinson. With the scores level, five wickets standing and 20 balls left, Wasim Akram dismissed Pringle and Garnham with successive deliveries, but Prichard smote the first ball of the next over for four.

Northamptonshire, who were placed as favourites to win the Cup when the quarter-final draw was made, were most surprisingly beaten by Kent, who had not been finding the season easy. Put in to bat, Kent reached a modest 208 and were greatly aided by Curtly Ambrose, who bowled 11 no-balls and conceded 66 runs in his 11 overs. The highlight of the Kent batting was an unbroken ninth-wicket stand of 52 in seven overs between Penn and Ellison, and it was these two who were to give their side a glimpse of victory.

Larkins and Cook got Northamptonshire off to a good start with a partnership of 61. Larkins drove loosely at Fleming and was caught by Penn, and Ellison, who had conceded 19 runs in his first two overs, now found his rhythm to capture the vital wickets of Bailey, Lamb and Wild. Geoff Cook batted 41 overs for 46 runs, and when he was bowled by Penn the innings fell apart and Kent snatched a remarkable victory.

With Chris Broad hitting a century against his old county, Nottinghamshire seemed in an impregnable position when, having made 222, they reduced Gloucestershire to 147 for 7 in the 44th over. At this point, Athey, who was batting with some difficulty because of the thumb injury he had sustained while playing against Essex, was joined by Russell. They added 43 in eight overs and, when Athey was leg before to Cooper, 33 were needed from

Mark Waugh took the Gold Award in the Benson and Hedges quarter-final at Chelmsford. (USPA)

three overs. Russell and Graveney attacked bravely, and the last over arrived with just seven to make. Russell hit Hemmings' first ball high to long-off where Broad took the catch, and Lawrence swung massively at the third and was bowled.

Most eyes and ears were turned towards events at Taunton where Combined Universities, having reached the knock-out stage of the competition for the first time, faced a grim task as Cook and Roebuck put on 109 for Somerset's first wicket. Atherton, a fine leader and outstanding all-round cricketer, broke the stand, and Tolley accounted for Tavare, but 200 was passed for the loss of only two wickets. Peter Roebuck, having hit 97 before lunch, was the backbone of the Somerset batting, and the total of 252 seemed to be beyond the reach of the students who, commendably, had bowled their overs at a rate of 20 an hour.

Examinations had cruelly robbed the Universities of the services of opener James, and his replacement, O'Gorman, was out for 9. After 11 overs they were 27 for 1, and Crawley was being X-rayed in hospital, where a cracked knuckle was revealed. Atherton and Hussain showed no sign of panic as they fought to restore their side's fortunes, and the score was 78 when Atherton was caught on the long-leg boundary shortly before tea.

Speight played breezily but briefly, and the score was 109 for 3 when Longley joined Hussain. Now came the stand which brought romance to the game and kept the crowd buzzing with excitement. Longley hit 49 off 39 balls as he helped Hussain to add 114 in 17 overs. He was out on the first ball of the 50th over when he hit Jones to backward point. Four balls later, Atkinson was caught behind. The score was now 222 for 4. Dale was needlessly run out, and the Universities had lost their way just as Hussain, at the last, seemed to lose his timing as he pressed for victory.

Roebuck had been brought into the attack to bowl four of the last eight overs at gentle medium pace. It was he who was to bowl the final over with nine runs needed for victory. Tolley was stumped off the first ball, and Hussain's glorious innings ended on the third ball when he hit hard to Bartlett at long-off. The injured Crawley returned and was promptly run out, and six off the last ball was more than Boiling could manage.

Roebuck's contribution to Somerset's victory and to the match was immense. He hit 102, held a vital catch to get rid of Longley and took 2 for 19 in four crucial overs. In

Combined Universities 1989
Benson and Hedges Cup

BATTING	v. Surrey (Cambridge) 26 April	v. Middlesex (Oxford) 9 May	v. Worcestershire (Worcester) 11 May	v. Gloucestershire (Bristol) 13 May	v. Somerset (Taunton) 31 May	Runs
S.P. James	9	16	65	15		105
M.P. Speight	30	20	29	19	12	110
M.A. Atherton	14	66	20	34	26	160
N. Hussain	23	4	67	25	118	237
J.C.M. Atkinson	1	16		7	1	25
J. Longley	20	0	14*	36	49	119
A. Dale	9	15	—	21*	0	45
C. Tolley	1	22	—	1*	6	30
A.R. Hansford	1	8*	—	—	1*	10
T.R. Parker	0					0
J. Boiling	2*	0*	—	—	2*	4
M.A. Crawley		16	8*	54	13	91
T.J.G. O'Gorman			0	9	9	9
Byes				2	2	
Leg-byes	3	3	3	4	6	
Wides		2	7	3	2	
No-balls	3	2	4	2	2	
Total	116	190	217	223	249	
Wickets	10	9	5	7	9	
Result	W	L	W	L	L	
Points	2	0	2	0	—	

Fielding Figures
5 – M.G. Speight (ct 4/st 1)
3 – M.A. Atherton
2 – C. Tolley, T.J.G. O'Gorman, M.A. Crawley and A. Dale
1 – S.P. James, N. Hussain, T.R. Parker and A.R. Hansford

BOWLING	A.R. Hansford	C. Tolley	T.R. Parker	J. Boiling	A. Dale	M.A. Atherton	M.A. Crawley
v. Surrey (Cambridge) 26 April	8-4-11-2	7-1-12-1	4-0-30-0	8-3-9-3	7-0-24-3	3-0-21-0	
v. Middlesex (Oxford) 9 May	11-3-26-0	11-2-22-1		8.4-1-53-0	11-2-28-1	4-0-23-0	8-0-37-0
v. Worcestershire (Worcester) 11 May	11-3-39-2	11-4-32-0		11-1-32-1	11-2-35-3		11-1-72-2
v. Gloucestershire (Bristol) 13 May	11-2-41-1	11-0-61-1		10.5-0-67-1	11-0-35-1		11-3-18-1
v. Somerset (Taunton) 31 May	11-0-50-0	9-1-40-1		11-2-28-0	7-0-46-0	9-0-42-4	8-0-43-0
Wickets	5	4	0	5	8	4	3

any other game he would have won the Gold Award, but, rightly it went to Nasser Hussain. He hit 11 fours in his 118, which came from 145 balls, and there were times when he hinted at greatness. More importantly, he, Atherton, Longley and the rest showed that the future of English cricket was in good hands, and that was a tonic that everyone needed.

3, 4 and 5 June

at Derby

Australians 200 (O.H. Mortensen 4 for 40, S.J. Base 4 for 49) and 180 (D.E. Malcolm 4 for 68)
Derbyshire 228 (K.J. Barnett 76) and 141 (T.M. Alderman 4 for 32)

Australians won by 11 runs

3, 5 and 6 June

at Tunbridge Wells

Hampshire 213 (M.D. Marshall 61, R.M. Ellison 4 for 45)
Kent 276 for 3 (M.R. Benson 114, N.R. Taylor 104 not out)

Match drawn
Kent 7 pts, Hampshire 3 pts

at Northampton

Surrey 175 (K.T. Medlycott 69, W.W. Davis 4 for 40) and 207 for 9 (D.J. Bicknell 74)
Northamptonshire 425 for 5 dec (A.J. Lamb 171, W. Larkins 89, D.J. Capel 76 not out)

Match drawn
Northamptonshire 8 pts, Surrey 3 pts

at Trent Bridge

Yorkshire 223 (P.E. Robinson 57, J.D. Love 53, K.E. Cooper 5 for 72) and 250 for 9 dec (P.W. Jarvis 59 not out, J.A. Afford 5 for 63)
Nottinghamshire 214 (E.E. Hemmings 58 not out, P.W. Jarvis 7 for 74) and 84 for 1

Match drawn
Nottinghamshire 6 pts, Yorkshire 6 pts

at Edgbaston

Sussex 259 (A.I.C. Dodemaide 52, D.M. Smith 50, G.C. Small 4 for 70) and 85 for 0

The hero of the Combined Universities in their brave bid to reach the Benson and Hedges Cup semi-finals, Nasser Hussain, 118 at Taunton. (Steve Lindsell)

Warwickshire 277 (P.A. Smith 66, A.M. Babington 5 for 59, A.I.C. Dodemaide 4 for 75)

Match drawn
Warwickshire 7 pts, Sussex 7 pts

at Worcester

Worcestershire 127 (S.R. Barwick 6 for 40) and 246 for 3 dec (T.S. Curtis 140 not out)
Glamorgan 134 (P.J. Newport 4 for 37) and 20 for 0

Match drawn
Worcestershire 4 pts, Glamorgan 4 pts

The Australians earned a narrow and welcome victory on the eve of the first Test match. Put in to bat on the inevitable seamers' wicket at Derby, they struggled against Mortensen, Malcolm and Base. West Indian Ian Bishop was less effective. By the end of the first day, Derbyshire were only 47 runs behind with six wickets standing, but the loss of four quick wickets on the Sunday restricted their lead to 28. For a second time the Australians struggled against the Derbyshire seam attack, and it was only a fighting stand of 71 between Moody and Healy that saved them from complete humiliation. Derbyshire were left to make 153 to gain a first historic win over the tourists, and when Barnett and Bowler began the quest with a stand of

Byes	Leg-byes	Wides	No-balls	Total	Wkts
		2		107	9
	5	1		194	2
	6	3		216	8
	5	3	1	227	7
	3	1		252	6

31 it seemed that history would be made. Then, in four overs on the Sunday evening, Alderman and Campbell captured five wickets while five runs were scored. Morris and Sharma stood firm until the close, and on the last morning they took the score to 90 before Morris was caught at slip off Campbell. Sharma and Bishop added 32, but a burst from Rackemann gave the Australians victory.

Rain blighted all the county matches. There was a sad mishap at Worcester, where Botham received a blow in the face that was to delay his return to the England Test side. The seamers thrived in the first innings. Fourteen wickets fell on the first day, and Newport celebrated his call up for the England side by restricting Glamorgan's lead on the Monday. Curtis played quite splendidly in difficult circumstances to hit 140 in 313 minutes, but the rain returned to close the match.

Having dismissed Hampshire cheaply, Kent could only bat for first-innings points. Benson and Taylor put on 195 for Kent's second wicket and then a thunderstorm ended play after three overs on the last day.

The Warwickshire–Sussex match at Edgbaston ended in farce as part-time bowlers lobbed the ball at Smith and Lenham in an effort to improve the home county's over rate.

Paul Jarvis had an excellent all-round match at Trent Bridge, hitting his maiden championship fifty and taking 7 for 74, but Nottinghamshire spurned the task of scoring 260 in 64 overs, and the match was brought to a premature close by bad light and drizzle.

Northamptonshire came closest to winning. Surrey, weakened by injury, were asked to bat first and were bowled out for 175 on the Saturday. By the close of play, Northamptonshire had established a lead of 95 for the loss of only two wickets. On the Monday, Allan Lamb added 114 to his overnight score in just over two hours. In all, he batted for 171 minutes and hit a six and 28 fours. Darren Bicknell batted with soundness and sense until run out in a mix-up with Thorpe, and Surrey entered the last day with only three wickets standing and needing 72 to avoid an innings defeat. Nineteen overs were all that was possible on the last day, and Murphy and Frost held out for the final 11 of them to deny Northamptonshire.

Robert Bailey hit 106 not out for Northamptonshire in the Refuge Assurance League match against Surrey, 4 June. It was Northamptonshire's first Sunday league century for two years. (Ken Kelly)

Refuge Assurance League

4 June

at Leicester

Lancashire 149 for 9
Leicestershire 152 for 3

Leicestershire (4 pts) won by 7 wickets

at Lord's

Hampshire 138 (S.P. Hughes 4 for 20)
Middlesex 138 for 8 (D.L. Haynes 52)

Match tied
Middlesex 2 pts, Hampshire 2 pts

at Northampton

Northamptonshire 201 for 4 (R.J. Bailey 106 not out, W. Larkins 63)

Surrey 159 for 9 (G.S. Clinton 56)

Northamptonshire (4 pts) won by 42 runs

at Trent Bridge

Nottinghamshire 183 for 7 (D.W. Randall 63)
Somerset 184 for 7

Somerset (4 pts) won by 3 wickets

at Edgbaston

Sussex 165 for 5
Warwickshire 169 for 4 (A.I. Kallicharran 66)

Warwickshire (4 pts) won by 6 wickets

at Worcester

Worcestershire 262 for 4 (I.T. Botham 70, G.A. Hick 50)
Glamorgan 119 (P.J. Newport 4 for 18)

Worcestershire (4 pts) won by 143 runs

Lancashire were surprisingly beaten at Leicester and so lost the chance to move to the top of the Refuge Assurance League. Northamptonshire had the most significant win and, by beating Surrey, they took over third place from the southern county. Surrey were dreadfully depleted by injuries and had to call upon 44-year-old coach Geoff Arnold. The former England pace bowler took 1 for 7 in six overs, a magnificent performance, before his shoulder gave out. It was his first appearance in county cricket for seven years. Larkins and Bailey put on 102 for the home county's second wicket. Worcestershire, with Botham and Curtis opening with a partnership of 123, overwhelmed Glamorgan, and Kallicharran steered Warwickshire to victory after Dodemaide and Pigott had shared an unbroken stand of 97 in 17 overs for Sussex's sixth wicket. Chasing a target of 184, Somerset looked beaten when they slipped to 116 for 6 against Nottinghamshire, but Burns and Rose added 55 in 12 overs. The last ball of the match arrived with the scores level, and Burns and Palmer scrambled a bye to give Somerset the points. There was also a pulsating finish at Lord's. Cowans took 3 for 6 in his eight overs, and Hampshire were restricted to a meagre 138. Gatting took a fine catch to dismiss Turner, but in doing so, he damaged a thumb and had to withdraw from the Test side. He came in at number ten and added 10 with Fraser, including a bye off the last ball to tie the match.

7, 8 and 9 June

at Cardiff

Somerset 330 for 8 dec (N.D. Burns 86 not out, C.J. Tavare 70, S.J. Cook 61) and 0 for 0 dec
Glamorgan 0 for 0 dec and 277 for 9 (M.J. Cann 109, V.J. Marks 4 for 73)

Match drawn
Glamorgan 3 pts, Somerset 3 pts

at Basingstoke

Surrey 291 (G.P. Thorpe 115, I.A. Greig 90 not out, P.J. Bakker 4 for 55) and 116 (M.D. Marshall 5 for 39, P.J. Bakker 5 for 48)
Hampshire 251 for 4 dec (K.D. James 83 not out, D.R. Turner 56 not out, M.C.J. Nicholas 51) and 157 for 2 (M.C.J. Nicholas 76 not out)

Hampshire won by 8 wickets
Hampshire 22 pts, Surrey 6 pts

at Tunbridge Wells

Kent 243 (M.R. Benson 57) and 82 for 1 dec
Sussex 99 for 2 dec and 228 for 7 (D.M. Smith 67, A.C.S. Pigott 54 not out)

Sussex won by 3 wickets
Sussex 20 pts, Kent 2 pts

at Leicester

Yorkshire 246 (D. Byas 67, M.D. Moxon 54, G.J. Parsons 5 for 48) and 112 for 2 dec

Leicestershire 108 for 6 dec and 201 (N.E. Briers 57, P.W. Jarvis 4 for 86)

Yorkshire won by 49 runs
Yorkshire 20 pts, Leicestershire 4 pts

at Lord's

Middlesex 296 (D.L. Haynes 84) and 107 for 7 dec
Nottinghamshire 179 (A.R.C. Fraser 5 for 37) and 97 for 5

Match drawn
Middlesex 7 pts, Nottinghamshire 3 pts

at Northampton

Gloucestershire 118 (D.J. Capel 4 for 14, W.W. Davis 4 for 31) and 186
Northamptonshire 236 (D.J. Capel 84, W. Larkins 74, K.M. Curran 7 for 69) and 69 for 1

Northamptonshire won by 9 wickets
Northamptonshire 22 pts, Gloucestershire 4 pts

at Nuneaton

Warwickshire 155 (A.J. Moles 53, O.H. Mortensen 6 for 38) and 199 for 6 dec (A.J. Moles 79)
Derbyshire 135 and 212 for 8 (P.D. Bowler 78, A.R.K. Pierson 6 for 82)

Match drawn
Warwickshire 5 pts, Derbyshire 4 pts

at Oxford

Lancashire 301 for 3 dec (G. Fowler 112, G.D. Lloyd 108) and 103 for 0 (N.H. Fairbrother 71 not out)
Oxford University 210 for 8 dec (A.N.S. Hampton 55, D.A. Hagan 53)

Match drawn

With the weather again uncertain, captains had to improvise to obtain a result. At Cardiff, both sides forfeited an innings, and Glamorgan were set a target of 331 in 94 overs. They began slowly, but the young left-hander Michael Cann gained in confidence as the innings progressed, and he and Shastri scored at a brisk rate to raise hopes of victory. Cann reached his maiden first-class century before being bowled, and Marks brought about a collapse with four wickets in 15 balls. Metson and Bastien held out for a draw.

Graham Thorpe, one of Surrey's several very promising young players, hit a career-best 115 against Hampshire at Basingstoke. The left-hander batted for nearly five hours, and it was left to skipper Ian Greig to boost the run rate with 90 off 87 balls late on the first day. A stubborn innings by Kevan James on the second day kept Hampshire in touch, but it was not until Turner joined him in an unbroken partnership of 107 in 25 overs that the home side wrested the initiative. Nicholas declared as soon as his side had earned the third batting point, and Surrey ended the second day at 66 for 2. They collapsed against Marshall and the ever-improving Bakker on the last morning, and Hampshire, brilliantly led by the example of their captain, romped to victory.

The rain again marred the festival at that most beautiful of grounds, Tunbridge Wells, and declarations left Sussex with the task of scoring 227 in 64 overs. Igglesden was in particularly good form, and seven wickets went down for

ABOVE: *Graham Thorpe, an exciting prospect for Surrey, a career-best 115 against Hampshire, 7 June. (Tom Morris)*

ABOVE RIGHT: *Paul-Jan Bakker – an outstanding season for Hampshire. (Stuart Franklin/ASP)*

160 so that Kent looked favourites to win, especially as five wickets had fallen for 25 runs. At this point, Tony Pigott attacked the bowling furiously and finished the match when he hit the second ball of the penultimate over for six.

Yorkshire gained their first Championship victory of the season when Jarvis bowled Agnew with just 15 balls of the match remaining. Leicestershire began confidently enough in their attempt to score 251 in 69 overs, but Sidebottom dismissed Boon and Willey in quick succession, and Jarvis gnawed at the middle order before Whitticase and Parsons offered late resistance.

Nottinghamshire again lost a few friends by their refusal to attempt to chase a target, and the match at Lord's was drawn. So, too, was the game at Nuneaton, but in more thrilling circumstances. Fine bowling by Ole Mortensen had given Derbyshire the edge on the opening day, but

then they collapsed against the varied Warwickshire attack. Lloyd's declaration left the visitors to make 220 in 56 overs, and fortunes fluctuated throughout the last afternoon. At 195 for 5, Derbyshire seemed set for victory, but three wickets fell for four runs. Warner and Bishop revived their hopes, but Derbyshire finished eight short of their target. Warwickshire's heroes were skipper Andy Lloyd, who handled his bowling with great intelligence, and off-break bowler Adrian Pierson, who returned the best bowling figures of his career in a 23-over spell.

Northamptonshire increased their lead at the top of the table when they demolished Gloucestershire with great efficiency. Their seam attack was particularly effective, and David Capel enjoyed a fine all-round match. Kevin Curran was again a lone hero for Gloucestershire.

Lancashire used the match in The Parks for batting practice. Rain restricted play on the first day, but on the second, Fowler and Graham Lloyd extended their opening partnership to 219. Both batsmen reached centuries. In Lloyd's case it was the first of his first-class career.

First Cornhill Test Match
ENGLAND v. AUSTRALIA

Kim Barnett came into the England side as a late replace-

upon the series. He was watchful in defence, but never dull. He punished the loose ball, and his straight-driving was a delight. Above all, he and Border demonstrated a quality that was to shine for the rest of the summer in that their running between the wickets was a joy to behold. Throughout the series the Australians did not appear to miss the chance of a run, and they ran two where England settled for one.

Taylor quickly completed his maiden Test century on the second morning in what was only his third Test match, his first against England. He was out to an uncharacteristic shot, swinging across the line at Foster, but he had batted for 6½ hours with strong discipline and a wealth of shots. He hit 16 fours. His dismissal was England's only success of the morning session, during which Australia scored 120 runs.

Steve Waugh was soon cracking the ball to the boundary in majestic fashion. In 32 overs, he and Jones put on 138 runs, and the series was alight. Waugh overtook Jones, so forceful was his cricket. He would rock onto the back foot and send the ball scorching to the cover boundary or move into the drive with the elegance of the ancients. Here was glory. Jones went to a nasty rising ball from Newport, and Healy offered a simple return catch on the stroke of tea. The afternoon session had produced 114 runs.

Waugh had reached his hundred, his first in Test cricket, off 124 balls with 16 fours, but his appetite was unsatiated. In the last session of the day, he and Hughes, more rustic in manner, scored 139 runs. Much of the England bowling

LEFT: *The Ashes series begins. Gower and Border toss. (Adrian Murrell/Allsport)*

BELOW: *Mark Taylor acknowledges the applause as he reaches his maiden Test century. (Adrian Murrell/Allsport)*

ment for the injured Botham while Australia gave a first Test cap to Greg Campbell as Rackemann was in hospital undergoing surgery. Neither side included a front-line spinner. Emburey was twelfth man for England.

Gower won the toss and asked Australia to bat first. It was not a surprising decision, for most of the pundits had predicted that the wicket would aid the seam bowlers, particularly in the early stages of the match when the weather, too, was a little uncertain. Indeed, the start was delayed, and there was a short break for bad light, but Marsh and Taylor took the score to an untroubled 44 at lunch.

Gower's decision to ask Australia to bat first seemed justified when, immediately after lunch, Marsh was lbw to DeFreitas. Thirteen runs later, Boon, having survived two confident appeals for leg before, was caught behind off a fine ball from Foster. Border's response at this crucial stage of the game was to attack. He hit 66 off 118 balls and shared a partnership of 117 with Taylor. Border's innings included a six and 9 fours and he was ever eager to attack the bowling. He batted for 141 minutes and was out when he top-edged a pull against DeFreitas. Jones stayed with Taylor until the close at 207 for 3.

Taylor was 96 not out on the Thursday evening, and he had already stamped his authority upon the game and

TOP LEFT: *One of the great glories of the summer – Steve Waugh square cuts to the boundary during his innings of 177 not out, his maiden Test century. (Ben Radford/ Allsport)*

LEFT: *Dean Jones in violent mood against Derek Pringle. (David Munden)*

ABOVE: *Gooch lbw to Alderman. (Adrian Murrell/Allsport)*

TOP RIGHT: *Another wicket for Alderman – Barnett is leg before wicket. (Adrian Murrell/Allsport)*

BELOW RIGHT: *The end of Pringle's second innings resistance – caught Border, bowled Alderman. (David Munden)*

was deplorable, and in the field England wilted, but Waugh showed us splendour. By the end of the day he had made 174. Hughes was on 63, and the game was out of England's reach with Australia 580 for 6.

Border delayed his declaration until five overs and three balls into the third morning, by which time Foster had reared three deliveries at Hughes, one of which he had parried with his glove so that it looped over his head into Russell's gloves and Australia had passed 600. Waugh remained undefeated on 177. He had batted for 308 minutes, faced 243 balls and hit 24 fours. The mere statistics can tell nothing of the grandeur, the memory of which will warm many a long winter.

The first task that faced England was to score the 402 that they needed to avoid the follow-on. They did not start well, Gooch being leg before to Alderman as he

groped half-forward. Broad looked totally at ease, and it came as a great shock when Hughes bowled him with what was, in effect, a slow leg-break, off-break to the left-hander. Barnett, ever on the move, and Lamb reacted to the situation positively and put on 114 at nearly five runs an over. The merry spree was ended when Alderman, always dangerous because he bowled so straight, trapped Barnett leg before. Lamb completed an exciting hundred just before the close with his 19th four, but by then England had lost Gower, who touched a ball down the leg-side to the wicket-keeper. Smith began positively, and at 284 for 4 on the Saturday evening, England looked safe.

Lamb and Smith resumed their partnership in sultry conditions on the Monday and extended it to 80 before Lamb was taken at short-leg off Alderman, who bowled in an exemplary manner. Lamb hit 24 fours in his pugnacious

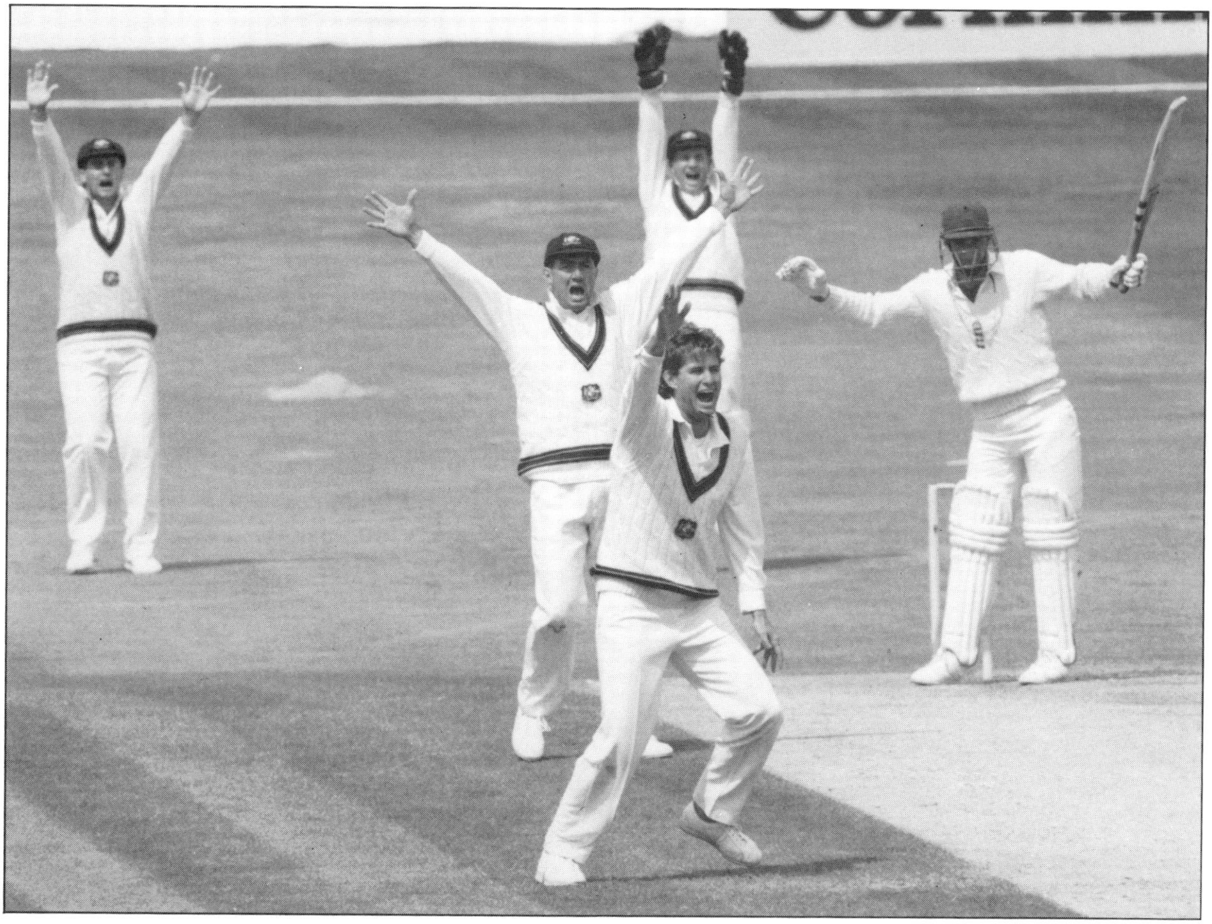

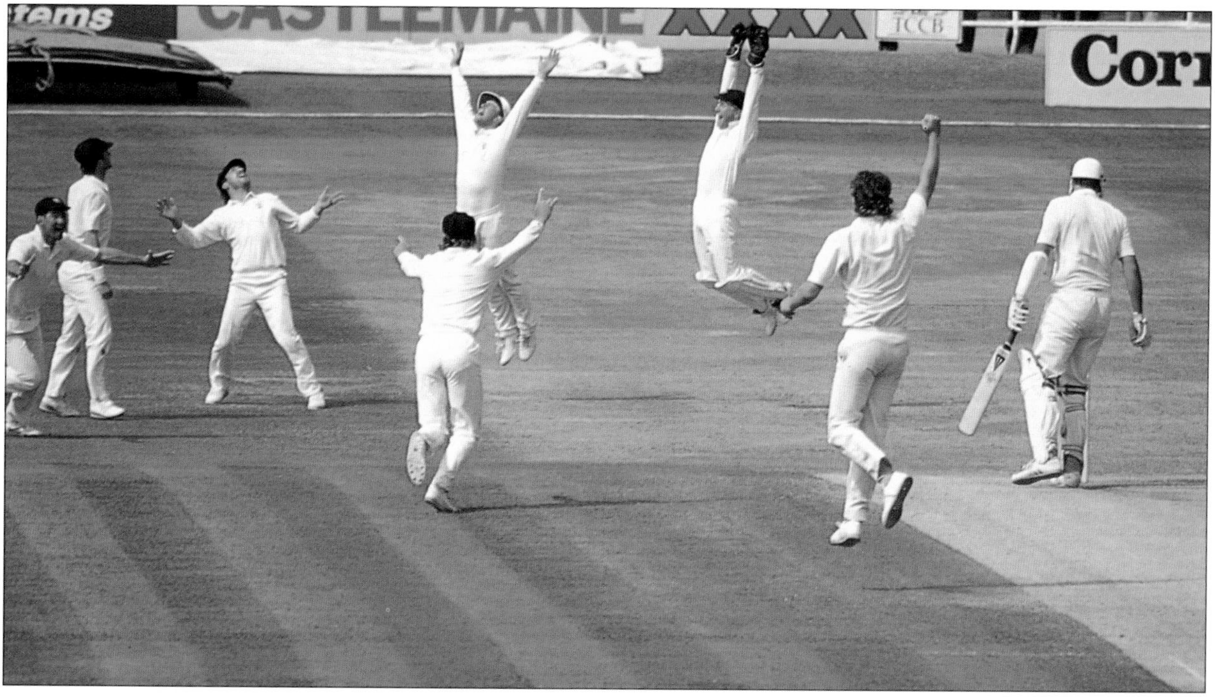
CASTLEMAINE
XXXX
TCCB
Cor

205-ball innings. Pringle became Campbell's first Test victim when he played a rather diffident shot.

England were still 10 short of saving the follow-on when Smith was out to the seventh ball after lunch, but the vital runs came without further alarms, and eventually England trailed by 171 runs. In dismissing Newport, Lawson claimed his 150th Test wicket.

It looked as though the game was certain to be drawn, but Border was determined to keep it alive, and from 45

overs at the end of the fourth day, Australia hit 158 for 3. Taylor showed his adaptability, but it was Border and Jones who forced the pace. In 43 minutes on the last morning, they scored 72 runs against bowling which was quite dreadful and fielding which capitulated. Border was true to his word and declared, leaving England a target of 402 at 4.8 runs an over, or, more realistically, leaving his bowlers most of the last day in which to bowl out England.

The only success that came Australia's way before lunch was when Broad was leg before to a ball which kept very low. With Gooch and Barnett together there was even a chance that England might chase the runs they needed, but Barnett was out to the fifth ball after lunch, and Lamb was quickly taken at short-leg. The resting of Alderman allowed Gooch and Gower to prosper temporarily, but Lawson opened a chink in the England armour when he had Gower splendidly and leapingly caught behind on the leg-side and Smith taken at third slip within the space of four balls. Pringle played passive defence for 39 minutes before prodding to slip.

Border's captaincy was vibrant and imaginative and the Australian cricket dynamic as fielders crowded the bat. Gooch had gone to the energetic and enthusiastic Hughes just before Pringle's departure, and six wickets fell in the afternoon session on a pitch on which only 21 wickets had previously fallen in 13 sessions spread over more than four days.

LEFT: *Allan Lamb restoring England's pride. (Adrian Murrell/Allsport)*

FIRST CORNHILL TEST MATCH – ENGLAND v. AUSTRALIA
8, 9, 10, 12 and 13 June 1989 at Headingley, Leeds

AUSTRALIA

	FIRST INNINGS		SECOND INNINGS	
G.R. Marsh	lbw, b DeFreitas	16	(2) c Russell, b Foster	6
M.A. Taylor	lbw, b Foster	136	(1) c Broad, b Pringle	60
D.C. Boon	c Russell, b Foster	9	lbw, b DeFreitas	43
A.R. Border†	c Foster, b DeFreitas	66	not out	60
D.M. Jones	c Russell, b Newport	79	not out	40
S.R. Waugh	not out	177		
I.A. Healy*	c and b Newport	16		
M.G. Hughes	c Russell, b Foster	71		
G.F. Lawson	not out	10		
G.D. Campbell				
T.M. Alderman				
Extras	lb 13, w 1, nb 7	21	b 2, lb 5, w 9, nb 5	21
	(for 7 wkts, dec)	601	(for 3 wkts, dec)	230

ENGLAND

	FIRST INNINGS		SECOND INNINGS	
G.A. Gooch	lbw, b Alderman	13	lbw, b Hughes	68
B.C. Broad	b Hughes	37	lbw, b Alderman	7
K.J. Barnett	lbw, b Alderman	80	c Taylor, b Alderman	34
A.J. Lamb	c Boon, b Alderman	125	c Boon, b Alderman	4
D.I. Gower†	c Healy, b Lawson	26	c Healy, b Lawson	34
R.A. Smith	lbw, b Alderman	66	c Healy, b Lawson	0
D.R. Pringle	lbw, b Campbell	6	c Border, b Alderman	0
P.J. Newport	c Boon, b Lawson	36	c Marsh, b Alderman	8
R.C. Russell*	c Marsh, b Lawson	15	c Healy, b Hughes	2
P.A.J. DeFreitas	lbw, b Alderman	1	b Hughes	21
N.A. Foster	not out	2	not out	1
Extras	b 5, lb 7, w 1, nb 10	23	b 4, lb 3, nb 5	12
		430		191

	O	M	R	W	O	M	R	W
DeFreitas	45.3	8	140	2	18	2	76	1
Foster	46	14	109	3	19	4	65	1
Newport	39	5	153	2	5	2	22	–
Pringle	33	5	123	–	12.5	1	60	1
Gooch	9	1	31	–				
Barnett	6	–	32	–				

	O	M	R	W	O	M	R	W
Alderman	37	7	107	5	20	7	44	5
Lawson	34.5	6	105	3	11	2	58	2
Campbell	14	–	82	1	10	–	42	–
Hughes	28	7	92	1	9.2	2	36	3
Waugh	6	2	27	–				
Border	2	1	5	–	5	3	4	–

FALL OF WICKETS
1–44, 2–57, 3–174, 4–273, 5–411, 6–441, 7–588
1–14, 2–97, 3–129

FALL OF WICKETS
1–35, 2–81, 3–195, 4–243, 5–323, 6–338, 7–392, 8–421, 9–424
1–17, 2–67, 3–77, 4–134, 5–134, 6–153, 7–153, 8–166, 9–170

Umpires: J.W. Holder & D.R. Shepherd

Australia won by 210 runs

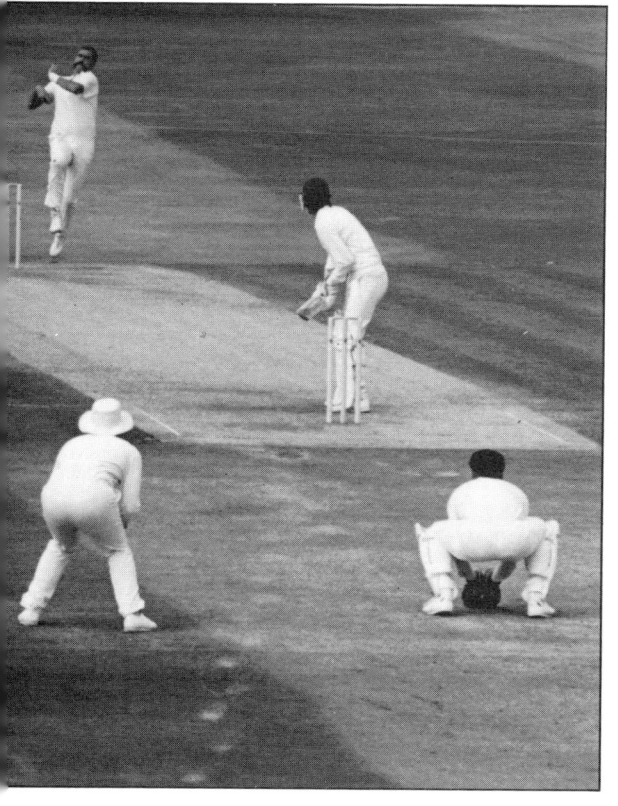

LEFT: *England under pressure as Hughes bowls to Russell. (Adrian Murrell/Allsport)*

ABOVE: *A spectacular catch by Geoff Marsh to dismiss Newport. (Adrian Murrell/Allsport)*

The end came at 4.45 p.m., with 28 overs left unused. England's last seven wickets had fallen for 57 runs. Alderman finished with 10 wickets in a Test match for the first time and took the individual award, but the Australian success stemmed from a magnificent team effort. They outplayed England in every department of the game.

Hughes bowls DeFreitas and Australia go one up in the series. (Adrian Murrell/Allsport)

10, 12 and 13 June

at Abergavenny

Glamorgan 302 for 7 dec (R.J. Shastri 127, A.R. Butcher 101) and 311 for 6 dec (R.J. Shastri 101 not out, A.R. Butcher 51)
Middlesex 263 for 4 dec (D.L. Haynes 85, M.A. Roseberry 51) and 345 for 8 (P.R. Downton 100, M.R. Ramprakash 62, M.A. Roseberry 61, S.R. Barwick 4 for 144)

Match drawn
Middlesex 5 pts, Glamorgan 4 pts

at Leicester

Leicestershire 145 (C.A. Walsh 4 for 37) and 238 (G.J. Parsons 69, L. Potter 52 not out, C.A. Walsh 4 for 63, K.M. Curran 4 for 78)
Gloucestershire 306 (J.P. Agnew 4 for 101) and 78 for 1 (J.W. Lloyds 52 not out)

Gloucestershire won by 9 wickets
Gloucestershire 24 pts, Leicestershire 4 pts

at Trent Bridge

Nottinghamshire 377 for 7 dec (R.T. Robinson 128, P. Pollard 83, C.L. Cairns 58, D.W. Randall 56) and 287 for 2 dec (R.T. Robinson 146 not out, P. Pollard 131)
Kent 354 for 7 dec (R.F. Pienaar 119, C.S. Cowdrey 101 not out) and 311 for 6 (N.R. Taylor 78, S.G. Hinks 70)

Kent won by 4 wickets
Kent 21 pts, Nottinghamshire 6 pts

at Taunton

Yorkshire 239 (M.D. Moxon 51) and 275 for 5 dec (C.S. Pickles 66, D.L. Bairstow 51 not out, R.J. Blakey 51)
Somerset 299 (P.M. Roebuck 103, P. Carrick 5 for 53)

Match drawn
Somerset 6 pts, Yorkshire 4 pts

at The Oval

Surrey 395 for 5 dec (A.J. Stewart 206 not out, G.S. Clinton 70) and 186 for 1 dec (D.J. Bicknell 105 not out, K.T. Medlycott 61)
Essex 303 for 9 dec (J.P. Stephenson 114, A.W. Lilley 67, K.T. Medlycott 4 for 95) and 279 for 2 (B.R. Hardie 142 not out, M.E. Waugh 58 not out)

Essex won by 8 wickets
Essex 21 pts, Surrey 7 pts

at Hove

Northamptonshire 223 (D.J. Capel 102, A.C.S. Pigott 5 for 52) and 355 for 5 dec (G. Cook 138, D.J. Capel 126)
Sussex 350 for 5 dec (A.P. Wells 89, C.M. Wells 84 not out, A.I.C. Dodemaide 54) and 158 for 8 (P. Moores 60)

Match drawn
Sussex 8 pts, Northamptonshire 4 pts

at Worcester

Worcestershire 220 (T.S. Curtis 58) and 227 for 8 dec (P. Bent 62, I.R. Bishop 4 for 50, S.J. Base 4 for 82)
Derbyshire 157 (G.R. Dilley 5 for 42) and 145 (N.V. Radford 6 for 59)

Worcestershire won by 145 runs
Worcestershire 22 pts, Derbyshire 5 pts

at Oxford

Hampshire 254 for 4 dec (C.L. Smith 143 not out) and 113 for 2 dec (T.C. Middleton 55 not out)
Oxford University 93 (C.A. Connor 6 for 19) and 147 (K.D. James 5 for 41)

Hampshire won by 127 runs

Three batsmen, Shastri, Capel and Robinson, had the distinction of scoring a century in each innings in the round of Britannic Assurance County Championship matches that coincided with the first Test match. Capel's hundred on the first day at Hove saved the Championship leaders from total collapse as only one other batsman, Nick Cook, reached 20. The Wells brothers took Sussex to a substantial first-innings lead. Batting again, Northamptonshire lost three wickets for 87 runs before Geoff Cook and David Capel added a marvellous 226 in 50 overs. Set to make 229 at more than six runs an over, Sussex slumped to 84 for 7, but Moores and Parker saved them from defeat.

Essex moved closer to the leaders with a fine win over Surrey at The Oval. Alec Stewart reached the first double century of his career as Surrey batted on to Monday morning before declaring. Cautious at first, Stewart batted with great elegance that left one wondering why this gifted batsman does not score runs more consistently. John Stephenson launched Essex's reply with his third century of the season, but the visitors had only just avoided the follow-on at the end of the second day. They went on to claim four batting points the following morning and then offered Surrey some friendly bowling in an effort to encourage a declaration. The result was that Darren Bicknell hit the season's fastest century, his hundred coming from 69 balls with 4 sixes and 12 fours. Greig declared at lunch, leaving Essex to score 279 from 71 overs. He was later criticized for the generosity of his declaration, but surely he was valid in offering his bowlers

ABOVE RIGHT: *Alec Stewart combined the duties of batsman and wicket-keeper to good effect and hit the first double century of his career, Surrey v. Essex, 10–13 June. (USPA)*

RIGHT: *Darren Bicknell – consistently fine form as Surrey's opening batsman and the fastest century of the season, against Essex at The Oval on 13 June. (Adrian Murrell/ Allsport)*

Paul Downton maintained a high standard behind the stumps for Middlesex and hit a thrilling century at Abergavenny, 13 June, which came close to giving his side victory. (George Herringshaw/ASP)

the last ball of the penultimate over, but he was spectacularly caught and bowled by Barwick off the first ball of the last over when Middlesex still needed 14 to win. Fraser and Hughes could manage just eight from the last five balls, and so ended a last day on which 529 runs were scored.

Gloucestershire brushed aside Leicestershire with remarkable ease to gain their first Championship win of the season, but Kent gained their first win in a more dramatic fashion. Robinson and Pollard began the match with a partnership of 222 for Nottinghamshire's first wicket. Chris Cowdrey and Roy Pienaar responded by adding 182 in 46 overs for Kent's fifth wicket on the second day. Then Pollard and Robinson etched their names in the record book by putting on 282 for the home county's first wicket in the second innings, so becoming only the second pair in history to share two double-century opening stands in the same match. Robinson hit his second century of the match and Pollard the second of his career, the first was also against Kent. Robinson's declaration left Kent to make 311. Benson went quickly, but Hinks, 70 off 79 balls, and Taylor put on 136. As the tempo flagged Chris Cowdrey hit 46 off 34 balls, and Fleming won the game with eight balls to spare with a cascade of boundaries, so justifying Cowdrey's first-day decision to make Notts bat first.

There were no such high jinks at Taunton, where night-watchman Pickles hit a career-best 66 to save Yorkshire from any embarrassment after Peter Roebuck had hit a patient century for Somerset.

On the seamers' paradise at New Road, Neal Radford and fit-again Graham Dilley bowled Worcestershire to a comfortable victory and moved the reigning champions menacingly up the table.

In The Parks, Chris Smith hit a welcome century, Cardigan Connor produced a fine spell of bowling and Adrian Aymes equalled Bobby Parks' Hampshire wicket-keeping record by taking 10 catches in the match. Kevan James also bowled well as Oxford University were beaten in what was their last first-class game before the Varsity match.

sufficient time in which to bowl out the opposition. Unfortunately the Surrey attack was below par, and Medlycott, in particular, had a bad afternoon, nor was he helped by some moderate fielding and catching. Hardie, the acting captain of Essex, relished the occasion to bludgeon an unbeaten century and take his side to victory.

Ravi Shastri hit a century in each innings for Glamorgan against Middlesex in a splendid match at Abergavenny. Glamorgan were 30 for 3 on the opening day, but Shastri and the veteran Alan Butcher put on 216, both batsmen making hundreds. Middlesex declared 39 runs behind on the second day, when Cann's off-breaks earned him three wickets. Shastri reached his second hundred of the match off 117 balls on the last morning, and he on-drove Emburey for 4 sixes. Morris' declaration meant that Middlesex had 68 overs in which to score 351. A dazzling century by Paul Downton brought Middlesex tantalizingly close to victory. He reached his hundred off 80 balls from

Refuge Assurance League

11 June

at Merthyr Tydfil

Glamorgan 209 for 6 (R.J. Shastri 92)
Middlesex 172

Glamorgan (4 pts) won by 37 runs

at Basingstoke

Warwickshire 158 for 9 (A.I. Kallicharran 55)
Hampshire 160 for 4 (V.P. Terry 53)

Hampshire (4 pts) won by 4 wickets

at Leicester

Gloucestershire 214 for 6 (A.J. Wright 81, P. Bainbridge 72, J.P. Agnew 4 for 25)
Leicestershire 155

Gloucestershire (4 pts) won by 59 runs

at Trent Bridge

Kent 206 (S.G. Hinks 54)
Nottinghamshire 207 for 7 (P. Pollard 100, A.P. Igglesden 4 for 41)

Nottinghamshire (4 pts) won by 3 wickets

at Taunton

Yorkshire 184 for 9 (R.J. Blakey 78)
Somerset 165 (P.W. Jarvis 6 for 27)

Yorkshire (4 pts) won by 19 runs

at The Oval

Surrey 192 (G.S. Clinton 57, A.J. Stewart 50, J.K. Lever 4 for 29)
Essex 160

Surrey (4 pts) won by 32 runs

at Hove

Northamptonshire 189 for 6 (D.J. Capel 63)
Sussex 190 for 7 (A.C.S. Pigott 51 not out)

Sussex (4 pts) won by 3 wickets

at Worcester

Worcestershire 207 for 6 (M.J. Weston 72)
Derbyshire 177 for 9

Worcestershire (4 pts) won by 30 runs

Essex suffered their first defeat in 17 matches in the various competitions when they were beaten by the eager young Surrey side at The Oval. Clinton and Stewart put on 109 for Surrey's second wicket, but fine bowling by Lever restricted the home county until Thorpe hit 40 off 27 balls. Against accurate bowling, particularly by Bullen, and dynamic fielding, Essex could never meet the required rate, and only a late flurry by Miller brought them close. Shastri's splendid all-round cricket gave Glamorgan their first Sunday league win of the season at the expense of Middlesex, and Hampshire maintained their challenge

with a comfortable victory against Warwickshire. Pollard's century set Nottinghamshire on the path to victory over Kent, but seven were needed off the last three balls. Mike swung a six and then the batsmen ran a leg-bye to give Nottinghamshire the points, but an ankle injury to Johnson clouded the celebrations. Some fierce hitting by Pigott gave Sussex victory over Northamptonshire, while Paul Jarvis produced some devastating fast bowling for Yorkshire and gave the England selectors a prod.

14, 15 and 16 June

at Old Trafford

Lancashire 184 (G.F. Lawson 4 for 44) and 185 (G.D. Campbell 5 for 54)
Australians 288 (T.M. Moody 74, D.M. Jones 59, B.P. Patterson 4 for 48) and 84 for 1

Australians won by 9 wickets

Some lively pace bowling dominated the tourists' match at Old Trafford. Geoff Lawson had match figures of 7 for 92.

Benson and Hedges Cup
Semi-Finals

14 June

at Taunton

Essex 293 for 5 (P.J. Prichard 73 not out)
Somerset 289 (C.J. Tavare 104 not out, P.M. Roebuck 53)

Essex won by 4 runs
(Gold Award – C.J. Tavare)

at Trent Bridge

Nottinghamshire 296 for 6 (R.T. Robinson 80, P. Pollard 77, B.C. Broad 66)
Kent 227 (M.R. Benson 65, J.A. Afford 4 for 38)

Nottinghamshire won by 69 runs
(Gold Award – J.A. Afford)

Nottinghamshire and Kent met each other for the fifth day in succession, and Chris Cowdrey adopted the policy that had proved successful in the County match in that he asked the home side to bat first when he won the toss. This time it proved to be a far from successful move. Broad and Pollard began the Nottinghamshire innings with a stand of 141 and, with Robinson scoring 80 at number three, Notts had 226 on the board before the fourth wicket fell. Pollard, who had hit two centuries in four days against the Kent bowling, made 77 off 100 balls and, although only Mike and French of the later batsmen made significant contributions, Nottinghamshire reached a formidable 296 for 6 in their 55 overs.

Injury had deprived the home county of both the overseas all-rounders, Stephenson and Cairns, as well as of

Benson and Hedges Cup Semi-Final at Trent Bridge, jubilation for Bruce French as Mark Benson is bowled and Nottinghamshire move closer to the final. (Adrian Murrell/ Allsport)

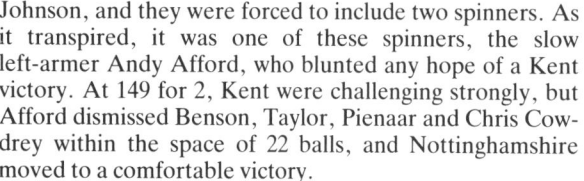

Gregory Mike celebrates as Kevin Evans takes a spectacular catch, Nottinghamshire v. *Kent, Benson and Hedges Cup Semi-Final. (Adrian Murrell/Allsport)*

RIGHT: *Neil Burns is exultant as Peter Roebuck breaks the Hardie–Lilley stand, Benson and Hedges Cup Semi-Final at Taunton. (Jon Nicolson/Allsport)*

Johnson, and they were forced to include two spinners. As it transpired, it was one of these spinners, the slow left-armer Andy Afford, who blunted any hope of a Kent victory. At 149 for 2, Kent were challenging strongly, but Afford dismissed Benson, Taylor, Pienaar and Chris Cowdrey within the space of 22 balls, and Nottinghamshire moved to a comfortable victory.

The match at Taunton was a much closer affair and produced some excellent cricket. Gooch won the toss, Essex batted and Gooch crashed the first ball of the day through the covers for four. He looked as if he would destroy Somerset single-handed until he missed a straight ball from Jones and was leg before. Jones was to prove the enigma of the match, cast one minute as hero and the next as villain. He bowled well early on, but Marks tended to chop and change his bowling, and when Jones returned later in the innings he began with three leg-side wides. Hardie and Lilley revived Essex after the dismissal of Gooch, but they, like Waugh, were cut down just as they were promising a big innings.

It was the Essex young lions, Prichard and Stephenson, who took their side to what seemed to be an awesome, match-winning total by adding 87 in nine overs for the fifth wicket. Essex plundered 108 runs from the last 10 overs of their innings, and 20 of them came from the final over

bowled by Mallender. Pringle hit the last ball into the crowd for six to give him a remarkable 15 off four balls. He also had a brush with some Somerset members who jibed at him.

It did not seem to be the required run rate that would deny Somerset, but the sheer number of runs that they were required to score. Roebuck and Marks had been the most effective of the Somerset bowlers and Childs, too rarely used in one-day cricket, was to prove the most meaningful bowler in the Essex attack.

Roebuck and Cook were quickly into their stride, undaunted by the magnitude of their task, and Roebuck reached his fifty out of 87 in the 22nd over. Cook was bowled by Gooch next ball, and when Childs took a tumbling return catch to dismiss Roebuck on the last ball before tea the game had tilted decidedly in favour of Essex. Burns, promoted in the order to deal with Childs because his eye, having been hit in practice, was swollen and closing, was bowled by the slow left-arm spinner, and Somerset, 97 for 3, were sinking rapidly.

Bartlett and Harden fluttered briefly, but Tavare was in supremely confident mood and while others came and went he remained firm and prospered. Marks offered good companionship in a stand of 44, but he skied Foster to mid-on, and the England bowler quickly accounted for

Rose and Mallender so that, at 233 for 8, Somerset looked beaten. Jones now entered to roars of approval from the Essex supporters, who were soon to be wishing he would bat as erratically as he had bowled. He middled the ball from the start and gave Tavare the support he needed. Tavare was magnificent, driving and pulling without the least hint of fuss or excitement. In six overs, he and Jones put on 53 for the ninth wicket, and Essex began to lose their composure.

The temperamental Foster remonstrated with Stephenson for a throw which went for two overthrows although he was as much to blame as the fielder. Unsettled, he bowled a wide and a long-hop which Tavare crashed for four, and it needed the combined counselling of Gooch and Hardie to soothe the bowler and remind him of the basics of the game. Somerset needed 24 from the last two overs, but Tavare hit Pringle for six to reach his hundred off 89 deliveries. From the last over, bowled by the old warrior Lever, 10 were needed, and this was reduced to seven with four balls remaining and Tavare at the striker's end.

The running between the wickets had been exhilarating, but now Tavare tested Foster's arm at long-on, and Jones was run out as he went for the second run. Jones had hit a massively brave 25. Tavare missed the chance of a leg-side hit off the next ball, and then clipped the penultimate down the leg-side, only to see Garnham make a fine stop. The batsmen crossed for a single which left Darren Foster, a batsman of most moderate accomplishment, the task of hitting the last ball of the match for six if Somerset were to win. He swung, but his off stump rocked back, and Essex had won by four runs.

It had been a pulsating game, and when one pondered on the heroes – Roebuck, Tavare, Jones, Childs, Prichard, Stephenson – one reflected what the result might have been had Pringle not hit the last ball of the Essex innings for six.

Tilcon Trophy

Semi-Finals

14 June

at Harrogate

Worcestershire 249 for 6 (M.J. Weston 100, G.A. Hick 80)
Sussex 170

Worcestershire won by 79 runs

15 June

at Harrogate

Surrey 234 for 5 (J.D. Robinson 68)
Yorkshire 200 (D.L. Bairstow 64)

Surrey won by 34 runs

Final

16 June

at Harrogate

Surrey 225 for 7 (D.M. Ward 117 not out)
Worcestershire 226 for 5 (T.S. Curtis 96)

Worcestershire won by 5 wickets

A highly entertaining three days at Harrogate saw two centuries scored, a fine innings and some good bowling by Hick, and an exciting final which Worcestershire won with 2.2 overs to spare.

17, 18 and 19 June

at Northampton

Australians 329 (A.R. Border 135, D.C. Boon 54, N.G.B. Cook 5 for 76) and 229 for 5 dec (M.A. Taylor 69, D.M. Jones 68 not out)
Northamptonshire 180 (W. Larkins 84, M.G. Hughes 5 for 37) and 106

Australians won by 272 runs

at Cambridge

Nottinghamshire 351 for 7 dec (P. Pollard 153, D.J.R. Martindale 60) and 229 for 5 dec (G.W. Mike 56 not out)
Cambridge University 308 for 8 dec (S.P. James 117, R.A. Pyman 69, J.A. Afford 5 for 91) and 100 for 2 (S.P. James 50)

Match drawn

17, 19 and 20 June

at Derby

Derbyshire 342 (B.J.M. Maher 97, J.E. Morris 67, A.I.C. Dodemaide 5 for 112) and 223 for 9 dec (K.J. Barnett 86, C. Gladwin 59, A.C.S. Pigott 4 for 69)
Sussex 417 (N.J. Lenham 62, I.J. Gould 62, A.P. Wells 60, C.M. Wells 58, D.E. Malcolm 4 for 94)

Match drawn
Derbyshire 6 pts, Sussex 6 pts

at Chelmsford

Leicestershire 377 for 8 dec (J.J. Whitaker 138, L. Potter 71, P. Willey 58) and 251 for 5 dec (J.J. Whitaker 92 not out, T.J. Boon 72)
Essex 262 for 2 dec (G.A. Gooch 124 not out, M.W. Waugh 89 not out) and 216 for 4 (P.J. Prichard 80 not out)

Match drawn
Essex 5 pts, Leicestershire 4 pts

at Old Trafford

Glamorgan 297 for 9 dec (H. Morris 69, A.R. Butcher 68, Wasim Akram 5 for 45) and 252 for 6 dec (A.R. Butcher 69, M.P. Maynard 52, I. Smith 51 not out)
Lancashire 196 (W.K. Hegg 73, S.L. Watkin 7 for 65) and 344 (G.D. Mendis 67, N.H. Fairbrother 65, P.A.J. DeFreitas 59, S.L. Watkin 6 for 94)

Glamorgan won by 9 runs
Glamorgan 23 pts, Lancashire 5 pts

at Bath

Kent 526 for 7 dec (M.R. Benson 157, T.R. Ward 104, R.F. Pienaar 87, C.S. Cowdrey 65, V.J. Marks 4 for 146) and 108 for 0 dec (S.G. Hinks 52 not out, M.R. Benson 50)
Somerset 274 for 5 dec (R.J. Harden 102 not out, V.J. Marks 89 not out) and 276 for 6 (P.M. Roebuck 107, S.J. Cook 72, R.P. Davis 4 for 96)

Match drawn
Kent 6 pts, Somerset 4 pts

Congratulations for Penberthy, who has just taken a wicket with his first ball in first-class cricket, Northamptonshire v. Australians, 17–19 June. (David Munden)

at The Oval

Surrey 226 (K.T. Medlycott 86 not out) and 305 for 6 dec (A.J. Stewart 148 not out, I.A. Greig 67)
Middlesex 225 (D.L. Haynes 64, K.T. Medlycott 5 for 93) and 243 for 9 (D.L. Haynes 102, M.A. Roseberry 79, M.P. Bicknell 4 for 63)

Match drawn
Surrey 6 pts, Middlesex 6 pts

at Harrogate

Yorkshire 220 (C.A. Walsh 5 for 86) and 312 for 6 dec (M.D. Moxon 95, P. Carrick 65 not out)
Gloucestershire 279 (C.W.J. Athey 81) and 163 for 8 (A.J. Wright 52, I.G. Swallow 4 for 58)

Match drawn
Gloucestershire 7 pts, Yorkshire 6 pts

The Australians sharpened their knives for the second Test match with a resounding win over Northamptonshire, who had both consolations and disappointments. A consolation was that Tony Penberthy took the wicket of Taylor with his first ball in first-class cricket. He had the left-hander caught behind and went on to capture two more wickets. The disappointments were that Capel had declared himself unfit and thereby ruled himself out of consideration for selection for the second Test, while Lamb so badly damaged a finger that it was to cause his withdrawal from the England side and to plague him for much of the rest of the season.

Paul Pollard's amazing run of success continued with a career-best 153 for Nottinghamshire against Cambridge University. Stephen James played two fine innings for the University.

The sunshine and flat wickets enabled batsmen to prosper and tedious draws to multiply. As is their custom, Derbyshire batted on into the second day against Sussex, who responded by batting into the third, and, inevitably, the match was drawn.

Briers won no friends at Chelmsford. Leicestershire occupied the first day in scoring 377 for 8 on a placid wicket. Gooch hit 124 not out on the second day and shared an unbroken third-wicket partnership of 192 with Mark Waugh before declaring 115 runs behind in order to keep the game alive. Essex's runs had come in 76 overs, so that Gooch's challenge was a bold one. It found no response in a rather ragged Leicestershire side. Whitaker played his second notable innings of the match, but Briers delayed his declaration until well into the afternoon, asking Essex to make 367 from 52 overs. Strongly criticized, Briers defended his action by saying that Leicestershire had lost their previous three matches and did not want to lose another. The philosophy of cricket is that if you are not brave enough to risk losing a match, you do not deserve to win one.

The Bath wicket took its usual toll of bowlers. Batsmen gorged themselves, and even the agreements between the captains could not produce a result.

The greatest excitement was at Old Trafford, where Glamorgan won a splendid match. Morris and Butcher began the match with a stand of 133 for Glamorgan, who then lost their way somewhat against Wasim Akram and missed a fourth batting point by three runs. This was more than compensated for by the fact that, in six overs before the close, Lancashire lost four wickets, three of them to Watkin, for 11 runs. The decline continued on the Monday, when Lancashire were reduced to 59 for 8 with Watkin again the main destroyer. Hegg and DeFreitas stopped the rot with a stand of 133 in 22 overs, but Glamorgan were able to build on their impressive lead, and Morris' declaration left Lancashire to make 354 in four hours plus 20 overs. It was a well-judged declaration, for the wicket was sound and the target tempting. The home side began slowly, but Wasim Akram tried to raise the tempo with 37 off 28 balls. He and Hegg fell to successive deliveries from the splendid Watkin, and at 194

Paul Pollard struck a rich vein of batting form in mid-season and played an important part in Nottinghamshire's successes. (Stuart Franklin/ASP)

for 7, Lancashire looked well beaten. Fairbrother and DeFreitas put on a rapid 92 for the eighth wicket, and Lancashire hoped again. Fairbrother ran himself out, and DeFreitas became Watkin's 13th victim of the match. When Allott joined Hughes for the last wicket 56 were needed from 10 overs. Shastri dropped a skier from Hughes off his own bowling, and Allott should have been stumped by Metson. The last over, bowled by Shastri, began with 14 runs needed for a Lancashire victory. Allott tried to hit the penultimate ball for six, but Alan Butcher took a diving catch on the boundary to give Glamorgan their first victory at Old Trafford for 28 years. Watkin was immediately awarded his county cap.

Gloucestershire were less successful in their efforts at Harrogate and were thankful to hang on for a draw at the end and deny the Yorkshire spinners.

It was a combination of pace and spin which nearly brought Surrey victory in a fine game at The Oval. Surrey, 91 for 6 on Saturday afternoon, were lifted by Keith Medlycott's fine innings, and it was Medlycott's left-arm spin that bowled them to a one-run lead on the Monday. Alec Stewart produced another excellent innings on the last day, dealing with the Middlesex spinners, Emburey and Tufnell, in the severest manner. He and the unquenchable Greig hit 145 at four runs an over so that Greig was able to declare and set Middlesex to score 307 in 54

overs. Haynes and Roseberry gave Middlesex a splendid start with a stand of 155, but Medlycott dismissed them both, and Martin Bicknell destroyed the middle order. Nine wickets went down in 24 overs for 88 runs, and it was left to Norman Cowans to grope his way through Medlycott's final over to save the game for Middlesex.

Refuge Assurance League

18 June

at Derby

Sussex 130
Derbyshire 134 for 7 (P.D. Bowler 55 not out)

Derbyshire (4 pts) won by 3 wickets

at Chelmsford

Leicestershire 192 for 6
Essex 193 for 1 (G.A. Gooch 111 not out, B.R. Hardie 67)

Essex (4 pts) won by 9 wickets

at Blackpool

Lancashire 244 for 5 (N.H. Fairbrother 100 not out)
Glamorgan 110

Lancashire (4 pts) won by 134 runs

at Bath

Somerset 249 for 8 (C.J. Tavare 110, R.P. Davis 5 for 52)
Kent 169 (V.J. Marks 4 for 48)

Kent (4 pts) won by 80 runs

at Edgbaston

Worcestershire 194 for 5 (M.J. Weston 63)
Warwickshire 172 for 8

Worcestershire (4 pts) won by 22 runs

at Leeds

Yorkshire 196 for 7 (R.J. Blakey 73, D.L. Bairstow 52)
Gloucestershire 184 for 8 (J.W. Lloyds 65)

Yorkshire (4 pts) won by 12 runs

The two leading sides in the Sunday league, Essex and Lancashire, had resounding victories. Gooch hit another massive century and shared an opening partnership of 178 with Hardie. Essex won with three overs to spare. Neil Fairbrother hit 100 off 75 balls as Lancashire trounced Glamorgan by 134 runs. Worcestershire moved into a challenging position by virtue of their win at Edgbaston, and Chris Tavare's run of success continued with a century against his old county. A large crowd at Harrogate were cheered by Yorkshire's success, while at Derby the home side, needing only 131 to win, became nervous and lost three wickets with the score on 112. Bowler kept his head and saw them to victory with one over to spare.

21, 22 and 23 June

at Ilford

Essex 277 (M.A. Garnham 54, G. Miller 51) and 234 for 9 dec (M.E. Waugh 109, G. Miller 50)

Hampshire 244 (J. H. Childs 5 for 36) and 165 (J. H. Childs 7 for 38)

Essex won by 102 runs
Essex 23 pts, Hampshire 6 pts

at Southport

Lancashire 336 (G. Fowler 92, N.H. Fairbrother 81, N.G.B. Cook 6 for 56)
Northamptonshire 144 (P.A.J. DeFreitas 5 for 46, M. Watkinson 4 for 30) and 407 for 7 dec (R.J. Bailey 134, G. Cook 128)

Match drawn
Lancashire 8 pts, Northamptonshire 3 pts

at Bath

Somerset 73 (C.A. Walsh 7 for 19) and 364 (S.J. Cook 147, J.W. Lloyds 7 for 134)
Gloucestershire 402 for 4 dec (C.W.J. Athey 108, K.M. Curran 101 not out, A.J. Wright 68, M.W. Alleyne 58 not out) and 36 for 2

Gloucestershire won by 8 wickets
Gloucestershire 22 pts, Somerset 1pt

at Edgbaston

Glamorgan 290 (I. Smith 105, A.A. Donald 4 for 53) and 378 for 2 dec (A.R. Butcher 171 not out, H. Morris 133)
Warwickshire 365 for 4 dec (G.W. Humpage 183, A.J. Moles 130 not out) and 84 for 0

Match drawn
Warwickshire 8 pts, Glamorgan 4 pts

at Sheffield

Yorkshire 249 (D. Byas 82 not out, M.D. Moxon 69, N.V. Radford 5 for 86) and 280 for 4 dec (D. Byas 80, A.A. Metcalfe 76)
Worcestershire 389 for 7 dec (G.A. Hick 150, P.A. Neale 62 not out)

Match drawn
Worcestershire 8 pts, Yorkshire 4 pts

at Hove

Cambridge University 229 (R.A. Pyman 55, A.R. Hansford 4 for 46) and 67 (R.A. Bunting 4 for 18, A.R. Hansford 4 for 25)
Sussex 371 for 9 dec (A.M. Green 94, R.A. Pyman 4 for 81)

Sussex won by an innings and 75 runs

With Lancashire and Northamptonshire locked in a drawn match at Southport, Essex moved to the top of the Britannic Assurance County Championship with a splendid and dramatic win over Hampshire at Ilford. An Essex side depleted by injury and Test calls had struggled on the first day and had slipped to 96 for 6 before being rescued by the combined efforts of Garnham, Miller and the elegantly impressive Nadeem Shahid, who was appearing in only his second county match. Nevertheless, Hampshire finished the day on 71 for 1 and seemed in complete command. John Childs transformed the match on the second day as he bowled 34.5 overs and took 5 for 36, maintaining a perfect line and length and turning the ball appreciably. A belligerent century from Mark Waugh, who added 161 for the fifth wicket with Miller after Essex floundered again to 43 for 4, made possible Hardie's declaration. Hampshire, needing 268 from a minimum of

63 overs, lost wickets regularly to Childs after Topley had made the early breakthroughs, but Cowley and Parks defied the Essex bowlers for 30 overs, having come together at 107 for 7. It seemed that they had thwarted Essex, but Childs dismissed them both in the 16th and 18th overs of the last hour. He then had Bakker taken at short-leg by Shahid, and Essex had won with two minutes to spare. Childs, 12 for 74 in the match, bowled magnificently and was supported by fielding and catching of the highest quality.

Lancashire prospered to four batting points on the opening day at Southport, and DeFreitas and Watkinson routed Northamptonshire on the second. Following-on, the visitors lost Larkins and Felton for 68, but Geoff Cook and Bailey put on 201 and saved their side from defeat. The partnership spanned 67 overs, and both batsmen showed great resolution.

Gloucestershire achieved a most surprising win at Bath. On a pitch which was totally without malice, Somerset were shot out for 73 in 43.3 overs. Their destroyer was the hostile Courtney Walsh, who took 4 for 5 in a three-over spell after lunch, to finish with 7 for 19. Somerset's one consolation was that Jim Cook became the first batsman in the country to reach a thousand runs in first-class cricket. It was Cook who came close to saving Somerset after Athey and Curran had taken Gloucestershire to a first-innings lead of 329. Cook batted for 335 minutes and faced 301 balls in his effort to save Somerset. He was eighth out, having made 147 out of 268. Lloyds had taken six wickets,

Ian Smith. Exciting all-round cricket for Glamorgan.
(George Herringshaw/ASP)

and Gloucestershire seemed on the brink of victory, but Gard, deputizing for the injured Burns, and Mallender added 80. Gard became Lloyds' seventh victim, and eventually Gloucestershire had just six overs in which to score 36 to win. They reached their target with five balls to spare.

There was a glut of runs in the draw at Edgbaston. Ian Smith, the Glamorgan all-rounder, hit an enterprising maiden first-class century on the opening day. On the second, Moles and Humpage shared a fourth-wicket stand of 279 in 75 overs for Warwickshire. On the last day, Butcher made his highest score for Glamorgan and put on 269 for the first wicket with Morris.

At Sheffield, Graeme Hick ended a barren spell with his first championship century of the season. His 150 came off 156 balls and contained 2 sixes and 25 fours, but Metcalfe and Byas ground out a draw for Yorkshire on the last day.

Hansford of Surrey University bowled his medium pace impressively for Sussex against Cambridge University, and took his first eight wickets in first-class cricket at a personal cost of 71 runs. With the Varsity match looming, Cambridge gave a wretched batting display in their second innings.

Second Cornhill Test Match
ENGLAND v. AUSTRALIA

England were without the injured Lamb, but Gatting returned to the fold, and a much changed attack saw Dilley, Jarvis and Emburey come in for Pringle, Newport and DeFreitas. Angus Fraser was named in the England twelve, but he was omitted on the day. Botham was still unfit. Australia brought in leg-spinner Hohns for Campbell.

At a sunlit Lord's, filled to capacity, Gower won the toss, and Gooch and Broad marched out to open the England innings. They began soberly enough, but there was no hint of discomfort until, in the 13th over, Broad was leg before to Alderman's late in-swinger. Barnett was soon busy, but he turned Hughes into the hands of short-leg and when, two overs later, Gatting gave Boon a second, simple catch off the first ball he received, England, 58 for 3, were in deep trouble. That trouble would have been even greater had Jones held on to a

BELOW: *HM the Queen is introduced to the Australian team. She meets Merv Hughes. (Adrian Murrell/Allsport)*

BOTTOM: *The five hundred is posted. Lawson and Waugh in partnership before a full house at Lord's. (Ken Kelly)*

difficult chance from Gower at fine-leg, but the fielder got his hands to the ball only to see it escape over the line for four. Gower was on seven at the time, and by lunch he had advanced to 14, and England were 88 for 3 with Gooch on 36.

Gooch had suggested solidity and purpose and reached his fifty in the 38th over, but, just as he seemed set for a big score, he flashed at Waugh's massive away swinger and was caught behind. Robin Smith began with a flurry of exciting strokes. One over from Waugh produced 15 runs, a no-ball and a raucous appeal. Briefly, it was all heady stuff for England, and at 180 for 4, Smith and Gower in full flow, they looked likely to reach an impressive score. Then Gower chopped a ball from Lawson onto his off-stump and Emburey was bowled by Alderman's leg-cutter second ball. The sight of Emburey coming in at number seven had underlined the length of England's tail, but Russell belied his record and his place in the Gloucestershire order with an innings of great good sense and no little skill.

At 191, Smith hit tamely and disappointingly to mid-on. In the afternoon session England scored a hectic 124 runs, but they lost the cream of their batting at the same time.

After tea Foster gave Russell good support until he was superbly caught by Jones on the boundary ropes at long-leg. Jarvis went four overs later, and Dilley helped to add a valuable 33 for the last wicket, before Alderman ended the innings with the second new ball. Russell, unbeaten on 64 with 9 fours to his credit, had brought some dignity to the England score. It was some 50 or 60 more than had at one time looked likely, but some 200 short of what it should have been after Gower had won the toss.

Australia had one over before the close of the first day, from which they scored four runs, but they lost Marsh early on the second morning. Taylor and Boon passed unruffled to lunch at 83 for 1. In the post-lunch period we saw the worst of Dilley. His spirits and his head seem to droop so readily, and he frequently stopped in the middle of his run-up. He was replaced by the wayward and inconsistent Jarvis.

In the 55th over of the innings, Mark Taylor, who had exuded confidence and class, was leg before on the back foot to Foster. At tea, Australia were 168 for 2, Border having given an immediate injection of quick scoring.

It was after tea that it all began to go wrong for Australia. Boon, solid as a rock and looking certain to reach a century, steered Dilley to second slip when he had made 94. Border swept carelessly and needlessly at Emburey and was taken at short fine-leg. Jones began to fret, played across the line and was leg before, and Healy was caught behind off Jarvis, who had now worked up a lively pace and looked very aggressive. Australia closed on 276 for 6, and the game was very evenly balanced.

Waugh, of course, was still there, 35 not out with 5 fours in 66 minutes, and it was on the third morning that he began to take the game firmly into Australia's grasp. He and Hughes, who was proving a thorn in England's flesh as both batsman and bowler, took their stand to 66 before Hughes edged to slip. Hohns, a wealthy batsman to have coming in at number nine, played with complete assurance

A model for all. A lesson for England. Steve Waugh in defence. (Adrian Murrell/Allsport)

before driving rashly at Emburey, who was to finish with four wickets and be the pick of the England bowlers even though there was no logical reason for his selection in the first place.

Waugh moved on with a grace and authority that will light the memory of this Australian summer for many years to come. Nothing had seemed surer from the first ball that he faced than that he would make a hundred, and it arrived shortly after lunch. What surprised England, and most of those who were watching, was the batting of Geoff Lawson. He matched Waugh run for run and stroke for stroke in a ninth-wicket stand of 130 which left England in disarray. Lawson passed his highest score in Test cricket before hitting Emburey high to mid-on, but by then he and Waugh had effectively ended England's hopes of winning the match.

Trailing by 242 on the first innings, England could now think only of saving the match. The last four Australian wickets had realized 263 runs. Inevitably Gower came in for criticism, but it is hard to see what a captain can do when his bowlers are firing with blank cartridges. What England needed in their second innings was a good start; what they got was Gooch leg before wicket second ball to give Alderman his 100th Test wicket. Barnett was taken at silly mid-off and Broad had his off stump knocked back, and at 28 for 3 the chances of survival seemed remote. Gower and Gatting took the score to 58 by the close.

Gatting was leg before, offering no shot on the Monday. He gestured quite plainly that he thought the umpire was wrong, but he was one of very few who believed so. The pugnacious Smith now joined Gower in what, for much of the day, promised to be a match-saving stand. Gower was ready to walk when he cut Lawson to Marsh in the gully, but the fielder signalled that he had not taken the catch. So the England captain stayed and played some sweet shots. There was a serenity about his batting, if not quite the zest of yesteryear, and it was a defiant 15th Test century that he reached, a fitting answer to some of the nonsense with which he had been abused from the press box. He had

ABOVE: *David Boon, brilliant at short-leg, catches 'Jack' Russell. (Adrian Murrell/Allsport)*

ABOVE RIGHT: *Broad is bowled by Lawson. (Adrian Murrell/Allsport)*

RIGHT: *The dreaded finger of Harold Bird. Gooch is leg before, and the England second innings begins in dismay. (Adrian Murrell/Allsport)*

never seemed quite at ease with the leg-stump attack of the Australian pace bowlers, and it was Hughes who dismissed him with a ball which Gower flicked quietly to backward of square. He and Smith had put on 139 in 167 minutes, and the England captain well deserved his ovation.

Soon after tea Russell square drove Hohns for four, and England were in the lead, but Lawson had the England wicket-keeper caught at short-leg in his first over with the second new ball.

Smith had batted magnificently, a mixture of great concentration and awesome power, and he was within sight of a maiden Test century when Alderman bowled him with a fine delivery which moved back at him and clipped the off stump. Two balls later, Alderman trapped Foster and, when Jarvis fell to the same bowler, like Gatting offering no shot, England faced defeat.

Emburey and Dilley prolonged England's innings on the last morning and took the lead to 117. Uncertain weather was causing Australia some anxiety, and the anxiety increased when Marsh was bowled without offering a shot, a disease which had become infectious.

Rain extended the lunch interval to cause Australia more concern, but Taylor and Boon batted with a comforting solidity. The fifty had just been passed when Taylor was taken low at slip. Border received one incredible three-bounce delivery outside the leg stump from Foster, which he swatted at and missed, and then he hit the next ball straight into the hands of deep fine-leg, where a member of the MCC groundstaff, Robert Sims, was fielding. Jones perished six runs later, mis-hooking and skying to the keeper. Australia were 67 for 4, three quick wickets to Foster, and there was a spectre of Bob Willis

SECOND CORNHILL TEST MATCH – ENGLAND v. AUSTRALIA
22, 23, 24, 26 and 27 June 1989 at Lord's

ENGLAND

	FIRST INNINGS		SECOND INNINGS	
G.A. Gooch	c Healy, b Waugh	60	lbw, b Alderman	0
B.C. Broad	lbw, b Alderman	18	b Lawson	20
K.J. Barnett	c Boon, b Hughes	14	c Jones, b Alderman	3
M.W. Gatting	c Boon, b Hughes	0	lbw, b Alderman	22
D.I. Gower†	b Lawson	57	c Border, b Hughes	106
R.A. Smith	c Hohns, b Lawson	32	b Alderman	96
J.E. Emburey	b Alderman	0	(8) not out	36
R.C. Russell*	not out	64	(7) c Boon, b Lawson	29
N.A. Foster	c Jones, b Hughes	16	lbw, b Alderman	4
P.W. Jarvis	c Marsh, b Hughes	6	lbw, b Alderman	5
G.R. Dilley	c Border, b Alderman	7	c Boon, b Hughes	24
Extras	lb 9, nb 3	12	b 6, lb 6, nb 2	14
		286		359

	O	M	R	W	O	M	R	W
Alderman	20.5	4	60	3	38	6	128	6
Lawson	27	8	88	2	39	10	99	2
Hughes	23	6	71	4	24	8	44	2
Waugh	9	3	49	1	7	2	20	–
Hohns	7	3	9	–	13	6	33	–
Border					9	3	23	–

AUSTRALIA

	FIRST INNINGS		SECOND INNINGS	
G.R. Marsh	c Russell, b Dilley	3	(2) b Dilley	1
M.A. Taylor	lbw, b Foster	62	(1) c Gooch, b Foster	27
D.C. Boon	c Gooch, b Dilley	94	not out	58
A.R. Border†	c Smith, b Emburey	35	c sub (Sims), b Foster	1
D.M. Jones	lbw, b Foster	27	c Russell, b Foster	0
S.R. Waugh	not out	152	not out	21
I.A. Healy*	c Russell, b Jarvis	3		
M.G. Hughes	c Gooch, b Foster	30		
T.V. Hohns	b Emburey	21		
G.F. Lawson	c Broad, b Emburey	74		
T.M. Alderman	lbw, b Emburey	8		
Extras	lb 11, nb 8	19	b 3, lb 4, nb 4	11
		528	(for 4 wkts)	119

	O	M	R	W	O	M	R	W
Dilley	34	3	141	2	10	2	27	1
Foster	45	7	129	3	18	3	39	3
Jarvis	31	3	150	1	9.2	–	38	–
Emburey	42	12	88	4	3	–	8	–
Gooch	6	2	9	–				

FALL OF WICKETS
1–31, 2–52, 3–58, 4–131, 5–180, 6–185, 7–191, 8–237, 9–253
1–0, 2–18, 3–28, 4–84, 5–223, 6–274, 7–300, 8–304, 9–314

FALL OF WICKETS
1–6, 2–151, 3–192, 4–221, 5–235, 6–265, 7–331, 8–381, 9–511
1–9, 2–51, 3–61, 4–67

Umpires: H.D. Bird & N.T. Plews

Australia won by 6 wickets

*England despair – Gower chops the ball on to his wicket.
(Adrian Murrell/Allsport)*

and Headingley 1981. Waugh, indeed, might have been caught, but neither he nor Boon are men who give their wickets lightly, and, as expected, Australia triumphed. It was no more than their rich cricket over five days had deserved.

Waugh's 21 not out brought his total of runs in three innings to 350 without being dismissed, an Australian record. Border had become the first Australian captain to win twice at Lord's, and the discipline, dedication and obvious joy of his side were a delight to behold.

24, 26 and 27 June

at Ilford

Warwickshire 338 (D.A. Reeve 97 not out, J.D. Radcliffe 72, J.H. Childs 4 for 96) and 145 (D.R. Pringle 7 for 44)
Essex 335 (N. Hussain 141, B.R. Hardie 56, A.A. Donald 5 for 103, A.R.K. Pierson 5 for 129) and 149 for 5

Essex won by 5 wickets
Essex 24 pts, Warwickshire 8 pts

at Southampton

Hampshire 356 for 8 dec (V.P. Terry 91, C.L. Smith 83, J.R. Wood 58) and 171 for 3 dec
Sussex 287 (A.P. Wells 153) and 116 for 5 (A.P. Wells 53 not out)

Match drawn
Hampshire 8 pts, Sussex 4 pts

at Old Trafford

Kent 296 (S.A. Marsh 59, B.P. Patterson 4 for 65) and 42 for 3

Lancashire 298 (G.D. Mendis 75, G. Fowler 65, T.E. Jesty 55 not out, A.P. Igglesden 6 for 73)

Match drawn
Kent 7 pts, Lancashire 6 pts

at Leicester

Leicestershire 352 for 6 dec (L. Potter 121 not out, P. Willey 85, T.J. Boon 57)
Nottinghamshire 116 (J.P. Agnew 5 for 37, C.C. Lewis 5 for 51) and 135 (J.P. Agnew 6 for 56)

Leicestershire won by an innings and 101 runs
Leicestershire 23 pts, Nottinghamshire 1 pt

at Luton

Somerset 274 (P.M. Roebuck 70, C.J. Tavare 59, N.G.B. Cook 5 for 28, J.G. Thomas 4 for 76) and 346 for 7 dec (R.J. Harden 115 not out, C.J. Tavare 89, J.J.E. Hardy 65)
Northamptonshire 300 for 5 dec (G. Cook 126, N.A. Felton 60 not out) and 308 (R.J. Bailey 100, D.J. Capel 58, W. Larkins 50)

Somerset won by 12 runs
Somerset 21 pts, Northamptonshire 8 pts

at The Oval

Surrey 275 (I.A. Greig 61, C.A. Walsh 5 for 83, P. Bainbridge 4 for 39) and 128 for 2 (D.J. Bicknell 58 not out, G.P. Thorpe 54 not out)
Gloucestershire 113 (M.P. Bicknell 6 for 47) and 289 (I.P. Butcher 68, A.J. Wright 55, G.A. Tedstone 50)

Surrey won by 8 wickets
Surrey 23 pts, Gloucestershire 4 pts

at Worcester

Worcestershire 142 (A.R.C. Fraser 4 for 34) and 172 (P.A. Neale 75 not out, A.R.C. Fraser 4 for 39)
Middlesex 221 (M.R. Ramprakash 54) and 96 for 1

Middlesex won by 9 wickets
Middlesex 22 pts, Worcestershire 4 pts

at Leeds

Yorkshire 308 for 9 dec (A.A. Metcalfe 113, R.J. Blakey 97, S.L. Watkin 5 for 53)
Glamorgan 214 for 2 (M.J. Cann 95, A.R. Butcher 87)

Match drawn
Yorkshire 3 pts, Glamorgan 3 pts

Ashley Metcalfe fashioned a welcome century for Yorkshire on the opening day at Headingley, but rain on the last day prevented play against Glamorgan.

Middlesex and Leicestershire needed only two days to win their matches. Leicestershire did well on the Saturday at Grace Road. On a dry pitch which gave some encouragement to the spinners, Boon, Willey and Potter batted with caution to take their side to 310 for 5. Briers decided to continue the Leicestershire innings on the Monday morning for another 13 overs before declaring. His critics were soon silenced when Agnew and Lewis bowled out a feeble Nottinghamshire side in 37 overs. The visitors did not last as long in their second innings, and Jonathan Agnew, who had been struggling to find form for most of the season, bowled unchanged from the pavilion end all day to return the best match figures of his career, 11 for 93.

The uncertain wicket at New Road saw 17 wickets fall on the first day. Worcestershire were saved from total

humiliation by Botham and Weston in the middle order, but Middlesex were given the edge by their young lions, Hutchinson and Ramprakash. Fraser and Cowans bowled out Worcestershire on the Monday, and Haynes and Hutchinson took Middlesex to a surprisingly comfortable victory.

Rain badly disrupted the game at Old Trafford, where a spell of 5 for 10 by Alan Igglesden during what little play was possible on the last day gave Kent four bowling points.

Choosing to bat first at The Oval, Surrey went to lunch at an uncomfortable 103 for 5, but Ian Greig's 61 off 60 balls put them on the right road. Greig was particularly severe on Lawrence but, when he was out, Surrey were 199 for 9 in 55 overs. A remarkable last-wicket stand of 76 between Tony Murphy and Martin Bicknell, both of whom hit the highest scores of their careers, took Surrey to a third batting point. Martin Bicknell was the main reason for the destruction of Gloucestershire on the Saturday and Monday and, although the visitors did better when they followed-on, Surrey moved to a comfortable and welcome victory. They are a young side, superbly led, and they could well prove to be the team of the 1990s.

Hampshire's top order batted with consistency to take them to a commanding position against Sussex on the opening day. Stricken by a mysterious stomach upset on the Monday, Sussex slumped to 185 for 9, still 22 short of saving the follow-on, but, astonishingly, Andy Babington, although far from well, helped Alan Wells to add 102 for the last wicket. Babington finished with a career-best 18

John Childs spun Essex to success at Ilford. (Sporting Pictures UK Ltd)

An outstanding season for Sussex – Alan Wells. (George Herringshaw/ASP)

not out, while Alan Wells moved from 74 to 153 during the course of the last-wicket stand before falling to newcomer Wood, who had impressed with the bat. A last-afternoon target of 241 off 55 overs proved more than the stricken Sussex wanted to attempt.

Northamptonshire's title hopes took another set-back when they were beaten by Somerset in a splendid contest at Luton. Northamptonshire led by 26 on the first innings, thanks to another century from Geoff Cook. That Marks was able to set the home side the task of scoring 321 off 61 overs was thanks mainly to an innings of 115 from 106 balls by Harden. Well as Harden played, however, he was encouraged by some occasional bowling from Felton as Lamb nudged his opponents to declare. Northamptonshire looked well set to succeed in their run chase when they reached 248 for the loss of only three wickets. Bailey and Capel had added 115 in 22 overs and seemed to be driving their side to victory, but Capel was caught off Foster, and Bailey was out as soon as he had reached a beautiful hundred. Only 40 runs were needed from the last six overs, but Northamptonshire were in a state of collapse which saw their last seven wickets go down in 12 overs for 60 runs. The game ended on the first ball of the last over, when Robinson moved down the wicket after playing forward to Marks and was run out.

Essex meanwhile moved 26 points clear at the top of the table. They survived Dermot Reeve's onslaught on the Saturday to come to near parity on the first innings. It had not looked as if they would do so when they lost seven wickets for 159 runs, and eight for 186, but then Nasser Hussain, playing his first championship match of the season after coming down from Durham University, found a good partner in Don Topley. The pair added 136 before Hussain was bowled by Pierson for 147. He hit 2 sixes and 21 fours and reached his hundred off 122 balls. To have such a batsman of quality coming in at number six in a side from which Gooch was absent suggested immense richness

in Essex cricket. Acting captain Pringle bowled splendidly to take 7 for 44 and rout Warwickshire when they batted again. Essex's only worry was time and a gathering storm, as they needed 149 to win at 4½ runs an over. Stephenson and Lilley hit lavishly, and Hussain scored the winning runs with three overs to spare to complete a highly successful Ilford week for Essex.

Refuge Assurance League
25 June

at Ilford

Warwickshire 216 for 7 (D.A. Reeve 70 not out)
Essex 218 for 6 (N. Hussain 63 not out)

Essex (4 pts) won by 4 wickets

at Southampton

Sussex 192 for 5 (D.M. Smith 56)
Hampshire 193 for 7

Hampshire (4 pts) won by 3 wickets

at Old Trafford

Kent 172 for 9
Lancashire 174 for 2 (N.H. Fairbrother 82 not out, G. Fowler 68)

Lancashire (4 pts) won by 8 wickets

at Luton

Northamptonshire 81 (L.B. Taylor 5 for 20)
Leicestershire 82 for 2

Leicestershire (4 pts) won by 8 wickets

at Trent Bridge

Nottinghamshire 170 for 8
Derbyshire 128 (K.P. Evans 4 for 28)

Nottinghamshire (4 pts) won by 42 runs

at Bath

Somerset 226 for 5 (S.J. Cook 124 not out)
Gloucestershire 128 (D.J. Foster 4 for 26)

Somerset (4 pts) won by 98 runs

at Worcester

Worcestershire 143 (S.P. Hughes 5 for 23)
Middlesex 144 for 5

Middlesex (4 pts) won by 5 wickets

at Hull

Yorkshire 211 for 7 (R.J. Blakey 92 not out)
Glamorgan 162 (A.R. Butcher 76 not out)

Yorkshire (4 pts) won by 49 runs

Essex and Lancashire maintained their places at the top of the Sunday league with comfortable victories. Reeve completed a fine weekend against Essex, scoring 167 runs without being dismissed, but Childs bowled an economic spell, and Hussain's precocious talent took Essex to victory. Lancashire brushed Kent aside with 3.5 overs to spare as Fowler and Fairbrother shared a stand of 125. Ambrose began with five wides at Luton. Northamp-

Alan Butcher was the first English-born batsman to reach a thousand runs in the season, and he later assumed the responsibility of the captaincy of Glamorgan. (George Herringshaw/ASP)

tonshire gave a miserable display and were well beaten by Leicestershire, for whom the veteran Les Taylor returned the best Sunday bowling figures of his career. Jim Cook continued to score runs in all types of cricket, and James hit a single off the last ball of the match to give Hampshire victory over Sussex.

NatWest Bank Trophy

Round One

28 June

at March

Cambridgeshire 202 for 4 (I.S. Lawrence 74, N.J. Adams 50)
Worcestershire 206 for 1 (T.S. Curtis 91 not out, G.A. Hick 86 not out)

Worcestershire won by 9 wickets
(Man of the Match: I.S. Lawrence)

at Darlington

Middlesex 215 for 7 (D.L. Haynes 83)
Durham 161 (S.P. Hughes 4 for 20)

Middlesex won by 54 runs
(Man of the Match: D.L. Haynes)

at Hitchin

Hertfordshire 154 for 7
Nottinghamshire 155 for 5 (B.C. Broad 63)

Nottinghamshire won by 5 wickets
(Man of the Match: B.C. Broad)

at Canterbury

Kent 359 for 4 (R.F. Pienaar 90, T.R. Ward 83, C.S. Cowdrey 69 not out, S.G. Hinks 62)
Dorset 161 (S.J. Legg 66)

Kent won by 198 runs
(Man of the Match: T.R. Ward)

at Christ Church, Oxford

Gloucestershire 269 for 3 (I.P. Butcher 71, C.W.J. Athey 56 not out)
Oxfordshire 226 (S.N.V. Waterton 92, K.B.S. Jarvis 5 for 32)

Gloucestershire won by 43 runs
(Man of the Match: S.N.V. Waterton)

at St George's, Telford

Shropshire 220 for 7 (J. Abrahams 79, M.R. Davies 89)
Leicestershire 221 for 4 (D.I. Gower 101 not out)

Leicestershire won by 6 wickets
(Man of the Match: D.I. Gower)

28 and 29 June

at Derby

Derbyshire 145
Ireland 82 (O.H. Mortensen 6 for 14)

Derbyshire won by 63 runs
(Man of the Match: O.H. Mortensen)

at Taunton

Somerset 276 for 6 (P.M. Roebuck 102, C.J. Tavare 101)
Essex 221 (G.A. Gooch 94)

Somerset won by 55 runs
(Man of the Match: P.M. Roebuck)

at Bury St Edmunds

Northamptonshire 265 for 5 (A.J. Lamb 103, D.J. Capel 92 not out)
Suffolk 224 (M.S.A. McEvoy 61, A.D. Brown 51)

Northamptonshire won by 32 runs
(Man of the Match: D.J. Capel)

at Hove

Sussex 235 for 8 (D.M. Smith 99 not out)
Berkshire 200 for 6

Sussex won by 35 runs
(Man of the Match: D.M. Smith)

at Edgbaston

Warwickshire 270 for 4 (J.D. Radcliffe 59, G.W. Humpage 59, T.A. Lloyd 57)
Wiltshire 84 (A.A. Donald 5 for 12)

Warwickshire won by 186 runs
(Man of the Match: A.A. Donald)

at Leeds

Scotland 210 for 3 (I.L. Philip 73)

Yorkshire 212 for 7 (D. Byas 54, A.A. Metcalfe 50)

Yorkshire won by 3 wickets
(Man of the Match: O. Henry)

29 June

at Boughton Hall, Chester

Hampshire 306 for 2 (C.L. Smith 159, V.P. Terry 99)
Cheshire 159 (M.D. Marshall 4 for 40)

Hampshire won by 147 runs
(Man of the Match: C.L. Smith)

at Kendal

Cumberland 84 (P.A.J. DeFreitas 5 for 13)
Lancashire 86 for 6

Lancashire won by 4 wickets
(Man of the Match: P.A.J. DeFreitas)

at Cardiff

Glamorgan 318 for 4 (H. Morris 154 not out, M.P. Maynard 56)
Staffordshire 151 (H.V. Patel 63)

Glamorgan won by 167 runs
(Man of the Match: H. Morris)

at Jesmond

Surrey 313 for 5 (D.M. Ward 97, G.P. Thorpe 74, A.J. Stewart 55)
Northumberland 245 for 6

Surrey won by 68 runs
(Man of the Match: D.M. Ward)

Ole Mortensen routed Ireland to win the match for Derbyshire in the first round of the NatWest Bank Trophy. (Chris Raphael/Allsport)

Hugh Morris – brave batting for Glamorgan throughout the season and individual award winner in the NatWest Bank Trophy match against Staffordshire. (Sporting Pictures UK Ltd)

The first round of the NatWest Bank Trophy produced some brave performances but no surprises. Scotland, Cumberland and, above all, Ireland came close to beating their first-class opponents. When play was ended on the Wednesday at Derby the home side were 66 for 5 from 21.3 overs. They slipped to 85 for 7 on the Thursday morning, and it was only some hard hitting from Michael Holding that lifted them to 145. Ireland seemed to have every chance of victory, but the bowling of Ole Mortensen soon had their batting in tatters, and they could make no effective recovery from the depths of 13 for 5.

Kent, Glamorgan and Surrey hit their highest scores in limited-over cricket, and Hugh Morris' 154 not out was the highest score made by a Glamorgan player in one-day cricket.

Paul Terry and Chris Smith established a new first-wicket record for the 60-over competition with a partnership of 228 for Hampshire against Cheshire, and J.A. Hartley and D.A. Hale created an eighth-wicket record with a stand of 83 for Oxfordshire against Gloucestershire. This match was noted for the performances of two former Kent players, pace bowler Jarvis and wicket-keeper batsman Waterton, who found themselves on opposite sides.

David Gower equalled Glenn Turner's record for the 60-over competition when he hit his fifth century while Allan Lamb's century and his 167-run partnership with David Capel rescued Northamptonshire after they had lost their first three wickets for 14 runs.

The main interest was centred on Taunton where Essex, dominant in three competitions, met Somerset in a vital

Peter Roebuck – increasingly effective with both bat and ball and Man of the Match as Somerset beat Essex in the first round of the NatWest Bank Trophy. (Jon Nicholson/ Allsport)

A thousand runs in the Minor Counties competition for Oxfordshire and the individual award for his innings of 92 in the NatWest Bank Trophy match with Gloucestershire – Stuart Waterton. (Simon Miles/Allsport)

one-day match for the second time in a fortnight. Only 10.1 overs were possible on the Wednesday, but Foster dismissed both the prolific Cook and Hardy in that time as Somerset laboured to 24 before bad light ended play. That was virtually the end of Essex's success. On the following day, Roebuck and Tavare extended their partnership to 195, both men hitting centuries. Some lusty blows from Vic Marks supplemented the good work of Roebuck and Tavare, and Somerset reached an impressive 276 for 6 in their 60 overs. Essex were soon in trouble when Hardie and Waugh were out cheaply. As long as Gooch stayed Essex had hopes of victory, but no one could offer him sufficient support and once he fell to Marks Essex were a beaten side. The Somerset triumph was built upon not only the batting of Roebuck and Tavare, but also the spin bowling of Marks, Trump and Roebuck. That Essex did not include Childs in their side was an incomprehensible decision.

28 June

at Oxford

Australians 215 for 5 (G.R. Marsh 73)
Oxford and Cambridge Universities 116 for 4

Australians won by 99 runs

Rain caused the game to be reduced to 35 overs an innings.

1, 2 and 3 July

at Neath

Australians 373 for 4 dec (M.R.J. Veletta 134 not out, A.R. Border 91) and 216 for 5 dec (M.R.J. Veletta 83, D.M. Jones 56)
Glamorgan 301 for 5 dec (H. Morris 94, I. Smith 61 not out, A.R. Butcher 54) and 135 for 5

Match drawn

The easy-paced pitch at Neath proved a paradise for batsmen, and Glamorgan acquitted themselves well. Viv Richards arrived in order to play for Glamorgan in the second half of the season, but he was found to be still unwell and returned to the Caribbean for treatment without appearing for the county.

1, 3 and 4 July

at Derby

Derbyshire 444 for 9 dec (J.E. Morris 127, K.J. Barnett 118, R. Sharma 70, P.D. Bowler 54, H.R.J. Trump 4 for 80) and 87 for 2 dec

Somerset 231 for 5 dec and 240 for 7 (S.J. Cook 85, P.M. Roebuck 54)

Match drawn
Derbyshire 6 pts, Somerset 2 pts

at Gloucester

Gloucestershire 101 (F.D. Stephenson 5 for 32, K.E. Cooper 4 for 28) and 147 (C.W.J. Athey 52, K.E. Cooper 6 for 37)
Nottinghamshire 252 (F.D. Stephenson 81, D.W. Randall 76, K.M. Curran 4 for 51, K.B.S. Jarvis 4 for 69)

Nottinghamshire won by an innings and 4 runs
Nottinghamshire 23 pts, Gloucestershire 4 pts

at Southampton

Hampshire 144 (A. Sidebottom 5 for 35) and 153 (A. Sidebottom 4 for 41)
Yorkshire 107 (C.A. Connor 5 for 20) and 191 for 7 (R.J. Blakey 53)

Yorkshire won by 7 wickets
Yorkshire 20 pts, Hampshire 4 pts

at Hinckley

Warwickshire 196 (D.A. Reeve 55, W.K.M. Benjamin 6 for 70) and 193 for 8 (G.W. Humpage 55)
Leicestershire 371 for 6 dec (J.J. Whitaker 138, P. Willey 96, G.C. Small 4 for 95)

Match drawn
Leicestershire 8 pts, Warwickshire 3 pts

at Lord's

Lancashire 161 (N.G. Cowans 4 for 29) and 196 (G.D. Mendis 50)
Middlesex 96 (B.P. Patterson 5 for 48) and 43 (P.A.J. DeFreitas 7 for 21)

Lancashire won by 218 runs
Lancashire 21 pts, Middlesex 4 pts

at Northampton

Northamptonshire 256 (A.J. Lamb 55, N.A. Felton 52 not out, I.T. Botham 6 for 99) and 158 (W. Larkins 56, D.J. Capel 53, I.T. Botham 5 for 76, G.R. Dilley 4 for 66)
Worcestershire 433 (G.A. Hick 111, T.S. Curtis 80, P.A. Neale 62, G.J. Lord 54, D.J. Capel 4 for 82)

Worcestershire won by an innings and 19 runs
Worcestershire 24 pts, Northamptonshire 4 pts

at Horsham

Essex 185 (C.M. Wells 4 for 33, A.I.C. Dodemaide 4 for 58) and 350 for 6 dec (M.A. Garnham 90 not out, D.R. Pringle 81 not out, P.J. Prichard 60)
Sussex 285 (I.J. Gould 58, N.A. Foster 4 for 53) and 240 for 9 (D.M. Smith 71, J.H. Childs 5 for 84)

Match drawn
Sussex 7 pts, Essex 3 pts

Twenty-three wickets fell on the opening day at Southampton as a result of vagaries of batting rather than vagaries of pitch. Yorkshire struggled to victory on the Monday afternoon with Arnie Sidebottom claiming the individual laurels. He followed his 9 for 76 bowling figures in the match with 45 not out as he and Phil Carrick scored 70 in 12 overs to win the match.

Nottinghamshire were also two-day winners as they brushed aside the limp Gloucestershire side, a shadow of the team that had challenged strongly in competitions in 1988. Kevin Cooper bowled splendidly to take 10 for 65 in the match.

Barnett and Morris hit centuries for Derbyshire who, as is their custom, batted into the second day. Marks made a challenging declaration, and Barnett eventually set Somerset the task of scoring 301 in 70 overs to win the match. At 173 for 1, Somerset looked set for victory, but three wickets in 22 balls by Michael Holding shifted the balance, and the match was drawn.

Warwickshire batted dourly on the last day to stave off defeat at Hinckley. Humpage batted for three hours for 55 to provide the necessary backbone. Earlier, James Whitaker had hit a century of quality to prompt the memories of England selectors, who had once considered him to be a Test-match prospect.

Another cricketer more recently discarded by the England side gave a magnificent display of fast bowling at Lord's. Eighteen wickets fell on the Saturday when Mid-

Phillip DeFreitas – fast and furious as Lancashire bowled out Middlesex for 43 at Lord's, 4 July. (Stuart Franklin/ASP)

Cambridge University 1989
First-Class Matches

BATTING

	v. Glamorgan (Cambridge) 15–17 April	v. Gloucestershire (Cambridge) 19–21 April	v. Leicestershire (Cambridge) 27–9 April	v. Warwickshire (Cambridge) 4–6 May	v. Kent (Cambridge) 17–19 May	v. Essex (Cambridge) 24–6 May	v. Nottinghamshire (Cambridge) 17–19 June	v. Sussex (Hove) 21–3 June	v. Oxford University (Lord's) 5–7 July
S.P. James	38 —	36 —	35 —	151* 8	15 5	13 60	117 50	3 16	23 5
J.M.G. Willatt	5 —	3 —	0 —	1 12	3 18	10 44	11 0*	45 4	16 —
M.A. Atherton	36 —	42 —	2 —	43 24	27 79	12 7	1 29*	27 2	56 30
R. Heap	19 —	42* —	0 —	4 35	46 43	14 19	6 12	0 6	7 25*
J.C.M. Atkinson	16 —	51 —	37 —	36 2	57 0	15 0	9 —	1 0	39 —
M.J. Morris	6* —	2 —	33 —	3 18*	0 4	9 0			
R. Bate	0 —								
R.J. Turner	0* —	1 —	36 —	15* 0*	58 5		32* —	43 6	57 —
R.A. Pyman	— —	1* —	9* —	— —	3 37	13 0	69 —	55 18	10* —
D.J. Bush	— —	— —	0 —	— —	28 3*	13* 8*	0 —	5 0	— —
M.F. Mullins	— —	— —	— —	— —	0* 0	0 3			
A.J. Buzza		— —	— —	— —	0 8		25* —	1* 3	— —
A. Davies						16 29			
D.C. Cotton						4 0	— —	0 0*	
M.T. Alban							10 —	36 2	86 —
D.H. Shufflebotham									28 —
Byes	6		4	3 7	3 4	3 1	5 4	6 4	1
Leg-byes	8	6	2	16 6	10 6	8 12	14 2	5 3	7
Wides				6	4 3	3 1	2 1	1 1	1
No-balls	1	3	1	4 2	3 4		7 1	2	10 1
Total	135	187	159	276 114	259 220	133 184	308 100	229 67	340 62
Wickets	6	6	8	5 5	10 10	10 10	8 2	10 10	8 2
Result	D	D	D	D	L	L	D	L	D

Fielding Figures
12 – R. J. Turner (ct 7/st 5)
7 – J.C.M. Atkinson
6 – M.A. Atherton and R. Heap
4 – M.J. Morris
3 – D.J. Bush, A.J. Buzza and A. Davies
2 – R.A. Pyman
1 – J.M.G. Willatt and M.F. Mullins

BOWLING

	D.J. Bush	M.F. Mullins	J.C.M. Atkinson	R.A. Pyman	M.A. Atherton	A.J. Buzza	D.C. Cotton	M.T. Alban
v. Glamorgan (Cambridge) 15–17 April	21–7–66–0	29–7–77–5	2–0–24–0	21–4–70–1	27.5–5–60–3			
v. Gloucestershire (Cambridge) 19–21 April	19–4–53–1	32–11–88–3		9–2–43–0	23–3–74–1	23–3–83–2		
v. Leicestershire (Cambridge) 27–9 April	23–4–71–0	22–6–75–2		21.2–8–60–2	28–7–67–3	15–1–66–1		
v. Warwickshire (Cambridge) 4–6 May	15.4–4–52–2 / 10–0–43–0	13–2–48–0 / 10–1–57–0		19.1–5–41–0 / 5–1–27–0	18.5–4–50–1 / 21–3–59–1	25–4–83–3 / 15–0–72–0		
v. Kent (Cambridge) 17–19 May	12–4–36–0 / 6–0–33–0	9–2–33–0		22–4–51–1 / 12–2–47–0	36.1–13–77–3 / 9–0–58–3	36–5–102–6 / 3–0–26–0		
v. Essex (Cambridge) 24–6 May	19–6–64–3	13–1–60–0		26–4–71–0	25–4–80–2		11–0–58–1	
v. Nottinghamshire (Cambridge) 17–19 June	13–2–59–2 / 8–2–21–0			14–2–65–0	22–4–69–2 / 26–5–69–3	21.3–2–98–2 / 26–4–77–2	13–0–52–1 / 7–0–30–0	2–0–21–0
v. Sussex (Hove) 21–3 June	20–4–51–0			27–4–81–4	31–9–74–1	35–5–108–3	14–3–48–1	
v. Oxford University (Lord's) 5–7 July	14–4–22–1			23–7–43–5	29–10–40–1	21–7–41–1		
	180.4–41– / 571–9 / av. 63.44	128–30– / 438–10 / av. 43.80	2–0– / 24–0 / —	199.3–43– / 599–13 / av. 46.07	296.5–67– / 777–24 / av. 32.37	220.3–31– / 756–20 / av. 37.80	45–3– / 188–3 / av. 62.66	2–0– / 21–0 / —

M	Inns	NOs	Runs	HS	Av
9	15	1	575	151*	41.07
9	14	1	172	45	13.23
9	15	1	417	79	29.78
9	15	2	278	46	21.38
9	13	—	263	57	20.23
6	9	2	75	33	10.71
1	1	—	0	0	0.00
8	11	4	253	58	36.14
9	10	3	215	69	30.71
9	8	3	57	28	11.40
6	4	1	3	3	1.00
7	5	2	37	25*	12.33
1	2	—	45	29	22.50
3	4	1	4	4	1.33
3	4	—	134	86	33.50
1	1	—	28	28	28.00

Cricket at Horsham – Sussex v. Essex, 1–4 July. (Sporting Pictures UK Ltd)

D.H. Shufflebotham

Byes	Leg-byes	Wides	No-balls	Total	Wkts
6	4	4	4	307	10
	4		4	345	7
3	2	1		344	8
1	9	5	2	284	6
	5			263	2
3	2	6	1	304	10
5	7	1		176	3
4	10	1	3	347	6
	8		3	351	7
10	1	1		229	5
5	4	1		371	9
7	5		3	192	9

5–3–34–1

5–3–
4–1
/. 34.00

dlesex, having asked Lancashire to bat first, were 66 for 8 at close of play. They finished the second day in even greater disarray at 12 for 4 in their second innings. The game was all over just after noon on the Tuesday, when Middlesex were bowled out for 43. Phillip DeFreitas bowled as quickly as any English bowler did all season and returned the best figures of his career. He maintained great hostility throughout his spell, and one must only wish that he will soon achieve the consistency and discipline that are needed to realize his immense potential.

Lancashire's win took them to second place in the table as Northamptonshire were crushed by a Worcestershire side that at last began to play like champions. Ian Botham turned back the clock to take 11 for 175 in the match, and Graeme Hick hit 2 sixes and 16 fours in another championship century. He was badly dropped at slip when 26, but there is an almost shy command in the man once he is under way. Curtis and Lord had laid the basis for a big score with an opening partnership of 121, and, as ever, Neale gave substance to the middle order. There was little to halt Worcestershire's progress to a comfortable win on the last day.

Meanwhile Essex looked in danger of their first cham-

Oxford University 1989
First-Class Matches

BATTING

BATTING	v. Northamptonshire (Oxford) 15–18 April		v. Surrey (Oxford) 19–21 April		v. Derbyshire (Oxford) 27–9 April		v. Nottinghamshire (Oxford) 17–19 May		v. Middlesex (Oxford) 24–6 May		v. Lancashire (Oxford) 7–9 June		v. Hampshire (Oxford) 10–13 June		v. Cambridge University (Lord's) 5–7 July	
S.A. Almaer	11	—	18	39*	22	—	0	5	0	62	14	—	4	6	0	—
D.A. Hagan	33	—			45	—	0	26	2	33	53	—	5	0	0	—
M.J. Kilborn	52	—	20	26	4	—										
R.E. Morris	9	—	14	17	17	—	55	2	16	3	6	—	4	19	76	
S. Chauhan	2	—	10	0							10	—				
P.D. Lunn	7	—	61	7		—	30	0	14	20*	45	—	17	24	22	—
A.N.S. Hampton	25	—	10	19*	0	—	53	4	19	1*	55	—	8	5	36	—
C.W. Timms	5	—							5	—						
I.M. Henderson	0	—									0	—	6	26	20*	
E.D. Hester	5	—					5	0	0	—	2*	—			4	
J.M.E. Oppenheimer	0*	—	0	—	0	—			0	—			0	7		
G.J. Toogood			19	—												
G.D. Reynolds			1	—	16	—	13	20			13	—	37*	40	7	—
M. Munro			12*	—												
P.G. Edwards			1	—	4*		4	0*	6*	—	—		0	10*	3*	—
M.A. Crawley					60	—	17	4	14	29					5	—
J.D. Nuttall					4	—	1*	13							4	—
J. Higgo							2	4	3	9			0	0		
R.M. Jackson																
C. Crocker													7	2		
Byes	1		1		4				9					4	7	
Leg-byes	9		11	1	5		4	5	4		8	10	3	3	5	
Wides	1						2				2		1			
No-balls	17		23	11			5				9		2		3	
Total	177		201	120	181		191	83	92		174	210	93	147	192	
Wickets	10		10	4	9		10	10	10		5	8	10	10	9	
Result	D		D		D		L		D		D		L		D	

Fielding Figures
8 – A.N.S. Hampton
6 – G.D. Reynolds (ct 4/st 2)
4 – M.A. Crawley and D.A. Hagan
2 – S. Chauhan, R.E. Morris, S.A. Almaer and J. Higgo
1 – M.J. Kilborn, P.D. Lunn, P.G. Edwards, J.D. Nuttall,
    J.M.E. Oppenheimer, C.W. Timms (ct 0/st 1) and sub

BOWLING

BOWLING	E.D. Hester	I.M. Henderson	A.N.S. Hampton	J.M.E. Oppenheimer	P.D. Lunn	S. Chauhan	M.J. Kilborn	G.J. Toogood
v. Northamptonshire (Oxford) 15–18 April	24–4–66–2 / 6–0–22–0	4–1–25–0	32–9–91–4	15–1–58–0 / 6–0–16–0	24–3–73–0	1–0–1–0	7–1–32–0	
v. Surrey (Oxford) 19–21 April			8–0–50–0	17–5–77–0 / 10–3–42–0	15–1–76–1		10–0–62–1	27–4–107–1
v. Derbyshire (Oxford) 27–9 April			14–3–49–0 / 4–1–10–0	20–7–57–0 / 14–1–51–3	6–0–24–0		3–0–10–0	2–1–8–0
v. Nottinghamshire (Oxford) 17–19 May	26–4–100–4 / 23–3–72–1		2–0–14–0		7–2–23–0 / 2–2–0–0			
v. Middlesex (Oxford) 24–6 May	15–2–73–0 / 15–7–35–0		4–0–17–0 / 7–0–32–0	16–4–78–0 / 13–2–50–1	3–0–25–0 / 1–0–9–0			
v. Lancashire (Oxford) 7–9 June	20–4–88–1 / 3–0–17–0	21.5–4–93–2 / 5–1–11–0			1–0–4–0 / 4–0–25–0			
v. Hampshire (Oxford) 10–13 June		28–9–80–1 / 13–3–40–2	4–1–14–0	23–2–102–1 / 7–3–12–0				
v. Cambridge University (Lord's) 5–7 July	23–4–95–3 / 2–1–4–0	15–1–64–1 / 4–1–12–1	6–0–26–1 / 2–0–16–0		7–1–12–0 / 4–0–20–0			
	157–29– 572–11 av. 52.00	90.5–20– 325–7 av. 46.42	83–14– 319–5 av. 63.80	141–28– 543–5 av. 108.60	74–9– 291–1 av. 291.00	1–0– 1–0 —	20–1– 104–1 av. 104.00	29–5– 115–1 av. 115.00

M	Inns	NOs	Runs	HS	Av
8	12	1	181	62	16.45
7	10	—	197	53	19.70
3	4	—	102	52	25.50
8	12	—	238	76	19.83
3	4	—	22	10	5.50
8	11	1	247	61	24.70
8	12	2	235	55	23.50
2	2	—	10	5	5.00
4	5	1	52	26	13.00
5	6	1	16	5	3.20
5	6	1	7	7	1.40
1	1	—	19	19	19.00
6	8	1	147	40	21.00
1	1	1	12	12*	—
7	8	5	28	10*	9.33
4	6	—	129	60	21.50
3	4	1	22	13	7.33
3	6	—	18	9	3.00
—					—
1	2	—	9	7	4.50

pionship defeat of the season at the close of play on the second day. Put in to bat, they had struggled against some lively seam bowling on the Saturday, and Sussex's late order had performed well on the Monday to give their side a first-innings lead of 100. Again the Sussex seamers troubled Essex and Gooch, Stephenson, Miller and Waugh were all back in the pavilion before the arrears had been cleared. The Essex side has depth and resilience, however, and a stand of 174 in 35 overs either side of lunch between Pringle and Garnham made it possible for Gooch to declare and ask Sussex to make 251 in just under three hours if they wanted to win the match. To their credit, Sussex challenged to the last. With sixteen needed from two overs and with three wickets to fall, Colin Wells was brilliantly caught at long-on by Stephenson off Childs, whose bowling brought his side close to victory. Moores needed to hit the last two balls of the match for six, but he was caught off the penultimate ball and Babington had to survive one ball from Miller to save his side from defeat.

Refuge Assurance League

2 July

at Derby

Somerset 155 for 6
Derbyshire 161 for 5 (P.D. Bowler 64)

Derbyshire (4 pts) won by 5 wickets

at Gloucester

Gloucestershire 154 for 8
Nottinghamshire 157 for 8 (K.M. Curran 4 for 27)

Nottinghamshire (4 pts) won by 2 wickets

at Southampton

Yorkshire 179 for 7
Hampshire 183 for 4 (R.J. Scott 116 not out)

Hampshire (4 pts) won by 6 wickets

M. Munro	P.G. Edwards	J.D. Nuttall	M.A. Crawley	R.M. Jackson	C. Crocker	R.E. Morris	Byes	Leg-byes	Wides	No-balls	Total	Wkts
							3	7		2	356	6
							1			1	39	0
7–1–15–1	28–6–114–3						4	4	7	2	447	6
1–0–6–0									1	5	119	1
	25–6–86–2	21–3–65–2	14–5–27–0				4	8	1		320	5
	9–1–36–2	9–1–35–0					1				143	5
	17–5–46–0	22.5–6–78–1	17–4–48–1				4	7	4		320	6
	14–4–44–1	13–2–51–1	7–0–19–0				5	3	2	1	194	3
	22–0–94–1		22–8–66–0				4	1		1	358	1
	9.3–1–39–2						2	6			173	3
	8–1–41–0			12–2–64–0			1	10	4		301	3
	10–3–25–0			9–1–23–0				2			103	0
	6–1–15–2				20–9–35–0			8	1		254	4
	12–2–42–0				7–4–15–0		1	3			113	2
	24.4–5–79–3	14–3–46–0	3–0–10–0				1	7		10	340	8
	1.3–0–5–1					1–0–5–0			1	1	62	2
8–1–	186.4–35–	79.5–15–	63–17–	21–3–	27–13–	1–0–						
21–1	666–17	275–4	170–1	87–0	50–0	5–0						
av. 21.00	av. 39.17	av. 68.75	av. 170.00	—	—	—						

at Leicester

Leicestershire 215 for 6 (D.I. Gower 82, J.J. Whitaker 81)
Warwickshire 194 (D.A. Reeve 64)

Leicestershire (4 pts) won by 21 runs

at Lord's

Middlesex 136 for 8
Lancashire 139 for 6 (N.H. Fairbrother 59 not out)

Lancashire (4 pts) won by 6 wickets

at Tring

Northamptonshire 168
Worcestershire 169 for 4 (T.S. Curtis 63)

Worcestershire (4 pts) won by 6 wickets

at Horsham

Sussex 154 for 7 (I.J. Gould 63)
Essex 157 for 4

Essex (4 pts) won by 6 wickets

Essex and Lancashire maintained their fierce pace at the top of the Refuge Assurance League. Both sides won with ease and stayed eight points clear of the field. At Horsham, Sussex could never throw off the burden of losing their first four wickets for 29 runs, while at Lord's, Middlesex never recovered from the indignity of being 74 for 6 against Lancashire. Hampshire, in third place, owed much to a spectacular innings by Richard Scott, who hit 116 off 86 balls. He and Robin Smith added 150 in 25 overs. Scott hit 9 sixes and 6 fours.

5, 6 and 7 July

at Derby

Derbyshire 191 (J.E. Morris 93, J.H. Childs 5 for 47, T.D. Topley 4 for 47) and 114 for 5 (P.D. Bowler 56 not out)
Essex 292 (J.P. Stephenson 93, R. Sharma 5 for 60)

Match drawn
Essex 7 pts, Derbyshire 5 pts

at Gloucester

Gloucestershire 399 for 9 dec (A.J. Wright 80, P. Bainbridge 69, J.W. Lloyds 59, C.W.J. Athey 50)
Sussex 232 (I.J. Gould 58 not out, N.J. Lenham 50, C.A. Walsh 5 for 44, M.C.J. Ball 4 for 84) and 21 for 0

Match drawn
Gloucestershire 7 pts, Sussex 3 pts

at Maidstone

Kent 156 (W.W. Davis 5 for 55, D.J. Capel 4 for 32) and 191 for 2 (N.R. Taylor 98, R.F. Pienaar 77 not out)
Northamptonshire 378 (W. Larkins 116, D.J. Capel 105, C. Penn 4 for 109)

Match drawn
Northamptonshire 8 pts, Kent 4 pts

at Leicester

Lancashire 411 for 9 dec (W.K. Hegg 86, G.D. Mendis 80, P.A.J. DeFreitas 69, N.H. Fairbrother 65)
Leicestershire 187 (P. Willey 85, P.J.W. Allott 5 for 24) and 91 for 2

Match drawn
Lancashire 8 pts, Leicestershire 5 pts

at Guildford

Nottinghamshire 475 for 8 dec (R.T. Robinson 136, D.W. Randall 101, D.J.R. Martindale 78, F.D. Stephenson 56, K.T. Medlycott 4 for 169)
Surrey 275 (D.J. Bicknell 70, G.P. Thorpe 62, E.E. Hemmings 6 for 87, J.A. Afford 4 for 39) and 146 for 1 (G.S. Clinton 65, D.J. Bicknell 59 not out)

Match drawn
Nottinghamshire 8 pts, Surrey 5 pts

at Worcester

Warwickshire 265 (P.A. Smith 140, R.K. Illingworth 4 for 33) and 47 for 0
Worcestershire 232 (T.A. Merrick 6 for 67)

Match drawn
Warwickshire 7 pts, Worcestershire 6 pts

at Lord's

Cambridge University 340 for 8 dec (M.T. Alban 86, R.J. Turner 57, M.A. Atherton 50) and 62 for 2
Oxford University 192 for 9 dec (R.E. Morris 76, R.A. Pyman 5 for 43)

Match drawn

Rain hampered all matches, and no play was possible on the last day at Maidstone or Worcester. Kent had suffered rather severely at Maidstone. Winston Davis and David Capel bowled out Kent by early afternoon on the first day after Larkins had won the toss and asked the home side to bat first. The acting Northamptonshire captain then blasted his first championship century of the season, and his side finished the day 90 runs ahead with only three wickets down. David Capel reached a forceful hundred on the second day, and Northamptonshire were well in command when Hinks was out without scoring at the start of the Kent second innings. Taylor and Pienaar restored Kent's pride with a stand of 189 before rain washed out the last day.

Lancashire scored consistently and bowled well to force Leicestershire to follow-on, but they were denied victory when only 22 overs were possible on the last day.

Paul Smith, an all-rounder of tantalizing talent as yet not completely fulfilled, hit his first century for three seasons and lifted Warwickshire's spirits after they had been 29 for 4. Small and Merrick reduced Worcestershire to 49 for 4 before the end of the first day, and although Rhodes and Lampitt effected a recovery on the second afternoon, Warwickshire still held the edge before rain brought a premature closure.

Gloucestershire were very much on top against Sussex, who were forced to follow-on, but only 38 balls could be bowled on the last day.

Centuries by Randall and Robinson and some hard hitting by the middle order brought Nottinghamshire 475 runs in 110 overs on the opening day at Guildford. Surrey could not match this. Only Thorpe offered significant resistance to the Nottinghamshire spinners, and the home side were forced to follow-on. Rain did not come to their rescue, but Darren Bicknell shared an opening stand of

101 with Clinton and battled grimly through the last day to save the match.

The controlled spin of John Childs and the medium pace of Don Topley combined to destroy Derbyshire, who lost their last eight wickets for 51 runs. Newman and Malcolm bowled them back into the game, however, and Essex were 71 for 5 and had lost Stephenson, who had been forced to retire hurt after being hit by a ball from Bishop. Stephenson returned to score a brave and aggressive 93. He and John Lever put on 88 for the eighth wicket and Essex took a first-innings lead of 102. They looked well set for victory as Derbyshire struggled painfully to survive against some accurate bowling and tenacious fielding, but only 11 overs were possible on the Friday, in which time Derbyshire lost two wickets and scored nine runs. Childs had figures of 1 for 11 in 18.5 overs before the rain came.

Sadly, rain washed out the last day's play in the Varsity match, which was one of the most enterprising of recent times. Crawley won the toss and asked Cambridge to bat. He had no great success with this venture, but at 152 for 5, Cambridge had lost their main batting. Then Alban, in what was only his third first-class match, shared a stand of 149 with Turner to take Cambridge to a position of total superiority, which was emphasized when they took three Oxford wickets for 24 before the close. Morris, elected captain for 1990, hit 76 and, with the late efforts of Hampton and Henderson, was responsible for Oxford saving the follow-on. Oxford's hopes of coming back into the game increased when James and Atherton were dismissed before the end of the second day, but rain claimed the finale.

Third Cornhill Test Match
ENGLAND v. AUSTRALIA

Not surprisingly, Australia were unchanged, but a series of misfortunes caused several alterations in the England side from the team originally selected. Lamb, Smith and Foster were all forced to withdraw through injury, while Gatting stood down because of the death of his mother-in-law. Curtis and Tavare were late replacements in the batting and Jarvis won the recall in the bowling. Angus Fraser won his first Test cap, and Ian Botham returned to Test cricket.

For the first time in 11 outings against David Gower, Allan Border won the toss and Australia batted first. Marsh and Taylor gave their side a bristling start with 48 runs coming from the first 15 somewhat ragged overs by Dilley and Jarvis. The introduction of Fraser and Botham slowed the run rate as 11 overs produced 12 runs, but the two openers had given Australia a solid start.

Immediately after lunch the game tilted in favour of

BELOW LEFT: *Dean Jones in all his glory. (Adrian Murrell/ Allsport)*

BELOW: *Mopping up after the torrential rain and violent storm. (Ken Kelly)*

Steve Waugh loses his wicket for the first time in the series, bowled by debutant Angus Fraser. (Adrian Murrell/ Allsport)

Healy becomes another Fraser victim. (Adrian Murre. Allsport

England. Taylor moved down the wicket to Emburey, but the ball turned sharply to beat the outside edge and Russell, who had an outstanding match, completed the stumping. Ten minutes later, Marsh played across a straight ball from Botham and was leg before. This was Botham's 374th Test wicket, and it was greeted with a roar of approval by the crowd, who were in need of an English hero.

Border became the fourth man to reach 8,000 runs in Test cricket, and then he offered no shot to a ball from Emburey which, inexplicably, clipped his leg stump. Australia were 105 for 3, and England had seized the initiative.

Dean Jones oozed confidence from his very first shot. He was positive in all that he did, and he and David Boon began to repair Australia's fortunes. They had added 96 when Jones drove hard and straight at Jarvis, who deflected the ball onto the stumps with Boon out of his ground. Jones was visibly shaken by this mishap, but he and Waugh took Australia to 232 for 4 by the close, which came 45 minutes early because of bad light. No sooner had the players left the field than a tremendous storm broke.

For a time visibility was down to 20 yards and the grou was awash.

Only 66 minutes play was possible on the Friday. Aft the downpour on the Thursday evening it was remarkab that any play at all was possible on the second day, but start was made at 4.30 pm, which says much for the wo of the groundstaff at Edgbaston. The shortened day w not without event. Dean Jones reached a fine century 3½ hours, and Waugh, uncharacteristically indecisi neither forward nor back, was bowled by a ball of perfe length. It was Fraser's first Test wicket, and it was the fir time that Waugh had been dismissed in the series. He ha scored 393 runs.

Fraser had well deserved his wicket and he quick added another when he bowled Healy. Australia beg the third day on 294 for 6, and soon after the start they lo Hughes, who edged Dilley to slip, but that was to be t only success that England enjoyed on a day when ra again restricted play. In the 37 overs that were possibl Australia scored 97 runs, and Hohns batted with su confidence as to mock his number nine position. He ar

Jones added 92, but Hohns was out without addition on the Monday morning, by which time, of course, the match seemed drawn and dead.

Australia's innings did not end until 50 minutes into the fourth morning, when Jones pulled to substitute Folley at square-leg. His innings had lasted for 327 minutes, and he

BELOW: *Gooch is leg before to Lawson for eight. (David Munden)*

RIGHT: *Russell is caught at slip by Taylor off leg-spinner Hohns. (Adrian Murrell/Allsport)*

had faced 293 balls and hit 17 fours. The fractured nature of the innings did nothing to detract from its quality. Fraser claimed four wickets on his Test debut, and he had earned them with his accuracy, control and aggression.

If we had thought the match was dead, we were mistaken. Gooch was frustrated by the attacking leg-side field that Border set for him and, erring across the line, he was leg before as he played back to Lawson. In the

THIRD CORNHILL TEST MATCH – ENGLAND v. AUSTRALIA
6, 7, 8, 10 and 11 July 1989 at Edgbaston, Birmingham

AUSTRALIA

	FIRST INNINGS		SECOND INNINGS	
G.R. Marsh	lbw, b Botham	42	b Jarvis	42
M.A. Taylor	st Russell, b Emburey	43	c Botham, b Gooch	51
D.C. Boon	run out	38	not out	22
A.R. Border†	b Emburey	8		
D.M. Jones	c sub (Folley), b Fraser	157		
S.R. Waugh	b Fraser	43		
I.A. Healy*	b Fraser	2	(4) not out	33
M.G. Hughes	c Botham, b Dilley	2		
T.V. Hohns	c Gooch, b Dilley	40		
G.F. Lawson	b Fraser	12		
T.M. Alderman	not out	0		
Extras	lb 20, nb 17	37	b 4, lb 4, nb 2	10
		424	(for 2 wkts)	158

ENGLAND

	FIRST INNINGS	
G.A. Gooch	lbw, b Lawson	8
T.S. Curtis	lbw, b Hughes	41
D.I. Gower†	lbw, b Alderman	8
C.J. Tavare	c Taylor, b Alderman	2
K.J. Barnett	c Healy, b Waugh	10
I.T. Botham	b Hughes	46
R.C. Russell*	c Taylor, b Hohns	42
J.E. Emburey	c Boon, b Lawson	26
A.R.C. Fraser	run out	12
G.R. Dilley	not out	11
P.W. Jarvis	lbw, b Alderman	22
Extras	b 1, lb 2, nb 11	14
		242

	O	M	R	W	O	M	R	W
Dilley	31	3	123	2	10	4	27	–
Jarvis	23	4	82	–	6	1	20	1
Fraser	33	8	63	4	12	–	29	–
Botham	26	5	75	1				
Emburey	29	5	61	2	20	8	37	–
Gooch					14	5	30	1
Curtis					3	–	7	–

	O	M	R	W
Alderman	26.3	6	61	3
Lawson	21	4	54	2
Hughes	22	4	68	2
Waugh	11	3	38	1
Hohns	16	8	18	1

FALL OF WICKETS
1–88, 2–94, 3–105, 4–201, 5–272, 6–289, 7–299, 8–391, 9–421
1–81, 2–109

FALL OF WICKETS
1–17, 2–42, 3–47, 4–75, 5–75, 6–171, 7–171, 8–185, 9–215

Umpires: H.D. Bird & J.W. Holder

Match drawn

post-lunch period, Alderman bowled an intelligent, probing spell that broke the back of the England innings. Gower was defeated by the in-swinger after being tested by a series of out-swingers, and Tavare marked an unhappy return after five years of Test exile when he was caught off the out-swinger after being probed by a series of in-swingers. He survived nine balls.

Hughes and Curtis seemed to be engaged in discussion before Curtis became the third leg before wicket victim of the innings. Barnett, limping and hopping, swatted at Waugh and was appropriately caught behind. Suddenly, England, 75 for 5, faced the humiliating prospect of failing to save the follow-on. Botham, full of determination, and Russell, showing all the resource he had shown at Lord's, added 96 invaluable runs, but both were out at the same score. Botham was too early into the drive against Hughes, and Russell edged high to slip. The bowler was Hohns, who was teasing and frustrating. Emburey was fortunate to survive, but survive he did until close of play, when England, 185 for 7, still needed to score 40 more runs to save the follow-on.

The last day began disastrously for England, when Fraser was run out in the first over, sent back after contemplating a rash single. Emburey looked as if he would score the required number of runs himself, but, 10 short of the safety mark, he hit a long-hop into the hands of mid-on. The watchful Dilley and the belligerent Jarvis did save the follow-on, the saving runs coming when Jarvis clouted the ball back over Lawson's head.

England were still afloat in the series, but only just. The afternoon of practice was noted for Botham's blinding catch that dismissed Taylor.

One of the happiest aspects of the Edgbaston Test. An MCC touring blazer which veteran Bob Wyatt had lost when he moved to Cornwall some years ago is returned to him by rival skippers David Gower and Allan Border. (Ken Kelly)

8, 9 and 10 July

at Dublin

Scotland 261 (B.M.W. Patterson 89, A.N. Nelson 5 for 27) and 193 (I.L. Philip 69, G.D. Harrison 6 for 75)
Ireland 249 (O. Henry 6 for 88) and 186 for 8 (O. Henry 7 for 86)

Match drawn

8, 10 and 11 July

at Swansea

Essex 174 (P.J. Prichard 81 not out, S.R. Barwick 5 for 59, S.L. Watkin 4 for 59) and 213 for 2 dec (B.R. Hardie 101 not out)
Glamorgan 65 (D.R. Pringle 7 for 18) and 134 (T.D. Topley 4 for 22)

Essex won by 188 runs
Essex 21 pts, Glamorgan 4 pts

at Maidstone

Gloucestershire 251 for 1 dec (A.J. Wright 118, I.P. Butcher 105 not out) and 207 for 6 dec (M.W. Alleyne 60 not out)
Kent 209 for 1 dec (M.R. Benson 102 not out) and 202 (S.A. Marsh 90 not out, M.C.J. Ball 4 for 53)

Gloucestershire won by 47 runs
Gloucestershire 19 pts, Kent 2 pts

at Lord's

Middlesex 223 (M.R. Ramprakash 65, D.E. Malcolm 4 for 111)

and 215 for 2 dec (I.J.F. Hutchinson 106, D.L. Haynes 80)
Derbyshire 177 for 5 dec (J.E. Morris 50) and 191 (P.D. Bowler 62, P.C.R. Tufnell 5 for 78)

Middlesex won by 70 runs
Middlesex 20 pts, Derbyshire 5 pts

at Northampton

Northamptonshire 166 (G. Cook 53, M.D. Marshall 4 for 20) and 253 (W. Larkins 97, R.J. Bailey 78, M.D. Marshall 5 for 36 P.J. Bakker 4 for 66)
Hampshire 366 for 6 dec (M.C.J. Nicholas 140, J.R. Wood 96 C.L. Smith 56) and 57 for 1

Hampshire won by 9 wickets
Hampshire 24 pts, Northamptonshire 2 pts

at Trent Bridge

Nottinghamshire 147 (T.A. Merrick 4 for 38) and 196 for 6 (B.C. Broad 63, D.W. Randall 56 not out)
Warwickshire 292 (T.A. Lloyd 100, P.A. Smith 68, J.A. Afford 4 for 74)

Match drawn
Warwickshire 7 pts, Nottinghamshire 4 pts

at Guildford

Surrey 177 (I.A. Greig 85 not out, A.N. Jones 5 for 62, V.J Marks 4 for 44) and 143 for 6
Somerset 297 (S.J. Cook 105, M.A. Feltham 4 for 108)

Match drawn
Somerset 6 pts, Surrey 3 pts

at Kidderminster

Leicestershire 180 (N.E. Briers 54, N.V. Radford 4 for 57) an 80 (S.M. McEwan 6 for 34)
Worcestershire 245 (S.J. Rhodes 73 not out, L.B. Taylor 4 fo 55) and 16 for 0

Worcestershire won by 10 wickets
Worcestershire 22 pts, Leicestershire 5 pts

at Middlesbrough

Yorkshire 260 for 8 dec (A.A. Metcalfe 64) and 0 for 0 dec
Sussex 0 for 0 dec and 252 (I.J. Gould 63, M.P. Speight 53, A. Sidebottom 5 for 56)

Yorkshire won by 8 runs
Yorkshire 19 pts, Sussex 3 pts

Worcestershire moved menacingly into second place in the Britannic Assurance County Championship when they disposed of Leicestershire at Kidderminster. Neale won the toss, asked the visitors to bat first and his seam bowlers Radford and McEwan bowled out Leicestershire for 180 on an abbreviated first day. On the Monday, a mid-order collapse saw Worcestershire slip from 83 for 1 to 130 for 8. The redoubtable Rhodes then found an able partner in Richard Illingworth, and the pair added 79. When Leicestershire batted again they collapsed before Steve McEwan, who produced a career-best bowling performance of 6 for 34. Leicestershire were 68 for 3 when McEwan bowled an amazing spell of 5 for 10 in 22 deliveries. The 27-year-old brisk medium-pace bowler had match figures of 9 for 87.

Essex made a remarkable recovery to overwhelm Glamorgan. Put in to bat when play eventually began on a lively pitch at 4.00 p.m. on Saturday afternoon, Essex collapsed to 101 for 8 in 41 overs before the close, but on the Monday Paul Prichard batted splendidly, and he and the courageous Childs shared a last-wicket stand of 62. When Glamorgan batted, Lever and Pringle bowled unchanged and the home side were shot out in 31.3 overs for a miserable 65. Pringle, leading Essex in the absence of Gooch, bowled his seamers with sustained accuracy and aggression to return the best bowling figures of his career, 7 for 18. It was the second time in the season that he had improved on his previous best. Essex romped to a substantial lead with Brian Hardie, ever-dependable, hitting his second hundred of the season. Glamorgan gave another inept performance against a varied attack which was excellently supported in the field. Essex's margin of victory, 188 runs, was a true reflection of the difference between the two sides.

Chris Cowdrey won the toss at Maidstone and asked Gloucestershire to bat first. As in all other matches, play was limited on the opening day, but on the Monday Wright and Ian Butcher took their first-wicket partnership to 236 before being separated. Chris Cowdrey kept the game alive by declaring as soon as Kent had gained a second batting point and Benson had reached his hundred. Athey eventually asked Kent to make 250. He was helped towards his declaration by some big hitting from Courtney Walsh, who hit 5 sixes in a whirlwind 47. Kent began wretchedly as they chased their target, losing their first five wickets for 23 runs. Chris Cowdrey and Steve Marsh added 93, and Richard Ellison aided Marsh in a stand of 54, but the last four wickets fell for 32 runs. Marsh was left unbeaten on 90, and the bowler who was most responsible for bringing about Gloucestershire's victory was the young off-spinner Ball.

Young left-arm spinner Phil Tufnell, a bowler of im-

Steve McEwan, a career-best bowling performance of 6 for 34 took Worcestershire to victory over Leicestershire at Kidderminster. McEwan's splendid form as deputy for Dilley, Radford or Botham played a vital part in Worcestershire's success and earned him his county cap at the end of the season. (Simon Bruty/Allsport)

mense promise, took Middlesex to victory over a motley Derbyshire side at Lord's. A delightful fifty by John Morris was the redeeming feature of the Derbyshire cricket. On the last day Ian Hutchinson hit his first championship hundred, but he was fed some laughable bowling in an attempt to encourage a declaration. Needing 272 to win, Derbyshire lost their way when Tufnell took three wickets in seven balls.

Ian Greig roused his side in the first innings with a belligerent 85 not out and saved them in the second, in spite of injury, when he and Feltham batted out time. Somerset had lacked enterprise in their cricket. Cook's century was a tedious affair, and Somerset's runs came at little more than two an over.

Nottinghamshire finished a shortened first day on 52 for 5 and made no effective recovery. Warwickshire skipper Andy Lloyd hit his first century of the season on the Monday and gave his side hope of recording their first championship win of the season, but, led by Broad and Randall, Nottinghamshire saved the match on the last day.

There was no play on the first day at Middlesbrough and both sides forfeited innings in an attempt to force a result. Yorkshire eventually set Sussex the task of scoring 261 in 62 overs. They were handicapped when Speight had to be

Scotland 1989
Limited-Over Matches

BATTING	v. Lancashire (Perth) 2 May (B&H)	v. Leicestershire (Leicester) 9 May (B&H)	v. Warwickshire (Edgbaston) 11 May (B&H)	v. Northamptonshire (Glasgow) 13 May (B&H)	v. Yorkshire (Leeds) 28 & 29 June (NW)	v. Australians (Glasgow) 15 July	Runs
I.L. Phillip	0	62	10	21	73	24	190
G.B.J. McGurk	5	5	29	0			39
R.G. Swan	2	1	40	40	6	8	97
C.E.B. Rice	2	0	2	0	29*		33
B.M.W. Patterson	7				39	70	116
O. Henry	58*	21	5	42	47*	3	176
D.L. Snodgrass	0			28	—	3	31
W. Morton	0	0*	—	18*			18
J.W. Govan	16			38*		32*	86
D.J. Haggo	0	0	—		—	7	7
D. Cowan	6*				—		6
A.C. Storie		4	6				10
M.J. Smith		12	21*	2		24	59
M.W. Burnett		3	6*				9
A.W. Bee		0	—				0
P.G. Duthie				—			—
A. Goram					—	4	4
J.D. Moir					—	14*	14
J.G. Williamson					—		
D.R. Brown						2	2
Byes	1		1				
Leg-byes	4	10	20	11	11	14	
Wides	9	3	18	6	2	4	
No-balls	1	7		1	3	1	
Total	111	128	158	207	210	210	
Wickets	9	10	6	7	3	9	
Result	L	L	L	L	L	L	
Points	0	0	0	0	—	—	

Fielding Figures 3 – D.J. Haggo and D.L. Snodgrass
2 – I.L. Phillip
1 – J.W. Govan, W. Morton, G.B.J. McGurk and R.G. Swan

BOWLING	C.E.B. Rice	D. Cowan	D.L. Snodgrass	J.W. Govan	W. Morton	O. Henry	A.W. Bee	M.J. Smith
v. Lancashire (Perth) 2 May (B&H)	5–1–11–0	5–0–18–0	8–0–25–1	6–1–24–0	6.2–1–24–2	5–2–7–0		
v. Leicestershire (Leicester) 9 May (B&H)	11–3–39–0				11–1–42–2	4–0–22–0	11–4–21–1	9–0–74–2
v. Warwickshire (Edgbaston) 11 May (B&H)	9–0–34–3				6–1–33–0		8–1–26–1	7.4–1–30–0
v. Northamptonshire (Glasgow) 13 May (B&H)	9–0–18–0		2–0–21–0	11–2–38–0	6–0–37–1	6–1–29–0		7.4–0–34–0
v. Yorkshire (Leeds) 28 & 29 June (NW)	11–4–27–0	11.5–1–47–2	2–0–8–2			12–1–35–2		
v. Australians (Glasgow) 15 July				5–0–44–0		11–0–70–0		11–0–53–0
Wickets	3	2	3	0	5	2	2	2

Derek Pringle was among the foremost bowlers in the country throughout the season and returned career-best bowling figures of 7 for 18 for Essex against Glamorgan at Swansea, 10 July. (Alan Cozzi)

More play was possible at Northampton on the first day than anywhere else, and Marshall gave Hampshire a firm grip on the match with a lively four-wicket spell. Having bowled out the home side for 166, Hampshire finished the day on 83 for 2, and on the Monday they took total charge. Mark Nicholas hit his first century of the season, and the left-handed Wood, playing in only his third first-class match, hit 96 and shared a fifth-wicket stand of 183. Larkins and Bailey kept Northamptonshire alive on the final day. Larkins put aside his usual flamboyant role to play a four-hour captain's innings which came close to saving his side. Bailey, too, batted with fluency, and the pair added 163 for the third wicket. The stand was broken by Nicholas, but it was Marshall, with a 44-ball spell either side of tea, in which he took 5 for 11, who broke the Northamptonshire innings. Hampshire won with 19 balls to spare.

Refuge Assurance League

9 July

at Neath

Essex 205 for 3 (M.E. Waugh 112 not out, B.R. Hardie 58)
Glamorgan 158 (R.J. Shastri 57)

Essex (4 pts) won by 47 runs

at Maidstone

Gloucestershire 85 (C. Penn 4 for 15)
Kent 86 for 4

Kent (4 pts) won by 6 wickets

at Lord's

Derbyshire 148 for 7
Middlesex 89 for 4

Middlesex (4 pts) won on faster scoring rate

taken to hospital for an X-ray on a finger, although he returned later to bat well. The main threat to the Sussex cause came from Sidebottom, who accounted for the Wells brothers in the space of three balls, and both without scoring. Ian Gould clumped the ball fiercely to keep Sussex's challenge alive, but he fell to Carrick, who also accounted for the dangerous Pigott. Yorkshire won with nine balls to spare when Fletcher dismissed Clarke and Babington with first and third balls of the penultimate over. In a nervous fielding display, Yorkshire were well served by wicket-keeper Blakey, who had taken over the position when a broken finger ruled out Bairstow for the rest of the season.

M.W. Burnett	P.G. Duthie	J.G. Williamson	J.D. Moir	A. Goram	D.R. Brown	Byes	Leg-byes	Wides	No-balls	Total	Wkts
						5	7	1		114	3
9–1–33–1						2	6	8	2	239	6
6–0–31–0						1	4	9		159	4
		3–0–21–0					12	1	2	210	1
		3–0–9–0	12–2–39–0	7–0–32–1		1	14	2	1	212	7
			11–3–33–5	6–0–30–0	11–0–68–2	4	5		5	307	7
1	0	0	5	1	2						

at Northampton

Northamptonshire 135 for 1 (N.A. Felton 58 not out, R.J. Bailey 53)
v. Hampshire

Match abandoned
Northamptonshire 2 pts, Hampshire 2 pts

at Trent Bridge

Warwickshire 139 (K. Saxelby 5 for 24)
Nottinghamshire 141 for 2

Nottinghamshire (4 pts) won by 8 wickets

at The Oval

Surrey 258 for 7 (A.J. Stewart 72, G.P. Thorpe 56)
Somerset 137 (K.T. Medlycott 4 for 45)

Surrey (4 pts) won by 121 runs

at Worcester

Leicestershire 156 for 9 (C.C. Lewis 50)
Worcestershire 157 for 4

Worcestershire (4 pts) won by 6 wickets

at Middlesbrough

Sussex 161 for 5 (M.P. Speight 60)
Yorkshire 151 for 8

Sussex (4 pts) won by 10 runs

With Lancashire idle, Essex increased their lead at the top of the Sunday league table to six points when they trounced Glamorgan at Neath. Hardie and Mark Waugh put on 117 in 26 overs for Essex's second wicket, and Waugh went on to score an unbeaten 112 off 125 balls. Essex savaged 94 from the last 10 overs. Maynard and Shastri gave Glamorgan a glimmer of hope, but it was never more than a glimmer.

Hampshire were thwarted by the weather, but Surrey and Worcestershire maintained a strong challenge. The game at Middlesbrough was restricted to 20 overs, and rain also reduced Middlesex's target at Lord's.

NatWest Bank Trophy

Round Two

12 July

at Cardiff

Glamorgan 189 (H. Morris 53)
Hampshire 190 for 3 (R.A. Smith 69 not out)

Hampshire won by 7 wickets
(Man of the Match: R.A. Smith)

at Gloucester

Gloucestershire 174 for 7 (P.J.W. Allott 4 for 31)
Lancashire 179 for 9

Lancashire won by 1 wicket
(Man of the Match: P.J.W. Allott)

at Canterbury

Warwickshire 272 for 5 (A.I. Kallicharran 93 not out, G.W. Humpage 65)
Kent 223 (M.R. Benson 64, C.S. Cowdrey 52)

Paul Allott – mighty deeds for Lancashire as they beat Gloucestershire in the second round of the NatWest Bank Trophy, 12 July. (George Herringshaw/ASP)

Warwickshire won by 49 runs
(Man of the Match: A.I. Kallicharran)

at Uxbridge

Middlesex 203 for 7 (P.R. Downton 69)
Nottinghamshire 167 (R.M. Ellcock 4 for 43)

Middlesex won by 36 runs
(Man of the Match: P.R. Downton)

at Taunton

Somerset 210 (C.J. Tavare 79, M.A. Robinson 4 for 32)
Northamptonshire 211 for 5 (R.J. Bailey 86 not out)

Northamptonshire won by 5 wickets
(Man of the Match: R.J. Bailey)

at The Oval

Surrey 256 for 4 (D.J. Bicknell 135 not out, D.M. Ward 80)
Yorkshire 255 for 9 (M.D. Moxon 59, M.P. Bicknell 4 for 49)

Surrey won by 1 run
(Man of the Match: D.J. Bicknell)

at Hove

Sussex 300 for 2 (P.W.G. Parker 87 not out, A.P. Wells 86 not out, D.M. Smith 59)
Leicestershire 232 (P. Willey 89, A.I.C. Dodemaide 4 for 37)

Sussex won by 68 runs
(Man of the Match: P.W.G. Parker)

at Worcester

Worcestershire 278 for 7 (S.J. Rhodes 61, I.T. Botham 53)
Derbyshire 240 (B. Roberts 64 not out, K.J. Barnett 55, R. Sharma 50, I.T. Botham 4 for 62)

Worcestershire won by 38 runs
(Man of the Match: I.T. Botham)

At Gloucester, Hughes won the toss, put Gloucestershire in to bat and was immediately rewarded with three wickets for 10 runs. The home side achieved some respectability through a cautious 47 from Kevin Curran, but their total of 174 did not look likely to trouble Lancashire. Batting was still a problem, however, and, when off-spinner Ball accounted for Hegg and DeFreitas with successive deliveries and then had Mendis caught, Lancashire were 123 for 4 in the 39th over. This became 147 for 7 in the 51st over, when Jarvis sent back Fairbrother, Jesty and Watkinson, and a tense finish was in prospect. Wasim Akram hit Bainbridge for six but was caught behind next ball, and Hughes fell to Curran to make it 168 for 9 in the 58th over. The last pair, Simmons and Allott, needed to score six from the last over to win. Four singles were scrambled before Allott was faced with the task of hitting the last ball of the match for two. He made quite sure of victory by pulling a mighty six over mid-wicket.

Robin Smith showed a welcome return after injury, and he and Nicholas shared an unbroken partnership of 102 to take Hampshire to victory with three overs to spare. Earlier Maru had frustrated Glamorgan by bowling his 12 overs for 19 runs and one wicket.

Warwickshire were somewhat surprising winners at Canterbury. Put in to bat, they flourished when Humpage and Kallicharran put on 109 in 25 overs for the third wicket, and later Dermot Reeve hit powerfully. Kent made a good start through Benson and Taylor, but the innings lost momentum as four wickets fell for 36 runs. Chris Cowdrey tried to breathe life into a dying cause, but his efforts were in vain.

Sussex gave an exhilarating batting display against Leicestershire as, of the four batsmen who got to the wicket, only Speight, 48, failed to reach 50. Dodemaide took two quick wickets when the visitors batted, and there was never any doubt as to who would win the tie.

Middlesex made an horrendous start against Nottinghamshire at Uxbridge. They lost openers Hutchinson and Haynes with only one scored, and Gatting and Ramprakash were also out before the score reached 40. It was the middle order of Carr, Downton and Emburey that gave the innings substance, and Downton's responsible 69 and his wicket-keeping were to win him the individual award. The Nottinghamshire innings began shakily, but Johnson and Randall raised hopes momentarily before the Middlesex pace attack again asserted superiority.

Although Tavare continued with his excellent one-day batting form, Somerset were bowled out for 210 in 55.4 overs at Taunton. Their innings was brought to an abrupt end by Robinson, who took three wickets in the space of nine deliveries. Adrian Jones gave his side a ray of hope when he had Cook caught at slip with his fourth ball, but Bailey and Felton righted matters. Jones was spoken to by umpire Julian for his verbal dissent after Bailey had been

Martin Bicknell, a most exciting young fast bowler, who shared the honours with his brother in Surrey's victory over Yorkshire, 12 July. (Tom Morris)

adjudged not out to an appeal for a catch behind. Jones was later cautioned and fined. Lamb's return to cricket after injury was brief, but both Capel and Ripley batted sensibly, and Northamptonshire moved to success with three overs to spare.

Ian Botham gave a remembrance of things past with an exciting all-round display for Worcestershire against Derbyshire. Put in to bat, Worcestershire lost Curtis at 46, but Rhodes, promoted to number three, batted with immediate authority. It was Botham at number six, however, who took Worcestershire to a commanding score. He hit Warner for 6, 4, 6, and then drove Newman for two more sixes. He moved from 16 to 50 off nine deliveries. He was then quickly among the wickets, sending back Bowler and Morris. There was some spirited middle-order batting from Sharma and Roberts, but Derbyshire were never really in the hunt. The main reason for their defeat was some poor fielding. Four catches, none of them difficult, went begging early in the day, and they were to pay dearly for these errors.

The match at The Oval began in rather distressing circumstances, when Clinton collapsed at the wicket in the third over of the day. He was taken to hospital, where no illness was diagnosed, but he was forbidden to take any further part in the match. Darren Bicknell did not allow this shock to disturb his concentration and was soon playing a wide range of authoritative shots. Stewart insanely ran himself out, and the promising Thorpe fell to Moxon, who bowled well. The soft belly of the Yorkshire bowling was Fletcher and later the erratic Jarvis, and both were savaged mercilessly. Ward helped Darren Bicknell to add 141 in 31 overs, and Ian Greig played a couple of lusty blows before skying a ball from Jarvis. Darren Bicknell carried out his bat for 135, a most worthy innings which rightly earned him the individual award. Yorkshire began most confidently, and Moxon and Metcalfe had 100 on the board after 29 overs. The younger of the Bicknell brothers, Martin, returned to dismiss them both. Blakey, Byas, Sharp and Neil Hartley all promised more than they achieved. Hartley and Carrick raised hopes of a Yorkshire victory, but Martin Bicknell claimed both of them in his final spell and, when Sidebottom fell to Murphy in the 56th over, Yorkshire looked a beaten side. Jarvis hit Feltham for six and was bowled next ball to make Yorkshire 228 for 9, 29 runs short of their target, with 20 balls remaining. Fletcher, not a noted batsman, suddenly began to lay about him, and 13 runs came from the 58th over. Seven, including a leg-bye, came from the next, so that when the last over began Yorkshire needed eight runs to win. Murphy kept the ball right in the block-hole, and Fletcher and Swallow could scramble only five from the first five deliveries. The final ball was again well up to the bat, and Swallow could only squirt it away on the leg side to leave Surrey victors by one run.

15 July

at Glasgow (Hamilton Crescent)

Australians 307 for 7 (M.R.J. Veletta 101, T.M. Moody 101, D.J. Moir 5 for 33)
Scotland 210 for 9 (B.M. Patterson 70)

Australians won by 97 runs

Jerry Moir, the pace bowler from Aberdeen who is close to seven feet tall, took five wickets, but the main honour in this 55-over game went to Veletta and Moody, who put on 184 for the second wicket. Jim Govan hit 3 fours in the final over to take a brave Scotland side past 200. Jerry Moir is the twin brother of Dallas Moir, the former Derbyshire spin bowler.

Benson and Hedges Cup Final
ESSEX v. NOTTINGHAMSHIRE

Glorious sunshine and a capacity crowd welcomed the season's first domestic highlight, the 18th Benson and Hedges Cup Final. Gooch won the toss and Essex batted first. Essex had chosen Miller ahead of Childs, and this was a decision that was to cost them dearly. For their part, Nottinghamshire played two spinners and omitted Saxelby.

There was an early shock for Essex when Hardie seemed to lose sight of a slower ball from Stephenson, operating from the Pavilion End. He offered no shot, and the ball flattened his off stump. Lilley gave Gooch solid

TOP: *Early delight for Nottinghamshire – Brian Hardie is bowled by Franklyn Stephenson's slower ball. (Adrian Murrell/Allsport)*

ABOVE: *Gooch falls to an inglorious shot. (USPA)*

support without ever suggesting command or confidence. Robinson used his spinners, and Afford, bowling at the Nursery End, showed an ability to turn the ball, although not always to maintain accuracy. Gooch had just seemed to have got the measure of him, when he aimed to hit a ball through mid-wicket and was bowled. The delivery was a long-hop, and very similar to one which Waugh later hit for six, but it came through too slow and too low for Gooch's rather wild shot.

Mark Waugh, capped on the eve of the game, was upright, authoritative and clean-hitting, yet, like so much of the Essex innings, his knock was not totally satisfactory. He suggested so much more than he achieved, before hitting Evans limply to mid-wicket after he and Lilley had put on 82. Waugh had survived one glaring stumping chance when he charged at Afford, the ball hitting French on the shoulder, and his 41 had come off 58 balls.

TOP LEFT: *Mark Waugh escapes as French misses the chance of a stumping. (Adrian Murrell/Allsport)*

ABOVE: *Essex stalwart Alan Lilley looking for runs. (USPA)*

TOP RIGHT: *Paul Johnson – the end of a fighting innings. (Adrian Murrell/Allsport)*

RIGHT: *The end of an innings that brought victory within the reach of Nottinghamshire, Tim Robinson is run out. (Adrian Murrell/Allsport)*

Prichard went quickly after lunch, and both Stephenson and Pringle were run out, the first by Lilley, the second by himself. Garnham also went cheaply in the final dash, and much rested on Lilley. He had done an admirable job, but he had never attained fluency, and at a time when Essex were looking to put the game out of Nottinghamshire's reach, he still found run-scoring a difficult task. His place in the order at number three cast another doubt on Essex's tactics and preparation for the match. For some years Alan Lilley, a brilliant fielder and a fine team man, has been only a fringe member of the Essex side, and had Hussain not been cup-tied, Lilley would not have played in the final. 'Why then,' Trevor Bailey asked, 'was a lesser batsman batting ahead of better batsmen, one of whom was an opener, in a limited-over game?'

Essex's total was adequate rather than daunting, and that it was restricted to 243 was thanks to some excellent fielding by Nottinghamshire, and to good support bowling by Evans and Hemmings.

If Essex's total had not seemed too vast, it soon took immense proportions as Lever accounted for both Pollard and Broad and the first 10 overs produced only 17 runs. Neither Robinson nor Johnson was able to disrupt the superiority of Foster and Lever, but the advent of Miller gave them the encouragement that they needed. So loose was Miller's bowling that Essex immediately surrendered the initiative. Miller was hit for 13 in one over, and 25 came from his first five. Gooch also conceded 11 in one over, and one sighed for what Childs might have achieved at this stage. The Nottinghamshire players revealed afterwards that they felt that his absence turned the game in their favour.

Johnson, wearing an ankle brace to support the bone he had fractured four weeks earlier, and Robinson added 132

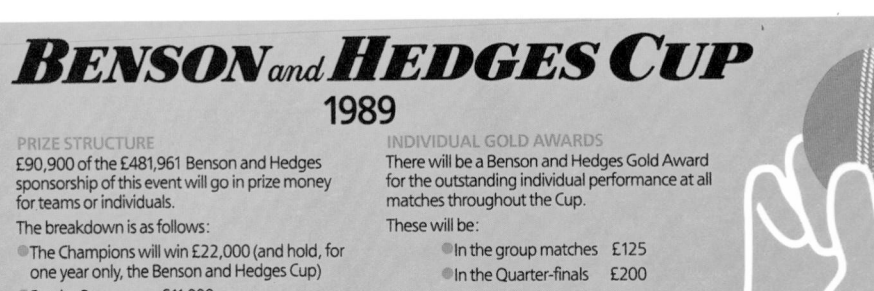

BENSON and HEDGES CUP
1989

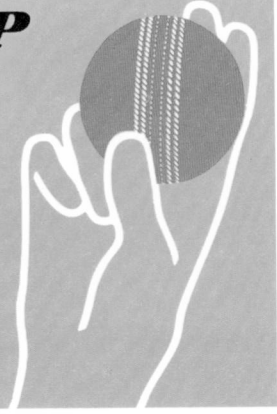

PRIZE STRUCTURE
£90,900 of the £481,961 Benson and Hedges sponsorship of this event will go in prize money for teams or individuals.

The breakdown is as follows:
- The Champions will win £22,000 (and hold, for one year only, the Benson and Hedges Cup)
- For the Runners-up £11,000
- For the losing Semi-finalists £5,250
- For the losing Quarter-finalists £2,625

ADDITIONAL TEAM AWARDS
The winners of all matches in the group stages of the Cup will receive £750.

INDIVIDUAL GOLD AWARDS
There will be a Benson and Hedges Gold Award for the outstanding individual performance at all matches throughout the Cup.

These will be:
- In the group matches £125
- In the Quarter-finals £200
- In the Semi-finals £275
- In the Final £550

The playing conditions and Cup records are on the reverse.

HOLDERS: HAMPSHIRE COUNTY CRICKET CLUB

MARYLEBONE CRICKET CLUB

20p   20p

FINAL
ESSEX v. NOTTINGHAMSHIRE
at Lord's Ground, Saturday, July 15th, 1989

Any alterations to teams will be announced over the public address system

ESSEX
†1 G. A. Gooch	b Afford	48
2 B. R. Hardie	b Stephenson	0
3 A. W. Lilley	not out	95
4 M. E. Waugh	c Robinson b Evans	41
5 P. J. Prichard	l b w b Cooper	1
6 J. P. Stephenson	run out	9
7 D. R. Pringle	run out	15
*8 M. A. Garnham	c Johnson b Evans	0
9 N. A. Foster	not out	2
10 G. Miller		
11 J. K. Lever		
B 1, l-b 26, w 4, n-b 1,		32
	Total...	243

FALL OF THE WICKETS
1...4 2...74 3...156 4...162 5...185 6...220 7...235 8... 9... 10...

Bowling Analysis	O.	M.	R.	W.	Wd.	N-b
Stephenson	11	0	61	1	...	1
Cooper	11	3	30	1	2	...
Evans	11	0	28	2	2	...
Afford	11	0	50	1	...	...
Hemmings	11	0	47	0	...	...

NOTTINGHAMSHIRE
1 B. C. Broad	c Garnham b Lever	6
2 P. Pollard	l b w b Lever	2
†3 R. T. Robinson	run out	86
4 P. Johnson	b Foster	54
5 D. W. Randall	c Waugh b Pringle	49
6 F. D. Stephenson	c Gooch b Miller	0
7 K. P. Evans	run out	26
*8 B. N. French	not out	8
9 E. E. Hemmings	not out	6
10 K. E. Cooper		
11 J. A. Afford		
B 1, l-b 3, w 2, n-b 1,		7
	Total...	244

FALL OF THE WICKETS
1...5 2...17 3...149 4...162 5...162 6...221 7...234 8... 9... 10...

Bowling Analysis	O.	M.	R.	W.	Wd.	N-b
Lever	11	2	43	2	1	...
Foster	11	1	40	1	...	...
Gooch	11	0	57	0	...	...
Pringle	11	1	38	1	...	1
Miller	9	0	50	1	1	...
Stephenson	2	0	12	0	...	...

† Captain   * Wicket-keeper

Umpires—K. E. Palmer & D. R. Shepherd

Scorers—C. F. Driver, L. Beaumont & E. Solomon

Toss won by—Essex

RESULT—Nottinghamshire won by 3 wickets

The playing conditions for the Benson & Hedges Cup Competition are printed on the back of this score card.

Total runs scored at end of each over :—

Essex
	1	2	3	4	5	6	7	8	9	10	11	12	13	14	15	16	17	18	19	20
	21	22	23	24	25	26	27	28	29	30	31	32	33	34	35	36	37	38	39	40
	41	42	43	44	45	46	47	48	49	50	51	52	53	54	55					

Notts.
	1	2	3	4	5	6	7	8	9	10	11	12	13	14	15	16	17	18	19	20
	21	22	23	24	25	26	27	28	29	30	31	32	33	34	35	36	37	38	39	40
	41	42	43	44	45	46	47	48	49	50	51	52	53	54	55					

Reproduced by kind permission of MCC

ABOVE: *Andy Afford bowled Gooch and showed the power of the spinner in the limited-over game. Lilley is the batsman. (Adrian Murrell/Allsport)*

ABOVE RIGHT: *Derek Randall as exuberant as ever. (David Munden)*

RIGHT: *'The greatest day of my life', Tim Robinson holds the Benson and Hedges Cup and signals triumphantly to the Nottinghamshire supporters. (Adrian Murrell/Allsport)*

in 29 overs. It was a stand that transformed a seemingly beaten side into one with the scent of victory in their nostrils. Nottinghamshire had needed 185 to win from 30 overs, but 63 in the next 10 brought the target to within a measurable distance. Johnson was out in a strange manner. He walked down the wicket to Foster, seemingly offered no shot and was bowled off his boot.

Robinson had batted as well as one can remember seeing him bat. He gave the match a sense of style, occasion and urgency, and while he was at the wicket Nottinghamshire looked likely winners. He and Randall showed no slackening of the run rate, but Randall was at his most fidgety. He called Robinson for an improbable single, and the Nottinghamshire captain was beaten by Stephenson's throw to the wicket-keeper. It was a wretched waste and a sad end to a quite beautifully positive innings.

Stephenson lofted the next ball tamely to Gooch at mid-on, and the game had swung dramatically back in favour of Essex.

It is really bread and butter cricketers who win club trophies, and so it was to be with Nottinghamshire when Kevin Evans, who had contributed so decisively with the

ball, helped Randall to restore the tenor of the innings. In 10 overs, they added 59 to take Nottinghamshire to within striking distance of their goal. Evans was run out when Prichard fielded finely in front of the pavilion, and Gooch gathered and broke the wicket as Evans attempted a third run.

Randall was twice dropped, and the Essex fielding throughout, like most of their cricket, was below their usual high standard. At times, indeed, it was slovenly. Evans had fallen in the 53rd over, and Randall was out to the fifth ball of the penultimate over when he hit high and rashly to leg. Nine runs were needed from the last over. John Lever, in the last of his 23 seasons in first-class cricket, was the bowler.

Scrambled singles, a bye to the wicket-keeper, two to the Tavern boundary, and a ball from which nothing could be scored and which drew a roar of approval, brought Hemmings to face the last ball with Nottinghamshire needing four for victory. At this point the odds were very

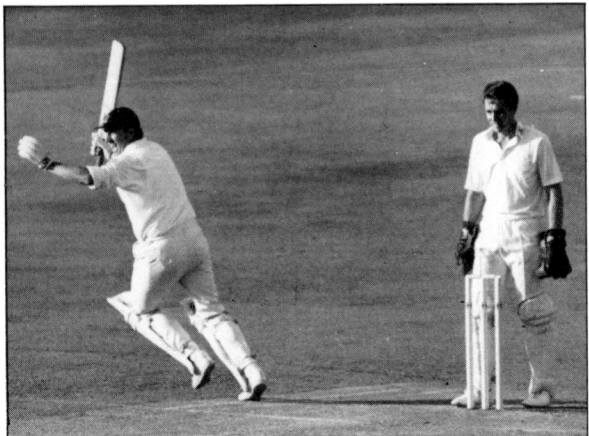

Hemmings wheels away as he hits Lever's last ball of the match for four to give victory to Nottinghamshire. Garnham looks stunned. (Adrian Murrell/Allsport)

much in favour of an Essex victory, but Gooch, in consultation with his entire team, took over three minutes to set a field for the final delivery, and even then he did not have four players in the circle when Lever was ready to bowl.

The non-committed in the crowd were angered by the delay, and Essex were roundly and rightly booed. Some of the field changes were hard to accept, notably the banishment of Lilley, one of the fleetest and most able of the Essex fielders, from the off side to fine-leg. The boundary fielders were packed on the leg side, while the off was left comparatively untenanted. Lever essayed a leg-stump yorker, but Hemmings, giving himself room, sliced the ball past Hardie, square at cover and just inside the circle. Hardie went after the ball in hot pursuit, but it had strength enough to beat him to the rope in front of the Grand Stand, and Nottinghamshire had won a famous and deserved victory.

The veteran and most popular Hemmings and his partner French did a dance of joy in the middle of the pitch before being engulfed by excited fans. Robinson said later that it was most probably the best day of his cricketing life, and Ted Dexter gave him the Gold Award for his innings of 86, a knock of charm and quality.

Refuge Assurance League

16 July

at Trowbridge

Gloucestershire 184 for 8 (M.C.J. Nicholas 4 for 30)
Hampshire 163 (K.D. James 66)

Gloucestershire (4 pts) won by 21 runs

at Canterbury

Derbyshire 164
Kent 139 (M.A. Holding 4 for 18)

Derbyshire (4 pts) won by 25 runs

at Old Trafford

Northamptonshire 133
Lancashire 136 for 7 (G. Fowler 53 not out)

Lancashire (4 pts) won by 3 wickets

at Leicester

Nottinghamshire 182 for 8 (B.C. Broad 71)
Leicestershire 146 (K. Saxelby 6 for 30)

Nottinghamshire (4 pts) won by 36 runs

at Taunton

Somerset 249 for 6 (S.J. Cook 114, P.M. Roebuck 63 not out)
Glamorgan 168 for 8 (V.J. Marks 4 for 27)

Somerset (4 pts) won by 81 runs

at The Oval

Surrey 225 for 4 (A.J. Stewart 100 not out)
Sussex 201 for 8 (I.J. Gould 84 not out)

Surrey (4 pts) won by 24 runs

at Scarborough

Yorkshire 204 for 7 (K. Sharp 80)
Worcestershire 208 for 4 (T.S. Curtis 79, I.T. Botham 68)

Worcestershire (4 pts) won by 6 wickets

Kevin Saxelby, relegated to twelfth man for the Benson and Hedges Cup Final, gave a statement of his qualities when he returned his career-best Sunday league bowling figures, 6 for 30, to give Nottinghamshire a celebratory victory over Leicestershire. Lancashire moved to within two points of Essex although they laboured somewhat in beating Northamptonshire. Needing 134 to win, they lost seven wickets for 114 runs before Fowler found a resolute partner in Austin. Alec Stewart led a violent assault on the Sussex bowling at The Oval and reached a century as Surrey plundered 126 runs from the last 12 overs to put the game out of the reach of the visitors. Surrey's win took them into fourth place, while Worcestershire maintained third place with a thrilling win at Scarborough. Curtis and Botham put on 138 in 28 overs as Worcestershire went in search of 205 to win. The reigning champions then lost their way, and the final over arrived with seven runs still needed. Neale drove Pickles through the covers for four off the first ball. The next ball was a wide, but three more deliveries yielded only a single before D'Oliveira sliced to cover. So the scores were level when Pickles bowled the last ball to Neale. The bowler essayed a slowish yorker on leg stump, but Neale turned it into a full toss and glanced it for four.

17 July

at Trowbridge

Australians 229 for 4 (G.R. Marsh 110, D.C. Boon 61)
Minor Counties 202 (N.A. Folland 51)

Australians won by 27 runs

Australians won this pleasant 55-over contest easily enough, but lost Mike Veletta through a broken finger in the process. Carl Rackemann, returning after his knee operation, bowled his 11 overs in comfort.

19, 20 and 21 July

at Southend

Kent 112 (D.R. Pringle 6 for 42) and 229 (T.R. Ward 91, D.R. Pringle 4 for 60)
Essex 347 (N. Hussain 127, A.P. Igglesden 4 for 66, H.L. Alleyne 4 for 92)

Essex won by an innings and 6 runs
Essex 24 pts, Kent 3 pts

at Bristol

Glamorgan 89 (K.B.S. Jarvis 5 for 15, V.S. Greene 4 for 36) and 171 (V.S. Greene 6 for 101)
Gloucestershire 383 for 9 dec (P. Bainbridge 98, M.W. Alleyne 88, A.J. Wright 85)

Gloucestershire won by an innings and 123 runs
Gloucestershire 23 pts, Glamorgan 3 pts

at Old Trafford

Worcestershire 191 (P.A. Neale 62, B.P. Patterson 4 for 61) and 199 (I.T. Botham 73, M. Watkinson 7 for 69)
Lancashire 125 (G.R. Dilley 5 for 30) and 229 (G.D. Mendis 70, M.A. Atherton 59, G.R. Dilley 5 for 94)

Worcestershire won by 36 runs
Worcestershire 21 pts, Lancashire 4 pts

at Leicester

Northamptonshire 198 (N.A. Stanley 75, G.J. Parsons 4 for 56) and 312 for 7 dec (G. Cook 105, D.J. Capel 77, R.J. Bailey 52)
Leicestershire 300 (J.J. Whitaker 99, D.I. Gower 50, C.E.L. Ambrose 5 for 52) and 206 for 7 (D.I. Gower 91, N.G.B. Cook 4 for 54)

Match drawn
Leicestershire 6 pts, Northamptonshire 3 pts

at Trent Bridge

Somerset 186 (S.J. Cook 120 not out, M.G. Field-Buss 4 for 33) and 218 (S.J. Cook 131 not out, P.M. Roebuck 50, J.A. Afford 5 for 90, F.D. Stephenson 4 for 60)
Nottinghamshire 471 for 7 dec (R.T. Robinson 128, P. Pollard 91, B.C. Broad 70, B.N. French 55 not out, K.P. Evans 51 not out, H.R.J. Trump 4 for 130)

Nottinghamshire won by an innings and 67 runs
Nottinghamshire 24 pts, Somerset 2 pts

at Leeds

Yorkshire 179 (R.M. Ellcock 5 for 35) and 189 (A.A. Metcalfe 81, A.R.C. Fraser 5 for 47)
Middlesex 294 (M.R. Ramprakash 128, A. Sidebottom 6 for 79) and 75 for 7 (A. Sidebottom 4 for 32)

Middlesex won by 3 wickets
Middlesex 23 pts, Yorkshire 4 pts

at Southampton

Australians 343 for 6 dec (S.R. Waugh 112, D.C. Boon 103) and 246 (S.R. Waugh 67, T.V. Hohns 58 not out, R.J. Maru 5 for 44)
Hampshire 275 for 6 dec (M.C.J. Nicholas 102 not out, J.R. Wood 65) and 81 for 0

Match drawn

Few overseas cricketers can have made such an impact in their first season in county cricket as Somerset's South

Jim Cook, a century in each innings for Somerset against Nottinghamshire at Trent Bridge, 19–21 July, and the most prolific run-getter in English cricket in 1989. (George Herringshaw/ASP)

African opening batsman Jim Cook. A century in the Sunday league game against Glamorgan was followed by a not out century in each innings of the match against Nottinghamshire at Trent Bridge, where his side was beaten by an innings. It was only the second time in the history of the game that a batsman had carried his bat through each innings while scoring a century. He batted for nine hours five minutes in the match, and hit 251 of Somerset's 404 runs. In the second innings, Somerset lost their last eight wickets for 39 runs, and Cook and Roebuck had given them a splendid start in an effort to save the match by putting on 127. Nottinghamshire, too, had their heroes. Michael Field-Buss, deputizing for the injured Hemmings, returned the best bowling figures of his career with his off-breaks. Broad and Pollard began the Nottinghamshire innings with a partnership of 159. Robinson scored 128 of the 195 runs scored while he was at the wicket, and there were late, bright contributions from Evans and French.

For Glamorgan troubles were coming heaped one upon another. Rodney Ontong had been forced to retire from first-class cricket because of injury, and now Hugh Morris announced that he was relinquishing the captaincy. Alan Butcher was named as his successor. Glamorgan, with spirits very low, were bowled out for 89 and 171 and lost by an innings to Gloucestershire, for whom Vibert Greene had match figures of 10 for 137. It was the first occasion on which he had taken 10 wickets in a match.

Ricardo Ellcock, Middlesex's surprise signing from Worcestershire shortly before the start of the season, produced the best figures of his career on the opening day at Headingley when, on a pitch of doubtful quality, Yorkshire were bowled out for 179. The second day belonged to the talented young Mark Ramprakash, who showed tenacity and great powers of concentration as he registered his maiden first-class century. The Middlesex innings was also boosted by the eccentric batting of John Emburey, who clubbed a six and 9 fours in his 47 off 33 balls. Fraser's second-innings bowling appeared to have made a Middlesex victory a formality, for the visitors needed only 75 to win, and there was ample time in which they could score the runs. As Jarvis and Sidebottom tore into them on a pitch which had deteriorated rapidly, but which, ironically, was to escape censure, Middlesex slumped to 34 for 7, and the improbable looked distinctly possible. The determined Gatting at last found a useful ally in Fraser, and Middlesex scraped home with three wickets to spare.

Another pitch to cause some concern was the one at Old Trafford, where the ball flew so alarmingly on the opening day that five batsmen had to receive treatment, including Jesty, who was taken to hospital, and 19 wickets fell. Patterson, Allott, Dilley and Botham found particular enjoyment in the proceedings, and only the courage, sometimes tempered with discretion, of Neale gave any hint of permanence to the batting. On the second day, Botham hit 73 off 84 balls and helped to take Worcestershire's lead over Lancashire to 265. That it was not greater was thanks to fine seam bowling by Watkinson. Mendis and Atherton gave Lancashire every hope of victory, but once Mendis was caught off Botham the home side collapsed before Dilley, who was able to make the ball lift frighteningly, and the last six wickets fell for 24 runs.

Northamptonshire trailed by 102 runs on the first innings at Leicester, where the home side owed much to a pleasant knock by Whitaker, who was caught behind off Thomas one short of his century. Geoff Cook, Bailey and Capel brought Northamptonshire back into the game, and Lamb, whose injury prevented him from batting, declared and set Leicestershire to make 211 in 42 overs. Gower hit a brisk 91, and with seven wickets in hand and only 118 needed from the last 20 overs, Leicestershire seemed in sight of victory, but Gower fell to Bailey, and Nick Cook took four middle-order wickets. With five overs left, 42 runs were wanted, and eventually Leicestershire fell five runs, and Northamptonshire three wickets, short of their respective targets.

TCCB's inspector of pitches, Harry Brind, was called to Southchurch Park, where Essex beat Kent in two days to extend their lead at the top of the Britannic Assurance County Championship to 36 points. Brind said that the pitch was dry, and acknowledged that the groundsman had had difficulty in preparation because of the hot, dry weather, but he could hardly condemn a pitch on which 688 runs were scored in two days and on which Nasser

Ricardo Ellcock, who moved from Worcestershire to Middlesex and bowled with such pace and fire as to win a place in the party to tour West Indies. (USPA)

Hussain made an exciting hundred. A spiritless Kent side fell to Pringle on the opening day, and by close of play, Essex were already 76 ahead with five wickets in hand. Hussain led the later-order batsmen through difficult periods on the second morning and his confidence and willingness to take responsibility ensured Essex of maximum batting points. He then took a catch at short-leg off the first ball of the Kent second innings, and from that point, in spite of Ward's positive knock, the visitors were always struggling as Pringle moved towards 10 wickets in the match.

Waugh and Boon exploited a good wicket at Southampton to hit centuries, and Nicholas responded for Hampshire, but the Australians' game against the southern county always looked likely to be drawn.

22, 23 and 24 July

at Bristol

Gloucestershire 200 (T.M. Alderman 4 for 39, G.D. Campbell 4 for 47) and 92 (G.F. Lawson 6 for 30)
Australians 438 (D.M. Jones 167 not out, M.A. Taylor 141)

Australians won by an innings and 146 runs

22, 24 and 25 July

at Derby

Glamorgan 191 (M.A. Holding 6 for 57) and 241 (M.A.

Holding 4 for 66)
Derbyshire 338 (J.E. Morris 134, P.D. Bowler 53) and 97 for 1 (K.J. Barnett 51 not out)

Derbyshire won by 9 wickets
Derbyshire 23 pts, Glamorgan 4 pts

at Southend

Yorkshire 115 (T.D. Topley 5 for 46) and 239 (N.A. Foster 4 for 94)
Essex 248 (J.P. Stephenson 85, P.W. Jarvis 6 for 76) and 107 for 7 (A. Sidebottom 4 for 48)

Essex won by 3 wickets
Essex 22 pts, Yorkshire 4 pts

at Uxbridge

Middlesex 458 for 1 dec (D.L. Haynes 206 not out, I.J.F. Hutchinson 177)
Kent 164 and 231 for 9 (N.R. Taylor 99, A.R.C. Fraser 4 for 23)

Match drawn
Middlesex 8 pts, Kent 1 pt

at Portsmouth

Lancashire 475 for 4 dec (N.H. Fairbrother 159, G. Fowler 130, T.E. Jesty 71 not out) and 147 for 6 dec (T.E. Jesty 73 not out)
Hampshire 336 for 4 dec (R.A. Smith 119 not out, C.L. Smith 66) and 287 for 7 (C.L. Smith 97, V.P. Terry 95, I.D. Austin 4 for 60)

Hampshire won by 3 wickets
Hampshire 21 pts, Lancashire 5 pts

at Northampton

Northamptonshire 322 (A. Fordham 84, W. Larkins 78, J.A. Afford 4 for 79) and 174 for 9 dec (D.J. Capel 51, J.A. Afford 4 for 30, F.D. Stephenson 4 for 52)
Nottinghamshire 289 (B.C. Broad 76, R.T. Robinson 68, B.N. French 51 not out) and 147

Northamptonshire won by 60 runs
Northamptonshire 23 pts, Nottinghamshire 6 pts

at Taunton

Somerset 449 (S.J. Cook 148, R.J. Bartlett 54)
Leicestershire 250 (T.J. Boon 51) and 152 (G.D. Rose 4 for 35)

Somerset won by an innings and 47 runs
Somerset 23 pts, Leicestershire 3 pts

at Hove

Worcestershire 320 (T.S. Curtis 102, M.J. Weston 70, N.V. Radford 66 not out) and 230 for 4 dec (G.A. Hick 110 not out, D.B. D'Oliveira 55)
Sussex 301 (C.M. Wells 81, P.W.G. Parker 66, I.T. Botham 7 for 85) and 250 for 6 (P.W.G. Parker 86)

Sussex won by 4 wickets
Sussex 22 pts, Worcestershire 6 pts

The Australians brushed aside Gloucestershire in two days, with Geoff Lawson striking his best form of the tour on the eve of the fourth Test match. Taylor and Jones hit centuries and added 227 for the fourth wicket, Taylor becoming the first of the tourists to reach a thousand runs in the season.

Put in to bat at Derby, Glamorgan, their morale and fortunes at low ebb, were bowled out by Holding and Malcolm. Derbyshire lost Barnett at 2, but Bowler and Morris put on 125. Morris continued in his rich vein of batting form with another century of quality. Overcoming the problems of a sluggish pitch, he hit 16 fours and reached his century off 184 balls. He perished as he tried to win his side a fourth batting point when others were struggling. Glamorgan offered sterner resistance when they batted for a second time, but their last five wickets fell for 50 runs, and Holding finished with match figures of 10 for 123. With ample time in which to score the necessary runs, Derbyshire moved to their second championship win of the season without trouble.

Middlesex were thwarted at Uxbridge after having the game totally in their command from the first day, on which Hutchinson and Haynes shared an opening stand of 361. Haynes reached the first double century of his career on the Monday, and Kent duly succumbed with little sign of resistance. Following-on, they lost Hinks before the close of the second day, and Ward, Longley and Chris Cowdrey went early on the last morning so that, at 65 for 4, Kent faced defeat. Taylor batted 5½ hours for a defiant 99. He faced 321 balls, hit 16 fours and made no hint of an error. He was finally bowled by Fraser, the ball keeping low, and the last pair, Ellison and Alleyne, survived the final three overs to save the game and restore some self-esteem to Kent cricket.

Like Middlesex, Lancashire scored heavily on the opening day but failed to win the match. Mendis and Fowler hit centuries and combined in a third-wicket partnership of 144. Runs came at four an over, and Hughes was happy to declare on his side's Saturday evening score. On the Monday, Robin Smith confirmed his return to full fitness with his fourth championship hundred of the season. He was given capable support by his elder brother, Chris. Having avoided the follow-on, Hampshire declared 139 runs in arrears, and they soon reasserted themselves by capturing six Lancashire wickets for 96 runs. Jesty scored brightly and briskly, and Hughes declared, leaving Hampshire to score 287 in 65 overs. They cruised to 188 before Terry fell to Watkinson; this was the first of five wickets to fall for 29 runs. Marshall set Hampshire back on course with a violent innings of 48 off 37 balls, and victory came with 11 balls to spare.

Northamptonshire, for so long title contenders, ended a bleak period with a win over Nottinghamshire. They set the visitors the moderate target of 208 in 48 overs and bowled them out with 20 balls to spare.

Jim Cook became the first Somerset batsman to score four first-class hundreds in succession when he hit 148 against Leicestershire. In the space of 13 days he had scored 504 runs in first-class matches alone. His century against Leicestershire was his seventh in first-class games and his 10th in all competitions during the season. It took Somerset to a commanding position, which they did not relinquish over the next two days.

Lord suffered a broken knee-cap at Hove, but his opening partner, Curtis, played a durable innings, and Worcestershire, with a late flourish from Radford, batted until Monday to reach 320. Ian Botham produced his best bowling performance in the championship for 11 years, but Dilley had a dreadful day, conceding 62 runs in nine wayward overs, and Sussex were able to come within 19 runs of the Worcestershire score. On the last morning,

Hick hit his fourth century of the season and passed 1,000 runs. He and the neat D'Oliveira added 144 for the third wicket. Neale's declaration meant that Sussex had 51 overs in which to score 250 runs. A sparkling 86 off 87 balls by skipper Parker seemed to set Sussex on course for victory, but they fell further and further behind the asking rate and needed 100 off the last 10 overs. With two overs left, and Pigott and Dodemaide batting, 23 runs were needed. Dodemaide hit a six off his first ball, and when the last over began 12 runs were needed. This was reduced to two from the final ball, which Pigott swung high. In going for the catch Radford misfielded, and the batsmen went through for two runs to win the match. Pigott's 27 came from 13 deliveries.

In spite of losing at Hove, Worcestershire remained in second place, and, indeed, the Essex lead over them was reduced to 27 points. This came about because of the unfortunate events at Southchurch Park, Southend where, incidentally, more than 25,000 people paid to watch cricket during the festival week. Yorkshire won the toss and batted first on the Saturday. They were bowled out shortly after lunch for 115, the Essex seam attack of Foster, Pringle and Topley being in dominant mood. Only one batsman, Carrick caught at short-leg first ball off Topley, could lay any blame on the wicket for his dismissal. Yorkshire were bowled out because they batted poorly and without confidence while Essex, supremely confident, bowled and caught well. The wicket began to show signs of deterioration as the day wore on, but Jarvis bowled as inconsistently and as inaccurately as he had done for England, and he was severely punished by the eager Stephenson. Essex, 205 for 8 on the Saturday evening, took their score to 248 on the Monday. Their last two wickets realized 60 runs as Pringle and Topley hit well. Moxon and Metcalfe began Yorkshire's second innings with a stand of 56 after which the later batsmen struggled to survive against Childs, became becalmed and succumbed to the seam bowlers. Another large crowd flocked to see the last day although the state of the game promised them little play. In fact, they had a share of excitement as Essex, needing 107 to win, lost six wickets for 61 runs before Hussain and Pringle ended the nervousness.

Ken Palmer and Nigel Plews, the umpires, had again reported the wicket on the Monday, and the committee responsible for decisions on sub-standard wickets gathered at Southend on the Tuesday. It was the first time that the committee had met. If Harry Brind had accepted the reasons for the dryness and less than perfect state of the wicket two days earlier, it was difficult to understand how those same reasons were no longer valid. The pitch was not under the direct control of Essex County Cricket Club, but was prepared by the Southend Borough Council. Although Essex were held to be innocent of any malpractice and were not held responsible for the state of the Southchurch Park wicket, they were punished by the deduction of 25 points, a shattering blow to their championship aspirations.

That the Southchurch Park wicket was not up to the standard expected for a first-class match is undeniable. Southend Cricket Club themselves had complained bitterly that, although the Borough Council was constantly

raising the charges, the standard of pitches that were being provided for the Club was deteriorating. At one period, they had been expected to play on the same strip for three matches in succession. What angered the Essex Club, however, was that the standard of the pitch at Southend for the Yorkshire game was no worse than they had encountered elsewhere, and that culprits at county grounds at Headingley, Northampton, Worcester and Old Trafford had gone unpunished. Essex's 248 in the first innings against Yorkshire, for example, was two runs more than Worcestershire had made in any first-class game at New Road, where only Warwickshire, at the beginning of July, had passed 250. It seemed that the reigning champions had made themselves immune from punishment by declaring after the early season debacle with the Australians that they were having trouble with their pitch and were calling on Brind for advice.

The other factor, given credibility by *The Times*' cricket correspondent's furthering of the theme, was that Southend had been picked upon because it was a festival ground rather than a county ground and that it was likely to be one of those grounds at which first-class cricket would cease to be played if some at the TCCB had their way and reduced the County Championship to 16 four-day matches, a scheme which has all the popularity and appeal of the Channel Tunnel.

The incident at Southend was one which was to sour the tone of the rest of the season and to cast a shadow on the Britannic Assurance County Championship.

Refuge Assurance League

23 July

at Heanor

Glamorgan 243 for 3 (A. Dale 67 not out, M.P. Maynard 61 retired hurt)
Derbyshire 245 for 1 (K.J. Barnett 100 not out, J.E. Morris 100 not out)

Derbyshire (4 pts) won by 9 wickets

at Southend

Yorkshire 213 for 6 (R.J. Blakey 66 not out, K. Sharp 50)
Essex 217 for 2 (G.A. Gooch 106 not out, M.E. Waugh 62)

Essex (4 pts) won by 8 wickets

at Portsmouth

Hampshire 166 for 9 (M.C.J. Nicholas 50)
Lancashire 168 for 4 (T.E. Jesty 51)

Lancashire (4 pts) won by 6 wickets

at Finedon

Northamptonshire 173 (K. Saxelby 5 for 45)
Nottinghamshire 149 (D.J.R. Martindale 53)

Northamptonshire (4 pts) won by 24 runs

at Lord's

Kent 211 for 7 (C.S. Cowdrey 78, J.I. Longley 57, S.A. Marsh 53)
Middlesex 205 for 7 (D.L. Haynes 56, M.W. Gatting 54)

Kent (4 pts) won by 6 runs

at Taunton

Leicestershire 183 (J.J. Whitaker 50)
Somerset 186 for 3

Somerset (4 pts) won by 7 wickets

at Hove

Sussex 239 for 5 (M.P. Speight 74, C.M. Wells 56 not out)
Worcestershire 225 (A.M. Babington 4 for 48)

Sussex (4 pts) won by 14 runs

at Edgbaston

Surrey 175 for 7 (D.M. Ward 76)
Warwickshire 156 for 9 (K.T. Medlycott 4 for 18)

Surrey (4 pts) won by 19 runs

Essex and Lancashire continued their march at the top of the Sunday league with convincing victories. Gooch and Mark Waugh put on 126 for Essex's second wicket, and Gooch reached a hundred on his 36th birthday, to lead his side to victory with a ball to spare. Lancashire had 3.5 overs to spare when they beat Hampshire. Morris and Barnett hit centuries for Derbyshire and put on 182 in 20 overs. Morris hit the quickest century of the summer, reaching his hundred with his fourth six, a shot which won the match. He hit 11 fours and his hundred came off 61 balls. Worcestershire's challenge received a set-back at Hove although O'Shaughnessy, Illingworth and McEwan did their best to rouse their side from 170 for 8. Surrey moved above Worcestershire into third place with a win at Edgbaston. The win was based upon a hard-hit 76 by David Ward, and upon the combined spin bowling talents of Chris Bullen and Keith Medlycott, who conceded only 40 runs in their 16 overs.

26, 27 and 28 July

at Cardiff

Glamorgan 228 (R.J. Shastri 67, P. Willey 5 for 45) and 118 (P. Willey 4 for 48)
Leicestershire 247 (J.J. Whitaker 99, K.A. Somaia 5 for 87) and 100 for 1 (T.J. Boon 60 not out)

Leicestershire won by 9 wickets
Leicestershire 22 pts, Glamorgan 6 pts

at Portsmouth

Gloucestershire 240 (C.W.J. Athey 60) and 48 (C.A. Connor 7 for 31)
Hampshire 406 for 9 dec (C.L. Smith 107, M.C.J. Nicholas 101, K.D. James 56)

Hampshire won by an innings and 118 runs
Hampshire 24 pts, Gloucestershire 3 pts

at Uxbridge

Essex 390 (M.E. Waugh 110, G. Miller 61)
Middlesex 195 (M.A. Roseberry 55, J.H. Childs 4 for 78) and 341 for 2 dec (M.W. Gatting 158 not out, I.J.F. Hutchinson 143 not out)

Match drawn
Essex 7 pts, Middlesex 4 pts

at Northampton

Northamptonshire 283 (R.J. Bailey 116, D.J. Capel 60, O.H.

Mortensen 6 for 105) and 165 (W. Larkins 73 not out)
Derbyshire 420 (T.J.G. O'Gorman 113 not out, P.D. Bowler 71) and 29 for 2

Derbyshire won by 8 wickets
Derbyshire 24 pts, Northamptonshire 6 pts

at Worksop

Nottinghamshire 327 for 8 dec (D.W. Randall 130, K.P. Evans 58, P. Johnson 51, M. Watkinson 4 for 99) and 211 (I.D. Austin 4 for 60)
Lancashire 230 (M. Watkinson 60, K. Saxelby 4 for 66) and 309 for 4 (G.D. Lloyd 117, M.A. Atherton 90, T.E. Jesty 59 not out)

Lancashire won by 6 wickets
Lancashire 21 pts, Nottinghamshire 8 pts

at Hove

Sussex 316 for 9 dec (P.W.G. Parker 110, I.J. Gould 53, V.J. Marks 4 for 65) and 245 for 4 dec (P. Moores 116, A.P. Wells 78 not out)
Somerset 266 for 7 dec (C.J. Tavare 83) and 292 for 6 (S.J. Cook 130)

Match drawn
Somerset 7 pts, Sussex 6 pts

at Edgbaston

Warwickshire 352 (D.A. Reeve 97 not out, S.D. Fletcher 4 for 88) and 237 for 3 dec (A.I. Kallicharran 70, G.W. Humpage 66 not out)
Yorkshire 301 for 4 dec (A.A. Metcalfe 112, R.J. Blakey 88, K. Sharp 51 not out) and 171 for 2 (R.J. Blakey 73 not out)

Match drawn
Yorkshire 7 pts, Warwickshire 4 pts

at Worcester

Worcestershire 284 (S.J. Rhodes 83, R.K. Illingworth 70, M.P. Bicknell 4 for 101) and 256 for 6 dec (G.A. Hick 85, M.J. Weston 74)
Surrey 153 (S.M. McEwan 4 for 57, N.V. Radford 4 for 66) and 285 (G.P. Thorpe 78, R.I. Alikhan 50, N.V. Radford 4 for 108)

Worcestershire won by 103 runs
Worcestershire 23 pts, Surrey 5 pts

It looked as though Essex had shaken off the disappointment of their 25-point deduction when they outplayed fellow title-contenders Middlesex for the first two days at Uxbridge. Mark Waugh steered them past 300, and energetic batting by Miller and Topley took them to a formidable 390 on the second morning. Middlesex then floundered against the left-arm spin of John Childs and were forced to follow-on 195 runs in arrears. When, on the last morning, Hughes and Hutchinson were out for 22 an Essex win seemed inevitable, but Haynes and Gatting batted throughout the rest of the day adding 319 and saving the match. Both batted in masterly fashion and offered no semblance of a chance.

Worcestershire meanwhile had a convincing win over Surrey in spite of some stubborn resistance on the last day by the middle and late order batsmen of the Surrey side. Although pace bowlers had dominated for much of the game, it was the left-arm spin of Richard Illingworth which was decisive. He accounted for both Thorpe and Alikhan, who had offered such a stern challenge.

Tim O'Gorman – a maiden first-class century, Derbyshire v. Northamptonshire, 26–8 July. (Chris Raphael/Allsport)

Hampshire, too, maintained their challenge when, following centuries by Chris Smith and Mark Nicholas, they bowled out Gloucestershire for 48 in the second innings, the second lowest score of the season. Cardigan Connor, enjoying the finest spell of his career, took a career-best 7 for 31 to bring about the rout.

The Cardiff pitch came under scrutiny, but Glamorgan escaped the penalty imposed upon Essex. Their misery was great enough in any case as they were outplayed by Leicestershire, for whom James Whitaker again batted impressively and for whom Peter Willey gave one of his best bowling performances of the season. The one consolation for Glamorgan was the performance of new spin bowler Somaia.

Derbyshire at last turned to their own talent instead of scouring the country for other counties' rejects and were rewarded with a surprisingly easy win over Northamptonshire. Bailey batted with customary elegance, and he and David Capel, another of England's forgotten men, added 140 for the home side's fourth wicket on the opening day. On the second day, Tim O'Gorman, in his first innings since coming down from Durham University, hit a maiden first-class century, dominating a seventh-wicket stand of 127 with Maher. This helped Derbyshire to reach their highest score against Northamptonshire for 56 years, and the Derbyshire pace attack then routed the home side to give Derbyshire the platform for a comfortable second win in succession.

Lancashire made a remarkable come-back to beat Nottinghamshire at Worksop. Randall's century had put the home side in command, and Lancashire were eventually left the task of scoring 309 in 91 overs. Their victory was founded most happily on a second-wicket partnership of 139 in 40 overs between the two young batsmen, Graham Lloyd and Mike Atherton. Lloyd hit his first century in the championship, and with a flourish from Trevor Jesty, Lancashire won a splendid victory with nine overs to spare.

There was no such enterprise or excitement at Edgbaston where, in spite of good individual performances from Dermot Reeve and Ashley Metcalfe in particular, the game ended in a drab draw. Asked to make 289 in 220 minutes, Yorkshire showed no interest in the task, even though Warwickshire offered them spin for most of the time.

Paul Parker's grace and charm were rewarded with a fine century at Hove, and this was supplemented by Peter Moores' maiden century off 108 balls as Sussex pressed for runs in their second innings. Invited to score 296 at approximately five runs an over, Somerset were given a splendid start by Jim Cook, who hit his fifth century in the last four championship matches. He hit 14 fours, but none of his early partners could find the necessary sense of urgency. Somerset needed 116 from the last 16 overs, but a surge of scoring between Harden and Cook brought the target within sight. Marks kept up the tempo, but 14 were needed from the last over, and Marks and Rose could manage only 12.

Fourth Cornhill Test Match
ENGLAND v. AUSTRALIA

At 5.40 p.m. on Tuesday 1 August, David Boon swept a ball from Nick Cook to the square-leg boundary, and Australia, victors by nine wickets, had regained the Ashes. It was a game in which, from first to last, little had gone right for England. While Australia remained unchanged, England, inevitably, made several changes. Robin Smith was welcomed back, and Robinson, presumably on the strength of his innings in the Benson and Hedges Cup Final, was recalled. Nick Cook was brought in as the second spinner although Childs, the best spinner in the country, Maru and Medlycott could consider themselves very unlucky to be passed over. The last stages of the game were played by England under a cloud of brooding melancholy and resentment.

Gower won the toss, and England batted. They were soon in trouble. Lawson, having found his best form and confidence at Bristol, bowled better than at any other time in the series. He brought a ball back sharply at Gooch to clip the off stump, and then had Robinson palpably lbw. There followed an arid period in which, at one time, only three runs were scored in 75 minutes, and which ended with Curtis having his stumps scattered by Lawson.

Robin Smith had been quietly establishing himself, and in the afternoon he and Gower gave a hint of enterprise. They had added 75 when Gower was deceived by Hohns' top spinner, which pitched short and kept a trifle low. Gower swept across the line and was leg before. Worse was to follow as Botham moved down the wicket to Hohns, attempted to hit him high and hard, missed, and

Robin Smith pulls Lawson to the boundary during his innings of 143. (Adrian Murrell/Allsport)

RIGHT: *Botham hoiks at Hohns and is bowled. (Adrian Murrell/Allsport)*

was bowled. It was a dismissal without dignity. For once Russell failed, leg before playing back to Lawson, and Emburey, frustrated by Hohns, essayed a grotesque clout to mid-wicket and was ingloriously leg before. At 158 for 7 and not for the first time in the summer, England were in deep trouble.

Foster stayed with Smith until the close, by which time the score had reached 224 and Smith was 112. No praise can be too high for Smith. His maiden Test century was of the highest quality. He built his innings with great care, but once settled his shots off his legs and his cover-driving provided a thrilling spectacle. He is a batsman of twin delights, power and pleasure.

He and Foster took their stand to 74 before being separated on the second morning. Foster had equalled his highest score in a Test match when he hit Lawson to Border at extra cover. The Australian captain allowed a simple catch to slip from his grasp, but grabbed the ball before it reached the ground. Fraser became Lawson's sixth victim and, after nearly six hours at the wicket, Robin Smith sliced Hughes hard and high to deep third man, where Hohns took a fine catch. Smith's 143 had come from 285 balls and included 15 fours. The South African-born batsman had given a masterly display.

The advantage which Lawson and Hohns had given the Australians was not to be dissipated by Marsh and Taylor. There was a great sense of purpose about them from the start, and it was not long before England began to look ragged. Botham came on as the fifth bowler to be used and was hit for three successive fours, and at one time 34 runs came in four overs. It was Botham, however, who broke the opening stand. Marsh tickled a ball down the leg side and Russell held a splendid catch standing up to the

Australians in England, 1989
First-Class Matches

BATTING	Worcs 1	Worcs 2	Som 1	Som 2	Mdx 1	Mdx 2	Warks 1	Warks 2	Derby 1	Derby 2	1st Test 1	1st Test 2	Lancs 1	Lancs 2	Northants 1	Northants 2	2nd Test 1	2nd Test 2	Glam 1	Glam 2	3rd Test 1	3rd Test 2	Hants 1	Hants 2
G.R. Marsh	21	0	10	57	100*	12*			34	27	16	6	46	27*	32	9	3	1	21	33	42	42	15	5
M.A. Taylor	6	11	97	58	35	24	30	67	5	28	136	60			28	69	62	27			43	51	46	38
T.M. Moody	9	9	17	2*	60*	7	144*	—	0	34			74	—					29	—			7	5
A.R. Border	8	48	0	—	—	77	—	69	17	5	66	60*			135	—	35	1	91		8	—		
M.R.J. Veletta	0	2	46	—	—	7			0	22									134*	83				
S.R. Waugh	0	63							14	9	177*	—	42	—	13	2	152*	21*	34*	—	43	—	112	67
I.A. Healy	25*	26				2			30	39	16	—			20	39	3	—	—		13	2	33*	
T.V. Hohns	3	6				7	—	14	11	2			12	—			21	—	15		40	—	2*	58*
G.F. Lawson	8	17				5*	—	—			10*	—			0	—			74	—	12	—	7	
M.G. Hughes	2	3	21*	15*				27*			71	—			12	12*	30	—			2	—		
T.M. Alderman	6	3*					—	—	0	5*	—	—			4*	—	8	—			0*	—		
C.G. Rackemann			—	0					0*	5													—	11
D.C. Boon			61	—	20	86	0	—	34	6	9	43	0	23*	54	22	94	58*			38	22*	103	24
T.J. Zoehrer			48	—			—	0					30	—									42	1
T.B.A. May			13*	—									—	0*					—	10*			—	7
G.D. Campbell			10	—				8*	31	11			—		0				2	—			—	15
D.M. Jones							248	—			79	40*	59	—	7	68*	27	0	37	56	157	—		
Byes			4		4	4	5				6		2	3			3		4	1	4		1	
Leg-byes	8	7	7	7	11	7	14	10	11	5	13	5	11		9	4	11	4	12	3	20	4	9	5
Wides			3	1		2			5	3	1	9								5				4
No-balls	7	3	8	1	1	4	8		2	1	7	5	11	7	9	4	8	4	7	2	17	2	6	3
Total	103	205	339	144	233	243	444	195	200	180	601	230	288	84	329	229	528	119	373	216	424	158	343	246
Wickets	10	10	8	3	2	7	3	4	10	10	7	3	10	1	10	5	10	4	4	5	10	2	6	10
Result	L		D		D		W		W		W		W		W		W		W		D		D	

Fielding Figures

36 – I.A. Healy (ct 34/st 2)
24 – M.A. Taylor
22 – D.C. Boon
18 – A.R. Border
16 – T.J. Zoehrer
15 – G.R. Marsh
8 – T.M. Moody, D.M. Jones and T.V. Hohns

6 – S.R. Waugh and M.R.J. Veletta
5 – T.M. Alderman
4 – G.F. Lawson
3 – G.D. Campbell and subs
2 – C.G. Rackemann
1 – T.B.A. May and M.G. Hughes

Robin Smith is caught behind down the leg side in England's second innings. (Adrian Murrell/Allsport)

wicket. At tea, Botham had taken 1 for 15, but he did not bowl again in the day.

Emburey had first bowled with fielders clustered round the bat. When he moved them back and offered the batsmen more temptation with his flight his wisdom was rewarded. Taylor advanced down the pitch, was beaten and stumped with ease. Boon shouldered arms to a ball from Fraser which moved back at him sharply and bowled him. England had enjoyed the luxury of two Australian wickets in six overs while just 11 runs were scored. The joy was short-lived. Jones hit a six off Cook, and there were also 6 fours in the 49 he scored before the close. Border was more sedate, and Australia ended the day on 219 for 3.

The Australian captain took his side to a position of total authority on the Saturday morning. He was particularly severe on Foster when the fast bowler overpitched, and one glorious off-drive to the boundary took Australia into the lead. The stand between Border and Jones had realized 120 before Botham slanted a ball between Jones' bat and pad and bowled him.

Rain caused a loss of 13 overs around lunch-time, but at

v. Gloucestershire (Bristol) 22–4 July		FOURTH TEST MATCH (Old Trafford) 27 July–1 Aug		v. Nottinghamshire (Trent Bridge) 2–4 Aug		v. Leicestershire (Leicester) 5–7 Aug		FIFTH TEST MATCH (Trent Bridge) 10–15 Aug		v. Kent (Canterbury) 16–18 Aug		v. Essex (Chelmsford) 19–21 Aug		SIXTH TEST MATCH (The Oval) 24–9 Aug		*M*	*Inns*	*NOs*	*Runs*	*HS*	*Av*
5	—	47	31	16	66	22	27*	138	—	2	—			17	4	18	33	4	934	138	32.20
141	—	85	37*	33	30	70	—	219	—	14	—			71	48	17	30	1	1669	219	57.55
				7	11	6	36			14		80	13*			12	20	4	564	144*	35.25
25	—	80	—			0	22*	65*				40	—	76	51*	16	22	4	979	135	54.38
																5	8	1	294	134*	42.00
92	—	46*	13*	7	—	0		1	—	1	100*			14	7*	16	24	8	1030	177*	64.37
21	—	0	—			73*	—	5	—	6*	45			44	—	14	19	4	442	73*	29.46
2	—	17	—			95	—	19*	—	39*	—			30	—	15	18	4	393	95	28.07
22	—	17	—	0	—									2	—	14	12	2	174	74	17.40
14	—	3	—	0	—	7	—			6	—			21	—	15	16	4	246	71	20.50
0	—	6*	—					—	—					6*	—	11	10	6	38	8	9.50
				2	—	4	—									8	6	1	22	11	4.40
16	—	12	10*	76	102*	73	—	86	—	151	—			46	37	17	28	5	1306	151	56.78
				0	—					32	—	13	93			7	9	—	259	93	28.77
				1	—	0	—			24	—					10	8	3	59	24	11.80
3	—	7	—					0*	—	—	—					11	10	2	87	31	10.87
167*	—	69	—	82	22	22	—	128	—	70	—			122	50	14	20	3	1510	248	88.82
2		5			6	4	8	6				1	5	1	2						
9		7		12	5	15	5	23		8		4	1	9	7						
3		1						3				4									
8		6	3	2		2	1	29		8		11	1	9	13						
438		447	81	284	255	305	99	602		356		387	258	468	219						
10		10	1	10	4	10	1	6		8		7	2	10	4						
W		W		W		W		W		D		W		D							

tea Australia had reached 351 for 4, and Waugh was cracking the ball about with disdainful ease. Uncharacteristically, Border dabbed at a ball from Foster and was caught behind. Healy was leg before first ball, and England's spirits leapt momentarily. Hohns and Waugh soon reasserted Australia's superiority, and, in truth, for much of the day England's cricket was quite dreadful. Cook's limp effort to stop a ball on the boundary line with his boot seemed to epitomize the attitude of many in the field, although Smith and Russell were shining exceptions.

Hohns was caught at silly-point, and Hughes played a dreadful swipe to be bowled. Waugh was moving towards his third century of the series when he hooked too hastily and too carelessly at a Fraser bouncer and was splendidly caught at square-leg by Curtis. The catch reduced Waugh's average in the series to 242.50.

The Australian innings ended early on Monday morning, and England began their second innings 187 runs in arrears. The next 90 minutes were, for England, among the most horrific of the summer. Gooch hit 10 off Lawson's opening over, but in the next, bowled by Alderman, Curtis survived a very confident appeal for leg before first ball and was caught at short-leg second ball. Robinson hit a four, faced 28 balls and was again palpably lbw. Gooch was beautifully caught low down at slip, and Smith touched a ball down the leg-side for Healy to take an

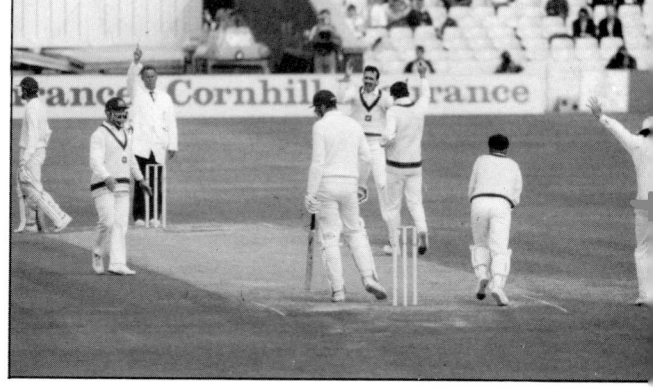

Fraser caught by Marsh off Hohns – Australia celebrate. (Adrian Murrell/Allsport)

excellent catch. Botham, having survived appeals, was unquestionably lbw, and Gower slashed a Lawson away-swinger into the hands of gully. England were 59 for 6, and a four-day defeat looked inevitable. Russell and Emburey survived until tea, however, when, with England on 123, rain ended play for the day.

Before the start of play on the last day the news broke of

BOWLING	T.M. Alderman	G.F. Lawson	M.G. Hughes	S.R. Waugh	C.G. Rackemann	G.D. Campbell	T.B.A. May	A.R. Border
v. Worcestershire (Worcester)	14–4–33–4	14.4–1–50–3	11–4–31–1	6–1–23–2				
13–15 May	17–4–61–4	18.4–6–44–1	4–1–23–0	6–0–25–2				
v. Somerset (Taunton)			16–7–26–2		13–3–33–3	9.4–1–25–1	28–15–48–3	
17–19 May			15–4–44–2		14–6–29–0	12–5–26–0	21–5–63–0	
v. Middlesex (Lord's)	15–6–31–2	22–5–59–2			21–5–85–4			25–8–55–1
20–2 May	21–2–73–3	19–7–48–5			11.5–1–39–1			3–0–14–0
v. Warwickshire (Edgbaston)		7–1–20–1	19–5–62–2			18–4–41–3		6–3–5–0
31 May–2 June		11–3–30–1	5–3–8–0			7–3–15–1		
v. Derbyshire (Derby)	18–6–38–3			11.2–2–35–2	17–2–60–2	18–3–70–2		
3–5 June	21–5–32–4			13–5–18–0	13–3–36–3	16–1–44–3		
First Test Match (Leeds)	37–7–107–5	34.5–6–105–3	28–7–92–1	6–2–27–0		14–0–82–1		2–1–5–0
8–13 June	20–7–44–5	11–2–58–2	9.2–2–36–3			10–0–42–0		5–3–4–0
v. Lancashire (Old Trafford)		17–2–44–4		9–2–28–2		12–2–48–2	15.3–6–29–2	
14–16 June		18–4–48–3		5–1–13–1		20.2–4–54–5	12–3–32–0	
v. Northamptonshire (Northampton)	10–3–35–1		11–2–37–5	11–1–40–2		3–0–15–0	15.3–1–35–1	
17–19 June	6–3–10–3		8–2–23–1	4.5–1–10–3		8–1–31–1	6–1–17–1	
Second Test Match (Lord's)	20.5–4–60–3	27–8–88–2	26–3–71–4	9–3–49–1				9–3–23–0
22–7 June	38–6–128–6	39–10–99–2	24–8–44–2	7–2–20–0				
v. Glamorgan (Neath)			15–5–42–0		21–3–61–1	15–1–67–1	16–5–61–1	
1–3 July					10–2–32–3	9–1–31–1	9–2–39–0	
Third Test Match (Edgbaston)	26.3–6–61–3	21–4–54–2	22–4–68–2	11–3–38–1				
6–11 July								
v. Hampshire (Southampton)		21–8–55–1		7–1–28–2	20–4–79–1	7–2–25–0	24–10–52–2	
19–21 July		6–3–13–0		3–2–8–0	10–1–29–0	6–2–8–0	3–0–4–0	
v. Gloucestershire (Bristol)	13–3–39–4	13–3–55–1	10–1–33–1			13.1–4–47–4		
22–4 July	7–0–31–1	13–5–30–6	6–1–26–0			2–1–1–2		
Fourth Test Match (Old Trafford)	26–13–49–0	33–11–72–6	17–6–55–1	6–1–23–0				8–2–12–0
27 July–1 August	27–6–66–5	31–8–81–3	14.4–2–45–1	4–0–17–0				
v. Nottinghamshire (Trent Bridge)			20–8–38–5	5–2–13–0	11–3–59–2	12–2–34–0	16–6–40–3	
2–4 August			9–4–35–1		18–3–65–5		10.4–1–43–4	
v. Leicestershire (Leicester)		15–5–38–4	14–3–48–0		10–2–19–3		10.1–2–21–2	3–0–14–0
5–7 August		17–9–30–2	9–2–18–1		11–2–41–2		29–7–79–2	
Fifth Test Match (Trent Bridge)	19–2–69–5	21–5–57–2	7.5–0–40–1	11–4–23–0				
10–15 August	16–6–32–2	15–3–51–2	12.3–1–46–3					
v. Kent (Canterbury)				7–1–29–1	10–3–39–2	23.1–5–78–4	15–5–40–3	
16–18 August					20–7–36–2	18–7–46–1	29–10–42–2	
v. Essex (Chelmsford)		18–6–52–3	20–4–69–2			14–3–51–0	11–2–45–0	7–1–22–0
19–21 August		15–4–40–3	17.4–5–64–5			7–0–41–0	17–5–50–2	
Sixth Test Match (The Oval)	27–7–66–5	29.1–9–85–3	23–3–84–1	3–0–11–0				
24–9 August	13–3–30–2	15.1–2–41–2	8–2–34–0					
	412.2–103–	522.3–140–	401.1–99–	176.1–39–	223.5–47–	250.2–50–	287.5–86–	68–21–
	1095–70	1447–69	1242–47	571–23	747–32	824–30	740–28	154–1
	av. 15.64	av. 20.97	av. 26.42	av. 24.82	av. 23.34	av. 27.46	av. 26.42	av. 154.00
	a A.J. Lamb absent hurt		b I.T. Botham absent hurt					

England's hero 'Jack' Russell leaves the field to a standing ovation. (Adrian Murrell/Allsport)

the 16 cricketers who had agreed to tour South Africa. As nine of the men involved had represented England in the Ashes series, and three were currently playing at Old Trafford, there was an immediate sense of shock and betrayal although a maturer reflection was to make followers of the game realize that those who were defecting would have had little future in Test cricket.

Ironically, the last day was to produce some of England's best fighting cricket of the series. Russell and Emburey withstood all that the Australians could do in the first session of the last day, and the ignominy of an innings defeat was avoided. It was not until 1.55 p.m. that Alderman, with the second new ball, brought one back sharply to hit Emburey's middle and off stumps. Emburey and Russell had added 142 runs, the highest seventh-

T.M. Moody	T.V. Hohns	D.M. Jones	D.C. Boon	T.J. Zoehrer	Byes	Leg-byes	Wides	No-balls	Total	Wkts
					3	6	5	2	146	10
					3	7		4	163	7
7–2–13–0					2	6	2	3	140	10
6–1–10–1	17.5–5–52–1				1	4	2	6	235	3
3–1–3–0	13–3–36–1					8	1	2	245	10
	27.3–4–87–4				4	10		5	227	10
	14–2–45–1				10	10	1	4	235	10
						7		1	105	3
5–1–18–0					5	2	1	11	228	10
					4	7	2	3	141	10
					5	7	1	10	430	10
					4	3		5	191	10
	8–3–27–0				1	7		6	184	10
	9–2–30–1					8		9	185	10
					9	9	1	4	180	9a
					5	10		1	106	9
	7–3–9–0					9		3	286	10
	13–6–33–0				6	6		2	359	10
4–0–17–0	20–6–44–2					9		2	301	5
9–2–32–1						1		2	135	5
	16–8–18–1				1	2		11	242	10
	13–7–23–0				7	6		2	275	6
	10–3–15–0				4				81	0
	6–3–7–0				12	7		8	200	10
	1–0–4–1							8	92	10
	27–7–59–3					2			260	10
	26–15–37–1					6	2	5	264	10
					1	10	1	3	195	10
					4	1		2	148	10
	18–9–26–1				1	4		6	157	10
	5.2–0–49–3				2	10		8	243	10
	18–8–48–2					18		13	255	10
	12–3–29–2				3	6	1	6	167	9b
	2–1–4–0					1		1	191	10
21–11–30–4	23–7–60–0	1–0–13–0			4	6		1	237	9
8–1–28–0			1–1–0–0	3–0–9–1	6	8		5	290	6
					4	6		2	205	10
	10–1–30–1				2	7	1	13	285	10
	10–2–37–1					1	1	5	143	5
63–19–	326.4–105–	1–0–	1–1–	3–0–						
151–6	809–26	13–0	0–0	9–1						
av. 25.16	*av.* 31.11	—	—	*av.* 9.00						

Jubilation. The Ashes are back with Australia. (Adrian Murrell/Allsport)

wicket stand for England against Australia at Old Trafford and only one run short of Vine and Woolley's record for an Ashes series.

Foster batted soundly for half an hour before Alderman bowled him with a delivery similar to the one that had accounted for Emburey. Fraser offered sound defence as Russell tried to keep the strike, and they added 32 before Fraser was taken at silly mid-off. At 3.30 p.m. England were all out when Cook touched Hughes to Healy. Russell, who had faced 260 balls and batted for 320 minutes, remained unbeaten on 128. His innings included 14 fours, and it was the first time that he had scored a century in first-class cricket. He batted with the utmost concentration and determination, and his innings was one of tenacity, courage and character such as would give hope

FOURTH CORNHILL TEST MATCH – ENGLAND v. AUSTRALIA
27, 28, 29, 31 July and 1 August 1989 at Old Trafford, Manchester

ENGLAND

	FIRST INNINGS		SECOND INNINGS	
G.A. Gooch	b Lawson	11	c Alderman, b Lawson	13
T.S. Curtis	b Lawson	22	c Boon, b Alderman	0
R.T. Robinson	lbw, b Lawson	0	lbw, b Lawson	12
R.A. Smith	c Hohns, b Hughes	143	c Healy, b Alderman	1
D.I. Gower†	lbw, b Hohns	35	c Marsh, b Lawson	15
I.T. Botham	b Hohns	0	lbw, b Alderman	4
R.C. Russell*	lbw, b Lawson	1	not out	128
J.E. Emburey	lbw, b Hohns	5	b Alderman	64
N.A. Foster	c Border, b Lawson	39	b Alderman	6
A.R.C. Fraser	lbw, b Lawson	2	c Marsh, b Hohns	3
N.G.B. Cook	not out	0	c Healy, b Hughes	5
Extras	lb 2	2	lb 6, w 2, nb 5	13
		260		264

AUSTRALIA

	FIRST INNINGS		SECOND INNINGS	
M.A. Taylor	st Russell, b Emburey	85	not out	37
G.R. Marsh	c Russell, b Botham	47	c Robinson, b Emburey	31
D.C. Boon	b Fraser	12	not out	10
A.R. Border†	c Russell, b Foster	80		
D.M. Jones	b Botham	69		
S.R. Waugh	c Curtis, b Fraser	92		
I.A. Healy*	lbw, b Foster	0		
T.V. Hohns	c Gower, b Cook	17		
M.G. Hughes	b Cook	3		
G.F. Lawson	b Fraser	17		
T.M. Alderman	not out	6		
Extras	b 5, lb 7, w 1, nb 6	19	nb 3	3
		447	(for 1 wkt)	81

	O	M	R	W	O	M	R	W
Alderman	26	13	49	–	27	7	66	5
Lawson	33	11	72	6	31	8	81	3
Hughes	17	6	55	1	14.4	2	45	1
Hohns	27	7	59	3	26	15	37	1
Waugh	6	1	23	–	4	–	17	–
Border					8	2	12	–

	O	M	R	W	O	M	R	W
Foster	34	12	74	2	5	2	5	–
Fraser	36.5	4	95	3	10	–	28	–
Emburey	45	9	118	1	13	3	30	1
Cook	26	6	85	2	4.5	–	18	–
Botham	24	6	63	2				

FALL OF WICKETS
1–23, 2–23, 3–57, 4–132, 5–140, 6–147, 7–158, 8–232, 9–252
1–10, 2–25, 3–27, 4–28, 5–38, 6–59, 7–201, 8–223, 9–255

FALL OF WICKETS
1–135, 2–143, 3–154, 4–274, 5–362, 6–362, 7–413, 8–423, 9–423
1–62

Umpires: B.J. Meyer & J.H. Hampshire

Australia won by 9 wickets

to English cricket at one of its darkest periods. At this bleak time, the cricket of Russell, Smith and Fraser was most heartening.

Australia needed 78 to win and had ample time in which to score the runs. Marsh and Taylor batted as if they were determined to be there at the finish, but Marsh hit Emburey to square-leg when 16 runs were still needed. The loss did not ruffle Australia, and they moved serenely to victory.

Taylor and Boon danced in the middle of the wicket as the Ashes were regained. It was the first time for 55 years that Australia had regained them in England. Lawson, whose wonderful bowling in the first innings had brought about the England decline, was named Man of the Match, and Alderman had once again given a splendid exhibition of fast medium-pace bowling, but the Australian victory was a triumph of team-work and good organization.

29 and 31 July and 1 August

at Derby

Derbyshire 320 (P.D. Bowler 106, D.E. Malcolm 51, K.J. Barnett 50, A.J. Murphy 6 for 97) and 10 for 1
Surrey 110 (I.R. Bishop 4 for 31) and 217 (G.S. Clinton 60, G.P. Thorpe 53 not out)

Derbyshire won by 9 wickets
Derbyshire 24 pts, Surrey 4 pts

at Cardiff

Glamorgan 208 (M.J. Cann 70, C.A. Connor 4 for 40, S.T. Jefferies 4 for 61) and 254 (I. Smith 67, C.A. Connor 5 for 74)
Hampshire 370 for 6 dec (K.D. James 162, T.C. Middleton 69) and 86 for 7

Match drawn
Hampshire 8 pts, Glamorgan 3 pts

at Lord's

Middlesex 287 (M.W. Gatting 80, M.R. Ramprakash 58) and 127 for 1 dec (J.D. Carr 68 not out)
Leicestershire 203 for 6 dec (N.E. Briers 50, N.F. Williams 4 for 39) and 184 for 8 (T.J. Boon 60, P.R. Tufnell 5 for 68)

Match drawn
Middlesex 5 pts, Leicestershire 4 pts

at Trent Bridge

Nottinghamshire 308 (D.W. Randall 76, B.C. Broad 53, D.R. Pringle 4 for 79) and 165 for 6 dec (D.W. Randall 60)
Essex 210 (N. Hussain 61, F.D. Stephenson 7 for 59) and 148 (F.D. Stephenson 8 for 47)

Nottinghamshire won by 115 runs
Nottinghamshire 24 pts, Essex 6 pts

at Edgbaston

Gloucestershire 279 (P. Bainbridge 101, J.W. Lloyds 71, A.A. Donald 5 for 67, G.C. Small 4 for 84) and 188 for 4 dec (J.W. Lloyds 54)
Warwickshire 218 for 8 dec (A.J. Moles 76) and 250 for 7 (D.A. Reeve 86 not out)

Warwickshire won by 3 wickets
Warwickshire 22 pts, Gloucestershire 8 pts

Franklyn Stephenson, wrecker of Essex at Trent Bridge, 29 July–1 August. (David Munden)

at Worcester

Worcestershire 402 for 6 dec (G.A. Hick 147, P. Bent 144, C. Penn 4 for 81) and 27 for 0
Kent 232 (C.S. Cowdrey 56, N.V. Radford 4 for 73) and 196 (S.A. Marsh 53, S.R. Lampitt 5 for 32)

Worcestershire won by 10 wickets
Worcestershire 24 pts, Kent 4 pts

Essex's unbeaten run in the Britannic Assurance County

Championship came to an end when they were beaten at Trent Bridge. Derek Pringle, later to say that the wicket at Trent Bridge was worse than any that he had played on at Southend, won the toss and asked Nottinghamshire to bat first. There was good reason for his decision, but Essex did not bowl well, and the home side were impressively served by Randall, who batted with his usual verve, and by Broad. In contrast, Essex struggled against the bowling of Franklyn Stephenson and, on a wicket that was deteriorating rapidly, a first-innings deficit of 98 was always going to be an immense liability. Hopes were raised when Essex captured the first three Nottinghamshire second-innings wickets before a run was scored, but Randall and Johnson improvised intelligently, and when French declared eight overs after lunch there was only one side with a hope of winning the match. Stephenson bowled at a lively pace and with thoughtful variety. He exploited the vagaries of the pitch to the full to finish with match figures of 15 for 106. These were better than the figures he had produced at the beginning of the season and were the best by a Nottinghamshire bowler in a championship match for 22 years.

As Essex were being comprehensively beaten, Worcestershire overwhelmed Kent on a much improved New Road wicket. Paul Bent, deputizing for Tim Curtis, hit a splendid maiden first-class hundred, and he and Tolley, another Worcestershire reserve of quality, put on 113 for the first wicket. This set the stage for Graeme Hick, but Bent outscored the young maestro in a second-wicket stand of 135. Bent was out after hitting 24 boundaries and scoring his 144 off 202 deliveries. Hick continued in majestic fashion, hitting 4 sixes and 14 fours. Neale was able to declare at 402 for 6 after 100 overs, and in the next two days his seam bowlers did the rest. Worcestershire's win took them seven points ahead of Essex.

Derbyshire scored briskly, and their quick bowlers performed well to earn their third victory in succession. They gave Surrey a sound drubbing and were in control of the game from beginning to end.

Although both sides pressed for victory until the end, the match at Lord's was drawn, a victim of much time lost to rain. Leicestershire's ultimate target was 212 in 44 overs, and they fought hard until Tuffnell, who had an excellent match, bowled Hepworth in the 41st over when 32 were still needed. Nixon and Taylor played out time after that.

A career-best innings of 162 by the likeable and enthusiastic Kevan James put Hampshire in a commanding position at Cardiff. James and Middleton shared a fifth-wicket stand of 203 in 59 overs, and James, who drove powerfully, hit a six and 18 fours in his 5¼-hour innings. On the final day, Hampshire found Smith and Dale hard to dislodge, and by the time they captured the last Glamorgan wicket they had just 16 overs in which to score 93 to win. They made a bold bid but finished seven short.

Warwickshire reached their target of 250 with one over to spare to beat Gloucestershire by three wickets at Edgbaston. The win ended a sequence of 21 first-class matches since they had last tasted success. Gloucestershire, put in to bat, occupied a shortened first day, scoring 268 for 7. They lost their last three wickets early on the Monday morning, and Warwickshire began a solid reply with a stand of 120 between Andy Lloyd and Andy Moles. All was going well until Paul Smith was forced to retire hurt after being hit in the face by a ball from Courtney Walsh. The Warwickshire batting fell apart after this, and the home side finished the second day 61 runs behind with two wickets in hand, one of them being Paul Smith, who had to be taken to hospital with a broken nose. Lloyd offered Gloucestershire some friendly bowling on the last morning in an attempt to induce a declaration, and he was rewarded, Athey demanding less than four an over from his opponents. Warwickshire looked most unlikely to reach their target when they lost their first four batsmen for 72, had Paul Smith unable to bat and Asif Din back in the pavilion tending a bruised thumb. Dermot Reeve continued in the splendid batting form that he had shown in the second half of the season, however, and struck the ball to all parts of the ground. Asif Din returned to give good support over the last 25 runs.

Kevan James who hit 162 for Hampshire against Glamorgan at Cardiff, 31 July. (David Munden)

Refuge Assurance League

30 July

at Derby

Surrey 125 (D.E. Malcolm 4 for 21)
Derbyshire 127 for 6

Derbyshire (4 pts) won by 4 wickets

at Swansea

Glamorgan 193 for 9 (R.J. Shastri 60)
Hampshire 156 (M.C.J. Nicholas 52)

Glamorgan (4 pts) won by 37 runs

at Lord's

Leicestershire 95 for 9
Middlesex 96 for 4

Middlesex (4 pts) won by 6 wickets

at Northampton

Northamptonshire 150 (D.J. Wild 54)
Somerset 152 for 7 (G.D. Rose 61 not out)

Somerset (4 pts) won by 3 wickets

at Trent Bridge

Nottinghamshire 197 for 4 (D.W. Randall 70 not out)
Essex 113 (K. Saxelby 5 for 36)

Nottinghamshire (4 pts) won on a faster scoring rate

at Edgbaston

Warwickshire 162 for 5 (A.I. Kallicharran 76, P.A. Smith 61)
Gloucestershire 144 for 8 (K.M. Curran 54)

Warwickshire (4 pts) won by 18 runs

at Worcester

Kent 123 for 8
Worcestershire 126 for 3

Worcestershire (4 pts) won by 7 wickets

A last-over hat trick by Kevin Curran could not help Gloucestershire to avoid defeat by Warwickshire, for whom Alvin Kallicharran and Paul Smith shared a second-wicket stand of 119. Smith was to suffer a broken nose the following day. Glamorgan lifted some of their gloom with their second win of the season. They beat Hampshire comfortably and owed much to an entertaining fifth-wicket stand of 91 between Morris and Shastri. Worcestershire easily disposed of hapless Kent and, in doing so, jumped above Surrey into third place in the league. Surrey were disturbed by the pace of Devon Malcolm and were surprisingly beaten by Derbyshire. Graham Rose played a fine innings of 61 not out to lead Somerset from 82 for 7 to 152 and victory at Northampton, but the most significant victory was that of Nottinghamshire over Essex at Trent Bridge. Inevitably, Randall had led Nottinghamshire to some prosperity, but rain intervened and the Essex target was reduced to 123 in 23 overs. Lilley and Waugh rejected an offer to leave the field and batted through the rain, but Lilley was immediately caught behind off Kevin Saxelby, who produced another excellent Sunday bowling performance, and the middle-order batting began to fall apart. Hussain hit 41, but Essex fell nine runs short of their target. They remained two points clear at the top of the table, but Lancashire now had a game in hand.

2, 3 and 4 August

at Trent Bridge

Australians 284 (D.M. Jones 82, D.C. Boon 76, D.J. Millns 4 for 86) and 255 for 4 dec (D.C. Boon 102 not out, G.R. Marsh 66)
Nottinghamshire 195 (M.G. Hughes 5 for 38) and 148 (C.G. Rackemann 5 for 65, T.B.A. May 4 for 43)

Australians won by 196 runs

The Castlemaine Challenge has given more meaning to the matches between the counties and the tourists than they have had for several years, and the Australians continued their serene journey of overwhelming the opposition. They were indebted to some fine bowling by Rackemann and May, who had not featured in the Test matches.

NatWest Bank Trophy

Quarter-Finals

2 August

at Lord's

Middlesex 266 for 3 (M.W. Gatting 132 not out, D.L. Haynes 88)
Sussex 188 (A.P. Wells 58, P.W.G. Parker 54)

Middlesex won by 78 runs
(Man of the Match: M.W. Gatting)

at Northampton

Northamptonshire 191 for 8 (D.J. Capel 54, A.A. Donald 4 for 26)
Warwickshire 194 for 7 (T.A. Lloyd 57)

Warwickshire won by 3 wickets
(Man of the Match: T.A. Lloyd)

at The Oval

Surrey 228 for 8 (I.A. Greig 75)
Hampshire 229 for 5 (R.A. Smith 125 not out, M.C.J. Nicholas 71)

Hampshire won by 5 wickets
(Man of the Match: R.A. Smith)

at Worcester

Lancashire 237 for 9 (M. Watkinson 62, I.T. Botham 5 for 51)
Worcestershire 241 for 3 (G.A. Hick 90 not out, T.S. Curtis 51, M.J. Weston 50)

Worcestershire won by 7 wickets
(Man of the Match: M.J. Weston)

Gatting shrugged off a faintly hostile reception to play one of his most beefy and sturdy innings. He reached his highest score in the NatWest competition, 132 not out off 157 balls. He was especially severe on leg-spinner Clarke, who had dropped him when he was on 59. Gatting and Haynes added 201 for the second wicket in 47 overs. Middlesex's 266 always looked as if it would be too many for Sussex. The visitors suffered an early blow when Speight was run out in bizarre fashion. He attempted a second run when the wicket was broken and Hutchinson

had the ball in his hand. The fielder pulled out a stump and Speight was gone. Smith followed with the score on 42, but Paul Parker and Alan Wells raised spirits with a stand of 100 in 26 overs. Once they were separated, Sussex collapsed, and Emburey returned the remarkable figures of 3 for 11 in his 12 overs.

On the other side of London, Surrey struggled through the opening overs against Hampshire. Darren Bicknell and Alec Stewart both promised substantial scores, but both were cut short just as they began to strike the ball cleanly. At lunch, Surrey were 93 for 4, and they lost their fifth wicket soon after the break. Maru held two good slip catches, and Hampshire were well on top until Ian Greig took command. He has never shirked responsibility or challenge, and his batting form throughout the season had been excellent. Now he hit 75 off 73 balls before being run out with just three overs remaining. Martin Bicknell and Tony Murphy bowled splendidly at the start of the Hampshire innings. Chris Smith fell to Murphy without scoring, and Terry was leg before to Martin Bicknell for six. Ian Greig brought himself on as first change, and James hit him for four. There were mutters that the Surrey skipper had erred, but he responded by having James caught at slip, and Hampshire were 23 for 3 in the 15th over. Robin Smith had arrived to a tumultuous reception, and he and Nicholas now set about winning the game for

Mike Gatting, a powerful innings and the individual award as Middlesex beat Sussex in the NatWest Bank Trophy quarter-final. (Alan Cozzi)

Alec Stewart is bowled by Cardigan Connor, a great blow for Surrey in their NatWest Bank Trophy quarter-final against Hampshire. (Tom Morris)

A captain's innings in vain. Ian Greig is run out for 75, and his Surrey side lose their NatWest Bank Trophy quarter-final to Hampshire. (Tom Morris)

Hampshire. They added 176 in 40 overs before Nicholas was caught behind off Murphy.

Hampshire needed 30 off five overs, and Marshall was prompted to raise the tempo, but he was caught and bowled by the admirable Martin Bicknell for one. It did not matter, for Robin Smith, who had played with his might and delight, hit 3 fours, and Hampshire won with two overs to spare. Smith's grandeur was the feature of the match, but Surrey suffered in that their support bowlers, particularly Feltham, had a poor day. Most would have suffered against Robin Smith in this form.

The match at Worcester began in a gloomy, humid atmosphere, and the Lancashire batting reflected the weather. After 30 overs the visitors had scored 71 for 1, and the usually free-scoring Mendis had made only 21. It was Watkinson who gave the innings some momentum with 62 off 54 balls. He hit 3 sixes and 6 fours. In contrast to Lancashire's slow start, Worcestershire's innings began with a flourish. This was mainly thanks to Weston, who hit 50 off 59 balls in a first-wicket stand of 80. Such a good platform made it easier for Hick, and Worcestershire romped to victory with 7.4 overs to spare. Weston took two fine catches, bowled eight economical overs and was rightfully named Man of the Match. Weston was caught by

Jack Simmons. It was Simmons' 25th and last catch in the competition before his retirement, and established a new record, taking him one ahead of Geoff Cook and Phil Sharpe. In bowling Curtis, Simmons took his 77th wicket in the competition. Only Geoff Arnold, 79, has taken more.

Put in to bat, Northamptonshire lost a wicket off the third ball of Donald's first over when Larkins flicked the ball into the hands of Lloyd, backward of square-leg. Felton edged to the wicket-keeper, and the home side were 27 for 2. Geoff Cook, Bailey, Capel and Wild all hinted at long innings which never reached fulfilment. Cook was bowled by an off-break from Neil Smith which turned sharply, and Bailey was caught behind off a rash shot. Capel and Wild added 87, but both fell when Donald returned to the attack. Warwickshire were given an exciting start by skipper Andy Lloyd and were 108 before the second wicket fell. Miserable conditions and two interruptions did not aid the visitors' cause. They were 165 for 6 with seven overs left, and victory did not come until Small hit the fourth ball of the last over for four.

Martin Weston. Man of the Match in the NatWest Bank Trophy quarter-final at Worcester and Worcestershire's Player of the Season. (David Munden)

3 August

at Jesmond

Rest of World XI 257 for 8 (P.J.L. Dujon 87 not out, R.J. Shastri 56)
England XI 261 for 6 (G.A. Gooch 88, M.P. Maynard 81, C.J. Sharma 4 for 38)

England XI won by 4 wickets

4 August

at Jesmond

England XI 272 for 9 (N. Hussain 88, K.J. Barnett 61, C.A. Walsh 4 for 40)
Rest of World XI 273 for 7 (M.J. Greatbatch 115 not out)

Rest of World XI won by 3 wickets

5, 6 and 7 August

at Leicester

Leicestershire 157 (G.F. Lawson 4 for 38) and 243
Australians 305 (T.V. Hohns 95, I.A. Healy 73, M.A. Taylor 70, W.K.M. Benjamin 7 for 54) and 99 for 1

Australians won by 9 wickets

5, 7 and 8 August

at Derby

Derbyshire 178 (C.A. Connor 5 for 50) and 326 for 9 (K.J. Barnett 106, J.E. Morris 65, B.J.M. Maher 56 not out, M.D. Marshall 6 for 69)
Hampshire 472 for 6 dec (V.P. Terry 180, M.C.J. Nicholas 121, C.L. Smith 52)

Match drawn
Hampshire 7 pts, Derbyshire 2 pts

at Colchester

Essex 208 (G.A. Gooch 51, G.A. Hick 5 for 52) and 323 for 9 (M.E. Waugh 76, N.A. Foster 50 not out, G.A. Hick 5 for 131, R.K. Illingworth 4 for 115)
Worcestershire 447 for 9 dec (T.S. Curtis 156, G.A. Hick 72, P. Bent 55, D.B. D'Oliveira 55, T.D. Topley 4 for 76)

Match drawn
Worcestershire 7 pts, Essex 3 pts

at Cheltenham

Lancashire 93 (C.A. Walsh 6 for 40, K.B.S. Jarvis 4 for 37) and 278 (T.E. Jesty 68, D.A. Graveney 4 for 51, C.A. Walsh 4 for 64)
Gloucestershire 394 (P. Bainbridge 128, M.W. Alleyne 111, P.A.J. DeFreitas 5 for 123)

Gloucestershire won by an innings and 23 runs
Gloucestershire 24 pts, Lancashire 2 pts

at Canterbury

Kent 287 (C.S. Cowdrey 56, S.G. Hinks 53, S.A. Marsh 53, A.A. Donald 5 for 57) and 141 (R.F. Pienaar 53, A.A. Donald 4 for 41)
Warwickshire 250 for 8 dec and 181 for 0 (T.A. Lloyd 109 not out, A.J. Moles 64 not out)

Warwickshire won by 10 wickets
Warwickshire 21 pts, Kent 6 pts

at Weston-super-Mare

Somerset 212 (R.J. Harden 76 not out, J.E. Emburey 6 for 38) and 254 for 6 dec (C.J. Tavare 81, S.J. Cook 50)
Middlesex 116 (A.N. Jones 4 for 30) and 223 for 7 (J.E. Emburey 77 not out, G.D. Rose 4 for 22)

Match drawn
Somerset 6 pts, Middlesex 4 pts

at The Oval

Surrey 357 (G.P. Thorpe 82, A.J. Stewart 68, K.T. Medleycott 53) and 232 for 4 dec (A.J. Stewart 99, R.I. Alikhan 84 not out)
Glamorgan 227 (A.R. Butcher 61, S.P. James 53, K.T. Medlycott 7 for 68) and 205 for 3 (A.R. Butcher 88 not out)

Match drawn
Surrey 8 pts, Glamorgan 5 pts

at Eastbourne

Sussex 325 for 6 dec (D.M. Smith 184, C.M. Wells 65) and 264 for 9 dec (C.M. Wells 79, P.W.G. Parker 72, F.D. Stephenson 5 for 86)
Nottinghamshire 303 for 7 dec (P. Pollard 82, F.D. Stephenson 64 not out) and 287 for 7 (B.C. Broad 90, R.T. Robinson 57)

Nottinghamshire won by 3 wickets
Nottinghamshire 22 pts, Sussex 7 pts

Winston Benjamin – a hat trick against the Australians and capped for Leicestershire as he finished the season strongly. (David Munden)

Mark Nicholas – a century at Derby, 7 August, and leadership of Hampshire by example throughout the season. (David Munden)

at Sheffield

Northamptonshire 379 (A. Fordham 199, R.J Bailey 98, A. Sidebottom 4 for 75, P.W. Jarvis 4 for 89) and 147 for 3 dec (W. Larkins 83, R.J. Bailey 59 not out)
Yorkshire 259 for 3 dec (R.J. Blakey 87 retired hurt, K. Sharp 78 not out, A.A. Metcalfe 56) and 225 (K. Sharp 78, M.D. Moxon 53, N.G.B. Cook 4 for 49)

Northamptonshire won by 42 runs
Northamptonshire 21 pts, Yorkshire 3 pts

The Australians withstood a fierce spell of bowling by Winston Benjamin to register another emphatic victory in the Castlemaine Challenge; and in the Britannic Assurance County Championship, Worcestershire took most of the honours in the top of the table clash with Essex. Electing to bat first on a wicket in which there seemed a little help for the spinners but no real spite, Essex floundered against the bowling of Illingworth and Hick, who took five wickets in an innings for the first time with his off-breaks. Bent and Curtis put on 98 for the first wicket, and Curtis and Hick took Worcestershire to a point of total domination on the Monday. Curtis batted over 7½ hours to reach the highest score of his career. He added 113 in 36 overs with Hick, and 102 in 34 overs with D'Oliveira. Essex were 239 behind on the first innings, and to add to their miseries they lost Gooch and Topley in the last half hour of the second day. Defeat seemed a formality, but Waugh, Pringle, Miller and Foster were the heroes of a last day rearguard action which saw them deny victory to Worcestershire. Hick and Illingworth sent down 107 overs in the second innings, and Hick finished with career-best match figures of 10 for 183.

Hampshire were similarly frustrated at Derby. Cardigan Connor enjoyed another successful spell of bowling on the Saturday, and Terry, who hit his best championship score, and Nicholas added 148 for the fourth Hampshire wicket on the Monday, but, led by Barnett, Derbyshire saved the game on the last day.

Bainbridge, at his most reliable and best in his benefit year, and Alleyne put on 245 for Gloucestershire's fifth wicket after Walsh and Jarvis had routed Lancashire for 93 on the opening day. The visitors showed greater determination in their second innings, but, with Mendis forced to retire hurt with a damaged finger, Lancashire lost to Gloucestershire for the first time in 24 years.

A rather inept Kent side twice succumbed to the pace of Alan Donald and were beaten by ten wickets by the

hours and he hit 2 sixes and 29 fours. Yorkshire gave a dour reply on the second day and declared 120 runs behind in order to keep the game alive. Larkins' declaration eventually left Yorkshire to make 268 in 69 overs to win, but the home side fell to the spin of Nick Cook and Robert Bailey.

One-Day Series
England Young Cricketers v. New Zealand Young Cricketers

5 August

---

at Edgbaston

Young New Zealand 163
Young England 164 for 2 (N.V. Knight 65 not out)

Young England won by 8 wickets

LEFT: *Tim Curtis hit the highest score of his career in the crucial match between Worcestershire and Essex at Colchester, 5–7 August. (David Munden)*

BELOW: *Keith Medlycott advanced his claims as a slow left-arm bowler and right-handed batsman worthy of consideration by the England selectors with an excellent all-round performance for Surrey against Glamorgan at The Oval, 5–7 August. (Tom Morris)*

revitalized Warwickshire side. Andy Lloyd continued his excellent run of form and led his side most ably.

John Emburey had a fine all-round match for Middlesex against Somerset. He produced his best bowling figures of the season on the first day, and battled grimly to preserve his wicket on the final day, when Middlesex faced defeat.

Glamorgan did not respond to Greig's challenge at The Oval, but Nottinghamshire were happy to accept the offer to make 287 at under five an over to beat Sussex at Eastbourne. Broad and Robinson made victory possible with a second-wicket stand of 118. Broad was the early-innings hero. He strained a thigh muscle and had to employ Pollard as a runner. He made 90 in excellent fashion and was just beginning the final onslaught when Pollard became involved in a mix-up over a run. Nottinghamshire reached the last over needing 12 to win. As in the Benson and Hedges Final, Hemmings was the batsman upon whom the fate of Nottinghamshire rested. He made the vital blow when he hit the second ball of the last over, bowled by Donelan, for six, and victory came with a leg-bye off the final ball.

A career-best 199 by Alan Fordham on the opening day at Sheffield put Northamptonshire in a strong position against Yorkshire. Fordham, who was one of several batsmen to benefit from Yorkshire's inability to catch, shared a third-wicket stand of 252 with Bailey, who hit 10 fours and a six in his 96. Fordham's innings lasted 5¼

6 August

at Northampton

Young England 250 for 7 (N.V. Knight 118, P.C.L. Holloway 54)
Young New Zealand 220

Young England won by 30 runs

8 August

at Lord's

Young England 203 (M.R. Ramprakash 51, W.M. Noon 51, C.L. Cairns 5 for 38)
Young New Zealand 181 for 9 (B. Pocock 71, A.L. Penberthy 4 for 50)

Young England won by 22 runs

Young England, led by Mark Ramprakash of Middlesex, won the 55-over series by three matches to nil. Nick Knight, a left-handed opening batsman on the Essex staff, but one of only two players in the side without first-class experience, was the outstanding batsman. Edmunds and Ball took the bowling honours.

Refuge Assurance League

6 August

at Derby

Derbyshire 148 (P.D. Bowler 71, P.J. Bakker 5 for 17)
Hampshire 149 for 6

Hampshire (4 pts) won by 4 wickets

at Colchester

Essex 193 for 9
Worcestershire 197 for 4 (D.B. D'Oliveira 60 not out, G.A. Hick 54)

Worcestershire (4 pts) won by 6 wickets

at Cheltenham

Gloucestershire 143 (A.J. Wright 52 not out, M. Watkinson 4 for 29)
Lancashire 144 for 4

Lancashire (4 pts) won by 6 wickets

at Canterbury

Warwickshire 201 for 5 (M. Asif Din 89)
Kent 202 for 3 (S.G. Hinks 80 not out, T.R. Ward 54)

Kent (4 pts) won by 7 wickets

at Weston-super-Mare

Somerset 205 for 8 (C.J. Tavare 65)
Middlesex 108

Somerset (4 pts) won by 97 runs

at The Oval

Surrey 254 for 8 (A.J. Stewart 119, G.P. Thorpe 80)
Glamorgan 157 (K.T. Medlycott 4 for 20)

Surrey (4 pts) won by 97 runs

at Eastbourne

Nottinghamshire 169 for 9 (R.T. Robinson 55)

Another young batsman of talent, Chris Adams: aggressive batting for Young England and a vital reason for the rejuvenation of Derbyshire, when he won a regular place in the county side in mid-season. (Chris Raphael/Allsport)

Sussex 170 for 3

Sussex (4 pts) won by 7 wickets

at Sheffield

Northamptonshire 198 for 4 (G. Cook 77, R.J. Bailey 58 not out)
Yorkshire 186 (A.A. Metcalfe 75, M.D. Moxon 59, A. Walker 4 for 39)

Northamptonshire (4 pts) won by 12 runs

Lancashire beat Gloucestershire with contemptuous ease at Cheltenham, and, with Essex's misery continuing as they were soundly defeated by Worcestershire, Lancashire moved to the top of the table. Lancashire also had the advantage of a game in hand. Surrey kept on course for a place in the Refuge Assurance Cup with a huge win over Glamorgan at The Oval. Stewart and Thorpe shared a third-wicket stand of 200 in 30 overs. A fine bowling performance from Bakker, his best in the league, set up Hampshire's victory over Derbyshire.

9, 10 and 11 August

at Chesterfield

Lancashire 372 (N.H. Fairbrother 161, G. Fowler 83, M.

Jean-Jacques 4 for 93) and 201 (G. Fowler 58, S.J. Base 4 for 80)

Derbyshire 354 (P.G. Newman 86 not out, C.J. Adams 79, P.A.J. DeFreitas 6 for 116, Wasim Akram 4 for 103) and 193 for 8 (P.D. Bowler 63)

Match drawn
Derbyshire 8 pts, Lancashire 8 pts

at Colchester

Essex 391 for 6 dec (P.J. Prichard 128, G.A. Gooch 75) and 0 for 0 dec
Northamptonshire 131 for 1 dec (W. Larkins 76 not out) and 140 (N.A. Felton 53, N.A. Foster 4 for 46, D.R. Pringle 4 for 49)

Essex won by 120 runs
Essex 20 pts, Northamptonshire 2 pts

at Cheltenham

Middlesex 222 (M.W. Gatting 110 not out) and 206 for 7 dec (M.A. Roseberry 51)
Gloucestershire 122 (J.E. Emburey 7 for 27) and 118 (J.E. Emburey 5 for 39)

Middlesex won by 188 runs
Middlesex 22 pts, Gloucestershire 4 pts

at Bournemouth

Warwickshire 229 (M. Asif Din 57, G.W. Humpage 51) and 110 for 2 dec
Hampshire 103 for 5 dec and 176 (R.J. Parks 52 not out, A.A. Donald 4 for 47)

Warwickshire won by 60 runs
Warwickshire 20 pts, Hampshire 4 pts

at Canterbury

Kent 346 (N.R. Taylor 118, R.F. Pienaar 51, A.J. Murphy 5 for 94) and 184 for 2 dec (S.G. Hinks 104 not out)
Surrey 302 for 9 dec (A.J. Stewart 87, I.A. Greig 69) and 230 for 3 (G.P. Thorpe 85 not out, M.A. Lynch 63 not out)

Surrey won by 7 wickets
Surrey 24 pts, Kent 8 pts

at Weston-super-Mare

Somerset 240 (P.M. Roebuck 99, R.J. Harden 59, S.R. Lampitt 4 for 60) and 145 (S.M. McEwan 5 for 28)
Worcestershire 302 for 6 dec (G.A. Hick 72, D.B. D'Oliveira 52) and 87 for 1

Worcestershire won by 9 wickets
Worcestershire 24 pts, Somerset 4 pts

at Eastbourne

Sussex 258 (M.P. Speight 88, W.K.M. Benjamin 4 for 63, J.P. Agnew 4 for 84) and 191 for 6 dec (A.P. Wells 56)
Leicestershire 167 (J.J. Whitaker 53, A.I.C. Dodemaide 5 for 77) and 134 for 0 (T.J. Boon 80 not out)

Match drawn
Sussex 7 pts, Leicestershire 5 pts

Worcestershire kept a firm grip on the Britannic Assurance County Championship with an impressive maximum-point win at Weston-super-Mare. Batting first, Somerset were held together by Peter Roebuck, who batted with sense and freedom until he was caught behind off Lampitt when one short of his century. He was given responsible support by Harden, but Worcestershire took control of the game on the second day, when night-watchman McEwan,

Hick, D'Oliveira and Neale all batted in a manner suggesting confidence and purpose. Neale declared as soon as his side had claimed their fourth batting point, and by the end of the second day, Somerset had lost three wickets and were still seven runs behind. A spell of four wickets in 18 balls by Steve McEwan after lunch on the last day ended Somerset's resistance and underlined the strength and talent of Worcestershire's reserves. McEwan and Lampitt had served them most capably in this match.

Essex maintained their challenge, but, hampered by the weather, they lost a little ground. Paul Prichard is among the most talented batsmen in the country, technically sound, rich and aggressive in stroke, yet, hindered by injury, he has failed to score the runs his talent merits. His exciting and eminently charming 128 against Northamptonshire was, bewilderingly, only his third century in first-class cricket. His innings included 21 fours. Gooch and Stephenson had given the innings a fine start with a stand of 134. Most of the second day was lost to rain, so that it needed a declaration and a forfeiture of Essex's second innings to breathe life into the game on the Friday. There was nothing contrived about Essex's victory, however, for Pringle and Foster quickly reduced Northamptonshire to 18 for 4. Felton offered resistance but, when Pringle dismissed Ripley, bowled playing back, and Davis, caught high at short-leg, within the space of three balls at the beginning of the last 20 overs, Essex were set for victory.

If Essex's win had depended upon their pace bowling, Middlesex were thankful for the off-spin of John Emburey at Cheltenham. He returned the outstanding figures of 12 for 66 in the match. Gloucestershire had no answer to him, nor could they boast a batsman with the unrelenting application of Gatting, who carried Middlesex through a most difficult time on the first day. He batted in masterly fashion for 3½ hours and hit a six and 12 fours.

Centuries by Taylor and Hinks could not compensate for Kent's lack of penetration in bowling. The loss of play before lunch on the last day meant that Chris Cowdrey was forced to offer Surrey a target of 229 in 42 overs. The visitors were 91 for 3, but Graham Thorpe hit 85 off 74 balls and Lynch hit 63 off as many deliveries to add 139 in 20 overs and take Surrey to victory with two balls to spare.

Warwickshire's appetite for victory remained unabated. Acting captain Humpage set Hampshire a target of 237 off 72 overs, but Donald, Munton and Benjamin proved far too hostile and accurate, and only Wood and Parks offered serious resistance as the midland county moved to their third championship victory in succession.

There was no excitement at Eastbourne, where the loss of the last morning's play made both sides accept a draw. Martin Speight, another of England's young hopefuls, brightened the first day with 88 before lunch.

An incredible third-wicket stand of 256 in 39 overs between Fowler and Fairbrother set the pattern for an exhilarating opening day at Chesterfield. Fairbrother, felled by a ball from Bishop early on, hit 161 off 124 balls. His innings included 6 sixes and 21 fours, and the last 11 overs before lunch produced 104 runs. At lunch, Lancashire were 171 for 2. They were finally bowled out in 75.2 overs, and Derbyshire scored 60 for 1 in 10 overs before

A young batsman of immense promise, who played magnificently for Young England against New Zealand: Nick Knight of Essex. (Sporting Pictures UK Ltd)

ABOVE RIGHT: *Twelve wickets for John Emburey as Middlesex overwhelmed Gloucestershire at Cheltenham, 9–11 August. (David Munden)*

RIGHT: *Warren Hegg – 11 catches for Lancashire against Derbyshire at Chesterfield, 9–11 August, to equal the world record. (USPA)*

the close. DeFreitas claimed six wickets in the Derbyshire innings, but the Lancashire hero was Warren Hegg, who equalled a county record with seven catches behind the wicket. When Derbyshire chased a target of 220 in 53 overs on the last afternoon he took four more catches to equal the world record held by Arnold Long, David Bairstow and Rodney Marsh. Derbyshire, who had survived by some hard hitting from Newman and some excitingly aggressive batting from the promising Adams in their first innings, lost five wickets for 10 runs after being 159 for 3, and abandoned the chase.

Fifth Cornhill Test Match
ENGLAND v. AUSTRALIA

The England selectors were restricted in their choice in that several players who had represented England during the series had announced their intention of going to South Africa, yet it is as well to consider how great a part any of those players would have had in the future of the England side.

Gatting had had a miserable run at Test level. He was reported to believe that he had been badly treated, but as he and his team had received the full bonus after the wretched tour of Pakistan, and as he had survived that tour and the dreadful one of New Zealand which followed, it was hard to see what grounds he had for complaint. Moreover, Gatting had failed to keep his place throughout three series against West Indies, albeit he suffered injury in one of them. If Ted Dexter was serious about his new era for English cricket, surely there was no place for Gatting in the new order.

The same must apply to John Emburey. A determined and likeable man, Emburey has never been among the great off-spinners, and his hold on a place in the England side in recent series has been tenuous, earned more by his tenacious batting and defensive qualities as a bowler than by an ability to bowl a side out.

Like Gatting, Emburey seemed to be part of a caucus whose places in the England side were secure come what may. It was this caucus which, one believed, Dexter would break. Now it had begun to break of its own accord.

Robinson had been recalled to the England side for the Test against Sri Lanka after others had taken a battering against West Indies. His selection had been incomprehensible, just as it had been when he was brought back for the Old Trafford Test, for it was generally accepted that he was vulnerable against anything much above medium pace. French, his county colleague, had been displaced by Russell and Rhodes, and their obvious advance left French with no future at Test level.

The third Nottinghamshire player, Chris Broad, is a tough, durable and ambitious man. His decision to go to South Africa was hard to understand, for he had fought hard to win an England cap and had survived impressively at the top level. His ability to come back had suggested that he could yet re-establish himself in the England side, but obviously he felt otherwise.

Barnett, on the other hand, once, for totally incomprehensible reasons considered to be a candidate for the England captaincy, had revealed himself to be technically deficient at Test level, and neither Athey nor Graveney were of international quality.

The same must be said of the Kent pair, Richard Ellison and Chris Cowdrey. Ellison, once an integral part of the England side and able to swing the ball more than any other bowler in the country, had lost form completely since being injured, and Cowdrey, so badly treated by May and his selectors, was, by his own admission, short of Test class. He alone of the party had the right to feel embittered at the treatment he had received.

Foster and Dilley, the current England opening bowlers, had also opted to go on the tour. Dilley's frequent loss of heart and lack of fitness had always clouded his career. He was 30 years old and could have little Test cricket ahead. Foster seemed to be a loss, but he had become increasingly more bad-tempered, reacted strongly to any hint of criticism and was an unhappy blend of an angry young man and a rebel without a cause. His Test record had been disappointing, and he will now go

down in cricket history as a nearly-man. It is an indictment of the present system that he has played in 28 Test matches, which is seven more than Harold Larwood played. Undoubtedly, Foster would have played more Test cricket but for his defection, although his long-term fitness is in doubt, and at least one observer, John Woodcock, to whom we should always pay attention, suggested that Foster was too much associated with the failures and discord of the past two years to be any part of England's immediate plans.

Paul Jarvis, one felt, may have had a future as an England bowler if he were able to achieve discipline and harmony, but, like Maynard, a batsman who had promised much and achieved little, he had condemned himself to a future without ambition.

DeFreitas and Butcher, who had originally been named as members of the party, withdrew after more mature consideration. Butcher's withdrawal came too late to repair much of the damage he had done to his benefit.

There were some crass statements by members of the party about ignorance of apartheid and building bridges. The reasons for agreeing to tour South Africa were purely financial ones, as some were honest enough to admit, at least in private.

The defections left many England supporters in high hopes that at last they would see a new England side begin to take shape, but few were excited with Dexter's choice for the fifth Test. The recall of Moxon and Hemmings, and

The heroes leave the field – Mark Taylor and Geoff Marsh on their way to their record-breaking partnership of 329. (Adrian Murrell/Allsport)

AUSTRALIA   Total 3 0 1   for   0

MARSH 1 2 5   extras 3 5

TAYLOR 1 4 1   overs 1 3

OVERS REMAINING   last man

bowler	10	11	6	9	12	5
overs	2 4	1 8	2 0	1 9	1 5	5
wickets						
runs	5 4	6 5	6 8	4 3	2 6	2 1
	1	2	3	4	5	

End of play on the first day at Trent Bridge. Australia 301 for 0. (Adrian Murrell/Allsport)

the retention of Cook, Curtis and even, sadly, Botham, were not easy to understand. The selection of the wayward Malcolm ahead of the so promising Martin Bicknell was also hard to follow, and Atherton, of the younger crop of batsmen which included Hussain, Darren Bicknell, Stephenson and Bailey, was the only selection to find favour.

Australia, unchanged for the fourth time, won the toss and batted. Marsh and Taylor struggled through the first session with much determination and skill and a little luck. Luck had not accompanied England throughout the summer; much of the time they had not deserved it, but they would not have been flattered by two wickets before lunch on the first day. Thereafter Marsh and Taylor grew in stature over by over. By the close, both batsmen had completed centuries and Australia were 301 for no wicket.

There is little to add to the praise and admiration that Taylor had earned at the beginning of the tour, and that Marsh would score a century during the series had seemed to be without question. The only surprise was that it had taken him until the fifth Test. Marsh and Taylor became the first pair of batsmen to bat through the whole day of a Test match in England, and they had established a new first-wicket record for Australia against England. Early on Friday morning, it became the highest opening partnership for either side in an England–Australia Test match. It was also the highest partnership for any wicket in a Test match at Trent Bridge.

The stand was brought to an end when, after 426 minutes at the crease, Marsh swept loosely and tiredly at Cook and edged the ball high over slip where Botham, running back, took the catch. Marsh had faced 382 balls and hit 15 fours in what was his highest Test score.

The England agony was far from over. Boon helped Taylor to add 101 for the second wicket before the left-handed opener moved down the wicket to Cook, was left stranded and was stumped for the third time in four innings. By then he had been at the crease for 554 minutes, had faced 461 deliveries, hit 23 fours and hit his first double century in Test cricket. No praise can be too high for this splendidly correct batsman. Not only does he face the bowler with impenetrable defence, but he is ever looking for runs. His 219, the highest score of his career, took him to 720 runs in the series. Only Bradman has scored more for Australia in a series against England, and that is a mighty yardstick.

Border also reached a landmark when he passed Boycott's record of 8,114 runs in Test cricket to move into second place behind Gavaskar. Boon played the brightest innings of the day although he was twice dropped, once by Botham off Malcolm, when the great all-rounder sustained

An early escape for Taylor as he edges past Moxon. (Adrian Murrell/Allsport)

a dislocated finger which was to put him out of the final Test.

Boon was stumped, and Jones was caught, bat and pad, at point. Waugh clipped Malcolm to square-leg to give the Derbyshire bowler his first Test wicket, and Australia ended the day on 560 for 5. To their credit the England bowlers and fielders had not wilted over the first two days.

Healy was out without addition on the third morning, and Border declared when his side had reached 600.

After so long and arduous a time in the field, England's early set-back came as no surprise, but few were prepared for the shocks that were in store. Curtis took a single off Alderman's first delivery. The fourth found the edge of Moxon's bat and Waugh took a fine low catch at slip. Two balls later, Atherton, of whom too much was being asked one feels, was leg before wicket so that England were 1 for 2 at the end of the first over. Curtis, balance and angle of the bat at odds it seemed, was leg before to a ball that came back at him, and England were 14 for 3.

Smith and Gower survived until lunch without further alarm, but immediately after the break Gower flashed at Lawson to give Healy a straightforward catch which the wicket-keeper fumbled and turned into a spectacular catch as he held it at the second attempt. Inevitably it was Russell and Smith who lifted England. Smith began to attack the bowling with awesome power. He crashed Hughes to the boundary square of the wicket on the off side, and, in all, he was to hit 16 thunderous fours.

Russell, outstanding in his first Test series, gave Smith splendid support and the pair added 82 in 91 minutes before Russell fell to the Lawson away swinger. Hemmings, in belligerent mood, became the yeoman of the England innings, and the crowd warmed to him as Smith thundered on.

The Hampshire batsman had just reached an exciting hundred when he made an error of judgement. He essayed a rash square cut at a ball from Alderman that was too close to him and was caught behind. His 101 had come out of 158 made while he was at the wicket, and he had faced

only 150 balls and batted for 205 minutes. Nothing could more emphasize the correctness of his attitude than the fact that he left the wicket angry and distraught that he had been dismissed.

Eddie Hemmings had been thumping the ball with great enthusiasm before he dragged a ball from Alderman on-to his wicket. It was the fifth wicket of the innings for Alderman, and it was the fifth time in the series that he had taken five wickets in an innings.

Fraser, another who shows great resolution, batted doggedly and courageously. He was joined by Botham, who was in obvious discomfort from his dislocated finger but who showed admirable determination. The pair offered a hint of solidity before both falling to Hohns within one run of each other. Fraser was bowled by the googly, and Botham was taken at silly point. England closed at 246 for 9 on the Saturday evening, Smith's century a beacon in the gloom.

The innings ended after eleven balls of the Monday morning. Malcolm clouted Hohns for six, and then swatted at Hughes and was caught behind. By 11.30 a.m. on the fourth morning, England were following-on.

There was a surprise when Gower came out to open with Curtis. The England captain came in first in an effort to provide the left-hander/right-hander combination as a counter to Alderman and Lawson. He began with a flourish, but in Lawson's first over he offered no shot to a ball which moved back at him and hit his off stump. Curtis, seemingly off balance, was again leg before, but Atherton and Smith added 54 in 14 heartening overs before Hughes hit Smith's middle and leg stumps with a yorker.

Moxon could not cope with a ball that kept low, and Russell, for once, failed. Atherton's innings occupied 172 minutes and gave much encouragement for the future. It ended when he was very well caught and bowled by Hohns

Fight back. Robin Smith drives his way to a century. (Adrian Murrell/Allsport)

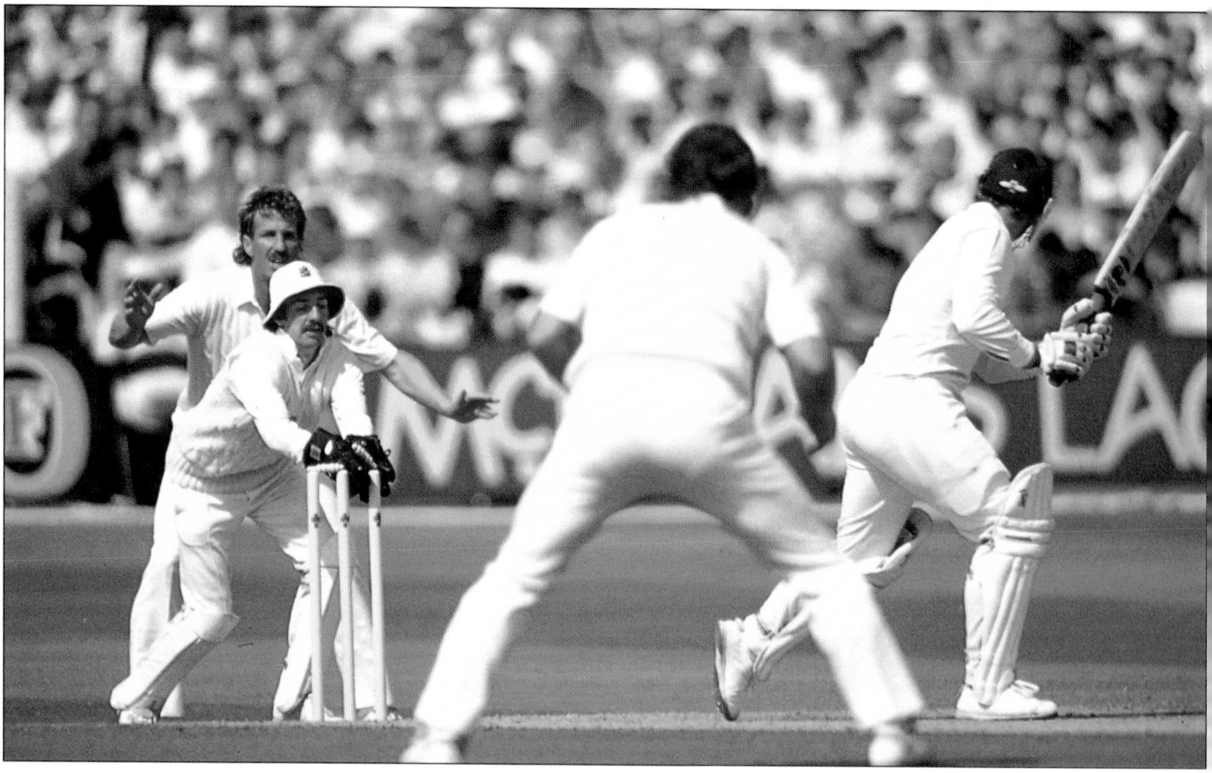

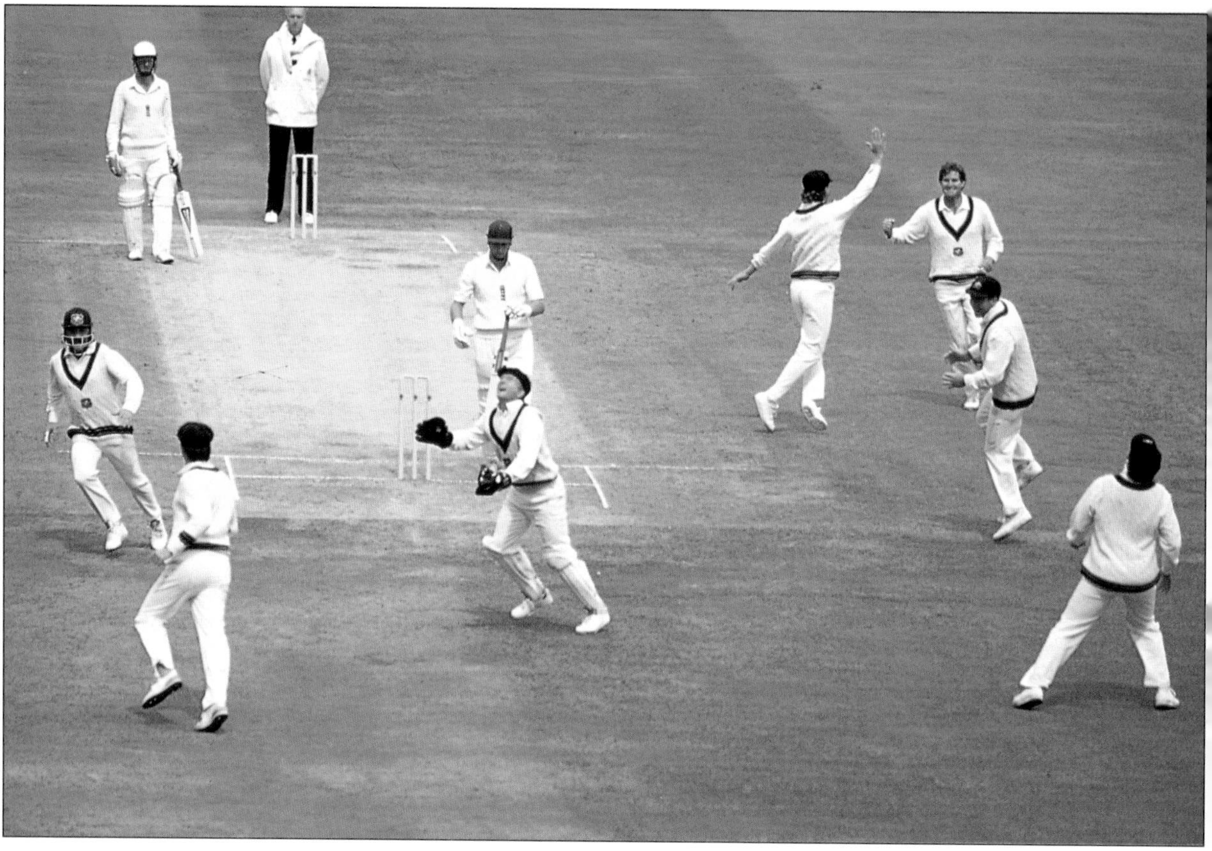

diving to his left. Hemmings had survived an appeal when he edged to slip off Lawson, and Waugh claimed the catch. The batsman stood his ground, and the umpires could do nothing but rule in the batsman's favour as they were undecided. Lawson reacted angrily, and harsh words were exchanged, but Border quickly silenced his team.

It was Hughes who finally claimed Hemmings, and Hohns bowled Fraser with the flipper. When Hughes wrecked Malcolm's stumps Australia were victors by an innings and 180 runs. The margin of defeat was the biggest England have ever suffered in a Test match in this country against Australia.

In winning for the fourth time in the series Australia equalled the record of Don Bradman's side of 1948. The triumph of Border's men was no more than they deserved. They were a splendidly organized group. Opponents had been studied and weaknesses exploited. The success of the

TOP LEFT: *Mark Taylor's innings finally comes to an end, stumped Russell, bowled Cook for 219. (Adrian Murrell/ Allsport)*

BOTTOM LEFT: *Moxon is caught at slip in the first over of the innings and another England disaster looms. (Adrian Murrell/Allsport)*

RIGHT: *Mike Atherton – second-innings promise for England. (Adrian Murrell/Allsport)*

FIFTH CORNHILL TEST MATCH – ENGLAND v. AUSTRALIA
10, 11, 12 and 14 August 1989 at Trent Bridge, Nottingham

AUSTRALIA

	FIRST INNINGS	
G.R. Marsh	c Botham, b Cook	138
M.A. Taylor	st Russell, b Cook	219
D.C. Boon	st Russell, b Cook	73
A.R. Border†	not out	65
D.M. Jones	c Gower, b Fraser	22
S.R. Waugh	c Gower, b Malcolm	0
I.A. Healy*	b Fraser	5
T.V. Hohns	not out	19
M.G. Hughes		
G.F. Lawson		
T.M. Alderman		
Extras	b 6, lb 23, w 3, nb 29	61
	(for 6 wkts, dec)	602

	O	M	R	W
Fraser	52.3	18	108	2
Malcolm	44	2	166	1
Botham	30	4	103	–
Hemmings	33	8	81	–
Cook	40	10	91	3
Atherton	7	–	24	–

FALL OF WICKETS
1–329, 2–430, 3–502, 4–543, 5–553, 6–560

ENGLAND

	FIRST INNINGS		SECOND INNINGS	
T.S. Curtis	lbw, b Alderman	2	(2) lbw, b Alderman	6
M.D. Moxon	c Waugh, b Alderman	0	(5) b Alderman	18
M.A. Atherton	lbw, b Alderman	0	c and b Hohns	47
R.A. Smith	c Healy, b Alderman	101	b Hughes	26
D.I. Gower†	c Healy, b Lawson	11	(1) b Lawson	5
R.C. Russell*	c Healy, b Lawson	20	b Lawson	1
E.E. Hemmings	b Alderman	38	lbw, b Hughes	35
A.R.C. Fraser	b Hohns	29	b Hohns	1
I.T. Botham	c Waugh, b Hohns	12	absent hurt	–
N.G.B. Cook	not out	2	(9) not out	7
D.E. Malcolm	c Healy, b Hughes	9	b Hughes	5
Extras	lb 18, nb 13	31	b 3, lb 6, w 1, nb 6	16
		255		167

	O	M	R	W	O	M	R	W
Alderman	19	2	69	5	16	6	32	2
Lawson	21	5	57	2	15	3	51	2
Hohns	18	8	48	2	12	3	29	2
Hughes	7.5	–	40	1	12.3	1	46	3
Waugh	11	4	23	–				

FALL OF WICKETS
1–1, 2–1, 3–14, 4–37, 5–119, 6–172, 7–214, 8–243, 9–244
1–5, 2–13, 3–67, 4–106, 5–114, 6–120, 7–134, 8–160, 9–167

Umpires: D.R. Shepherd & N.T. Plews

Australia won by an innings and 180 runs

Australians was built on intelligent management and leadership and team-work of the highest quality. One will remain ever grateful for the joy and zest that they brought to the English summer of 1989.

12, 14 and 15 August

at Swansea

Sussex 240 (M.P. Speight 69, C.M. Wells 57 not out) and 223 for 3 (A.P. Wells 72 not out, P.W.G. Parker 63)
Glamorgan 308 (A.R. Butcher 67, M.P. Maynard 65)

Match drawn
Glamorgan 7 pts, Sussex 4 pts

at Cheltenham

Derbyshire 448 for 9 dec (T.J. O'Gorman 124, J.E. Morris 121, R. Sharma 77, P.D. Bowler 57, C.A. Walsh 4 for 62)
Gloucestershire 175 for 6

Match drawn
Derbyshire 6 pts, Gloucestershire 2 pts

at Bournemouth

Worcestershire 325 (P.A. Neale 98, R.K. Illingworth 71)
Hampshire 137 (S.R. Lampitt 5 for 38) and 97 (R.K. Illingworth 5 for 23, S.M. McEwan 4 for 32)

Worcestershire won by an innings and 91 runs
Worcestershire 22 pts, Hampshire 3 pts

at Lytham

Lancashire 95 (N.A. Foster 4 for 31, T.D. Topley 4 for 33) and 381 (G.D. Lloyd 100, N.J. Speak 64, N.H. Fairbrother 60, P.A.J. DeFreitas 50, J.H. Childs 4 for 80)
Essex 400 for 4 dec (J.P. Stephenson 171, N. Hussain 105 not out, G.A. Gooch 68) and 79 for 3

Essex won by 7 wickets
Essex 23 pts, Lancashire 1 pt

at Lord's

Northamptonshire 363 (D.J. Capel 90, W. Larkins 80, R.J. Bailey 65) and 142 (P.C.R. Tufnell 5 for 60)
Middlesex 302 for 1 dec (J.D. Carr 153 not out, D.L. Haynes 76, M.R. Ramprakash 53 not out) and 204 for 3 (M.W. Gatting 83 not out)

Middlesex won by 7 wickets
Middlesex 22 pts, Northamptonshire 4 pts

at Edgbaston

Somerset 316 for 8 dec (N.D. Burns 90, V.J. Marks 75, C.J. Tavare 52) and 170 for 7 dec (J.C.M. Atkinson 53)
Warwickshire 250 for 7 dec (J.D. Ratcliffe 67 not out) and 107 for 3

Match drawn
Warwickshire 6 pts, Somerset 6 pts

at Scarborough

Yorkshire 400 for 5 dec (P.E. Robinson 147, D. Byas 117, K. Sharp 53) and 147 for 2 dec (A.A. Metcalfe 87 not out)
Kent 271 for 6 dec (N.R. Taylor 111, C.S. Cowdrey 80) and 277 for 5 (R.F. Pienaar 125, S.G. Hinks 69)

Kent won by 5 wickets
Kent 20 pts, Yorkshire 5 pts

Essex seemed set for the easiest of victories when Lancashire, having chosen to bat first, were bowled out just after

John Stephenson – a career-best 171 for Essex against Lancashire at Lytham, 12–15 August. (Alan Cozzi)

lunch on the first day for 95. Lancashire were devastated by the Essex seam bowlers, Pringle, Foster and Topley, and lost their last nine wickets for 45 runs. Gooch and Stephenson began the Essex innings with a stand of 120, and on the Monday, Stephenson, who batted for more than seven hours and hit the highest score of his career, reached the first century to be made in a championship match on the Lytham ground. He was soon followed by Nasser Hussain, with whom he shared a fourth-wicket partnership of 162 in 49 overs and who hit his 105 off 159 balls. When Lancashire batted again Mendis was out at 15, but Graham Lloyd and Nick Speak added 146 in 56 overs. Lloyd, son of the former England and Lancashire left-hander, hit his third century of the season off 220 balls. His innings included 12 fours, and he was bowled by Childs the ball after he reached his century. Fairbrother, Fowler and later DeFreitas were savage on the bowling of Foster, and DeFreitas was aided by Fitton in a ninth-wicket stand which realized 79 in 16 overs. This stand ate its way into the last 20 overs and left Essex with the difficult task of scoring 77 in 14 overs. There were alarms, but they raced to a thrilling victory with 13 balls to spare.

This win, however, was able to reduce Worcestershire's lead at the top of the table by only one point. The leaders endured a hard first day at Bournemouth, and they were

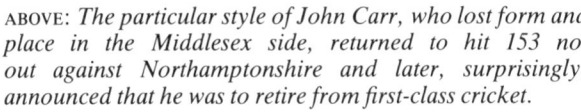

ABOVE: *The particular style of John Carr, who lost form and place in the Middlesex side, returned to hit 153 not out against Northamptonshire and later, surprisingly, announced that he was to retire from first-class cricket.*

ABOVE RIGHT: *Phil Robinson . . . (Dan Smith/Allsport)*

RIGHT: *. . . and David Byas, who hit career-best scores for Yorkshire against Kent at Scarborough. (Iain Duck/ASP)*

rescued from the embarrassment of 158 for 7 by Neale and Illingworth. Illingworth continued to bat sensibly on the Monday morning and led Worcestershire to a commendable 325. The home side then collapsed before Dilley and Lampitt, and, following-on, they fared even worse against McEwan and Illingworth to give the champions the easiest of victories.

Middlesex maintained their challenge with an excellent win over Northamptonshire, who dominated the first day's play by scoring at a consistently brisk rate. A shortened second day belonged entirely to Middlesex. Carr and Haynes put on 181 for the first wicket, and Carr reached his first century of the season. Gatting declared as soon as Middlesex had claimed their fourth batting point on the last day, and then, unexpectedly, Northamptonshire collapsed before the spin of Tufnell and Emburey. Needing 204 to win in 2¾ hours, Middlesex were given a fine example by skipper Gatting, and their victory, accomplished with five and a half overs to spare, was never in doubt.

At the other end of the table Kent gained their first victory for two months and moved off the bottom of the championship table. Robinson and Byas completed centuries on the opening day and shared a fourth-wicket stand of 258. Carrick did not declare until his side had reached 400 on the Monday morning, but Kent batted with considerably more zest. Taylor provided a solid base and Cowdrey the enterprise, and, in order to keep the game alive, he declared Kent's first innings closed when they still trailed Yorkshire by 129. Kent then offered Yorkshire some friendly bowling and fielding, and they were rewarded by being offered a target of 277 in 72 overs. Two wickets fell for 29 runs, but a dashing century from Pienaar and good foundation work by Simon Hinks took them to victory with 10 balls to spare.

There was no such excitement at Swansea, where nothing could be contrived that would compensate for some rather dour batting. At Cheltenham, too, there was little to gratify the paying customers. John Morris' excellent form continued with another stylish century, but even more gratifying for Derbyshire was the purposeful and accomplished batting of Tim O'Gorman. Drizzle and cold condemned the match to an inevitable draw.

There was a draw at Edgbaston also. Somerset occupied the first day, when Neil Burns showed that his left-handed batting is as stylish and correct as his immaculate wicket-keeping. Jason Ratcliffe displayed sound technique and solid defence on a shortened second day, and the home side eventually declined the offer to score 237 in 44 overs.

Middlesex (4 pts) won by 6 wickets

at The Oval

Surrey 233 for 5 (A.J. Stewart 77, G.S. Clinton 60, G.P. Thorpe 51)
Nottinghamshire 234 for 1 (P. Pollard 123 not out, R.T. Robinson 50)

Nottinghamshire (4 pts) won by 9 wickets

at Edgbaston

Somerset 207 for 8 (J.C.M. Atkinson 69, C.J. Tavare 51, G.C. Small 4 for 36)
Warwickshire 187 for 7

Warwickshire (4 pts) won on faster scoring rate

at Scarborough

Kent 225 for 7 (C.S. Cowdrey 68 not out)
Yorkshire 228 for 6 (A.A. Metcalfe 73, J.D. Love 65)

Yorkshire (4 pts) won by 4 wickets

Lancashire needed only to beat Essex at Old Trafford to win the Refuge Assurance League. As it was, they were thankful that rain saved them from defeat. Rain delayed the start and reduced the match to 28 overs a side. Only some fierce hitting by Wasim Akram rescued Lancashire from total disaster, and Essex were 53 for 0 in 10.4 overs when the umpires called a halt. Needing to hit the last ball of the match at Bournemouth for four, Tim Tremlett could manage only two, so that Worcestershire finished narrow victors over Hampshire and made certain of a place in the Refuge Assurance Cup. Surrey's hopes of maintaining their place in the last four suffered a severe blow when

Refuge Assurance League

13 August

at Ebbw Vale

Glamorgan 117 for 5
v. Sussex

Match abandoned
Glamorgan 2 pts, Sussex 2 pts

at Cheltenham

Gloucestershire 127
Derbyshire 130 for 6

Derbyshire (4 pts) won by 4 wickets

at Bournemouth

Worcestershire 149
Hampshire 147 for 9 (S.R. Lampitt 4 for 30)

Worcestershire (4 pts) won by 2 runs

at Old Trafford

Lancashire 135 for 9 (D.R. Pringle 4 for 31)
Essex 53 for 0

Match abandoned
Lancashire 2 pts, Essex 2 pts

at Lord's

Northamptonshire 157 for 8
Middlesex 160 for 4

Man of the Match at Edgbaston in the NatWest Bank Trophy semi-final, Asif Din, 94 not out. (Ken Kelly)

they were comprehensively beaten by Nottinghamshire at The Oval. After losing Darren Bicknell at six, Surrey took total command and scored consistently and briskly to reach 233 in 39 overs. Nottinghamshire were undaunted by this score, however, and were given a splendid start by Pollard and Robinson, who put on 119. Robinson's 50 came off 59 balls, and Pollard hit his century off 116 balls. With Randall also making a bright contribution, Nottinghamshire won by nine wickets with four balls to spare. It was Surrey's last home Sunday league game of the season and their first Sunday defeat at The Oval.

16, 17 and 18 August

at Canterbury

Australians 356 for 8 dec (D.M. Jones 128, D.C. Boon 86, D.J.M. Kelleher 4 for 82)
Kent 191 (S.G. Hinks 85, G.D. Campbell 4 for 78) and 237 for 9 (M.R. Benson 106, T.M. Moody 4 for 30)

Match drawn

The tourists were an embarrassing 35 for 3, all three wickets to Danny Kelleher, after being put in to bat, but Jones and Boon restored order with a stand of 189 in 49 overs. Interruptions for rain helped Kent's cause when they were forced to follow-on, but Benson played a determined innings to earn his side a draw.

NatWest Bank Trophy

Semi-Finals

16 August

at Southampton

Middlesex 267 for 7 (J.D. Carr 83, D.L. Haynes 80)
Hampshire 264 for 7 (C.L. Smith 114)

Middlesex won by 3 runs
(Man of the Match: C.L. Smith)

at Edgbaston

Warwickshire 220 for 9 (M. Asif Din 94 not out, A.J. Moles 61)
Worcestershire 120

Warwickshire won by 100 runs
(Man of the Match: M. Asif Din)

Put in to bat, Middlesex survived without alarm or loss until the fourth over after lunch. Haynes and Carr batted with a confidence and purpose that mocked Nicholas' understandable decision to ask his opponents to bat first. The openers negotiated a difficult first eight overs after which they began to score freely to give their side the base, 165 in 43 overs, from which a huge score should have been made. Hampshire played with great resource to keep the visitors in check, however, and Middlesex contributed somewhat to their own frustrations. The opening partnership was broken when Carr was stumped off Cowley, and Haynes, caught by Nicholas off a skier, followed 10 runs later. Gatting, shrugging off a generally hostile reception, cut his first ball for four and reversed swept the second for three. He looked to be in awesome form when Ramprakash called him for a suicidal single and Terry hit the stumps with his throw. Emburey, promoted to raise the

Man of the Match at Southampton, but no NatWest Cup Final place for Chris Smith of Hampshire. (David Munden)

tempo, suffered the same fate. He had not scored when Ramprakash called him, and Terry again hit the stumps with Emburey stranded. These were blots on an otherwise excellent innings by Ramprakash, who hit 43 off 39 balls. Roseberry, too, batted well until he became a third run out victim, but with Marshall bowling so economically at the close, Middlesex scored fewer runs than had looked probable early in the day. Hampshire's chase for runs suffered early set-backs with the loss of Terry and James, but the Smith brothers injected a sense of urgency into the batting with a partnership of 78 in 19 overs. Robin Smith was at his most powerful, hitting as cleanly and as hard as he had done in the quarter-final at The Oval and in the Test match at Trent Bridge. He had just driven Emburey back over his head when he was caught in two minds and bowled. Emburey's relief and jubilation were obvious to all. Nicholas and Scott did their best to keep the run rate going, and Scott once pulled Fraser for six, but Hampshire's hopes rested squarely on Chris Smith. As long as he remained, Hampshire were likely to win. He reached a most praiseworthy century and showed no sign of slackening his control over the bowling when he was hit a nasty blow on the right hand by a ball from Fraser. It was later revealed to have caused a broken thumb, but in the immediate context it reduced his power of hitting. In the 58th over, with 20 runs required for a Hampshire victory, he was caught half-way to the mid-wicket boundary. His 114 had occupied 177 balls and had brought his side to the brink of success. The next seven balls produced five runs, so that Cowley and Marshall needed to hit a formidable 15 off the last over. Eight runs came off the first four balls of the over, bowled by Fraser, and seven of them were scored by Cowley, but the last ball arrived with Marshall needing to hit a six to win the match. The West Indian all-rounder swung hard, and the ball went high, but there was trajectory without the necessary distance, and Middlesex were in the NatWest Final for the second year in succession.

There was less excitement, but more surprise at Edgbaston. Worcestershire, already handicapped by the absence of Botham and Newport, suffered a further blow when Dilley was ruled unfit just before the start. It later became obvious that Radford, too, was not fully fit for such an encounter. None of this seemed to matter when Worcestershire, having won the toss and put Warwickshire in to bat, quickly claimed the wicket of Andy Lloyd. There was an unfortunate mishap when Kallicharran was forced to retire hurt before he had scored when he was hit in the face by a return from Neale. Humpage drove loosely at Radford, who limped through his 12 overs at the outset and conceded only 18 runs, and was bowled. Warwickshire, 21 for 2 and Kallicharran retired hurt, were in trouble, and the game seemed to be following a predictable pattern. Moles and Asif Din disturbed the tenor of the Worcestershire success when, in their differing styles, they added 104 in 32 overs. Moles was the rock, pushing and nudging, while Asif Din provided most of the flair, being particularly aggressive square of the wicket. When Moles was bowled by Illingworth, as he gave himself too much room to hit the ball on the off side, and Reeve went cheaply, beaten in the flight by the same bowler and stumped by Rhodes, it seemed that Worcestershire had again grasped the initiative, but Kallicharran returned to help Asif Din add a sparkling 39 in five overs. The Smiths disappointed, and, in spite of Small helping Asif Din to add 30 in three overs, Warwickshire's 220 did not look as if it would be enough to deny Worcestershire. Rain, delay and early tea all appeared to add to Warwickshire's problems as they were now faced with the prospect of a long, unrelieved session of bowling. They had early encouragement when Donald's second ball beat Curtis' hesitant defence and had him leg before although the batsman clearly thought otherwise. Rhodes was promoted to number three to spare Hick for later, but he was bowled by Small without offering a shot, and Worcestershire were 7 for 2. Hick could be spared no longer and he showed his pedigree with a sumptuous four through the off-side field. Reeve's third ball was to see the end of him, however, as he drove lazily at an outswinger and was caught behind by the gleeful Humpage. Weston and D'Oliveira gave hint of recovery with a stand of 26 which doubled the score, but the worthy Weston was bowled by Paul Smith, who then ran out Neale, and dismissed D'Oliveira in extraordinary fashion. The batsman drove hard at Paul Smith, who got

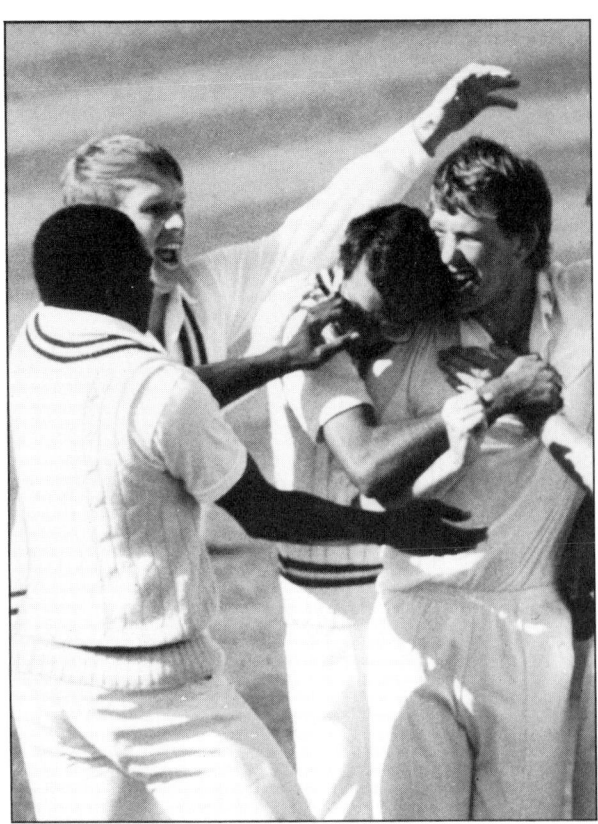

Warwickshire exultant. Gladstone Small, skipper Andy Lloyd and Asif Din congratulate Dermot Reeve, who has just had Graeme Hick caught behind, and Warwickshire are on their way to victory over Worcestershire. (Ken Kelly)

his hands to the ball and parried it in the manner of a goalkeeper. He succeeded in knocking it into the covers, where Neil Smith completed the catch. With the run out of Neale, Worcestershire's hopes of victory faded, and Warwickshire, underdogs in every round bar the first, strode easily to Lord's.

International Matches
HOLLAND v. ENGLAND XI

As part of the celebrations of the Dutch Cricket Association an England XI composed of players on the short list to tour West Indies but not involved in the NatWest Bank Trophy semi-finals played two international matches against Holland. The cosmopolitan Dutch side snatched a narrow victory in the first game when West Indian Noel Clarke hit 7 sixes in his innings of 77. England seemed set for victory as Bailey and Stephenson took the score past 100 with only one wicket down, but Lubbers, the Dutch captain and off-break bowler, bowled Stephenson and had Stewart caught at short-leg within the space of three deliveries. England reached the last over, bowled by Sri Lankan Aponso in near darkness, needing 12 to win. Pringle was out to the first ball, and Bailey and Medlycott could only drive singles to the deep set field.

FIRST ONE-DAY INTERNATIONAL – HOLLAND v. ENGLAND XI
16 August 1989 at Amstelveen, Amsterdam

HOLLAND				ENGLAND XI			
E. Gouka	b Pringle		18	P.M. Roebuck†	c Gomes, b Aponso		19
P. Holland	c Capel, b Base		0	J.P. Stephenson	b Lubbers		43
R. Lifman	c Bailey, b Pringle		18	R.J. Bailey	not out		68
N. Clarke	c Medlycott, b Base		77	A.J. Stewart*	c Gomes, b Lubbers		0
R. Lefebvre	c Hussain,			N. Hussain	b Edwards		21
	b Medlycott		7	D.J. Capel	c Holland, b Jansen		5
R. Gomes	c Roebuck,			M. Watkinson	c Ruskamp, b Jansen		0
	b Thomas		18	D.R. Pringle	c Gomes, b Aponso		1
S. Lubbers†	c Capel, b Thomas		6	K.T. Medlycott	not out		2
F. Aponso	not out		12	J.G. Thomas			
C. Ruskamp*	not out		5	S.J. Base			
F. Jansen				Extras	b 4, lb 4, w 4, nb 2		14
R. Edwards							
Extras	b 1, lb 8, w 4, nb 2		15	(40 overs)	(for 7 wkts)		173
(40 overs)	(for 7 wkts)		176				

	O	M	R	W		O	M	R	W
Thomas	8	3	32	2	Jansen	8	1	25	2
Base	8	1	22	2	Edwards	8	–	41	1
Pringle	8	–	35	2	Aponso	8	–	44	2
Capel	4	–	23	–	Lubbers	8	–	33	2
Medlycott	7	–	32	1	Lefebvre	8	1	22	–
Watkinson	5	1	23	–					

FALL OF WICKETS
1–2, 2–29, 3–57, 4–105, 5–137, 6–151, 7–159

FALL OF WICKETS
1–46, 2–101, 3–101, 4–145, 5–159, 6–162, 7–165

Umpires: R. Dukker & W. van Dijk

Holland won by 3 runs

SECOND ONE-DAY INTERNATIONAL – HOLLAND v. ENGLAND XI
17 August 1989 at Amstelveen, Amsterdam

ENGLAND XI				HOLLAND			
P.M. Roebuck†	c Jansen, b Aponso		60	R. Vos	lbw, b Watkin		10
J.P. Stephenson	b Lefebvre		121	F. Aponso	c Capel, b Medlycott		9
R.J. Bailey	run out		18	R. Lifman	c Stewart, b Capel		12
A.J. Stewart*	c Lefebvre, b Lubbers		5	N. Clarke	b Capel		12
N. Hussain	c Gomes, b Lubbers		11	R. Lefebvre	c Bailey, b Base		11
M. Watkinson	b Lubbers		6	R. Gomes	c Roebuck, b Pringle		22
D.R. Pringle	not out		24	P. Holland	b Pringle		5
D.J. Capel	run out		2	S. Lubbers†	c Base, b Medlycott		32
K.T. Medlycott	not out		0	C. Ruskamp*	not out		21
S.L. Watkin				F. Jansen	b Capel		0
S.J. Base				J. Coster	run out		6
Extras	b 2, lb 6, w 4, nb 2		14	Extras	lb 5, w 9, nb 9		23
(55 overs)	(for 7 wkts)		261	(48.3 overs)			163

	O	M	R	W		O	M	R	W
Jansen	11	–	82	–	Base	8	3	12	1
Lefebvre	11	1	32	1	Watkin	9	–	37	1
Aponso	11	–	38	1	Medlycott	8.3	1	25	2
Coster	11	–	48	–	Capel	7	–	39	3
Lubbers	11	–	53	3	Roebuck	2	–	10	–
					Pringle	8	1	23	2
					Watkinson	6	–	12	–

FALL OF WICKETS
1–112, 2–156, 3–179, 4–214, 5–231, 6–244, 7–261

FALL OF WICKETS
1–22, 2–22, 3–41, 4–53, 5–87, 6–92, 7–101, 8–154,
9–154

Umpires: H. Poederbach & J.O. Wilts

England XI won by 98 runs

England in Amsterdam. Left to right: Base, Watkin, Capel, Stewart, Stephenson, Pringle, M.J. Stewart, P.M. Lush, Roebuck, Watkinson, Hussain, Bailey, Thomas and Medlycott. (Pascal Rondeau/Allsport)

In the second game, a fine century by John Stephenson of Essex, who reached both his fifty and his hundred with sixes, put England in a strong position, and Holland, having lost early wickets, could never match the required run rate.

19, 20 and 21 August

at Chelmsford

Australians 387 for 7 dec (D.C. Boon 151, T.M. Moody 80, D.M. Jones 70) and 258 for 2 dec (S.R. Waugh 100 not out, T.J. Zoehrer 93)
Essex 290 for 8 dec (M.E. Waugh 100 not out, P.J. Prichard 86, G.A. Gooch 58) and 205 (M.E. Waugh 57, P.J. Prichard 52, M.G. Hughes 5 for 64)

Australians won by 150 runs

19, 21 and 22 August

at Canterbury

Kent 372 for 9 dec (R.F. Pienaar 132, C.S. Cowdrey 57, M.C. Dobson 52, S.J. Dennis 5 for 83) and 218 for 4 dec (T.R. Ward 78 not out, C.S. Cowdrey 53)
Glamorgan 311 (I. Smith 116, H. Morris 56) and 178 (H. Morris 68, R.P. Davis 4 for 57, A.P. Igglesden 4 for 58)

Kent won by 101 runs
Kent 24 pts, Glamorgan 6 pts

at Old Trafford

Lancashire 293 (M.A. Atherton 115 not out, P. Carrick 4 for 85) and 228 for 3 dec (G.D. Mendis 103 not out, M. Watkinson 51 not out)
Yorkshire 192 (R.J. Blakey 56, Wasim Akram 5 for 44) and 148 (R.J. Blakey 62, Wasim Akram 5 for 51)

Lancashire won by 181 runs
Lancashire 23 pts, Yorkshire 5 pts

at Leicester

Leicestershire 297 (N.E. Briers 63, L. Potter 55, A.J. Murphy 4 for 66) and 182 (M. Frost 5 for 40)
Surrey 184 (W.K.M. Benjamin 5 for 83) and 296 for 6 (G.S. Clinton 84, A.J. Stewart 77)

Surrey won by 4 wickets
Surrey 21 pts, Leicestershire 7 pts

at Northampton

Northamptonshire 51 (T.A. Munton 5 for 13) and 109 (P.A. Smith 4 for 9)
Warwickshire 191 (A.I. Kallicharran 100, C.E.L. Ambrose 6 for 22)

Warwickshire won by an innings and 31 runs
Warwickshire 21 pts, Northamptonshire 4 pts

at Trent Bridge

Nottinghamshire 185 (B.C. Broad 57, R. Sharma 4 for 31, S.J. Base 4 for 33) and 114 (O.H. Mortensen 4 for 21, K.J. Barnett 4 for 36)
Derbyshire 165 (K.J. Barnett 80, E.E. Hemmings 4 for 57, F.D.

Stephenson 4 for 59) and 64 (E.E. Hemmings 5 for 20)

Nottinghamshire won by 70 runs
Nottinghamshire 21 pts, Derbyshire 5 pts

at Taunton

Hampshire 257 (M.C.J. Nicholas 121 not out, K.D. James 56, A.N. Jones 6 for 37) and 138 (J.R. Wood 55 not out, N.A. Mallender 5 for 55)
Somerset 303 for 8 dec (V.J. Marks 89 not out, N.D. Burns 78) and 93 for 2

Somerset won by 8 wickets
Somerset 23 pts, Hampshire 5 pts

at Hastings

Sussex 249 (A.P. Wells 66, A.I.C. Dodemaide 61 not out) and 216 (A.P. Wells 51)
Middlesex 370 (M.W. Gatting 121, K.R. Brown 90, A.M. Babington 4 for 94) and 97 for 1

Middlesex won by 9 wickets
Middlesex 23 pts, Sussex 5 pts

First Youth Test Match

20, 21, 22 and 23 August

---

at Scarborough

England 156 (C.L. Cairns 5 for 26) and 268 (A.L. Penberthy 83 not out, C.L. Cairns 5 for 61)
New Zealand 440 for 9 dec (C. Harris 125, A. Parore 96, S. Wilson 51, C. Ross 51, R.H. Edmunds 4 for 78)

New Zealand won by an innings and 16 runs

The Australians' last match against a county side provided them with their eighth win and brought their share of the Castlemaine XXXX challenge to more than £63,000. While some may deplore the increasing commercialization of cricket it cannot be denied that the matches between the tourists and the counties in 1989 were of more import and interest than they had been for many years. The most remarkable thing about the game at Chelmsford, which saw much good cricket, was that the Waugh twins created a record for a first-class match by scoring centuries on successive days for the opposing sides.

The seven matches in the Britannic Assurance County Championship all produced results. The matches at Trent Bridge and Northampton both ended in two days. The game at Nottingham caused much controversy. Twenty wickets fell on the Saturday, and so disturbed were the umpires about the pitch and the dangers that it presented to the batsmen that they moved to the strip of turf that had been used for the Test match. This proved to be no more encouraging, and 18 wickets fell to bring the match to an end on the Monday afternoon. Michael Holding protested at the umpires' action on a matter of principle and refused to bat in Derbyshire's second innings. It surprised no one that Nottinghamshire were penalized 25 points for an unsatisfactory pitch.

Northamptonshire, whose pitches had caused critical comment from several counties during the course of the season, were bowled out shortly before lunch on the first day. The reliable and accurate Tim Munton did most of the damage, but Dermot Reeve had the astonishing figures

Tim Munton, a reliable bowler for Warwickshire throughout the season and 5 for 13 in the rout of Northamptonshire, 19 August. (David Munden)

of 3 for 3 in 7.3 overs, six of which were maidens. In the afternoon Alvin Kallicharran played an innings of high quality while all about him fell, and Northamptonshire collapsed depressingly on the Monday to leave Warwickshire victors by an innings in a match in which they had failed to score 200.

Kent enjoyed the heady success of two championship victories in succession when Igglesden bowled Barwick with only three balls of the match remaining. Another excellent century by Roy Pienaar was the feature of the first day's play, but Glamorgan fought back splendidly when all-rounder Ian Smith hit the highest score of his career. Smith's innings, full of zest and enthusiasm, contained 16 boundaries and much intelligent aggression. Quick scoring by Ward and Chris Cowdrey set up a Kent declaration, and after early resistance Glamorgan wilted before Davis and Igglesden.

The Roses match at Old Trafford seemed very much in favour of Yorkshire until mid-afternoon on the first day. Lancashire stumbled to 145 for 6, but Atherton, having stood firm to reach 50 off 46 overs, organized the later batting in mature fashion to take his side to 293 and reach his first century of the season in four hours. The Yorkshire

Derbyshire CCC
Limited-Over Matches, 1989

BATTING

BATTING	Northamptonshire (Derby) 23 April (RA)	Somerset (Derby) 25 & 26 April (B&H)	Leicestershire (Leicester) 30 April (RA)	Nottinghamshire (Trent Bridge) 2 May (B&H)	Essex (Chelmsford) 7 May (RA)	Minor Counties (Derby) 11 May (B&H)	Yorkshire (Leeds) 13 May (B&H)	Lancashire (Leek) 14 May (RA)	Worcestershire (Worcester) 11 June (RA)	Sussex (Derby) 18 June (RA)	Nottinghamshire (Trent Bridge) 25 June (RA)	Ireland (Derby) 28 & 29 June (NW)	Somerset (Derby) 2 July (RA)	Middlesex (Lord's) 9 July (RA)	Worcestershire (Worcester) 12 July (NW)	Kent (Canterbury) 16 July (RA)
K.J. Barnett	0	77	50	2	75	101	11		13		16	49			55	27
P.D. Bowler	17	4	6	58	8	11	35	12	55*	11	8	64	1		9	17
B.J.M. Maher	27	39	21	17	42*	21	11	0	0	1	14	0*	49*		3	3
J.E. Morris	0			1	—	13	32	3*	1	45	4	7	35		0	41
B. Roberts	20	35*	30	5	—	26*	0	24	16	24	13				64*	31
S.C. Goldsmith	13	15	32	37*	—	1*	14	49								
R. Sharma	0	1	5	10				6	28	0	10	15		0	50	17
P.G. Newman	26*		3	3	11	—	8		24	0*	18	4	—	0*	25	0*
M.A. Holding	12	0	5	2	—	6	0		5	11	32	18*			6	4
S.J. Base	4	—	6*	—	—	—	6*				1	—	—			0
O.H. Mortensen	1	—	0*	—	—	—	6*	11	—		4*	4*	—	—	1	2
A.E. Warner		—			5*	0	11	8					—	5	0	
F.A. Griffith			10						1	0	5					1
I.R. Bishop									16*							
C. Gladwin										3	8			20		
D.E. Malcolm											4				6	
C.J. Adams														0		
I. Redpath														9		
K.M. Krikken														16		
T.J.G. O'Gorman																
M. Jean-Jacques																
Byes	5	1			4				1	4		1				2
Leg-byes	15	12	7	8	5	14	10	17	8	2	10	5	11		8	12
Wides	1		2	5	2	6	9	5	3	1	17		2	2	10	6
No-balls		3	1	1	2	2			1		2	1			3	1
Total	141	187	178	153	150	201	153	177	134	128	145	161	148		240	164
Wickets	10	6	9	8	3	6	9	9	7	10	10	5	7		10	10
Result	Ab.	L	W	L	L	W	L	L	L	W	L	W	W	W	L	W
Points	2	0	4	0	0	2	0	0	0	4	0	—	4	4	—	4

Fielding Figures
27 – B.J.M. Maher
10 – R. Sharma
8 – K.J. Barnett
7 – M.A. Holding
5 – P.G. Newman
4 – S.C. Goldsmith and P.D. Bowler
3 – B. Roberts, S.J. Base and J.E. Morris
2 – O.H. Mortensen
1 – A.E. Warner

BOWLING

BOWLING	M.A. Holding	O.H. Mortensen	P.G. Newman	S.J. Base	R. Sharma	B. Roberts	A.E. Warner
v. Northamptonshire (Derby) 23 April (RA)							
v. Somerset (Derby) 25 & 26 April (B&H)	11–3–25–1	11–1–19–0	11–3–17–0	11–0–48–1	2.2–0–12–0	5–2–10–1	
v. Leicestershire (Leicester) 30 April (RA)	4–0–14–1	8–0–23–3	7.5–1–20–2	5–0–14–2	4–1–12–2		3–0–10–0
v. Nottinghamshire (Trent Bridge) 2 May (B&H)	11–2–31–2	11–0–35–2	11–2–25–0	11–1–37–0	4–0–15–0	3.1–0–28–0	
v. Essex (Chelmsford) 7 May (RA)	8–0–30–0	8–1–38–1	8–0–22–2	8–1–20–1	6–0–17–2	2–0–12–1	
v. Minor Counties (Derby) 11 May (B&H)	6.4–1–17–3	11–6–21–2	8–3–30–1	8–1–47–1			11–1–30–3
v. Yorkshire (Leeds) 13 May (B&H)	11–1–44–0	11–2–33–2	11–1–53–1	11–2–40–0			11–3–32–2
v. Lancashire (Leek) 14 May (RA)	8–0–41–0	8–2–19–2	8–1–51–1	8–1–31–1			8–0–29–2
v. Worcestershire (Worcester) 11 June (RA)		6–0–24–0	7–1–43–0			7–0–24–2	8–1–35–2
v. Sussex (Derby) 18 June (RA)	7–1–11–1	8–2–16–3	8–1–25–1	7.4–0–29–3			
v. Nottinghamshire (Trent Bridge) 25 June (RA)	7–0–32–2	8–1–26–1	8–0–37–2	8–0–34–1			
v. Ireland (Derby) 28 & 29 June (NW)	9–1–29–1	12–6–14–6	3–0–18–0		0.4–0–0–1		
v. Somerset (Derby) 2 July (RA)	8–2–26–0	8–3–11–2	8–1–45–0	8–0–28–2			8–0–37–0
v. Middlesex (Lord's) 9 July (RA)		8–2–19–2	4–0–18–1	8–0–23–0			3.4–0–23–0
v. Worcestershire (Worcester) 12 July (NW)	12–3–20–2	12–0–46–0	12–1–79–2				12–2–60–1
v. Kent (Canterbury) 16 July (RA)	7–1–18–4	8–2–23–1	7.3–0–27–3	8–0–30–0	4–0–23–0		
v. Glamorgan (Heanor) 23 July (RA)	8–0–33–2			8–0–52–1	4–0–24–0		8–0–55–0
v. Surrey (Derby) 30 July (RA)	8–0–24–1	8–0–29–0		7.4–0–24–3			8–0–22–2
v. Hampshire (Derby) 6 August (RA)	8–1–22–0	8–2–14–2		7.2–0–37–3			8–0–32–0
v. Gloucestershire (Cheltenham) 13 August (RA)	8–2–21–3		8–3–17–1	8–0–35–1	8–3–24–1		
v. Warwickshire (Edgbaston) 20 August (RA)	8–0–34–2	8–1–27–1	3.4–0–16–1	5–0–35–0	8–1–44–3		
v. Yorkshire (Chesterfield) 27 August (RA)	8–2–15–0	8–1–25–1		8–1–17–3	5–0–33–2	3–0–20–0	8–0–34–1
Wickets	25	31	18	23	13	2	13

innings began well enough, but Wasim Akram brought about a decline which put Lancashire in command. Mendis hit his third century in Roses matches, and Hughes' declaration left Yorkshire 81 overs in which to score 330 runs. They lost their first six wickets for 64 runs to end all hope of victory, and only Blakey saved them from total ignominy. Wasim Akram finished with his best figures for Lancashire, 10 for 95, and led his county to their first victory in a Roses match for eight years.

Having struggled for much of the first two days, Surrey gave a fine display on the last day to beat Leicestershire at Grace Road. They took the last four Leicestershire wickets for 19 runs in 37 balls on the final morning and then went boldly in search of their target, 296 runs off 92 overs on a pitch that was far from easy. Clinton and Darren Bicknell gave them a sound start with a stand of

English Counties Form Charts

The statistics of all limited-over cricket matches are given on pages 370–407. The games covered are:

Refuge Assurance League (RA)
Refuge Assurance Cup (RC)
Tilcon Trophy (TT)
Benson and Hedges (B&H)
Four Counties Tournament (FC)
National Westminster Bank Trophy (NW)
Seeboard Trophy (SB)

Once again averages are not produced as it is felt that they have little relevance in limited-over cricket where batsmen often sacrifice wickets for quick runs and bowlers are ordered to contain rather than capture wickets.
In the batting tables a blank indicates that a batsman did not *play* in a game, a dash (—) that he did not *bat*.

Batting

v. Glamorgan (Heanor) 23 July (RA)	v. Surrey (Derby) 30 July (RA)	v. Hampshire (Derby) 6 August (RA)	v. Gloucestershire (Cheltenham) 13 August (RA)	v. Warwickshire (Edgbaston) 20 August (RA)	v. Yorkshire (Chesterfield) 27 August (RA)	Runs
00*	14	2	6	3	13	614
36	22	71	3	13	66*	527
—	5	7	9*	—		269
00*		0	35	112*	7	436
—			0		10	298
						161
—	0	5	3	15	—	165
			—			122
—	1	1	22	33*	—	158
—	—	3	—	—	—	20
	—	2*	—	—	—	31
—	31*	40		—		100
—						17
						16
						31
—		0			—	10
	1		46*		—	47
						9
						16
	35*	0	2	3	46*	86
					—	
				2		
8	12	11	3	9	3	
1	6	3	1	5	2	
			3		1	
45	127	148	130	195	148	
1	6	10	6	5	3	
W	W	L	W	W	W	
4	4	0	4	4	4	

Bowling

I.R. Bishop	F.A. Griffith	D.E. Malcolm	K.J. Barnett	M. Jean-Jacques	Byes	Leg-byes	Wides	No-balls	Total	Wkts
										Ab.
						11	4	2	142	3
					5	7	1		105	10
						8	2		179	5
					2	13	3	1	154	8
					1	3	9	4	149	10
					1	5	9	5	208	5
						5	5		176	8
8-0-51-1	4-0-23-0					7	6	3	207	6
	7-0-41-2					8	4	5	130	10
	8-2-32-2					9	8	3	170	8
			7-1-18-2			3	3	2	82	10
						8	7	2	155	6
						6		2	89	4
		12-0-62-2			5	6	6	6	278	7
	4-0-14-2					4	1	2	139	10
	4-0-35-0	8-0-35-0			2	7	4	1	243	3
		8-0-21-4				5	3	1	125	10
		8-0-34-0			1	9	10	3	149	6
			7-1-20-2	1-0-7-0		3	2		127	10
		7.2-0-28-0			1	7	5		192	7
					1	2	6		147	8
1	6	8	2	0						

Essex CCC
Limited-Over Matches, 1989

BATTING

BATTING	v. Kent (Canterbury) 23 April (RA)	v. Sussex (Hove) 25 & 26 April (B&H)	v. Middlesex (Chelmsford) 30 April (RA)	v. Hampshire (Chelmsford) 2 May (B&H)	v. Derbyshire (Chelmsford) 7 May (RA)	v. Kent (Canterbury) 9 May (B&H)	v. Glamorgan (Chelmsford) 11 May (B&H)	v. Hampshire (Chelmsford) 14 May (RA)	v. Gloucestershire (Bristol) 21 May (RA)	v. Somerset (Chelmsford) 28 May (RA)	v. Lancashire (Chelmsford) 31 May (B&H)	v. Surrey (The Oval) 11 June (RA)	v. Somerset (Taunton) 14 June (B&H)	v. Leicestershire (Chelmsford) 18 June (RA)	v. Warwickshire (Ilford) 25 June (RA)	v. Somerset (Taunton) 28 & 29 June (NW)	v. Sussex (Horsham) 2 July (RA)	v. Glamorgan (Neath) 9 July (RA)	v. Nottinghamshire (Lord's) 15 July (RA)	v. Yorkshire (Southend) 23 July (RA)
G.A. Gooch	34	18	76*	100*	22	8	69*	63	76	—	1	—	20	111*	—	94	41	—	48	106*
B.R. Hardie	31	5	18	20	36	24	20*	12	73*	49	65	10	41	67	28	7	38	58	0	13
P.J. Prichard	6	73	11	12*	1	22	—	18	—	35*	19	73*	—	5	17	37*	4	1	27*	—
M.E. Waugh	40*	0	16*	20	6	22	—	22	6*	81*	93	20	36	2*	48	0	32	112*	41	62
D.R. Pringle	10	44*	—	—	13	6	—	3	—	—	1	15*	—	—	0	4	—	15	—	—
J.P. Stephenson	0*	38	—	—	25	63*	—	12	—	16	28	4	31	—	30	6	2*	—	9	—
A.W. Lilley	—	20	—	3	13	3	—	14*	—	21	10	0	43	—	18	—	—	3	95*	—
D.E. East	—	1*																		
T.D. Topley					7*							9								
N.A. Foster							2*										7		2*	
J.K. Lever																	3*			
G. Miller		20	—	—	4				29*	0*			44*		0*	15				
M.A. Garnham				8*	27*			3		3	0	10				18		0		
K. Butler																				
J.H. Childs																				
N. Hussain												23				63*	24	0	15*	
M.C. Ilott												4								
Nadeem Shahid																				
Byes				2	1				8		2	2	1		6	5			1	2
Leg-byes	8	8	10	11	13	13	4	5	10	10	9	4	20	6	13	9	7	11	26	6
Wides	4	1	1	3	3	2	5	2	2		4	8	10	4	5	10		2	4	
No-balls	3	4	2	6	1	5	1	1	1	4	1	2	2	2	2	2			1	1
Total	136	232	134	175	154	196	99	157	168	218	250	160	293	193	218	221	157	205	243	217
Wickets	4	7	2	3	8	6	0	7	1	5	7	10	5	1	6	10	4	3	7	2
Result	W	W	W	W	W	W	W	W	W	W	W	L	W	W	W	L	W	W	L	W
Points	4	2	4	2	4	2	2	4	4	4	—	0	—	4	4	4	—	4	—	4

Fielding Figures

24 – M.A. Garnham (ct 20/st 4)	10 – B.R. Hardie
14 – G.A. Gooch	9 – D.R. Pringle and P.J. Prichard
13 – M.E. Waugh	8 – J.P. Stephenson and G. Miller
7 – J.K. Lever	5 – N. Hussain and T.D. Topley
3 – D.E. East	4 – N.A. Foster and A.W. Lilley
1 – J.H. Childs	

BOWLING

BOWLING	J.K. Lever	N.A. Foster	D.R. Pringle	T.D. Topley	G.A. Gooch	J.P. Stephenson	M.E. Waugh
v. Kent (Canterbury) 23 April (RA)	8–1–16–1	8–0–25–3	8–1–28–2	8–0–24–2	8–0–33–2		
v. Sussex (Hove) 25 & 26 April (B&H)		8.4–0–25–2	10–3–35–3	11–3–26–2	9–3–19–1	6–2–18–2	2–0–20–0
v. Middlesex (Chelmsford) 30 April (RA)		8–2–12–2	8–0–32–3	8–1–20–1	8–1–20–1	8–0–27–3	
v. Hampshire (Chelmsford) 2 May (B&H)		11–2–34–1	11–0–39–2	11–4–23–1	11–2–22–2	7–0–24–0	
v. Derbyshire (Chelmsford) 7 May (RA)	8–1–17–0		8–1–23–3	8–0–42–2	8–1–37–1		
v. Kent (Canterbury) 9 May (B&H)	11–5–23–1	11–2–44–2	11–1–44–2	11–3–37–1	6–2–24–0	5–1–16–1	
v. Glamorgan (Chelmsford) 11 May (B&H)	8–2–19–1	10.3–6–5–3	10–3–22–3	7–2–15–2	9–0–28–1		
v. Hampshire (Chelmsford) 14 May (RA)	8–2–17–1	8–1–16–1	8–2–30–3	8–0–47–1	8–0–36–0		
v. Gloucestershire (Bristol) 21 May (RA)	7–3–21–1	8–2–28–1	8–0–34–2	2–0–14–1	8–0–33–2	7–0–22–0	
v. Somerset (Chelmsford) 28 May (RA)	7–1–22–2				8–0–38–0	8–0–30–1	
v. Lancashire (Chelmsford) 31 May (B&H)	11–2–35–1	11–0–67–0	11–2–43–3		9–0–29–1	11–0–37–3	
v. Surrey (The Oval) 11 June (RA)	8–1–29–4				8–1–44–3	8–0–46–1	
v. Somerset (Taunton) 14 June (B&H)	11–1–55–1	11–1–56–3	11–0–58–1		11–0–56–2		
v. Leicestershire (Chelmsford) 18 June (RA)	8–3–36–1	8–0–30–3	8–1–52–0		8–1–19–2	4–0–22–0	
v. Warwickshire (Ilford) 25 June (RA)	8–0–44–2		8–0–53–0			8–1–40–0	1–0–9–0
v. Somerset (Taunton) 28 & 29 June (NW)	12–1–42–0	12–1–50–2	12–1–53–1		11–1–42–1	4–1–22–0	
v. Sussex (Horsham) 2 July (RA)	8–1–28–1	8–2–24–3		8–0–11–2	8–1–27–0	4–0–30–0	
v. Glamorgan (Neath) 9 July (RA)	6–2–16–3			6.5–0–27–3	6–0–29–1	8–0–27–2	4–0–18–0
v. Nottinghamshire (Lord's) 15 July (B&H)	11–2–43–2	11–1–40–1	11–1–38–1		11–0–57–0	2–0–12–0	
v. Yorkshire (Southend) 23 July (RA)	8–2–35–2	8–0–44–1	8–0–36–0		5–0–21–0	4–0–28–1	
v. Nottinghamshire (Trent Bridge) 30 July (RA)	8–2–36–1		8–0–40–0	7–0–26–0		5–0–18–1	6–0–44–2
v. Worcestershire (Colchester) 6 August (RA)	7–0–28–1	8–0–31–0	8–0–43–1		6–0–30–1	3–0–15–0	
v. Lancashire (Old Trafford) 13 August (RA)	6–0–28–0	7–0–33–2	6–1–31–4		2–0–11–1		
v. Northamptonshire (Northampton) 27 August (RA)	8–4–16–1	7.4–0–34–0		8–1–33–0			8–0–33–2
v. Worcestershire (Scarborough) 4 September (FC)		6–2–12–0	10–1–27–1	6–0–24–0			4–0–31–0
v. Yorkshire (Scarborough) 5 September (FC)	10–2–40–3	5–0–38–0			9–1–23–0	8–0–42–1	8–0–49–1
v. Worcestershire (Worcester) 6 September (RC)	5–2–12–2	8–1–23–1	6–2–19–1		6–1–13–3	8–0–27–2	1.1–0–4–1
v. Nottinghamshire (Edgbaston) 17 September (RC)		8–0–48–1	7.4–0–20–4		8–1–34–2		
Wickets	32	32	40	22	26	18	6

a J. Derrick absent ill

v. Nottinghamshire (Trent Bridge) 30 July (RA)	v. Worcestershire (Colchester) 6 August (RA)	v. Lancashire (Old Trafford) 13 August (RA)	v. Northamptonshire (Northampton) 27 August (RA)	v. Worcestershire (Scarborough) 4 September (FC)	v. Yorkshire (Scarborough) 5 September (FC)	v. Worcestershire (Worcester) 6 September (RC)	v. Nottinghamshire (Edgbaston) 17 September (RC)	Runs
	24	21*		76	42	11	31	1092
7	5	27*	8	86	12	8	18	786
2	27	—	1	38*	34	82*	56	602
14	2	—	31	2*	28	31	4	771
16	46*	—		—		31	—	204
4	5	—		—	14	10	2*	299
10			33		1			287
								1
2	3		12*	—				33
	44	—	9	—	30	—	—	94
0*	—	—	5*		0*	—	—	10
10		—	3	—	14	—	—	139
2	1	—	14	—	41	12	—	139
								—
41	21	—	0	—	31	2	32	252
								4
			11					11

Extras and match summary (Byes / Leg-byes / Wides / No-balls / Total / Wkts / Result / Points):

	v. Notts (Trent Bridge)	v. Worcs (Colchester)	v. Lancs (Old Trafford)	v. Northants (Northampton)	v. Worcs (Scarborough)	v. Yorks (Scarborough)	v. Worcs (Worcester)	v. Notts (Edgbaston)
Byes					4	4	6	1
Leg-byes	3	8	3	10	3	7	13	13
Wides	1	5	2	6	10	2	5	
No-balls	1	2		1	6			3
Total	113	193	53	144	225	260	211	160
Wkts	10	9	0	9	2	10	7	5
Result	L	L	Ab.	L	W	L	W	W
Points	0	0	2	0	—	—	—	—

Vic Marks – who has announced his retirement to take up a career in journalism. (Jon Nicholson/Allsport)

G. Miller	J.H. Childs	K. Butler	M.C. Ilott	Byes	Leg-byes	Wides	No-balls	Total	Wkts
					9		2	135	10
4–0–20–0					6	4	7	169	10
					6	4	1	130	10
4–0–16–0				1	14	5	3	173	6
8–1–22–0				4	8	5	1	153	8
					4	12		192	7
				1	8	10	3	98	10
					10	4		156	9
8–0–45–1	8–0–28–0	1–0–5–0		5	10	9	1	167	7
2–0–8–0					3	1	3	171	7
8–0–37–1			8–0–27–0		27	2	1	246	9
				2	7	5	2	192	10
	11–0–46–2				18	8		289	10
	4–0–22–0				11	3	1	192	6
7–0–35–1	8–0–23–2				12	5	1	216	7
9–0–52–1				1	14	8	2	276	6
4–0–20–0				1	13	10		154	7
6–0–32–0					9	2		158	9a
9–0–50–1				1	3	2	1	244	7
7–1–41–2				1	7	1	1	213	6
3–0–20–0					13	8	3	197	4
				1	4	9		197	4
7–0–26–2					6	5		135	9
8–0–24–1					5	7		145	7
10–0–52–0				8	12			221	4
10–0–56–0				1	12		2	261	6
					12	2		110	10
8–0–20–1	8–0–26–2				7	3		155	10
11	**6**	**0**	**0**						

Glamorgan CCC
Limited-Over Matches, 1989

BATTING

BATTING	v. Leicestershire (Leicester) 23 April (RA)	v. Kent (Cardiff) 25 April (B&H)	v. Gloucestershire (Newport) 7 May (RA)	v. Hampshire (Southampton) 9 May (B&H)	v. Essex (Chelmsford) 11 May (B&H)	v. Sussex (Swansea) 13 & 14 May (B&H)	v. Northamptonshire (Cardiff) 21 May (RA)	v. Nottinghamshire (Llanelli) 28 May (RA)	v. Worcestershire (Worcester) 4 June (RA)	v. Middlesex (Merthyr Tydfil) 11 June (RA)	v. Lancashire (Blackpool) 18 June (RA)	v. Yorkshire (Hull) 25 June (RA)	v. Staffordshire (Cardiff) 29 June (NW)	v. Essex (Neath) 9 July (RA)	v. Hampshire (Cardiff) 12 July (NW)	v. Somerset (Taunton) 16 July (RA)
A.R. Butcher	5	52	24	22	41	16	8	4	27	6		76*	42	10	11	35
H. Morris	8	25	143*	3	0	3		6	4	44	4		154*	7	53	0
P.A. Cottey	4	34*	68	0	4	16										15
M.P. Maynard	3	5	43*	22	12	42	4	20	18	10	11	56	35	12		15
M.J. Cann	15	1	—	10*	12						0	5	2*			2
I. Smith	9						16		8	21				11	33	16
J. Derrick	0	3				15	8*	0					—			
C.P. Metson	6	1*	—	1	12	21*	—	2	0*	4	4	—	7	6		6
S.J. Dennis	0			1	0				0	1				4	1	—
S.L. Watkin	3*	—	—	1	1*	1*		16	—	0*	0	—			2*	28*
S.R. Barwick	4	—	—	0	0	—	—	48*	—	0	10	—		2*		
S. Bastien		—	—	7								1				
R.C. Ontong		15				40	33	44	1	34*						
R.J. Shastri			—		9	25	1	13	8	92	2	11	13	57	4	
G.C. Holmes							63*	9	9	7	0	25	9	26	17	
A. Dale												34	—	5	10	9*
K.A. Somaia																0
S.P. James																
M.L. Roberts																
R.D.B. Croft																
Byes	4				1	1	2	4								4
Leg-byes		20	6	8	9	3	4	3	6	11	3	5	9		20	10
Wides	10	14	4	10	3	3	6	2	11	3	3	17	2	4	5	8
No-balls	11	1	2	3			6	2			1		4		5	5
Total	82	171	290	98	160	162	172	119	209	110	162		318	158	189	168
Wickets	10	6	2	10	10	7	5	10	6	10	10		4	9†	10	8
Result	Ab.	L	L	W	L	L	L	L	L	W	L	L	W	L	L	L
Points	2	0	0	2	0	0	0	0	0	4	0	0	—	0	—	0

Fielding Figures
15 – C.P. Metson (ct 13/st 2)
7 – H. Morris
5 – S.L. Watkin, I. Smith and S.J. Dennis
4 – M.P. Maynard, R.C. Ontong and G.C. Holmes
3 – M.J. Cann and R.J. Shastri
2 – A.R. Butcher
1 – S. Bastien, S.R. Barwick, A. Dale, S.P. James and R.D.B. Croft

† J. Derrick absent ill

BOWLING

BOWLING	S.L. Watkin	S.R. Barwick	S.J. Dennis	J. Derrick	R.C. Ontong	S. Bastien	R.J. Shastri
v. Leicestershire (Leicester) 23 April (RA)							
v. Kent (Cardiff) 25 April (B&H)	9.3–2–29–2	9–2–16–1	5–0–19–0	9–2–14–1			
v. Gloucestershire (Newport) 7 May (RA)	8–1–30–3		7.1–0–28–1	8–1–48–2	8–0–34–0	8–0–28–0	
v. Hampshire (Southampton) 9 May (B&H)	11–5–33–0		11–1–37–2			6–0–43–0	11–0–45–0
v. Essex (Chelmsford) 11 May (B&H)	5–0–31–0	4.2–0–23–0	9–1–20–0			5–1–21–0	
v. Sussex (Swansea) 13 & 14 May (B&H)	10–3–28–1	11–2–33–2	11–3–28–0		6–0–36–0		11–0–37–0
v. Northamptonshire (Cardiff) 21 May (RA)	7.1–1–33–2	8–0–18–0	7–1–32–1	5–0–25–0	4–0–28–1		7–1–24–0
v. Nottinghamshire (Llanelli) 28 May (RA)	8–0–36–1	7–1–24–2	7.1–1–22–1	7–0–35–0	7–0–34–0		2–0–19–0
v. Worcestershire (Worcester) 4 June (RA)	8–0–38–1	8–0–75–0	8–0–52–0	6–0–28–1	8–0–49–2		2–0–10–0
v. Middlesex (Merthyr Tydfil) 11 June (RA)	7–1–37–1	6.5–2–10–2			7–0–32–3	4–0–23–0	8–1–33–3
v. Lancashire (Blackpool) 18 June (RA)	8–0–53–0	8–0–54–2	8–1–35–0				8–0–40–1
v. Yorkshire (Hull) 25 June (RA)	7–0–45–2	8–1–35–1				3–0–14–0	8–0–33–2
v. Staffordshire (Cardiff) 29 June (NW)	6–3–10–1	8–1–28–1	6–1–22–0				12–3–16–3
v. Essex (Neath) 9 July (RA)		8–0–35–1	8–0–36–0	3–0–16–0			4–0–19–0
v. Hampshire (Cardiff) 12 July (NW)			12–5–34–0				12–2–40–0
v. Somerset (Taunton) 16 July (RA)	8–2–27–0		8–0–32–2				
v. Derbyshire (Heanor) 23 July (RA)	7–0–35–0		8–0–42–0				
v. Hampshire (Swansea) 30 July (RA)	6.3–0–16–2	7–1–24–2	7–0–36–1				8–0–29–1
v. Surrey (The Oval) 6 August (RA)	8–0–63–0	8–0–34–3	7–0–39–2				8–0–44–0
v. Sussex (Ebbw Vale) 13 August (RA)							
v. Kent (Canterbury) 20 August (RA)		8–0–44–1	8–0–44–3				
v. Warwickshire (Aberystwyth) 27 August (RA)	8–1–40–1	7–1–23–1	6.5–0–61–0	8–0–32–1			
Wickets	18	19	13	5	6	0	10

63, but it was the second-wicket partnership of 133 between Clinton and Stewart that took the pressure off the batsmen who followed. Thorpe also batted well, and, in spite of a nervous collapse when four wickets fell for 39 runs, Medlycott and Martin Bicknell saw Surrey home with seven balls to spare.

Hampshire's season showed further signs of fading to disappointment when they were well beaten by Somerset. Mark Nicholas made a most courageous century on the opening day as his colleagues stumbled. He and Kevan James added 100 for the fourth wicket, but there was little else of substance. Adrian Jones bowled with impressive hostility for Somerset, whose captain, Vic Marks, had announced that he would retire at the end of the season to become cricket correspondent of *The Observer*. Marks celebrated his impending retirement with an excellent innings and a partnership with Neil Burns which realized 109 for the seventh wicket at a time when Somerset were in a difficult position. Hampshire collapsed to 41 for 4 before the close of the second day and slumped to a heavy defeat by mid-afternoon on the Tuesday.

The last match to be played on the Hastings ground before it became part of a redevelopment plan went entirely in favour of Middlesex, for whom Mike Gatting hit his third century within a month. He was at his most pugnacious and impressive, and there was able support from Keith Brown, whose opportunities had become increasingly limited.

In the youth Test at Scarborough, New Zealand were easy winners and owed much to the pace bowling of skipper Chris Cairns.

v. Derbyshire (Heanor) 23 July (RA)	v. Hampshire (Swansea) 30 July (RA)	v. Surrey (The Oval) 6 August (RA)	v. Sussex (Ebbw Vale) 13 August (RA)	v. Kent (Canterbury) 20 August (RA)	v. Warwickshire (Aberystwyth) 27 August (RA)	Runs
39	0	5	6	34	17	480
6	49	40	16*	62*	83	710
						126
61*	17	4	15	10	2	417
—						47
25*	3	4	9	17	56*	228
			—		—	26
—	5*	15		9		99
—	8	8	—	—	2*	25
—	0	5	—	—	—	57
	2*	8*	—	—	—	74
						8
						167
	60	39	28			362
31			29	18	21	264
67*	14	1	—	9	—	149
—						0
	13	9		8		30
			1*			1
				3*		3
2		2		3	8	
7	10	11	7	12	7	
4	11	6	5	2	7	
1		1		1		
243	193	157	117	187	203	
3	9	10	5	7	4	
L	W	L	Ab.	L	L	
0	4	0	2	0	0	

A.R. Butcher	M.P. Maynard	G.C. Holmes	I. Smith	A. Dale	M.J. Cann	K.A. Somaia	R.D.B. Crott	Byes	Leg-byes	Wides	No-balls	Total	Wkts
													Ab.
								5	1	2		83	4,
								5	2	2		173	7,
3-0-29-0	2-0-26-0							5	7	1		286	3
								4	5	1		99	0
6-0-32-3								13	6			207	7
								3	4			163	4
								4	4			174	4
								10	6			262	4
		3-0-20-1	2-0-12-0					5	11	1		172	10
		8-0-55-1						7	5	1		244	5
		6-0-37-1		8-0-35-0				3	9	2		211	7
				10.4-1-32-2	11-2-40-3			1	2	7		151	10
		5-0-33-1	4-1-20-1	8-0-35-0				11	2			205	3
		4-0-22-1	8-0-25-0	9-0-38-1				1	7	3		190	3
5-0-31-1			5-0-49-0	6-0-45-2		8-0-52-1		13	7	2		249	6
		6-0-55-0	6-0-26-0	5-0-43-1		4-0-36-0		8	1			245	1
			3-0-22-3	4-0-27-1				2	4			156	10
			5-0-44-1	4-0-28-0				1	1	7		254	8
													Ab.
3-0-24-0			8-0-47-0	8-0-58-2			5-0-28-0		3			245	6
			2-0-14-1	6-1-28-0									
4	0	5	6	9	3	1	0						

Gloucestershire CCC
Limited-Over Matches, 1989

BATTING

	v. Surrey (The Oval) 23 April (RA)	v. Middlesex (Bristol) 2 May (B&H)	v. Glamorgan (Newport) 7 May (RA)	v. Worcestershire (Worcester) 9 May (B&H)	v. Surrey (The Oval) 11 May (B&H)	v. Combined Universities (Bristol) 13 May (B&H)	v. Middlesex (Bristol) 14 May (RA)	v. Essex (Bristol) 21 May (RA)	v. Worcestershire (Bristol) 28 May (RA)	v. Nottinghamshire (Bristol) 31 May (B&H)	v. Leicestershire (Leicester) 11 June (RA)	v. Yorkshire (Leeds) 18 June (RA)	v. Somerset (Bath) 25 June (RA)	v. Oxfordshire (Oxford) 28 June (NW)	v. Nottinghamshire (Gloucester) 2 July (RA)	v. Kent (Maidstone) 9 July (RA)
C.W.J. Athey	4	0	21	35	15	40	36	16		54	1	11	6	56*	21	11
A.J. Wright	11	49	35	4	48	27	66	2	49*	8	81	1	17		9	1
K.M. Curran	13	10*	27	36	0	27*	0	34	26	12		25	3	45*	46	0
P. Bainbridge	8	47	24	53	7	38	17	26	24	2	72	24	21	—	13	
J.W. Lloyds	9	9*	2							8	65	13		28	14	31
R.C. Russell	14	—	6*	0*	6*	6*	15*	2	39	44	1*			—		4
M.W. Alleyne	6	—	4	23*	17*	7	15	33			5*	8	17	—	8	14
V.S. Greene	14	—	32*	1			10	10*				13		—	18*	
D.V. Lawrence	0	—		—	—	—	—			0						
M.W. Pooley	2*	—										1*	8	—	6*	6*
D.A. Graveney	0								—	11*						
A.W. Stovold		15		23	90	45			24	24	29	38	1	49		
P.W. Romaines			13	12	76	0	2	11	31	21	1				7	11
K.B.S. Jarvis			—						—		—		11		—	1
C.A. Walsh					0	28				13*	15	—	1			0
K.B.K. Ibadulla							9*	8*			0					
I.P. Butcher											—			71		3
G.A. Tedstone											—			5*		0
M.C.J. Ball																
G.D. Hodgson																
N.M. Pritchard																
S.N. Barnes																
Byes				4	7		3	5	2	1	8	2	4	2		1
Leg-Byes	5	11	5	4	11	5	10	10	6	15	9	7	8	13	7	4
Wides	1	8	2	1	5	3	3	9	4	6			1	5	1	1
No-balls	3	1	2	4	4	1	2	1	3	4						1
Total	81	150	173	200	286	227	188	167	221	217	214	184	128	269	154	85
Wickets	10	4	7	7	7	7	7	7	5	10	6	8	10	3	8	10
Result	L	W	W	W	W	W	L	L	L	L	W	L	L	W	L	L
Points	0	2	4	2	2	2	0	0	0	—	4	0	0	0	0	0

Fielding Figures

23 – R.C. Russell (ct 21/st 2)
12 – C.W.J. Athey
7 – M.W. Alleyne and A.J. Wright
6 – K.B.S. Jarvis
5 – P.W. Romaines

4 – J.W. Lloyds
3 – M.W. Pooley and P. Bainbridge
2 – K.M. Curran, V.S. Greene, I.P. Butcher and G.A. Tedstone
1 – D.A. Graveney, C.A. Walsh and G.D. Hodgson

BOWLING

	D.V. Lawrence	V.S. Greene	K.M. Curran	M.W. Pooley	M.W. Alleyne	P. Bainbridge	J.W. Lloyds
v. Surrey (The Oval) 23 April (RA)	7-1-23-1	7-0-23-1	8-0-43-0	8-1-18-2	8-0-41-1		
v. Middlesex (Bristol) 2 May (B&H)	8-0-42-1	9.4-1-27-2	8-0-16-1	11-1-33-1	5-1-12-2	11-4-12-1	1-0-3-0
v. Glamorgan (Newport) 7 May (RA)		8-1-26-1	8-0-37-1	8-0-37-3	8-1-24-0		
v. Worcestershire (Worcester) 9 May (B&H)	9-1-31-0	9.1-2-15-4	11-5-15-3	11-1-42-0	1-0-2-1	10-1-34-1	
v. Surrey (The Oval) 11 May (B&H)	5-1-12-2		6-0-25-1	8-1-30-2	5-0-40-1	6-1-15-2	
v. Combined Universities (Bristol) 13 May (B&H)	11-2-36-2		11-1-41-0	11-0-51-0	11-0-49-2		
v. Middlesex (Bristol) 14 May (RA)	8-0-37-1	8-0-42-0	8-0-30-0	4-0-20-1	4-0-20-0	8-0-39-3	
v. Essex (Bristol) 21 May (RA)		8-0-31-0	8-0-33-0		8-0-32-1	3.1-0-22-0	
v. Worcestershire (Bristol) 28 May (RA)			7.5-0-64-2			8-0-43-0	
v. Nottinghamshire (Bristol) 31 May (B&H)	11-0-43-0		11-1-41-4			11-0-34-0	
v. Leicestershire (Leicester) 11 June (RA)	6-0-15-2				8-0-34-1	8-0-42-2	
v. Yorkshire (Leeds) 18 June (RA)				8-0-32-1	8-0-49-2	8-1-40-1	
v. Somerset (Bath) 25 June (RA)		8-0-27-1		8-0-34-1	2-0-25-0	8-1-57-2	6-0-36-0
v. Oxfordshire (Oxford) 28 June (NW)		12-2-43-2		12-2-35-0	10-2-43-1	12-0-46-2	3-0-15-0
v. Nottinghamshire (Gloucester) 2 July (RA)		8-3-29-2	8-1-27-4	7-1-50-1		8-2-13-1	
v. Kent (Maidstone) 9 July (RA)				3.5-0-22-0	6-1-26-0		
v. Lancashire (Bristol) 12 July (NW)			12-2-41-1			5-0-18-1	7-1-24-0
v. Hampshire (Trowbridge) 16 July (RA)		7-3-17-2		8-1-29-2	8-0-36-2	7.1-1-38-3	
v. Warwickshire (Edgbaston) 30 July (RA)			5-0-33-3	4-1-28-1		5-0-30-0	
v. Lancashire (Cheltenham) 6 August (RA)	8-1-48-1		4-0-30-0			2-1-10-0	
v. Derbyshire (Cheltenham) 13 August (RA)			8-1-34-2	5-1-21-1		3-0-26-0	
v. Northamptonshire (Moreton-in-Marsh) 20 August (RA)			8-0-35-2	8-0-33-0		5-0-36-1	3-0-18-0
v. Sussex (Hove) 27 August (RA)				8-0-45-2	8-1-39-2		
Wickets	10	15	24	19	15	20	0

a P.D Atkins retired hurt

	v. Lancashire (Bristol) 12 July (NW)	v. Hampshire (Trowbridge) 16 July (RA)	v. Warwickshire (Edgbaston) 30 July (RA)	v. Lancashire (Cheltenham) 6 August (RA)	v. Derbyshire (Cheltenham) 13 August (RA)	v. Northamptonshire (Moreton-in-Marsh) 20 August (RA)	v. Sussex (Hove) 27 August (RA)	Runs
	25	39	0	14	5	65	19	494
	1	41*	2	52*	5	1*	46	556
	47	3	54	14	6	36		464
	13	26	32	15	6	0		468
	5	12	1	0		32	46	266
	42*	8		4		—		191
	0	3	41*	7	29	5*	1	243
		10						108
				16				16
								338
		8*	0					193
	—		1	6	—	—		19
	9*		1	4	18*	—		89
								17
	2	26		0	14		11*	116
			0	12		4		28
								4
			16	39		8		63
								9
						11*		11
Total	174	184	144	143	127	195	172	
Wkts	7	8	8	10	10	5	8	
Result	L	W	L	L	L	L	L	
Points	—	4	0	0	0	0	0	

Refuge Assurance League

20 August

at Moreton-in-Marsh

Gloucestershire 195 for 5 (C.W.J. Athey 65)
Northamptonshire 198 for 3 (W. Larkins 101)

Northamptonshire (4 pts) won by 7 wickets

at Canterbury

Kent 245 for 6 (R.F. Pienaar 119)
Glamorgan 187 for 7 (H. Morris 62 not out)

Kent (4 pts) won by 58 runs

at Old Trafford

Yorkshire 201 for 5 (K. Sharp 76, P.E. Robinson 51 not out)
Lancashire 169

Yorkshire (4 pts) won by 32 runs

at Leicester

Leicestershire 219 for 4 (J.J. Whitaker 55)
Surrey 215 for 6 (D.J. Bicknell 56)

Leicestershire (4 pts) won by 4 runs

at Trent Bridge

Hampshire 254 for 4 (R.A. Smith 131, J.R. Wood 66)
Nottinghamshire 222 (F.D. Stephenson 69)

Hampshire (4 pts) won by 32 runs

at Hastings

Sussex 170 for 9 (A.P. Wells 72, J.E. Emburey 4 for 28)
Middlesex 172 for 6 (M.A. Roseberry 83 not out)

Middlesex (4 pts) won by 4 wickets

K.B.S. Jarvis	C.A. Walsh	K.B.K. Ibadulla	D.A. Graveney	M.C.J. Ball	C.W.J. Athey	A.J. Wright	S.N. Barnes	Byes	Leg-byes	Wides	No-balls	Total	Wkts
									16	14	1	164	5
8-1-27-0									4	8	4	149	10
									20	14	1	171	6
									13		5	152	10
		7-3-12-0							8	1	2	142	9a
		11-2-40-2						2	4	3	2	223	7
									14	1		202	6
8-0-26-0			4-1-14-0						10	2	1	168	1
8-1-36-0	7-0-36-1		8-0-34-1					1	8	5	1	222	4
		11-1-41-1	4-0-22-0	7-1-32-0				1	8	4	1	222	6
8-1-38-2	5.3-1-16-3							1	9	3	1	155	10
8-1-26-0	8-0-45-2								4			196	7
8-0-38-1								1	8	1		226	5
10.4-0-32-5									12	5	1	226	10
6-0-30-0									8	3		157	8
8-3-23-2	8-2-9-1								6		1	86	4
12-2-25-3	12-2-27-1			12-1-42-3					2	5		179	9
						8-0-36-1			7	2		163	10
5-0-14-0	5-0-51-1								6	2		162	5
5.4-1-29-1	8-0-21-2								6	5	2	144	4
4-0-22-0	8-1-20-3						0.2-0-4-0		3	1		130	6
6-1-36-0	6.2-0-36-0								4	5	2	198	3
8-0-85-3				8-0-49-0			8-0-54-0		7	3		279	7
17	17	0	1	3	1	0	0						

Hampshire CCC
Limited-Over Matches, 1989

BATTING

BATTING	v. Somerset (Southampton) 23 April (RA)	v. Surrey (The Oval) 30 April (RA)	v. Essex (Chelmsford) 2 May (B&H)	v. Kent (Southampton) 7 May (RA)	v. Glamorgan (Southampton) 9 May (B&H)	v. Sussex (Hove) 11 May (RA)	v. Kent (Southampton) 13 May (B&H)	v. Essex (Chelmsford) 14 May (RA)	v. Leicestershire (Bournemouth) 28 May (RA)	v. Middlesex (Lord's) 4 June (RA)	v. Warwickshire (Basingstoke) 11 June (RA)	v. Sussex (Southampton) 25 June (RA)	v. Cheshire (Chester) 29 June (NW)	v. Yorkshire (Southampton) 2 July (RA)	v. Northamptonshire (Northampton) 9 July (RA)	v. Glamorgan (Cardiff) 12 July (NW)	v. Gloucestershire (Trowbridge) 16 July (RA)	v. Lancashire (Portsmouth) 23 July (RA)	v. Glamorgan (Swansea) 30 July (RA)
M.C.J. Nicholas	57	1	0	52	2	15	32	7	40*	13	49	11	14*	13	—	46*	2	50	52
V.P. Terry	45	6	73	79*	76	4	31	3	15	2	53	6	99	2	—	2	12	20	5
R.A. Smith	14	9	21	14*	155*	96*	20	21		1						69*	3	20	
C.L. Smith	41*		4				.		11*	0	9*	14	159	45	—	20	8	0	17
R.J. Scott	31	2	—	—	0	69	54	10	13		7	46	—	116*					
S.T. Jefferies	26	24*	3*	—	—	7	4	20											
R.J. Parks	2*	4	—	—	—	—	4*	0		3	—	0*	—	—	—	—	10	1	4
K.D. James	—	12	45	—	—	18*	31	4	—	31	2*	48*	—	0*	—	42	66	14	12
N.G. Cowley	—	6	4*	—	—	—	6	7	—	9	—	3	—	—	—	—			2
S.J.W. Andrew	—																		
C.A. Connor	—	6	—	—	—	—	4*	3*	—	0	—	—	—	—	—	—	19	8	8
D.R. Turner		26	0	—	40*	20	21	66	15	28	34	13	22*	1	—		0*		24
P.J. Bakker		1*	—		—	—	1*		1*	—						0*	—		2*
T.M. Tremlett																			
M.D. Marshall									—	36	—	31	—	—	—		14	14	24
J.R. Wood																—	19	5	0
R.J. Maru																—	1	8*	
T.C. Middleton																			
S.D. Udal																			
Byes		1				4					2	3	1				1		
Leg-byes	3	6	14	4	5	6	17	10	2	5	2	17	6	5		1	7	12	2
Wides	1	7	5	6	7	2	11	4	7	5	1	1	5	1		7	2	11	4
No-balls	1	4	3	3	1	1		7		4	1					3		2	
Total	221	114	173	158	286	242	235	156	110	138	160	193	306	183		190	163	166	156
Wickets	5	9	6	1	3	5	8	9	3	10	4	7	2	4		3	10	9	10
Result	W	L	L	W	L	W	L	L	W	Tie	W	W	W	W	Ab.	W	L	L	L
Points	4	0	0	4	0	2	0	0	4	2	4	4	—	4	2	—	0	0	0

Fielding Figures

27 – R.J. Parks (ct 23/st 4)
10 – V.P. Terry
9 – R.A. Smith
6 – C.A. Connor and S.T. Jefferies
5 – D.R. Turner, M.C.J. Nicholas and M.D. Marshall
4 – K.D. James, N.G. Cowley and R.J. Maru

3 – R.J. Scott and P.J. Bakker
2 – J.R. Wood
1 – C.L. Smith, T.M. Tremlett, T.C. Middleton and sub

BOWLING

BOWLING	K.D. James	C.A. Connor	S.J.W. Andrew	S.T. Jefferies	M.C.J. Nicholas	N.G. Cowley	P.J. Bakker
v. Somerset (Southampton) 23 April (RA)	8-3-10-1	8-3-28-2	6-0-35-0	8-0-59-1	3-0-24-0	7-0-48-1	
v. Surrey (The Oval)	7-0-18-1	8-1-25-1		8-2-31-1	2.1-1-3-1	6-0-17-0	8-1-11-1
v. Essex (Chelmsford) 2 May (B&H)	8-2-23-0	6-1-24-0		7.1-0-34-1	8-1-30-1	6-0-24-0	11-1-29-1
v. Kent (Southampton) 17 May (RA)	8-1-26-0	7-0-18-2		7-0-28-2		8-1-43-2	
v. Glamorgan (Southampton) 9 May (B&H)	10-1-44-0	9.1-0-66-1		11-0-53-0	2-0-16-0	10-0-45-1	11-1-60-0
v. Sussex (Hove)	7.5-0-34-3	8-2-19-4		9-0-37-2	3-0-17-0	11-2-33-0	11-3-20-1
v. Kent (Southampton) 13 May (B&H)	9.3-2-48-0	11-1-46-2		11-0-47-2	8-0-26-1	4-0-17-0	11-3-37-1
v. Essex (Chelmsford) 14 May (RA)	8-0-17-0	8-1-32-0		8-0-39-4		8-0-33-2	8-1-31-1
v. Leicestershire (Bournemouth) 28 May (RA)	3-0-17-0	6-2-18-3			4-0-11-0	8-1-22-3	6-0-20-1
v. Middlesex (Lord's) 4 June (RA)	8-1-22-2	8-0-19-1			1-0-2-0	7-0-31-0	8-0-35-3
v. Warwickshire (Basingstoke) 11 June (RA)	8-1-23-3	6-1-35-0			1-0-9-0	8-0-30-1	8-0-29-2
v. Sussex (Southampton) 25 June (RA)	8-0-39-1	8-2-38-2				8-0-49-1	8-1-28-0
v. Cheshire (Chester) 29 June (NW)	8-1-26-2	12-3-38-2				9-0-39-0	8-2-13-0
v. Yorkshire (Southampton) 2 July (RA)	8-1-23-2	8-0-32-2				8-0-37-2	8-1-40-1
v. Northamptonshire (Northampton) 9 July (RA)		4-0-18-0			6-0-39-1	1.2-0-16-0	6-0-37-0
v. Glamorgan (Cardiff) 12 July (NW)	12-3-46-2	11.4-1-43-3					12-3-30-2
v. Gloucestershire (Trowbridge) 16 July (RA)	6-1-22-0	8-0-48-1			8-1-30-4	1-0-8-0	4-1-5-0
v. Lancashire (Portsmouth) 23 July (RA)	8-0-53-0	5-0-28-0			1-0-8-0		8-2-15-1
v. Glamorgan (Swansea) 30 July (RA)	8-0-40-1	7-0-27-2			1-0-15-0	7-0-42-0	8-1-31-3
v. Surrey (The Oval) 2 August (RA)	12-2-39-2	12-3-61-3				12-2-44-1	
v. Derbyshire (Derby) 6 August (RA)	8-1-17-3	8-2-25-1		8-2-41-1	1-0-4-0		7-0-17-5
v. Worcestershire (Bournemouth) 13 August (RA)	8-2-19-1	8-2-26-3		7.4-0-34-1		8-2-17-2	
v. Middlesex (Southampton) 16 August (NW)	10-0-56-0	12-0-62-2			2-0-17-0	12-0-62-1	12-3-42-0
v. Nottinghamshire (Trent Bridge) 20 August (RA)	7.3-0-33-2	8-1-42-3		7-0-52-2	8-1-30-1		
v. Sussex (Hove) 3 September (SB)	9-0-43-1	10-1-39-0	10-0-61-2				
Wickets	27	40	2	17	9	16	24

v. Surrey (The Oval) 2 August (NW)	v. Derbyshire (Derby) 6 August (RA)	v. Worcestershire (Bournemouth) 13 August (RA)	v. Middlesex (Southampton) 16 August (NW)	v. Nottinghamshire (Trent Bridge) 20 August (RA)	v. Sussex (Hove) 3 September (SB)	Runs
71	7	12	24	16	1	587
6	47	37	3	—	7	633
125*	13		46	131	12	770
0	4	6	114			452
		18	22	6	21	415
	7	9		10*		110
—	6*	25	0	—	0	59
10	39*	1	18	14*	100	507
			0	8*		45
						—
—	—	14	—	—	—	62
	3					313
—			—			5
		7*			36*	43
3			17*			139
3*				66	53	146
—			—			9
		4*				4
				—	8*	8
	1	1	2			
4	9	8	3	7	9	
4	10	3	4	3	1	
3	3	2	3	1		
229	149	147	264	254	248	
5	6	9	7	4	7	
W	W	L	L	W	L	
—	4	0	—	4	—	

at Edgbaston

Warwickshire 192 for 7 (P.A. Smith 70)
Derbyshire 195 for 5 (J.E. Morris 112 not out)

Derbyshire (4 pts) won by 5 wickets

at Worcester

Worcestershire 202 for 5 (G.A. Hick 81)
Somerset 190 for 7 (V.J. Marks 67 not out)

Worcestershire (4 pts) won by 12 runs

Still the Refuge Assurance League championship eluded Lancashire. Having lost two cheap wickets, Yorkshire recovered strongly through Sharp, Love and Robinson, but their total of 201 seemed well within Lancashire's reach. Mendis and Fowler gave the home side the right start with a stand of 50, but thereafter the innings fell apart. Wickets fell, the asking rate increased and Yorkshire were comfortable winners. Another fierce hundred by Robin Smith kept alive Hampshire's hopes of qualifying for the Refuge Assurance Cup, particularly as Surrey were beaten at Leicester. Facing a target of 220, Surrey were rallied by Greig and Robinson, but their brave stand fell five short of the target. Emburey hit a six in the last over to win the game for Middlesex, and centuries by Larkins, Pienaar and Morris brought victories to their sides. Hick hit 81 off 77 balls to guide Worcestershire to victory in their final Sunday league game. They finished on 46 points and were left to rue their wretched start to the season.

24, 25, 26 and 27 August

at Worcester

Somerset 338 (C.J. Tavare 89, G.D. Rose 50 not out, S.R.

T.M. Tremlett	M.D. Marshall	R.J. Maru	S.D. Udal	R.J. Scott	Byes	Leg-byes	Wides	No-balls	Total	Wkts
						16	2	4	220	8
						10	2	1	115	5
						11	3	6	175	3
8-1-29-2						12	5		156	10
						6	4	2	290	2
						17	3		177	10
						16	10	1	237	6
						5	2	1	157	7
	4.5-0-13-3					6	3	4	107	10
	8-1-18-2				1	10	8		138	8
	8-0-29-0					3	2		158	9
	8-0-27-1				4	7			192	5
	10.1-1-40-4				1	2		5	159	10
	8-1-37-0				4	6	1		179	7
	6-1-15-0				2	8	4		135	1
	12-3-31-1	12-1-19-1				20	4	5	189	10
	8-0-40-0	6-1-32-1				7	1		184	8
	8-1-17-2	6.1-1-33-1			1	13	2		168	4
	8-0-28-2					10	11	1	193	9
12-3-40-1	12-0-35-0					9	8	5	228	8
				8-0-33-0		11	3	3	148	10
8-0-43-1						10		4	149	10
	12-2-25-1					3	2	1	267	7
6-0-27-1		2-0-15-0	5-0-36-1		4	10	4	2	222	10
			10-0-43-2	5-0-26-0	1	12	4		252	6
4	17	3	3	0						

Kent CCC
Limited-Over Matches, 1989

BATTING

BATTING	v. Essex (Canterbury) 23 April (RA)	v. Glamorgan (Cardiff) 25 April (B&H)	v. Sussex (Hove) 30 April (RA)	v. Sussex (Canterbury) 2 May (B&H)	v. Hampshire (Southampton) 7 May (RA)	v. Essex (Canterbury) 9 May (B&H)	v. Hampshire (Southampton) 13 May (B&H)	v. Surrey (Canterbury) 14 May (RA)	v. Northamptonshire (Canterbury) 28 May (RA)	v. Northamptonshire (Northampton) 31 May (B&H)	v. Nottinghamshire (Trent Bridge) 11 June (RA)	v. Nottinghamshire (Trent Bridge) 14 June (B&H)	v. Somerset (Bath) 18 June (RA)	v. Lancashire (Old Trafford) 25 June (RA)	v. Dorset (Canterbury) 28 June (NW)	v. Gloucestershire (Maidstone) 9 July (RA)	v. Warwickshire (Canterbury) 12 July (NW)	v. Derbyshire (Canterbury) 16 July (RA)
S.G. Hinks	7	28	27	25	44	0	0	6			54	49	9	3	62			
M.R. Benson	13	19	27	41	11	9	48	8		55	11	65	45				64	
N.R. Taylor	27	15	27*	0	34	46	64	38	20	15	37	19		23	13	1	29	56
C.S. Cowdrey	29	4	20*	9	21	0	2	34*	12	7	21	3	10	39	69*	11	52	10
G.R. Cowdrey	5	6*	—	37	6				40	7				15	34*	5*		17
T.R. Ward	22	3*	10	22	1	37	37	47	34	8	14	11	3	26	83		18	9
S.A. Marsh	9	—	—	4	1	41*	15*	17	15	3	1	12	40	14	—	—	6	9
R.M. Ellison	5	—		2	9*	29	16*	4*	3	23*							14	
D.J.M. Kelleher	4	—	—	4*	10	—	—	—	2*			11*	4	7				
A.P. Igglesden	1	—	—	2*		—	—	—	—		0*	1	0*	1*			2	0
H.L. Alleyne	2*	—	—		0									1*				2
C. Penn		—	11		0*			2*	24*	12	8	18					3	1
R.P. Davis			—	2							16		9	0			1*	1
M.V. Fleming						14	28	30	37	13	10	24	7			22*	12	14*
R.F. Pienaar										7	36	15	7	6	90		10	
M.A. Ealham														24				2
M.C. Dobson																21		
J.I. Longley																19		12
N.J. Llong																		
P. Farbrace																		
K.D. Masters																		
Byes			1	1				6	1					4	1			
Leg-byes	9	5	2	8	12	4	16	12	17	9	11	11	7	10	3	6	7	4
Wides		1	6	5		12	10	1	5	3	4	6	9	2	3		4	1
No-balls	2	2		1		1			1	4			2	3	1	1	1	2
Total	135	83	114	173	156	192	237	197	201	208	206	227	169	172	359	86	223	139
Wickets	10	4	3	9	10	7	6	6	8	8	10	10	10	9	4	4	10	10
Result	L	W	W	L	L	L	W	W	L	W	—	—	L	L	W	W	L	L
Points	0	2	4	0	0	0	2	4	0	0	—	0	—	0	0	—	4	—

Fielding Figures

35 – S.A. Marsh (ct 32/st 3)
10 – C.S. Cowdrey
8 – S.G. Hinks

7 – G.R. Cowdrey
6 – M.V. Fleming
5 – A.P. Igglesden and N.R. Taylor

4 – M.R. Benson and C. Penn
2 – H.L. Alleyne, R.F. Pienaar, R.P. Davis, D.J.M. Kelleher and M.A. Ealham
1 – M.C. Dobson and J.I. Longley

BOWLING

BOWLING	A.P. Igglesden	D.J.M. Kelleher	H.L. Alleyne	R.M. Ellison	C.S. Cowdrey	C. Penn	G.R. Cowdrey	R.P. Davis
v. Essex (Canterbury) 23 April (RA)	8-2-21-1	8-0-24-0	8-0-35-2	5.4-1-22-1	6-0-26-0			
v. Glamorgan (Cardiff) 25 April (B&H)	10-2-15-1		9.3-0-23-3	3-0-4-1	9-2-14-1	9-3-14-2	5-2-8-1	
v. Sussex (Hove) 30 April (RA)	8-3-13-5	8-4-11-0	5-0-28-0		5-0-18-3		2-0-12-0	7-1-19-1
v. Sussex (Canterbury) 2 May (B&H)	9-1-45-3	11-4-23-1			8-1-38-0	7-1-25-1	9-3-27-0	2.4-0-14-0
v. Hampshire (Southampton) 7 May (RA)		6-0-17-0	8-2-32-1		5.3-0-29-0	4-1-20-0	6-0-24-0	6-0-32-0
v. Essex (Canterbury) 9 May (B&H)					11-2-28-2	7-0-40-0	10.3-1-39-2	5-0-21-1
v. Hampshire (Southampton) 13 May (B&H)	11-1-43-3	11-0-42-1			3-0-15-1	11-0-46-1	10-0-36-0	
v. Surrey (Canterbury) 14 May (RA)	8-0-32-2	8-0-34-1			4-0-19-2	7-0-50-1	8-2-18-0	
v. Northamptonshire (Canterbury) 28 May (RA)	8-0-37-2	3-0-15-0			8-0-44-0	3-0-14-0	7.3-0-25-0	1-0-11-0
v. Northamptonshire (Northampton) 31 May (B&H)	11-0-42-1				11-0-45-3	11-1-33-1	11-5-27-1	
v. Nottinghamshire (Trent Bridge) 11 June (RA)	8-0-41-4				8-0-45-0	7.5-0-48-1		8-0-36-1
v. Nottinghamshire (Trent Bridge) 14 June (B&H)	11-1-68-0	10-0-48-1			11-1-45-2	11-0-54-0		
v. Somerset (Bath) 18 June (RA)	8-0-32-1	8-0-49-1			7-0-58-0	7-0-40-0		8-0-52-5
v. Lancashire (Old Trafford) 25 June (RA)	8-0-29-0	5-0-18-0	5-0-37-1		5.1-0-23-1			7-0-39-0
v. Dorset (Canterbury) 28 June (NW)	7-1-17-1			2-0-5-0		6-1-8-2		12-4-21-1
v. Gloucestershire (Maidstone) 9 July (RA)	8-3-13-3		7.2-1-20-1	6-1-18-1	2-0-14-1	8-1-15-4		
v. Warwickshire (Canterbury) 12 July (NW)	10-0-50-1				12-1-55-2	2-0-15-0	12-0-61-0	12-3-43-1
v. Derbyshire (Canterbury) 16 July (RA)	7-0-17-1		6.4-0-25-3		4-0-20-1	6-0-29-0		
v. Middlesex (Lord's) 23 July (RA)	8-0-19-1		7-1-35-2		3-0-28-0			
v. Worcestershire (Worcester) 30 July (RA)	5-0-39-1		3.4-0-27-0		2-0-13-0			
v. Warwickshire (Canterbury) 6 August (RA)	8-0-43-2				1-0-4-1	8-2-34-0		8-0-41-2
v. Yorkshire (Scarborough) 13 August (RA)		8-0-18-1			8-0-56-2	7.1-0-47-0		2-0-14-0
v. Glamorgan (Canterbury) 20 August (RA)	5-0-11-0	6-0-28-0						8-0-29-1
v. Leicestershire (Folkestone) 27 August (RA)		8-1-20-0						5-0-16-2
v. Surrey (Hove) 4 September (SB)	8-0-33-2		4-0-12-0		8-0-56-1	8-1-42-1		4-0-36-2
v. Sussex (Hove) 5 September (SB)	10-0-42-1		9.4-0-60-0		10-0-70-3	10-0-54-0		9-0-50-1
Wickets	37	6	13	13	20	13	1	18

v. Middlesex (Lord's) 23 July (RA)	v. Worcestershire (Worcester) 30 July (RA)	v. Warwickshire (Canterbury) 6 August (RA)	v. Yorkshire (Scarborough) 13 August (RA)	v. Glamorgan (Canterbury) 20 August (RA)	v. Leicestershire (Folkestone) 27 August (RA)	v. Surrey (Hove) 4 September (SB)	v. Sussex (Hove) 5 September (SB)	Runs
0	45	80*	19	5	7	31	108	609
						39	30	485
1	7*					99*	88	659
78	1	22	68*	25	5	4	0	556
		10*	13	38	102*			335
0	41	54	11	29	0		12	532
53			9	20*	29	2	5*	305
	0							105
								42
—								7
—	3		—		—	—	—	8
		—	15*			0*	3	96
							1*	30
1	2	—	32	5	16			267
		24	37	119	30	58	38	477
9*	3	—	5	1*	1*			45
								21
57	8							96
0*								0
	1*							1
								—
						5		
9	8	4	11		7	5	8	
3	4	6	5	3	2	10	5	
		2						
211	123	202	225	245	199	253	298	
7	8	3	7	6	6	5	7	
W	L	W	L	W	W	W	L	
4	0	4	0	4	4	—	—	

Graeme Hick – an innings of breathtaking brilliance to take Worcestershire to victory over Somerset at New Road on 27 August. (Ben Radford/Allsport)

M.V. Fleming	T.R. Ward	M.A. Ealham	N.R. Taylor	R.F. Pienaar	N.J. Llong	T. Wren	K.D. Masters	Byes	Leg-byes	Wides	No-balls	Total	Wkts
									8	4	3	136	4
								4	10		11	82	10
									9	4	2	110	10
								1	3	2	5	176	5
10–2–24–0									4	6	3	158	1
9–0–36–1								1	13	2	5	196	6
5–0–30–0									17	11		235	8
5–0–26–0	4–0–20–0							2	10	5	1	195	7
11–2–25–1									13	7	1	205	2
8–0–32–1								5	10	7	3	187	8
10–1–58–2	2–0–10–0								5	2	1	207	7
2–0–12–1									13	1	5	296	6
		6–1–25–0						1	5	4	1	249	8
									3	2		174	2
	12–0–58–1		6.5–0–29–3	5–1–16–2				3	4	2	8	161	10
								1	4	1	1	85	10
12–2–37–1									11	3	1	272	5
8–0–33–2		6–0–26–3						2	12	6	1	164	10
7–0–33–2	4–0–22–0	8–1–30–0			3–0–20–1			5	13	7	4	205	7
4–0–18–1	1–0–5–0	5–0–17–1							7	1		126	3
6–1–32–0	5–0–21–0	4–0–16–0							10	2	5	201	8
5–0–37–0	1–0–10–0	7–1–27–2						1	18	3	1	228	6
7–0–43–1	8–0–20–3	6–0–41–2						3	12	2		187	7
8–1–26–3		8–1–40–3				7.3–0–41–1			4	3		147	10
							8–0–54–3	1	4	6	2	238	9
	1–0–12–0								14	6	2	302	5
16	4	11	3	2	1	1	3						

Lancashire CCC
Limited-Over Matches, 1989

BATTING

BATTING	v. Warwickshire (Edgbaston) 23 April (RA)	v. Leicestershire (Old Trafford) 25 April (RA)	v. Nottinghamshire (Old Trafford) 30 April (RA)	v. Scotland (Perth) 2 May (B&H)	v. Worcestershire (Worcester) 7 May (RA)	v. Northamptonshire (Northampton) 9 May (B&H)	v. Warwickshire (Old Trafford) 13 May (B&H)	v. Derbyshire (Leek) 14 May (RA)	v. Somerset (Taunton) 21 May (RA)	v. Sussex (Old Trafford) 28 May (RA)	v. Essex (Chelmsford) 31 May (B&H)	v. Leicestershire (Leicester) 4 June (RA)	v. Glamorgan (Blackpool) 18 June (RA)	v. Kent (Old Trafford) 25 June (RA)	v. Cumberland (Kendal) 29 June (NW)	v. Middlesex (Lord's) 2 July (RA)	v. Gloucestershire (Bristol) 12 July (NW)	v. Northamptonshire (Old Trafford) 16 July (RA)	v. Hampshire (Portsmouth) 23 July (RA)	v. Worcestershire (Worcester) 2 August (NW)
G.D. Mendis	82*		27		26	0			46	23	28	40	19	1	19	46	0		8	34
G. Fowler	78	26	42	39		41	35	74	6	28	6	36	68	0		22	53*		29	8
A.N. Hayhurst	1	29	13	5	6				22	17				9*						
N.H. Fairbrother	11	53	18*	64	3	69*	31	38	25	47	2	100*	82*	7	59*	31	31	40*		25
Wasim Akram	5*	14*	–	3	52	30	0	24*	44*	39	0	29	–	19	3	15	3	–		4
M. Watkinson	–	–	–	38	7	1	44	57	1	2	25	5	0*	16*	31	4	9		3*	62
D.P. Hughes	–	–	–	0	2	3*	8	11*	6	12	32	–	–	0*	5	6	0		21	3
P.A.J. DeFreitas	–	–	–	25	30	–	0	0			29*	9	12	–	–	0*	0	11		25
W.K. Hegg	–	–	–	1*	5	10*	–	–	0*	13	8	–	–	26	1	29	8			10
P.J.W. Allott	–	–	–	22	–		2*	1	6*		1	6*					11*			0*
J. Simmons	–	–				7*	–										2*			0*
T.E. Jesty		45*	1*	8	20	34	17	7	6	22	23			13		4	6		51	
I.D. Austin		–							7*	3									5*	–
M.A. Atherton																				35
Byes		1		4	1				2	1									5	1
Leg-byes	3	10	5	13	10	10	5	10	7	27	8	7	3	2	10	2	7	13		13
Wides	2	8	7		6	3	5	2	1	2		5	2		5	5	3	2		14
No-balls	5		1	2		2		3		1	2	1		2	2		1			4
Total	187	186	114	202	197	203	176	245	146	246	149	244	174	86	139	179	136	168		237
Wickets	3	3	3	8	10	5	8	6	7	9	9	5	2	6	6	9	7	4		9
Result	Ab.	W	W	W	W	L	W	W	W	W	L	L	W	W	W	W	W	W	W	L
Points	2	2	4	2	4	0	2	4	4	4	–	0	4	4	–	4	–	4	4	–

Fielding Figures

30 – W.K. Hegg (ct 28/st 2)
8 – G.D. Mendis
6 – G. Fowler
5 – N.H. Fairbrother, D.P. Hughes, P.J.W. Allott, J. Simmons and Wasim Akram
4 – I.D. Austin
3 – M. Watkinson and T.E. Jesty

BOWLING

BOWLING	P.A.J. DeFreitas	P.J.W. Allott	Wasim Akram	M. Watkinson	J. Simmons	A.N. Hayhurst	I.D. Austin
v. Warwickshire (Edgbaston) 23 April (RA)							
v. Leicestershire (Old Trafford) 25 April (B&H)	11–1–44–0	9.1–2–24–2	11–2–36–2	10–2–38–0	11–3–23–1	2.5–0–11–1	
v. Nottinghamshire (Old Trafford) 30 April (RA)	8–0–44–1		8–0–35–1	8–1–21–1	7–0–37–1	1–0–7–0	8–0–26–0
v. Scotland (Perth) 2 May (B&H)	11–5–13–4		11–4–27–5	11–2–28–0	9–4–19–0	9–3–16–0	
v. Worcestershire (Worcester) 7 May (RA)	8–1–27–2	8–3–9–2	8–0–28–2	8–0–61–1	8–0–54–2		
v. Northamptonshire (Northampton) 9 May (B&H)	11–0–56–1	10–3–25–1	11–0–60–0	11–2–49–0	11–0–29–1		
v. Warwickshire (Old Trafford) 13 May (B&H)	11–3–40–2	11–1–33–1	11–2–40–2	11–2–38–1	11–2–39–1		
v. Derbyshire (Leek) 14 May (RA)	8–0–26–1	8–2–36–1	8–0–18–2	8–0–35–1			8–0–28–4
v. Somerset (Taunton) 21 May (RA)	8–0–56–1	8–0–31–1	7–1–32–2	6–0–44–1	8–0–50–1		
v. Sussex (Old Trafford) 28 May (RA)		8–0–33–2	8–1–32–3	8–0–15–0	8–0–38–3		8–1–17–1
v. Essex (Chelmsford) 31 May (B&H)	10.1–1–35–2	11–1–33–0	11–0–54–4	9–0–68–1	11–0–51–0		
v. Leicestershire (Leicester) 4 June (RA)	7–1–19–0	8–2–20–1	8–0–38–2	6.2–0–29–0	8–1–27–0		
v. Glamorgan (Blackpool) 18 June (RA)	5–0–15–2	6–0–16–0	5–0–12–1	1.4–0–7–2	8–1–21–2		6–0–28–2
v. Kent (Old Trafford) 25 June (RA)	7–1–24–2	6–1–25–2	6–0–26–1	8–0–24–0	8–0–34–1		4–0–25–2
v. Cumberland (Kendal) 29 June (NW)	10.3–5–13–5	12–7–7–2	8–4–20–2	8–1–26–1	6–3–11–0		
v. Middlesex (Lord's) 2 July (RA)	8–0–25–1	8–2–19–2	8–1–20–2	8–0–27–1			8–1–25–2
v. Gloucestershire (Bristol) 12 July (NW)	12–1–35–2	12–5–31–4	12–2–42–0	12–1–36–0	12–5–13–1		
v. Northamptonshire (Old Trafford) 16 July (RA)	7–1–18–2	6–0–18–0	5.3–2–16–2	6–1–26–0	8–0–31–3		
v. Hampshire (Portsmouth) 23 July (RA)		8–0–41–3	8–0–30–3	8–0–30–1	8–0–29–2		8–0–23–0
v. Worcestershire (Worcester) 2 August (NW)	10–3–22–0	11.2–0–52–1	9–0–52–0	8–0–52–1	12–0–44–1		
v. Gloucestershire (Cheltenham) 6 August (RA)	8–0–32–1	8–3–20–2	8–1–23–1	8–1–29–4			7.5–0–30–2
v. Essex (Old Trafford) 13 August (RA)	4–0–20–0	5–0–15–0	1–0–8–0	0.4–0–7–0			
v. Yorkshire (Old Trafford) 20 August (RA)	6–0–21–1	6–1–9–1	8–0–51–1	6–0–34–0	6–0–38–1		8–0–28–0
v. Surrey (Old Trafford) 27 August (RA)		8–1–25–0	8–0–30–4	8–0–41–1	8–0–39–1		8–0–41–1
v. Nottinghamshire (Old Trafford) 6 September (RC)	6.2–0–37–1	5–0–20–0	8–0–28–1	8–1–33–1	8–0–41–1		4–0–22–0
Wickets	31	28	43	18	23	1	15

v. Gloucestershire (Cheltenham) 6 August (RA)	v. Essex (Old Trafford) 13 August (RA)	v. Yorkshire (Old Trafford) 20 August (RA)	v. Surrey (Old Trafford) 27 August (RA)	v. Nottinghamshire (Old Trafford) 6 September (RC)	Runs
48	8	18	66	12	551
0	30	32	26	3	682
					102
45	0	7	5	59	852
23*	33	21	13	56	430
13*	11	9	3	0	341
2	14*	27	20	7	179
—	3	15	—	16	175
—	3	4	—	4	122
—	9	1	12*	13*	77
—	—	1*	—	5*	15
			10		267
—	13	10	19*	1	58
					35
		4	1	1	
6	6	14	10	6	
5	5	6	3	4	
2					
144	135	169	188	187	
4	9	10	7	9	
W	Ab.	L	W	L	
4	2	0	4	—	

T.E. Jesty	M.A. Atherton	Byes	Leg-byes	Wides	No-balls	Total	Wkts
							Ab.
			2	8	6	186	6
		1	13	11	1	184	5
4–2–3–0		1	4	9	1	111	9
			9	1	2	188	9
–0–4–0		5	7	7	5	235	5
			9		2	199	8
			10	9		153	9
–0–22–0			9	10	2	244	7
		1	9	8	3	145	9
			9	4	4	250	7
–0–9–0		2	8	6	2	152	3
			11	3	1	110	10
		4	10	2	3	172	9
			7	2	5	84	10
		2	18	2	2	136	8
		3	14	6	7	174	7
		2	6	1	2	133	10
		1	12	11	2	166	9
	2–0–12–0		7	9	3	241	3
			9	6	1	143	10
			3	2		53	0
		4	16	5	1	201	5
			10	5		186	10
			7	4	2	188	5
0	0						

Lampitt 4 for 89, S.M. McEwan 4 for 111) and 161 for 6 dec (C.J. Tavare 62)
Worcestershire 200 for 5 dec (G.A. Hick 86, D.B. D'Oliveira 63) and 302 for 5 (G.A. Hick 136 not out, T.S. Curtis 84)

Worcestershire won by 5 wickets
Worcestershire 20 pts, Somerset 4 pts

24, 25, 26 and 28 August

at Chesterfield

Yorkshire 136 (S.J. Base 7 for 60) and 184 (S.J. Base 5 for 93)
Derbyshire 102 (P.W. Jarvis 6 for 27, A. Sidebottom 4 for 47) and 219 for 7 (K.J. Barnett 74, A. Sidebottom 5 for 92)

Derbyshire won by 3 wickets
Derbyshire 20 pts, Yorkshire 4 pts

at Swansea

Warwickshire 430 (T.A. Lloyd 183, A.I. Kallicharran 119, S.L. Watkin 6 for 106) and 31 for 2
Glamorgan 131 (T.A. Munton 4 for 33) and 329 (H. Morris 108, R.J. Shastri 56)

Warwickshire won by 8 wickets
Warwickshire 24 pts, Glamorgan 1 pt

at Folkestone

Leicestershire 498 (J.J. Whitaker 116, P. Willey 99, L. Potter 96, C.C. Lewis 69, P. Whitticase 61, C.S. Cowdrey 4 for 33, C. Penn 4 for 116)
Kent 264 (T.R. Ward 78, R.F. Pienaar 72) and 267 for 2 (R.F. Pienaar 134 not out, N.R. Taylor 63 not out)

Match drawn
Leicestershire 8 pts, Kent 4 pts

at Old Trafford

Lancashire 305 and 20 for 1 dec
Surrey 24 for 1 dec and 204 (M.A. Lynch 50, Wasim Akram 5 for 52, J.D. Fitton 5 for 72)

Lancashire won by 97 runs
Lancashire 20 pts, Surrey 4 pts

at Northampton

Essex 324 (M.A. Garnham 91, M.E. Waugh 53, J.G. Thomas 5 for 74) and 166 for 7 dec (N. Hussain 64)
Northamptonshire 227 (A. Fordham 75, N.A. Foster 7 for 105) and 264 for 6 (W. Larkins 73, N.A. Felton 55, R.J. Bailey 50)

Northamptonshire won by 4 wickets
Northamptonshire 22 pts, Essex 8 pts

at Trent Bridge

Nottinghamshire 308 (B.C. Broad 144, D.W. Randall 78, R.M. Ellcock 4 for 63, P.C.R. Tufnell 4 for 72) and 136 (R.M. Ellcock 4 for 23)
Middlesex 204 for 2 dec (M.W. Gatting 83, D.L. Haynes 75 not out) and 160 for 6

Match drawn
Middlesex 4 pts, Nottinghamshire 3 pts

at Hove

Gloucestershire 133 (C.M. Wells 4 for 39) and 363 (K.M. Curran 117 not out)
Sussex 323 (D.M. Smith 115, A.I.C. Dodemaide 80) and 175 for 7

Sussex won by 3 wickets
Sussex 23 pts, Gloucestershire 3 pts

Leicestershire CCC
Limited-Over Matches, 1989

BATTING

BATTING	v. Glamorgan (Leicester) 23 April (RA)	v. Lancashire (Old Trafford) 25 April (B&H)	v. Derbyshire (Leicester) 30 April (RA)	v. Warwickshire (Leicester) 2 May (B&H)	v. Scotland (Leicester) 9 May (B&H)	v. Northamptonshire (Northampton) 11 & 12 May (B&H)	v. Yorkshire (Leicester) 14 May (RA)	v. Sussex (Hove) 21 May (RA)	v. Hampshire (Bournemouth) 28 May (RA)	v. Lancashire (Leicester) 4 June (RA)	v. Gloucestershire (Leicester) 11 June (RA)	v. Essex (Chelmsford) 18 June (RA)	v. Northamptonshire (Luton) 25 June (RA)	v. Shropshire (Telford) 28 June (NW)	v. Warwickshire (Leicester) 2 July (RA)	v. Worcestershire (Worcester) 9 July (RA)
T.J. Boon	11	6	12	40	4*	—			3				39*	24		
N.E. Briers	4	7	71	5	0	5	28	20	6*	9	10		13	15	4	20
D.I. Gower	19	42	36	11	2*	35*	5		10				101*	82		6
P. Willey	23	1	41		8		20	2	31	6		25	43	9		6
J.J. Whitaker	33	0	26	48			3*	10	22	48*	23	46	0	6	81	2
L. Potter	21	12	22*	23			34	16	16	14	5	0	0	4*	4	50
C.C. Lewis	23*	7	8*	17			3	21		19	32*	—			17*	50
P. Whitticase	36*	0		14*			11	5		4	10				1*	23
G.J. Parsons	—	7*	—	63*			8	0		14	—	—	—		1*	5*
J.P. Agnew	—	4	—				14	0*		11*				—		0
G.J.F. Ferris	—	6	—						0							
W.K.M. Benjamin				—			—	5		—	9	41*			2	0
P.M. Such				—							—					2*
L.B. Taylor							3*									2*
J.D.R. Benson									5	25*	41	13	—			6
P.A. Nixon										—						—
R.H. Edmunds												0				
P.N. Hepworth													20*			
L. Tennant																
Byes	2	5		2			1		2	1				4	1	1
Leg-byes	8	7	7	6	4	5	6	6	8	9	11	1	7	9	3	14
Wides		1	5	8	1	2	1	3	6	3	3			14	9	17
No-balls	6		8	2				4	2	1	1	2	1			2
Total	186	105	236	239		11	92	131	107	152	155	192	82	221	215	156
Wickets	6	10	5	6		1	3	10	10	3	10	6	2	4	6	9
Result	Ab.	L	L	W	W	Ab.	W	L	L	W	L	L	W	W	W	L
Points	2	0	0	2	2	1	4	0	0	4	0	0	4	—	4	0

Fielding Figures

17 – P. Whitticase (ct 16/st 1)   †L.B. Taylor absent hurt
9 – L. Potter
7 – C.C. Lewis
6 – N.E. Briers
4 – G.J. Parsons and J.J. Whitaker
3 – J.D.R. Benson and J.P. Agnew
2 – T.J. Boon, P. Willey, D.I. Gower and P.A. Nixon
1 – G.J.F. Ferris and L. Tennant

BOWLING

	G.J.F. Ferris	J.P. Agnew	C.C. Lewis	G.J. Parsons	P. Willey	L. Potter	W.K.M. Benjamin	P.M. Such
v. Glamorgan (Leicester) 23 April (RA)								
v. Lancashire (Old Trafford) 25 April (B&H)	10-1-26-0	11-1-47-1	9.3-0-47-1	11-4-26-1	11-1-38-0			
v. Derbyshire (Leicester) 30 April (RA)	7-1-19-2	5-1-23-0	8-0-36-0	8-0-39-0	8-0-31-2		4-0-26-1	
v. Warwickshire (Leicester) 2 May (B&H)	11-1-42-3	10-4-19-2	11-1-49-3	10-0-41-1	11-2-42-1		2-0-9-0	
v. Scotland (Leicester) 9 May (B&H)		6-0-11-1	9-0-18-1	8-3-12-4		6-3-13-1	9-1-29-2	11-2-35-1
v. Northamptonshire (Northampton) 11 & 12 May (B&H)		11-3-22-0	11-1-48-1	11-1-67-0	11-1-24-1		11-4-28-1	
v. Yorkshire (Leicester) 14 May (RA)		8-2-15-1	8-3-9-3	8-3-13-0	6-2-15-2	2-1-2-1	8-1-28-2	
v. Sussex (Hove) 21 May (RA)		8-0-41-1	8-1-45-2	4-0-27-1	8-1-24-0		8-1-30-0	
v. Hampshire (Bournemouth) 28 May (RA)	5-1-18-1	6.4-2-32-0	5-0-19-1	7-0-30-0	4-1-9-1			
v. Lancashire (Leicester) 4 June (RA)		8-2-31-3	8-1-38-3	8-2-26-2	8-1-22-0		8-1-24-1	
v. Gloucestershire (Leicester) 11 June (RA)		8-1-25-4		8-0-59-1	8-0-55-0		8-0-31-0	
v. Essex (Chelmsford) 18 June (RA)		7-1-26-0	3-0-16-0	8-0-32-0	5-0-30-0	2-0-16-1	7-0-32-0	5-0-34-0
v. Northamptonshire (Luton) 25 June (RA)		6-1-14-1	8-0-16-2	5-0-13-1			7-1-13-0	
v. Shropshire (Telford) 28 June (NW)		12-2-30-2			12-1-54-0		12-3-39-2	
v. Warwickshire (Leicester) 2 July (RA)		7-2-25-1	2-0-18-0	7-0-45-1	8-0-31-3		7.1-1-32-3	
v. Worcestershire (Worcester) 9 July (RA)		6.3-1-19-0		8-0-38-1	8-0-28-1		7-0-20-0	
v. Sussex (Hove) 12 July (NW)		12-2-49-0		8-0-64-0	12-2-31-1	5-0-33-0	12-4-39-0	
v. Nottinghamshire (Leicester) 19 July (RA)		6-0-24-2			7-1-36-1	6-1-18-1		
v. Somerset (Taunton) 23 July (RA)	7-0-38-0	8-0-35-1		8-0-52-0		0.2-0-4-0		7-1-29-0
v. Middlesex (Lord's) 30 July (RA)		7-1-18-0		5-0-25-0	7-0-18-1			
v. Surrey (Leicester) 20 August (RA)		8-0-34-2		8-1-42-1			8-1-41-0	8-0-45-2
v. Kent (Folkestone) 27 August (RA)		8-2-22-0	4-1-34-0	7-0-41-1			6-2-14-3	5-0-26-1
v. Yorkshire (Scarborough) 3 September (FC)		9.2-4-28-1	10-0-52-3	10-0-37-1	6-0-26-0		9-1-33-1	
Wickets	6	23	20	16	15	5	15	4

a D. Ripley retired hurt   b G.C. Small absent hurt

As the Britannic Assurance County Championship entered its final stages with the first of four rounds of four-day matches Worcestershire moved a step closer to retaining their title with a most thrilling and impressive win over Somerset. Rain restricted play to 18 overs on the second day and carried Somerset's first innings into the third morning. Showing great enterprise, Phil Neale declared when his side had reached two hundred and avoided the follow-on. Marks could offer no easy target in the circumstances, and none of the contenders could complain when he offered Worcestershire the chance to score 300 in 57 overs. Few counties would have contemplated such a task, but Worcestershire attacked with sense and purpose from the start. Curtis and Bent put on 51 before Bent was run out, and Hick and Curtis then added 128. D'Oliveira was caught without scoring, but Hick had asserted complete authority over the bowling. He took nine off an over from Pringle and pulled Mallender for six. He and Neale added 75 in 11 overs and, although Neale and Weston were dismissed, Worcestershire always looked likely to reach their target while Hick remained. Victory came with five balls to spare, and Hick was left

Mike Garnham took over as Essex wicket-keeper early in the season when David East broke a finger. He kept wicket efficiently and scored many useful runs. (USPA)

v. Sussex (Hove) 12 July (NW)	v. Nottinghamshire (Leicester) 19 July (RA)	v. Somerset (Taunton) 23 July (RA)	v. Middlesex (Lord's) 30 July (RA)	v. Surrey (Leicester) 20 August (RA)	v. Kent (Folkestone) 27 August (RA)	v. Yorkshire (Scarborough) 3 September (FC)	Runs
			20		1	76	236
8	13	45	0	37	24	11	355
23	5	14		32			417
89	8		3			28	343
36	19	50	16	55	38	52	614
17	19	0	19	11*	22	5	274
5	22	17	0	40	10	13	304
0	21	22		—	2		148
16*		20	17	—	7	2*	160
6	1	2	4	—	17	—	59
		1*					7
17				27*	2	9	112
		0		—	8*		8
—	2	0	1*	—		—	8
							90
			1			7*	8
	5*				9		14
							20
	13		1*				14
1				4		1	
	14	5	2	11	4		
12	4	7	8	2	3	1	
2			3				
32	146	183	95	219	147	205	
9†	10	10	9	4	10	7	
L	L	L	L	W	L	L	
—	0	0	0	4	0	—	

L.B. Taylor	R.H. Edmunds	L. Tennant	Byes	Leg-byes	Wides	No-balls	Total	Wkts
								Ab.
				3	2	5	187	3
			1	12		3	187	6
				3	4	4	205	10
				10	3	7	128	10
				15	3	3	204	10
				7	3	6	89	9
4-0-24-0			6	11	5	2	208	4
				2	7	7	110	3
				8		2	149	9
	8-0-36-0		8		9		214	6
			1	6	4	2	193	1
8-0-20-5				5	2		81	9a
12-0-40-1				16	4	4	220	7
8-1-37-1			2	4	3	1	194	9b
8-0-42-1			4	6	8		157	4
11-0-67-1			5	12	2	1	300	2
7-0-29-2	7-3-27-2	5-0-34-0		14	13	3	182	9
6-0-18-2				10	7	2	186	3
6-1-25-2		1-0-5-0		5	7	4	96	4
8-0-37-0			2	14	5		215	6
	7-0-55-0			7	2		199	6
5-1-17-0				12	2	2	205	7
15	2	0						

unbeaten on 136, which had come off 120 balls. He hit 3 sixes and 10 fours, and there were those among the Somerset players who considered it a better innings than the 405 he had scored against them at Taunton a year earlier.

In contrast, Essex failed against Northamptonshire and thereby seriously weakened their challenge for the title. Solid batting by the middle order with more useful runs from Mike Garnham took Essex to maximum batting points in spite of losing three men to the England side. Foster, aggressive if expensive, then helped his side to claim four bowling points, and Essex were still on top even though most of the third day was lost to rain. Hardie's declaration eventually left the home side to 264 in 73 overs on a wicket which many had predicted would increasingly favour the bowler. Cook and Larkins gave Northamptonshire a fine start in their bid for victory with a partnership of 101, but Essex dropped vital catches to make their opponents' task easier. Larkins was dropped by Shahid off Childs, and the fielder sustained a broken nose as he lost the ball in the sun. Bailey and Felton maintained the momentum, and Northamptonshire won with an over to spare.

There was play only on the first and last days at Old Trafford, where Wasim Akram and Dexter Fitton were the main reasons for Lancashire's success after enterprising declarations by both captains.

It was only rain which extended play at Chesterfield into

David Smith in belligerent mood for Sussex. (USPA)

the fourth day, for 21 wickets fell on the first day. Barnett led Derbyshire to a narrow victory, but their real hero was medium-pace bowler Simon Base, who furthered his England claims with his career-best figures for both innings, 7 for 60, and match, 12 for 153. It seemed strange that Derbyshire had ignored his talents for most of the season.

Chris Broad provided the backbone to the Nottinghamshire innings at Trent Bridge, where rain also interfered with play. Eventually, Middlesex were left to make 241 in 40 overs, but after the departure of Gatting they called off the chase and their chances of winning the championship vanished.

Warwickshire's winning run continued with an emphatic win at Swansea. Andy Lloyd, 91 runs before lunch on the opening day, and Alvin Kallicharran shared a second-wicket partnership of 241. Lloyd's hundred came out of 134 runs scored in 2½ hours. He was eventually out when he lofted a ball from Barwick to cover. Kallicharran moved at a more sedate pace, but Warwickshire scored at a rate of more than 3½ runs an over. Glamorgan wilted before the Warwickshire seam bowlers and, although Hugh Morris almost succeeded in frustrating the visitors with his third championship hundred of the season, Warwickshire were comfortable winners.

A century from James Whitaker and consistent batting throughout the order took Leicestershire to a formidable

Simon Base – 12 wickets for Derbyshire against Yorkshire at Chesterfield, 24–8 August. (George Herringshaw/ASP)

total at Folkestone, but Roy Pienaar hit his third century in successive championship matches to save the game for Kent after they had been forced to follow-on.

Sussex's seam attack shot out Gloucestershire on the opening day at Hove, and, thanks to David Smith and Tony Dodemaide, they recovered from 95 for 5 to take a commanding lead on the Friday. Gloucestershire's second innings, built around Curran's century, revealed greater consistency and resilience on the part of the west country batsmen, but they were only 11 runs ahead when their sixth wicket fell. The tail wagged fiercely, and Sussex eventually needed 174 to win. At 12 for 3, they were in dire straits, but Parker and Colin Wells rescued them and they moved to a nervous victory.

Sixth Cornhill Test Match
ENGLAND v. AUSTRALIA

It is difficult to remember what the England side was as originally chosen, so many were the changes forced upon the selectors through injuries and withdrawals. Devon Malcolm and Ian Botham were unfit, and Greg Thomas, who had once seemed a young man of eagerness and ambition to play for England, announced that he had joined the rebel tour to South Africa. Watkin was approached, but, like DeFreitas, now back in favour, he was pronounced unfit for a five-day Test. Gooch, having exiled himself from the fifth Test through lack of form, returned

The wicket of Steve Waugh for Alan Igglesden in his first Test match. (Adrian Murrell/Allsport).

SIXTH CORNHILL TEST MATCH – ENGLAND v. AUSTRALIA
24, 25, 26, 28 and 29 August 1989 at The Oval, Kennington, London

AUSTRALIA

	FIRST INNINGS		SECOND INNINGS	
G.R. Marsh	c Igglesden, b Small	17	(2) lbw, b Igglesden	4
M.A. Taylor	c Russell, b Igglesden	71	(1) c Russell, b Small	48
D.C. Boon	c Atherton, b Small	46	run out	37
A.R. Border†	c Russell, b Capel	76	not out	51
D.M. Jones	c Gower, b Small	122	b Capel	50
S.R. Waugh	b Igglesden	14	not out	7
I.A. Healy*	c Russell, b Pringle	44		
T.V. Hohns	c Russell, b Pringle	30		
M.G. Hughes	lbw, b Pringle	21		
G.F. Lawson	b Pringle	2		
T.M. Alderman	not out	6		
Extras	b 1, lb 9, nb 9	19	b 2, lb 7, nb 13	22
		468	(for 4 wkts, dec)	**219**

	O	M	R	W	O	M	R	W
Small	40	8	141	3	20	4	57	1
Igglesden	24	2	91	2	13	1	55	1
Pringle	24.3	6	70	4	16	–	53	–
Capel	16	2	66	1	8	–	35	1
Cook	25	5	78	–	6	2	10	–
Atherton	1	–	10	–				
Gooch	2	1	2	–				

ENGLAND

	FIRST INNINGS		SECOND INNINGS	
G.A. Gooch	lbw, b Alderman	0	c and b Alderman	10
J.P. Stephenson	c Waugh, b Alderman	25	lbw, b Alderman	11
M.A. Atherton	c Healy, b Hughes	12	b Lawson	14
R.A. Smith	b Lawson	11	not out	77
D.I. Gower†	c Healy, b Alderman	79	c Waugh, b Lawson	7
D.J. Capel	lbw, b Alderman	4	c Taylor, b Hohns	17
R.C. Russell*	c Healy, b Alderman	12	not out	0
D.R. Pringle	c Taylor, b Hohns	27		
G.C. Small	c Jones, b Lawson	59		
N.G.B. Cook	c Jones, b Lawson	31		
A.P. Igglesden	not out	2		
Extras	b 2, lb 7, w 1, nb 13	23	lb 1, w 1, nb 5	7
		285	(for 5 wkts)	**143**

	O	M	R	W	O	M	R	W
Alderman	27	7	66	5	13	3	30	2
Lawson	29.1	9	85	3	15.1	2	41	2
Hughes	23	3	84	1	8	2	34	–
Hohns	10	1	30	1	10	2	37	1
Waugh	3	–	11	–				

FALL OF WICKETS
1–48, 2–130, 3–149, 4–345, 5–347, 6–386, 7–409, 8–447, 9–453
1–7, 2–100, 3–101, 4–189

FALL OF WICKETS
1–1, 2–28, 3–47, 4–80, 5–84, 6–98, 7–169, 8–201, 9–274
1–20, 2–27, 3–51, 4–67, 5–138

Umpires: H.D. Bird & K.E. Palmer

Match drawn

Middlesex CCC
Limited-Over Matches, 1989

BATTING

BATTING	Yorkshire (Lord's) 23 April (RA)	Worcestershire (Lord's) 26 April (B&H)	Essex (Chelmsford) 30 April (RA)	Gloucestershire (Bristol) 2 May (B&H)	Surrey (Lord's) 7 May (RA)	Combined Universities (Oxford) 9 May (B&H)	Surrey (Lord's) 13 May (B&H)	Gloucestershire (Bristol) 14 May (RA)	Warwickshire (Edgbaston) 28 May (RA)	Hampshire (Lord's) 4 June (RA)	Glamorgan (Merthyr Tydfil) 11 June (RA)	Worcestershire (Worcester) 25 June (RA)	Durham (Darlington) 28 June (NW)	Lancashire (Lord's) 2 July (RA)	Derbyshire (Lord's) 9 July (RA)	Nottinghamshire (Uxbridge) 12 July (NW)	Kent (Lord's) 23 July (RA)	Leicestershire (Lord's) 30 July (RA)
J.D. Carr	23	16	12	43	86	26	29		39	2	41	20		7	40*	44	20	0
P.R. Downton	16	13	7	0	—		34	7	3	11	0	7*	31*	31*	10*	69	17*	—
M.W. Gatting	81*	15	25	30	80	123*	30	32		3*			37	1		16	54	34*
M.R. Ramprakash	29*	19	8	2	13	24*	3	26	16		14	47*	1	6	21	11	11	29*
R.O. Butcher	—	7	29	5	16	15	25	44	27	8	32	28	3	0	—			
K.R. Brown	—	12	4		—			20*	2	8								
J.E. Emburey	—	4	1	5	5	—	18	6*		10	3		—	13		36	0	
S.P. Hughes	—	1*	5	4	—	—	15*		4*	3		—	11	0*	—	9*	4*	—
J.F. Sykes	—	16*	13	38	0*	—	38	35			18	8						
A.R.C. Fraser	—	—	11*	3*	—	—		—	2*	2*	25		19	12		8*	3	
N.G. Cowans	—	—	4	1	—	—	0		—		0							
N.F. Williams				2	—	—	4	—	22									
D.L. Haynes							59	14	2	52	2	19	83	35	3	0	56	8
M.A. Roseberry											20	7	7	17		7		2
P.C.R. Tufnell												13*						
R.M. Ellcock													—		0*			
I.J.F. Hutchinson														7	0	1	11	7
A.G.J. Fraser																		
Byes	2			4					7	1			3	2			5	
Leg-byes	6	6	6	4	11	5	12	14	2	10	5	3	3	18	6	7	13	5
Wides	5	5	4	8	5	1	3	1	6	8	11	5	5	2	2	1	7	7
No-balls			1	4	1				1				2	2	2	1	4	4
Total	162	114	130	149	221	194	232	202	167	138	172	144	215	136	89	203	205	96
Wickets	2	7	10	10	5	2	9	6	8	8	10	5	7	8	4	7	7	4
Result	W	L	L	L	W	W	W	W	L	Tie	L	W	W	L	W	W	L	W
Points	4	0	0	0	4	2	2	4	2	0	—	4	—	0	4	—	0	4

Fielding Figures

41 – P.R. Downton (ct 34/st 7)
10 – J.D. Carr
9 – M.W. Gatting
8 – N.G. Cowans
7 – M.R. Ramprakash and I.J.F. Hutchinson
6 – R.O. Butcher, D.L. Haynes and R.M. Ellcock
3 – J.E. Emburey and S.P. Hughes
1 – A.R.C. Fraser, J.F. Sykes, N.F. Williams, P.C.R. Tufnell, M.A. Roseberry and sub

BOWLING

BOWLING	N.G. Cowans	A.R.C. Fraser	J.D. Carr	S.P. Hughes	J.E. Emburey	J.F. Sykes	M.W. Gatting
v. Yorkshire (Lord's) 23 April (RA)	8-2-16-0	8-0-28-1	6-0-26-1	8-0-51-2	8-0-37-3	2-1-7-1	
v. Worcestershire (Lord's) 26 April (B&H)	7-2-20-1	6-0-19-0	2-0-4-0	6-0-38-3	6-2-14-0	4-0-18-1	
v. Essex (Chelmsford) 30 April (RA)	6-4-3-0	8-0-35-2	8-1-28-0	6.4-1-29-0	8-1-29-0		
v. Gloucestershire (Bristol) 2 May (B&H)	11-4-28-0			5-0-15-0	8-0-20-2	3-1-16-0	2-0-10-0
v. Surrey (Lord's) 7 May (RA)		7.3-0-34-1	8-2-21-4	4-0-10-0	7-0-29-0	4-0-30-2	
v. Combined Universities (Oxford) 9 May (B&H)	9-1-36-0	11-3-26-2	7-1-17-1	8-1-36-2	11-1-39-3		
v. Surrey (Lord's) 13 May (B&H)	7-1-23-2	10.1-0-39-2		6-0-32-3	8-3-16-2		
v. Gloucestershire (Bristol) 14 May (RA)		8-0-32-0		7-0-27-0	8-0-60-2		8-1-30-4
v. Warwickshire (Edgbaston) 28 May (RA)	8-1-38-1	8-0-26-2	3-0-14-0	7-0-48-0		5-0-27-1	
v. Hampshire (Lord's) 4 June (RA)	8-5-6-3	7-1-23-1	6-0-46-0	7.4-0-20-4	8-1-29-2		2-0-9-0
v. Glamorgan (Merthyr Tydfil) 11 June (RA)	8-2-45-2	8-0-22-0	8-0-23-0		8-0-62-2	1-0-13-0	
v. Worcestershire (Worcester) 25 June (RA)	8-1-36-1	8-2-23-1	8-0-24-2	7.2-1-23-5			
v. Durham (Darlington) 28 June (NW)	12-3-29-2	12-2-45-1		10.2-2-20-4	10-5-18-0		
v. Lancashire (Lord's) 2 July (RA)	8-4-18-1	8-3-25-1	5-0-32-0	7.4-0-28-1	8-1-18-2		2-0-8-1
v. Derbyshire (Lord's) 9 July (RA)	8-1-30-1		8-1-19-1	8-0-33-1			
v. Nottinghamshire (Uxbridge) 12 July (NW)	7.4-0-24-1	12-1-27-3	3-0-8-0	10-4-25-2	12-1-36-0		
v. Kent (Lord's) 23 July (RA)	8-2-18-2	8-4-16-1	5-0-32-1	4-0-43-0	7-0-43-2		
v. Leicestershire (Lord's) 30 July (RA)	5-2-14-1		3-0-14-2	7-1-21-2			
v. Sussex (Lord's) 2 August (NW)	12-1-49-0	11-1-32-1		10-0-37-3	12-6-11-3		
v. Somerset (Weston-super-Mare) 6 August (RA)	8-0-17-1	8-0-38-2		8-0-50-3	8-0-47-0		
v. Northamptonshire (Lord's) 13 August (RA)	8-1-17-0			8-2-38-3	8-0-31-1		
v. Hampshire (Southampton) 16 August (NW)	12-2-48-1	12-4-56-1		12-1-55-1	12-2-38-2		
v. Sussex (Hastings) 20 August (RA)			3-0-12-0	8-0-48-1	8-0-28-4		
v. Nottinghamshire (Trent Bridge) 27 August (RA)	8-3-17-1			6-0-26-0	7-0-36-0		
v. Warwickshire (Lord's) 2 September (NW)	12-4-23-1	12-3-30-2	3-0-11-1	10.4-2-45-0	12-2-46-1		
Wickets	22	26	13	42	29	5	5

and had his Essex partner John Stephenson to open with him, a brave and imaginative choice. Nasser Hussain was also in the party, but he was omitted from the final eleven. David Capel, Derek Pringle, the country's leading wicket-taker, and Gladstone Small, injured at Trent Bridge, were brought back to Test cricket while Alan Igglesden, a surprise replacement, earned his first Test cap. Australia were unchanged.

Border won the toss, and Australia batted, and only Pringle, once, passed the bat in the opening session. It was Small, however, who captured the first wicket when Marsh mis-hit to mid-wicket where Igglesden slid to take a good low catch. Taylor looked as unbreachable and as dominant as ever until he gave Igglesden his first Test wicket when he played rashly at a ball slanted across him. Border cover-drove the next ball for four to announce his arrival, but he became more sedentary after that, content to play the anchor role.

Boon was looking most menacing when he drove at a widish ball from Small and was taken at slip. That was England's last success of the day, for Dean Jones was at once in imperious mood. In 162 minutes before the close, he and Border added 176, and Jones made 114 of them. Sixteen times Jones had hit the ball to the boundary. It was hard to believe that his selection for the tour had been in doubt throughout most of the Australian season and that only his innings in the final Test against West Indies had clinched his place, so dominant, so assured, so unquestionably a batsman of the highest class did he look.

Neither Jones nor Border could recapture the Thursday evening form on the Friday morning. Jones added one more four to his overnight score, and the stand was worth 196 when Border looped a mis-pull to Russell off Capel's

Batting

v. Sussex (Lord's) 2 August (NW)	v. Somerset (Weston-super-Mare) 6 August (RA)	v. Northamptonshire (Lord's) 13 August (RA)	v. Hampshire (Southampton) 16 August (NW)	v. Sussex (Hastings) 20 August (RA)	v. Nottinghamshire (Trent Bridge) 27 August (RA)	v. Warwickshire (Lord's) 2 September (NW)	Runs
3	2	23	83	27	8	17	611
—	6	9*	0	5	8	43*	327
132*	0	40	29	3	26	1	792
2		44	43			24	393
				15	67		321
				20	5		71
20*	17	—	0	6*	13	21*	168
—	8	—	5*	—	4*	—	73
							166
—	10		0*			—	95
—	1*	—	—		0	—	6
		—		0	0		28
88	7		80			50	558
	34	15*	21	83*	24	26	263
—							13
	13		—	—	5	—	18
—	0	13					39
		—		—			—
1		1					
16	8	10	3	5	5	16	
3		5	2	2	2	9	
1	2		1	6		3	
266	108	160	267	172	167	210	
3	10	4	7	6	10	5	
W	L	W	W	W	L	L	
—	0	4	—	4	0	—	

Bowling

N.F. Williams	P.C.R. Tufnell	D.L. Haynes	R.M. Ellcock	A.G.J. Fraser	K.R. Brown	Byes	Leg-byes	Wides	No-balls	Total	Wkts
							5	4		170	9
							2	3	4	115	6
							10	1	2	134	2
							11	8	1	150	4
7.2-2-33-0						4	9		1	161	10
8-0-24-2							3	2	2	190	9
9-2-33-1							4	1	3	156	10
7-0-42-1						3	10	2	3	188	7
8-0-18-1						1	6	5	1	196	4
8-0-36-0							5	5	4	138	10
	4-0-19-0	3-0-19-0					6	11		209	6
			8-1-26-1			4	7	1		143	10
			12-3-38-2			4	7	3	1	161	10
							10	5	2	139	6
8-1-46-2			8-1-9-2				11	2		148	7
			10-2-43-4				4	4	5	167	10
			8-0-50-0				9	3		211	7
7-2-19-3	6-0-25-1						2	8	3	95	9
	12-1-50-1						9	1	4	188	10
			8-0-39-2				14	10	3	205	8
8-1-24-1				8-0-35-2		4	8		3	157	8
			12-0-62-2			2	3	4	3	264	7
8-1-36-1			8-2-19-2	5-0-22-1			5	5	2	170	9
7-0-38-0			6-0-41-1		0.2-0-6-0		4	1	3	168	2
			10-1-45-0								
12	2	0	16	3	0						

Northamptonshire CCC
Limited-Over Matches, 1989

BATTING

BATTING	v. Derbyshire (Derby) 23 April (RA)	v. Warwickshire (Edgbaston) 25 & 26 April (B&H)	v. Warwickshire (Northampton) 7 May (RA)	v. Lancashire (Northampton) 9 May (B&H)	v. Leicestershire (Northampton) 11 & 12 May (B&H)	v. Scotland (Glasgow) 13 May (B&H)	v. Glamorgan (Cardiff) 21 May (RA)	v. Kent (Canterbury) 28 May (RA)	v. Kent (Northampton) 31 May (B&H)	v. Surrey (Northampton) 4 June (RA)	v. Sussex (Hove) 11 June (RA)	v. Leicestershire (Luton) 25 June (RA)	v. Suffolk (Bury St Edmunds) 28 & 29 June (NW)	v. Worcestershire (Tring) 2 July (RA)	v. Hampshire (Northampton) 9 July (RA)	v. Somerset (Taunton) 12 July (NW)
G. Cook	57		66	25	72*	53	66*	46	3	20	8	4				4
W. Larkins	15	6	49	2	54	11	6	33	63	44	0	1		17	10	19
R.J. Bailey	0	27	39	30	69*	0	96	13	106*	7	20	0		32	53*	86*
A.J. Lamb	84*	80*	38	87*					11	21		0	103	10		4
D.J. Capel	3	40*	15*	5	—	25	16*	21	2	63	0		92*	32	—	31
R.G. Williams	8	—	2*	30	—											
D. Ripley	22*	—	—	1*	—	—		9	—	5*	18*	4*	5	—		21*
N.G.B. Cook	14	—						7*		—		13*		10*		
J.G. Thomas	—		2	3				2				5		0		
W.W. Davis	—															
M.A. Robinson	—							—	—	—		2		0		
D.J. Wild		3				—	52*	—	3	0*	0			25	—	
A. Walker		—														
W.M. Noon						—										
N.A. Felton							15*	—				7	23	18	58*	41
C.E.L. Ambrose								—	17*			13*	1	2		—
A. Fordham												23				
G. Smith						—										
N.A. Stanley																
A.L. Penberthy																
J.W. Govan																
Byes						5		5	1				3	2		
Leg-byes	19	5	7	15	12	3	13	10	5	4	5	14	10	8	2	
Wides	1	9	7	3	1	4	7	7	7	2			13	4	4	2
No-balls	2	2	5	3	2		1			3			3	2		1
Total	225	172	235	204	210	163	205	187	201	189	81	256	168	135		211
Wickets	6	3	5	6	1	4	2	8	4	6	9†	5	10	1		5
Result	Ab.	W	W	W	Ab.	W	W	W	L	W	L	L	W	L	Ab.	W
Points	2	2	4	2	1	2	4	4	—	4	0	0	0	—	2	—

Fielding Figures

28 – D. Ripley (ct 27/st 1)
12 – W. Larkins
7 – G. Cook
6 – M.A. Robinson
5 – D.J. Capel
4 – J.G. Thomas, R.J. Bailey, N.A. Felton and N.G.B. Cook
3 – D.J. Wild and A. Fordham
2 – A.J. Lamb, A. Walker, C.E.L. Ambrose and subs
1 – R.G. Williams, W.W. Davis and A.L. Penberthy
† D. Ripley retired hurt

BOWLING

BOWLING	W.W. Davis	J.G. Thomas	M.A. Robinson	D.J. Capel	R.G. Williams	A. Walker	N.G.B. Cook
v. Derbyshire (Derby) 23 April (RA)							
v. Warwickshire (Edgbaston) 25 & 26 April (B&H)	11–0–65–1	11–3–25–1	11–1–42–1	11–0–35–2	11–3–43–2		
v. Warwickshire (Northampton) 7 May (RA)	8–0–32–0	8–0–34–3		3–0–20–0	8–0–33–2	5–2–14–1	8–0–24–1
v. Lancashire (Northampton) 9 May (B&H)	8–2–11–0	9–0–36–3	11–1–19–1	11–0–47–3	10–2–66–1		2.1–0–7–1
v. Leicestershire (Northampton) 11 & 12 May (B&H)	3–1–5–0	2.2–1–2–1					
v. Scotland (Glasgow) 13 May (B&H)	11–0–48–0	10–1–34–1	11–1–20–3	7–0–32–1	5–0–38–1		11–2–24–1
v. Glamorgan (Cardiff) 21 May (RA)		8–1–41–3	8–0–28–1	8–0–19–1			8–0–35–2
v. Kent (Canterbury) 28 May (RA)	8–0–38–4	8–0–50–0	8–1–28–0	8–0–42–1			8–1–20–3
v. Kent (Northampton) 31 May (B&H)		11–2–38–2	11–2–29–0	11–0–30–2			11–1–35–3
v. Surrey (Northampton) 4 June (RA)	8–0–18–2	8–0–28–2	8–0–31–2	8–0–40–2			8–0–31–0
v. Sussex (Hove) 11 June (RA)			8–0–34–0	8–0–44–1			8–0–27–2
v. Leicestershire (Luton) 25 June (RA)		5–0–15–2	4–0–10–0	6.3–1–25–0			2–1–7–0
v. Suffolk (Bury St Edmunds) 28 & 29 June (NW)		7–0–24–2	12–2–30–1	12–1–54–3			11–2–49–1
v. Worcestershire (Tring) 2 July (RA)		7.4–0–32–1	8–0–32–0	8–0–30–0			8–0–28–2
v. Hampshire (Northampton) 9 July (RA)							
v. Somerset (Taunton) 12 July (NW)		10–0–36–3	11.4–2–32–4	12–1–52–2			12–1–53–0
v. Lancashire (Old Trafford) 16 July (RA)			5–0–30–0	8–0–33–3		7–1–24–0	7–2–22–2
v. Nottinghamshire (Finedon) 23 July (RA)		7.2–0–31–1	8–1–40–2	8–0–28–3			8–0–32–1
v. Somerset (Northampton) 30 July (RA)	7–0–20–2	8–0–31–0		8–0–20–3		7.5–1–20–2	
v. Warwickshire (Northampton) 2 August (NW)		11–0–54–3		10.4–1–42–1		12–4–29–1	12–1–29–0
v. Yorkshire (Sheffield) 6 August (RA)		7–0–45–2		8–0–63–0		8–0–39–4	8–2–22–2
v. Middlesex (Lord's) 13 August (RA)		8–1–19–0	8–1–30–2	5–0–24–1		4.5–1–12–0	
v. Gloucestershire (Moreton-in-Marsh) 20 August (RA)		7–1–32–1	8–1–22–1	8–1–33–1			8–0–40–0
v. Essex (Northampton) 27 August (RA)		8–0–36–2	8–0–24–0				
Wickets	9	33	18	30	6	8	21

Batting

v. (Old Trafford) 16 July (RA)	v. Nottinghamshire (Finedon) 23 July (RA)	v. Somerset (Northampton) 30 July (RA)	v. Warwickshire (Northampton) 2 August (NW)	v. Yorkshire (Sheffield) 6 August (RA)	v. Middlesex (Lord's) 13 August (RA)	v. Gloucestershire (Moreton-in-Marsh) 20 August (RA)	v. Essex (Northampton) 27 August (RA)	Runs
			45	77	0			568
	1	0	19	6		101	1	458
25	22	30	58*	46	46		3	813
								448
40	1	54	24	30	25*			567
								40
4	1	3	—		1*	—	16*	115
4		0*	—					49
18*	10	1	—		11		23	75
	2							2
0					—	—	—	2
	54	38	5*	30		—	22	251
	0*	—			1*			5
								—
2	29	6			17	5*	24	250
4		—			0			40
10	12				6	10	31	92
								—
13								13
35	7						4	46
						9*		9
1	2	1			4			
10	7	9	8	8	4	5		
4	1	4	1			5	7	
3	1			3	2			
173	150	191	198	157	198	145		
10	10	8	4	8	3	7		
W	L	L	W	L	W	W		
4	0	—	4	0	4	4		

Border and Jones contemplate the destruction of the England bowling in the last session of the first day. (Adrian Murrell/Allsport)

Bowling

C.E.L. Ambrose	G. Smith	W. Larkins	A.L. Penberthy	D.J. Wild	R.J. Bailey	J.W. Govan	Byes	Leg-byes	Wides	No-balls	Total	Wkts
												Ab.
								11	2	7	221	7
							1	13	3	1	171	9
							1	10	6		197	10
								4	1		11	1
–0–34–0								11	6	1	207	7
–0–66–1							2	3	6	3	162	7
1–1–17–2	7–0–63–0						6	17	5	1	201	8
–0–24–0							1	9	3	4	208	8
1.5–1–31–3		6–0–26–0					1	10	2		159	9
–1–38–1							1	4		4	190	7
												Ab.
0–0–36–1							1	6		1	210	10
–0–15–2							5	7	3	1	136	7
–2–15–3								3	4		149	10
			4–0–24–0	3–0–29–0				8	3	5	152	7
2–4–24–2					2–0–6–0			10	5		194	7
3–4–12–1								5	1	6	186	10
5–1–26–0		3–0–12–1				3.1–0–26–0	1	10	5		160	4
–0–48–1		1–0–6–0					2	12	2	1	195	5
–3–25–0			8–1–26–3			8–2–23–3		10	6	1	144	9
17	0	1	3	0	0	3						

ABOVE: *Allan Border. The master of the situation and of the series. (Adrian Murrell/Allsport)*

BELOW: *The end of Dean Jones, Gladstone Small celebrates the wicket. (Ben Radford/Allsport)*

first ball of the day. In Small's next over, Jones edged to slip. Gower was moving to his right, but realigned to take a superb catch low with his left hand. Waugh jabbed a ball from Igglesden into his stumps, and Healy, after a most impressively aggressive innings which contained six fours, was caught behind off Pringle.

Hughes and Hohns made their customary useful runs and Australia lasted an hour after lunch before Pringle, who bowled an excellent spell, claimed the last three wickets. In all, he had taken the last four for 25 runs. The last seven Australian wickets had fallen for 123 runs. It was the England bowlers' best 2½ hours of the summer.

Gloom quickly descended again. Gooch and Stephenson began the England innings in worsening light. Gooch allowed two outswingers from Alderman to pass. The third ball, an inswinger, trapped him leg before, although some felt the ball would have missed leg stump. England had one no-ball on the board when Gooch was out, and seven balls later, with still just one no-ball on the board, the players trooped off for bad light and did not return as the rain set in.

There was little to lift the England gloom on the Saturday when play was again brought to an early end by bad light and rain. Stephenson began encouragingly, pulling Lawson hard through mid-wicket, and both he and Atherton gave hope for the future before the Lancastrian played loosely to edge to the wicket-keeper. Stephenson looked secure and ready to build a big innings when he received a nasty blow on the arm from a ball by Hughes. A large swelling was immediately visible. Stephenson received treatment at the end of the over, but he was out to the next ball he faced when he guided Alderman to slip.

Smith had his stumps totally wrecked by Lawson, and Capel, having hit a four, was leg before third ball. Russell, England's Man of the Series, was caught behind, and, at 98 for 6, England again faced the embarrassment of having to follow-on.

Gower and Pringle stayed until the premature closure at 3.24 p.m., and on Monday morning they batted with complete confidence. Gower played with the certainty of timing and the eloquent fluency of stroke that have made him one of the great delights of Test cricket in the past decade. When the criticism and burden of his term as England captain is long forgotten, Gower will always be remembered as one of the most beautiful of batsmen that this country has produced since the war.

Gower caught behind on the leg-side off Alderman, the end of a delightful innings. (Adrian Murrell/Allsport)

CORNHILL TEST MATCH AVERAGES – ENGLAND v. AUSTRALIA

ENGLAND BATTING

	M	Inns	NOs	Runs	HS	Av	100s	50s
R.A. Smith	5	10	1	553	143	61.44	2	3
R.C. Russell	6	11	3	314	128*	39.25	1	1
D.I. Gower	6	11		383	106	34.81	1	2
J.E. Emburey	3	5	1	131	64	32.75		1
K.J. Barnett	3	5		141	80	28.20		1
N.G.B. Cook	3	5	3	45	31	22.50		
G.R. Dilley	2	3	1	42	24	21.00		
B.C. Broad	2	4		82	37	20.50		
G.A. Gooch	5	9		183	68	20.33		2
M.A. Atherton	2	4		73	47	18.25		
N.A. Foster	3	6	2	68	39	17.00		
I.T. Botham	3	4		62	46	15.50		
T.S. Curtis	3	5		71	41	14.20		
P.W. Jarvis	2	3		33	22	11.00		
D.R. Pringle	2	3		33	27	11.00		
A.R.C. Fraser	3	5		47	29	9.40		

Played in one Test: A.J. Lamb 125 & 4; M.D. Moxon 0 & 18; P.J. Newport 36 & 8; P.A.J. DeFreitas 1 & 21; M.W. Gatting 0 & 22; E.E. Hemmings 38 & 35; C.J. Tavare 2; R.T. Robinson 0 & 12; D.E. Malcolm 9 & 5; J.P. Stephenson 25 & 11; D.J. Capel 4 & 17; G.C. Small 59; A.P. Igglesden 2*

AUSTRALIA BATTING

	M	Inns	NOs	Runs	HS	Av	100s	50s
S.R. Waugh	6	8	4	506	177*	126.50	2	1
M.A. Taylor	6	11	1	839	219	83.90	2	5
A.R. Border	6	9	3	442	80	73.66		6
D.M. Jones	6	9	1	566	157	70.75	2	3
D.C. Boon	6	11	3	442	94	55.25		3
T.V. Hohns	5	5	1	127	40	31.75		
G.R. Marsh	6	11		347	138	32.54	1	
G.F. Lawson	6	5	1	115	74	28.75		1
M.G. Hughes	5	5		127	71	25.40		1
T.M. Alderman	6	4	3	20	8	20.00		
I.A. Healy	6	7	1	103	44	17.16		

Played in one Test: G.D. Campbell did not bat

ENGLAND BOWLING

	Overs	Mds	Runs	Wkts	Av	Best	10/m	5/inns
N.A. Foster	167	42	421	12	35.08	3/39		
A.R.C. Fraser	144.2	30	323	9	35.88	4/63		
J.E. Emburey	152	37	342	8	42.75	4/88		
A.P. Igglesden	37	3	146	3	48.66	2/91		
G.C. Small	60	12	198	4	49.50	3/141		
D.J. Capel	24	2	101	2	50.50	1/35		
N.G.B. Cook	103.5	23	282	5	56.40	3/91		
D.R. Pringle	86.2	12	306	5	61.20	4/70		
G.R. Dilley	85	12	318	5	63.60	2/123		
G.A. Gooch	31	9	72	1	72.00	1/30		
P.A.J. DeFreitas	63.3	10	216	3	72.00	2/140		
I.T. Botham	80	15	241	3	80.33	2/63		
P.J. Newport	44	7	175	2	87.50	2/153		
P.W. Jarvis	69.2	8	290	2	145.00	1/20		
M.A. Atherton	8	–	34	–	–			

Bowled in one innings: T.S. Curtis 3–0–7–0; K.J. Barnett 6–0–32–0; D.E. Malcolm 44–2–166–1; E.E. Hemmings 33–8–81–0

AUSTRALIA BOWLING

	Overs	Mds	Runs	Wkts	Av	Best	10/m	5/inns
T.M. Alderman	270.2	68	712	41	17.36	6/128	1	6
T.V. Hohns	139	53	300	11	27.27	3/59		
G.F. Lawson	277.2	68	791	29	27.27	6/72		1
M.G. Hughes	189.2	41	615	19	32.36	4/71		
S.R. Waugh	57	15	208	2	104.00	1/82		
G.D. Campbell	24	–	124	1	124.00	1/82		
A.R. Border	24	9	44	–	–			

ENGLAND FIELDING FIGURES

18 - R.C. Russell (ct 14/st 4); 4 - G.A. Gooch and D.I. Gower; 3 - I.T. Botham; 2 - B.C. Broad and subs; 1 - R.A. Smith, A.P. Igglesden, P.J. Newport, M.A. Atherton, N.A. Foster, T.S. Curtis and R.T. Robinson

AUSTRALIAN FIELDING FIGURES

14 - I.A. Healy; 9 - D.C. Boon; 5 - A.R. Border, M.A. Taylor and G.R. Marsh; 4 - S.R. Waugh and D.M. Jones; 3 - T.V. Hohns; 2 - T.M. Alderman

Nottinghamshire CCC
Limited-Over Matches, 1989

BATTING

BATTING	v. Worcestershire (Trent Bridge) 23 April (RA)	v. Lancashire (Old Trafford) 30 April (RA)	v. Derbyshire (Trent Bridge) 2 May (B&H)	v. Yorkshire (Leeds) 7 May (RA)	v. Minor Counties (Oxton) 9 May (B&H)	v. Yorkshire (Trent Bridge) 11 May (B&H)	v. Somerset (Taunton) 13 May (B&H)	v. Glamorgan (Llanelli) 28 May (RA)	v. Gloucestershire (Bristol) 31 May (B&H)	v. Somerset (Trent Bridge) 4 June (RA)	v. Kent (Trent Bridge) 11 June (RA)	v. Kent (Trent Bridge) 14 June (B&H)	v. Derbyshire (Trent Bridge) 25 June (RA)	v. Hertfordshire (Hitchin) 28 June (NW)	v. Gloucestershire (Gloucester) 2 July (RA)	v. Warwickshire (Trent Bridge) 9 July (RA)	v. Middlesex (Uxbridge) 12 July (NW)	v. Essex (Lord's) 15 July (B&H)	v. Leicestershire (Leicester) 16 July (RA)
B.C. Broad	54	4	18	31	53	78	4	106	2		66		63	44		34	4	6	71
R.T. Robinson	8	15	4	6	8	30	76*	38	11	24	80	29	24	29		42*	9	86	1
D.W. Randall	18	57*	55	52	22	18	1	21	63	24	0	5	0	1			29	49	
P. Johnson	34	7	2			33	2	41	12*							18*	47	54	0
F.D. Stephenson	35*	54	14	33*	0	3	37*	25*		1		18	11*	11	—		22	0	37
M.G. Field-Buss	5		0																
K.P. Evans	4*	—	8	—	13			2	19*	9	1	5	0*	4	—		8	26	2
B.N. French	—	25*	21	4*	6	13					22*	15	—	3			5	8*	2
D.J. Millns																			
K. Saxelby	—	—	3*	0					0*	—	—		—			1			6*
K.E. Cooper	—	—	0	—	17*	1	—	—	—		9*	—	28*		6				8
M. Newell		7		30	3	39	15	12	13	4	2*	8		19*				6*	
E.E. Hemmings		—	4	0		2*	2		4	2*	8		19*			—		6*	
R.A. Pick			6	—	1	2*	—	—											
P. Pollard		0	12	4				100	77	12	4		36			23	2	1	
J.A. Afford			1*	—	—		—	0*											
C.W. Scott		—	11*	0															
C.L. Cairns		4																	
G.W. Mike	—		25*	29	0		0												24
D.J.R. Martindale			49*	47	7	—		24											
Byes	1			1	3				1							4		1	
Leg-byes	13	8	7	11	4	9	4	8	6	5	13	9	2	7	2	4	3	14	
Wides	11	2	2	2	1	2	4	4	11	2	1	8	4	1	5	4	2	13	
No-balls	1			3		2		1			1	5	3			5	1	3	
Total	184	179	141	175	144	202	174	222	183	207	296	170	155	154	141	167	244	182	
Wickets	5	5	10	5	10	9	4	6	7	7	6	8	5	8	2	10	7	9	
Result	Ab.	L	W	L	W	W	L	W	W	L	W	W	W	W	W	W	L	W	W
Points	2	0	2	0	2	2	0	4	—	0	4	—	4	—	4	4	—	4	

Fielding Figures

25 – B.N. French (ct 24/st 1)
14 – R.T. Robinson
9 – B.C. Broad
7 – F.D. Stephenson and P. Johnson
6 – D.W. Randall, P. Pollard and K.P. Evans
5 – D.J.R. Martindale
4 – K. Saxelby
3 – K.E. Cooper
2 – J.A. Afford, E.E. Hemmings and C.W. Scott
1 – M. Newell, G.W. Mike and sub

BOWLING

BOWLING	K. Saxelby	F.D. Stephenson	K.E. Cooper	K.P. Evans	M.G. Field-Buss	G.W. Mike	E.E. Hemmings	R.A. Pick
v. Worcestershire (Trent Bridge) 23 April (RA)								
v. Lancashire (Old Trafford) 30 April (RA)	7–0–35–0	6–1–16–0	7.4–0–37–1	8–0–38–2	6–0–26–0	3–0–23–0		
v. Derbyshire (Trent Bridge) 2 May (B&H)	11–0–50–1	11–1–34–4	11–2–23–2	11–2–39–1			11–2–25–1	
v. Yorkshire (Leeds) 7 May (RA)	7–1–40–0	8–3–22–3	8–1–20–0	8–0–44–1	3–1–28–0			6–0–37–0
v. Minor Counties (Oxton) 9 May (B&H)		9.2–3–19–3	10–2–20–1	11–0–52–1			11–4–16–0	9–1–29–2
v. Yorkshire (Trent Bridge) 11 & 12 May (B&H)		10–3–25–2	9.5–3–9–4	10–1–28–2			11–2–31–1	10–1–46–1
v. Somerset (Taunton) 13 May (B&H)		11–2–35–0	9.2–0–43–0					
v. Glamorgan (Llanelli) 28 May (RA)		8–2–25–1	8–0–30–1	8–0–31–0			8–1–27–1	8–0–51–2
v. Gloucestershire (Bristol) 31 May (B&H)		3.4–1–9–0	11–3–25–2	11–2–37–1			10.3–0–47–4	11–1–57–2
v. Somerset (Trent Bridge) 4 June (RA)			8–0–36–1	8–1–31–2			8–1–36–2	8–1–38–0
v. Kent (Trent Bridge) 11 June (RA)	7.3–0–38–2	8–0–52–1		8–0–27–2		2–0–12–1	8–1–30–1	
v. Kent (Trent Bridge) 14 June (B&H)	8.4–1–46–2		10–0–42–1	9–0–51–2			10–0–39–0	
v. Derbyshire (Trent Bridge) 25 June (RA)	3–0–19–0		5–0–21–0	8–1–28–4		5.3–0–23–1	8–1–18–2	
v. Hertfordshire (Hitchin) 28 June (NW)		12–2–26–1	12–1–23–1	12–1–29–0			12–5–27–1	
v. Gloucestershire (Gloucester) 2 July (RA)	6–0–29–1	8–1–26–3	6–0–19–1	8–1–31–0		4–0–16–0	8–0–26–2	
v. Warwickshire (Trent Bridge) 9 July (RA)	8–0–24–5	8–0–26–0	8–1–28–1	8–0–26–0				8–0–30–2
v. Middlesex (Uxbridge) 12 July (NW)	12–0–70–3	12–2–22–1	12–4–31–1	12–1–45–1				
v. Essex (Lord's) 15 July (B&H)		11–0–61–1	11–3–30–1	11–0–28–2			11–0–47–0	
v. Leicestershire (Leicester) 16 July (RA)	7–0–30–6	7–0–18–1	8–0–28–1	7–1–28–1				
v. Northamptonshire (Finedon) 23 July (RA)	8–0–45–5	8–1–25–1	8–2–27–1	8–0–33–2				
v. Essex (Trent Bridge) 30 July (RA)	6.4–0–36–5	8–0–38–3	8–0–36–1					
v. Sussex (Eastbourne) 6 August (RA)	6.4–0–33–1	8–1–16–2	8–1–36–0				8–1–42–0	
v. Surrey (The Oval) 13 August (RA)	8–0–60–1	8–1–31–1	8–0–48–1	7–0–26–0				
v. Hampshire (Trent Bridge) 20 August (RA)	8–0–57–1	8–0–51–0	8–0–31–1				8–0–47–0	8–0–61–0
v. Middlesex (Trent Bridge) 27 August (RA)	8–0–27–2	7.5–0–33–4	8–0–25–1				8–0–48–0	8–1–29–3
v. Lancashire (Old Trafford) 6 September (RC)	8–0–58–0	8–1–32–3	8–0–38–1				8–0–27–0	8–1–25–4
v. Essex (Edgbaston) 17 September (RC)	8–1–25–1	8–1–37–0	8–2–34–0				8–2–24–1	8–2–26–1
Wickets	36	35	27	24	0	2	19	19

v. Northamptonshire (Finedon) 23 July (RA)	v. Essex (Trent Bridge) 30 July (RA)	v. Sussex (Eastbourne) 6 August (RA)	v. Surrey (The Oval) 13 August (RA)	v. Hampshire (Trent Bridge) 20 August (RA)	v. Middlesex (Trent Bridge) 27 August (RA)	v. Lancashire (Old Trafford) 6 September (RC)	v. Essex (Edgbaston) 17 September (RC)	Runs
38		2				49	39	766
13	55		50	0	97*	44	22	801
	70*	13	43*	23	26	32*	14	636
0	9	11	—		20*		1	291
10	20*	12	—	69	—	2	16	430
								5
5	—		—					106
6	—	4	—	12	—			146
		0*						0
4*		0	—	2	—	—	5	21
9	—	0	—	25	—	—	10	113
	47			7				173
		20*		5		5*	24	101
				0*	—	—	1*	10
4	16	29	123*	12	17	42	12	526
0	—		—					1
							1	12
								4
								54
53	11		—	47	—		1	239
		4		4				
3	13	19	11	10	4	7	7	
4	8		6	4	1	4	3	
		3		1	2	3	2	
149	197	169	234	222	168	188	155	
10	4	9	1	10	2	5	10	
L	W	L	W	L	W	W	L	
0	4	0	4	0	4	—	—	

John Stephenson cracks Geoff Lawson to the mid-wicket boundary for his first four in Test cricket. (Adrian Murrell/ Allsport)

BELOW: *Lawson wrecks Smith's stumps. (Adrian Murrell/ Allsport)*

J.A. Afford	B.C. Broad	C.L. Cairns	D.J. Millns	Byes	Leg-byes	Wides	No-balls	Total	Wkts
									Ab.
				1	10	8		186	3
					7	2	1	178	9
					10	3	2	201	4
					15	7	1	172	10
					4	3	2	111	10
11–1–32–1					16	4	7	203	3
				4	4	6	2	172	5
	7.2–0–26–1			1	15	6	4	217	10
			8–0–38–2	2	3	5	1	184	7
6–1–36–1					11	4		206	10
11–2–38–4					11	6		227	10
					2	1	2	128	10
12–3–32–3				1	16	9		154	7
					7	1		154	8
					5	6		139	10
12–2–28–1					7	1	1	203	7
11–0–50–1				1	26	4	1	243	7
7–1–28–1					14	4		146	10
8–1–20–0				1	10	4	3	173	10
					3	1	1	113	10
			6–0–34–0	1	8	12		170	3
8–0–58–0				4	6	8		233	5
					7	3	1	254	4
					5	2		167	10
				1	6	4		187	9
				1	13	3		160	5
12	1	2	0						

Somerset CCC
Limited-Over Matches, 1989

BATTING

BATTING	v. Hampshire (Southampton) 23 April (RA)	v. Derbyshire (Derby) 25 & 26 April (B&H)	v. Minor Counties (Taunton) 2 May (B&H)	v. Sussex (Taunton) 7 May (RA)	v. Yorkshire (Leeds) 9 May (B&H)	v. Nottinghamshire (Taunton) 13 May (B&H)	v. Lancashire (Taunton) 21 May (RA)	v. Essex (Chelmsford) 28 May (RA)	v. Combined Universities (Taunton) 31 May (B&H)	v. Nottinghamshire (Trent Bridge) 4 June (RA)	v. Yorkshire (Taunton) 11 June (RA)	v. Essex (Taunton) 14 June (B&H)	v. Kent (Bath) 18 June (RA)	v. Gloucestershire (Bath) 25 June (RA)	v. Essex (Taunton) 28 & 29 June (NW)	v. Derbyshire (Derby) 2 July (RA)
S.J. Cook	2	27	55	0	62	79	123	20	61	28	30	28	2	124*	1	10
P.M. Roebuck	6	65	10	52	25	11	22	58	102	2	3	53	14		102	1
J.J.E. Hardy	1	12	7		12									1		
C.J. Tavare	120*	17*	78	19	65	59*	13	6	23	20	11	104*	110	20	101	11
R.J. Bartlett	32	4*	11	0		10	26	8	36	26	26	15		21		
V.J. Marks	31	—	13	28	15*	—	5	20	13*	5	9	15	5	11	36*	40
G.D. Rose	0	—	7*	0	—	—	7	—	—	30	19*	4				
N.D. Burns	6	—	8	1	0*	—	12*	22*	6	34*	6	5		4*	—	38*
N.A. Mallender	0	—	1*	—	—	—	0*	13*	—	—	1	1	3*			
A.N. Jones	0*	—	—	0	—	—	—	—	—	2	25	6		—	7	4*
D.J. Foster	—	—	—	0*	—	—	—	—	—		0			0	—	—
R.J. Harden				61	44	17*	15	14	7	20	36	13	49	30	0	10
G.V. Palmer			2*					3	8*				9*			
J.G. Wyatt													40	6		24
H.R.J. Trump													0	—		
T. Gard													—			
M.W. Cleal														—	3*	
J.C.M. Atkinson																
Byes			9		1					2	1		1	1	1	
Leg-byes	16	11	6	13	12	16	9	3	3	3	16	18	5	8	14	8
Wides	2	4	3	6	4	10	1	1		5	3	8	4	1	8	7
No-balls	4	2	3		1	7	2	3		1	2		1		2	2
Total	220	142	205	182	243	203	244	171	252	184	165	289	249	226	276	155
Wickets	8	3	7	9	5	3	7	7	6	7	10	10	8	5	6	6
Result	L	W	W	Tie	W	W	L	L	W	W	L	L	W	W	W	L
Points	0	2	2	2	2	2	0	0	—	4	0	—	4	4	—	0

Fielding Figures
36 – N.D. Burns (ct 30/st 6)
10 – S.J. Cook, R.J. Bartlett and C.J. Tavare
9 – P.M. Roebuck
7 – V.J. Marks
5 – N.A. Mallender and R.J. Harden
4 – J.J.E. Hardy and A.N. Jones
3 – G.D. Rose
2 – D.J. Foster, H.R.J. Trump and J.G. Wyatt
1 – G.V. Palmer

BOWLING

BOWLING	N.A. Mallender	D.J. Foster	G.D. Rose	A.N. Jones	V.J. Marks	G.V. Palmer	P.M. Roebuck
v. Hampshire (Southampton) 23 April (RA)	8-0-33-1	8-0-48-0	8-0-29-2	7.2-0-53-1	8-0-55-0		
v. Derbyshire (Derby) 25 & 26 April (B&H)	11-0-27-3	11-2-32-2	10.2-1-19-2	11-3-25-2	11-3-18-0		
v. Minor Counties (Taunton) 2 May (B&H)	11-2-22-1	11-3-51-1	11-1-35-0	11-4-33-2	11-3-24-1		
v. Sussex (Taunton) 7 May (RA)		5-1-20-0	8-1-33-0	7-0-43-1	8-3-12-2	5-0-30-1	7-0-34-2
v. Yorkshire (Leeds) 9 May (B&H)	9-3-31-0	11-3-26-2	10-1-38-2	9.3-1-47-4	11-4-31-1		
v. Nottinghamshire (Taunton) 13 May (B&H)	11-2-36-2	11-1-27-0	11-1-43-0	11-1-53-5	11-1-34-1		
v. Lancashire (Taunton) 21 May (RA)	8-0-28-1	7-0-58-0	8-1-43-2	7.2-0-57-0	8-0-47-1		
v. Essex (Chelmsford) 28 May (RA)	8-0-51-1	4-0-17-0		7-0-44-1	8-1-21-0	7-1-40-2	6-0-27-1
v. Combined Universities (Taunton) 31 May (B&H)	11-1-56-1	7-1-28-0	11-1-50-0	11-1-36-2	11-0-52-2		4-0-19-2
v. Nottinghamshire (Trent Bridge) 4 June (RA)	8-0-18-2		8-1-20-2	8-3-34-1	8-0-52-2	7-0-41-0	1-0-12-0
v. Yorkshire (Taunton) 11 June (RA)	8-0-28-2	8-0-36-1	8-2-36-2	8-0-33-3	8-0-38-1		
v. Essex (Taunton) 9-1-56-2	11-2-33-0		11-2-42-2				
v. Kent (Bath) 18 June (RA)	5-0-12-1				5-0-27-1	4-0-26-0	4.4-0-26-1
v. Gloucestershire (Bath) 25 June (RA)		7.5-2-26-4		6-0-23-2	8-1-24-3		
v. Essex (Taunton) 28 & 29 June (NW)		7-0-17-0		9.5-1-32-3	12-0-38-3		6-0-34-1
v. Derbyshire (Derby) 2 July (RA)		5-0-20-0		6.5-0-37-0	8-0-32-0		6-0-23-3
v. Surrey (The Oval) 9 July (RA)		8-0-45-2		8-0-49-2	8-0-47-0		2-0-24-2
v. Northamptonshire (Taunton) 12 July (NW)		8-3-15-1		12-1-62-1	12-1-38-1		4-0-21-1
v. Glamorgan (Taunton) 16 July (RA)		8-2-40-0		5-2-11-2	8-1-27-4		4-0-14-0
v. Leicestershire (Taunton) 23 July (RA)			7-1-27-2	7-0-40-1	8-0-36-1		6-0-26-3
v. Northamptonshire (Northampton) 30 July (RA)	8-1-15-2		7.1-1-21-3	8-1-37-3	8-0-35-1		
v. Middlesex (Weston-super-Mare) 6 August (RA)	7-0-17-1		5-1-9-2	5-3-8-2	7.2-0-35-3		
v. Warwickshire (Edgbaston) 13 August (RA)	7.4-0-36-1		8-0-36-1	8-1-42-3	8-0-35-1		
v. Worcestershire (Worcester) 20 August (RA)	8-1-31-0		8-2-30-3	8-2-49-1	8-0-29-1		
Wickets	20	13	23	45	33	3	18

v. Surrey (The Oval) 9 July (RA)	v. Northamptonshire (Taunton) 12 July (NW)	v. Glamorgan (Taunton) 16 July (RA)	v. Leicestershire (Taunton) 23 July (RA)	v. Northamptonshire (Northampton) 30 July (RA)	v. Middlesex (Weston-super-Mare) 6 August (RA)	v. Warwickshire (Edgbaston) 13 August (RA)	v. Worcestershire (Worcester) 20 August (RA)	Runs
18	33	114	37	18	16	0	14	902
9	18	63	40*			0	2	648
0								33
	79*	9	0	7	65	51	5	993
			36	12	47			310
4	19	18	5*	0	6	28	67*	393
			—	61*	14	4	25	171
13	3	—	—	8	8*	13	19	206
1				21*	1	11*	19*	72
37	2	0*	—		4*	2*	—	89
8*	0	—						8
13	14	4	49*	9	17	11	4	437
								22
12	9	11		0				102
2	0	—	—	—	—	—	—	2
								—
	25	8*	—				15	51
						69	6	75
								1
3								
7	1	13	10	8	14	11	10	
10	6	7	7	3	10	5	5	
	1	2	2	5	3			
137	210	249	186	152	205	207	190	
10	10	6	3	7	8	8	7	
L	L	W	W	W	W	L	L	
0	—	4	4	4	4	0	0	

H.R.J. Trump	M.W. Cleal	Byes	Leg-byes	Wides	No-balls	Total	Wkts
			3	1	1	221	5
		5	15	1		141	10
			5	5	3	170	6
			10	2	1	182	7
			8	2	8	181	10
			9	2	2	202	9
		2	10	2	3	245	6
		8	10			218	5
		2	6	2	2	249	9
			6	11		183	7
		3	10	1	5	184	9
		2	20	10	2	293	5
8–0–23–2			7	9	2	169	10
8–0–27–1	6–1–16–0		8	1		128	10
12–0–44–2	8–0–42–1	4	9	10	2	221	10
8–0–19–0	5–0–24–0	5	5	2		161	5
6–0–54–0		1	4	6	1	258	7
9–0–29–0	12–0–44–1		2	2	1	211	5
8–0–27–2	7–1–35–0	4	10	8	5	168	8
8–1–33–1	4–0–16–0		5	7		183	10
8–0–33–0			7	1	1	150	10
8–1–31–2		2	8		2	108	10
4–0–22–0			16	4	1	187	7
4–0–32–0	4–0–30–0		1	1		202	5
10	2						

He had hit 79 off 120 balls, found the boundary 11 times, when he touched a ball from Alderman down the leg side. It was the sixth time in the series that Alderman had taken five wickets in an innings. Small might have been caught second ball, but Healy obscured first slip and the chance was lost. It was to prove costly.

Pringle had batted with discipline and intelligence for 147 minutes before he was caught high at slip off a leg-break by Hohns. At 201 for 8, England still needed 68 to avoid the follow-on. Small and Cook got the necessary runs. Small became the hero of the day as he clouted the ball to all parts of The Oval in an uninhibited manner. He hit 8 fours and reached fifty in a Test match for the first time before offering an uncharacteristic gentle catch to cover. Cook and Igglesden ate up another 39 valuable minutes before Cook fell to Lawson.

Australia lost Marsh almost immediately, but Taylor and Boon were in command again at the close. The final morning's play became rather unreal as Jones and Border hit fifties, and the crowd and the media speculated as to when Border would declare. To the surprise of all, he delayed the declaration until lunch-time and left England to score 403 at six an over. The delay in the declaration was perhaps Border's one error of the series.

It seemed no error when Stephenson offered no shot at Alderman's in-swinger and Gooch offered the same bowler a simple caught and bowled. This made Alderman the first bowler to take 40 wickets in two separate Ashes series. Atherton batted for an hour before he was bowled by a ball from Lawson which came back at him.

Gower fell to the penultimate ball before tea when he cut uppishly to slip. Capel fell after tea, and Robin Smith was thumping away joyously and defiantly as he had done all summer when bad light descended and brought an end to the series.

For Border and Simpson and their men it had been a total triumph. The planning and organization of the side could not have been better, nor could the happy, meaningful and courteous way in which they had played their cricket. One feels privileged to have watched them.

Taylor catches Capel off Hohns, but dark clouds are looming to end England's unhappy summer. (Adrian Murrell/Allsport)

Surrey CCC
Limited-Over Matches, 1989

BATTING

	v. Gloucestershire (The Oval) 23 April (RA)	v. Combined Universities (Cambridge) 26 April (B&H)	v. Hampshire (The Oval) 30 April (RA)	v. Worcestershire (The Oval) 2 May (B&H)	v. Middlesex (Lord's) 7 May (RA)	v. Gloucestershire (The Oval) 11 May (B&H)	v. Middlesex (Lord's) 13 May (B&H)	v. Kent (Canterbury) 14 May (RA)	v. Worcestershire (Worcester) 21 May (RA)	v. Yorkshire (The Oval) 28 May (RA)	v. Northamptonshire (Northampton) 4 June (RA)	v. Essex (The Oval) 11 June (RA)	v. Yorkshire (Harrogate) 15 June (TT)	v. Worcestershire (Harrogate) 16 June (TT)	v. Northumberland (Jesmond) 29 June (NW)	v. Somerset (The Oval) 9 July (RA)	v. Yorkshire (The Oval) 12 July (NW)	v. Sussex (The Oval) 16 July (RA)	v. Warwickshire (Edgbaston) 23 July (RA)
G.S. Clinton	23	36	45	74	35	6	27	4	78	76	56	57			40	9	1*	47	37
J.D. Robinson	10	0	3*							8*	4	68	4						3
A.J. Stewart	8	4	12	44	17	4	23	43	55	15	27	50	38	0	55	72	5	100*	5
D.M. Ward	57	8	15	9	1	14	3	62*	30	22	14	3	6	117*	97	40	80	11	76
Zahid Sadiq	34	9	16	1	2			10	7	3	13	2							
I.A. Greig	1*	2	4*	5	11	33	9	8	9*	61*	7	11	28*	15	23*	25	15	4*	15
K.T. Medlycott		2	7		4	11		33	1*		3	4	23*	32	7*	12	2*	—	5*
M.A. Feltham		2	—	1	35	26	29	14	24	31					—	1	—	17	2
C.K. Bullen	—	35*	—	7*	28*	20*	5	0*	—	0	4			16	—	8*	—	—	3*
A.J. Murphy	—	5*	—		3	0	0		—	0	0	—			—				
M.P. Bicknell	—	2	—	6	1	9	11*	—			—				—				
D.J. Bicknell				11		8	13					40	26		5		22*	135*	12
P.D. Atkins				9		0*	6												
S.T. Clarke				2*															
G.P. Thorpe					10		22	3		13*	14	40	10	1	74	56	8	29	
G.G. Arnold											4*								
N.H. Peters													1*		—	3*		—	
G.E. Brown																			
M.A. Lynch															—				
Byes				1	4		2		2	1	2	1			1	2		4	6
Leg-byes	16		10	6	9	8	4	10	11	9	10	7	14	8	7	4	7	7	7
Wides	14	2	2	14		1	1	5	3	4	2	5	6	3	4	6	3	4	3
No-balls	1		1	1	1	2	3	1	3	2		2				1		2	1
Total	164	107	115	191	161	142	156	195	221	238	159	192	234	225	313	258	256	225	175
Wickets	5	9	5	9	10	9†	10	7	5	5	9	10	5	7	5	7	4	4	7
Result	W	L	W	W	L	L	L	L	W	W	L	W	W	L	W	W	W	W	W
Points	4	0	4	2	0	0	0	0	4	4	0	4	—	—	—	4	4	4	4

Fielding Figures

25 – A.J. Stewart (ct 20/st 5)
17 – C.K. Bullen
15 – D.M. Ward
8 – I.A. Greig and G.P. Thorpe
7 – M.P. Bicknell and K.T. Medlycott
6 – M.A. Feltham
3 – G.S. Clinton, D.J. Bicknell, Zahid Sadiq, N.H. Peters and A.J. Murphy
2 – J.D. Robinson
1 – G.E. Brown
† P.D. Adkins retired hurt

BOWLING

	M.P. Bicknell	A.J. Murphy	M.A. Feltham	I.A. Greig	C.K. Bullen	K.T. Medlycott	J.D. Robinson	S.T. Clarke
v. Gloucestershire (The Oval) 23 April (RA)	5.1-0-31-1	8-0-22-4	6-0-23-3					
v. Combined Universities (Cambridge) 26 April (B&H)	8-0-24-1	5-1-10-0	7-0-28-5	6-1-26-0	8-2-14-2	2.3-0-11-2		
v. Hampshire (The Oval) 30 April (RA)	8-2-18-1	8-2-26-2	8-3-16-3	8-1-19-1	6-0-16-1		2-0-13-1	
v. Worcestershire (The Oval) 2 May (B&H)	11-4-33-2		11-3-36-2	11-0-44-1	11-1-31-1			11-2-29-1
v. Middlesex (Lord's) 7 May (RA)	8-0-43-2	8-0-39-0	8-0-34-1	7-0-29-1	3-0-20-0			
v. Gloucestershire (The Oval) 11 May (B&H)	11-1-54-1	11-0-34-0	11-0-50-1	9-0-52-1	11-2-52-1	2-0-26-0		
v. Middlesex (Lord's) 13 May (B&H)	11-1-44-1	11-1-52-0	11-1-37-2	11-1-52-2				
v. Kent (Canterbury) 14 May (RA)	8-1-26-2	8-0-30-1	7-1-31-0	4-0-22-0	7-0-50-2			
v. Worcestershire (Worcester) 21 May (RA)	8-0-43-1	8-0-41-1	8-0-45-2	8-0-40-1	8-0-33-2			
v. Yorkshire (The Oval) 28 May (RA)	7.2-0-37-2	8-0-46-1	8-0-54-2		8-0-31-5	8-0-30-0		
v. Northamptonshire (Northampton) 4 June (RA)		8-0-36-1		7-0-42-1	8-0-48-0	7-0-42-1		
v. Essex (The Oval) 11 June (RA)		8-0-26-3		7.2-0-34-1	8-3-18-1	8-1-22-1		
v. Yorkshire (Harrogate) 15 June (B&H)		10.4-2-30-2		9-0-48-3	11-0-24-2	11-1-43-0		
v. Worcestershire (Harrogate) 16 June (TT)		11-2-35-1		4-0-16-0	11-1-49-3	11-0-44-1		
v. Northumberland (Jesmond) 29 June (NW)	9-2-24-2	12-1-49-1	11-0-61-2	12-0-46-0	12-0-31-1	2-0-8-0		
v. Somerset (The Oval) 9 July (RA)		5-0-21-1	3.5-1-5-2	1-0-5-0	8-0-44-3	8-0-45-4		
v. Yorkshire (The Oval) 12 July (NW)	12-0-49-4	12-2-51-1	12-2-46-2		12-0-47-0	12-3-45-1		
v. Sussex (The Oval) 16 July (RA)	6-1-21-1	5-0-17-1	8-0-43-0	5-0-23-1	8-0-38-1	8-0-54-3		
v. Warwickshire (Edgbaston) 23 July (RA)	8-0-30-0	8-0-52-1	8-0-29-2		8-2-22-1	8-1-18-4		
v. Derbyshire (Derby) 30 July (RA)	8-2-14-3	8-3-22-1	6-0-27-0	8-0-33-1	0.5-0-6-0			
v. Hampshire (The Oval) 2 August (NW)	12-3-32-2	11-1-34-2	6-0-45-0	5-0-37-1	12-1-36-0	12-2-41-0		
v. Glamorgan (The Oval) 6 August (RA)	4-0-10-0	4-0-9-2		8-0-41-1	5-0-30-1	6-1-20-4	8-0-34-0	
v. Nottinghamshire (The Oval) 13 August (RA)	7.2-0-46-0		8-0-47-0	3-0-20-0	8-0-41-0	8-0-52-1	4-0-17-0	
v. Leicestershire (Leicester) 20 August (RA)	6-0-42-0	8-1-45-1		8-1-29-2	6-1-29-0	4-0-24-0	8-0-35-0	
v. Lancashire (Old Trafford) 27 August (RA)	7.1-0-27-1	8-0-35-1		3-0-16-0	8-0-31-2	6-0-28-1	7-0-40-1	
v. Kent (Hove) 4 September (SB)	8-0-43-2	7-0-54-0		8-0-34-1	7-0-33-1	2-0-22-0		
Wickets	29	28	29	19	30	23	2	1

v. Derbyshire (Derby) 30 July (RA)	v. Hampshire (The Oval) 2 August (NW)	v. Glamorgan (The Oval) 6 August (RA)	v. Nottinghamshire (The Oval) 13 August (RA)	v. Leicestershire (Leicester) 20 August (RA)	v. Lancashire (Old Trafford) 27 August (RA)	v. Kent (Hove) 4 September (SB)	Runs
1	1	9	60	15	33	7	777
	2	—	18*	9			129
17	20	119	77	18	56	27	911
18	21	2	19*	36	3	42	806
							97
1	75	3	4	40*	0	29	438
23	18	4	0*	0	6	13	210
13	19*						214
8	8	0*	—	—	13*	29*	184
1*	—	—	—		0	6*	15
7	—	1*	—	—	4	6	47
24	43	25	4	56	8		432
							15
							2
3	1	80	51	11	39	19	484
							4
							4
						0	—
						47	47
		1	4	2		1	
5	9	1	6	14	10	4	
3	8	7	8	5	5	6	
1	5					2	
125	228	254	233	215	186	238	
10	8	8	5	6	10	9	
L	L	W	L	L	L	L	
0	—	4	0	0	0	—	

A triumphant farewell for Jack Simmons – victory in the Refuge Assurance League for Lancashire . . . (George Herringshaw/Allsport)

. . . and for John Lever, 7 for 48 in his last championship match for Essex. (Adrian Murrell/Allsport)

G.P. Thorpe	G.G. Arnold	N.H. Peters	Byes	Leg-byes	Wides	No-balls	Total	Wkts
				5	1	3	81	10
				3		3	116	10
				6	7	4	114	9
			3	14	2	1	190	7
6–0–41–1			4	11	5	1	221	5
			7	11	5	4	286	7
11–2–35–3				12	3		232	9
5–0–26–0				12	1		197	6
			4	10		1	216	8
			1	7	7		206	10
4–0–20–0	6–3–7–1		1	5			201	4
		7–0–44–1	2	4	8	1	160	10
5–0–20–1	7–2–19–1		6	10	1		200	10
7–0–36–0	8.4–1–41–0		1	4			226	5
2–0–12–0			8	6	1		245	6
	3–0–7–0		3	7	10		137	10
			1	16	1		255	9
			1	4	5		201	8
			1	4	2		156	9
2–0–13–1				12	6		127	6
				4	4	3	229	5
			2	11	6		157	10
				11	6	1	234	1
			4	11	2		219	4
			1	10	3		188	7
		8–0–57–0	5	5	10		253	5
6	1	2						

Sussex CCC
Limited-Over Matches, 1989

BATTING

BATTING	v. Essex (Hove) 25 & 26 April (B&H)	v. Kent (Hove) 30 April (RA)	v. Kent (Canterbury) 2 May (B&H)	v. Somerset (Taunton) 7 May (RA)	v. Australians (Hove) 9 May	v. Hampshire (Hove) 11 May (B&H)	v. Glamorgan (Swansea) 13 & 14 May (B&H)	v. Leicestershire (Hove) 21 May (RA)	v. Lancashire (Old Trafford) 28 May (RA)	v. Warwickshire (Edgbaston) 4 June (RA)	v. Northamptonshire (Hove) 11 June (RA)	v. Worcestershire (Harrogate) 14 June (TT)	v. Derbyshire (Derby) 18 June (RA)	v. Hampshire (Southampton) 25 June (RA)	v. Berkshire (Hove) 28 & 29 June (NW)	v. Essex (Horsham) 2 July (RA)	v. Yorkshire (Middlesbrough) 9 July (RA)	v. Leicestershire (Hove) 12 July (NW)
D.M. Smith	1	17	0	35	22	13	41	43		36	22*	7	9	56	99*		26	59
A.M. Green	4	28	5	15	0										18	3		
P.W.G. Parker	3	10	85*	32	48	57		24*	12		5							87*
A.P. Wells	17	0	4	20	17	20	14	69	19	0	48	0	5	27	30	5	32	86*
C.M. Wells	11	1	40	28	1	20	117	10	7	15	19	38	3	32	2	4	0	—
I.J. Gould	16	5	0	26*	12	3		12*	16	10	1		5	49*	14	63	20	—
A.I.C. Dodémaide	38	21	31*	10	17*	32	6	—	1	40*	9	7	21	17	1	38*	4*	—
P. Moores	3	10	—	—	—	1	0*	—	21	—	4	23	0	—	20	5	7*	—
A.C.S. Pigott	49*	3*	—	3	28*	6	9*	—	27	49*	51*	6	46	—	13	—	—	—
A.R. Clarke	1	0	—	—	—	0	—	—	0	—	—	—	1	—	2*	9*	—	—
A.M. Babington	9	0	—	—	—	1*	—	—	1	—	—	0	0	—	—	—	—	—
N.J. Falkner						4	1			1								
K. Greenfield								0			22	34	16	0				
N.J. Lenham								26	8			6				17	3	—
I.D.K. Salisbury								12*	—			6*	7*					
S.J.S. Kimber												20						
A.R. Hansford																		
M.P. Speight																0	60	48
B.T.P. Donelan																		
C.C. Remy																		
Byes		1		5			6	1		1	5			4	1	1	2	5
Leg-byes	6	9	3	10	4	17	13	11	9	7	4	17	8	7	5	13	9	12
Wides	4	4	2	2	1	3	6	5	8	6		1	4		8	10	1	2
No-balls	7	2	5	1	3			2	3	1	4		5		5			1
Total	169	110	176	182	158	177	207	208	145	165	190	170	130	192	235	154	161	300
Wickets	10	10	5	7	6	10	7	4	10	5	7	10	10	5	8	7	5	2
Result	L	L	W	Tie	W	L	W	W	L	L	W	L	L	L	W	L	W	W
Points	0	0	2	2	—	0	2	4	0	0	4	0	0	0	—	0	4	—

Fielding Figures

34 – P. Moores (ct 25/st 9)
7 – A.C.S. Pigott, P.W.G. Parker, D.M. Smith, C.M. Wells and A.P. Wells
6 – I.J. Gould and A.M. Babington
5 – A.I.C. Dodemaide

4 – M.P. Speight
3 – A.R. Clarke
2 – A.M. Green
1 – K. Greenfield and B.T.P. Donelan

BOWLING

BOWLING	A.C.S. Pigott	A.I.C. Dodemaide	C.M. Wells	A.M. Babington	A.R. Clarke	A.M. Green	I.D.K. Salisbury
v. Essex (Hove) 25 & 26 April (B&H)	11-2-60-2	9-1-45-0	11-4-24-3	11-2-41-1	11-2-46-1	2-0-8-0	
v. Kent (Hove) 30 April (RA)	8-0-35-0	8-1-20-0	6-2-12-1	7.1-0-20-1	8-1-24-1		
v. Kent (Canterbury) 2 May (B&H)	11-0-35-1	11-0-34-2	11-1-45-3	11-4-21-2	11-1-29-1		
v. Somerset (Taunton) 7 May (RA)	8-1-41-3	8-0-35-1	8-1-22-0	8-0-38-2	8-0-33-0		
v. Australians (Hove) 9 May	9-3-20-2	11-0-59-2	9-1-25-2	8.3-0-30-2	7-1-15-1		
v. Hampshire (Hove) 11 May (B&H)	11-3-43-1	11-2-18-2	11-1-52-0	11-0-63-1			
v. Glamorgan (Swansea) 13 & 14 May (B&H)	8-1-14-1	11-3-26-3	9-0-57-1	10.2-2-36-3	10-2-17-1		
v. Leicestershire (Hove) 21 May (RA)	8-0-33-1	7.1-1-20-1	8-2-19-2	8-1-26-3	7-0-26-2		
v. Lancashire (Old Trafford) 28 May (RA)	6-1-25-1	8-0-31-2	2-0-13-0	4.1-0-17-1	8-3-27-2		8-0-25-1
v. Warwickshire (Edgbaston) 4 June (RA)	8-0-31-2	6.3-0-32-0	3-0-13-0	5-0-25-0	8-1-27-0		8-0-37-1
v. Northamptonshire (Hove) 11 June (RA)	7-0-33-0	8-1-21-0	8-0-46-0	8-0-33-3	8-0-52-2		
v. Worcestershire (Harrogate) 14 June (TT)	11-3-44-2	11-2-37-2	8-1-40-0	3-0-24-0			11-1-42-2
v. Derbyshire (Derby) 18 June (RA)	8-1-21-2	7-1-21-0	4-0-9-1	6-1-25-0	8-2-18-1		6-0-28-1
v. Hampshire (Southampton) 25 June (RA)	8-0-49-1	6-0-34-1	2-0-13-0	8-1-14-1	8-0-44-1		
v. Berkshire (Hove) 28 & 29 June (NW)	12-1-37-1	12-2-24-0	12-1-51-0	12-1-32-1	12-3-41-3		
v. Essex (Horsham) 2 July (RA)		7-0-43-0	7-0-21-0	8-0-38-1	6-1-18-2		
v. Yorkshire (Middlesbrough) 9 July (RA)		4-0-23-2	4-0-28-2	4-0-27-1	4-0-30-1		
v. Leicestershire (Hove) 12 July (NW)	12-1-71-1	10.4-1-37-4	10-0-29-0	11-0-53-3	12-1-41-0		
v. Surrey (The Oval) 16 July (RA)		8-1-41-0	8-2-17-0	8-0-56-1	8-0-48-2		
v. Worcestershire (Hove) 23 July (RA)	8-0-27-1	8-0-32-2	8-0-43-2	6.4-0-48-4	8-0-48-1		
v. Middlesex (Lord's) 2 August (NW)	12-2-54-1	12-2-41-0	12-0-41-0		12-2-65-0		
v. Nottinghamshire (Eastbourne) 6 August (RA)	8-0-44-1	8-1-19-3	8-1-24-0	8-0-27-0			
v. Glamorgan (Ebbw Vale) 13 August (RA)	5-0-21-2	3-0-7-1	6-0-32-0	3-0-8-0			
v. Middlesex (Hastings) 20 August (RA)	8-1-33-3	8-1-34-3	8-0-31-0	8-0-45-0			
v. Gloucestershire (Hove) 27 August (RA)	4-0-12-0		8-1-21-1	8-0-28-0	8-0-36-0		
v. Hampshire (Hove) 3 September (SB)	10-0-51-3				10-1-34-2		
v. Kent (Hove) 5 September (SB)	6-0-37-0		10-1-44-0	10-0-52-0			
Wickets	32	31	19	32	23	0	5

a L.B. Taylor absent hurt

v. Surrey (The Oval) 16 July (RA)	v. Worcestershire (Hove) 23 July (RA)	v. Middlesex (Lord's) 2 August (NW)	v. Nottinghamshire (Eastbourne) 6 August (RA)	v. Glamorgan (Ebbw Vale) 13 August (RA)	v. Middlesex (Hastings) 20 August (RA)	v. Gloucestershire (Hove) 27 August (RA)	v. Hampshire (Hove) 3 September (SB)	v. Kent (Hove) 5 September (SB)	Runs
1		17	49			2			555
									73
	26	54	0	—	7	67	52	20	589
12	20	58	26	—	72	38	32	3	674
28	56*	8	46*	—	2	63		67	618
84*	17	5	—	—	30	47	63*	38*	536
18	3*	7	—	—	14*				335
0		5	—		4	0*	9		112
	18	5	—		18	19	1	5*	356
3	—	3			—				19
—	—			—	0*	—	—	—	11
									6
									72
8				—		4	39	128	239
									25
									20
2*		5*	—		1	—	—	—	8
35	74	7	28*	—	8	31	39	19	349
	—					—	—	—	—
1			1						
4	17	9	8		5	7		14	
5	7	1	12		5	3		6	
		1	4		2			2	
201	239	188	170		170	279		302	
8	5	10	3		9	7		5	
L	W	L	W	Ab.	L	W	W	W	
0	4	—	4	2	0	4	—	—	

David Hughes holds a glass of champagne in one hand and the Refuge Assurance League Trophy in the other after Lancashire have beaten Surrey at Old Trafford on the last Sunday of the season. (Ben Radford/Allsport)

S.J.S. Kimber	A.R. Hansford	N.J. Lenham	B.T.P. Donelan	P.W.G. Parker	C.C. Remy	Byes	Leg-byes	Wides	No-balls	Total	Wkts
							8	1	4	232	7
						1	2			114	3
						1	8	6	1	173	9
							13	3	3	182	9
						2	3	4	7	154	10
						4	6	2	1	242	5
						1	9	3		160	10
						1	6	1		131	10
						1	7	1		146	7
							4	2	5	169	4
							4	7	3	189	6
11–0–49–0						9	4		4	249	6
						4	8	3	1	134	7
	8–1–19–1					3	17	1		193	7
	8–0–30–1					1	14	18	1	200	6
		4–0–29–1					7			157	4
							4	2		151	8
	7–0–41–0	1–0–11–0				1		12	2	232	9a
			1–0–14–0			4	7	4	2	225	4
							13	5		225	10
12–0–48–2						1	16	3	1	266	3
8–0–32–2						4	19			169	9
5.3–0–42–2							7	5	1	117	5
7.3–0–24–0							5	2	6	172	6
8–1–32–5		3–0–19–2		1–0–10–0		1	13	1	2	172	8
10–0–62–1			10–1–37–0		10–0–55–1		9	1		248	7
10–0–56–3	10–1–61–3	4–0–40–0					8	5		298	7
0	17	6	0	0	1						

Warwickshire CCC
Limited-Over Matches, 1989

BATTING

	v. Lancashire (Edgbaston) 23 April (RA)	v. Northamptonshire (Edgbaston) 26 & 27 April (B&H)	v. Leicestershire (Leicester) 2 May (B&H)	v. Northamptonshire (Northampton) 7 May (RA)	v. Scotland (Edgbaston) 11 May (B&H)	v. Lancashire (Old Trafford) 13 May (B&H)	v. Yorkshire (Leeds) 21 May (RA)	v. Middlesex (Edgbaston) 28 May (RA)	v. Sussex (Edgbaston) 4 June (RA)	v. Hampshire (Basingstoke) 11 June (RA)	v. Worcestershire (Edgbaston) 18 June (RA)	v. Essex (Ilford) 25 June (RA)	v. Wiltshire (Edgbaston) 28 & 29 June (NW)	v. Leicestershire (Leicester) 2 July (RA)	v. Nottinghamshire (Trent Bridge) 9 July (RA)	v. Kent (Canterbury) 12 July (NW)	v. Surrey (Edgbaston) 23 July (RA)	v. Gloucestershire (Edgbaston) 30 July (RA)
T.A. Lloyd	37	7	25	8	9		9	28	38	2	6	24	57	29	30	21	38	7
A.J. Moles	2	14	8		10	65						19	26	7		26		
M. Asif Din	10			0	27		33	11*	6	44	3	41*	0				49*	0
A.I. Kallicharran	50	62	30	31	32	104	0	66	55					38	19	93*	9	76
D.A. Thorne	3	37	22	57*	24.*	8				8				28	4	2*	0	
P.A. Smith	74	20	30	39*	10		26	93*	28	41	45	23			33	5	6	61
G.W. Humpage	17	13	14		7			25	0	6	2	26	59	1	11	65		
G.C. Small	3*	5	10	—	11		8*	—	—	9	—	2	—	—	4	—	4	—
A.A. Donald	5*	23*	7	—	2*	—	—	14*	0	17*	—	8	0	—	17			
A.R.K. Pierson	—	0	2*	—	1	—			6*				9		—			
T.A. Munton	—	13	4*	—	—	—	—	1*	—	—	—		0*	1*	—	4*	—	
S.J. Green	0																	
D.A. Banks			1															
R.G. Twose							1	—	—	9								0
D.A. Reeve							15	4*	15*	4	24	70*	2*	64	15	45	22	9*
N.M.K. Smith							5	—		6	14				0			—
K.J. Piper							5*				20		—	—	11		0	
J.E. Benjamin										9*								
J.D. Ratcliffe														59				
T.A. Merrick																		1*
Byes			1	1				1					5	2			1	
Leg-byes	11	3	13	4	9		7	6	4	3	6	12	12	4	5	11	4	6
Wides	2	4	3	9			1	5	2	2	1	5	9	3	6	3	2	2
No-balls	7	4	1		2		2	1	5		1	1	1		1		1	
Total	221	201	171	159	199	191	196	169	158	172	216	270	194	139	272	156	162	
Wickets	7	10	9	4	8	7	4	4	9	8	7	4	9†	10	5	9	5	
Result	Ab.	L	L	W	L	L	W	W	L	L	L	W	L	L	W	L	W	
Points	2	0	0	2	0	0	4	4	0	0	0	0	—	0	0	0	4	

Fielding Figures
18 – G.W. Humpage (ct 17/st 1)
7 – G.C. Small
5 – K.J. Piper, T.A. Lloyd and D.A.Thorne
4 – D.A. Reeve and T.A. Munton
2 – M. Asif Din, A.R.K. Pierson, R.G. Twose, A.A. Donald, P.A. Smith, N.M.K. Smith and A.I. Kallicharran
1 – J.D. Ratcliffe

†G.C. Small absent hurt

BOWLING

	G.C. Small	A.A. Donald	P.A. Smith	T.A. Munton	A.R.K. Pierson	A.J. Moles	N.M.K. Smith
v. Lancashire (Edgbaston) 23 April (RA)							
v. Northamptonshire (Edgbaston) 25 & 26 April (B&H)	11-3-36-1	10.5-1-51-0	11-3-34-2	10-0-39-2	11-0-46-0		
v. Leicestershire (Leicester) 2 May (B&H)	11-1-61-2	11-2-44-1	8-0-36-2	11-1-41-0	11-2-29-0	3-0-18-0	
v. Northamptonshire (Northampton) 7 May (RA)	8-0-29-0	8-1-23-0	7-0-49-0	7-1-17-2	8-0-49-1		
v. Scotland (Edgbaston) 11 May (B&H)	11-4-15-3	11-1-35-0	11-3-16-0	11-3-20-2	7-0-33-0	4-0-18-0	
v. Lancashire (Old Trafford) 13 May (B&H)	10-2-44-1	10-2-28-1	7-0-53-1	9-1-40-1	11-3-28-1		
v. Yorkshire (Leeds) 21 May (RA)	8-1-24-1	8-1-26-0	4-0-21-1	7-0-32-1			8-0-46-0
v. Middlesex (Edgbaston) 28 May (RA)	8-0-32-1	8-0-32-4	7-0-33-0	8-0-26-1			8-0-35-2
v. Sussex (Edgbaston) 4 June (RA)	8-1-20-0	8-1-36-1	8-0-25-1	8-1-34-0	8-1-43-1		
v. Hampshire (Basingstoke) 11 June (RA)	4-0-18-0	8-1-18-0	3.1-0-18-0	8-1-33-1			8-0-37-0
v. Worcestershire (Edgbaston) 18 June (RA)		8-0-53-1	8-1-29-1	8-1-29-1	8-0-40-2		
v. Essex (Ilford) 25 June (RA)	8-0-34-1	7-0-32-2		6.3-0-22-1			3-0-27-0
v. Wiltshire (Edgbaston) 28 & 29 June (NW)	6-3-14-1	7-2-12-5		3-0-6-1	8-3-20-3		
v. Leicestershire (Leicester) 2 July (RA)	8-0-62-0	8-2-30-2		8-2-27-2	8-0-53-2		
v. Nottinghamshire (Trent Bridge) 9 July (RA)	8-1-33-1	8-1-28-0		6-1-22-0			8-1-20-1
v. Kent (Canterbury) 12 July (NW)	12-1-26-1	10.4-0-41-3	10-0-55-2	11-1-36-3	9-0-35-1		
v. Surrey (Edgbaston) 23 July (RA)	8-1-29-1	8-0-31-2	8-0-36-1	8-3-33-1			
v. Gloucestershire (Edgbaston) 30 July (RA)	5-0-25-2		4-0-29-1	5-0-26-0			5-0-17-2
v. Northamptonshire (Northampton) 2 August (NW)	12-0-44-1	12-1-26-4		12-1-42-0			2-0-6-1
v. Kent (Canterbury) 6 August (RA)	8-0-32-0	8-0-33-2		7-0-51-0			7-0-37-0
v. Somerset (Edgbaston) 13 August (RA)	8-1-36-0			8-0-34-1			8-0-46-0
v. Worcestershire (Edgbaston) 16 August (NW)	10-1-15-2	6-1-17-1	11-0-39-3	7-2-11-1			
v. Derbyshire (Edgbaston) 20 August (RA)	8-0-54-1		8-0-35-1	7-2-25-0			8-1-41-1
v. Glamorgan (Aberystwyth) 27 August (RA)			8-0-54-0	8-2-18-1			3-0-28-0
v. Middlesex (Lord's) 2 September (NW)	12-3-35-1	12-1-41-1	4-0-21-0	11-3-37-1			9-0-33-1
Wickets	24	30	15	23	11	0	8

v. Northamptonshire (Northampton) 2 August (NW)	v. Kent (Canterbury) 6 August (RA)	v. Somerset (Edgbaston) 13 August (RA)	v. Worcestershire (Edgbaston) 16 August (NW)	v. Derbyshire (Edgbaston) 20 August (RA)	v. Glamorgan (Aberystwyth) 27 August (RA)	v. Middlesex (Lord's) 2 September (NW)	Runs
57	0		0	20	56*	34	542
8		17	61			10	273
17	89	18	94*		4	34*	480
48	26	7	21	34	32	0	833
							193
		2	70	23		24	653
5			10		19	36	316
4*	—	—	15	—		—	75
			0				93
							18
—	—	—	1*	—	—	—	24
							0
							2
		1				4	88
9	28	23		18*	—		486
15	27	31	7	19	56*	42	79
16*	9*	11*	0	3		15*	46
			10*				9
	5*	37		5	—		106
		21*		0			22
10	10	16	7	7	9	7	
5	2	4	2	5	8	5	
	5	1					
194	201	187	220	192	207	211	
7	5	7	9	7	4	6	
W	L	W	W	L	W	W	
—	0	4	—	0	4	—	

Refuge Assurance League

27 August

at Chesterfield

Yorkshire 147 for 8
Derbyshire 148 for 3 (P.D. Bowler 66 not out)

Derbyshire (4 pts) won by 7 wickets

at Aberystwyth

Glamorgan 203 for 4 (H. Morris 83, I. Smith 56 not out)
Warwickshire 207 for 4 (T.A. Lloyd 56 not out, D.A. Reeve 56 not out)

Warwickshire (4 pts) won by 6 wickets

at Folkestone

Kent 199 for 6 (G.R. Cowdrey 102 not out)
Leicestershire 147

Kent (4 pts) won by 52 runs

at Old Trafford

Surrey 186 (A.J. Stewart 56, Wasim Akram 4 for 30)
Lancashire 188 for 7 (G.D. Mendis 66)

Lancashire (4 pts) won by 3 wickets

at Northampton

Essex 144 for 9
Northamptonshire 145 for 7

Northamptonshire (4 pts) won by 3 wickets

at Trent Bridge

Middlesex 167 (R.O. Butcher 67, F.D. Stephenson 4 for 33)
Nottinghamshire 168 for 2 (R.T. Robinson 97 not out)

Nottinghamshire (4 pts) won by 8 wickets

R.G. Twose	D.A. Reeve	J.E. Benjamin	M. Asif Din	A.I. Kallicharran	T.A. Merrick	J.D. Ratcliffe	Byes	Leg-byes	Wides	No-balls	Total	Wkts
												Ab.
								19	1	2		225	6
								7	5	8		236	5
								5	9	2		172	3
							1	20	18			158	6
4-0-25-1								10	3	2		203	5
							1	17	1	1		192	5
							7	2	6			167	8
5-0-18-1	2-0-14-0							7	6	1		165	5
		8-0-23-0					2	2	1	1		160	4
	5-0-24-1		8-0-60-1				1	13	4			194	5
	6-1-25-0						6	13	5	2		218	6
	8-0-39-0							7	7			84	10
	3.4-0-16-0			2-0-16-0			1	3	9	2		215	6
	5-0-23-1						4	2	5			141	2
	5-0-18-0		3-0-15-0					7	4	1		223	10
					5-0-38-2		6	7	3	1		175	7
10-0-31-1	12-2-32-1							9	3			144	8
2-0-19-0				2-0-18-0		1.1-0-8-1	1	9	4			191	8
5-0-41-0					8-2-18-2	3-0-21-1		4	6	2		202	3
	12-4-24-1							11	5			207	8
					6.2-0-29-1			14	6			120	10
8-0-25-1		8-0-34-0				5-0-29-0	2	9	5			195	5
	12-4-27-1						8	7	7			203	4
								16	9	3		210	5
4	5	0	1	0	5	2						

Worcestershire CCC
Limited-Over Matches, 1989

BATTING

BATTING	v. Nottinghamshire (Trent Bridge) 23 April (RA)	v. Middlesex (Lord's) 26 April (B&H)	v. Surrey (The Oval) 2 May (B&H)	v. Lancashire (Worcester) 7 May (RA)	v. Gloucestershire (Worcester) 9 May (B&H)	v. Combined Universities (Worcester) 11 May (B&H)	v. Surrey (Worcester) 21 May (RA)	v. Gloucestershire (Bristol) 28 May (RA)	v. Glamorgan (Worcester) 4 June (RA)	v. Derbyshire (Worcester) 11 June (RA)	v. Sussex (Harrogate) 14 June (TT)	v. Surrey (Harrogate) 16 June (TT)	v. Warwickshire (Edgbaston) 18 June (RA)	v. Middlesex (Worcester) 25 June (RA)	v. Cambridgeshire (March) 28 June (NW)	v. Northamptonshire (Tring) 2 July (RA)	v. Leicestershire (Worcester) 9 July (RA)	v. Derbyshire (Worcester) 12 July (NW)	v. Yorkshire (Scarborough) 16 July (RA)
T.S. Curtis	6	38	22	26	9	43	50	47	18	0	96	40	11	91*	63			13	79
I.T. Botham	10	31	0	37	0	31		70					8		—	39		53	68
G.A. Hick	21	24	4	16	109	1	84	50	6	80	43	35*	5	86*		4	13	45	18
D.B. D'Oliveira	28	12	6	7	15	91*	29	1	15	7	8	15	43			27	45	1	14
P.A. Neale	3					3	3*	49*	25	—	6*	18	20	—		23*	36*	43*	12*
S.J. Rhodes	10	42*	14	21	1	4			—	—			7				—	61	0*
M.J. Weston	19*	15		0			7	16		72	100	33	63	2	23	2*	19	43	
N.V. Radford	9*			37	0	39*	2	25*	29*	38*	4	—	4	3				0*	
P.J. Newport	—	1	1	12	1	10*	—												
G.R. Dilley	—	—		0*															
A.P. Pridgeon	—		4*		—														
G.J. Lord		0				18													
R.K. Illingworth		7*	16*	11		1*								0*		6			
S.R. Lampitt			3												6			0	
S.J. O'Shaughnessy			69	4		14	9			17	7	34*	1*		26			15	
S.R. Bevins						—													
D.A. Leatherdale											34*	1						11*	
S.M. McEwan																			
C.M. Tolley																			
P. Bent																			
Byes		3				4	1			9	1	1	4	2			4	5	
Leg-byes		2	14	9	13	6	10	8	10	7	4	4	13	7	4	9	6	6	9
Wides		3	2	1		3		5	6	6			4	1		2	8	6	6
No-balls		4	1	2	5		1	1		3	4							2	2
Total		115	190	188	152	216	216	222	262	207	249	226	194	143	206	169	157	278	208
Wickets		6	7	9	10	8	8	4	4	6	6	5	5	10	1	4	4	7	4
Result	Ab.	W	L	L	L	L	L	W	W	W	W	W	W	L	W	W	W	W	W
Points	2	2	0	0	0	0	0	4	4	4	—	—	4	0	—	4	4	—	4

Fielding Figures

- 32 – S.J. Rhodes (ct 20/st 12)
- 12 – P.A. Neale
- 11 – I.T. Botham
- 9 – T.S. Curtis
- 7 – G.A. Hick, D.B. D'Oliveira and S.J. O'Shaughnessy
- 5 – M.J. Weston and R.K. Illingworth
- 4 – S.R. Lampitt
- 3 – N.V. Radford

BOWLING

BOWLING	G.R. Dilley	N.V. Radford	A.P. Pridgeon	P.J. Newport	I.T. Botham	M.J. Weston	R.K. Illingworth
v. Nottinghamshire (Trent Bridge) 23 April (RA)							
v. Middlesex (Lord's) 26 April (B&H)	6-0-23-1	6-1-21-1	6-1-16-0	7-1-20-1	5-0-17-3	1-0-11-1	
v. Surrey (The Oval) 2 May (B&H)	11-1-28-3		11-2-31-1	11-1-39-1	11-0-44-4		9-1-27-0
v. Lancashire (Worcester) 7 May (RA)		8-0-29-2	8-1-30-1	8-0-27-2	5-0-34-1		6-0-37-2
v. Gloucestershire (Worcester) 9 May (B&H)	10-1-40-2	11-2-30-1		11-2-33-2	10-2-41-2	11-1-28-0	2-0-20-0
v. Combined Universities (Worcester) 11 May (B&H)		11-0-38-4	9.1-0-41-0	9-0-46-0	5-0-25-0		11-2-29-1
v. Surrey (Worcester) 21 May (RA)		8-0-41-0	7-0-46-1	8-0-38-1	7-0-33-2	8-1-37-1	
v. Gloucestershire (Bristol) 28 May (RA)		8-0-31-2	8-0-57-2	8-0-26-1		8-0-32-0	2-0-21-0
v. Glamorgan (Worcester) 4 June (RA)			8-0-40-3	6.2-0-18-4	8-2-31-3		
v. Derbyshire (Worcester) 11 June (RA)	5-0-11-0	8-2-15-2				8-0-38-2	8-1-21-2
v. Sussex (Harrogate) 14 June (TT)	9-2-13-1	9-1-30-1				8-1-20-1	5.5-0-22-2
v. Surrey (Harrogate) 16 June (TT)	11-0-65-2	11-3-24-1				11-0-38-2	11-1-34-1
v. Warwickshire (Edgbaston) 18 June (RA)	8-0-30-3	7-0-29-2				8-0-26-0	8-0-32-2
v. Middlesex (Worcester) 25 June (RA)		7.2-1-21-2			8-0-29-2	8-0-28-1	8-2-21-0
v. Cambridgeshire (March) 28 June (NW)		11-2-33-0			11-1-44-2	11-0-32-1	12-2-22-1
v. Northamptonshire (Tring) 2 July (RA)		8-1-30-3			8-0-33-1	8-2-20-2	7.4-0-28-3
v. Leicestershire (Worcester) 9 July (RA)		8-2-16-3				8-2-21-2	7-0-36-1
v. Derbyshire (Worcester) 12 July (NW)	10-4-38-1	9-3-23-1			12-1-62-4	6-0-31-0	12-2-43-1
v. Yorkshire (Scarborough) 16 July (RA)	8-0-45-0				7-0-56-0	8-0-25-2	8-0-28-3
v. Sussex (Hove) 23 July (RA)		8-1-59-1			7-1-27-1	5-0-24-0	6-0-41-0
v. Kent (Worcester) 30 July (RA)		5-0-29-2					4-0-18-3
v. Lancashire (Worcester) 2 August (NW)	12-3-47-0	12-3-31-1			12-1-51-5	8-1-22-0	11-0-55-2
v. Essex (Colchester) 6 August (RA)					8-0-39-2	8-1-21-3	8-0-29-1
v. Hampshire (Bournemouth) 13 August (RA)		8-1-14-3			6-0-18-0		8-1-37-0
v. Warwickshire (Edgbaston) 16 August (NW)		12-5-18-1			5-0-19-0	12-0-45-2	
v. Somerset (Worcester) 20 August (RA)						6-0-23-0	8-1-25-2
v. Essex (Scarborough) 4 September (FC)		8-1-33-1			7-0-35-0		10-1-44-1
v. Essex (Worcester) 6 September (RC)		8-0-40-2			6-1-23-0	8-0-37-1	3-0-16-1
Wickets	13	36	8	12	32	19	33

v. Sussex (Hove) 23 July (RA)	v. Kent (Worcester) 30 July (RA)	v. Lancashire (Worcester)	2 August (NW)	v. Essex (Colchester) 6 August (RA)	v. Hampshire (Bournemouth) 13 August (RA)	v. Warwickshire (Edgbaston) 16 August (NW)	v. Somerset (Worcester) 20 August (RA)	v. Essex (Scarborough) 4 September (FC)	v. Essex (Worcester) 6 September (RC)	Runs
16	51	34		0	14	95	10			872
3		11					16	3		380
35	15	90*	54	30	7	81	7	0		963
31	32		60*	14	32	47	14*	17		611
43	22*	20*	6	3	11	22*	—	22		390
2	48*		—	33	3	—	—	16		262
13		50	18*	2	26	35	64	5		627
11	—	—		13	0		—	1		215
										25
										0
										4
										18
22			—	11	1	—	—	6		75
—	—		—	21	9*		5*	15*		59
24	1									221
										—
—	11		6	5	1					69
7*			—	0*	6		—	1		14
—				—						—
			2							2
		1				8				
13	7	7	4	10	14	1	12	12		
5	1	9	9		6	1		2		
		3		4						
225	126	241	197	149	120	202	221	110		
10	3	3	4	10	10	5	4	10		
L	W	W	W	W	L	W	L	L		
0	4	—	4	4	—	4	—	—		

2 – G.R. Dilley, P.J. Newport,
  S.M. McEwan and D.A. Leatherdale
1 – C.M. Tolley and S.R. Bevins

at Hove

Sussex 279 for 7 (P.W.G. Parker 67, C.M. Wells 63)
Gloucestershire 172 for 8 (A.R. Hansford 5 for 32)

Sussex (4 pts) won by 107 runs

After two weeks of unsuccessful attempts to clinch the title Lancashire won the Refuge Assurance League with a thrilling win over Surrey at Old Trafford before a near capacity crowd. Put in to bat, Surrey lost their way after passing 125 with only two wickets down, but the tail plundered useful runs and their 186 off 40 overs was by no means a disappointing score. Mendis and Fowler gave Lancashire a most solid start with a partnership of 68, but Bullen and Medlycott bowled accurately and Lancashire, having lost five men, needed 66 from the last 10 overs. With the hard-hitting Wasim Akram caught behind off Robinson, 41 were needed from the final five overs. At this point Surrey faltered. David Hughes should have been run out twice, but once Robinson was ill-positioned to gather the throw, and once Martin Bicknell's throw was too fierce and wild for Stewart, who flattened the stumps without the ball. Hughes steadied the innings and hit cleanly to score 20 before being bowled by Martin Bicknell, by which time 17 were wanted from 16 balls. Austin stepped across his wicket and smote the ball hard to fine leg for 2 fours, and the last over arrived with four runs wanted. Martin Bicknell's first ball was of full length, but Paul Allott hit it high over long-off for six to give Lancashire the title. Surrey's defeat cost them a place in the Refuge Assurance Cup, for Nottinghamshire beat Middlesex with ease to move into fourth place. Essex

G.A. Hick	S.R. Lampitt	S.J. O'Shaughnessy	S.M. McEwan	C.M. Tolley	P.A. Neale	Byes	Leg-byes	Wides	No-balls	Total	Wkts
											Ab.
							6	5		114	7
2-0-15-0						1	6	14	1	191	9
	5-0-28-0					4	13		2	202	8
						4	4	1	4	200	7
8-0-35-0							3	7	4	217	5
		2-0-15-0					11	3	3	221	5
	6-0-46-0					2	6	4	3	221	5
	5-0-27-0						3	2		119	10
7-0-44-2		5-0-30-1				1	17	5		177	9
11-1-41-3		7-0-22-0				5	17	1		170	10
8-1-46-0		3-0-10-1					8	3		225	7
6-0-30-0		3-0-19-0					6	1	1	172	8
5-0-29-0		2-0-13-0					3	5		144	5
3-0-24-0	8-1-24-0	4-0-14-0				5	4	6		202	4
		8-0-44-1				3	10	4		168	10
	8-0-21-2	4-0-29-0	5-0-18-0			1	14	17		156	9
	7-0-35-2						8	10	3	240	10
	2-0-13-0		7-0-32-1			1	4	3		204	7
4-0-24-2		2-0-13-0	8-0-34-1				17	7	1	239	5
	1-0-8-0	4-0-30-2	3-0-11-0	5-0-19-0			8	4		123	8
	5-0-18-0						13	14	4	237	9
	8-0-43-2		8-0-53-0				8	5	2	193	9
8-0-24-1	6-0-30-4		4-0-15-1			1	8	3	2	147	9
12-0-43-0	8-0-37-2		11-3-51-3				7	2		220	9
6-0-46-1	4-0-20-1		8-0-47-2	8-1-18-1		1	10	5		190	7
9-0-42-0	7-0-26-0		5-0-34-0		0.5-0-4-0	4	3	10	6	225	2
	7-0-40-2		8-1-36-0			6	13	5		211	7
9	15	5	8	1	0						

Yorkshire CCC
Limited-Over Matches, 1989

BATTING

BATTING	v. Middlesex (Lord's) 23 April (RA)	v. Minor Counties (Jesmond) 25 & 26 April (B&H)	v. Nottinghamshire (Leeds) 7 May (RA)	v. Somerset (Leeds) 9 May (B&H)	v. Nottinghamshire (Trent Bridge) 11 & 12 May (B&H)	v. Derbyshire (Leeds) 13 May (B&H)	v. Leicestershire (Leicester) 14 May (RA)	v. Warwickshire (Leeds) 21 May (RA)	v. Australians (Leeds) 23 May	v. Surrey (The Oval) 28 May (RA)	v. Somerset (Taunton) 11 June (RA)	v. Surrey (Harrogate) 15 June (TT)	v. Gloucestershire (Leeds) 18 June (RA)	v. Glamorgan (Hull) 25 June (RA)	v. Scotland (Leeds) 28 & 29 June (NW)	v. Hampshire (Southampton) 2 July (RA)	v. Sussex (Middlesbrough) 9 July (RA)	v. Surrey (The Oval) 12 July (NW)	v. Worcestershire (Scarborough) 16 July (RA)
D. Byas	9	22	6	0	5	27*	2	12	13	47	19	7	19*	3	54	47*	30	17	8
A.A. Metcalfe	76	18	19	35	14	77	0	0	2	12	0		18	22	50	22	8	40	11
P.E. Robinson	55	37	0	7	12	11	11	24		5			13	15		22	4		16
D.L. Bairstow	5	48*	65*	51*	7	26*	8	21	46	3	13	64	52	22	—				
J.D. Love	14	9	35*	2	30	3	12					25	6	3	8	2	1		
R.J. Blakey	1	7	61	19	16	39	5	94*	2	50	78		73	92*	17	43	46	22	5
S.N. Hartley	0	—	—	39	13*	—	13	5*	5	3	5							20	8
P. Carrick	0	18*	—	1	1	—	1	—	17	0	31	3	4	0	33*	11	16	17	48*
P.W. Jarvis	0	—	—	4	0	15*	—	15	—	2			7*		15*	7		6	—
C.S. Pickles	1*	—	—	5	4	—	2	—	5*	19	1*	2	—	3	—				
P.A. Booth	—																		
S. Oldham			—	0	0	—	4*												
K. Sharp						5		16	6		12	47					14	15	80
A. Sidebottom								—	2		20	9*	1*	—	0	4*	0*	8	2*
M.D. Moxon								55	23	2	4		0	40	14	10	26	59	18
S.D. Fletcher											2*		0	—	—	—	—	—	16*
S.A. Kellett											24								
I.G. Swallow											6								17*
N.G. Nicholson																			
S.C. Gough																			
Byes		4				1		1	5	1	3	6		3	1	4		1	1
Leg-byes	5	10	10	8	4	5	7	17	1	7	10	10	4	9	14	6	4	16	4
Wides	4	8	3	2	3	9	3	1	1	7	1	1		2	2	1	2	1	3
No-balls			2	8	2	5	6	1	13		5			1					
Total	170	181	201	181	111	208	89	192	188	206	184	200	196	211	212	179	151	255	204
Wickets	9	5	4	10	10	5	9	5	10	10	9	10	7	7	7	7	8	9	7
Result	L	W	W	L	L	W	L	W	L	L	W	L	W	W	W	L	L	L	L
Points	0	2	4	0	0	2	0	4	—	0	4	—	4	4	—	0	0	—	0

Fielding Figures

13 – D.L. Bairstow (ct 11/st 2)
8 – P. Carrick
7 – R.J. Blakey (ct 6/st 1), P.E. Robinson and P.W. Jarvis
6 – J.D. Love
5 – K. Sharp and A. Sidebottom

4 – C.S. Pickles and A.A. Metcalfe
3 – D. Byas, S. Oldham and N.G. Nicholson
1 – M.D. Moxon, S.N. Hartley and S.D. Fletcher

BOWLING

BOWLING	C.S. Pickles	S.N. Hartley	P.W. Jarvis	D. Byas	P. Carrick	P.A. Booth	S. Oldham
v. Middlesex (Lord's) 23 April (RA)	7–0–49–0	7–0–23–0	7.1–0–38–1	5–0–18–1	5–0–16–0	3–0–10–0	
v. Minor Counties (Jesmond) 25 & 26 April (B&H)	11–3–24–0		11–4–28–3	8–0–25–1	11–1–33–2	4–0–19–0	10–3–38–0
v. Nottinghamshire (Leeds) 7 May (RA)	5–1–11–1	5.4–0–36–2	6–0–20–0	4–0–19–3	8–2–19–2		8–0–28–1
v. Somerset (Leeds) 9 May (B&H)	8–2–49–0	6–1–24–0	11–1–35–2	11–1–38–2	11–0–36–0		8–0–48–0
v. Nottinghamshire (Trent Bridge) 11 May (B&H)	8–0–27–0	7–0–29–1	11–4–21–3	4.1–0–18–1	11–2–32–0		11–5–13–4
v. Derbyshire (Leeds) 13 May (B&H)	11–3–42–1	11–2–32–4			11–2–40–1		11–0–49–0
v. Leicestershire (Leicester) 14 May (RA)	7.4–0–32–2		8–3–11–1	2–0–7–0	6–1–12–0		8–2–25–0
v. Warwickshire (Leeds) 21 May (RA)	7–0–22–0	6–0–33–1	8–1–43–2	3–0–20–1	8–2–28–1		
v. Australians (Leeds) 23 May	11–2–48–1	4–1–31–0	11–1–62–1	3–0–18–0	11–1–47–0		
v. Surrey (The Oval) 28 May (RA)	8–0–56–0	8–0–34–0			8–0–33–2		
v. Somerset (Taunton) 11 June (RA)	8–0–41–1		7.4–1–27–6	8–1–25–1	8–0–34–1		
v. Surrey (Harrogate) 15 June (TT)	7–1–30–1			10–0–49–1	11–2–37–0		
v. Gloucestershire (Leeds) 18 June (RA)	8–0–39–0		8–1–26–2	2–0–23–1	6–0–31–2		
v. Glamorgan (Hull) 25 June (RA)	4–0–26–1			2–0–22–1	8–0–38–0		
v. Scotland (Leeds) 28 & 29 June (NW)	12–1–41–1		12–0–48–0		12–2–30–1		
v. Hampshire (Southampton) 2 July (RA)	6–0–35–1		7.3–1–38–1		7–0–35–0		
v. Sussex (Middlesbrough) 9 July (RA)	4–0–39–0			2–0–16–1	2–0–24–0		
v. Surrey (The Oval) 12 July (NW)			12–1–50–1		12–0–47–0		
v. Worcestershire (Scarborough) 16 July (RA)	7–1–40–3		8–0–37–0	7–0–28–0	2–1–11–0		
v. Essex (Southend) 23 July (RA)			8–0–45–0		7–0–48–0		
v. Northamptonshire (Sheffield) 6 August (RA)	8–1–46–1		8–1–34–0		5–0–23–0		
v. Kent (Scarborough) 13 August (RA)	6–0–20–2		8–0–37–3	2–0–22–0	8–1–45–2		
v. Lancashire (Old Trafford) 20 August (RA)	8–0–46–3		7–2–21–1	8–0–34–1	8–2–30–1		
v. Derbyshire (Chesterfield) 27 August (RA)	7–1–27–2		8–2–18–0	6.1–0–28–1	4–0–21–0		
v. Leicestershire (Scarborough) 3 September (FC)	10–0–54–0		10–2–30–2		10–0–30–1		
v. Essex (Scarborough) 5 September (FC)	7–0–44–3		10–0–48–1	3–0–11–0	10–1–49–2		
Wickets	24	8	30	16	18	0	5

	v. Essex (Southend) 23 July (RA)	v. Northamptonshire (Sheffield) 6 August (RA)	v. Kent (Scarborough) 13 August (RA)	v. Lancashire (Old Trafford) 20 August (RA)	v. Derbyshire (Chesterfield) 27 August (RA)	v. Leicestershire (Scarborough) 3 September (FC)	v. Essex (Scarborough) 5 September (FC)	Runs
	25	11	10	12	0	6	7	418
	29	75	73	2	0	27	42	672
	0	0	12	51*	39*	57	27	418
						23	57	511
			65	32	27			274
	66*	8	15	1	17	1	2	780
								111
	3	7	11*	—	11	0	—	233
	0*	6*	—	—	—	—	—	77
	0		16*	—	0	36*	2*	96
								4
	50	5	3	76				329
	—	3	—		9*	4*	—	62
	30	59			35		108	483
	—	0	—	—				18
								24
	—			1*	0	37	1*	23
								39
								—
	1		1	4	1		1	
	7	5	18	16	2	12	12	
	1	1	3	5	6	2	2	
	1	6	1	1		2		
	213	186	228	201	147	207	261	
	6	10	6	5	8	7	6	
	L	L	W	W	L	W	W	
	0	0	4	4	0	—	—	

needed to beat Northamptonshire to take advantage of any lapse by Lancashire, but they were restricted to 144 in their 40 overs. They bowled and fielded splendidly to reduce Northamptonshire to 119 for 7, but news came through of Lancashire's victory, heads went down and Ripley and Givan steered Northamptonshire to victory. Essex's defeat pushed them down to third place and cost them home advantage in the Cup semi-final.

Refuge Assurance League – Final Table

	P	W	L	T	N/R	Pts
Lancashire (3)	16	12	2	0	2	52
Worcestershire (1)	16	11	4	0	1	46
Essex (10)	16	11	4	0	1	46
Nottinghamshire (17)	16	9	6	0	1	38
Derbyshire (12)	16	9	6	0	1	38
Hampshire (9)	16	8	6	1	1	36
Surrey (5)	16	9	7	0	0	36
Northamptonshire (14)	16	8	6	0	2	36
Middlesex (4)	16	8	7	1	0	34
Somerset (12)	16	7	8	1	0	30
Yorkshire (8)	16	7	9	0	0	28
Kent (7)	16	7	9	0	0	28
Sussex (14)	16	6	8	1	1	28
Leicestershire (14)	16	5	10	0	1	22
Warwickshire (10)	16	5	10	0	1	22
Gloucestershire (2)	16	3	13	0	0	12
Glamorgan (5)	16	2	12	0	2	12

(1988 positions in brackets)
The top four sides qualified for the Refuge Assurance Cup.

A. Sidebottom	M.D. Moxon	S.D. Fletcher	I.G. Swallow	S.C. Gough	Byes	Leg-byes	Wides	No-balls	Total	Wkts
					2	6	5		162	2
					2	10	10		179	6
					1	7	2		141	10
					1	12	6	1	243	5
						4	1		144	10
						14	6	2	201	6
8-0-38-1						5	2		92	3
11-1-64-1	4-0-24-0					7	1	2	191	7
8-0-33-2		8-0-71-1				3	3	2	297	3
7-0-21-0					2	9	2	4	238	5
7-0-18-0	4-1-11-0	11-1-53-2	5-1-21-0		1	16	3	2	165	10
	8-0-27-0	8-1-29-3			1	14	6		234	5
6.3-4-4-3	8-1-37-3	8-0-32-2			2	7			184	8
12-4-27-1		12-0-53-0				3	3		162	10
8-2-29-2		8-0-41-0			11		2	3	210	3
4-0-21-1	4-0-22-1	4-0-28-2				5	1		183	4
12-2-39-0	11-4-34-2	9-1-63-0	4-0-16-0		2	9	1		161	5
8-0-29-0	8-0-54-1					7	3		256	4
8-0-40-0	7.5-0-47-0	8-0-29-2				9	6	2	208	4
8-0-26-1	4-0-17-1	7-0-44-1			2	6		1	217	2
8-0-48-0		7-0-42-0				8	1		198	4
		6.5-0-20-3				11	5		225	7
8-2-28-0	4.4-0-23-0				4	14	6		169	10
10-0-46-2				10-0-44-2		3	2	1	148	3
10-0-46-1	10-0-51-1				1		1		205	7
15	9	16	0	2						

Derbyshire CCC
First-Class Matches, 1989

Each cell shows both innings (1st 2nd); a blank = did not play, a dash (—) = did not bat.

BATTING	v. Northamptonshire (Derby) 20–4 April	v. Oxford University (Oxford) 27–9 April	v. Essex (Chelmsford) 4–8 May	v. Leicestershire (Chesterfield) 17–19 May	v. Kent (Dartford) 20–2 May	v. Yorkshire (Leeds) 24–6 May	v. Australians (Derby) 3–5 June	v. Warwickshire (Nuneaton) 7–9 June	v. Worcestershire (Worcester) 10–13 June	v. Sussex (Derby) 17–20 June	v. Somerset (Derby) 1–4 July	v. Essex (Derby) 5–7 July	v. Middlesex (Lord's) 8–11 July	v. Glamorgan (Derby) 22–5 July
K.J. Barnett	36 74	— —		9 16	36 8		76 23			14 86	118 —			1 51*
P.D. Bowler	4 35	157 —	16 20	0 16	0 31	41 17	4 9	6 78	16 26	48 12	54 33	26 56*	6 62	53 17
B.J.M. Maher	15 18	25 53*	0 0	6 15	0 25*	1 20	17 0	1 23	17 0	97 15*	9* 2*	8 3	18 10	22 —
J.E. Morris	13 13	42* —	10 2	0 77	55 15*	31 70	7 34	25 24	48 47*	67 4	127 —	93 29	50 15	134 16*
B. Roberts	30 0	24 —	0 63	2 25	102 —	0 4	31 1	23 12	2 0	1 11				40 —
S.C. Goldsmith	4 11	46 47*	18 4	24 4	88 —	3 7	31 0	0 0	0 20	19 17	70 —	29 24	13 15	10 —
R. Sharma	17 11	— 21	10 4		45 —	39 53*	28 37*	36* 23	6 14					
P.G. Newman	0 13	2* 1	26* 57	4 0	13 —	13 0		7 1	10 12		27 2	4 —		5 —
A.E. Warner	17 3	— 7		1* 29	46 —	20 8*			0 9*	14 10*	10 —	0 —	— 32	17* —
S.J. Base	14 0	0 12	1 10	4 0			7 6			0* 0	10 —			2 —
O.H. Mortensen	20* 12*	8 0*		0 0*			0 1	2 —		— —	5 0		— 0	
D.E. Malcolm		11* 1			2 —	8* —	4* 4			13* 0*		10* —	— 12*	25 —
C.J. Adams			5 22			5* —	0 —					0 —		8 —
M.A. Holding			1 3								4 —		— 2	
I.R. Bishop			4 20				4 10	13 3*	0 1	8 0		0 —		
C. Gladwin							12 0				21 59	0 1	6 28	
F.A. Griffith									12 22	30 4				
I. Redpath											4 43*	0 0	41* 0	
K.M. Krikken											10 1	1 1*	36* 1	
T.J.G. O'Gorman														
M. Jean-Jacques														
A. Brown														
Byes	1 2	4 1	2 4	1	1	2 1	5 4	1		1 4	5 8	9	9	7 4
Leg-byes	3 16	8	15 8	13	13 1	1 1	2 7	9 16	10 6	12 3	15 7	8	7 9	16 6
Wides		1		1	4		1 2		1	3			1	1 2
No-balls	9 8		1	3 12	10 6	3 8	11 3	1 1	2 1	5 3	4 1	3		4 5
Total	183 216	320 143	113 197	57 228	416 87	178 189	228 141	135 212	157 145	342 223	444 87	191 114	177 191	338 97
Wickets	10 10	5 5	10 10	10 10	10 2	10 7	10 10	10 8	10 9†	10 9	9 2	10 5	5 10	10 1
Result	D	D	L	L	W	D	L	D	L	D	D	D	L	W
Points	5	—	0	4	24	4		4	5	6	6	5	5	23

Fielding Figures

- 59 – B.J.M. Maher (ct 57/st 2)
- 23 – P.D. Bowler (ct 22/st 1)
- 18 – B. Roberts
- 16 – R. Sharma and K.J. Barnett
- 11 – P.G. Newman
- 10 – C.J. Adams
- 8 – J.E. Morris and M.A. Holding
- 7 – S.J. Base
- 6 – S.C. Goldsmith and subs
- 5 – K.M. Krikken (ct 4/st 1)
- 4 – O.H. Mortensen, A.E. Warner and F.A. Griffith
- 2 – I.R. Bishop, C. Gladwin and T.J.G. O'Gorman
- 1 – D.E. Malcolm and A. Brown

English Counties Form Charts

The statistics of all first-class matches are given on pages 408–79. The games covered are:

Britannic Assurance County Championship
Matches against touring and representative sides

In the batting table a blank indicates that a batsman did not *play* in a game, a dash (—) that he did not *bat*. A dash (—) is placed in the batting averages if a player had 2 innings or less, and in the bowling figures if no wicket was taken.

29, 30 and 31 August and 1 September

at Chelmsford

Surrey 250 (A.J. Stewart 120, N.A. Foster 4 for 50) and 183 (G.P. Thorpe 55, J.K. Lever 7 for 48)
Essex 207 (N. Shahid 52, M.P. Bicknell 6 for 55) and 227 for 8 (N. Hussain 70)

Essex won by 2 wickets
Essex 22 pts, Surrey 7 pts

at Leicester

Derbyshire 204 (W.K.M. Benjamin 5 for 51) and 78 (W.K.M. Benjamin 5 for 25, C.C. Lewis 5 for 40)
Leicestershire 241 (P. Willey 96, I.R. Bishop 6 for 67) and 42 for 0

Leicestershire won by 10 wickets
Leicestershire 22 pts, Derbyshire 6 pts

at Hove

Sussex 430 (I.J. Gould 125, A.C.S. Pigott 91, A.P. Wells 91, P.J. Bakker 5 for 83, C.A. Connor 4 for 90) and 45 for 1
Hampshire 233 (A.R. Hansford 5 for 79) and 241 (V.P. Terry 61, A.C.S. Pigott 4 for 58)

Sussex won by 9 wickets

v. Northamptonshire (Northampton) 26–8 July	v. Surrey (Derby) 29 July–1 August	v. Hampshire (Derby) 5–8 August	v. Lancashire (Chesterfield) 9–11 August	v. Gloucestershire (Cheltenham) 12–15 August	v. Nottinghamshire (Trent Bridge) 19–22 August	v. Yorkshire (Chesterfield) 24–8 August	v. Leicestershire (Leicester) 29 Aug.–1 Sept.	v. Nottinghamshire (Derby) 8–11 September	v. Lancashire (Old Trafford) 13–16 September	M	Inns	NOs	Runs	HS	Av
30 2	50 —	33 106	42 29	9 —	80 0	0 74	3 36	5 14	3 —	18	30	1	1064	118	36.68
71 3	106 0	0 0	4 63	57 —	14 0	1 0	17 4	11 58	81 4	24	46	1	1337	157	29.71
46 —	11 —	15 56*	36 0	5 —	3 0	6 0		2 1		22	40	6	601	97	17.67
22 11*		20 65	16 28	121 —	1 24	7 16		3 1	12 66	23	43	5	1638	156	43.10
					24 18*			15 7	15 75	15	27	1	541	102	20.80
								30 17	16 6	11	21	1	376	88	18.80
8 10*	23 4*	5 2	7 0	77 —	4 0	6 43	22 3			21	37	5	755	77	23.59
	0 —	6 12	86* 6*	2 —						15	25	4	309	86*	14.71
	0 —	0 23						0 2	0 5*	15	23	6	253	46	14.88
25 —			6 —	— —	17 0	0* —	8* 0	0 8*	32* 19*	16	25	6	181	32*	9.52
9 —	2* —				1* 11				8 —	13	19	8	79	20*	7.18
30 —	51 —				— 1					11	14	7	172	51	24.57
21 —	25 —		79 4	5 —		24 38*			38 0	7	11	1	261	79	26.10
		34 10		4* —	6 —			0* 13*		10	13	4	90	34	10.00
4 —	25 —		8 0			7 28*	27 4		14 —	12	20	2	180	28*	10.00
										4	8	—	127	59	15.87
		2 13				1 5	5 8			5	10	—	102	30	10.20
										3	6	2	88	43*	22.00
							37 1*			4	8	3	88	37	17.60
113* —	4 6*	43 15	39 29	124 —	2 7	44 1	29 6			8	14	2	462	124	38.50
			1 16*	0 —		0 —	11 3	1 2		5	8	1	34	16*	4.85
								65 2	23 19	2	4	—	109	65	27.25
3	4			6	6		4	1	14 10						
18	16	10 18	13 5	27	6 2	4 8	14 1	13 7	11 3						
2	1	1 1	1 2	5			1	1	3						
18 3	2	9 5	16 11	6	1	2 6	8 4	6 2	22 2						
420 29	320 10	178 326	354 193	448	165 64	102 219	204 78	293 160	292 209						
10 2	10 1	10 9	10 8	9	9‡ 9§	10 7	10 10	10 9	10 6						
W	W	D	D	D	L	W	L	W	D						
24	24	2	8	6	5	20	6	23	7						

† A.E. Warner retired hurt
‡ D.E. Malcolm absent injured
§ M.A. Holding absent

Sussex 24 pts, Hampshire 5 pts

at Worcester

Worcestershire 248 (T.S. Curtis 98) and 213
Gloucestershire 206 (M.W. Alleyne 55, S.M. McEwan 5 for 61) and 124 (G.R. Dilley 4 for 22, S.R. Lampitt 4 for 32)

Worcestershire won by 131 runs
Worcestershire 22 pts, Gloucestershire 6 pts

at Leeds

Yorkshire 426 for 9 dec (A.A. Metcalfe 138, D. Byas 95, N.G. Nicholson 56)
Warwickshire 248 (T.A. Lloyd 61, P. Carrick 6 for 70) and 296 for 3 dec (N.M.K. Smith 161, M. Asif Din 82 not out)

Match drawn
Yorkshire 6 pts, Warwickshire 3 pts

Triumph, too, for Phil Neale, who led Worcestershire to the Britannic Assurance County Championship title for the second year in succession and was named as the championship's Player of the Year. (David Munden)

Derbyshire CCC
First-Class Matches, 1989

BOWLING	P.G. Newman	O.H. Mortensen	S.J. Base	A.E. Warner	D.E. Malcolm	R. Sharma	K.J. Barnett	M.A. Holding	B. Roberts
v. Northamptonshire (Derby) 20–4 April	28.5–8–45–5 11–4–31–2	18–6–34–1 21–4–52–3	24–3–61–4 19–4–61–2	14–5–11–0 8–1–22–1					
v. Oxford University (Oxford) 27–9 April	7–1–26–0		15.4–6–21–4	6–2–15–0	15–3–49–3	17–7–34–2	11–2–27–0		
v. Essex (Chelmsford) 4–8 May	31–5–92–2	28–4–75–0	27–3–92–0			21–3–62–0		26–4–96–1	5–0–22–0
v. Leicestershire (Chesterfield) 17–19 May	14–2–46–1	26–4–71–3	14–2–38–1	19–3–53–2 3.1–1–6–0					
v. Kent (Dartford) 20–2 May	10–0–35–0 11–2–44–3			11–2–27–1 10.3–1–30–2	16.2–2–69–4 16–0–61–2	18–6–54–2	1–0–5–0 6–2–18–0	18–3–71–4 12–1–53–0	
v. Yorkshire (Leeds) 24–6 May	16–4–39–1			26.2–10–58–2	21–1–94–3	14–4–37–2		27–5–79–2	
v. Australians (Derby) 3–5 June		12.4–0–40–4 8–0–34–1	12–0–49–4 13–3–41–2		13–2–50–2 18.3–1–68–4				
v. Warwickshire (Nuneaton) 7–9 June	20–8–31–2 9–0–51–1	20.5–6–38–6 11–1–48–1		16–5–28–1 10–2–24–1					
v. Worcestershire (Worcester) 10–13 June	17–6–30–3 10–4–36–0		21.4–4–63–2 18–2–82–4	16–5–32–2 10–4–24–0			1–0–5–0 11–4–20–0		
v. Sussex (Derby) 17–20 June	24–5–85–1	13–2–31–1			18.1–2–94–4	19–3–68–0	11–2–35–1		
v. Somerset (Derby) 1–4 July		21–1–56–1 16–3–46–2	14–4–40–2 13–3–47–1	13–1–41–1 12–0–42–1		10–3–23–0	2–0–2–0 12–2–31–0	18–3–61–1 17–3–64–3	
v. Essex (Derby) 5–7 July	19–5–55–2			17–7–45–1	16–3–48–2	15.3–4–60–5			
v. Middlesex (Lord's) 8–11 July		26–10–47–3		8.1–3–13–3	23–3–111–4			8–0–43–0	
v. Glamorgan (Derby) 22–5 July	13–2–25–0		11–1–40–0 18–4–59–3	15–6–23–1 17–5–40–1	18–6–37–3 21.5–9–55–2		3–0–10–0	15.1–3–57–6 23–6–66–4	
v. Northamptonshire (Northampton) 26–8 July		25.2–2–105–6 8.3–1–23–2	14–4–34–2 10–0–54–2		14–0–81–2 10–1–46–3				
v. Surrey (Derby) 29 July–1 August	6–1–18–0 20–3–68–0	7–1–13–1 18.3–5–39–3		9–1–26–2 16–2–45–3	8–3–19–3 9–0–24–3		1–0–3–0		
v. Hampshire (Derby) 5–8 August	31–8–107–0	12–4–21–0		31–9–78–0		11–3–44–2	6–0–35–0	30–9–76–2	
v. Lancashire (Chesterfield) 9–11 August	18–1–88–2 9–1–36–1		15–1–88–0 22.3–5–80–4			10.2–2–46–1			
v. Gloucestershire (Cheltenham) 12–15 August	9–3–26–1		4–0–18–0			12–4–23–2	9–3–23–1	23.1–8–62–1	
v. Nottinghamshire (Trent Bridge) 19–22 August		10–2–29–0 11.5–2–21–4	7.5–1–33–4 2–0–9–1		12–2–50–2	18–6–31–4 8–0–18–0	17.2–5–36–4	9–0–31–0 4.4–0–12–1	4–0–8–0
v. Yorkshire (Chesterfield) 24–8 August			19.5–5–60–7 18–2–93–5						
v. Leicestershire (Leicester) 29 Aug.–1 Sept.			23–4–53–1 6–1–20–0			6–1–22–0	3–0–12–1		
v. Nottinghamshire (Derby) 8–11 September			24–2–106–2 7–1–34–1	18–4–53–3 9.4–1–18–4				17–1–59–0 10–1–33–3	
v. Lancashire (Old Trafford) 13–16 September		14–3–46–1 6–3–9–0	24–8–75–2	11–0–50–2 4.2–0–17–1			19–6–33–3 4–2–2–1		
	333.5–73–1014–27 av. 37.55	333.4–64–878–43 av. 20.41	417.3–73–1451–60 av. 24.18	331.1–80–821–35 av. 23.45	249.5–38–956–46 av. 20.78	191.5–50–547–20 av. 27.35	105.2–24–272–11 av. 24.72	258–47–863–28 av. 30.82	9–0–30–0 —

a S.G. Hinks retired hurt, absent hurt   b K. Krikken 6–0–40–0   c K. Sharp retired hurt

P.D. Bowler	I.R. Bishop	J.E. Morris	F.A. Griffith	M. Jean-Jacques	B.J.M. Maher	I. Redpath	Byes	Leg-byes	Wides	No-balls	Total	Wkts
							1	9			161	10
								11	1	1	177	9
							4	5			181	9
10–1–57–0							2	24	2	8	522	3
2–1–1–2	17–4–54–1						4	7	2	6	274	10
	4–2–6–1										12	1
							1	2	2	8	210	9a
2–0–12–0							7	13		8	292	9
								6	1	1	313	10
	12–2–44–0						6	11	5	2	200	10
	15–4–32–3							5	3	1	180	10
	17–3–48–1								10	1	155	10
	13–1–54–3	1–0–14–0						8	1	1	199	6
	21–0–61–1		10–3–18–2				2	9	9	8	220	10
	19–6–50–4							15	1	1	227	8
	25–3–86–2						9	9	3	3	417	10
							4	4		14	231	5
							2	8	1	9	240	7
	21–3–52–0						5	28		6	293	10
							4	5	1	5	223	10b
15–3–52–1		9–2–24–0			12–0–83–1	5–2–11–0	2	3	5	3	215	2
								9		14	191	10
							5	6		5	241	10
	16–0–54–0						1	8		3	283	10
	9–1–36–3						2	4	1	2	165	10
	12.5–2–31–4						1	2	1	1	110	10
	11–3–27–1						1	10	1		217	10
3–0–16–0			18–1–81–2				7	7	2	10	472	6
	16–3–39–3			16–0–93–4			5	13	2	12	372	10
	22–9–41–2			10–3–33–1			6	5	4	5	201	10
				7–1–17–1			1	5	1	9	175	6
								11			185	10
							1	9		2	114	10
	12–2–24–2			8–1–35–1			6	11		11	136	10
	19–5–47–3		7–1–23–0	7–1–15–1				6	3	9	184	9c
	22.3–6–67–6		6–1–30–1	10–0–49–1			6	2	1	11	241	10
	6.4–0–17–0			1–1–0–0			4	1		2	42	0
				24.2–4–84–4			9	19	2	24	330	10
				7–0–33–2			1		1	12	119	10
	17–5–32–1						11	4	1	2	251	9
	7–0–18–0						5	2		1	53	2
32–5– 138–3 av. 46.00	335–64– 920–41 av. 22.43	10–2– 38–0 —	41–6– 152–5 av. 30.40	90.2–11– 359–15 av. 23.93	12–0– 83–1 av. 83.00	5–2– 11–0 —						

Essex CCC
First-Class Matches 1989

BATTING

	v. Kent (Canterbury) 20–4 April	v. Middlesex (Chelmsford) 27 April–1 May	v. Derbyshire (Chelmsford) 4–8 May	v. Gloucestershire (Bristol) 20–3 May	v. Cambridge University (Cambridge) 24–6 May	v. Somerset (Chelmsford) 27–30 May	v. Surrey (The Oval) 10–13 June	v. Leicestershire (Chelmsford) 17–20 June	v. Hampshire (Ilford) 21–3 June	v. Warwickshire (Ilford) 24–7 June	v. Sussex (Horsham) 1–4 July	v. Derbyshire (Derby) 5–7 July	v. Glamorgan (Swansea) 8–11 July	v. Kent (Southend) 19–21 July
G.A. Gooch	32 55	65 0	148 —	63 3				124* 42			29 25			7 —
J.P. Stephenson	0 109*	0 49*	94 —	9 0	63 —	102 34*	114 36	35 10	20 3	27 43	34 0	93 —	0 30	16 —
A.W. Lilley	65 14	0 19*	113* —	23 0	16 —	9 9	67 35	1 48	7 1	6 49	11 —		1 —	
M.E. Waugh	4 17	39 —	77 —	11 9	92 —	26 79	13 58*	89* 15	20 109	1 2	0 8	26 —	21 —	29 —
P.J. Prichard	11 12*	9 —	54* —	18 32	88 —	40 —	13 —	— 80*	0 3	0 2	9 60	1 —	81* 26	40 —
B.R. Hardie	26 —		— —	0 24	0 —	46 80	21 142*		33 30	56 17		1 —	13 101*	15 —
D.R. Pringle	20 —	15 —		4 2						14 9*	13 81*	17 —	2 —	15 —
D.E. East	0 —	2 —												
T.D. Topley	4 —	6 —		2 10		8 —	18 —		25 0	35* —	3 —	0 —	1 —	15 —
N.A. Foster	20* —	3 —		22* 5							13* —			6* —
J.H. Childs	0 —	0* —		16 2*			0* —	1 —	0 2	8 —	4 —	7* —	24 —	2 —
G. Miller		0 —				5 —	41* 4*	24* —		51 50	7 —	11 21		24 —
M.A. Garnham			— —	0 1		55* —	41 —	1 —	9*	54 0	18 90*	43 —	0 48*	37 —
K. Butler						10* —								
M.C. Ilott								13* —		2* 0*				
J.K. Lever							0 —	5 —				27 —	10 —	
Nadeem Shahid									— —	40 27*				
N. Hussain									141 16*	32 23	28 —		8 —	127 —
Byes			2	— 4	4	— 1	3 4	— 1	8	8 9	4 18	5		4
Leg-byes	8 7	5	24	3 4	10	10 6	7 4	8 9	15 8	8 2	11 21	28	11 6	9
Wides	4 5		2		1		1 1	1		1	2		1 1	3
No-balls	9 5	5 1	8	7 12	3	4 3	2	5 1	2 1	4	2 3	6	1 1	13
Total	203 224	149 69	522	178 108	347	327 217	303 279	262 216	277 234	335 149	185 350	293	174 213	347
Wickets	10 3	10 1	3	10 10	6	8 3	9 2	2 4	10 9	10 5	10 6	10	10 2	10
Result	D	W	W	W	W	D	W	D	W	W	D	D	W	W
Points	6	20	24	21	—	4	21	5	23	24	3	7	21	24

Fielding Figures

51 – M.A. Garnham (ct 48/st 3)
31 – M.E. Waugh
25 – B.R. Hardie
23 – N. Hussain
21 – G.A. Gooch and P.J. Prichard
14 – T.D. Topley
13 – N.A. Foster
11 – J.P. Stephenson and A.W. Lilley
7 – G. Miller
6 – Nadeem Shahid and D.R. Pringle
5 – J.H. Childs

Second Youth Test Match

at Canterbury

New Zealand 395 for 9 dec (S. Wilson 91, L. Howell 87, J. Aiken 65, A. Parore 63) and 271 for 9 dec (B. Pocock 65, J. Aiken 53, L. Howell 51, M.C.J. Ball 5 for 69)
England 335 (C.J. Adams 71, M. Keech 58) and 59 for 1

Match drawn

30 and 31 August and 1 September

at Scarborough

Michael Parkinson's World XI 398 for 4 dec (M.D. Crowe 138 not out, C.A. Best 100) and 273 for 7 dec (S.P. O'Donnell 96)
MCC XI 333 for 8 dec (W. Larkins 108, N.D. Burns 58, M.W. Pringle 53, E.E. Hemmings 53) and 81 (Wasim Akram 7 for 42)

World XI won by 257 runs.

Only the Britannic Assurance County Championship matches at Chelmsford and Headingley lasted until the fourth day, but by then the championship had been decided and Worcestershire had retained their title. A slightly shortened first day saw Worcestershire reach 240 for 8 in 95 overs. It was a grim day's batting, and Worcestershire owed much to Tim Curtis' patient and effective batting. He hit 11 fours and was seventh out, by which time he had faced 265 balls. He did not give a chance and was out when he was bowled by a ball from Walsh which came back at him sharply. Worcestershire added only eight runs on the second morning, but they quickly reduced Gloucestershire to 130 for 7. Alleyne and Walsh offered defiance, and Worcestershire's first-innings lead was restricted to 42. By the close, this had been increased to 104 for the loss of Bent and Curtis. It was consistent team-work rather than individual brilliance that took Worcestershire to 213 on the third day and left Gloucestershire the task of scoring 256 to win on a wicket that was never easy. They reached 43 before Hodgson was bowled by Lampitt, but after that the decline was rapid, with only Bainbridge offering resistance to Dilley and Lampitt. Worcestershire's triumph was testimony to their wise policies of team-building and strength in depth. They had been hard hit by both Test calls and injury during the season, Newport and Lord, with a broken knee-cap, being out for long periods, but such players as Bent, McEwan and Lampitt had performed admirably to compensate for

v. Yorkshire (Southend) 22–5 July	v. Middlesex (Uxbridge) 26–8 July	v. Nottinghamshire (Trent Bridge) 29 July–1 August	v. Worcestershire (Colchester) 5–8 August	v. Northamptonshire (Colchester) 9–11 August	v. Lancashire (Lytham) 12–15 August	v. Australians (Chelmsford) 19–21 August	v. Northamptonshire (Northampton) 24–8 August	v. Surrey (Chelmsford) 29 Aug.–1 Sept.	v. Leicestershire (Leicester) 8–11 September	M	Inns	NOs	Runs	HS	Av
11 1		51 17	75 —	68 20	58 21				158 —	13	22	1	1073	158	51.09
85 0	2 —	26 29	8 20	41 —	171 7	3 3			2 —	22	37	3	1318	171	38.76
	40 —	9 10				20 1	21 18			16	27	2	613	113*	24.52
27 0	110 —	46 26	12 76	24 —	24 23*	100* 57	53 1	40 8	165 —	24	39	4	1537	165	43.91
0 13		14 12	28 0	128 —	19 10	86 52	1 3	2 0	2 —	23	36	4	949	128	29.65
5 11	26 —	0 2				9 8	29 41	23 48	0 —	17	27	2	792	142*	31.68
37 16*	26 —	0 9	19 42	25* —	— —				22 —	17	20	4	388	81*	24.25
										2	2	—	2	2	1.00
25* —	49 —	9 16	6 1	— —	— —	— 9	1 5*	2 17	6 4*	23	26	4	277	49	12.59
0 4*			27 50*	— —	— —		11 0	12* 0*	5 —	14	15	8	178	50*	25.42
7 —	2 —	0* 2*	0* 3*	— —	— 1*		5* —	0 —	0* —	24	23	11	86	24	7.16
	61 —		1 46							10	14	3	346	61	31.45
13 0	21 —	33 0	2 20	26* —	3* —	1* 1	91 3	16 22*	32 3*	22	32	9	703	91	30.56
										1	1	1	10	10*	—
	7* —									5	4	4	22	13*	—
		3 1				— 0	10 —	0 0		9	10	—	56	27	5.60
				28 —	— —	0 10	33 34*	52 31		7	9	2	255	52	36.42
21 45	23 —	61 37	47 17	5 —	105* 14*	14 31	42 64	19 70	0 —	15	24	3	990	141	47.14
4 3		1		10	4	2	6 4	2 1	4						
5 9	13	8 4	4 16	13	2 4	8 6	11 6	11 7	10 1						
1			1	3		1			1						
11 4	7		2 5	19	6	5 2	17 6	8 5	9						
248 107	390	210 148	208 323	391 0	400 79	290 205	324 166	207 227	415 8						
10 7	10	10 10	10 9	6 0	4 3	6 10	10 7	10 8	10 0						
W	D	L	D	W	W	L	L	W	W						
22	7	6	3	20	23	—	8	22	24						

3 – J.K. Lever
2 – D.E. East and subs
1 – M.C. Ilott

the loss of first choice players. Indeed, McEwan and Lampitt, medium-pace bowlers, had been outstanding, and their achievements were recognized when they were both awarded their county caps amid the celebrations at winning the county championship.

Essex, who had led the table for so long, struggled against Surrey over the first two days. Alec Stewart's century and some enterprising late batting by Martin Bicknell took Surrey to a third batting point on the second morning, and Martin Bicknell then bowled most impressively to take six wickets and give his side a first-innings lead of 43. He owed something to some rather careless batting on the Essex side. In his last home match before retirement, John Lever, long held in affection by all who have played with him and against him as well as by those who have watched him, shattered the Surrey second-innings batting by taking 7 for 48. It was a marvellous performance by the 40-year-old left-arm medium-pace bowler and earned him a standing ovation which, one feels, would have been his anyway. He took the last four wickets in 20 balls. He received another moving ovation on the last day. Hardie's tenacity and Hussain's sparkle had laid the foundations of an Essex victory, but the outcome of the match was in doubt until Garnham and Nadeem Shahid, who had batted with maturity and style in the first innings, stood firm and stayed together until the scores were level. Shahid was then leg before, and Lever was sent in to make the winning run. He was given a welcoming guard of honour by the Surrey players and the umpires, but, having been dropped, he was out for nought. It did not matter. His place in the history of Essex cricket and in the hearts of all those who love the game had long been secure.

A doubtful wicket and limp batting brought the game at Leicester to an end within three days. Winston Benjamin, having thrown off illness and injury, confirmed his return to form and fitness with match figures of 10 for 46 and was awarded his county cap.

Sussex also won in three days. On the opening day, Ian Gould and Tony Pigott added 184 in 45 overs for the seventh wicket. Gould hit 20 fours in his spectacular 208-minute innings while Pigott hit 13. Earlier Alan Wells had come close to scoring a century before lunch, and it was very sad news that he had decided to join the rebel tour to South Africa. Hampshire had no answer to Sussex's bombardment and were well beaten, another

Essex CCC
First-Class Matches, 1989

BOWLING	N.A. Foster	D.R. Pringle	T.D. Topley	M.E. Waugh	G.A. Gooch	J.H. Childs	M.C. Ilott	J.K. Lever	J.P. Stephenson
v. Kent (Canterbury) 20–4 April	19.3–6–38–4	21–4–38–2	12–3–39–4						
	11–3–29–0	16.3–3–36–4	12–1–40–3	8–1–28–1					
v. Middlesex (Chelmsford) 27 April–1 May	22–9–28–1	22.5–5–42–5	18–6–40–2		3–1–6–0				
	14–3–42–4	13.3–1–38–5	1–0–1–0						
v. Derbyshire (Chelmsford) 4–8 May	18–5–39–4	12–2–27–1	15.5–6–30–5						
	28–9–72–3	28.5–10–63–4	12–5–23–1			24–17–27–2			
v. Gloucestershire (Bristol) 20–3 May	11.4–5–14–4	14–6–22–2	15–4–39–4						
	12–1–35–4	12–5–13–1	8–1–28–3	3–0–11–1					
v. Cambridge University (Cambridge) 24–6 May				12–4–23–3		20–11–24–0	11–3–26–4	9–2–23–1	13–5–18–2
				8–4–14–0		19–11–35–7	7–1–25–0	12–5–26–1	17–5–37–0
v. Somerset (Chelmsford) 27–30 May			9–1–30–1			40–11–86–2	14–0–57–0	17.5–5–25–0	
				5–1–25–1		16–8–14–0	10–3–29–2	6–0–21–0	
v. Surrey (The Oval) 10–13 June			25–6–74–0	12–1–55–0		11–5–15–0	26–7–74–1	32–5–99–2	11–3–41–2
			3–0–37–0				3–0–15–0	4–0–9–0	
v. Leicestershire (Chelmsford) 17–20 June	26–6–77–2	21–7–62–1	13–4–49–1	4–0–24–0		34–8–97–2			2–0–3–0
	20–5–35–1		14–3–38–1	4.2–0–9–2	4–0–26–0	16–4–41–0			2–0–8–0
v. Hampshire (Ilford) 21–3 June			21–3–74–0			34.5–17–36–5	11–2–50–1		13–3–46–2
			11–2–34–2	1–1–0–0		29.1–16–38–7	4–0–20–0		
v. Warwickshire (Ilford) 24–7 June		22.4–2–73–2	28–4–92–2	2–0–8–0		28–4–96–4		5–1–13–0	
		30–13–44–7	24.4–6–44–3			11–5–31–0			
v. Sussex (Horsham) 1–4 July	28.5–8–53–4	21–5–46–2	20–7–63–2		6–2–7–0	16–7–38–2		4–0–12–0	
	4–1–29–1	17–1–62–2	7–1–25–0			20–3–84–5			
v. Derbyshire (Derby) 5–7 July		22–7–62–1	21.2–8–47–4			32–15–47–5		10–3–18–0	
		18–5–42–2	10–1–28–1			18.5–12–11–1		8–1–33–1	
v. Glamorgan (Swansea) 8–11 July		15.3–8–18–7						16–2–47–3	
		13–2–29–2	9.1–4–22–4			17–6–55–2		6–0–17–2	
v. Kent (Southend) 19–21 July	15–3–38–2	16.2–3–42–6	7–2–27–1						
	20–6–53–1	17.4–6–60–4	16–2–68–2			10–2–31–1			
v. Yorkshire (Southend) 22–5 July	15–5–30–3	13–5–33–2	13.4–0–46–5						
	36–10–94–4	24.1–5–67–3	19–7–43–2			23–13–24–1			
v. Middlesex (Uxbridge) 26–8 July		22–10–42–3	13.2–7–35–2			24–7–78–4	9–2–21–1		
		13–5–45–1	15–3–46–0	8–0–42–0		24–9–53–0	14–4–48–1		10–2–57–0
v. Nottinghamshire (Trent Bridge) 29 July–1 August		27–6–79–4	27–3–91–3	2–0–11–1		8–1–13–0		22–4–72–1	10–1–40–1
		14–3–56–2	10–1–35–1	1–0–5–0				17–2–65–3	
v. Worcestershire (Colchester) 5–8 August	31–10–94–1	28–6–50–2	23–5–76–4		4–1–20–0	34–11–115–0			
v. Northamptonshire (Colchester) 9–11 August	6–2–13–1	6–0–20–0			6–0–41–0				
	20.5–5–46–4	17–6–49–4	8–2–24–1		5–1–21–0				
v. Lancashire (Lytham) 12–15 August	15–5–31–4	11–2–27–2	10.5–2–33–4			3–1–2–0			
	34–5–134–2	22–2–75–2	12–2–23–1		2–1–3–0	43–15–80–4			
v. Australians (Chelmsford) 19–21 August			12–1–40–0	20–3–68–1	7–0–49–0	18–2–69–3		17–4–43–1	5–0–30–0
			11–2–48–0	7–0–40–1		12–1–53–0		13–1–56–0	1–0–2–0
v. Northamptonshire (Northampton) 24–8 August	35–7–105–7		17–6–62–2					17–5–54–1	
	17–0–68–1		19–4–81–2			22–5–64–1		14–4–34–1	
v. Surrey (Chelmsford) 29 Aug.–1 Sept.	28.4–12–50–4		23–6–60–1	12–2–34–2		14–10–24–1		19–3–64–2	
	24–8–41–2		17–5–58–0	8–2–18–1		8–4–11–0		23.2–8–48–7	
v. Leicestershire (Leicester) 8–11 September	8–1–29–2	12–4–28–2	17–6–35–3			20–10–45–3			
	25.5–4–98–3	18–2–57–2	5–1–23–0			32–12–84–5			
	546.3–144–	582–151–	605.5–143–	117.2–19–	37–6–	681.5–263–	109–22–	263.1–54–	93–20–
	1415–73	1447–89	1851–77	415–14	173–0	1521–67	365–10	754–26	307–7
	av. 19.38	av. 16.25	av. 24.03	av. 29.64	—	av. 22.70	av. 36.50	av. 29.00	av. 43.85

a C.W.J. Athey absent hurt

G. Miller	A.W. Lilley	P.J. Prichard	Nadeem Shahid	N. Hussain	Byes	Leg-byes	Wides	No-balls	Total	Wkts
						4		6	119	10
							2	2	133	8
					1	12		2	129	10
					1	3		3	85	10
					2	15		1	113	10
					4	8			197	10
						5		5	80	10
						3		8	90	9a
9–6–8–0					3	8	3		133	10
17.4–8–34–2					1	12	1		184	10
28–6–72–0					5	5	1		280	3
14–8–25–0					2			3	116	4
9–2–26–0						11	1	3	395	5
	6–0–53–1	7–0–66–0			1	5	2		186	1
			15–2–40–2		4	21	4	10	377	8
		4–1–16–0	20–3–69–1		1	8	2	3	251	5
11–2–20–2					4	14	1	15	244	10
21–8–33–0			6–2–30–1		8	2		4	165	10
13–1–42–2					4	10		11	338	10
2–0–10–0					10	6			145	10
17–7–35–0					6	25	1	3	285	10
3–0–23–1					4	13		2	240	9
					9	8		3	191	10
									114	5
									65	10
					8	3			134	10
						5	1	1	112	10
5–1–9–2					5	3		1	229	10
						6		2	115	10
					7	4		3	239	10
5–1–11–0					6	2	1		195	10
10–3–31–0				1–0–1–0	13	5	1	3	341	2
						2	1	6	308	10
					1	3		4	165	6
27–7–85–1					1	6	4	6	447	9
		5–0–46–0			1	10		1	131	1
								5	140	10
						2		2	95	10
			17–3–51–1		10	5	1	3	381	10
			14–2–83–2		1	4	4	11	387	7
			9.1–1–53–1		5	1		1	258	2
					1	5	2	1	227	10
					5	12	1	1	264	6
					6	12	1	2	250	10
						7	1	4	183	10
					1	7			145	10
					4	8		4	274	10
191.4–60–	6–0–	16–1–	81.1–13–	1–0–						
464–10	53–1	128–0	326–8	1–0						
av. 46.40	av. 53.00	—	av. 40.75	—						

Glamorgan CCC
First-Class Matches, 1989

BATTING	v. Cambridge University (Cambridge) 15-17 April		v. Leicestershire (Leicester) 20-4 April		v. Somerset (Taunton) 28 April-1 May		v. Gloucestershire (Cardiff) 4-8 May		v. Northamptonshire (Swansea) 20-3 May		v. Nottinghamshire (Cardiff) 27-30 May		v. Worcestershire (Worcester) 3-6 June		v. Somerset (Cardiff) 7-9 June		v. Middlesex (Abergavenny) 10-13 June		v. Lancashire (Old Trafford) 17-20 June		v. Warwickshire (Edgbaston) 21-3 June		v. Yorkshire (Leeds) 24-7 June		v. Australians (Neath) 1-3 July		v. Essex (Swansea) 8-11 July	
A.R. Butcher	37	—	19	84*	14	10	69	—	0	1	107*	10	32	3*	—	46	101	51	68	69	14	171*	87	—	54	14	5	2
H. Morris	102	—	0	30	7	96	90	—	35	45	—	7	21	16*	—	12	7	0	69	16	10	133	0*	—	94	5	0	19
P.A. Cottey	24	—	2	12	8	10	0	—																				
M.P. Maynard	4	—	18	14	5	22	191*	—	38	39	49	65	11	—	—	22	5	43	24	52	41	41*	13*	—	42	26	0	13
M.J. Cann	58	—	0	3	13	65	34	—	75*	45*	26	34	11	—	—	109	2	1	39	1	38	20	95	—	3	5	19	0
I. Smith	11	—	11	—	3	1											0	47	25*	51*	105	—	—	—	61*	38*	16	31
J. Derrick	47	—	67	—	1	22	0	—	23	—	—	22*																
C.P. Metson	0	—	6	—	29	16	0	—	15	—	—	0*	3	—	—	7*	14	22*	19	1*	6	—					0	6*
P.D. North	0	—	0	—	17	0	15	—																				
S.L. Watkin	0	—	31	—	4	2*	0	—	0	—			0	—	—	9			1	—	22	—					11*	0
S.R. Barwick	6*	—	0*	—	10*	—	1	—					0*	—	—	0	0*	—	0*	—	0*	—					0	0
R.C. Ontong							2	—	0	—	48	0			—	4												
S.J. Dennis							0	—	13	—			13	—					4	—	15	—					0	1
R.J. Shastri									50	48	54*	80	11	—	—	44	127	101*	0	11	8	—	10*	—	10	44*	11	20
G.C. Holmes															19	—	7	28*	33	1	28	4	—	—	26*	0	3	31
S. Bastien																												
S.P. James																												
A. Dale																												
K.A. Somaia																												
R.D.B. Croft																												
Byes	6				1	5	1		12	6	8				1		1		9		8	6	4				8	
Leg-byes	4		4	8	4	9	19		5	7	5	3	10	1		10	5	4	18	2	11	6			9	1	3	
Wides	4		1		1		1		4	3	1	2	1						3	6	4		1					
No-balls	4		9	14	2	1	13		19	11	8	7	2				5		13	8	17	15	4	1	4		2	2
Total	307		167	166	118	260	435		290	214	250	286	134	20	0	277	302	311	297	252	290	378	214		301	135	65	134
Wickets	10		10	4	10	10	10		10	4	2	6	10	0	0	9	7	6	10	2	10	2	2		5	5	10	10
Result	D		D		D		D		W		D		D		D		D		W		D		D		D		L	
Points	—		5		4		4		23		5		4		3		4		23		4		3		—		4	

Fielding Figures

63 – C.P. Metson (ct 57/st 6)
23 – M.P. Maynard
18 – H. Morris
11 – A.R. Butcher and R.J. Shastri
10 – S.P. James
8 – I. Smith
7 – J. Derrick and S.L. Watkin
6 – S.R. Barwick, M.J. Cann and G.C. Holmes
3 – R.C. Ontong and P.D. North
2 – P.A. Cottey and S.J. Dennis
1 – K.A. Somaia, R.D.B. Croft and sub

indication that their season was falling apart. Remy, from the Haringey cricket school, made his first-class debut for Sussex and was out first ball, but he did capture the wicket of Scott in the second innings.

There was little entertainment at Headingley, where bad light and a slow pitch produced a rather tedious, if shortened, first day. Carrick's policy was to bat for most of the first two days and to attempt to bowl Warwickshire out twice. He himself was mainly responsible for them being bowled out in the first innings, but Neil Smith hit the first century of his career when Warwickshire followed-on. His 161 occupied 366 balls and included 24 fours. He and Asif Din added 184 for the third wicket.

The youth Test at Canterbury produced a tedious draw with New Zealand intent on holding what they had, and there were the customary fireworks in the festival game at Scarborough.

2 September

at Scarborough

Michael Parkinson's World XI 214 for 9 (P.J. Dujon 67, C.S. Pickles 4 for 39)

Yorkshire 156 (D. Byas 54)

World XI won by 58 runs

National Westminster Bank Trophy Final
MIDDLESEX v. WARWICKSHIRE

Mike Gatting could not hide his delight at winning the toss, and he had no hesitation in deciding to bat first on a wicket which he predicted would get increasingly slower and lower in bounce. Haynes and Carr began in a most confident fashion. Small troubled both batsmen with the occasional delivery, but Donald tended to overpitch, and the first few overs were mostly serene for the batsmen. Runs came in a gentle flow, and the first 10 overs realized 31.

The advent of Reeve and Munton tended to blunt the scoring, and in the 15th over, Reeve moved a ball away from Carr, flicked the outside edge and Humpage took a fine plunging catch. Gatting entered to a mixture of boos and cheers. Three overs later he left in silence to the protests of one demonstrator after he had attempted to cut a ball from Munton that was too close to him and succeeded only in chopping the ball into his stumps. After

Match columns (each with two innings):
v. Gloucestershire (Bristol) 19–21 July · v. Derbyshire (Derby) 22–5 July · v. Leicestershire (Cardiff) 26–8 July · v. Hampshire (Cardiff) 29 July–1 August · v. Surrey (The Oval) 5–8 August · v. Sussex (Swansea) 12–15 August · v. Kent (Canterbury) 19–22 August · v. Warwickshire (Swansea) 24–8 August · v. Hampshire (Southampton) 8–11 September · v. Worcestershire (Pontypridd) 13–16 September

Glos 1	Glos 2	Der 1	Der 2	Leic 1	Leic 2	Ham(C) 1	Ham(C) 2	Sur 1	Sur 2	Sus 1	Sus 2	Kent 1	Kent 2	War 1	War 2	Ham(S) 1	Ham(S) 2	Wor 1	Wor 2	M	Inns	NOs	Runs	HS	Av
		37	43	24	1	7	30	61	88*	67	—	7	46	1	34	65	1	43	—	23	40	5	1632	171*	46.62
4	29	26	37	2	20	6	1	25	50	0	—	56	68	2	108	40	4	7	—	24	41	2	1299	133	33.30
																				4	6	—	56	24	9.33
1	0	3	21	14	1	11	0	25	—	65	—	0	21	16	15	0	20	44	—	24	40	3	1035	191*	27.97
6	1	1	40			70	12	1	22	37	—	9	0							20	34	2	895	109	27.96
1	1			9	15	38	67	18	—	1	—	116	7	26	33	40	14	0	—	18	28	4	786	116	32.75
																				6	7	1	182	67	30.33
2	27*	40	8	28	0	2	4	12	—	26	—	28	0	0	5	14*	12*	47	—	24	33	8	399	47	15.96
																				4	5	—	32	17	6.40
0	0	7	3	2*	15*			0	—	3	—	6	2	4	0	7	0	2*	—	23	27	5	131	31	5.95
5	23	0*	0	0	0	0*	0*	8	—	0*	—	0*	0	0*	12	0	0			22	27	13	65	23	4.64
																				5	5	—	54	48	10.80
		38	5			5	7	35	—			36	1	0	9*	0	0	5	—	15	19	1	187	38	10.38
				67	44			46	35	15	14*	9	—	27	56			22	—	16	26	5	964	127	45.90
37*	8	6	21	38	12									5	1	7	22			13	21	3	337	38	18.72
																		0*	—	4	2	2	1	1*	—
9	16					3	45	53	21	42	—			31	38	40	46	3	—	7	12	—	347	53	28.91
4	44	4	41*	2	2			0	37											4	8	1	134	44	19.14
11	15	6	6	11	1															3	6	—	50	15	8.33
								5*	—			16	24*	11	1	22	5	45	—	5	8	2	129	45	21.50

Glos 1	Glos 2	Der 1	Der 2	Leic 1	Leic 2	Ham(C) 1	Ham(C) 2	Sur 1	Sur 2	Sus 1	Sus 2	Kent 1	Kent 2	War 1	War 2	Ham(S) 1	Ham(S) 2	Wor 1	Wor 2
	2				5	17	5	4	5	7		6		9		2	1		
6	3	9	6	11	2	5	2	3	2	9		10	5	8	9	7	4	11	
								1	3	3				3				1	
3	2	14	5	3		10	6	1	1	5		12	2	5	6	3	4		
89	171	191	241	228	118	208	254	227	205	308		311	178	131	329	247	133	230	
10	10	10	10	10	10	10	10	10	3	10		10	10	10	10	10	10	9	
L		L		L		D		D		D		L		L		W		D	
3		4		6		3		5		7		6		1		22		2	

20 overs Middlesex were 46 for 2, and they had lost the initiative that they had seized early on.

They would have been in deeper trouble had Lloyd hung on to a high chance at cover that Ramprakash offered off the naggingly accurate Reeve. The batsman was on two at the time, and the chance came in the 23rd over, but he survived for another 17 overs.

Shortly before lunch Lloyd introduced his sixth bowler, off-spinner Neil Smith. His third delivery nipped back at Haynes, who was uncomfortably tucked and knocked back the off stump. At lunch, after 34 overs, Middlesex were 101 for 3, and honours were even.

Ramprakash and Roseberry found run-getting difficult, and Ramprakash was bowled by Donald, who was much happier bowling from the Pavilion end than he had been from the Nursery end. Roseberry and Downton put on 37 before Roseberry, flat-footed, hit Small high to square-leg, where Asif Din, who had not excelled in that position, took the catch.

Humpage shouts in glee as Neil Smith bowls Desmond Haynes just before lunch. (Adrian Murrell/Allsport)

Glamorgan
First-Class Matches, 1989

BOWLING	S.L. Watkin	S.R. Barwick	J. Derrick	P.D. North	I. Smith	M.P. Maynard	M.J. Cann	A.R. Butcher	S.J. Dennis
v. Cambridge University (Cambridge) 15–17 April	16–7–19–1	20–11–23–2	24–12–41–3	6–3–16–0	4–2–14–0	3–1–8–0			
v. Leicestershire (Leicester) 20–4 April	27.3–7–53–6 / 38–7–130–4	24–12–30–1 / 35–8–101–1	21–4–47–2 / 26–3–95–2	1–0–9–0 / 9–1–25–0	13–2–49–1 / 19–2–57–2				
v. Somerset (Taunton) 28 April–1 May	20–2–50–2 / 7–0–29–0	35.1–16–47–7 / 31–16–40–3	5–0–24–0 / 5–1–20–0	17–5–29–0 / 18.3–4–54–3	5–3–12–0		11–6–12–1 / 1–0–4–0	1–1–0–0	
v. Gloucestershire (Cardiff) 4–8 May	30–15–56–2 / 17–4–31–0		36.1–18–61–3 / 12–2–35–0	20–8–33–0 / 37–13–63–2		11–3–20–0	8–0–30–0	4–0–17–0 / 9–2–30–1	31–8–56–4 / 10–6–14–0
v. Northamptonshire (Swansea) 20–3 May	13–2–37–1 / 11–3–42–6	24–10–31–4					1–0–2–1		14–2–40–1 / 6–4–7–1
v. Nottinghamshire (Cardiff) 27–30 May	17–2–49–2 / 12–2–47–1	26–5–71–1 / 19–4–47–0	12–1–53–1 / 14.4–1–63–0				1–0–10–0	1–0–10–0	15–2–34–0 / 16–1–65–2
v. Worcestershire (Worcester) 3–6 June	25–11–54–1 / 29–8–75–3	22–9–40–6 / 31–10–80–0							16.1–10–2 / 20–4–63–0
v. Somerset (Cardiff) 7–9 June	33–7–90–3	31–14–73–3				3–0–18–0			
v. Middlesex (Abergavenny) 10–13 June	16–2–42–0 / 18–1–92–2	26–7–68–0 / 28–3–144–4			8–0–44–0		8–2–30–3		
v. Lancashire (Old Trafford) 17–20 June	22–5–65–7 / 24–3–94–6	12–1–58–1 / 23–3–83–0							12.2–2–64 / 7–2–29–0
v. Warwickshire (Edgbaston) 21–3 June	23–6–57–2 / 4–0–7–0	11–5–11–0			18–1–94–2 / 4–0–23–0	6–1–16–0	6–0–36–0 / 6–0–37–0		12–3–42–0
v. Yorkshire (Leeds) 24–7 June	25.4–6–53–5	32–10–72–3			12–2–53–1		6–2–20–0		
v. Australians (Neath) 1–3 July	24–5–81–2 / 14–2–36–0	16–2–41–1			18–3–75–1 / 18.2–2–66–2		4–1–22–0 / 1–0–8–0		28–8–69–0 / 25–4–65–2
v. Essex (Swansea) 8–11 July	25–7–59–4 / 13–1–59–0	19.2–2–59–5 / 1–0–5–0			5–1–18–1 / 8–1–37–0		3–1–7–1		13–6–17–0 / 21–2–76–1
v. Gloucestershire (Bristol) 19–21 July	33–9–84–3	35.3–9–85–3			16–0–93–1		1–0–1–0		
v. Derbyshire (Derby) 22–5 July	19–2–62–0 / 5–0–24–0	25–4–72–2 / 9.5–5–26–0							26–10–65 / 5–2–19–0
v. Leicestershire (Cardiff) 26–8 July	8–1–35–1 / 2–0–12–0	26–11–45–1 / 10–3–26–1							
v. Hampshire (Cardiff) 29 July–1 August		27–8–76–0			20–3–64–1 / 8–0–48–3			11–1–45–1	27–9–80–2 / 8–0–35–3
v. Surrey (The Oval) 5–8 August	25–3–96–2 / 11–0–41–1	21.3–6–50–2 / 11–0–50–0			20–2–86–3 / 12–0–56–2		1–0–4–0	2–1–3–1 / 4–0–31–0	
v. Sussex (Swansea) 12–15 August	19–2–52–2 / 12–4–49–1	18–7–47–3 / 11–2–36–0			13–2–45–2 / 6–1–9–0	3–0–10–0	16–2–74–1	3–0–15–0	16–3–54–3 / 7–1–19–1
v. Kent (Canterbury) 19–22 August	23–6–92–2 / 16–1–47–2	22–6–55–1 / 12–0–50–1			11–0–46–1 / 2–0–19–0			4–1–7–0	23–2–83–5 / 12–1–47–1
v. Warwickshire (Swansea) 24–8 August	32.5–8–106–6 / 3–0–11–1	33–6–82–3			8–0–50–1			2.1–0–19–1	24–7–69–0
v. Hampshire (Southampton) 8–11 September	27.1–8–73–6 / 16.5–4–46–5	39–14–75–2 / 14–3–49–3			3–0–8–0 / 6–1–25–2				16–7–34–2 / 8–3–28–0
v. Worcestershire (Pontypridd) 13-16 September									
	757–163– 2237–92 av. 24.31	781.2–232– 1948–64 av. 30.43	155.5–42– 439–11 av. 39.90	108.3–34– 229–5 av. 45.80	257.2–28– 1091–26 av. 41.96	26–5– 72–0 —	74–14– 297–7 av. 42.42	41.1–6– 177–4 av. 44.25	418.3–110 1196–35 av. 34.17

a P.A. Cottey 1–0–6–0; H. Morris 1–0–1–0   b G. Cook absent   c H. Morris 3.5–0–16–0

R.C. Ontong	R.D.B. Croft	A. Dale	R.J. Shastri	G.C. Holmes	S.R. Bastien	K.A. Somaia	Byes	Leg-byes	Wides	No-balls	Total	Wkts
							6	8		1	135	6
								2		3	190	10
								7			415	9
							8	4		1	186	10
								5		1	152	6
21–6–53–1							1	5	1	3	282	10
46–5–128–2							10	13	1	5	381	5a
15–5–23–1			32.3–9–61–2					6		6	200	10
			4–0–11–2								60	9b
20.5–4–55–2			6–0–20–0					8		3	300	6
17–0–64–0							4	2	1	4	302	3
			2–0–8–0				2	1	1		127	10
			1–0–1–0	9–4–12–0			6	9		1	246	3
14–2–38–0			10–2–29–0	2–0–4–0	20–7–52–1		1	9	1		330	8c
											0	0
			7–2–23–0		13–2–41–1		4	11		9	263	4
			6–0–23–0		16–1–70–2		1	15	3	4	345	8
			1–1–0–0				6	3			196	10
			32.5–4–128–2					10	2	1	344	10
			25–5–60–0	13–2–58–0			1	6	1	8	365	4
								1		2	84	0
			32–14–59–0	2–1–1–0	10–2–39–0			11	1	9	308	9
			4–0–20–0	12–0–49–0			4	12	4	7	373	4
			2–0–16–1	6–0–21–0			1	3		2	216	5
			2–0–10–0					11	1	1	174	10
			14–4–23–0					6	1	1	213	2
		20–5–62–1				22–7–51–1		7		2	383	9
		7–1–26–0		10.4–2–28–3		20–6–69–2		16	1	4	338	10
				9–1–22–1				6	2	5	97	1
			38–11–77–3			26–5–87–5		3		3	247	10
			8–1–22–0			10.4–1–38–0		2		4	100	1
		12–4–41–1	9–1–36–0				12	16		6	370	6
								3		4	86	7
	31–9–72–0		5–0–33–0				3	10	10	1	357	10
	7–0–35–1		5–1–14–0					5	2		232	4
			6–1–21–0					6		7	240	10
			13–9–8–0					2	4	1	223	3d
	27–8–81–0							8			372	9
	11–1–51–0						2	2	3		218	4
	17–3–71–0		11–1–41–0					11	2	1	430	10
							1			1	31	2
	1–0–2–0							9	2	1	201	10
							1				149	10
												Ab.
133.5–22–	94–21–	39–10–	276.2–6–	63.4–10–	59–12–	78.4–19–						
361–6	312–1	129–2	744–10	195–4	202–4	245–8						
av. 60.16	av. 312.00	av. 64.50	av. 74.40	av. 48.75	av. 50.50	av. 30.62						

d H. Morris 4–0–16–0

National Westminster Bank Trophy 1989

The County winning the Trophy will receive a prize of £22,000, the losing Finalist £11,000, the losing Semi-finalist £5,250 each and the losing Quarter-finalists £2,625 each.

MARYLEBONE CRICKET CLUB

NatWest Bank Trophy Final

20p   20p

MIDDLESEX v. WARWICKSHIRE

at Lord's Ground, †Saturday, September 2nd, 1989

MIDDLESEX		
1 J. D. Carr	c Humpage b Reeve	17
2 D. L. Haynes	b N. Smith	50
‡3 M. W. Gatting	b Munton	1
4 M. R. Ramprakash	b Donald	24
5 M. A. Roseberry	c Asif Din b Small	26
*6 P. R. Downton	not out	43
7 J. E. Emburey	not out	21
8 S. P. Hughes		
9 A. R. C. Fraser		
10 N. G. Cowans		
11 R. M. Ellcock		

B , l-b 16, w 9, n-b 3, ... 28

Total... 210

WARWICKSHIRE		
‡1 T. A. Lloyd	b Emburey	34
2 A. J. Moles	b Fraser	10
3 A. I. Kallicharran	c Downton b Fraser ...	0
*4 G. W. Humpage	c Gatting b Cowans	36
5 P. A. Smith	b Carr	24
6 D. A. Reeve	run out	42
7 Asif Din	not out	34
8 N. M. K. Smith	not out	15
9 G. C. Small		
10 A. A. Donald		
11 T. A. Munton		

B 4, l-b 7, w 5, n-b , ... 16

Total.. 211

FALL OF THE WICKETS

1...40 2...41 3...98 4...111 5...148 6... 7... 8... 9... 10...

Bowling Analysis	O.	M.	R.	W.	Wd.	N-b
Donald	12	1	41	1	6	2
Small	12	3	35	1	...	
Reeve	12	4	27	1	2	...
Munton	11	3	37	1	...	1
P. Smith	4	0	21	0	...	...
N. Smith	9	0	33	1	1	...
	...	...	...	...	...	...

FALL OF THE WICKETS

1...16 2...26 3...66 4...99 5...122 6...191 7... 8... 9... 10...

Bowling Analysis	O.	M.	R.	W.	Wd.	N-b
Ellcock	10	1	45	0	2	...
Cowans	12	4	23	1	...	...
Fraser	12	3	30	2	...	...
Hughes	10.4	2	45	0	3	...
Emburey	12	2	46	1	...	...
Carr	3	0	11	1	...	...
	...	...	...	...	...	...

Any alterations to teams will be announced over the public address system

RULES—1 The Match will consist of one innings per side and each innings is limited to 60 overs.

2 No one bowler may bowl more than 12 overs in an innings.

3 Hours of play : 10.30 a.m. to 7.10 p.m. In certain circumstances the Umpires may order extra time.

Luncheon Interval 12.45 p.m.—1.25 p.m.   Tea Interval will be 20 minutes and will normally be taken at 4.30 p.m.

‡Captain   * Wicket-keeper

Umpires—H. D. Bird & N. T. Plews   Scorers—H. P. H. Sharp, P. Austin & E. Solomon

†This match is intended to be completed in one day, but three days have been allocated in case of weather interference.

Middlesex won the toss

Warwickshire won by 4 wickets

Total runs scored at end of each over:

First Innings	1	2	3	4	5	6	7	8	9	10	11	12	13	14	15	16	17	18	19	20
	21	22	23	24	25	26	27	28	29	30	31	32	33	34	35	36	37	38	39	40
	41	42	43	44	45	46	47	48	49	50	51	52	53	54	55	56	57	58	59	60

Second Innings	1	2	3	4	5	6	7	8	9	10	11	12	13	14	15	16	17	18	19	20
	21	22	23	24	25	26	27	28	29	30	31	32	33	34	35	36	37	38	39	40
	41	42	43	44	45	46	47	48	49	50	51	52	53	54	55	56	57	58	59	60

Today's Adjudicator is Tom Graveney O.B.E. (Gloucestershire, Worcestershire and England)

'Man of the Match' Award

In each match in the National Westminster Bank Trophy a 'Man of the Match' was given a medal, a tie and a cheque. In the first round the cheque was for £100. In the second round £125, Quarter-Finals £200, the Semi-Finals £275 and £550 in the Final. The selection was made by a team of Test cricketers, one at each game.

The panel was as follows: David Allen (Gloucestershire), Trevor Bailey (Essex), Alec Bedser (Surrey), Freddie Brown (Northamptonshire), Basil D'Oliveira (Worcestershire), Godfrey Evans (Kent), Farokh Engineer (Lancashire), Don Kenyon (Worcestershire), Roy Marshall (Hampshire), Colin Milburn (Northamptonshire), Arthur Milton (Gloucestershire), Chris Old (Yorkshire/Warwickshire), Jim Parks (Sussex), Geoff Pullar (Lancashire), Phil Sharpe (Yorkshire), Reg Simpson (Nottinghamshire), Brian Statham (Lancashire), Roy Tattersal (Lancashire), Fred Titmus (Middlesex), Cyril Washbrook (Lancashire).

The Warwickshire players run to congratulate Neil Smith after he has bowled Haynes. Smith was to play a significant role in Warwickshire's victory. (Adrian Murrell/Allsport)

RIGHT: *Mike Roseberry tries to push the score along for Middlesex. (Adrian Murrell/Allsport)*

The real impetus to the Middlesex innings came from the veterans Downton and Emburey, who shared an unbeaten sixth-wicket partnership of 62 off as many balls. Their running between the wickets and their reliance on placing the ball as much as hitting hard was an example to younger, less experienced players.

While Middlesex's total of 210 was by no means a formidable one, it provided a difficult enough target for Warwickshire on a slowish wicket. There was no hurry at the beginning of the Warwickshire innings, and it was not until the ninth over that Moles struck a boundary, pulling Fraser emphatically through mid-wicket. The bowler had his revenge immediately, yorking Moles next ball. Kallicharran seemed ill at ease from the start, but he remained until the 15th over when, in frustration, he flicked at Fraser and was caught behind for nought.

Humpage and Lloyd tried to raise the tempo, but tea arrived with Warwickshire on 47 for 2 from 25 overs. Lloyd was just finding his rhythm and helped to take 11 runs in one over from Ellcock, a surprisingly expensive weakness in the Middlesex attack, when he was bowled by Emburey.

Paul Smith was promoted in order to give momentum to the Warwickshire innings, and he did his job admirably. He hit the suffering Ellcock for three fours in four balls, and his 24 was made off 25 balls. He became over-ambitious, and wastefully chopped on to the seemingly innocuous Carr, pressed into service because of Ellcock's vagaries.

The splendidly controlled and disciplined Cowans had Humpage caught by Gatting at mid-off in the 42nd over, by which time Warwickshire needed 89 to win. This brought Reeve and Asif Din together. Reeve's batting form throughout the season, which had begun late for him because of injury, was the best of his career, and he was full of confidence. Asif Din rarely suggested confidence at the outset, but he adopted the more orthodox style while Reeve worked busily for runs. Gradually they increased the tempo, moving certainly towards their target. By the 52nd over they had begun to plunder. Ramprakash and Cowans tripped each other up on the boundary in front of the Warner Stand and the ball went for four. Suddenly Warwickshire were winning. In the 57th over, with the score on 191, Asif Din sent Reeve back, but the non-striker had advanced too far, and Haynes ran him out. Reeve left cursing himself, believing that he had thrown away the game he had come so close to winning.

Delight in the Warwickshire dressing-room. (Adrian Murrell/Allsport)

Gloucestershire CCC
First-Class Matches, 1989

BATTING	v. Cambridge University (Cambridge) 19–21 April	v. Northamptonshire (Bristol) 27 April–1 May	v. Glamorgan (Cardiff) 4–3 May	v. Essex (Bristol) 20–3 May	v. Worcestershire (Bristol) 27–30 May	v. Northamptonshire (Northampton) 7–9 June	v. Leicestershire (Leicester) 10–13 June	v. Yorkshire (Harrogate) 17–20 June	v. Somerset (Bath) 21–3 June	v. Surrey (The Oval) 24–7 June	v. Nottinghamshire (Gloucester) 1–4 July	v. Sussex (Gloucester) 5–7 July	v. Kent (Maidstone) 8–11 July	v. Glamorgan (Bristol) 19–21 July
A.W. Stovold	27 —	16 36	0 24	5 15	5 23	16 7				0 10				
A.J. Wright	55 —	10 130	4 100	8 4	46 0	0 21	32 2	4 52	68 12*	4 55	4 4	80 —	118 7	85 —
P.W. Romaines	64 —	13 0	22 77	20 10	2 10	2 0								
C.W.J. Athey	14 —	2 63	30 93*	3 —	5 10	5 5	17 —	81 0	108 13*	11 37	8 52	50 —	— 39	6 —
P. Bainbridge	97 —	59 0	56 7	3 2	20 12	5 5	33 —		6 18	15 29	35 8	69 —		98 —
K.M. Curran	0 —	65 1	93 27	11 5	6 116*	46 33	43 —	10 31	101* 7	19 4	17 34	30 —	— 47	0 —
J.W. Lloyds	9 —	61 14	27 24*		31 19	0 37	43 52*	42 5	30 1	23 7	12 1	59 —	9* 2	44 —
R.C. Russell	59* —	0 0	26 —	15 14	0 0				12 0		10 24*			41* —
D.A. Graveney	12* —	9 0	3* —	0 11	8 15	0 16			6 1*					
D.V. Lawrence	— —	4* 1*	8 —	4 11*	1* 12	13 6*	20 —			0 20				
K.B.S. Jarvis	— —						10 —	4* —		0 0*		0 0		
V.S. Greene		13 4	3 —									5 0		0 —
M.W. Pooley			1 3									2* —		
C.A. Walsh				0* 4	3 19	13* 6	30* —	38 26		4 0		21 —	— 47	
M.W. Alleyne						21 9	26 —	20 18*	58* —	12 0	4 5	27 —	60* —	88 —
G.A. Tedstone						5 30	30 —			6* 50		9 —		2
I.P. Butcher							7 21*		49 3	2 —	13 68	26 —	105* 0*	10 —
M.J.C. Ball										0* 0				2 —
G.D. Hodgson														
Byes		13	1 10		2		1		6	4	4 11	2	10	2
Leg-byes	4	7 13	5 13	5 3	3 7	7 13	9 2	6 3	19 3	5	2 9	12	8 3	7
Wides			1 1		1 6					1	1	1	5	
No-balls	4	6 16	3 5	5 8	1 7	6 2	5 1	1	11	2 3	1	3	4	2
Total	345	265 291	282 381	80 90	148 257	118 186	316 78	279 163	402 36	113 289	101 147	399	251 207	383
Wickets	7	10 10	10 5	10 9†	10 10	10 10	10 1	10 8	4 2	10 10	10 10	9	1 6	9
Result	D	L	D	L	L	L	W	D	W	L	L	D	W	W
Points	—	4	4	4	4	4	24	7	22	4	4	7	19	23

Fielding Figures

38 – R.C. Russell (ct 35/st 3)	21 – A.J. Wright
32 – C.W.J. Athey	19 – J.W. Lloyds
30 – M.W. Alleyne	9 – D.A. Graveney
27 – G.A. Tedstone (ct 24/st 3)	8 – K.M. Curran
	7 – D.V. Lawrence
	5 – A.W. Stovold and M.J.C. Ball
	4 – P. Bainbridge and I.P. Butcher

Neil Smith, fresh from a maiden first-class century the previous day, joined Asif Din. He began circumspectly. Five runs came from the 58th over and five from the 59th, although how Emburey escaped being called for a wide, it was difficult to imagine. So the last over arrived with Warwickshire needing 10 to win, a task which surely was beyond them.

Simon Hughes bowled to Asif Din on whose shoulders Warwickshire hopes rested, but Asif Din pushed the first ball for a single to put the responsibility on young Neil Smith. Then came the improbable. To a ball of full length on or outside the off stump, Smith swung his bat in a wide arc, and the ball soared over long-off for six. Middlesex looked stunned. Gatting failed to react to the situation and re-set his field to prevent the single. Hughes reacted by

LEFT: *Man of the Match Reeve acknowledges the cheers of the crowd. (Ken Kelly)*

RIGHT: *The NatWest Trophy for Warwickshire. Andy Lloyd, Tim Munton and Andy Moles cannot hide their delight. In the background are Gladstone Small and Angus Fraser. (Ken Kelly)*

v. Australians (Bristol) 22-4 July		v. Hampshire (Portsmouth) 26-8 July		v. Warwickshire (Edgbaston) 29 July-1 August		v. Lancashire (Cheltenham) 5-8 August		v. Middlesex (Cheltenham) 9-11 August		v. Derbyshire (Cheltenham) 12-15 August		v. Sussex (Hove) 24-8 August		v. Worcestershire (Worcester) 29 Aug.-1 Sept.		v. Somerset (Bristol) 8-11 September		v. Hampshire (Bristol) 13-16 September		M	Inns	NOs	Runs	HS	Av
																				7	13	—	184	36	14.15
0	21	8	5	4	33	12	—	2	11	23	—	17	33	34	27	7	17	—	—	24	41	1	1159	130	28.97
																				6	11	—	220	77	20.00
34	0	67	14	21	49	13	—	2	14	10	—	36	11	1	11	22	1	—	—	23	36	2	948	108	27.88
		5	6*	101	—	128	—	24	3	24*	—	19*	3	4	45	16	0	—	—	22	33	3	955	128	31.83
46	4	8	2	4	36*	9	—	0	29	30	—	36	117*	40	1	0	128	—	—	24	39	4	1236	128	35.31
46	36	36	4	71	54	26	—	19	3	30	—	0	43	12	5	58	37	—	—	23	39	3	1032	71	28.66
16	9					4	—									15	27*	—	—	12	18	4	272	59*	19.42
1*	1*			15*	—	0	0					3	25	11*	0	27*	—	—	—	15	22	8	164	27*	11.71
								—	—			6	14	4	4	45	—	—	—	13	17	5	173	45	14.41
0	0	32	0	0	—	14	—	4*	1											13	14	3	65	32	5.90
4	1																			5	8	—	30	13	3.75
																				3	3	1	6	3	3.00
		27	6	16	—	4	—	3	2			6	29	30	6*	10	10*	—	—	18	25	5	360	47	18.00
22	0	12	3	17	—	111	—	29	9	2*	—	0	41	55	2	14	56	—	—	19	28	4	721	111	30.04
		11	2	1	—			12	10*	19	—	0	12	4	3					12	17	2	206	50	13.73
0	8	0	3	5	2	40	—	21	19	21	—	5	9							14	23	3	437	105*	21.85
4	4	17*	0	4*	—															8	8	3	31	17*	6.20
														4	16	15	25	—	—	3	4	—	60	25	15.00
12		4		9	4	1		1		1				8		9									
7		9	3	18	9	5		10		5		1	11	5	3	12	8								
		2		1						1				1	7	5	1								
8	8	2		7	1	12		6	6	9		3		2	1	4									
200	92	240	48	279	188	394		122	118	175		133	363	206	124	259	310								
10	10	10	10	10	4	10		10	10	6		10	10	10	10	10	7								
L		L		L		W		L		D		L		L		W		D							
—		3		6		24		4		2		3		6		23		3							

3 – K.B.S. Jarvis

2 – P.W. Romaines, C.A. Walsh and subs

1 – V.S. Greene

†C.W.J. Athey absent hurt

A memorable weekend for Neil Smith. On the Friday he hit 161 against Yorkshire, and on the Saturday he took the vital wicket of Desmond Haynes and hit a last-over six to help Warwickshire to win the NatWest Trophy. He shows the bat with which he hit the six to his father, M.J.K. Smith, the former Warwickshire and England captain. (Ken Kelly)

Gloucestershire CCC
First-Class Matches, 1989

BOWLING	D.V. Lawrence	K.M. Curran	K.B.S. Jarvis	D.A. Graveney	P. Bainbridge	J.W. Lloyds	V.S. Greene	C.A. Walsh	M.W. Pooley
v. Cambridge University (Cambridge) 19–21 April	10–2–45–1	6–3–7–0	13–6–22–3	10–4–23–0	8–2–39–1	5–1–45–1			
v. Northamptonshire (Bristol) 27 April–1 May	34–7–101–3 3.5–0–11–0	27–7–71–0		47.1–18–78–3	25–6–72–0	27–7–51–3	37–9–93–1 3–0–37–0		
v. Glamorgan (Cardiff) 4–8 May	22–6–41–1	18–5–49–0		50–13–128–6	10–1–38–0	35–10–91–1	20–5–68–2		
v. Essex (Bristol) 20–3 May	17–4–61–4 12.1–3–23–3	9–2–15–0 10–4–23–2		1–0–1–0	9–1–17–3 11–4–23–3			17.1–2–57–3 13–2–31–2	3–0–24–0
v. Worcestershire (Bristol) 27–30 May	19–5–62–4 11–0–58–1	18.5–4–53–6 20–2–75–1		8–2–21–0 35–12–66–3	6–2–16–0 3–0–10–0	3–0–10–0		19–2–42–0 20–6–47–1	
v. Northamptonshire (Northampton) 7–9 June	14–3–46–1 7–0–35–0	26–6–69–7		5–3–17–0	12–1–39–0 6–3–11–1	5–3–8–0		27.1–4–57–2 7–1–14–0	
v. Leicestershire (Leicester) 10–13 June	10–1–32–1 16–8–26–1	13–4–35–3 19.1–3–78–4	11.4–1–39–2 15–2–57–1			1–0–6–0		23–9–37–4 30–6–63–4	
v. Yorkshire (Harrogate) 17–20 June			14–7–37–2 4–0–14–0	20–11–30–1 38–12–111–1	17–4–43–1	11–4–17–1 29–6–103–2		24.3–5–86–5 8–4–22–0	
v. Somerset (Bath) 21–3 June			16.3–6–27–2 7–2–18–0	3–2–1–0 47–13–96–2	5–3–9–0	1–0–5–0 45–6–134–7		16–4–19–7 28–6–88–1	
v. Surrey (The Oval) 24–7 June	14–0–61–1		16–1–53–0 16–5–54–2		14–1–39–4 5–1–12–0	2–1–6–0 2–0–14–0		23.2–2–83–5 12–4–20–0	
v. Nottinghamshire (Gloucester) 1–4 July		20–3–51–4	19–2–69–4		9–2–24–0			23.1–4–85–2	
v. Sussex (Gloucester) 5–7 July		16–3–38–0 5.3–3–13–0				1–0–1–1		17.2–4–44–5 6–3–6–0	15–3–46–
v. Kent (Maidstone) 8–11 July		11–3–33–0 7–0–37–2	12.1–2–39–0 14–3–37–2					15–4–38–0 14.3–3–59–1	14–2–32– 3–1–11–0
v. Glamorgan (Bristol) 19–21 July			10.2–3–15–5 15–6–29–0		6–0–18–0 7.2–1–13–1		16–4–36–4 26–8–101–6		
v. Australians (Bristol) 22–4 July			25–7–77–3	26–3–112–2			4.2–0–22–1 20–1–65–2		
v. Hampshire (Portsmouth) 26–8 July		6–2–19–0	27–7–105–2		14.5–0–59–2	6–0–24–1		31–4–91–2	
v. Warwickshire (Edgbaston) 29 July–1 August		13.3–2–45–2 18–0–60–3	12–3–42–0 10–2–43–1		15–3–41–3 7–2–16–0			18–3–50–1 21–2–73–1	
v. Lancashire (Cheltenham) 5–8 August		3–1–16–0 16–3–67–1	9–1–37–4 11–2–44–0	21–7–51–4	4–0–14–0	6–1–21–0		12–5–40–6 19–3–64–4	
v. Middlesex (Cheltenham) 9–11 August		16–4–36–1 3–1–6–0	18–2–51–3 3–0–19–0	14–1–44–2 25–5–63–2	10–1–25–1	25–7–60–3		20–5–50–3 14–3–44–2	
v. Derbyshire (Cheltenham) 12–15 August	21–3–68–3	14–1–64–0			17–5–49–0	11–2–30–0		25.3–6–62–4	
v. Sussex (Hove) 24–8 August	19.1–4–85–3 11.2–1–41–2	20–5–52–2 2–0–14–0		23–7–48–2 13–4–33–0	15–4–29–1 3–1–15–0	2–1–1–0		26–6–74–2 20–3–59–3	
v. Worcestershire (Worcester) 29 Aug.–1 Sept.	12.4–1–47–1 19–2–84–3	17–4–45–3 12–1–27–2		33–15–65–3 1–1–0–0	15–8–25–1 13–2–43–2			21–4–60–2 21.4–4–45–2	
v. Somerset (Bristol) 8–11 September	11–0–48–0 14–0–81–1	14–3–37–2 17–5–59–1		23.3–10–37–4 23.4–14–25–2	3–1–7–0 9–4–16–1	6–4–8–0		18–7–33–4 20–6–68–4	
v. Hampshire (Bristol) 13–16 September	15–4–48–1	17–1–64–1		21–8–45–2		18–2–69–1		18.4–5–49–1	
	313.1–54– 1104–34 av. 32.47	415–85– 1258–47 av. 26.76	298.4–70– 928–36 av. 25.77	488.2–165– 1095–39 av. 28.07	279.1–63– 762–25 av. 30.48	245.2–55– 726–22 av. 33.00	145.1–31– 485–17 av. 28.52	626.5–137– 1675–81 av. 20.67	35–6– 113–0 —

a G.D. Mendis retired hurt   b V.J. Marks retired hurt

M.W. Alleyne	C.W.J. Athey	A.J. Wright	I.P. Butcher	M.J.C. Ball		Byes	Leg-byes	Wides	No-balls	Total	Wkts
							6		3	187	6
						3	36	1	20	505	10
						4	1			53	0
						1	19	1	13	435	10
							3		7	178	10
						4	4		12	108	10
						2	5	1	14	201	10
						5	12		10	283	6
						2	6	1		236	10
						1		1		69	1
2–1–5–0							2	1	1	145	10
						1	2		8	238	10
4–3–1–0	2–2–0–0						6		3	220	10
	8.4–4–19–1	4–0–16–1	3–0–15–0			9	3		3	312	6
	2–0–9–1						3	1	2	73	10
	1–0–5–0					10	13		6	364	10
2–0–20–0						10	3		1	275	10
4.5–0–20–0			1–1–0–0			5	3	1	1	128	2
				2–1–1–0			22	2	3	252	10
				29–2–84–4		3	16		2	232	10
							2		1	21	0
	7–3–11–0			13–2–45–1		4	7	1	1	209	1
				12–1–53–4		1	4		1	202	10
	2–0–3–0			5–2–11–1			6		3	89	10
1–1–0–0		2–2–0–0		13–5–23–2		2	3		2	171	10
13–2–60–1	9–3–27–0			15–1–64–1		2	9	3	8	438	10
8–0–40–1				23–6–60–1		2	6	1	4	406	9
				11–4–23–2		8	9		4	218	8
				12–0–49–1		2	7	4	8	250	7
									1	93	10
	4–1–10–0						7	4	7	278	9a
						4	12		7	222	10
						10	4	1	1	206	7
11–0–41–2	1–0–10–0			20–2–91–1		6	27	5	6	448	9
	2–0–18–0					5	11	1	6	323	10
							13		5	175	7
							6		5	248	10
						9	5		7	213	10
							3	1	4	165	10
							6		2	263	9b
							12		10	287	7
45.5–7– 187–4 av. 46.75	38.4–13– 112–2 av. 56.00	6–2– 16–1 av. 16.00	4–1– 15–0 —	155–26– 504–18 av. 28.00							

Hampshire CCC
First-Class Matches, 1989

BATTING	v. Somerset (Southampton) 20–4 April		v. Surrey (The Oval) 27 April–1 May		v. Kent (Southampton) 4–8 May		v. Middlesex (Lord's) 17–19 May		v. Nottinghamshire (Trent Bridge) 20–2 May		v. Leicestershire (Bournemouth) 27–30 May		v. Kent (Tunbridge Wells) 3–6 June		v. Surrey (Basingstoke) 7–9 June		v. Oxford University (Oxford) 10–13 June		v. Essex (Ilford) 21–3 June		v. Sussex (Southampton) 24–7 June		v. Yorkshire (Southampton) 1–4 July		v. Northamptonshire (Northampton) 8–11 July		v. Australians (Southampton) 19–21 July	
V.P. Terry	0	—	63	88	3	96	30	11	12	82*	5	68	9	—	1	18			41	20	91	39	35	0	1	5	19	28*
C.L. Smith	45	—	14	94*			2	30	22	13	7	38	30	—	25	29	143*	—	25	0	83	35	14	7	56	13*	32	49*
M.C.J. Nicholas	0	—	2	14*	0	5	71	0	32	43	12	—			51	76*	37	—	9	4	40	41*	7	25	140	—	102*	—
R.A. Smith	127	—	16	—	182	29	31	46	148	20			8	—													9	—
R.J. Scott	0	—	30	—	19	21							77	32*			5	—	18	6	0	27						
K.D. James	2	—	10	—					0	36	68	40	19	—			83*	30*	3	21	48	20	45	14	4	0	6	35*
R.J. Parks	76*	—	2	—	12	—	18	3*			26	—			2	—			9	26	2*	—	44	12*	0*	—	0	—
S.T. Jefferies	42	—	12	—	41	8*	33	7	5*	0																	28*	—
R.J. Maru	1	—	11*	—	6*	0	29	0			6	—			4	—	—	27*	7	0*	8	—			9	12		
S.J.W. Andrew	6	—	14	—	0	—																						
P.J. Bakker	0	—	1	—			5	—	20	7	4*	—			1	—			0*	0			0*	22				
D.R. Turner					12	65*	13	53	24	0	15	1*			5	—	56*	—	45	6			8	38*	2	1	20	—
T.M. Tremlett					12	40*	5	5	4*	10*	2	—			32*	—												
K.J. Shine							26*	3																				
M.D. Marshall											25	—			61	—			0	6	0	—			2	0	10*	—
T.C. Middleton																	20	55*										
A.N. Aymes																	24*	—										
S.D. Udal																			—	—								
C.A. Connor																							4*	—	11	19		
N.G. Cowley																			26	42								
J.R. Wood																					58	—	1	45	96	—	65	—
I.J. Turner																												
Byes	4			4		5	2			2		1			13			1	4	8					5		7	4
Leg-byes	6		7	7	8	6	7	6	11	7	9	3	7		13	2	8	3	14	2	14	3	3	6	7	4	6	
Wides			2						4	1	11				4	1			1				3		2			
No-balls	9		14	8	15	9	1		3	2	8	12	12				2		15	4	3	1	9	4	23		2	
Total	318		198	215	358	280	217	176	300	172	288	239	213		251	157	254	113	244	165	356	171	144	153	366	57	275	81
Wickets	10		10	1	10	5	10	10	6	6	10	4	10		4	2	4	2	10	10	8	3	10	10	6	1	6	0
Result	D		D		W		L		D		W		D		W		W		L		D		L		W		D	
Points	4		5		22		5		5		23		3		23				6		8		4		24		—	

Fielding Figures

71 – R.J. Parks (ct 67/st 4)
40 – V.P. Terry
21 – M.C.J. Nicholas and R.J. Maru

18 – C.L. Smith
11 – R.A. Smith
10 – A.N. Aymes

8 – T.C. Middleton
7 – S.T. Jefferies
6 – R.J. Scott, K.D. James and J.R. Wood

---

bowling a massive leg-side wide. Then Smith pushed the ball back past him for two and Warwickshire had won a memorable victory with two balls to spare.

It was not a great encounter, for the best cricket was crammed into the last 10 overs, and the match had produced no innings of significance, but it was a very thrilling one. Dermot Reeve deservedly won the individual award for his economic bowling and his contribution to the partnership of 69 off 94 balls with Asif Din, but it is also a match, and 48 hours, that Neil Smith will remember for a long time.

Seeboard Trophy

at Hove

3 September

Sussex 252 for 6 (I.J. Gould 63 not out, P.W.G. Parker 52)
Hampshire 248 for 7 (K.D. James 100, J.R. Wood 53)

Sussex won by 4 runs

4 September

Kent 253 for 5 (N.R. Taylor 99 not out, R.F. Pienaar 58)

Surrey 238 for 9

Kent won by 15 runs

Final

5 September

Kent 298 for 7 (S.G. Hinks 108, N.R. Taylor 88)
Sussex 320 for 5 (N.J. Lenham 128, C.M. Wells 67)

Sussex won by 5 wickets

The first Seeboard Trophy proved to be an immense success, providing some scintillating and entertaining cricket and much revenue. A large crowd saw the inaugural match on the Sunday, when Ian Gould hit 63 off 47 deliveries, carving boundaries in all directions. Hampshire began badly, losing Terry, Nicholas, Robin Smith and Scott with only 43 scored. James and Wood added 114, and Man-of-the-Match Kevan James hit 100 off 108 balls. Hampshire needed nine runs off the last over, but Hansford bowled an over of full length deliveries, and Sussex won by four runs.

Some ferocious hitting by Kent proved too much for Surrey in the other semi-final, but the final was a magnifi-

v. Lancashire (Portsmouth) 22–5 July		v. Gloucestershire (Portsmouth) 26–8 July		v. Glamorgan (Cardiff) 29 July–1 August		v. Derbyshire (Derby) 5–8 August		v. Warwickshire (Bournemouth) 9–11 August		v. Worcestershire (Bournemouth) 12–15 August		v. Somerset (Taunton) 19–22 August		v. Sussex (Hove) 29 Aug.–1 Sept.		v. Glamorgan (Southampton) 8–11 September		v. Gloucestershire (Bristol) 13–16 September		M	Inns	NOs	Runs	HS	Av
25	95	1	—	20	4	180	—	13	7	8	8	4	2	24	61	11	0	17	—	22	41	2	1245	180	31.92
66	97	107	—	26	4	52	—	4	12	38	18									19	33	4	1230	143*	42.41
22	9	101	—	0	10	121	—	28	0	17	12	121*	0	39	19	0	15	0	—	24	40	5	1269	140	36.25
119*	10					40	—					4	17			47	47	68	—	12	18	1	968	182	56.94
										25	0	1	1	9	27	15	52	34	—	12	20	1	399	77	21.00
47	0	56	—	162	35	1	—	19	12	0	0	56	19	8	1	13	4	60	—	22	37	3	982	162	28.88
—	8*	18*	—	10*	2	4*	—	—	52*	9	1*	26	2	1	30	14	0*	18	—	23	29	12	427	76*	25.11
				7*	7*									15	40*					8	13	6	245	42	35.00
—	1*	3	—	—	0*	—	—	—	7	5	23	0	6	24*	3			0*	—	23	25	8	192	29	11.29
												0	1							6	5	—	21	14	4.20
—	—	—	—	—	—	—	—	—	1	0	0			11	10	10	4	—	—	21	18	3	96	22	6.40
																				10	17	4	364	65*	28.00
																				6	8	4	110	40*	27.50
																				2	2	1	29	26*	29.00
41*	48	21	—			27*	—	8*	46	11	23	2	0			13	0	68*	—	15	21	5	412	68*	25.75
		33	—	69	—			0	14					22	2	33	26	0	—	7	11	1	274	69	27.40
																				1	1	1	24	24*	—
																				1					—
—	—	17	—	—	1	—	—	—	0	5*	0	13	17	14	4	24	0	—	—	15	14	2	129	24	10.75
																				1	2	—	68	42	34.00
—	11	36	—	42	16	21	—	25*	11	13	2	20	55*	36	35					12	18	2	588	96	36.75
																9*	0			1	2	1	9	9*	9.00
4	4	2		12		7				1		3		4	4			1							
10	4	6		16	3	7	7	3	9	2	7	3	12	13	5	9		12							
1				1				2		1		3		1		2		1							
1		4		6	4	10		2	4	1		7	2	13	3	1		10							
336	287	406		370	86	472		103	176	137	97	257	138	233	241	201	149	287							
4	7	9		6	7	6		5	10	10	10	10	10	10	10	10	10	7							
W		W		D		D		L		L		L		L		L		D							
21		24		8		7		4		3		5		5		4		3							

4 – S.J.W. Andrew
3 – P.J. Bakker
2 – D.R. Turner and M.D. Marshall

cent game, 600 runs being scored off 100 overs.

Hinks hit 108 at a run a ball, but Lenham's well-paced 128 and three wickets earned him the individual award and set up Sussex's last-ball victory.

Four Counties Trophy

at Scarborough

3 September

Leicestershire 205 for 7 (T.J. Boon 76, J.J. Whitaker 52)
Yorkshire 207 for 7 (P.E. Robinson 57)

Yorkshire won by 3 wickets

4 September

Worcestershire 221 for 4 (T.S. Curtis 95, M.J. Weston 64)
Essex 222 for 2 (B.R. Hardie 86, G.A. Gooch 76)

Essex won by 8 wickets

Final

5 September

Yorkshire 261 for 6 (M.D. Moxon 108, D.L. Bairstow 57)

Essex 260

Yorkshire won by 1 run

The Scarborough Festival gave immense pleasure to the home supporters when Yorkshire won the Four Counties Trophy, sponsored by Ward. They narrowly beat Leicestershire in the opening match thanks to some good hitting by Chris Pickles. In the other semi-final Weston and Curtis began Worcestershire's innings with a partnership of 148 in 34 overs, but the later batsmen failed to capitalize on this. Gooch, badly missed on 48, hit 76 off 92 balls, and he and Hardie put on 169 in 34 overs to set Essex on course for an easy victory, which came with 3.1 of their 50 overs to spare.

Moxon's hundred put Yorkshire in a strong position in the final, and Essex looked lost at 135 for 5, but Garnham and Hussain added 52 in nine overs. The last over arrived with Essex needing 13 to win. Foster hit Pickles' fourth ball for six, but he was out next ball. Miller needed four off the last ball, but he was run out, to leave Yorkshire the winners.

Hampshire CCC
First-Class Matches, 1989

BOWLING	S.J.W. Andrew	S.T. Jefferies	P.J. Bakker	K.D. James	R.J. Maru	M.C.J. Nicholas	R.A. Smith	T.M. Tremlett	K.J. Shine
v. Somerset (Southampton) 20–5 April	28–6–73–0 6–0–28–0	34–6–92–2 9.1–1–20–1	33–8–81–1 3–0–17–0	25–5–58–0	24–6–51–1 6–1–6–0	15–2–37–6			
v. Surrey (The Oval) 27 April–1 May	10–1–34–1 10.3–1–29–1	13–4–24–0 4–0–18–1	26–3–81–6 11–3–26–1	13–0–55–1 6–0–20–0	7–3–8–1 11–2–18–3	4.4–0–12–1			
v. Kent (Southampton) 4–8 May	32–7–76–1 12–2–25–0	18–1–81–0 4–0–30–0	23–7–75–2 16–6–40–2		29.3–11–64–4 23.4–8–41–8	2–0–5–0	1–1–0–0 1–1–0–0	25–7–60–3	
v. Middlesex (Lord's) 17–19 May		8–0–52–0 6–2–9–0	20.1–3–52–5 16–3–52–3		20–10–27–1 2–0–9–0	2–0–13–0		34–16–51–3 16–7–22–1	20–3–75–1 6–3–6–1
v. Nottinghamshire (Trent Bridge) 20–2 May		21–4–65–0 8–1–26–0	18–3–61–1 13–6–25–2	9–1–40–0 6–2–11–0	31–10–76–0 19–6–46–1	15–2–37–3 6–1–16–1	6–0–31–0	17–2–39–2 3–0–12–0	
v. Leicestershire (Bournemouth) 27–30 May			24–4–63–3 8–1–27–2	16–5–42–0 8–1–24–4	20–4–73–2 8–3–25–0	3–2–3–0		19–5–67–4 8–4–5–0	
v. Kent (Tunbridge Wells) 3–6 June			17–1–48–0	18–1–44–1	13–3–51–0	2–0–17–0		16–4–45–0	
v. Surrey (Basingstoke) 7–9 June			26–10–55–4 15–2–48–5	17–4–31–0 6–3–18–0	18–3–63–0	8–2–19–0		21–4–51–3 1–0–4–0	
v. Oxford University (Oxford) 10–13 June	10–3–21–2 16–5–29–2			13.4–4–32–1 17–7–41–5	7–3–9–0 6.2–2–9–1				6.2–2–7–1
v. Essex (Ilford) 21–3 June			21–4–51–2 13–2–45–2	11–4–28–2 19–5–51–2	26–5–73–3 15–2–41–1	1–0–1–0			
v. Sussex (Southampton) 24–7 June			25–8–74–3 12–5–15–1	15–2–44–2 3–1–9–0	9–2–21–0 13.3–6–26–3	4–1–7–0			
v. Yorkshire (Southampton) 1–4 July			11.1–3–39–3 13–4–49–2	7–0–23–0 10–4–19–3	4–0–16–0				
v. Northamptonshire (Northampton) 8–11 July			13–2–34–1 20.1–5–66–4	10–4–28–1 10–1–47–0	9–5–10–1 13–2–35–0	2–0–7–0 4–1–6–1			
v. Australians (Southampton) 19–21 July	14.5–3–60–2 10–0–68–1	15–2–59–1 11–1–26–1		14–4–39–1 9–0–32–1	21–2–85–0 23–10–44–5	9–0–39–1			
v. Lancashire (Portsmouth) 22–5 July			14–5–50–0 13–7–14–1	18–3–85–1	25–1–100–0 8–1–23–2	15–0–81–1	5–1–36–0		
v. Gloucestershire (Portsmouth) 26–8 July			18–5–37–2 1–1–0–0	9–2–30–1	15–6–44–1				
v. Glamorgan (Cardiff) 29 July–1 August		14.3–3–61–4 15–3–50–1	22–3–68–2 21–6–58–1	5–0–13–0 6–1–15–2	7–3–17–0 22.3–7–45–1	4–1–5–0			
v. Derbyshire (Derby) 5–8 August			19–5–53–4 25–7–60–1	5–1–12–0 18–6–35–1	8–2–12–0 24–7–58–1	6–1–19–0			
v. Warwickshire (Bournemouth) 9–11 August			13–4–32–2	17–2–61–2 11–5–20–0	22.3–7–49–2 1–0–2–0	5–0–11–1 8–3–17–0			
v. Worcestershire (Bournemouth) 12–15 August			29–7–73–1	15–3–38–2	32–11–63–1	1–0–7–0			
v. Somerset (Taunton) 19–22 August	19.3–1–70–3 2–0–10–0			13–5–44–2 1.5–0–16–0	19–3–67–1	1–0–1–0			
v. Sussex (Hove) 29 August–1 September		16–2–64–1 3–0–25–0	23.1–2–83–5 4–0–20–1	11–0–56–0	23–5–84–0	5–0–24–0			
v. Glamorgan (Southampton) 8–11 September			20–9–33–1 10–2–27–1	14–5–27–0 9–0–34–2			2–0–5–0		
v. Gloucestershire (Bristol) 13–16 September									
	170.5–29– 523–13 av. 40.23	199.4–30– 702–12 av. 58.50	629.4–156– 1732–77 av. 22.49	415.3–91– 1222–37 av. 33.02	586–162– 1491–44 av. 33.88	122.4–16– 384–15 av. 25.60	15–3– 72–0 —	160–49– 356–16 av. 22.25	32.2–8– 88–3 av. 29.33

a D.R. Turner 4.2–1–11–0   b T.C. Middleton 3–0–26–1   c R.J. Scott 2–0–17–0

C.L. Smith	*I.J. Turner*	*M.D. Marshall*	*C.A. Connor*	*S.D. Udal*	*N.G. Cowley*	*J.R. Wood*	*Byes*	*Leg-byes*	*Wides*	*No-balls*	*Total*	*Wkts*
								21	3	8	413	10
										1	71	1
							2	3	2	7	219	10
							4	13		6	128	6
								8		7	369	10
									1	7	136	10
							5	15	2	1	290	10
							1	7	2	1	106	6
								13	4	6	331	6
8–1–31–0								5	1		214	4a
		16.3–7–38–1					3	4		5	293	10
		11.1–4–33–4						1		1	115	10
		21–3–64–2					2	5		6	276	3
		20–4–67–2					1	4	1	3	291	10
		13.2–1–39–5					4	3			116	10
			21–14–19–6	3–1–2–0				3		2	93	10
			19–5–42–2	8–5–19–0			4	3	1		147	10
		21–8–49–1			13–0–52–1		8	15		2	277	10
1–1–0–0		15–3–39–3			14–1–50–1			8		1	234	9
		15–3–53–2	24–5–65–2			1.4–0–5–1	8	10		2	287	10
		6–1–23–0	14–2–40–1					3		2	116	5
		9–2–16–2	12–3–20–5					9			107	10
		17–1–45–1	16–3–46–1				6	10		4	191	7
		14.2–6–20–4	20–5–59–3				5	3	2	6	166	10
		25–11–36–5	17–3–40–0			2–0–9–0	6	8		3	253	10
			15–2–51–0				1	9		6	343	6
2–0–3–0			14.1–1–68–2					5		3	246	10
1–0–1–0		18–1–63–2	19–4–80–0					15	2	2	475	4
		9–3–18–1	8–1–40–2			0.5–0–7–0	4	5		3	147	6
		28–7–64–3	22–5–52–3				4	9	2	2	240	10
		12–3–14–3	10.5–3–31–7					3			48	10
			19–10–40–4				4	5	1	10	208	10
1–1–0–0			20–4–74–5				5	2	3	6	254	10
		10–1–41–1	20.1–3–50–5					10	1	9	178	10
11–8–10–0		30–9–69–6	15–1–57–0					18	1	5	326	9
		17–8–26–2	19–4–38–1					12		1	229	10
9–3–23–1		3–3–0–0	2–0–10–0				4	8		1	110	2b
2–0–4–1		29–7–67–2	25.1–4–64–2				1	8	2	4	325	10
		18–5–60–2	18–4–53–0					8	1	7	303	8
		9–3–33–2	9–0–33–0					1	1	2	93	2
			26–2–90–4				1	11	4	7	430	10c
								1		7	45	1
	18–8–28–1	25.2–6–68–5	27–6–68–3				2	7		3	247	10d
	17–13–20–3	15.5–5–22–3	11–4–25–1				1	4		4	133	10
												Ab.
35–14– 72–2 *av.* 36.00	35–21– 48–4 *av.* 12.00	428.3–115– 1067–64 *av.* 16.67	443.2–98– 1255–59 *av.* 21.27	11–6– 21–0 —	27–1– 102–2 *av.* 51.00	4.3–0– 21–1 *av.* 21.00						

d R.J. Scott 5–1–9–0

Kent CCC
First-Class Matches, 1989

BATTING	v. Essex (Canterbury) 20–4 April	v. Sussex (Hove) 27 April–1 May	v. Hampshire (Southampton) 4–8 May	v. Cambridge University (Cambridge) 17–19 May	v. Derbyshire (Dartford) 20–2 May	v. Leicestershire (Leicester) 24–6 May	v. Hampshire (Tunbridge Wells) 3–6 June	v. Sussex (Tunbridge Wells) 7–9 June	v. Nottinghamshire (Trent Bridge) 10–13 June	v. Somerset (Bath) 17–20 June	v. Lancashire (Old Trafford) 24–7 June	v. Northamptonshire (Maidstone) 5–7 July	v. Gloucestershire (Maidstone) 8–11 July	v. Essex (Southend) 19–21 July
S.G. Hinks	12 6	30 56	9 14	86 —	1* —				37 70		43 52*	4 7	35 0	
M.R. Benson	3 8	45 74*	53 4		3 16	75 37*	114 —	57 45*	17 1	157 50*			102* 8	0 21
N.R. Taylor	47 63	1 23	78 43		74 23	4 18*	104* —	48 32*	2 78		13 10	10 98	47 0	3 0
C.S. Cowdrey	1 1	40 —	9 38	59 5*	2 0	9 —			46 —	101* 46	65 —	13 —	9 —	8 27
D.J.M. Kelleher	0 4*			8 16	0 53*				4 —		38 —			
G.R. Cowdrey	1 3	5 —	2 4	78 13*		108* —	17* —	4 —				9 —	0	
T.R. Ward	12 25	64 87*	91 4	30 54	27 57	11 69	28 —	4 2	35 18	104 —	24 10*	7 —	— 1	16 91
S.A. Marsh	7 6	0 —	0 13*	8 —	52 23	12 —		33 —	26 7*	1 —	59 —	18* 0*	90* 4	27 4
R.M. Ellison	0 11		10 0	7 —		24 —		5 —	5 —		0 —	0 —	30	39* 12
C. Penn	16 2*	21 —	24 0		29 60	0 —		15 —			0* —	1 —	9	
H.L. Alleyne	10* —	2 —												2 28
R.P. Davis		12* —	67 8	14 —	1* 14	6 —		6* —			34 —	18 —	7	1 2
A.P. Igglesden		0 —	11* 0		6 17	5 —		0 —			0* —	4 —	0	0 10*
R.F. Pienaar				0 75		35 —	0 —	11 —		119 40	87 0	23 0	30 77*	47* 8
M.V. Fleming				2 —						6 36*	35 —			
M.D. Harman				0* —										
V.J. Wells				2 1							22 12*			
M.A. Ealham											45 —			
J.I. Longley														9 17
M.C. Dobson														0 8
P. Farbrace														
M. Patel														
Byes		1		3 5	1 7	2	2	3	2	7	2		4 1	5
Leg-byes	4	3 6	8		2 7	2 13	9 6	5	7 2	5 11	13 4	18 3	2 2	5 3
Wides		2	1	6 1	2	2 1		1 2		1		1	1	1
No-balls	6 2	10 6	7 7	1	8 8	7 3	6	2	3 2	14 2		12 14	1 1	1 1
Total	119 133	234 252	369 136	304 176	210 292	307 133	276	243 82	354 311	526 108	296 42	156 191	209 202	112 229
Wickets	10 8	10 2	10 10	10 3	9† 9	10 1	3	10 1	7 6	7 0	10 3	10 2	1 10	10 10
Result	D	D	L	W	L	D	D	L	W	D	D	D	L	L
Points	4	5	5	—	5	5	7	2	21	6	7	4	2	3

Fielding Figures

41 – S.A. Marsh (ct 40/st 1)
19 – C.S. Cowdrey
15 – R.P. Davis
13 – T.R. Ward
9 – N.R. Taylor

8 – S.G. Hinks and R.F. Pienaar
7 – P. Farbrace (ct 5/st 2)
4 – G.R. Cowdrey, A.P. Igglesden and R.M. Ellison

3 – C. Penn and D.J.M. Kelleher
2 – Subs
1 – M.R. Benson, V.J. Wells, M. Patel and M.V. Fleming

Refuge Assurance Cup

Semi-Finals

6 September

at Old Trafford

Lancashire 187 for 9 (N.H. Fairbrother 59, Wasim Akram 56, R.A. Pick 4 for 25)
Nottinghamshire 188 for 5

Nottinghamshire won by 5 wickets

at Worcester

Essex 211 for 7 (P.J. Prichard 82 not out)
Worcestershire 110

Essex won by 101 runs

Essex gained some consolation for the disappointment of the past few weeks when they trounced Worcestershire to enter the Refuge Assurance Cup final. Put in to bat, Essex lost Hardie, bowled by Weston, and Gooch, who ran himself out when he attempted a second leg-bye to McEwan. Waugh and Prichard steadied the innings after these early disasters, and Prichard played an excellent innings. He was aided over the closing overs by Derek Pringle, who hit a blistering 31. John Lever wrecked the Worcestershire innings when he sent back Weston and Hick in quick succession. Hick failed to score, and with the first four Worcestershire batsmen offering simple catches to fielders within the circle, the innings disintegrated. Gooch took 3 for 13, and all six Essex bowlers captured a wicket as their side swept into the final with ease.

Lancashire were also put in to bat, but they fared disastrously, with four wickets falling for 20. Fairbrother and Wasim Akram repaired the innings with a partnership of 110, but the later batsmen made little impact. Broad and Pollard gave Nottinghamshire an excellent start, putting on 84 in 20 overs. Both were dismissed, but Robinson maintained a sense of urgency before being leg before attempting a big hit. Randall was slow to settle, but once he found his touch the result was never in doubt. He was involved in a mix up with Stephenson, which cost the West Indian his wicket, but the last over arrived with Nottinghamshire needing only two for victory. An overthrow gave them the win with four balls to spare and symbolized Lancashire's rather shoddy fielding in the later stages of the match.

	v. Middlesex (Uxbridge) 22–5 July		v. Worcestershire (Worcester) 29 July–1 August		v. Warwickshire (Canterbury) 5–8 August		v. Surrey (Canterbury) 9–11 August		v. Yorkshire (Scarborough) 12–15 August		v. Australians (Canterbury) 16–18 August		v. Glamorgan (Canterbury) 19–22 August		v. Leicestershire (Folkestone) 24–8 August		v. Surrey (The Oval) 8–11 September		v. Middlesex (Canterbury) 13–16 September		M	Inns	NOs	Runs	HS	Av
	8	10	0	13	53	16	33	104*	13	69	85	16	5	13	9	23	16	6	7	67*	19	36	4	1028	104*	32.12
									14	8	3	106			42	31	149	56			15	29	5	1299	157	54.12
	10	99	45*	12	20	5	118	45	111	6			42	32	4	63*	10	0	5	49*	21	41	6	1495	118	42.71
	38	5	56	21	56	22	1	—	80	24			57	53	7	—	—	146*	69	—	23	33	3	1157	146*	38.56
					0	0	30	—	—	—	8	12*	25	—	0	—	—	—			11	14	3	194	53*	17.63
																					9	12	3	244	108*	27.11
	0	15	12	30	8	1	3	10*			32	36	36	78*	78	—	22*	4	21	—	23	40	5	1257	104	35.91
	16	20	5	53	53	6	31	—	10	19*			4	—			—	8	3	—	22	31	6	614	90*	24.56
	34	26*	30	36															0	—	12	16	2	264	39*	18.85
	42	11	0	7	13	—	—	—			0	—	24*	—			0*	—	43	—	19	21	4	317	60	18.64
	0*	0*	6	0																	5	8	3	48	28	9.60
	12	16	25	0	5*	4			—	—	0*	11	0*	—	0	—	—	—	9*	—	21	23	6	263	67	15.47
	0	4	1	5*	4	0*	32*	—					7*	—			—	—	20	—	19	21	8	115	32*	8.84
					33	53	51	16	38	125	0	7	132	35	72	134*	53*	0	29	—	17	29	4	1321	134*	52.84
					45	6	23	—	0*	15*	7	0									8	12	3	204	45	22.66
																					2	1	1	0	0*	—
											7	4*									2	4	1	37	22	12.33
											10	0									2	3	1	56	45	28.00
	1	1	4	0																	4	8	—	42	17	5.25
	28	13					0	—	0*	—	2	33	52	—	1	—					7	10	1	137	52	15.22
											35	1	8	—							2	3	—	44	35	14.66
																			3	—	1	1	—	3	3	3.00
	6	8	2	4	2	5	5	5		5		4		2		1	8	4	8	3						
	5	5	4	10	5	9	5	2	5	4	1	6	8	2	10	8	6	1	11							
	1				1		1	2					3			2				1						
	6	8			2	7				2	1	1			13	5	5	3	13							
	164	231	232	196	287	141	346	184	271	277	191	237	372	218	264	267	269	228	241	120						
	10	9	10	10	10	10	10	2	6	5	10	9	9	4	10	2	3	6	10	0						
	D		L		L		L		W		D		W		D		D		D							
	1		4				6		20		—		24		4		5		6							

†S.G. Hinks retired hurt, and absent hurt

7 September

at Scarborough

Yorkshire 203 for 6 (N.G. Nicholson 63)
Yorkshire Exiles 200 for 7 (S.J. Rhodes 64, C.W.J. Athey 52)

Yorkshire won by 3 runs

The Yorkshire committee, being pressed on all sides, not least from their own players who wanted to break with tradition and import an overseas player, were no doubt relieved that the County beat a side of players born in Yorkshire but playing for other counties by three runs in this 50-over match.

8, 9, 10 and 11 September

at Derby

Nottinghamshire 330 (D.W. Randall 70, C.W. Scott 51, M. Jean-Jacques 4 for 84) and 119 (A.E. Warner 4 for 18)

Andy Pick bowled Nottinghamshire into the Refuge Assurance Cup Final. (David Munden)

Kent CCC
First-Class Matches, 1989

BOWLING	C. Penn	H.L. Alleyne	R.M. Ellison	D.J.M. Kelleher	C.S. Cowdrey	G.R. Cowdrey	A.P. Igglesden	R.P. Davis	M.V. Fleming
v. Essex (Canterbury) 20–4 April	20.4–7–57–4 17–7–45–0	18–2–71–2 12–1–52–0	14–4–24–1 20–7–34–1	22–7–43–3 18–6–51–2	5–0–28–0	2–0–7–0			
v. Sussex (Hove) 27 April–1 May	27–4–62–2	28.4–3–101–2			17–3–46–2	4–0–22–1	25–2–78–1	17–5–37–2	
v. Hampshire (Southampton) 4–8 May	35–9–96–2 26–4–71–1		34.3–4–98–5 21–9–49–3		23–9–36–0 7–0–34–0		34–6–88–2 9–1–28–0	11–3–32–0 37–12–87–1	
v. Cambridge University (Cambridge) 17–19 May			15–2–43–1 10–3–28–0	15–6–41–1 9–2–18–1				31–17–64–2 34.4–17–68–4	11–3–42–2 5–1–16–0
v. Derbyshire (Dartford) 20–2 May	20–1–93–1 10–2–31–0			16–2–67–3	3–0–13–0		21–1–90–4 7–2–24–1	39–11–90–2 1–0–9–0	
v. Leicestershire (Leicester) 24–6 May	15–1–35–0 11–1–39–1		13–1–41–1 9–3–14–3		8–2–31–1		13–5–16–1 12.4–5–33–3	26–10–47–3 26–6–90–0	
v. Hampshire (Tunbridge Wells) 3–6 June	25–6–53–2		20–5–45–4		3–0–10–1		23.2–2–83–3	4–0–15–0	
v. Sussex (Tunbridge Wells) 7–9 June	11–3–23–2 14–2–48–1		13–5–34–0 5–0–11–1		2–0–5–0 8–1–26–0		8–1–24–0 17.2–2–76–3	7–4–11–0 23–9–61–2	
v. Nottinghamshire (Trent Bridge) 10–13 June	16–3–74–0 10–1–42–0				13.4–1–44–2		18–3–64–1 6–0–24–0	36–9–109–2 26–4–101–1	12–4–47–0 9–2–29–0
v. Somerset (Bath) 17–20 June	20–2–79–0				5–1–14–0 11–0–54–0		23–8–70–3 15–2–63–0	26–9–46–1 30–5–96–4	
v. Lancashire (Old Trafford) 24–7 June				16–2–70–1	4–1–8–0		28–7–73–6	41–13–105–3	
v. Northamptonshire (Maidstone) 5–7 July	31–3–109–4		22–5–77–1		21–3–58–2		26.5–3–131–3		
v. Gloucestershire (Maidstone) 8–11 July	22–3–60–0 11–4–19–1		20–4–49–1 5–3–15–0		5–2–15–0		27–6–62–0 11–4–18–2	22–7–55–0 20.5–4–67–3	
v. Essex (Southend) 19–21 July		25–0–92–4	20–5–50–1		7–2–21–0		26–8–66–4	20–3–68–0	
v. Middlesex (Uxbridge) 22–5 July		18–2–69–0	15–0–47–0		9–0–56–0		24–6–72–0	30–3–121–1	
v. Worcestershire (Worcester) 29 July–1 August	22–6–81–4	16–4–49–1	11–0–50–0		6–0–26–0		20–0–82–0	23–4–93–1 2.5–0–16–0	
v. Warwickshire (Canterbury) 5–8 August	26–6–61–3 12.4–3–53–0			22.4–6–57–1 4–0–24–0	7–0–31–0		22.2–3–92–1 8–1–20–0	5–3–2–1 4–0–29–0	14.2–5–34– 7–1–16–0
v. Surrey (Canterbury) 9–11 August	24–3–85–3 10.4–2–50–1			21–5–61–2 8–1–46–2	6–1–25–0		25–3–74–2 4–0–24–0		14–6–27–1 12–1–59–0
v. Yorkshire (Scarborough) 12–15 August	24–3–57–2			30–3–117–1 7–3–27–0	7–0–30–0			31.2–11–61–1 10–2–45–0	23–3–75–0 9.4–1–33–1
v. Australians (Canterbury) 16–18 August				26.1–7–82–4				21–3–75–1	19–3–55–0
v. Glamorgan (Canterbury) 19–22 August	18–3–51–3 6–1–15–0			13–3–43–2 7–2–23–0	6–0–43–0		22.5–3–75–3 14.3–3–58–4	23–7–53–1 24–10–57–4	
v. Leicestershire (Folkestone) 24–8 August	36–6–116–4			33–5–123–0	14.5–1–33–4			40–4–129–1	
v. Surrey (The Oval) 8–11 September	31–3–138–0			16–3–88–1	14–4–57–0		33–7–100–4	24–4–84–1	
v. Middlesex (Canterbury) 13–16 September	15–3–49–0		24.4–11–43–6				23–4–99–2		4–0–12–0
	567–102– 1792–41 av. 43.70	117.4–12– 434–9 av. 48.22	292.1–71– 752–29 av. 25.93	283.5–63– 981–24 av. 40.87	212.3–31– 744–12 av. 62.00	6–0– 29–1 av. 29.00	547.5–98– 1807–53 av. 34.09	716.4–199– 2023–42 av. 48.16	139.2–30– 445–6 av. 74.16

a N.R. Taylor 2–0–13–0   b R.F. Pienaar 11–3–43–0   c S.A. Marsh 4–0–37–0

M.D. Harman	V.J. Wells	M.R. Benson	T.R. Ward	M.C. Dobson	S.G. Hinks	M.A. Ealham	Byes	Leg-byes	Wides	No-balls	Total	Wkts
								8	4	9	203	10
								7	5	5	224	3
							4	11	3	21	361	10
								8		15	358	10
							5	6		9	280	5
24.4–6–56–4							3	10	6	3	259	10
35–12–80–5							4	6	4	4	220	10
	9–0–50–0							13	1	10	416	10
	5–2–11–1	1–0–6–0	0.3–0–4–0				1	1		6	87	2
			1.4–0–7–0				,2	9	1	7	201	7a
								8		1	184	7
								7	11	12	213	10
							1	1		6	99	2
							3	3	1	2	228	7
			4–0–11–0	4–0–18–2			4	6	2	3	377	7
			13.4–0–84–1				2	5		3	287	2
22–9–54–1							5	6		2	274	5
12–2–58–0							1	4			276	6
			1–1–0–0			5–0–26–0	11	5		8	298	10
			5–4–1–0					2	1	5	378	10
		4–0–42–0					2	8	5	4	251	1
								3			207	6b
				9–3–37–0			4	9	3	13	347	10
			9–2–23–0	19–3–62–0			7	1	6	13	458	1
			2–1–1–0				4	16	1	2	402	6
			2–0–11–0								27	0
								4	1	13	250	8
							3	5			181	0
				6.3–2–21–1			4	5		12	302	9
			2–0–11–0	5–0–34–0			1	5		3	230	3
				12–0–45–0			6	9		3	400	5
				7–2–40–1			1	1	2		147	2
				12–0–44–2		24–5–92–1		8		8	356	8
				10–2–27–1			9	10	1	12	311	10
				13–7–20–2				5	1	2	178	10
			1–0–4–0	25–3–87–1			1	5		7	498	10
							1	9	2	28	477	6
		4–0–18–0						1	2		56	0c
							3	11	1	19	251	10d
93.4–29–	14–2–	9–0–	41.5–8–	118.3–22–	4–0–	29–5–						
248–10	61–1	66–0	157–1	417–8	18–2	118–1						
av. 24.80	av. 61.00	—	av. 157.00	av. 52.12	av. 9.00	av. 118.00						

d M. Patel 10–2–34–1

Lancashire CCC
First-Class Matches, 1989

BATTING	War (Edgbaston) 20–4 April		Notts (Old Trafford) 27 Apr–1 May		Worcs (Worcester) 4–8 May		War (Old Trafford) 17–19 May		Som (Taunton) 20–3 May		Surrey (The Oval) 24–6 May		Sussex (Liverpool) 27–30 May		Oxford Univ (Oxford) 7–9 June		Australians (Old Trafford) 14–16 June		Glam (Old Trafford) 17–20 June		Northants (Southport) 21–3 June		Kent (Old Trafford) 24–7 June		Middlesex (Lord's) 1–4 July		Leics (Leicester) 5–7 July	
G.D. Mendis	22	47	118	81*	0	69			35	59	11	40	10	84			25	28	1	67	27	—	75	—	0	50	80	—
G. Fowler	56	22	4	4	60	5	30	4	96	20	20	52	7	49	112	—	0	19	92	—	65	—	6	—				
A.N. Hayhurst	10	12	22	33	26	9	2	9	0*	—						30*	40	13	7	34	11	—						
N.H. Fairbrother	4	9			1	31	23	62	1	47	26	62*	10	24		71*	49	2	4	0	18	—	16	—	0	24	65	—
M. Watkinson	9	2	61*	1	0	45	7	1	1	59*	2	10*	35	4			—	—	4	0	18	—	15	—	47	22	27	—
D.P. Hughes	33	5	13	23	6	1					42*	—	50*	—	13	2	0	2	18	37	3	—	0	—	38	15	0	—
Wasim Akram	18	36	9*	24	5	14	21*	2					2	—					0	2								
W.K. Hegg	31*	1	13	50	31*	1	4	13	58	2	59	28	19	1			0	23	73	0	31	—	11	—	18	15	86	—
P.A.J. DeFreitas	11	19	—	11*	26	18	78	0	10	—	9	—	2*	18*					59	59	13	—			5	15	69	—
P.J.W. Allott	5	5					26	0	0	—	9	—	2*	18*					2*	20	1*	—	26	—	1	17	14	—
J. Simmons	16	0*	—	—	1	12*	5*	13	5*	—							0	2										
T.E. Jesty			44	4			7	8	1	7	28	93*	38	23	48	50	0	12	21	4	31	—	55*	—	4	17	15	—
J.D. Fitton	—	—											19	—	16	12*	28*	—	2	44	1	—			24	15	23*	—
N.J. Speak							39	6*									28*	—	26	12								
I.D. Austin											0	—	29	1	38	—	4	—										
B.P. Patterson													4	—			—	—	4*	1*			0	—	0*	1*		
G.D. Lloyd																	108	—									11	—
J. Stanworth																			8	27								
I. Folley																	—	—										
P.J. Martin																	16	4										
M.A. Atherton																												
Byes	9			4		3	8	11	13	3	13	2		2	1		1		6				11				5	
Leg-byes	24	7	13	12	8	10	12	2	8	16	5	12	10	17	10	2	7	8	3	10	1		5		12	3	15	
Wides	4						1		1		1	2			4				2	1								
No-balls	7	6	3	3		5	4	3	5	3	2	1	1	2			6	9	1	8	8		6	2			1	
Total	259	171	300	250	171	231	261	133	303	302	257	232	204	266	301	103	184	185	196	344	336		298		161	196	411	
Wickets	10	10	6	7	10	10	9†	10	8	4	10	4	10	8	3	0	10	10	10	10	10		10		10	9‡	9	
Result	D		D		W		W		W		D		D		D		L		L		D		D		W		D	
Points	7		7		21		23		23		4		4						5		8		6		21		8	

Fielding Figures

79 – W.K. Hegg (ct 77/st 2)	12 – M. Watkinson	6 – T.E. Jesty
24 – P.J.W. Allott	9 – M.A. Atherton	5 – G.D. Mendis
18 – D.P. Hughes	8 – N.H. Fairbrother	4 – J. Simmons and N.J. Speak
17 – G. Fowler	7 – J.D. Fitton	3 – Wasim Akram

Derbyshire 293 (J.E. Morris 156, A. Brown 65) and 160 for 9 (P.D. Bowler 58, R.A. Pick 4 for 41)

Derbyshire won by 1 wicket
Derbyshire 23 pts, Nottinghamshire 8 pts

at Bristol

Gloucestershire 259 (J.W. Lloyds 58, A.N. Jones 4 for 56) and 310 for 7 dec (K.M. Curran 128, M.W. Alleyne 56, G.D. Rose 4 for 82)
Somerset 165 (C.A. Walsh 4 for 33, D.A. Graveney 4 for 37) and 263 (P.M. Roebuck 117, C.A. Walsh 4 for 68)

Gloucestershire won by 141 runs
Gloucestershire 23 pts, Somerset 5 pts

at Southampton

Glamorgan 247 (A.R. Butcher 65, M.D. Marshall 5 for 68) and 133
Hampshire 201 (S.L. Watkin 6 for 73) and 149 (R.J. Scott 52, S.L. Watkin 5 for 46)

Glamorgan won by 30 runs
Glamorgan 22 pts, Hampshire 4 pts

at Leicester

Essex 415 (M.E. Waugh 165, G.A. Gooch 158, J.P. Agnew 5 for 89) and 8 for 0
Leicestershire 145 and 274 (D.I. Gower 109, J.H. Childs 5 for 84)

Essex won by 10 wickets
Essex 24 pts, Leicestershire 2 pts

at Lord's

Sussex 438 (P.W.G. Parker 136, D.M. Smith 129) and 137 for 4 dec (D.M. Smith 51 not out)
Middlesex 302 (M.W. Gatting 139 not out, A.C.S. Pigott 4 for 71) and 202 for 5 (K.R. Brown 53 not out, D.L. Haynes 51)

Match drawn
Sussex 6 pts, Middlesex 3 pts

at The Oval

Surrey 477 for 6 dec (M.A. Lynch 172 not out, G.P. Thorpe 154, A.P. Igglesden 4 for 100) and 56 for 0 dec
Kent 269 for 3 dec (M.R. Benson 149, R.F. Pienaar 53 not out) and 228 for 6 (C.S. Cowdrey 146 not out, M.R. Benson 56, M.P. Bicknell 4 for 64)

Match drawn
Surrey 5 pts, Kent 5 pts

v. Worcestershire (Old Trafford) 19-21 July	v. Hampshire (Portsmouth) 22-5 July	v. Nottinghamshire (Worksop) 26-8 July	v. Gloucestershire (Cheltenham) 5-8 August	v. Derbyshire (Chesterfield) 9-11 August	v. Essex (Lytham) 12-15 August	v. Yorkshire (Old Trafford) 19-22 August	v. Surrey (Old Trafford) 24-8 August	v. Yorkshire (Scarborough) 8-11 September	v. Derbyshire (Old Trafford) 13-16 September	M	Inns	NOs	Runs	HS	Av
0 70	34 5		8 30*		24 10	28 103*	38 —	22 66		19	34	3	1367	118	44.09
30 12	130 16	8 25	0 12	83 58	23 8	25 —		58 123	24 12	21	37	—	1370	130	37.02
										9	15	2	258	40	19.84
0 39	159 —		30* 14	161 17	0 60	1 40	0 —	161 67	28 6*	22	38	4	1458	161	42.88
18 7	25* 8	70 4*	0 43	2 22	16 21	48 51*	1 —	0 10	17 —	23	39	6	733	70	22.21
10 7*	— —	37 —	7 2			15 —	40* —		17 —	17	24	5	413	50*	21.73
					16 42		4 —		49 —	12	19	2	336	49	19.76
0 9	— 9	0 —	0 9	15 9	0 1	4 —	28 11	7* 13*	11 —	23	39	4	694	86	19.82
14 0			4 0	28 1	15 50	12 —		26 0	15* —	16	26	2	558	78	23.25
0 5		14* —	5 28		7 —		2 —	8 —		16	23	5	215	28	11.94
					2* 2					6	9	5	56	16	14.00
32* 7	71* 73*	2 59*	17 68	12 5*			47 —	26 35	66 —	21	35	7	1030	93*	36.78
	— 2	0 —	0 18*	8 12	0 32*	16 6	43 —	11 0	4* —	18	25	6	336	44	17.68
		15 7		1 8	8 64					5	10	1	186	64	20.66
	— 20*	23 —		13* 2	0 14		13 1*		17 —	9	13	3	171	38	17.10
0* 1								4 —		8	9	5	15	4*	3.75
		31 117		1 5	3 100		41 8*		2 15	7	12	1	442	117	40.18
										1					—
										2	2	—	35	27	17.50
	— —									2	2	—	20	16	10.00
0 59	37 2	21 90	21 36			115* 16		3 39	0 12*	7	14	2	451	115*	37.58
4	4			5 6	10	2 2	1	12 5	11 5						
11 5	15 5	9 7	7	13 5	2 5	7 10	13	4 8	4 2						
1	2			4	2 4	1	4		1 1						
5 8	2 3		1 7	12 5	2 3	5	4	5 2	2 1						
125 229	475 147	230 309	93 278	372 201	95 381	293 228	305 20	347 369	251 53						
9†† 10	4 6	10 4	10 9§	10 10	10 10	10 3	10 1	10 8	9 2						
L	L	W	L	D	L	W	W	W	D						
4	5	21	2	8	1	23	20	24	7						

2 – I.D. Austin, J. Stanworth, G.D. Lloyd, P.A.J. DeFreitas and subs
1 – A.N. Hayhurst, B.P. Patterson,, I. Folley and P.J. Martin

†† Wasim Akram retired hurt
‡ G. Fowler absent ill
†† T.E. Jesty retired hurt
§ G.D. Mendis retired hurt

---

at Edgbaston

Northamptonshire 179 (A. Fordham 50, G.C. Small 4 for 49) and 79 for 1 dec (A. Fordham 55 not out)
Warwickshire 0 for 0 dec and 217 for 8 (A.J. Moles 50)

Match drawn
Warwickshire 4 pts, Northamptonshire 1 pt

at Scarborough

Lancashire 347 (N.H. Fairbrother 161, G. Fowler 58, P. Carrick 4 for 69) and 369 for 8 dec (G. Fowler 123, N.H. Fairbrother 67, G.D. Mendis 66, J. Batty 5 for 118)
Yorkshire 237 (C.S. Pickles 62, M.D. Moxon 54, J.D. Fitton 5 for 53) and 295 (P.E. Robinson 117)

Lancashire won by 184 runs
Lancashire 24 pts, Yorkshire 6 pts

Third Youth Test Match

at Old Trafford

England 420 (N.V. Knight 160, K. Butler 72, M. Keech 63, M. Hart 4 for 98)
New Zealand 205 and 390 for 9 (B. Pocock 106 not out, A. Parore 90, C.L. Cairns 55, I.D.K. Salisbury 5 for 131)

Match drawn

With the championship already decided and the teams to tour West Indies and Zimbabwe selected, the last two rounds of matches in the Britannic Assurance County Championship were played with something of a sense of unreality if not anti-climax. Hampshire's miserable end to the season continued with defeat by bottom-place Glamorgan, for whom Watkin took 11 for 119 in the match. Many felt that Watkin should be in the party to go to the Caribbean rather than in the 'B' side destined for Pakistan.

Derbyshire gained revenge over Nottinghamshire with a thrilling one-wicket victory at Derby. John Morris continued with the batting form which, had it come earlier in the season and more often, must have won him a place in the national side. Rain thwarted the efforts of Warwickshire and Northamptonshire at Edgbaston and also hampered progress at The Oval and Lord's.

At The Oval, Graham Thorpe celebrated his selection for the England 'B' side with a gloriously aggressive innings of 154. The left-hander's innings included 29 fours, and he and Monte Lynch added 216 for the fourth wicket.

Lancashire CCC
First-Class Matches, 1989

BOWLING	Wasim Akram	P.A.J. DeFreitas	P.J.W. Allott	M. Watkinson	J. Simmons	J.D. Fitton	D.P. Hughes	A.N. Hayhurst	T.E. Jesty
v. Warwickshire (Edgbaston) 20–4 April	20–7–51–3 5–1–22–0	23–6–68–2 16.5–6–37–3	19.4–5–44–4 13–4–20–1	13–5–42–1					
v. Nottinghamshire (Old Trafford) 27 April–1 May	29–3–70–6 13–4–21–0	32–5–81–2 11–1–39–0		18–1–40–0 6–1–27–0	24–7–58–1 9–1–34–0	6–1–30–0	4–0–21–0		
v. Worcestershire (Worcester) 4–8 May	28–10–52–5 24–5–59–1	27.4–9–61–4 29–6–53–3		11–5–23–0 22.2–6–44–5				5–0–13–1	
v. Warwickshire (Old Trafford) 17–19 May	26–7–58–3	30–10–65–4 27–7–47–4	17–2–42–1 14.2–3–24–2	22–3–45–5 16–8–22–1					
v. Somerset (Taunton) 20–3 May		17–2–51–0 10–2–24–0	17–6–42–0 9–2–23–1	15–0–46–1 4–0–17–0	33–4–122–1 9–2–28–1		12–0–70–1 5–0–25–2	16–3–52–1	9–1–23–0
v. Surrey (The Oval) 24–6 May	14–2–33–0 13–2–31–2		16–6–43–0 10–2–14–0	10–2–45–1 10–0–21–0		13–2–58–1 13–5–39–1			
v. Sussex (Liverpool) 27–30 May			16–5–54–0 11–0–36–1	13–3–28–0 11–2–29–2		38–11–87–3 23–4–65–1			
v. Oxford University (Oxford) 7–9 June				18–3–44–3		20–5–58–1			
v. Australians (Old Trafford) 14–16 June	12.3–2–35–2 8–2–21–1					18–2–59–1 3.3–1–13–0		5–1–14–0	
v. Glamorgan (Old Trafford) 17–20 June	28–8–45–5 17–2–50–0	21–4–52–0 17–3–57–1	22–3–69–2 17–5–33–3	19–2–79–1 13–4–33–0			3–0–6–1	10–4–25–0 12–2–57–1	0.5–0–14–0
v. Northamptonshire (Southport) 21–3 June	15–3–40–1 31–5–95–1	21–7–46–5 11–1–43–0	5–2–16–0 24–9–37–0	14–6–30–4 19–4–61–1		2–0–8–0 42–8–125–2	19–6–34–3		
v. Kent (Old Trafford) 24–7 June			19–1–67–0 4–2–6–0	15.1–7–32–3 4–0–6–0		40–11–98–3 6–4–5–2	8–2–14–0 7–5–4–0	4–2–5–1	3–1–6–0
v. Middlesex (Lord's) 1–4 July		16–3–41–3 10.2–4–21–7	3–2–3–2	3–2–1–0					
v. Leicestershire (Leicester) 5–7 July		20–5–49–2 14–4–41–0	17.4–6–24–5 14–4–23–1	6–2–12–1 1–0–5–0		11–2–48–0			
v. Worcestershire (Old Trafford) 19–21 July		18–3–46–2 2–0–13–0	18–4–51–3 20–4–55–0	11.3–3–25–1 25–7–69–7					
v. Hampshire (Portsmouth) 22–5 July				20–5–70–1 16–1–67–0		28–5–99–2 3–0–14–0	18.1–1–93–2		
v. Nottinghamshire (Worksop) 26–8 July			27–8–66–3 11–3–25–2	24–9–99–4 15.5–4–59–3		14–3–53–0 13–2–57–1			
v. Gloucestershire (Cheltenham) 5–8 August		29–2–123–5	27–4–73–2	20.4–4–78–3		24–6–81–0			
v. Derbyshire (Chesterfield) 9–11 August	28–0–103–4 15–4–50–1	29.3–5–116–6 18–2–63–3		7–2–39–0 6–0–30–0		8–1–30–0			
v. Essex (Lytham) 12–15 August		26–5–94–2 6–0–44–0		29–5–103–1 5.5–0–31–1	25–3–67–0	25–4–76–0			
v. Yorkshire (Old Trafford) 19–22 August	28.5–9–44–5 22–6–51–5	8–1–29–0 4–0–10–1	15–8–24–3	5–0–17–0		20–5–48–1 4–0–20–0	21–10–30–3 5–3–6–0		
v. Surrey (Old Trafford) 24–8 August	7–4–9–1 24.4–3–52–5		4–1–7–0 15–6–35–0	8–3–26–0		2–1–2–0 26–7–72–5			
v. Yorkshire (Scarborough) 8–11 September		10–1–44–0 17–5–58–1	17–5–37–2 20–3–59–3	6–0–18–1 6.3–1–36–3		20–2–53–5 22–6–70–2			
v. Derbyshire (Old Trafford) 13–16 September	26.3–3–57–2	28–6–76–4 2–0–10–1		8–1–32–0 6–3–9–1		21–4–89–3 5–1–18–1			
	435.3–92– 1049–53 av. 19.79	551.2–115– 1602–65 av. 24.64	442.4–115– 1052–41 av. 25.65	503.5–109– 1540–55 av. 28.00	100–17– 309–3 av. 103.00	470.3–103– 1475–35 av. 42.14	102.1–27– 303–12 av. 25.25	52–12– 166–4 av. 41.50	12.5–2– 43–0 —

a G.D. Mendis 2–0–5–0   b W.K. Hegg 1–0–7–0   c G.D. Lloyd 5–0–55–0

G. Fowler	N.H. Fairbrother	M.A. Atherton	I.D. Austin	B.P. Patterson	I. Folley	P.J. Martin	Byes	Leg-byes	Wides	No-balls	Total	Wkts
								5	5	2	210	10
								2			81	4
								4	1	17	283	9
							1	4	3	6	147	0
								17	1	7	166	10
								14	3	7	170	10
							3	3	1	1	158	10
							3	20	1	13	174	10
							5	11		3	399	4
4–0–24–0	5–0–29–0						4	1		2	203	4a
		7–4–15–1					1	5		8	200	3
1–0–1–0		3–1–2–0					8	3	1	12	119	3
		28–7–59–3		26–2–91–1			4	11		2	334	7
		3–0–8–0		9–0–42–0				5		3	185	4
		14–4–24–2		17–2–37–2	7–0–37–0			10	2		210	8
				16–4–48–4	17–3–72–2	17–3–46–1	3	11		11	288	10
				4–0–16–0	4–0–19–0	4–0–15–0			5	7	84	1
							9	18	3	17	297	9
								2	6	15	252	6
								4	2	11	144	10
	1–1–0–0							12	1	19	407	7
				28–9–65–4			2	18	1		296	10
								3			42	3b
				16.2–4–48–5				3		2	96	10
				11–2–20–3				2		4	43	10
				17–5–45–2			1	8		4	187	10
				7–1–22–1					1		91	2
		1–0–1–0		19–4–61–4				7	1	10	191	10
		9.5–2–25–0		12.1–3–28–3			4	5	1	7	199	10
		22–7–73–0	17–6–29–1			17–3–51–0	4	10	1	1	336	4
		3–0–24–0	18–1–60–4			5–0–21–0	4	4			287	7
		15–0–59–1	15–4–43–0				1	6		1	327	8
		1–0–6–0	17–3–60–4				2	2			211	10
		12–3–33–0					1	5		12	394	10
			17–5–53–0					13	1	16	354	10
			13.5–2–45–3					5	2	11	193	8
			25–5–56–1				2	2		6	400	4
								4	1		79	3
		13–3–26–1					5	10	1	6	192	10
		4–1–5–1					5	10	4	8	148	10
							1	5			24	1
			3–1–7–0				8	4	2	7	204	10
		8–4–22–0		16–3–58–2			5		4	8	237	10
		6–2–25–0		12–4–37–1			4	6		2	295	10
		3–0–13–1					14	11	3	22	292	10
8–1–36–0	6–0–42–1	3–0–14–0	7–3–12–2				10	3		2	209	6c
13–1– 61–0	12–1– 71–1	100.5–22– 326–4	187.5–46– 473–21	210.3–43– 618–32	28–3– 128–2	43–6– 133–1						
—	av. 71.00	av. 81.50	av. 22.52	av. 19.31	av. 64.00	av. 133.00						

Leicestershire CCC
First-Class Matches, 1989

BATTING	v. Glamorgan (Leicester) 20–4 April		v. Cambridge University (Cambridge) 27–9 April		v. Northamptonshire (Northampton) 4–8 May		v. Derbyshire (Chesterfield) 17–19 May		v. Kent (Leicester) 24–6 May		v. Hampshire (Bournemouth) 27–30 May		v. Yorkshire (Leicester) 7–9 June		v. Gloucestershire (Leicester) 10–13 June		v. Essex (Chelmsford) 17–20 June		v. Nottinghamshire (Leicester) 24–7 June		v. Warwickshire (Hinckley) 1–4 July		v. Lancashire (Leicester) 5–7 July		v. Worcestershire (Kidderminster) 8–11 July		v. Northamptonshire (Leicester) 19–21 July	
T.J. Boon	11	37	39	—	1	14	27	9	2	25	35	23	0	19	15	11	20	72	57	—	33*	—	28	44*			4	15
N.E. Briers	30	20	54	—	5	41	73	3*	26	32	49	0	0	57	48	1	0	23	3	—	25	—	1	33	54	0	46	1
D.I. Gower	4	228	—	—	26	2	14	0*			52	0	45*	3	8	9	58	2	85	—	27	—					50	91
P. Willey	46	8	—	—	0	0	10	—	38	18											96	—	85	8*	33	0	12	20
J.J. Whitaker	39	6	89	—	92*	4	5	—	8	36	48	31	10	4	12	11	138	92*			138	—	2	—	6	23	99	7
L. Potter	29	37	28	—	8	23	41	—	56	28*	41	15	0	2	0	52*	71	1	121*	—	0	—	1	—	22	12	49	5
C.C. Lewis	4	7	54	—	0	27	0	—	0	0	4	8	42	7							12	—						
P. Whitticase	21	37	30	—	16	56*	15	—	7*	6			0*	49	8	46			16*	—	26	—	40	2	0	0	0	5
G.J. Parsons	1	14*	29*	—	0	35	33*	—			3	21	—	30*	13	69			13	—			30	—	0	0	0	41*
J.P. Agnew	0*	13	14	—	25	8	0	—	0*	—	2	0	—	0	5*	0			8*	—			0*	—	8	7	25	5*
G.J.F. Ferris	0	1*	—	—	30	15					14	9*													1*	0		
L.B. Taylor			1	—																			0	—	0	0*	4*	—
W.K.M. Benjamin							37	—	—	14*			—	10	30	4	1	—			4*	—	8	—	13	—		
J.D.R. Benson									45	16	1	6	2	2											0	—		
P.M. Such							—	—	—	—											—	—						
R.A. Cobb															2	7			13	47	33	—	14	5	2	34		
R.H. Edmunds																			0	17								
P.A. Nixon																							0	—				
P.N. Hepworth																									7	0		
M. Gidley																												
Byes			3		4		4		2		3		2		1		4		1		2		1		1		5	
Leg-byes	2	7	2		6		7		9	8	4	1	2	11	2	2	21	8	8		18		8		4		11	10
Wides			1				2		1						1				4	2			1		2		1	
No-balls	3				5	15	6		7	1	5	1	5	7	1	8	10	3			1		3		4	2	1	
Total	190	415	344		208	250	274	12	201	184	293	115	108	201	145	238	377	251	352		371		187	91	180	80	300	206
Wickets	10	9	8		10	10	10	1	7	7	10	10	6	10	10	10	8	5	6		6		10	2	10	10	10	7
Result	D		D		L		W		D		L		L		L		L		D		W		D		L		D	
Points	5		—		6		23		4		6		4		4		4		4		23		8		5		6	

Fielding Figures

43 – P. Whitticase (ct 41/st 2)	13 – T.J. Boon	7 – W.K.M. Benjamin
25 – L. Potter	12 – G.J. Parsons and C.C. Lewis	6 – N.E. Briers
15 – J.J. Whitaker	11 – P. Willey	5 – R.A. Cobb
14 – P.A. Nixon (ct 12/st 2)	9 – D.I. Gower	4 – L.B. Taylor

John Morris ended the season with a flourish for Derbyshire. (Chris Raphael/Allsport)

Lynch emphasized the loss that he had been to Surrey for most of the season by playing a splendid innings of 172 not out. Kent scored well, if not so attractively, thanks to Benson's century, and Chris Cowdrey declared in arrears so that a last day target could be set. Needing 265 in 59 overs, Kent lost four wickets for 22 runs, but Chris Cowdrey reached his highest score of the season, 146 not out off 152 balls, to bring his side to within 37 runs of victory in the gloom.

There were no such thrills at Lord's. Gatting's determined century answered the splendour of Parker and Smith on the opening day, when they added 191 in 76 overs for Sussex's second wicket. It was the highest Sussex stand of the season, but rain reduced the probability of a result after the second day.

Troubled Gloucestershire beat Somerset with surprising ease at Bristol, but the one match of significance was at Leicester, where Essex trounced the home side. There was little play on the first day because of rain, but Gooch and Mark Waugh added 272 for Essex's third wicket and both reached their highest scores of the season when play resumed on the Saturday. Leicestershire were bowled out for 145 and forced to follow-on. David Gower, deprived of

	v. Somerset (Taunton) 22–5 July	v. Glamorgan (Cardiff) 26–8 July	v. Middlesex (Lord's) 29 July–1 August	v. Australians (Leicester) 5–7 August	v. Sussex (Eastbourne) 9–11 August	v. Surrey (Leicester) 19–22 August	v. Kent (Folkestone) 24–8 August	v. Derbyshire (Leicester) 29 Aug.–1 Sept.	v. Essex (Leicester) 8–11 September	v. Nottinghamshire (Trent Bridge) 13–16 September	M	Inns	NOs	Runs	HS	Av
	51 2	45 60*	1 60	14 20	36 80*	29 30		31 12*	26 7		21	39	5	1045	80*	30.73
	16 25	2 25	50 31	15 41	13 48*	63 13	28 —	4 23*	5 4	4 26	24	44	3	1061	73	25.87
	48 19			9 46		13 4		0 109	27 2		11	19	1	719	228	39.94
	10 4	38 —	16 30		2 —	15 39	99 —	96 —	4 14	0 10	23	37	2	1013	99	28.94
	0 12	99 9*	46 0	6 17	53 —	0 28	116 —	7 —	6 44	15 6	23	39	3	1364	138	37.88
	42 22	10 —	20 13	41 18	4 —	55 2	96 —	14 —	29* 7	19 59*	24	39	5	1093	121*	32.14
						69 —		18 —	16 6	3 0*	12	19	1	277	69	15.38
	19 29					32 47	61 —	5 —	16 17	46* —	18	29	6	684	61	29.73
	24 23*		31* 19			9 2	10 —	3 —			18	26	8	474	69	26.33
	4 0	9 —	— 2	30 39	10 —	21 3	4* —	3* —	10 24		23	31	8	279	39	12.13
		10 —									5	9	3	80	30	13.33
	27 14	0* —	— 0*	0* 0	0 —	11* 0*		0 —	2 0*	1 —	14	18	8	60	27	6.00
		0 14	1 —	41 5	2 —	40 —	23 26	0 —			15	19	2	273	41	16.05
										31 7	4	8	—	110	45	13.75
	0* 0	14 —	— —	1 2*	1 —	0 —					10	8	2	18	14	3.00
											5	9	—	157	47	17.44
						0 —					2	3	—	17	17	5.66
		10 —	10* 2*	24 17	24* —	0 —					6	7	3	87	24*	21.75
		4 —	10 10	6 9	17 —						5	8	—	63	17	7.87
										15 —	1	1	—	15	15	15.00
	1 2		8 4	1 2	4	2	1	6 4	1 4	5						
	7	3 2	2 8	4 10	4 2	4 4	5	2 1	7 8	2 8						
			1				2		1	1						
	1	3 4	8 5	6 8	2	2 3	7	11 2	4	3 1						
	250 152	247 100	203 184	157 243	167 134	297 182	498	241 42	145 274	166 125						
	10 10	10 1	6 8	10 10	10 0	10 10	10	10 0	10 10	10 5						
	L	W	D	L	D	L	D	W	L	D						
	3	22	4	—	5	7	8	22	2	5						

3 – J.P. Agnew and P.N. Hepworth
2 – G.J.F. Ferris and P.M. Such
1 – J.D.R. Benson and M. Gidley

the England captaincy and even of a place in the party to tour West Indies, answered Dexter, Stewart, and his successor Gooch, with an elegant century; but John Childs, who, sadly, had declined the invitation to tour West Indies, nagged away at the Leicestershire middle order, and Essex claimed maximum points. This brought them to within two points of Worcestershire who, therefore, had to gain maximum points in their last game at Pontypridd to eradicate the belief that they had won the title only by default.

The gloom over Yorkshire deepened when they were severely beaten by Lancashire, for whom Neil Fairbrother played an exhilarating innings on the opening day, reminding England selectors that he was still a young man hopeful of recognition. The only consolations for Yorkshire in the depression which followed were the performance of debutant off-spinner Batty, and the batting of Robinson.

Pocock rose from a sick bed to defy Young England at

Bill Athey, who resigned the captaincy of Gloucestershire at the end of a troubled season. (USPA)

Leicestershire CCC
First-Class Matches, 1989

BOWLING	G.J.F. Ferris	J.P. Agnew	C.C. Lewis	G.J. Parsons	P. Willey	L. Potter	L.B. Taylor	W.K.M. Benjamin	P.M. Such
v. Glamorgan (Leicester) 20–4 April	23–6–44–4 / 12.1–4–29–1	19–2–57–1 / 19–6–42–1	16–8–35–3 / 19–4–41–0	6–2–14–0 / 16–7–44–2	5.2–1–7–2 / 4–3–2–0	2–0–6–0			
v. Cambridge University (Cambridge) 27–9 April		12–2–33–1	14–5–20–0	14–7–14–1	9.1–5–17–2	9–2–25–1	12–5–44–3		
v. Northamptonshire (Northampton) 4–8 May	16–7–30–3 / 17–6–42–2	21–3–58–1 / 22–7–80–4	19.3–4–47–4 / 20.5–4–58–1	12–3–46–2 / 12–1–61–1	9–1–28–0				
v. Derbyshire (Chesterfield) 17–19 May		12.2–2–31–4 / 10–2–44–0	20.5–6–69–5	13–2–43–2	4–2–9–0			13–5–26–6 / 21–9–49–3	
v. Kent (Leicester) 24–6 May		29–2–101–0 / 7–1–40–0	29–5–79–2 / 3–0–8–0		18–5–31–1 / 14–1–31–0	5.4–1–17–1		14–5–28–2 / 3–0–19–0	28–11–40–3 / 15–4–29–0
v. Hampshire (Bournemouth) 27–30 May	20–4–76–3 / 3–0–20–0	24.2–6–71–2 / 12–2–38–0	21–8–50–2 / 10–0–38–1	17–4–42–3 / 9–1–34–0	19–6–40–0	1–1–0–0 / 10–1–20–1			
v. Yorkshire (Leicester) 7–9 June		24–4–82–2 / 9–1–38–0	18–1–65–3 / 1–0–8–0	20.2–7–48–5 / 6–1–22–1	6–1–19–0			20–8–47–0 / 11–5–20–1	
v. Gloucestershire (Leicester) 10–13 June		36–5–101–4 / 8–1–39–1		18–2–70–0 / 5–1–13–0	1–0–3–0 / 5–1–10–0	2.5–0–9–1 / 2.4–1–14–0		27–6–75–3	
v. Essex (Chelmsford) 17–20 June		18–5–60–1 / 12–0–69–1		19–6–59–1 / 10–1–45–1	8–0–20–0 / 6–0–21–0	8–1–31–0		16–3–52–0 / 11–1–46–2	7–0–32–0 / 7–2–25–0
v. Nottinghamshire (Leicester) 24–7 June		18–6–37–5 / 17.5–5–56–6	9–0–51–5 / 7–0–29–3					10–2–26–0 / 11–4–40–1	
v. Warwickshire (Hinckley) 1–4 July		26–5–62–1 / 16–4–50–2		13–3–29–2 / 12–7–11–0	2–2–0–0 / 34–16–63–3	3–3–0–0	15–2–30–1 / 12–2–32–1	25.4–3–70–6 / 25–13–28–2	
v. Lancashire (Leicester) 5–7 July		22–5–75–3		15.3–0–83–1	22–7–73–3	4–0–21–0	17–1–78–0	19–7–61–1	
v. Worcestershire (Kidderminster) 8–11 July	18–5–54–3	24–5–81–2		14–2–48–1 / 1.4–0–5–0			19.5–5–55–4 / 2–0–10–0		
v. Northamptonshire (Leicester) 19–21 July		19–5–50–3 / 20–4–39–2		18.4–4–56–4 / 4–0–9–0	1–1–0–0 / 27–10–66–1	21.2–3–88–3	19–5–56–3 / 11–1–32–0		12–4–29–0 / 26–8–71–1
v. Somerset (Taunton) 22–5 July		31–2–105–2		5–1–37–0	43–9–96–3		32–9–120–3		23.2–5–71–2[a]
v. Glamorgan (Cardiff) 26–8 July	10–4–20–0 / 5–3–12–1	6–1–34–1 / 1–0–3–0			18.5–8–45–5 / 15.3–5–48–4	5–3–37–1 / 16–7–20–2	6–1–10–0		22–8–54–3 / 19–9–28–3
v. Middlesex (Lord's) 29 July–1 August		12–0–45–1 / 9–1–27–0		17–5–66–1 / 11–1–47–0	30–16–40–3	16.2–1–50–3 / 3–0–13–0	18–7–33–0 / 4–1–7–0		18–5–42–2 / 9–0–33–1
v. Australians (Leicester) 5–7 August		23–3–64–2 / 7–0–39–0				10–0–42–0	14–1–49–1 / 7–1–31–1	23–6–54–7 / 6–3–7–0	24–4–77–0 / 6–2–9–0
v. Sussex (Eastbourne) 9–11 August		22–2–84–4			28–12–60–2 / 11–2–33–0	6–2–11–2	9–1–30–0 / 13.5–2–61–1	23.4–7–63–4 / 17–4–55–3	5–1–16–0 / 6–1–24–0
v. Surrey (Leicester) 19–22 August		15–1–45–1 / 21–3–52–2		6–2–19–0 / 5–1–26–0	14–5–22–2 / 32–5–91–3	6–1–21–0	4–1–10–1 / 5–1–21–0	24–6–83–5 / 21.5–5–60–0	
v. Kent (Folkestone) 24–8 August		19–3–72–2 / 18–4–59–0	10–2–45–2	12–1–52–2 / 12–3–40–0	17–7–28–1	19–7–35–0		18–7–37–2 / 18–10–33–1	1–1–0–0 / 16–5–36–0
v. Derbyshire (Leicester) 29 Aug.–1 Sept.		22–3–58–2 / 3–0–12–0	6–1–17–0 / 10–0–40–5	10–4–17–1	2–2–0–0		16–3–43–2	23.1–6–51–5 / 13.5–4–25–5	
v. Essex (Leicester) 8–11 September		33–10–89–5	28–3–137–2		16.2–2–53–1		13–0–50–0	29–7–72–2	
v. Nottinghamshire (Trent Bridge) 13–16 September			16.2–4–69–4 / 21.4–6–80–3		9–1–29–1		21–4–69–3	17–5–42–6 / 23–4–69–2	
	124.1–39– / 327–17 / av. 19.23	699.3–123– / 2222–69 / av. 32.20	300.3–61– / 986–45 / av. 21.91	334.1–79– / 1100–31 / av. 35.48	431.1–136– / 985–37 / av. 26.62	150.5–34– / 460–15 / av. 30.66	270.4–53– / 871–24 / av. 36.29	484.1–145– / 1238–69 / av. 17.94	244.2–70– / 616–15 / av. 41.06

a J.D. Robinson retired hurt

J.D.R. Benson	T.J. Boon	R.H. Edmunds	P. Whitticase	M. Gidley	Byes	Leg-byes	Wides	No-balls	Total	Wkts
						4		9	167	10
						8	1	14	166	4
					4	2		1	159	8
					1	3		7	185	10
					1	6		10	276	9
								3	57	10
					1	13		12	228	10
					2	9		7	307	10
						6		3	133	1
9.3–0–44–1	7–0–41–1					9	4	8	288	10
					1	3	1	12	239	4
						4		16	246	10
						5		3	112	2
		11–0–38–2			1	9		5	306	10
						2		1	78	1
						8		5	262	2
					1	9	1	1	216	4
						2		4	116	10
						10	1		135	10
						5		4	196	10
					5	4		7	193	8
					5	15		1	411	9
					1	6	7	7	245	10
						1	1		16	0
					1	6	1	2	198	10
					4	3			312	7
					9	11	1	14	449	10
					17	11		3	228	10
					5	2			118	10
					1	10		9	287	10
								4	127	1
	0.5–0–0–0				4	15		2	305	10
					8	5		1	99	1
					3	2			258	10
					4	3			191	6
					1	4	1	3	184	9a
					12	13		4	296	6
		15–2–48–1				10		13	264	10
		11–3–27–0			1	8	2	2	267	2
					4	14	1	8	204	10
						1		4	78	10
			0.5–0–7–0		4	10		9	415	10
						1			8	0
						10		1	121	10
				8–0–23–1		8		2	278	10
9.3–0– 44–1 av. 44.00	7.5–0– 41–1 av. 41.00	37–5– 113–3 av. 37.66	0.5–0– 7–0 —	8–0– 23–1 av. 23.00						

Middlesex CCC
First-Class Matches, 1989

BATTING	v. Yorkshire (Lord's) 20-4 April	v. Essex (Chelmsford) 27 April-1 May	v. Surrey (Lord's) 4-8 May	v. Hampshire (Lord's) 17-19 May	v. Australians (Lord's) 20-2 May	v. Oxford University (Oxford) 24-6 May	v. Warwickshire (Edgbaston) 27-30 May	v. Nottinghamshire (Lord's) 7-9 June	v. Glamorgan (Abergavenny) 10-13 June	v. Surrey (The Oval) 17-20 June	v. Worcestershire (Worcester) 24-7 June	v. Lancashire (Lord's) 1-4 July	v. Derbyshire (Lord's) 8-11 July	v. Yorkshire (Leeds) 19-21 July
J.D. Carr	0 31	6 7	19 1	4 4	22 13	50 —	9 19*	37 13	23 23				0 —	
P.R. Downton	17 40	2 23	5 15	17 6	8 6	— 39	1 —	13 17*	34* 100	15 11*	10 —	5 0	20 —	15 6
M.W. Gatting	72 4	26 0	54 83	30 19	65 79					0 1		19 0		34 33*
M.R. Ramprakash	34 14	22 3	69 12	6 3	46* 33	— 21	32 —	48 2	32* 62	35 13	54 —	9 7	65 1*	128 0
R.O. Butcher	22 17*	17 6	14 126	39 2	31 21		58 41*	8 27	14 9	6 16	11 —		34 —	
K.R. Brown	47 9*	4 15	37 38			— 91								
J.E. Emburey	10 —	9 15	3 21*	7 20*	4 0					— 5	9 1	16 2		47 1
S.P. Hughes	14 —	21 1*	2 6	1 —	0 5		14* 12	13 2*	— 5*	31 0		22* 4	2 —	5 5
N.F. Williams	13 —	0 1		69* 19*	28 36*		12 —	9 0			16 —			
A.R.C. Fraser	8* —	2 0	3 2	26 —	0 3		12 —	2* —	— 43*	29 2	7 —	0 0		4 16*
N.G. Cowans	4 —	5* 7	21* 0	1 —	17 0		0 —	4 —	— 10	12 0*	10* —	7 7	0 —	0* —
P.C.R. Tufnell			3 7*							3* 2			9* —	
D.L. Haynes					67 22	13 12		27 9	84 34	85 4	64 102	0 39*	0 0	10 5
J.F. Sykes						— 14*			6 2		19 —			
I.J.F. Hutchinson						201* —		12 17*			42 40*	5 13	28 106	
M.A. Roseberry						101* —		2 —	48 4	51 61	2 79	35 13	49 15*	20 1
D. Boden														
R.M. Ellcock												5 4*	1 —	8 —
J.C. Pooley														
Byes	4	1 1	6	5 1	4	4 2	4 4	5		4 1	6	3	4 2	
Leg-byes	14 4	12 3	1 15	15 7	8 10	1 6	9 2	12 5	11 15	13 5	8 1	3 2	5 3	4 4
Wides	1		4	2 2	1			2			3 1		1 5	
No-balls		2 3	12 16	1 1	2 5	1	5 4	7 1	9 4	5 5	1 3	2 4	5 3	14 4
Total	260 119	129 85	247 348	290 106	245 227	356 173	199 108	296 107	263 345	225 243	221 96	96 43	223 215	294 75
Wickets	10 4	10 10	10 10	10 6	10 10	1 3	10 2	10 7	4 8	10 9	10 10	10 10	10 2	10 7
Result	D	L	W	W	L	D	W	D	D	D	W	L	W	W
Points	7	4	22	23	—	—	21	7	5	6	22	4	20	23

Fielding Figures

69 – P.R. Downton (ct 63/st 6)
25 – M.W. Gatting
20 – J.D. Carr

14 – M.R. Ramprakash, J.E. Emburey, I.J.F. Hutchinson and M.A. Roseberry
13 – R.O. Butcher

12 – D.L. Haynes
10 – K.R. Brown
9 – P.C.R. Tufnell

Old Trafford and give Young New Zealand the three-match series by virtue of one victory and two draws.

13, 14, 15 and 16 September

at Pontypridd

Glamorgan 230 for 9 (S.M. McEwan 4 for 38)
v. Worcestershire

Match drawn
Worcestershire 4 pts, Glamorgan 2 pts

at Bristol

Hampshire 287 for 7 (R.A. Smith 68, M.D. Marshall 68 not out, K.D. James 60)
v. Gloucestershire

Match drawn
Gloucestershire 3 pts, Hampshire 3 pts

at Canterbury

Kent 241 (C.S. Cowdrey 69, A.R.C. Fraser 7 for 77) and 120 for 0 (S.G. Hinks 67 not out)
Middlesex 251 (K.R. Brown 76, M.R. Ramprakash 64, R.M. Ellison 6 for 43)

Match drawn
Middlesex 7 pts, Kent 6 pts

at Old Trafford

Derbyshire 292 (P.D. Bowler 81, Wasim Akram 4 for 76) and 209 for 6 dec (B. Roberts 75, J.E. Morris 66)
Lancashire 251 for 9 dec (T.E. Jesty 66) and 53 for 2

Match drawn
Lancashire 7 pts, Derbyshire 7 pts

at Trent Bridge

Nottinghamshire 121 (W.K.M. Benjamin 6 for 42, C.C. Lewis 4 for 69) and 279 (P. Johnson 79, F.D. Stephenson 72 not out)
Leicestershire 166 (F.D. Stephenson 7 for 65) and 125 for 5 (L. Potter 59 not out)

Match drawn
Leicestershire 5 pts, Nottinghamshire 4 pts

at Taunton

Somerset 141 (A.A. Donald 5 for 40)
Warwickshire 119 for 1 (T.A. Lloyd 58 not out, A.J. Moles 50)

Match drawn
Warwickshire 4 pts, Somerset 0 pts

	v. Kent (Uxbridge) 22–5 July	v. Essex (Uxbridge) 26–8 July	v. Leicestershire (Lord's) 29 July–1 August	v. Somerset (Weston-super-Mare) 5–8 August	v. Gloucestershire (Cheltenham) 9–11 August	v. Northamptonshire (Lord's) 12–15 August	v. Sussex (Hastings) 19–22 August	v. Nottinghamshire (Trent Bridge) 24–8 August	v. Sussex (Lord's) 8–11 September	v. Kent (Canterbury) 13–16 September	M	Inns	NOs	Runs	HS	Av
		11 —	33 68*	11 4	22 22	153* 11	0 26	13 27	12 8		18	33	3	702	153*	23.40
		0 —	38 —	0 18	6 10	— —	42 —	— 0	25 8		23	34	3	572	100	18.45
		25 158*	80 —	4 8	110* 35	— 83*	121 21*	83 46	139* 45	4 —	18	31	6	1481	158*	59.24
		35 —	58 —		0 21	53* 43		26* 1		64 —	21	34	5	1052	128	36.27
											11	20	2	519	126	28.83
							90 —	— 32*	30 53*	76 —	8	12	3	522	90	58.00
				9 77*	5 16	— —	14 —	— 4	21 12*	5 —	17	25	4	333	77*	15.85
	22* 11	4 —			0 3*		5 —			6 —	21	28	7	221	31	10.52
	20 —	10 —		0 30	6 8*		36 —	— 4*			15	19	5	317	69*	22.64
				15* 12*	0 —		0* —		27 —	4 —	17	23	7	217	43*	13.56
	4 —	8* —		0 —	0 —				0 —	10* —	20	24	7	127	21*	7.47
	8 —	5 —		1 —			4 —	— —	12 —	0 —	14	11	3	54	12	6.75
206* —	4 143*	2 —	17 38	20 24	76 21	0 46*	75* 36	13 51	17 —		20	37	5	1446	206*	45.18
											3	4	1	41	19	6.33
177	2 7	29 39	7 1								10	18	3	731	201*	48.73
48* —	55 —	0 16*	41 9	21 51	— 14*	32 —		0 16	17 —		18	29	5	804	101*	33.50
											1	—		—	—	—
			9 —					0 —			8	6	1	27	9	5.40
									14 —		1	1	—	14	14	14.00

Bowling / match details:

v. Kent	v. Essex	v. Leicestershire	v. Somerset	v. Gloucestershire	v. Northamptonshire	v. Sussex	v. Nottinghamshire	v. Sussex	v. Kent
7	6 13	1	4 8	4 10	8	3 2	1	12 1	3
1	2 5	10	2 10	12 4	9 17	11 1	1 7	9 7	11
6	1 1			1		1			1
13	3	9 4	5 8	7 1	11 7	11 1	5 3	2 1	19
458	195 341	287 127	116 223	222 206	302 204	370 97	204 160	302 202	251
1	10 2	10 1	10 7	10 7	1 3	10 1	2 6	10 5	10
D	D	D	D	W	W	W	D	D	D
8	4	5	4	22	22	23	4	3	7

4 – S.P. Hughes and N.F. Williams   1 – J.F. Sykes and sub.
3 – N.G. Cowans, A.R.C. Fraser and R.M. Ellcock
2 – D. Boden

at The Oval

Surrey 385 (A.J. Stewart 199 not out, I.A. Greig 71, C.M. Wells 7 for 82) and 53 for 3 dec
Sussex 153 for 2 dec (N.J. Lenham 81 not out, D.M. Smith 62) and 128 for 4 (P.W.G. Parker 74 not out)

Match drawn
Surrey 4 pts, Sussex 3 pts

The first-class season came to a soggy end and so decimated matches that not one could produce a result. There was no play after the first day at Taunton nor after the second at Pontypridd. There was no more play after nine overs had been bowled on the second day at Bristol, and all other matches were affected.

At Canterbury, Angus Fraser capped a magnificent season with the best bowling figures of his career, Mark Ramprakash reached a 1,000 runs for the season and Richard Ellison rekindled memories of past feats. Benjamin and Lewis shot out Nottinghamshire at Trent Bridge, but Franklyn Stephenson bowled and hit the home side back into the match, and Leicestershire were none too well placed when rain brought the match to a close on the last day.

Britannic Assurance County Championship – Final Table (1988 positions in brackets)

	P	W	L	D	Bonus pts Bt	Bonus pts Bl	Pts
Worcestershire (1)	22	12	3	7	44	83	319
Essex (3)	22	13	2	7	59	71	313
Middlesex (8)	22	9	2	11	50	72	266
Lancashire (9)	22	8	5	9	57	65	250
Northamptonshire (12)	22	7	8	7	47	63	222
Hampshire (15)	22	6	8	8	55	65	216
Derbyshire (14)	22	6	6	10	45	75	216
Warwickshire (6)	22	5	4	13	44	75	207
Gloucestershire (10)	22	6	11	5	38	70	204
Sussex (16)	22	4	4	14	60	68	192
Nottinghamshire (5)	22	6	6	10	54	65	190
Surrey (4)	22	4	7	11	50	69	183
Leicestershire (7)	22	4	8	10	43	74	181
Somerset (11)	22	4	6	12	50	54	168
Kent (2)	22	3	8	11	53	53	154
Yorkshire (13)	22	3	9	10	41	60	149
Glamorgan (17)	22	3	6	13	38	59	145

Warwickshire's total includes 8 points as the side batting second in a match where the scores finished level. Essex and Nottinghamshire deducted 25 points for sub-standard pitches at Southend and Trent Bridge.

Middlesex CCC
First-Class Matches, 1989

BOWLING	N.G. Cowans	A.R.C. Fraser	N.F. Williams	S.P. Hughes	P.C.R. Tufnell	J.E. Emburey	J.D. Carr	M.W. Gatting	D. Boden
v. Yorkshire (Lord's) 20–4 April	14–5–31–2	14.3–6–28–4	11–1–40–1	11–5–16–2					
v. Essex (Chelmsford) 27 April–1 May	17.3–7–34–5 / 5–1–12–1	13–2–53–2 / 4–0–14–0	8–0–37–0 / 2–0–32–0	12–3–20–3 / 2.5–1–11–0					
v. Surrey (Lord's) 4–8 May	16–8–24–3 / 14–1–45–3	22–8–42–2 / 21.2–2–87–1		10–3–25–2 / 13–3–33–2	22.4–5–48–2 / 22–4–61–3	17–8–36–1 / 35–19–45–0			
v. Hampshire (Lord's) 17–19 May	15–3–49–3 / 14.2–3–33–2	23.4–12–49–4 / 23–9–62–3	12–2–53–1 / 12–2–25–2	14–0–52–2 / 16–6–29–3		1–0–1–0 / 10–4–21–0	1–0–4–0		
v. Australians (Lord's) 20–2 May	14–3–40–0 / 13–2–35–1	17–4–42–0 / 30.3–5–89–4	12–1–35–1 / 8–1–23–0	11–5–41–1		20–7–49–0 / 21–4–84–2		4–0–11–0	
v. Oxford University (Oxford) 24–6 May			8–4–13–0 / 8–1–37–1	6–4–3–1 / 11–3–22–0	16–7–21–1 / 24–5–61–3		5–2–9–1 / 2–1–6–0		10.5–6–11– / 4–1–15–0
v. Warwickshire (Edgbaston) 27–30 May	19.4–3–43–3 / 9–2–28–0	27–13–41–0 / 16–6–20–5	20–4–52–3 / 13–1–40–0	24–9–44–3 / 9.5–3–23–4			4–1–6–1		
v. Nottinghamshire (Lord's) 7–9 June	16–3–45–1 / 9–3–29–1	21–6–37–5 / 14–1–26–2	13–2–45–1 / 7–0–18–0	15.1–3–45–3 / 8–3–14–2			2–1–3–0		
v. Glamorgan (Abergavenny) 10–13 June	12–5–29–2 / 6–1–17–1	25–3–76–2 / 18–4–64–2		10–0–31–0 / 8–1–25–1	30–4–77–2 / 22–4–79–1	29.3–9–84–1 / 20–6–70–1			
v. Surrey (The Oval) 17–20 June	19–5–61–1 / 12–2–33–1	22–5–40–3 / 14–3–30–1		18–3–47–2 / 5–0–19–0	13–3–27–2 / 27–4–115–1	20–10–29–1 / 39–7–103–2		6–3–16–0	
v. Worcestershire (Worcester) 24–7 June	15–5–50–3 / 18–4–49–3	15–2–34–4 / 19–5–39–4	5–0–32–0 / 11–1–37–1	7.5–1–25–2 / 10–0–39–2					
v. Lancashire (Lord's) 1–4 July	15–1–29–4 / 9–1–32–1	18–4–38–2 / 16–3–31–1		15–4–38–2 / 11–0–20–1		3–1–12–0 / 32.1–12–48–3		2–2–0–0	
v. Derbyshire (Lord's) 8–11 July	11–4–20–1 / 10–1–30–2			15–3–47–1 / 13–7–29–1	34–14–54–2 / 26.3–7–78–5		11–2–22–0 / 5–0–15–0		
v. Yorkshire (Leeds) 19–21 July	12–2–43–2 / 17–4–47–3	15–2–40–3 / 22.3–7–47–5		8–2–21–0 / 8–1–40–1		13–3–36–0 / 8–1–17–0			
v. Kent (Uxbridge) 22–5 July		18–4–46–2 / 18–7–23–4		8–2–28–1 / 17–7–26–0	11–3–37–1 / 46–19–77–3	23.4–15–23–3 / 48–27–62–2		1–1–0–0	
v. Essex (Uxbridge) 26–8 July	25–2–74–2		30–5–77–1	29.4–7–74–3	38–8–122–3		12–3–22–0	4–3–5–0	
v. Leicestershire (Lord's) 29 July –1 August	12–6–23–0 / 7–1–17–1		24–9–39–4 / 7–0–43–0	18.5–7–53–0 / 12–3–44–2	38–19–71–2 / 19–2–68–5		7–3–7–0		
v. Somerset (Weston-super-Mare) 5–8 August	15–4–43–1 / 17–2–56–2	21–6–55–2 / 19–1–71–2	16–2–48–1 / 7–1–24–0		6–2–13–0 / 30–8–59–1	20.5–9–38–6 / 19–8–38–1	6–1–10–0		
v. Gloucestershire (Cheltenham) 9–11 August	7–1–26–0 / 3–1–5–0		6–0–17–1 / 13.2–7–19–3	1–0–10–0 / 5–3–7–2		14.3–2–27–7 / 26–8–39–5			
v. Northamptonshire (Lord's) 12–15 August	19–5–60–1		19–3–45–3		21–4–77–3 / 28–6–60–5	34.5–9–88–3 / 26–10–39–3	6–2–19–0 / 3–0–12–0	4–0–16–0	
v. Sussex (Hastings) 19–22 August		26–9–52–1 / 5–1–19–1	21–4–48–3 / 16.5–3–58–3	20–4–58–2 / 15–2–65–3	19–8–40–1 / 6–2–16–1	18–11–34–1 / 14–2–40–2	4–1–8–1 / 5–2–11–0		
v. Nottinghamshire (Trent Bridge) 24–8 August			17.1–4–33–1	15–4–42–1 / 14–5–24–3	24–2–72–4 / 22–7–55–2	33–11–70–0 / 13–3–29–1		1–0–10–0	
v. Sussex (Lord's) 8–11 September	20–3–60–3 / 7–4–3–1	29–9–60–2 / 10–2–38–2			36–7–106–2 / 8–1–35–0	47–14–95–1 / 10.4–2–27–0	1–1–0–0		
v. Kent (Canterbury) 13–16 September	28–9–66–2	34.2–10–77–7 / 3–2–4–0		11–1–41–0 / 4–2–11–0	3–0–10–0 / 10–4–25–0	12–5–24–1 / 6–2–8–0		4–3–4–0	
	492.3–117–1321–62 av. 21.30	614.5–163–1474–82 av. 17.97	327.2–58–970–31 av. 31.29	463.1–120–1242–58 av. 21.41	602.1–159–1564–55 av. 28.43	635.1–229–1316–47 av. 28.00	74–20–154–3 av. 51.33	26–12–62–0 av. —	14.5–7–26–4 av. 6.50

a G. Fowler absent ill

J.F. Sykes	M.R. Ramprakash	M.A. Roseberry	R.M. Ellcock	D.L. Haynes	Byes	Leg-byes	Wides	No-balls	Total	Wkts
					5	10		1	130	10
						5		5	149	10
								1	69	1
					7	8	1	9	190	10
						9	1	7	280	10
					2	7		1	217	10
						6			176	10
					4	11	2	1	233	2
					5	7		4	243	7
12–5–22–3					9	4			92	10
18–9–25–1	1–1–0–0					8		9	174	5
					2	6		8	194	10
						1	1	5	112	10
						7	1	8	179	10
						7	1	2	97	5
	3–0–29–0	2.5–0–22–0				5		13	302	7
					1	4		8	311	6
						6		7	226	10
						5		7	305	6
						1		6	142	10
					4	4		10	172	10
			10.2–2–32–2			12		6	161	10
			16–4–62–3			3		2	196	9a
			14–3–27–1			7			177	5
			10–2–26–2		4	9	1		191	10
			12–2–35–5		2	2	2	2	179	10
			10–0–34–1			4		3	189	10
			7–3–19–3		6	5		6	164	10
			10–3–30–0		8	5	1	8	231	9
					3	13		7	390	10
					8	2	1	8	203	6
					4	8		5	184	8
						5		9	212	10
					1	5	1	9	264	6
			11–1–42–2					6	122	10
			11–4–37–0		1	10		6	118	10
			11–1–60–0		4	10		4	363	10
			2.5–1–4–2		1	10		1	142	10
					5	4	1	7	249	10
					4	3		7	216	10
			17–3–63–4		2	16	1	13	308	10
			13–2–23–4			5	1	4	136	10
			23–4–98–2		3	16		2	438	10
			4–0–23–1		7	4		1	137	4
					8	11		13	241	10
	11–1–31–0	12–5–25–0		6–3–13–0	3		1		120	0
30–14–	15–2–	14.5–5–	182.1–35–	6–3–						
47–4	60–0	47–0	615–32	13–0						
av. 11.75	—	—	*av.* 19.21	—						

Neil Fairbrother finished the season strongly for Lancashire but did not catch the attention of the England selectors. (Sporting Pictures UK Ltd)

Lancashire recovered through Jesty, and were engaged in a good tussle with Derbyshire when rain returned. Rain also thwarted the efforts of the two captains at The Oval. Alec Stewart hit the season's last century, and he was only one short of his second double century of the season when Surrey's last wicket fell. Ian Greig reached 1,000 runs for the season during a typically virile innings.

Refuge Assurance Cup Final
ESSEX v. NOTTINGHAMSHIRE

The uncertain weather kept the attendance for the last match of the season to half what it had been for the inaugural final in 1988. Bruce French was unfit to play for Nottinghamshire and was replaced by Chris Scott while, most unhappily, John Lever was unable to play in what would have been his last game for Essex before retirement, because of a back strain. Essex's decision to bring in slow left-arm bowler John Childs as Lever's replacement proved to be a most happy one.

Robinson won the toss and asked Essex to bat first. It was a sensible decision in the circumstances, for the wicket was damp after heavy overnight rain and was expected to pose problems for the batsmen. Gooch and Hardie played with much sense and a little luck, however, and began the Essex innings with a partnership of 52 in 15 overs. The stand was broken when Hardie edged on to Saxelby, and Waugh went cheaply, bowled by the naggingly accurate Hemmings. When Gooch, who had become becalmed, was bowled by Pick as he tried to force the ball through mid-wicket, Essex were 75 for 3 in 27 overs, and the advantage was very much with Nottinghamshire.

Prichard had started uncertainly, but he began to measure the pace of the pitch and after a watchful start he and Hussain scored at a brisk rate. In 13 overs, they added 83 before both perished in a suicidal one-day fashion in the final over. The last 10 overs of the Essex innings had produced 72 runs, an incredible rate in the conditions. Hussain had hit Stephenson back over his head for six, and Prichard's 56 had come off 84 balls. It was an innings that was to win him the individual award.

Broad looked magnificently solid at the start of the Nottinghamshire innings, and he and Pollard gave their side a firm foundation. Pollard was leg before as he moved across his stumps, and Robinson was very close to suffering the same fate to the accurate Miller, but at the half-way mark Nottinghamshire were 63 for 1.

It was the introduction of Childs that began to bring the game back in favour of Essex. Miller, who bowled well, accounted for Broad in his final over, and Robinson, frustrated by Childs, skied Pringle to Hussain at the start of the 27th over. On the last ball of the next over, Johnson moved down the wicket to Childs, was beaten by the turn and stumped, and when, in Childs' next over, Randall was bowled as he tried to sweep, Nottinghamshire had slumped to 95 for 5 in 30 overs.

Stephenson hit out from the beginning of his innings and was twice dropped by Gooch in the space of three overs. The first chance was a skier at mid-wicket off Foster, and the second a hard, low hit to mid-on off Childs.

It was third time lucky for Gooch when he held a simple return catch in the 34th over. Eight balls later, Scott was caught behind off Foster, but by then Hemmings had announced his presence with a massive six off Foster. Another six by Hemmings off the same bowler and some cheeky running made the Essex fielding look vulnerable, and Cooper was joining in the fun most effectively until he was leg before to Pringle in the 38th over.

The dismissal of Cooper left Nottinghamshire needing 14 to win off 17 balls with two wickets standing. Pringle had bowled splendidly, and Gooch now produced an accurate over to compensate for the less controlled bowling of Foster earlier. The last over began with Pringle bowling to Saxelby and Nottinghamshire needing seven to win.

Pringle's first ball lifted sharply outside the off stump; his second induced a simple caught and bowled. Pick tucked the third ball away for a single to give the strike to Hemmings, the hero of the Benson and Hedges Cup Final victory and now cast again in the role, but this time he was to be denied. Pringle produced a carefully disguised slower delivery which Hemmings hit high to long-on, where Waugh, 15 yards inside the boundary, safely took the catch.

So the season ended, and for Essex there was some consolation.

First-Class Averages

BATTING

	M	Inns	NOs	Runs	HS	Av	100s	50s
S.J. Cook	23	41	4	2241	156	60.56	8	8
R.A. Smith	18	29	2	1577	182	58.40	6	5
K.R. Brown	8	12	3	522	91	58.00		4
G.A. Hick	24	38	6	1824	173*	57.00	6	8
M.W. Gatting	19	33	6	1503	158*	55.66	4	8
M.A. Lynch	6	9	2	383	172*	54.71	1	2
M.R. Benson	15	29	5	1299	157	54.12	5	6
R.F. Pienaar	17	29	4	1321	134*	52.84	4	7
A.P. Wells	22	38	7	1629	153	52.54	2	13
A.J. Lamb	11	15	1	733	171	52.35	3	2
I.J.F. Hutchinson	10	18	3	731	201*	48.73	3	
N. Hussain	15	24	3	990	141	47.14	3	3
A.R. Butcher	23	40	5	1632	171*	46.62	3	11
R.J. Shastri	17	27	5	1004	127	45.63	2	5
G.P. Thorpe	18	30	5	1132	154	45.28	2	8
D.L. Haynes	20	37	5	1446	206*	45.18	3	8
D.M. Smith	19	35	6	1305	184	45.00	4	6
D.A. Reeve	14	17	4	581	97*	44.69		4
A.J. Stewart	23	42	5	1637	206*	44.24	4	5
G.D. Mendis	19	34	3	1367	118	44.09	2	10
M.E. Waugh	24	39	4	1537	165	43.91	4	8
T.S. Curtis	21	35	2	1430	156	43.33	4	8
J.E. Morris	23	43	5	1638	156	43.10	4	8
N.H. Fairbrother	22	38	4	1458	161	42.88	3	8

Paul Prichard, Man of the Match in the Refuge Assurance Cup Final as Essex gain some consolation from their season. (USPA)

REFUGE ASSURANCE CUP FINAL – ESSEX v. NOTTINGHAMSHIRE
17 September 1989 at Edgbaston, Birmingham

ESSEX

G.A. Gooch†	b Pick	31
B.R. Hardie	b Saxelby	18
M.E. Waugh	b Hemmings	4
P.J. Prichard	run out	56
N. Hussain	run out	32
J.P. Stephenson	not out	2
M.A. Garnham*		
D.R. Pringle		
N.A. Foster		
G. Miller		
J.H. Childs		
Extras	b 1, lb 13, w 3	17
(40 overs)	(for 5 wkts)	160

	O	M	R	W
Cooper	8	2	34	–
Pick	8	2	26	1
Stephenson	8	1	37	–
Saxelby	8	1	25	1
Hemmings	8	2	24	1

FALL OF WICKETS
1–52, 2–59, 3–75, 4–158, 5–160

NOTTINGHAMSHIRE

B.C. Broad	b Miller	39
P. Pollard	lbw, b Gooch	12
R.T. Robinson†	c Hussain, b Pringle	22
D.W. Randall	b Childs	14
P. Johnson	st Garnham, b Childs	1
F.D. Stephenson	c and b Gooch	16
E.E. Hemmings	c Waugh, b Pringle	24
C.W. Scott*	c Garnham, b Foster	1
K.E. Cooper	lbw, b Pringle	10
K. Saxelby	c and b Pringle	5
R.A. Pick	not out	1
Extras	lb 7, w 3	10
(39.4 overs)		155

	O	M	R	W
Foster	8	–	48	1
Pringle	7.4	–	20	4
Miller	8	–	20	1
Gooch	8	1	34	2
Childs	8	–	26	2

FALL OF WICKETS
1–35, 2–69, 3–81, 4–90, 5–95, 6–118, 7–131, 8–147, 9–154

Umpires: B.J. Meyer & J.W. Holder

Man of the Match: P.J. Prichard

Essex won by 5 runs

Northamptonshire CCC
First-Class Matches, 1989

Main scorecard — each match cell shows both innings (1st 2nd); a dash (—) = did not bat that innings, blank = did not play.

BATTING	v. Oxford University (Oxford) 15–18 April	v. Derbyshire (Derby) 20–4 April	v. Gloucestershire (Bristol) 27 April–1 May	v. Leicestershire (Northampton) 4–8 May	v. Yorkshire (Northampton) 16–19 May	v. Glamorgan (Swansea) 20–3 May	v. Surrey (Northampton) 3–6 June	v. Gloucestershire (Northampton) 7–9 June	v. Sussex (Hove) 10–13 June	v. Australians (Northampton) 17–19 June	v. Lancashire (Southport) 21–3 June	v. Somerset (Luton) 24–7 June	v. Worcestershire (Northampton) 1–4 July	v. Kent (Maidstone) 5–7 July
G. Cook	16 —	53 27	76 10*		83 4	21 —	23 —	17 17*	6 138		4 128	126 18	42 1	15 —
W. Larkins	126 —	15 11	4 38*	50 6	32 10	22 0	89 —	74 42	16 13	84 21	12 5	21 50	45 56	116 —
R.J. Bailey	27 19*	0 9	100 —	16 8	15 0	45 0	27 —	11 8*	11 25	2 17	15 134	20 100	17 13	35 —
D.J. Capel	30 —	24 6	81 —	1 39	2 9*	13 1	76* —	84 —	102 126		34 22	21 58	1 53	105 —
D.J. Wild	38 —		45 —	6 17	121 2	17 0	13 —		0 —	13 5				
R.G. Williams	48 —	8 28	71 —	7 2	1 1*		19 7	5* —	25* —	12 4*		0 16	3 4	7 —
D. Ripley	46* —	27* 24	22 —	40 18	123 —		5* —							
J.G. Thomas	13* —	9 7	19 —	35 11	11 —	28 22		10 —				4 0	10* 11	1 10
N.G.B. Cook	— 18*	5 3		1 3	14 —	0 7*		0 —		21 —	2 14	2 7*	— 6* / 5 0	1 —
G. Smith									0 —					
M.A. Robinson	— —	0 0*	0* —	0* 0*	0* —			0 —	9 —	1 0	0* —	— 2	2 0*	1 —
S.J. Brown	— —													5* —
A.J. Lamb		6 22	16 —	16 148		15 1	171 —		6 —	24 0	19 —	32 24	55 —	
W.W. Davis		4 27*	11 —	2 7*	4 —			6 —						9 —
A. Roberts						8* 7								
C.E.L. Ambrose						0 15		16* —		3 20*		— 0	22 11	
A. Fordham									0 —		4 0	0 37*		30
N.A. Felton										26 1	37 26	60* 23	52* 0	46
A.L. Penberthy										0 0				
W.M. Noon										0 37				
A. Walker										14* 0*				
N.A. Stanley														
J.W. Govan														
Byes	3 1	1	3 4	1 1	1			11	2 1		9 5		5	4
Leg-byes	7	9 11	36 1	3 6	7	6	6	6		4 12	9 10	4 12	4 7	2 4 / 2
Wides		1	1		3	6	3		1 1	4 1	1	2 1	1	1
No-balls	2 1	1	1 20	7 10		6		1	6 11	4 1	1	11 19 / 5 1	4 6	5
Total	356 39	161 177	505 53	185 276	418 26	200 60	425	236 69	223 355	180 106	144 407	300 308	256 158	378
Wickets	6 0	10 9	10 0	10 9	10 4	10 9†	5	10 1	10 5	9‡ 9	10 7	5 10	10 9‡	10
Result	D	D	W	W	W	L	D	W	D	L	D	L	L	D
Points	—	5	23	21	22	6	8	22	4	—	3	8	4	8

Fielding Figures
63 – D. Ripley (ct 57/st 6)
23 – R.J. Bailey
20 – W. Larkins
19 – N.G.B. Cook
11 – A.J. Lamb and N.A. Felton
8 – A. Fordham
7 – D.J. Wild, G. Cook and D.J. Capel
5 – J.G. Thomas
4 – W.W. Davis, A.L. Penberthy and W.M. Noon (ct 3/st 1)

First-Class Averages continued

BATTING

	M	Inns	NOs	Runs	HS	Av	100s	50s
N.R. Taylor	21	41	6	1495	118	42.71	3	7
W. Larkins	24	45	3	1787	126	42.54	3	13
C.L. Smith	19	33	4	1230	143*	42.41	2	6
I.A. Greig	22	34	10	1013	107*	42.20	1	8
R.T. Robinson	23	42	6	1516	146*	42.11	4	8
G.A. Gooch	18	31	1	1256	158	41.86	3	9
P.M. Roebuck	22	37	3	1399	149	41.14	5	6
V.J. Marks	20	32	12	822	89*	41.10		4
G.D. Lloyd	7	12	1	442	117	40.18	3	
D.W. Randall	25	43	6	1485	130	40.13	3	8
P.A. Neale	22	32	8	961	98	40.04		8
C.S. Cowdrey	24	34	4	1169	146*	38.96	2	8
B.C. Broad	22	41	2	1512	144	38.76	3	10
T.J.G. O'Gorman	8	14	2	462	124	38.50	2	
G.W. Humpage	23	34	7	1039	183	38.48	1	5
D.I. Gower	17	30	1	1102	228	38.00	3	4
J.J. Whitaker	23	39	3	1364	138	37.88	3	6
P.W.G. Parker	16	29	3	984	136	37.84	2	5
J.P. Stephenson	23	39	3	1354	171	37.61	4	4
G. Fowler	21	37		1370	130	37.02	3	9
D.A. Banks	4	7	3	148	60*	37.00		1
T.E. Jesty	21	35	7	1030	93*	36.78		8
J.R. Wood	12	18	2	588	96	36.75		4
T.A. Lloyd	22	33	2	1138	183	36.70	3	3

	M	Inns	NOs	Runs	HS	Av	100s	50s
Nadeem Shahid	7	9	2	255	52	36.42		1
D.J. Capel	23	39	3	1311	126	36.41	3	9
C.J. Tavare	22	39	2	1343	153	36.29	1	9
M.R. Ramprakash	21	34	5	1052	128	36.27	1	7
M.C.J. Nicholas	24	40	5	1269	140	36.25	5	3
R.J. Turner	8	11	4	253	58	36.14		2
T.R. Ward	23	40	5	1257	104	35.91	1	9
D.J. Bicknell	23	45	6	1392	119	35.69	4	6
J.D. Ratcliffe	11	20	4	571	127*	35.68	1	2
M.D. Moxon	19	34	1	1174	162*	35.57	1	7
G. Cook	20	36	3	1174	138	35.57	4	6
K.J. Barnett	22	36	1	1244	118	35.54	2	8
S.P. James	16	27	1	922	151*	35.46	2	3
K.M. Curran	24	39	4	1236	128	35.31	4	2
S.T. Jefferies	8	13	6	245	42*	35.00		
P.A. Smith	19	26	4	762	140	34.63	1	3
S.J. Rhodes	22	31	13	623	83	34.61		2
R.J. Harden	20	34	6	969	115*	34.48	3	2
A.J. Moles	21	38	5	1138	130*	34.48	2	8
A.A. Metcalfe	21	37	1	1230	138	34.16	3	6
K. Sharp	11	19	4	512	78	34.13		5
M.T. Alban	3	4		134	86	33.50		1
M.A. Roseberry	18	29	5	804	101*	33.50	1	5
R.J. Bailey	25	44	4	1337	134	33.42	4	6

v. Hampshire (Northampton) 8–11 July	v. Leicestershire (Leicester) 19–21 July	v. Nottinghamshire (Northampton) 22–5 July	v. Derbyshire (Northampton) 26–8 July	v. Yorkshire (Sheffield) 5–8 August	v. Essex (Colchester) 9–11 August	v. Middlesex (Lord's) 12–15 August	v. Warwickshire (Northampton) 19–22 August	v. Essex (Northampton) 24–8 August	v. Warwickshire (Edgbaston) 8–12 September	M	Inns	NOs	Runs	HS	Av
53 5	0 105		23 0	35 0	36* 2	5 12	4 11	18 40		20	36	3	1174	138	35.57
1 97		78 4	21 73*	5 83	76* 14	80 28	15 3	9 73	18 14	23	43	3	1650	126	41.25
11 78	9 52	9 10	116 17	98 59*	— 36	65 5	15 26	5 50	1 —	24	43	3	1336	134	33.40
4 16	4 77	23 51	60 11	5 1*	— 0	90 9	3 2		46 —	22	37	3	1290	126	37.94
				0 —	— 8				8 —	11	15	—	293	121	19.53
										5	8	1	166	71	23.71
0 18	12 6	32 22	12 0	0 —	— 3	24 5	2 5*	49* 16*	25 —	23	36	9	636	123	23.55
5 1	5 13*	16 1	3 28	10 —		2 4	0 14	20 11	12 —	20	32	3	346	35	11.93
10 8	0* —	1 2*		0 —		6 7		6 0*	0 —	19	27	6	143	21	6.80
								2 —		2	3	1	6	6	3.00
0 0*			0* 0			0* 0		0* 0	0 —	18	23	10	17	9	1.30
								6 0*		2	1	1	5	5*	—
	31 —							2 —		9	12	—	537	171	44.75
40* 2			0 5		— 0	0 6*			0 —	14	19	4	166	40*	11.06
					— 7					2	3	1	22	8*	11.00
	13 2*	23* 2*		7* —	— 1	29 12	1 0	15 —		9	14	5	127	23*	14.11
14 0		84 16		199 0	— 53	43 41	5 13	75 0	50 55*	13	23	3	647	199	32.35
12 11	25 0	1 28	0 0				0 16	15 55	0 8*	14	26	3	579	60*	25.17
	14 7	27 8	9 10							4	8	—	75	27	9.37
										1	2	—	37	37	18.50
				6 —	7 11*	7* 1		4 —		4	7	4	46	14*	15.33
	75 43	15 15	27 12							3	6	—	187	75	31.16
						0 7				2	3	—	11	7	3.66

5 6	1 4	4 4	1 2		1	4 1		1 5	4
3 8	6 3	8 8	8 4	8 3	10	10 10	11	5 12	13 2
2	1	1	1	1				2 1	
6 3	2	1 2	3 2	5 1	1 5	4 1	1	1 1	2
166 253	198 312	322 174	283 165	379 147	131 140	363 142	51 109	227 264	179 79
10 10	10 7	10 9	10 3	10 3	1 10	10 10	10 10	10 6	10 1
L	D	W	L	W	L	L	L	W	D
2	3	23	6	21	2	4	4	22	1

3 – R.G. Williams, M.A. Robinson, A.Walker and subs
2 – C.E.L. Ambrose and J.W. Govan
1 – A. Roberts

† G. Cook absent
‡ A.J. Lamb absent hurt

First-Class Averages continued

BATTING

	M	Inns	NOs	Runs	HS	Av	100s	50s
P. Pollard	18	32		1064	153	33.25	2	4
H. Morris	25	43	2	1351	133	32.95	3	7
C.M. Wells	22	36	4	1054	84*	32.93		8
I. Smith	18	28	4	786	116	32.75	2	3
A.I.C. Dodemaide	20	30	9	683	80	32.52		4
A. Fordham	13	23	3	647	199	32.35	1	4
R.J. Blakey	22	39	3	1159	97	32.19		8
L. Potter	24	39	5	1093	121*	32.14	1	6
S.G. Hinks	19	36	4	1028	104*	32.12	1	8
V.P. Terry	23	41	2	1245	180	31.92	1	8
P. Bainbridge	22	33	3	955	128	31.83	2	5
B.R. Hardie	17	27	2	792	142*	31.68	2	2
G. Miller	10	14	3	346	61	31.45		3
M.A. Atherton	18	33	3	941	115*	31.36	1	4
N.A. Stanley	3	6		187	75	31.16		1
K.T. Medlycott	24	38	8	928	86*	30.93		7
T.J. Boon	21	39	5	1045	80*	30.73		6
C.L. Cairns	6	8	1	215	58	30.71		1
R.A. Pyman	9	10	3	215	69	30.71		2
M.A. Garnham	22	32	9	703	91	30.56		4
J. Derrick	6	7	1	182	67	30.33		1
N.D. Burns	22	33	6	818	90	30.29		5
M.W. Alleyne	19	28	4	721	111	30.04	1	5
C.M. Tolley	5	6	2	120	37	30.00		
I.J. Gould	22	33	4	870	125	30.00	1	7
M. Asif Din	18	28	3	748	82*	29.92		4
P. Whitticase	18	29	6	684	61	29.73		2
P.D. Bowler	24	46	1	1337	157	29.71	2	10
P.J. Prichard	23	36	4	949	128	29.65	1	7
A.J. Wright	24	41	1	1159	130	28.97	3	6
P. Willey	23	37	2	1013	99	28.94		7
P.E. Robinson	18	31	4	781	147	28.92	2	1
K.D. James	22	37	3	982	162	28.88	1	5
R.O. Butcher	11	20	2	519	126	28.83	1	1
P. Johnson	20	36	3	949	109*	28.75	1	5
J.W. Lloyds	23	39	3	1032	71	28.66		6
A.M. Green	5	7		198	94	28.28		1
D.R. Turner	10	17	4	364	65*	28.00		3
M.P. Maynard	24	40	3	1035	191*	27.97	1	3
M.J. Cann	20	34	2	895	109	27.96	1	5
C.W.J. Athey	23	36	2	948	108	27.88	1	6
N.M.K. Smith	9	11	2	248	161	27.55	1	
T.M. Tremlett	6	8	4	110	40*	27.50		
T.C. Middleton	7	11	1	274	69	27.40		2
A.M. Brown	2	4		109	65	27.25		1
D. Byas	20	33	2	844	117	27.22	1	5
G.R. Cowdrey	9	12	3	244	108*	27.11	1	1
R.C. Russell	19	29	7	586	128*	26.63	1	2

Northamptonshire CCC
First-Class Matches, 1989

BOWLING	J.G. Thomas	S.J. Brown	D.J. Capel	M.A. Robinson	N.G.B. Cook	R.G. Williams	W.W. Davis	C.E.L. Ambrose	A. Roberts
v. Oxford University (Oxford) 15–18 April	13–2–40–1	12–3–38–1	12–2–33–4	14–1–35–1	13–5–18–2	6.2–3–3–1			
v. Derbyshire (Derby) 20–4 April	16–1–53–3 16–3–43–0		19–9–39–1 23–8–53–5	18–6–44–2 17.3–4–26–1			19.1–4–43–4 23–3–76–3		
v. Gloucestershire (Bristol) 27 April–1 May	26.3–6–87–5 19–3–68–2		16–2–49–0 23–3–67–4	25–5–60–4 17.4–6–29–3		3–1–5–0	18–3–62–1 26–2–96–1		
v. Leicestershire (Northampton) 4–8 May	15–2–53–6 22–3–79–3		13–2–45–1 14–6–32–2	9–1–22–0 19–5–52–1	10–4–12–0 12.1–8–10–2	0.5–0–5–1 6–1–16–0	19–2–71–2 18–3–51–2		
v. Yorkshire (Northampton) 16–19 May	13–1–59–2 20.3–5–58–3		17–1–59–1 16–3–50–1	5.1–1–15–1 17–9–25–1	4–3–1–2 19–9–14–3	6–2–15–0	13–2–48–4 20–1–73–2		
v. Glamorgan (Swansea) 20–3 May	19–3–52–1 10–0–46–1		18–1–76–3 5–1–16–0		23.4–10–62–4 20–5–49–0			26–2–72–2 8.2–1–25–1	3–0–7–0 7–1–40–1
v. Surrey (Northampton) 3–6 June	15–1–69–2 23–2–64–3		9–1–27–2 16–5–33–3	9–1–28–2 12–5–21–0	9–6–13–0		17–3–40–4 27–9–66–2		
v. Gloucestershire (Northampton) 7–9 June	11–4–45–2 14–2–46–2		5.1–2–14–4 17–3–64–2	7–1–21–0 8–5–6–1	4.5–3–4–2		13–6–31–4 23–8–53–3		
v. Sussex (Hove) 10–13 June			17–4–60–0 5.5–0–48–1	22–4–78–2 12–0–49–3	25–7–57–0			28–5–106–2 14–5–43–2	
v. Australians (Northampton) 17–19 June				16–2–39–0 8–1–33–2	30–8–76–5 14–3–43–0		11–1–45–0 9–1–29–2		
v. Lancashire (Southport) 21–3 June	13–3–46–0		14–2–47–0	20–6–72–2	27.1–8–56–6		23–1–91–1		
v. Somerset (Luton) 24–7 June	19–3–76–4 8–2–27–0		13–2–27–0 6–1–20–0	13–5–27–0 6–1–19–0	15.2–7–28–5 26–8–67–3			23–3–94–1 11–3–41–0	
v. Worcestershire (Northampton) 1–4 July	18–2–100–1		23.2–3–82–4	24–2–59–1	29–9–79–2			24–4–84–1	
v. Kent (Maidstone) 5–7 July		4–1–27–0 15–2–62–0	11–2–32–4 7–1–26–0	13–0–40–1 7–1–23–0	16–8–25–1		14.4–2–55–5 13–2–43–1		
v. Hampshire (Northampton) 8–11 July	29–5–87–2 4.5–1–31–1		17–1–67–0	18–2–69–0	20–10–35–1 1–0–5–0		23.5–4–82–3 4–0–17–0		
v. Leicestershire (Leicester) 19–21 July	24–5–89–3 7–1–31–1		18–3–58–0 7–0–47–0		33–13–63–2 14–1–54–4			30.3–10–52–5 8–3–17–0	
v. Nottinghamshire (Northampton) 22–5 July	16.5–1–57–2 14.4–1–73–3		21–3–66–2 6–0–25–2		29–9–95–3 15–6–28–2			23–10–38–2 9–2–16–3	
v. Derbyshire (Northampton) 26–8 July	21–3–86–2 2–0–2–1		27–5–99–3	20.3–3–59–2			28–2–101–1 5–2–11–1		
v. Yorkshire (Sheffield) 5–8 August	21–2–76–0 5–0–31–0		8–1–23–1 7–2–17–0		37–16–50–1 22–7–49–4			21–7–31–0 5–1–20–0	
v. Essex (Colchester) 9–11 August			27–3–59–2				23–4–81–3		24–1–110–
v. Middlesex (Lord's) 12–15 August	13–1–68–0 9–0–39–1		6–1–21–0 5–1–26–0				19–0–65–1 10–1–40–1		
v. Warwickshire (Northampton) 19–22 August	12–3–26–2		8–2–40–0	14–1–51–0	8–1–40–2			13.1–4–22–6	
v. Essex (Northampton) 24–8 August	20–1–74–5 15–5–38–2			16.1–2–52–2 10–0–47–3				24–8–94–1 13–2–40–2	
v. Warwickshire (Edgbaston) 8–12 September	11–2–27–1		16–4–45–3	13–2–38–2	6–3–13–0		20–3–74–1		
	536.2–79– 1946–67 av. 29.04	31–6– 127–1 av. 127.00	493.2–90– 1592–55 av. 28.94	411–82– 1139–37 av. 30.78	483.1–177– 1046–56 av. 18.67	22.1–7– 44–2 av. 22.00	439.4–69– 1444–52 av. 27.76	281–70– 795–28 av. 28.39	34–2– 157–2 av. 78.50

a A. Fordham 1–0–6–0   b G. Cook 1–0–5–0, 1–0–10–0

R.J. Bailey	G. Smith	A. Walker	A.L. Penberthy	J.W. Govan	W. Larkins	N.A. Felton	Byes	Leg-byes	Wides	No-balls	Total	Wkts
							1	9	1	17	177	10
							1	3		9	183	10
							2	16		8	216	10
								7		6	265	10
							13	13		16	291	10
										5	208	10
							4	6		15	250	10
							2	7		4	191	10
							3	13		11	251	10
1–0–4–0							12	5	4	19	290	10
7–1–25–1							6	7	3	11	214	4
							4	7	1	8	175	10
							2	8		15	207	9
								7		6	118	10
								13		2	186	10
2–0–9–0	6–1–27–0							13		8	350	5
	4–0–8–2						4	6		4	158	8
15.2–4–40–2		11–0–64–0	15–1–56–3					9		9	329	10
8–0–29–0		17–1–57–1	10–0–28–0					4		4	229	5a
7–0–23–0								1	1	8	336	10
2–0–14–0								8	1	4	274	10
21.5–3–104–2					4–1–9–0	7–0–58–1		1		1	346	7
								29		8	433	10
								2	1	12	156	10
7–3–10–0								2		14	191	2
3–0–14–0							5	7	2	23	366	6
								4			57	1
2–0–6–0			7–2–21–0					11			300	10
6–0–42–1							5	10	1		206	7
3–1–7–0			3–0–15–0				4	7	3	1	289	10
								5	2	1	147	10
7–1–28–1			10–3–26–0				3	18	2	18	420	10
			3–1–16–0							3	29	2
18–4–43–0		12–4–31–1						5		1	259	3
10.3–0–70–3		13–5–32–3					4	2			225	10
7–0–34–0		22–3–90–0					4	13	3	19	391	6
											0	0
10–1–41–0				27.2–8–55–0	10–1–38–0			9		11	302	1b
1.3–0–9–0				13–0–55–1			8	17		7	204	3
							4	8	1	4	191	10
	14–4–44–0			14–2–49–2				11		17	324	10
	7–0–33–0						2	6		6	166	7
											0	0
							7	13	1	7	217	8
139.1–18–552–10 av. 55.20	31–5–112–2 av. 56.00	75–13–274–5 av. 54.80	48–7–162–3 av. 54.00	54.2–10–159–3 av. 53.00	14–2–47–0 —	7–0–58–1 av. 58.00						

Nottinghamshire CCC
First-Class Matches, 1989

BATTING	v. Worcestershire (Trent Bridge) 20–4 April	v. Lancashire (Old Trafford) 27 April–1 May	v. Yorkshire (Leeds) 4–8 May	v. Oxford University (Oxford) 17–19 May	v. Hampshire (Trent Bridge) 20–2 May	v. Worcestershire (Worcester) 24–6 May	v. Glamorgan (Cardiff) 27–30 May	v. Yorkshire (Trent Bridge) 3–6 June	v. Middlesex (Lord's) 7–9 June	v. Kent (Trent Bridge) 10–13 June	v. Cambridge University (Cambridge) 17–19 June	v. Leicestershire (Leicester) 24–7 June	v. Gloucestershire (Gloucester) 1–4 July	v. Surrey (Guildford) 5–7 July
B.C. Broad	30 61	1 56*	23 54*		64 15	26 40	132 113	29 31				18 36	30 —	7 —
R.T. Robinson	6 4	66 77*	1 55*	26 24	36 73*	54* 19	37 63*	24 —	32 5	128 146*		8 0	11 —	136 —
M. Newell	35 0	99 —	32* —	43 28	41 1	8 62	31 4	0 24*	3 9		29 35	4 0		
P. Johnson	38 35	2 —	0 —	7 109*	43 69	18 6	52 87	0 29*	0 11*	17 —				
D.W. Randall	73* 32	0 —	1 —	100* —	45 46*	35* 18	8 24*	13 —	17 25	56 0		12 36	76 —	101 —
F.D. Stephenson	1 1	0 —	6 —		12 —							5 24	81 —	56 —
B.N. French	2 27	5 —	7 —		43* —							6 —	12 0	5 —	14 —
K.P. Evans	13 11	55 —	0 —	10 8		— 25*			39 6*	8 —			0 —	17* —
E.E. Hemmings	0 4	3 —	0 —	34 14*	24* —	— 16	2* —	58* —	29* —	— —		9 4	4 —	18 —
K. Saxelby	4 6*	7* —	12 —								8* —	11* 4	0* —	
K.E. Cooper	0 1	23* —	0 —			— 2		21 —	12 —			13 24*	4 —	1* —
P. Pollard				72 —					24 28	83 131	153 27	1 24	7 —	36 —
C.W. Scott				13* —		— 7	1* —	15 —	7 —		1* —			
R.A. Pick				— —	— 4	— 1*			0 —			2 1		
J.A. Afford				— —				0 —						
C.L. Cairns						— 11	26 —	41 —	0 3	58 —	47* 29			
D.J. Millns									0 —					
D.J.R. Martindale											11 —	60 2	33 7	78 —
M. Saxelby												4 32*		
G.W. Mike												15 56*		
M.G. Field-Buss														
Byes		1		4 5		7 12		4		4 2	10			
Leg-byes	13 6	4 4	2 6	7 3	13 5	2 12	8 2	5	7 7	6 5	8 1	2 10	22	7
Wides	1	1 3	2 4	4 2	4 1		1		1 1	2	1	1	2	1
No-balls	3 9	17 6		1	6		7	3 4	8	8 2	3 3	3	4	3
Total	218 198	283 147	86 119	320 194	331 214	150 238	300 302	214 84	179 97	377 287	351 229	116 135	252	475
Wickets	10 10	9 0	10 0	6 3	6 4	3 9	6 3	10 1	10 5	7 2	7 5	10 10	10	8
Result	L	D	W	W	D	D	D	D	D	L	D	L	W	D
Points	5	5	20	—	5	5	4	6	6	2	—	1	23	8

Fielding Figures
34 – B.N. French (ct 27/st 7)   18 – M. Newell and C.W. Scott (ct 16/st 2)   7 – K.E. Cooper
29 – R.T. Robinson   13 – D.W. Randall and K.P. Evans   6 – E.E. Hemmings, D.J.R. Martindale and subs
22 – B.C. Broad   8 – F.D. Stephenson
19 – P. Pollard and P. Johnson

First-Class Averages continued

BATTING

	M	Inns	NOs	Runs	HS	Av	100s	50s
M.P. Speight	9	17	1	425	88	26.56		3
N.J. Lenham	15	27	3	633	116	26.37	1	3
K.P. Evans	14	21	6	395	58	26.33		3
G.J. Parsons	18	26	8	474	69	26.33		1
P. Moores	22	30	6	629	116	26.20	1	2
C.J. Adams	7	11	1	261	79	26.10		1
N.E. Briers	24	44	3	1061	73	25.87		6
M.D. Marshall	15	21	5	412	68*	25.75		2
M.J. Kilborn	3	4		102	52	25.50		1
A.I. Kallicharran	16	26	2	610	119	25.41	2	1
D.M. Ward	15	26	2	608	145	25.33	1	
A.C.S. Pigott	21	27	5	556	91	25.27		3
N.A. Felton	14	26	3	579	60*	25.17		4
R.J. Parks	23	29	12	427	76*	25.11		2
M.J. Weston	14	22	3	473	74	24.89		2
P.D. Lunn	8	11	1	247	61	24.70		1
J.D. Carr	19	34	3	766	153*	24.70	1	3
S.A. Marsh	22	31	6	614	90*	24.56		5
A.W. Lilley	16	27	2	613	113*	24.52	1	2
B.N. French	17	27	5	537	55*	24.40		2
P. Bent	13	22		530	144	24.09	1	2
R.G. Williams	5	8	1	166	71	23.71		1
R. Sharma	21	37	5	755	77	23.59		3
D. Ripley	23	36	9	636	123	23.55	1	

BATTING

	M	Inns	NOs	Runs	HS	Av	100s	50s
G.S. Clinton	22	40	3	870	90*	23.51		5
A.N.S. Hampton	8	12	2	235	55	23.50		2
R.I. Alikhan	9	17	2	351	84*	23.40		3
D.L. Bairstow	11	17	3	327	101*	23.35	1	1
S.M. McEwan	11	9	3	139	28*	23.16		
R.G. Twose	5	9	3	139	37	23.16		
J.J.E. Hardy	13	23	4	435	65	22.89		2
C.S. Pickles	18	24	7	388	66	22.82		2
M. Newell	14	26	2	545	99	22.70		2
M.V. Fleming	8	12	3	204	45	22.66		
N.F. Williams	15	19	5	317	69*	22.64		1
N.A. Foster	17	21	10	246	50*	22.36		1
J.C.M. Atkinson	13	20		447	57	22.35		3
P.A.J. DeFreitas	17	28	2	580	78	22.30		5
M. Watkinson	23	39	6	733	70	22.21		4
D.R. Pringle	19	23	4	421	81*	22.15		1
F.D. Stephenson	18	30	3	597	81	22.11		4
I.P. Butcher	14	23	3	437	105*	21.85	1	1
D.P. Hughes	17	24	5	413	50*	21.73		1
G.R. Dilley	15	17	11	130	31	21.66		
R.D.B. Croft	5	8	2	129	45	21.50		
M.A. Crawley	4	6		129	60	21.50		1
R. Heap	9	15	2	278	46	21.38		
D.B. D'Oliveira	24	37	1	766	63	21.27		5

v. Warwickshire (Trent Bridge) 8-11 July	v. Somerset (Trent Bridge) 19-21 July	v. Northamptonshire (Northampton) 22-5 July	v. Lancashire (Worksop) 26-8 July	v. Essex (Trent Bridge) 29 July-1 August	v. Australians (Trent Bridge) 2-4 August	v. Sussex (Eastbourne) 5-8 August	v. Derbyshire (Trent Bridge) 19-22 August	v. Middlesex (Trent Bridge) 24-8 August	v. Derbyshire (Derby) 8-11 September	v. Leicestershire (Trent Bridge) 13-16 September	M	Inns	NOs	Runs	HS	Av
5 63	70 —	76 19	11 3	53 0		16 90	57 11	144 5	13 17	0 11	20	37	2	1430	144	40.85
6 11	128 —	68 30			37 5	22 57	0 8	26 39	30 2	2 2	22	40	6	1504	146*	44.23
				11 0	12 4		12 18				14	26	2	545	99	22.70
	0 —	6 4	51 43	25 36	0 23	47 37	5 16	4 9	6 24	11 79	20	36	3	949	109*	28.75
10 56*	44 —	25 3	130 29	76 60	0 48	24 38	0 0	78 8	70 27	22 9	24	41	6	1475	130	42.14
28 8	7 —	15 23	37 17	0 22*	47 13	64* 1	30 2	1 7	11 6	0 72*	18	30	3	597	81	22.11
28 2*	55* —	51* 32	14 40	23 25	20 9	26 19	1 20	9 42*			17	27	5	537	55*	24.40
18 14	51* —	1 1	58 20*	26 14*							14	21	6	395	58	26.33
21 —			5* 5	19 —	4 6	8 9*	8* 15	9 0	47 2	16 14	20	28	7	378	58*	18.00
											10	11	6	81	19	16.20
4 —	— —	4 15		33* —	9 10	8* 0*	21 1	0 0	12 2	8 23	21	27	6	251	33*	11.95
7 25	91 —	10 12	7 45	33 0	35 11	82 4	39 10	5 1	26 7	10 18	18	32	—	1064	153	33.25
									51 14	4 23	8	10	3	136	51	19.42
						1 1*		0 14	7 4	15 17	10	13	2	64	17	5.81
1* —	— —	18 0*	— 0	0 —	9 3*	— —		0* 1	3* 0*	22* 0	18	16	7	60	22*	6.66
					7* 9	— —					6	8	1	215	58	30.71
											4	3	1	16	9	8.00
8 11			0 4								7	11	—	221	78	20.09
											1	2	1	36	32*	36.00
											1	2	1	71	56*	71.00
	5 —		6* 1								2	3	1	12	6*	6.00
	1	4	1 2	1	1 4	14	1	2	9 1							
4 3	14	7 5	6 2	2 3	10 1	6 18	11 9	16 5	19	10 8						
5 2	1	3 2		1		1		1 1	2 1							
2 1	4		1		6 4	3 2	2	13 4	24 12	1 2						
147 196	471	289 147	327 211	308 165	195 148	303 287	185 114	308 136	330 119	121 278						
10 6	7	10 10	8 10	10 6	10 10	7 7	10 10	10 10	10 10	10 10						
D	W	L	L	W	L	W	W	D	L	D						
4	24	6	8	24	—	22	21	3	8	4						

4 – K. Saxelby and J.A. Afford
2 – D.J. Millns
1 – C.L. Cairns, M.G. Field-Buss and R.A. Pick

First-Class Averages continued

BATTING

	M	Inns	NOs	Runs	HS	Av	100s	50s
R.J. Scott	12	20	1	399	77	21.00		2
G.D. Reynolds	6	8	1	147	40	21.00		
B. Roberts	15	27	1	541	102	20.80	1	2
N.J. Speak	5	10	1	186	64	20.66		1
D.E. Malcolm	12	16	7	186	51	20.66		1
Wasim Akram	13	20	3	350	49	20.58		
J.D. Love	9	15	2	264	53	20.30		1
E.E. Hemmings	22	32	7	505	58*	20.20		2
D.J.R. Martindale	7	11		221	78	20.09		2
P.W. Romaines	6	11		220	77	20.00		2
G.D. Rose	16	20	7	258	50*	19.84		1
A.N. Hayhurst	9	15	2	258	40	19.84		
R.E. Morris	8	12		238	76	19.83		2
W.K. Hegg	23	39	4	694	86	19.82		5
D.A. Hagan	7	10		197	53	19.70		1
D.J. Wild	11	15		293	121	19.53	1	
J.D. Robinson	7	11	2	175	38*	19.44		
C.W. Scott	8	10	3	136	51	19.42		1
A. Dale	4	8	1	134	44	19.14		
M.A. Feltham	14	21	2	361	64	19.00		1
R.M. Ellison	12	16	2	264	39*	18.85		
S.C. Goldsmith	11	21	1	376	88	18.80		1
G.C. Holmes	13	21	3	337	38	18.72		
G.J. Lord	10	16	2	262	80	18.71		2
C. Penn	19	21	4	317	60	18.64		1
J.E. Emburey	20	30	5	464	77*	18.56		2
P.R. Downton	23	34	3	572	100	18.45	1	
I.T. Botham	17	24	1	419	73	18.21		1
A. Sidebottom	19	24	5	344	45*	18.10		
C.A. Walsh	18	25	5	360	47	18.00		
J.D. Fitton	18	25	6	336	44	17.68		
B.J.M. Maher	22	40	6	601	97	17.67		3
D.J.M. Kelleher	11	14	3	194	53*	17.63		1
R.A. Cobb	5	9		157	47	17.44		
P. Carrick	22	31	3	483	65*	17.25		2
I.D. Austin	9	13	3	171	38	17.10		
N.N. Radford	18	21	2	325	66*	17.10		1
K. Greenfield	5	8		132	48	16.50		
S.A. Almaer	8	12	1	181	62	16.45		1
W.K.M. Benjamin	15	19	2	273	41	16.05		
K.J. Piper	12	15	2	208	41	16.00		
C.P. Metson	24	33	8	399	47	15.96		
I.G. Swallow	13	20	2	287	64	15.94		1
C. Gladwin	4	8		127	59	15.87		1
R.P. Davis	21	23	6	263	67	15.47		1
G.C. Small	18	23	4	293	59	15.42		1
C.C. Lewis	12	19	1	277	69	15.38		2
M.C. Dobson	7	10	2	137	52	15.22		1

Nottinghamshire CCC
First-Class Matches, 1989

BOWLING	F.D. Stephenson	K.E. Cooper	K.P. Evans	K. Saxelby	E.E. Hemmings	M. Newell	R.A. Pick	J.A. Afford	C.L. Cairns
v. Worcestershire (Trent Bridge) 20–4 April	29.1–5–71–2 14.2–0–77–2	31.2–12–67–3 12–4–33–1	20.5–6–46–1 2–0–11–0	25–4–72–3	9.4–3–16–1				
v. Lancashire (Old Trafford) 27 April–1 May	21–5–80–0 11–4–21–2	21.1–7–46–0 6.3–4–13–1	13–2–36–2 9–1–23–1	15–1–68–1 13–4–39–2	22–5–57–3 28–7–94–1	8–0–44–0			
v. Yorkshire (Leeds) 4–8 May	19–11–38–7 11.1–1–37–6	11–7–11–0 9–1–19–2	9.1–4–20–3 7–2–28–2	7–2–16–0 5–1–24–0	2–0–5–0				
v. Oxford University (Oxford) 17–19 May			15–3–49–3	21–8–50–1 6–2–18–2	4–1–4–0 10.4–2–18–3		19.3–6–52–6 4–2–7–2	15–0–32–0 13–3–35–3	
v. Hampshire (Trent Bridge) 20–2 May	21–2–84–4 9.3–4–20–1	16–3–56–0 9–1–26–1			21.2–1–59–1 14–3–37–0		16–2–62–0 10–1–43–3	15–6–28–0 12–2–37–0	
v. Worcestershire (Worcester) 24–6 May		28–9–53–3 11–4–25–2	10–6–18–1		34–14–60–4 10–4–18–1		17.2–8–30–1 3–0–25–0		7–1–37–1
v. Glamorgan (Cardiff) 27–30 May		11–1–40–0			17.3–3–59–1 29–1–145–2		12–2–39–1 15–2–32–1	19–4–55–0 23–4–81–1	8–1–52–0 8–1–17–1
v. Yorkshire (Trent Bridge) 3–6 June		26–7–72–5 22–11–42–2			5–1–10–0 21–2–62–1		12–1–56–1 6–1–14–0	7–2–29–1 28.5–11–63–5	15–3–50–3 8–1–50–1
v. Middlesex (Lord's) 7–9 June		15.3–5–25–0	21.3–5–51–3 13–2–60–2		31–14–55–2 6.3–1–25–3				24.2–7–79 7–2–17–2
v. Kent (Trent Bridge) 10–13 June			13–2–45–2 6–1–22–0	19–7–54–1 12.4–0–82–1	29–7–71–1 11–1–70–0			24.2–7–99–3 14–1–73–2	15–4–78–4 9–0–53–2
v. Cambridge University (Cambridge) 17–19 June				18–7–28–0				36–11–91–5	
v. Leicestershire (Leicester) 24–7 June	22–6–66–1	32–8–69–1		16–7–51–0	32–9–66–2			31–10–90–2	
v. Gloucestershire (Gloucester) 1–4 July	20–9–32–5 15–4–44–3	18.3–8–28–4 15.1–7–37–6	7–4–11–1 3–0–11–0	6–1–26–0 9–4–27–0	9–4–19–1				
v. Surrey (Guildford) 5–7 July	17–3–63–0 13–2–34–1	12–1–44–0 5–2–11–0	14–3–35–0 3–0–20–0		38.5–9–87–6 27–10–32–0			20–6–39–4 26–11–41–0	
v. Warwickshire (Trent Bridge) 8–11 July	26–7–66–3	23–7–79–2	12–1–43–1		5–1–13–0			16.2–1–74–4	
v. Somerset (Trent Bridge) 19–21 July	9.3–1–29–2 20–4–60–4	17–5–42–2 9–4–20–0	16–1–48–2					9–2–30–0 37.3–11–90–5	
v. Northamptonshire (Northampton) 22–5 July	24–5–59–3 22–4–52–4	17–3–64–0 18–9–33–1	16–4–64–3 6–0–13–0				16–2–44–0 7–1–34–0	35.3–7–79–4 12–5–30–4	
v. Lancashire (Worksop) 26–8 July	23–2–71–2 20–3–69–2		5.2–1–17–1 17–4–58–0	26–10–66–4 12–2–49–1				14–3–39–2 24–4–98–0	
v. Essex (Trent Bridge) 29 July–1 August	25.1–12–59–7 18.5–5–47–8	21–5–59–1 10–2–34–1	13–4–31–1 7–3–21–0	16–4–46–1 9–1–42–1				4–2–6–0	
v. Australians (Trent Bridge) 2–4 August	10–4–16–0 10–3–12–1	17.3–7–47–3 9–2–25–1			17–4–48–2 20.4–3–86–0			13–2–75–0 19–4–68–2	
v. Sussex (Eastbourne) 5–8 August	15–1–77–0 27–7–86–5	22–5–62–1 24–5–68–2			33–12–75–3 13–2–40–1			17–4–60–0 8–3–20–1	
v. Derbyshire (Trent Bridge) 19–22 August	15–2–59–4 15–5–23–3	9–1–16–1 6–1–19–1			19–6–57–4 8.1–2–20–5		4–0–21–0		
v. Middlesex (Trent Bridge) 24–8 August	14–3–33–0 12–2–39–1	24.1–3–81–2 8–1–33–1			9–2–20–0 4–0–10–2		16–3–66–0 4–0–26–0	3–1–2–0 11–3–45–2	
v. Derbyshire (Derby) 8–11 September	19–2–75–1 8–0–34–0	19–4–53–3 4–0–23–1			15–7–17–2 19–8–29–1		15.2–1–50–2 12–1–41–4	24–8–85–0 12–2–25–3	
v. Leicestershire (Trent Bridge) 13–16 September	19–2–65–7 15–5–29–1	19.1–5–32–3 20–6–46–2			4–2–2–0 13–4–20–2		11–0–65–0 5–1–17–0	2–2–0–0	
	590.4–135– 1727–92 av. 18.77	609–177– 1553–59 av. 26.32	258.5–59– 781–29 av. 26.93	235.4–65– 758–18 av. 42.11	592.2–155– 1506–55 av. 27.38	8–0– 44–0 —	205.1–34– 724–21 av. 34.47	545.3–142– 1619–53 av. 30.54	101.2–20– 433–13 av. 33.30

a D.E. Malcolm absent injured   b M.A. Holding absent

R.T. Robinson	P. Johnson	D.J. Millns	G.W. Mike	M. Saxelby	D.W. Randall	M.G. Field-Buss	Byes	Leg-byes	Wides	No-balls	Total	Wkts
								19		6	291	10
							8		1	1	129	3
								13		3	300	6
							4	12		3	250	7
								2			92	10
								1			109	10
								4	2	5	191	10
								5			83	10
								11		3	300	6
							2	7		2	172	6
6–0–46–0	4.2–0–64–0						5	6		3	209	10
								2			180	3
								5	1	8	250	2
							8	3	2	7	286	6
								6	1	3	223	10
							8	11	2	1	250	9
		20–2–69–1					5	12		7	296	10
								5		1	107	7
							2	5	1	3	354	7
								11	2	2	311	6
		23–4–83–1	20–4–62–2	7–2–25–0			5	14	2	7	308	8
		10–3–24–0	8–1–45–0	9–1–25–2			4	2	1	2	100	2
							2	8		1	352	6
							2	2	1	1	101	10
								9			147	10
								7		3	275	10
					1–0–3–0		2	3		1	146	1
							6	11	1		292	10
						16–6–33–4		4			186	10
						20–8–39–1	3	6	1		218	10
							4	8		1	322	10
							4	8	1	2	174	9
						3–0–28–1		9			230	10
						9–1–28–1		7			309	4
							1	8			210	10
								4			148	10
		25–5–86–4						12		2	284	10
		14–2–53–0					6	5			255	4
		15–3–45–2						6			325	6
		11–3–39–0					4	7	2	2	264	9
							6	6		1	165	9a
								2	1		64	9b
							1	1		5	204	2
								7		3	160	6
								13		6	293	10
							1	7		2	160	9
								2		3	166	10
							5	8	1	1	125	5
6–0– 46–0 —	4.2–0– 64–0 —	118–22– 399–8 av. 49.87	28–5– 107–2 av. 53.50	16–3– 50–2 av. 25.00	1–0 3–0 —	48–15– 128–7 av. 18.28						

Somerset CCC
First-Class Matches, 1989

BATTING

Legend of match columns (opponent / venue / dates):
H = v. Hampshire (Southampton) 20–4 April · GlaT = v. Glamorgan (Taunton) 27–30 April · Sus = v. Sussex (Taunton) 4–8 May · Aus = v. Australians (Taunton) 17–19 May · Lan = v. Lancashire (Taunton) 20–3 May · Ess = v. Essex (Chelmsford) 27–30 May · GlaC = v. Glamorgan (Cardiff) 7–9 June · Yor = v. Yorkshire (Taunton) 10–13 June · Kent = v. Kent (Bath) 17–20 June · Glos = v. Gloucestershire (Bath) 21–3 June · Nor = v. Northamptonshire (Luton) 24–7 June · Der = v. Derbyshire (Derby) 1–4 July · Sur = v. Surrey (Guildford) 8–11 July · Not = v. Nottinghamshire (Trent Bridge) 19–21 July

(each cell shows both innings where played)

BATTING	H	GlaT	Sus	Aus	Lan	Ess	GlaC	Yor	Kent	Glos	Nor	Der	Sur	Not
S.J. Cook	85 44*	42 79	91 36	11 57	156 17	147* 10	61 —	34	49 72	12 147	25 46	44 85	105 —	120* 131*
P.M. Roebuck	149 26	19 12	18 36	13 100*	20 66	20 65*	26 —	103 —	19 107	4 25	70 —	7 54	13 —	0 50
J.J.E. Hardy	1 0*	51 0	12 34			8* 24*		0 —	1 12	3 31	0 65	35 29	35* —	6 13
J.G. Wyatt	2 —												2 —	
R.J. Bartlett	5 —	18 0	0 5	0 18	20 48	0 4	0 —							
N.D. Burns	62 —	12 17	4 1	27 —		— 38*	6*	86* —	4 —		33 20	38* 10	15 —	4 0
V.J. Marks	35 —	1 11*	59* 25*	14 —	0 —			17 —	89* 17	6 3	19 5	23* 14*		6 0
G.D. Rose	0 —	13 5*	14 —	0 —			16 —	4 —						
N.A. Mallender	31 —	6 —	7 —	0 —			2 —	0 —		5 48*	6 0			
A.N. Jones	0 —	6* —	4 —	15 —				20* —		6*	0* 8	19* 2*	12 —	4 0
D.J. Foster	11* —	0 —	1 —	6 —									5 —	6 0
C.J. Tavare		5 22	3 90*	6 43	153 1	1 18	70 —	42 —	1 23	5 25	59 89	28 5		21 11
R.J. Harden				45 4*	23* —	101* 8	10 —	25 —	102* 22	25 5	16 115*	34 7	41 —	14 1
P.D. Unwin				4* —	—									
T.J.A. Scriven					—									
H.R.J. Trump							31* —	23 —		0 0	14 2	0* —	9 —	1 2
N.J. Pringle									0 12*	7 3				
T. Gard									— —	0 40				
M.W. Cleal													16	0 0
J.C.M. Atkinson														
Byes		8	5	2 1	5 4	5 2	1		5 1	10		4 2		3
Leg-byes	21	4 5	9 4	6 4	11 1	5	9	8	6 4	3 13	8 1	4 8	10	4 6
Wides	3		1	2 2	2	1	1	1	1	1	1	1	1	1
No-balls	8 1	1 1	7 1	3 6	3 2	3	4		2 6	4 1	14 9			1
Total	413 71	186 152	229 238	140 235	399 203	280 116	330 0	299	274 276	73 364	274 346	231 240	297	186 218
Wickets	10 1	10 6	10 5	10 3	4 4	3 4	8 0	10	5 6	10 10	10 7	5 7	10	10 10
Result	D	D	W	D	L	D	D	D	D	L	W	D	D	L
Points	6	5	22	—	7	5	3	6	4	1	21	2	6	2

Fielding Figures
51 – N.D. Burns (ct 45/st 6)
18 – C.J. Tavare
13 – S.J. Cook
10 – R.J. Bartlett and R.J. Harden
8 – P.M. Roebuck, N.A. Mallender and A.N. Jones
7 – V.J. Marks
6 – J.J.E. Hardy and H.R.J. Trump
5 – N.J. Pringle
4 – G.D. Rose

First-Class Averages continued

BATTING

	M	Inns	NOs	Runs	HS	Av	100s	50s
A.E. Warner	15	23	6	253	46	14.88		
P.G. Newman	15	25	4	309	86*	14.71		2
D.V. Lawrence	14	17	5	173	45	14.41		
A.N. Jones	23	23	10	186	43*	14.30		
A.W. Stovold	7	13		184	36	14.15		
C.E.L. Ambrose	9	14	5	127	23*	14.11		
R.K. Illingworth	24	26	2	333	71	13.87		2
P.J. Newport	9	12	2	138	36	13.80		
G.A. Tedstone	12	17	2	206	50	13.73		1
A.A. Donald	19	22	6	215	40	13.43		
D.A. Thorne	5	10		134	41	13.40		
N.A. Mallender	18	18	4	186	48*	13.28		
J.M.G. Willatt	9	14	1	172	45	13.23		
M.P. Bicknell	18	24	6	234	40*	13.00		
T.D. Topley	23	26	4	277	49	12.59		
A.R.C. Fraser	21	28	7	264	43*	12.57		
J.P. Agnew	24	31	8	279	39	12.13		
R.J. Bartlett	11	19		228	54	12.00		1
K.E. Cooper	21	27	6	251	33*	11.95		
P.J.W. Allott	16	23	5	215	28	11.94		
J.G. Thomas	20	32	3	346	35	11.93		
P.W. Jarvis	18	25	5	236	59*	11.80		1
D.A. Graveney	15	22	8	164	27*	11.71		
R.J. Maru	23	25	8	192	29	11.29		

BATTING

	M	Inns	NOs	Runs	HS	Av	100s	50s
W.W. Davis	14	19	4	166	40*	11.06		
C.A. Connor	15	14	2	129	24	10.75		
S.P. Hughes	21	28	7	221	31	10.52		
S.J. Dennis	15	19	1	187	38	10.38		
F.A. Griffith	5	10		102	30	10.20		
I.R. Bishop	12	20	2	180	28*	10.00		

(Qualification – 100 runs, average 10.00)
(Also batted – M.D. Crowe 100 not out, C.A. Best 100 & 39)

BOWLING

	Overs	Mds	Runs	Wkts	Av	Best	10/m	5/inns
O. Henry	59	9	174	13	13.38	7/86	1	2
D.A. Reeve	97.4	35	163	11	14.81	3/3		
A.A. Donald	537.1	122	1398	86	16.25	7/66		6
M.D. Marshall	428.3	115	1067	64	16.67	6/69		4
S.R. Lampitt	219.5	56	526	31	16.96	5/32		2
Wasim Akram	463.3	103	1117	63	17.73	7/42	2	7
W.K.M. Benjamin	484.1	145	1238	69	17.94	7/54	1	7
D.R. Pringle	668.2	163	1753	94	18.64	7/18	2	5
F.D. Stephenson	590.4	135	1727	92	18.77	8/47	2	7

v. Leicestershire (Taunton) 22-5 July	v. Sussex (Hove) 26-8 July	v. Middlesex (Weston-super-Mare) 5-8 August	v. Worcestershire (Weston-super-Mare) 9-11 August	v. Warwickshire (Edgbaston) 12-15 August	v. Hampshire (Taunton) 19-22 August	v. Worcestershire (Worcester) 24-7 August	v. Gloucestershire (Bristol) 8-11 September	v. Warwickshire (Taunton) 13-16 September	M	Inns	NOs	Runs	HS	Av
148 —	6 130	25 50	9 44	4 16	25 3	10 3	18 35	9 —	23	41	4	2241	156	60.56
36 —		18 0	99 6	1 11	14 32*	22 —	0 117	21 —	22	37	3	1399	149	41.14
							40 0	35 —	13	23	4	435	65	22.89
	23 19								3	4	—	46	23	11.50
54 —	7 37	0 0	12 0						11	19	—	228	54	12.00
13 —	38* —	0 32	3 23	90 13	78 —	5 38	5 9	36 —	21	31	5	760	90	29.23
18 —	33 32*	16 26*	0 20	75 1*	89* —	45 24*	15 18*		20	32	12	822	89*	41.10
33 —	— 3*	3 21*	6 14*	27* —	8 —	50* 19*	0 15	7 —	16	20	7	258	50*	19.84
		23 —	5 3	12* —	— —	20 —	0* 9	9* —	18	18	4	186	48*	13.28
43* —	— 1	13 —	6* 0		4* —	13 —	0 1*	9 —	23	23	10	186	43*	14.30
									9	8	1	29	11*	4.14
9 —	83 25	24 81	18 1	52 42	11 46*	89 62	39 36	2 —	21	38	2	1341	153	37.25
30 —	39 39	76* 28	59 15	3 1	8 8	27 0	23 10	5 —	20	34	6	969	115*	34.60
									1	1	1	4	4*	—
									1					
0 —	— —	0 —	12 0					0 —	14	15	2	94	31*	7.23
				8 6	10 —	4 0			5	9	1	50	12*	6.25
									2	2	—	40	40	20.00
30 —	20 —							2 —	6	7	—	68	30	9.71
				17 53	40 —	46 6	17 5		4	7	—	184	53	26.28
9	4	1	6	10 10										
11	6 3	5 5	4 4	16 12	8 1	4 7	3 6							
1	1	1	2 1	1 1	1 1	1								
14	7 2	9 9	5 8	1 5	7 2	3 1	4 2	6						
449	266 292	212 254	240 145	316 170	303 93	338 161	165 263	141						
10	7 6	10 6	10 10	8 7	8 2	10 6	10 9†	10						
W	D	D	L	D	W	L	L	D						
23	7	6	4	6	23	4	5	0						

3 – Subs

2 – T. Gard and M.W. Cleal

1 – J.C.M. Atkinson and D.J. Foster

† V.J. Marks retired hurt

First-Class Averages continued

BOWLING

	Overs	Mds	Runs	Wkts	Av	Best	10/m	5/inns
S.M. McEwan	368.3	82	999	52	19.21	6/34		3
R.M. Ellcock	182.1	35	615	32	19.21	5/35		1
G.J.F. Ferris	124.1	39	327	17	19.23	4/44		
B.P. Patterson	210.1	43	618	32	19.31	5/48		1
G.A. Hick	214.4	65	519	26	19.96	5/52	1	2
A.R.C. Fraser	797.1	203	1861	92	20.22	7/77		4
O.H. Mortensen	334.4	64	878	43	20.41	6/38		2
C.A. Walsh	626.5	137	1675	81	20.67	7/19	1	5
C.A. Connor	443.2	98	1255	59	21.27	7/31	1	5
N.G. Cowans	492.3	117	1321	62	21.30	5/34		1
S.P. Hughes	463.1	120	1242	58	21.41	4/23		
N.A. Foster	713.3	186	1836	85	21.60	7/105		1
N.G.B. Cook	587	200	1328	61	21.77	6/56		3
R.K. Illingworth	444.5	179	893	41	21.78	5/23		1
C.C. Lewis	300.3	61	986	45	21.91	5/40		3
P.J. Newport	279.5	42	902	41	22.00	6/43	1	3
T.M. Tremlett	160	49	356	16	22.25	4/67		
I.R. Bishop	335	64	920	41	22.43	6/67		1
P.J. Bakker	629.4	156	1732	77	22.49	6/81		4
I.D. Austin	187.5	46	473	21	22.52	4/60		
J.H. Childs	681.5	263	1521	67	22.70	7/35	1	6
N.V. Radford	572.4	119	1725	75	23.00	6/59		3
A. Sidebottom	574	129	1590	68	23.38	6/79	1	5
A.E. Warner	331.1	80	821	35	23.45	4/18		

BOWLING

	Overs	Mds	Runs	Wkts	Av	Best	10/m	5/inns
D.E. Malcolm	293.4	40	1122	47	23.87	4/68		
M. Jean-Jacques	90.2	11	359	15	23.93	4/84		
G.R. Dilley	422.2	73	1438	60	23.96	5/28	1	5
T.D. Topley	605.5	143	1851	77	24.03	5/30		2
S.J. Base	417.3	73	1451	60	24.18	7/60	1	2
A.R. Hansford	167.2	39	485	20	24.25	5/79		1
G.D. Rose	418.2	104	1143	47	24.31	4/12		
M.D. Harman	93.4	29	248	10	24.80	5/80		1
S.L. Watkin	792	170	2359	94	25.09	7/65	3	8
D.P. Hughes	102.1	27	303	12	25.25	3/30		
I.T. Botham	496.4	109	1417	56	25.30	7/85	1	3
P.W. Jarvis	617.3	137	1924	76	25.31	7/74		4
G.C. Small	537	134	1400	55	25.45	5/55		1
M.C.J. Nicholas	122.4	16	384	15	25.60	6/37		1
P.J.W. Allott	442.2	115	1052	41	25.65	5/24		1
K.B.S. Jarvis	298.4	70	928	36	25.77	5/15		1
R.M. Ellison	292.1	71	752	29	25.93	6/43		2
T.A. Munton	613.4	178	1538	59	26.06	5/13		1
K.E. Cooper	609	177	1553	59	26.32	6/37	1	2
M.P. Bicknell	622.3	137	1717	65	26.41	6/47		4
P. Willey	431.1	136	985	37	26.62	5/45		1
T.A. Merrick	110.4	29	320	12	26.66	6/67		1
P.A.J. DeFreitas	614.5	125	1818	68	26.73	7/21	1	4
K.M. Curran	415	85	1258	47	26.76	7/69		2

Somerset CCC
First-Class Matches, 1989

BOWLING	A.N. Jones	N.A. Mallender	G.D. Rose	D.J. Foster	V.J. Marks	P.M. Roebuck	P.D. Unwin	R.J. Harden	T.J.A. Scriven
v. Hampshire (Southampton) 20–4 April	23–4–87–2	26–4–58–4	19–3–37–2	20–4–75–1	23–8–50–0	1–0–1–1			
v. Glamorgan (Taunton) 27–30 April	13–4–27–0 18–4–33–1	16–5–36–1 19–9–31–1	14–8–12–4 26.2–9–46–4	6–0–18–0	27.2–13–38–5 55–24–96–1	14–7–22–2			
v. Sussex (Taunton) 4–8 May	17–3–51–3 17–4–53–2	16.2–6–30–5 21.5–4–62–7	16–4–40–0 19–2–51–1	17–2–57–2 11–1–50–0	15–2–44–0 10–5–13–0	3–0–4–0			
v. Australians (Taunton) 17–19 May	21–2–83–2 5–0–15–0	20–5–55–2 6–1–25–0	16–5–45–1 6–1–18–0	16–2–49–0 4–0–17–0		7–1–27–0 4–1–15–1	24–5–73–3 12–1–43–2		
v. Lancashire (Taunton) 20–3 May	23–1–97–3 14.5–2–73–1	20–9–34–1 13–0–70–1	7–2–24–1			14–5–35–1 11–1–52–0		8.3–1–25–0	27.1–5–67– 16–3–88–2
v. Essex (Chelmsford) 27–30 May	14–3–45–1 6–1–20–0	17–5–48–2 8–0–35–0		10–2–34–0 8–0–36–1	40–12–86–1 16–1–80–0	9–1–25–2			
v. Glamorgan (Cardiff) 7–9 June	16–1–42–3	20–7–35–1	20–4–57–1		21–2–73–4				
v. Yorkshire (Taunton) 10–13 June	15–3–57–2 13–0–48–1	19–4–60–3 18–6–34–0	20.2–6–51–3 5–2–4–0		15–6–29–1 31–5–75–1	6–1–10–1 13–3–33–0		1–0–10–0	
v. Kent (Bath) 17–20 June	17–3–94–2 3–1–9–0	24–2–93–0 3–1–7–0			38.1–5–146–4 11–6–15–0				
v. Gloucestershire (Bath) 21–3 June	20–6–49–1 3–0–16–1	24–5–47–1 1–0–8–0			50–14–149–1 1.1–0–9–0	16–4–27–1		1–0–2–0	
v. Northamptonshire (Luton) 24–7 June	17–3–83–1 13.1–0–71–2	16–2–58–1 5–0–27–1		17–3–48–2 10–0–43–2	24.3–8–70–1 20–1–95–1				
v. Derbyshire (Derby) 1–4 July	25–5–55–1 4–2–2–1			22–1–97–0 5–0–10–0	41–12–115–3 10–3–11–1	6–3–17–0		2–0–6–0	
v. Surrey (Guildford) 8–11 July	18–5–62–5 11–4–22–1			10–2–22–0 10–1–31–0	27–10–44–4 26–12–31–3	1–0–1–0 4–0–10–0			
v. Nottinghamshire (Trent Bridge) 19–21 July	19–4–64–2			13–3–60–0	52.1–19–136–1	4–1–13–0			
v. Leicestershire (Taunton) 22–5 July	25–13–38–3 8–1–30–2		18–7–41–1 10.4–1–35–4		28–5–85–2 12–3–25–1				
v. Sussex (Hove) 26–8 July	15–5–48–3 10–5–23–0		19–3–74–0 14–1–69–3		23.1–6–65–4 14–4–45–0			5–2–14–0 6–1–32–0	
v. Middlesex (Weston-super-Mare) 5–8 August	13.2–4–30–4 14.4–0–64–1	14–2–42–2 14–5–32–0	15–4–33–3 20–10–22–4		4–2–5–1 23–9–48–1	13–3–23–1			
v. Worcestershire (Weston-super-Mare) 9–11 August	14–2–57–0 4–0–15–0	21–2–62–2 7–2–13–1	14–3–42–2 6–1–25–0		25–4–81–1 8–3–21–0	7–2–14–1			
v. Warwickshire (Edgbaston) 12–15 August	16–2–42–1 8–2–21–2	18–6–42–2 8–2–25–0	19.2–5–47–2 4–0–19–0		24–6–91–1 12–2–39–1	6–2–11–0			
v. Hampshire (Taunton) 19–22 August	17–5–37–6 14–4–53–3	19.1–6–54–1 19.3–6–55–5	24–5–57–1 6–3–14–1		35–18–68–1	2–0–7–0			
v. Worcestershire (Worcester) 24–7 August	15–1–55–3 14.1–1–77–1	15–4–18–2 9–1–47–0	15–2–51–0 15–1–69–2		11.2–2–42–0 18–1–99–1				
v. Gloucestershire (Bristol) 8–11 September	23.1–5–66–4 19–2–71–0	27–5–69–2 23–4–59–2	24–7–48–3 18–4–82–4		18–5–43–1 34–8–90–0				
v. Warwickshire (Taunton) 13–16 September	7–1–29–0	7–1–18–0	7.4–1–30–0						
	603.2–118– 2014–71 av. 28.36	514.5–121– 1389–50 av. 27.78	418.2–104– 1143–47 av. 24.31	179–21– 647–8 av. 80.87	843.5–246– 2252–47 av. 47.91	141–35– 347–11 av. 31.54	36–6– 116–5 av. 23.20	23.3–4– 89–0 —	43.1–8– 155–4 av. 38.75

H.R.J. Trump	N.J. Pringle	M.W. Cleal	J.J.E. Hardy	J.C.M. Atkinson	Byes	Leg-byes	Wides	No-balls	Total	Wkts
					4	6		9	318	10
					1	4		2	118	10
					5	9	1	1	260	9
					2	6		11	234	10
						3		9	232	10
						7	1	8	339	8
					4	7		1	144	3
					13	8	1	5	303	8
					3	16		3	302	4
29–4–79–1						10		4	327	8
13–2–39–2					1	6	1	3	217	3
									0	0
17–2–59–0					1	10		5	277	9
10–3–28–0						4		4	239	10
34–11–50–2					15	6	7	1	275	5
35–6–119–0	10–0–54–0				7	13		14	526	7
14–2–40–0	8–2–33–0					4		2	108	0
38.3–9–82–0	5–0–23–0				4	19	1	11	402	4
						3			36	2
14–3–37–0						4	1	5	300	5
12–0–60–3					5	7		1	308	10
32.2–12–80–4		17–3–56–1			9	15		4	444	9
13–2–28–0		5–0–17–0	1.4–0–6–0			7		1	87	2
11–4–21–0		10–3–23–1				4		3	177	10
22–8–31–2					11	7		3	143	6
32–5–130–4		13–3–53–0			1	14	1	4	471	7
23–7–38–2		11.4–4–40–2			1	7		1	250	10
14–3–39–3		5–1–21–0			2				152	10
11–4–42–0		17–1–62–2				11		2	316	9
8–0–37–1		10–3–33–0				6		2	245	4
					4	2		5	116	10
7–1–16–0					8	10		8	223	7
15.5–4–38–0						8		6	302	6
3.2–0–12–0						1		3	87	1
					6	11	1	5	250	7
						3	1	1	107	3
				9–3–31–0		3		7	257	10
					4	12		2	138	10
	3–0–12–0			2–0–3–0	11	8	2	7	200	5
						10		1	302	5
				2–0–12–0	9	12	5	4	259	10
						8	1		310	7
7–1–20–1		7–1–22–0						2	119	1
416–93–1125–25 av. 45.00	26–2–122–0 —	95.4–19–327–6 av. 54.50	1.4–0–6–0 —	13–3–46–0 —						

Surrey CCC
First-Class Matches, 1989

BATTING

	v. Oxford University (Oxford) 19–21 April		v. Hampshire (The Oval) 27 April–1 May		v. Middlesex (Lord's) 4–8 May		v. Sussex (Hove) 17–19 May		v. Warwickshire (Edgbaston) 20–3 May		v. Lancashire (The Oval) 24–6 May		v. Yorkshire (The Oval) 27–30 May		v. Northamptonshire (Northampton) 3–6 June		v. Hampshire (Basingstoke) 7–9 June		v. Essex (The Oval) 10–13 June		v. Middlesex (The Oval) 17–20 June		v. Gloucestershire (The Oval) 24–7 June		v. Nottinghamshire (Guildford) 5–7 July		v. Somerset (Guildford) 8–11 July	
G.S. Clinton	16	—	6	14	0	3	0	90*	38	0	15	8	30	27	15	15	1	6	70	—	19	7	26	0	42	65	16	19
D.J. Bicknell	82	—	2	34	12	93	10	101	34	1	100*	2	119	26	0	74	37	6	0	105*	5	10	32	58*	70	59*	9	29
J.D. Robinson	29	38*	3	1													9	4	29	—								
A.J. Stewart	4	—	46	13	0	1	26	13	60	14	31	29	39	42	0	30	0	29	206*	12*	33	148*	3	6	26	16*	1	0
D.M. Ward	145	—	0	1	31	9	45	3	14	10	24*	26*	1	10	37	15	23	8	38	—	23	43	0	—	22	—	27	28
Zahid Sadiq	36	—	6	12	20	4																						
I.A. Greig	107*	—	69*	9*	26	4	87*	10	35	0	—	—	4*	2*			90*	11	—	—	5	67	61	—	13	—	85*	20*
K.T. Medlycott	11*	56*	1	21*	22	77	5	6*	48	7	—	—	71	7	69	11	3	0	37*	61	86*	11	12	—	6	—	2	4
M.A. Feltham	—	19	64	—	3	0	40	1	13	11	—	—	—	32*	0	2							13	—	17	22*		
D. Tazelaar	—	—	4	—	18*	29	14	—																				
M. Frost	—	—													0	0*	0	4										
M.P. Bicknell			4	—	7	13	16	—	0	6	—	—	—	—	8	24					10	—	40*	—				
P.D. Atkins					26	30*	2	—	17	16																		
R.I. Alikhan							4	—	9	35	16	30*	51	9	2	0												
A.J. Murphy									1*	4*	—	—	—	—	3*	0*	1	0			0	—	38	—	2	—	8	—
G.P. Thorpe											—	—	64*	17	21	11	115	22	0	—	0	7	29	54*	62	—	2	0
C.K. Bullen																	3	19*			31	—						
N.H. Peters																			—	—	1	—			0	—		
N.F. Sargeant																							16	—	9*	—	1	—
N.M. Kendrick																							4	—			2	—
J. Boiling																												
M.A. Lynch																												
Byes	4		2	4	7		3	3			1	8			4	2	1	4	1				10	5	2		11	
Leg-byes	4	1	3	13	8	9	7	6	4	3	5	3	10	2	7	8	4	3	11	5	6	5	3	3	7	3	4	7
Wides	7		2		1	1		2	13		1		5		1		1		1	2			1					
No-balls	2	5	7	6	9	7			7	1	8	12	6	3	8	15	3		7	7	1	1	3	1			3	3
Total	447	119	219	128	190	280	259	235	293	108	200	119	400	177	175	207	291	116	395	186	226	305	275	128	275	146	177	143
Wickets	6	1	10	6	10	10	10	5	10	10	3	3	6	7	10	9	10	10	5	1	10	6	10	2	10	1	10	6
Result	D		D		L		D		W		D		D		D		L		L		D		W		D		D	
Points			6		5		5		23		6		6		3				7		6		23		5		3	

Fielding Figures

58 – A.J. Stewart (ct 55/st 3)	8 – M.A. Feltham	3 – Zahid Sadiq, N.H. Peters, P.D. Atkins and N.M. Kendrick
24 – D.M. Ward	7 – I.A. Greig and R.I. Alikhan	2 – J.D. Robinson and C.K. Bullen
18 – K.T. Medlycott	6 – G.S. Clinton and M.A. Lynch	1 – D. Tazelaar, A.J. Murphy, M. Frost, J. Boiling and sub
15 – D.J. Bicknell	5 – N.F. Sargeant (ct 4/st 1) and M.P. Bicknell	
11 – G.P. Thorpe		

First-Class Averages continued

BOWLING

	Overs	Mds	Runs	Wkts	Av	Best	10/m	5/inns
K.P. Evans	258.5	59	781	29	26.93	3/20		
P.A. Smith	272.4	37	898	33	27.21	5/82		1
R. Sharma	191.5	50	547	20	27.35	5/60		1
C.M. Wells	564.5	151	1351	49	27.57	7/65		2
W.W. Davis	439.4	69	1444	52	27.76	5/55		1
N.A. Mallender	514.5	121	1389	50	27.78	7/62	1	3
M. Watkinson	503.5	109	1540	55	28.00	7/69		3
M.C.J. Ball	155	26	504	18	28.00	4/53		
D.A. Graveney	488.2	165	1095	39	28.07	6/128		1
P. Carrick	693.1	242	1603	57	28.12	6/70		2
A.N. Jones	603.2	118	2014	71	28.36	6/37		2
C.E.L. Ambrose	281	70	795	28	28.39	6/22		2
P.C.R. Tufnell	602.1	159	1564	55	28.43	5/60		3
K.J. Barnett	113.2	24	313	11	28.45	4/36		
V.S. Greene	145.1	31	485	17	28.52	6/101	1	1
J.K. Lever	263.1	54	754	26	29.00	7/48		1
J.G. Thomas	536.2	79	1946	67	29.04	6/53		3
M.E. Waugh	117.2	19	415	14	29.64	3/23		
E.E. Hemmings	663.2	171	1720	58	29.65	6/87		2
D.J. Capel	517.2	92	1693	57	29.70	5/53		1
J.E. Emburey	787.1	266	1658	55	30.14	7/27	1	3
A.I.C. Dodemaide	672.1	133	1971	65	30.32	5/77		2
M.J. Weston	141.3	44	365	12	30.41	3/21		
S.R. Barwick	781.2	232	1948	64	30.43	7/47	1	3

BOWLING

	Overs	Mds	Runs	Wkts	Av	Best	10/m	5/inns
P. Bainbridge	279.1	63	762	25	30.48	4/39		
J.A. Afford	545.3	142	1619	53	30.54	5/63		3
L. Potter	150.5	34	460	15	30.66	3/50		
M.A. Robinson	411	82	1139	37	30.78	4/60		
M.A. Holding	258	47	863	28	30.82	6/57	1	1
A.J. Murphy	623	127	2008	65	30.89	6/97		2
M.A. Feltham	388.3	81	1124	36	31.22	4/68		
N.F. Williams	327.2	58	970	31	31.29	4/39		
P.M. Roebuck	141	35	347	11	31.54	2/22		
A.C.S. Pigott	679.1	130	2084	66	31.57	5/52		1
A.M. Babington	511.4	97	1541	47	32.78	5/37		2
J.W. Lloyds	245.2	55	726	22	33.00	7/134		1
K.D. James	415.3	91	1222	37	33.02	5/41		1
J.P. Agnew	732.3	132	2322	70	33.17	6/56	1	3
C.L. Cairns	101.2	20	433	13	33.30	3/50		
K.T. Medlycott	724.4	181	2166	65	33.32	7/68		2
R.J. Maru	586	162	1491	44	33.88	8/41	1	2
S.J. Dennis	418.3	110	1196	35	34.17	5/83		1
R.A. Pick	205.1	34	724	21	34.47	6/52		1
A.P. Igglesden	584.5	101	1953	56	34.87	6/73		1
D.V. Lawrence	353.1	60	1186	34	34.88	4/61		
G.J. Parsons	334.1	79	1100	31	35.48	5/48		1
J.E. Benjamin	177	44	505	14	36.07	3/55		
L.B. Taylor	270.4	53	871	24	36.29	4/55		

	v. Worcestershire (Worcester) 26–8 July	v. Derbyshire (Derby) 29 July–1 August	v. Glamorgan (The Oval) 5–8 August	v. Kent (Canterbury) 9–11 August	v. Leicestershire (Leicester) 19–22 August	v. Lancashire (Old Trafford) 24–8 August	v. Essex (Chelmsford) 29 Aug.–1 Sept.	v. Kent (The Oval) 8–11 September	v. Sussex (The Oval) 13–16 September	M	Inns	NOs	Runs	HS	Av
	3 9	0 60	47 —		28 84	9* 2	0 15	30 34*	1 —	22	40	3	870	90*	23.51
	34 5	9 16	25 13	6 20	29 22	5 3	0 10	5 19*	38 23*	23	45	6	1392	119	35.69
			23 15	10 —	14* —					7	11	2	175	38*	19.44
	0 37	0 0	68 99	87 45	21 77	— 35	120 8	13 —	199* —	23	42	5	1637	206*	44.24
	4 21									15	26	2	608	145	25.33
										3	5	—	78	36	15.60
	22 2	43 9	8 2*	69 —	3 2	— 19	8 32	7 —	71 11	22	34	10	1013	107*	42.20
	29 24	1 35	53 —	17 —	12 26*	— 24*	3 11	45 —	14 0	23	38	8	928	86*	30.93
	12 38	0 21					11 16		26 —	14	21	2	361	64	19.00
										4	4	1	65	29	21.66
		0 0			3 —			— —	4 —	9	9	1	11	4	1.37
	3 0*	6 0	5 —	18* —	18* 10*	4* 0	32 0	— —	1 9	18	24	6	234	40*	13.00
										3	5	1	91	30*	22.75
	11 50	2 11	6 84*	23 8						9	17	2	351	84*	23.40
	1* 0	0* 0	1* —	5* —	0 —	— 0	4 10		0 —	19	21	8	78	38	6.00
	23 78	44 53*	82 12	4 85*	34 43	— 44	5 55	154 —	4 8*	18	30	5	1132	154	45.28
			15 —							2	3	1	53	31	26.50
										4	3	—	16	15	5.33
										3	3	1	26	16	13.00
								11* —		3	3	1	17	11*	8.50
			15 —			— 6	6* 2*			3	4	2	29	15	14.50
				27 63*	13 3	— 50	40 12	172* —	3 —	6	9	2	383	172*	54.71

	v. Worcestershire	v. Derbyshire	v. Glamorgan	v. Kent (C)	v. Leicestershire	v. Lancashire	v. Essex	v. Kent (O)	v. Sussex
	7 10	1 1	3	4 1	1 12	1 8	6	1	1
	3 10	2 10	10 5	5 5	4 13	5 4	12 7	9 1	18 2
	1	1 1	10 2		1		2 1	2 2	1
	1	1	1	12 3	3 4	7	2 4	28	4
	153 285	110 217	357 232	302 230	184 296	24 204	250 183	477 52	385 53
	10 10	10 10	10 4	9 3	9† 6	1 10	10 10	6 0	10 3
	L	L	D	W	W	L	L	D	D
	5	4	8	24	21	4	7	5	4

† J.D. Robinson retired hurt

First-Class Averages continued

BOWLING

	Overs	Mds	Runs	Wkts	Av	Best	10/m	5/inns
M.C. Ilott	109	22	365	10	36.50	4/26		
A.R.K. Pierson	383.5	77	1197	32	37.40	6/82		2
P.G. Newman	333.5	73	1014	27	37.55	5/45		1
A.J. Buzza	220.3	31	756	20	37.80	6/102		1
N.M.K. Smith	130.4	26	427	11	38.81	3/62		
P.G. Edwards	186.4	35	666	17	39.17	3/79		
J. Derrick	155.5	42	439	11	39.90	3/41		
S.J.W. Andrew	170.5	29	523	13	40.23	3/70		
C.S. Pickles	347.2	79	1177	29	40.58	4/92		
M.A. Atherton	405.4	89	1137	28	40.60	3/58		
D.J.M. Kelleher	283.5	63	981	24	40.87	4/82		
P.M. Such	244.2	70	616	15	41.06	3/28		
D. Tazelaar	127.4	24	417	10	41.70	3/88		
I. Smith	257.2	28	1091	26	41.96	3/48		
K. Saxelby	235.5	65	758	18	42.11	4/66		
J.D. Fitton	470.3	103	1475	35	42.14	5/53		2
C. Penn	567	102	1792	41	43.70	4/57		
M.F. Mullins	128	30	438	10	43.80	5/77		1
H.R.J. Trump	416	93	1125	25	45.00	4/80		
B.T.P. Donelan	193	42	633	14	45.21	3/51		
M. Frost	185.2	36	679	15	45.26	5/40		1
I.G. Swallow	225	56	728	16	45.50	4/58		
R.A. Pyman	199.3	43	599	13	46.07	5/43		1
G. Miller	191.4	60	464	10	46.40	2/9		

BOWLING

	Overs	Mds	Runs	Wkts	Av	Best	10/m	5/inns
V.J. Marks	843.5	246	2252	47	47.91	5/38		1
R.P. Davis	716.4	199	2023	42	48.16	4/57		
S.D. Fletcher	230	37	772	15	51.46	4/88		
E.D. Hester	157	29	572	11	52.00	4/100		
I.A. Greig	181	33	596	11	54.18	2/15		
R.J. Bailey	139.1	18	552	10	55.20	3/70		
S.T. Jefferies	199.4	30	702	12	58.50	4/61		
I.D.K. Salisbury	277.4	61	932	15	62.13	3/75		
C.S. Cowdrey	227.3	32	798	12	66.50	4/33		
R.J. Shastri	282.2	66	780	11	70.90	3/77		

(Qualification – 10 wickets)

LEADING FIELDERS

79 – W.K. Hegg (ct 77/st 2); 71 – R.J. Parks (ct 67/st 4); 69 – P.R. Downton (ct 63/st 6); 67 – S.J. Rhodes (ct 61/st 6); 63 – C.P. Metson (ct 57/st 6) and D. Ripley (ct 57/st 6); 59 – B.J.M. Maher (ct 57/st 2); 58 – R.C. Russell (ct 51/st 7), A.J. Stewart (ct 55/st 3) and P. Moores (ct 56/st 2); 54 – N.D. Burns (ct 48/st 6); 51 – M.A. Garnham (ct 48/st 3); 45 – G.W. Humpage (ct 41/st 4) and R.J. Blakey (ct 43/st 2); 43 – G.A. Hick and P. Whitticase (ct 41/st 2); 41 – S.A. Marsh (ct 40/st 1); 40 – V.P. Terry; 34 – B.N. French (ct 27/st 7); 32 – C.W.J. Athey; 31 – M.E. Waugh; 30 – M.W. Alleyne and R.T. Robinson; 27 – K.J. Piper (ct 26/st 1) and G.A. Tedstone (ct 24/st 3); 25 – G.A. Gooch, B.R. Hardie, L. Potter, M.W. Gatting and R.J. Bailey.

Surrey CCC
First-Class Matches, 1989

BOWLING	D. Tazelaar	M. Frost	M.A. Feltham	I.A. Greig	K.T. Medlycott	J.D. Robinson	M.P. Bicknell	R.I. Alikhan	A.J. Stewart
v. Oxford University (Oxford) 19–21 April	22–5–58–2 / 7–0–21–1	12.4–6–27–3 / 9–2–34–0	10–3–19–2 / 14–2–35–3	14–3–36–1 / 6–2–24–0	21–8–46–2 / 6–3–5–0	2–0–3–0			
v. Hampshire (The Oval) 27 April–1 May	15–4–43–1 / 15–3–44–0		11–0–34–2 / 17–2–67–0	9–2–24–1 / 11–2–41–1	12.3–3–24–3 / 3–1–13–0		22–7–66–3 / 12–3–39–0		
v. Middlesex (Lord's) 4–8 May	9.4–1–34–0 / 26–5–88–3		18.2–2–64–3 / 18–8–45–0	10–2–31–1 / 3–0–16–0	26.2–7–49–3 / 31–12–79–1		24–6–68–3 / 39–10–99–5		
v. Sussex (Hove) 17–19 May	21–4–89–2 / 12–2–40–1		25–6–62–2 / 18–3–67–2	18–2–43–0	13–3–47–1 / 19–4–56–2		24–10–51–2 / 18–4–44–1	1–0–2–0	1–0–8–0
v. Warwickshire (Edgbaston) 20–3 May			13–3–56–2 / 27.2–7–68–4	4–0–16–0	15–8–22–0		24.2–5–64–6 / 29–9–46–3		
v. Lancashire (The Oval) 24–6 May			17–5–33–2 / 2–0–8–0	2–0–18–1	23–9–42–4 / 14–1–59–3		27.1–6–67–1 / 14–3–44–0	1.1–0–17–0	1–0–4–0
v. Yorkshire (The Oval) 27–30 May			26–8–46–2 / 12–2–21–0	3–0–15–0	25.5–6–74–1 / 19–4–72–1		6–0–16–1	2–0–3–1	1–0–13–0
v. Northamptonshire (Northampton) 3–6 June		20–4–94–1	5–1–31–0		23–1–106–0		15–4–24–1		
v. Hampshire (Basingstoke) 7–9 June		19.4–5–48–1 / 11–0–45–1		20–5–61–2 / 5–0–24–0	6–0–20–0 / 7.2–2–17–0	8–3–29–0			
v. Essex (The Oval) 10–13 June		13–2–45–0 / 13–2–53–0		4–0–23–0	34–14–95–4 / 27–0–92–1	2–0–12–0			
v. Middlesex (The Oval) 17–20 June					28–9–93–5 / 22–4–86–3		19–5–38–1 / 16–1–63–4		
v. Gloucestershire (The Oval) 24–7 June				10–2–31–2 / 16–4–44–0	35–11–74–2		16.2–3–47–6 / 24–7–40–1		
v. Nottinghamshire (Guildford) 5–7 July			18–1–81–0	4–0–20–0	43–5–169–4				
v. Somerset (Guildford) 8–11 July			43.5–9–108–4		14–5–16–1				
v. Worcestershire (Worcester) 26–8 July			31–10–85–3 / 13–1–44–1	6–1–16–0 / 4–0–16–0	2–0–17–0 / 5–0–23–3		23.1–3–101–4 / 10–0–61–1		
v. Derbyshire (Derby) 29 July–1 August		10–1–50–1	13–4–35–1	8–3–15–2	5–0–34–0		16–1–69–0 / 3–2–1–1		
v. Glamorgan (The Oval) 5–8 August					30.4–8–68–7 / 34–12–69–1	6–2–21–1	15–1–41–1 / 15–3–46–1	1–0–2–0	
v. Kent (Canterbury) 9–11 August				7–2–20–0	19–4–66–1	5–0–18–0	31–8–81–2 / 2–0–6–0		16–0–88–1
v. Leicestershire (Leicester) 19–22 August		21–6–61–2 / 13–2–40–5			17–8–47–2 / 16–5–50–0	7.2–0–37–2	27–11–79–0 / 18.1–1–55–3		
v. Lancashire (Old Trafford) 24–8 August		11–2–31–1			28–4–94–3 / 2–0–13–0		24–3–64–1		2.4–0–7–1
v. Essex (Chelmsford) 29 Aug.–1 Sept.			14–1–39–1 / 16–3–50–2	3–1–6–0 / 5–0–23–0	9–3–25–0 / 6–1–13–3		20.5–6–55–6 / 25–5–74–2		
v. Kent (The Oval) 8–11 September		18–3–85–0 / 3–0–21–0		2–0–15–0	25–6–63–3 / 12–2–64–0		19.3–5–37–0 / 18–3–64–4		
v. Sussex (The Oval) 13–16 September		10–1–37–0 / 1–0–8–0	4–0–10–0 / 2–0–16–0	1–0–1–0 / 6–2–17–0	7–3–23–0		17–2–48–0 / 8–0–19–1		
	127.4–24–417–10 av. 41.70	185.2–36–679–15 av. 45.26	388.3–81–1124–36 av. 31.22	181–33–596–11 av. 54.18	685.4–176–2025–64 av. 31.64	30.2–5–120–3 av. 40.00	622.3–137–1717–65 av. 26.41	5.1–0–24–1 av. 24.00	21.4–0–120–2 av. 60.00

a M.A. Lynch 1–1–0–0

A.J. Murphy	G.P. Thorpe	D.J. Bicknell	C.K. Bullen	N.H. Peters	N.M. Kendrick	J. Boiling	Byes	Leg-byes	Wides	No-balls	Total	Wkts
							1	11		23	201	10
								1		11	120	4
								7	2	14	198	10
							4	7		8	215	1
								1	4	12	247	10
							6	15		16	348	9
							6			15	300	7
							14	4		12	233	6
16–5–41–2							4	9		6	190	10
33–9–62–3							3	6		2	207	10
20–3–62–2	2–0–17–0						13	5	1	2	257	10
15–1–76–1	4–0–10–0						2	12	2	1	232	4
24–5–84–3	10–1–33–0						16	6		7	303	8
24–2–73–2	10–1–34–2						6	8			217	6
30–5–116–3	7–0–37–0						11	6	3	1	425	5
23–8–62–1	6–0–17–0		2–0–17–0				13	13	4		251	4
16–5–34–1			4–0–6–0					2		2	157	2
15.3–1–51–2	13–3–31–2			13–3–36–0			3	7	1	2	303	9
11–0–56–0	1–0–11–0			16.1–3–59–1			4	4			279	2
17–6–35–2				14–2–46–2				13	1	5	225	10
10–1–60–1			6–1–23–0				6	5		5	243	9
17–4–31–2							4			2	113	10
19.5–5–45–3					22–5–70–3		11	5		3	289	10
25–1–104–3				20–1–94–1				7	1	3	475	8
37–8–98–2	2–0–15–0				31–13–50–3			10		1	297	10
25–9–53–3							1	11		5	284	10
21–3–106–1								6	1		256	6
24.3–6–97–6							4	16	1	2	320	10
2.4–1–9–0											10	1
8–1–28–0					25–7–66–1			3		1	227	10
6–0–32–0					24–17–47–1		7	2		1	205	3
27.4–7–94–5				19–2–57–2			5	5	1		346	10
2–0–10–0		15.4–1–73–1					5	2	2		184	2
26–8–66–4		1–0–1–0					2	4		2	297	10
10–2–33–1								4	2	3	182	10
18–5–62–1						12.4–2–40–3	1	13		4	305	10
											20	1
23–5–70–3							1	11		8	207	10
23–5–51–1						1–0–9–0		7	1	5	227	8
14–3–45–0				6–3–10–0			8	6		5	269	3a
16.1–1–65–2				3–0–9–0			4	1		3	228	6
11.4–1–54–2								3		4	153	2
11–1–43–3								2		1	128	4
623–127–2008–65 av. 30.89	55–5–205–4 av. 51.25	16.4–1–74–1 av. 74.00	12–1–46–0 —	82.1–11–292–6 av. 48.66	64–21–139–6 av. 23.16	62.4–26–162–5 av. 32.40						

Sussex CCC
First-Class Matches, 1989

BATTING	v. Kent (Hove) 27 April–1 May	v. Somerset (Taunton) 4–8 May	v. Surrey (Hove) 17–19 May	v. Lancashire (Liverpool) 27–30 May	v. Warwickshire (Edgbaston) 3–6 June	v. Kent (Tunbridge Wells) 7–9 June	v. Northamptonshire (Hove) 10–13 June	v. Derbyshire (Derby) 17–20 June	v. Cambridge University (Hove) 21–3 June	v. Hampshire (Southampton) 24–7 June	v. Essex (Horsham) 1–4 July	v. Gloucestershire (Gloucester) 5–7 July	v. Yorkshire (Middlesbrough) 8–11 July	v. Worcestershire (Hove) 22–5 July
A.M. Green	34 —	5 7							94 —		39 15	4 —		
D.M. Smith	68 —	14 5	4 1	101 10	50 46*	44* 67	22* 12	34 —		24 14	46 71	4 9*		12 24
P.W.G. Parker	16 —	1 39		9 17			45 28*						— 42	66 86
A.P. Wells	7 —	48 58	103 54*	52 63*	29 —	16* 46	89 4	60 —		153 53*	1 49	31 —	— 0	15 40
C.M. Wells	25 —	9 50	8 36	66 46	6 —	— 15	84* 2	58 —	33 —	10 4	20 27	28 —	— 0	81 26
I.J. Gould	49 —	84 24	4 3	20 16*	8 —	— 5			62 —	1 —	11 12	58 20	63	4 6
A.I.C. Dodemaide	10 —	32 13	29* 0*	1 —	52 —	— 14*	54 13	29 —	29 —	1 2*	35 0	24 —	3	36 7*
P. Moores	10 —	6 21	1* 44	38* 43	22* 26	— 54*	— 0	8* 60	8* —	6 —	5* 4	2 —	26*	12 —
A.C.S. Pigott	64 —	2 0	4 —	22* 26		— 54*				26 —		0 32	24	32 27
A.R. Clarke	36* —	13 0	— —		0* —				12 —				8	
A.M. Babington	3 —	1* 3*			0* —				1* —	18* —	5 0*	0 —	0	6 —
N.J. Falkner		10 17							48 —					
N.J. Lenham		116 48	8 25	12 38*	1 7	14 17	62 —	25 —		14 2	4 0	50 9*	20	
I.D.K. Salisbury		— —		5 —		— —	— 4*	4* —	48 —	2 —	37 3*	1 —		
K. Greenfield							30 11	13 4	0 —	48 —	2 24			
S.J.S. Kimber									25 —	21 —				
R.A. Bunting									73 —					
A.R. Hansford									5* —					
M.P. Speight													53	7 26
B.T.P. Donelan														10* —
C.C. Remy														
Byes	4	2	6 14	4		1 3		4	9	5	8	6 4	3	8 2
Leg-byes	11	6 3	4	11 5	25 1	1 3	13 6	9	4	10 3	25 13	16 2	6	3 5
Wides	3						1	1 3		1			1 1	1 1
No-balls	21	11 9	15 12	2 3	2	6 2	8 4	3			2 2	3 2	2	5 8 1
Total	361	234 232	300 233	334 185	259 85	99 228	350 158	417	371	287 116	285 240	232 21	0 252	301 250
Wickets	10	10 10	7 6	7 4	10 0	2 7	5 8	10	9	10 5	10 9	10 0	0 10	10 6
Result	D	L	D	D	D	W	D	D	W	D	D	D	L	W
Points	7	6	7	7	7	20	8	6	—	4	7	3	3	22

Fielding Figures:
58 – P. Moores (ct 56/st 2)
21 – A.C.S. Pigott
14 – D.M. Smith
13 – P.W.G. Parker
11 – A.I.C. Dodemaide
10 – C.M. Wells and A.P. Wells
9 – M.P. Speight
7 – N.J. Lenham
4 – A.M. Babington, K. Greenfield, I.D.K. Salisbury and B.T.P. Donelan

REVIEW OF THE SEASON

We were promised a new era, and it was heralded with press conferences and a fanfare of trumpets. When the noise died down the players looked distinctly similar to those who had lost Test series to all bar Sri Lanka in recent years, and at the end of the summer, having lost overwhelmingly to an Australian side we had been expected to beat, we were promised another new era, only this time there were some new faces, for several of the losers had opted to go to South Africa where they were promised greater rewards.

The South African venture would, of course, mean that players would be excluded from Test cricket for the next five years, but then money had been an important topic from the start of the first new era. It was not difficult to grow cynical about a game where many knew the price of everything and the value of nothing and where the award of a Test cap had become so cheapened by excess that to represent one's country was no longer the great event it used to be but a weekly occurence. Graham Dilley, a useful pace bowler prone to injury, goes into exile knowing that he has played twice as many Test matches as Harold Larwood did.

The domestic competitions were played against this back-drop of national failure and navigational uncertainty, and they, too, were not without their peculiarities. In the Britannic Assurance County Championship, the team who won the most matches and scored the most points was placed second. We have explained the reasons for this and the injustice of those reasons earlier in this volume. It remains only to say that the inconsistency of the application of the rule whereby 25 points were deducted for a sub-standard pitch made a mockery of the county championship in 1989.

In spite of these vagaries, the paying-customer, who is long-suffering in his acceptance of what those who administer the game do to him, enjoyed a summer when there was much sun and some cricket to remember.

It was a season that those at Kent would best forget. After the joys of 1988, last season was dross indeed. The loss of Tavare obviously had an effect, but the batting presented fewer problems than the bowling. Ellison missed much of the season. We still await the development of Kelleher's potential, and even Igglesden, though he won

	v. Somerset (Hove) 26-8 July	v. Nottinghamshire (Eastbourne) 5-8 August	v. Leicestershire (Eastbourne) 9-11 August	v. Glamorgan (Swansea) 12-15 August	v. Middlesex (Hastings) 19-22 August	v. Gloucestershire (Hove) 24-8 August	v. Hampshire (Hove) 29 Aug.-1 Sept.	v. Middlesex (Lord's) 8-11 September	v. Surrey (The Oval) 13-16 September	M	Inns	NOs	Runs	HS	Av
	6 24	184 26	5 —		13 3	115 1		129 51*	62 4*	5	7	—	198	94	28.28
	110 4	24 72	45 0	0 63	5 24	2 49	0 12*	136 0	3 74*	19	35	6	1305	184	45.00
	37 78*	17 20	47 56	33 72*	66 51	37 4	91 —	27 0	0* 22	15	28	3	972	136	38.88
	44 9*	65 79	35 15	57* 19*	11 12	5 46		7 15	— 1	22	38	7	1629	153	52.54
	53 —	3 7	13 26*	1 —	30 38	0 5	125 —	4 51*	— 6	22	36	4	1054	84*	32.93
	21 —	16* 26	0 27*	18 —	61* 6	80 27*		46 —		22	33	4	870	125	30.00
	29 116	— 1	11 8	25 —	1 50	29 11	17 —	0 —	— 16*	20	30	9	683	80	32.52
		9* 15	3 9	10 —	3 11	7 14*	91 —	32 —	— —	22	30	6	629	116	26.20
	— —		— 0*		3 1*		9* —		— —	20	27	5	556	91	25.27
										5	5	1	69	36*	17.25
										18	15	9	50	18*	8.33
										3	4	—	76	48	19.00
	0* —		2 —	7 14	4 —		28 4	17 8	81* 2	15	27	3	633	116	26.37
					6* —					11	10	4	62	37	10.33
					18 —	16 —		14* —	— —	5	8	—	132	48	16.50
										2	2	—	46	25	23.00
										2	2	1	79	73	79.00
										5	4	2	53	18	26.50
	1 6	1 0	88 43	69 48	35 6		20 21*			9	17	1	425	88	26.56
	2 —		3* 4*	3 —	4 0		10 —	5 —		9	9	3	41	10*	6.83
							0 —			1	1	—	0	0	0.00
		4	3 4		5 4	5	1	3 7							
	11 6	6 7	2 3	6 2	4 3	11 13	11	16 4	3 2						
			2		4 1		4 1								
	2 2		2	7 1	7 7	6 5	7 7	2 1	4 1						
	316 245	325 264	258 191	240 223	249 216	323 175	430 45	438 137	153 128						
	9 4	6 9	10 6	10 3	10 10	10 7	10 1	10 4	2 4						
	D	L	D	D	L	W	W	D	D						
	6	6	7	4	5	23	24	6	3						

3 – A.M. Green

2 – A.R. Hansford and subs

1 – C.C. Remy

an England cap, could hardly be satisfied with his season. Of the spin bowling department it is best to say nothing. The decline in spirit and performance of the Kent side was one of the saddest aspects of 1989.

If Kent were desperately short of class bowling, Worcestershire seemed to have an abundance of it. With Dilley and Botham on Test duty and Newport injured, much work fell on the shoulders of Lampitt and McEwan, and they responded magnificently. Phil Neale, a wise leader of men, was quick to pay tribute to them when Worcestershire won the title, and he was right to do so. Worcestershire had proved the policy advocated by Duncan Fearnley and Don Kenyon that a strong squad is essential if a county is to maintain the highest standards. The Champions' batting was neither as consistent nor as strong in depth as their bowling. Damian D'Oliveira's final record was bitterly disappointing, and there was a sense of uncertainty about the middle order, but there was always Hick, who played some marvellous innings, and Neale himself. Rhodes made valuable contributions and kept wicket well, but special praise should go to Curtis. He received much scrutiny and criticism from the media because of his failures at Test level, but he was a tower of strength to his county and played a most significant part in their success.

Nottinghamshire were another side to enjoy success. A trip to Trent Bridge was an unwelcome hazard for most batsmen, but Nottinghamshire also performed well away from home. Their batting was solid and their bowling generally good enough to bowl sides out, not a quality which all county attacks can claim. Had they shown a greater sense of adventure earlier in the season, they might well have challenged more strongly for the championship, but they were worthy winners of the Benson and Hedges Cup, and they enjoyed a good year.

If Nottinghamshire surprised many of us, Northamptonshire disappointed. Their wickets seemed tailored to suit their battery of fast bowlers, but none performed quite up to expectations, and the Northamptonshire middle-order batting looked most vulnerable at times. In the absence of Lamb and Williams for most of the season, this was perhaps not unexpected.

Somerset were another side with middle-order batting problems. Cook and Roebuck were outstanding as an opening pair, but they were followed by more fragile play. Tavare was at his best in the one-day game, and more use

BOWLING	A.C.S. Pigott	A.I.C. Dodemaide	C.M. Wells	A.R. Clarke	A.M. Babington	A.P. Wells	P.W.G. Parker	I.D.K. Salisbury	N.J. Lenham
v. Kent	16–5–36–0	22–8–44–2	20.4–6–65–7	4–1–7–0	21–1–78–1				
(Hove) 27 April–1 May	20–5–72–2	23–5–53–0	18–4–48–0		10–3–34–0	6–1–34–0	5–2–5–0		
v. Somerset	29.4–3–68–3	24–6–50–2	23–10–39–1	8–2–11–2	16–2–52–0				
(Taunton) 4–8 May	18.5–2–46–1	22–4–61–1	22–7–37–0	23–7–53–2	15–2–32–1				
v. Surrey	23.4–2–91–4	29–5–61–3	14–3–28–1	12–5–34–1	14–4–35–1				
(Hove) 17–19 May	4–1–18–0	17–2–65–2	6–0–39–0	14–0–68–2	10–0–36–0				
v. Lancashire	12–3–45–2	12–3–28–0	7–2–12–0		18.3–5–37–5			23–6–72–2	
(Liverpool) 27–30 May	18–1–63–3	7–1–31–0	8–2–21–0		9–2–23–4			25.5–4–109–1	
v. Warwickshire	29–3–93–1	31–9–75–4	9–3–34–0		21.1–5–59–5			3–1–6–0	
(Edgbaston) 3–6 June									
v. Kent	20–7–39–1	24–5–74–3	15–5–31–3		16–2–58–1			11–2–31–2	
(Tunbridge Wells) 7–9 June						5–1–14–0			5–1–25–1
v. Northamptonshire	18–3–52–5	23–3–55–2	17–6–37–0		23–4–65–3			12–8–10–0	
(Hove) 10–13 June	11–0–53–0	9–1–45–1	6–1–15–0		19.1–3–52–2		2–0–12–0	35–3–147–1	4–0–19–1
v. Derbyshire	30–7–83–2	41–8–112–5	24–6–59–1					12–3–26–1	
(Derby) 17–20 June	21–6–69–4	19–4–64–2	4–2–5–0					20–6–58–2	
v. Cambridge University				12–3–33–1	21–7–45–4				3–0–7–0
(Hove) 21–3 June			2.5–0–6–2	1–1–0–0	5–3–3–0				
v. Hampshire	22–3–63–4	20–1–97–1	19–3–47–0		26–6–66–2			23–6–69–1	
(Southampton) 24–7 June	7–0–28–0	13.5–2–41–2	12–2–40–1		15–4–45–0			4–0–14–0	
v. Essex	15.2–4–34–1	19.4–4–58–4	14.4–4–33–4		21–2–45–0				
(Horsham) 1–4 July	7–0–35–0	31–6–108–2	23–6–62–2		20–1–54–2			9–0–52–0	
v. Gloucestershire	11–1–22–0	16–3–39–2	16–5–43–1		30–11–63–2			27.3–5–92–1	7–1–25–0
(Gloucester) 5–7 July									
v. Yorkshire	15–6–30–2	27–3–71–2	16–2–30–1	7–3–16–1	26–4–91–2	0.1–0–6–0			
(Middlesbrough) 8–11 July									
v. Worcestershire	26–7–77–2	26.3–7–56–3	22–6–48–0		20–5–66–0				
(Hove) 22–5 July	15–2–69–1	13–3–51–1			6–0–21–0				
v. Somerset		24–7–55–2	18–5–44–2		18–2–64–0			31.2–9–75–3	
(Hove) 26–8 July		18–1–79–2	9–4–13–1		6–0–25–1			19–2–113–0	
v. Nottinghamshire	23–5–92–3	16–2–97–1	18–5–38–2		15–3–56–1				
(Eastbourne) 5–8 August	19–3–73–3	7–1–21–0	10–0–33–0		4–0–33–1				
v. Leicestershire	18–6–30–0	26.2–5–77–5	17–7–29–3					2–1–8–0	
(Eastbourne) 9–11 August	8–1–32–0	6–1–20–0	8–2–1⚓–0					13–4–32–0	
v. Glamorgan	29–7–69–0	26.2–4–75–3	35–10–69–3					7–1–18–1	3–0–15–0
(Swansea) 12–15 August									
v. Middlesex	21–2–93–2	23.1–4–78–3	24–4–69–1		27–7–94–4				
(Hastings) 19–22 August	4–0–20–0	7–1–14–0	7–1–21–1		3–0–26–0				
v. Gloucestershire	14.4–3–37–3	8–1–22–2	14–5–39–4						
(Hove) 24–8 August	37–9–129–3	12.2–5–30–1	19–9–45–1						
v. Hampshire	21–5–53–2				17–6–39–1				2–0–3–0
(Hove) 29 August–1 September	22–5–58–4				22.5–2–82–3				
v. Middlesex	24–7–71–4	21–4–51–2	22–6–48–0						10–3–16–2
(Lord's) 8–11 September	14–0–46–2	7–4–13–0	8–1–25–0						1–0–3–0
v. Surrey	35–6–95–2		34.4–7–82–7		16–1–62–1				3–0–14–0
(The Oval) 13–16 September			2–0–3–0						
	679.1–130–	672.1–133–	564.5–151–	81–22–	511.4–97–	11.1–2–	7–2–	277.4–61–	38–5–
	2084–66	1971–65	1351–49	222–9	1541–47	54–0	17–0	932–15	127–4
	av. 31.57	av. 30.32	av. 27.57	av. 24.66	av. 32.78	—	—	av. 62.13	av. 31.75

a I.J. Gould 4–0–27–0   b P. Moores 1–0–10–0   c G.J. Lord retired hurt   d C.C. Remy 8–2–11–0; 7–1–22–1

K. Greenfield	D.M. Smith	B.T.P. Donelan	S.J.S. Kimber	A.R. Hansford	R.A. Bunting	A.M. Green	Byes	Leg-byes	Wides	No-balls	Total	Wkts
							1	3		10	234	10
								6		6	252	2
								9		7	229	10
							5	4	1	1	238	5
							3	7			259	10
							3	6	2		235	5
								10		1	204	10
							2	17		2	266	8
							5	5		11	277	10
							3	7	2	2	243	10
3–0–11–0	1–0–3–0							2	1		82	1a
								4	4	6	223	10
								12	1	11	355	5
			15–2–45–1				5	12		5	342	10
	1–0–2–0		4–1–14–1				8	3	3	3	223	9
			8–2–24–0	18.5–5–46–4	10–2–45–0	4–1–18–0	6	5	1	1	229	10
			3–1–8–0	14–3–25–4	9–3–18–4		4	3	1	2	67	10
								14		3	356	8
								3		1	171	3
							4	11	2	2	185	10
							18	21		3	350	6
					34–5–93–3		10	12	1	3	399	9
							2	4		5	260	8b
											0	0
		28–11–51–3					4	18		5	320	9c
		17–3–78–2					4	7	1		230	4
		12–5–18–0					4	6		7	266	7
		11–0–59–1						3	1	2	292	6
		2–0–14–0						6			303	7
		19–2–95–2					14	18			287	7
		16–9–19–2						4		2	167	10
		11–1–30–0					4	2			134	0
		11–0–47–1					6	9	3	5	308	10
		11–4–22–0					3	11	1	11	370	10
	0.1–0–4–0	3–0–9–0					2	1		1	97	1
				5–1–14–0	3–1–20–0			1	1	3	133	10
				31.4–8–70–3	14–0–70–1		8	11	7		363	10
		11–1–31–1		32–9–79–5			4	13		13	233	10d
		16–4–46–2		13–5–28–0				5	1	3	241	10
		3–0–12–0		24–5–83–2			12	9		2	302	10
		7–0–34–0		11.5–2–69–2			1	7		1	202	5e
		11–1–42–0		17–1–71–0			1	18	1	4	385	10
	2–0–12–0	4–1–26–0						2			53	3f
3–0–11–0	4.1–0–21–0	193–42–633–14 av. 45.21	30–6–91–2 av. 45.50	167.2–39–485–20 av. 24.25	36–6–153–5 av. 30.60	38–6–111–3 av. 37.00						
—	—											

e I.J. Gould 1–0–4–0   f I.J. Gould 4–1–10–3

Warwickshire CCC
First-Class Matches, 1989

BATTING	v. Lancashire (Edgbaston) 20–4 April		v. Worcestershire (Edgbaston) 27–30 April		v. Cambridge University (Cambridge) 4–6 May		v. Lancashire (Old Trafford) 17–19 May		v. Surrey (Edgbaston) 20–3 May		v. Middlesex (Edgbaston) 27–30 May		v. Australians (Edgbaston) 31 May–2 June		v. Sussex (Edgbaston) 3–6 June		v. Derbyshire (Nuneaton) 7–9 June		v. Glamorgan (Edgbaston) 21–3 June		v. Essex (Ilford) 24–7 June		v. Leicestershire (Hinckley) 1–4 July		v. Worcestershire (Worcester) 5–7 July		v. Nottinghamshire (Trent Bridge) 8–11 July	
T.A. Lloyd	65	36	11	21			4	3	15	35	26	7	22	—	35	—	5	5	—	—	14	23	6	28	24	—	100	—
A.J. Moles	1	23	2	85	66	—	0	10	4	100	5	4	14	9	13	—	53	79	130*	46*	42	2	38	0	0	34*	6	—
M. Asif Din	10	16*					67	15	6	0	36	39	50	38	36	—	18	46	9	—	10	32	0	17				
A.I. Kallicharran	1	2	3	19			29	5	37	6	30	0	30	0	5	—	17	23										
D.A. Thorne	32	1	1	30	41	2	6	1					20	0														
P.A. Smith	26	1*	4	5	61	—	19	24	45	20	5	29			66	—	18	5	20*	—	37	2			140	—	68	—
G.W. Humpage	30	—	31*	5*	8	97	9	42			14	5	58	—	38	—	16	8*	183	—	18	7	31	55	0	—	13	—
G.C. Small	13	—	11	7*			2	10	3	10	5	5*	5	5*	34	—	4	13*					13	5	15	—	17	—
A.A. Donald	8	—	12	—			0	9	9*	0	19*	1			15	—	9	—			1	7*	5	—				
A.R.K. Pierson	8	—	3	—	—	—	8	18	0	5	11	10	4	—	14*	—	3	—	3	—	13	1	3*	0	0	—	7*	—
T.A. Munton	4*	—	0	—	—	—	6*	0*	3	0*	7	5	3	—	0	—	1*	—					0	1*	2*	—	6	—
S.J. Green			7	11	1	—																						
J.D. Ratcliffe					30	127*							6	17					4	35*	72	1	36	32	3	8*	23	—
D.A. Banks					60*	32*									28	18*	0	—	0	10								
J.E. Benjamin					—	—									8*	—												
T.A. Merrick					—	—									0	—									31	—	9	—
D.A. Reeve									8	7											97*	42	55	19	33	—	15	—
K.J. Piper									41	13											1	8	0	20*	2	—	10	—
R.G. Twose															17	15*												
N.M.K. Smith																					8	4						
Byes				6	1		3	3	4	3	2		10		5				1		4	10			5		3	6
Leg-byes	5	2	7	13	9	5	3	20	9	6	6	1	10	7	5		10	8	6	1	10	6	5	4	14	2	11	
Wides	5				5	1	1	1			1		1						1	1							1	
No-balls	2		7	2	2		1	13	6	2	8	5	4	1	11		1	1	8	2	11		4	7	1			
Total	210	81	99	204	284	263	158	174	190	207	194	112	235	105	277		155	199	365	84	338	145	196	193	265	47	292	
Wickets	10	4	10	6	6	2	10	10	10	10	10	10	10	3	10		10	6	4	0	10	10	10	8	10	0	10	
Result	D		D		D		L		L		L		D		D		D		D		L		D		D		D	
Points	6		12		—		5		5		5		—		7		5		8		8		3		7		7	

Fielding Figures

45 – G.W. Humpage (ct 41/st 4)	10 – T.A. Munton	6 – P.A. Smith
27 – K.J. Piper (ct 26/st 1)	9 – T.A. Lloyd and A.R.K. Pierson	5 – D.A. Thorne and J.D. Ratcliffe
17 – A.J. Moles	8 – M. Asif Din	4 – Subs
14 – D.A. Reeve	7 – A.I. Kallicharran	3 – G.C. Small and A.A. Donald

could have been made of the admirable Burns, an accomplished wicket-keeper and equally stylish left-handed batsman. Adrian Jones showed aggression as a pace bowler that could win him an England cap, and Rose at last began to suggest that he could come to fruition as a most capable all-rounder.

For Leicestershire, at present, one sees little hope. There is talent in the county – Lewis and Benjamin ended very strongly – but there is a lack of sparkle and joy. Gower's involvement with the England side and the disgraceful way in which he was treated by sections of the press, and ultimately by the selectors, could not have helped. At the time of writing his position as Leicestershire captain is undecided, but one sees no obvious successor unless Willey returns to the job. Whatever happens, one hopes that Gower will delight and entertain for several years to come. The failures and controversies of 1989 should never be allowed to obscure the grace and charm that this man has brought to cricket.

Another county where all is not well is Gloucestershire. We commented last year that Athey hardly seemed an appropriate choice as captain to replace the dismissed Graveney, and he has lasted only one year in the post. There is obvious unhappiness in the county, and one feels that it may be two or three seasons before the gloom is dispersed.

Glamorgan, on the other hand, in spite of their bottom place in the championship and an apparent loss of morale, suggest that they may soon experience better times. There is some exciting young talent in the county – James, Cann, Smith, Watkin – and if it can be properly nurtured, Glamorgan could do well. They need a taste of success to lift morale and boost confidence, and that initial success may be the hardest thing to attain.

If they cast their eyes in the direction of Warwickshire, Glamorgan will see what a vast change is brought about by confidence. Intelligent and enthusiastic leadership by Andy Lloyd, and the stability of team selection, made Warwickshire formidable opponents in the closing weeks of the season and brought them the NatWest Bank Trophy. In Small and Donald, they have probably the best pair of opening bowlers in the country. They are short on spin and they need a batsman of class and substance, particularly as Kallicharran must be nearing the end of his career, but they have laid good foundations, and these are exciting times at Edgbaston after the traumas of recent seasons.

	v. Yorkshire (Edgbaston) 26–8 July	v. Gloucestershire (Edgbaston) 29 July–1 August	v. Kent (Canterbury) 5–8 August	v. Hampshire (Bournemouth) 9–11 August	v. Somerset (Edgbaston) 12–15 August	v. Northamptonshire (Northampton) 19–22 August	v. Glamorgan (Swansea) 24–8 August	v. Yorkshire (Leeds) 29 Aug–1 Sept.	v. Northamptonshire (Edgbaston) 8–11 September	v. Somerset (Taunton) 13–16 September	M	Inns	NOs	Runs	HS	Av
	49 46	44 12	48 109*	12 —		2 —	183 1	61 —	— 28	58* —	22	33	2	1138	183	36.70
	13 5	76 10	12 64*	23 35	18 16				0* 50	50 —	21	38	5	1138	130*	34.48
	39 —	25 32*	18 —	57 —	37 1			12 82*	— 0		18	28	3	748	82*	29.92
	15 70	16 1	38 —	0 12*		100 —	119 1	23 —	— 31	7* —	16	26	2	610	119	25.41
	33 42*	4* —				0 —	35 —	31 —	— 22		5	10	—	134	41	13.40
	15 66*	16 19	39 —	51 13*	34 29*	10 —	19 3*	46 —	— 11		19	26	4	762	140	34.63
	0 —	0 24	23* —		13* —	0 —			— 20		23	34	7	1039	183	38.48
	40 —	4 15	11* —	13 —	13* —	1 —	17 —		— 6*		17	22	4	234	34	13.00
	12 —	3* —									19	22	6	215	40	13.43
				0* —		0* —	5* —	0* 0			16	20	4	126	18	7.87
				5 —			5 —	7 —			21	20	11	43	7	4.77
											2	3	—	19	11	6.33
					67 30	0 —	1 24*	14 41			11	20	4	571	127*	35.68
											4	7	3	148	60*	37.00
											6	4	1	25	8*	8.33
											4	3	—	40	31	13.33
	97* —	8* 86*	18 —		41 —	15 —	1 —	33 —	— 6		14	17	4	581	97*	44.69
	1 —	1 30	14 —	22 —	17* —	28 —					12	15	2	208	41	16.00
					14 37	0 26*		25 —	3 2*		5	9	3	139	37	23.16
			11 ·	19 —	0 —	18 —	6 —	6 161	0* 15*		9	11	2	248	161	27.55

	v. Yorkshire	v. Gloucestershire	v. Kent	v. Hampshire	v. Somerset	v. Northamptonshire	v. Glamorgan	v. Yorkshire	v. Northamptonshire	v. Somerset
	5	8 2	3	4	6	4	1	3 2	7	
	15 8	9 7	4 5	12 8	11 3	8	11	8 6	13	2
	3	4	1	1 1	1 1	1	2 1	1	1 2	2 2
	15	4 8	13	1 1	5 1	4	1 1	2	7 2	7 2
	352 237	218 250	250 181	229 110	250 107	191	430 31	248 296	0 217	119
	10 2	8 7	8 0	10 2	7 3	10	10 2	10 3	0 8	1
	D	W	W	W	D	W	W	D	D	D
	4	22	21	20	6	21	24	3	4	4

2 – J.E. Benjamin, S.J. Green and R.G. Twose
1 – N.M.K. Smith

Lancashire are another county for whom fortunes have changed for the better. Ably and firmly led by David Hughes, they have a strong pace attack and a most reliable pair of opening batsmen, Mendis and Fowler. Fairbrother has days when he thrills, and Atherton shows immense promise, but there is doubt as to the depth of batting in the Lancashire side. Lloyd could be the answer and, if he is, the Red Rose county will be very strong indeed.

Across the Pennines there is less cause for optimism. So many talents have failed to flourish in the way in which one had anticipated. Metcalfe should be an England player by now, and Jarvis should have had such a permanent grip on the new ball in a Test match as to make his South African venture unnecessary, but they have flattered only to deceive. Now the players cry for an infusion of overseas blood, but their first task should be unrelenting self-questioning as to why they have failed to live up to the traditions of a noble county.

Sussex are on the mend in every respect. Parker has proved to be a sensitive and sensible captain. There are still obvious lacks in the side, but there is a better spirit abroad. Future success revolves around imponderables, not the least of which is whether or not Neil Lenham is ever going to perform to his full capabilities at first-class level.

Their neighbour, Hampshire, had an enigmatic season. At the beginning Hampshire looked as if they had achieved the balance in their side that they had sought for so long, but defeat in the NatWest Bank Trophy semi-final and the loss of Chris Smith hit them badly, and they finished the season in wretched form. For a side which, on paper, looked so strong in batting, there were days of improbable collapse. One still feels that the highest honours are only just out of reach and that if Wood, Scott or Middleton could mature sufficiently to fill the gaps left by the departure of Greenidge and the decline of Turner, and if James could find more consistency, Hampshire would be an outstanding side. Bakker and Connor have developed splendidly, and Ayling, a superb all-rounder who missed the entire season through injury, will be back next year. Marshall is still the most feared bowler in the country, and Tremlett will press to recapture a first team place. Nicholas' leadership is positive and ambitious. The Benson and Hedges Cup triumph of 1988 served only to whet the appetite for more success.

It would be surprising if Essex did not add to their

Warwickshire CCC
First-Class Matches, 1989

BOWLING	A.A. Donald	G.C. Small	T.A. Munton	P.A. Smith	A.R.K. Pierson	T.A. Merrick	J.E. Benjamin	J.D. Ratcliffe	D.A. Reeve
v. Lancashire (Edgbaston) 20–4 April	21–5–55–3 19–4–41–3	22.4–3–61–2 25.1–6–55–5	20–5–63–2 14–4–32–1	15–0–35–2 4–0–22–0	4–2–12–1 4–0–14–1				
v. Worcestershire (Edgbaston) 27–30 April	15–1–37–3 11–1–37–2	17–7–42–3 18–4–43–0	20.3–7–39–4 23–4–63–3	3–1–15–0					
v. Cambridge University (Cambridge) 4–8 May			9–3–20–0 5–4–6–1	15.3–1–61–2 4–2–7–0	36–8–72–1 19–7–30–3	16–6–41–1 7–2–14–0	20–6–56–1 10–2–31–1	4–1–7–0	
v. Lancashire (Old Trafford) 17–19 May	20.4–4–58–1 17–8–23–4	21–10–39–3 18–2–52–3	22–3–74–3 6–1–16–0	16–5–43–2 10–2–29–3	3–0–27–0				
v. Surrey (Edgbaston) 20–3 May	23–5–74–3 16–6–18–5	21–4–61–1 11.4–3–27–3	25–8–44–1 19–5–43–0	19.5–1–82–5 5–0–14–1	6–1–28–0 3–1–3–1				
v. Middlesex (Edgbaston) 27–30 May	23.5–7–66–7 15–2–43–1	18–2–60–1	8–0–29–0 12–3–35–1	10–1–31–2 2.4–0–16–0	2–0–8–0				
v. Australians (Edgbaston) 31May–2 June			21–6–85–0 21–7–60–2		27–5–98–1 22–7–51–0	22–4–107–1 8–0–23–0	14–2–81–0 7–1–31–1		
v. Sussex (Edgbaston) 3–6 June	17.2–4–49–2	26–4–70–4	14–5–24–1	14–1–39–0	23–6–52–3				
v. Derbyshire (Nuneaton) 7–9 June	18.4–5–38–3 9–2–29–2	11–2–24–2 5–1–15–0	6–5–4–1 9–1–28–0		20–7–40–2 23–1–82–6				
v. Glamorgan (Edgbaston) 21–3 June	25–8–53–4 10–1–21–0	18.1–1–49–3 10–5–18–0	25–9–61–1 4–1–13–0	21–7–55–2 6–0–21–0	6–0–42–0 23–6–68–0			4–0–19–0	
v. Essex (Ilford) 24–7 June	30.5–2–103–5 17–4–52–3			3–0–13–0	29–4–129–5 12–2–49–2			3–0–22–0	3–1–3–0
v. Leicestershire (Hinckley) 1–4 July	14–2–50–0	36–6–95–4	32–9–97–1		36–6–109–1				
v. Worcestershire (Worcester) 5–7 July		26–6–62–1	12–6–23–0	13–0–36–1	3.5–0–24–2	28–8–67–6			
v. Nottinghamshire (Trent Bridge) 8–11 July		26–8–50–3 11–2–28–0	17–5–55–3 15–2–37–3		24–4–98–2	15.4–3–38–4 14–6–30–0			
v. Yorkshire (Edgbaston) 26–8 July	17–2–60–0 7–3–14–0	18–8–36–0 10–4–26–0		17–1–70–3 11–0–43–1	20–2–63–0 16–3–41–1				7–1–19–0
v. Gloucestershire (Edgbaston) 29 July–1 August	23.5–6–67–5 6–0–23–1	22–4–58–4 4–3–8–0		18–4–62–1	22–7–57–0				
v. Kent (Canterbury) 5–8 August	21.5–4–57–5 22–6–41–4	21–7–55–0 3.2–3–3–0	32–9–80–2 10.4–3–27–1						16.2–7–29–1
v. Hampshire (Bournemouth) 9–11 August	12–4–21–2 17.1–4–47–4		15.2–2–43–1 17–4–44–2				16–7–21–1 14–3–46–2		
v. Somerset (Edgbaston) 12–15 August	15–4–45–1 10–2–32–1		32–14–65–2 12–2–37–2				25–7–55–3 10–4–23–1	6–2–19–0	5–0–9–0
v. Northamptonshire (Northampton) 19–22 August	6–4–4–1 16–4–37–3	9–1–31–1 18–7–45–2	11–4–13–5 6–4–7–1	3.4–0–9–4					7.3–6–3–3
v. Glamorgan (Swansea) 24–8 August	11–3–26–1		15.1–2–33–4 36–11–76–3	2–0–3–0 24–4–78–3			15–3–34–2 14–1–33–1		13–2–27–3 18.1–7–26–
v. Yorkshire (Leeds) 29 Aug.–1 Sept.			31–11–68–2	20–3–67–1			32–8–94–1	10–3–15–1	16–6–33–0
v. Northamptonshire (Edgbaston) 8–11 September	16–4–37–2	20–8–49–4	20–4–46–3 8–2–37–1	6–2–16–0					11.4–5–14–
v. Somerset (Taunton) 13–16 September	13–1–40–5	10–1–40–2	8–3–11–2	9–2–31–0					
	537.1–122– 1398–86 av. 16.25	477–122– 1202–51 av. 23.56	613.4–178– 1538–59 av. 26.06	272.4–37– 898–33 av. 27.21	383.5–79– 1197–32 av. 37.40	110.4–29– 320–12 av. 26.66	177–44– 505–14 av. 36.07	27–6– 82–1 av. 82.00	97.4–35– 163–11 av. 14.81

a D.A. Thorne 6–2–13–0   b Wasim Akram retired hurt   c D.A. Banks 5–1–13–0

R.G. Twose	M. Asif Din	T.A. Lloyd	A.I. Kallicharran	A.J. Moles	G.W. Humpage	N.M.K. Smith	Byes	Leg-byes	Wides	No-balls	Total	Wkts
							9	24	4	7	259	10
								7		6	171	10
								10	1	5	143	10
							1	16	5	5	160	5
							3	16		4	276	5
							7	6		2	114	5a
							8	12	1	4	261	9b
							11	2		3	133	10
								4	13	7	293	10
								3		1	108	10
							4	9	2	5	199	10
							4	2		4	108	2
3–0–23–0	6.4–0–36–1							14		8	444	3
	3–0–20–1							10			195	4
		18–7–29–0	18–8–25–0	5–1–17–0				25		2	259	10
								1			85	0c
	6–0–20–2							9		1	135	10
	10–1–42–0							16		1	212	8
	3–0–11–0						8	11	4	4	290	10
	15–0–61–0	11–0–82–1		14–2–63–1			6	6		1	378	2
	9–1–42–0					5–1–29–0	8	8	1	4	335	10
	2–0–15–0						9	2			149	5
							2	18		3	371	6
							3	17	6	7	232	10
								4	5	2	147	10
								3	2	1	196	6
		7.3–0–35–1					1	17	2	4	301	4
		10–0–42–0						5		1	171	2
	3–0–8–0						9	18	1	7	279	10
	6–1–39–0		10.5–0–30–2	4–0–47–0	11–2–28–1		4	9		1	188	4
				16–5–28–2		18–3–60–1	2	5	1	2	287	10
						9–1–27–2	5	9		7	141	10
						8–3–15–1		3	1	2	103	5
						7–1–29–1	1	9		4	176	10
10–1–33–0	6–1–26–1					17–3–57–1	10	16		1	316	8
	4.2–0–13–2					6–2–24–0	10	12		5	170	7
											51	10
								11		1	109	10
								8		5	131	10
8–0–33–0						29–5–74–1		9	3	6	329	10
17.5–2–54–1	3–0–12–0					17–2–62–3	5	16	3	4	426	9
							4	13		2	179	10
				1–0–9–0		6–1–31–0		2			79	1
						8.4–4–19–1						
38.5–3–143–1 av. 143.00	94.3–4–422–8 av. 52.75	29–7–111–1 av. 111.00	28.5–8–55–2 av. 27.50	23–3–127–1 av. 127.00	27–7–56–3 av. 18.66	130.4–26–427–11 av. 38.81						

Worcestershire CCC
First-Class Matches, 1989

BATTING	v. MCC (Lord's) 15–18 April		v. Nottinghamshire (Trent Bridge) 20–4 April		v. Warwickshire (Edgbaston) 27–30 April		v. Lancashire (Worcester) 4–8 May		v. Australians (Worcester) 13–15 May		v. Nottinghamshire (Worcester) 24–6 May		v. Gloucestershire (Bristol) 27–30 May		v. Glamorgan (Worcester) 3–6 June		v. Derbyshire (Worcester) 10–13 June		v. Yorkshire (Sheffield) 21–3 June		v. Middlesex (Worcester) 24–7 June		v. Northamptonshire (Northampton) 1–4 July		v. Warwickshire (Worcester) 5–7 July		v. Leicestershire (Kidderminster) 8–11 July	
T.S. Curtis	92	—	68	24	8	55*	4	10	46	8	50	19	23	102	1	140*	58	14	43	—	3	16	80	—				
G.J. Lord	80	—	6	8	16	1	14	9	0	12													54	—	5	—	33	4*
G.A. Hick	173*	—	56	55*	7	5	15	2	13	43	9	90*	8	53	43	0	17	42	150	—	5	6	111	—	4	—	41	—
D.B. D'Oliveira	38	—	1	8	19	2	33	58	1	4	43	4	6	22	4	33	26	47	30	—	11	2	26	—	0	—	0	—
P.A. Neale	50*	—	14	24*	11	—					0	51*	70	34	22	10*	22	17	62*	—	8	75*	62	—	26	—	18	—
I.T. Botham	—	—	8	—	5	7	17	0	39	42					0	10*			41	—	47	6	0	—				
S.J. Rhodes	—	—	40*	—	24	42*	9	43	18	16			3	5*	6	10*	22*	15*	1	0	5	13	4	—	44	—	73*	—
P.J. Newport	—	—	16	—	18	—	2	2	3	5*	27	—	6	10*	5	—												
R.K. Illingworth	—	—	6	—	1	21	13	3	0	12*	1	—	0	—	11	—	4	5*	4	—	0	8	14	—	0	—	34	—
N.V. Radford	—	—	47	—	16	—	9	9	6*	—	39	—	28	9	6	—	36	5			0	3	13	—	4	—	0	—
G.R. Dilley	—	—	4	—	2*	—	0*	5*									8*	11*							1*	—		
M.J. Weston							25	5			9	—	14	26*			3	7	21	—	45	6	31	—	37	—	11	10*
S.J. O'Shaughnessy									4	7																		
A.P. Pridgeon									0	—			2		19*		2	—	1	—								
P. Bent									9	14			0	0	7	22	16	62	20	—	9	1						
S.R. Bevins													6*	—	5	—												
S.M. McEwan																			—	—	2*	18			28*	—	9	—
D.A. Leatherdale																									5	—	0	—
S.R. Lampitt																									46	—	5	—
C.M. Tolley																												
Byes	3			8		1			3	3	5		2	5	2	6	2					4			3		1	
Leg-byes	21		19		10	16	17	14	6	7	6	2	5	12	1	9	9	15	9		1	4	29		17		6	1
Wides				1	1	5	5				1				1		9	1							6		7	1
No-balls	17		6	1	5	5	7	7	2	4	3		14	10	1		8	1	8		6	10	8		7		7	
Total	474		291	129	143	160	166	170	146	163	209	180	201	283	127	246	220	227	389		142	172	433		232		245	16
Wickets	3		10	3	10	5	10	10	10	7	10	3	10	6	10	3	10	8	7		10	10	10		10		10	0
Result	D		W		D		L		W		D		W		D		W		D		L		W		D		W	
Points	—		22		4		5		—		3		22		4		22		8		4		24		6		22	

Fielding Figures

67 – S.J. Rhodes (ct 61/st 6)	13 – N.V. Radford and D.A. Leatherdale	7 – S.R. Bevins
43 – G.A. Hick	11 – T.S. Curtis, R.K. Illingworth and I.T. Botham	5 – P.A. Neale and S.R. Lampitt
21 – D.B. D'Oliveira	8 – M.J. Weston	4 – Subs

honours in the next two or three years although their bowling raises queries, mainly because of the continued uncertainty of Foster's fitness and form. Having said this, one must emphasize the great advance made by players like Topley. There is a wealth of talent in Essex, and the policy of the County in fostering this talent is an example to all. Hussain and Stephenson are young players on the verge of the England side, and jostling them for places in the Essex side are other youngsters like Shahid, Knight and Seymour. The blend of youth and experience in the side is excellent, and they will remain the team to beat for several years to come.

Middlesex, too, have a reservoir of talent. Carr has retired, prematurely, but Hutchinson, Pooley and Brown, if he remains, will be vying for his place. The bowling is as strong as any in the country. Cowans remains grossly under-rated and should have played for England in 1989. Ellcock's advance was extraordinary, and Williams could not gain a regular place. Tufnell and Barnett are young spinners of quality, and the fact that Middlesex won the second eleven championship posted a warning to all.

If one had to select a team to shine in the nineties, however, it would be Surrey. No county is better led nor better administered. Greig has fashioned a side of youth, eager and eminently capable. They play half of their matches on the best wicket in the country so that their bowlers have had to learn to bowl without the aid of a track on which it is only necessary to pitch the ball to capture wickets. They survived last season without an overseas bowler and, for a long period, without Monte Lynch, their most experienced batsman. More than any other county they represent the great hope for English cricket.

One wishes one could say the same for Derbyshire, but while they persist with their policy of permutating pace bowlers, ignoring their own talent for much of the season and relying on doubtful pitches to get them wickets, they will not succeed as they would wish. Even so, there is some exciting talent at Derbyshire – Morris, still only 25 years old, Malcolm, and the virtually untried O'Gorman and Adams. More thoughtful guidance could see Derbyshire become a power in the land.

Adams, Shahid, Hussain, Hutchinson, Hansford, Thorpe – it was, amid the gloom, a season of much hope. The sun shone, and there were the wonderfully exciting performances of the Combined Universities side in the

v. Lancashire (Old Trafford) 19–21 July	v. Sussex (Hove) 22–5 July	v. Surrey (Worcester) 26–8 July	v. Kent (Worcester) 29 July–1 August	v. Essex (Colchester) 5–8 August	v. Somerset (Weston-super-Mare) 9–11 August	v. Hampshire (Bournemouth) 12–15 August	v. Somerset (Worcester) 24–7 August	v. Gloucestershire (Worcester) 29 Aug–1 Sept.	v. Glamorgan (Pontypridd) 13–16 September	M	Inns	NOs	Runs	HS	Av
0 21	102 12			156 —			1 84	98 21	— —	18	30	2	1359	156	48.53
13 3	4* —									10	16	2	262	80	18.71
21 16	0 110*	9 85	147 —	72 —	72 39*	44 —	86 136*	19 20	— —	24	38	6	1824	173*	57.00
11* 10	2 55	17 14	19 —	55 —	52 —	4 —	63 0	29 17	— —	24	37	1	766	63	21.27
62 14	16 33*	29 28	11 —	7 —	44* —	98 —	4 25	4 10		22	32	8	961	98	40.04
1 73	8 4			7 —				13 29		14	20	1	357	73	18.78
8 13	11 —	83 5*	8* 16*	27 —	30* —	1 —	7* 13*	9 22*		22	31	13	623	83	34.61
										8	10	2	94	27	11.75
0 10	8 —	70 —	— —	11 —		71 —		0 26		24	26	2	333	71	13.87
14 0*	66* —	11 4	— —							18	21	2	325	66*	17.10
31 0*	6 —			9* —		4* —		6* 1		13	14	10	88	31	22.00
12 22	70 4	22 74					11* 8			14	22	3	473	74	24.89
										1	2	—	11	7	5.50
		0 22	144 —	55 —	30 18	28 —	0 25	21 27		5	5	1	24	19*	6.00
										13	22	—	530	144	24.09
		7* —	— —		25 —	28 —		15 7		2	2	1	11	6*	11.00
		5 17*	9 —	25 —	12 —	20 —				11	9	3	139	28*	23.16
			4* —	6* —	— —	3 —		23 12	— —	7	8	1	93	25	13.28
		14 —	37 11*		23 26*	9 —			— —	9	7	2	99	46	19.80
										5	6	2	120	37	30.00

v. Lancashire	v. Sussex	v. Surrey	v. Kent	v. Essex	v. Somerset (W)	v. Hampshire	v. Somerset (Worc)	v. Gloucestershire
4	4	4	1	4	1		1	11 9
7 5	18 7	11 6	16	6	8 1	8	8 10	6 5
1 1		1	1	1	4	2	2	
10 7	5	5	2	6	6 3	4	7 1	5 7
191 199	320 230	284 256	402 27	447	302 87	325	200 302	248 213
10 10	9† 4	10 6	6 0	9	6 1	10	5 5	10 10
W	L	W	W	D	W	W	W	W
21	6	23	24	7	24	22	20	22

3 – S.M. McEwan and P.J. Newport   † G.J. Lord retired hurt
2 – G.J. Lord and G.R. Dilley
1 – P. Bent and A.P. Pridgeon

Benson and Hedges Cup, the thrilling finish to that competition, and to the NatWest Bank Trophy and the two Sunday competitions, and there were the Australians. The summer really belonged to them. As the evenings draw in one can still see Waugh driving the ball through the off side and Alderman bowling relentlessly straight and probing.

Border's Australians reminded us of the intrinsic worth of cricket in their commitment, harmony, team-spirit, planning and good management. The 1989 season will remain an unhappy memory only if we take no heed of the principles of which they gave us so firm and eloquent a reminder.

Book Reviews

THE HAROLD RHODES AFFAIR. *Harold Rhodes*; Breedon Books; 208pp; £7.95

This is a sad story by an honest and most capable county cricketer whose Test career was brief because his bowling action was suspect. The son of a professional cricketer, Harold Rhodes was, and is, dedicated to the game, and he tells his story simply and honestly. His punishment went beyond being no-balled by Gibb in 1961 and by Buller in 1965, for, at a time when England were in search of a pace bowler and Rhodes was top of the first-class bowling averages, he was never considered even though his action was declared fair after close scrutiny. He tells his story without bitterness but there is regret that his honesty and endeavour have not enabled him to remain involved in the game.

CHEERFUL CHARLIE. *Jan Kemp*; privately published; 152pp; £10.95

While applauding the attempt to fill a gap in cricket biographies, one cannot recommend this book. It tells us nothing of Charlie McGahey, the Essex and England cricketer, that we did not know before and we are left with no clear picture of why or how he could be called 'Cheerful'. This book is short on anecdotes that would reveal character, and the editing and proof-reading are dreadful.

WAITING FOR CHELTENHAM. *Nico Craven*; privately published; 58pp; £3.25

Always one of the delights of the summer is the arrival of Nico Craven's

Worcestershire CCC
First-Class Matches, 1989

BOWLING	G.R. Dilley	N.V. Radford	P.J. Newport	I.T. Botham	R.K. Illingworth	T.S. Curtis	A.P. Pridgeon	G.A. Hick	M.J. Weston
v. MCC (Lord's) 15–18 April	16–6–58–0	17–4–60–1	17–1–75–1	20–5–36–1	16–3–36–1	1–0–2–0			
v. Nottinghamshire (Trent Bridge) 20–4 April	20.3–0–42–5 14.4–4–40–2	22–5–56–1 17–0–56–4	24–2–64–2 15–2–47–3	16–7–37–2 13–0–49–1	3–1–6–0				
v. Warwickshire (Edgbaston) 27–30 April	12–5–28–5 14–2–45–1	14.4–1–43–4 4–2–8–0	6–1–12–1 12–1–39–1	4–0–9–0 16–2–70–1	6–0–23–1				
v. Lancashire (Worcester) 4–8 May	13–2–41–3 16.1–2–62–4	8–2–28–1 16–2–50–1	13.5–3–41–2 15–0–45–1	18–4–53–4 27–10–61–4					
v. Australians (Worcester) 13–15 May		11–2–32–3 28.2–8–58–4	10.5–2–43–6 27–4–84–5	10–3–18–1			9–1–20–1 9–2–34–0		
v. Nottinghamshire (Worcester) 24–6 May		13–2–41–0 14–1–54–2	9–2–32–1 17–1–64–4		23–9–37–2 23–7–68–3		7–4–10–0 5–1–10–0	7–2–21–0 2–0–18–0	
v. Gloucestershire (Bristol) 27–30 May		22–8–57–5 27–6–88–2	22.5–5–52–3 26–8–73–5		13.4–2–53–2		10–3–18–1 13–5–30–1		8–4–18–1 1–0–4–0
v. Glamorgan (Worcester) 3–6 June		18–3–36–3 3.4–3–0–0	16.2–3–37–4 4–0–19–0	10–1–29–2			11–1–22–1		
v. Derbyshire (Worcester) 10–13 June	21.2–9–42–5 14.1–1–51–1	20–3–51–2 25–6–59–6			9.1–3–27–0 8–4–4–0		1.5–0–5–0		15–7–21–3 13–5–21–1
v. Yorkshire (Sheffield) 21–3 June		31.4–5–86–5 23–6–76–2		24–8–45–2 24–7–68–1	6–1–16–0 16–4–35–0	4–0–5–0		10–3–22–1	20–10–33–2 6–1–25–0
v. Middlesex (Worcester) 24–7 June		16.2–5–61–2 11–2–49–1		20–1–59–3 5.2–1–14–0	19–10–40–3			4–2–6–1	7–0–26–1
v. Northamptonshire (Northampton) 1–4 July	19–1–90–1 16–3–66–4	18–2–61–3		28.5–7–99–6 19–5–76–5	1–1–0–0				5–2–12–0
v. Warwickshire (Worcester) 5–7 July		16–2–68–1 5–0–26–0			22.2–12–33–4			4–0–16–0	13–3–36–0 1–1–0–0
v. Leicestershire (Kidderminster) 8–11 July		21–8–57–4 15.3–7–24–3			9–5–9–2 5–1–8–0				11–4–31–1 7–2–14–1
v. Lancashire (Old Trafford) 19–21 July	12.2–0–30–5 27.1–4–94–5	13–4–41–1 17–1–63–2		15–1–39–3 19–4–55–3					4–0–12–0
v. Sussex (Hove) 22–5 July	9–0–62–0	5–1–18–0 6–0–26–0		40–10–85–7 25–4–92–2	20–5–56–0 9–1–42–1			14–4–35–3 11–0–83–2	6–0–34–0
v. Surrey (Worcester) 26–8 July		28.1–5–66–4 28.2–4–108–4			4–3–4–1 35–15–53–3			16–5–29–1	6–1–8–1
v. Kent (Worcester) 29 July–1 August		26–8–73–4 11–1–45–0			25–6–58–1 20.5–13–22–3			6.4–2–7–1 2–1–1–0	
v. Essex (Colchester) 5–8 August	7–2–14–1 16.2–3–47–0			16–4–42–1 2–1–4–0	19.4–7–57–3 52–21–115–4			17–5–52–5 55–15–131–5	
v. Somerset (Weston-super-Mare) 9–11 August	25–5–101–3 14–2–44–0				1–1–0–0 23–14–13–1			27–11–40–3	
v. Hampshire (Bournemouth) 12–15 August	11–3–32–3 7–2–18–0				17–10–23–5			11–4–19–1 7–4–6–1	
v. Somerset (Worcester) 24–7 August					20–11–22–0	0.3–0–5–0		13–5–21–1	11–4–32–1 5–0–26–0
v. Gloucestershire (Worcester) 29 Aug.–1 Sept.	13–2–51–3 8.4–2–22–4			14–2–47–0 17–5–39–2	7–3–12–1				
v. Glamorgan (Pontypridd) 13–16 September	10–1–40–0			13.3–2–50–2	12–6–21–0			8–2–12–1	2.3–0–12–0
	337.2–61– 1120–55 av. 20.36	572.4–119– 1725–75 av. 23.00	235.5–35– 727–39 av. 18.64	416.4–94– 1176–53 av. 22.18	445.5–179– 893–41 av. 21.78	5.3–0– 12–0 —	65.5–17– 149–4 av. 37.25	214.4–65– 519–26 av. 19.96	141.3–44– 365–12 av. 30.41

a A.E. Warner retired hurt   b A.J. Lamb absent hurt

S.M. McEwan	S.R. Lampitt	C.M. Tolley	P.A. Neale	Byes	Leg-byes	Wides	No-balls	Total	Wkts
				2	12	4	13	281	4
					13		3	218	10
					6	1	9	198	10
					7		7	99	10
				6	13		2	204	6
					8			171	10
				3	10		5	231	10
					8		7	103	10
				4	7	3	3	205	10
				7	2			150	3
				12	12		7	238	9
					3	1	1	148	10
				2	7	6	7	257	10
					10	1	2	134	10
					1			20	0
				1	10	1	2	157	10
				4	6			145	9a
25–8–65–1				2	2	2	1	249	10
13–4–35–0				4	10	4	3	280	4
5–0–18–0				3	8		1	221	10
5–0–32–0					1		3	96	1
				4	2	1	4	256	10
					4		6	158	9b
17–1–62–4	15–4–36–1				14		1	265	10
7–0–12–0	3.2–0–4–0			3	2			47	0
20–7–53–3	6–0–25–0			1	4		2	180	10
14–5–34–6						2		80	10
				4	11	1	5	125	9
					5		8	229	10
				8	3	1	8	301	10
				2	5		1	250	6
21–8–57–4		5–2–8–0		7	3	1		153	10
25–7–61–2		6–2–14–0		10	10		1	285	10
28–8–50–1	15–5–29–2	4–1–9–0		2	4			232	10
24–4–73–2	23–13–32–5	6–3–9–0		4	10	1		196	10
	8–2–39–0				4	1	2	208	10
				10	16		5	323	9
23.3–5–57–3	23–2–60–4	7–0–18–0			4	2	5	240	10
11.2–2–28–5	7–3–10–1			6	4	1	8	145	10
15–3–46–1	11.4–1–38–5				2	3	1	137	10
16–4–32–4	10–4–8–0			3	7			97	10
38–4–111–4	36.5–8–89–4	27–8–59–0			4		3	338	10
16–5–46–3	16–3–48–2	6–0–21–1	1–0–8–0		7	1	1	161	6
20.2–4–61–5	12–2–30–1				5		2	206	10
9–1–28–0	16–6–32–4				3		1	124	10
15.2–2–38–4	17–3–46–2				11	1		230	9
368.3–82–	219.5–56–	61–16–	1–0–						
999–52	526–31	138–1	8–0						
av. 19.21	av. 16.96	av. 138.00	—						

Yorkshire CCC
First-Class Matches, 1989

BATTING	v. Middlesex (Lord's) 20–4 April	v. Nottinghamshire (Leeds) 4–8 May	v. Northamptonshire (Northampton) 16–19 May	v. Derbyshire (Leeds) 24–6 May	v. Surrey (The Oval) 27–30 May	v. Nottinghamshire (Trent Bridge) 3–6 June	v. Leicestershire (Leicester) 7–9 June	v. Somerset (Taunton) 10–13 June	v. Gloucestershire (Harrogate) 17–20 June	v. Worcestershire (Sheffield) 21–3 June	v. Glamorgan (Leeds) 24–7 June	v. Hampshire (Southampton) 1–4 July	v. Sussex (Middlesbrough) 8–11 July	v. Middlesex (Leeds) 19–21 July
D. Byas	30 —	15 3	1 50	30 —	10 11		67 —		16 15	82* 80	7 —	7 15	43 —	23 5
A.A. Metcalfe	0 —	7 19	49 10	60 —	4 12	31 18	2 41	0 7		0 76	113 —	1 1	64 —	10 81
R.J. Blakey	24 —	33 39	13 12	0 —	13 40	10 1	26 48*	7 51	15 38	26 16	97 —	17 53	9 —	47 0
P.E. Robinson	31 —	13 17	46 15			57 18	10 7*	28 15	19 28	4 32*	1 —			9 0
J.D. Love	1 —	0 14				53 7	17 —	39 39*	18 0	2 40*	32 —	0 2		
D.L. Bairstow	0 —	9 0	9 44	0 —	2 101*		0 7	0 —	28 51*	1 42*	5 —			
P. Carrick	13 —	5 10	3 10	22 —	51 15	9 30	8 —	25 —	4 65*	13 —	0 —	10 22*	47* —	19 30
C.S. Pickles	5 —	7 2	4 20*	4 —	19* —	0 28*	34* —	1 66	4 —		4* —	0 45*		1 5
A. Sidebottom	8 —			22 —	7 12*	4 21	3 —	6* —	39 —	12 —	4 —		7* —	
P.W. Jarvis	0 —	0 3	19 0			11* 59*	5 —	25 —	20* —		7 —			12* 12*
D. Gough	2* —													
I.M. Priestley		0* 0	2* 23											
S.D. Fletcher		1 1*			— —						13 —	1* —		4 5
K. Sharp			6 39	51 —	4 3*								27 —	23 18
I.G. Swallow			26 1	64 —	2 9	1 0		21 —	37 14	17 —		20 18	16 —	2 1
M.D. Moxon				50 —	162* 0	37 39	54 8	51 17	38 95	69 15	24 —	35 10	18 —	21 25
P.A. Booth				2* —										
S.A. Kellett												0 5	0 —	
I.J. Houseman													18 —	
P.J. Hartley														
N.G. Nicholson														
J. Batty														
Byes	5		2 3		16 5		8		15	9	2 4		6	2
Leg-byes	10	2 1	7 13	6	6 8	6 11	4 5	4 6	6 3	2 10	11	9 10	4	2 4
Wides				1		1 2		7		2 4	1			2
No-balls	1		4 11	1	7	3 1	16 3	4 1	3 3	1 3	9	4 5		2 3
Total	130	92 109	191 251	313	303 217	223 250	246 112	239 275	220 312	249 280	308	107 191	260	179 189
Wickets	10	10 10	10 10	10	8 6	10 9	10 2	10 5	10 6	10 4	9	10 7	8	10 10
Result	D	L	L	D	D	D	W	D	D	D	D	W	W	L
Points	3	4	3	8	6	6	20	4	6	4	3	20	19	4

Fielding Figures

45 – R.J. Blakey (ct 43/st 2)	11 – P.E. Robinson	8 – A.A. Metcalfe
23 – D.L. Bairstow (ct 22/st 1)	10 – C.S. Pickles and A. Sidebottom	6 – J. D. Love
21 – M.D. Moxon	9 – K. Sharp	5 – P. Carrick, I. G. Swallow and N. G. Nicholson
14 – D. Byas		

latest offering. *Waiting for Cheltenham*, with a foreword by David Foot and illustrations by Frank Fisher, is no disappointment. It is written with Craven's usual combination of gentle wit and loving observation of all that is good in the game. Long may Nico Craven prosper. His books should be compulsory reading for those who have grown cynical on a surfeit of international cricket, for Craven's interests are the club and county game and the joys of friendships at Cheltenham and elsewhere.

RISING TO THE CHALLENGE. *Roland Butcher and Bridgette Lawrence*; Pelham Books; 165pp; £12.95

Roland Butcher had a benefit year in 1989, and the benefit was welcomed by the publication of this book. It is unfortunate that Bridgette Lawrence had so little matter at her disposal in telling the Butcher story. He grew up and played cricket, and that does not make a sensational story. The book could not have been aided by the fact that Butcher lost his place in the Middlesex side and was originally destined for South Africa with Gatting's side, a decision he recanted, but not before it had seriously damaged his benefit.

F.S. JACKSON: A CRICKETING BIOGRAPHY. *James P. Coldham*; Crowood Press; 208pp; £12.95

James Coldham has completed the work begun by his late father and offers us a competent and well-written study of the great Yorkshire all-rounder. There is no great advance on Alan Gibson's admirable work of 24 years ago, and the real fascination of Jackson is the life he lived outside cricket, but this is a worthy book, and it does not ignore the social background of the Edwardian period.

FROM THE SEA END. *Christopher Lee*; Partridge Press; 322pp; £15.00

This is the official history of Sussex County Cricket Club, published to commemorate its first 150 years. As such, it is a great disappointment, for it is so unbalanced. While the distant past is lavishly and lovingly treated and extravagantly written, the closer past, the era of Greig and Barclay, is cursorily dealt with. Surely an official history must offer hope for the present and future and a balanced assessment of all periods, not simply a wallowing nostalgia for things past. One also feels that an official history deserves a better production job than this book has been given.

VIJAY MERCHANT – IN MEMORIAM. *Edited by Marcus Couto*; Association of Cricket Statisticians of India; distributed by Marine Sports of Bombay; 122pp

This is a collection of memories of the great Indian batsman by whose who knew him, from Mushtaq Ali to Sunil Gavaskar

C.K. NAYUDU. *Vasant Raiji*; Marine Sports; 101pp

An interesting account of the career of one of India's greatest cricketers. The book is well illustrated and there are comments from many who knew and saw him, as well as a good statistical section. Also from India comes *ANKA*, the official newsletter of the Association of Cricket Statisticians and Scorers of India. This was first published in 1987 when the association was founded, and it contains much fascinating statistical information about Indian cricket and cricket in general.

Details and copies of these Indian publications can be obtained from: The Marine Sports, 63-A Gokhale Road (North), Dadar, Bombay 400 028.

v. Essex (Southend) 22–5 July	v. Warwickshire (Edgbaston) 26–8 July	v. Northamptonshire (Sheffield) 5–8 August	v. Kent (Scarborough) 12–15 August	v. Lancashire (Old Trafford) 19–22 August	v. Derbyshire (Chesterfield) 24–8 August	v. Warwickshire (Leeds) 29 Aug.–1 Sept.	v. Lancashire (Scarborough) 8–11 September	M	Inns	NOs	Runs	HS	Av
15 20	0 18*	10 9	117 —	3 7	0 40	95	0 0	20	33	2	844	117	27.22
9 30	112 40	56 45	7 87*	44 4	0 3	138	19 30	21	37	1	1230	138	34.16
12 1	88 73*	87* 3	33 30	56 62	6 27	9	15 22	22	39	3	1159	97	32.19
8 47	16* —	9* 16	147 —	2 2	34 23	0	10 117	18	31	4	781	147	28.92
								9	15	2	264	53	20.30
		— 1		1 11	3 5	1	15 0	10	16	3	299	101*	23.00
0 35	— —			0 5	24 0	30	62 25	22	31	3	483	65*	17.25
13* 27*	— —						40 40*	18	24	7	388	66	22.82
21 0		— 9		4 1	13 6	19		19	24	5	344	45*	18.10
2 5		— 4			0 12		0 2	16	22	5	203	59*	11.94
						9		2	2	1	11	9	11.00
								2	4	2	25	23	12.50
0 7		— 0*		1 0*	9 15*	9		11	11	4	33	13	4.71
0 16	51* —	73* 78	53 26	20 0		41	54 41	11	19	4	512	78	34.13
	— 1	— 1	1* —	18* 18				13	20	2	287	64	15.94
27 37	10 34	18 53		21 11	14 27			18	32	1	1156	162*	37.29
					5* 8*			2	3	3	15	8*	—
								2	3	—	5	5	1.66
								1	1	—	18	18	18.00
								1	—	—	—	—	—
			24* —			56*	1 6	3	4	2	87	56*	43.50
							4* 0	1	2	1	4	4*	4.00
7	1		4	6 1	5 5	6	5	5 4					
6 4	17 5	5 2		9 1	10 10	11 6	16	6					
	2			2	1 4	3	3	4					
2 3	4 1	1	3	6 8	11 9	4	8 2					
115 239	301 171	259 225	400 147	192 148	136 184	426	237 295						
10 10	4 2	3 10	5 2	10 10	10 9	9	10 10						
L	D	L	L	L	L	D	L						
4	7	3	5	5	4	6	4						

3 – Subs

2 – P.A. Booth and P.W. Jarvis

1 – I.M. Priestley, S.D. Fletcher and S.A. Kellett

† K. Sharp retired hurt

THE MEN AND THE MATCHES THAT CHANGED THE GAME. *Allen Synge*; St Michael; 192pp; £8.95

This is a beautifully produced book, lavishly illustrated. It is, in effect, a potted history of the game, with emphasis on certain players and periods. It is an easy read and a pleasant gift book.

FAMOUS WRITERS ON CRICKET. *Compiled by Roger Adams*; Partridge Press; 107pp; £9.95

This is offered as an anthology with a difference by which the publishers mean, no doubt, that photographs by Adrian Murrell and Patrick Eagar are given captions from Socrates, Johnson and Shakespeare. In a small book, there are nine pages of text taken from Ranjitsinhji's *Jubilee Book of Cricket* and the word 'famous' is used rather liberally. A scant offering.

TREASURES OF LORD'S. *Tim Rice*; Collins Willow; 160pp; £16.95

The new MCC Cricket Library series is launched in splendid fashion with this magnificently produced book. Tim Rice has chosen 120 pieces from the collection of cricketana housed at Lord's and presents them with succinct and intelligent comment. The items range from the plate which W.G. Grace commissioned for the dinner given him by the Century Club at Bristol in 1896 to the balls with which Laker took his 19 wickets in the Old Trafford Test of 1956. Bats, balls, portraits, tankards, busts and tumblers jostle each other in this admirable selection, and the author and the publishers are to be congratulated on giving us such a fine record of the MCC collection. If the rest of the series maintains this standard, the MCC Cricket Library will itself become a treasure.

WEST INDIAN SUMMER. *Patrick Eagar and Alan Ross*; Hodder & Stoughton; 112pp; £12.95

The annual offering of photographs by Patrick Eagar with text by Alan Ross is of the usual high standard and presents us with an interesting photographic record of the international matches played between England and West Indies in 1988.

THE PAVILION LIBRARY 1989 – all published by Pavilion Books at £7.99:
SORT OF A CRICKET PERSON. *E.W. Swanton*; 318pp
DOUBLE CENTURY: CRICKET IN *THE TIMES*: VOL. I, 1785–1934. *Edited by Marcus Williams*; 301pp
CRICKET ALL HIS LIFE. THE CRICKET WRITING OF E.V. LUCAS. *Introduced by John Arlott*; 218pp
THE CRICKET CAPTAINS OF ENGLAND. *Alan Gibson*; 242pp

The four additions to the Pavilion Library for the current year are worthy ones and of a higher literary standard than some of the offerings in recent years. It is particularly good to see a work by Jim Swanton included in the series, and one hopes that his *As I Said at the Time* and other works will also find a place in the library, for he is one we should value.

Alan Gibson has brought his study of the cricket captains of England up to date by commenting upon the achievements of Botham, Willis, Gower, Gatting and the fiasco of 1988.

The most interesting of the four books in that it gives us writing not readily obtainable elsewhere is *Cricket All His Life*, yet becoming reacquainted with the work of E.V. Lucas is a less pleasurable experience than one had anticipated. He is not the great literary figure one had seemed

Yorkshire CCC
First-Class Matches, 1989

BOWLING

	P.W. Jarvis	A. Sidebottom	D. Gough	C.S. Pickles	P. Carrick	D. Byas	S.D. Fletcher	I.M. Priestley	I.G. Swallow
v. Middlesex (Lord's) 20–4 April	32–12–77–5 / 6–2–16–0	15.2–5–38–0	16–4–44–3 / 13–0–47–2	28.4–9–67–2 / 11–3–22–0	9–3–16–0 / 8–2–24–2	5–2–6–0			
v. Nottinghamshire (Leeds) 4–8 May	9.4–3–10–3 / 10.2–2–44–0			8–0–26–3 / 3–0–16–0			6–1–21–0 / 9–2–34–0	11–4–27–4 / 5–1–19–0	
v. Northamptonshire (Northampton) 16–19 May	46–12–104–3 / 5.2–4–12–2			34.3–8–92–4 / 5–1–14–2	53–22–75–3	9–3–21–0		14–1–73–0	26–10–45–
v. Derbyshire (Leeds) 24–6 May		24.4–14–40–5 / 26–3–71–3		15–6–37–1 / 19–3–67–1	25–6–60–4 / 32–27–28–3				9–5–16–0 / 4–0–17–0
v. Surrey (The Oval) 27–30 May		26–3–89–0 / 9–2–37–0		17.2–4–60–2 / 11–1–49–3	30–7–75–1	7–0–39–2	21–5–75–1		27–4–81–2
v. Nottinghamshire (Trent Bridge) 3–6 June	23.4–5–74–7 / 9–2–28–0	25–3–77–1 / 9–0–24–0		3–0–15–0	10–3–26–1 / 12–6–17–1				3–0–17–1 / 6–1–15–0
v. Leicestershire (Leicester) 7–9 June	16–3–33–3 / 23.3–1–86–4	16–5–37–2 / 17–4–44–2		6–3–13–0 / 8–5–8–1	7–1–11–0 / 18–7–52–3				
v. Somerset (Taunton) 10–13 June	13–4–31–2	23–6–53–2		18–5–55–0	29.2–14–53–5				26–5–83–1
v. Gloucestershire (Harrogate) 17–20 June	26–2–84–3 / 8–2–17–0	14–4–44–1 / 2–1–4–0		0.5–0–0–1	36–8–96–2 / 23–10–55–2				21–7–49–3 / 18–8–58–4
v. Worcestershire (Sheffield) 21–3 June		26–4–91–1		18–4–99–1	25–14–39–1	5–0–25–2	28–7–85–2		5–1–17–0
v. Glamorgan (Leeds) 24–7 June		15–1–43–0		13.1–2–63–1	13–2–36–0		15–3–50–1		
v. Hampshire (Southampton) 1–4 July	17–2–73–2 / 13.5–4–51–3	18–4–35–5 / 14–3–41–4					12.3–4–33–2 / 7–0–31–0		
v. Sussex (Middlesbrough) 8–11 July		20–3–56–5			22–3–83–3		11.3–0–45–2		
v. Middlesex (Leeds) 19–21 July	28.1–11–77–2 / 18–7–29–3	30–8–79–6 / 16.4–5–32–4			11–4–49–1		21–2–50–1 / 1–0–10–0		1–0–7–0
v. Essex (Southend) 22–5 July	26–8–76–6 / 11–0–35–3	11–2–40–1 / 10.2–1–48–4		5–0–22–0	30.4–13–62–3 / 1–0–3–0		10–0–43–0 / 1–0–8–0		
v. Warwickshire (Edgbaston) 26–8 July		24–3–58–1		27.5–2–90–2 / 7–1–50–1	24–9–45–3 / 8–0–51–0	6–1–32–1	34–5–88–4 / 11–2–44–1		
v. Northamptonshire (Sheffield) 5–8 August	24.3–5–89–4 / 7–1–25–1	27–2–75–4 / 10–3–28–1			19–5–61–0 / 8–1–29–1	2–1–13–0	21–0–79–1 / 4–0–33–0		14–3–46–1 / 7–1–29–0
v. Kent (Scarborough) 12–15 August	13–5–35–0 / 14.2–2–69–1	12–3–28–1 / 25–5–71–3		15–4–37–2 / 7–0–30–0	30.3–3–79–2 / 21–4–73–1				26–7–83–1 / 3–0–25–0
v. Lancashire (Old Trafford) 19–22 August	21.5–5–61–3 / 11–2–35–1			5–2–4–0 / 14–3–47–1	39–17–85–4 / 15–5–39–0	4.4–0–40–0	15–5–38–0 / 2–1–5–0		20–3–96–2 / 9–1–44–1
v. Derbyshire (Chesterfield) 24–8 August	13–4–27–6 / 18–1–66–1	12–2–47–4 / 27–4–92–5		5–1–16–0 / 6–1–28–0	3–1–8–0 / 1–1–0–0				
v. Warwickshire (Leeds) 29 Aug.–1 Sept.	18–7–30–0 / 16–5–63–1	23–10–37–3 / 16–7–18–0	20–6–46–1 / 16–3–36–0	17–7–54–0 / 8–1–39–0	42.4–17–70–6 / 26–11–56–1	3–3–0–1			
v. Lancashire (Scarborough) 8–11 September	18–1–74–2 / 31–5–103–3	15–3–56–0 / 15–6–57–0		11–3–57–1	28–9–69–4 / 33–7–78–0				
	548.1–129– 1634–74 av. 22.08	574–129– 1590–68 av. 23.38	65–13– 173–6 av. 28.83	347.2–79– 1177–29 av. 40.58	693.1–242– 1603–57 av. 28.12	41.4–10– 176–6 av. 28.33	230–37– 772–15 av. 51.46	30–6– 119–4 av. 29.75	225–56– 728–16 av. 45.50

a P.E. Robinson 7–0–22–0; N.G. Nicholson 5–0–25–0   b J. Batty 26–9–75–3; 38.1–8–118–5

P.A. Booth	M.D. Moxon	K. Sharp	A.A. Metcalfe	J.D. Love	I.J. Houseman	P.J. Hartley	Byes	Leg-byes	Wides	No-balls	Total	Wkts
							4	14		1	260	10
								4			119	4
								2	2		86	10
								6	4		119	0
							1	7	3	1	418	10
											26	4
9–2–22–0							2	1	4	3	178	10
5–4–4–0							1	1		8	189	7
	2–0–10–0							10	5	6	400	6
	8–0–31–1	1–0–15–0	0.4–0–4–0					2		3	177	7
								5		8	214	10
											84	1
	5–1–10–1						2	2		5	108	6
								11		7	201	10
	9–2–16–0							8	1	4	299	10
								6		1	279	10
				4–1–20–2			6	3			163	8
	4–0–24–0							9		8	389	7
	3–1–18–0						4		1	4	214	2
								3	3	9	144	10
	6–3–24–3							6		4	153	10
											0	0
					9–1–61–0		1	6	1	5	252	10
	12–2–28–0							4		14	294	10
								4		4	75	7
								5	1	11	248	10
							4	9		4	107	7
						12–1–51–0	5	15	3	15	352	10
								8			237	3
		8–0–52–0						8	1	5	379	10
		2–0–8–0						3		1	147	3
		2–0–4–0						5			271	6
							5	4		2	277	5
							2	7	4	5	293	10
		1–0–6–0					2	10			228	3
								4		2	102	10
12–5–21–1	1–0–4–0							8		6	219	7
							3	8	1		248	10
			13–3–29–0				2	6		2	296	3a
							12	4		5	347	10 b
							5	8	1	2	369	8
26–11–	50–9–	14–0–	13.4–3–	4–1–	9–1–	12–1–						
47–1	165–5	85–0	33–0	20–2	61–0	51–0						
av. 47.00	*av.* 33.00	—	—	*av.* 10.00	—	—						

to remember, and his writing has neither the depth and clarity nor the lyrical charm of Swanton, Woodcock or Gibson. Nevertheless, this is a valuable publication and Pavilion are to be commended for their bravery. It should teach us to value more the giants of today.

THE HISTORY OF DERBYSHIRE CCC. *John Shawcroft*; Christopher Helm; 336pp; £14.95
THE HISTORY OF GLAMORGAN CCC. *Andrew Hignell*; Christopher Helm; 256pp; £15.95
THE HISTORY OF LANCASHIRE CCC. *Peter Wynne-Thomas*; Christopher Helm; 290pp; £14.95
THE HISTORY OF SURREY CCC. *David Lemmon*; Christopher Helm; 373pp; £15.95
THE HISTORY OF WORCESTERSHIRE CCC. *David Lemmon*; Christopher Helm; 288pp; £14.95
THE HISTORY OF YORKSHIRE CCC. *Anthony Woodhouse*; Christopher Helm; 618pp; £17.95

The impressive series of county histories, beautifully produced and well illustrated, saw six new titles in 1989 so that nine of the 17 county histories have now been published by Christopher Helm, and more are promised for next year. Four of the histories published this year, Derbyshire, Glamorgan, Surrey and Worcestershire have the seal of approval from the counties concerned and are the official histories.

John Shawcroft's history of Derbyshire is an accurate, factual account of the trials, triumphs and tribulations of the county. The author concerns himself with events rather than characters, and there are occasions where one feels his criticism should have been sharper, but this is a worthy addition to the series. Andrew Hignell's history of Glamorgan is a delight. It is well researched and presents a rich tapestry of memorable characters. For a county that has struggled for the past few years, this book should present something of a tonic. It is balanced, objective and eminently readable.

If Peter Wynne-Thomas' history of Lancashire has not quite the warmth of Hignell's work, it cannot be faulted for the accuracy of the information it offers and the scrupulousness of the research. Peter Wynne-Thomas has established himself as one of the foremost authorities on the game, and his study of Lancashire cricket gives further credibility to his status.

Anthony Woodhouse is the chairman of the Association of Cricket Statisticians and a life-member of Yorkshire. His massive history of the county he loves is his first book. It is an achievement which merits the highest praise. It is direct in approach, but it is never laboured, and it is coloured by some brief and perceptive character studies of those who have played for the county. The balanced, chronological, factual approach never oppresses the warmth that the author has for his subject nor dwarfs the humanity with which he deals. It is an excellent addition to the series.

The official histories of Surrey and Worcestershire were written by the present reviewer.

MIDDLESEX COUNTY CRICKET CLUB REVIEW 1988/89. *Edited by Alvan Seth-Smith*; Middlesex CCC; 136pp; £4.50

The ninth year of this excellent publication sees it maintain the high standard of previous years both in content and production. There is clarity in presentation of score-cards and all else. Highly recommended for all followers of the game.

THE SKILLS OF CRICKET. *Keith Andrew*; Crowood Press; 136pp

This is a re-issue of this excellent and highly acclaimed coaching manual. It is clear, precise and never dull, a great merit for a book that attempts to instruct young people how to play the game.

THE HANDBOOK OF CRICKET. *Keith Andrew*; Pelham Books; 230pp; £14.95

The Handbook of Cricket is an expansion of Keith Andrew's earlier coaching manual. It contains a brief history of the game and the author's comments on players and writers as well as a comprehensive section of instruction. It forms an excellent introduction to the game and a fine companion for young players and all interested in cricket.

ACSSI CRICKET YEARBOOK 1987–88. *Edited by Anandji Dossa*; The Marine Sports; 220pp

After being in existence for only a year the Association of Cricket Statisticians and Scorers of India have found it possible to produce an excellent yearbook. It contains full score-cards of all first-class matches played in India, a statistical who's who of Indian cricketers and much else. It is an important publication, and one hopes that it will prosper. Like other Indian publications, it is obtainable from Marine Sports.

NEW ZEALAND IN INDIA 1988. *Edited by Pradeep Vijayakar*; Marine Sports; 80pp

Another publication from India, this brochure gives full details of the New Zealand and Indian players and there are several interesting articles. The statistics are provided by Sudhir Vaidya, who makes an invaluable contribution to *Benson and Hedges Cricket Year*.

ESSEX COUNTY CRICKET CLUB YEARBOOK 1989. *Edited by Peter Edwards*; Essex CCC; 280pp; £4.00

Once again Essex provides the fattest and the fullest of the yearbooks with reports and score-cards of all matches. One cannot think that there is any aspect of Essex cricket past and present that is not touched upon. The book is excellent value for money.

THE JOURNAL OF THE CRICKET SOCIETY. *Edited by Clive W. Porter*; The Cricket Society

This quarterly publication continues to delight. It is packed with articles that are erudite and fascinating. It teases with the questions it poses and never lapses from a high standard in the quality of writing that it publishes. Would that all publications followed its example.

SURREY COUNTY CRICKET CLUB YEARBOOK 1989. *Edited by Anne Bickerstaff*; Surrey CCC; 160pp; £4.50

The Oval is a lively and exciting place, and the attitude of the Surrey staff is reflected in this bubbling publication. It is carefully compiled and produced, vital and entertaining. The standard of county yearbooks seems to be getting higher and higher.

THE ASHES CAPTAINS. *Gerry Cotter*; Crowood Press; 320pp; £16.95

Graced by Ken Kelly's photographs, *The Ashes Captains* is a beautiful publication. Much of the writing is witty and elegant, but the author's original intention has become blurred. What purports to be a study of England and Australia Test captains subsides into a ramble through the various series. This is a book which lost its direction somewhere along the way.

WISDEN CRICKETERS' ALMANACK 1989. *Edited by Graeme Wright*; John Wisden; 1264pp; £16.95 (cased), £14.95 (softcover)

The 126th edition of *Wisden* inevitably gives us much to savour and enjoy, not least the forthright, refreshing views of its editor. Graeme Wright's vision of English cricket in the context of our society echoes my own views on the attitudes of players, and one cannot but applaud such a statement as: 'There is no reason why, in a country where it is often impossible to have building work done or a motor car serviced properly, its sporting tradesmen should perform any better.' Mr Wright has put his finger on the pulse; there are many cricketers who do not know their trade. My only quarrel with this annual joy of a book is that I feel that it deserves a better standard of contribution than some of the articles offered in the 1989 edition.

100 GREAT BOWLERS. *Phil Edmonds, with Scyld Berry*; Macdonald Queen Anne Press; 256pp; £16.95

This is the companion book to Arlott's *100 Great Batsmen*, which was published a couple of years ago. Inevitably there are choices and omissions which will cause debate, the inclusion of John Emburey, for example, but it is a stimulating book which has been put together well and is pleasantly presented.

CRICKET'S SECOND GOLDEN AGE *Gerald Howat*: Hodder & Stoughton; 300pp; £14.95

Gerald Howat can be an infuriating author. He can produce important works such as the studies of Constantine and Hutton and less satisfactory biographies such as the bitterly disappointing book on Hammond. Unfortunately his latest offering comes into the second category. It is a potted history of cricket in the thirties, but it is a dense, unselective book that tries to embrace so wide a field and so many subjects that it examines nothing with sufficient depth or value. It has all the marks that one associates with book-making, and Gerald Howat is too good an author to descend to that.